SOCIAL PROBLEMS

A CANADIAN PERSPECTIVE
Second Edition

Lorne Tepperman
James Curtis
Albert Kwan

OXFORD
UNIVERSITY PRESS

OXFORD
UNIVERSITY PRESS

70 Wynford Drive, Don Mills, Ontario M3C 1J9
www.oup.com/ca

Oxford University Press is a department of the University of Oxford.
It furthers the University's objective of excellence in research, scholarship,
and education by publishing worldwide in

Oxford New York

Auckland Cape Town Dar es Salaam Hong Kong Karachi
Kuala Lumpur Madrid Melbourne Mexico City Nairobi
New Delhi Shanghai Taipei Toronto

With offices in

Argentina Austria Brazil Chile Czech Republic France Greece
Guatemala Hungary Italy Japan Poland Portugal Singapore
South Korea Switzerland Thailand Turkey Ukraine Vietnam

Oxford is a trade mark of Oxford University Press
in the UK and in certain other countries

Published in Canada
by Oxford University Press

Library and Archives Canada Cataloguing in Publication

Tepperman, Lorne, 1943-
Social problems : a Canadian perspective / Lorne Tepperman, James Curtis,
and Albert Kwan. — 2nd ed.

ISBN-13: 978-0-19-542500-0
ISBN-10: 0-19-542500-6

1. Social problems. 2. Canada—Social conditions. I. Curtis, James E., 1943–2005
II. Kwan, Albert, 1979- III. Title.

HN103.5.T46 2008   361.1   C2006-905197-6

1 2 3 4 –10 09 08 07

Cover Design: Joan Dempsey
Cover Photo: John Foxx

This book is printed on permanent (acid-free) paper ∞.
Printed in Canada

Contents

Each chapter includes, at the beginning, Learning Objectives, and, at the end, Questions for Critical Thought, Recommended Readings, Recommended Websites, Glossary, and References.

Preface

Welcome to the second edition of *Social Problems: A Canadian Perspective*. We were very pleased with the reception readers gave the first edition and have tried to make this new edition even better. To do so, we have added new topics for discussion in each chapter, yet maintained the manageable size. Two new chapters—on health and on sexual orientation—have been added. To make space for these, we have combined two earlier chapters into one—on population and environment—and shortened most of the other chapters. We have updated the examples and references and made the book's layout more attractive. Yet, for all this, the book has remained the same in its fundamental approach. So, we need to spend a little time talking about our basic assumptions in writing the book.

First, we assume there is such a thing as a 'social problem'. A social problem is any circumstance that many people experience and that has both social causes and social consequences. The social problem in each case actually exists. We can verify that fact with our own eyes and with the measurement tools of social science. Yet the social problem is also socially constructed, in the sense that people think it exists and tend to agree on this. They define it as a social problem. The condition in question has become a problem for people, and if they did not think it was a problem, it would cease being one, at least at the level of consciousness, social definition, and social action.

Because of this socially constructed aspect of social problems, we can trace historically the rise and fall of social problems over time. We can study when people came to share the understanding that it was a problem. To take a simple example, few people in Canada today consider the so-called promiscuity of young women to be a social problem, although this was not the case in the past. Likewise, few Canadians today are troubled by miscegenation—couples from two different races having sexual relations—although in earlier times many people considered this a serious social problem.

Sociologists study why certain behaviours, and not others, come to occupy our concern and evoke the label of 'social problem'. This takes us into the areas of changing morality and moral panics—sudden, intense, widespread, and often fleeting concerns about the immorality of one particular group. Also of interest to sociologists, though, are social problems that can be shown to do major harm to our quality of life but that only a few people see as a problem and that government and other powerful agencies are doing little to address.

The social problems that are longest lasting and evoke concern among the largest numbers of people are those that are not merely socially constructed and, in that sense, are not simply problems 'in people's minds'. They are also serious matters of health, and of life and death. Poverty, racial discrimination, bad working conditions, domestic violence—these are all serious social problems because, at the extremes, they hurt or kill people. In less extreme circumstances, they increase illness and reduce people's well-being and quality of life. Increasingly, we live in what Ulrich Beck (1992) has called a 'risk society', in which we are all, always, in danger of harm from sources that are often hidden from view and beyond human control. Often these risks are a result of human activity, especially the applications of science and technology to the natural environment. Often they are a result of what we are taught to regard fondly as 'progress'.

So apart from the perceived immorality, injustice, or unfairness of the problems we will discuss in this book, serious social problems cost our society many human lives and many days lost from work and family life, as well as shattered families, workplace conflict, and destroyed hopes. These problems are not merely 'in people's minds'. In fact, the job of the sociologist, in these cases, is to bring them to people's conscious attention.

To summarize to this point, we are particularly interested in issues that are both potentially and actually social problems: they cause people trouble and are seen as causing trouble. We will pay no attention whatever to the more pleasant sides of life—making this a somewhat dark-hued book. And we will pay only passing attention to issues that people may briefly consider problems but, in the long run, prove not to be. Actual and potential problems that lurk below the consciousness of most people will make intermittent appearances in this book, especially in the final chapter.

Sometimes people are unaware of the risks surrounding them because they have been disciplined to view the harmful as safe, the inhumane and dangerous as normal. To some degree, we are all victims of techniques of management and moral regulation that some, following Michel Foucault (2000), have called 'governmentality'. Our trained unawareness and secret but effective regulation ensure that we will usually abide by the rules of society, thus protecting the advantage of those in power.

Social science has a poor batting average in solving human problems. It has not done well at bringing about change, as we will see. The problem here is in part the complexity of the roots of social problems and in part the will and ability (or lack thereof) of society's agencies of power to address the problems. Yet we, as authors of this book, believe that the purpose of sociology today, just as in the nineteenth century when sociology began, is to use knowledge to improve social life. Thus, our goal in a book like this is to aid the understanding of the roots of social problems, their health consequences for individuals and society as a whole, and how these can be addressed. For this task, it is important to explore facts and theories concerning how problems develop and are maintained, and how they are interrelated. We believe that these theories help us organize our facts and help us work towards solving our problems.

We will see that sociologists, like other social scientists, have a variety of theories about society and its social problems. Throughout this book, we will return to three sociological theories—structural functionalism, conflict theory, and symbolic interactionism—as well as to two other important perspectives for understanding problems in society—feminism, which varies in its analysis and solutions from liberal to radical points of view, and social constructionism, an outgrowth of symbolic interactionism that posits that groups of people create and recreate their own realities. Each contributes important elements to our understanding of society and social problems. None rules out the validity or contribution of any other. Each of the theories approaches social life from a different standpoint, asking different questions and looking at different kinds of evidence. Therefore, each pays off for our understanding of social problems, in different ways. These approaches compete for our attention and loyalty. Sociologists tend to prefer and attach themselves to one approach rather than another. At the same time, applied sociologists go about analyzing and solving real-life problems in families, workplaces, organizations, and societies by combining insights from all of these perspectives.

We also introduce an additional perspective—the population health perspective—and employ it in each chapter. This perspective focuses attention on the physical and psychological harm caused by social problems to individuals and, thereby, on the harm caused to society. This perspective also emphasizes the social sources and consequences of people's illness and health. The population health perspective complements the other perspectives: it not so much contradicts them as it adds to and extends them. It simply has a more explicit focus on the issues of the health of individuals and societies. All of the theoretical approaches will be discussed in further detail in the Introduction and in the ensuing chapters.

We have organized this book to reflect our assumptions about social problems. We begin each chapter with a brief general introduction to the problem at hand. We then follow with a section containing some facts about the problem, setting the stage for our understanding of it. This section is not meant to replace other information about the problem from, for example, academic reports, newspapers, magazines, or television reportage. Facts in books such as this one must be somewhat selective, and they tend to age quickly. We therefore urge the reader to seek additional facts about all of the problems discussed in this book from other sources.

Next in each chapter, we review a range of theoretical approaches to the problem under discussion. We show how these approaches ask different questions and come to different conclusions. These theories help us organize our understanding of the problem. Since the theory sections are invariably brief, we urge the reader to explore further the assumptions and implications of the different approaches, as with much else in this book. Critical thinking questions at the end of each chapter will help the reader do this.

After the theoretical approaches follows, in each chapter, a section on the social consequences of the social problem in question. As we shall see throughout this book (often by way of mild repetition), most of the social problems we discuss are connected to one another, some more closely than others. For example, there is no adequate way to discuss work and unemployment without discussing poverty, no way to discuss family problems without also considering aging, gender inequality, and sexual orientation, and no way to discuss ageism without discussing stereotypes. A few general principles related to social inequality and social exclusion return time and again to inform our discussion.

Many serious social problems share a similar range of consequences. Problems such as exploitation, discrimination, and exclusion tend to impoverish people, isolate them, and give them less stake in the future of the community. The results of some social problems also commonly include crime, violence, addiction, stress, mental illness (for example, depression), and physical illness. We view these consequences as problems in their own right, and our goal would be for societies to solve them or at least reduce their prevalence. We therefore need to deal with the root causes of the social problems. These root causes are very much social in nature. As sociologists, we need to explain what occurs and why, and suggest how this situation might be improved. As citizens, we should try to understand the problems and their roots, and do what we can to improve the situation—for ourselves and for future generations.

We should say a few final words about the purpose of a book as general as this one. This text duplicates some of what students may have learned in an Introduction to Sociology course. The duplication is intentional. We want to refresh your memory of the basic principles of sociology before proceeding to a close discussion of social problems. Some instructors may even find that this book can substitute for a book that introduces first-time students to the field of sociology. In addition, this book covers a variety of problems, each briefly. This brevity is also intentional. We want to get students thinking in a particular way so that they can study these same problems, new problems, or changed problems on their own. We do not offer the last word on any social problem presented here—only the beginnings of a discussion informed by sociological principles.

We do not offer sociology as a cure-all. We emphasize how very difficult many social problems have been to solve and how little has been done about some of them. Like many of our colleagues in sociology, we understand the concerns of postmodernity. The 'project' of modernization that engaged thinkers and social practitioners for much of the last three centuries has taken a new turn. The horrors of the twentieth century shook our faith in reason and in the power of humans to build a better world using science and technology, social legislation, mass media, higher education, and secular values. No one who spends a few moments thinking about the Holocaust, the two world wars, the terrorism of September 2001 and the ensuing wars in Afghanistan, Iraq, and Lebanon, not to mention recurring crises in Darfur and the Congo and other parts of Africa, environmental degradation in many parts of the world, and continued practices of imperialist domination will readily indulge fantasies about the perfection, or even the perfectibility, of human societies. Part of the reason for this is that the solutions to social problems are often complex and costly. Another reason is that the solutions are political matters requiring strong commitment from society's elites.

In this respect, one of sociology's three founders was particularly prescient. Sociologist Max Weber saw the nightmare of modern society coming. His eyes were open to the 'iron cage' of modernity, especially to how bureaucracies and governments can enslave and torment humans more effectively than had ever been known before. Weber believed that bureaucracies would become all-powerful in society, and that their elites would end up largely serving their own interests, very often contrary to the interest of average people. Only those problems and solutions seen as important by powerful interests would be addressed in societies of the future (that is, in our time now). Another founder of sociology, Karl Marx, believed that communism would solve all problems of the human condition. He appears to have been wrong, although some still argue that his theories have never been put to a proper test in any society. Émile Durkheim was, of sociology's three leading figures during its developing years, the most optimistic, and therefore the most wrong about the twentieth century. He believed that societies change in a progressive direction, solving social problems over time through the differentiation and specialization of tasks, with modest negative side effects of anomie, or alienation, on the part of individuals because of the processes of social change.

Yet, despite having been shaken by the twentieth century and its horrors, we persist in our efforts. As long as we live, most of us strive to build a better world for our children, our community, and ourselves. It is in the hopes of continuing this optimistic effort that we, the authors, have written this book. We believe that social problems really do exist and do great harm. Furthermore, we believe that knowledge and purposeful informed action may still improve human life. This, then, is where we begin our study of social problems.

We dedicate this book to the memory of one of the two authors of the first edition, Jim Curtis, who passed away in May 2005. Though Albert Kwan, who assisted on the first edition, took over his role in revising the book for this edition, Jim's absence was felt at every stage. Jim, like sociology's founders, was profoundly optimistic about the ability of sociological research and teaching to improve the world. We hope this edition has lived up to his standards of scholarship and would have pleased him.

Pedagogical Features and Ancillaries

Pedagogical Features

A number of pedagogical features have been incorporated into the text to make it a more effective learning tool for students. Each chapter includes the following components:

- learning objectives;
- an introduction that sets the contents of the chapter in a wider context;
- a conclusion that summarizes key points discussed in the chapter;
- questions for critical thought;
- annotated recommended readings;
- annotated recommended websites;
- a glossary;
- references.

An appendix about research methods in sociology is included at the end of the text.

The text's well-developed art program is designed to make the book more accessible and engaging. Twenty-three photographs, 41 figures and charts, 19 tables, and 44 boxed inserts covering the full range of subject matter help clarify important concepts and make the subject come alive.

Ancillaries

TEST BANK

A Test Bank is available to instructors adopting the text. Each chapter in the Test Bank contains the following: 20 multiple-choice questions, 10 true/false questions, 10 short-answer questions, and 10 discussion questions.

INSTRUCTOR'S MANUAL

An Instructor's Manual is also available to adopters. Each chapter in the Instructor's Manual contains the following: chapter table of contents, summary, 5–10 learning objectives, 10 key concepts, and 10 audiovisual materials and teaching aids.

Instructors should contact their Oxford University Press representative regarding ancillary materials.

References

Beck, Ulrich. 1992. *Risk Society: Towards a New Modernity*, trans. Mark Ritter. London: Sage.

Foucault, Michel. 2000. *Power*, trans. Robert Hurley et al. New York: New Press.

Acknowledgements

Our first thank you is to the outstanding University of Toronto undergraduate students who helped us research this book. They include (in alphabetical order) Monica Beron, Gregory Brown, Dana Gore, Maygan Jorge, Weeda Mehran, Miranda Ng, Cheryl Pe, Ingrid Seo, Amy Umpleby, Wen Xiao, Hannah Yang, and Jing Jing Zeng. We want to single out undergraduate Leemauve Patrontasch, who produced large chunks of material for the new sexual orientation chapter. It's been a privilege and a pleasure to work with these talented young people—one of the two best parts of working on this book.

The other best part of this project was working with the people at Oxford University Press and their associates. Lisa Meschino, the acquisitions editor, has been a constant support on this project and many others; her unflagging good cheer has energized and encouraged us. Lisa Berland, the developmental editor, gave us a roadmap of changes we needed to make and pushed us hard to make them; her experience and wisdom was much appreciated. Richard Tallman, the copy editor, provided many wise insights and provocative challenges that forced us further to rethink our work. Finally, we want to thank Phyllis Wilson for taking care of the backstage practical matters at Oxford—making sure that all the pieces come together when and where they are supposed to.

We want to also thank our anonymous reviewers and our students who have read and responded to material in the first edition. They have all given us new ideas about what to discuss and how to discuss it most effectively. We've learned a lot writing this book, and it's been fun, too. All we can say now is, read the book and let us know what *you* think. We want this book to make your world clearer and more meaningful. If you have some ideas about how we can do that better in the next edition, send us an e-mail at: <lorne.tepperman@utoronto.ca>.

Lorne Tepperman
Albert Kwan
August 2006

What Are Social Problems?

What Is a 'Social Problem'?

When you hear the words **social problem**, what do you think of? Juvenile delinquents? Drug addicts? Homeless people? Sex workers? Or do you think about insider trading, tax fraud, arms sales, and the mass marketing of junk food? How about witchcraft, devil worship, interplanetary abduction, celebrity sex scandals, and the secret lives of powerful people? The words *social problem* are often applied to each of these topics and more.

Sociologists sometimes differ in what they believe makes up a social problem. The definition of 'social problem' is neither static nor absolute, and it has changed according to social and historical contexts. Moreover, even within a specific context, the definition people accept is based on both objective and subjective factors.

Objective factors refer to the existence of a social condition. The condition is a reality; it exists, and we can see that it is hurting people. We can study its effects without necessarily making any moral judgement. Cases of sexual abuse, environmental pollution, and racially motivated hate crimes in society are examples, however sobering, of such problems. They happen. As sociologists, we study what changes in social life cause the numbers or rates of these events to go up and down.

Subjective factors are people's *evaluations* of the situation. These factors include people's application of moral labels ('wrong', 'immoral', and so on) to particular acts or situations, as well as people's accounts of the reasons for these acts and situations. These definitions and accounts are accompanied by the belief that something should be done about the problems, that we should try to change these circumstances for the better. For example, most people in Canadian society today view rape, deforestation, and lynching as wrong and in need of eradication. This reflects their subjective estimate of these acts and situations as inappropriate in their society.

Thinking only of the subjective or evaluative dimension, one response to the question 'What is a social problem?' would be 'It depends'—on historical and cultural contexts, on people's values and beliefs. Taking this approach, although the specifics may vary from one group to the next, most sociologists would define a social problem as a social condition or behavioural pattern that a sizable portion of society views as harmful and warranting collective action to remedy. Bringing together both the objective and subjective elements, we can define a social problem as both a condition—an empirically observed condition that threatens the well-being of a significant segment of society—and as a process—the sequence of events by which members of society come to see a condition as a social problem.

So, in response to the question 'Do social problems exist?' there are two answers: Yes, and yes. Yes, many social conditions have observably harmful effects. And yes, people believe the conditions they have singled out as social problems cause harm and should be prevented or remedied.

Why Study Social Problems?

To anyone concerned with the state of the society in which we live, the answer to this question should be obvious. If social problems harm our social environment, a sense of civic duty directs us to be at least aware of these conditions or, better yet, to be actively involved in their correction.

Beyond this, studying social problems from a sociological perspective helps people to understand the complex ways in which social structure interacts with and influences members of society. It allows people to move beyond a purely common-sense approach to understanding their social environment. It allows them to use more powerful methods of investigation that reveal the multi-layered, multi-faceted, and elaborate ways that the social world around them—local, national, and global—is interconnected.

Through systematic research (discussed in the Appendix), researchers produce hypotheses, carry out experiments in controlled conditions (as much as possible), gather objective evidence, and draw careful and sound conclusions. We can then create theories or explanations from which we can hope to gain practical solutions and policies. Further, at the bottom of this research is an approach we call the 'sociological imagination'. In addition to being at the heart of the sociological discipline, this approach can be of great use to us in most aspects of our everyday lives.

Social Problems and the Sociological Imagination

According to sociologist C. Wright Mills (1959), the **sociological imagination** is the ability to see connections between one's own life and the social world in which one lives. This relationship between close-to-home aspects of social life and broad social trends, between private troubles and public issues, is the core subject matter of sociology. Further, this relationship is one of the most important things we need to know about if we want to understand how social problems affect our lives.

To use Mills's example, unemployed people may view their lack of employment as a private trouble that involves only them, their immediate family members, and their friends. They brought the problem on themselves, they may think. In fact, however, widespread unemployment—often the source of the individual's own private trouble, multiplied many thousands of times across other people's lives, too—is caused by factors such as economic recession, corporate downsizing, and advances in technology that replace people with machines. Indeed, plant closings and the resulting unemployment are part of a centuries-old workplace struggle between workers and the people who own and manage workplaces (Zipp and Lane, 1987).

Thus, unemployment is not merely a private trouble; it is also a public issue. The same is true of other social problems—crime and victimization, family issues, poverty, drug abuse, pollution, racism, and so on. The sociological imagination means stepping back to consider one's own place in the big picture, to make the connection between the conditions of one's own life and the larger social context in which that life is played out.

Sociologists make these connections by considering two levels of analysis, that is, by looking closely at two kinds of things. Microsociology, or *micro-level analysis*, focuses on the interaction between individuals in small groups. This approach, which studies people's understanding and experience of social problems at the local, personal level, is similar to that used by social psychologists. Macrosociology, or *macro-level analysis*, focuses on the societal level. It explores the ways in which social trends occurring within major bureaucratic organizations and social institutions, such as the economy or the government, affect the population as a whole. We need both levels of understanding for a proper understanding of social problems, and to see that many private troubles are essentially public issues.

Social Problems Research as a Moral Enterprise

Sociology is, for the most part, an engaged, progressive, and optimistic discipline founded on the notion that people can improve society through research and the application of research-based knowledge. So, many sociologists focus on research aimed, for example, at preventing genocide, fighting hunger, ending violence, reducing inequalities, and expanding democratic choices to create more freedom, pleasure, and power in individual lives (Risman and Tomaskovic-Devey, 2000).

Paradoxically, people's efforts to improve society sometimes backfire. Modernization itself and its associated social systems and products, such as the economic market system and bureaucratic organization, not only leave fundamental problems unresolved, they lack enough problem-solving mechanisms to ensure that we preserve life and quality of life. The cost may be mass deaths and even genocide—realities in the twentieth century (Wallimann, 1994). As others have remarked, modernization also carries harsh costs for the natural environment; we will discuss these costs in later chapters.

According to Montgomery (1998), five social innovations of the past millennium that people designed to solve problems have brought new problems that threaten all of our lives. These are the amoral state, the imperialistic corporation, the feudal crime organization, relativistic culture, and the self-interested individual. We will discuss each of these in the chapters that follow. As we will see, it will take more than a single unified policy of action to correct these five innovations and the problems they create.

Sociologists who study social problems often think of themselves as engaged in a moral enterprise whose goal is to improve human societies through social change (Alvarez, 2001). Much of the research that sociologists do on social problems is guided by seven value preferences:

Mills on 'the Sociological Imagination'
Neither the life of an individual nor the history of a society can be understood without understanding both. ... The sociological imagination enables its possessor to understand the larger historical scene in terms of its meaning for the inner life and the external career of a variety of individuals. ... The first fruit of this imagination—and the first lesson of the social science that embodies it—is the idea that the individual can understand his own experience and gauge his own fate only by locating himself within this period, that he can know his own chances in life only by becoming aware of those of all individuals in his circumstances.
Source: Mills (1959: 3-10).

- life over death;
- health over sickness;
- knowing over not knowing;
- co-operation over conflict;
- freedom of movement over physical restraint;
- self-determination over direction by others;
- freedom of expression over restraint of communication.

As a result, much of the research on social problems criticizes the existing social order. Much of the social problems literature shows a wish to change society, protect the vulnerable, and redress injustices. So, for example, Jim MacLaughlin (1996) writes about the ideological roots of anti-traveller (that is, anti-gypsy) sentiment in Ireland and its outcomes for the health and social exclusion of these people, and Emery Castle (1995) writes about the hidden complexity and vulnerability of rural society in North America and the tendency to ignore rural problems because of stereotypes and mythology about rural life.

Like much research into social problems, these authors are concerned with myths, ideologies, and stereotypes that perpetuate harmful conditions for vulnerable peoples. A related concern is the noted tendency for 'public issues' to be turned into 'private troubles'. The public and public officials often wrongly see a social problem as the responsibility of the sufferers, who are blamed for having these problems. Consider depressive disorders, which are a major public health problem today. They occur often and produce severe suffering for the people affected and their families, leading to higher risks of death, disability, and secondary illness. For various reasons, including the aging of the population and the extended life expectancy of people suffering from chronic physical disorders, the frequency of depressive disorders will increase in years to come (Sartorius, 2001).

Social problems researchers often express concern that sufferers are dealing with their problems in idiosyncratic ways that may not work as desired. Michael Montagne (1992), for example, notes the medicalization of poorly defined health disorders— depression, chronic pain, and chronic fatigue, but also male pattern baldness, small women's breasts, and obesity—have led to increased self-medication. When biomedical explanations and cures fail to help, consumers are prompted to self-medicate to achieve symptomatic relief. Self-medication may include the excessive use of drugs and alcohol, often with harmful outcomes. For example, alcoholism, birth defects, drunk driving, fighting, and rowdy behaviour, with health problems such as liver disease, are all common results of drinking too much distilled spirits and beer. Even excessive wine consumption has these effects, though fewer people recognize it (Klein and Pittman, 1998).

The social costs of self-medication are huge, especially when they include the use of addictive drugs, such as illegal opium derivatives and legal substances such as Valium, Prozac, and other feel-good anti-depressants. Though most people view the regular use of opiates as a social and health problem, they rarely stop to estimate the cost. One survey aimed at estimating the social costs of untreated opiate addiction in Toronto (Wall et al., 2000) showed that the annual social cost caused by a sample of 114 regular opiate users amounted to more than $5 million. The costs break down as follows: crime victimization (45 per cent), law enforcement (42 per cent), productivity losses (7 per cent), and healthcare use (6 per cent). Given roughly 8,000 to 13,000 opiate users in Toronto, the estimated social cost of this addiction is between $43 and $69 per Toronto resident per year.

Some social problems researchers criticize society's dominant institutions for their failure to recognize or deal adequately with important problems. They argue that actions should be taken, and the right actions at the right time can have enormous effects. As an example of the latter, consider workplace smoking bans. Where these have been carried out, they have succeeded in bringing about changes in the behaviour and attitudes of smokers. Also, smokers' levels of acceptance of these rules increase following their adoption, and attitude changes follow changes in behaviour. Thus, large-scale patterns of constraints and opportunities that influence choices and actions *do* affect harmful behaviours and attitudes (Owen et al., 1991).

However, dominant institutions often fail to act as effectively as they should. For example, they insufficiently fund useful programs. Lisbeth Schorr (1991) notes that the kinds of programs that work best in reducing problems of teenagers—high rates of school dropout, pregnancy, violent crime, and the beginnings of long-term dependency on welfare—give access to various services, stress trust and respect, are community-based, and recognize the needs of those most at risk. However, such programs are often at odds with the health, mental health, social service, and educational institutions that might provide such services, as well as the institutions that fund them.

Social problems researchers point out the social-structural conditions that make people vulnerable. Consider medical patients and their needs for social support. Some suffer from *social insufficiency*—inadequate networks of social support and the incapacity of their familiar surroundings to guarantee and satisfy all their needs (Carmona et al., 1999). Homeless people are another vulnerable population with too few social supports. They typically suffer from a variety of problems, including unemployment, poverty, physical impairments, substance abuse, and mental illness. Mental disorders are a major factor leading to (as well as resulting from) homelessness—by one estimate, two-thirds of homeless people suffer from mental illness. No less important is their social isolation and the insufficiency of help they receive as outpatients (Kellinghaus et al., 1999).

Social problems researchers also point out social-structural factors that increase the likelihood of problem behaviours. For example, peer influences are associated with health-risk behaviours, including early and risky sexual activity, tobacco use, alcohol use, and marijuana use (Beal et al., 2001). Risky sexual behaviour may lead to teenage parenthood, which reduces the likelihood of school completion and financial independence (Hoffman et al., 1993). Dropping out of school early also substantially increases the risk of early parenthood (Gest et al., 1999), as do low socio-economic status, low academic achievement, and low popularity.

Furthermore, social problems researchers also point out new concerns that, if left unattended, may become serious social problems in the future. Here are a few examples:

- *Genetic engineering.* Potential problems include the creation and later escape from the laboratory of dangerous biological forms, uncontrollable experimentation, and the emergence of a new eugenics movement (McFalls et al., 1987).
- *Unregulated antibiotics.* The misuse of antibiotics by physicians, pharmacists, and the public, the emergence of poor-quality drugs, and conditions such as crowding, lack of hygiene, and poor hospital infection control may lead to the evolution and global spread of new, resistant bacteria (Isturiz and Carbon, 2000).
- *Manufactured longevity.* Advances in biomedical sciences that add more years to life expectancy in industrial countries have resulted in unprecedented rates of survival into older ages. Although longer life is in itself a positive social development, higher life expectancies have also produced new issues of caregiving (including family organization) and quality of life (Hassan, 2000).

■ *Global refugees.* More than 15 million refugees are scattered around the world, most of them in poor developing or underdeveloped countries. Suffering from various social, financial, psychological, and health problems, they threaten to destabilize the countries that have granted them asylum (Clinton-Davis and Fassil, 1992). As well, refugee camps may serve as seedbeds for violent terrorism.

Social Construction

This book is organized on the idea that there is wide agreement about the most pressing problems in our society. In fact, most 'social problems' or 'social issues' textbooks talk about all of the topics in this book, suggesting there is a consensus in the sociological research and teaching community about what the most serious or urgent social issues are. Further, this consensus is stable over time. Most of the same topics—with a few exceptions—were viewed and discussed as social problems 50 or more years ago. Finally, we will note repeatedly throughout this book that the social problems we are discussing often have significant social effects for their victims. They even have significant health effects, and that is telling. Though people sometimes imagine or exaggerate social (or psychological) concerns, they are less likely to imagine or exaggerate health concerns; and in any event, health claims are open to clinical verification. We can readily confirm that a given problem causes death, illness, malnutrition, addiction, depression, or any of several other health effects of bad social conditions.

So, for all these reasons, we often feel comfortable talking about social problems as though they 'really' exist. However, this approach to problems is not the only possible approach. It is just one approach to reality—an approach based on the view that an external world exists separate from the way we represent it in thoughts, language, beliefs, pictures, maps, and so on. This 'realist' position is sometimes called the 'essentialist' position, meaning that social problems are problems-in-their-essence—self-evidently and demonstrably problems, with real and serious outcomes.

Yet, there are weaknesses to this approach. First, we know that social 'reality' in general is a social construct—a set of ideas, beliefs, and views that is infinitely flexible and open to interpersonal influence. This is the central finding of social science research on religion, culture, ideology, mass communication, propaganda, and the like. The widely varying ways people think about reality are amply clear in historical and cross-national research on any topic. Human beings invent all kinds of 'stories' about reality. These stories may be real in their consequences—that is, people will act as though they are true, and these actions will have real effects—but the stories themselves are not necessarily or demonstrably factual.

Second, we know that some social 'problems' of the past are no longer considered problems. Behaviour that in the past would have been considered immoral, and for that reason considered problematic—for example, premarital sex, drinking, cursing, failing to respect one's elders—is no longer considered immoral or, at least, no longer considered a social problem. Finally, we have all become familiar with the work of professional 'spin doctors'—in politics, advertising, and elsewhere—whose job it is to promote a self-interested concern, belief, or wish, often at the expense of the truth. Lying has become full-time professional work for many of the most successful people in our society. Only the most naive person would believe everything she or he hears or reads.

So, it takes no stretch of the imagination to realize that at least some of the supposed social problems we will discuss are not really problems—they are merely 'social constructions'. This approach to understanding reality, called social constructionism, rests on a sociological theory of knowledge stated by Peter L. Berger and Thomas Luckmann in *The Social Construction of Reality* (1966). Social construction often involves stereotyping and classifying some people as deviants (Goode and Ben Yahuda, 1994). People whom sociologists call **moral entrepreneurs** do this construction work; they may be members of the grassroots community, elites, or interest groups. Constructing problems involves **claims-making**, a procedure that describes, explains, and blames people who are involved with the problem.

The goal of **social constructionism** is to examine the ways people interact to create a shared social reality. Berger and Luckmann argue that *all* knowledge—including the most taken-for-granted knowledge of everyday life—is created, preserved, and spread by social interaction. However natural or obvious an idea may seem to the people who accept it, that idea, according to the social constructionist approach, is just an invention of a particular culture or society.

It is easy to see that this approach grows out of symbolic interactionism and the early twentieth-century work of George Herbert Mead. Mead (1934) wrote that children learn to interact with others by learning a shared system of symbols, including language, which allows them to share and negotiate meanings. With shared meanings, they can play together, perform complementary roles, and relate to the social group as a 'generalized other'. For Mead, this capability is the basis of all social order. Shared meanings (including shared symbols) make social interaction possible, and interaction allows people to co-operate and influence one another.

A generation later, another symbolic interactionist, Erving Goffman (1959), proposed that we can usefully think of society as a theatre in which people compose and perform social scripts together. We even come to believe in the truth of the roles we are asked to play; often, we become the person people think we are. In the end, social life is little more than a set of constructed, directed performances. Inside our social roles, we struggle to find and express (or hide and protect) our true identities.

In the eyes of social constructionists, human beings react not to physical objects and events themselves, but to the shared meanings of objects and events. These meanings are not essential features of the objects and events, but socially imposed or constructed meanings. In our society, a red rose is considered beautiful and romantic, while a daisy is simple and a cabbage, ugly. That's a social construction. (If you doubt the social power of this construction, give your loved one a dozen cabbages on Valentine's Day.) Thus, the meaning of anything, including a social problem, is the product of the dominant cultural and symbolic practices in a group or society.

Burr (1995) identifies four basic assumptions of the social constructionist position:

- *A critical stance is made towards taken-for-granted knowledge.* The world does not present itself objectively to the observer but is known through human experience, which is largely influenced by language.
- *Historical and cultural specificity is recognized.* The categories in language used to classify things emerge from the social interaction within a group of people at a particular time and in a particular place. Categories of understanding, then, are situational.
- *Knowledge is sustained by social process.* How reality is understood at a given moment is determined by the conventions of communication in force at that time. The stability of social life determines how concrete our knowledge seems to be.
- *Knowledge and social action go together.* Reality is socially constructed by interconnected patterns of communication behaviour. Within a social group or culture, real-

Goffman on Constructed Realities

The past life and current round of activity of a given performer typically contain at least a few facts which, if introduced during the performance, would discredit or at least weaken the claims about self that the performer was attempting to project . . . . These facts may involve well-kept dark secrets or negative-valued characteristics that everyone can see but no one refers to. When such facts are introduced, embarrassment is the usual result. . . . [S]uch disruptions of projections may be called 'faux pas'. Where a performer unthinkingly makes an intentional contribution which destroys his own team's image we may speak of 'gaffes' or 'boners'. Source: Goffman (1959: 209-10).

ity is defined not so much by individual acts, but by complex and organized patterns of ongoing actions.
(source: www.psy.dmu.ac.uk/michael/soc_con_disc.htm)

In short, when people interact, they share their views of reality and act on these shared views. Since people negotiate their shared common-sense knowledge, it can be said that reality is socially constructed. As an approach, social constructionism looks at the ways people create and institutionalize social reality. And when people act on their interpretations and their knowledge of this 'reality', they reinforce it or lock it in. It becomes habit and seems natural, even inevitable.

As for social problems: the social constructionist position is that social problems 'exist' when 'claims-makers' or 'moral entrepreneurs' succeed in persuading the public that they do. The social constructionist position is interested in answering questions like: How do claims-makers make successful claims? What kinds of problems or situations support claims-making? What kinds of people, with what kinds of motives, make claims? What leads people to hold certain kinds of belief, not others; and under what circumstances (if any) is it possible to argue with or disprove these beliefs?

The social constructionist position is built on a weak foundation, however, and we must admit it. The view that belief and perception are socially constructed is, ultimately, an attack on empiricism and the authority of science to say what is real or unreal. In our culture, scientific 'facts' are given more credibility than religious or artistic or personal opinion, because they are supposedly grounded in rationality and empirical observation. Perhaps some (or many) scientific theories—even scientific facts—are wrong, biased, misconceived, or ill-measured. Perhaps water doesn't boil at 100 degrees Celsius, and apples actually fall upward into the sky. However, if we chip away at the principle of a fixed, scientifically knowable reality, all views of reality become equally good and all equally bad. Then, no view or course of action is privileged or legitimate. Under this condition, we become paralyzed by an inability to decide; we may give in to the will of the most powerful. So, the social constructionist position has no anchor, and therefore it is socially dangerous even as it is socially liberating. Yet we study social constructionism because it is partly right.

The social constructionist approach to social problems gained major ground with Spector and Kitsuse's (1977) theory of social problems as claims-making activities. These authors proposed a natural history or chronological model that has proved especially useful, since it reminds us of the stages of problem development. Some recent uses of this approach include the following:

■ Wagner (2001) shows the change in ideas about disability and rehabilitation between 1950 and 1990. Following Spector and Kitsuse, she identifies the (a) primary stakeholders in disability discourse, (b) time periods when critical changes occurred in rehabilitation practice, and (c) emerging new concepts that can describe changes in rehabilitation practice. Four categories of stakeholders are described as care providers, consumers, government officials, and investors.

■ Bohon and McPherson (2006) note that though estimates of the undocumented immigrant population in the United States are always tentative, governmental and non-governmental agencies have reported similar estimates in recent years. On the other hand, the numbers reported by major newspapers in the Southeast are sometimes almost 2 million higher than official estimates. The authors argue that such overestimation is part of the print media's effort to socially construct an emerging illegal immigration problem in the Southeast US.

■ Swygart-Hogaugh (2005) analyzes anti-prostitution crusades in Chicago during the Progressive Era, using a social constructionist approach to explore how crusaders created a discourse of prostitution as a social problem. She finds that larger debates during the Progressive Era shaped the claims crusaders made. However, often crusaders' claims also reflected their particular values, interests, and agendas.

■ Coltrane and Adams (2003) note that divorce rates have been stable or dropping for two decades, yet Americans continue to worry about the state of marriage. The authors study how the divorce 'problem' has been framed by organizations promoting conservative family values who are inclined to portray divorce as a symptom of breakdown of the moral order. Today, some social science experts portray children as victims of divorce. Such portrayals serve to legitimate the political goals of specific interest groups and hide basic issues of gender inequality.

Early social constructionists in the tradition of Spector and Kitsuse often did little to situate claims-making in its social context. They paid little attention to the motives, meanings, and intentions that went into claims-making activity. More recent research has treated ideologies and interests as causes of claims-making and critical factors that make some claims more saleable than others. Another development has been the growing interest among social constructionists in the use and abuse of statistical data to provide claims with an aura of precision and accuracy (on this, see Best, 2004). In this respect, we can view social statistics as a kind of rhetoric in a scientific, supposedly fact-obsessed age.

Throughout this book we will have to ask ourselves, about any particular problem, is this a real problem or is it merely (or in large part) a social construction? We will have several reasons for doing this. First, as sociologists, we need to have the clearest possible understanding of reality, even if our own understanding challenges 'common sense', prevailing wisdom, or the dominant ideology on a given issue. Second, as sociologists, we are curious to learn as much as we can about the social processes by which real social problems, and imagined social problems, come into being. We need to be able to make theories about these historical or developmental issues, since by doing so we learn a great deal about how society and social theory work.

Finally, and most importantly, we need to know which social problems need immediate, concerted action and which ones can be safely ignored. Poverty, for example, continues to interfere with the health, education, and social integration of hundreds of thousands of young Canadians and it cannot be ignored. We need to help solve the problem of poverty in Canada because doing so is fair and just. Equally important, a failure to help solve this problem will mean millions of added person-years of misery, unemployment, crime, addiction, and violence during your own lifetime. We can choose to ignore this problem now and pay for it continuously over the next 50 years, or try to solve the problem now. By contrast, it is less obvious that we need to act as decisively to stem the outbreaks of, say, devil worship or witchcraft. Though some people may feel concerned about the dangers posed by devil worship, witchcraft, UFOs, premarital sex, and rude behaviour by young people, there is—so far—no proof that a failure to take action will mean millions of added person-years of misery. In a world of pressing concerns, some are simply less pressing than others; we need to prioritize our concerns and our efforts.

So, we will need to keep asking, is X a 'real' problem or just a 'socially constructed' problem. More precisely, we will have to ask, to what degree is problem X 'real' and to what degree is it 'socially constructed'? And, even if X is a real problem, in what ways do the usual techniques of social construction help to put the problem on the public agenda for discussion, debate, and legislative action?

Warnings, Panics, and Claims

While many issues that we are concerned about today are issues that concerned people 50 years ago, others have gained our attention in a way they did not a couple of generations ago. For example, today we consider family violence (Walker, 1990) and child sexual abuse (Scott, 1995) to be legitimate social problems that need public attention. They 'became' problems not because their occurrence increased, but because people became more concerned about them. Social issues are constructed by claims-making to invoke intense feelings towards perceived harm done to people of the community.

Some sensed problems create intense feelings of concern that, viewed from a distance, are more than one might expect from the harm posed by the threat. In some parts of the population, abortion and welfare fraud fall into that category. Another example is the recent concern over witchcraft, devil worship, and satanic rituals (see, e.g., Lippert, 1990). Sociologists refer to short-lived, intense periods of concern as **moral panics**, and to the people held responsible for the sensed threats as *folk devils*. Though moral panics, like fads, are short-lived, they leave a legacy, whether as laws, stereotypes, cultural beliefs, or changed attitudes (Goode and Ben Yahuda, 1994).

Claims-making, intended to bring a perceived problem to the public agenda, relies on common rhetorical idioms and claims-making styles that reflect and legitimize core cultural values (McMullan and Eyles, 1999). Often the rhetoric used invokes certain types of risk and risk avoidance as pre-eminent goals. For example, we often call on people to take action to protect their country, their children's health, or their community. Particular images or icons may be used to sway public opinion. The media play a large part in shaping public opinion of a problem. In fact, popular opinions and beliefs today are more often shaped by media depiction than by first-hand experience, so how the media depict a problem plays a crucial part in how the public will respond (Szasz, 1995).

Part of the media's influence comes through putting 'problems' on the agenda for repeated discussion in news reports. Some comes through portraying the problem in particular ways, with heroes and villains in fictionalized stories. Some media portrayal is implicit, as in talk shows. We learn community standards of behaviour—what is deviant and normal, praiseworthy and shocking—as members of the audience (Abt and Seesholtz, 1994). Here, the hosts are moral entrepreneurs and claims-makers, but the studio audience (and the home audience) is the court of public opinion.

Sometimes, ordinary people make the claims. We learn how to tell stories that describe or explain problems, and how to blame others for these problems; however, some people learn these skills especially well. For example, high school debaters learn how to take both sides of an argument, express ideas with which they do not necessarily agree, and present powerful if sometimes questionable evidence. This teaches them how to engage in social problem discourse and trains them for moral entrepreneurship (Fine, 2000). They then hone these skills in law schools across the nation.

Sometimes interest groups are successful at bringing issues into the social realm by redefining and renegotiating previously sinful acts, thus making them a more acceptable social practice. Interest groups that have a particular view of the problem and its solution make some of the claims. For example, COYOTE (Call Off Your Old Tired Ethics) has sought to redefine prostitution as a social problem, removing it from the arenas of sin and crime. COYOTE proposes that prostitution should be considered work, not crime; that prostitutes choose to work at their occupation; and that we should protect that occupation, as work that people have a right to choose, like any other respectable service occupation. This organization has achieved success by becoming a link between public health agencies and sex workers, connecting the problems of prostitutes to women's rights issues, and engaging law enforcement groups in debate over criminal laws (Jenness, 1990).

The organization FARM has been less successful in influencing public opinion. With the final goal of cutting out the use of cows, pigs, and chickens as human food, FARM (Farm Animal Reform Movement) adopted the short-term goal of reducing the suffering of farm animals by closing down factories that use modern intensive farming techniques. However, claims about the suffering of animals did not persuade the public, so FARM began, in the early 1990s, to focus attention on health, longevity, and environmental endangerment in their reason for rejecting factory farming. These claims gained wider support for the organization, though it has not yet succeeded in its long-term goals (Kunkel, 1995).

In the past, religious leaders were heavily involved in moral claims-making. Today, they have an ever-diminishing influence, at least in Canada. People with professional and scientific expertise are much more often allowed to make claims. For example, increasingly since the 1980s, police elites (for example, chief constables) have gained the power to legitimately name, diagnose, and classify social problems (Loader and Mulcahy, 2001).

Medical doctors have continued to exercise control over defining many personal and social problems. Medical claims-makers concentrate on detecting, diagnosing, and treating problems of vulnerable people. In emergency homeless shelters, for example, they teach homeless people to look within themselves for the cause of their homelessness, and 'treatment' concentrates on reforming and governing the self (Lyon-Callo, 2000). Adolescent episodes of 'acting up' and 'acting out' have been medicalized under the rubric of *conduct disorder*, a psychiatric category with broad professional diagnostic criteria (Potter, 2000). Implicit in such a medical assessment is the notion that we can study and fix teen misbehaviour without reference to the social or interaction context within which it occurs.

Sometimes, organization insiders (for example, in nuclear power or tobacco)—called **whistle-blowers**—aid in claims-making. Whistle-blowers are unusual claims-makers in that they gain credibility for speaking out contrary to their own interests and those of their employer, but they lack the organizational power to promote their definitions of the social problem. A few prominent whistle-blowers, blacklisted in their industries, turn to social movement organizations for employment (Bernstein, 1991).

Today, other problems are under construction, including concerns about workplace violence (Mullen, 1997), stalking (Emerson et al., 1998; Morewitz, 2001), money laundering (Nichols, 1997), the failure to disclose homosexuality (Cain, 1989), and drowsiness or sleep disorder (Kroll-Smith, 2000). Since social problems arise out of claims-making, and since claims-making is a social activity that occurs within a historical context, we must understand the construction and spread of social problems within their historical context.

The Historical Context of Social Problems

Many issues that were considered social problems a century ago have changed since then. This is most clear in areas of human activity that give pleasure (such as sex) or alter consciousness (such as drugs). The definition of *social problems* has changed dramatically in these battlegrounds.

The Beginnings of Alcohol

While no one knows when beverage alcohol was first used, it was presumably the result of a fortuitous accident. The discovery of late Stone Age beer jugs has established the fact that intentionally fermented beverages existed at least as early as the Neolithic period (c. 10,000 BC) . . . . The earliest alcoholic beverages may have been made from berries or honey . . . and wine-making may have originated in the wild grape regions of the Middle East. The Old Testament (Genesis 9:20) asserts that Noah planted a vineyard on Mt Ararat in what is now Saudi Arabia. In Sumeria, beer and wine were used for medicinal purposes as early as 2,000 BC.

Source: Adapted from Hanson (1995).

In England during the early Industrial Revolution, for example, there was a surge in gin drinking that some called a 'gin epidemic'. The underlying problems were overcrowding and poverty, both of which led to social unrest. This unrest led to increased drunkenness when cheap gin became available after Parliament did away with the distilling monopolies that had kept prices high. Reformers, ignoring the social causes of unrest, focused their attention on gin drinking by the poor. They feared it would endanger England's wealth by weakening and reducing its workforce. The response was to pass a Gin Act in 1743 and a Tippling Act in 1751 that raised gin prices and lessened consumption (Abel, 2001).

In the United States, attitudes towards alcohol also varied over time. In the seventeenth and eighteenth centuries, almost everyone held alcohol in high regard and consumed it. Campaigns against alcohol began in the nineteenth century, with temperance supporters holding alcohol responsible for most major social problems. They were briefly successful in having alcohol banned in the 1920s, a topic we discuss in Chapter 3, on alcohol and drug abuse.

Since the 1930s, the focus of national concern has been on treating alcoholics. As in eighteenth-century England and nineteenth-century United States, most people today continue to blame drinking and individual weaknesses for many problems that have broader political and economic causes (Levine, 1984).

In North America today, many people still fear epidemics of drug-induced misbehaviour. Two centuries ago in England, it was the gin epidemic. In the 1980s and 1990s, it was the 'crack attack', a supposed epidemic of drug abuse. Drug scares today are characterized by anti-drug extremism, by the association of a certain drug with various social problems, and by linking that same drug to a subordinate minority group. In the crack scare, between 1986 and 1992, drug use was used as a scapegoat to account for lower-class unemployment, poverty, violence, and crime. This served to explain away growing urban poverty and relieved politicians of having to address the real issues. The scare had secondary outcomes, including increases in drug use resulting from exaggerated and dramatized media coverage, declines in health services aimed at helping addicts, and neglect of the social problems that inspire drug use (Reinarman and Levine, 1995).

Abortion is another area in which the definition of a social problem has changed over time. In the mid-nineteenth century, the United States criminalized the previously unregulated practice of abortion; in the early twentieth century, Sweden liberalized a previously harsh law against abortion. These different policies may have been based on opposed understandings of abortion or may both have stemmed from the same concern that unlicensed abortionists were killing women through botched abortions. Today, Sweden remains one of the most liberal countries where abortion—and sexuality more generally—is concerned (Linders, 1998). The United States has decriminalized abortion, but abortion is still hard to access in some regions and the topic remains morally charged in many parts of the country.

Along similar lines, out-of-wedlock pregnancy changed its public meaning in Canada and the United States in the last half of the twentieth century. Today, most people no longer view the pregnancy of single women as morally disgraceful; however, views and policies still vary depending on the pregnant woman's race (Solinger, 1992). Poor black US women are viewed more critically than poor white women, let alone middle-class white women, and teenage mothers are viewed most critically of all.

Rates of teenage pregnancy are high and increasing in the United States compared to other industrial nations. Americans, therefore, are much more likely than Canadians or Dutch to view unplanned pregnancy as a 'very big problem' (Delbanco et al., 1997).

Two-thirds of Americans mistakenly believe that more women have unplanned pregnancies today than 10 years ago (Mauldon and Delbanco, 1997); in fact, only the teenage portion is increasing. Researchers relate this latter trend to poverty, hopelessness, and an absence of sex education in the schools.

Considering these changes in sexual behaviour, social conservatives have called for a renewal of 'family values'. For example, David Popenoe (1993) states that American family decline since 1960 has been extraordinarily steep and its social outcomes serious, especially for children. He argues that families have lost their purpose, power, and authority, that familism as a cultural value has diminished, and that people have become less willing to invest time, money, and energy in family life, turning instead to investment in themselves. Some commentators have responded by saying that such diagnoses of moral and social decline are wrong and have harmful results. These diagnoses divide people into righteous 'us' and wicked 'them', and when these lines are drawn, they throw progressive thinking and social justice out the window (Morone, 1996).

These brief examples show that historical changes in the perception and treatment of social issues—changes in their problematization and normalization over time—are often connected to social and cultural conflicts in the society. Often these conflicts are over social inequality, whether in regard to social class, ethnicity and 'race', age, or gender. As groups conflict, people use moral rhetoric to exclude, punish, and blame one another. The powerful most often penalize the least powerful.

The rhetoric used is particular to the culture and period. So, for example, themes involving health and purity were common to many movements against alcohol, drugs, smoking, and sex in the last century or two (Wagner, 1995). Increasingly, with the rise to dominance of science and medicine, we have seen social problems become medicalized: social problems are often cast in an individualistic medical model. The patient is blamed for his or her sickness and then told to change. Occasionally, solutions to social problems are cast in the public health mode: the goal is to prevent the illness through social or personal action and, if necessary, lessen the harm associated with it.

The tendency to medicalize problems fits the individualistic tendency in our culture that holds people responsible for their own success and failure. For many, 'self-esteem' and 'self-help' are seen as the keys to overcoming both personal problems and social problems. In pop psychology, all social problems are thought to stem from relationships and from problems between individuals (Cravens, 1997). This approach stresses self-efficacy and self-esteem as personal qualities, independent of such aspects of social structure as control over and access to power and the social assets that individuals need to take certain actions (Franzblau and Moore, 2001).

In this book, we will see that to understand social problems and their history, we must understand the social structures within which they rise, flower, and fall.

Social Organization, Culture, and Social Problems

Sociology is the study of social organization and culture. *Social organization* is any enduring, predictable pattern of social relations among people in society. This is the basic organization of a society, and it takes form in social institutions, formal organizations, smaller **social groups**, and **roles**. *Social institutions*—stable, well-acknowledged large-scale social relationships that endure over time—include family, the economy, education, politics, religion, mass media, medicine, and science and technology. They provide the bedrock on which people base the rest of social life.

Social institutions are made up of *social groups*, two or more individuals who have a specific, common identity and who interact in a reciprocal *social relationship*. The associations between politician and constituent member, doctor and patient, teacher and student, and parent and child are examples of social relationships that characterize political, medical, educational, and family social groups and organizations. In turn, these social groups and organizations sum across whole populations to form their respective social institutions.

Social organization refers to how society is organized, from a dyadic (two-person) relationship all the way up to a broad social institution. *Culture*, meanwhile, refers to the meanings and lifestyles set up by human populations. These include beliefs, values, **symbols**, and **norms**. Together, these divide human populations into unique societies.

Social organization and culture are double-edged swords with respect to social problems. They are centrally involved in the development and maintenance of social problems, and they hold hope, in the form of socio-cultural change directed by human collective action, for solutions to social problems. Society and culture also define how we come to think about our own troubles and the social problems that they represent.

Four aspects of social organization and culture limit people's opportunities to get what they want out of life, whether it is to get out of poverty and continue to avoid it or to escape other negative situations. These mechanisms that cause an individual's continued involvement with social problems are *exclusion*, *disability*, *decoupling*, and *scarcity*.

Exclusion

Power is often used to exclude people from desirable situations, and exclusion rewards people unequally for equal performances. Organizations practise exclusion against other organizations, ethnic groups practise it against other ethnic groups, social classes practise it against other classes, and individuals practise it against other individuals. Every exclusion, whether motivated by fear, stereotyping, or mere economic interest, is an exercise of power.

If power is nothing else, it is the ability to make rules about who will get the biggest share of social goods: wealth, authority, and prestige (Murphy, 1982). Every group has an elite; the top few percentages in a society, business, university, or political party is that group's elite. The idea of a fixed group of people dominating politics and economics may go against the view that Canadians are equal, but nevertheless that is the reality. As John Porter (1965) and Wallace Clement (1975) have showed, there is a socially cohesive Canadian ruling class. The corporate elite own and control the largest businesses. They contribute to political campaigns, lobby elected officials, and influence the media—which the corporate elite also own. The elite can also embarrass politicians by publicly questioning their competence or honesty.

We also find exclusion in the job market, where professional associations and unions use exclusionary practices to protect their members, their jobs, and their salaries. Degrees from medical schools are especially valuable in this way since almost no doctors are unemployed or poorly paid. We see exclusion at work in the continuing battles over health care—the debates about who shall pay and who is entitled to receive how much, and the exclusion of such competitors as chiropractors, homeopaths, and midwives from public recognition and coverage under public health plans. Professional associations help middle-class people protect middle-class incomes; unions help working-class people protect working-class incomes. Professional associations use special means to protect their members. The example of medicine shows that successful professionalization gives restricted groups the power to exclude others and to control public and private spending on specialized services (see Chapter 10). The very notion of a 'career' implies processes of exclusion. It has occurred because of the growth of a new middle class, the expansion of higher education, and the spread of a new demand for more credentials for more people (Bledstein, 1976).

Ethnic and religious communities also use exclusion to protect themselves and advance their own interests. Despite Canada's official policies of multiculturalism and equality, minority ethnic group members often face serious discrimination on their arrival in this country. So, they organize themselves into ethnic communities, using **institutional completeness** to keep their identity and preserve group survival (Breton et al., 1991). For some groups, residential or occupational segregation may be most important. However, retention and use of the ethnic language also plays a key part in keeping the community together.

The expectation that ethnic occupational inequality would dwindle or disappear as ethnic groups gained educational credentials and became culturally assimilated into Canadian society has proved illusory. Investing in human capital (for example, higher education) has not led to equality for racial minorities. Many, especially Native peoples, who have been the targets of aggressive policies intended to result in their assimilation, have resisted and survived as distinct peoples. Most ethnic and racial minorities are still not represented among the economic elite.

This is not to deny that some ethnic communities and some individuals within those communities have prospered. The strategy the most successful among them have employed, both to insulate their members and to promote their interests in the wider community, is the practice of exclusion. Aboriginal people, however, have little opportunity to practise exclusion in their own interest. Although there has been much progress in educational achievement, employment, and income, their social status and outcomes continue to lag significantly behind those of white Canadians. While the number of Aboriginal people completing high school has increased since the 1960s, racial differences at the post-secondary level remain large. Further, education does not produce the same income returns for Aboriginal people as for whites. Thus, although more Aboriginal men and women have moved into the middle class, economic opportunities for Aboriginal and white Canadians remain unequal.

Disability

Socialization teaches us how and why to conform to cultural values and social norms. Some people receive socialization that teaches them *not* to compete for society's most valued goals. This crippling socialization is *social disability—disability* for short. For many people, disability means learning ways of thinking about themselves that make them less than they might otherwise be. This socialization leads to lower goals, a lack of assertiveness, even withdrawal from competition.

The common element is our society's *dominant ideology*—specifically, the ideas that our culture promotes about success and failure. For instance, when asked whether they think hard work or good luck or help from others accounts for success, about two-thirds of respondents in a national Canadian survey say 'hard work' (Curtis and Grabb, 1999). People's thinking is largely *ideological*, based on beliefs that we keep insulated from reality and from everyday experience. Others have called these same beliefs the principles of 'laissez-faire capitalism', 'liberal democracy', and the 'liberal ideology'.

Liberal democracy rests on (supposedly) free choice, free competition, and a free market in labour, goods, and ideas (Macpherson, 1965). We find freedom of this kind in societies with a capitalist economy, universal suffrage, and two or more political parties. This is why a person who is unable to find work is likely to blame his or her own failings rather than the high unemployment rate, discrimination, business mismanagement, or poor handling of the economy by the government. It explains why a dual-income family struggling unsuccessfully to pay its bills may turn its aggression inward, one spouse against the other spouse, parent against child, child against parent. In this way, family members end up destroying their family rather than blaming exploitative employers or bad government—not easy targets to attack.

Michael Mann (1970) argues that false consciousness, a Marxist concept whereby the ruling ideology is accepted and espoused by those who do not benefit from it, disables voters. The main political parties lead voters to believe in vague political philosophies that contradict voters' everyday experience and support the status quo; the politicians appeal to patriotism, tradition, harmony, and national unity to mask their failings to achieve greater economic opportunities for the broad base of citizens. Thus, voters are disabled by misdirection and by their own optimism and gullibility.

People are also disabled by failed attempts to change their circumstances. Below these types of false consciousness—a willingness to blame oneself, a readiness to reinvest in the status quo, a tendency to see public issues as personal problems—we find a more general set of illusory beliefs about social inequality. This 'split personality' defence gives many people temporary relief from the effects of a cruel social order. Defences they erect against feelings of worthlessness and powerlessness allow life to go on; however, these defences also keep people from fighting the structured inequality that is at the root of their troubles.

Marxists—whose views are strongly allied with those of a sociological theoretical perspective known as conflict theory (described below)—believe that people are also disabled by religion. Their ideological father, Karl Marx, characterized religion as an 'opiate' of the people in that it deadened them to the pain of inequality and injustice. For example, Mohammed Fazel and David Young (1988) found that Tibetan refugees in India display more life satisfaction than local Indian Hindus, despite language problems and fewer financial assets. Though both the Hindus and the Tibetans subscribe to a fatalistic attitude, called 'karma' by both, the Tibetans adopt a 'proactive' posture, compared with the 'reactive fatalism' of the Hindus.

A similarly effective (if equally self-deluding) strategy is sketched by Bruce Headey and Alex Wearing (1988). They write that as a group, Australians report a high level of satisfaction, or subjective well-being. They attribute this to the tendency of Australians to experience a sense of relative superiority in every area of their lives. For example, about 86 per cent of Australians report that they perform above average in their main job; only 1 per cent report performing below average. They achieve this feat of self-congratulation by giving particular weight (in their own minds) to things that are going smoothly and by comparing themselves with reference groups that are, as Headey and Wearing say, 'restricted'. This attitude deters them from seeing problems with their own performance and taking corrective action.

Decoupling

A third limit on opportunity is *decoupling*. This word makes us think of a disconnected railway car that has been shunted onto a sidetrack. For example, the job vacancy created by a death or retirement may set off a chain reaction leading to the upward movement of dozens of others in an organization (White, 1970). So, career advancement is as much the result of 'vacancy chains' as of the accomplishment of the individuals promoted. Depending on economic conditions, an early change (such as retirement or death) may produce a longer or shorter chain of reactions.

Some people are decoupled by a lack of useful social contacts. Social contacts are important in every social setting. A survey of managers showed that people typically find the best white-collar jobs through personal contacts (Granovetter, 1974). That is because employers know that hiring through networks of personal contact is the simplest, most trust-worthy approach. As well, the most valuable job information is passed on by acquaintances rather than close friends or family. Because we have a great many more acquaintances than close friends, we are more likely to get useful information from an acquaintance. Further, people who begin moving between organizations early in their careers and who have more social contacts than others benefit most. This creates a 'snowballing' of career opportunities over time. By contrast, people who stay with the same organization for much of their working life have trouble finding a new job when forced to do so.

Research shows, however, that people seeking careers within ethnic communities might do better by keeping contact with old friends and kin than by seeking new acquaintances. Working-class people may also need to rely on friends and kin. They are likely to find their first job through friends and relatives in a similar line of work. Later in life, they start finding jobs by answering advertisements and other formal means. Middle-class people do the opposite: they use their educational credentials to find a first job, and then they find later jobs through acquaintances they have met at work.

As we shall see in Chapter 9, networking works against groups who are under-represented in the most desirable fields of work and socially decoupled from the dominant group. For example, whites tend to make the acquaintance of other whites, men the acquaintance of other men. When asked to recommend people for jobs, white men will tend to recommend other white men (Mark Granovetter, personal communication). Even without people intending to 'discriminate', the outcome is discriminatory, in that the organization remains racially or sexually unbalanced.

A final point is that decoupling affects more than your chances of getting a better quality of life; it also directly affects your life satisfaction. Ronald Burt (1987) has shown that people with larger networks of acquaintances are happier than people with smaller networks, even after differences in socio-economic status, age, sex, race, and marital status are considered. Burt found the presence of close relations has no positive effect on people's happiness, while the presence of strangers has a negative effect.

Scarcity

A fourth reason for limited opportunity is that often there are too few assets to go around—what people want is scarce. One obvious way to reduce scarcity is to increase the supply of goods to be shared out. However, some resources are finite and cannot be increased. As well, sharing requires co-operation, and, for those who already have access to a disproportionate share of the society's wealth, voluntary sacrifice. More often, the elite choose to protect what they already own and use their political, economic, and social power to ensure that they continue to have privileged access. Since *scarcity* varies with the ratio of competitors to desired goods, cutting out competitors through the practice of exclusion, disability, and decoupling can lessen scarcity, at least for those doing the cutting out. Usually, this means that the rich get even richer, the rest get poorer, and even the traditional middle class declines as well.

Often scarcity is a result of exclusion—the monopolization of desired goods by people powerful enough to control access to them. Capitalists want a large 'reserve army of the unemployed' to keep down wages, and they want shortages to keep prices up. Besides, with the technical improvements in capitalist production, certain jobs are bound to disappear. According to this theory, capitalism creates too few jobs—indeed, ever fewer jobs. Prices rise, and inequality increases steadily. Typically, high rates of economic growth give most people more of the goods they want without breaking the existing monopolies.

Beyond material scarcity, we find 'social limits to growth' (Hirsch, 1978) expressed in a growing sense of scarcity. Increasingly, people value scarce items—the unique vacation, the unusual home, designer clothing—*because they are scarce*. This relative feeling of scarcity can never be removed as long as those who control our consumer culture continually invent and give out new objects of desire to show that some people have more money, leisure, or taste than other people.

Diffusion of Information and Other Valuable Assets

The four types of structural and cultural constraints we have just discussed are all in part problems with the easy diffusion of information and other forms of scarce assets to those who need them to avoid negative circumstances. Simply put, **diffusion** is the spread of information and other assets through a population. This includes the spread of cultural information from one society to another, the spread of investment information, the communication of safecracking techniques or informal rules in a prison, the telling of false stories and nasty gossip among friends, the passing along of job information and the 'inside dope' on job candidates, advice about birth control or safe sex, the distribution of income and wealth, and the distribution of all manner of goods and services.

In the chapters that follow, we will see different types of diffusion and constraints to diffusion, in different concrete settings. As sociologists, we will be looking for answers to certain general questions about the ways societies work. These questions include but are not limited to the following: How does the thing we call 'social structure' influence how quickly people get information and other assets, who gets the assets, and how many people in total get them? What kinds of socially harmful, irrational, or inefficient outcomes are caused by limited flows of assets? How can we overcome these limits?

For example, we find in most universities a relative abundance of professors who are white, able-bodied males. What is there about the flow of job information and people with different types of job credentials that is likely to work against hiring women, visible minorities, Native people, or the physically disabled? What sorts of things, besides enacting employment equity policies, are likely to change this situation? This topic, and others, will be discussed throughout this book.

Broad Theories about Social Problems

Social problems are not the exclusive domain of sociologists. In fact, both the natural and social sciences have contributed their own unique understandings and perspectives to the study of social problems. It is important for the student of sociology (and of any other academic field) to note that where finding truth is concerned, disciplines are not in competition with each other. For example, the contributions made by psychologists are not 'right' and those by anthropologists 'wrong'; both are correct, according to their own designs and self-imposed limits. Each approach can further our understanding of the problems we are considering.

The study of social problems is best understood as a complementary, multi-level co-operative action in which the findings of one field or discipline corroborate or elaborate on the research and theories of the others. This is not to suggest an absence of conflicting data or results in areas of study. The contradictory findings likely mean a flaw in one or another theory, calling for closer scrutiny and further refinement of ideas on both sides.

With this mind, consider three of the more prominent contributors to the theories of social problems: biology, psychology, and sociology.

Biological Perspectives

Biologists who study social problems try to uncover the biological bases for socially harmful behaviour. To this end, their focus of study is centred on the individual and on the genetic, hormonal, neurological, and physiological factors that contribute to that individual's dysfunction in society.

An example is biology's contribution to understanding violence in society. A proponent of the biological approach might cite evidence showing that increases in hormonal levels (for example, of testosterone) or in neurotransmitter levels (for example, of serotonin) are associated with increased aggression in both human and animal subjects. Other biologists might add there is a genetic component to violence, pointing out how many primate species, including humans and chimpanzees, our closest evolutionary relatives, typically 'go to war against one another' over limited assets or position on the social dominance hierarchy.

Psychological Perspectives

Like biological perspectives, psychological perspectives centre on individuals. Unlike biologists, though, psychologists are concerned mainly with cognitive, perceptual, and affective (that is, emotional) processes.

Much of the contribution made by psychology to understanding various social problems has come from social psychologists, who study the ways in which social and mental forces control social action, and vice versa. Social psychologists distinguish themselves conceptually from sociologists by limiting their research to the thoughts and personalities of individuals as they are influenced by and represented in a social context. For example, a social-psychological approach to the Holocaust might focus on how a charismatic authority can create unwavering obedience among subordinates, as a way of explaining why Nazi soldiers would carry out the atrocities ordered by Adolf Hitler against the Jews in the concentration camps. Notice how this perspective stresses the individual soldier and his thinking rather than the entire National Socialist (Nazi) party as a social group or the political ideology of German society. In practice, however, social psychological and sociological approaches often overlap.

Sociological Perspectives

Unlike the explanations put forward by researchers working within a biological or psychological framework, sociological theories focus on group relations and culture. Even

Diffusion and Innovation

The diffusion of information is a key societal process in the creations and maintenance of social problems. Nothing diffuses more quickly or completely than information, often with the result that people change their behaviour—or innovate.

According to sociologist Everett Rogers, people do not adopt an innovation at the same time. Rather, they adopt in an over-time sequence, so that individuals can be classified into adopter categories on the basis of when they first begin using an idea. We know more about innovativeness (the degree to which an individual or other unit of adoption is relatively earlier in adopting new ideas than other members of the system) than about any other concept in diffusion research. Source: Adapted from: <studentweb.tulane.edu/ ~mtruill/diss/AppendixA.pdf>.

**Durkheim and
Social Regulation**
As Robert Nisbet has shown
convincingly, such key terms
as *cohesion, solidarity, integration, authority, ritual,*
and *regulation* indicate that
[Durkheim's] sociology is
anchored upon an anti-atom-
istic set of premises.
In this respect he was like his
traditionalist forebears, yet it
would be a mistake to classify Durkheim as a traditionalist social thinker. Politically
he was a liberal—indeed, a
defender of the rights of individuals against the state. . . .
Anomie, he argued, was as
detrimental to individuals as
it was to the social order at
large.
Source: Coser (1977: 133).

so, within the field of sociology, different perspectives specialize in different aspects of group relations and culture, with some preferring macroanalysis at the societal level and others opting to concentrate on microanalysis at the small-group level. The two major macroanalytical approaches that have emerged in sociology are the structural-functional and conflict perspectives, while the major microanalytical approach is the symbolic interactionist perspective.

THE STRUCTURAL-FUNCTIONALIST PERSPECTIVE

Structural functionalism views society as a set of interconnected elements that work together in equilibrium to preserve the overall stability and efficiency of the whole. The individual social institutions—families, the economy, government, education, and others—each make a contribution to the larger functioning of society. Families, for instance, work to reproduce and nurture members of society, while the economy regulates the production, distribution, and consumption of goods and services.

Robert Merton (1968), a key figure in developing this perspective, argued that social institutions perform both manifest and latent functions. *Manifest functions* are those that are intended and easily recognized; *latent functions* are unintended and often hidden from participants. Education, for example, is manifestly responsible for providing students with the knowledge, skills, and cultural values that will help them to work effectively in society. Both the school and its participants formally recognize these roles. At a latent level, however, education also works as an institutional 'babysitter' for young children and teenagers not yet ready to take a full-time job or roam the streets independently while their parents are at work, and as a 'matchmaker' where older high school and university students socialize with potential future lovers or marriage partners. These functions, though important to society and carried out with equal success, are considered latent because they are not the intended results imagined by designers of the educational system, nor are they admitted in any official way by school administrators, students, or parents.

The functionalists' emphasis on the interconnectedness of society has also been useful in highlighting the ways in which one part of the overall social system influences other parts. For example, recent changes to the family, such as the rise in divorces and in single-parenting, have important consequences for work and education, especially for time constraints among those juggling the dual—and often conflicting—roles of employee and parent.

According to functionalists, the cause of most social problems is a failure of institutions to fulfill their roles during times of rapid change. This *social disorganization* view of social problems holds that sudden cultural shifts disrupt traditional values and common ways of doing things. For example, during the phases of industrialization and urbanization in Western Europe and North America in the late nineteenth and early twentieth centuries, crime, poverty, unsanitary living conditions, environmental pollution, and other forms of social disorganization increased sharply. French sociologist Émile Durkheim (see, e.g., 1964 [1893], 1964 [1897], 1965 [1912]) introduced the term *anomie*, or normlessness, to reflect this condition in which social norms are weak or in conflict with one another. As traditional forms of guidance break down, social control declines and people experience less cohesion and bonding with one another; they become more likely to engage in non-conforming, deviant types of behaviour (crime, drug use, and so on). The general solution to social problems, according to this perspective, is to strengthen social norms and slow the pace of social change.

CONFLICT THEORY

Conflict theory has its roots in the basic division between the 'haves' and the 'have-nots'. Conflict theorists take exception to the structural-functionalist explanation of social problems, criticizing its assumption of consensus among members of society and its limited attention to power struggles and competing interests within the population. The conflict perspective instead views society as a collection of varied groups—especially, social classes—struggling over a limited supply of assets and power.

Conflict theory has its origins in the works of German economic-political philosopher Karl Marx (see, e.g., 1970 [1843], 1965 [1867]) and others. Marx believed that as societies make the transition from an agricultural to an industrial economy, the main social concerns of the people shift from survival to earning a living wage. In an industrialized, capitalist system, two broad groups emerge: the *bourgeoisie*, the elite owners of the means of production, and the *proletariat*, the working class who must sell their labour power in exchange for a livable wage. As the social class with control over the economic system, the bourgeois minority holds a superior position to the proletariat within the society. Also, they use their great economic power and political influence to ensure that they remain in a position of dominance.

Marxist conflict theories argue that social problems stem from the economic inequalities that exist between these two groups. Obviously, to hold wealth and power is to be in an enviable position, since one reaps the financial, political, and social benefits of a system that works for one's own group over others. However, for the capitalist class to uphold its wealthy, privileged status, it must also ensure that those below it in power do not have an opportunity—and if possible, even the wish—to encroach on bourgeois power. Because the bourgeoisie reap so much economic gain from the system without giving much back in the form of social welfare support, there are often sizable minorities who live in poverty. This poverty of the less fortunate working and lower classes is a social problem in itself since it is unjust and produces conflict. It is also associated with many other social problems, including crime, drug use, underemployment and unemployment, homelessness, environmental pollution, gender issues, and racism, as well as physical and mental health problems.

Marxists also contend that labourers in a capitalist system often experience a feeling of alienation from the processes and products of their labour, which are fragmented and specialized; they have narrow job roles and are therefore powerless to control or change the conditions of their work. The plight of the working class as imagined by Marx is illustrated in the opening vignette of the classic film *Modern Times* (1936), in which Charlie Chaplin plays a hapless and beleaguered factory worker who becomes so overwhelmed by the pace of the assembly line that he eventually goes insane and himself becomes a part of the machinery.

Besides exploiting their workers, boardroom executives—the post-industrial successors to the factory owners of the industrial era—sometimes increase profits through the perpetration of corporate violence, harm caused to workers, consumers, and the public for the sake of the company's efficiency or success. Examples of these corporate crimes include the failure to correct unsafe working conditions, exposing employees to dangerous materials, knowingly marketing dangerous or inferior products, and releasing industrial pollution into the environment.

Given its emphasis on economic inequality, the Marxist solution to social problems, not surprisingly, calls for the abolition of class differences. As well, it proposes that work should be altered so labourers have more control of their workplace and a wage scale on par with supervisors and executives.

Critics of the Marxian conflict theory approach have noted that, historically, communist societies founded on Marxism have failed either to prosper or to erase inequality. As well, the Marxist approach has overemphasized the importance of economic inequality at the expense of other types of inequality and social injustice. Non-Marxist conflict theories argue that many social conflicts are based on non-class-based interests, values, and beliefs. While they recognize the value people place on differences in income and social class, proponents of these perspectives believe that other divergent interests and characteristics can also lead to conflict and oppression. Thus, feminist conflict theorists have noted that women and men often have competing interests and that this is as much a cause of some social problems as is economic inequality. Others cite the conflicting interests of various groups within society, for example, Aboriginal and non-Aboriginal, whites and non-whites, heterosexuals and homosexuals, the young and the old, liberals and conservatives, urbanites and rural dwellers, and environmentalists and industrialists. We will have more to say about all of these conflicts in this book.

THE SYMBOLIC INTERACTIONIST PERSPECTIVE

While the structural-functionalist and conflict perspectives focus on large elements of society, such as social institutions and major demographic groups, **symbolic interactionism** focuses on the opposite end of the sociological spectrum: small-group interactions. Taking an approach that overlaps considerably with parts of social psychology, the interactionist sees society as being essentially made up of the shared meanings, definitions, and interpretations held by interacting individuals. In studying social problems, followers of this perspective analyze how certain behaviours and conditions come to be defined or framed as social problems and how people learn to engage in such activities.

One of the forerunners of the interactionist approach was the German sociologist Georg Simmel (1997 [1943]), who studied the effects of urbanization on group relations at the community level. He found the urban lifestyle to be relentless and eventually alienating, with inhabitants numbing their emotional contacts with others to cope with the excessive stimulation that city life offered. The fragmentation of urban life leads to a decrease in shared experience. It is within such a framework of distinct, isolated, and isolating experiences that urban people must work out their social lives.

Labelling theory, a major social theory originating in the symbolic interactionist tradition, rests on the premise that a given activity is viewed as a social problem simply because groups of people define it this way. In this sense, labelling theory is a close cousin of the social constructionist viewpoint discussed earlier. Howard Becker (1963), for example, argued that moral entrepreneurs extend their own beliefs about right and wrong into social rules and norms. Those who violate these guidelines are labelled as 'deviant', and their actions are defined as social problems. Among their concerns, symbolic interactionists are interested in why some people violate guidelines and others do not.

Consistent with the basic premise of labelling theory, Herbert Blumer (1971) proposed that social problems develop in stages. The first stage is *social recognition*, the point at which a given condition or behaviour—say, drug use—is first identified as a potential social concern. Second, *social legitimating* takes place when society and its various institutional elements formally recognize the social problem as a serious threat to social stability. With drug use, this stage might occur, for example, when high-profile drug-related deaths make news headlines or when public officials discover a connection between drug abuse and crime and violence. The third stage is termed *mobilization for action*; it marks the point at which various social organizations begin planning strategies for remedial action. The final stage is the *development and implementation of an official plan*, such as a government-sanctioned 'war on drugs'.

Critics of the symbolic interactionist perspective argue that social problems still exist even when they are not recognized as problems. Date rape and spousal abuse, for example, were not considered problematic behaviours before a few decades ago, but physical and emotional harm still hurt the victims, regardless of the historical or social context. As well, symbolic interactionism is often criticized for not making detailed connections between microsociological and macrosociological forces.

POPULATION HEALTH PERSPECTIVE

Common sense tells us that many conditions in society are correctly identified as social problems. For example, few would dispute the claim that violent crime, say, or homelessness fits the necessary criteria for such a label. In each case, the issue in question (1) is a social condition or behaviour, (2) is harmful to society and its members, and (3) warrants and needs collective remedial action. Beyond that, there is a moral ingredient to our view and understanding of social problems. A vague feeling of indignation or distress on hearing about young children dying of malnutrition or the effects of industrial water pollution on a small residential community reminds us that, at least according to the values and beliefs in our culture, global health inequality and corporate environmental negligence are indeed worthy of social concern.

Still, this common-sense approach to distinguishing legitimate social problems from private concerns or unsubstantiated and unchecked moral reactions becomes problematic for social scientists trying to study social problems systematically. The basis for proper scientific study is an operational definition of the topic (which was given at the start of this chapter) and a means for measuring it. The common-sense approach fails to offer any concrete, measurable criteria for labelling a given condition as a social problem beyond the claim that it violates some popularly held value.

Consider inequality, whether economic, racial, or gender-based. Many people would consider it a social problem because it benefits some people at the expense of others. However, not everyone agrees that unfairness alone is enough to define a condition as a social problem. Many people—especially those who benefit most from social inequality— might argue that differences between social classes, racial groups, or genders occur because some people work harder or are more deserving than others. Therefore, without denying the subjective part of social problems, it would be useful to devise some form of objective criteria that could be used to settle what is and what is not a social problem.

Increasingly, social scientists have noted that many social problems are associated with health outcomes. From these observations has emerged the *population health perspective*, a broad approach to health whose goals are to improve the health of the entire population and to reduce health inequalities between social groups. According to this perspective, health includes not only the traditional genetic or biological foundations, but also socio-economic, environmental, material, cultural, psychosocial, and health system characteristics (Starfield, 2001). As a Health Canada study says, 'These factors, referred to as "determinants of health", include income and social factors, social support networks, education, employment, working and living conditions, physical environments, social environments, biology and genetic endowment, health practices, coping skills, healthy child development, health services, gender and culture' (Health Canada,

2001). Further, the understanding is that 'these determinants do not act in isolation of each other. It is the complex interactions among these factors that have an even more profound impact on health' (ibid.). In turn, health status indicators should be recast to go beyond the traditional measures of disease, disability, and death. Ideally, they would also include factors such as 'mental and social well-being, quality of life, life satisfaction, income, employment and working conditions, education and other factors known to influence health' (ibid.).

As Chapter 10 on health and health care will discuss, some researchers have also suggested changing the notion of 'disease' commonly held by the medical establishment to admit the fluidity and variability that exist in the idea, depending on historical and cultural contexts. A new definition should recognize both biological and environmental factors (Brean, 2001). It has also been argued that the cultural and economic influences on health are so great that social gradients in health status are 'surprisingly independent of diagnostic categories of illness, tending to persist across shifts in disease pattern and in hazardous exposures over time, and across societies' (Frank, 1995: 162).

Because of complex interactions among the determinants of health, the population health perspective employs a multidisciplinary approach to theory and research, combining insights from various government divisions, such as health, justice, education, social services, finance, agriculture, and environment, with input from academic fields such as medicine, social work, psychology, cultural anthropology, and sociology.

This book takes as the proper criteria for the study of social problems the effects that social conditions have on the overall physical and mental health of the population. There are several advantages to this approach. The first is that health outcomes can be more easily measured than some other criteria being used in the study of social problems. Because they are tangible and directly observable phenomena, physical and mental illness and death are easier to study. Second, many people take health seriously, as they should.

To show that certain family issues are a social problem because they disrupt family relationships may spark interest and action in some, but not in all. Conversely, to show that those same family issues are a social problem because they can lead to suppressed immune functioning, cognitive damage in children, or a significant three-year decline in life expectancy is both a more concrete argument and more likely to result in enthusiastic collective action to achieve a solution. Almost everyone wants good health and would agree the spread of preventable illnesses is a serious problem. Therefore, social conditions that have harmful health effects should be taken seriously.

Solutions to Social Problems

Each chapter in this book will contain a section on solutions to the social problems under discussion, some of which have been tried with varying degrees of rigour and success in Canada. These are solutions that individuals, groups, and organizations are using to address the problems, or solutions that should be undertaken to address them. We should be careful to distinguish between solutions of two broad types: *individual solutions* and *group-based or organization-based solutions*. We will see examples of many of each of these types of solutions as we move through the chapters that follow.

C. Wright Mills's point in describing 'the sociological imagination' in the way he did (1959) was that 'knowledge can be power'—if individuals choose to act on it. When we know what is going on in society, then act appropriately and in our best interests, we stand some chance of increasing our opportunities. Under individual-level solutions, we can act to 'work the system' to our benefit. For example, if you learn that some sections of the workforce are shrinking while others are expanding, you can consider preparing yourself for a job you would like in one of the expanding sectors. We have choices of this type to make. Your power to choose means that while society and culture may constrain your choices, they do not determine your life altogether. What you choose to do at certain points in life can make a difference. Opportunities can be exploited or squandered, difficulties overcome or compounded. The trick is to know what is occurring and how to help your chances. Information and understanding can lead us to some solutions for some problems, as we will see in the remaining chapters.

You can also consider getting involved in groups or organizations—there are political parties and interest groups of all sorts. Some of them will have goals for social changes that you would like to see realized. Here, too, knowledge of your society and culture is a condition for making good decisions about which groups and organizations are most suitable to your interests. Your values and ideologies (which are gained through social interaction, remember) will also influence your choices of goals and organizations.

People acting in groups and organizations make history. The chapters that follow will demonstrate this many times over for different areas, especially around social policy changes. Consider, for example, the changes in family law (discussed in Chapter 8) that have been forced by reform groups, and the changes that are yet to come. However, this strategy of political action through groups and organizations can be a slow road. And many of your journeys may be unsuccessful. The analyses to come will show that dominant groups often oppose certain solutions to certain social problems because they are not especially in their interests. As Marx and Max Weber, with other scholars, have underlined, such groups will have great organizational and ideological power.

However, political struggles can be won. There are many examples in Canada and the United States alone of successful protest movements by subordinate groups: the civil rights movement in the United States, the Quiet Revolution in Quebec, and the women's movement in both countries, to name only three. Another important example is the success of the labour movement in Canada and the United States, fighting over many decades to secure better wages and job conditions for the working class. We will have occasions to discuss many such group-based strategies for solving social problems, including many launched by government agencies. Such developments should give us heart about the possibilities of political action to resolve social problems. Many problems are formidable, but there is room to effect change.

Concluding Remarks

The authors of this book assume that the purpose of sociology today, just like it was almost two centuries ago when the discipline of sociology began, is to use knowledge to improve social life. We are concerned about all social problems that cause harm to people. However, we attend here especially to social problems that can be shown to do major harm to our health and quality of life but that only a few people see as a problem and that government and other powerful agencies are doing little to address.

As stated before, this book approaches the study of social problems in terms of their effects on the overall physical and mental health of the population. Thus, our goal here is to aid our understanding of the roots of social problems, their health outcomes for individuals and society as a whole, and how these can be addressed. For this task, it is important to explore facts and theories about how problems develop and are preserved and about how problems are interrelated. After all, this bridge between private troubles and public issues is at the heart of sociological study.

So, this book explores how processes and social trends occurring within major bureaucratic organizations and social institutions, such as the economy or the government, affect the population as a whole. As we have seen, sociology is the study of social structure and culture, roles and statuses, institutions, networks, and organizations. Social structure constrains people through various mechanisms—exclusion, decoupling, disabling, and scarcity—that are involved in many social problems. These four types of structural and cultural constraints all are problems in the easy diffusion of information and other rare assets to people who need them. Therefore, we will have repeated occasion to discuss flows and diffusion of information and other assets.

The two major macroanalytical approaches that have emerged in sociology are the structural-functional and conflict perspectives, while the major microanalytical model is the symbolic interactionist perspective. The individual social institutions—families, the economy, government, education, and others—each make a contribution to the larger functioning of society, according to functionalists. In their view, the cause of most social problems is a failure of institutions to fulfill their roles during times of rapid change. As we shall note, sociologists who support competing explanatory approaches hotly debate this view. The controversial search for suitable explanations and solutions for each problem makes the study of social problems fascinating to newcomers and professional sociologists alike. The great harm caused by many social problems, their continuing threat to individuals and society, gives this area of study a pressing importance.

QUESTIONS FOR CRITICAL THOUGHT

1. It is stated that what is defined as a social problem is constantly in a state of change. Are people inclined to evaluate social issues in a critical way before deciding that they are truly problems? Justify your answer using real-life examples.

2. To what extent do you agree with C. Wright Mills's ideas about the usefulness of the 'sociological imagination'? Relate your answer to personal experiences. How is this imagination useful in studying social problems?

3. More often than not, moral entrepreneurs are male, white, and middle-aged. Do these moral entrepreneurs have the right to use the claims-making process on behalf of society, despite their not being a fair representation of the population at large?

4. What makes something a social problem? And what are some characteristics of a *real* social problem? What is the most severe social problem affecting society today? Include clear arguments and examples in your answer.

5. Social constructionism is a sociological approach that looks at how people create and institutionalize social reality. When people act on their interpretations and their knowledge of this 'reality', they reinforce it or lock it in. Why do you think people do this and what do you think influences their perspectives?

6. To what extent and in what ways do the media influence the creation of social problems?

RECOMMENDED READINGS

Diana Kendall, *Social Problems in a Diverse Society* (Boston: Allyn & Bacon, 2006). This American textbook focuses on the significance of race, class, and gender when discussing social problems. The author also examines how the media shape our perceptions of problems.

Helena Z. Lopata and Judith A. Levy, eds, *Social Problems across the Life Course* (Lanham, Md: Rowman & Littlefield, 2003). This book offers accessible readings that examine the societal construction of social problems out of the personal troubles that people confront at major life stages.

Social Problems, ed. Amy Wharton. This quarterly journal publishes articles that tackle the most difficult of contemporary society's issues. *Social Problems* brings to the fore influential sociological findings and theories that help us better understand—and better deal with—our complex social environment.

RECOMMENDED WEBSITES

Society for the Study of Social Problems

www.sssp1.org/index.cfm

The Society for the Study of Social Problems promotes research on and serious examination of problems of social life.

Working for Change

www.workingforchange.com/

This website allows individuals to speak out on urgent issues of the day, such as gun violence and environmental degradation. It provides direct links to the decision-makers who can make a difference on these issues.

International Sociological Association

www.ucm.es/info/isa/

The goal of the ISA is to represent sociologists everywhere, regardless of their school of thought, scientific approaches, or ideological opinion, and to advance sociological knowledge throughout the world. Its members come from 109 countries.

Culture.ca

www.culture.ca/explore-explorez-e.jsp?category=224

This site offers access to hundreds of other websites providing support to Canadians facing social problems or interested in learning more about social issues in Canada.

GLOSSARY

Claims-making The process by which groups assert grievances about the troublesome character of people or their behaviour; claims-making thus involves the promotion of a particular moral vision of social life and, thus, is anything anybody does to propogate a view of who or what is deviant and what should be done about it.

Conflict theory A theoretical paradigm, derived from the writings of Marx and Engels, that emphasizes conflict and change as the regular and permanent features of society, because society is made up of various groups and classes who wield varying amounts of power; a macrosociological research approach that focuses on processes within the whole society.

Diffusion The spread of information throughout a population.

Institutional completeness A measure of the degree to which a community offers a range of services to its members.

Moral entrepreneurs Term coined by Howard Becker to describe those who 'discover' and attempt to publicize deviant acts. Becker says that moral entrepreneurs are crusading reformers who are disturbed by some evil that they see in the world and who will not rest until something is done to correct it.

Moral panics Mass movements based on the false or exaggerated perception that some cultural behaviour or group of people, frequently a minority group or a subculture, is dangerously deviant and poses a menace to society.

Norms The rules and expectations of appropriate behaviours under various social circumstances. Norms create social consequences that have the effect of regulating appearance and behaviour.

Roles The specific duties and obligations expected of one who occupies a specific status.

Social constructionism Research approach that examines the ways people interact to create a shared social reality.

Social group A number of individuals, defined by formal or informal criteria of membership, who share a feeling of unity or are bound together in stable patterns of interaction; two or more individuals who have a specific common identity and who interact in a reciprocal social relationship.

Sociological imagination A term used by sociologist C. Wright Mills in his 1959 book, *The Sociological Imagination*, that describes the ability to connect seemingly impersonal and remote historical forces to the most basic incidents of an individual's life. The term suggests that people look at their own personal problems as social issues and try to relate their own individual experiences to the workings of society. The sociological imagination enables people to distinguish between personal troubles and public issues.

Structural functionalism A theoretical paradigm emphasizing the way each part of society functions to fulfill the needs of society as a whole; also called 'functionalism'; a macrosociological approach that focuses on the societal, as opposed to the individual, level.

Symbolic interactionism A theoretical paradigm that studies the process by which individuals interpret and respond to the actions of others and that conceives of society as the product of this continuous face-to-face interaction; a microsociological approach that focuses on individuals and small groups.

Symbols The heart of cultural systems, from which we construct thoughts, ideas, and other ways of representing reality to others and to ourselves; gestures, artifacts, and language that represent something else.

Whistle-blowers Employees in a bureaucratic organization who bring forward valid information about wrongdoing or illegal conduct by their organization and who are often punished for doing so. Even organizations that say publicly that they want employees to 'participate' and that they hold high ethical standards move to discredit whistle-blowers and to fire them as soon as they report information about waste, fraud, or abuses of power in the organization.

REFERENCES

Abel, E.L. 2001. 'The Gin Epidemic: Much Ado About What?', *Alcohol and Alcoholism* 36: 401–5.

Abt, Vicki, and Mel Seesholtz. 1994. 'The Shameless World of Phil, Sally and Oprah: Television Talk Shows and the Deconstructing of Society', *Journal of Popular Culture* 28: 171–91.

Alvarez, Rodolfo. 2001. 'The Social Problem as an Enterprise: Values as a Defining Factor', *Social Problems* 48, 1: 3–10.

Beal, A.C., J. Ausiello, and J.M. Perrin. 2001. 'Social Influences on Health-Risk Behaviors among Minority Middle School Students', *Journal of Adolescent Health* 28: 474–80.

Becker, Howard. 1963. *Outsiders: Studies in the Sociology of Deviance*. New York: Free Press.

Bell, R.F., B. Schjødt, and A.G. Paulsberg. 2000. 'Childhood Trauma and Chronic Pain', *Tidsskr Nor Laegeforen* 120: 2759–60.

Berger, Peter L., and Thomas Luckmann. 1966. *The Social Construction of Reality: A Treatise on the Sociology of Knowledge*. Garden City, NY: Anchor Books.

Bernstein, Mary. 1991. 'Whistle Blowing As Claims-Making in Technological Controversies', American Sociological Association, conference paper.

Best, Joel. 2004. *More Damned Lies and Statistics*. Berkeley: University of California Press.

Bledstein, Burton J. 1976. *The Culture of Professionalism: The Middle Class and the Development of Higher Education in America*. New York: Norton.

Blumer, Herbert. 1971. 'Social Problems as Collective Behavior', *Social Problems* 8: 298–306.

Bohon, Stephanie A., and Heather Macpherson. 2006. 'The Myth of Eleven Million: The Social Construction of the Illegal Immigration in the South', conference paper, Southern Sociological Society, New Orleans.

Brean, Joseph. 2001. 'Semantics of Disease', *National Post*, 3 Aug., A16.

Breton, Raymond, Wsevolod W. Isajiw, and J. Myles. 1991. *Ethnic Identity and Equality: Varieties of Experience in a Canadian City*. Toronto: University of Toronto Press.

Burr, Vivienne. 1995. 'What Is Social Constructionism?', in Burr, *An Introduction to Social Constructionism*. London: Routledge, 1–16.

Burt, Ronald S. 1987. 'A Note on Strangers, Friends and Happiness', *Social Networks* 9: 311–32.

Cain, Roy. 1989. 'Disclosure and Secrecy among Gay Men: A Shift in Views', Society for the Study of Social Problems, conference paper.

Carmona, Saez T., F. Garcia, Mayoral P. Romero, C. Roman Fernandez, A.J. Jimenez Alvarez, and I. Rodrigo Santos. 1999. 'Social Failure: The Concept and a Method for Its Clinical Assessment', *Medicina Interna* 16: 442–6.

Castle, Emery N. 1995. 'The Forgotten Hinterlands', in Emery N. Castle, ed., *The Changing American Countryside: Rural People and Places*. Lawrence: University Press of Kansas, 3–9.

Clement, Wallace. 1975. *The Canadian Corporate Elite: An Analysis of Economic Power*. Toronto: McClelland & Stewart.

Clinton-Davis, Lord Stanley, and Yohannes Fassil. 1992. 'Health and Social Problems of Refugees', *Social Science and Medicine* 35: 507–13.

Coltrane, Scott, and Michele Adams. 2003. 'The Social Construction of the Divorce "Problem": Morality, Child Victims, and the Politics of Gender', *Family Relations* 52, 4: 363–72.

Coser, Lewis A. 1977. *Masters of Sociological Thought: Ideas in Historical and Social Context,* 2nd edn. New York: Harcourt Brace Jovanovich.

Cravens, Hamilton. 1997. 'Postmodernist Psychobabble: The Recovery Movement for Individual Self-Esteem in Mental Health Since World War II', *Journal of Policy History* 9, 1: 141–54.

Curtis, James, and Edward Grabb. 1999. 'Social Status and Beliefs about What's Important for Getting Ahead', in James Curtis, Edward Grabb, and Neil Guppy, eds, *Social Inequality in Canada*, 3rd edn. Scarborough, Ont.: Prentice-Hall, 330–46.

Delbanco, Suzanne, Janet Lundy, Tina Hoff, Molly Parker, and Mark D. Smith. 1997. 'Public Knowledge and Perceptions about Unplanned Pregnancy and Contraception in Three Countries', *Family Planning Perspectives* 29, 2: 70–5.

Durkheim, Émile. 1964 [1893]. *The Division of Labor in Society*, trans. George Simpson. Glencoe, Ill.: Free Press.

————.1964 [1897]. *Suicide*, trans. John A. Spaulding and George Simpson. Glencoe, Ill.: Free Press.

————.1965 [1912]. *The Elementary Forms of Religious Life*, trans. Karen E. Fields. New York: Free Press.

Emerson, Robert M., Kerry O. Ferris, and Carol Brooks Gardner. 1998. 'On Being Stalked', *Social Problems* 45, 3: 289–314.

Fazel, Mohammed K., and David M. Young. 1988. 'Life Quality of Tibetans and Hindus: A Function of Religion', *Journal for the Scientific Study of Religion* 27: 229–42.

Fine, Gary Alan. 2000. 'Games and Truths: Learning to Construct Social Problems in High School Debate', *Sociological Quarterly* 41: 103–23.

Frank, John W. 1995. 'Why "Population Health"?', *Canadian Journal of Public Health* 86, 3: 162–4.

Franzblau, Susan H., and Michael Moore. 2001. 'Socializing Efficacy: A Reconstruction of Self-Efficacy Theory within the Context of Inequality', *Journal of Community and Applied Social Psychology* 11, 2: 83–96.

Gest, S.D., J.L. Mahoney, and R.B. Cairns. 1999. 'A Developmental Approach to Prevention Research: Configural Antecedents of Early Parenthood', *American Journal of Community Psychology* 27: 453–65.

Goffman, Erving. 1959. *The Presentation of Self in Everyday Life*. Garden City, NY: Doubleday Anchor.

Goode, Erich, and Nachman Ben Yehuda. 1994. 'Moral Panics: Culture, Politics, and Social Construction', *Annual Review of Sociology* 20: 149–71.

Granovetter, Mark. 1974. *Getting a Job: A Study of Contacts and Careers*. Cambridge, Mass.: Harvard University Press.

Hanson, David J. 1995. *Preventing Alcohol Abuse: Alcohol, Culture and Control*. Westport, Conn.: Praeger.

Hassan, R. 2000. 'Social Consequences of Manufactured Longevity', *Medical Journal of Australia* 173: 601–3.

Headey, Bruce, and Alex Wearing. 1988. 'The Sense of Relative Superiority—Central to Well-Being', *Social Indicators Research* 20: 497–516.

Health Canada. 2001. *Population Health Approach*. Available at: <www.hc-sc.gc.ca/hppb/phdd/index.html>; accessed 10 Jan. 2003.

Hirsch, Fred. 1978. *The Social Limits to Growth*. Cambridge, Mass.: Harvard University Press.

Hoffman, Saul D., E. Michael Foster, and Frank F. Furstenberg. 1993. 'Reevaluating the Costs of Teenage Childbearing', *Demography* 30, 1: 1–13.

Isturiz, R.E., and C. Carbon. 2000. 'Antibiotic Use in Developing Countries', *Infection Control and Hospital Epidemiology* 21: 394–7.

Jenness, Valerie. 1990. 'From Sex as Sin to Sex as Work: COYOTE and the Reorganization of Prostitution as a Social Problem', *Social Problems* 37: 403–20.

Kellinghaus, C., B. Eikelmann, P. Ohrmann, and T. Reker. 1999. 'Homeless and Mentally Ill: Review of Recent Research and Results on a Doubly Disadvantaged Minority', *Fortschritte der Neurologie-Psychiatrie* 67, 3: 108–21.

Klein, Hugh A., and David J. Pittman. 1998. 'Perceived Consequences Associated with the Use of Beer, Wine, Distilled Spirits, and Wine Coolers', Society for the Study of Social Problems, conference paper.

Kroll-Smith, Steve. 2000. 'The Social Production of the "Drowsy Person"', *Perspective on Social Problems* 12: 89–109.

Kunkel, Karl R. 1995. 'Down on the Farm: Rationale Expansion in the Construction of Factory Farming as a Social Problem', in Joel Best, ed., *Images of Issues: Typifying Contemporary Social Problems*, 2nd edn. Hawthorne, NY: Aldine de Gruyter, 239–56.

Levine, Harry Gene. 1984. 'The Alcohol Problem in America: From Temperance to Alcoholism', *British Journal of Addiction* 79: 109–19.

Linders, Annulla. 1998. 'Abortion as a Social Problem: The Construction of "Opposite" Solutions in Sweden and the United States', *Social Problems* 45: 488–509.

Lippert, Randy. 1990. 'The Construction of Satanism as a Social Problem in Canada', *Canadian Journal of Sociology* 15: 417–40.

Loader, Ian, and Aogan Mulcahy. 2001. 'The Power of Legitimate Naming: Part I—Chief Constables as Social Commentators in Post-War England', *British Journal of Criminology* 41, 1: 41–55.

Lyon-Callo, Vincent. 2000. 'Medicalizing Homelessness: The Production of Self-Blame and Self-Governing within Homeless Shelters', *Medical Anthropology Quarterly* 14: 328–45.

McFalls, Joseph A., Jr, Marguerite Harvey McFalls, Brian Jones, and Bernard J. Gallagher III. 1987. 'Genetic Engineering: Social Problems and Social Policy', *Sociological Viewpoints* 3, 1: 1–22.

MacLaughlin, Jim. 1996. 'The Evolution of Anti-Traveller Racism in Ireland', *Race and Class* 37, 3: 47–63.

McMullan, Colin, and John Eyles. 1999. 'Risky Business: An Analysis of Claims-Making in the Development of an Ontario Drinking Water Objective for Tritium', *Social Problems* 46: 294–311.

Macpherson, C.B. 1965. *The Real World of Democracy*. The Massey Lectures. Toronto: Canadian Broadcasting Corporation.

Mann, Michael. 1970. 'The Social Cohesion of Liberal Democracy', *American Sociological Review* 35: 423–39.

Marx, Karl. 1965 [1867]. *Capital: A Critical Analysis of Capitalist Production*, vol. 1. New York: International.

———. 1970 [1843]. *Critique of Hegel's 'Philosophy of Right'*, trans. Annette Jolin and Joseph O'Malley. Cambridge, Mass.: Harvard University Press.

Mauldon, Jane, and Suzanne Delbanco. 1997. 'Public Perceptions about Unplanned Pregnancy', *Family Planning Perspectives* 29, 1: 25–9.

Mead, George Herbert. 1934. *Mind, Self and Society*, ed. Charles W. Morris. Chicago: University of Chicago Press.

Merton, Robert K. 1968. *Social Theory and Social Structure*. New York: Free Press.

Mills, C. Wright. 1959. *The Sociological Imagination*. London: Oxford University Press.

Montagne, Michael. 1992. 'The Promotion of Medications for Personal and Social Problems', *Journal of Drug Issues* 22: 389–405.

Montgomery, John D. 1998. 'The Next Thousand Years', *World Policy Journal* 15, 2: 77–81.

Morewitz, Stephen J. 2001. 'The Psychosocial Effects of Stalking: A Social Problem', Society for the Study of Social Problems, conference paper.

Morone, James A. 1996. 'The Corrosive Politics of Virtue', *American Prospect* no. 26 (May/June): 30–9.

Mullen, Elizabeth A. 1997. 'Workplace Violence: Cause for Concern or the Construction of a New Category of Fear?', *Journal of Industrial Relations* 39, 1: 21–32.

Murphy, Raymond. 1982. 'The Structure of Closure: A Critique and Development of the Theories of Weber, Collins and Parkin', *British Journal of Sociology* 35: 547–67.

Nichols, Lawrence T. 1997. 'Social Problems as Landmark Narratives: Bank of Boston, Mass Media, and "Money Laundering"', *Social Problems* 44: 324–41.

Owen, Neville, Ron Borland, and David Hill. 1991. 'Regulatory Influences on Health-Related Behaviours: The Case of Workplace Smoking-Bans', *Australian Psychologist* 26, 3: 188–91.

Popenoe, David. 1993. 'American Family Decline, 1960–1990: A Review and Appraisal', *Journal of Marriage and the Family* 55: 527–55.

Porter, John. 1965. *The Vertical Mosaic: An Analysis of Social Class and Power in Canada.* Toronto: University of Toronto Press.

Potter, Deborah Anne. 2000. '"Acting Up" and "Acting Out": "Conduct Disorder" and the Medicalization of Adolescent Aggressive Behaviours', Society for the Study of Social Problems, conference paper.

Reinarman, Craig, and Harry G. Levine. 1995. 'The Crack Attack: America's Latest Drug Scare, 1986–1992', in Joel Best, ed., *Images of Issues: Typifying Contemporary Social Problems*, 2nd edn. Hawthorne, NY: Aldine de Gruyter, 147–86.

Risman, Barbara, and Donald Tomaskovic-Devey, eds. 2000. 'Utopian Visions: Engaged Sociologies for the 21st Century', special issue, *Contemporary Sociology* 29, 1 (Jan.).

Sartorius, N. 2001. 'The Economic and Social Burden of Depression', *Journal of Clinical Psychiatry* 62, suppl. 15: 8–11.

Schorr, Lisbeth B. 1991. 'Children, Families, and the Cycle of Disadvantage', *Canadian Journal of Psychiatry* 36: 437–41.

Scott, Dorothy. 1995. 'The Social Construction of Child Sexual Abuse: Debates about Definitions and the Politics of Prevalence', *Psychiatry, Psychology, and Law* 2, 2: 117–26.

Simmel, Georg. 1997 [1943]. 'The Metropolis and Mental Life', in Donald N. Levine, ed., *On Individuality and Social Forms: Selected Writings.* Chicago: University of Chicago Press, 324–39.

Solinger, Rickie. 1992. *Wake Up Little Susie: Single Pregnancy and Race before Roe v. Wade.* New York: Routledge.

Spector, Malcolm, and John Kitsuse. 1977. *Constructing Social Problems.* Menlo Park, Calif.:. Benjamin/Cummings.

Starfield, Barbara. 2001. 'Basic Concepts in Population Health and Health Care', *Journal of Epidemiology and Community Health* 55: 452–4.

Swygart-Hogaugh, Amanda Jo. 2005. 'Constructing the "Social Evil": An Analysis of Anti-Prostitution Crusades in Progressive-Era Chicago, 1907–1915', *Dissertation Abstracts International, A: The Humanities and Social Sciences* 65, 10, (Apr.): 3998–A

Szasz, Andrew. 1995. 'The Iconography of Hazardous Waste', in Marcy Darnovsky, Barbara Epstein, and Richard Flacks, eds, *Cultural Politics and Social Movements.* Philadelphia: Temple University Press, 197–222.

Wagner, David. 1995. 'Historicizing Social Constructionist Perspectives: The Example of Temperance Movements', Society for the Study of Social Problems, conference paper.

Wagner, Marilyn B. 2001. 'Transformation of Disability and Rehabilitation: 1950–1990', *Dissertation Abstracts International, A: The Humanities and Social Sciences* 61, 7 (Jan.): 2947–A.

Walker, Gillian A. 1990. *Family Violence and the Women's Movement: The Conceptual Politics of Struggle.* Toronto: University of Toronto Press.

Wall, R., J. Rehm, B. Fischer, B. Brand, L. Gliksman, J. Stewart, W. Medved, and J. Blake. 2000. 'Social Costs of Untreated Opioid Dependence', *Journal of Urban Health* 77: 688–722.

Wallimann, Isidor. 1994. 'Can Modernity Be Sustained? Prevention of Mass Death and Genocide', *Population Review* 38, 1–2: 36–45.

White, Harrison C. 1970. *Chains of Opportunity: System Models of Mobility in Organizations.* Cambridge, Mass.: Harvard University Press.

Zipp, John F., and Katherine E. Lane. 1987. 'Plant Closing and Control over the Workplace', *Work and Occupations* 14, 1: 62–87.

CHAPTER ONE

POVERTY AND ECONOMIC INEQUALITY

LEARNING OBJECTIVES

- To understand the difference between 'relative' and 'absolute' poverty.
- To learn about the different theoretical perspectives on economic inequality.
- To know about the policies that Canada and other countries have tried to lessen inequalities.
- To discover different definitions of poverty, including LICOs and poverty lines.
- To appreciate the concentration of wealth that exists in capitalist societies today.
- To see how poverty is related to other social problems discussed in this book.
- To know the effects of poverty on youth and the elderly.
- To understand the problem of homelessness.
- To appreciate the health consequences of poverty and inequality.

Poverty: A Social Problem and a Cause of Problems

This chapter is about rich and poor people, individuals and families, households, communities, and nations. It is about being absolutely poor, being only relatively poor, and suffering not from poverty at all but from inequality. Finally, it is about the harsher results of poverty and inequality. These results include crime, bad living conditions, and poor health. As we will see throughout this book, the major social problems are in one way or another all related to economic inequality, and most of them have vital health consequences. **Economic inequality** includes large differences in income and wealth across individuals and groups, and large differences in the economic power of nations.

As early as 1759, Adam Smith—the father of modern economics—recognized that poverty is a thorny problem. He, and many scholars since, saw that poverty is not merely an absence of money, but also a cause of social isolation, illness, and mental unease (Gilbert, 1997). Research shows that these personal experiences of need are the strongest influences of poverty on psychosocial health (Piko and Fitzpatrick, 2001; Sennett and Cobb, 1993). Yet societies and their governments have not found a way to sever the link between poverty and health.

Sociologists study social problems from a variety of perspectives. In this chapter, we will discuss three main sociological outlooks on, or theories of, poverty and economic

Inequality and Health
The major social problems, in one way or another, all are related to economic inequality, and most of them have vital health consequences.

inequality: structural-functional theories, conflict theories, and symbolic interactionist theories. We will also discuss a theory related to the symbolic interactionist approach—the 'culture of poverty' theory. Each theoretical approach points to important aspects of economic inequality. Each provides an understanding of how people become rich or poor. Each yields a different recipe for action—what to do about economic inequality—and each deserves criticism for failing to address certain issues, as we will see.

Some have called poverty the world's leading health problem. With all other things held constant, higher income usually means better health and poverty means worse health. Beyond that, economic inequality itself is a major source of health problems.

Economic inequality includes both differences in income and wealth across individuals and groups, and differences in the economic power of nations. Both inequality and poverty cause social problems. Social problems are also a result of the division of power and authority, which are related to economic inequality. In the end, most social problems are due to the unequal sharing of power and wealth and the failure by powerful elites to address the problems inequality produces. As sociologists, we have to help conquer ignorance and narrow-mindedness about poverty. As Table 1.1 demonstrates, many prevailing beliefs about the poor are grounded in myth rather than fact.

Definitions and Measurements of Poverty and Economic Inequality

Some think that poverty has always been with us. Others think that capitalism and the class relationships it produces give poverty a unique historical and social context (Novak, 1996). Certainly, we cannot discuss, or even define, poverty without understanding its social and historical background (Pritchard, 1993). With so complicated an idea as poverty, we are bound to have problems of meaning and measurement. Let us consider, first, some of these issues of types of poverty and how to measure them.

Table 1.1 Myths versus Facts about Canada's Poor	
Myth	**Fact**
The poor are lazy and careless, more interested in seeking pleasure than in working hard.	Being poor is in many instances not by choice; instead, being poor is a product of a number of sociological influences, e.g., family structure, as evidenced by the fact that two in five single-parent women in Canada are poor (National Council of Welfare, 2004).
The well-educated never wind up on welfare.	Education offers no absolute protection from welfare: one in five unattached adults with a university bachelor's degree lives in poverty (National Council of Welfare, 2004).
The poor use welfare cheques to fund extravagant lifestyles.	Welfare payments do not provide a free-rider incentive. Across Canada, welfare income rates hover significantly below low-income cut-off lines (LICOs; see below), regardless of family type and region (National Council of Welfare, 2005).

Relative and Absolute Poverty

Sociologists agree that people who live in poverty have much less than the average standard of living. However, we can view poverty in two ways: as absolute and as relative. People who live in **absolute poverty** do not have enough of the basic requirements—food, shelter, and medicine, for example—for physical survival. By contrast, people who live in **relative poverty** can survive, but their living standards are far below the general living standards of the society or social group to which they belong.

Researchers disagree about how to measure poverty. Although you may think that it is easy to decide whether a particular lifestyle qualifies as 'poor', in practice, determining what constitutes poverty is difficult. Cross-national evidence from the United States, Great Britain, Canada, and Australia shows that the **poverty line** is elastic, responding both to changes in real income and to the success of advocates fighting to increase social welfare by redefining or remeasuring poverty (Fisher, 1998).

Measuring Poverty

Until recently, Statistics Canada, the primary data-gathering agency for all of Canada, has relied on two different measurement strategies when compiling statistical data on poverty: LICOs and LIMs. The first method, **low-income cut-offs** (**LICOs**), is based on the percentage of income devoted to daily necessities such as food, shelter, and clothing (see Figure 1.1 and Box 1.1 for more on how LICOs are calculated). Although some consider LICOs to be equivalent to poverty lines, Statistics Canada stresses that they are not.

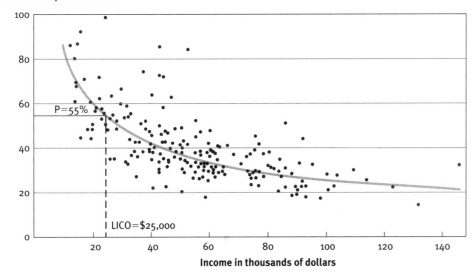

FIGURE 1.1 Calculation of a Low-Income Cut-off (LICO)

Source: Cotton et al. (2000). Adapted from Statistics Canada, 'Income Research Paper Series', *Should the Low Income Cutoffs Be Updated? A Discussion Paper*, Catalogue no. 75F0002MIE1999009, no. 9, available at http://www.statcan.ca/english/research/75F0002MIE/75F0002MIE1999009.pdf

---

Box 1.1   Historical Perspective: The Development of the LICO

A Statistics Canada survey of family expenditures in 1959 determined that the average Canadian family spent about one-half its income on the three essentials: food, clothing, and shelter. Statistics Canada concluded that a family that spent significantly more (i.e., 20 percentage points more) than half its income on these essentials was living in straitened circumstances. As a result, it adopted 70 per cent of income as the cut-off point: families that spent more than 70 per cent of their income on food, clothing, and shelter would have little or no income left to spend on other needs, such as transportation, health, personal care, education, household operation, recreation, or insurance.

. . . Since 1971, Statistics Canada has conducted its income survey annually. The agency began to conduct the family expenditure survey annually in 1997; this survey is used for updating the cut-offs. . . . The most recent estimate of the proportion of income spent on essentials is carried forward until a new expenditure survey reveals a different proportion. The 70 per cent standard based on the 1959 expenditure survey was reduced in subsequent years to:

- a 62 per cent standard based on the 1969 survey;
- a 58.5 per cent standard based on the 1978 survey;
- a 56.2 per cent standard based on the 1986 survey;
- the current 54.7 per cent based on the 1992 survey.

. . . Statistics Canada has always varied its cut-off levels with the number of family members, capped by seven or more. Since 1973, it has also distinguished among five different-sized urban and rural communities (a distinction that it has applied retroactively to its data for 1969 through 1972). The larger the community, the higher the low-income cut-off for any family size. The accommodation of these two factors—family size and community size—results in 35 separate low-income cut-offs.

Source: Adapted from Ross et al. (2000: 14–15).

LICO varies with the size of the family and the size of the community of residence because of geographic differences in the cost of living for families of different sizes (see Figure 1.2). Thus, LICO is higher in a large city than a rural area, and higher for a large family than for a small one. In a community with a population of 500,000 or more, if 'the average family' of four spends 35 per cent of its income on food, shelter, and clothing, then any four-person household that spends 55 per cent or more of its income on these necessities is considered 'low-income'. Using this method, one first calculates an income that covers the basic needs of one adult, and then assumes that need increases in proportion to family size. Each added adult requires 40 per cent more and each added child 30 per cent more of the resources required by the first adult.

The second methodology used by Statistics Canada has been the **low-income measures** (**LIMs**)—a set of figures representing 50 per cent of the median 'adjusted family income', which is based on a consideration of the varying needs of families of differing sizes. Each family's actual income is compared with the corresponding LIM for their particular family size; those that fall below are considered 'low-income'.

A third, alternative measure, the **market-basket measure**, has been years in the making—a result of work by the Federal/Provincial/Territorial Working Group on Social Development Research and Information—and is designed to define and measure poverty

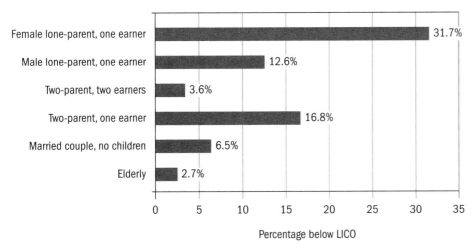

FIGURE 1.2 Low Income Rates after Tax, by Family Type, 2003
Note: Elderly families are those whose major income earner is age 65 or over; married couples and two-parent and lone-parent families are non-elderly; children are under age 18.
Source: Adapted from Statistics Canada, 'Income in Canada', 2003, Catalogue no. 75-202, available at http://www.statcan.ca/english/freepub/75-202-XIE/75-202-XIE2003000.pdf.

in absolute, not relative, terms. This working group proposed a preliminary market-basket measure (MBM) of poverty based on an imaginary basket of market-priced goods and services. This measure, then, is based on the income needed to purchase the items in the basket (Pellegi, 1997).

The MBM measure signals a change in our perceived obligations to the poor because it replaces a relative (or comparative) measure of poverty—the LICO—with an absolute market-basket measure. Human Resources and Development Canada (HRDC) officials were instructed by politicians to create a measure 'related to changes in the cost of consumption rather changes in income' (HRDC, Mar. 1998, cited in Shillington, 1999). Implicit in the market-basket approach is the idea that our obligations to low-income people consist of a particular basket of goods, not a share of Canada's wealth. In establishing an MBM in May 2003, HRDC officials acknowledged that many children will be socially excluded and isolated but not, by their measure, poor (Shillington, 1999; Brooks, 2004: 74).

At the population level, poverty does not simply depend on the national income or gross domestic product (GDP). Other socio-economic variables also contribute to the absolute and relative well-being of a country. The United Nations Development Program (2005), for example, monitors social and economic progress through a broad measure known as the **human development index (HDI)**. The HDI is a combined measure of achievement in three basic areas of human development: a long and healthy life, as measured by life expectancy at birth; knowledge, as measured by adult and youth literacy; and a decent standard of living, as measured by GDP per capita. When assessed by this measure, Canada performs well, ranking fifth out of 177 countries in 2005, behind only Norway, Iceland, Australia, and Luxembourg.

However, the HDI may not accurately reflect the extent of important differences among the world's most developed countries, which all score similarly high in the three dimensions of the index. So, for these nations, population-level well-being is measured by the second variant of the human poverty index (HPI-2). The HPI-2 assesses relative

The Burden of Debt in Africa

- African governments spend an average of $14 per person a year on debt service and just $5 per capita on health care.
- Between 1970 and 2002, the poorest African countries received $294 billion in loans, paid back $298 billion in interest and principal, but still owed more than $200 billion.
- Zambia spends twice as much repaying debts as it does on education.
- In Tanzania, debt relief enabled the government to abolish primary school fees, leading to a 66 per cent increase in attendance.

Source: Make Poverty History (2005).

deprivation in these same dimensions: vulnerability to premature death, as measured by the probability at birth of not surviving to age 60; exclusion from the world of reading and communications, as measured by adult (ages 16–65) illiteracy; a deprived standard of living, as measured by the percentage of the population living below the income poverty line (defined as 50 per cent of the country's median household income); and social exclusion, as measured by the rate of long-term unemployment (12 months or more). When this measure is used, Canada's ranking falls to ninth in the world. Although our country provides a very high average standard of living, this standard of living is not equally distributed across all levels of society (UNDP, 2005).

While the topic of measurement is specialized and may seem dry to the beginner, the exact measurement of poverty is complicated and politically contentious. Errors can make a huge difference to needy people, taxpayers, and program administrators. Moreover, as in any area of social science, if you cannot measure something, you cannot make good theories about how it varies.

Global Poverty

About two billion people—40 per cent of the world's population—live on less than two dollars per day. Yet, as UN Secretary-General Kofi Annan noted recently, 'even this statistic fails to capture the humiliation, powerlessness and brutal hardship that is the daily lot of the world's poor' (UN, 2000). It also ignores the millions more who live in poverty in more developed nations such as Canada, where the standard of living surpasses the two-dollar-per-day threshold. Eradicating extreme poverty is the first of the United Nations Millennium Development Goals, yet as Box 1.2 indicates, the problems of global poverty do not get much sustained attention in the public view.

The distribution of global wealth is massively unequal. The richest 20 per cent of the world's population control 75 per cent of the wealth. The world's richest 10 per cent control 103 times more income than the poorest 10 per cent. Progress has been made in the developing countries of South Asia, which now account for one-third of the world's poorest 20 per cent. However, conditions in sub-Saharan Africa continue to deteriorate, largely because of the AIDS crisis, crushing foreign debt, and government corruption. Currently, one in two residents of the region is among the poorest 20 per cent of the world's population (UNDP, 2005).

Living in extreme poverty means living in substandard housing, often in a slum district. It also means that clean water is scarce, as is indoor plumbing; electricity, if available at all, is erratic and unreliable. Infectious disease outbreaks are common. Few opportunities for dignified work present themselves. These impoverished social and economic conditions also mean constant exposure to the threat of victimization by environmental disasters. The tsunami in South Asia in December 2004, the flooding of New Orleans by Hurricane Katrina in 2005, the mudslide in early 2006 that buried the village of Guinsaugon in the Philippines—in these and countless other environmental catastrophes, the victims were overwhelmingly among society's poorest members.

Income inequalities between nations parallel health inequalities between nations. These inequalities are particularly visible among children. In 2004, for example, the under-five mortality rate per 1,000 live births in the least developed countries was 155, compared to the world average of 79. Worldwide, 29,000 children under five die every day from easily preventable causes—a level of mortality equal to a jumbo jet

Box 1.2   Social Construction: Coverage of Major North American News Topics during One Week in September 2002

Public opinion polls conducted in Canada find that one in two Canadians shows a genuine desire for international poverty relief through private donations. So why do the news media, among other institutions, not reflect this public concern over issues of poverty here and abroad? Table 1.2 shows news coverage on various topics, including poverty, for three major Canadian newspapers and one American paper.

Veteran journalist John Stackhouse, in the 2002 David Hopper Lecture in International Development at the University of Guelph, noted that '[i]nstitutions, notably churches, once told people that poverty was important, that the poor deserved their consideration. But today that role of directing the public conscience has been left to the media, an institution that some argue to be unaccountable, directionless and amoral. . . . News has to be stark, dramatic, or emotive. Yet [international] development is diffuse. It unfolds slowly and undramatically, and it often meanders rather than following the linear lines of an election or sporting match' (Stackhouse, 2002).

Table 1.2   Coverage of Major News Topics during One Week in September 2002

Newspaper	Politics (%)	War & Terrorism (%)	Crime (%)	Environment (%)	Health (%)	Poverty (%)
Globe and Mail	24	31	17	8	13	8
Toronto Star	21	38	18	7	11	6
National Post	30	36	13	5	14	2
New York Times	18	55	2	9	7	8

In North America, news broadcasts often only briefly mention the plight of the developing world before moving on to the next item of the day, without any meaningful discussion of how these problems can be solved. As such, many Canadians may be saddened by the suffering of others and moved perhaps to donate to a charity, but few are correctly informed about the state of the world and of international development efforts, and fewer still feel a deeper connection to the global community.

airplane crashing every 21 minutes every day of the year (UNICEF Canada, 2006). One in three young children living in the least developed countries is underweight. Compared to the world average, children living in the poorest countries are less likely to be immunized, less likely to receive health care when sick, less likely to attend school, less likely to learn to read, at higher risk of contracting HIV/AIDS, and more likely to die prematurely (UNICEF, 2005).

Those Most Likely To Be Poor

The face of poverty and economic inequality in Canada has been described as 'racialized, destitute, and young' (Curry-Stevens, 2004: 31). In addition, poverty is on the rise in urban areas, in some cities more than others. Cities in Quebec tend to have the highest rates of poverty, while those in southern Ontario tend to have the lowest. Three-fifths of all high-poverty neighbourhoods are located in Toronto and Montreal (CCSD, 2000b).

Poverty is also more common among racial minorities, both non-white visible minority immigrants and Aboriginal communities. Racial minorities earn much less on average than their white counterparts and are also more likely to experience unemployment and underemployment. Frenette and Morisette (2003; cited in Curry-Stevens, 2004) have shown that immigrant males who arrived in Canada within the past five years earned on average 28 per cent less than their Canadian-born counterparts, and recent immigrant females earned 31 per cent less. Over time, this gap between immigrants and native-born Canadians narrows, but not by much, and in some groups equity is never reached. Even after 15 years in Canada, minority immigrants on average still earn 15–24 per cent less than whites.

The disadvantaged social and economic status of Aboriginals in Canada is also well documented. For example, the median pre-tax income of all persons indicating Aboriginal identity during the 2001 census was $13,526, or 61 per cent of the national average (CCSD, 2003). At 1.5 per cent of Canada's urban population but 3.4 per cent of the urban poor, they are over-represented among the nation's impoverished urban populations. On reserves, the situation is equally bad, if not worse. A lack of employment opportunities combined with a sense of cultural isolation has resulted in economic, social, and health conditions that are in some instances as bad or worse than those found in the least developed countries of the world.

In October 2005, the Ontario government ordered the evacuation of the Kashechewan First Nation reserve in northern Ontario after the water supply was found to be contaminated with high levels of E. coli. This may have come as a surprise to the public and government leaders, but it was nothing new for reserve residents, who had been under a boil-water alert for the past two years and had experienced water purity issues for the past eight years. E. coli levels had been so high for so long that Kashechewan residents had taken to drinking, cooking, and bathing with bottled water, since the concentration of chlorine needed to purify the water was so high that it caused skin rashes. The dramatic evacuation may have made Kashechewan momentarily newsworthy, but its underlying economic and social conditions are far from unique. According to the CBC, as of February 2006, 76 reserves across the country were under boil-water alerts, some of which have been in place for years (CBC, 2006).

Worse yet, poverty is in many ways self-perpetuating. Structural mechanisms ensure that the poorest Canadians remain poor. The poorest of the poor tend to lose proportionally the most during economic recessions and gain the least during times of prosperity. Curry-Stevens (2001) estimates that upward of 90 per cent of the total income of the poorest tenth of the Canadian population comes from Employment Insurance, welfare, and other government transfers, which are usually among the first social programs on the chopping block during economic slowdowns.

Wealth

At the wealthy end of the income scale, economic resources are concentrated in the hands of very few people. This is because private wealth is usually gained from corporate wealth, which is also concentrated. And as mergers and buyouts further combine corporate ownership in a smaller number of huge, multi-industry conglomerates, wealth will become even more concentrated within a small circle of business elites. Of the world's 100 largest economic entities, 51 are corporations and 49 are countries (Anderson and Cavanagh, 2000). Michael Parenti (1995) points out that more than 80 per cent of the output of the US private sector originates in fewer than 1 per cent of all corporate businesses. According to an Institute for Policy Studies report on the rise of global corporate dominance, each of the world's top five corporations—General Motors, Wal-Mart, Exxon Mobil, Ford Motor, and DaimlerChrysler—earned more in sales dollars than the gross domestic products of at least 182 countries (Anderson and Cavanagh, 2000).

The fastest-growing segment of millionaires is made up of baby boomers, who in the United States alone stand to inherit roughly $20 trillion (US) within the next two decades (Davidson, 1997). Currently, the richest man in the world is Bill Gates, chairman of Microsoft, with a personal net worth of over $45 billion in 2005. With five members among the world's 15 richest people, the richest family is undoubtedly the Waltons, whose patriarch, Sam Walton, founded the mega-retailer Wal-Mart. Before his death in June 2006, Kenneth Thomson, chairman of Thomson Corporation, was the richest Canadian, with $19.6 billion (US) in holdings (Forbes, 2006).

Social Problems Associated with Poverty and Economic Inequality

As we said, most social problems are related to poverty and economic power. In this section we introduce several of the social problems associated with poverty and income inequality. Each of these topics will be addressed more fully in later chapters. We begin with reminders that poverty and inequality are associated with all of the following: work and unemployment, crime and violence, drug and alcohol abuse, gender, ethnicity, age discrimination, homelessness, and relative social isolation.

Work and Unemployment

No matter how we measure them, *poverty* is about having too little money and *wealth* is about having plenty of money. Both poverty and wealth are closely related to employment, the main source of money for most people. More and better jobs mean more money. Today in Canada, most families have trouble living comfortably on a single income. To avoid poverty, many households need two or more incomes, so two or more adult household members have paying jobs. Yet even this is no guarantee of prosperity. Often, even the gainfully employed live on the edge of poverty.

Many work lives—particularly those of people who work in the secondary sector of the dual-labour market—are characterized by periods of employment followed by stretches of unwanted idleness. (Jobs in the secondary labour market, such as unskilled labourer, cab driver, and salesperson, feature poor pay, low status, low security, high turnover, and easy entry.) Moreover, low wages prevent many people from saving part of their income to provide a safety net during times of unemployment. As a result, many must rely on social assistance programs, such as Employment Insurance, welfare, and workfare. These programs, though helpful and well intentioned, help the poor survive but rarely help them improve their lives.

Crime and Violence

Many believe that the poor, desperate to improve their financial state, are more likely than other people to commit opportunistic crimes, such as petty theft, muggings, or burglary. Research bears out this belief, at least in part (Braun, 1995; Hagan, 1994; Kennedy et al., 1998). The poor have fewer legitimate opportunities to achieve the economic and social goals our culture teaches us to value. So, rises in the crime rate may reflect more desperation or even an increase in self-destructive attitudes among those who are poor; or they may reflect a decrease in community social cohesion.

Still, this is only half of the story. The poor do not commit all of society's crimes. As Chapter 2 will point out, violations of the law committed wholly by the wealthy—so-called corporate crimes and white-collar crimes—are equally challenging and may harm many more people's lives. However, because these crimes are often hidden, the wrongdoers powerful, and the legal code more tolerant, white-collar infractions remain low on most law enforcement agencies' list of priorities. By contrast, the police target certain high-profile crimes—homicides, robberies, drug trafficking, and so on—that receive much more media attention and, so, cause much more public concern.

Drug and Alcohol Abuse

Another consequence of poverty and inequality is the excessive use of alcohol and drugs, whether for pleasure or to dull pain. This type of behaviour, like crime, is found in all social classes and is not limited to the poor. Nor is it caused only by social inequality. However, the desperately poor, deprived of legitimate opportunities to achieve wealth and success, are more likely to use alcohol and drugs to deal with what Robert Merton (1957b), and before him Émile Durkheim, called 'anomie', the gap between what they have been taught to want and what they are able to get, which leads to a lack of social standards or normlessness. Rhonda Jones-Webb and colleagues (1997), for instance, found that people living in poor neighbourhoods are more likely to suffer from alcoholism. Not only does poverty affect the occurrence of drug and alcohol use, it also increases the influence of drug and alcohol use on people's lives. One study found that poverty accounts for 69 per cent of the variance in the cocaine and opiate overdose mortality rates in New York City (Marzuk et al., 1997). Said another way, by far the single best predictor of death from a drug is the poverty of the drug user. Drugs do their worst harm when people are already leading lives stressed by low income, poor health, bad nutrition, and inadequate housing. All of these conditions reduce the immunity to disease that helps us survive and, likewise, reduce the individual's sense of care about oneself or others.

Is there a 'drug problem' in North America today? Part of the so-called drug problem is due to labelling and to prejudice in the enforcement of drug laws. As we will see in the chapter on drug and alcohol abuse, the justice system tends to unduly condemn drug and alcohol use by poor and marginalized people. Crack cocaine users, who are often poor and non-white, are punished more severely by the law than powder cocaine users, who are more often middle- or upper-class and white.

Children and Their Development

Poverty is also age-related in most societies. People without an income (for example, children) or with a fixed income (for example, elderly people) are more susceptible to the risks of poverty and inequality than other members of society. For children, longer durations of poverty produce a larger number of harmful outcomes. Children who grow up continuously poor develop higher rates of anti-social behaviour than children who are poor only briefly or not at all (McLeod and Shanahan, 1993, 1996). Timing also matters: poverty during the earlier years of life (that is, preschool and elementary school) is most harmful, causing lower school-completion rates (Brooks-Gunn and Duncan, 1997). Poverty is particularly harmful for the cognitive development of preschoolers, who need a rich learning environment to reach their human potential (Duncan and Brooks-Gunn, 1997b).

An Ontario study found that children in families with lower socio-economic status—for example, with poorly educated mothers—are more likely to have trouble with school, and even more psychiatric difficulties. The change to living in a female-headed household, after separation or divorce, is a strong predictor of poor academic performance and of emotional and behavioural problems, particularly if the change occurs later in a child's life. However, the associations among poverty, family status, and child morbidity are lower in Ontario than in the United States, suggesting the possibility of US–Canadian differences with respect to poverty, social safety nets, and other contextual factors (Lipman and Offord, 1997).

Poor conditions in childhood, especially low socio-economic status, are often related to poor health behaviours and mental states in adulthood (Lynch et al., 1997). However, this is not always certain or enduring (see, e.g., Hauser and Sweeney, 1997). Good parenting, for example, can limit the effects of childhood poverty on adult self-esteem, depression, and loneliness (De Haan and MacDermid, 1998; Jones et al., 2002). Finally, poverty is not the only important influence on childhood development. Peers are important, as are mass media and the schools. Some researchers even find that the childhood experience of divorce is a stronger predictor of behavioural problems than is low income during childhood, probably because of the correlation between divorce and family conflict (Pagani et al., 1997).

Teenage pregnancy can also increase the risk of living in poverty, largely because it disrupts educational progress. Earning power increases as educational achievement increases, and in today's knowledge economy, people who lack educational qualifications often become trapped in low-paying, dead-end jobs. The pressures of balancing work obligations with parental responsibilities further prevent the families of teen mothers from breaking out of the cycle of poverty (Ehrenreich, 2001).

Research on children who grow up poor leads to three conclusions about poverty: (1) raising the income level of poor families, even just barely above the poverty line, will improve the learning ability and performance of young children; (2) raising the educational status of poor parents will have a similar effect; and (3) raising both the income and the education level of poor parents will have the most effect (Smith et al., 1999). However, it may be easier to raise family incomes (for example, through transfer payments) than to raise parental education levels.

Human Trafficking and the Global Sex Trade

One of the world's most serious threats to healthy child development is the underground trafficking of minors, for cheap labour and especially for the purposes of commercial sexual exploitation. The illegal sex trade is a shadowy business and reliable

---

Affordable Housing Shortages for Canada's Children

- 21.4 per cent of Canadian families with children live in unaffordable housing (where the cost of shelter accounts are more than 30 per cent of total income).
- Among low-income families with children, 66 per cent live in unaffordable housing.
- Higher housing costs can mean difficult choices between paying the rent and buying other necessities, such as nutritious foods or clothing.

Source: Campaign 2000 (2005).

statistics about the extent of the problem are hard to find. However, the International Labour Organization (ILO, 2002) has conservatively estimated that human trafficking affects at least 1.2 million children per year. Another 2 million children are currently exploited in the commercial sex industry.

The purpose and extent of underage human trafficking vary from one region to another. In East Asia, for instance, trafficked children, the vast majority of whom are girls, are used largely as child prostitutes. The demand is created mainly by tourists coming from wealthy neighbouring and Western nations. In Europe, minors are trafficked from east to west across the open borders of the European Union for similar purposes.

In South Asia and West and Central Africa, too, children are recruited to take part in the exploitative child labour market, though many are still destined for the sex trade. Here, boys and girls suffer similar fates. UNICEF (2005) estimates that 41 per cent of boys and girls under age 14 in West and Central Africa and 14–15 per cent of boys and girls in South Asia were forced to work full-time between 1999 and 2004. For those between the ages of 5 and 11, child labour is defined by UNICEF as participation in at least one hour of economic activity or 28 hours of domestic work per week, and for those between the ages of 12 and 14, at least 14 hours of economic activity or 42 hours of economic and domestic work combined per week. Frequently, debt bondage—where children are forced to work off money given to their parents—is the route by which children enter the downward spiral of exploitation (UNICEF, 2001). In African nations experiencing civil or tribal conflicts, children may also be abducted and forced to fight in the militia.

Many girls and women who live in poverty in the developing world are limited to a few tough choices: chiefly, domestic subservience, sex work, forced labour, or a handful of other grim options. One way to break the cycle of exploitation and poverty, then, is to empower women rather than marginalize them. Groups such as the Durbar Mahila Samanwaya Committee (2004)—'Durbar' is the Bengali word for unstoppable or indomitable—a forum of 65,000 sex workers based in West Bengal, India, have demanded workers' rights and a secure life for sex workers and their children. They argue that the best way to end the exploitation of children and young women is to recognize sex work as a legitimate form of work, remove the barriers that perpetuate their material deprivation, normalize the industry through decriminalization, regulation, and monitoring, and target sex traffickers and pimps rather than persecuting the workers and clients. It should be noted that neither Durbar nor other sex workers' rights groups support the participation of minors in sex work.

The Elderly

At the other end of the age distribution, the fight against poverty among elderly people was one of Canada's biggest success stories in the latter part of the twentieth century. Poverty rates for people 65 and older have fallen noticeably over the years and continue to fall. In 1998, the poverty rate for women 65 and older fell to an all-time low of 21.7 per cent. That pushed the overall poverty rate for seniors down to a near-record low of 17.5 per cent. Mainly, better pensions for men and women who had been in the workforce could claim credit for these improvements. Still, very few old people are wealthy.

Researchers have proposed two hypotheses to connect age, poverty, and poor health; one predicts a decrease in wealth with aging, the other an increase in wealth.

One hypothesis, the **affluence-trajectory hypothesis**, argues that as people get older, they typically earn higher incomes until late middle age, when most people reach their maximum earning potential. Then, the combination of inflation and a fixed income begins to create economic hardship and poorer health. Another hypothesis, the **adequacy-gradient hypothesis**, likewise argues that as people get older, they accumulate wealth and other resources. However, after a certain point, especially after children leave the household, their needs start to decline. In relative terms, they become better off than they were at an earlier age, and though their health condition declines, it declines more slowly than before.

Studies testing these two theories for the United States have found support for the latter theory (Cairney and Avison, 1999; Mirowsky and Ross, 1999). The health gap between rich and poor people does not appear to increase as people age, perhaps because older people enjoy more similar levels of income adequacy than younger people. As well, rich and poor people suffer equally from many of the same infirmities of old age. However, poor health in old age reflects a lifetime of harm, often related to life-long experiences of low income. Compared with the more economically advantaged, the less advantaged on each post-retirement measure have high lifetime exposure scores on a variety of environmental health hazards (Berney et al., 2000).

Poverty as an Urban Problem

The incidence of urban poverty in Canada is rising (National Anti-Poverty Organization, 2003). One of the most serious problems associated with urban poverty is the lack of affordable housing for low-income families and individuals. Economists argue that, as a rule, housing is 'affordable' if either the monthly rent or mortgage payments consume no more than one-third of household income. Currently, affordable housing is scarce in many major Canadian cities (see Table 1.3 and Figure 1.3). In 2001, for instance, 44 per cent of Vancouver's population were spending more than 30 per cent of their household

Table 1.3 Rental Vacancy Rates (Percentages), Selected Major Cities, 1995–2004					
	Vancouver	Winnipeg	Toronto	Montreal	St John's
1995	1.2	5.4	0.8	6.2	10.8
1996	1.1	6.0	1.2	5.7	15.4
1997	1.7	5.9	0.8	5.9	16.6
1998	2.7	4.0	0.8	4.7	15.4
1999	2.7	3.0	0.9	3.0	9.2
2000	1.4	2.0	0.6	1.5	3.8
2001	1.0	1.4	0.9	0.6	2.5
2002	1.4	1.2	2.5	0.7	2.7
2003	2.0	1.3	3.8	1.0	2.0
2004	1.3	1.1	4.3	1.5	3.1

Note: Data reflect rental vacancy rates in privately initiated apartment structures with at least three units.

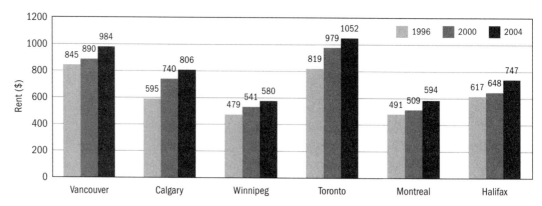

FIGURE 1.3 Average Rent for Two-Bedroom Apartments, Selected Major Cities, 1996-2004

income on housing; 23 per cent were spending more than half of their income (RBC Economics, 2005). There are several reasons for this scarcity. First, the ownership of rental housing is being concentrated in the hand of a few property owners. Second, developers stand to make larger profits by investing in housing solely for the middle and upper classes. As a result, upscale homes are abundant for people who can afford them, while low-income housing remains scarce.

When affordable housing is available, it is often found in city neighbourhoods that are economically stagnant and physically decayed. In these areas, rates of crime, violence, and drug use are typically higher than anywhere else in the city. People who are unable to afford even the most modest places to live increasingly come to rely on urban shelters for places to sleep at night. Although 'the poor' are often stereotyped as shiftless and unattached, two-parent families with children are the most rapidly increasing category of shelter-using poor. Still, as desperate and humbling as reliance on shelters may be for poor people, the alternative—homelessness—is even worse.

The Homeless

One of Canada's most pressing social problems today is homelessness, a growing problem in the country's urban centres. Most low-income families are renters, not homeowners. So, when rent prices increase or owners change rental units into owner-occupied condominiums, many families are forced onto the streets and into shelters, while others end up in crowded conditions living with parents, other relatives, or friends.

Although the exact number of homeless people in Canada is unknown, some estimates illustrate the size of the problem. In 2002, 32,000 Torontonians—including 4,800 children—used the city's shelter system. The demand for shelter space has increased 21 per cent since 1990. The waiting list for social housing reached nearly 72,000 in 2003 (Toronto Homelessness Action Task Force, 2003). In Calgary, a biannual count by the municipal government found 2,597 homeless persons in May 2004. This figure, based on a one-night enumeration, likely underestimates the extent of the problem (City of Calgary, 2004). The Greater Vancouver Homeless Count estimated 2,174 homeless persons in the Greater Vancouver Regional District in 2005, an increase of 94 per cent from 2002 (Social Planning and Research Council of BC, 2005).

Box 1.3   Personal Experience: Being Homeless

At age 47, Lynn's description of what home means comes out of a lifelong history of abuse that started when she was young and subject to very nasty custody battles. As an adult she has tried valiantly to cope with her past and to make a home for herself. She currently finds refuge in living with an older male roommate while working as his homemaker and cleaner. Lynn describes the feelings and consequences of her former homelessness:

It doesn't feel very good, you feel frustrated and everything is totally useless because you have nothing. . . . The more useless you feel the more useless you become and it becomes an ongoing circle. . . . Circumstances put people where they are. . . . You're living in a cockroach-infested, one-room place that is not as big as half of the room we are sitting in now, about the size of a jail cell. And you are supposed to live twelve months of the year like this? And not go out and beat each other up? And rob each other? And go and steal, and do this and do that? Because what else have you got, what else have you got to lose? At least when you are in jail you get three meals a day and comfortable bed and don't have to be on the street. . . . People change on their own when they've got a little bit of self-respect and a place to be, to live. They don't act badly just because they like it.

Source: Neal (2004).

The homeless are a varied mix of single men and women, young people, families, Aboriginal people, and some individuals with serious health problems (such as HIV/AIDS). Many are able-bodied, free from substance or alcohol abuse, and willing to work. Some even have jobs but lack enough income to pay the rent on the cheapest city apartment. And in large cities, many of the homeless are young people who have run away from home because they would rather live on the street than under the same roof with an abusive parent. Gerald Adams, Thomas Gullotta, and Mary Anne Clancy (1985) identify three categories of homeless adolescents: runaways (those who run away from home), throwaways (those who have been thrown out of the home by parents or others), and societal rejects (those who have been rejected by societal institutions, such as the school system or the mental health system).

Most street youth are from families suffering serious emotional, mental, or substance abuse problems. These youth are not essentially on the street because of socio-economic pressures (Price, 1989), though family financial difficulties increase the chance of physical abuse. Research shows that runaways overlap, in experience and background, with a variety of other social types. To their parents, they are 'missing children'.

In a similar classification scheme to that of Adams et al., Malcolm Payne (1995) identifies five different kinds of young people who go missing: runaways, pushaways, throwaways, fallaways, and take-aways. Les Whitbeck, Danny Hoyt, and Kevin Ackley (1997) conclude that families of runaways tend to give their children less support, supervision, and acceptance than other families. Even the parents of runaways sometimes concede they may have been guilty of minor abusive acts, though they are less willing to report severe forms of abuse. Abused runaways are even more likely than other runaways to describe their parents in ways that suggest serious anti-social personality and drug problems (Stiffman, 1989a). Evidence also suggests that the parents of runaways themselves had a history of running away from home when they were children (Plass and Hotaling, 1995).

Runaways run a heightened risk of suicide attempts: 30 per cent of runaways report having attempted suicide in the past. Those who attempt suicide have many more behavioural and mental health problems than average, and report having more family members and friends with mental problems than do other runaways (Stiffman, 1989b). Suicide attempts by runaway youth are most commonly a result of trouble at home, arguments, disappointments, humiliations, trouble at school, assault, and sexual abuse (Rotherham-Borus, 1993).

So, the main reason that runaways remain on the street, refusing to return home or try foster care, is their stated belief that family conflict is inevitable. Runaways develop their own substitute families on the street, among other street people, rather than risk further rejection or abuse (Holdaway and Ray, 1992). Many chronic runaways grow up to be homeless adults. As a result, homeless adults with higher than average rates of criminal behaviour, substance abuse, and other forms of deviant behaviour tend to report more abusive and deprived childhoods (Simons and Whitbeck, 1991). A history of foster care, group-home placement, and running away is particularly common among homeless adults (Susser et al., 1991).

Social Involvement and Social Support

Research has shown that people who are poor have less social contact with others in the community—whether friends, acquaintances, or relatives. We only need to think about poor elderly people and homeless people, the two social categories just discussed, to know that this is accurate, at least at the extremes of poverty. Poverty means more limited contact with others—indeed, sometimes it means almost complete social isolation. There is ample research evidence, though, that the relationship between income and social involvement extends beyond the low-income extremes. It appears that the higher one's income, the greater one's level of social contact with others. If social contact means more chance of receiving social support when one needs it, people with more income also have more opportunity for social support.

Data from a large national survey of the social involvement of adult Canadians support these conclusions. Using data gathered by Statistics Canada, Hall and colleagues (1998) showed that people with lower incomes and education were less likely to volunteer their time and assist others in the past year than people with higher income and education. Both informal volunteering—help given to relatives, neighbours, friends, and others on an ad hoc, personal basis—and formal volunteering—help given under the auspices of some group or organization—increased as the income and education of the respondent increased. Also, this study found that the frequency of visiting friends outside the neighbourhood was positively correlated with how much money the respondent or his or her household earned.

In Canada and 30 other countries, people's income and education also predict how many affiliations they have with voluntary community organizations and how active they are in organizations (Curtis et al., 2001; see also Curtis et al., 1999, for further results for Canada). Robert Putnam drew a similar conclusion based on US studies: 'People with lower incomes and those who feel financially strapped are much less engaged in all forms of social and community life than those who are better off' (2000:

193). Reasons for these patterns may include (1) the amount of financial resources available for use in social involvement, (2) the amount of free, flexible time available for this purpose, and (3) available opportunities.

Nan Lin (2000) has stressed that similar patterns hold for gender, racial, and ethnic differences in social involvement. With some exceptions for specific ethnic groups, men and the majority ethnic group have more extensive and varied social contacts with others than women and minority groups. Here, again, differences in financial resources, available time, and opportunities for participation probably play a part in explaining these patterns of social involvement.

Theories of Poverty

We noted earlier that sociologists differ in the ways they explain poverty and inequality, and in how they explain the correlation of other social problems with social inequality. The basic theories can be distinguished as follows.

The Structural-Functionalist Perspective

The sociological perspective or theory called structural functionalism argues that society consists of a connected network of groups, organizations, and institutions that work together to maintain the well-being of a society. In the eyes of a structural-functionalist, everything in a society has a purpose or function that, when fulfilled, permits society to continue, or 'survive', in its present form.

Accordingly, the structural-functionalist perspective argues that poverty and inequality also serve important functions in society. Inequality comes to be defined as a graded ladder of people with different occupational roles and income levels. Poverty motivates people to work harder to move up the ladder. The jobs at the top of this ladder require much more investment in education and effort, and they therefore carry greater rewards. They are also, according to this theory, the most socially useful and socially valued jobs.

Consider, as an example, the job of physician. Doctoring requires a great deal of skill and expertise. Physicians need many years of education to develop their skills. After obtaining a medical degree, physicians then face a highly stressful career filled with long shifts and hard, challenging work. Noble intentions alone may not inspire enough people to become physicians. Few would likely subject themselves to such a tiring life were it not for the rewards society attaches to doctoring, this theory says. These rewards—a high salary, social prestige, respected community standing, among others—suit the social importance of the job and the study and sacrifice required to prepare for the job.

By contrast, consider the job of serving coffee and donuts at Tim Horton's. The training required to do this job is virtually zero; likewise, the job complexity and associated stress and responsibility are perceived to be minimal. Almost anyone could do this job on five minutes' notice. So there is little need for the donut store to pay high salaries to induce people to take the job or stay in it. As a result, the pay for this work is low. Again, the rewards suit the social importance of the occupation and the study and sacrifice required to prepare for the job.

When skill and effort are consistent with compensation, as with doctors and donut servers, the functional theory of inequality works well. However, structural-functionalists are hard-pressed to explain the inflated salaries received by professional athletes, entertainers, and criminals, or the much lower salaries of nurses, teachers, and child-care workers. In these cases, the rewards do not obviously suit the social importance of the job and the study and sacrifice required to do it.

Conflict Theory

The conflict theory of poverty and inequality relies heavily on ideas first developed by Karl Marx and Max Weber. This sociological approach, which concerns class conflict in industrial economies and has always been popular outside North America, enjoyed a surge of popularity everywhere in the late twentieth century.

According to Marxist theory, the bourgeoisie is the social class comprising the owners of the means of production. As the controllers of factories and business establishments, the bourgeoisie can decide the nature of the work for the second, less powerful class of society, the proletariat. This latter group, lacking the means to produce goods on their own, must resort to selling the only commodity they possess: their labour power. The bourgeoisie, recognizing the proletariat's dependence on the wages earned from work, are free to exploit the labour of the working class and collect more wealth for themselves. They keep wages low to ensure that their workers remain dependent on them for economic survival. By manipulating the schools and mass media, they ensure that popular thinking— ideology—continues to support the unequal distribution of wealth and power.

This practice continues in the present era, this theory argues. Those who control the means of production continue to control the market system, although in a post-industrial economy the controllers are no longer just local factory owners. Today, multinational corporations—or, more precisely, the powerful executives who run them—continue to build up huge annual profits that are grossly out of line with the payments offered to their employees. In developed nations, owing to the influence of unions and labour legislation, employers are more likely to pay workers a reasonable wage for work done under safe conditions. In developing nations, however, employers are less constrained. Transnational corporations enjoy great freedom to raise their profits by reducing costs and exploiting workers almost without limit, thanks to their influence on the global political and economic systems.

Conflict theorists also recognize the biased nature of laws and policies that favour the rich, such as low-interest government loans to bail out failing businesses and giving tax breaks to corporations. As might be expected, conflict theories are more likely to discuss the types of social-structural and cultural causes of continued poverty that we discussed in the introductory chapter. Many of the mechanisms of exclusion, disability, decoupling, and scarcity that create and maintain poverty and maintain economic inequality are familiar to conflict theorists.

Symbolic Interactionism

The symbolic interactionist approach developed out of a combination of European and American philosophical approaches and took its current form at the University of Chicago in the mid-twentieth century. It is particularly concerned with the ways people work together to 'make sense' of social reality.

In relation to poverty, symbolic interactionists focus on the ways that people construct the labels 'wealthy' and 'poor' through social interaction. The typical though unspoken stereotype of a poor person in North American society runs as follows: a lazy, irresponsible, undeserving, freeloading ethnic minority (probably black, Latino, or Aboriginal) who would rely on welfare and social assistance rather than find a steady job to support himself or herself; a person who probably dabbles in petty crime and spends much of his or her money on alcohol and drugs; possibly a violent and dangerous threat, and a nuisance to society. On the other hand, the stereotyped depiction of a rich person is this: greedy, shallow, snobbish, egotistical, callous, wasteful, and probably white; has no qualms about stepping on others for personal gain; born with a silver spoon in his or her mouth and accustomed to living a life of sheltered privilege; inherited the already sizable wealth of mommy or daddy, and therefore has not had to expend any personal effort to build or increase the family fortune; and willing to take advantage of an unjust economic and social system that favours the privileged few at the expense of the disadvantaged many.

Like all stereotypes, these ones are exaggerations. Still, even if such labels are arbitrary and unfounded, their consequences are real enough. Being labelled 'poor' creates many problems that contribute to further poverty. Employers, mindful of these stereotypes, are less likely to offer poor people well-paying, stable jobs. Poor people are more likely to be the targets of unwarranted police scrutiny and harassment. Members of the public will see any reliance on government assistance by the poor as proving the validity of the applied stereotype. These are some ways in which the poor become excluded and decoupled from normal social and economic activity.

Table 1.4 summarizes the three main theoretical approaches to poverty.

Table 1.4 Summary of Theoretical Perspectives on Poverty

Theoretical Perspective	Main Points
Structural Functionalism	■ Inequality and poverty serve important functions in society. ■ Poverty motivates people to work harder to improve their life conditions. ■ Those who invest the most receive the best-paying jobs and working conditions (e.g., physicians). ■ Such a view is most applicable in situations where effort corresponds with rewards.
Conflict Theory	■ A structural power imbalance exists between capitalists and employees. ■ Employees are dependent on wages for survival and are therefore vulnerable to exploitation. ■ By exploiting workers through poor working conditions and poor pay, owners amass more wealth for themselves, leading to unequal distribution of wealth.
Symbolic Interactionism	■ This approach focuses on the labels attributed to the 'wealthy' and the 'poor'. ■ Labels attached to the poor, such as 'lazy', are often unjustified exaggerations. ■ However, widespread subscription to these stereotypes makes them real in their consequences.

The Growing Income Gap
The income gap between the rich and poor has stretched since the late 1970s. In 2001, the average income of Canadian families in the top 20 per cent of the income distribution was $145,580, more than 17 times greater than the poorest 20 per cent of families (Canadian Labour Congress, 2003).

Culture versus Economic Inequality as Explanations of Poverty

THE 'CULTURE OF POVERTY' THEORY

The result of years of studying urban ghettos in Mexico, Puerto Rico, the continental United States, and elsewhere, Oscar Lewis's (1959, 1966) controversial **culture of poverty** theory characterizes the urban poor as having a distinct set of values and norms, developed over time as adaptations to their impoverished state. These values and norms include a short-sighted view of the future, an impulsive and hedonistic attitude that lacks discipline and restraint, a failure to participate in mainstream culture, and a tendency to accept their marginalized status in society. These urban poor, many of them from a rural background that provided little in the way of coping skills for city life, struggle to build an understanding of an otherwise chaotic social world. Most group members lack the skills to escape to better lives and better communities. In these ways, they remain decoupled and disabled.

This summary, though too brief to capture the richness of Lewis's analysis, highlights the reasons why the theory polarizes opinion. Some say it portrays the poor as deserving their poverty because they do not make enough effort to escape it. It supports stereotypical characterizations of poor people as 'naturally' lazy or incapable—an idea that has long since fallen out of favour with most sociologists and anthropologists. However, the idea that certain types of culture prevent people from achieving their potential, and therefore act to keep their members—groups, or even whole societies—in poverty, still enjoys a considerable currency in popular thinking.

ECONOMIC INEQUALITY AS A CAUSE OF POVERTY

What if we view poverty not as a personal failure or commitment to a flawed value system, but instead as a result of the uneven distribution of resources within society? If we do, we come to see the poor in a different light.

The sheer physical fact of poverty has implications for the people who deal with it on a daily basis. When money is scarce and uncertain, it makes little sense to speak of 'improvidence'. Daily survival preoccupies people's attention. For example, children from poor families have to deal with conditions that their wealthier peers do not face: underequipped classrooms, crowded home conditions, the lack of a place to study, even hunger during the day, which prevents children from giving full attention to their classwork. To say that a culture of poverty and the people who share it are responsible for this uneven distribution of physical resources is to blame the victim (Ryan, 1976).

For example, the 'culture of poverty' theory implies that people in poverty will remain there passively and that even the children of poor families will themselves stay poor, having made no real attempts at improving their lots in life. In reality, this is not the case. While the poverty cycle often lasts across generations, many individuals and families nevertheless strive—sometimes successfully—to move up the socio-economic hierarchy (e.g., Dominguez and Watkins, 2003). The mechanisms for this upward **social mobility** are talent, effort, luck, social connections, and formal education. There is very little evidence that occupational aspirations are unchangeable, that high educational aspirations are restricted to the rich, or that religious and cultural values (for example, Catholicism versus Protestantism) affect mobility. Mainly, opportunities for good jobs affect mobility. A generation's worth of research on social mobility is this: children who get the same amount of education get the same kinds of jobs and incomes, regardless of the class they start out in. The goal for society, then, should be to ensure equal access to higher education and the creation of good jobs.

It is true that some poor people do not seek work, for good reasons. Some live in areas where there is little work to seek. Moving out may not be an option that makes much sense, particularly if people can support their families in other ways than by directly earning a wage—for example, by taking care of children or elderly relatives and by participation in the underground and subsistence economies. Moving without the guarantee of a job may merely mean that the expenses for another household have to be found. As we will see in Chapter 4, migration is a high-risk activity.

If the only jobs poor people can find pay a minimum wage, earnings may still fall below the poverty line for a household with one or more children to support, especially in an expensive city. Some may have sought work so often that they are dispirited and injured by the experience. This is not a cultural fact so much as it is a normal reaction to the material difficulties of their lives and the ways other people treat them. Rather than blaming the victim, sociologists ask how labelling comes about and how society is involved in it, how society constructs dependency in people so labelled, and how some groups manage to break free of it.

Health Consequences of Poverty and Economic Inequality

Poverty is not only hard and depressing, it also harms your health. What is more, poor health is sometimes a cause of poverty, not vice versa. For chronically ill people, for example, poverty and inequality may be continuing problems they cannot handle on their own. However, changes in health do not appear to influence changes in income as much as changes in income influence changes in health (Thiede and Traub, 1997). Poor people are often caught in a downward cycle of low food quality, low income, poor health, malnutrition, poor environmental sanitation, and infectious disease.

Poverty and Health

Studies show that, everywhere, poverty directly hinders access to food of high quality—food that contains essential nutrients, vitamins, minerals, and so on—which then leads to poorer health (Akinyele, 1997; Bakken et al., 1999; Dowler, 1998; Kusumayati and Gross, 1998). For example, iodine deficiency among pregnant mothers can result in cretinism and other forms of mental retardation in children. Iron deficiency—which affects 2 billion people globally—in youth can cause problems with co-ordination and balance. It has been estimated that because of poor nutrition, one-quarter of children under the age of five who live in the developing world—more than 150 million people—are underweight (UN, 2005). Chronic hunger leads to serious health problems, including rickets, scurvy, intestinal infections or damage, a depressed immune system, and impaired cognitive development. As well, hungry children are more likely to be hyperactive, have problems concentrating in school, and have other serious behavioural problems (Akinyele, 1997; Bakken et al., 1999; Dowler, 1998; Kusumayati and Gross, 1998).

Poverty is also likely to worsen health problems through the social problems to which it is related, such as crime (see Figure 1.4) and substance abuse. These other problems can also lead to poverty and the health problems that poverty entails. We discuss the specific health consequences of these other social problems in their respective chapters.

In all countries, income inequalities are also correlated with the chances of dying early (see, e.g., Kawashi and Kennedy, 1997). In the popular mythology, people with 'important' jobs—bankers, judges, politicians, and Donald Trump-like businessmen—suf-

The Relative Income Hypothesis
Income inequality alone (as opposed to absolute deprivation) is enough to bring on serious health problems within a population.

Rate per 1,000 population

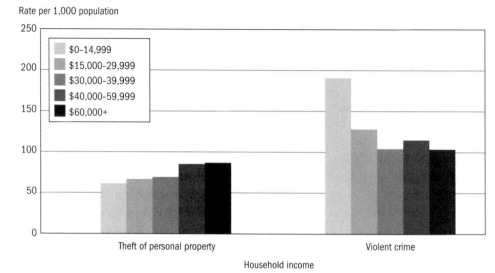

FIGURE 1.4 Household Income in Relation to Violent Victimization
Note: Violent crime—sexual assault, assault, and robbery—includes incidents of spousal physical and sexual assault.
Source: Statistics Canada (2001). Available at http://www.statcan.ca/english/freepub/85F0033MIE/
85F0033MIE2001004.pdf

fer terribly from their hard, important work and die from the stress of it at younger than average ages. This view is, generally, false. In Canada, for almost every cause of death we can examine in national statistics, the rates of early death are higher for people of low socio-economic status and lower for people of high socio-economic status (see, e.g., Health Canada, 1999). This mortality gradient is most notable in deaths from hypertensive heart disease, tuberculosis, asthma, pneumonia, and bronchitis. Early mortality is also much higher for Aboriginal people than for other Canadians (ibid.). So, from the standpoint of sheer survival—let alone quality of life—it is better to be rich than poor.

Effects of Inequality

In short, inequality—like poverty—is bad for our health. Surprisingly, there is evidence that being at the bottom end of a hierarchy—no matter how affluent that hierarchy may be—leads to health problems. The world's poorest populations, whether they live in Sudan or Canada, experience worse health than people within the same country who are not so poor. In less developed countries like Sudan the causes of ill health are obvious: a lack of clean water, famine, infectious disease, and so forth. In more developed countries like Canada, however, these conditions are not significant health threats except in some northern Aboriginal communities. Something else is therefore at the root of much of the disparity in health outcomes in Canada, and this 'something' appears to be inequality itself.

Much of the relevant research has revolved around the **relative income hypothesis**, which proposes that income inequality alone (as opposed to absolute deprivation) is enough to bring on various health problems, including premature mortality, within a population. This theory argues that the fact of inequality itself has real and measurable health outcomes for people at the lower end of the hierarchy. One influential study (Wilkinson, 1994) found a correlation between life expectancy and the proportion of income received by the poorest 70 per cent of the population. The author showed that the greater the difference in income distribution between the least well-off 70 per cent and the most well-off 30 per cent, the higher the levels of early mortality in an entire society or community.

The best-known investigations of the relationship between inequality and health are the Whitehall studies, which involved 18,000 male British civil servants in the late 1960s and the 1970s. A major finding was that mortality rates, particularly from coronary heart disease (CHD), were three times higher among workers in the lowest civil service positions (messengers, doorkeepers, and so on) than among workers in the highest positions (such as top administrators). This difference remained even after taking into account risk factors such as obesity, smoking habits, amount of leisure time and physical activity, other illnesses, baseline blood pressure, and height (Marmot et al., 1984).

One explanation of this variation in CHD mortality is the difference in control and support workers' experience along the job hierarchy (Marmot et al., 1987). Briefly, people in low-status jobs have less control over their work; this lack of control produces more stress; and more stress appears to produce higher blood pressure and higher risks of heart disease (for example, strokes and heart attacks).

To further test the hypothesis that inequality in occupational settings contributes directly to health problems and increased mortality, researchers in 1985 undertook a second Whitehall study, involving more than 10,000 male and female British civil servants. Findings from that research have confirmed that, indeed, low work control—characteristic of low-status occupations such as clerical and office support workers—increases the risk of developing CHD (Bosma et al., 1997). Even those working *near* the top of the civil service hierarchy had poorer health outcomes than those working at the *very top*. Not surprisingly, low levels of work control are associated with more frequent absences from work (North et al., 1996).

Further evidence showing the importance of relative—not absolute—deprivation comes from the finding that GNP (gross national product) per capita is correlated with health only up to a boundary of $5,000 GNP per capita per year. Beyond this threshold, increases in standard of living have little effect on a population's health. Thus, in developed countries, people's disadvantage *in relation to others*, rather than their absolute deprivation, leads to health inequalities. As Norman Daniels, Bruce Kennedy, and Ichiro Kawachi note, 'the health of a population depends not just on the size of the economic pie but on how the pie is shared. . . . Differences in health outcomes among developed nations cannot be explained by the absolute deprivation associated with low economic development' (Daniels et al., 2000: 9).

George Kaplan and colleagues (1999) found that income inequality influences a variety of health-related measures, including homicide rates, violent crime rates, the frequency of low-birth-weight children, the incidence of sedentary behaviour, and rates of smoking. Thus, social inequality contributes directly to poor health and social problems; the question is how and why?

Two Sociological Explanations

Researchers have offered two complementary avenues of interpretation to explain how income inequality causes poor health. First, according to one macro-level sociological explanation, income inequality breaks down social cohesion. Also, as we have said, within societies, people's levels of income predict the extent of their social involvement and types of contact with others. The final part of this explanation is evidence that social integration and social support networks are vital resources supporting good health. The latter may be due to a mix of factors, including a buffering effect on stress, reduction of high-risk behaviours, more sources of financial and social assistance, and greater emotional and spiritual support. At the macro level, social inequality influences the provision of health-care information and health-care access to members of a society.

Robert Putnam (2000) finds in many studies a link between social cohesion and social connectedness (on the one hand) and health and longevity (on the other). People with higher levels of social involvement are healthier and live longer; also, communities with more social integration have better health and mortality records. Cross-national comparisons find better health experiences and greater longevity in the countries with higher social integration (OECD, 2001; Putnam, 2000; Wilkinson, 1996).

Also, the breakdown in social cohesion is associated with higher levels of crime and violence, which, in turn, have direct consequences for health status (for example, exposure to drugs, physical injury) and indirect consequences (for example, lowered social capital and property values within the community, greater unemployment, lower quality or absence of health-care services). As David Coburn (2000) points out, neo-liberal economic policies are often at the root of this problem, by producing both higher income inequality and lower social cohesion while undermining social supports historically provided by the welfare state.

According to a second, socio-biological analysis, income inequality may have physiological consequences for people, by creating dangerous stress and other harmful environmental factors. Bruce McEwan (1999) calls the problem one of 'allostatic load', where allostasis is defined as 'the ability to achieve stability through change'. According to this theory, health decline under stressful conditions results from the overuse of natural bodily processes. In an indirect way, the Whitehall studies support this theory through their findings on the importance of control and social support.

Explanations from Biology and Chemistry

To complete the causal pathway, researchers have shown that the experience of stress results in significant levels of physiological and psychological harm. Studies of primate subjects in laboratory and field settings have shown that inferior status in the group (presumably a stressful experience) is associated with coronary artery atherosclerosis (Shively and Clarkson, 1999), depression (Shively et al., 1999), and raised levels of the stress hormone cortisol (Sapolsky et al., 1999). Kristenson and colleagues (1998) reported that cortisol levels are related to differential rates of CHD among men in Lithuania (high rates of occurrence) and Sweden (low rates of occurrence), and presumably in other countries as well.

Cortisol is the body's major response agent to chronic stress. Our bodies release cortisol in 'fight-or-flight' situations, and it prepares the individual for vigilance and long-term action. We also know that the chemical induces measurable physiological responses, including raised blood pressure, disrupted circadian rhythms (sleep patterns), and the suppression of the immune system.

These bodily reactions are all evolutionarily important, as they assign the body's resources and allow for greater levels of physical action. However, researchers are coming to believe that the bodily responses to raised cortisol levels, if repeated often, will do more harm than good, leading to problems such as heart ailment (resulting from high blood pressure and cholesterol levels) and increased receptiveness to various diseases (resulting from a suppressed immune system and sleep deprivation) (Sapolsky, 1998).

So, we now have evidence that social inequality has not only social and psychological but also biological and health consequences. Experiencing social inequality over long periods can harm your health if you are near the bottom of the hierarchy. In this way, relative deprivation (i.e., inequality), as well as absolute deprivation (i.e., poverty), affects people's life chances—their health and longevity.

Solving the Problems of Poverty and Inequality

Solutions to the problems of poverty and inequality have been debated for centuries. They fall into two main categories—individual and collective. Individuals, usually in their own interest, undertake individual solutions. Collective solutions require the cooperation of many individuals for their mutual benefit. Let us begin by considering some of the ways that individuals deal with their own personal experience of poverty and/or inequality in North American society.

Individual Solutions

As an individual, you may best solve the problem of exclusion by getting whatever credentials allow you to enter the group you hope to spend your life in. Higher education is the single best investment you can make if your goals are material, and perhaps even if they are creative. However, racial and ethnic discrimination continue to limit people's educational and economic opportunities. For example, members of groups that suffer discrimination may not do as well in work settings controlled by those from other ethnic groups as they would by remaining within their own ethnic community, even with less education. The decision to be made here—and it is a complex one—depends on several factors: the actual extent of discrimination against your ethnic or racial group, the chance of a significant reduction in that discrimination during your lifetime, the range of attractive occupational opportunities within your own racial or ethnic community, and the chance of a significant increase in these opportunities during your lifetime.

Alone, a person can do little to influence any of these factors. An individual can only choose between getting a higher education (and possibly cutting him/herself off from the ethnic community) and getting less education (and building contacts within the ethnic community). The first choice risks discrimination outside the community; the second limits opportunities for selecting a career and advancing within the community. The individual's contribution to a group solution, to be discussed shortly, will be much more important.

The problem of personal disability can be resolved by changing the way one thinks about oneself—not an easy task, but one that a great many people manage to accomplish. This is partly what the major social movements of our time—for example, feminism, Native rights, and gay rights—are all about. People learn more about the history of their oppression as members of a despised or belittled group, discuss this problem with others, find mentors and role models within the community who have done what the majority society would have them think cannot be done. Most important of all, this consciousness-raising enterprise rejects the victim-blaming ideology that oppressed peoples use against themselves. Those who are oppressed have enough problems without being their own worst enemies.

Again, individual remedies are less likely to succeed than group remedies. Women, for example, will only be able to demonstrate that they can succeed in activities previously thought to be outside their competence if they are given a chance. Opening up new opportunities often requires that an excluded group mobilize. Personal contributions, therefore, might best be made towards a group remedy. Still, results most often are a long time in coming. Aboriginal peoples in Canada did not suddenly discover their plight when the infamous 1969 White Paper, which proposed the dismantling of the Indian Act and assimilation to the majority Canadian society, was released. They had formed organizations to seek rights and petition governments from early in the twentieth century, and in previous centuries had demanded, but not received, equitable treatment. Similarly, the modern civil rights movement in the United States during the 1950s, 1960s, and 1970s was the outcome of centuries of oppression and protest.

The problem of decoupling can be addressed by building and making use of social networks. That is how people find good jobs—the size and variety of one's network of acquaintances can be improved by getting to know people who have larger and 'better' networks. People who are themselves mobile and widely acquainted, who are (typically) higher in status, or who operate within institutions that encourage interpersonal contact are valuable people to know. As we have seen, this social connectedness seems to be related to later health and the ability to deal with illness.

Social institutions that break down traditional gender, class, and ethnic barriers to interpersonal contact include colleges, universities, and government. Thus, higher education and involvement in civic affairs are doubly beneficial: they allow self-improvement and they encourage contact with others. However, both activities leave less time for participation in one's own community. Here, wrong choices are potentially costly. Thus, one should try to become a 'cosmopolitan' member of her or his community, with feet in both camps (Merton, 1957a). This connects the individual and the community into the larger networks of influence and opportunity beyond.

Finally, coping with real scarcity as an individual can be achieved by producing more of what people need, by adjusting one's thinking downward from the imaginary to the possible, and by seeking creative alternatives to scarce goods. It is the human ability to do this that has kept our species alive for a million years.

The danger here lies in confusing scarcity with inequality, considering scarcity beyond remedy, or lowering our heads rather than raising the bridge. French demographer Alfred Sauvy (1969: 391) has called this approach the 'Malthusian Spirit . . . a state of mind characterised by the fear of excess—faced with two quantities that need adjusting, it tends to lower the highest instead of boosting the lowest. It is the opposite of courage and generosity.' The Malthusian is the person who, at a dinner party with too little food for all the guests, tries to send guests home rather than find more food in the pantry.

When what appears to be scarcity is really a result of inequality or of a temporary shortage that could be remedied through innovation and higher productivity, group remedies are called for. But group remedies depend on the personal commitment of individuals who are willing to accept the effects that these remedies will have on their lives along with the solutions that they offer.

Collective Solutions

The chief actors in a large, modern society are groups and organizations, not individuals. That is why we must look beyond individuals for adequate solutions to inequality.

REDUCING MATERIAL INEQUALITY

Karl Marx and Friedrich Engels (1955 [1848]) contended that a revolution that would eliminate ruling classes forever by eliminating private property—by putting the means of production in the hands of the state—would bring better conditions for all. With the eventual 'withering away' of the state, communism would end history as we have known it, for it would end social classes and class conflict.

There are two problems with this formulation. First, a reading of history shows that every society of any size has had a class structure and a ruling class. This would not lead sociologists to the confident conclusion that a society with no class structure and no ruling class is truly possible. Rather, it would lead in the opposite direction—in the direction most often associated with the name of Robert Michels (1962 [1916]), who stated the 'iron law of oligarchy'. Michels's principle, based on a socialist's study of the German socialist party—a sympathetic observer studying a radically democratic organization—holds that in every social grouping a dominant group will struggle to perpetuate its power, whatever its original ideology. That is, inequality is inevitable in human groupings, whatever their size or their members' ideology.

Michels's 'iron law' has not proven completely unbreakable. For example, a sociological study of the International Typographical Union, a democratic printers' union in the United States and Canada, found some of the conditions that prevent or minimize oligarchy (Lipset et al., 1963). So, not every organization must be oligarchic. Yet oligarchic organizations in our own society and elsewhere far outnumber the democratic organizations. There is no evidence of a society that has broken the hold of oligarchy. At best, there is only a slim chance that Marx was right about the possibility of a fully democratic society.

Second, the premise that history can end with a democratic, class-free society is far from supported by empirical evidence. History does not show that communist revolutions have succeeded in bringing about either equality or democracy. In the century and a half since Marx and Engels's *Communist Manifesto*, a number of groups in different countries have experimented with communism. Some attempts have been utopian or anarchistic, based in a small community or region (see Hobsbawm, 1959; Kanter, 1972). But, except for Cuba, the Israeli kibbutzim, and Hutterite communities, these have all failed, for various reasons. Some have been forcibly overturned; others have lacked a sufficient material base; still others have suffered from demographic pressures from within and attack from without. Even the relatively successful kibbutzim and Hutterite communities have suffered serious losses of population, as native-born members deserted. For its part, Cuba's revolution has produced neither prosperity nor democracy.

Contrary to Marx's expectation, attempts at communistic equality at the state level have produced new kinds of inequality. In every instance—in Russia, China, Albania, Cuba, Vietnam, Nicaragua, and so on—rule based on ownership of the means of production has merely been replaced by political and bureaucratic control. So inequality has lived on in a new form. In many places, communism has greatly reduced material inequality and the worst effects of this inequality. But a certain inequality—rule by a political elite, or 'vanguard of the proletariat', as Lenin called it—never disappeared.

Many believe that the excesses of control under communism were due to an overcentralization of planning and political power. That is why throughout Eastern Europe and the former Soviet Union, people have rejected communism as unworkable. Communism has collapsed as a system of organization. In the end, citizens' behaviour in rejecting communism suggests that Marx's remedy does not work as he thought it would.

The communist alternative has proven more attractive in less developed parts of the world. In fact, the benefits of capitalism and liberalism have meant little to many people in developing countries. They consider European nations unsuitable models to imitate, since they carry the stigma of colonialism. Further, 'free enterprise' seems less likely to succeed in the developing world than large-scale economic planning. As Geoffrey Barraclough (1967: 223) wrote many years ago, 'one of the outstanding attractions of communism to Asian and African eyes [is] that it [offers] the underdeveloped peoples a blueprint for development.'

On the other hand, material inequality within a society can be significantly reduced without communism, as it has been in the democratic socialist countries of Scandinavia and, to a smaller degree, in certain other countries. Moreover, many people in the industrial capitalist countries—and not simply the very rich and powerful—do not want to give up private property in favour of communism. Values justifying acquisitiveness and free enterprise arise whenever personal acquisition becomes possible. People offered the chance to improve their wealth and status seize that opportunity almost without fail. They do not easily give it up.

As we will see throughout this book, liberal democracy does not give people an equal chance to get what they want out of life. So it would be satisfying to believe that some alternative (such as communism) could do so. However, researchers have been unable to show that Marx's proposed remedies lie within the realm of the possible, or that they satisfactorily link the advancement of group and individual interests. That is not to say that more modest socialist remedies would also fail to meet our needs. Indeed, any remedies that equalize income and power will benefit the majority. So let us turn to some truly possible remedies and see whether they meet our requirements.

OTHER GROUP REMEDIES

Wherever opportunity is limited, any wholly individual remedies are no more than quick fixes with temporary effects. In the long run, the chance of getting more opportunity is greater for a group working together than for an individual working alone. But if we rule out the revolutionary option, what remains? Again, what follows is merely schematic. It would be impossible to encompass all remaining scenarios within the scope of this book.

Two group remedies to exclusion are truly possible: legislation and group action. To bring this about requires banding together with others who suffer discrimination, joining forces across ethnic, class, gender, and regional boundaries where necessary. It also means electing sympathetic legislators to push for changes. If successful, the result will be a more assimilated, less discriminatory society. A second remedy is to mobilize within one's own group—whether class, ethnic, religious, or regional—to increase community organization. This has the effect of discriminating in one's own favour to counter the discrimination of the larger society. Many groups use this tactic today, notably class-based political parties, unions, lobbies, and associations.

Group mobilization carries the risks of increasing inter-group conflict without eliminating the underlying conditions that gave rise to it. By pitting one group against another—women against men, blacks against whites, gays against heterosexuals—this tactic increases the risk of misunderstanding and injustice. A society torn by such disputes is no further ahead than a society marked by smouldering resentment. Events in

Box 1.4   Social Policy: Canadian Debt Relief Efforts

When the governments of developing countries are burdened by massive foreign debt, the result is more money being spent on interest payments than on domestic investments that could help lift these countries out of poverty. Debt relief by affluent loaning countries goes a long way to relieving this burden. Canada supports debt relief and debt elimination in three ways:

1. The Heavily Indebted Poor Countries (HIPC) Initiative. Proposed by the World Bank and International Monetary Fund (IMF) in 1996, the HIPC Initiative is open to poor nations that:
   i.   face an unsustainable debt burden;
   ii. have established a track record of reform and sound policies through IMF- and World Bank-supported programs; and
   iii. have developed a plan to pull their country out of poverty.
2. Participation in the Paris Club. The Paris Club was formed in 1956 as an informal group of countries that assist other nations with unsustainable debt burdens, primarily through the establishment of debt treatment agreements.
3. The Canadian Debt Initiative (CDI). Established in 1999, the CDI promises 100 per cent debt cancellation to countries completing the HIPC process and a debt service moratorium during the HIPC interim period.

Source: From *Helping the Poorest: An Update on Canada's Debt Relief Efforts*. Reproduced by permission of the Minister of Public Works and Government Services Canada, 2007.

the Balkans, Somalia, Israel, Northern Ireland, and the former Soviet Union show that civil war is considerably worse than smouldering resentment.

Group mobilization also narrows people's field of vision. People become less available for solving problems that cut across groups: international problems of peace and scarcity, national problems of cultural unity and political or economic independence, problems of class and gender inequality, and others. The first solution—a frontal group assault on privilege—is the only one that will benefit everyone in the long run.

Social education and re-education can reduce disability; the schools and the mass media are key vehicles for such a change. As already noted, the strengthening of individual identities is best done collectively, since nothing changes people's minds more readily than the evidence that change is possible.

The benefits of slow, incremental individual change are much more limited (Kanter, 1977). For example, a sole woman given the opportunity to 'model' executive abilities in a large organization is under unusual pressures to succeed 'on behalf of all women' and is judged by criteria quite unlike those applied to men. Confusion will arise between the unique characteristics of the individual and the 'type' she represents. Consequently, we really do not learn what excluded groups can do until we see many group members performing in common, emotionally neutral situations. Achieving this requires legislation that ensures inclusion for as many representatives of a social 'type' as may seek it. Laws against discrimination not only break down traditional patterns of exclusion, they also reduce disability and decoupling. Again, governments will not pass and enforce such laws without group mobilization.

Groups can remedy decoupling by building bridges to other groups—for example, to other racial, ethnic, regional, and occupational groups. Typically, increased communication among the leaders of these groups is the key to success. But everyone can play a part in this process by participating in broadly based activities and organizations.

Finally, material scarcity can be reduced if more of what people want and need is produced. This requires an international commitment to economic growth and redistribution and the breaking up of monopolies that restrict productivity as well as sharing.

These solutions to inequality are group remedies, not individual remedies. All are truly possible. However, they do not systematically address the question of how people might link their own advancement with that of society as a whole. C. Wright Mills (1959) maintained that personal lives are linked with public issues; another way of putting it is that personal troubles are shared and socially structured. This implies that personal and social problems must be solved at the same time.

Concluding Remarks

Poverty has many definitions. Typically, the government decides where to draw the poverty line, so the meaning of poverty varies by society and, within societies, varies over time. Some think that poverty is caused by the continuation of economically damaging cultural habits (this is the 'culture of poverty' approach), while others believe it is simply caused by an unfair distribution of resources (the conflict approach). Functionalists believe that economic rewards are merit-based and inequality and poverty are mostly inevitable. It is not clear, however, from this standpoint, why women and ethnic minorities have the most poverty.

Oscar Lewis's 'culture of poverty' argument, which has a kinship with functional theory as well as symbolic interactionism, is often interpreted as blaming poor people for their problems. Although Lewis himself never made such a claim, his thesis fails to adequately explain poverty for various reasons. In particular, it does not directly address the role of structural elements—laws, social policies, institutionalized discrimination, and so on—that contribute to the maintenance of a marginalized subset of the population, the presence of which ultimately benefits the powerful ruling class. Further, this theory ignores the fact that people's ability to 'get ahead' depends less on their values and motivation than it does on the job structure: the opportunities for good jobs in the community where a person lives and the non-discriminatory willingness of employers to hire into these jobs.

Widespread poverty is evident in Canada and throughout the world. For this country, we could classify nearly 18 per cent of the population (5.3 million people) as 'low-income' individuals or households. Yet many people move in and out of poverty. Longer durations of poverty produce more harmful outcomes, and children who are continuously poor have higher rates of anti-social behaviour than transiently poor or non-poor children. Sometimes, poor health is a cause of poverty, not vice versa. However, for most people, the reverse is true. Poverty and inequality will be continuing problems they cannot handle on their own.

As we have seen, both inequality and poverty are thorny ideas—not merely conditions of economic insufficiency, but also causes of physical and mental health problems. Further, lower income means a higher probability of dying relatively young. These patterns make it especially important—for both individuals and for society—that we attempt to lessen economic inequality and try to discover ways of unlinking health and death from income level. Much of the research discussed in the remainder of this book is directed to these two ends.

QUESTIONS FOR CRITICAL THOUGHT

1. What particular insights do structural functionalism, conflict theory, and symbolic interactionism offer to our understanding of the sources of poverty? How would each theory approach this problem?

2. Is poverty unique to capitalism? Why or why not? Consider information on communal societies such as Hutterite colonies and Israeli kibbutzim, and discuss whether or not experiences of economic inequality occur there.

3. This text emphasizes that poverty and inequality are matters of life and death. Discuss this statement, drawing on articles in the newspaper that show how mortality rates are often related to income distribution and social class.

4. In your opinion, what is the government's proper role in dealing with the health problems associated with economic inequality? Should policies focus more on dealing with poverty on the individual level, or should efforts be focused more on redistribution issues? If neither, what is your proposed solution?

5. Consider the very high salaries that top athletes and movie stars make and the lower incomes of teachers and social workers. Do you agree with the structural-functional explanation of the discrepancy, or do you prefer alternative interpretations? Discuss.

RECOMMENDED READINGS

Naomi Dachner and Valerie Tarasuk, 'Homeless "Squeegee Kids": Food Insecurity and Daily Survival', *Social Science and Medicine* 54 (2002): 1039–49. What is the food experience of homeless people? In developed nations such as Canada few people go hungry. This study uses ethnographic data from a drop-in centre in downtown Toronto to address this question. Food access was found to be insecure and dependent on sources such as charity and the more desirable option: squeegeeing for money to buy their own food.

Linda Gordon, *Pitied but Not Entitled: Single Mothers and the History of Welfare* (Cambridge, Mass.: Harvard University Press, 1994). Gordon looks at responses to poverty in the United States and contrasts New Deal anti-poverty values with policies in place during the late 1980s and early 1990s. The book is written from the standpoint of the single mother and focuses on the cultural meanings of the welfare system.

Joan Kendall, 'Circles of Disadvantage: Aboriginal Poverty and Underdevelopment in Canada', *American Review of Canadian Studies* 31, 1–2 (2001): 43–59. This article connects the lower living standard of Aboriginal Canadians to social problems such as family violence, educational failure, poverty, ill health, and violence. Policy suggestions are made, along with warnings that emphasize the importance of self-determination.

Evelyn Lau, *Runaway: Diary of a Street Kid* (Toronto: Harper Collins, 1989). Written by Lau at the age of 18, this book is an autobiographical account of her experiences as a teenage runaway, drug abuser, and prostitute on the streets of Vancouver.

Roxanne Rimstead, *Remnants of Nation: On Poverty Narratives by Women* (Toronto: University of Toronto Press, 2001). This book is compiled from women's narratives regarding their own poverty. It could be used as case examples, as exploratory research, or as mini-ethnographies. Rimstead suggests that a 'poverty narrative' informs national, cultural, and community identity.

Benedetto Saraceno and Corrado Barbui, 'Poverty and Mental Illness', *Canadian Journal of Psychiatry* 42 (1997): 285–90. This is a literature review of studies that use poverty, cultural poverty, and service delivery inadequacy as risk factors in the development of mental illness. Saraceno and Barbui compare poverty and mental health rates in developing countries to those in developed countries.

D.L. Williamson, 'The Role of the Health Sector in Addressing Poverty', *Canadian Journal of Public Health* 92, 3 (2001): 178–83. The Canadian health-care system has undertaken various initiatives, varying regionally, regarding poverty. These initiatives have included awareness of poverty, prevention of poverty, skills development and education, awareness of the consequences of poverty, and policy changes to alter economic and social conditions that contribute to poverty. These strategies are evaluated, and it is found that they do little to alleviate poverty.

RECOMMENDED WEBSITES

National Council of Welfare

www.ncwcnbes.net

The National Council of Welfare oversees this website, which contains reports on poverty and on related social issues as well as statistical information and policy materials.

National Anti-Poverty Organization

www.napo-onap.ca

The National Anti-Poverty Organization represents the interests of low-income Canadians. This website provides information on key issues, statistics, and lists of publications with the goal of educating and informing the public on the plight of low-income Canadians.

GLOSSARY

Absolute poverty   Lack of the basic necessities (food, shelter, medicine) for easy basic survival. Starvation is an example of absolute poverty.

Adequacy-gradient hypothesis   The hypothesis that economic hardship consistently decreases as age increases.

Affluence-trajectory hypothesis   The hypothesis that economic difficulties should decline as age increases up until late middle age, after which economic hardship should begin to rise.

Culture of poverty   Theory developed by Oscar Lewis characterizing the urban poor as having a distinct set of values and norms, including short-sightedness, impulsiveness, and a tendency to accept their marginalized status in society, and as remaining poor because they pass on these values to future generations.

Economic inequality   Large differences in income and wealth across individuals and groups; differences in the economic power of nations.

Human development index (HDI)   A combined measure of achievement in three basic areas of human development—life expectancy at birth; literacy; and GDP per capita—used by the United Nations Development Program to monitor social and economic progress across countries.

Low-income cut-offs (LICOs)   A formal definition used by Statistics Canada for measuring relative poverty based on the percentage of income devoted to daily necessities (food, shelter, clothing) and determined both regionally and by population (size of city or rural).

Low-income measures (LIMs)   A set of figures representing 50 per cent of the median 'adjusted family income'. Actual incomes are compared with LIMs to determine whether or not a family can be considered 'low-income'.

Market-basket measure (MBM)   A way of measuring income and poverty in absolute, not relative, terms that was added in 2003 to Statistics Canada's methods of measuring income and poverty. It is based on an imaginary basket of market-priced goods and services and on the income needed to purchase the items in the basket. The determination of what goes into this imaginary basket, however, is subjective and tends to exclude all but the absolute essentials of bare survival.

Poverty line   Also called the human poverty index. It represents a usual standard of living and differs between countries. The definition of poverty varies by society, within societies, and also over time.

Relative income hypothesis   Proposal that income inequality alone (as opposed to absolute deprivation) is enough to bring on various health problems, including premature mortality, within a population.

Relative poverty   Survival, but far below the general living standards of the society or social group in which the poor live; affects people's lives in dramatic ways.

Social mobility   The movement of individuals from one social class to another during the course of one's lifetime.

REFERENCES

Adams, Gerald R., Thomas Gullotta, and Mary Anne Clancy. 1985. 'Homeless Adolescents: A Descriptive Study of Similarities and Differences between Runaways and Throwaways', *Adolescence* 20: 715–24.

Akinyele, Isaac O. 1997. 'Household Food Security in Africa', *Development* 40, 2: 71–3.

Anderson, Sarah, and John Cavanagh. 2000. *Top 200: The Rise of Corporate Global Power*. Washington: Institute for Policy Studies. Available at: <www.ipsdc.org/downloads/Top_200.pdf>; accessed 10 Jan. 2003.

Bakken, Rosalie, Marzena Jezewska-Zychowicz, and Mary Winter. 1999. 'Household Nutrition and Health in Poland', *Social Science and Medicine* 49: 1677–87.

Barraclough, Geoffrey. 1967. *An Introduction to Contemporary History*. Harmondsworth, UK: Penguin.

Berney, Lee, David Blane, George Davey Smith, David J. Gunnell, Paula Holland, and Scott M. Montgomery. 2000. 'Socioeconomic Measures in Early Old Age as Indicators of Previous Lifetime Exposure to Environmental Health Hazards', *Sociology of Health and Illness* 22: 415–30.

Bosma, Hans, Michael G. Marmot, Harry Hemingway, Amanda C. Nicholson, Eric Brunner, and Stephen A. Stansfeld. 1997. 'Low Job Control and Risk of Coronary Heart Disease in Whitehall II (Prospective Cohort) Study', *British Medical Journal* 314: 558–65.

Braun, Denny. 1995. 'Negative Consequences to the Rise of Income Inequality', *Research in Politics and Society* 5: 3–31.

Brooks-Gunn, Jeanne, and Greg J. Duncan. 1997. 'The Effects of Poverty on Children', *Future of Children* 7, 2: 55–70.

Cairney, John, and William R. Avison. 1999. 'Age, Social Structure and Perceived Health', paper presented at the annual meeting of the American Sociological Association.

Campaign 2000. 2005. *Decision Time for Canada: Let's Make Poverty History—2005 Report Card on Child Poverty in Canada*. Available at: <www.campaign2000.ca/rc/rc05/05NationalReportCard.pdf>; accessed 25 Feb. 2006.

Canadian Broadcasting Corporation. 2006. 'Aboriginal waters: a slow boil—the state of drinking water on Canada's reserves', 20 Feb. Available at: <www.cbc.ca/slowboil>; accessed 26 Feb. 2006.

Canadian Council on Social Development (CCSD). 2000a. *Canadian Fact Book on Poverty*. Ottawa: CCSD.

———. 2000b. *Urban Poverty in Canada: A Statistical Profile*. Ottawa: CCSD.

———. 2003. 'Aboriginal Children in Poverty in Urban Communities: Social Exclusion and the Growing Racialization of Poverty in Canada'. Available at: <www.ccsd.ca/research.htm>; accessed 26 Feb. 2006.

Canadian Labour Congress. 2003. *Economy: Economic Review and Outlook* 14, 2. Ottawa: Canadian Labour Congress.

Canadian Mortgage and Housing Corporation (CMHC). 2005. *Canadian Housing Observer: Rental Market Survey*. Ottawa: CMHC.

City of Calgary. 2004. *Biennial Count of Homeless Persons in Calgary: Enumerated in Emergency and Transition Facilities, by Service Agencies, and On the Streets—2004 May 12*. Calgary: Policy and Planning, Community Strategies, City of Calgary.

Coburn, David. 2000. 'Income Inequality, Social Cohesion and the Health Status of Populations: The Role of Neo-Liberalism', *Social Science and Medicine* 51, 1: 135–46.

Cotton, Cathy, Yves St-Pierre, and Maryanne Webber. 2000. *Should the Low Income Cutoffs Be Updated? A Discussion Paper*. Income Research Paper Series, Catalogue no. 75F0002MIE1999009. Ottawa: Statistics Canada.

Curry-Stevens, Ann. 2001. *When Markets Fail People: Exploring the Widening Gap between Rich and Poor in Canada*. Toronto: CSJ Foundation for Research and Education.

———. 2004. 'Income Security and Employment in Canada', in Dennis Raphael, ed., *Social Determinants of Health: Canadian Perspectives*. Toronto: Canadian Scholars' Press, 21–38.

Curtis, James, Douglas Baer, and Edward Grabb. 2001. 'Nations of Joiners: Explaining Voluntary Association Membership in Democratic Societies', *American Sociological Review* 66: 783–805.

———, Edward Grabb, and Tina Chui. 1999. 'Public Participation, Protest and Social Inequality', in Curtis, Grabb, and Neil Guppy, eds, *Social Inequality in Canada: Patterns, Problems, and Policies*. Scarborough, Ont.: Prentice-Hall, 371–86.

Daniels, Norman, Bruce Kennedy, and Ichiro Kawachi. 2000. 'Justice Is Good for Our Health', in Daniels, Kennedy, and Kawachi, eds, *Is Inequality Bad for Our Health?* Boston: Beacon Press, 3–33.

Davidson, Paul. 1997. 'So, How Much Money Does It Take To Be Rich?', *USA Today*, 20 June, A1.

De Haan, Laura G., and Shelley MacDermid. 1998. 'The Relationship of Individual and Family Factors to the Psychological Well-Being of Junior High School Students Living in Urban Poverty', *Adolescence* 33: 73–89.

Department of Finance Canada. 2005. 'Helping the Poorest—An Update on Canada's Debt Relief Efforts.' Available at: <www.fin.gc.ca/toce/2005/cdre0105_e.html>; accessed 28 Feb. 2006.

Dominguez, Silvia, and Celeste Watkins. 2003. 'Creating Networks for Survival and Mobility: Social Capital among African-Americans and Latin-American Low-Income Mothers', *Social Problems* 50, 1: 111–35.

Dowler, Elizabeth. 1998. 'Food Poverty and Food Policy', *IDS Bulletin* 29, 1: 58–65.

Duncan, Greg J., and Jeanne Brooks-Gunn, eds. 1997a. *Consequences of Growing Up Poor*. New York: Russell Sage Foundation.

————— and —————. 1997b. 'Income Effects across the Life Span: Integration and Interpretation', in Duncan and Brooks-Gunn (1997a: 596–610).

Durbar Mahila Samanwaya Committee. 2004. Available at: Durbar.org; accessed 28 Feb. 2006.

Ehrenreich, Barbara. 2001. *Nickel and Dimed: On (Not) Getting By in America*. New York: Henry Holt.

Fisher, Gordon M. 1998. 'Using a Little-Known Body of Historical Knowledge: What Can the History of U.S. Poverty Lines Contribute to Present-Day Comparative Poverty Research?', paper presented at the annual meeting of the International Sociological Association.

Forbes. 2006. 'The World's Billionaires'. Available at: <www.forbes.com/billionaires/>; accessed 24 Feb. 2006.

Gilbert, Geoffrey. 1997. 'Adam Smith on the Nature and Causes of Poverty', *Review of Social Economy* 55: 273–91.

Hagan, John. 1994. *Crime and Disrepute*. Thousand Oaks, Calif.: Pine Forge Press.

Hall, Michael, Tamara Knighton, Paul Reed, Patrick Bussiere, D. McRae, and Paddy Bowen. 1998. *Caring Canadians, Involved Canadians: Highlights from the 1997 National Survey of Giving, Volunteering, and Participation*. Ottawa: Statistics Canada, Catalogue no. 71–542–XIE.

Hauser, Robert M., and Megan M. Sweeney. 1997. 'Does Poverty in Adolescence Affect the Life Chances of High School Graduates?', in Duncan and Brooks-Gunn (1997a: 541–95).

Health Canada. 1999. *Toward a Healthy Future: Second Report on the Health of Canadians*. Ottawa: Government Services.

Hobsbawm, E.J. 1959. *Primitive Rebels: Studies in Archaic Forms of Social Movement in the 19th and 20th Centuries*. New York: Norton.

Holdaway, Doris M., and JoAnn Ray. 1992. 'Attitudes of Street Kids toward Foster Care', *Child and Adolescent Social Work Journal* 9: 307–17.

International Labour Organization (ILO). 2002. *A Future without Child Labour*. Geneva: ILO.

Jones, Charles, Linn Clark, Joan Grusec, Randle Hart, Gabriele Plickert, and Lorne Tepperman. 2002. *Poverty, Social Capital, Parenting and Child Outcomes in Canada*. Ottawa: Applied Research Branch, Strategic Policy, Human Resources Development Canada.

Jones-Webb, Rhonda, Lonnie Snowden, Denise Herd, Brian Short, and Peter Hannan. 1997. 'Alcohol-Related Problems among Black, Hispanic and White Men: The Contribution of Neighborhood Poverty', *Journal of Studies on Alcohol* 58: 539–45.

Kanter, R.M. 1972. *Commitment and Community: Communes and Utopias in Sociological Perspective*. Cambridge, Mass.: Harvard University Press.

—————. 1977. *Men and Women of the Corporation*. New York: Basic Books.

Kaplan, George A., Elsie R. Pamuk, John W. Lynch, Richard D. Cohen, and Jennifer L. Balfour. 1999. 'Inequality in Income and Mortality in the United States: Analysis of Mortality and Potential Pathways', in Kawachi et al. (1999: 50–9).

Kawachi, Ichiro, and Bruce P. Kennedy. 1997. 'The Relationship of Income Inequality to Mortality: Does the Choice of Indicator Matter?', *Social Science and Medicine* 45: 1121–7.

—————, —————, and Richard G. Wilkinson, eds. 1999. *The Society and Population Health Reader*, vol. 1, *Income Inequality and Health*. New York: New Press, 50–9.

Kennedy, Bruce P., Ichiro Kawachi, Deborah Prothrow-Stith, Kimberly Lochner, and Vanita Gupta. 1998. 'Social Capital, Income Inequality, and Firearm Violent Crime', *Social Science and Medicine* 47, 1: 7–17.

Kristenson, M., Z. Kucinskiene, B. Bergdahl, H. Calkauskas, V. Urmonas, and K. Orth-Gomer. 1998. 'Increased Psychosocial Strain in Lithuanian versus Swedish Men: The LiVicordia Study', *Psychosomatic Medicine* 60, 3: 277–82.

Kusumayati, Agustin, and Rainer Gross. 1998. 'Ecological and Geographic Characteristics Predict Nutritional Status of Communities: Rapid Assessment for Poor Villages', *Health Policy and Planning* 13: 408–16.

Lewis, Oscar. 1959. *Five Families: Mexican Case Studies in the Culture of Poverty*. New York: Basic Books.

—————. 1966. 'The Culture of Poverty', *Scientific American* 2, 5: 19–25.

Lin, Nan. 2000. 'Inequality in Social Capital', *Contemporary Sociology* 29: 785–95.

Lipman, Ellen L., and David R. Offord. 1997. 'Psychosocial Morbidity among Poor Children in Ontario', in Duncan and Brooks-Gunn (1997a: 239–87).

Lipset, Seymour Martin, James S. Coleman, and Martin A. Trow. 1963. *Union Democracy: The Internal Politics of the International Typographical Union*. New York: Simon & Schuster.

Lynch, John W., George A. Kaplan, and Sarah J. Shema. 1997. 'Cumulative Impact of Sustained Economic Hardship on Physical, Cognitive, Psychological, and Social Functioning', *New England Journal of Medicine* 337: 1889–95.

McEwan, Bruce S. 1999. 'Protective and Damaging Effects of Stress Mediators', in Kawachi et al. (1999: 379–92).

McLeod, Jane D., and Michael J. Shanahan. 1993. 'Poverty, Parenting, and Children's Mental Health', *American Sociological Review* 58: 351–66.

——— and ———. 1996. 'Trajectories of Poverty and Children's Mental Health', *Journal of Health and Social Behavior* 37: 207–20.

Make Poverty History. 2005. 'Poverty Facts and Stats'. Available at: <www.makepovertyhistory.ca/e/elections/kit/facts-stats.pdf>; accessed 25 Feb. 2006.

Marmot, M.G., M. Kogevinas, and M.A. Elston. 1987. 'Social/Economic Status and Disease', *Annual Review of Public Health* 8: 111–35.

———, M.J. Shipley, and G. Rose. 1984. 'Inequalities in Death—Specific Explanations of a General Pattern?', *Lancet* no. 1: 1003–6.

Marx, Karl, and Friedrich Engels. 1955 [1848]. *The Communist Manifesto*, trans. Samuel Moore. New York: Appleton Century Crofts.

Marzuk, Peter M., Kenneth Tardiff, Andrew C. Leon, Charles S. Hirsch, Marina Stajic, Laura Portera, and Nancy Hartwell. 1997. 'Poverty and Fatal Accidental Drug Overdoses of Cocaine and Opiates in New York City: An Ecological Study', *American Journal of Drug and Alcohol Abuse* 23: 221–8.

Merton, Robert K. 1957a. 'Patterns of Influence: Local and Cosmopolitan Influentials', in Merton, *Social Theory and Social Structure*, rev. edn. New York: Free Press, 387–420.

———. 1957b. 'Social Structure and Anomie', in Merton, *Social Theory and Social Structure*, rev. edn. New York: Free Press, 131–60.

Michels, Robert. 1962 [1916]. *Political Parties: A Sociological Study of the Oligarchical Tendencies of Modern Democracy*, trans. Eden Paul and Cedar Paul. New York: Free Press.

Mills, C. Wright. 1959. *The Sociological Imagination*. New York: Oxford University Press.

Mirowsky, John, and Catherine E. Ross. 1999. 'Economic Hardship across the Life Course', *American Sociological Review* 64: 548–69.

National Anti-Poverty Organization. 2003. *The Face of Poverty in Canada*. Ottawa: National Anti-Poverty Organization.

National Council of Welfare. 2004. *Poverty Profile 2001*. Ottawa: Minister of Public Works and Government Services Canada.

———. 2005. *Welfare Incomes 2004*. Ottawa: Minister of Public Works and Government Services Canada.

Neal, Rusty. 2004. *Voices: Women, Poverty, and Homelessness in Canada*. Ottawa: National Anti-Poverty Organization. Available at: <www.napo-onap.ca/en/resources/Voices_English_04232004.pdf>; accessed 28 Feb. 2006.

North, F.M., L.S. Syme, A. Feeney, M. Shipley, and M. Marmot. 1996. 'Psychosocial Work Environment and Sickness Absence among British Civil Servants: The Whitehall II Study', *American Journal of Public Health* 86: 332–40.

Novak, Tony. 1996. 'The Class Analysis of Poverty: A Response to Erik Olin Wright', *International Journal of Health Services* 26, 1: 187–95.

Organization for Economic Co-operation and Development (OECD). 2001. *The Well-Being of Nations: The Role of Human and Social Capital*. Paris: OECD.

Pagani, Linda, Bernard Boulerice, and Richard E. Tremblay. 1997. 'The Influence of Poverty on Children's Classroom Placement and Behavior Problems', in Duncan and Brooks-Gunn (1997a: 311–39).

Parenti, Michael. 1995. *Democracy for the Few*, 6th edn. New York: St Michael's Press.

Payne, Malcolm. 1995. 'Understanding "Going Missing": Issues for Social Work and Social Services', *British Journal of Social Work* 25: 333–48.

Pellegi, Ivan P. 1997. 'On Poverty and Low Income'. Statistics Canada. Available at: <www.statcan.ca/english/concepts/pauv.htm>; accessed 17 Mar. 2003.

Piko, Bettina, and Kevin M. Fitzpatrick. 2001. 'Does Class Matter? SES and Psychosocial Health among Hungarian Adolescents', *Social Science and Medicine* 53: 817–30.

Plass, Peggy S., and Gerald T. Hotaling. 1995. 'The Intergenerational Transmission of Running Away: Childhood Experiences of the Parents of Runaways', *Journal of Youth and Adolescence* 24: 335–48.

Price, Virginia Ann. 1989. 'Characteristics and Needs of Boston Street Youth: One Agency's Response', *Children and Youth Services Review* 11: 75–90.

Pritchard, Alice M. 1993. 'A Common Format for Poverty: A Content Analysis of Social Problems Textbooks', *Teaching Sociology* 21, 1: 42–9.

Putnam, Robert D. 2000. *Bowling Alone: The Collapse and Revival of American Community*. New York: Simon & Schuster.

RBC Economics. 2005. 'Housing Affordability'. Available at: <www.rbc.com/economics/market/pdf/house.pdf>; accessed 25 Feb. 2006.

Ross, David P., Katherine J. Scott, and Peter J. Smith. 2000. *The Canadian Fact Book on Poverty 2000*. Ottawa: Canadian Council on Social Development.

Rotherham-Borus, Mary J. 1993. 'Suicidal Behavior and Risk Factors among Runaway Youths', *American Journal of Psychiatry* 150: 103–7.

Ryan, William. 1976. *Blaming the Victim*. New York: Vintage Books.

Sapolsky, Robert M. 1998. *Why Zebras Don't Get Ulcers: An Updated Guide to Stress, Stress Related Diseases, and Coping*. New York: W.H. Freeman.

———, Susan C. Alberts, and Jeanne Altmann. 1999. 'Hypercortisolism Associated with Social Subordinance or Social Isolation among Wild Baboons', in Kawachi et al. (1999: 421–32).

Sauvy, Alfred. 1969. *General Theory of Population*, trans. Christopher Campos. New York: Basic Books.

Sennett, Richard, and Jonathan Cobb. 1993. *The Hidden Injuries of Class*. New York: Norton.

Shillington, Richard. 1999. 'What Do We Mean by Poverty? Or HRDC Reduces Our Obligations to Poor Children'. Available at: <www.shillington.ca/poverty/mbm.htm>; accessed 17 Mar. 2003.

Shively, Carol A., and Thomas B. Clarkson. 1999. 'Social Status and Coronary Artery Atherosclerosis in Female Monkeys', in Kawachi et al. (1999: 393–404).

———, Kathy Laber-Larid, and Raymond F. Anton. 1999. 'Behavior and Physiology of Social Stress and Depression in Female Cynomolgus Monkeys', in Kawachi et al. (1999: 405–20).

Simons, Ronald, and Les Whitbeck. 1991. 'Running Away during Adolescence as a Precursor to Adult Homelessness', *Social Science Review* 65: 224–47.

Smith, George Davey, Danny Dorling, David Gordon, and Mary Shaw. 1999. 'The Widening Health Gap: What Are the Solutions?', *Critical Public Health* 9, 2: 151–70.

Social Planning and Research Council of BC. 2005. *On Our Streets and in Our Shelters: Results from the 2005 Greater Vancouver Homeless Count*. Vancouver: Social Planning and Research Council of BC.

Stiffman, Arlene R. 1989a. 'Physical and Sexual Abuse in Runaway Youths', *Child Abuse and Neglect* 13: 417–26.

———. 1989b. 'Suicide Attempts in Runaway Youths', *Suicide and Life-Threatening Behavior* 19: 147–59.

Stackhouse, John. 2002. 'Why No One Cares about the Poor: The Mass Media's Role in Poverty and Its Perceptions', David Hopper Lecture in International Development, University of Guelph, 22 Oct. Available at: <www.uoguelph.ca/cip/PDFS/HopperLectures/stackhouse2002.pdf>; accessed 28 Feb. 2006.

Statistics Canada. 2001. *Canadians with Low Incomes*. Canadian Centre for Justice Statistics Profile Series, Catalogue no. 85F0033MIE2001004. Ottawa: Statistics Canada.

———. 2005. *Income in Canada 2003*. Ottawa: Statistics Canada, Catalogue no. 75–202–XIE.

Susser, Ezra S., Shang P. Lin, Sarah A. Conover, and Elmer L. Struening. 1991. 'Childhood Antecedents of Homelessness in Psychiatric Patients', *American Journal of Psychiatry* 148: 1026–30.

Thiede, Michael, and Stefan Traub. 1997. 'Mutual Influences of Health and Poverty: Evidence from German Panel Data', *Social Science and Medicine* 45: 867–77.

Toronto Homelessness Action Task Force. 2003. *The Toronto Report Card on Housing and Homelessness 2003*. Toronto: City of Toronto.

United Nations (UN). 2000. 'Message of the United Nations Secretary-General, Kofi Annan, on the International Day for the Eradication of Poverty, 17 October 2000'. Available at: <www.un.org/events/poverty2000/messages.htm>; accessed 14 July 2006.

———. 2005. *The Millennium Development Goals Report 2005*. New York: UN.

United Nations Children's Fund (UNICEF). 2001. *Profiting from Abuse: An Investigation into the Sexual Exploitation of Our Children*. New York: UNICEF.

———. 2005. *State of the World's Children 2006*. New York: UNICEF.

UNICEF Canada. 2006. *Global Child Survival and Health: A 50-Year Progress Report from UNICEF Canada*. Toronto: UNICEF Canada.

United Nations Development Program (UNDP). 2005. *Human Development Report 2005: International Cooperation at a Crossroads—Aid, Trade, and Security in an Unequal World*. New York: UNDP.

Whitbeck, Les B., Danny R. Hoyt, and Kevin A. Ackley. 1997. 'Families of Homeless and Runaway Adolescents: A Comparison of Parent/Caretaker and Adolescent Perspectives on Parenting, Family Violence, and Adolescent Conduct', *Child Abuse and Neglect* 21: 517–28.

Wilkinson, Richard G. 1994. 'Income Distribution and Life Expectancy', *British Medical Journal* 304: 165–8.

———. 1996. *Unhealthy Societies: The Afflictions of Inequality*. London: Routledge.

World Health Organization (WHO). 1997. *Fact Sheet No. 170: Health and Environment in Sustainable Development*. Available at: <www.who.int/inf-fs/en/fact170.html>; accessed 12 June 2001.

CHAPTER TWO

CRIME AND VIOLENCE

LEARNING OBJECTIVES

- To know the definitions of 'crime', 'laws', and 'social order'.
- To understand how crime is measured and the problems associated with these measures.
- To be able to distinguish among different types of crime.
- To appreciate the demography of crime.
- To learn about theories explaining criminal activities.
- To understand the economic, social, and psychological consequences of crime.
- To discover the impact of crime on health.
- To know about possible solutions to the crime problem and debates about capital punishment.

Introduction

This chapter is about crime and its victims. It discusses violence, murder, assault, homicide, and robbery, and also the more common, less dramatic criminal acts. Finally, it is about offenders and the reasons they commit their offences. Therefore, it is also about responsibility, guilt, and economic payoffs to crime.

Crime is a social problem for several reasons. First, as we will see, crime has real effects on people's health, safety, and sense of well-being. Victimization can be traumatic. It can cause people to withdraw from normal social life. Second, and as a result, victimization on a large scale can reduce people's trust in social institutions and their willingness to take part in community life. Thus, fear of crime can reduce a community's vitality and cohesion. Third, crime and its aftermath can damage the central institutions of society—families, workplaces, and schools, for example—and in this way hinder our ability to carry out the most basic social activities of learning, earning, and raising children.

As we shall see, crime is a social activity, with social causes and effects. Men are more likely to be involved in violent crimes than women, both as victims and as offenders—more likely than women to commit acts of murder, forcible rape, armed robbery, aggravated assault, and arson, for example (see Figure 2.1). Many researchers believe that differential socialization provides the best explanation for this pattern.

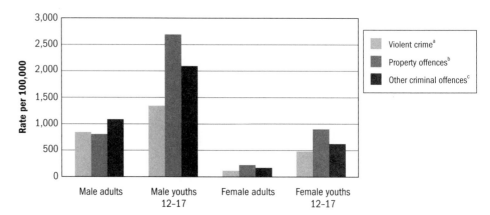

FIGURE 2.1 Adults and Youths Charged, by Offence Category and Gender, Canada, 2001

[a] Violent crimes involve offences that deal with the application, or threat of application, of force to a person. These include homicide, attempted murder, various forms of sexual and non-sexual assault, robbery, and abduction. Traffic incidents that result in death or bodily harm are included under Criminal Code traffic incidents.

[b] Property crimes involve unlawful acts with the intent of gaining property but do not involve the use of threat of violence against an individual. Theft, breaking and entering, fraud, and possession of stolen goods are examples of property crimes.

[c] Other Criminal Code offences involve the remaining offences that are not classified as violent or property crimes (excluding traffic offences). Examples are mischief, bail violations, disturbing the peace, arson, prostitution, and offensive weapons.

Source: Adapted from Statistics Canada, 'Health Indicators', Catalogue no. 82-221 October 2002, vol. 2002, no. 2, p. 11, available at http://www.statcan.ca/english/freepub/82-221-XIE/01002/tables/pdf/22142.pdf.

Theorists differ in their views on criminal causation and responsibility. Some argue that criminal behaviour, especially where property crimes are concerned, is a result of rational calculation that takes into account the profitability and risk of a crime. Others argue that crime will result whenever groups possess different amounts of power and influence. As a result, criminal activity will increase whenever social inequality increases. Some argue that strict law enforcement and harsh prisons will solve the 'crime problem'. Others argue that prisons cause as many problems as they solve—in fact, they teach crime and harden criminals. Let us now look more closely at these beliefs and at the relevant evidence.

Defining Crime, Laws, and Social Order

All industrial societies make formal rules about what their members can and cannot do, and Canadian society is no exception. We know these formal rules as **laws**, and when someone breaks a law we say that he or she has committed a **crime**. Such laws are important tools for promoting good behaviour—if people know that the police and courts will enforce these laws. The regularity of enforcement and the harshness of the punishment applied to lawbreakers depend, in turn, on how seriously a society takes the offending behaviour.

The breaking of rules makes crime a social problem because of the symbolic meaning of social order and disorder. **Social order** exists when people obey rules. Social order is better than **social disorder**: with social order, life is predictable and 'safe'. The rules in place not only serve to show which behaviours are acceptable, they also allow people to predict the behaviour of others. Social order does not emerge routinely out of kindly impulses and spontaneous co-operation—there are simply too many people and too many competing interests. Order must be manufactured and protected. Under the best circumstances, the social order that emerges is fair and accepted.

In other words, laws and other rules help create an orderly society that is safe for those within it. They limit the risk of harm from others, and they influence how comfortable people will feel in public situations. When rules are broken routinely, disorder prevails. Because disorder is ill-defined and unpredictable, it is unsafe. Disorder proves that control has been lost, that the system of rules that defines the boundaries of acceptable behaviour has broken down. Then people no longer control their actions. They are free to pursue their own interests without considering the costs for other members of society. They do so not because people are innately anti-social or vicious, but because they are protecting themselves. Under conditions of total uncertainty, nothing is more rational than preventive self-interest.

Law and order signal to people that there is some certainty in the society. As we have said, social order is important because it symbolizes safe predictability and, by symbolizing it, maintains it. Once this safe predictability starts to break down, it is liable to break down more rapidly and seriously. If a broken window in a building is left unrepaired, all the rest of the windows will soon be broken. Window-breaking blossoms because an unrepaired broken window signals that no one cares. Since no one cares and since breaking more windows costs them nothing, people are likely to break them (Wilson and Kelling, 1982; Zimbardo, 1969).

Crime in Canada and Elsewhere

A few crimes that are common, easily investigated, and cheaply prosecuted make up the bulk of our criminal statistics at any given time. As a result, changes in the recorded rates of crime reflect mainly changes in the reporting and prosecution of particular crimes. Changes in the crime rate also reflect changes in victims' willingness to report crimes and the willingness of police to investigate them. Measuring the total rate of crime is difficult since this sort of **self-reporting** may not be accurate. **Victimization surveys** may yield a truer account. In these surveys, samples of people report how often, within a given period, they have been victims of particular crimes. However, these surveys, too, are subject to distortion. Most often, we rely for our information on official statistics on arrest, conviction, and imprisonment, knowing that this information is incomplete and possibly biased.

In 2004, over 2.6 million Criminal Code and drug offences were recorded across Canada, approximately 8,000 incidents per 100,000 people. These offences ranged from illegal gambling to theft to murder (Statistics Canada, 2005b). Of these offences in 2004, 47 per cent were property crimes, making them the most often occurring offences, as they have been for many years. We know a great deal more, however, about the prevalence of certain crimes such as murder, robbery, and kidnapping. That is because people are more likely to report occurrences of these crimes to the police and because such reports are more likely to lead to investigations, arrests, and convictions. As well, these types of crimes tend to grab headlines in the news media.

People are much less willing to report other crimes. Sexual assault is an example. Many women (who make up most of the victims) fear the psychological, legal, and public humiliations that have often accompanied such reporting in the past. Also, of the sexual assaults reported, only a small fraction result in convictions—judges and juries are often unwilling to believe the victim—and convictions often result in less than the maximum sentence. The victim may also fear revenge by the criminal or, if the offender is an intimate, may want to spare him a criminal record. Some victims may even feel they are to blame in some way.

Other crimes that are likely to go unreported are committed for gain by professional criminals, such as robbery, arson, and the trafficking of drugs, simply because professionals are better able than amateurs to cover their tracks and avoid arrest and conviction.

Crimes of Violence

Contrary to the impression presented on the nightly news, violent crimes accounted for only about 11 per cent of total crimes reported in Canada in 2004. Yet criminologists refer to these types of offences as **conventional crimes** because they are the illegal behaviours that most people think of as crime. Also, they are crimes that people agree are serious and deserving of harsh punishment.

The most headline-grabbing violent crime is **homicide**, the killing of one person by another. It can be subdivided into two categories, murder and manslaughter, depending on whether the homicide involves malicious intent. Typically, men are more likely to be involved in homicides than women, both as victims (67 per cent of all victims are men) and as offenders (88 per cent of those charged with homicide are men). Victims of homicide are more likely to be killed by a family member or acquaintance than by a stranger. Still, homicides are on the whole a rare occurrence in Canada— they, along with attempted murder charges, accounted for only 0.4 per cent of all crimes of violence in 2004.

In contrast, *assault* charges accounted for nearly 90 per cent of all violent crimes reported (Statistics Canada, 2005b). Assault can be differentiated depending on whether a weapon was involved or if major bodily harm was inflicted. *Sexual assault*, most seriously rape but also sexual harassment, is another form of violent crime. Social science and law enforcement experts agree that most sexual assault victims probably do not report their experience to the police.

Stalking has recently emerged as a new social problem. This crime has gained a great deal of notice in recent years because it is common and is associated with gendered harassment, abuse, and violence. Surveys have found that repeated stalking is reported by up to 62 per cent of young adults, although results vary depending on the sample and on the precise definition of 'stalking' used (Davis and Frieze, 2000). In a study of US college students, for example, 25 per cent of the women and 11 per cent of the men had been stalked at some point in their lives, and 6 per cent were currently being stalked (Bjerregaard, 2000: 401). Most legally defined stalking incidents, in which victim fear is a key component, involve men stalking women (Davis and Frieze, 2000).

Stalking is a type of relationship abuse that may evolve into other physical, psychological, and sexual forms, including violence against women. It has various determinants— socio-cultural, interpersonal, dyadic, situational, and intrapersonal (White et al., 2000), often with deep roots in the history of the stalker. For example, men who experienced parental divorce or separation show more extreme stalking behaviours than men who did not experience parental divorce or separation (Langhinrichsen-Rohling and Rohling, 2000). Often, stalking follows a relationship breakup. The recipient of the breakup (that is, the person dumped) feels anger and jealousy, anxious attachment, and a need for control, and may express these feelings by intensified courtship and stalking (Davis et al., 2000).

Most stalkers are former, rather than current, intimates. Typically, stalking involves efforts to re-establish a relationship in the face of the other's resistance. Usually, the victim recognizes that she is being followed and learns that someone is seeking detailed information about her life and routines. She may have to turn away frequent efforts to escalate the relationship. Sometimes the stalker's attentions may turn hostile and even violent (Emerson et al., 1998). Stalked women often seek a restraining order so that police can charge the stalker with violating the restraining order (Tjaden and Thoennes, 2000).

As we will see in a later chapter, violence between intimates is common, with men especially likely to carry out the most extreme types of violence, up to and including intimate-partner homicide (Browne et al., 1999). The combination of violence with stalking is lethal. Compared to battered women who are only occasionally stalked, women who are relentlessly stalked report more severe simultaneous physical violence, sexual assault, and emotional abuse after separation, as well as higher rates of depression and post-traumatic stress disorder (Mechanic et al., 2000).

Non-Violent Crimes

Most crimes committed in Canada are non-violent in nature. The major non-violent crimes include theft, mischief and property damage, drug production and trafficking, and breaking and entering.

Vice crimes include the use of illegal drugs, illegal gambling, communication for prostitution, and the possession, distribution, or sale of child pornography. These crimes provide the greatest opportunities for organized crime, since most societies bar legal access to these goods and services, yet many people are willing to pay for them nevertheless. We will discuss organized crime shortly.

White-collar crimes can be defined as crimes 'committed by a person of respectability and high social status in the course of his occupation' (Sutherland, 1949). These include fraud, bribery, insider trading, embezzlement, computer crime, and forgery, and they can amount to anywhere from hundreds to millions of dollars. Fraudulent practices rely on the ignorance, fear, or greed of others. Often, white-collar criminals take advantage of gaps in the social structure—for example, loopholes or uncertainties about new laws or economic conditions—to profit from their crimes (Tillman and Indergaard, 1999). They prosper wherever governments have decided they have no important role to play in supervising the economic marketplace. Governments typically give white-collar crime a lower priority than conventional crime, despite much evidence that white-collar crime does great economic and physical harm (Friedrichs, 1995).

However, in recent years white-collar crimes in corporations and governments have come under strong public and legal scrutiny, following a series of high-profile exposés of bold criminal activity among the business elite, particularly in the US. For many average citizens, the well-documented downfall and conviction of executives at Enron, Worldcom, Tyco, and Cendant Corporation, among others, merely confirmed what they had suspected all along—that in spite of rhetoric about their commitment to workers, shareholders, and the broader community, corporate boardrooms are too often ruled by greed, self-interest, and a lust for power. Nor was Canada without its fraudulent practices: in the 2004 federal sponsorship scandal, for example, $100 million in public funds was diverted by members of the Liberal government to Liberal-friendly advertising agencies in Quebec. The public outrage over perceived widespread political corruption in Ottawa helped to oust the Liberal Party from power in the 2006 federal election.

The financial damage caused by white-collar crime is tremendous; yet, worse still, these crimes can also result in injury or death. For example, the same ignorance, self-interest, and fraud that underpin the majority of corporate crimes caused seven deaths and hundreds of hospitalizations during the Walkerton, Ontario, water contamination scandal in 2000. A classic case of deadly fraud involved General Motors two decades ago. When an internal report uncovered a gas-tank defect in one of GM's cars, the authors of the study noted that it would be cheaper to settle the lawsuits that might result from accidents in which the victim burned to death because of the defect (estimated to cost US$2.40 per car produced) than to recall and correct the design flaw (estimated to cost $8.59 per car produced). So although General Motors knew that the gas tanks on some of their vehicles were unsafe, likely to cause accidental deaths, and, in turn, likely to produce lawsuits, a cost-benefit analysis convinced executives to ignore the problem instead (White, 1999). As predicted, people died.

Offences against occupational health and safety laws are acts of workplace deviance—typically, regulatory offences rather than crimes—that are widespread and potentially harmful, though not always well recorded (Hutter, 1999). Employee safety and health are often sacrificed for the sake of corporate profit, as in the case of the Westray coal mine in Pictou County, Nova Scotia. There, 26 workers were killed when the mine exploded in 1992. A study found that the explosion resulted directly from the carelessness of managers responsible for the workers' safety. Justice Peter Richard, during an official inquiry into the Westray accident, stated that managers at the site 'displayed a certain disdain for safety and appeared to regard safety-conscious workers as the wimps in the organization' (Hamilton, 1997).

Other types of corporate crime include price-fixing, antitrust violations, and tax fraud. Others still, discussed in Chapter 11, include toxic waste disposal, pollution violations, and intentional destruction of the environment. As is evident from this list, corporate and white-collar crime, like organized crime, is widespread, costly, and dangerous. It is also well-hidden, owing to the power and social standing of the criminals and their high degree of organization and influence.

Organized Crime: A Window on Our Culture?

North Americans are fascinated by the glamour and excitement of organized crime, as shown by the many books, movies, television programs, and music videos that feature organized crime figures. Organized crime rings that currently exist in Canada include the Hong Kong Triad, the Colombian Mafia, the Russian Mafia, and motorcycle gangs like the Hell's Angels. These groups have been variously mixed up in drug trafficking, prostitution, extortion, bribery, money laundering, assaults, and homicides. The conventional image of organized crime, however, is the Italian Mafia, as headed by a patriarchal, raspy-voiced Don Corleone figure making various 'offers that we cannot refuse'. Other portrayals of the organized criminal put him—it is always a 'him'—in the role of a modern-day Robin Hood, crazed psychopath, or ambitious and creative manager. We have many images of organized crime today, some more positive than others.

Early sociologists believed that crime results from poverty and that crime in poor neighbourhoods of the United States results from social disorganization: the more disorganization, the more crime. After roughly 1940, however, with the publication of William Whyte's classic *Street Corner Society* (1981 [1943]), sociologists changed their views. They came to recognize that crime—especially crime in poor neighbourhoods—

was often highly organized. It was also closely connected with the social, political, and economic life of the people in the community. It was a basic part of city life—indeed, of national corporate and political life.

Research shows that modern organized crime operates at the crossroads of legitimate and illegitimate business, family, and formal organization (see, e.g., Ianni, 1972). It has as strong connections to white-collar crime as it does to vice crimes (such as drug trafficking, pornography, and prostitution). Organized crime draws on the talents of professionals and amateurs, older and younger criminals. What organized crime shows us vividly is that crime is a learned, organized social activity with historical cultural roots. It is often grounded in traditional notions of kinship and friendship, honour and duty. Organized crime is a social form, not the mere result of a biological genetic peculiarity, as early criminologists such as Cesar Lombroso (e.g., Lombroso-Ferrero, 1972 [1911]) believed. Organized crime is not a departure from mainstream society; it is fully a part of it, and plays a crucial role in the world's economic and political activities.

However, the need for secrecy means criminal organizations cannot be structured quite like other large formal organizations, such as the Catholic Church, the Canadian Forces, or IBM. Every secret organization depends, to an unusual degree, on friendship and kinship relations, which help to maintain order and conformity (on this, see Erickson, 1981; and Simmel, 1950 [1906], on secret societies).

At the base of organized crime is an organizing principle that sociologists have variously called *patronage* or **clientelism**. Tony Soprano, the 'Godfather' figure on a recent television series, might be surprised to learn that his 'boss' role in the cities and suburbs of modern New Jersey goes back hundreds of years to the agricultural organization of Mediterranean Europe. There, Tony would have been called the 'patron', and his collaborators would have been called 'clients'. From a functionalist perspective, organized crime exists because a criminal underworld provides certain services—whether in breaking union strikes, stealing elections, or providing drugs and prostitutes—that law-abiding citizens cannot do—or be seen to do—for themselves. In this way, the traditional forms of organized crime suit modern business and politics to a tee.

Organized crime in urban North America prospers under four key conditions. First, organized crime flourishes under conditions of scarcity and inequality. It is most common in poor communities with a wide range of economic inequality and, often, strong family traditions. Second, it is common where poverty and prejudice keep people from moving easily to find work elsewhere. Third, organized crime provides protection in communities that lack equal legal or human rights or equal access to welfare, health care, and good-quality education. Finally, organized crime flourishes among people who lack human capital and cultural capital. North American capitalism is one type of economic and social system that produces these conditions, though it is not the only one. In these respects, South American neo-feudalism and Russian neo-capitalism do just as well.

The Demography of Crime

Gender: Offenders

The gender gap in crime—whether organized, professional, or amateur crime—is nearly universal: women commit fewer criminal acts than men (Steffensmeier and Allan, 1996). There are a few small exceptions to this rule, however. One exception is the rate of females killing intimate partners, which is almost as high as that of men killing intimate partners (0.75:1), at least in North America (Wilson and Daly, 1992). As well, women are twice as likely as men to be arrested for prostitution (Wrangham and Peterson, 1997).

Otherwise, the statistics for crimes are mainly about men. Of the more than 566,000 Canadians adults charged with a Criminal Code offence in 2004, only 18 per cent were female. Among youths, the female percentage is slightly higher, at 23 per cent.

The gender gap is particularly pronounced with respect to violent crimes. In Canada, for example, the ratio of males to females charged with violent crimes in 2004 was more than 4.5:1. However, this gap is closing, particularly among youths. In 1984, for instance, females 17 and under accounted for 19 per cent of all violent offence charges laid; by 2004, that figure had increased to 26 per cent (Statistics Canada, 2005b). Other research has found that men are 7 times more likely than women to commit arson, 9 times more likely to commit murder, 10 times more likely to commit armed robbery, 35 times more likely to discharge a firearm with the intent to harm, 54 times more likely to commit sexual assault, and 78 times more likely to commit forcible rape (ibid.; Wrangham and Peterson, 1997).

A similar gender pattern emerges for non-violent offences, with men committing property crimes, for example, at a ratio of nearly 4:1 compared to women. North American data indicate that men are more than twice as likely than women to commit fraud, 7 times more likely to engage in illegal gambling, 8 times more likely to vandalize, 8.5 times more likely to be arrested for drunkenness, 9 times more likely to steal a car, and 11 times more likely to commit a break-and-enter offence (Statistics Canada, 2005b; Wrangham and Peterson, 1997). Again, however, the gender gap has been growing smaller in recent decades (Statistics Canada, 2005b; Canadian Centre for Justice Statistics, 1995).

Explanations of these gender differences vary. Some researchers say that biology is the answer, that men's higher levels of testosterone incline them towards aggression and hostile actions. Others say that **differential socialization** is the cause: that the male subculture is more violent and that young males are encouraged to use aggressive and violent behaviours to solve problems.

Gender: Victims

Just as criminal offenders are primarily male, so too are victims of crime. This is true for most criminal offence categories, including homicide, robbery, and assault. There are, however, several exceptions. For example, men are disproportionately the perpetrators of domestic and sex-based crimes, and women are disproportionately their victims.

Domestic abuse is a serious social problem throughout the world, and it is particularly problematic in cultures that subscribe to a patriarchal world view in which wives and daughters are inferior to husbands and sons. Canada, like some other nations populated to a considerable extent by immigrants of hundreds of ethnicities and numerous faiths, is caught in a dilemma for this reason. On the one hand, Canada wants to provide its citizens with free religious, cultural, and ethnic expression; on the other hand, it wants to protect the rights and safety of its more vulnerable members, including women and children. In households where women are abused by men who use cultural norms to justify their criminal behaviour, the victims may be too frightened to seek help or, through physical confinement or language and other social barriers, may not even be aware that help is available.

Victims of sex-based crimes, including sexual assault and rape, are also mainly female. One social explanation for this is the continued ambivalence that (male-dominated) North American society holds towards sex and, in particular, female sexuality. On the one hand, the female body is endlessly displayed on television, in films, and in marketing campaigns as a sexual object for male consumption. At the same time, women who take control of their sexuality are often accused of being overly aggressive and characterized as 'tramps' or 'sluts'. Despite the sexual revolution of the 1960s, remnants of Victorian prudery still remain. The result is an uneasy and conflicted attitude towards sex, which can sometimes show itself in violence. It would be tempting to dismiss sexual predators as psychopaths, but in important ways their behaviour merely reflects the hypocrisy and ambivalence of our broader society, which still reflects patriarchal power differentials despite the inroads of the women's movement over the past half-century. Our culture unwittingly promotes sexually violent behaviour.

Age

Stated simply, young people are more likely to commit criminal acts than old people. This is above all true for property crimes, where there is a large drop in the number of people accused after the age of 18. People under the age of 25 committed 37 per cent of all violent crimes in 1997, for example. Accordingly, as Rebecca Kong (1999) notes, as the Canadian population has become older, the crime rate has dropped. An aging society is a more law-abiding society.

One explanation is that young people are more likely to be unemployed or to work in low-wage jobs. Thus, as the sociologist Robert K. Merton (1938) has argued, they are more likely to use 'innovations' to achieve their culturally desired goals (that is, money and material goods). They have less investment in the old, conventional ways of doing things. As a result, wherever social events or occasions bring together large numbers of young men—especially unemployed or underemployed young men—there will be high rates of crime. This will be especially true of cities with high unemployment rates and high rates of recent immigration from less developed countries. Moreover, juveniles are protected from many of the legal penalties of criminal activity; they may be arrested and convicted without any lasting legal consequence.

Victimization from Crime

Crime produces victims, and some people are more likely than others to become victims. To some degree, this has to do with involvement in criminal activities: people who commit crimes are more likely to have crimes committed against them. At the same time, more is involved than just criminals victimizing criminals. It is important, then, to understand where and against whom crimes are committed.

Demographic and Community Correlates of Criminal Victimization

At an individual level, many characteristics have been said to predispose some people to higher risks of victimization than others. These include demographic variables, such as being male, young, unmarried, or unemployed (Arnold et al., 2005). However, as we saw above, females are at an unduly high risk of being victims of certain types of crimes, specifically sex-based offences and domestic violence. Risky behaviours, such as high levels of alcohol consumption or living on the street, also increase a person's risk of being victimized (Hoyt et al., 1999).

Crime Victimization Patterns in Canada

- The risk of self-reported violent victimization is highest among young people aged 15-24, single people, those who frequently participate in evening activities, and those who live in an urban area.

- In general, people living west of the Manitoba-Ontario border are also at higher overall risk of victimization, but there were some exceptions.

- The self-reported rate of violent victimization for the 1 per cent of Canadians who self-identify as gay or lesbian is about 2.5 times higher than the rate for heterosexuals.

- People who frequently participate in evening activities have a victimization rate of 174 incidents per 1,000 population, four times the rate for people who participate in few evening activities.

Source: Canadian Centre for Justice Statistics (2005). Available at: <www.statscan.ca/daily/english/051124/d051124b.htm>; accessed 28 Feb. 2006.

At the community level, the nature of one's neighbourhood plays an obvious but important role in victimization patterns. Many ingredients go into determining the attractiveness and safety of a community, including socio-economic vitality, social cohesion and trust, community resources and infrastructure, and mechanisms of informal social control. In general, crime rates go up when certain neighbourhood characteristics, such as household income and home ownership, decline, and a vicious cycle is established with the increase in crime.

Routine Activities Theory

Besides studying the demographic and neighbourhood explanations of victimization, researchers have examined the social process of victimization. Routine activities theory states that victimization requires the convergence of likely offenders, suitable targets, and the absence of capable guardians. That is, to be victimized, vulnerable people need to pass through unsafe environments in the absence of protectors. No wonder, then, that victimization reflects our routine activities—criminal and otherwise—and the increased opportunities for victimization in modern urban life. Automobiles, vacations, college enrolment, female labour force participation, and new consumer goods all improve our lives, but they also provide new occasions for criminal behaviour and victimization.

To repeat, for victimization to occur, an 'offender' and 'suitable target' must converge in a 'hot spot', or suitable locale, where 'effective guardians' are absent (Felson and Cohen, 1980). Hot spots where the risks of crime are particularly great include downtown entertainment districts (Cochran et al., 2000) and tourist attractions abroad (Mawby et al., 2000). Figure 2.2 shows the range of crime rates by province.

SUITABLE TARGETS

Suitable targets are people who are routinely exposed to criminal activity or who, for other reasons, have heightened vulnerability. For example, taxi drivers have a greater than average risk of victimization because of their repeated interaction with strangers at night (Elzinga, 1996). Gay men and lesbians have a greater than average risk because of hostile public attitudes towards them in some quarters (Tiby, 2001). Generally, people who are powerless or vulnerable run higher risks of victimization. Thus, tourists are more likely than natives of the same class background to experience victimization while on holiday in a strange place (Mawby et al., 1999). For example, the risk of victimization is 8 to 10 times higher for foreign visitors to the (relatively safe) Netherlands than it is for natives of the country (Hauber and Zandbergen, 1996).

Three characteristics, identified as putting youth at risk of victimization, probably apply to older people as well. They are the target's (i.e., victim's) vulnerability (for example, physical weakness or psychological distress), gratifiability (for example, female gender for the crime of sexual assault), and antagonism (for example, ethnic or group identities that may spark hostility or resentment) (Finkelhor and Asdigian, 1996). Repeat victimization—that is, crimes targeting the same victim over time—may be of sociological interest because they identify people who are particularly susceptible to targeting (Gallagher, 2000).

Socio-demographic factors (such as age, race, and sex) and economic factors (such as income) predict victimization in a wide variety of situations, including homicide (Caywood, 1988). With some exceptions, poor and powerless people are more vulnerable than rich and powerful people, with one exception: people with more and better property—larger homes, newer cars—are more likely to have their property stolen (Mesch, 1997).

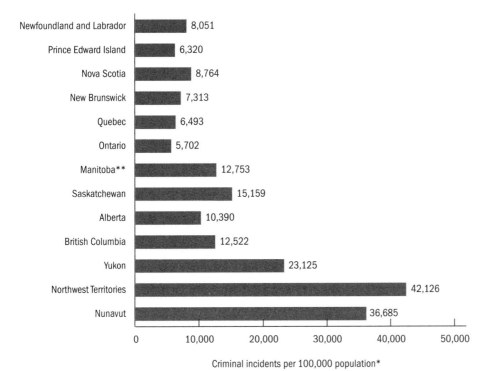

FIGURE 2.2 Crime Rates, Canadian Provinces and Territories, 2004
*Total Criminal Code offences also include other Criminal Code offences (excluding traffic) not shown in this figure.
**Crime data from April to December 2004 for Winnipeg are estimates (except for homicide and motor vehicle theft) due to the implementation of a new records management system.
Source: Adapted from Statistics Canada (2005c).

As we have noted several times, women risk certain kinds of victimization more than men. Female homicide victims, for example, tend to be killed by a spouse, another family member, or an intimate partner as a result of domestic violence; men are more likely to be killed by a stranger in a public place (Pratt and Deosaransingh, 1997). Thus, 'home' and the routine activities associated with home have a different meaning for women and men. Women and men have different risks of victimization at home than they do in school and at places of public leisure (Mustaine and Tewksbury, 1997). However, public places also carry their own risks for women. Women run higher than usual risks, for example, when using public transportation, living near a park, or drinking alcohol. Women are 46 per cent more likely to be victims than men, especially if they eat out often and spend time socializing. Risk of victimization is due, in these and other cases, to increased exposure to offenders and lack of protectors (Mustaine and Tewksbury, 1998).

Elderly people run higher risks of victimization than middle-aged people, especially for crimes of robbery, intimidation, vandalism, and forgery or fraud (McCabe and Gregory, 1998). Robbery is the most serious offence committed against elderly victims of a violent incident, and men and women are equally likely to experience it (Bachman et al., 1998). Most such robberies take place outside the home during routine activities. Elderly people robbed in this way run higher risks of serious physical injury and even death than younger people who are robbed (Faggiani and Owens, 1999). This is not primarily because they lead dangerous lifestyles. Their risk of theft-related homicide is relatively high because they are more likely than younger people to lack capable guardianship and to be perceived as suitable targets. This risk increases with age, and is especially high when victims and offenders are socially distant (that is, unconnected) (Nelsen and Huff-Corzine, 1998).

At the other end of the age distribution, juveniles aged 12–17 are more likely than adults to be victims of violent crimes and to suffer from crime-related injuries. Juvenile victims are also more likely than adult victims to know their offenders (Hashima and Finkelhor, 1999). A Canadian study of high school students in Calgary found that, except for sexual victimization, males report higher victimization rates, in and out of school, than females. Younger students report higher rates of victimization at school than older students. Finally, students who report moderate to high levels of victimization are also more likely to report moderate to high levels of delinquency (Paetsch and Bertrand, 1999), confirming the link between criminal activity and criminal victimization.

Immigrants and ethnic minorities are also at higher than average risk of victimization, especially in respect to crimes against persons. We sometimes refer to these as 'hate crimes'. In Sweden, for example, immigrants with a non-European appearance are more often victims of personal crimes than are other immigrants (Martens, 2001). The victimization of minority persons is higher than average in the Netherlands, too; their risk depends on their age and length of residence in the country (Junger-Tas, 1997). In the United States, blacks are also the victims of hate crimes by whites, and there is some evidence that the number of hate crimes has risen in the last decade (Torres, 1999; but compare Cohen, 1999; Miller and Myers, 2000).

Gay men and lesbian women are sometimes victims of hate crimes, too. Recent debates about the cultural and legal status of sexual-orientation minorities have increased the awareness of violence against gays and lesbians (Tewksbury et al., 1999). It is not clear whether this anti-gay violence itself has increased, however. Our information about the extent of hate crimes against these groups is hindered by the reluctance of gays and lesbians to report victimization because of concerns about police homophobia (Peel, 1999).

Inmates of 'total institutions' are also liable to suffer victimization on a day-to-day basis. Common offences against prisoners include assault, robbery, threats of violence, theft of property from cells, verbal abuse, and exclusion (O'Donnell and Edgar, 1998; Wooldredge, 1998). The main perpetrators are other prisoners.

HOT SPOTS

Often, situational context—the where and when of a sexually violent crime—is an even better predictor of the outcome of rape attempts than victim or offender characteristics (Clay-Warner, 2000). That is because targets of crime and violence are at greater risk in some places than others. As we have just mentioned, prisons are very risky places for prisoners, for example. Public places generally increase the risk of rape for women, and women who are highly mobile—working women, students, and younger women overall—are at a much higher risk of rape than women who are less mobile (Ploughman and Stensrud, 1986).

Crime on college campuses is a relatively unstudied phenomenon. We can be certain that crimes are going on there as everywhere else in society. However, colleges often use alternative strategies to resolve disputes and internal procedures to deal with, or hide, the offences that occur (Konradi, 1999). As a result, we know little about who is victimized on campus, or how (Fernandez-Lanier, 1999).

Fear of Crime

Much has been written about the near-epidemic levels of fear of crime and anxiety over potential victimization. Although the overall crime rate—as well as the rates for most types of Criminal Code offences in Canada—has decreased dramatically since the early 1990s, many Canadians continue to think that crime, and especially violent crime, is occurring more often than in the past. This error is important because it influences decisions about the use of public funds for justice and public safety issues (e.g., hiring more police officers versus investing in crime prevention social programs). For this and other reasons, some have believed for a long time that the fear of crime has become a problem as grave as crime itself (Clemente and Kleiman, 1977).

A common finding is that various forms of media influence the fear of crime. For example, television viewing is correlated with fear of crime (Sparks and Ogles, 1990). People who watch a lot of television become more fearful. Coupled with social isolation, televised information about crime intensifies fears of victimization, regardless of the viewer's personal experience (Taschler-Pollacek and Lukesch, 1990). Newspaper coverage also intensifies the fear of crime (Romer et al., 2003; Williams and Dickinson, 1993). In particular, the many crime stories in which the crimes are local, random, and sensational increase people's fear. Researchers find that people who express the most fear over crime are not necessarily people who are most vulnerable, but are often just isolated people. Isolated people have less independent information about the conditions outside their home, so they are more suggestible and rely more on biased but apparently objective news reports.

People typically learn about crime events through the mass media (see, for example, Box 2.1). The media exploit people's feelings of insecurity when they highlight random and impersonal violent attacks (Lagrange, 1993). This increased fear of crime, in turn, can hinder the development of community programs designed to help people with criminal records. Mary Holland Baker and colleagues (1983) suggest that the fear of crime elicits avoidance behaviour, reduces normal social interaction, and alters everyday routines unnecessarily.

Secondary Victimization

Being the victim of a criminal act is painful and stressful enough. Often, however, the trauma does not stop with the criminal act itself. The victim may suffer additional harm as she/he navigates the complex and often frustrating criminal and civil court system in hopes of seeing justice done.

Secondary victimization refers to 'the victimization which occurs, not as a direct result of the criminal act, but through the response of institutions and individuals to the victim' (Canadian Resource Centre for Victims of Crime, 2005). Examples of secondary victimization include the refusal by law enforcement officers and/or the public to recognize an individual's experience as criminal victimization; intrusive or inappropriate conduct by police or judicial officers; psychological stress associated with the criminal investigation and trial process; and criminal justice processes and procedures that ignore, marginalize, or discount the role and input of the victim.

Box 2.1   Social Policy: Voters More Trusting of Tories on Crime

Stephen Harper's Conservatives have emerged as the favoured choice of Canadian voters to grapple with the growing threat of gangs and gun violence, a major new poll has found.

During the recent federal election campaign, Ipsos Reid surveyed 8,336 Canadian voters via the Internet over the period 30 December 2005 to 2 January 2006. Canadians were asked: 'Thinking of the current federal election, which federal party and leader has, in your view, the best ideas and policies for dealing with gangs and gun violence?'

The Conservatives came out on top (36 per cent), followed by the Liberals (24 per cent), the NDP (19 per cent), and the Bloc Québécois (6 per cent). As well, a further 16 per cent chose 'other' as their response.

Ipsos Reid president Darrell Bricker said in an interview . . . that people tend to perceive the Conservatives as being 'a little more hard-nosed' on crime.

In addition to a handgun ban, the Liberals would impose tougher jail sentences by raising minimum jail terms to two years from the current one for firearms smuggling, trafficking, and illegal possession of loaded handguns in a public places. They would spend $50 million on community-based programs designed to keep young men from becoming gang members and would strengthen border controls by placing 75 new officers at Canadian border crossings.

The Conservatives promise automatic jail terms for gun, drug, and gang-related crimes. They would hire more police officers. Strengthened border and airport security and speedy deportation of criminals who are not Canadian citizens are also promised.

Source: Adapted from Kennedy (2006).

Theories of Crime

Let's turn now to sociological theories of why people get involved in deviant and criminal behaviour. There are several, which, again, can be grouped under the three broad sociological perspectives.

The Structural-Functionalist Perspective

The functionalist approach to deviance includes a variety of theories that unite around a few central views: namely, that crime is normal, universal, and inevitable, and that it is to be expected in any society. Here, we review one theory about the relationship between crime and social disorganization and three competing interpretations of the 'functions' served by crime: social bond theory, strain (anomie) theory, and subculture theory.

SOCIAL DISORGANIZATION THEORY

Durkheim's early work in *Suicide* (1951 [1897]) provides the basis for a theory that crime and other social pathologies (including suicide) result from a breakdown in social norms and social integration. This breakdown, in turn, typically results from rapid social change and from organizational problems associated with rapid change—for example, rapid increases in population, cultural diversity, and social mobility associated with the rise of urban industrial society. As the theory would predict, international data show that people in developing and transitional countries have higher victimization rates, express less satisfaction with law enforcement, and support a more punitive approach to controlling crime than people in fully industrialized societies (Zvekic, 1996).

Social disorganization leads to a loss of social cohesion—a central concern of functionalist theory. Other things being equal, a loss of social cohesion increases the likelihood of robbery and assault near the home and of robbery and assault by strangers (Lee, 2000). Areas with high crime rates also have higher mortality rates from all causes, suggesting that crime rates mirror the quality of the social environment (Kawachi et al., 1999). Also, random violence and exposure to the continual use of guns and knives in the community produces children who are more likely to act violently themselves (Scott, 1999). Further supporting the validity of social disorganization theory is evidence that we reduce crime by increasing cohesion.

SOCIAL BOND THEORY

Some members of society are constantly being exposed to external factors—poverty, lack of educational opportunities, poor living conditions—and internal factors—feelings of aggression or jealousy—that tempt them to break society's rules. However, not every member of a disadvantaged or disorganized community becomes a delinquent or a criminal.

Travis Hirschi's **social bond theory** (1969) argues that strong social bonds can keep people from giving in to the temptation to commit criminal acts. When social bonds are weak and the individual is exposed to anti-social opportunities, the chance of participating in criminal behaviour increases.

Social bond theory can be viewed as an addition to social disorganization theory on the micro-sociological level. The theory directs our attention to the importance of childhood socialization and the relationships we establish with family members. Disorganized families hinder the formation of early attachments and commitments and make it less likely that young people will hold conventional norms and values. As a result, children from conflictual families—families marked by neglect, abuse, violence, separation, or divorce—run a higher than average risk of delinquent behaviour (see, e.g, Cox, 1996; Ruchkin et al., 1998; Simons and Chao, 1996).

STRAIN THEORY

As we saw in the previous chapter, Merton (1938) theorizes that **anomie** and strain arise whenever unequal social opportunities prevent some people from using legitimate means (such as a job) to achieve culturally defined goals (such as money).

One way that people confront a gap between culturally approved ends and the culturally approved means to achieve them is by innovating. They accept society's goals but pursue them through socially disapproved means, such as theft, robbery, tax fraud, embezzlement, and organized crime. From Merton's standpoint, crime is a creative way to get what our society values. In that sense, crime supports social order by allowing people to continue believing in the competitive and unequal capitalist system.

Implicit in **strain theory** is the idea that criminals hold the same values and goals as everyone else; they just use alternative means to pursue those goals and values. Choosing between legal and illegal work means rationally assessing the likely returns and risks, punishment costs, and personal preferences. Besides, many criminals take part in both forms of work, sequentially or at the same time. One kind of work does not rule out the other (Fagan and Freeman, 1999). This anomie approach, however, does not work as well to explain crimes against persons (such as assault, rape, or murder of an intimate) or crimes against property that yield no gain (such as vandalism). For this, we must turn to subculture theory.

SUBCULTURE THEORY

Subculture theory has been applied to delinquents and criminals to explain how their values and belief systems contribute to unlawful behaviour. Contrary to Merton's anomie theory, not everyone wants to get a college degree, land a responsible nine-to-five job in a large organization, spend his or her life paying off the mortgage on a suburban home, and retire to a condominium in Florida. Some people want to get the most possible fun, fame, relaxation, sex, drinking—even, the most possible respect or community service.

For example, inner-city gang members often live by a street code that justifies violence to gain respect from others. Guns—which symbolize respect, power, identity, and manhood—play a central role in initiating, sustaining, and escalating youth violence (Fagan and Wilkinson, 1998). Violence becomes expected behaviour for youth who are regularly exposed to violence, are gang members (see also Figure 2.3), have family or friends who are gang members, and have peer support for violence (Katz and Marquette, 1996; Powell, 1997). In gang subcultures, men who behave fearfully are likely to be threatened (Vander Ven, 1998).

Violent subcultures are nothing new, nor merely a result of social disorganization caused by industrialism. Many cultures in the past valued heroic male violence, self-assertion, and elitism, and stressed obedience to the communal honour code. However, the subculture of honour and violence is not universal. Therefore, it is not genetic, biological, or otherwise inevitable, even among young men, peasants, or embattled ethnic minorities. For the Semai, a Malaysian aboriginal group, for example, violent crime is completely absent. They have socialized their young to react to frustrating stimuli in a way that prevents them from committing violent criminal acts: they become fearful when frustrated, not violent (Moss, 1997). More relevant to modern industrial societies, we teach our young men to enact their aggressive impulses in sports, business, or even war; or to channel them into verbal or other symbolic jousting. Thus, rap music is not

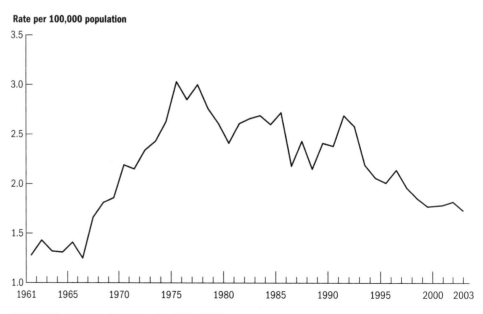

FIGURE 2.3 Homicide Rate, Canada, 1961–2003
Sources: Statistics Canada (2001, 2005d).

only a form of poetry and social protest; it is also a mainly male channelling of pride and aggression into verbal taunts and putdowns.

Conflict Theory

Conflict theories of crime and violence point to inequalities in society as the cause of such deviant behaviour. They would predict that, as inequality increases in a society, criminal activity will also increase. They would also predict that people who are economically disadvantaged will react to inequality by getting money through unlawful means, such as robbery or embezzlement. For similar reasons, they would predict that declining wages will lead to increased rates of 'quick cash' crimes, especially in societies lacking a safety net of unemployment benefits, universal health insurance, and income security provisions (Gaylord and Lang, 1997).

For less obvious reasons, people who are disadvantaged are also more likely to embrace violent subcultures of honour and respect, leading to higher rates of crimes against persons. As a result, homes in poor neighbourhoods are more likely to be repeatedly burglarized than are homes in wealthy areas (Ratcliffe and McCullagh, 1999). Homicide rates are the highest in poor communities marked by a high percentage of female-headed families, a high dropout rate from schools, and low welfare payment levels. This last variable may seem counterintuitive at first glance, but research finds that welfare payments serve as an 'investment in youth', buffering them against the temptations of criminal activity (Hannon, 1997). On release from psychiatric hospitals, mentally ill people are more likely to be violent if they live in poor areas than in wealthy areas (Silver, 1999). These offences against persons, not property, appear to support the idea that social inequality produces 'hidden injuries of social class', which in turn promote anti-social behaviour (Sennett and Cobb, 1975).

The conflict perspective also notes that people in privileged positions work to maintain their status. One way of doing this is by defining what is considered a 'serious' criminal offence. Both dominant ideology and formal laws—social constructs shaped and maintained by the ruling class—help the powerful to stay on top. They ensure, for example, that most people in society will view street crimes—for example, public drug use and vagrancy, which are more common among the disadvantaged—as deviant and undesirable behaviours. At the same time, corporate crimes that profit the wealthy but harm the environment and place the public in needless danger continue to be hidden from the mass media, the general public, and policy-makers.

Conflict theory also focuses on power differences between men and women in a male-dominated society. One example of such inequality is the perpetuation of 'rape myths', which depict women as responsible for their own victimization. The beliefs that 'no' means 'yes', that a revealing style of dress is like 'asking for' sex, and that 'good girls' do not get raped are examples of sexist myths that occasionally help acquit men of wrongdoing.

Symbolic Interactionism

SOCIAL CONSTRUCTIONISM

As we noted in the first chapter, social constructionism looks at how deviant behaviours come to be defined as 'deviant' in the first place. This perspective stresses that behaviours are not inherently right or wrong: they only become wrong, deviant, or criminal when someone in power attaches a moral value to them. So, for example, we can view hate-motivated violence, or hate crime, as a social construct. Some deny that hate crimes are different from, or require different treatment than, equally severe crimes of violence. The concept of hate crime was originally developed to combat expressions of racial, ethnic, and religious prejudice. In recent years, gays, lesbians, children, and women have also been depicted as potential victims of hate crimes. The enlargement of this umbrella to protect more types of victims has resulted from claims-making by special interest groups that have documented such crimes and called for legal remedies (Jenness, 1995). The mode of news presentation in the media plays a crucial role in promoting claims about crime and victimization (Sacco, 2000). In this way, the media contribute to the social construction of crimes and 'crime waves'—false perceptions that a crime problem is getting worse and worse.

LABELLING THEORY

Another symbolic interactionist approach is labelling theory. From the labelling point of view, deviance is not a quality of the act a person commits, but rather an outcome of the application by others of rules and sanctions to an 'offender'. Labelling theorists who study criminal behaviour distinguish between primary deviance—the initial acts of deviant behaviour committed by people before they are labelled 'deviant'—and secondary deviance—further deviant activity that results from having been labelled 'deviant' or 'criminal'.

Being labelled a deviant or criminal may promote further deviance if the labelled person is unable to escape stigmatization. Stigmatized people have fewer legitimate opportunities and so must rely more on illegitimate means for survival. Also, the labelled person begins to internalize and live out the identity of 'deviant'. It is often through this labelling and self-identification that the 'career criminal' is born (Hartjen, 1978).

DIFFERENTIAL ASSOCIATION THEORY

Differential association theory, first proposed by Edwin Sutherland (1939), states that deviance and criminality are behaviours learned through frequent and extended interaction with people who lead an anti-social lifestyle. Living in a high-crime neighbourhood and merely seeing others benefit from a criminal lifestyle are enough to raise the likelihood of engaging in similar illegitimate activities. Seeing criminals operate, without seeing them condemned or punished, is likely to teach a person not only the techniques of deviance, but also the motives for, rationalizations of, and attitudes of such a lifestyle. In a similar vein, time spent in jail or prison for a first-time offender can foster acquaintanceships, dependencies, and interests that lead to continued anti-social behaviours upon release from incarceration.

Social Aspects of Crime and Violence

Poverty and Inequality

Of all the people arrested for violent street crimes, most are undereducated, poor, unemployed, or working in low-wage, low-status jobs. Other kinds of crimes and criminals receive less attention.

The police are less energetic in pursuing white-collar crimes, which are mainly committed by middle-class and upper-class people. Yet, from a victimization standpoint, white-collar crimes are much worse: they affect many more people than street crimes. Also, the police (like the public in general) tend to assume that lower-class people are

Table 2.1 Summary of Theoretical Perspectives on Crime

Theory	Main Points
Structural Functionalism	
Social Disorganization Theory	■ Crime results from a breakdown in social norms and social integration following rapid social change. ■ Social disorganization leads to a loss of social cohesion, which in turn increases the likelihood of criminal behaviours such as robbery and assault. ■ Exposure to chronic random violence produces individuals who are more likely to act violently themselves. ■ Increased cohesion reduces crime.
Social Bond Theory	■ Travis Hirschi's social bond theory (1969) argues that developing a strong social bond, established in childhood, can prevent people from giving in to the temptation to commit criminal acts. ■ Four elements are involved in a strong social bond: an attachment to other people, a commitment to conventional goals, an involvement in conventional activities, and a belief in the legitimacy of conventional values, norms, and moral standards encouraged by society. ■ Criminal activities increase where bonds are weak and individuals are exposed to anti-social values and activities.
Anomie Theory	■ Merton (1938) theorizes that anomie and strain arise whenever unequal social opportunities prevent some people from achieving the culturally defined goals (such as money) by using legitimate means (such as a job). ■ One way to circumvent the gap between culturally approved ends and the culturally approved means to achieve them is through *innovation* (e.g., theft, robbery, tax fraud, embezzlement, and organized crime). ■ Assumes that criminals hold the same values and goals as everyone else.
Subculture Theory	■ Violent subcultures, such as gangs, provide minority youth with an alternative community for achieving social status, friendship, and economic mobility. ■ Using violence to right a wrong or defend one's honour may be considered justifiable under the value and belief system of delinquents and criminals.
Conflict Theory	■ Conflict theories of crime and violence point to inequalities in society as the cause of such deviant behaviour. ■ Criminal activity increases as inequality increases. ■ Dominant ideology and formal laws protect the privileged status of the ruling class and mask white-collar crimes that benefit the social elite.
Symbolic Interactionism	
Social Constructionism	■ Looks at how deviant behaviours come to be defined as 'deviant'. ■ Stresses that behaviours are not innately right or wrong; they only become wrong, deviant, or criminal when someone in power ascribes a moral value to them.
Labelling Theory	■ Deviance is not a quality of the act a person commits, but rather a consequence of the application by others of rules and sanctions to an 'offender'. ■ Being labelled as deviant or criminal may promote further deviancy because the labelled person is unable to escape stigmatization and internalizes the 'deviant' identity.
Differential Association Theory	■ Deviancy and criminality are behaviours learned from frequent and extended interaction with people who live an anti-social lifestyle. ■ Exposure to criminal influences, without effective condemnation of such elements by mainstream society, can teach a person not only the techniques of deviance, but also the motives for, rationalizations of, and attitudes of such a lifestyle.

more likely to commit crimes. Consequently, they assign more personnel to watch low-income neighbourhoods, and closer police attention to lower-income individuals inevitably results in higher arrest rates for street crimes. Laws against crimes that are mainly committed by the poor—drug-related crimes, assault, and robbery, for example—are also more strictly enforced and severely punished (for example, with prison time) than corporate and occupational crimes, which often result only in fines.

Conflict theories have a lot to say about this tendency to target lower-class criminals and overlook upper-class crimes. They suggest that if police investigated corporate, occupational, and political crimes nearly as energetically, they would find equally high rates of crime among the wealthy and, as a result, 'the wealthy might even be convicted and punished more than the poor' (Pepinsky and Jesilow, 1984: 81).

However, the arrest and conviction of poor people are not merely a result of bias in the police and courts. The existing social order does treat the poor worse than it treats the rich and well-educated. John Braithwaite (1993) provides a useful distinction between what he calls 'crimes of poverty', which are largely motivated by the need to obtain goods for personal use, and 'crimes of wealth', which are motivated by a greedy desire to obtain goods for exchange—that is, goods beyond those needed for personal use. Both types of crimes are promoted by social and economic inequality. A system of wide inequality and extreme competitiveness results in a class of needy poor and a class of greedy rich; a large middle class strives mightily to avoid falling into the former and to succeed in rising into the latter.

Living in poverty encourages the commission of crimes. As Merton's anomie theory argues, people who live in poverty still desire socially approved goals, such as money, though their economic position keeps them from the means of achieving their objectives legally. This temptation to crime is further exacerbated by the materialism of North American culture, which often measures human success in terms of the size of one's income, the prestige of one's job, and the market value of one's material possessions. Under such immense pressure to 'succeed', many who live in deprived conditions commit criminal acts they see as being profitable for a fast, easy escape from their life of poverty.

The Racial Dimension

Over the last several decades, researchers in Canada have paid more attention to the unduly large number of Aboriginal people arrested and convicted of law violations (see Figure 2.4). Although Aboriginal adults make up only 2 per cent of the Canadian population according to the 1996 census, they made up 19 per cent of those sentenced to provincial custody and 17 per cent of those sent to federal penitentiaries in 2000–1 (Reed and Roberts, 1999: 10). In other words, they were about eight or nine times more likely to end up in jail than their numbers in the population would lead one to expect.

The discrepancy between actual and expected numbers is especially striking in the Prairie provinces of Manitoba and Saskatchewan. In Manitoba, for example, Aboriginal people make up only 9 per cent of the population but 69 per cent of the prison population. One study found that, compared to non-Aboriginal inmates, Aboriginal inmates are younger, more likely to come from dysfunctional backgrounds, and likely to have had more run-ins with the criminal justice system, i.e., more previous arrests (LaPrairie et al., 1996).

One common explanation is that, like some other ethnic groups, Aboriginal people are mostly poor, and poverty drives them to criminal activity. Other explanations include a racially prejudiced law enforcement and correctional system; a conflict

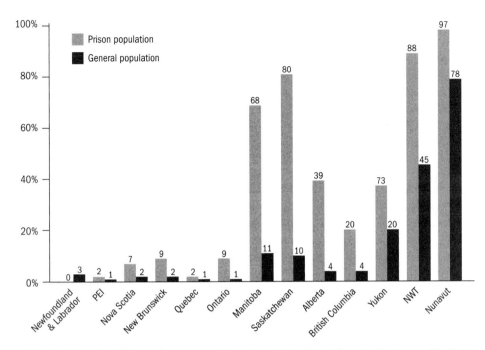

FIGURE 2.4 Aboriginal Adults as Percentage of General and Prison Populations, by Province and Territories, 2003–4

Source: Adapted from Statistics Canada, 'Juristat', *Adult Correctional Services in Canada 2003/04*, Vol. 25, No. 8, Catlogue no. 85-002, p.14. Available at: <http://www.statcan.ca/english/freepub/85-002-XIE/ 0080585-002-XIE.pdf>.

between the values of Aboriginal culture and mainstream Canadian culture; social and economic consequences of colonization and oppression by European settlers; and a breakdown in the traditional social fabric of Aboriginal communities. These explanations are not mutually exclusive. In fact, these factors tend to support and interact with one another. However, the multiplicity of theories makes it difficult to generate the political will and co-ordinate the efforts required to begin solving the problem of Aboriginal crime and conviction. It is likely that any solution will require greater cultural sensitivity on the part of non-Aboriginal policy-makers than has been shown in the past. Indeed, many of the more promising initiatives—healing and sentencing circles, First Nation police forces, elders courts, etc.—are being developed and pursued at the grassroots level by Aboriginal communities themselves.

Because Canadian authorities do not tabulate crime statistics by the race of the offender, the connection between race and crime is hard to flesh out quantitatively. Many police forces across the country are against collecting statistics based on race, since doing so may cause their officers to practise the kind of racial profiling of suspects that is a constant issue in law enforcement, or would attract the negative attention of the public and the media. Others believe that collecting and publishing race-based crime data would serve to reinforce existing racial stereotypes.

However, there is reason to believe that racial profiling is already a conventional practice of Canadian police. In a recent study of possible racial bias within the police force in Kingston, Ontario—described as the first of its kind in Canada—the data showed that between October 2003 and September 2004, blacks were much more likely to be stopped and questioned by police than members of any other racial group. Young black males aged 15–24 were the demographic group most likely to be pulled over by officers (Wortley and Marshall, 2005). Although, as the authors note, these results do not 'prove' the existence of racial profiling, they suggest that at least some 'routine' police stops are racially motivated.

Since the study focused only on a single police force in a single province, we would be reckless to generalize beyond the results of this study. More research is needed in this area. Still, these Canadian data are corroborated by international studies of policing. In Britain and the US, for example, where racial statistics are routinely recorded by police, young black men are again far more likely than other demographic groups to get the attention of legal authorities. Some think the high arrest and prosecution rates of certain ethnic groups prove that law enforcement officers, prosecutors, judges, and the criminal justice system in general are racially prejudiced. Others in the US argue that the police target blacks, along with Latinos and Native Americans, because they are often poor, and that law enforcement agencies focus on crimes committed by all lower-class people rather than by blacks alone (Walker, 1989). It is not clear whether the public would condone class profiling any more than it condones racial profiling.

Profiling does not begin or end with the police. The media, as well as police, rely on stereotypes to portray criminals in television dramas and movies, including the inner-city black or Latino gang member, the Arab terrorist, the Italian or Russian mafioso, and the Chinese Triad member. Not by accident is fictional crime boss Tony Soprano Italian-American. Not by accident are the relentless fictional terrorists in *24* Arabs and Arab look-alikes. By contrast, blond, Nordic criminals are disproportionately rare in the mass media, compared with their presence in the general population. These biased images, when distributed to wide audiences, perpetuate inaccurate and prejudicial notions about entire ethnic groups.

Drug Abuse

Another social problem closely linked with crime is drug abuse. There are several reasons for this. First, as we discuss in the next chapter, some criminal offences are drug-related. The possession, cultivation, production, and sale of controlled substances are all against the law. Public intoxication, drunken and disorderly conduct, and driving while intoxicated are all behaviours that are clearly forbidden by the Criminal Code. Second, there is a well-established link between alcohol abuse and domestic violence; generally, drug use often loosens inhibitions and may lead to aggressive and violent behaviour. Finally, as we note in the next chapter, alcohol and drug addiction may lead to criminal activities aimed at raising money to feed the addiction.

Economic Consequences of Crime

Crime costs a society a lot. For example, many financial costs result from crime. These include costs resulting from the loss of property through bank robberies, auto theft, breaking and entering, embezzlement schemes, and copyright violations. In 1995, for example, $250 million worth of compact disks and cassette tapes were illegally copied in China, according to one reported estimate (Faison, 1996). Other costs of crime result

Box 2.2   Social Construction: Reporting on Diversity in Canada

The following journalistic guidelines are from 'Reporting on Diversity: A Checklist', a set of principles for achieving racially and ethnically balanced news reportage developed by journalists, journalism professors, and diversity advisers at a Carleton University workshop in June 1995.

FOR BEAT AND GENERAL REPORTERS

Am I covering all aspects, including positive and negative, of diverse communities?

Am I aware of the power of images, and do I avoid furthering stereotypes by seeking a diverse representation when interviewing people, no matter what the story?

Are the *labels* I use to describe people appropriate and necessary, and do they meet the guidelines of my news organization?

Do I research diverse groups thoroughly, to avoid perpetuating stereotypes?

Do I include questions/allegations of systemic racism as context to specific stories, whenever I can do so fairly and responsibly?

Am I aware of factions and agendas within groups so that I do not fall prey to manipulation by prominent sources?

FOR DESK AND ASSIGNMENT EDITORS

Do our story and photo ideas and our content perpetuate cultural or other stereotypes? Am I assessing whether our photographs and visuals accurately reflect the entire community?

Am I watching our use of language for bias?

Am I aware of minority sensitivities before setting and reviewing a style to describe groups or communities?

Are we under-playing or over-playing a story because of its diversity content?

Is our coverage of the actions of a few stereotyping an entire group?

Am I regularly reviewing the accumulative impact of our coverage?

Source: Adapted from Canadian Race Relations Foundation (1995).

from criminal violence; they include the loss of productivity by injured workers and the medical costs of treating crime victims. Also, unrecorded or illegal spending on drugs, prostitution, gambling, and other underground activities diverts cash away from legitimate businesses and goes untaxed.

Besides victims' financial losses, crime also imposes an economic burden on the broader public through government spending on law enforcement, the criminal court system, and correctional services. Total Canadian spending on corrections was estimated at $2.7 billion in 2003–4, despite that year having the lowest imprisonment rate in over two decades. The federal system accounted for slightly more than half of all expenditures, with the various provincial/territorial systems accounting for the rest. On average, it costs taxpayers $240.18 per day to house one inmate in a federal penitentiary (though only $141.75 per inmate in a provincial/territorial prison) (Statistics Canada, 2005a). For $240 per day—$87,665 a year—two or three readers of this book could pay their entire year's costs of tuition, room, board, books, clothing, and recreation at a college or university. Some might consider that a better way to spend the money.

Social and Psychological Consequences of Crime

Personal lives can be shattered by violent crime. Box 2.3 describes some of the rights and recourses available to victims. In addition to the impact on individuals and families, crime and disorder harm societies in a number of subtle ways. We have seen, for example, the shocking economic toll that corporate and white-collar crime has on society; but that's not all. Such crimes also, according to Elizabeth Moore and Michael Mills (2001: 54), may create '(a) diminished faith in a free economy and in business leaders, (b) loss of confidence in political institutions, processes and leaders, and (c) erosion of public morality'. At the societal level, violent crimes breed fear and wear down neighbourhood cohesion. People grow suspicious of one another; with greater isolation and social distance, prejudicial stereotypes based on race, gender, and age are reinforced. As the National Research Council (1994: 5–6) concluded, 'If frightened citizens remain locked in their homes instead of enjoying public spaces, there is a loss of public and community

---

Box 2.3   Personal Experience: Rights of Crime Victims

Becoming a victim of crime is a frightening and devastating experience for thousands of Canadians each year. As recently as 25 years ago, almost no services were available to help crime victims or their survivors repair the damage to their lives or cope with the trauma and frustration associated with the criminal justice system. Today, however, because of victim services programs offered by each province and territory, and the dedicated efforts of advocates, lawmakers, and crime victims, an extensive range of services and resources is available to help victims of crime. The Canadian Resource Centre for Victims of Crime wants you to know that you do have rights if you or someone you love is a victim of crime. You can get help and you can work for positive change.

YOU HAVE RIGHTS

Both the federal and provincial governments play an equally important role with regard to victims of crime. While the federal government enacts and reforms criminal law (mainly in the Criminal Code), the provinces have the responsibility of the enforcement, administration, and prosecution of those laws.

The federal government has given victims the following rights:

■ The right to have input at sentencing (e.g., victim impact statements presented orally or in writing). Judges are required to ask Crowns if the victim has been informed of his/her right to complete an impact statement. If the victim chooses to prepare a victim impact statement, it must be taken into consideration by the sentencing judge.

■ Police and judges must consider the safety of victims in all bail decisions.

■ Young victims and witnesses are protected from personal cross-examination by accused persons representing themselves.

■ Victims and witnesses are permitted to have a support person present when giving testimony.

■ Judges are permitted to ban the publication of the identity of victims and witnesses in appropriate circumstances.

■ Victims have the right to obtain information about the conviction, sentence, imprisonment, and release of the offender. They may also attend federal parole hearings and submit victim impact statements to the parole board (in writing, orally, or by audio/video tape).

Source: Adapted from Canadian Resource Centre for Victims of Crime, *What you can do if you become a victim of crime* (pamphlet) (Ottawa: CRCVC, n.d.). Available at: <www.crcvc.ca/docs/What%20to%20do%20if%20you%20are%20a%20victim.pdf>.

life, as well as a loss of "social capital"—the family and neighbourhood channels that transmit positive social values from one generation to the next.'

There are consequences for the criminal as well, especially the psychological and social issues that must be dealt with after one is labelled a 'criminal'. Crimes, as we have seen, are committed for a variety of reasons, including boredom (for example, automobile theft for the sake of joyriding), psychopathological disorders (for example, some serial killers), and despair (for example, robbery for the sake of economic need).

Not all criminals are inevitably destined to be repeat offenders after having been prosecuted, incarcerated, and released. However, having been labelled a criminal, and having a criminal record, means losing many opportunities. Convicts returning to the community are sometimes greeted with unease and fear. Many are denied employment; the jobs they do find are often degrading and menial. At the least, an ex-convict carries the social stigma of having once been a criminal. For some, a return to the criminal lifestyle seems like the only available means of survival. This produces a vicious circle, in which an initial act of (primary) deviance results in the expectation by society of further acts of (secondary) deviance, and in which the fulfillment of such expectations is nonetheless the only means of survival.

Health Consequences of Crime and Violence

Crimes have consequences, and criminal victimization harms people's health. Victims of crime consistently report lowered levels of well-being after their victimization, and victims of violent crimes are especially likely to suffer psychological distress (Denkers and Winkel, 1998). Controlling for measures of injury and for socio-demographic characteristics, victims of violent crime also report lower levels of perceived health and physical well-being. Younger victims of violent crime report the largest decreases in their health. Victims of property crime also report lowered levels of health and physical well-being, but older victims suffer the most negative effects (Britt, 2001).

Violent crimes often result in physical pain and suffering due to injuries. Violent victimization also results in lowered self-esteem. The victims of violent crimes report more distress and more stressful life events than do non-victims and victims of non-violent crimes (Johnson, 1997). Rape especially exacts an overwhelming psychological and social toll. Because of the traumatic nature of rape, fear of retaliation by the rapist, and fear of stigmatization, victims of rape have often been unwilling to report rape incidents to the police. Many have trouble trusting men again and establishing or resuming intimate relationships.

However, criminal victimization affects different people in different ways, even when the crime is the same. Resources such as social support, time, money, education, and the presence of other life stressors affect a victim's resistance or vulnerability to stress (Gifford, 2001). In terms of both physical and emotional trauma, the health effect of a crime also depends on the social meaning of the violence (Gilbert, 1996). For example, lesbians, gay men, and bisexuals who have been victimized by hate crimes report higher than average levels of depression, anxiety, anger, and symptoms of post-traumatic stress.

The emotional consequences of criminal victimization can be very serious. Victims of crimes are more likely than non-victims to suffer from post-traumatic stress disorder, major depressive episodes, and a variety of phobias. The reaction depends largely on the crime. Completed rape, for example, produces a variety of deep emotional disturbances, while robbery and burglary produce none that are lasting (Boudreaux et al., 1998).

Though victims are affected most, everyone in the community is affected by a high risk of homicide or assault. The family and friends of victims of homicide and other violent acts suffer a great deal. However, the social consequences are more general than that. As Catherine Ross (2000) reports, merely living in a poor, high-crime neighbourhood can heighten one's level of stress, including depression. Research on homeless adults, for example, finds a significant relationship between witnessing violence and reporting symptoms of poor mental health (Fitzpatrick et al., 1999).

The Health of Criminals

Some forms of crime are more often associated with health problems than others. For example, the drug abuser who commits crimes to support his or her habit is likely to be much less healthy than other people in the general population. Alcohol, which is also associated with criminal behaviour, has serious health consequences when taken to excess. Whether health problems originate from the criminal behaviour or from the drug or alcohol use, however, is hard to determine.

For most offenders, a life of crime is stressful. Constantly looking over one's shoulder, being always on guard against the authorities, leads to an unhealthy level of stress that may harm a person's health over time. The health of prisoners has been widely studied by sociologists and health practitioners, who, not unexpectedly, have concluded that prisons are harmful to health. The criminal justice system, with its reliance on punishment and coercive social control, produces many harmful effects that include human rights violations, drug abuse, the spread of HIV/AIDS, and racism (Welch, 1999). Violent assaults, rapes, unsanitary and overcrowded conditions, and staff brutality also harm the prisoners' health. Prisons, lacking the facilities to do otherwise, often ignore all but the most severe mental illnesses, such as schizophrenia or other psychotic disorders. Post-traumatic stress disorder, often from rape and violent assaults, can go undiagnosed or untreated because of insufficient treatment resources, fears of stigmatizing the inmates, and lack of anonymity and safety (Kupers, 1996).

Some aspects of prison life are intended to pose health risks to inmates. For example, Michael Vaughn and Linda Smith (1999) list six forms of ill treatment in prison facilities: (1) the use of medical care to humiliate prisoners (e.g., invasive procedures that may not be necessary); (2) the withholding of medical care from prisoners with HIV and AIDS; (3) the withholding of medical care from other prisoners; (4) the subjection of inmates to sleep deprivation and extreme temperature changes; (5) the use of dental care as a means of torture; and (6) the falsification of prisoners' medical records. The authors argue that since prisons are run with efficiency in mind, not prisoners' health, some health-care providers in the penal system ignore their professional ethics.

These problems are only going to worsen as prison populations, like the rest of society, age. Already, aging prisoners are placing a greater burden on medical and hospice care. A growing number are showing the symptoms of ill health often associated with aging: disorientation, heart disease, diabetes, asthma, emphysema, and terminal illnesses such as cancer. Unlike the general population, however, inmates have neither the resources nor, in many cases, the desire to keep up their health or diet, or to seek the special medical care they need. Also, many have a history of alcohol and drug abuse, while others have a history of mental disorders. The cost of treating all these illnesses has not yet been discussed with taxpayers.

Solutions to the Crime and Violence Problem

Reducing Crime

Other things being equal, a community is better off preventing crime than punishing it. Investments in improving education, creating jobs, supplying daycare, upgrading low-income housing, increasing access to health care, and otherwise supporting poor families—all of these front-end strategies to prevent crime are likely to work better, in the long run, than trying to remedy crime through imprisonment after a criminal has been trained and hardened by an unequal society. Other useful strategies may include more use of probation, better gun control, and expanding drug treatment (Anderson, 1994). As John Irwin and James Austin argue, reducing crime means addressing those factors that are most directly related to producing crime. This means reducing teenage pregnancies, high school dropout rates, youth unemployment, drug abuse, and lack of meaningful job opportunities.

Although opinions differ on how best to address these factors, the first step is to admit that these factors have more to do with reducing crime than the use of imprisonment after the fact. This is especially true of the crimes committed by frustrated, marginalized youths and those that induce fear in the community—violent assaults, robberies, and homicides.

The Criminal Justice System

Part of the crime problem is that, in many societies, people feel dissatisfied with and distrustful of public officials and institutions—especially politicians, police, lawyers, and courts. Though they dislike crime and criminals, they also dislike and distrust people in authority. This distrust may lead them to avoid reporting crimes or giving information to the police and courts; they may even use violence—taking action into their own hands—to settle disputes. Such problems are evident, for example, in Brazil (Noronha et al., 1999) and the former Yugoslavia (Nikolic-Ristanovic, 1998). Preventing crime in these societies might mean more effectively controlling migration, planning urbanization, and seeking more citizen participation in criminal justice matters (Seetahal, 1997).

As we have seen, biases intrude into the criminal justice system, even in Canada, where Aboriginal and black minorities are over-represented in the prison population. Research has found discrimination against blacks in bail hearings and in sentencing, especially for drugs, sexual assault, and bail violations. The discrimination against Aboriginal and black people is strongest at the point of contact with the police (Roberts and Doob, 1997). Likewise, in the United Kingdom, Afro-Caribbeans are seven times more highly represented in the prison population than other groups, given their number in the general population. Blacks in the UK are the targets of proactive policing and suffer a disadvantage when neutral criteria are applied in judgement, though these biases do not fully account for the high rates of arrest and conviction (Smith, 1997).

As we have seen, criminal behaviour is not fully rational. Yet the criminal justice system is based on the principle of **deterrence**. This principle assumes that most crimes are rational acts in which the offender weighs the perceived benefits of committing the crime against the probability of being caught and the severity of the punishment.

The United Nations International Criminal Tribunal for the Former Yugoslavia

- The International Criminal Tribunal for the Former Yugoslavia (ICTY) was established by Resolution 827 of the United Nations Security Council in May 1993. It is based in The Hague, Netherlands.
- The ICTY's mandate is to prosecute and try war crimes and crimes against humanity committed since 1991 in the territory of the former Yugoslavia under the leadership of former president Slobodan Milošević.
- It is the first international body for the prosecution of war crimes since the Nuremberg and Tokyo trials held in the aftermath of World War II, and has jurisdiction over individuals responsible for genocide, war crimes, and crimes against humanity in the territory of the former Yugoslavia after 1 January 1991.

Source: <http://edition.cnn.com/2004/WORLD/europe/08/31/milosevic.keyfacts>.

The 'get tough on crime' approach often discussed in North America calls for maximizing punishment to increase its deterrent effects and thereby lower crime rates. However, a criminal justice system based on deterrence assumes that the likelihood of being punished is high—that is, that law enforcement agencies are efficient in apprehending offenders. This assumption may be unwarranted. Finally, a deterrence-based approach to criminal justice fails to admit and address societal, economic, and political factors that encourage crime in the first place: unemployment, racial inequality, poverty, and the unequal distribution of resources and opportunities.

The Capital Punishment Debate

Capital punishment—taking an offender's life as punishment for a crime—is the most extreme punishment a state has at its disposal. (Some might argue that torture—an increasingly used practice in the interrogation of suspected terrorists by US operatives—may be an even more extreme punishment, though it is not admitted to be.) Before 1961, the sentence for murder in Canada was death by hanging. Between 1867 and 1962, 710 people were executed. However, by the mid-twentieth century, capital punishment had lost its support among urban Canadians, who no longer saw it as an appropriate form of criminal punishment. In 1976, after decades of debate, the House of Commons replaced capital punishment in the Criminal Code with a mandatory life sentence with no possibility of parole for 25 years for all first-degree murder convictions (Amnesty International Canada, 2000). For a more detailed history of Canada's death penalty policy, see Box 2.4.

Among Western countries today, only the United States currently retains the use of capital punishment. According to Amnesty International data, 74 countries worldwide have retained the death penalty as of October 2005, while 86 have abolished it for all crimes. Eleven nations have retained capital punishment only for extraordinary circumstances or for crimes under military law, and another 25 have abolished it in practice (i.e., though capital punishment remains a legal option, the courts have not sentenced anyone to death in at least 10 years, and informal policies are believed to deter its future use) (Amnesty International, 2005). A suspension of the death penalty and/or its ultimate abolition is supported by many influential national and international bodies, including many national constitutional courts, Amnesty International, the European Court of Human Rights, and the United Nations Human Rights Committee.

Supporters of the practice, particularly those in the US, argue that capital punishment is the most vital deterrent, since all but the most reckless individuals would reconsider participating in a crime if faced with the possibility of their own death. Other supporters argue that irrespective of its deterrent effects, the death penalty symbolically expresses the public's rejection of criminal violence. Also, putting a murderer to death ensures that he or she cannot, through a legal technicality or a breakdown in prison security, escape and repeat the offence.

Opponents to capital punishment in the US point out that most research shows that the threat of capital punishment has little if any effect on violent crime rates (e.g., Radalet and Akers, 1996). Although we might imagine that the threat of death would deter violent crime, in practice it is unlikely to influence the behaviour of people acting out of rage or panic, people who are intoxicated at the time, or people suffering from a mental illness. In each of these cases, offenders are unlikely to fully understand the seriousness of their criminal actions and act accordingly.

Box 2.4   Historical Perspective: Capital Punishment in Canada

1865: Crimes of murder, treason, and rape carry the death penalty in Upper and Lower Canada.

1961: Murder is classified into capital and non-capital offences. Capital murder offences in Canada include premeditated murder and murder of an on-duty police officer, guard, or warden, and have a mandatory sentence of hanging.

1962: The last executions take place in Canada. Arthur Lucas, convicted of the premeditated murder of an informer and witness in racket discipline, and Robert Turpin, convicted of the unpremeditated murder of a policeman to avoid arrest, are hanged at the Don Jail in Toronto, Ontario.

1966: Capital punishment in Canada is limited to the killing of on-duty police officers and prison guards.

1976: Capital punishment is removed from the Criminal Code, to be replaced with a mandatory life sentence without possibility of parole for 25 years for all first-degree murders. Capital punishment remains authorized in the Canadian National Defence Act for the most serious military offences, including treason and mutiny.

1987: A motion to reintroduce capital punishment is debated in the Canadian House of Commons and defeated on a free vote.

1998: The Canadian National Defence Act is amended to replace the death penalty with life imprisonment without eligibility for parole before 25 years. Capital punishment is fully abolished in Canada.

2001: The Supreme Court of Canada rules, in *United States v. Burns*, that in extradition cases it is constitutionally required 'in all but exceptional cases' that the Canadian government seek assurances that the death penalty will not be imposed or, if imposed, not carried out.

Source: Susan Munroe, 'History of Capital Punishment: Timeline of the Abolition of Capital Punishment in Canada', at: <canadaonline.about.com/cs/crime/a/cappuntimeline.htm?terms=capital+punishment+in+canada>.

Alarmingly, research suggests that racial prejudices within the justice system may influence the use of capital punishment laws. Evidence indicates, for instance, that the race of a homicide victim influences the likelihood an offender will receive the death penalty. Analysis of persons executed for interracial murders in the US since 1976 found that 209 cases involved a black defendant and a white victim, compared to only 12 cases involving a white defendant and a black victim (Death Penalty Information Center, 2006).

Also, opponents of capital punishment note that court proceedings are often filled with error, so any justice system that supports the death penalty risks putting an innocent person to death.

The debate over capital punishment is related to a larger discussion about the role of the criminal justice system. Is its purpose, as some believe, the healing of offenders to make them productive, law-abiding members of society? Are criminals the supple product of social and psychological influences? If the answer to these questions is yes, then the criminal justice system should focus on identifying the circumstances that led to criminal behaviour so that rehabilitation experts can effect changes in the offender to prevent recidivism (i.e., repeat offending).

The conflict theory of crime and deviance has argued that crimes are prosecuted differently according to the socio-economic class of the offender. In effect, it argues that people from all social classes commit crimes, but that the police and the courts expend greater effort in apprehending and prosecuting those from the lower classes. If so, the proper course of action would be to prevent further crimes from being committed and to support reformed offenders so that they need not return to the environment that led them into crime in the first place. Programs based on this notion of treatment include job training and education classes, individual and group therapy, and substance abuse counselling.

In contrast, others feel that the main concern of the justice system should be to protect law-abiding citizens from criminals and punish people who break the law for their personal gain. These goals can supposedly be achieved by increasing the length of imprisonment to reduce the risk of recidivism. Supporters of this view believe that in the end crime is a matter of free choice. While they may admit that poverty and hardship lure people into crime, they believe that, in the end, offenders commit crimes because they have failed to take responsibility for their own lives. They note that many people grow up in poverty yet choose to uphold the law and work themselves out of poverty. Where there is variation, there is choice; and where there is choice, there is personal responsibility and blame.

The Victims' Rights Movement

Western social norms concerning the behaviour and treatment of crime victims have developed in at least three distinct stages. In the first, individualistic stage, the injured party is expected to seek vengeance on his own. The matter is between the perpetrator and the victim, and the right of the victim to exact revenge is taken for granted. The old practice of duelling reflects this individualistic notion, as does the Biblical injunction an eye for an eye, a tooth for a tooth. The second stage moves beyond the victim to include his/her kinship network; retribution is sought through 'blood feuds' or in the form of material compensation. Both the Old Testament and Hammurabi's code—humanity's first written legal code—specify the price of different injuries a victim has suffered (10 shekels for a lost hand, five cows for a violated wife, and so on). The third, and current, stage moves the locus of action away from the victim to the state, and views criminal acts as violations of 'the king's peace'—therefore, matters to be handled by state authorities (Smith and Huff, 1992).

At present, the Canadian criminal justice system is focused on two parties: the defendant, who stands accused of the crime, and the state, which prosecutes the crime. For the most part, the victimized individual has a marginal and passive role to play, mainly providing testimony about the facts of the criminal incident. In other words, when a person commits a criminal act, he/she is said to have done so against the state, not specifically against the injured party. This is to ensure that the accused is granted a fair and neutral trial—a right that would be difficult to assure if the victim served as judge, jury, and executioner (Canadian Resource Centre for Victims of Crime, 2006).

In the past few decades, however, a victims' rights movement has emerged in Canada and elsewhere that seeks to expand the rights of crime victims to balance out the rights of the offender (Carrington and Nicholson, 1984). This movement grew out of the feminist movement, in particular, in response to domestic violence and sexual abuse. All of Canada's 13 provinces and territories have now established a victim's Bill of Rights that is similar to statutes enacted by other jurisdictions worldwide. Though the precise entitlements vary from one jurisdiction to another, they all include access to information throughout the trial; the right to submit a victim impact statement at sentencing; compensatory damages for victimization; offender restitution; notification of parole hearings; and the right to submit a victim impact statement at parole hearings (Smith et al., 1990). Though these are not binding 'rights', they serve as guidelines for judicial officers to keep in mind as they conduct their cases. Only in Manitoba are victims' rights rigorously enforced in the legislation, and a complaints mechanism is in place should those rights be violated (Canadian Resource Centre for Victims of Crime, 2006).

As mentioned, the original goal of the victims' rights movement was to restore the balance between protecting the rights of accused (i.e., presumption of innocence, a fair trial in a court of law, etc.) and allowing the victim to play a more active role in the prosecution of the person who harmed her or him. However, some critics have argued that, rather than minimizing 'secondary victimization' and giving the injured party an equal voice in the criminal justice process, the movement has prioritized the demand for harsher and more punitive verdicts. So, while pretending to advocate on behalf of crime victims, some groups—mainly a subset of the conservative 'get tough on crime' proponents—are more concerned about lobbying for more severe penalties (Sanborn, 2001; Smith and Huff, 1992).

Individual Strategies

Victims cope with crime in various ways consistent with their gender, their experience, and the nature of the crime. Some withdraw, practise denial, or reduce risks, while others cope more actively. Women are more likely to do the former and men the latter (Yee et al., 1998).

Friends and family are the most usual sources of victim assistance. Though victim services programs help a large number of victims with counselling-related needs, they are little help in dealing with crime prevention, household needs, or property replacement (Davis et al., 1999). Intimate partners are the most important supporters. Victims whose partners give too little support suffer further reduced well-being (Denkers, 1999).

Many of us—especially women, but men, too—run a reasonably high risk of being victimized during our lifetimes. Thus, there is good reason for us to study the social and geographic distribution of victimization and to act in ways that lessen our risk whenever possible. This means, in part, that we should try to avoid being alone in places where violent attacks and robberies are common. We should avoid worrying too much about possible victimization and adversely affecting our health, but we should be wary.

It only makes good sense, as well as good sociology, for us to lessen the risk of thefts by raising the costs or hindrances for possible perpetrators. For example, locks (on doors, windows, desk drawers, and so on) and alarms are useful ways to protect our possessions, and we should use them. Also, we can join lobby groups calling for improvements in the criminal justice system, law enforcement, prisons, and the organization and safety of public places. Still other organizations are trying to improve the economic circumstances of those groups highly at risk of recruitment to crime. These organizations are likely to welcome anyone who wants to pitch in with volunteer hours and financial support.

Some individuals are more likely than others to practise preventive behaviours against violent crime. Not surprisingly, women, people who have experienced violent victimization, and people who see benefits to preventive measures are most likely to practise them (Hammig and Moranetz, 2000). Awareness of the facts of crime and victimization as a social problem not only reduces the danger and risk, it may also be personally empowering and contribute to a growth of community cohesion.

Concluding Remarks

Along with the state of the economy, crime has been among Canadians' top five concerns for most of the last 20 years. Considered the most serious form of deviance, a crime is any act formally banned by law, specifically by the Criminal Code of Canada. Defining certain acts as 'crimes' gives the state the authority to seek, arrest, try, convict, and punish offenders, and the Criminal Code specifies an allowable range of punishments for each crime.

Within the bounds of the Criminal Code, we find many different kinds of crime. Some are crimes considered very harmful by most people, such as murder, armed robbery, extortion, arson, sexual assault, and kidnapping. In general, there is widespread agreement in Canadian society—and in most other societies—that these behaviours are wrong and should be harshly punished. In contrast, there are crimes, such as the possession of marijuana, over which people disagree so much that the law has, in effect, lost control. Then there are the more standard crimes. Most people consider them wrong but do not wish to debate or increase the severity of punishment. These include offences against property, such as breaking and entering, automobile theft, and shoplifting; minor assaults; drunk driving; and 'white-collar' offences such as embezzlement and fraud. All of these offences have a victim or (as in the case of drunk driving) run a serious risk of harming someone.

Despite biases in reporting, criminologists know enough about crime to permit several inferences. First, crimes against property have increased over the last 20 years, but the rates of homicide and other crimes of violence have changed little. Contrary to what we might hear in the media, there is no wave of violent crime swamping our towns and cities. Second, crimes of violence are rarely committed for gain; they often result from fights between spouses or friends. This is especially true when women are the victims. Men are more likely than women to be attacked by mere acquaintances or even strangers. Third, crimes that are committed for gain—for example, drug peddling, solicitation for prostitution, illegal gambling, and extortion—are often tied (however indirectly) to organized crime.

Criminals, as we have seen, tend to be certain kinds of people—young, poor men, for example. The exact relationship between these demographic variables and criminal behaviour is complex and not well understood. As we have suggested, the connection is probably a result of the interaction of economic, social, and cultural variables. In many instances, criminals are more likely to be victimized than non-criminals, largely because of the factors discussed in connection with routine activities theory.

QUESTIONS FOR CRITICAL THOUGHT

1. 'Laws, as well as their means of enforcement, maintain social order based on the illusion of order.' Discuss this statement. Do you agree with this? Why or why not?

2. The figures and statistics on where crimes occur but are not reported are often termed the 'dark side' of crime. Seen most often with regard to sexual harassment and rape cases, the victim is often too afraid or traumatized to file a report. After reading about how crimes are (or aren't) reported, do you now question the authority and legitimacy of crime statistics? If so, when are they useful and valid pieces of evidence, and when should they be taken with a large grain of salt?

3. Canada, like other industrialized countries, is beginning to see a significant trend towards an older population. What are some of the major health consequences that prison and correctional facilities will experience as the Canadian population continues to grow older?

4. Don Corleone, the notorious mafioso of *The Godfather* movies, provides popular culture with a prototype by which to envision mobster activities. Then there is the recent Soprano family of prime-time television. What are the effects of such movies and shows with regard to stereotypes? Also include in your discussion how other inner-city ethnic 'gangs' (black, Latino, Italian, Russian, Arab) are portrayed either positively or negatively in the media.

5. List and discuss the different arguments for and against capital punishment as a deterrent for crime.

RECOMMENDED READINGS

Peter J. Carrington, 'Population Aging and Crime in Canada, 2000–2041', *Canadian Journal of Criminology* 43 (2001): 331–56. How will the rapidly aging Canadian population alter crime rates and criminal victimization rates? Generally, crime will continue to decline based on present demographics. Drinking and driving and sexual assault—crimes committed by older adults—will not change.

Jane Dickson-Gilmore and Carol LaPrairie, *'Will the Circle be Unbroken?' Aboriginal Communities, Restorative Justice, and the Challenges of Conflict and Change* (Toronto: University of Toronto Press, 2005). Dickson-Gilmore and LaPrairie examine the role of restorative justice programs in reducing the over-representation of Aboriginals in the Canadian criminal justice system. They evaluate initiatives such as conferencing and healing circles, and compare recent reform efforts in Canada with those in New Zealand, Australia, and the United States.

N. Chabanyi Manganyi and André du Toit, eds, *Political Violence and the Struggle in South Africa* (London: Macmillan, 1990). This book discusses ways in which prevailing discourses underscore the authority of the state and legitimize state repression and power. This collection shows the rich contribution that sociologists, psychologists, lawyers, criminologists, and political theorists have made to the study of such topics as policing, the operation of state judicial structures, social control, violence, gangsterism, and crowd behaviour.

Marc Ouimet, 'Crime in Canada and in the United States: A Comparative Analysis', *Canadian Review of Sociology and Anthropology* 36 (1999): 389–408. Although Canadians often proudly reflect on their relative crimelessness compared to their southern neighbours, this article examines this notion by controlling for mediating factors. The author finds that US crime rates appear higher than Canada's because of a few 'outliers'—cities with extremely high crime rates. Crime in these cities is explained by residential segregation and ease of acquiring firearms.

Vincenzo Ruggerio, Mick Ryan, and Joe Sim, eds, *Western European Penal Systems: A Critical Anatomy* (London: Sage, 1995). This text analyzes the criminal justice systems of European Union member states. A trend towards convergence is observed, characterized by heightened imprisonment, longer sentences, the evolution of alternatives to imprisonment, the increasing lack of welfare provisions and education within the penal system, and privatization.

Gresham M. Sykes, *The Society of Captives: A Study of Maximum Security Prison* (Princeton, NJ: Princeton University Press, 1958). This classic study of prisons deserves to be revisited in the changed prison context of the current period. Sykes's main idea was that maximum-security prisons are unstable institutional settings and should be avoided. The prison population in the United States is now close to triple the size it was in 1958; the United States is a relatively violent country and relies more on imprisonment than other Western countries.

RECOMMENDED WEBSITES

National Crime Prevention Strategy
www.psepc-sppcc.gc.ca/prg/cp/ncps-en.asp

The National Crime Prevention Strategy is a policy directive of the federal Department of Justice. The NCPS website provides information regarding policy implementation and various publications, programs, and services related to crime prevention, as well as links to other crime prevention sites.

CAVEAT
www.caveat.org

Canadians Against Violence (CAVEAT) is a non-profit charitable organization working for safety, peace, and justice. It provides news, publications, educational kits, and information regarding submissions made to government on legislation. Related resources and links are also supplied.

Department of Justice Canada
www.canada.justice.gc.ca

The Department of Justice website provides information regarding the justice system in general, programs and services, consultation, news, and pertinent events. Information on departmental priorities in terms of youth justice, victims of crime, and crime prevention can also be found here.

GLOSSARY

Anomie According to Durkheim, a condition characterized by a breakdown of norms and personal disorganization, which may lead to crime.

Clientelism A special relationship in which someone of influence or wealth continues to protect a subordinate client; seen traditionally as a single wealthy family or individual hiring socially or economically vulnerable wage labourers. In a more modern sense, though, clientelism can be seen when new immigrants are protected by individuals of wealth or influence from potentially hostile environments.

Conventional crimes The traditional illegal behaviours that most people think of as 'crime'. For example, homicide and sexual assault are given the most media coverage but account for only 12 per cent of all crimes.

Crime Any behaviour that, in a given time and place, is prohibited by applicable statutory law. When a law is violated, a crime is said to have been committed.

Deterrence A justice system based on deterrence assumes that crimes are rational acts in which the offender weighs the perceived benefits of committing the crime against the probability of being caught and the severity of the punishment. It assumes that the probability of being punished is high and that the law enforcement agencies are competent and efficient in apprehending offenders.

Differential socialization The processes whereby individuals learn to behave in accordance with prevailing standards of culture or gender. For example, boys and men learn to be less inhibited in using aggressive and violent actions, and this may account for the disproportionate number of males involved in criminal activity.

Homicide The killing of a human being by another, directly or indirectly, by any means; includes murder, i.e., the unlawful killing of another human being with malicious intent, and manslaughter, the unlawful killing of another person without sufficient intent to constitute murder.

Laws Orderly and dependable sequences of events, or rules of conduct that may provide for the punishment of violators. In other words, the formal rules about what a society's members can and cannot do.

Self-reporting The victim reports to authorities that a crime has occurred. This is the most direct method of measuring crime rates. However, it is not the most accurate, as changes in the crime rate reflect changes in victims' willingness to report.

Social bond theory A type of control theory. A strong social bond prevents most people from succumbing to the temptation to engage in criminal activities.

Social disorder The uncertain and unpredictable condition in which rules are not obeyed. It is generally unsafe, and the boundaries of acceptable behaviour have broken down.

Social order The prevalence of generally harmonious relationships; used synonymously with social organization. This condition exists when rules are obeyed and social situations are controlled and predictable. Rules serve not only to indicate which behaviours are acceptable, but also to allow participants to anticipate the behaviour of others.

Strain theory (anomie theory) Merton holds that strain is produced when social structure prevents people from achieving culturally defined goals through legitimate means. He outlines various adaptive strategies: conformity, ritualism, retreatism, rebellion, and innovation. Innovation is most commonly associated with criminal activities, which include theft, robbery, tax fraud, embezzlement, and organized crime.

Subculture theory Investigates the norms that set a group apart from mainstream society. Specifically, this approach gives special insight into the subculture of the criminal, looking into the values and belief systems that may be conducive to delinquent and criminal action.

Vice crimes Deviant behaviour that may be defined as immoral (for example, gambling, prostitution, drug trafficking). These crimes provide the greatest opportunity for organized crime.

Victimization surveys Samples of people are asked how many times within a given time period they have been the victim of particular crimes.

White-collar crimes The crimes committed by white-collar workers and management in the course of their occupations. They are always distinguished from conventional criminal offences such as robbery or murder. White-collar crimes are performed as part of normal work and usually occur in reputable organizations.

REFERENCES

Amnesty International. 2005. 'The Death Penalty: Abolitionist and Retentionist Countries'. Available at: <web.amnesty.org/pages/deathpenalty-countries-eng>; accessed 15 Feb. 2006.

Amnesty International Canada. 2000. 'The Death Penalty in Canada: Twenty Years of Abolition.' Available at: <www.amnesty.ca/deathpenalty/canada.php>; accessed 15 Feb. 2006.

Anderson, Elijah. 1994. 'The Code of the Streets: Sociology of Urban Violence', *Atlantic Monthly* (May): 80–91.

Arnold, Robert, Carl Keane, and Stephen Baron. 2005. 'Assessing Risk of Victimization through Epidemiological Concepts: An Alternative Analytic Strategy Applied to Routine Activities Theory', *Canadian Review of Sociology and Anthropology* 42, 3: 345–64.

Bachman, Ronet, Heather Dillaway, and Mark S. Lachs. 1998. 'Violence against the Elderly: A Comparative Analysis of Robbery and Assault across Age and Gender Groups', *Research on Aging* 20: 183–98.

Bjerregaard, Beth. 2000. 'An Empirical Study of Stalking Victimization', *Violence and Victims* 15: 389–406.

Boudreaux, Edwin, Dean G. Kilpatrick, Heidi S. Resnick, Connie L. Best, and Benjamin E. Saunders. 1998. 'Criminal Victimization, Posttraumatic Stress Disorder, and Comorbid Psychopathology among a Community Sample of Women', *Journal of Traumatic Stress* 11: 665–78.

Braithwaite, John. 1993. 'Crime and the Average American', *Law and Society Review* 27: 215–32.

Britt, Chester L. 2001. 'Health Consequences of Criminal Victimization', *International Review of Victimology* 8, 1: 63–73.

Browne, Angela, Kirk R. Williams, and Donald G. Dutton. 1999. 'Homicide between Intimate Partners', in M. Dwayne Smith and Margaret A. Zahn, eds, *Studying and Preventing Homicide: Issues and Challenges*. Thousand Oaks, Calif.: Sage, 55–78.

Canadian Centre for Justice Statistics. 1995. *Uniform Crime Reporting Survey*, 39.

———. 2005. 'Adult Correctional Services in Canada, 2003/04', *Juristat* 25, 8: 14.

Canadian Race Relations Foundation. 1995. 'Reporting on Diversity: A Checklist'. Available at: <www.crr.ca/Load.do?section=26&subSection=38&id=322&type=2>; accessed 1 Mar. 2006.

Canadian Resource Centre for Victims of Crime. 2005. 'Impact of Victimization'. Available at: <www.crcvc.ca/en>; accessed 15 July 2006.

———. 2006. 'Victims' Rights in Canada'. Available at: <www.crcvc.ca/en>; accessed 15 Feb. 2006.

Carrington, F., and G. Nicholson. 1984. 'The Victims' Movement: An Idea Whose Time Has Come', *Pepperdine Law Review* 11: 1–14.

Caywood, Tom. 1988. 'Routine Activities and Urban Homicides: A Tale of Two Cities', *Homicide Studies* 2, 1: 64–82.

Clay-Warner, Jody. 2000. 'Situational Characteristics of Sexually Violent Crime', paper presented at the annual meeting of the Southern Sociological Society.

Cochran, John K., Max L. Bromley, and Kathryn A. Branch. 2000. 'Victimization and Fear of Crime in an Entertainment District Crime "Hot Spot": A Test of Structural-Choice Theory', *American Journal of Criminal Justice* 24: 189–201.

Cohen, Howard. 1999. 'The Significance and Future of Racially Motivated Crime', *International Journal of the Sociology of Law* 27, 1: 103–18.

Cox, Ruth P. 1996. 'An Exploration of the Demographic and Social Correlates of Criminal Behavior among Adolescent Males', *Journal of Adolescent Health* 19: 17–24.

Davis, Keith E., April Ace, and Michelle Andra. 2000. 'Stalking Perpetrators and Psychological Maltreatment of Partners: Anger-Jealousy, Attachment Insecurity, Need for Control, and Break-up Context', *Violence and Victims* 15: 417–25.

——— and Irene Hanson Frieze. 2000. 'Research on Stalking: What Do We Know and Where Do We Go?', *Violence and Victims* 15: 473–87.

Davis, Robert C., Arthur J. Lurigio, and Wesley G. Skogan. 1999. 'Services for Victims: A Market Research Study', *International Review of Victimology* 6, 2: 101–15.

Death Penalty Information Center. 2006. 'Race of Death Row Inmates Executed Since 1976'. Available at: <www.death-penaltyinfo.org/article.php?scid=5&did=184>; accessed 15 Feb. 2006.

Denkers, Adriaan. 1999. 'Factors Affecting Support after Criminal Victimization: Needed and Received Support from the Partner, the Social Network, and Distant Support Providers', *Journal of Social Psychology* 139: 191–201.

Denkers, Adriaan J.M., and Frans Willem Winkel. 1998. 'Crime Victims' Well-Being and Fear in a Prospective and Longitudinal Study', *International Review of Criminology* 5, 2: 141–62.

Durkheim, Émile. 1938 [1895]. *The Rules of Sociological Method*, trans. Sarah A. Solovay and John H. Mueller. Chicago: University of Chicago Press.

———. 1951 [1897]. *Suicide*, trans. John A. Spaulding and George Simpson. New York: Free Press.

———. 1964 [1893]. *The Division of Labor in Society*, trans. George Simpson. New York: Free Press.

Elzinga, Anne. 1996. 'Security of Taxi Drivers in the Netherlands: Fear of Crime, Actual Victimization and Recommended Security Measures', *Security Journal* 7, 3: 205, 210.

Emerson, Robert M., Kerry O. Ferris, and Carol Brooks Gardner. 1998. 'On Being Stalked', *Social Problems* 45, 5: 289–314.

Erickson, Bonnie H. 1981. 'Secret Societies and Social Structure', *Social Forces* 60: 188–210.

Fagan, Jeffrey, and Richard B. Freeman. 1999. 'Crime and Work', *Crime and Justice* 25: 225–90.

——— and Deanna L. Wilkinson. 1998. 'Guns, Youth Violence, and Social Identity in Inner Cities', *Crime and Justice* 24: 105–88.

Faggiani, Donald, and Myra G. Owens. 1999. 'Robbery of Older Adults: A Descriptive Analysis Using the National Incident-Based Reporting System', *Justice Research and Policy* 1, 1: 97–117.

Faison, Seth. 1996. 'Copyright Pirates Prosper in China Despite Promises', *New York Times*, 20 Feb., A1, A6.

Felson, Marcus, and Lawrence E. Cohen. 1980. 'Human Ecology and Crime: A Routine Activity Approach', *Human Ecology* 8: 389–406.

Fernandez-Lanier, Adriana. 1999. 'Crime in the Ivory Tower (College Campuses, Medieval Universities, Colonial Colleges)', Ph.D. dissertation, State University of New York, Albany.

Finkelhor, David, and Nancy L. Asdigian. 1996. 'Risk Factors for Youth Victimization: Beyond a Lifestyles/Routine Activities Theory Approach', *Violence and Victims* 11, 1: 3–19.

Fitzpatrick, Kevin M., Mark E. LaGory, and Ferris J. Ritchey. 1999. 'Dangerous Places: Exposure to Violence and Its Mental Health Consequences for the Homeless', *American Journal of Orthopsychiatry* 69: 438–47.

Friedrichs, David O. 1995. 'Responding to the Challenge of White-Collar Crime as a Social Problem', Society for the Study of Social Problems, conference paper.

Gallagher, Catherine A. 2000. 'The Role of Victim Experience in Violent Situations: A Longitudinal Analysis of the National Crime Victimization Survey Data, 1992–1995', Ph.D. dissertation, University of Maryland.

Gaylord, Mark S., and Graeme Lang. 1997. 'Robbery, Recession and Real Wages in Hong Kong', *Crime, Law and Social Change* 27, 1: 49–71.

Gifford, Diane M. 2001. 'A Model for Analyzing the Effects of Neighbourhood Characteristics on Adolescent Depression', Southern Sociological Society, conference paper.

Gilbert, Leah. 1996. 'Urban Violence and Health: South Africa 1995', *Social Science and Medicine* 43: 873–86.

Hagan, John. 1985. 'Toward a Structural Theory of Crime, Race and Gender: The Canadian Case', *Crime and Delinquency* 31: 129–46.

Hammig, Bart J., and Christine A. Moranetz. 2000. 'Violent Victimization: Perceptions and Preventive Behaviors among Young Adults', *American Journal of Health Behavior* 24, 2: 143–50.

Hamilton, Graeme. 1997. 'Westray "Deceit" Deadly Mine Blast Preventable', *Montreal Gazette*, 2 Dec., A1.

Hannon, Lance. 1997. 'AFDC and Homicide', *Journal of Sociology and Social Welfare* 24, 4: 125–36.

Hartjen, Clayton A. 1978. *Crime and Criminalization*, 2nd edn. New York: Praeger.

Hashima, Patricia Y., and David Finkelhor. 1999. 'Violent Victimization of Youth versus Adults in the National Crime Victimization Survey', *Journal of Interpersonal Violence* 14: 799–820.

Hauber, Albert R., and Anke G.A. Zandbergen. 1996. 'Foreign Visitors as Targets of Crime in the Netherlands: Perceptions and Actual Victimization over the Years 1989, 1990, and 1993', *Security Journal* 7, 3: 211–18.

Hirschi, Travis. 1969. *Causes of Delinquency*. Berkeley: University of California Press.

Hoyt, D.R., K.D. Ryan, and A.M. Cauce. 1999. 'Personal Victimization in a High-Risk Environment: Homeless and Runaway Adolescents', *Journal of Research in Crime and Delinquency* 36, 4: 371–92.

Hutter, Bridget M. 1999. 'Controlling Workplace Deviance: State Regulation of Occupational Health and Safety', *Research in the Sociology of Work* 8: 191–209.

Ianni, Francis A.J., with Elizabeth Reuss-Ianni. 1972. *A Family Business: Kinship and Social Control in Organized Crime*. New York: Russell Sage Foundation.

Irwin, John, and James Austin. 1994. *It's About Time: America's Imprisonment Binge*. Belmont, Calif.: Sage.

Jenness, Valerie. 1995. 'Hate Crimes in the United States: The Transformation of Injured Persons into Victims and the Extension of Victim Status to Multiple Constituencies', in Joel Best, ed., *Images of Issues: Typifying Contemporary Social Problems*, 2nd edn. Hawthorne, NY: Aldine de Gruyter, 213–37.

Johnson, Knowlton W. 1997. 'Professional Help and Crime Victims', *Social Service Review* 71, 1: 89–109.

Junger-Tas, Josine. 1997. 'Ethnic Minorities and Criminal Justice in the Netherlands', in 'Ethnicity, Crime and Immigration: Comparative and Cross-National Perspectives', special issue of *Crime and Justice* 21: 257–310.

Katz, Roger C., and Joe Marquette. 1996. 'Psychosocial Characteristics of Young Violent Offenders: A Comparative Study', *Criminal Behaviour and Mental Health* 6: 339–48.

Kawachi, Ichiro, Bruce P. Kennedy, and Richard G. Wilkinson. 1999. 'Crime, Social Disorganization, and Relative Deprivation', *Social Science and Medicine* 48: 719–31.

Kennedy, Mark. 2006. 'Voters More Trusting of Tories on Crime: Poll', CanWest News Service, 2 Jan. Available at: <www.canada.com/national/features/decisioncanada/story.html?id=28e98047-0a7f-41bb-b1db-225450d6cde0>; accessed 1 Mar. 2006.

Kong, Rebecca. 1999. 'Canadian Crime Statistics, 1997', in Canadian Centre for Justice Statistics, *The Juristat Reader: A Statistical Overview of the Canadian Justice System*. Toronto: Thompson Educational Publishing, 117–37.

Konradi, Amanda. 1999. 'Campus Judiciaries and Sociological Inquiry', Society for the Study of Social Problems, conference paper.

Kupers, Terry A. 1996. 'Trauma and Its Sequelae in Male Prisoners: Effects of Confinement, Over-crowding and Diminished Services', *American Journal of Orthopsychiatry* 66: 189–96.

Langhinrichsen-Rohling, Jennifer, and Martin Rohling. 2000. 'Negative Family-of-Origin Experiences: Are They Associated with Perpetrating Unwanted Pursuit Behaviors?', *Violence and Victims* 15: 459–71.

LaPrairie, Carol, et al. 1996. *Examining Aboriginal Correction in Canada*. Ottawa: Solicitor General of Canada.

Lee, Matthew R. 2000. 'Community Cohesion and Violent Predatory Victimization: A Theoretical Extension and Cross-National Test of Opportunity Theory', *Social Forces* 79: 683–706.

Lombroso-Ferrero, Gina. 1972 [1911]. *Criminal Man, According to the Classification of Cesare Lombroso*. Montclair, NJ: Patterson-Smith.

McCabe, Kimberly, and Sharon S. Gregory. 1998. 'Elderly Victimization', *Research on Aging* 20: 363–72.

Martens, Peter L. 2001. 'Immigrants as Victims of Crime', *International Review of Victimology* 8: 199–216.

Mawby, R.I., P. Brunt, and Z. Hambly. 1999. 'Victimisation on Holiday: A British Survey', *International Review of Victimology* 6: 201–11

———. 2000. 'Fear of Crime among British Holidaymakers', *British Journal of Criminology* 40: 468–79.

Mechanic, Mindy B., Mary H. Uhlmansiek, Terri L. Weaver, and Patricia A. Resick. 2000. 'The Impact of Severe Stalking Experienced by Acutely Battered Women: An Examination of Violence, Psychological Symptoms and Strategic Responding', *Violence and Victims* 15: 443–58.

Merton, Robert K. 1938. 'Social Structure and Anomie', *American Sociological Review* 3, 5: 672–82.

Mesch, Gustavo S. 1997. 'Victims and Property Victimization in Israel', *Journal of Quantitative Criminology* 13: 57–71.

Miller, J. Kirk, and Kristen A. Myers. 2000. 'Are All Hate Crimes Created Equal?', Southern Sociological Society, conference paper.

Moore, Elizabeth, and Michael Mills. 2001. 'The Neglected Victims and Unexamined Costs of White-Collar Crime', in Neal Shover and John P. Wright, eds, *Crimes of Privilege: Readings in White-Collar Crime*. New York: Oxford University Press, 51–7.

Moss, Geoffrey. 1997. 'Explaining the Absence of Violent Crime among the Semai of Malaysia: Is Criminological Theory up to the Task?', *Journal of Criminal Justice* 25: 177–94.

Mustaine, Elizabeth Ehrhardt, and Richard Tewksbury. 1997. 'Obstacles in the Assessment of Routine Activity Theory', *Social Pathology* 3: 177–94.

——— and ———. 1998. 'Victimization Risks at Leisure: A Gender-Specific Analysis', *Violence and Victims* 13: 231–49.

National Research Council. 1994. *Violence in Urban America: Mobilizing a Response*. Washington: National Academy Press.

Nelsen, Candice, and Lin Huff-Corzine. 1998. 'Strangers in the Night: An Application of the Lifestyle-Routine Activities Approach to Elderly Homicide Victimization', *Homicide Studies* 2, 2: 130–59.

Nikolic-Ristanovic, Vesna. 1998. 'Victims and Police in Belgrade', *International Review of Victimology* 6, 1: 49–62.

Noronha, Ceci Vilar, Eduardo Paes Machado, Gino Tapparelli, Tania Tegina F. Cordeiro, Denise Helena P. Laranjeira, and Carlos Antonio Telles Santos. 1999. 'Violence, Ethnic Group and Color: A Study of Differences in the Metropolitan Region of Salvador, Bahia, Brazil', *Pan American Journal of Public Health* 5: 268–77.

O'Donnell, Ian, and Kimmet Edgar. 1998. 'Routine Victimization in Prisons', *Howard Journal of Criminal Justice* 37: 266–79.

Paetsch, Joanne J., and Lorne D. Bertrand. 1999. 'Victimization and Delinquency among Canadian Youth', *Adolescence* 34: 351–67.

Peel, Elizabeth. 1999. 'Violence against Lesbians and Gay Men: Decision-Making in Reporting and Not Reporting Crime', *Feminism and Psychology* 9, 2: 161–7.

Pepinsky, Harold E., and Paul Jesilow. 1984. *Myths That Cause Crime*. Cabin John, Md: Seven Locks Press.

Ploughman, Penelope, and John Stensrud. 1986. 'The Ecology of Rape Victimization: A Case Study of Buffalo, New York', *Genetic, Social, and General Psychology Monographs* 112: 303–24.

Powell, Kathleen B. 1997. 'Correlations of Violent and Nonviolent Behavior among Vulnerable Inner-City Youths', *Family and Community Health* 20, 2: 38–47.

Pratt, Carter, and Kamala Deosaransingh. 1997. 'Gender Differences in Homicide in Contra Costa County, California, 1982–1993', *American Journal of Preventive Medicine* 13, suppl.: 19–24.

Radalet, Michael, and Ronald L. Akers. 1996. 'Deterrence and the Death Penalty: The Views of Experts', *Journal of Criminal Law and Criminology* 87, 1: 1–16.

Ratcliffe, Jerry, and Michael McCullagh. 1999. 'Burglary, Victimization and Social Deprivation', *Crime, Prevention and Community Safety* 1, 2: 37–46.

Reed, Micheline, and Julian Roberts. 1999. 'Adult Correctional Services in Canada, 1997–98', in Canadian Centre for Justice Statistics, *The Juristat Reader: A Statistical Overview of the Canadian Justice System*. Toronto: Thompson Educational Publishing, 39–51.

Roberts, Julian V., and Anthony N. Doob. 1997. 'Race, Ethnicity, and Criminal Justice in Canada', in Michael Tonry, ed., *Ethnicity, Crime, and Immigration: Comparative and Cross-national Perspectives*. Chicago: University of Chicago Press, 469–522.

Romer, Daniel, Kathleen H. Jamieson, and Sean Aday. 2003. 'Television News and the Cultivation of Fear of Crime', *Journal of Communication* 53, 1: 88–104.

Ross, Catherine E. 2000. 'Neighborhood Disadvantage and Adult Depression', *Journal of Health and Social Behavior* 41: 177–87.

Ruchkin, Vladislav V., Martin Eisenmann, Bruno Hagglof, and C. Robert Cloninger. 1998. 'Aggression in Delinquent Adolescents vs Controls in Northern Russia: Relations with Hereditary and Environmental Factors', *Criminal Behaviour and Mental Health* 8, 2: 115–26.

Sacco, Vincent F. 2000. 'News That Counts: Newspaper Images of Crime and Victimization', *Criminologie* 33: 203–23.

Sanborn, Joseph B., Jr. 2001. 'Victims' Rights in Juvenile Court: Has the Pendulum Swung Too Far?', *Judicature* 85, 3: 140–6.

Scott, Bridget T. 1999. 'Chronic Community Violence and the Children Who Are Exposed To It', *Journal of Emotional Abuse* 1, 3: 23–37.

Seetahal, Dana. 1997. 'Urbanisation and Industrialization on Crime: The Commonwealth Caribbean in the 1990s', *Caribbean Journal of Criminology and Social Psychology* 2, 2: 115–45.

Silver, Eric. 1999. 'Violence and Mental Illness from a Social Disorganization Perspective: An Analysis of Individual and Community Risk Factors', Ph.D. dissertation, State University of New York, Albany.

Simmel, Georg. 1950 [1906]. 'The Sociology of Secrecy and of Secret Societies', in Kurt H. Wolff, ed., *The Sociology of Georg Simmel*. Glencoe, Ill.: Free Press, 305–76.

Simons, Ronald L., and Wei Chao. 1996. 'Conduct Problems', in Ronald L. Simons and Associates, eds, *Understanding Differences between Divorced and Intact Families: Stress, Interaction, and Child Outcome*. Thousand Oaks, Calif.: Sage, 125–43.

Smith, Brent L., and C. Ronald Huff. 1992. 'From Victim to Political Activist: An Empirical Examination of a Statewide Victims' Rights Movement', *Journal of Criminal Justice* 20: 201–15.

————, John J. Sloan, and Richard M. Ward. 1990. 'Public Support for the Victims' Rights Movement: Results of a Statewide Survey', *Crime and Delinquency* 36, 4: 488–502.

Smith, David J. 1997. 'Ethnic Origins, Crime, and Criminal Justice in England and Wales', in Michael Tonry, ed., *Ethnicity, Crime, and Immigration: Comparative and Cross-National Perspectives*. Chicago: University of Chicago Press, 101–82.

Statistics Canada. 2001. 'Homicide Statistics, 2000', *The Daily*, 31 Oct.

————. 2002. *Health Indicators*. Ottawa: Statistics Canada.

————. 2005a. 'Adult Correctional Services', *The Daily*, 16 Dec.

————. 2005b. *Crime Statistics, Canada, Provinces and Territories, 1977–2004*. Ottawa: Canadian Centre for Justice Statistics.

————. 2005c. *Juristat: Crime Statistics in Canada, 2004*. Ottawa: Statistics Canada, Catalogue no. 85–002–XIE.

————. 2005d. CANSIM data tables.

————. 2005e. *General Social Survey on Victimization, Cycle 18: An Overview of Findings*. Ottawa: Statistics Canada, Catalogue no. 85–565–XIE.

Steffensmeier, Darrell, and Emilie Allan. 1996. 'Gender and Crime: A Gendered Theory of Female Offending', *Annual Review of Sociology* 22: 459–87.

Sutherland, Edwin H. 1939. *Principles of Criminology*. Philadelphia: Lippincott.

————. 1949. *White Collar Crime*. New York: Dryden Press.

Tewksbury, Richard, Elizabeth L. Grossi, Geetha Suresh, and Jeff Helms. 1999. 'Hate Crimes against Gay Men and Lesbian Women: A Routine Activity Approach for Predicting Victimization Risk', *Humanity and Society* 23, 2: 125–42.

Tiby, Eva. 2001. 'Victimization and Fear among Lesbians and Gay Men in Stockholm', *International Review of Victimology* 8: 217–43.

Tillman, Robert, and Michael Indergaard. 1999. 'Field of Schemes: Health Insurance Fraud in the Small Business Sector', *Social Problems* 46: 572–90.

Tjaden, Patricia, and Nancy Thoennes. 2000. 'The Role of Stalking in Domestic Violence Crime Reports Generated by the Colorado Springs Police Department', *Violence and Victims* 15: 427–41.

Torres, Sam. 1999. 'Hate Crimes against African Americans: The Extent of the Problem', *Journal of Contemporary Criminal Justice* 15, 1: 48–63.

United States, Bureau of Justice. 1991. *Statistics Sourcebook*. Washington: US Government Printing Office.

Vander Ven, Thomas M. 1998. 'Fear of Victimization and the Interactional Construction of Harassment in a Latino Neighbourhood', *Journal of Contemporary Ethnography* 27: 374–98.

Vaughn, Michael S., and Linda G. Smith. 1999. 'Practicing Penal Harm Medicine in the United States: Prisoners' Voices from Jail', *Justice Quarterly* 16, 1: 175–231.

Walker, Samuel. 1989. *Sense and Nonsense about Crime: A Policy Guide*, 2nd edn. Pacific Grove, Calif.: Brooks/Cole.

Weaver, Greg S., Thomas A. Peete, Jay Corzine, Janice E. Clifford Wittekind, Lin Huff-Corzine, and Gregory S. Kowalski. 2001. 'Race, Gender, Context, and the Subcultures of Violence', Southern Sociological Society, conference paper.

Welch, Michael. 1999. *Punishment in America: Social Control and the Ironies of Imprisonment*. Thousand Oaks, Calif.: Sage.

White, Jacqueline, Robin M. Kowalski, Amy Lyndon, and Sherri Valentine. 2000. 'An Integrative Contextual Developmental Model of Male Stalking', *Violence and Victims* 15: 373–88.

White, Michael. 1999. 'GM Ordered to Pay Accident Victims $49 B', *National Post*, 10 July, A1.

Whyte, William Foote. 1981 [1943]. *Street Corner Society: Social Structure of an Italian Slum*, 3rd edn. Chicago: University of Chicago Press.

Wilkinson, Richard G., Ichiro Kawachi, and Bruce P. Kennedy. 1998. 'Mortality, the Social Environment, Crime and Violence', in Mel Bartley, David Blane, and George Davey Smith, eds, *The Sociology of Health Inequalities*. Oxford: Blackwell, 19–37.

Wilson, James Q., and George L. Kelling. 1982. 'Broken Windows', *Atlantic Monthly* (Mar.): 29–38.

Wilson, Margo, and Martin Daly. 1992. 'Who Kills Whom in Spouse Killings? On the Exceptional Sex Ratio of Spousal Homicides in the U.S.', *Criminology* 30: 189–215.

Wooldredge, John D. 1998. 'Inmate Lifestyles and Opportunities for Victimization', *Journal of Research in Crime and Delinquency* 35: 480–502.

Wortley, Scot, and Lysandra Marshall. 2005. *Bias-Free Policing: The Kingston Data Collection Project—Final Results*. Available at: <www.police.kingston.on.ca>; accessed 14 Feb. 2006.

Wrangham, Richard, and Dale Peterson. 1997. *Demonic Males: Apes and the Origins of Human Violence*. Boston: Houghton Mifflin.

Yee, Jennifer, Martin S. Greenberg, and Scott R. Beach. 1998. 'Attitudes toward Various Modes of Coping with Criminal Victimization: The Effects of Gender and Type of Crime', *Journal of Social and Clinical Psychology* 17: 273–94.

Zimbardo, Philip G. 1969. 'The Human Choice: Individuation, Reason, and Order versus Deindividuation, Impulse, and Chaos', *Nebraska Symposium on Motivation* 17: 237–307.

Zvekic, Ugliesa. 1996. 'The International Crime (Victim) Survey: Issues of Comparative Advantages and Disadvantages', *International Criminal Justice Review* 6: 1–21.

DRUGS AND ALCOHOL ABUSE

Are Alcohol and Drugs Social Problems?

In this chapter we discuss a variety of substances—tobacco, alcohol, marijuana, cocaine, heroin—that change a person's mental state. Taken to extremes, drugs can harm a person, and drug use is then considered substance abuse. Substance abuse can lead to serious health risks for the user and for others. As we will see, there are close connections between drug use and a variety of public issues, including traffic safety and crime. Poverty and inequality, which we discussed in Chapter 1, are also related to drug abuse.

Drug or alcohol use does not always look like a social problem. After all, many people use drugs or alcohol in one way or another, whether a beer with dinner or a Tylenol capsule for a headache, for example. However, drug use is more than a personal choice with personal consequences. By changing our consciousness chemically, we change the risks to which we are subjecting other people. Alcohol and drug use inevitably affect other members of society. An obvious example of one person's use affecting others is drunk driving, which can result in accidents; we will discuss this problem later in the chapter. Usually, however, the effects of drug use are less dramatic and less visible.

We begin by discussing the changing definitions of drugs and alcohol and the characteristics of the two types of substances.

Changing Social Definitions of Drugs and Drug Abuse

We can define a **drug**, generally, as any substance that causes a biochemical reaction in the body. However, it is against the law to induce some biochemical reactions inside your body. What people define as a legal drug or an illegal drug usually depends less on its chemical properties—less on the reactions in your body—and more on surrounding economic, social, and political factors.

In Canada, the use of legal drugs, such as alcohol, tobacco, and prescription medicine, is much more common than the use of illegal drugs, such as heroin, cocaine, and marijuana. Many members of society treat the use of illegal drugs as a major problem while ignoring the harm done by legal drugs. Society's response to drug use is, therefore, largely irrational. Some substances that harm public health, such as alcohol and tobacco, are welcomed or tolerated almost everywhere in society, while others that may not be as dangerous, such as marijuana, are often condemned and banned. Our attitudes towards specific drugs also vary over time. When social and cultural sensibilities shift, people start rejecting what they once accepted. So we cannot understand drug attitudes and drug laws without a historical account that explains how and why the attitudes have evolved over time.

Examples of such attitude changes abound. Consider opium, from which morphine and heroin are derived. Opium was a commonly used painkiller until the early 1900s (Witters et al., 1992). At some historical moment, opium and cocaine were deemed dangerous and subjected to strict regulation, if not an outright ban. The reason is sociological, not pharmacological—that is, the chemical properties of the drugs did not change, only the public's perception of their effects and those who used them.

In this and other instances, a commonly used drug was restricted or criminalized when prevailing attitudes changed. The new restrictions were rarely due to new medical research findings or even new discoveries that the drugs caused social problems. Often, as with cocaine and marijuana, the changes were due to new attitudes towards immigrants or racial minorities who were in some way associated with the drug. These attitudinal changes, in turn, often reflected new economic and social concerns. Typically, these changes penalized the least powerful members of society.

In the same vein, what constitutes **drug abuse** depends largely on what constitutes an 'acceptable' drug at a particular time and place. Overall, trends in alcohol, cigarette, and cannabis (marijuana) use are similar in the United States and Canada. A study of adolescents comparing Ontario with the United States finds that, in both places, alcohol use has steadily decreased since the late 1970s, while both cigarette and cannabis use peaked in the late 1970s, decreased throughout the 1980s, and then began to increase dramatically in the early 1990s. Cocaine use was consistently higher in the United States and LSD use consistently higher in Ontario over the period 1975–95. The similar trends in use of alcohol and cigarettes in the United States and Ontario suggest similar shifts in basic attitudes over time. Different trends in the use of less common drugs—cocaine and LSD—may reflect deeper cultural differences or national differences in drug policy or availability (Ivis and Adlaf, 1999).

The ideas of alcohol 'abuse' and drug 'abuse' begin with a notion of extreme or unsuitable use that results in social, psychological, and physiological harm. There are two

Coca-Cola and Cocaine
Cocaine, currently the object of a 'war on drugs' in the United States, was an active ingredient in Coca-Cola until 1906, when caffeine replaced it.

Box 3.1 Historical Perspective: When Heroin Was Legal

'The Case for Heroin'—so ran the headline for the *Times* [of London] of Tuesday, 14 June 1955. In the course of a short, lucid article the newspaper, which had long been the mouthpiece of Establishment Britain, set out its argument in favour of heroin.

In the context of all that has happened since, from heroin's link with violent crime to the transfer of HIV among users who share needles, as well as countless other social ills, such an article today would seem unthinkable in all but the most libertarian of newspapers. But in mid-1950s Britain, the spectre of drug addiction was a long way from the top of the public's concerns.

In fact, as the *Times* editorial states, in 1955 there were only 317 addicts to 'manufactured' drugs in the whole of Britain, of which just 15 per cent were dependent on heroin. That's a national total of 47.5 heroin addicts. History, regrettably, does not record the precise circumstances of the half-addict. By contrast, in the US, where heroin was outlawed in 1925, it was said to be a 'major social problem'.

But who were this handful of heroin addicts? According to Dr James Mills, a historian who has traced drug use through the twentieth century, they tended to be doctors or middle-class patients who could afford to sustain a habit.

'In the 1930s, it was really the well-to-do crowd. The working classes might have a bit of heroin in the medicine prescribed to them but it wouldn't be enough to form a dependency', says Dr Mills. Clearly, the fact heroin was legal and widely prescribed for common ailments such as coughs, colds, and diarrhea, as well as a pain killer, had not led to the sort of widespread dependency that opponents of legalization fear would occur if legalized today.

Source: From Duffy (2006).

aspects to this idea of abuse: objective and subjective. The objective aspect relies on physical, mental, or social evidence that the use of a drug harms the individual and society. For example, drug abuse may lead to **drug dependency**, the routine need for a drug for physical reasons (for example, to avoid withdrawal symptoms) and/or for psychological reasons (for example, to maintain a sense of well-being). Related to drug dependency is the notion of tolerance. Drug-dependent people experience increases in drug tolerance, meaning they need larger and larger doses of the drug to get the same effects that a smaller dose originally produced. Drug abuse can also lead to domestic violence, marriage breakdown, job loss, and bankruptcy; all of these are objectively visible and verifiable aspects of drug use.

The subjective aspect of drug use reflects society's beliefs about the effects of overuse and about the courses of action that we should take to tackle the problem. This subjectivity lends itself to change over time. A vivid illustration of this process is society's attitudes about alcohol, a drug that many people use today without a second thought. In the late nineteenth century, however, the English medical profession labelled habitual drunkenness 'dipsomania', portraying it as a disease of the will and moral sense. They stressed the harmful social effects of drunkenness, particularly among poorer members of society who were unable to support their families. Note that this shift from a moral to a medical definition of alcoholism, from vice to disease, mainly affected the poorest, least powerful members of society (Johnstone, 1996). Then as now, shifting conceptions of deviant behaviour had little effect on the rich and powerful.

The temperance movement of the late nineteenth and early twentieth centuries was driven both by a concern on the part of middle-class reformers regarding the negative effects of drink on working-class families and by a growth in the power of the medical establishment. Medicalization is the process through which behaviours—particularly those formerly defined as deviant, sinful, or immoral—are reconceived as instances of illness, that is, they are deemed no longer sinful since they are outside personal control. This process of medicalization, which we discuss further in Chapter 10 on health, has become increasingly important in the definition of social problems with the triumph of science over religion in the past century and a half. Where alcohol abusers were once deemed sinners or moral weaklings and subjected to scorn or criticism, with medicalization they became sick people in need of treatment. This was a new way of controlling the same deviant behaviour, but it put control in the hands of doctors rather than clergy. In the end, medicalization is a means by which the medical profession extends its turf and influence in society, to the point where medical doctors are deemed to be the ones who are able to declare people fit for society. Medicalization temporarily excuses the 'affliction'—a benefit to the drug abuser—and raises the power of physicians in society.

Alcohol abuse is one of many conditions that have evolved into diseases in this way. However, alcohol abuse does not conform perfectly to the processes of medicalization since organizations outside conventional medicine—for example, faith healers, social workers, politicians, and leaders of social movements—have also had a say in the redefinition of this behaviour previously regarded as deviant (Appleton, 1995).

Also, the redefinition of alcohol abuse as a disease is not merely a process of medicalization. The temperance and prohibition movements of the last two centuries also reflected deeper cultural themes—for example, the importance of purity, hygiene, and health. The specific targets of historical temperance movements have varied over time and have included alcohol, drugs, smoking, prostitution, and homosexuality (Wagner, 1995). The common element was an obsession with cleanliness (also purity, virtue, and hygiene) versus dirt (also sin, wickedness, and filth). Below the surface of this cultural dichotomy raged classic struggles between clean and dirty classes (middle and upper classes versus the working classes), clean and dirty communities (native-born versus immigrant), clean and dirty subcultures (rural versus urban), clean and dirty sexes (female versus male). These struggles provide excellent examples of the processes of exclusion and decoupling that we discussed in the introductory chapter.

A century later, groups and professions still fight over the right to define drug use and abuse. Currently, those who use alcohol in moderation are considered 'clean' but those who use illicit street drugs are considered 'dirty'. Consider current views about crack cocaine, spread mainly by the police and religious-moral leaders in their 'war on drugs'. Three prevailing views are that crack is instantly addictive, that it leads people to binge on drugs, and that it inevitably ruins their lives (Reinarman et al., 1997). Poor people are said to be more likely than others to use crack cocaine, while middle- and upper-class people are more likely to use powder cocaine (Alden and Maggard, 2000). Because of its class connotation, the label 'crack head' is intensely stigmatizing (Furst et al., 1999).

Thus, even today, we are repeating the same mistake people made in the early 1900s. Some people want to ban recreational drugs completely. This goal is not realistic since many people want to use these drugs; so, attempting such a ban serves mainly to enrich organized crime. What is more, a large amount of medical and social research confirms that the use of unlawful drugs carries far fewer social and public health costs than tobacco use or alcohol abuse (see, e.g., Fenoglio et al., 2003; Single et al., 1998).

However, many Canadians still believe that drug use is sinful, wrong, or dirty, and oppose publicly funded care for substance abusers, which may be the only practical way to deal with drug problems in our society. In practice, the laws against personal drug use in Canada are largely unenforced, though they remain on the books. Legislative amendments—most recently, in the form of Bill C-17, introduced by the government in November 2004—have sought to decriminalize the personal possession of small amounts of marijuana for recreational use, although to date Parliament has yet to enact any of these proposed laws. Further, majorities appear to be speaking out on drug issues: for example, Vancouver's population chose in 2002 to elect a mayor who ran on a much-publicized platform supporting liberalized care programs for substance abusers.

In short, ignorance and stereotyping have historically shaped people's attitudes to drugs and alcohol, and they continue to do so. These attitudes complicate the process of finding ways to solve the problems associated with alcohol and drug abuse. Emotion-charged beliefs continue to shape our understanding of drugs and drug users, and limit our ability to deal with drug problems in a sensible way.

Physical and Social Characteristics of Alcohol and Drugs

Alcohol

Like most other drugs, alcohol is relatively harmless when used moderately and responsibly. However, it is one of the most destructive substances when abused. People drink alcohol to achieve its chemical effects: to relax, smooth social events, reduce tension, and slow down perceptual, cognitive, and motor functioning. The goal of drinking, then, is to escape from the speed, boredom, stress, or frustration of everyday life and, often, to do so in the company of others, as part of a shared, sociable haze. Impaired judgement usually accompanies these chemical changes.

Many people drink responsibly, remaining below their tolerance limit, practising restraint around minors, and giving up their driving duties to a designated driver. However, some drinkers are not so responsible. Men are much more likely than women to drink heavily and to suffer the physical consequences (for example, injury or death). Women drink much more responsibly, as do university graduates: 'Canadians with university degrees are the least likely of all education groups to report regular heavy drinking. One-fifth (21 per cent) of Canadians with less than a high school education regularly drank heavily, compared with just 12 per cent of current drinkers with a university education' (Health Canada, 1999: 177).

Aside from sex, age is the most important determinant of alcohol use. According to data from the recent Canadian Addiction Survey, 'past year use' peaks between the ages of 18 and 24, with about 90 per cent of those in this age range consuming alcohol within the past year (Adlaf, Begin, and Sawka, 2005). The 2004 Canadian Campus Survey reveals that roughly one-third of undergraduate students engage in harmful drinking practices, such as binge drinking, and exhibit signs of alcohol dependency. Students who do not live with their families, students from the Atlantic region, and students who value recreational activities such as parties and athletics are more likely than average to join in risky levels of consumption. As well, 10 per cent report incidents of alcohol-related assault, 9.8 per cent report alcohol-related sexual harassment, and 14.1 per cent report having unplanned sexual encounters due to alcohol (Adlaf, Demers, and Gliksman, 2005). And, as Figure 3.1 illustrates, a significant number of young people who drink alcohol are also likely to use drugs or tobacco, or both.

These demographic variables provide a snapshot of drinking patterns in Canada and suggest that social factors affect drinking habits. Specifically, social factors shape alcohol use and abuse in at least two ways: by influencing the odds that a person will learn to use alcohol to cope with stress, and by influencing the opportunities a person has to use alcohol for any reason.

LEARNING TO USE ALCOHOL

Medical studies indicate that vulnerability to alcohol addiction may to a large degree be determined by genetic inheritance. Using twins, researchers found lifetime alcohol abuse to have a heritability of 71.4 per cent. This level is lower than for cigarette smoking but higher than for use of other drugs, especially marijuana, whose use is mainly due to environmental influences (Maes et al., 1999).

Still, this figure leaves room for family processes of imitation and learning to strongly affect alcohol consumption. According to primary socialization theory, children learn societal norms within the family, the school, and the peer group (Nurco and Lerner, 1999). Children often learn to drink by watching their parents. Alcohol abuse patterns pass from one generation to the next because, in part, children imitate their parents and siblings, and consequently, those whose parents have a drinking problem are more likely than other children to develop alcohol-related problems themselves, even in their adolescent years (Johnson, 1999). This is an example of disabling.

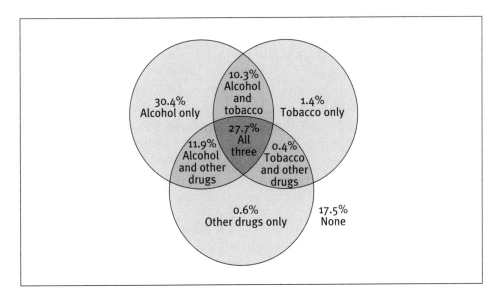

FIGURE 3.1 Drug Use among Manitoba High School Students, 2000

Source: Broszeit and Dhaliwal (2001). Figure reprinted by permission of the Vanier Institute of the Family.

In part, this 'learning' is due to the effects of alcohol abuse on family functioning. Marriages of alcoholic parents are more likely to be conflictual and to end in divorce—conditions that also increase drinking. Children of alcoholic parents are particularly likely to become alcohol abusers themselves if they have an alcoholic sibling. On the other hand, the children of alcoholic parents can lower the risk of alcohol abuse in adulthood by making a good marriage, based on good marital communication (Jennison and Johnson, 1998).

A family history of alcohol abuse also increases the learning of norms favourable to excess drinking. It reduces educational attainment, particularly among men, which increases the likelihood of excess drinking (Curran et al., 1999). Also, an alcoholic, abusive, or otherwise dysfunctional family increases the likelihood that an adolescent will link up with deviant peers and learn deviant norms from them (Whitbeck, 1999). Research found that street youths in Edmonton who use alcohol and hard drugs, for example, were more likely than average to come from families in which they witnessed parental substance abuse. Long-term homelessness and peers who use drugs and alcohol also increased the risks of drug abuse among these street youth (Baron, 1999). Parents who abuse or neglect their children increase the odds that their children will have higher-than-average rates of substance abuse (Widom and White, 1997). Abuse and neglect also increase the likelihood that a young person will end up living on the street.

The norms one learns from peers may be either socially acceptable or deviant, tending to discourage or encourage heavy drinking. Adolescents looking for thrills, for example, often seek out others with similar desires. Groups and subcultures form, made up of young people who drink and behave in similar ways. Persistent alcohol abusers in young adulthood (18–31) are mostly male and exhibit many problem behaviours (Bennett, McCrady, et al., 1999), including being problem drivers and getting involved in traffic accidents. The norms of peer culture may condone drinking to excess—for example, binge drinking (see, e.g., Bennett, Miller, and Woodall, 1999, who discuss binge drinking on a college campus).

Drinking patterns are heavily gendered; men and women use, and abuse, alcohol differently. They also often deal with their problems in different ways. For example, under stress, men are more likely to drink and/or fight, while women are more likely to suffer from depression. Also, friends play a more important part in women's lives, as sources of social support, than they do in men's lives (Skaff et al., 1999). Finally, women become abusers of alcohol in a 'telescoped' way, with a faster progression through the events in the development of alcohol abuse, from first getting drunk to this becoming a regular occurrence to encountering socially and physiologically significant drinking problems (Randall et al., 1999). Stress-related drinking is more common among women, and it becomes more prominent and problematic as the women age (Perkins, 1999).

Alcohol Use Opportunities

Social factors structure drinking by encouraging or discouraging drinking occasions. Drinking norms vary from one society to another and from one ethnic group to another. For example, binge drinking is a cultural tradition in Russia (Bobak et al., 1999). Drinking norms even vary among the workers from one workplace to another, with drinking subcultures existing among those in certain workplaces. Under the best circumstances, the norms regulate drinking on the job (Macdonald et al., 1999). Under the worst circumstances, a lax 'drinking climate', combined with low worker cohesion, increases the risk of job stress, job withdrawal, health problems, work accidents, and absences. In one study, 40 per cent of employees reported at least one negative consequence of co-worker substance abuse (alcohol or drugs). Teamwork and cohesion are needed to buffer the harmful effects on co-workers of a climate that condones and encourages excessive drinking (Bennett and Lehman, 1998).

The same is true in homes and schools. We have already noted that the children of heavy drinkers are much more likely to become heavy drinkers themselves. In addition to this, the odds of alcohol abuse are much greater than average among primary school-children who perceive no parental monitoring at all of their alcohol use, whose parents allow them to drink alcohol at home, and who perceive high levels of parental permissiveness. Efforts to forbid drinking, by contrast, have no apparent effect on children (Jackson et al., 1999). This tells us that the best parenting is authoritative, not lax or repressive. Among adolescents, both risk factors (such as low expectations of success, peer models for substance abuse, and poor school performance) and protective factors (such as intolerance of deviance, peer models for conventional behaviour, and participation in pro-social activities) affect the chances of drinking to excess. More risk and less protection are associated with more problematic use of alcohol (Costa et al., 1999).

Marriage also influences drinking opportunities. Overall, people drink less after they marry. People who never marry are more likely to drink heavily, in a way that contributes to higher risks of mortality. After divorce, people begin to drink more heavily than they did when they were married (Leonard and Rothbard, 1999). The heavy drinking of single, separated, and divorced adults is not due to selection effects (Power et al., 1994). Rather, as Émile Durkheim showed in his classic work *Suicide* (1951 [1897]), marriage sets limits to people's activities and in that way limits the harm they do to themselves.

Heavy drinking within marriage tends to harm marital quality and stability. At the same time, wives and husbands who are happily married tend to drink similarly, especially if they belong to higher socio-economic levels (Demers et al., 1999). Happily married couples with higher education and/or higher income levels likely do more of their drinking together, rather than with friends or alone. It is not clear whether heavy drinking harms a marriage when it is done in the company of a spouse.

Religiosity also affects opportunities for drinking, with more devout people drinking less and reporting fewer alcohol-related problems (Mason and Windle, 2000). Punjabi Canadians interviewed in the Peel Region of Ontario, for example, have a lower-than-average prevalence of drinking than the general Ontario population, especially among women. Despite this, and because of their high standards, most Punjabi respondents believe that alcohol problems are widespread in their community. The most devout Punjabi Canadians drink even less alcohol than other Punjabi Canadians (Kunz and Giesbrecht, 1999).

Again, this is likely for the reasons Durkheim outlined: like marriage, religion puts limits on people's lives and gives them meaning. In this way, religion not only serves to temper alcohol use, it can also help some people overcome addiction as well (see Box 3.2). It also integrates people into social groups that impose norms on drinking and other escapist behaviours. Similar tendencies are evident among the 'Straight Edge' subculture, youths who advocate the avoidance of drug use; this subculture is also characterized by vegetarianism, avoidance of promiscuous and casual sex, and a preference for hardcore punk music (Irwin, 1999).

Box 3.2   Personal Experience: The 12 Steps of Alcoholics Anonymous

Alcoholics Anonymous, today a vast worldwide organization of self-help that is operated by and for alcoholics, had its beginnings in Akron, Ohio, in 1935 through the meeting of two struggling alcoholics, a New York stockbroker, Bill W., and an Akron physician, Dr Bob. The basis of its program for overcoming personal addiction to alcohol is its 12-step program, an approach to self-discipline and mutual assistance that has been widely copied over the years by other groups organized to deal with personal problems and addictions.

1. We admitted we were powerless over alcohol—that our lives had become unmanageable.
2. Came to believe that a Power greater than ourselves could restore us to sanity.
3. Made a decision to turn our will and our lives over to the care of God *as we understood Him.*
4. Made a searching and fearless moral inventory of ourselves.
5. Admitted to God, to ourselves, and to another human being the exact nature of our wrongs.
6. Were entirely ready to have God remove all these defects of character.
7. Humbly asked Him to remove our shortcomings.
8. Made a list of all persons we had harmed, and became willing to make amends to them all.
9. Made direct amends to such people wherever possible, except when to do so would injure them or others.
10. Continued to take personal inventory and when we were wrong promptly admitted it.
11. Sought through prayer and meditation to improve our conscious contact with God *as we understood Him,* praying only for knowledge of His will for us and the power to carry that out.
12. Having had a spiritual awakening as the result of these steps, we tried to carry this message to alcoholics, and to practice these principles in all our affairs.

Source: Alcoholics Anonymous (1976: 59–60). The Twelve Steps are reprinted with permission of Alcoholics Anonymous World Services, Inc. (AAWS). Permission to reprint the Twelve Steps does not mean that AAWS has reviewed or approved the contents of this publication, or that AAWS necessarily agrees with the views expressed herein. A.A. is a program of recovery from alcoholism *only*—use of the Twelve Steps in connection with programs and activities which are patterned after A.A., but which address other problems, or in any other non-A.A. context, does not imply otherwise.

People with less access to alcohol, more access to other forms of activity, or friends who reject drinking are safer from the risks of alcohol abuse. Interestingly, these are instances in which forms of decoupling and scarcity have positive consequences for the individual; they work to the individual's advantage in staying away from alcohol. As we have seen, many forms of decoupling and scarcity yield negative outcomes for those affected by them.

Tobacco

Tobacco is Canada's other major legal drug. Like alcohol, nicotine is a highly addictive substance, a psychoactive drug to blame for many health problems, and a costly habit, both for the individual and for society. Tobacco is also hugely popular, though a concerted public health movement targeted at smoking reduction has led to steadily declining use in recent years. In 2005, approximately five million Canadians—20 per cent of the population 15 years and over—reported smoking daily or occasionally, a drop from nearly seven million Canadians in 1996–7 (Statistics Canada, 2005a; Health Canada, 1999: 164).

Most adult smokers develop their habit of smoking before the age of 20. As with alcohol, men are more likely than women to use tobacco, although the gender gap has been narrowing for the past quarter-century. Health Canada has found that girls are more likely to smoke than boys until age 18, when boys begin to outpace girls. Unlike alcohol use, there is a simple linear relationship between education and cigarette smoking: 'People with less than a high school education are almost three times more likely than university graduates to be current smokers' (Health Canada, 1999: 165).

A study of more than 22,000 Ontario high school students found that teenagers are at increased risk for smoking if they (a) have smoking friends, (b) have smoking family members, and/or (c) attend a school with a relatively high senior-student smoking rate (Leatherdale et al., 2005). Among adolescents who experiment with smoking, the development of a smoking habit is positively correlated with poor academic performance, parental smoking, and having more than half of one's friends smoking; it is negatively correlated with attending a school with a clear anti-smoking policy and having confidence in one's ability to succeed academically (Karp et al., 2005). European data also suggest that smoking is more common among teenagers in single-parent households and blended-family households than among those in intact families. The researchers suggest that these trends may be due to lower levels of attachment, a tendency towards rebellion, and less parental supervision in stepfamily and lone-parent homes (Griesbach et al., 2003).

Banned Drugs

Since the middle of the twentieth century, unlawful drug use has increased among Canada's youth population, though evidence suggests that usage rates may have peaked in recent years. Among Ontario youths, for example, the use of most forms of illegal

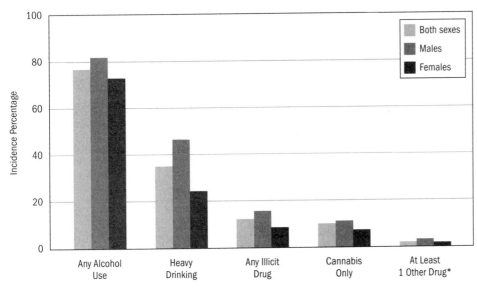

FIGURE 3.2 Alcohol and Illicit Drug Use in Past 12 Months, Ages 15 and Older, Canada excluding Territories, 2002

*'Heavy drinking' is defined as consuming five or more drinks on a single occasion.

Source: Statistics Canada, at: <www.statscan.ca/english/freepub/82-003-SIE/2004000/pdf/82-003-SIE20040007447.pdf>.

drugs declined throughout the 1980s, increased throughout the 1990s, and appears since 1999 to be on the decline once more. As the rates of use have dropped, more teenagers have reported a complete avoidance of drugs: 36 per cent of Ontario secondary-school students claimed to be completely drug-free (including alcohol and tobacco) in 2005, up from 32 per cent in 2003 (Centre for Addiction and Mental Health, 2006). Researchers have blamed the continued drug use on a weakened sense that it is harmful or immoral and an increased availability of drugs.

CANNABIS

Marijuana, or cannabis, is the most widely used drug in the world (UN Office on Drugs and Crime, 2000). Ninety-six per cent of all countries reporting a drug abuse problem report the use of cannabis in either its leaf form (marijuana) or its resin form (hashish). It is also the most widely used illegal drug in Canada, among youth in particular. In 1999, cannabis was used by 29.3 per cent of Ontario students in grades 7–13, up from 12.7 per cent in 1993 (Centre on Substance Abuse and Centre for Addiction and Mental Health, 1999).

Many health-care officials are worried about marijuana's possible role as a **gateway drug**, that is, as a drug that leads to the use of other banned drugs, such as cocaine or heroin (see, e.g., Kane and Yacoubian, 1999). However, others have pointed out that, for social and psychological reasons, people who are willing to try one type of drug may already be likely to try another drug, with no particular 'gateway' process involved. That is, some people are disposed to trying many drugs and they merely start with marijuana. Research finds that the most popular combination for so-called **polydrug use** is alcohol, nicotine, and marijuana.

Cannabis has been used as a traditional medicine for pain relief and anti-nausea for many millennia, and remained popular and socially accepted until at least the late 1800s. Only in the twentieth century was its medical and recreational use outlawed. For example, when the US passed the federal Marijuana Tax Act in 1937, which effectively criminalized cannabis, the only group opposing its enactment was the American Medical Association. Medicinal marijuana remained widely outlawed until the 1970s, when new medical research and increasingly liberalized societies emerged to challenge the rationale behind a universal ban.

Although marijuana for recreational use currently remains illegal in Canada, possession and use for medical purposes are legal under Health Canada's Marijuana Medical Access Regulations. These regulations were adopted in July 2001, making Canada the first country to control the medical use of marijuana. The change came about after numerous constitutional challenges in the late 1990s arguing that prohibiting access to the drug, when it is deemed a medically necessary treatment, was a violation of the Charter of Rights and Freedoms. As a result of these rulings, a federal program was developed allowing individuals to apply for authorization to buy, possess, and use marijuana as a medical drug. To qualify, patients must be diagnosed with one or more specified conditions, such as multiple sclerosis, HIV/AIDS, severe arthritis, or epilepsy. Supply is also strictly controlled—patients may either order prepared marijuana from a government-licensed pharmaceutical company or order seeds to grow their own. As of December 2005, 1,186 Canadians were allowed to possess marijuana for medical reasons, while 859 were authorized to cultivate medicinal marijuana (Health Canada, 2005b).

COCAINE

Cocaine is an inhaled stimulant; its effects include joy, excitement, self-confidence, and feelings of great well-being. It has been used for centuries, mainly for religious, social, and medicinal purposes. Anti-cocaine sentiment emerged in the United States and Canada only at the start of the twentieth century. At that time, the impetus for an attack on the use of the drug was more political and social than pharmacological. Urban blacks were the primary users of the drug, and the demonization of cocaine coincided 'with a wave of repressive measures defined to ensure the subordination of blacks' (Giffen et al., 1991: 14). A negative view of the drug has persisted, fuelling the worldwide 'war on drugs', despite reports that have questioned cocaine's addictive properties (Van Dyck and Byck, 1982). Less than 1 per cent of the population in Canada uses cocaine regularly, and, like most other drugs, Canadian men are more likely than Canadian women to be users (Health Canada, 1999: 184).

Crack cocaine is a crystallized derivative produced by boiling baking soda, water, and cocaine together. Its effect is more intense than powder cocaine, in part because people inhale it directly into the lungs. There, it can be more readily absorbed into the bloodstream than it can if taken through the mucous membrane in the nose. Research has not demonstrated that crack is more addictive than powder cocaine (Morgan and Zimmer, 1997).

HEROIN

Heroin is a modified form of morphine that delivers an intense and addictive effect. It is the most commonly injected drug in Canada for recreational use, although, again, only about 1 per cent of the population reports having used it in the past year. The RCMP estimates that regular users of heroin number between 28,000 and 50,000 in Canada (Lafranire and Spicer, 2002: 21). Still, because the preferred method of its delivery is injection, heroin poses particular risks to its users. Besides physiological hazards, which include collapsed veins, unplanned abortions, comas, and fatal overdoses, many heroin addicts are at risk of contracting HIV/AIDS, hepatitis B, and other diseases transmitted through the sharing of dirty needles. For example, Vancouver's Downtown Eastside, home to many intravenous drug users, has the highest rate of HIV infection in the Western world, according to one estimate by the members of the Killing Fields Campaign (Cernetig, 1997).

METHAMPHETAMINES AND CRYSTAL METH

Crystal 'meth', or methamphetamine hydrochloride, is a street variant of methamphetamine ('meth'), which itself is a modified form of amphetamine. The physiological effect of these various drugs is to stimulate the central nervous system, increase wakefulness, and suppress appetite. Psychologically, the experience is one of extreme euphoria, mental alertness, and focus. Amphetamines and methamphetamines have been used in low doses to treat attention deficit disorder (ADD), narcolepsy, and obesity, though a form of the latter is also sold illegally on the streets as 'speed'.

Production of meth and crystal meth is relatively simple; they can be concocted from common household products and over-the-counter medicines. Instructions are readily available on the Internet, resulting in a proliferation of illicit amateur 'meth labs', particularly in suburban and rural households. These labs are often hazardous, as production results in highly toxic by-products and fumes, and can lead to explosions if done

Cocaine Use among Ontario Youth and Adults

According to a 2001 survey of Ontario students in grades 7–12:

- 4 per cent had used cocaine at least once.
- 2 per cent had used crack cocaine at least once in the past year.

According to a 2000 survey of Ontario adults:

- 6.4 per cent had used cocaine at least once.
- 1.2 per cent had used it in the past year.

Source: Cited in Centre for Addiction and Mental Health (2003).

improperly. However, in North America, crystal meth is more often produced and sold in large quantities by organized crime, especially motorcycle gangs.

HALLUCINOGENS

The family of hallucinogens (psychedelics) includes both natural forms (for example, mescaline) and synthetic forms (for example, PCP, or phencyclidine). LSD (lysergic acid diethylamide) has been the most commonly used hallucinogenic drug since the 1960s, although in recent decades synthetic designer drugs have gained in popularity. MDMA (a.k.a. 'ecstasy' or simply 'E'), in particular, first became popular in underground rave parties and then spread among other groups in the wider society. The effects of hallucinogens include psychedelic illusions and altered perceptual and thought patterns. Less pleasant effects include paranoia, loss of bodily control, delusions, and slurred speech. One public health concern arises from the variable quality of the drug, which often contains substances entirely different from MDMA, ranging from caffeine to dextromethorphan (used in cough medicines) (NIDA, 2001). Although the medical establishment is still debating its health effects, ecstasy made headlines—and was the target of an extensive police crackdown—in the late 1990s after a series of overdoses and overdose-related deaths occurred among teenage party-goers during all-night rave parties (ibid.).

Social Influences on Illicit Drug Abuse

Much of what we have said about alcohol abuse applies equally to drug abuse. Factors that reduce the likelihood of drug use and abuse include strong family bonds, which reduce the use of all illegal drugs except marijuana (Ellickson et al., 1999); a strong religious commitment (Yarnold, 1999); and normative boundaries that separate adolescents who use drugs socially, on an occasional basis, from those who use them often or in isolation (Warner, Room, and Adlaf, 1999). Marriage and parenthood are also important influences (Liu and Kaplan, 1999). Married people and parents who adhere to conventional values may use illegal drugs when they come under stress, for the reasons Robert Merton (1957) has suggested: the control of stress (and, more generally, of anomie) with drugs allows them to continue to conform to dominant values. The drugs reduce stress in a private and non-disruptive fashion (Liu and Kaplan, 1999). People committed to conventional values may find their own failure in valued social roles more distressing than people less committed to these values.

Factors that increase the likelihood of drug use include friends who are users and parents who use tobacco or alcohol (Colson, 2000); early initiation into drug use (Dishion et al., 1999); and a history of parental abuse (Bensley et al., 1999). Working conditions also make a difference. Workers with low cognitive ability make more use of cigarettes, alcohol, and marijuana the more complex their jobs are; workers with high cognitive ability, on the other hand, make less use of these substances the more complex their jobs are (Oldham and Gordon, 1999).

Even more than alcohol use, drug use is a learned behaviour that depends on social opportunities and on inclusion in social occasions where drugs are being used. Opportunities to use drugs, and actual drug use, are more common as youths get older. The probability of trying drugs, given the opportunity, also increases with age. Ethnic and gender differences in adolescent drug use correspond to differences in opportunities to try drugs with acquaintances, dating partners, and even parents (Moon et al., 1999).

Males tend to have more opportunities to use marijuana, crack cocaine, and other forms of cocaine, and at a younger age. However, they are no more likely than females to begin using drugs once an opportunity has arisen (Delva et al., 1999; Van Etten et al., 1999). Normative boundaries restricting girls' access to and use of drugs are largely due to traditional gender roles that limit girls' access to certain types of leisure and sociability. Male peers enforce these norms in their capacity as drug dealers and distributors (Warner, Weber, and Albanes, 1999). While males are more likely to receive offers of drugs from other males and even parents, often in public settings, drug offers to females are more likely to come from other females or dating partners, often in private settings (Moon et al., 1999)

Theories of Drug and Alcohol Abuse

Several theories have been put forward by scholars concerning why drug and alcohol abuse occur. Here, as in other chapters, we discuss what the three major sociological traditions have to say about substance use.

The Structural-Functionalist Perspective

Structural-functionalists hold that alcohol and drug abuse, like all social problems, results from the way the social structure influences the individual. Some argue that recreational drug and alcohol use are common because these substances serve an important function as social lubricant. For example, alcohol use, for many people, is almost mandatory on certain occasions—for example, Mardi Gras in New Orleans or Carnival in Rio de Janeiro, or New Year's Eve anywhere—where it breaks down personal inhibitions and fosters communal conviviality.

Structural-functionalism also seeks to explain substance abuse. Two of the more influential camps within this perspective are social disorganization theory and anomie theory.

SOCIAL DISORGANIZATION THEORY

Social disorganization theory argues that institutions that have traditionally acted to discourage deviant behaviours become less effective during times of rapid social change. Rapid changes cause norms and values to become unclear. Without traditional sources of moral guidance to restrain behaviour, deviancy—including drug and alcohol use—becomes more common.

We can usefully apply this perspective, for example, to Canada's Aboriginal population and its problem with addictive substances, especially alcohol. For centuries after arriving in North America, Aboriginal peoples lived in many small communities or bands that varied widely but had certain features in common. Despite differences in language and culture, the Native communities were all highly cohesive. A strong sense of community, with cultural custodians who stood guard over the group's traditions, promoted the sharing and defence of communal values.

Forced off their traditional hunting lands and onto reserves by the arrival of whites, Aboriginal community norms and traditions broke down, speeded by the imposition of residential schooling. Alcohol abuse and suicide spread among Aboriginal peoples throughout the nineteenth and twentieth centuries. Few methods worked to stem this problem because they did not address the issue of social disorganization: the loss of traditional controls and values imparted by family, community, and religion.

The method of treatment that has worked best to control alcohol abuse has included addiction counselling by other Native people, sharing Aboriginal experiences, relearning the traditional culture, and practising Aboriginal rituals. Using this approach, the Shuswap people on the Alkali Lake Reserve in British Columbia went from 100 per cent addiction to 95 per cent sobriety in 15 years (Hodgson, 1987). With the reversal of social disorganization, alcohol abuse has begun to subside.

MERTON'S ANOMIE THEORY

According to Merton (1957), the cause of excessive drinking and other substance abuse lies not in an absence of values and institutions but in the conflict between them. According to this theory, excessive drinking is driven by a basic conflict or paradox—a gap between culturally defined goals and socially approved means for attaining those goals. Merton, using American society as his example, argues that one of the primary goals of that society is success, especially in obtaining money, material goods, and 'the good life'. Most people have been taught to value success. Yet social inequality ensures that most people will not succeed because they will not have access to the socially approved (that is, legal) means and resources that allow them to attain success—for example, higher education and good jobs.

Merton has called this gap between goals and means 'anomie'. This state of anomie allows for a variety of solutions, which Merton called possible adaptations. They include what he called ritualism, retreatism, rebellion, and innovation (see Table 3.1). Substance abuse results from adopting one such adaptation—retreatism.

However, the use of drugs and alcohol is not merely an individual adaptation; it is socially organized. Groups of individuals with higher levels of social capital, especially social network connections that offer them access to valued jobs, have less need for the numbing escapism that drugs and alcohol offer. Those exposed to adverse community-level conditions—poverty, unemployment, and other measures of social breakdown—are more likely to retreat from their oppressive realities.

Conflict Theory

Alcohol and drug use affect different socio-economic groups differently. The poor tend to suffer more harmful consequences than the rich (see, e.g., Makela, 1999). However, conflict theorists focus largely on the labelling and criminalization processes. They note that in a capitalist economic system that perpetuates inequality, the powerful members of society are in a position to define whether a substance is legal or illegal. The powerful are able to criminalize drug use by the powerless. Moreover, they are in a position to benefit from drug use at the same time as they may disavow it.

Alcohol and tobacco, for example, are produced and sold by the powerful. Both of these billion-dollar industries are regulated but not considered illegal. Both also heavily brand and market their addictive products (see Figure 3.3), reaping huge profits for wealthy stockholders while harming the heavy users, who tend to be poor.

Conflict theories also note that banned substances are often forbidden not only because of their harmful pharmacological properties, but also for social and political reasons. Box 3.3 describes the process whereby early Chinese immigrants to Canada were economically and socially marginalized under the pretense of an anti-drug morality.

Table 3.1 Merton's Adaptations to Anomie

Conformist	Recognizes that one has limited means and may never attain every idealized social goal. Instead, simply tries to live one's life as best as one can.
Ritualist	Appears to conform, but has given up all hope of personal success. Merely 'going through the motions'.
Retreatist	Recognizes that one will never achieve one's goals and gives up entirely. No pretense of conformity is preserved. Resorts to alcoholism, drug abuse, and perhaps suicide.
Rebel	Recognizes the inherent inequality within the existing system and rejects the norms and values upon which 'success' is based. May try to change the political order.
Innovationist	Internalizes social goals but not the legitimate norms and means for attaining them. Seeks innovative ways (i.e., crime) to achieve these goals.

Symbolic Interactionism

Symbolic interactionists focus on the social meanings and values associated with alcohol and drug use and on the labels people attach to others when they use drugs. What do you think of when you hear the term 'alcoholic'? Does it bring to mind a person who cannot control the harmful effects of alcohol use? A person who is less educated, unemployed, and trapped in the lower socio-economic strata of society? A person with various prior emotional difficulties—for example, an unhappy marriage—that precipitated his or her alcoholism?

Contrast that image with the 'social drinker'. Paradoxically, friendly social drinking is the drinking code of the modern, advanced capitalist society. The links between alcohol use and leisure have been omnipresent in our society as some indi-

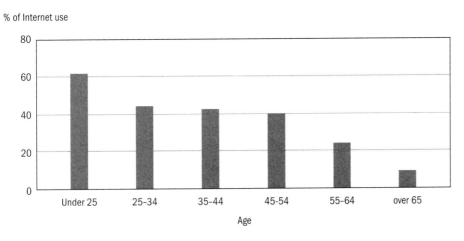

FIGURE 3.3 The Marketing of Alcohol and Tobacco on the Internet

Source: Moscovitch (1998). Reprinted by permission of the Vanier Institute of the Family.

Box 3.3   Social Construction: Opium and Early Chinese Canadians

Opium was brought to Canada by the Chinese, who themselves were brought over as a cheap labour source for building the Canadian Pacific Railway in the late nineteenth century. As long as the Chinese provided a useful service to the ruling white population, opium smoking was considered nothing more than 'an individual medical misfortune or personal vice, free of severe moral opprobrium' or, for that matter, legal sanction (Green, 1986: 25).

Once construction was completed in 1885, the Chinese began to establish inroads into other areas of the labour market and sought out a new life for themselves in their adopted homeland. However, as the economy declined and jobs became scarce, the Chinese came to be viewed as unwanted competitors for the limited positions that remained. Canadians demanded that Chinese immigration be limited or stopped, and they stigmatized the Chinese who already lived in Canada. Opium use (which in fact Britain had introduced into China in the 1840s) provided a handy excuse.

In Vancouver, the Reverend Dr Fraser asked, 'Is there harm in the Chinaman? In this city, that could be answered with one word, "Chinatown", with its wicked unmentionables'—of which opium was only one. The fact that many opium users at the time were white, far from undermining anti-Chinese sentiments, was viewed as evidence of the harmful effects of 'degenerate' and 'depraved' Chinese culture on the Canadian way of life.

Racist attitudes also reached the highest levels of public office. An 1885 resolution drafted by the BC government for transmission to Ottawa argued that 'the Chinese population chiefly consists of male adults, and thus they come into unfair competition with white labour. . . . They have a system of secret societies which encourages crime amongst themselves. . . . The use of opium has extended throughout the Province to the demoralization of the native races [i.e., whites]. . . . This House urgently requests that some restrictive legislation be passed to prevent our Province from being completely overrun by Chinese.' Over the next decades, Ottawa responded, first through a series of increasingly oppressive head taxes, before finally enacting the Chinese Immigration Act (also known as the Chinese Exclusion Act) in 1923, which virtually ended Chinese immigration into Canada for the next 24 years.

Source: Adapted from Anderson (1991).

viduals not only typically drink in their free time, but often do so to have a good time (Carruthers, 1992). Yet only 'alcoholics' and heavy drinkers are stigmatized and stereotyped in our society.

Joseph Gusfield's study of the symbolic crusade that led to Prohibition in the United States (1963) provides a good example of the social construction of deviant behaviour that benefits one group more than another. Prohibition consisted of a ban, from 1920 to 1933, on the sale and public use of alcohol in the United States. The successful lobbying effort organized by the American temperance movement that led to Prohibition was an example of what Gusfield calls *status politics*—'a struggle between groups for prestige and social position' (Gusfield, 1963: 3). Defending their position in the status order is as important to people as protecting or expanding their economic power; indeed, the two are often related.

Table 3.2 summarizes the major theoretical viewpoints on drug and alcohol abuse.

Table 3.2 Theoretical Viewpoints of Substance Abuse

Theoretical Perspective	Main Points
Structural Functionalism	Alcohol and drug abuse results from the social structure's influence on the individual.
	Drug and alcohol use is common because it serves social functions.
Social Disorganization Theory	Institutions that traditionally discourage deviant behaviour are rendered less effective by rapid social change.
	Breakdown in community norms and traditions deprives individuals of a sense of meaning and moral guidance.
	Relearning or re-establishing traditional institutions can reduce substance abuse.
Merton's (1957) Anomie Theory	Drug and alcohol abuse is the result of the incongruence between culturally defined goals and the socially approved means for attaining these goals (i.e., anomie).
	One adaptation to this gap is to retreat (abandon efforts to achieve goals, escape reality via substance abuse).
Conflict Theory	Alcohol and drug use affect different socio-economic groups differently.
	Powerful capitalist members of society are in a position to define whether a substance is legal or illegal.
	The poor tend to suffer harmful consequences of substance abuse more than the rich, due to labelling and the criminalization process.
Symbolic Interactionism	The social meanings and values associated with drug and alcohol use and with the labels attached to people when they use these substances are the focus for understanding.
	The term 'alcoholic' is laden with negative characterizations, judgements, and stereotypes in a way that 'social drinker' is not.

Social Consequences of Drugs and Drug Abuse

The adverse social consequences of drugs and alcohol reinforce the argument that excessive and/or unregulated drug and alcohol use is a real social problem and not merely a social construction. For instance, with respect to alcohol abuse, adverse social consequences may indicate a more serious form of problem drinking than do symptoms of dependency or other medical consequences (Bailey, 1999).

Crime and Violence

According to the Criminal Intelligence Service Canada (2005: 8), 'the illicit drug trade . . . is the most prominent criminal market for organized crime groups.' For example, Vietnamese criminal organizations and the Hell's Angels motorcycle gang each play

Homicide and Drugs

Eleven per cent (*n* = 684) of all homicides in Canada between 1992 and 2002 were drug-related.

Source: Statistics Canada (2004).

major roles in the Canadian domestic marijuana trade, while Southwest Asian crime groups are particularly active in heroin trafficking. Organized criminals typically use violence to assert and expand their respective territories, posing an obvious threat to public safety. In addition, violence and the threat of violence are frequently used to frighten community members and discourage co-operation with police. Just as Prohibition during the 1920s led to illegal gangster-operated speakeasies, the continued insistence on criminalizing drugs in high demand, such as marijuana, ensures that criminal organizations, sensing a potentially lucrative source of revenue, will continue to be active in their illicit production and trafficking.

In a study of young men in prison, men who said they used drugs during their last year of freedom prior to their imprisonment—particularly those who used a combination of drugs, alcohol, and tobacco—were especially likely to have ever participated in violent offending and to have done so that same year (Brownstein et al., 1999) (see also Figure 3.4). Another study found that chronic drug users are significantly more likely than non-drug users to have assaulted, shot, stabbed, or robbed someone, and also significantly more likely to have been both victims and observers of all violent acts (McCoy et al., 2000).

The link between alcohol use and crime, particularly violent crime, is well known. Canadian data suggest a moderate association between annual rates of alcohol consumption and unemployment and between alcohol consumption and annual rates of homicide. One explanation for this correlation is that unemployment leads to desperation and disillusionment, while alcohol use lessens inhibition and cognitive judgement—two factors that make the decision to commit homicide seem more rational (Statistics Canada, 2005b). Of course, driving while drunk is a criminal offence all on its own. Drunk drivers are involved in over one-third of all traffic accident-related deaths in North America.

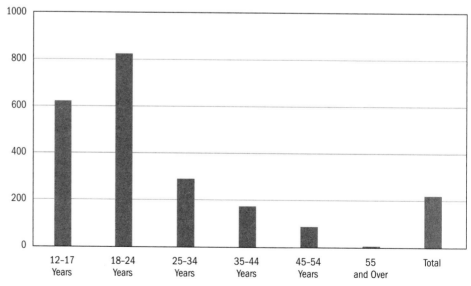

FIGURE 3.4 Drug-Related Crime Rate per 100,000 Population, by Age Group, 2002
Source: Statistics Canada (2004).

Alcohol use is more strongly and more consistently associated with both violent and non-violent offences than are marijuana and heroin use (Dawkins, 1997). Alcohol use and abuse are often involved in incidents of physical assault, both among the perpetrators and the victims (Scott et al., 1999). The research literature suggests that alcohol causes biochemical changes producing behaviours that would not have occurred otherwise; it also provides a convenient excuse to engage in violent behaviours (Patton and Baird, 2000). A review of the literature also reveals that 50 per cent of all homicide offenders and victims are intoxicated from drug or alcohol use at the time of the crime (Auerhahn and Parker, 1999).

Alcohol abuse is also unduly common among malfunctioning families and broken homes. First, alcohol has been implicated in roughly 75 per cent of all incidents of spousal violence (Greenfield, 1998), suggesting that alcohol use can act as the catalyst that ignites violence in an already explosive domestic environment. Such violence can also lead to other forms of family disruption and displacement, including divorce and child custody battles.

Female victims of domestic violence are excessively likely to be married to extremely heavy drinkers. Drunkenness, not drinking per se, is the main predictor for threatening behaviour and wife battering by husbands (Hutchison, 1999). Even among newlyweds, heavy drinking by the husband can degenerate into physical (versus verbal) aggression. Violent episodes are largely unrelated to the wife's drinking (Leonard and Quigley, 1999). Among male alcoholics, returns to drinking predict returns to domestic violence, even among men who have received treatment in a marital-therapy alcoholism treatment program (O'Farrell et al., 1999).

Poverty and Income

Although alcohol use rates are higher among well-educated, high-income people than among poorly educated, low-income people, alcohol abuse and problem drinking are reported more often among the latter group. Whether poverty causes drug abuse or drug abuse causes poverty is difficult to distinguish. A vicious circle may occur as well, with poverty leading to abuse and abuse, in turn, reinforcing joblessness and poverty.

Alcohol and drugs such as heroin and cocaine provide their users with a temporary feeling of well-being and contentment and at the same time relieve feelings of loneliness, depression, and pain. The appeal of drugs to the disadvantaged, desperate, and marginalized is therefore considerable. However, because of the addictive properties of banned substances, the buildup of physical and psychological tolerance, and the desire to avoid painful withdrawal symptoms, many drug users soon require larger and larger quantities of the drug. This translates into a costly habit, and many addicts—unless they are gainfully employed—resort to prostitution, theft, and robbery to continue their drug use. As addicts begin to gather together in a single area, other social consequences of banned drug use arise, including poverty, social disorganization, homelessness, gang activities, and invasive drug trafficking and distribution systems.

At the other end of the income spectrum, laundered drug funds have been used to subsidize the world economy, including war involving the major powers and armed insurgencies, since the economic crisis of the 1980s. The interdependence of the legal economy, state interests, and drug interests makes it almost impossible to distinguish between formal, informal, and criminal economies (Laniel, 1999).

Binge Drinking in the UK
The estimated total annual cost of Britain's binge drinking culture in 2003 was £20 billion (approximately Cdn$44 billion) (Prime Minister's Strategy Unit, 2003).

Racism

The 'war on drugs', particularly in the US but also to a degree in Canada, has increased racial and class injustice by targeting the poor and racial minorities unduly. It has focused on drug users and street traffickers, not others (such as money launderers) in the drug economy, and has attributed their drug abuse and criminal activity to moral weakness rather than to a loss of manufacturing jobs (Duster, 1997).

Legislators enact laws to govern behaviour in society and the criminal justice system seeks to punish people who violate these laws. However, the system undermines its own authority when it fails to follow the 'blind justice' doctrine upon which it is founded. Several lines of evidence suggest that justice is not blind, at least in relation to drug enforcement and prosecution.

Within each ethnocultural group, drug use is fairly similar. The US Substance Abuse and Mental Health Services Administration (1999) estimates that 10.4 per cent of American whites reported that they had used drugs in the past year; among African Americans, 13.0 per cent reported that they had used drugs in the past year, as did 10.5 per cent of Hispanic Americans. However, African Americans were four times more likely to be arrested for drug abuse violations and as much as 10 times more likely to be arrested in some major cities (Meddis, 1993). Even though the majority of crack cocaine users were white, about 96 per cent of the crack defendants in federal court were non-white. Equivalent race-based drug arrest data is not available in Canada. However, given recent concerns about racial profiling practices among Canadian law enforcement agencies, there is reason to believe that similar trends may exist here as well. More research is needed in this area.

Other Social Consequences

Because of the high rate of alcohol and drug use, both legal and illegal, many aspects of social life have been affected. The Canadian Centre on Substance Abuse (Rehm et al., 2006) estimates that the social costs of substance abuse in Canada—including direct economic costs such as health care, law enforcement, and prevention, and indirect costs such as lost productivity—totalled $40 billion in 2002. Losses in productivity and premature death accounted for over 60 per cent of the costs, while law enforcement and health care accounted for most of the remainder. Other economic costs of drug and alcohol abuse are associated with homelessness, the need for educational and rehabilitation treatment programs, and the medical treatment of drug addicts and of substance abuse-related injuries and fatalities.

Health Consequences of Substance Abuse

Because alcohol and other drugs are chemicals that have direct physiological effects on the human body, the health consequences arising from substance abuse are both widespread and severe.

Health Consequences of Alcohol and Drug Abuse

The physical consequences of alcohol abuse are extremely complex and varied. A report by the United Kingdom's Royal College of Physicians (1987) found that alcohol abuse is linked to disorders of the nervous system, strokes, paralysis and other nerve damage, liver damage, high blood pressure, heart failure, and many other health problems. However, the unique effects of alcohol on health are hard to parcel out since heavy drinkers tend to show other health-destroying characteristics as well: smoking, depression, unemployment, and so on (Fillmore et al., 1998).

Some evidence suggests that the volume of alcohol consumption per occasion has more harmful effects than the overall drinking volume; that is, binge drinking is more harmful in its social consequences than drinking or drunkenness per se (Rehm and Gmel, 1999). Overall, chronic drug users show greater health-care needs than non-users, and are less likely to receive appropriate health-care services (McCoy et al., 2000). Poor eating habits and malnutrition are positively related to heavy drinking, as are social and family disorganization (Santolaria et al., 2000). Even among youth aged 12–18, the regular use of alcoholic beverages (beer, wine, and distilled spirits) contributes significantly to gradual decreases in physical health, with no evidence that alcohol helps to cope with pre-existing psychological distress and physical symptoms (Hansell et al., 1999). Adolescent substance use, in turn, predicts poor physical health in adulthood (Spohn and Kaplan, 2000).

The risk of suicidal thinking is increased by a family history of alcohol abuse among men, though not among women (Grant and Hasin, 1999). In particular, an alcoholic father in the home places the child at high risk for later problems, including suicide, mortality, drug abuse, and social maladjustment (Mutzell, 1994). Cannabis abuse or dependence is significantly associated with serious suicide attempts, even after controlling for other factors that predict dependence and suicide (Beautrais et al., 1999). A longitudinal (17-year) study found that narcotic addicts are generally at high risk for mortality (including violent death) compared with the general population (Mutzell, 1996).

Early initiation into alcohol and marijuana use was found to predict earlier initiation of sexual activity and subsequent risky sexual behaviour among US adolescents and young adults, with males taking the greater risks (Staton et al., 1999). Parental monitoring mitigated later levels of alcohol misuse and sexual risk-taking (Thomas et al., 2000). The use of illicit drugs and alcohol appears to increase the likelihood that women will engage in sexual behaviour in which they would not have engaged if they had not been under the influence. The greater use of drugs and alcohol may be part of a wider pattern of sexual behaviour, including a higher number of sexual partners, although it does not typically result in unsafe or undesired sexual behaviour (Taylor et al., 1999). Some women who have worked in the sex trade found that the use of crack cocaine undermined their safety at work and in other relationships, including greater risk of ill health, loss of earnings, and violence through their drug use (Green et al., 2000).

Drug users run a higher risk of HIV infection, in part from unprotected sex with multiple partners (Inciardi et al., 1999). This practice is common in prisons, as well as outside. Women drug offenders are found to engage in numerous high-risk drug and sexual behaviours while in prison; on release, they are a major public health risk. Criminal justice policies, grounded in deterrence and based on imprisonment, may be contributing to the spread of HIV infection in the wider society (Marquart et al., 1999). Crack cocaine injectors are at the greatest potential risk for exposure to heterosexually transmitted HIV, followed by other injecting drug users, crack smokers, and then other drug users (Cotton Oldenburg et al., 1999). The connection between drug use and the spread of HIV/AIDS is found throughout the world (see, e.g., Bastos et al., 1999, on South America and the Caribbean).

Health consequences are not limited to the drug-using individual, however. Pregnant women who drink may also be placing their unborn children at risk. Fetal alcohol syndrome (FAS) occurs as a result of prenatal exposure to alcohol, and can result in facial abnormalities and stunted growth after birth. In addition, damage to the central nervous system can lead to attention deficits and to intellectual, memory, and learning disabilities. FAS occurs in approximately one to three live births per 1,000, which is unfortunate as it is considered one of the most preventable forms of birth defect in Canada (see Williams and Gloster, 1999).

Health consequences faced by users of illegal drugs include shortened lifespans, dietary irregularities, severe weight loss, vomiting, mucous membrane damage, and brain lesions. Among injection drug users, the risk of contracting HIV/AIDS from sharing contaminated needles is severe. A conservative estimate by the Canadian Centre on Substance Abuse and the Centre for Addiction and Mental Health (1999) indicates that one in every five AIDS cases in Canada was related in some way to intravenous drug use.

Alcohol and drug abuse can also lead to mental health problems. White and Labouvie (1994), for example, have shown that drug users are more likely to develop anxiety disorders, phobias, depression, and anti-social personalities. Suicide is also more common among drug users, particularly adolescents. Marijuana, the illicit drug of choice among teenagers, has been associated with short-term memory loss, impaired learning, amotivational syndrome, and emotional deficits. Further, of all students in Ontario who reported alcohol problems in 1998, 40 per cent reported impaired mental health as a direct result.

Health Consequences of Tobacco Smoking

Tobacco smoking is the primary cause of lung cancer, which is the leading cause of cancer death. In 2006, over 19,000 Canadians were expected to die from lung cancer and nearly 23,000 expected to develop the disease. Another 12,000 were expected to die from cancer to the mouth, larynx, esophagus, stomach, bladder, kidney, and pancreas, all of which have been linked to cigarette and cigar smoking (Canadian Cancer Society/National Cancer Institute of Canada, 2006). Further, smoking can lead to elevated risk of asthma, pulmonary disease, emphysema, heart disease, stroke and other cardiovascular diseases, spontaneous abortions, and premature births. (For detailed information on these and other smoking-related health problems, see the Action on Smoking and Health Web site at <http://ash.org/>.)

Smoking near infants and children can also increase the child's susceptibility to sudden infant death syndrome (SIDS), asthma, respiratory infection, and mental retardation. Annually, smoking kills more people than alcohol, AIDS, car collisions, illegal drugs, murders, and suicides combined. In the United States, the yearly number of tobacco-related deaths is equivalent to three 747 jumbo jets crashing every day for an entire year, with no survivors. Not surprisingly, then, smoking is the leading cause of preventable disease and death in Canada and elsewhere.

Withdrawal Symptoms

Contrary to popular belief, the most deadly withdrawal symptoms are those associated with long-term alcohol abuse, and not—despite what some may believe—heroin addiction. Sudden withdrawal by chronic alcoholics can result in nausea, vomiting, intense seizures, and delirium tremens, a state of disorientation and confusion with a 2–10 per cent fatality rate.

Addiction to the other main legal drug, nicotine, is also extremely difficult to beat. Anyone who has tried—or has been around someone who has tried—to quit smoking knows that irritability, frustration, depression, insomnia, and lack of concentration are common experiences. Typically, ex-smokers require several months before they can report feeling comfortable with their new lives.

Attempting to withdraw from heroin addiction is also a harrowing experience. Symptoms can appear as early as a few hours after the last injection; they include drug craving, restlessness, muscle and bone pain, insomnia, diarrhea and vomiting, cold sweats and goose bumps (hence the term 'quitting cold turkey'), kicking motions (hence 'kicking the habit'), tremors, cramps, and panic attacks. Symptoms peak at around 48 hours and subside after approximately one week.

Withdrawal from other illicit drugs varies in severity. Any attempt to end addiction to barbiturates, or 'downers', results in roughly the same withdrawal symptoms as from alcohol, and is therefore notoriously difficult and dangerous to accomplish.

Dangers of Recreational Drug Use

Some of the dangers associated with recreational drug use are illustrated by the findings of research on ecstasy (MDMA). Even seemingly harmless recreational drugs like ecstasy can have health costs, such as decreased levels of serotonin, a substance found in the brain that controls mood, pain perception, sleep, appetite, and emotions (Kish et al., 2000). Low levels of this chemical can result in slow speech, lethargy, and sluggish movement.

Many of the risks people face with MDMA use are similar to those found with the use of cocaine and amphetamines—psychological difficulties, including confusion, depression, sleep problems, drug craving, severe anxiety, and paranoia—and sometimes these effects can occur weeks after taking MDMA. Physical symptoms such as muscle tension, involuntary teeth clenching, nausea, blurred vision, rapid eye movement, faintness, and chills or sweating also occur. Increases in heart rate and blood pressure pose a special risk for people with circulatory or heart disease.

Research links MDMA use to long-term damage to those parts of the brain critical to thought and memory. One study, in primates, showed that exposure to MDMA for four days caused brain damage that was evident six to seven years later.

MDA, the parent drug of MDMA, is an amphetamine-like drug that has also been abused and is similar in chemical structure to MDMA. Research shows that MDA destroys serotonin-producing neurons in the brain. MDMA is also related in its structure and effects to methamphetamine, which has been shown to cause degeneration of neurons containing the neurotransmitter dopamine. Damage to these neurons is the underlying cause of the motor disturbances seen in Parkinson's disease. Symptoms of this disease begin with lack of co-ordination and tremors and can eventually result in a form of paralysis.

Solutions for Alcohol and Drug Abuse

At the policy level, several approaches—some complementary, some conflicting—have been put into practice by governments attempting to address drug and alcohol use.

These policies vary from punitive to progressive, depending on whether the threat to public health and safety is perceived to lie in substance use per se or in its lack of monitoring and regulation.

The 'War on Drugs'

The first approach, which has been the status quo for much of the past and is also the most punitive way of handling the drug problem, is summarized by Charles McCaghy (1976: 300): 'Pass a law; if that does not work make the sentences harsher, get more policemen, get better detection devices, loosen up the law to make arrests easier and so on. Whatever you do, refuse to recognize that making some behaviors criminal does not prevent them.'

This perspective forms the basis of the so-called 'war on drugs', which follows the belief that drugs pose an immediate threat to the safety and well-being of society and that every effort should therefore be made to prevent them from entering people's lives. Among Western nations, the most prominent supporter of this approach is the United States. Oddly, since 1960, gambling has been legalized and arrests on gambling charges decreased, virtually without comment, while arrests on drug charges have increased (Chilton, 1997). Arguing primarily from a moral standpoint, advocates of this approach call for severe laws intended to punish the producers, pushers, and users of illicit drugs. However, these strict regulations have largely failed for several reasons.

The seemingly whimsical designation of legal and illegal status for various substances further undermines the legitimacy of drug laws, making it easier for people to ignore them whenever it suits them. In the United States, the main victims of the war on drugs have been black males. Many young people have trouble understanding why tobacco is legal and marijuana is not, for example. They are unlikely to take laws against marijuana use seriously if they disrespect the law (especially if young people do not expect strict enforcement). Further, as **labelling** theorists would point out, placing labels such as 'drug dealer', 'drug user', 'drug abuser', or 'criminal' on a person only serves to increase the chance that a person will internalize that identity and behave accordingly.

As well, the threat of judicial action for drug use does not get rid of the demand. Instead, it pushes the supply underground, where a well-paid black market, typically run by organized crime rings, quickly develops. Users looking for an illicit substance will go to where the source is, that is, to the criminal underworld. As Clayton Hartjen (1977) explains, the interaction of drug peddlers and addicts, away from the interfering eyes of law enforcement, only serves to create a deviant subculture. Moreover, placing the international drug trade in the hands of criminals ensures a lack of quality control, resulting in impure drugs that are often more dangerous than they would be in their pure form.

Legalizing Drugs

At its heart, the failure of the war on drugs rests in the strategy's stubborn refusal to admit the realities of drug demand in society. By framing substance abuse as an enforcement issue rather than a health issue, countries that pursue this punitive approach continue to rely on the blunt instruments of fines and imprisonment to discourage addictive behaviours. Other governments, including Canada's, have recognized the flaws of this strategy, and are now experimenting with progressive, practical policies that focus on minimizing harm rather than punishing offenders.

Just like alcohol prohibition in the 1920s, drug prohibition in North America has produced a large, lucrative criminal industry. Research shows that decriminalization of the possession of marijuana elsewhere since the early 1970s has resulted in decreased costs of enforcement and prosecution of marijuana-related offences (for a detailed account of this, see Haans, n.d.). So long as drug use is illegal, we can do little to monitor the quality of drugs available to users or the conditions under which people use these drugs.

Where alcohol, caffeine, and prescription medicines, are concerned, food and drug regulations ensure that we do not consume dangerous or poor-quality substances. (The same cannot be said of cigarettes, which contain known carcinogens as well as nicotine.) Similarly, health protection rules would apply to recreational drugs if they were legalized.

One reason for repealing Prohibition was the realization that when quality-controlled alcoholic beverages are not in stock, people will drink just about anything. In the 1920s and 1930s, people died or went blind from drinking beverages that contained dangerous impurities or the wrong kind of alcohol (that is, methanol instead of ethanol). Similarly, some drug users have died from drug overdoses because they had no way of knowing the strength of the drug. Legalization could prevent this by regulating strength and quality so the user would be always aware of how much is a safe amount to use.

When drugs are illegal, users also take fewer health precautions. Needle-sharing among intravenous drug users, for example, is a primary factor in the spread of HIV/AIDS in many developing nations (see Chapter 10). By driving the drug culture underground, the law works against safety, good hygiene, and disease prevention. Programs in other countries have reduced the sharing of contaminated equipment without increasing drug use.

Canada's Drug Strategy

Survey evidence shows that many Canadians still oppose illicit drug use and sales, and some oppose legalization. However, many are also indifferent to legalizing non-addictive recreational drugs: they just do not care. They oppose efforts to construct a 'war on drugs', which they consider unnecessary. Some strongly favour legalization, for the reasons noted above.

Canada's current federal drug strategy was first conceived in 1987 and was most recently renewed in 2003. In its present form, the strategy is built on four pillars:

- *prevention* to teach about the dangers of harmful substance use and to provide information on how to adopt healthy behaviours;
- *treatment* for those with an unhealthy dependency on substances;
- *harm reduction* to limit the secondary effects of substance use, such as the spread of infectious diseases like HIV/AIDS and hepatitis C;
- *enforcement* to prevent the unlawful import, export, production, distribution, and possession of illegal drugs (Health Canada, 2005a).

The first three pillars—prevention, treatment, and harm reduction—recognize that drug abuse is a public, medical, and social health issue, and that it should be averted and discouraged where possible and treated where necessary. The last pillar—enforcement— recognizes that the supply of illicit drugs must be controlled and limited if the other pillars are to achieve their targeted goals. The government of Canada in May 2003 announced an investment of $245 million over five years to support various programs implemented under this federal initiative.

The Canadian effort towards prevention, treatment, and reduction of harm related to the use and distribution of psychoactive substances has gone through important changes in recent years. It builds on public health lessons learned from a variety of infectious diseases and pushes for an integrated approach to both legal and illegal drugs (Erickson, 1999). Methadone maintenance programs are good examples of harm-reduction efforts; heroin addicts stabilized on methadone can reduce illicit drug use and criminality and improve their life conditions even though they have not achieved abstinence (Cheung and Ch'ien, 1999).

Together, prevention, treatment, and harm reduction, with minimal application of criminal law, may be the most effective public health policy on drugs (for an innovative—and controversial—example of a harm reduction program, see Box 3.4). The government can license the production and sales of soft drugs to regulate their quality, explore the potential of access mechanisms for drugs (free market versus government monopoly versus medical control), and tax the profits on legalized drug sales, then use the taxes for drug education. From a legal standpoint, one can reduce the penalties for using hard drugs, treat unlicensed drug-selling as a regulatory or tax offence that is punishable by huge fines, develop a full public health approach to addressing illegal drug problems, and educate the public against too much drug use and against the use of harmful drugs.

Recently, the federal government has heard renewed calls from influential groups, including the Canadian Medical Association and a Senate Special Committee on Illegal Drugs (2002), to amend the Controlled Substances and Drugs Act to decriminalize the

---

Box 3.4   Social Policy: Harm Reduction in Action

Among Canadian cities, Vancouver has been a leader in embracing the idea of harm reduction as a central component of its progressive and innovative drug strategy. To address the serious problem of open heroin use on the streets of its Downtown Eastside 'skid row' neighbourhood, the city established North America's first supervised injection site (or 'safe injection site', SIS) in September 2003. These health-care settings allow users to inject drugs under supervised and sanitary conditions, and receive medical care, addiction counselling, drug treatment, and access to other social services. As of mid-2003, the SIS model had already been implemented in 33 cities in Switzerland, Germany, the Netherlands, Spain, and Australia (Kimber et al., 2003). Officially titled Insite, the clinic was a partnership of the Vancouver Coastal Health Network, the City of Vancouver, the Vancouver Police Department, the provincial and federal health ministries, and the Downtown Eastside community. To operate legally, Insite required a Health Canada-ordered exemption to section 56 of the federal Controlled Drugs and Substances Act.

A one-year evaluation found that the site supervised almost 600 injections per day (BC Centre for Excellence in HIV/AIDS, 2004). Additional studies have found that use of the SIS is associated with reduced rates of needle-sharing (Kerr et al., 2004), injecting and disposing of syringes in public (Wood et al., 2004), and drug-related fatalities (Kimber et al., 2003). As well, surveys suggest that local communities are generally positive towards SISs as long as the open drug scene is no longer visible in public and the facilities are located in appropriate social settings (Zurhold, 2001, cited in Kimber et al., 2003).

possession of small amounts (approximately 15 grams) of marijuana. Decriminalization is not the same as full legalization. While it would still be illegal to possess the drug for personal use, this would be considered a non-criminal offence similar to a parking violation, and likewise punishable by a ticketed fine. In other words, marijuana's legal status would not change, only the manner of the law's enforcement. However, decriminalization is opposed by other groups, including many municipal police agencies, who worry about increased drug trafficking, and the US government, which is concerned that wider use in Canada will trickle south across the border.

Internationally, the approach of the Netherlands to substance use continues to be the model for a comprehensive and rational national drug policy. That approach also focuses on prevention and harm reduction, and prioritizes practicality over ideology. Three principles serve as the cornerstones for the Dutch approach:

- a separation of the markets for hard and soft drugs;
- treating drug users as ordinary citizens entitled to government assistance, but also required to assume responsibility for their actions; and
- harm-reduction efforts directed at minimizing the damage done by drugs to users, communities, and the society as a whole (Korf et al., 1999).

The Netherlands, and Amsterdam in particular, is famously known for its liberal policies towards marijuana use. In fact, the production, possession, and sale (but not use) of cannabis is, like all other hard and soft drugs, illegal. However, 'coffee shops' are exempted from prosecution for selling marijuana and other soft drugs (e.g., hashish, but not ecstasy or alcohol) as long as the quantity is five grams or less. Like any other café, customers, who must be 18 or over, order from a menu. The purpose of this arrangement is to move the distribution of soft drugs off the streets, where monitoring and regulation are impossible, into establishments that must comply with strict regulations. In keeping with the strategy to reduce supply, criminal enforcement places a priority on dismantling large-scale trafficking operations (including those that supply soft drugs to coffee shops) over the sale and possession for personal use.

Though this approach may have increased both lifetime and last-month prevalence of cannabis use by young people since 1984, only a minority of students report using cannabis on a regular basis (Kuipers and De Zwart, 1999). The two main threats to Dutch society posed by drug users are petty crime and drug trafficking (Partanen, 1997). Even crack cocaine use poses no threat to Dutch society, given the more rational Dutch drug policy: effective social policy is effective drug policy (Cohen, 1997). For that matter, crack cocaine use poses no major problem in Canada either (Cheung and Erickson, 1997).

In the Netherlands, as in North America, drugs—even powder and crack cocaine—are used differently according to socio-economic background. Middle-class 'party youth' make experimental use of the drugs in clubs and discotheques for recreational purposes. Deprived 'problem youth', from minority backgrounds, add the drugs to already troubled multi-problem behaviour in the context of their marginalized lifestyles (Nabben and Korf, 1999). This demonstrates that the problem to be solved is not drug use but deprivation.

Imagine the benefits if these policies were implemented in Canada and the United States as an alternative to the 'war on drugs'. Currently, 47 US states make it illegal for injection drug users to possess syringes, a prohibition some say can lead to syringe sharing. Research finds that injection drug users concerned about being arrested are significantly more likely to share syringes and injection supplies. Thus, decriminalizing syringes and needles would likely result in reduction of behaviours that expose injection drug users to blood-borne viruses such as HIV (Blumenthal et al., 1999). A needle exchange would do more than reduce risks of infection; participants would also experience significant emotional benefits from the contact with needle-exchange workers (Larkins, 1999).

In Canada, despite a long history of empirical research pointing away from aggressive criminalization, the most recent law (the Controlled Drugs and Substances Act of May 1997) affirms both the seriously deviant status of illicit drug users and the primacy of the criminal justice model over the public health and social justice alternatives (Erickson, 1998).

Individual Responses

In terms of individual-level strategies, people should arm themselves and those around them with the facts on the health and social consequences of substance abuse, from both illegal and legal drug use (particularly tobacco and alcohol). The evidence, such as we have discussed here, gives more than sufficient reason for people to try to do whatever they can to guard against addiction, and, if addicted, to seek treatment. As we have seen, peers and family have a much greater effect on drinking behaviour than do schools, with the result that growing exposure to school prevention programs over the 1980s and 1990s had little influence on adolescent alcohol and other substance use (Welte et al., 1999). Networks of informal support for sobriety will play a large part in preventing and remedying individual addiction problems.

At the same time, people find it easier to avoid, control, and give up drug use if they have peers and friends with whom they do not use drugs. As we saw earlier, initiation into drug use depends on contacts with friends and family who use drugs. Cessation of drug use is also associated with having fewer friends and acquaintances who use drugs (Latkin et al., 1999). So controlling drug use means making a judicious selection of friends. Membership in support groups, self-help programs, or grassroots movements is also likely to help (Gundelach, 1994).

Concluding Remarks

Substances that are considered 'drugs' are not always defined as such by any absolute criteria. Instead, their definition depends partly on politics and culture. In this sense, drugs are social constructions. Laws that specify which drugs are legal and which are not are also socially constructed and influenced largely by politics. Laws are not consistently based on a drug's potential for harm. Many legal drugs, including nicotine and alcohol, may be more harmful to health than illegal drugs such as marijuana or even heroin.

The criminalization of drugs may cause more harm than good. Criminalization creates a black market, encourages organized crime, prevents quality control, and puts heroin drug users at higher risk of HIV/AIDS. People with a high socio-economic status are most likely to be heavy drinkers, yet they are safe from the law. How we view a drug, use it, and regulate it can have a large effect on how the person experiences and uses the drug. These perceptions tend to be influenced by one's peers and social milieu.

Substance abuse has many negative consequences for users and for individuals around them. These consequences involve other social problems and, often, severe health problems for users and their associates. For these reasons, substance abuse must be viewed, and pursued, as a social problem.

QUESTIONS FOR CRITICAL THOUGHT

1. The text outlines how attitudes to drugs changed historically in England and the United States. Search through microfilms of old newspapers and try to find evidence showing policy and/or attitude change regarding drug and alcohol use in Canada. Describe the patterns.
2. Do you agree that attitudes towards drugs and alcohol have been shaped as much by ignorance and stereotypes as by facts and first-hand experience? Is there a way to escape the social stigmatization of substance abusers and their lifestyles while addressing the social problems?
3. Merton argues that drug and alcohol abuse represents the individual retreating to 'alternate means'. Other scholars emphasize different macro-socio-cultural explanations.

Based on your readings, what is (or are) the best explanation(s) of drug abuse? Why?
4. A major controversy surrounds the topic of whether the legalization of drugs may be beneficial or harmful to society. Go onto the Internet to the Marijuana Party of Canada's website (www.marijuanaparty.org) and look over their platform. What, in their view, are the major advantages of legalization? Differentiate between responsible and irresponsible drug use. What, if anything, is wrong with their platform?
5. There has been a significant rise in use of party drugs such as ecstasy among teens and young adults. Research the rave culture and analyze the role the drug plays in their activities.

RECOMMENDED READINGS

James B. Bakalar and Lester Grinspoon, *Drug Control in a Free Society* (New York: Cambridge University Press, 1984). This book describes some of the legal and ethical issues around drugs in North America and the United Kingdom. Using a historical analysis of drug policies, the authors explain how factors such as a segregated youth culture have contributed to drug problems in society.

Jon Elster, *Strong Feelings: Emotion, Addiction, and Human Behavior* (Cambridge, Mass.: MIT Press, 1999). This text examines the relationship between emotion and addiction with a focus on the possibility of choice within compulsive behaviour. Chapter 3 includes a phenomenological analysis.

Patricia G. Erickson, 'Neglected and Rejected: A Case Study of the Impact of Social Research on Canadian Drug Policy', *Canadian Journal of Sociology* 23 (1998): 263–80. How does Canada create new drug laws? This article looks at the long-awaited creation of the Controlled Drugs and Substances Act, enacted in May 1997. Erickson asks how the Act responded to empirical and theoretical research on drugs and drug use and argues that the Act opted for a criminal justice model rather than a public health lens through which to view drug users.

M. Haden, 'Illicit IV Drugs: A Public Health Approach', *Canadian Journal of Public Health* 93 (2002): 431–4. Within the polarized views of legalization versus criminalization of intravenous drugs, one question is forgotten: how do Canadian drug laws harm individuals and society? This article takes a public health perspective towards the dichotomy, arguing for a middle ground in policy.

James A. Inciardi, *Handbook of Drug Control in the United States* (New York: Greenwood Press, 1990). This book looks at the intended and unintended consequences of drug laws, the history of drugs and drug policy, some constitutional issues in drug testing, links between drugs and crime, and the legalization of drugs. The text attacks current drug policy as ineffective, expensive, and intrusive but also presents arguments against legalization.

Jimmie Lynn Reeves and Richard Campbell, *Cracked Coverage: Television News, the Anti-Cocaine Crusade, and the Reagan Legacy* (Durham, NC: Duke University Press, 1994). Reeves and Campbell examine the role of major American TV news programs in promoting the war against drugs by analyzing 270 news stories aired between 1981 and 1988. Their analysis reveals that drugs were not a genuine grassroots concern of the public initially but that concern developed after a relentless sensationalist torrent of media news coverage.

Thomas Szasz, *Our Right to Drugs: The Case for a Free Market* (New York: Praeger, 1992). This book offers an alternative to the traditional arguments on drug policy. Szasz takes a rights-based approach that drug policies must maximize the responsibility of the individual rather than criminalize individual choice.

Franklin E. Zimring and Gordon Hawkins, *The Search for Rational Drug Control* (Cambridge: Cambridge University

Press, 1992). Zimring and Hawkins outline three ideal-type perspectives on the war on drugs. They propose that the government's strategy regarding drugs serves only to hide a political agenda.

RECOMMENDED WEBSITES

Centre for Addiction and Mental Health
www.camh.net

The Centre for Addiction and Mental Health (CAMH) provides information aimed at educating both the general public and those with health problems about addiction and mental health. A number of links to community events, volunteer opportunities, and current and future research are provided.

Canadian Centre on Substance Abuse
www.ccsa.ca

The Canadian Centre on Substance Abuse is a non-profit organization working to minimize the harm of tobacco, alco-

hol, and other drugs. Its website includes a resource database, statistics on substance abuse, and a network listing. Of considerable importance is the Topics/Issues link, which contains information on topics such as cannabis, gambling, seniors, the law, and policy and research.

MADD Canada
www.madd.ca

Mothers Against Drunk Driving provides facts about drunk driving. The site has up-to-date news about drunk driving as well as a listing of programs that the organization administers solely or in conjunction with other organizations.

GLOSSARY

Drug Any substance that causes a biochemical reaction in the body.

Drug abuse This concept begins with the notion of excessive or inappropriate drug use resulting in social, psychological, and/or physiological impairments. It stems from a chronic physical and psychological compulsion to continue taking a drug in order to avoid unpleasant withdrawal symptoms.

Drug dependency The routine need for a drug for physiological and/or psychological reasons.

Gateway drug Proponents of this concept suggest that, for example, marijuana is a substance that paves the way for the use of other illicit drugs, such as cocaine or heroin.

Others point out that someone who is willing to try one type of drug may be more likely to try any drug, with no particular 'gateway' process involved.

Labelling The process of defining and treating others as deviant. Labelling theory explores the effects of negative labels on individuals' self-conceptions and is interested in the development of a 'deviant identity'. Social reactions of condemnation and criminalization can lead actors to alter their individual characteristics and to adopt the values of their labelled identity.

Polydrug use Using drugs in combination, with the most popular combination being alcohol, nicotine, and marijuana. This concept is a cousin to the concept of gateway drugs.

REFERENCES

Adlaf, Edward M., Patricia Begin, and Ed Sawka, eds. 2005. *Canadian Addiction Survey (CAS): A National Survey of Canadians' Use of Alcohol and Other Drugs: Prevalence of Use and Related Harms: Detailed Report*. Ottawa: Canadian Centre on Substance Abuse.

———, Andrée Demers, and Louis Gliksman, eds. 2005. *Canadian Campus Survey 2004*. Toronto: Centre for Addiction and Mental Health.

Alcoholics Anonymous. 1976 [1939]. *Alcoholics Anonymous: The Story of How Many Thousands of Men and Women Have*

Recovered from Alcoholism, 3rd edn. New York: Alcoholics Anonymous World Services.

Alden, Helena, and Scott R. Maggard. 2000. 'Perceptions of Social Class and Drug Use', paper presented at the annual conference of the Southern Sociological Society.

Anderson, Kay J. 1991. *Vancouver's Chinatown: Racial Discourse in Canada, 1875–1980*. Montreal and Kingston: McGill-Queen's University Press.

Appleton, Lynn M. 1995. 'Rethinking Medicalization: Alcoholism and Anomalies', in Joel Best, ed., *Images of Issues:*

Typifying Contemporary Social Problems, 2nd edn. Hawthorne, NY: Aldine de Gruyter, 59–80.

Auerhahn, Kathleen, and Robert Nash Parker. 1999. 'Drugs, Alcohol and Homicide', in M. Dwayne Smith and Margaret A. Zahn, eds, *Studying and Preventing Homicide: Issues and Challenges*. Thousand Oaks, Calif.: Sage, 99–114.

Bailey, Susan L. 1999. 'The Measurement of Problem Drinking in Young Adulthood', *Journal of Studies on Alcohol* 60: 234–44.

Baron, Stephen W. 1999. 'Street Youths and Substance Use: The Role of Background, Street Lifestyle, and Economic Factors', *Youth and Society* 31, 1: 3–26.

Bastos, Francisco Imacio, Steffanie A. Strathdee, Monica Derrico, and Maria de Fatima Pina. 1999. 'Drug Use and the Spread of HIV/AIDS in South America and the Caribbean', *Drugs, Education, Prevention and Policy* 6, 1: 29–49.

BC Centre for Excellence in HIV/AIDS. 2004. *Evaluation of the Supervised Injection Site: Year One Summary*. Vancouver: BC Centre for Excellence in HIV/AIDS.

Beautrais, Annette L., Peter R. Joyce, and Roger T. Mulder. 1999. 'Cannabis Abuse and Serious Suicide Attempts', *Addiction* 94: 1155–64.

Bennett, Joel B., and Wayne E.K. Lehman. 1998. 'Workplace Drinking Climate, Stress, and Problem Indicators: Assessing the Influence of Teamwork (Group Cohesion)', *Journal of Studies on Alcohol* 59: 608–18.

Bennett, Melanie E., Barbara S. McCrady, Valerie Johnson, and Robert J. Pandina. 1999. 'Problem Drinking from Young Adulthood to Adulthood: Patterns, Predictors and Outcomes', *Journal of Studies on Alcohol* 60: 605–14.

Bennett, Melanie E., Joseph H. Miller, and W. Gill Woodall. 1999. 'Drinking, Binge Drinking, and Other Drug Use among Southwestern Undergraduates: Three-Year Trends', *American Journal of Drug and Alcohol Abuse* 25: 331–50.

Bensley, Lillian Southwick, Susan J. Spieker, Juliet van Eenwyk, and Judy Schoder. 1999. 'Self-reported Abuse History and Adolescent Problem Behaviors, II: Alcohol and Drug Use', *Journal of Adolescent Health* 24, 3: 173–80.

Blumenthal, Ricky N., Alex H. Kral, Elizabeth A. Erringer, and Brian R. Edlin. 1999. 'Drug Paraphernalia Laws and Injection-Related Infectious Disease Risk among Drug Injectors', *Journal of Drug Issues* 29, 1: 1–16.

Bobak, Martin, Martin McKee, Richard Rose, and Michael Marmot. 1999. 'Alcohol Consumption in a National Sample of the Russian Population', *Addiction* 94: 857–66.

Broszeit, Brian, and Jastej Dhaliwal. 2001. *Substance Abuse among Manitoba High School Students*. Winnipeg: Addictions Foundation of Manitoba. Available at: <www.afm.mb.ca/pdfs/HSSU.pdf>; accessed 15 Mar. 2003.

Brownstein, Henry H., Sean D. Cleary, Susan M. Crimmins, Judith Ryder, Raquel Warley, and Barry Spunt. 1999. 'The Relationship between Violent Offending and Drug Use in the Pre-prison Experience of a Sample of Incarcerated Young Men', paper presented at the annual meeting of the American Sociological Association.

Canadian Cancer Society/National Cancer Institute of Canada. 2006. *Canadian Cancer Statistics 2006*. Available at: <www.cancer.ca>; accessed 16 July 2006.

Canadian Centre on Substance Abuse and Centre for Addiction and Mental Health. 1999. *Canadian Profile 1999: Alcohol, Tobacco and Other Drugs*. Ottawa: Canadian Centre on Substance Abuse and Centre for Addiction and Mental Health.

Carruthers, Cynthia P. 1992. 'The Relationship of Alcohol Consumption Practices to Leisure Patterns and Leisure-Related Alcohol Expectancies', *Dissertation Abstracts International* 52, 7–A: 2700–1.

Centre for Addiction and Mental Health. 2003. 'Do You Know . . . Cocaine'. Available at: <www.camh.net/About_Addiction_Mental_Health/Drug_and_Addiction_Information/cocaine_dyk.html>; accessed 18 Mar. 2006.

———. 2006. *Drug Use among Ontario Students: Detailed OSDUS Findings*. Available at: <www.camh.net>; accessed 16 July 2006.

Cernetig, M. 1997. 'The HIV Epidemic in Vancouver's Lower East Side', *Globe and Mail*, 8 Oct.

Cheung, Yuet W., and James M.N. Ch'ien. 1999. 'Previous Participation in Outpatient Methadone Program and Residential Treatment Outcome: A Research Note from Hong Kong', *Substance Use and Abuse* 34: 103–18.

——— and Patricia G. Erickson. 1997. 'Crack Use in Canada: A Distant American Cousin', in Reinarman and Levine (1997: 175–93).

Chilton, Roland. 1997. 'Victimless Crime in the Twentieth Century: Drug Prohibition as the Folly of Our Time', paper presented at the annual meeting of the Society for the Study of Social Problems.

Cohen, Peter D.A. 1997. 'Crack in the Netherlands: Effective Social Policy is Effective Drug Policy', in Reinarman and Levine (1997: 214–24).

Colson, Tara A. 2000. 'Study of Marijuana Use among Young Adults', paper presented at the annual meeting of the Southern Sociological Society.

Costa, Frances M., Richard Jessor, and Mark Turbin. 1999. 'Transition into Adolescent Problem Drinking: The Role of Psychosocial Risk and Protective Factors', *Journal of Studies on Alcohol* 60: 480–90.

Cotton Oldenburg, Niki U., Kathleen B. Jordan, Sandra L. Martin, and Lawrence Kupper. 1999. 'Women Inmates' Risky Sex and Drug Behaviors: Are They Related?', *American Journal of Drug and Alcohol Abuse* 25: 129–49.

Criminal Intelligence Service Canada. 2005. *2005 Annual Report: Organized Crime in Canada.* Available at: <www.cisc.gc.ca/webpage/index_b_e.htm>; accessed 11 Feb. 2006.

Curran, Geoffrey M., Scott F. Stoltenberg, Elizabeth M. Hill, Sharon A. Mudd, Frederic C. Blow, and Robert A. Zucker. 1999. 'Gender Differences in the Relationships among SES, Family History of Alcohol Disorders and Alcohol Dependence', *Journal of Studies on Alcohol* 60: 825–32.

Dawkins, Marvin P. 1997. 'Drug Use and Violent Crime among Adolescents', *Adolescence* 32: 395–405.

Delva, Jorge, Michelle L. Van Etten, Gonzalo B. Gonzalez, Miguel A. Cedeno, Marcel Penna, Luis H. Caris, and James C. Anthony. 1999. 'First Opportunities to Try Drugs and the Transition to First Drug Use: Evidence from a National School Survey in Panama', *Substance Use and Misuse* 34: 1451–67.

Demers, Andree, Jocelyne Bisson, and Jezabelle Palluy. 1999. 'Wives' Convergence with Their Husbands' Alcohol Use: Social Conditions as Mediators', *Journal of Studies on Alcohol* 60: 368–77.

Dishion, Thomas J., Deborah M. Capaldi, and Karen Yoerger. 1999. 'Middle Childhood Antecedents to Progressions in Male Adolescent Substance Abuse: An Ecological Analysis of Risk and Protection', *Journal of Adolescent Research* 14: 175–205.

Duffy, Jonathan. 2006. 'When Heroin Was Legal', *BBC News Magazine*, 25 Jan. Available at: <news.bbc.co.uk/1/hi/magazine/4647018.stm>; accessed 18 Mar. 2006.

Durkheim, Émile. 1951 [1897]. *Suicide: A Study in Sociology*, trans. John A. Spaulding and George Simpson. New York: Free Press.

Duster, Troy. 1997. 'Pattern, Purpose, and Race in the Drug War: The Crisis of Credibility in Criminal Justice', in Reinarman and Levine (1997: 260–87).

Ellickson, Phyllis L., Rebecca L. Collins, and Robert M. Bell. 1999. 'Adolescent Use of Illicit Drugs Other Than Marijuana: How Important Is Social Bonding and for Which Ethnic Groups?', *Substance Use and Misuse* 34: 317–46.

Erickson, Patricia G. 1998. 'Neglected and Rejected: A Case Study of the Impact of Social Research on Canadian Drug Policy', *Canadian Journal of Sociology* 23: 263–80.

———. 1999. 'Introduction: The Three Phases of Harm Reduction: An Examination of Emerging Concepts, Methodologies, and Critiques', *Substance Use and Misuse* 32: 1–7.

Feldman, Linda, Bart Harvey, Philippa Holowaty, and Linda Shortt. 1999. 'Alcohol Use Beliefs and Behaviors among High School Students', *Journal of Adolescent Health* 24: 48–58.

Fenoglio, Philippe, Véronique Parel, and Pierre Kopp. 2003. 'The Social Cost of Alcohol, Tobacco and Illicit Drugs in France, 1997', *European Addiction Research* 9: 18–28.

Fillmore, Kaye Middleton, Jacqueline M. Golding, Karen L. Graves, Steven Kniep, E. Victor Leino, Anders Romelsjo, Carlisle Shoemaker, Catherine R. Ager, Peter Allebeck, and Heidi P. Ferrer. 1998. 'Alcohol Consumption and Mortality. I. Characteristics of Drinking Groups', *Addiction* 93: 183–203.

Furst, R. Terry, Bruce D. Johnson, Eloise Dunlap, and Richard Curtis. 1999. 'The Stigmatized Image of the "Crack Head": A Sociocultural Exploration of a Barrier to Cocaine Smoking among a Cohort of Youth in New York City', *Deviant Behavior* 20: 153–81.

Giffen, P.J., Shirley Endicott, and Sylvia Lambert. 1991. *Panic and Indifference: The Politics of Canada's Drug Laws.* Ottawa: Canadian Centre on Substance Abuse.

Grant, Bridget F., and Deborah S. Hasin. 1999. 'Suicidal Ideation among the United States Drinking Population: Results from the National Longitudinal Alcohol Epidemiological Survey', *Journal of Studies on Alcohol* 60: 422–9.

Green, Anna, Sophie Day, and Helen Ward. 2000. 'Crack Cocaine and Prostitution in London in the 1990s', *Sociology of Health and Illness* 22: 27–39.

Green, Melvyn. 1986. 'The History of Canadian Narcotics Control: The Formative Years', in Neil Boyd, ed., *The Social Dimensions of Law.* Scarborough, Ont.: Prentice-Hall, 24–40.

Greenfield, Lawrence A. 1998. *Alcohol and Crime: An Analysis of National Data on the Prevalence of Alcohol Involvement in Crime.* Washington: US Department of Justice.

Griesbach, Dawn, Amanda Amos, and Candace Currie. 2003. 'Adolescent Smoking and Family Structure in Europe', *Social Science and Medicine* 56: 41–52.

Gundelach, Peter. 1994. 'Communities, Grass-roots Movements, and Substance Abuse Problems: New Strategies', *Nordisk Alkohol and Narkotikatidskrift* 11: 5–12.

Gusfield, Joseph. 1963. *Symbolic Crusade: Status Politics and the American Temperance Movement.* Urbana: University of Illinois Press.

Haans, Dave. n.d. 'The Effects of Decriminalization of Marijuana'. Available at: <www.chass.utoronto.ca/~haans/misc/mjdcrim.html>; accessed 17 Mar. 2003.

Hansell, Stephen, Helene Raskin White, and Firoozeh Molaparast Vali. 1999. 'Specific Alcoholic Beverages and Physical and Mental Health among Adolescents', *Journal of Studies on Alcohol* 60: 209–18.

Hartjen, Clayton A. 1977. *Possible Trouble: An Analysis of Social Problems.* New York: Praeger.

Health Canada. 1999. *Statistical Report on the Health of Canadians.* Available at: <www.statcan.ca/english/freepub/82-570-XIE/free.htm>; accessed 20 Feb. 2003.

———. 2005a. 'Canada's Drug Strategy'. Available at: <www.hc-sc.gc.ca/ahc-asc/activit/strateg/drugs-drogues/index_e.html>; accessed 12 Feb. 2006.

———. 2005b. 'Drug and Health Products: Medical Use of Marijuana—Stakeholder Statistics'. Available at: <www.hc-sc.gc.ca/dhp-mps/marihuana/stat/index_e.html>; accessed 12 Feb. 2006.

Hodgson, Maggie. 1987. *Indian Communities Develop Futuristic Addictions Treatment and Health Approach*. Edmonton: Nechi Institute on Alcohol and Drug Education.

Hutchison, Ira W. 1999. 'Alcohol, Fear, and Woman Abuse', *Sex Roles* 40: 893–920.

Inciardi, James A., Hilary L. Suratt, Hector M. Colon, Dale D. Chitwood, and James E. Rivers. 1999. 'Drug Use and HIV Risks among Migrant Workers on the DelMarVa Peninsula', *Substance Use and Misuse* 34: 653–66.

Irwin, Darrell D. 1999. 'The Straight Edge Subculture: Examining the Youths' Drug-free Way', *Journal of Drug Issues* 29: 365–80.

Ivis, Frank J., and Edward M. Adlaf. 1999. 'A Comparison of Trends in Drug Use among Students in the USA and Ontario, Canada: 1975–1997', *Drugs, Education, Prevention, and Policy* 6: 17–27.

Jackson, Christine, Lisa Henriksen, and Denise Dickinson. 1999. 'Alcohol-Specific Socialization, Parenting Behaviors, and Alcohol Use by Children', *Journal of Studies on Alcohol* 60: 362–7.

Jennison, Karen M., and Kenneth A. Johnson. 1998. 'Alcohol Dependence in Adult Children of Alcoholics: Longitudinal Evidence of Early Risk', *Journal of Drug Education* 28: 19–37.

Johnson, Valerie. 1999. 'Alcohol Problems, Deviance and Negative Affect among Children from Alcoholic, Depressed and Comorbid Families', paper presented at the annual meeting of the Society for the Study of Social Problems.

Johnstone, Gerry. 1996. 'From Vice to Disease? The Concepts of Dipsomania and Inebriety, 1860–1908', *Social and Legal Studies* 5, 1: 37–56.

Kane, Robert J., and George S. Yacoubian Jr. 1999. 'Pattern of Drug Escalation among Philadelphia Arrestees: An Assessment of the Gateway Theory', *Journal of Drug Issues* 29: 107–20.

Karp, Igor, Jennifer O'loughlin, Gilles Paradis, James Hanley, and Joseph Difranza. 2005. 'Smoking Trajectories of Adolescent Novice Smokers in a Longitudinal Study of Tobacco Use', *Annals of Epidemiology* 15, 6: 445–52.

Kerr, Thomas, Mark Tyndall, Kathy Li, Julio Montaner, and Evan Wood. 2004. 'Safer Injection Facility Use and Syringe Sharing in Injection Drug Users', *Lancet* 366: 316–18.

Kimber, J., K. Dolan, I. van Beek, D. Hedrich, and H. Zurhold. 2003. 'Drug Consumption Facilities: An Update Since 2000', *Drug and Alcohol Review* 22: 227–33.

Kish, S.J., Y. Furukawa, L. Ang, S.P. Vorce, and K.S. Kalasinsky. 2000. 'Striatal Serotonin Is Depleted in Brain of a Human MDMA (Ecstasy) User', *Neurology* 55: 294–6.

Korf, Dirk J., Helene Riper, and Bruce Bullington. 1999. 'Windmills in Their Minds? Policy and Drug Research in the Netherlands', *Journal of Drug Issues* 29: 451–71.

Kuipers, S.B.M., and W.M. De Zwart. 1999. 'Trends and Patterns in Illicit Drug Use among Students aged 12 to 18 in the Netherlands', *Journal of Drug Issues* 29: 549–63.

Kunz, Jean Lock, and Norman Giesbrecht. 1999. 'Gender, Perceptions of Harm, and Other Social Predictors of Alcohol Use in a Punjabi Community in the Toronto Area', *Substance Use and Misuse* 34: 403–19.

Lafranire, Gerald, and Leah Spicer. 2002. *Illicit Drug Trends in Canada 1998–2001: A Review and Analysis of Enforcement*. Prepared for the Special Senate Committee on Illegal Drugs. Ottawa: Law and Government Division, Parliamentary Research Branch of the Library of Parliament.

Laniel, Laurent. 1999. 'Drugs and Globalization: An Equivocal Relationship', *International Social Science Journal* 51: 239–40.

Larkins, Sherry. 1999. 'The Emotional Health Benefits of Needle-Exchange Contact', paper presented at the annual meeting of the American Sociological Association.

Latkin, Carl A., Amy R. Knowlton, Donald Hoover, and Wallace Mandell. 1999. 'Drug Network Characteristics as a Predictor of Cessation of Drug Use among Adult Injection Drug Users: A Prospective Study', *American Journal of Drug and Alcohol Abuse* 25: 463–73.

Leatherdale, S.T., P.W. McDonald, R. Cameron, and K.S. Brown. 2005. 'A Multilevel Analysis Examining the Relationship between Social Influences for Smoking and Smoking Onset', *American Journal of Health Behavior* 29, 6: 520–30.

Leonard, Kenneth E., and Brian M. Quigley. 1999. 'Drinking and Marital Aggression in Newlyweds: An Event-based Analysis of Drinking and the Occurrence of Husband Marital Aggression', *Journal of Studies on Alcohol* 60: 537–45.

——— and Julie C. Rothbard. 1999. 'Alcohol and the Marriage Effect', *Journal of Studies on Alcohol* 60, suppl. 13: 139–46.

Liu, Xiaoru, and Howard Kaplan. 1999. 'Role Strain and Illicit Drug Use: The Moderating Influence of Commitment to Conventional Values', paper presented at the annual meeting of the American Sociological Association.

McCaghy, Charles H., ed. 1976. *Deviant Behavior: Crime, Conflict, and Interest Groups*. Boston: Allyn & Bacon.

McCoy, Clyde B., Lisa R. Metsch, Dale D. Chitwood, James E. Rivers, H. Virginia McCoy, and Sarah Messiah. 2000. 'Health Services for Chronic Drug Users in an Era of Managed Care: The University of Miami Community-based Health Services Research Centre', *Advances in Medical Sociology* 7: 151–74.

McCoy, H. Virginia, Sarah E. Messiah, Zhinuan Yu, Kerry Anne

McGeary, and Janvier Gasana. 2000. 'Drug Users as Perpetrators, Victims and Observers of Violence: Implications for Intervention', paper presented at the annual meeting of the Southern Sociological Society.

Macdonald, Scott, Samantha Wells, and T. Cameron Wild. 1999. 'Occupation Risk Factors Associated with Alcohol and Drug Problems', *American Journal of Drug and Alcohol Abuse* 25: 351–69.

Maes, Hermine H., Charlene E. Woodard, Lenn Murrelle, Joanne M. Meyer, Judy L. Silberg, John K. Hewitt, Michael Rutter, Emily Simonoff, Andrew Pickles, Rene Carbonneau, Michael C. Neale, and Lindon J. Eaves. 1999. 'Tobacco, Alcohol, and Drug Use in Eight- to Sixteen-Year-Old Twins: The Virginia Twin Study of Adolescent Behavioral Development', *Journal of Studies on Alcohol* 60: 293–305.

Makela, Pia. 1999. 'Alcohol-Related Mortality as a Function of Socio-economic Status', *Addiction* 94: 867–86.

Marquart, James W., Victoria E. Brewer, Janet Mullings, and Ben M. Crouch. 1999. 'The Implications of Crime Control Policy on HIV/AIDS-Related Risk among Women Prisoners', *Crime and Delinquency* 45: 82–98.

Mason, W. Alex, and Michael Windle. 2000. 'A Longitudinal Study of the Effects of Religiosity on Adolescent Alcohol Use and Alcohol-Related Problems', paper presented at the annual meeting of the Southern Sociological Society.

Meddis, Sam V. 1993. 'Is the Drug War Racist? Disparities Suggest the Answer Is Yes', *USA Today*, 23 July, 2A.

Mekolichick, Jeanne T. 1996. 'Anabolic-Androgenic Steroids: The Construction of a Social Problem', paper presented at the annual meeting of the Society for the Study of Social Problems.

Merton, Robert K. 1957. 'Social Structure and Anomie', in Merton, *Social Theory and Social Structure*, rev. edn. New York: Free Press, ch. 3.

Moon, Dreama G., Michael L. Hecht, Kristina M. Jackson, and Regina E. Spellers. 1999. 'Ethnic and Gender Differences and Similarities in Adolescent Drug Use and Refusals of Drug Offers', *Substance Use and Misuse* 34: 1059–183.

Morgan, John P., and Lynn Zimmer. 1997. 'The Social Pharmacology of Smokeable Cocaine: Not All It's Cracked Up to Be', in Reinarman and Levine (1997: 131–70).

Moscovitch, Arlene. 1998. 'Contemporary Family Trends: Electronic Media and the Family'. Available at: <www.vifamily.ca/cft/media/media.htm>; accessed 13 Jan. 2003.

Mutzell, Sture. 1994. 'Mortality, Suicide, Social Maladjustment and Criminality among Male Alcoholic Parents and Men from the General Population and Their Offspring', *International Journal of Adolescence and Youth* 4: 305–28.

——. 1996. 'The Use of Narcotic Drugs in Stockholm County, Sweden: A Follow-up after 17 Years', *International Journal of Adolescence and Youth* 6: 245–59.

Nabben, Tom, and Dirk J. Korf. 1999. 'Cocaine and Crack in Amsterdam: Diverging Subcultures', *Journal of Drug Issues* 29: 627–51.

Nagasawa, Richard, Zhenchao Qian, and Paul Wong. 1999. 'Theory of Segmented Assimilation and Patterns of Drug and Alcohol Use among Asian Pacific Youths', paper presented at the annual meeting of the American Sociological Association.

National Institute on Drug Abuse (NIDA). 2001. 'MMDA (Ecstasy)'. Available at: <www.nida.nih.gov/Infofax/ecstasy.html>; accessed 14 Feb. 2003.

Nurco, David N., and Monroe Lerner. 1999. 'A Complementary Perspective to Primary Socialization Theory', *Substance Use and Misuse* 34: 993–1003.

O'Farrell, Timothy J., Valerie Van Hutten, and Christopher M. Murphy. 1999. 'Domestic Violence before and after Alcoholism Treatment: A Two-Year Longitudinal Study', *Journal of Studies on Alcohol* 60: 317–21.

Oldham, Greg R., and Benjamin I. Gordon. 1999. 'Job Complexity and Employee Substance Use: The Moderating Effects of Cognitive Ability', *Journal of Health and Social Behavior* 40: 290–306.

Parsons, Talcott. 1951. 'Social Structure and Dynamic Process: The Case of Modern Medical Practice', in Parsons, *The Social System*. New York: Free Press, ch. 10.

Partanen, Juha. 1997. 'The Merchant, the Priest, and the Humble Engineer: Observations on the Drug Scene in Rotterdam', *Nordisk Alkohol och Narkotikatidskrift* 14, 3: 167–83.

Patton, Travis, and Anne Baird. 2000. 'Alcohol and Interpersonal Violence: Methodological Considerations', paper presented at the annual meeting of the Southern Sociological Society.

Perkins, H. Wesley. 1999. 'Stress-Motivated Drinking in Collegiate and Postcollegiate Young Adulthood: Life Course and Gender Patterns', *Journal of Studies on Alcohol* 60: 219–27.

Power, Chris, Bryan Rodgers, and Steven Hope. 1994. 'Heavy Alcohol Consumption and Marital Status: Disentangling the Relationship in a National Study of Young Adults', *Addiction* 94: 1477–87.

Prime Minister's Strategy Unit. 2003. *Strategy Unit Alcohol Harm Reduction Project: Interim Analytical Report*. Available at: <www.strategy.gov.uk/work_areas/alcohol_misuse/interim.asp>; accessed 18 Mar. 2006.

Randall, Carrie L., James S. Roberts, Frances K. Del Boca, Kathleen M. Carroll, Gerard J. Connors, and Margaret E. Mattson. 1999. 'Telescoping of Landmark Events Associated with Drinking: A Gender Comparison', *Journal of Studies on Alcohol* 60: 252–60.

Rehm, J., D. Baliunas, S. Brochu, B. Fischer, W. Gnam, J. Patra, S. Popova, A. Sarnocinska-Hart, and B. Taylor. 2006. *The Cost of Substance Abuse in Canada 2002: Highlights*. Ottawa: Canadian Centre on Substance Abuse.

Rehm, Jurgen, and Gerhard Gmel. 1999. 'Patterns of Alcohol Consumption and Social Consequences: Results from an 8-Year Follow-up Study in Switzerland', *Addiction* 94: 899–912.

Reinarman, Craig, and Harry G. Levine, eds. 1997. *Crack in America: Demon Drugs and Social Justice*. Berkeley: University of California Press.

———, Dan Waldorf, Sheila B. Murphy, and Harry G. Levine. 1997. 'The Contingent Call of the Pipe: Bingeing and Addiction among Heavy Cocaine Smokers', in Reinarman and Levine (1997: 77–97).

Royal College of Physicians. 1987. *Great and Growing Evil: The Medical Consequences of Alcohol Abuse* [working party report]. Cited by the Institute of Alcohol Studies, *The Nature of Alcohol Problems*, 2000, available at: <www.ias.org.uk/factsheets/medsoc3.htm>; accessed 12 Jan. 2003.

Santolaria, Francisco, Jose Luis Perez Manzano, Antonio Milena, Emilio Gonzalez Reimers, Maria Angeles Gomez Rodriguez, Antonio Martinez Riera, Maria Remedios Aleman Valls, and Maria Joe de la Vega Prieto. 2000. 'Nutritional Assessment in Alcoholic Patients: Its Relationship with Alcoholic Intake, Feeding Habits, Organic Complications and Social Problems', *Drug and Alcohol Dependence* 59: 295–304.

Scott, Kathryn D., John Schafer, and Thomas K. Greenfield. 1999. 'The Role of Alcohol in Physical Assault Perpetration and Victimization', *Journal of Studies on Alcohol* 60: 528–36.

Senate Special Committee on Illegal Drugs. 2002. *Cannabis: Our Position for a Canadian Policy*. 37th Parliament, 1st session.

Single, Eric, Lynda Robson, Xiaodi Xie, and Jurgen Rehm. 1998. 'The Economic Costs of Alcohol, Tobacco and Illicit Drugs in Canada, 1992', *Addiction* 93, 7: 991–1006.

Skaff, Marilyn McKean, John W. Finney, and Rudolf H. Moos. 1999. 'Gender Differences in Problem Drinking and Depression: Different "Vulnerabilities"?', *American Journal of Community Psychology* 27: 25–54.

Spohn, Ryan E., and Howard B. Kaplan. 2000. 'Adolescent Substance Use and Adult Health Status: A Critical Analysis of a Problematic Relationship', *Advances in Medical Sociology* 7: 45–65.

Statistics Canada. 2004. 'Trends in Drug Offences and the Role of Alcohol and Drugs in Crime', *The Daily*, 23 Feb. Available at: <www.statcan.ca/Daily/English/040223/d040223a.htm>; accessed 16 Mar. 2006.

———. 2005a. 'Canadian Tobacco Use Monitoring Survey', *The Daily*, 11 Aug.

———. 2005b. 'Study: Exploring Crime Patterns in Canada', *The Daily*, 29 June.

Staton, Michele, Carl Leukefeld, T.K. Logan, Rick Zimmerman, Don Lyman, Rich Milich, Cathy Martin, Karen McClanah, and Richard Clayton. 1999. 'Gender Differences in Substance Use and Initiation of Sexual Activity', *Population Research and Policy Review* 18, 1–2: 89–100.

Taylor, Jenny, Naomi Fulop, and John Green. 1999. 'Drink, Illicit Drugs and Unsafe Sex in Women', *Addiction* 94: 1209–18.

Thomas, Gerald. 2004. 'Alcohol-related Harms and Control Policy in Canada'. Ottawa: Canadian Centre on Substance Abuse. Available at: <www.ccsa.ca>; accessed 16 July 2006.

Thomas, George, Alan Reifman, Grace M. Barnes, and Michael P. Farrell. 2000. 'Delayed Onset of Drunkenness as a Protective Factor for Adolescent Alcohol Misuse and Sexual Risk Taking: A Longitudinal Study', *Deviant Behavior* 21: 181–210.

United Nations Office on Drugs and Crime. 2000. *World Drug Report 2000*. Available at: <www.undcp.org/world_drug_report.html>; accessed 13 Jan. 2003.

United States Bureau of Justice Statistics. 1999. *Substance Abuse and Treatment, State and Federal Prisoners, 1997*. NCJ 172871. Washington: US Department of Justice.

United States Substance Abuse and Mental Health Services Administration. 1999. *National Household Survey on Drug Abuse: Population Estimates 1998*. Washington: US Department of Health and Human Services.

Van Dyke, Craig, and Robert Byck. 1982. 'Cocaine', *Scientific American* 246: 128–141.

Van Etten, Michelle, Yehuda D. Neumark, and James C. Anthony. 1999. 'Male-Female Differences in the Earliest Stages of Drug Involvement', *Addiction* 94: 1413–19.

Wagner, David. 1995. 'Historicizing Social Constructionist Perspectives: The Example of Temperance Movements', paper presented at the annual meeting of the Society for the Study of Social Problems.

Warner, Jessica, Robin Room, and Edward M. Adlaf. 1999. 'Rules and Limits in the Use of Marijuana among High-School Students: The Results of a Qualitative Study in Ontario', *Journal of Youth Studies* 2: 59–76.

———, Timothy R. Weber, and Ricardo Albanes. 1999. '"Girls Are Retarded When They're Stoned": Marijuana and the Construction of Gender Roles among Adolescent Females', *Sex Roles* 40: 25–43.

Welte, John, Grace M. Barnes, Joseph H. Hoffman, and Barbara A. Dintcheff. 1999. 'Trends in Adolescent Alcohol and Other Substance Use: Relationships to Trends in Peer, Parent, and School Influences', *Substance Use and Misuse* 34: 1427–49.

Whitbeck, Les B. 1999. 'Primary Socialization Theory: It All Begins with the Family', *Substance Use and Misuse* 34: 1025–32.

White, Helene R., and Erich W. Labouvie. 1994. 'Generality versus Specificity of Problem Behaviour: Psychological and Functional Differences', *Journal of Drug Issues* 24: 55–74.

Widom, Cathy Spatz, and Helene R. White. 1997. 'Problem Behaviours in Abused and Neglected Children Grown Up: Prevalence and Co-occurrence of Substance Abuse, Crime and Violence', *Criminal Behaviour and Mental Health* 7, 4: 287–310.

Williams, Robert, and Susan P. Gloster. 1999. 'Knowledge of Fetal Alcohol Syndrome (FAS) among Natives in Northern Manitoba', *Journal of Studies on Alcohol* 60: 833–6.

Witters, Weldon, Peter Venturelli, and Glen Hanson. 1992. *Drugs and Society*, 3rd edn. Boston: Jones and Bartlett.

Wood, Evan, Thomas Kerr, Will Small, Kathy Li, David C. Marsh, et al. 2004. 'Changes in Public Order after the Opening of a Medically Supervised Safer Injecting Facility for Illicit Injection Drug Users', *Canadian Medical Association Journal* 171, 7: 731–4.

Yarnold, Barbara. 1999. 'Cocaine Use among Miami's Public School Students, 1992: Religion versus Peers and Availability', *Journal of Health and Social Policy* 11, 2: 69–84.

Zurhold, H. 2001. 'Drogenkonsumräume im Spannungsfeld zwischen gesundheitspolitischen und ordnungspolitischen Wirkungserwartungen', *Akzeptanz* 2.

CHAPTER FOUR

RACE AND ETHNIC RELATIONS

LEARNING OBJECTIVES

■ To learn that social distance is maintained between different ethnic and racial groups.

■ To understand how racial and ethnic conflict occurs in Canada.

■ To appreciate the varying intensities of prejudice.

■ To know about the process of chain migration.

■ To know what is meant by the 'vertical mosaic'.

■ To be able to define 'diaspora'.

■ To understand different theoretical perspectives on ethnic and racial inequality.

■ To discover the social and health consequences of racial and ethnic inequality.

■ To recognize possible solutions to problems of race and ethnic relations.

Introduction

This chapter is about racial and ethnic minority groups and the social relations between them and the majority group. Thus, it is about problems of exclusion and discrimination, racism, prejudice, and conflict.

Prejudice against minority groups is a social problem in Canada, for various reasons. First, most people view prejudice as unjust and unfair; Canadians tend to look for remedies to injustice. Second, because it is unfair, prejudice creates conflicts in our society—between minorities and the majority, and between people who are prejudiced and people who are not. Third, prejudice and its outcomes—discrimination, conflict, exclusion, hatred, distrust—are politically and economically wasteful. They make our society far less prosperous than it might be. A prejudiced society does not make the best possible use of its human resources.

Yet, in spite of our good intentions and our support for social equality, discrimination against racial and ethnic minority groups is evident in a wide variety of settings, in Canada and elsewhere. For example, even when members of minority groups find suitable work, they still often face bias when competing for promotions. Throughout this chapter we will see examples of exclusion, decoupling, disabling, and scarcity because of the discrimination against minority groups and the limitations placed on their opportunities for economic advancement.

Discrimination has health consequences, too. The most dramatic health consequences are injuries and deaths resulting from hate crimes. However, injuries to self-esteem and feelings of stress and low worth also carry health consequences for victims of racism. These hidden injuries make discrimination and prejudice important health problems, as well as social and moral problems.

Facts about Race and Ethnicity

Race

Is race a social construction? People who have the most difficulty accepting other races believe that race is a biological—and therefore unassailable—fact. For them, race is an essential feature of any human being; as such, it is not changeable and not debatable. They see each 'race' as possessing unique physiological characteristics, based in genetic differences that are absent in the other races. Further, they are likely to believe that certain cultural or personality dispositions are genetically based as well. People who take this approach believe there are at least three categories of people in the human species— Negroid ('black'), Caucasoid ('white'), and Mongoloid ('yellow')—from which all racial groups are derived.

However, scientists increasingly reject this view of race in light of growing genetic evidence showing that the so-called human races are more alike than they are different. For example, the Human Genome Project has shown that only a tiny fraction of our genetic makeup as human beings varies by characteristics typically associated with 'race'. Indeed, 85 per cent of the genetic variability that exists within the entire human species can be found within a single local population and approximately 90 per cent can be found within each continent (Barbujani et al., 1997). Thus, there could be as much or more genetic difference between, say, two randomly selected Cambodians than there is between a Cambodian and a Norwegian. Besides, the physical attributes commonly associated with race—skin colour, hair texture, eye colour, etc.—are not genetically associated. That is, the pieces of DNA that determine a person's skin colour are inherited separately from the pieces that determine if that person's hair is curly or straight.

Yet, many continue to believe that people can be usefully distinguished on the basis of race and that important human differences are biologically determined. So although many people reject racism in principle, many others continue to behave as though the concept of race is meaningful. Thus, from a sociological perspective, it is meaningful. As long as large numbers of people continue to think race really does make a difference, the idea of race will continue to influence the social order and social inequality. The job of the sociologist is to understand why people invent and preserve such exclusionary ideas as race and give them such social and emotional power. In other words, race may be a social construction, but it is far from unimportant. As the sociologist W.I. Thomas stated nearly a century ago, what people believe to be true is true in its consequences; or, rephrased, what people believe to be real will have real outcomes. The belief in race has real outcomes, even if it is an imagined construct.

Ethnicity

Some people believe that 'race' and 'ethnicity' are, if not the same, closely related: 'One race, one ethnicity—biologically Negroid, therefore culturally African'. To be sure, a broad and generalized understanding of ethnicity has some value. Cultural differences certainly exist between groups of people, sharpened by apparent differences in skin colour, height, facial structure, and other physical features. Differences in physical appearance are likely to make cultural differences seem more prominent and meaningful.

Typically, the physical features supposedly shared by members of only one race are a result of collective evolutionary adaptation to specific environmental influences (for example, the darkening of skin colour where strong sunlight shines most of the time, as it does near the equator). However, race and ethnicity are not necessarily connected. People who look different may have the same cultural values. Conversely, people who look the same may think in very different ways.

The cultural features people share as members of an ethnic group usually are a result of collective experiences with a particular historical and regional background. Differences do exist between members of different ethnic groups—for example, between Poles and Ukrainians, or Chinese and Koreans—and there are historical reasons for these differences. The divisive effects of ethnicity, however, result from the ways people interpret these differences.

The most useful way to think about ethnic groups is to see them as created social interactions. We form ethnic groups relationally, through processes of exclusion and inclusion around symbols of real or imagined common descent, such as a common language, common rituals, and common folklore. However, because these are social and cultural in nature, they can be learned, and hence, ethnic boundaries may be traversed over time. For example, Canadians of Northern European ethnicity (historically the dominant cultural group in Canada) have traditionally identified one another according to such characteristics as white skin colour, English language, Protestant or Catholic religious affiliation, and common cultural practices. Despite such criteria of inclusion, however, a Canadian of, say, Persian descent could gradually be (and many have been) accepted into this community by speaking English in a particular way and adopting local customs (for example, particular ways of celebrating Christmas, preparing meals, raising children, and so on). In similar fashion, an English-speaking white person might become accepted into the Canadian Greek community by learning the Greek language and adopting Greek customs such as music, particular ways of celebrating holidays, preparing meals, and raising children, and perhaps even embracing Greek Orthodox Catholicism.

The point is that ethnic boundaries are potentially fluid and non-exclusive, based more on shared cultural experiences and knowledge than on immutable biological traits, such as skin colour. Of course, the process of being accepted into a new ethnic community takes time—on the order of years, even lifetimes—and requires an earnest desire to learn about others. However, ethnicity need not be used as a tool of divisiveness.

Social scientists used to define culture as an inventory of visible characteristics. Today, they understand **culture** as the values and practices that frame people's lives. From this perspective, culture is not something constant or permanent. Most anthropologists would deny a fixed pattern of Chinese culture, for example, that is learned and enacted uniformly across generations and contexts by Asian people in Hong Kong,

Malaysia, Trinidad, South Africa, and Vancouver. We can neither deduce people's ethnic group affiliations from their skin colour, language, religion, or other markers people use to place themselves and each other in groups nor can we assume that being Chinese today is very similar to being Chinese a generation or a century ago.

Canadians should be familiar with such ideas by now. Of Canada's roughly 31 million citizens, over 13 per cent were classified as visible minorities in 2001, while another 3 per cent possessed an Aboriginal background (Statistics Canada, 2001; see also Figure 4.1). Canada has become multicultural by virtue of one of the highest rates of immigration in the world throughout the last century. In 2002, for example, Canada received 229,091 immigrants, including refugees (Citizenship and Immigration Canada, 2003). The majority settled in metropolitan areas, with 49 per cent choosing to live in Toronto. That city contains many ethnic communities, including Little India, Little Jamaica, Little Portugal, Little Vietnam, Greektown, Koreatown, and multiple Italian enclaves and Chinatowns. This pattern of settlement has led the United Nations to call Toronto 'the most multicultural city in the world'. Montreal and Vancouver also are home to large and diverse ethnic populations. In 2002, 14 per cent of new immigrants chose to live in Montreal, while 13 per cent chose Vancouver. These three major urban gateways display different immigration patterns within. China was the principal source nation for immigrants arriving in Vancouver in 2002, with 25 per cent from that country. In Toronto, the single largest group of new immigrants came from India (16.6 per cent), while in Montreal, 10 per cent arrived from Morocco (Citizenship and Immigration Canada, 2003). These differences reflect the relative proximity of each destination to the source country and also the linguistic factor in choice: for most in Morocco, French is a second language, while English is a second language in China and India.

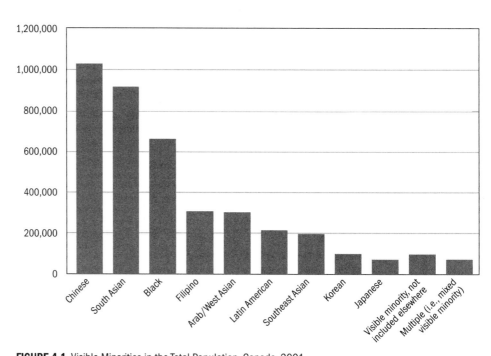

FIGURE 4.1 Visible Minorities in the Total Population, Canada, 2001
Source: Statistics Canada (2001).

Ethnic Nationalism

Nationalism—a sense of nationhood and a strong love of one's nation or ethnic group—grows out of the sense of a boundary between 'us' and 'them'. Some believe nationalism is a good thing because national unity is a good thing. The United States is often referred to as a 'melting pot', since people there are encouraged to hold strong nationalistic beliefs and to identify themselves as Americans first and ethnic group members second. This process of enculturation is supported strongly in the schools. So, in the US, nationalism includes assimilation and does tend to produce national unity. In contrast, Canada is described as a cultural mosaic, reflecting the country's support of difference and pluralistic cultural expression. As a decentralized—and decentralizing—federal state, Canada has a less unified national sentiment, and for many Canadians their strongest attachment is to a region or province. Relatively few symbols or rituals bind them together, apart from hockey, universal health care, and a (fading) tradition as an international peacekeeper; indeed, over the years various analysts have suggested that Canadians identify themselves in the negative, as *not* American (e.g., Gwyn, 1985; Brooks, 2007: chs 1, 2).

On the other hand, some believe that a lack of a strong Canadian identity is a good thing. They recognize that nationalism has acted as a mindless, dangerous force in history. Along similar lines, they deplore the possibility that multiculturalism, by fostering ethnic cultural identities within Canada, will promote feelings of nationalism and group identity for some Canadians and not for others. They believe that nationalism has done more harm than good in human history, and that encouraging pride in one particular people's ethnicity could engulf us in wars and genocidal acts. In the days since 11 September 2001, this issue has been on more people's minds.

The phrase 'ethnic nationalism' conjures up images of the horrors of 'ethnic cleansing' in the former Yugoslavia, of the struggle between the Hutu and Tutsi peoples in central Africa, of the 'jihad' by Islamic terrorists in many countries against the United States and its way of life. Ethnic nationalism can also describe the long-standing attempts of the Basques to have a separate and recognized political identity and of the Kurdish people of the Middle East to achieve international recognition. Michael Ignatieff, in his book *Blood and Belonging: Journeys into the New Nationalism* (1994), outlines two kinds of nationalism: civic and ethnic. In his view, *civic nationalism* refers to a community of citizens who as equals express loyalty and patriotic attachment to a shared set of social and political values. For some groups, this is a simple statement of identity, reflecting family ties, language, religion, tradition, and culture. It can also coexist with membership in a larger, multi-ethnic society and state.

Ethnic nationalism, by contrast, is a search for identity—a tracing of roots to a shared cultural past—as part of a search for political recognition. It is also a statement of resistance against being treated as an 'other', outside the bounds of society, by those who consider themselves the 'mainstream'. Ethnic nationalism is especially marked among peoples who do not have their own nation-state. All over Europe there have been movements seeking national autonomy. Basque, Scottish, and Welsh nationalism are only three of many examples.

In many parts of the world, people are calling for the right to govern themselves as they wish. They claim this right is based on their concept of nationhood, rooted in their culture and history. In claiming this right, they speak not only of the traditions and customs they share, but also of legal, educational, and political systems and institutions they consider uniquely their own. Within North America, too, groups that claim nationhood rather than ethnic group status include, most notably, the people of Quebec—many of whom feel that they constitute a distinct society—and the many Aboriginal nations who note that they had their own political and legal systems long before Europeans landed on North American soil.

Not all Québécois seek independence from Canada; just over half of those who voted in the Quebec referendum of 1995 voted to remain part of Canada. Many, including many of those who voted against separation, define themselves as Québécois rather than Canadian. However, where people with a geographical land base feel they form a nation, are strongly loyal to that nation, and preserve their own institutions, such as political, legal, and educational systems, there seems little reason to insist that they are not a nation. Nationhood is largely a state of mind, whether it is acknowledged by other nations or not.

At worst, ethnic nationalism denies basic human rights to others who do not belong. The rhetoric of nationalism can fuel fantasies of power and urge people to pick up weapons against their alleged enemies. This kind of ethnic nationalism, which focuses on power, is inherently destructive and cannot fit a liberal-democratic multicultural society like Canada. The only defence against such nationalistic destructiveness is to prevent a buildup of nationalism by denying demagogues a platform, while recognizing people's universal desire—even need—to celebrate their ancestry and build communities around it.

Canada Is Multicultural—and Conflictual

Canada's Population History

Few countries have been shaped by migration as rapidly and dramatically as Canada. The country has grown considerably in some periods and much less in others. The decades before World War I and after World War II were times of rapid growth; growth was slower during the late nineteenth century, during the 1930s, and after 1965. These demographic shifts have resulted from global events (wars), economic need and nation-building (Canada's National Policy of 1878–9 and the completion of the Canadian Pacific Railway line in 1885 meant both access to and political desire to populate western Canada), changing patterns of international migration, and natural increase.

When Europeans 'discovered' and later began to settle North America in the early 1600s, between 200,000 and 1,000,000 people already lived in what is now Canada. Their ancestors had arrived in the Americas from Asia at least 10,000 years earlier and possibly as much as 50,000 years earlier (Farb, 1978). Thus, all Canadians in one way or another are descended from or are immigrants.

Canada began as an outpost of the French and British empires. Missionaries, whose work suited the early forms of colonial governance, attempted to convert the Native people to 'civilized' Christianity. This process subdued the Native peoples, altered their cultures, and simplified the theft of their land (Peikoff, 2001). The conversion process was aided by the myth of a 'frontier' made up of vast, empty spaces from which the Native peoples were apparently absent (Furniss, 1999). Gradually, immigrants from France, Britain, and elsewhere filled up this supposedly empty country. Liberal capitalism, considered by some to be a neutral doctrine that promotes rights and citizenship, served as a genocidal tool for colonial domination and land appropriation (Samson, 1999, 2003).

By 1763, French, English, and other European immigrants and their descendants had increased the local population by 100,000. Greater numbers of immigrants, from a wider range of countries, arrived during the nineteenth and twentieth centuries. The population grew about 4 per cent annually during the century before Confederation, and 2 per cent annually during much of the century that followed. The growth of Canada's population to its present size—over 31 million—has taken more than two centuries. It is the result both of high rates of childbirth in earlier years and of immigration—two factors that have created an extremely high ratio of newcomers (immigrants and newborns) (see Bell and Tepperman, 1979; Li, 2003).

At the same time, emigration *from* Canada was so common that it often offset much of the effects of immigration. Since 1851, about 12 million immigrants have entered Canada and 7.5 million emigrants have left. Thus, the net gain through migration has been only about 4.5 million people. In the same period, there was a net gain through natural increase of some 20.5 million people—more than four times the gain through migration. So, especially in French Canada, fertility has influenced Canada's population history much more notably than immigration (Beaujot and McQuillan, 1982; Foot, 1982).

However, immigration has uniquely coloured Canada's history, culture, and social organization. Much more than any European, Asian, or African society, Canada is a nation of immigrants and descendants of immigrants—as John Porter (1965) said, a rail-

---

Box 4.1   Social Policy: The White Australia Policy

Canada is not the only country to have struggled with the immigration of visible minority groups. In 1901, Australia enacted the Immigration Restriction Act, which codified the so-called White Australia policy, a term that signified what many Australians then considered the 'ideal' vision of Australian nationalism.

At this time, parties across the political spectrum were openly against non-white immigration, especially from China and India. One important feature of the Act was a dictation test given selectively to immigrant applicants by immigration officers. This test required the applicant to write out a passage of 50 words in any European language the immigration officer might choose. This meant that immigration officers could exclude English-speaking applicants simply by choosing a language the applicant did not know, such as German or Dutch. This practice was employed even though Australia was and still is officially an English-speaking nation. Even when the test was given in English, the immigration officials could choose a complex passage to ensure that the applicant failed. As well, the dictation test, which was supposedly required of all immigration applicants (white or non-white), was actually administered only to non-whites. A great many 'undesired' minority group members were prevented from entering Australia during the first half of the twentieth century as a result of this strategy and others like it.

It took growing protest and an increased need for cheap labour to replace the Immigration Restriction Act with the Migration Act in 1958. The new Act removed the dictation test from entry requirements; however, the White Australia policy remained in place until 1966.

way station full of comings and goings; and as others have said, a hotel for the world. So, we cannot understand Canadian society without examining the contribution of migration to Canada's population history.

The Impacts of Immigration

The effects of migration to and from Canada have varied widely with time and place, while the effects of natural increase have not. Mirroring Western Europe's demographic transition, Canada's birth and death rates have dropped slowly and predictably since about 1851. While the economic depression of the 1930s pushed births below the expected level and the post–World War II baby boom pushed births above it, otherwise, the downward trend has been slow and steady.

By contrast, migration into and out of Canada has varied from one decade to another. Canadian economic development has veered from one resource-driven economic boom-and-bust cycle to another. With each resource discovery, a new portion of the country was opened for settlement. Willing workers arrived to extract the resource, whether fish, furs, timber, wheat, or minerals. Resource extraction creates new communities and new related jobs in manufacturing, services, communications, and transportation. Often, more jobs were created in this way than could be filled by native-born Canadians. So Canada opened its doors to immigrants, loosening the rules, increasing quotas, even searching out immigrants in preferred countries (Hawkins, 1972; Kalbach, 1970). Immigrant workers were needed both to extract resources and to build the infrastructure to make resource development and economic growth possible—Irish on the canals of early Ontario; Chinese on the CPR line to the west coast; Eastern and Southern Europeans in the mining communities that sprang up across the country through much of the twentieth century; Ukrainians and other Central and Eastern Europeans to farm the Prairie West; Italians on the Toronto subway system and in the construction industry in the 1950s.

Historically, whenever the demand for a natural resource has diminished, the need for immigrant labour has collapsed. Immigration laws tighten up again and fewer immigrants are admitted. The 'quality' and quantity of immigrants are controlled more systematically through, for instance, the tightening of medical inspection (Sears, 1990). As work opportunities within Canada vanish, more people leave the country, chiefly for the United States. Today, however, the vast majority of immigrants to Canada locate in major cities, principally Toronto, Vancouver, and Montreal, and are not involved in the resource sector.

In 1990, the federal government raised the ceiling on the number of immigrants allowed into Canada. This decision was influenced by a prediction based on current demographic trends that unless more immigrants were allowed in, Canada's population would start to shrink by the year 2025. This need for immigrants to prevent population shrinkage remains a basis for policy today, due to continued below-replacement fertility.

Multiculturalism in Canada Today

Today, Canada prides itself on its multicultural makeup. Yet multiculturalism is a complicated notion. Increasingly, Canadians have found it useful to distinguish between traditional, or liberal, multiculturalism and modern multiculturalism. **Traditional multiculturalism**, or pluralism, is concerned with protecting the rights of individuals.

It protects the rights of minority people through, for example, provincial human rights codes. By contrast, **modern multiculturalism** is concerned with the survival of cultural groups. In this case, the group, not the individual, is protected by law. Modern multiculturalism treats each of us as the member of an ethnic or racial group—we are viewed as proxies for the groups we belong to.

The difference between these two approaches is important. By its nature, traditional multiculturalism focuses on fostering civil liberties. Where the traditional multiculturalism protects individual job-seekers against bias, modern multiculturalism supports blanket preferences, such as employment equity, to promote the hiring of disadvantaged group members. People who are members of specifically protected groups will be advantaged under the new arrangement; members of other groups will struggle to gain entry into the protected domain. This, in turn, perpetuates a struggle over, for example, who we include under the label 'visible minority' or 'disabled person'.

This policy is also closely tied to employment equity (known in the US as affirmative action), which—other things being equal—gives preference to members of the specifically protected groups (e.g., females, visible minorities, disabled people) over otherwise blameless males, white people, and the able-bodied.

Some criticize the federal policy of multiculturalism (and employment equity) for emphasizing group differences, encouraging different value systems, and building isolated communities rather than promoting common interests and objectives. As long as Canada maintains diverse cultures within its borders, the argument goes, it will never build a national identity. The promotion of cultural differences splits Canadians into separate (and occasionally hostile) ethnic groups; racism is only one negative result. Without the social differences promoted by multiculturalism, there might be less exclusion, prejudice, or discrimination based on perceived ethnic or cultural differences.

For critics of multiculturalism, treating minority groups in a different, special way violates the former Canadian norm of equal treatment, for in modern multicultural societies the state does not treat people exactly the same. Different groups enjoy different rights. It is because multiculturalism is aimed at protecting diversity and difference that some groups—the more vulnerable ones—enjoy advantages.

This situation has its roots in four social revolutions that have occurred since 1960: the Quiet Revolution in Quebec, the acceleration of Aboriginal demands to settle Native land claims, the impact of higher rates of immigration from developing countries with different cultures, and the cross-border influence of the US civil rights movement (Duffy Hutcheon, 1998). The Quiet Revolution in Quebec raised the possibility of national separation, which reinforced a sense that Canada contains at least two distinct cultures. The conflict over Aboriginal land claims emphasized that other 'nations' besides Canada inhabit the Canadian land mass. High rates of immigration from countries with different cultures produced large, hard-to-assimilate communities in the heart of Canada's main cities. The US civil rights movement gave Canadian protestors a variety of models for civil disobedience and disruption by which to press their special claims.

The deepest roots of modern multiculturalism are located in the early European settlement of Canada, first by the French and then by the English, a fact reflected in Canada's founding document, the British North America (BNA) Act of 1867 (today called the Constitution Act, 1867). That document promotes regionalism, giving small provinces more political representation and clout per capita than large provinces receive. Some religions receive special treatment under law. Because of the BNA Act, in

Canada's Visible Minorities
By 2017, the 150th anniversary of Confederation, approximately one in five Canadians will be a member of a visible minority group. Approximately half of all visible minorities will be of South Asian or Chinese descent (Statistics Canada, 2005).

2007 we support Catholic schools out of public funds, though we do not support Jewish or Islamic schools in the same way. We require that French be available in all federal institutions, even when Chinese or other languages are spoken more often within the local community. These inequities and peculiarities—as well as a level of tolerance and compromise unimaginable in many other countries—arise out of Canada's early history and the BNA Act and are perpetuated in the policy of multiculturalism.

Federal–Aboriginal Relations in Canada

As noted, the Aboriginal peoples pose a big problem for Canadian multiculturalism. Some people believe that the political concerns of Canada's Aboriginal peoples will not be satisfied unless they achieve some degree of political autonomy (Warburton, 1997). Will Kymlicka (1995) argues that we should view Canadian Aboriginal peoples as 'national minorities'. He believes that their rights should include both individual equality and collective self-determination, within the framework of liberal democratic principles (see also Spaulding, 1997). So far, however, movement in that direction has been slow. The two demands—individual equality and collective self-determination—may not be compatible.

In a struggle to gain sovereignty over their land and to preserve it for future generations, the Aboriginal people of northern Quebec mounted a campaign to stop a major hydroelectric development. Ironically, provincial administrators declared the right to self-determination for the people of Quebec as a whole but not for the Aboriginal peoples within Quebec. Thus, the problems in Quebec reflect the province's own difficulties within Canada. Quebec claims to be a melting pot where minorities are assimilated into the francophone culture; however, Aboriginal and other ethnic voters helped prevent a separatist victory in the 1980 and 1995 referendums on Quebec's secession from Canada (Hunt, 1996).

Aboriginal efforts to achieve self-government have not been entirely without effect. Where they exist, for example, Canada's alternative Native justice systems stress collective, as opposed to individual, rights and give special priorities to Native principles and practices of justice. Participation is voluntary but limited to minor offences (Clairmont, 1996). Such power-sharing between judges and Native communities seems to be more acceptable to the federal government than the application of Aboriginal values to jury selection, trial location, and criminal liability (Melancon, 1997). Land claim settlements, though slow in coming, have also provided individual First Nations and peoples with the opportunity and the resources to govern themselves as nations within a nation. The recently created territory of Nunavut, where the Inuit of the eastern Arctic comprise 85 per cent of the population, is a prime example in this regard.

Can different groups coexist as a unified nation without falling into divisiveness and conflict? These were questions that sociologist Émile Durkheim asked over a century ago in his classic work, *The Division of Labor in Society* (1965 [1895]). He answered that in a modern society, people will learn to value one another and live together peacefully. To do this, they must recognize their interdependence. In Canada, we have not fully learned how to do that yet. Canadians are generally happy with their citizenship in a multicultural society, and elements of a distinct Canadian national identity do exist (Howard, 1998). However, prejudice, discrimination, and conflict persist, too.

Box 4.2   Personal Experience: Growing Up Aboriginal in Canada

Near dusk on a Wednesday evening, all the high school students on the Beausoleil First Nation file up from the ferry dock and make their way home somewhere on Christian Island.

It becomes cold and dark. After a 30-minute crossing over the waters of Georgian Bay by ferry, followed by a 45-minute bus ride to school in Midland—and then doing it all over again after school—no one wants to stop to talk or laugh on their way home.

An hour later a few arrive at the community health centre to talk about the pressures they feel as young people living on an island reserve. About 650 people live on the Georgian Bay island located three kilometres across from Cedar Point, a 40-minute drive northwest of Barrie.

'When you get older you start to question things', says 26-year-old Lawrence Copegog, who has lived on the island almost his entire life. 'Being on the island represents safety and security for a lot of the kids. But you eventually wonder if you're being treated like a refugee in your own land.'

He explains the dilemma faced by younger members of the Beausoleil First Nation: They can either succumb to the racism he says exists across the water and descend into a life of isolation and alcoholism on the island; or they can face the 'stereotyping' off the island and hopefully not get too deeply alienated by it.

. . .

'We already see it with some of the kids we grew up with', says 16-year-old Niki Monague (all Monagues in this story are not related). 'Some of the girls have already dropped out. When they turn 16, they know they can. And instead of leaving the island they just start having babies.'

. . .

If the kids already sound bitter, it's because [hundreds of] years of oppression, genocide, and alienation are in the 'memory chips of all the youth', says H. Neil Monague, an addiction prevention counsellor in the community. 'It will always be there. For some it makes them stronger, they want things to change and they are starting to change things. Others are just too scared.'

. . .

'Once you're locked in here, you're locked in', Monague says, explaining that it's more than a psychological feeling. 'When the ferry stops running in the evening around nine, there is no way off the island.'

Source: Adapted from Grewal (2005).

Patterns of Human Migration

The Vertical Mosaic

Despite Canada's global reputation for multicultural tolerance, the country has not always been as welcoming towards immigrants as one would imagine. Repeatedly, the majority group has excluded and devalued immigrant groups, with minority newcomers experiencing less-than-average access to better occupations and higher income. These facts led John Porter (1965) to describe Canadian society as a **vertical mosaic** in which English and French Canadians exist at the top of a patchwork hierarchy, with other ethnic minorities positioned below them.

Porter traced this stratification pattern to Canada's historical reliance on selective immigration as a means of fulfilling specific workforce needs during industrialization. Gradually, as Canada industrialized, a close relationship between ethnicity and social class developed. Ethnic groups took the best available roles in society and held on to them, leaving the less desirable roles for other ethnic groups—especially, for more recent immigrants. With economic growth and immigration, the less preferred ethnic groups assumed an 'entrance status' and stayed in it.

Here's how the process worked: with each decade, fewer of the desired kinds of immigrants—Northern European Protestants—were available for migration. Canada's new, hard, and dangerous jobs—such as mining in northern Ontario, farming in rural Saskatchewan, building the national railway, erecting the urban skyscrapers—required new 'kinds' of immigrants, from Northern, then Eastern, then Southern Europe, and then from Asia, the Caribbean, and countries in the southern hemisphere. New immigrants would arrive to find Canada's best jobs taken. They had to settle for what was left over, typically lower down the social hierarchy.

With few exceptions, their children and children's children were unable to move up the hierarchy with the passage of years because mechanisms for upward mobility—especially, institutions of higher education—were largely inaccessible. So, from generation to generation, particular ethnic groups remained stuck in their **entrance status**: the status attained when their group first arrived in Canada.

Most of Canada's minority groups have at some time held a low entrance status. By now, thanks to the continued expansion of educational opportunity, many, though not all, have moved out of it. Discrimination and a lack of educational opportunities have continued to make it difficult for the Canadian-born children of some ethnic minority immigrants to climb the economic ladder. This has left a stable base of labourers on which the dominant English/French group could perch itself. 'Ethnic differences', Porter concluded, 'have been important in building up the bottom layer of the stratification system in both agricultural and industrial settings' (1965: 73). In this way, a low-paid reserve army of labour was always available.

The vertical mosaic persisted not only because of exclusionary practices by the dominant English-French majority, but also because of the migration patterns and self-organization practices of the ethnic groups. For example, the continued practice of chain migration preserved linkages between Canada and the immigrants' countries of origin. The practice of building institutional completeness preserved a link with the ancestral culture across generations. The practice of diaspora built linkages with other comparable ethnic cultures around the world. Let us examine each of these briefly.

Chain Migration

For most ethnic groups, the process of migration to Canada has been gradual. Some immigrants came to escape war, bad living conditions, or an absence of human rights—so-called 'push factors'. Others came in hopes of finding better jobs and education for their children—so-called 'pull factors'. Typically, immigrants arrived, generation after generation, as links in a **chain migration** process. Family members would come, one or two at a time, establish a home, get work, and send for spouses, siblings, and children, gradually creating a chain (or sequence) of linked migrations. Eventually, these chains would extend outward to include grandparents and grandchildren, uncles and aunts, cousins, friends, neighbours, and even distant relatives or acquaintances. Many immigrants spent their first Canadian years in large old houses packed with family members who had just arrived and were looking for a foothold.

This pattern of chain migration is common throughout the world. People generally migrate to nearby places they know about, usually through people they knew at home. Like many other social processes, migration relies on processes of information flow. The amount of migration between two towns, cities, or countries is determined not only by distance and economic opportunity, as researchers originally thought, but also by the social networks linking potential migrants. Social networks channel migrants into particular areas, and they link people to particular distant communities. And this explains why some immigrants who, in the same given year, left a particular town in Poland (or Italy or Vietnam) ended up living in Winnipeg, while others ended up living in Montreal, Boston, Houston, Capetown, or Sydney.

Institutional Completeness

Most chain migrants receive help from either relatives or co-villagers. With each arrival, the immigrant community becomes larger and more differentiated, containing a wider variety of communal institutions. As Raymond Breton has written (1964, 1978; Breton et al., 1980), the growing communities often develop **institutional completeness**: they build schools, churches, newspapers, lending societies, shops, and so on. In turn, the community's degree of completeness increases community solidarity and cohesion. It does this by increasing the number of members who carry out most of their activities within the ethnic group and retain ethnic culture and ethnic social ties. By retaining its ancestral language, religion, and culture, an immigrant community remains cohesive.

Because visible minority groups are sometimes denied fair access to economic opportunities by some members of the host society, new immigrants are often forced to use their ethnic membership and assert their ethnic pride as a matter of economic and cultural survival. People who try to assimilate socially may find themselves marginalized—that is, accepted by neither the ethnic community nor the host culture. This is a particular problem for the children of immigrants, as sociologists W.I. Thomas and Florien Znaniecki (1971 [1919]) first pointed out in their classic work, *The Polish Peasant in Europe and America*. Often, intergenerational value conflicts arise in immigrant families. Immigrants' grandchildren find themselves fully accepted into the society; immigrants' children—their parents—are only partly accepted; and the immigrants themselves, often limited in education, language skills, and social capital, are least accepted of all. So, members of the same extended family can have very different experiences of the same society.

Diasporas

Viewed from within our own society, immigrant groups are either included or excluded. Viewed internationally, immigrant groups such as the Arabs of Montreal or the Sikhs of Edmonton are often the members of a much larger community: the global Arab or Sikh community to which they belong. Originally, the word 'diaspora' described the dispersal of the tribes of Israel and, in modern times, Jewish communities outside the state of Israel, especially as they were forced to flee the persecution of Nazi Germany. Today, we use **diaspora** to mean the global spread of migrants of any ethnic group or nationality and the global spread of cultures by means of these migrants. It is used as well to describe the global dispersion of any historically victimized minority, such as the Roma (gypsies) or Armenians, or visible and potentially victimized minorities (for example, Arabs in Africa, Sikhs in the West Indies, and Chinese people in Indonesia). Almost any migrant community—especially a community made up mainly of refugees, deportees, or former slaves—is now referred to as 'diasporic'.

Traditionally, sociologists viewed immigration and ethnicity in terms of social disorganization. They assumed that immigrants routinely suffered from the breakdown of their traditional culture and social organization in the adopted homeland. It is true that breakdowns of traditional family authority have led to intergenerational conflict in many communities. At the same time, however, immigrant groups in North America have usually organized themselves effectively for a new life in a new country, usually by building institutional completeness. As a result, immigrants have managed to exercise influence over their new homeland and still maintain a foothold in their homeland of origin.

The diasporic Jews illustrate this combination: a mixture of strong connections with their European, Asian, and African origin countries, with relatives who immigrated to other countries, with Israel—the historic 'homeland' of Jewry in Zionist thinking—and yet strong assimilation into all of the countries in which they reside, especially Canada and the United States. As a result of migration over generations, many Jewish families have links to other Jewish communities in South Africa, South America, and Europe as well as in North America.

The diasporic Chinese illustrate another, different pattern. The Chinese in Canada originally did heavy labour, helping to build the railways. Unlike the African migration, overseas Chinese migration was mainly voluntary and took place in three stages: migration from inland China to coastal areas in ancient times, migration to Southeast Asian regions in more modern times, and migration to places all over the world after World War II. Despite a continuing identification with Chinese culture in many diasporic communities, few but the most recent immigrants express a desire to return to China, Hong Kong, or Taiwan. However, like the Jews, the diasporic Chinese are likely to have family connections in many cities throughout the world.

In short, members of major diasporic groups are simultaneously members of the countries in which they live, which is often where they were born and grew up, and members of an international ethnic network that may span dozens of communities throughout the world. The resulting pattern—**transnationalism** among immigrant peoples—reflects the twentieth-century revolutions in communication and travel, the global expansion of human rights, and the maintenance of social networks that ease transnational migration. Today, to think meaningfully about race and ethnic relations, we can begin with the nation-state, but we must eventually think about the world as a whole.

Theories of Race and Ethnic Relations

The Structural-Functionalist Perspective

According to functionalists, even the inequality between racial or ethnic groups has a social purpose. As we noted in earlier chapters, functionalists stress that social inequality provides incentives in the form of status and material rewards that prompt people to take on the most important social roles. Also, functionalists see exclusion, prejudice, and discrimination as providing benefits for society as a whole. They point out the value of maintaining distinct ethnic identities in a pluralistic society such as Canada for the purposes of socially integrating members of the groups.

Ethnic identity provides people with roots and social connectedness in an otherwise individualistic, fragmented society. For many people, their ethnic heritage serves as a link both to a rich cultural past and to current members of their ethnic group. Although the complete dissolution of ethnic boundaries might reduce inter-group conflict, it would also mean the end of an ethnic basis for group identity and cohesion. As well, ethnoracial diversity benefits society as a whole, functionalists argue, since it allows for the discussion of a wider range of opinions, perspectives, and values and for the development of a wider range of skills than might be available in a homogeneous society. Even social conflict has value (see, e.g., Coser, 1965). By drawing and enforcing boundaries, conflict intensifies people's sense of identity and belonging and gives groups more cohesion and a heightened sense of purpose.

Conflict Theory

Unlike functionalists, conflict theorists focus on how one group benefits more than another from differentiation, exclusion, and institutional racism. They explore, for instance, how economic competition results in the creation and preservation of racial stereotypes and institutionalized racism. Conflict theory proposes that majority groups seek to dominate minorities because this makes them feel superior or because the minority threatens the majority's economic superiority.

For example, as we mentioned earlier, Chinese workers were brought to Canada in the nineteenth century as cheap labourers in building the transcontinental railway. Once the railroad was built, however, the same Asian workers—originally recognized and admired for their hard work and discipline—were seen by many Euro-Canadians, especially in British Columbia, as a threat to the economic well-being of the dominant white majority. A federal head tax was put in place in the hopes of preventing further immigrant flow. Then, the Chinese Exclusion Act was passed in 1923, which effectively reduced the number of Chinese immigrants entering Canada to a handful. This law remained in place until 1947.

Symbolic Interactionism

Symbolic interactionists focus on microsociological aspects of race and discrimination, such as the ways people construct ethnic differences and racial labels to subordinate minority groups.

'Nigger', 'dago', 'wop', 'chink', 'kike', 'jap', 'gook', and 'spic' are just a few of the many slang terms for race used sometimes casually, sometimes with cruel intent. Not only do such terms usually imply condescension intended to demean, which is hurtful, they can also create a self-fulfilling prophecy. If people come to believe slurs against their ethnic or national group—thinking themselves really stupid, lazy, cheap, underhanded, and so on—they may behave according to the negative labels. They may come to hate themselves, reject their own group, or give in to impulses to live up to others' worst expectations.

Redress for the Chinese Head Tax
On 22 June 2006 the government of Canada issued a formal apology to Chinese Canadians for the head tax, which cut off most Chinese immigration from 1923 to 1947. The government offered symbolic payments of redress to those still living who had paid the tax and to the living spouses of deceased payers.

Interactionists also point to **racial socialization** as another factor that contributes to ongoing racial conflicts in society. Racial socialization is a process of social interaction that exposes people to the beliefs, values, cultural history, language, and social and economic realities of their own and other people's racial or ethnic identities. In other words, it is the process of learning 'what it means' socially and culturally to be a Jew, a Chinese person, a Ukrainian, and so on.

A constant awareness of race (or ethnicity) in daily social interaction increases the likelihood of racial conflict. Whenever there is a conflict between people of different races or ethnicities—particularly where there is a troubled and volatile history (such as between Aboriginal people and whites in Canada)—the question of race and racism is never far from people's minds. Moreover, as the news story in Box 4.3. suggests, if the only form of exposure to other racial cultures is through stereotyped pop culture images, the result may be a distorted perception of ethnic minority group members.

Box 4.3   Social Construction: Hip-Hop Culture and Racial Stereotypes as Recreational Amusement

Hip hop has been accused of glorifying the stereotype of black youths as gangsters and thugs. The latest offshoot of 'gangsta' culture is 'Ghettopoly', an inner-city version of the board game 'Monopoly'. Is it an ironic commentary on the manufacture of hip-hop culture for a receptive white audience, or a cheap exploitation of racist stereotypes for commercial gain from all quarters?

In comes Ghettopoly, a takeoff on Monopoly. Unlike the Monopoly gent who sports a top hat, cane and mustache, the Ghettopoly 'bruh' is a thug wearing a bandanna. His bug eyes glare at you over dark glasses, and he clinches a marijuana cigarette between his teeth . . . an Uzi in one hand and a bottle of malt liquor in the other.

Charles Thomas, an announcer for WLS-TV in Chicago, describes Ghettopoly well: 'The game is played like Monopoly, but the object is to put crack houses or project buildings in some of the worst neighborhoods in America while trying to avoid being carjacked, shot, or addicted. There are ghetto stash and hustle cards, and the seven game pieces include a pimp, a prostitute, a machine gun, malt liquor bottle, basketball, marijuana leaf, and a rock of crack cocaine.'

Obviously, many African Americans, along with whites who care about such things, are outraged. To them, Ghettopoly is racist and offensive. . . . The Rev. Michael Pfleger of Chicago: 'It is not only insulting and ignorant, but it's shameful. I'd like to get hold of the person who is behind it because this is something that should be stopped. . . . It promotes the absolute worst of racism. It's racial pornography. It takes the worst element of race prejudice and begins to glorify it and raise it up.' . . .

[On the other hand], I cannot improve on the observations of *Chicago Sun-Times* columnist Mary Mitchell: 'The symbols found in Ghettopoly are an accurate reflection of what hip-hop heroes are selling to white America. Ironically, people are outraged about Urban Outfitters selling a foul board game, but few people of influence seem to care that every record store in America is selling music that glorifies the very stereotypes the game promotes. How can black people be outraged over a board game when black superstars have gotten rich by promoting those same stereotypes? These performers aren't boycotted. They are worshipped.'

Source: Maxwell (2003).

Structural Theory

Another perspective, structural theory, helps us understand the experiences of racial and ethnic minorities in job markets. Generally, people who are most similar—racially, culturally, and educationally—to members of the host society will enjoy the easiest, most rapid assimilation into the labour market. They will be able to compete more successfully for the better jobs and get them faster, particularly during economic growth. In recessionary times, everyone's assimilation will be slower and more conflictual. People's experiences will usually reflect the characteristics of the economy more than anything they do or believe.

The sorting of people into jobs in Canada usually begins in schools. Through the deliberate application of subtle and complex procedures like tracking and grade-weighting, some students are encouraged while others are discouraged, reducing the opportunities of the latter group following high school graduation. Once out of school and in the workforce, people of 'different kinds' are streamed into some types of jobs and away from others. For example, far more women and visible minorities are streamed into the secondary labour market, and far more white men into the primary labour market, than could have occurred by chance. However, even within these markets, there are important differences among jobs. For example, although both teachers and doctors are in the primary labour market, few teachers feel they have the sort of benefits and opportunities that doctors do. So, it is of interest to sociologists to know according to what criteria people become teachers or doctors.

Some job markets exclude or discourage people on the grounds of race, ethnicity, or gender, though this is becoming less common. One fact remains, however: immigration tends to level the playing field, whatever the immigrant's race or ethnicity, credentials or background experience. In Canada, new immigrants routinely hold similar positions in the labour market, and these are usually the lowest entrance statuses. In big cities especially, immigrants with a variety of advanced degrees—such as doctors, dentists, architects, engineers, professors, social workers, and nurses—can be found driving taxis, serving hamburgers, selling computers or television sets, and providing low-paid personal services. Even when they earn good wages, recent immigrants earn relatively less than native-born Canadians with equivalent education and experience (see Figure 4.2).

To compensate for these (hidden) structural barriers, immigrants often become middlemen—that is, entrepreneurs, agents, or brokers. Research on middleman minorities finds the following historical pattern is typical: a culturally or racially distinct group immigrates and suffers discrimination. Members of the group come to see themselves as 'strangers' in the country and, to protect themselves, settle in the larger towns and cities. There, they become self-employed as wholesalers, small merchants (e.g., shopkeepers), or even professionals. As a result, they come into competition with local capitalists of the dominant ethnic group. Their economic and social survival depends on thrift, a high degree of education and organization, and the use of family and community ties in business. By these means the group achieves a middle-class standard of living. No wonder family and community are so important in the lives of these immigrant groups.

Social Aspects of Racism and Prejudice

We have already touched on various aspects of racism and prejudice at several points in this chapter. In this section, we will focus specifically on these issues as social problems.

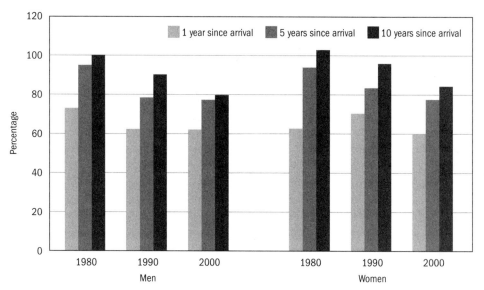

FIGURE 4.2 Percentage Earnings of Recent Immigrants Relative to Earnings of the Canadian-born, by Sex, Canada, 1980–2000
Source: Adapted from Statistics Canada website: http://www12.statcan.ca/english/census01/Products/ Analytic/companion/earn/tables/canada/earnimm.cfm

Defining and Measuring Racial Prejudice

Psychologist Gordon Allport (1954: 7) defined **prejudice** as 'an aversive or hostile attitude toward a person who belongs to a group, simply because he belongs to that group, and is therefore presumed to have the objectionable qualities ascribed to the group'. **Racial discrimination** has been characterized by the United Nations' Office of the High Commissioner for Human Rights as 'any distinction, exclusion, restriction or preference based on race, colour, descent, or national or ethnic origin which has the purpose or effect of nullifying or impairing the recognition, enjoyment or exercise, on an equal footing, of human rights and fundamental freedoms in the political, economic, social, cultural or any other field of public life' (Office for the High Commissioner for Human Rights, 1969). Racial prejudice can show itself in many ways and in many different areas of society.

Racism appears in society at multiple levels. Most broadly, **institutional (structural) racism** is any systemic bias embedded in an existing social structure, policy, or process that deprives some groups of equal access to goods, services, and rights because of their ethnic or racial membership. Examples of institutional racism include rental housing markets that try to keep 'undesirable' ethnic groups out of certain communities, and banks and insurance companies that deny loans to people in certain neighbourhoods based on crude economic (and racially tinged) criteria, a practice known as 'redlining'. These actions result in unequal educational opportunities for whites and some minority groups and an unequal distribution of material wealth in society by ethnic status. Eventually, this translates into an under-representation of visible minorities in political offices, corporate boardrooms, professional ranks (e.g., medicine and law), and other positions of power. Policies such as employment equity seek to offset the effects of institutional racism on oppressed groups.

Individual racism is the classic form of prejudice, in which a person makes groundless assumptions about the motives and abilities of others based on a stereotypical

Table 4.1 Summary of Theoretical Perspectives	
Theory	**Main Points**
Structural Functionalism	■ Ethnic identity provides social connectedness in an individualistic society. ■ Racial diversity provides a wide range of opinions, perspectives, and values that enrich society. ■ Social conflict enforces boundaries, which give groups more cohesion and a sense of identity.
Conflict Theory	■ Majority groups benefit from excluding and marginalizing minority groups, e.g., corporate leaders benefit by hiring minorities at low wages to secure shareholder profits; racial tension divides workers by setting up competition among them, diverting their anger from the exploitive capitalists.
Symbolic Interactionism	■ Ethnic differentiation is constructed by labelling process. ■ Racial slurs further undermine the inferior status of minority groups. ■ Racial labels and slurs can shape the way groups view themselves nega- tive racial slurs can make individuals hate themselves/reject their groups). ■ Constant awareness of race (racial socialization) in daily social interaction increases the likelihood of racial conflict.
Structural Theory	■ More visible minorities are streamed into the secondary labour market and more white men into the primary market. ■ Job markets sometimes exclude people on the grounds of race or ethnicity. ■ A general bias against hiring non-whites has made many visible minority immigrants become 'middlemen'.

Source: Adapted from Statistics Canada, 'Ethnocultural Portrait of Canada, 2001 Census', Catalogue no. 97F0010XIE2001002, available at http://www.statcan.ca/bsolc/english/bsolc?catno= 97F0010X2001002.

understanding of the person's racial or ethnic group characteristics. Its epitome is the dangerous and unrepentant bigot—the Ku Klux Klan member, say, or the neo-Nazi. However, it would be wrong (and dangerous) to suppose that the practice of racism is limited to these extremist groups. As we shall see, research has found that subtle expressions of racism persist among a majority of people (e.g., Gaertner and Dovidio, 2000; Reitz and Breton, 1999; Devine and Elliot, 1995).

Perhaps the most destructive form of racism is **internalized racism**, where members of an ethnic or racial group come to believe the stereotypes that others have imposed on them. This tragic consequence of institutional and individual racism leads people to devalue their own worth, compromise their life goals, and passively accept the racial barriers that carry on the cycle of oppression and inequality.

How do researchers measure racism? Many different tools have been developed and tested, but as yet no academic consensus exists on the best method for measuring people's levels of racial and ethnic bias. Asking people direct questions about the prejudices they hold against a particular ethnic or cultural group is unlikely to yield accurate results. People have a hard time admitting their biases to themselves, let alone to others, and may feel pressured to respond in a socially approved (i.e., non-prejudicial) way. Thus, social scientists often use indirect measures instead.

One way to do this is to measure the **social distance** between ethnic groups, which E.S. Bogardus did in 1928. He asked respondents whether they would be willing to accept members of specified ethnic groups into close kinship by marriage, their club as friends, their street as neighbours, their workplaces as colleagues, their country as citizens, and their country as visitors. The research found that people feel varying comfort levels when interacting with members of other cultures under different conditions. Generally, people are more willing to have close (e.g., kinship) relations with people they judge to be culturally and racially similar to themselves, though they may be willing to have distant relations—if any at all—with people they view as different.

So, for example, an Anglo-Saxon respondent may be more likely to see his daughter marry someone of German or French ancestry than someone of Japanese or Chinese ancestry. Conversely, a Chinese respondent may be more likely to see his daughter marry someone of Japanese or Korean ancestry than someone of German or French ancestry. However, this distance preference is not symmetrical: people are more likely to accept their daughter marrying a distant 'higher status' group member than an equally distant 'lower status' group member. Finally, distance preferences are cumulative: groups a respondent would accept as close relations would also be accepted as workmates, friends, and neighbours. Groups a respondent would reject as citizens or even visitors would surely be rejected as workmates, friends, or neighbours.

Through continued use of this scale, sociologists have learned that people who place other groups at a distance from themselves often hold prejudices about those other groups. They also sometimes act on those prejudices and practise discrimination against the other groups, at work and in the wider community. This creates hardship for members of minority groups, so named not only because they are few but because they are relatively powerless.

Other measures of racial prejudice are based on social psychological principles. The Modern Racism Scale (MRS) was designed in the 1980s as another way of indirectly tapping into respondents' prejudices about various ethnic groups (McConahay, 1986; McConahay et al., 1981). As a consequence of legal and social changes brought about by the civil rights movement in the US, some people assumed—based on the growing rejection of overt discrimination—that racist attitudes were declining. The MRS, developed along with other scales to test this assumption, shows that although adherence to explicitly racist notions (such as support for segregation or slavery) is considered socially unacceptable by almost everyone, racial ambivalence and prejudice persist in more subtle forms.

For example, so-called **aversive racists** sympathize with the victims of past injustice; support public policies that, in principle, promote racial equality and reduce the harm of racism; identify more generally with a liberal political agenda; and view themselves as non-prejudiced and non-discriminatory. However, they still harbour negative feelings about the members of other races: 'The negative affect that aversive racists have for blacks is not hostility or hate. Instead, this negativity involves discomfort, uneasiness, disgust, and sometimes fear, which tend to motivate avoidance rather than intentionally destructive behaviours' (Gaertner and Dovidio, 2000: 289–90).

More recently, researchers have developed the Implicit Association Test (IAT) as a cognitive measure of racial bias (Greenwald et al., 1998). In this procedure, two types of test stimuli are displayed in rapid succession on a computer screen—photographs of the faces of blacks and whites posed with neutral facial expressions, and positive and negative words, such as 'peace' and 'happy' or 'nasty' and 'failure'. Subjects are asked to quickly group each stimulus object into one of two headings, which are either consistent (i.e., 'black faces/negative words' and 'white faces/positive words') or inconsistent (i.e., 'black faces/positive words' and 'white faces/negative words') with popular racial stereotypes. A fast response is interpreted as an indication of a stronger mental association between the stimulus object and the category heading, and hence an implicit cognitive bias. That is, according to the test, racial prejudice may be signalled by a faster response time in assigning a photograph of a black person to the 'black faces/negative words' category than to the 'black faces/positive words' category, or conversely, by a faster response time in assigning a negative word to the 'black faces/negative words' category than to the 'white faces/negative words' category.

Although the IAT has gained a large following (and its fair share of media attention) in a relatively short time, it has also attracted much criticism from other academic circles (e.g., Arkes and Tetlock, 2004; Rothermund and Wentura, 2004; Ottaway et al., 2001). It remains a controversial measurement tool.

Racialization

Racism is the everyday outcome of a historic process called **racialization**, the tendency in a community to introduce racial distinctions into situations that can be understood and managed without such distinctions. Thus, race becomes a substitute for distinctions that otherwise would be based on class, education, age, or job experience, for example. In this way, race sometimes becomes the basis for decisions about hiring, purchasing, renting, befriending, and respecting others. Such changes of practice in the direction of racialization can happen easily unless people take pains to avoid them.

Racialization is common in a wide variety of situations. For example, sports commentators may praise a black athlete for his 'natural athletic ability' but praise a white athlete, under similar circumstances, for his 'determination', 'work ethic', 'intelligence', or 'extra effort'. Though both statements convey positive sentiments and may both be well intentioned, the praise of 'natural ability' plays to a traditional stereotype of blacks as being physically strong but mentally weak, gifted in physical areas (e.g., sports, sex) but not industrious or dedicated. In this way, the practice of racializing sports commentary—however unconscious—reveals deep and persistent racial prejudices.

In the police and judicial systems, racial profiling—a tendency to anticipate and interpret the acts of individuals differently on the basis of their race—can easily replace fair treatment. Police may pull over cars driven by young black or Aboriginal men but not by young white men in the expectation of finding alcohol, drugs, weapons, or other grounds for arrest there. Some evidence of this practice is reported by the Commission on Systemic Racism in the Ontario Criminal Justice System (1995) (see also Box 4.4 on a recent study of racial profiling conducted by the Kingston, Ontario, police force). Evidence also indicates that the US government practises racial profiling against dark-skinned men at its borders in the anticipation of finding Islamic terrorists in transit.

We can imagine various reasons why race, racism, and racialization have persisted. Ignorance and childhood learning are important reasons. Structured social inequality that pits one racial community against another is another reason—especially when two or more communities are in active conflict. A related reason is the absence of clearly understood national and ethnic distinctions. Americans in particular are poorly informed about other societies and cultures. They tend, therefore, to have trouble distinguishing between different kinds of Latin Americans, Africans, Asians, or Europeans. They have little understanding of the traditional rivalries, for example, between blacks

**Box 4.4   Social Policy: Racial Profiling in Canada?
A Case Study in Kingston, Ontario**

In October 2003, the Kingston, Ontario, police force voluntarily began to participate in what was later billed as the first racial profiling study of its kind in Canada. For one year, whenever a civilian was stopped and questioned by police, officers recorded the person's age, gender, and race in addition to standard information about the reason for the stop and the outcome of the incident. These data were then compared by researchers against Kingston's racial composition, as provided by the 2001 census.

The results were damning. Despite comprising only 0.6 per cent of the city's population, blacks accounted for 2.2 per cent of all stops. Even after controlling for age, gender, non-residents, and individuals with multiple stops, blacks were 3.7 times more likely to be stopped by police than any other members of the community. Disparities were particularly high for black males aged 15–24. Although the researchers stopped short of claiming proof that racial profiling was at play, they concluded that 'race may be an issue in police decision-making and [the study] documents the need for future research and monitoring.'

As a consequence of this study, and the frenzied media coverage following its publication, the Kingston police force implemented a new anti-racial profiling strategy, which included the continued recording of race data (to allow for follow-up analysis), diversity training for officers, and community outreach initiatives to bridge the gap between law enforcement and minorities in Kingston.

Sources: Wortley and Marshall (2005); Smith (2003).

from Jamaica and those from Barbados, or between blacks from the West Indies and those from the United States, or between blacks from Africa and blacks from the United Kingdom—though the differences and rivalries between these groups are real enough to blacks themselves.

The American belief in their society as a 'melting pot' has a tendency to blur national, ethnic, or cultural distinctions—not to mention class, educational, or other distinctions that exist within racial groups—and to exaggerate the magnitude of distinctiveness between racial groups. This has produced a kind of racialization based on ignorance more than on fear, and fosters an indifference to the consequences for those who are treated in this way. Finally, racialization is often convenient and advantageous to people in the lower middle of the status and class hierarchy—people who, because they have little, jealously guard what they have to maintain their own self-esteem. For those at the upper end of the class and status system, racialization provides an excuse, however invalid, for keeping down the price of labour.

The Social Exclusion of Minority Groups

The perception of social distance between groups produces the social exclusion of minorities. Selective ethnic and racial inclusion by the majority group only emphasizes the larger-scale exclusion. Inclusion usually implies exclusion, because inclusion is not total and homogeneous, but rather implies the creation and defence of group boundaries by one group against another.

We are all familiar with processes of exclusion and inclusion from our school days as children, when we had personal experience with cliques. Few escape childhood without becoming a member of a **clique** or feeling left out of—excluded from—a clique. And few forget the people who led the cliques that included or excluded them.

Exclusion is common in social life, but it is not something that people do all the time, since people are often sociable and co-operative. On the contrary, exclusion usually develops in situations in which one group wants to defend its social status or resources against others. Leaders play a key role in this process. In any clique, the leader is the most powerful or popular member and rules the other members through strategies of information control, threat, and shame. Leaders prey on the weaknesses of clique members and their need for belonging and admiration.

At the opposite end of the social continuum is 'the stranger', a person who belongs to no clique and is actively included in no community. According to Georg Simmel (1964 [1905]), a stranger is a person who physically exists within a community and may even affect the life of the group but who is not given social standing by 'natives' as one of the 'in' group. Insiders decide that the stranger is 'not one of us', a notion that may be justified in terms of different nationality, race, or culture. Strangers, for better or worse, are rootless and free to come and go. Because of their marginality, social distance, and mobility, strangers are free to accept or reject local values and conventions. As outsiders, strangers can be agents of change. For these reasons, they often meet with surprising openness and confidences. Such 'marginal' people enjoy certain freedoms denied to the native-born yet are also denied the right to participate that other community members enjoy.

Consider the Jewish peddler of 100 years ago. A young Jewish immigrant might have saved up to buy a cardboard suitcase, which he stocked with cloth, ribbons, small items of clothing, and kitchen items, and left Toronto to travel on foot for weeks at a time, to small rural communities where people rarely visited shops and where they never before had met Jews. The peddler would bring them what they needed, perhaps what they had ordered on an earlier visit. He was useful and necessary, but a stranger nonetheless. Were he to die of pneumonia after one of his trips, would he be missed?

Often, strangers are feared. That is because strangers are less well known and therefore less predictable, and because they are less connected to friends and relatives and therefore less controllable. By Simmel's definition, the 'stranger' or 'outsider' occupies a structural position in a community that arises from social marginality and lack of information-sharing. Put differently, anyone who is out of the information loop—for whatever reason—is effectively a stranger and, potentially, an enemy.

The rhetoric of inclusion and exclusion emphasizes the distinctiveness of insiders and of strangers. Differences in cultural identity, traditions, and heritage raise anxieties (Stolcke, 1999). Fears grow especially at times of increased immigration, unemployment, crime, xenophobia and insecurity, and depleted state resources for social services (Fontana, 1997). At times like these, we tend to see people as 'others' and build barriers against them when we feel they are competing with us for scarce resources. Through much of Canada's history, immigrants were shunned, tolerated only because we needed their labour. In times of distress, it was common to attack and exclude immigrants. Such was the experience of South Asians and Chinese in BC early in the twentieth century, of German Canadians during two world wars, and, perhaps most especially, of Japanese Canadians whose property was seized and who were sent to internment camps during

World War II. Since 'terrorism' became a watchword of the early twenty-first century, Muslims have become a target of those who fear difference in their midst.

Of course, even the appearance of competition and scarcity because of immigration, race, or ethnicity can be a social construction. A question of interest to sociologists, then, is: What are the social conditions that make race or ethnicity a basis for isolating and excluding others? How (and when and why) do people define some people as 'others', who are viewed as unlike themselves in significant ways? Answering this question brings us to a discussion of nationalism, which is to ethnicity as self-congratulation is to cliques.

Expressions of Racial Prejudice and Discrimination

The social problems associated with racial and ethnic conflict include prejudice and discrimination. As Allport (1954) noted, people act out their prejudices with varying degrees of intensity. At the most benign level is **antilocution**, the sharing of prejudiced beliefs among like-minded friends. Less benign is prejudice that shows itself in the *avoidance* of a disliked group. Even stronger prejudice produces *discrimination*, which involves active attempts to dominate the minority. Discriminatory actions can involve exclusion of the minority group from jobs, education, housing, and even political rights. Discrimination based on racial or ethnic prejudice, when left to fester, can grow into racial hate crimes, beginning with *physical attacks* such as the desecration of religious buildings and graveyards. Lastly, the 'ultimate degree of violent expression of prejudice', according to Allport, is extermination—including lynchings, pogroms, and genocides.

Hate crimes are among the most shocking signs of racism and ethnic intolerance. In a pilot study conducted between 2001 and 2002, 12 police forces of major Canadian cities reported 926 hate crimes motivated by race, ethnicity, or religion. Just under half of these incidents involved threats of violence; 34 per cent involved physical force; and 17 per cent involved the use of a weapon (Statistics Canada, 2004). Still, these statistics underestimate the true extent of the problem, since hate crimes have not been systematically reported on a national scale. Often, victims fail to report hate crimes to the police, choosing instead to deal with the physical and psychological costs on their own. The psychological costs to those victimized include fear, anger, and feelings of inferiority.

Conflict-laden relations between competing racial, ethnic, and tribal groups sometimes spill over into mass conflicts such as genocides and civil war, many instances of which can be found throughout human history. For example, in *Shake Hands with the Devil* (2003), Canadian Lieutenant-General Roméo Dallaire, the Force Commander of the ill-fated United Nations Assistance Mission for Rwanda (UNAMIR), recounts his witnessing of the massacre of more than 900,000 Rwandan Tutsis and Hutu moderates over 100 days in 1993 at the hands of extremist Hutus (see also Chapter 12 on warfare). Many of these conflicts are fought in the name of ethnic nationalism. However, some political theorists have said that many so-called 'ethnic wars' are misnamed, since the root causes of these conflicts are unjust institutional, economic, and political conditions rather than ethnic or tribal membership alone (Bowen, 1996). This distinction is important: by characterizing a conflict as being due to ethnic hatred alone is to imply that the groups in question are stuck in an unthinking primordial and never-ending blood feud. The more complex reality may be that systemic political and economic inequalities—which are subject to intervention and change—are the true basis for the violence.

Consider again the Hutu and Tutsi 'tribes', the present differences between whom are primarily economic rather than ethnic or genetic. Historically, what separated them was that the Tutsi were cattle-herders, which brought them economic superiority, while the Hutus were primarily agricultural peasants. When Belgian colonial administrators arrived in the region in the nineteenth century, they held a census and deemed anyone who owned 10 or more cows a Tutsi, while all farmers were deemed Hutus. ID cards were issued, and 'tribal memberships' were thus manufactured from this arbitrary distinction. Indeed, so fluid were the categories that a Hutu could become a Tutsi if he were able to acquire the required number of cattle. Given this fact, it is doubtful whether the recent conflicts between the two groups can still be considered to have an ethnic basis.

Social Consequences of Race and Ethnic Relations

Ethnic tensions and racial discrimination are associated with many adverse social consequences for their victims. In this section, we provide an overview of some of these problems.

Gender

The interaction of gender and racism leads to unique problems for women of some minority groups. Women continue to be consigned to a lesser status within almost all immigrant groups. However, in some cultures women face a higher degree of oppression than in others. Not only is this oppression a problem in itself, but it also creates further conflict when new immigrants find their notions of proper gender relations clashing with the gradually changing gender concepts in North America.

In some groups in which men dominate, for example, women are more exposed to health risks such as HIV/AIDS. A continued rise of HIV infection in the US Latina population underscores the failure of current preventive programs that target Latinas. Merely teaching the women sexual assertiveness is not enough. The spread of HIV is driven by a machismo subcultural dynamic that limits a woman's ability to demand safer (that is, contraceptive) sex from her partner (Gil, 1998–9).

Having to deal with unconcealed racism in the workplace and in society on a daily basis is hard enough. Having to deal with the constant sexism of a patriarchal social structure may be too hard an obstacle for many ethnic minority women to overcome. In particular, new immigrant women who belong to paternalistic cultures may find themselves isolated socially and linguistically at the same time as they are economically dependent on their husbands. These issues will be further detailed in Chapter 5 on gender and sexism.

Work and Unemployment

As we have already noted, discrimination in the workplace is often directed along racial and ethnic lines (see Table 4.2 and Figure 4.3). Aboriginal people, members of visible minority groups, and recent immigrants to Canada all experience lower employment and pay rates in almost every region of Canada. Aboriginal people in Canada are less likely than other Canadians to attend college or to finish a college degree (Johnson and

Table 4.2 Major Occupational Groups of Immigrants before and after Arriving in Canada, 2001

Occupation Group	Before Arriving	After Arriving
Management occupations	20.7	7.0
Occupations in business, finance, and administration	33.4	27.7
Natural and applied sciences and related occupations	55.4	25.6
Health occupations	13.5	6.0
Occupations in social science, education, government service, and religion	24.9	11.0
Occupations in art, culture, and recreation and sport	5.6	2.8
Sales and service occupations	22.3	62.2
Trades, transport and equipment operators, and related occupations	10.6	13.1
Occupations unique to primary industry	4.9	4.4
Occupations unique to processing, manufacturing, and utilities	8.5	40.2

Source: Adapted from Statistics Canada (2003). Available at: http://www.statcan.ca/english/ freepub/89-611-XIE/89-611-XIE2003001.pdf.

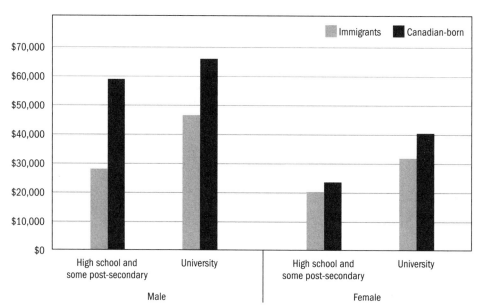

FIGURE 4.3 Average Annual Earnings of Immigrants and Canadian-born, Ages 25–54, by Highest Level of Schooling, 2000

Note: Immigrants are those who arrived in Canada from 1990 through 1999. Statistics Canada data included only those with education beyond high school.

Source: Adapted from Statistics Canada website: http://www12.statcan.ca/english/census01/Products/ Analytic/companion/earn/tables/canada/earnimm.cfm

Boehm, 1995). Differences in income between various immigrant and ethnic minorities also result from differences in human capital, such as education, experience, credentials, and scarce expertise (Rodlandt, 1996).

According to the Canadian Council on Social Development (CCSD, 2000), visible minorities continue to fall behind in employment and income levels despite their high educational attainment when compared to non-racialized groups. Foreign-born visible minorities experience even greater discrepancies between their education levels and their occupations than do other groups. Less than half of foreign-born visible minorities with a university degree work in jobs with a high skill level, especially during difficult economic times.

Many recent immigrants find that their educational and work credentials are not recognized in the Canadian employment system. They are forced into jobs that are below their level of training and expertise. In a longitudinal survey, it was found that six out of 10 immigrants to Canada did not work in the same field after their arrival (Statistics Canada, 2003). Reitz (1998) shows that four factors affect the entry-level job status of immigrants: (1) the specificity of skills required by the nation's immigration policy; (2) the educational competition experienced between immigrants and the native-born; (3) the labour market structure; and (4) the welfare state.

Race continues to play a role in people's work experiences. As one survey participant mentioned in an interview conducted by the CCSD:

> I've called about jobs and had people say 'come down for an interview', yet when I get there, I get the feeling they are surprised to see that I'm black because I sound like the average guy on the telephone. They've said 'Oh, the job has just been filled', or during the interview they'll say that I'm overqualified or ask me questions like 'Are you sure you want to work at this type of job?' (CCSD, 2000)

Frances Henry and Effie Ginzberg (1985; Henry, 1999) graphically showed such processes in operation in Toronto. In a first set of field experiments conducted in the mid-1980s, Henry and Ginzberg sent two job applicants (actually research confederates), matched with respect to age, sex, education, experience, style of dress, and personality, to apply for the same advertised job. The applicants differed in only one respect—one was white and the other black. Teams of applicants sought a total of 201 jobs in this way. Some applicants were young male or female students applying for semi-skilled or unskilled jobs—waitress, gas station attendant, busboy, or store clerk—that people might expect them to seek. Other applicants were middle-aged professional actors. Supplied with fake resumés, they applied for positions in retail management, sales jobs in prestigious stores, and serving and hosting jobs in fancy restaurants.

In a second set of experiments, the researchers asked their confederates to call 237 telephone numbers published in the classified job section of the newspaper and present themselves as applicants. The jobs they were seeking ranged widely from unskilled to highly skilled, well-paying jobs. Henry and Ginzberg report that callers phoned each number four times, using different voices. One voice had no apparent accent (it sounded like a white-majority Canadian), the second had a Slavic or Italian accent, the third had a Jamaican accent, and the fourth had a Pakistani accent. Men who did the calling (no women took part in this study) presented themselves as having the same

Income Rates of Recent Immigrants
The low-income rate among recent immigrants (living in Canada less than five years) is on the rise, even among the highly educated.

- All recent immigrants:
  - 1980: 24.6%
  - 1990: 31.3%
  - 2000: 35.8%
- Those with university degrees (ages 25-65):
  - 1980: 14.5%
  - 1990: 19.1%
  - 2000: 27.5%

Source: Picot and Hou (2003).

characteristics: the same age, education, years of job experience, and so on. As before, the applicants were suited in age and (imaginary) experience for the jobs they were seeking.

With data collected in this way, the researchers created an Index of Discrimination that combined the results of in-person and telephone testing. They found that in 20 calls, black applicants would be offered 13 interviews yielding one job. By contrast, in 20 calls, white applicants would be offered 17 interviews yielding three jobs. 'The overall Index of Discrimination is therefore three to one. Whites have three job prospects to every one that blacks have' (Henry and Ginzberg, 1985: 308).

This study and others like it (e.g., Beck et al., 2002; Austin and Este, 2001) prove that racial discrimination is not a result of the behaviour of a very few bigoted employers. These experiences are common. Also, even after members of minority groups find suitable employment, they are sometimes faced with discrimination when competing for promotions. Compared to non-visible minorities, members of visible racial groups and Aboriginal people with a university degree are less likely to enter managerial or professional positions. For those who do, more than half are self-employed, compared to only one-third in non-minority groups.

Poverty and Wealth

Although most of the people who live in poverty in Canada and the United States are white, higher proportions of minority groups are impoverished. As we said in Chapter 1, immigrants and visible minorities are over-represented in low-income groups, earning thousands of dollars less than the average income. In Canada, Aboriginal people and foreign-born visible minorities are over-represented at the bottom of the income scale, while other Canadian-born non-racialized groups are under-represented (cf. Gee and Prus, 2000; Hou and Balakrishnan, 1996). Among the top 20 per cent of income earners, the positions are reversed: Aboriginal people and visible minorities are under-represented among top earners and non-visible (ethnic) minorities are over-represented. It has been estimated that foreign-born visible minorities aged 35–44 earn only 79 cents for every dollar that a Canadian-born white individual earns. Similarly, wealthy Canadians are disproportionately members of non-visible minorities.

Social exclusion can also take the form of geographic segregation. Although less advanced than in the US, ethnic segregation is underway even in Canada. In 1981, only three visible minority neighbourhoods—defined as census tracts in which at least 30 per cent of the population belongs to a single visible minority group—were identified in Montreal, Vancouver, and Toronto. According to a recent Statistics Canada report, by 2001 this number had risen to 254. These communities are more likely than average to feature low household incomes and high rates of unemployment. Increasing segregation is confirmed by the 'isolation index', which measures the extent to which minority group members encounter only one another within their neighbourhoods (Hu and Picot, 2004). This index shows that, over time, the concentration of ethnic minorities has steadily increased. Many are concerned that, without policy interventions, the level of segregation will continue to rise to a dangerous level.

Much Canadian and international literature has shown that living in a poor neighbourhood increases exposure to crime, drugs, and other unhealthy environmental factors (e.g., Massey and Denton, 1993). For young males especially, a chronic lack of economic and life opportunities, combined with unrelenting social exclusion, can produce a sense of frustration that can boil over into violence. On 27 October 2005, a group of 10 high school teenagers were playing football in the Paris, France, suburb of Clichy-sous-Bois. The teenagers allegedly ran and hid when police officers arrived to check their identities. Thinking they were being chased by the police, three of the teens climbed a wall to hide in a power substation. Two of them—a 15-year-old of Malian background and a 17-year-old of Tunisian origin—were electrocuted by a transformer in the electric substation. The third, aged 17, whose parents are Turkish Kurds, was injured and hospitalized. A friend of the three remarked that Clichy-sous-Bois 'has three principal communities, the Arabs, the Turks and the blacks. The three victims represented each one a community.' The riots that ensued during the fall of 2005 centred on the three teens' neighbourhood—public housing complexes in Clichy-sous-Bois and nearby suburbs—and were perpetrated by young men similarly living at the economic margins of French society.

In Canada and elsewhere, the junction of ethnicity and poverty invariably raises the issue of Aboriginal populations. Unlike those in developing and less developed countries, people whose experience has been internal colonization, that is, indigenous peoples living in developed nations, cannot escape from imperial power because they are located within the boundaries of the imperialist nation. Therefore, indigenous people must either obtain equal access to the political and economic opportunities of the surrounding society or continue to struggle for political autonomy (Russell, 1996). As in many less industrialized societies, among Aboriginal people in recent years income inequality has increased, even more than among the non-Aboriginal population. As well, inequalities have increased between different Aboriginal groups. In terms of intra-Aboriginal inequality, Aboriginal groups rank from Inuit at the high end through status Indians to non-status Indians and, finally, to Métis (Maxim et al., 2001). Such a crude ordering of inequality misses the point, however—Inuit suicide rates are among the highest in the world, and the relative wealth or poverty of particular Aboriginal groups or First Nations depends to a great extent on whether a land claim has been successfully achieved and on the natural resource base of the people's reserve or claim area. In addition, such relative measurement of poverty is based on a Western, non-Aboriginal standard of individual material wealth, not on an Aboriginal understanding of community health and well-being.

Crime and Violence

As we saw in Chapter 2, blacks and Aboriginal people are over-represented in the criminal justice system, as perpetrators and as victims. In Canada, attention has been paid in the last several decades to the excessive numbers of Aboriginal people and blacks arrested and convicted for breaking the law. Explanations of this include unemployment, poverty, and substance abuse. There is also evidence of discrimination at the bail and sentencing stages (Roberts and Doob, 1997). Further, evidence suggests that law enforcement officers may racialize and stereotype ethnic minorities, particularly when dealing with street gangs (Symons, 1999).

Although Aboriginal adults make up only 2 per cent of the Canadian population, they represented 15 per cent of all the people sentenced to provincial custody and 17 per cent of those sent to federal penitentiaries in 1997–8 (Reed and Roberts, 1999; see also Frideres and Robertson, 1994). In the United States, although blacks account for only 13 per cent of the population, they represent 30 per cent of those people arrested and roughly half of those incarcerated in a state or federal penitentiaries. Aboriginal rates of violent victimization are higher than those for non-Aboriginal people because of their disadvantaged status (Weinrath, 1999). A study carried out in Australia, on Aborigine deaths in custody, likewise concludes that unemployment, poverty, poor health, homelessness, and disenfranchisement are the causes of over-representation at all stages of the criminal process (Broadhurst, 1996).

In short, disadvantage and poverty increase the likelihood of law-breaking by racial and ethnic minorities, while prejudice and discrimination increase the likelihood of arrest, conviction, and imprisonment.

Other Problems

Nowhere in North America are the problems resulting from exclusion, discrimination, and prejudice more evident than among the Aboriginal peoples. Severe socio-economic distress experienced by many Aboriginal families has led to serious social problems among adolescents, including substance abuse, school dropout, psychological problems, suicide, and violence (Beauvais, 2000).

Substance abuse is a major problem among Canada's Aboriginal people. Gasoline is the most common inhalant used, often accompanied by alcohol and drug abuse (Coleman et al., 2001). Similar problems are found among the indigenous peoples of the North in the former Soviet Union; even under Soviet rule, poverty, unemployment, and health problems, including alcoholism, suicide, high rates of infant mortality, and shortened life expectancy, were common (Ruttkay-Miklián, 2001) (see also Figure 4.4).

Homeless Aboriginal people of both genders—who have moved to urban areas from reserves and other rural locations in search of work or simply to escape their impoverished home environment—come from a variety of locales and represent a range

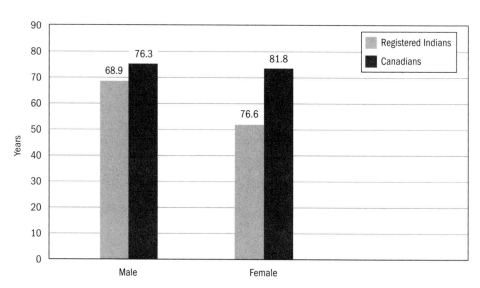

FIGURE 4.4 Life Expectancy of Registered Indians vs Other Canadians, 2000

Source: DIAND (2002). Source: 'Projected Life Expectancy at Birth by Gender, Registered Indian Population and Canadian Population, 1975-2016' Figure 2.1 in *Basic Departmental Data 2001*. Indian and Northern Affairs Canada. 2002. http://www.ainc-inac.gc.ca/pr/sts/bdd01/bdd01_e.pdf. *Reproduced with the permission of the Minister of Public Works and Government Services, 2006*. Adapted in part from Statistics Canada, 'Population Projections for Canada, Provinces and Territories', 2000 to 2026, Catalogue 91-520.

of ages. They may be without housing as the result of discriminatory treatment by land-lords and may feel culturally isolated from conventional services for the homeless. The resultant traumas associated with inadequate housing, both physical and emotional, may not be adequately met by standard intervention, i.e., they may have some distinctive needs, such as traditional healing techniques (Klos, 1997).

One analyst characterizes this as the historical trauma response—a collection of characteristics resulting from a huge group trauma accumulated over generations, similar to what is found among Jewish Holocaust survivors and their descendants. Trauma responses include higher-than-average mortality rates and health problems due to heart disease, hypertension, alcohol abuse, and suicidal behaviour. In the United States, an analysis of the Lakota (Teton Sioux) finds evidence of more men than women suffering trauma over the life course (Brave Heart, 1999).

Health Consequences

Effects of Disadvantage

Disadvantaged groups lead different lives from the rest of the population. So, for example, in Canada, though regional inequalities in health status are diminishing, the life expectancy of Aboriginal Canadians is still significantly shorter than that of other groups, as shown in Figure 4.4 (D'Arcy, 1998; see also Waldram et al., 1996). Similarly, in the US, Native Americans' lives are marked by long periods of chronic illness, and, of all racial groups, American blacks live the fewest years and they live a higher proportion of those years with chronic health problems (Hayward and Heron, 1999).

Studies of race and ethnicity as determinants of health have led to three different types of explanations: biological explanations that attribute differences in disease prevalence to genetic differences; cultural explanations that link differences in disease prevalence to cultural factors (such as diet); and socio-economic explanations that focus on the association between poor health, minority status, and economic disadvantage (Spencer, 1996). However, the link between poor health and material advantage is clear (Farmer and Ferraro, 1999; Fenton et al., 1995), and many of the health problems of ethnic minorities are due to socio-economic status. Accordingly, racial and ethnic differences in physical and mental health shrink significantly when we control for education and other factors related to income (Williams et al., 1997).

The current mortality conditions of Canadian Aboriginal people, American Indians, and New Zealand Maori reflect, in varying degrees, all of the problems associated with poverty, marginalization, and social disorganization. Of these three minority groups, Canadian Aboriginal people suffer most from these types of conditions and the Maori suffer least (Trovato, 2001). These differences can be explained, at least in part, by the greater isolation from economic opportunity of many Canadian Native peoples in northern communities, as well as by the fact that the Maori are constitutionally empowered and thus have a voice in the political mainstream.

Effects of Immigration

Institutional racism creates economic hardships with bad health consequences. Chiefly, racial and ethnic discrimination in the workplace forces many visible minority members into low-paying jobs, unemployment, and poverty. Though Canadian research has found that neither the health status of immigrants nor their use of health services differs much from those of the Canadian-born population (Laroche, 2000), immigration can have harmful health effects over and above the effects of poverty and discrimination. In fact, on arriving in North America, new immigrants typically have better health than the host population, largely due to strict immigration selection criteria. Within a generation or two, however, this health advantage disappears for many ethnic minorities, and some groups even experience worse health status than the native-born.

Immigrants often find employment in manual labour or unskilled work, as we noted earlier. In these low-paying jobs, they are often exposed to higher-than-average health risks. Second, immigrants often experience a lack of access to health-care information and services. Sometimes they hesitate to use health services because of a low level of English- or French-language literacy; for example, an elderly immigrant who does not speak English finds it difficult to communicate with English-speaking doctors.

Problems with their personal lives may also have health consequences for immigrants. For example, 80 per cent of refugees to Quebec from Africa and Latin America had experienced or were experiencing separations (averaging three years) from their partners and/or children (Moreau et al., 1999). Such separations, often associated with traumatic events, can cause emotional distress and hinder the process of adapting to a new country. In addition, immigrants may suffer from loneliness, boredom, and post-migration anxieties about discrimination. Asylum seekers may also suffer from pre-migration trauma, immigration difficulties, and racial discrimination, which together give rise to post-traumatic stress disorder (Allotey, 1998; Silove et al., 1997). People who have been displaced by war are even worse off than people who are impoverished, for they suffer over and above their material disadvantage. The trauma of displacement often results in fear, disorientation, and distrust—conditions that are not easily relieved (Segura Escobar, 2000).

Access to Health Care

Research indicates that, on the whole, Canadian immigrants, visible minorities, and Aboriginal populations are able to access adequate general care to meet their overall health needs (e.g., Quan et al., 2006; Wardman et al., 2005; Wu et al., 2005; Wen et al., 1996). However, these same studies also find evidence of systemic barriers in accessing specialized health-care services, such as surgery, emergency room visits, and dental care. Obstacles include a lack of knowledge about where to find appropriate assistance, language barriers between medical staff and patients, concerns about encountering institutional racial discrimination, and in the case of rural Aboriginal communities, a shortage of physicians, nurses, and facilities. Researchers have called upon governments and health-care practitioners to address these systemic barriers, for example, by ensuring availability of language interpreters in health-care settings (Tang, 1999).

Another issue pertains to cultural sensitivity of health-care professionals towards their patients. Different cultures have different views about health and illness. Indeed, they even have different beliefs about diet, personal hygiene, body alterations (body piercing, cosmetic surgery, tattooing, obesity, slimness), use of drugs (tea, coffee, alcohol, hallucinogens), and the use of non-traditional medical practitioners (Nakamura, 1999). As a result, every culture provides its members with a culturally relevant diagnosis or cause and a framework for appropriate intervention. Ethnic group members living in a Western culture often find that non-Western health-care alternatives are scarce or lacking. So, when forced to seek help from the only available caregiver—the modern hospital—they approach the experience with a worry and doubt that can only worsen the effects of the illness.

The Importance of Communication

Good communication plays an important role in ensuring good access to treatment. For cultural reasons, minority patients are much more likely to report having a minority physician as their regular doctor, especially when they regularly speak a language other than English (Gray and Stoddard, 1997; see also Callan and Littlewood, 1998; LaVeist et al., 2000). The results of matching for cultural similarity are impressive. In one study, ethnically matched therapists judged their clients to have higher mental health functioning than did mismatched therapists (Russell et al., 1996). In another study, when clients were matched with an ethnically similar clinician who was also proficient in the client's preferred language, they had fewer emergency service visits than did unmatched clients (Snowden et al., 1995). These results can be interpreted in two ways. First, therapists are more likely to underestimate the mental health of patients from another culture. Second, patients are likely to get better treatment and require fewer emergency visits if their doctor is from their own culture. These results, though different, are compatible; both point to the health disadvantage suffered by minority groups.

Some minority populations are particularly vulnerable. For example, Canada's ethnic elderly who speak neither English nor French are isolated from the mainstream of Canadian society. Serious communication problems with this group in the delivery of social and health services can lead to poor treatment, extended hospital stays, unnecessary testing, premature discharge, and problematic follow-up. Besides the language barrier are differences in cultural concepts about health and illness (Saldov, 1991). Ethnic elders from some cultures also go to healers or herbalists from their native culture as well as to Western health providers; this shows the need to better integrate Western and non-Western treatment systems for the elderly (Yeo, 1991).

The Health Effects of Racism

Both racial discrimination and socio-economic discrimination contribute to the poor health of minorities. Some of the effects are obvious: discrimination, by increasing stress, increases the likelihood of psychiatric symptoms and unhealthy addictions, such as cigarette-smoking (Landrine and Klonoff, 1996). To these, one must add the stress-related health consequences of discrimination itself (Krieger et al., 1993). The experiences of racial discrimination and resulting family stress also diminish the well-being of minority people. Other factors, such as alienation, poverty, inequality at work, and worries about unemployment, all contribute to the poor health of minority people. Shelly Harrell (2000: 45–6) has identified six sources of racism-related stress:

1. acute, intense, but relatively infrequent 'racism-related life events', such as being harassed by the police or discriminated against in the workplace;
2. 'vicarious racism experiences', including the transmission of specific incidents of prejudice and discrimination experienced by family members and friends, or through the news media;

3. 'daily racism micro-stressors', which are subtle and frequent reminders of one's racially and/or ethnically linked subordinate status in society, such as being ignored or overly scrutinized by sales staff;

4. 'chronic contextual stress', which arises from the need to adapt to the broad racial and ethnic inequalities in social structure, institutions, political systems, and resource distribution;

5. 'collective experiences', which reflect 'the idea that cultural-symbolic and sociopolitical manifestations of racism can be observed and felt by individuals' and which include the 'economic conditions of members of one's racial/ethnic group, the lack of political representation, or stereotypic portrayals in the media'; and

6. 'transgenerational transmission', or the historical context in which modern racial and ethnic discrimination has been bred and maintained, such as the removal of indigenous peoples from their lands throughout North America, African slavery in the United States, the internment of Japanese Canadians during World War II, and the experiences of current refugees.

The health outcomes of racism-related stress can be severe. Several researchers have found, for instance, that the resentment and distrust bred by racial victimization can raise a person's blood pressure and put other stress on the cardiovascular system (Franklin, 1998; Williams, 1999). David Rollock and Edmund Gordon (2000: 6) have also shown that 'racism can erode the mental health status of individual victims and dominate the institutional and cultural mechanisms through which it operates.' Merridy Malin (2000: 5) cites several studies showing how 'racism that is internalized by the victim can negatively impact on an individual's sense of ambition, self-assertion, [and] erosion of sense of self and can lead to depression, anxiety, substance abuse, and chronic physical health problems.'

Solutions to Problems of Prejudice and Racism

Multicultural Education

One of the means of overcoming racial discrimination is the educational system. Schools are important sources of socialization and provide their students with socially approved belief, value, and ideological systems. Informal socialization also takes place at school, since school gives most students their first big opportunity to interact with other people of the same age and interests.

The mixing of Canada's diverse young people at school leads to more interracial friendships and relationships, increases exposure to and acceptance of other cultural practices, and makes skin colour less of an issue in social life. However, the educational curriculum remains highly Eurocentric, putting an undue emphasis on Western European concepts, events, and ideas (see, e.g., Henry and Tator, 1994; McNaughton, 1990). Though an important part of a complete education, this material—when delivered at the exclusion of non-Western ideas and histories—can no longer speak meaningfully to a population with Canada's racial and ethnic diversity. Introducing more multicultural content into standard provincial curricula, beginning at the primary school level, may not only broaden all students' cultural knowledge, but also better engage those students who recognize little of their own heritage in classroom lessons and thus feel disconnected from the education institution (Dei, 1997).

Governmental and Organizational Intervention

The Employment Equity Act, passed in 1986, applies to the federal public service, Crown corporations and agencies, and private companies employing 100 employees or more, and it is intended to ensure that the proportion of visible minorities, Aboriginal people, women, and people with disabilities hired in the workplace reflects the proportion of these groups who are applying for work. To ensure that hiring practices are equitable, employers are obliged to submit annual reports on their employees to the federal government. Data from these reports are then summarized and made public.

As well, employers are obliged to identify and to make an effort to eliminate the barriers facing members of under-represented groups by planning initiatives to increase their representation. Employment equity is intended to tackle what many sociologists believe to be the cause of racial and ethnic inequality, that is, structural barriers erected by the dominant majority to support their advantage.

The Multiculturalism Act of 1988 made Canada the world's first officially multicultural nation. It also required all federal institutions and employers to act in accordance with the country's stated belief in the value of racial and ethnic diversity when making their economic, social, cultural, and political policies. In large part, this effort has succeeded. UNESCO (the United Nations Educational, Scientific and Cultural Organization) has cited Canada's approach to multiculturalism as the ideal model to be followed by other countries.

Canada's Charter of Rights and Freedoms (s. 15[1]) declares that 'Every individual is equal before and under the law and has the right to the equal protection and equal benefit of the law without discrimination and, in particular, without discrimination based on race, national or ethnic origin, colour, religion, sex, age or mental or physical disability.' In addition, the Criminal Code provides for strict enforcement against racist acts known as 'hate crimes'. However, to be meaningful, these commitments must be supported by sustained efforts to protect the rights of all ethnic groups.

Individual Solutions

Again, as is the case for issues studied in other chapters of this book, many of the problems that hinder race and ethnic relations are beyond the efforts of individuals to solve. The problems are structural and require the determined efforts of government, schools, the courts, and other institutions. Such efforts must begin with a widespread recognition that the differences between people—physical, cultural, and so on—are problematic only if they are used to justify prejudiced attitudes and discriminatory behaviour. Laws, strongly enforced, will go a long way towards promoting equality. However, they must build on a popular desire to support racial equality in everyday life.

To solve the problem, all Canadians will have to recognize the harm caused by structural inequality and discrimination. As well, they will have to speak out against inequality or discrimination directed at ourselves or others around us. Of course, there are laws and regulations against discrimination. There are also investigative bodies—the courts, grievance committees in the workplace, and human rights commissions in different provinces—that will pursue the cases of injustice brought to their attention. However, we as citizens must call attention to these problems as we discover them; to do so is our right and our responsibility.

Concluding Remarks

People often try to justify racist beliefs and behaviour by repeating misinformed views about a minority group's physical, psychological, and cultural inferiority. These views rest on a flawed understanding of humanity as a species. Commonly, 'racial groups' are thought to have similar genetic or inherent characteristics. However, research has shown us increasingly that the physical traits by which people are grouped into racial categories are not intrinsic at all; they reflect a particular way of dividing up people that is particular to a time and place. Ethnic groups, similarly, have common cultural traits and believe they are distinct. In different ways, both racial and ethnic groups are 'imagined communities'.

As we have seen, 'prejudice' refers to biased beliefs about individuals based on their presumed membership in a particular racial or ethnic group. Prejudice always starts with stereotyping. Some argue that prejudice is learned through socialization. Others emphasize that prejudice has evident economic benefits. Sometimes it is a practice used as part of a strategy by a dominant group to maintain its dominance.

We are a long way from achieving the society Durkheim imagined a century ago, built on organic solidarity and valuing different kinds of people for the different values, interests, and skills they contribute. Today Canada needs immigrants even more than ever—to make up for declining fertility, provide tomorrow's workers and taxpayers, and link us to other peoples and societies around the world. This means that we are likely to keep grappling with issues of racial and ethnic inequality, and with the topic of immigration, for a very long time. It is in Canada's national interest to solve these issues of inequality as quickly and fairly as possible.

QUESTIONS FOR CRITICAL THOUGHT

1. Can different ethnic groups live together harmoniously without conflict? Use the terms 'cultural mosaic', 'melting pot', and 'multiculturalism' in your answer.
2. Use Georg Simmel's definition of 'the stranger' and briefly outline how this applies to the experience of minority ethnic groups. Discuss with reference to 'otherness'.
3. Elaborate on the notion that perceptions of conflict and competition are social constructions.
4. There is a debate as to whether race should be considered biologically or socially constructed. Discuss the arguments each side would offer; which side would be more likely to justify racial inequality and discrimination.
5. This chapter briefly notes the role that Israel plays with regard to the diasporic Jews. Elaborate on how the Jews have maintained strong ties both to their birthplace and to their 'homeland' throughout history. In your answer, discuss the identity issues likely experienced by diasporic individuals and their children.

RECOMMENDED READINGS

Kay J. Anderson, *Vancouver's Chinatown: Racial Discourse in Canada, 1875–1980* (Montreal and Kingston: McGill-Queens University Press, 1991). This analysis examines how place is related to identity. The author uses government documents and other written evidence (such as letters to the editor) to document the changing role of Vancouver's Chinatown, from a ghetto to a slum to an advertised tourist attraction.

Raymond Breton, Wsevolod W. Isajiw, Warren E. Kalbach, and

Jeffrey G. Reitz, *Ethnic Identity and Equality: Varieties of Experience in a Canadian City* (Toronto: University of Toronto Press, 1990). Focusing on eight ethnic groups in Toronto, this book looks at how ethnicity works as a sustaining factor in Canada's socio-economic system. The book covers identity retention, residential segregation, concentrations in labour markets, and the ethnic group as a political resource.

Donald R. Kinder and Lynn M. Sanders, *Divided by Color: Racial Politics and Democratic Ideals* (Chicago: University of

Chicago Press, 1996). This book considers the historical context of and various arguments for and against affirmative action programs in the US. Using analysis of opinion polls, the authors see indications that a sizable majority of whites feel that enough has been done to redress past discrimination against minorities.

William F. Lewis, *Soul Rebels: The Rastafari* (Prospect Heights, Ill.: Waveland Press, 1993). An overview of Rastafarian culture is offered with specific attention to peasant roots, group heterogeneity, and the possible classification of Rastafarians as an ethnic group based on cultural identity. The Rastafarian world view sees capitalist society as an extension of Babylon. There is also mistrust of money and technology, and a belief in natural living and in the use of marijuana as sacrament.

Anthony H. Richmond, 'Socio-demographic Aspects of Globalization: Canadian Perspectives on Migration', *Canadian Studies in Population* 29, 1 (2002): 123–49. Immigration and emigration trends in Canada are studied in global context. The author constructs a typology of migrants who move for work reasons. Recent concerns over security and border control are debated in terms of human rights.

Julia Roberts, '"A Mixed Assemblage of Persons": Race and Tavern Space in Upper Canada', *Canadian Historical Review* 83, 1 (2002): 1–28. Whites, blacks, and Native people mixed together in public taverns in early Canadian history, but race boundaries were maintained through interactions in taverns in Upper Canada. This paper examines the ways that these boundaries were created.

Ella Shohat and Robert Stam, *Unthinking Eurocentrism: Multiculturalism and the Media* (London and New York: Routledge, 1995). It is suggested here that Eurocentrism perpetuates stereotypes of marginalized people in both Western and non-Western mass media. These are reinforced in the media by casting, linguistic decisions, and audience expectations.

Jace Weaver, *That People Might Live: Native American Literatures and Native American Community* (New York: Oxford University Press, 1997). This book deals with ethnic identity generally and looks at how identity is distinguished not only by blood, but also by both tribal and pan-Aboriginal identity.

RECOMMENDED WEBSITES

World Conference on Racism

www.un.org/WCAR/

The World Conference on Racism website provides a brief backdrop to the events leading up to the 2001 conference in Durban, South Africa. A great deal of information is also available relating to the conference itself and to its media coverage. This important conference was quickly forgotten because it was held just days before 9/11.

Canadian Race Relations Federation

www.crr.ca/EN/default.htm

This website deals with issues of racism in Canada. A number of publications, research reports, and fact sheets are available here. In conjunction with this, the CRRF provides recent news race relations and information on current events and programs.

Citizenship and Immigration Canada

www.cic.gc.ca

This site offers practical information, such as how to get a new passport. Also, it provides information on public policy. There are useful links, too.

GLOSSARY

Antilocution The sharing of prejudiced behaviours among like-minded friends; considered the most benign level of prejudiced attitudes.

Aversive racists Those who often sympathize with the victims of past injustice and support public policies that, in principle, promote racial equality but who, nonetheless, hold negative and prejudicial views towards those of other 'races' and ethnicities although they regard themselves as unprejudiced and undiscriminatory.

Chain migration The successful migration of one family member creates a chain of opportunities for the kin and community network. Migration is not random or disorganized, but is increasingly about networks, rational choices, economic opportunities, sponsorship, and kinship relations. Immigrants today are more likely to keep ties to their ethnic culture and homeland.

Clique A small exclusive group of friends or associates; also, a friendship circle within which members are identical to each other sociometrically and are mutually connected. Cliques are social structures that create and control an exclusive information flow.

Culture The way of life of a society, which includes codes of manners, dress, language, norms of behaviour, foods, tools, folklore, belief systems, etc. Humans are acted on by culture and act back, and so generate new cultural forms and meanings. Thus, this framework of values and practices adapt to the changing historical and regional circumstances.

Diaspora   The dispersal of any group of people, whether forcibly or voluntarily, throughout the world; originally applied to the tribes of Israel. Almost any migrant community with some degree of international linkage is referred to as diasporic.

Entrance status   The status attained when a particular immigrant group first arrives in a receiving country. Because of processes of assimilation laid down by dominant groups, less preferred immigrants enter Canada's labour force in lower-level occupational roles. The low-status groups are then compelled to accept their inferior position and subjection.

Exclusion   The selective ethnic and racial inclusion by a majority group delineates and defends group boundaries, thereby leaving out those who do not meet the criteria for inclusion and who, consequently, have diminished access to higher-level educational, employment, and income opportunities.

Institutional completeness   A measure of the degree to which an immigrant ethnic group gives its own members the services—medical, legal, shopping, worship, realty, finance, travel, etc.—they need through its own institutions. It usually gives off an impression of cohesiveness and solidarity among members of the group.

Internalized racism   When members of an ethnic or racial group come to believe the stereotypes that others have imposed on them.

Modern multiculturalism   Concerned for the survival of cultural groups, so that the group, not the individual, is protected by law.

Prejudice   A hostile or aversive attitude towards a person who belongs to a particular group simply because of the person's membership in the group; opinions and attitudes often unjustified by fact.

Racial discrimination   'Any distinction, exclusion, restriction or preference based on race, colour, descent, or national or ethnic origin which has the purpose or effect of nullifying or impairing the recognition, enjoyment or exercise, on an equal footing, of human rights and fundamental freedoms in the political, economic, social, cultural or any other field of public life' (Office for the High Commissioner for Human Rights, 1969).

Racialization   The tendency in a community to introduce racial distinctions into situations that can be understood and managed without such distinctions.

Racial socialization   The process of social interaction whereby a person is exposed to and over time internalizes his or her racial or ethnic identity, including its set of beliefs, values, cultural history, language, and social and economic implications; the constant awareness of race in daily social interaction.

Social distance   Feelings of aloofness and inapproachability often felt between members of different social strata or of different ethnic or 'racial' origins. People feel varying comfort levels when interacting with members of other cultures and in different circumstances and tend to be more willing to have close relations with others who are culturally and racially similar. Distance increases with prejudices and discriminatory practices.

Traditional multiculturalism   Concern for protecting the rights of individuals whereby the rights of minority people are protected through, for example, provincial human rights codes; pluralism.

Transnationalism   Marked by the globalization of capitalism and by a revolution in communication and transportation technologies, by decolonization and an expansion of human rights, and by the growth of social networks that facilitate transnational migration patterns.

Vertical mosaic   Coined by John Porter, a socio-economic hierarchy in which English and French Canadians live at the top and other ethnic minorities are positioned below. This economic ladder categorizes the Canadian experience of opportunity stratification.

REFERENCES

Allotey, Pascale. 1998. '"Travelling with "Excess Baggage": Health Problems of Refugee Women in Western Australia', *Women and Health* 28, 1: 63–81.

Allport, Gordon. 1954. *The Nature of Prejudice*. Reading, Mass.: Addison-Wesley.

Anderson, Kay J. 1991. *Vancouver's Chinatown: Racial Discourse in Canada, 1875–1980*. Montreal and Kingston: McGill-Queen's University Press.

Arfken, Cynthia L., and Cheryl A. Houston. 1996. 'Obesity in Inner-City African Americans', *Ethnicity and Health* 1: 317–26.

Arkes, H.R., and P.E. Tetlock. 2004. 'Attributions of Implicit Prejudice, or Would Jesse Jackson "Fail" the Implicit Association Test?', *Psychological Inquiry* 15: 257–78.

Austin, Christopher, and David Este. 2001. 'The Working Experiences of Underemployed Immigrant and Refugee Men', *Canadian Social Work Review* 18, 2: 213–29.

Barbujani, Guido, Arianna Magagni, Eric Minch, and L. Luca

Cavalli-Sforza. 1997. 'An Apportionment of Human DNA Diversity', *Proceedings of the National Academy of Science* 94, 9: 4516–19.

Beaujot, Roderic. 1991. *Population Change in Canada: The Challenges of Policy Adaptation.* Toronto: McClelland & Stewart.

Beauvais, Fred. 2000. 'Indian Adolescence: Opportunity and Challenge', in Raymond Montemayor, Gerald R. Adams, and Thomas P. Gullotta, eds, *Adolescent Diversity of Ethnic, Economic and Cultural Contexts.* Thousand Oaks, Calif.: Sage, 110–40.

Beck, J. Helen, Jeffrey G. Reitz, and Nan Weiner. 2002. 'Addressing Systemic Racial Discrimination in Employment: The Health Canada Case and Implications of Legislative Change', *Canadian Public Policy* 28, 3: 373–94.

Bell, David, and Lorne Tepperman. 1979. *The Roots of Disunity: A Look at Canadian Political Culture.* Toronto: McClelland & Stewart.

Bogardus, E.S. 1928. *Immigration and Race Attitudes.* Boston: D.C. Heath.

Bowen, John R. 1996. 'The Myth of Global Ethnic Conflict', *Journal of Democracy* 7, 4: 3–14.

Brave Heart, M.Y. 1999. 'Gender Differences in the Historical Trauma Response among the Lakota', *Journal of Health and Social Policy* 10, 4: 1–21.

Breton, Raymond. 1964. 'Institutional Completeness of Ethnic Communities and Personal Relations to Immigrants', *American Journal of Sociology* 70: 193–205.

———. 1978. 'Stratification and Conflict between Ethnolinguistic Communities with Different Social Structures', *Canadian Review of Sociology and Anthropology* 15: 138–57.

———, Jeffrey G. Reitz, and Victor Valentine. 1980. *Cultural Boundaries and the Cohesion of Canada.* Montreal: Institute for Research on Public Policy.

Broadhurst, Roderic. 1996. 'Aboriginal Imprisonment in Australia', *Overcrowded Times* 7, 3: 5–8.

Brooks, Stephen. 2007. *Canadian Democracy: An Introduction*, 5th edn. Toronto: Oxford University Press.

Callan, Alyson, and Roland Littlewood. 1998. 'Patient Satisfaction: Ethnic Origin or Explanatory Model?', *International Journal of Social Psychiatry* 44, 1: 1–11.

Canadian Council on Social Development (CCSD). 2000. 'Unequal Access: A Report Card on Racism', *Perception* 24, 3. Available at: <www.ccsd.ca/perception/243/racism.htm>; accessed 21 Jan. 2003.

Citizenship and Immigration Canada. 2003. 'Facts and Figures 2002: Immigration Overview'. Available at: <www.cic.gc.ca/english/pub/facts2002/index.html>; accessed 19 Feb. 2006.

Clairmont, Donald. 1996. 'Alternative Justice Issues for Aboriginal Justice', *Journal of Legal Pluralism and Unofficial Law* 36: 125–57.

Coleman, Heather, Grant Charles, and Jennifer Collins. 2001.

'Inhalant Use by Canadian Aboriginal Youth', *Journal of Child and Adolescent Substance Abuse* 10, 3: 1–20.

Commission on Systemic Racism in the Ontario Justice System. 1995. *Report of the Commission on Systemic Racism in the Ontario Justice System.* Toronto: The Commission.

Cooper, Helen, Chris Smaje, and Sara Arber. 1999. 'Equity in Health Service Use by Children: Examining the Ethnic Paradox', *Journal of Social Policy* 28: 457–78.

Coser, Lewis A. 1965. *The Functions of Social Conflict.* London: Routledge & Kegan Paul.

Curtis, James, Edward Grabb, and Neil Guppy, eds. 1999. *Social Inequality in Canada: Patterns, Problems, Policies*, 3rd edn. Scarborough, Ont.: Prentice-Hall.

D'Arcy, Carl. 1998. 'Social Distribution of Health among Canadians', in David Coburn, Carl D'Arcy, and George M. Torrance, eds, *Health and Canadian Society: Sociological Perspectives*, 3rd edn. Toronto: University of Toronto Press, 73–101.

Dallaire, Roméo A. 2003. *Shake Hands with the Devil: The Failure of Humanity in Rwanda.* Toronto: Random House of Canada.

Dei, George J.S. 1997. 'Afrocentricity and Inclusive Curriculum: Is There a Connection or a Contradiction', in S.H. Riggins, ed., *The Language and Politics of Exclusion: Others in Discourse.* Thousand Oaks, Calif.: Sage, 203–25.

Department of Indian Affairs and Northern Development (DIAND). 2002. *Basic Departmental Data 2001.* Ottawa: DIAND.

Devine, Patricia G., and Andrew J. Elliot. 1995. 'Are Racial Stereotypes Really Fading? The Princeton Trilogy Revised', *Personality and Social Psychology Bulletin* 21, 11: 1139–50.

Duffy Hutcheon, Pat. 1998. 'Multiculturalism, Good Intentions and a Clouded Vision?', paper presented at the annual meeting of the International Sociological Association.

Durkheim, Émile. 1964 [1895]. *Division of Labor in Society*, trans. George Simpson. New York: Free Press.

Farb, Peter. 1978. *Man's Rise to Civilization: The Cultural Ascent of the Indians of North America*, 2nd edn. New York: Bantam.

Farmer, Melissa M., and Kenneth F. Ferraro. 1999. 'Who Are the "Truly Disadvantaged" in Health? A 20-Year Examination of Race, Socioeconomic Status, and Health Outcomes', paper presented at the annual meeting of the American Sociological Association.

Farrales, Lynn L., and Gwen E. Chapman. 1999. 'Filipino Women Living in Canada: Constructing Meanings of Body, Food, and Health', *Health Care for Women International* 20: 179–94.

Fenton, Steve, Anthony O. Hughes, and Christine E. Hine. 1995. 'Self-assessed Health, Economic Status and Ethnic Origin', *New Community* 21, 1: 55–68.

Fontana, Barbara. 1997. *The State of Migration Research in South*

Africa. Foundation for Global Dialog Occasional Paper 8. Braamfontein, South Africa: Foundation for Global Dialog.

Foot, David K. 1982. *Canada's Population Outlook: Demographic Futures and Economic Challenges*. Toronto: Lorimer.

Franklin, Anderson J. 1998. 'Treating Anger in African American Men', in William S. Pollack and Richard F. Levant, eds, *New Psychotherapy for Men*. New York: Wiley, 239–58.

Frideres, J.S., and Boni Robertson. 1994. 'Aboriginals and the Criminal Justice System: Australia and Canada', *International Journal of Contemporary Sociology* 31: 101–27.

Furniss, Elizabeth. 1999. 'Indians, Odysseys and Vast, Empty Lands: The Myth of the Frontier in the Canadian Justice System', *Anthropologica* 41: 195–208.

Gaertner, Samuel L., and John F. Dovidio. 2000. 'The Aversive Form of Racism', in Charles Stangor, ed., *Stereotypes and Prejudice: Essential Readings*. Philadelphia: Psychology Press, 289–304.

Gee, Ellen M., and Steven G. Prus. 2000. 'Income Inequality in Canada: A Racial Divide', in Madeline A. Kalbach and Warren E. Kalbach, eds, *Perspectives on Ethnicity in Canada: A Reader*. Toronto: Harcourt Canada, 238–56.

Gil, Vincent E. 1998–9. 'Empowerment Rhetoric, Sexual Negotiation, and Latinas' AIDS Risk: Research Implications for Prevention Health Education', *International Quarterly of Community Health Education* 18: 9–27.

Gray, Bradley, and Jeffrey J. Stoddard. 1997. 'Patient-Physician Pairing: Does Racial and Ethnic Congruity Influence Selection of a Regular Physician?', *Journal of Community Health* 22: 247–59.

Greenwald, Anthony G., Debbie E. McGhee, and Jordan K.L. Schwartz. 1998. 'Measuring Individual Differences in Implicit Cognition: The Implicit Association Test', *Journal of Personality and Social Psychology* 74, 6: 1464–80.

Grewal, Sam. 2005. 'Island of Isolation', *Toronto Star*, 29 Nov. Available at: <www.thestar.com>; accessed 5 Dec. 2005.

Gwyn, Richard. 1985. *The 49th Paradox: Canada in North America*. Toronto: McClelland & Stewart.

Harrell, Shelly P. 2000. 'A Multidimensional Conceptualization of Racism-Related Stress: Implications for the Well-Being of People of Color', *American Journal of Orthopsychiatry* 70, 1: 42–57.

Hawkins, Freda. 1972. *Canada and Immigration: Public Policy and Public Concern*. Montreal and Kingston: McGill-Queen's University Press.

Hayward, Mark D., and Melanie Heron. 1999. 'Racial Inequality in Active Life among Adult Americans', *Demography* 36: 77–91.

Henry, Frances. 1999. 'Two Studies of Racial Discrimination in Employment', in Curtis et al. (1999: 226–35).

———— and Effie Ginzberg. 1985. *Who Gets the Work: A Test of Racial Discrimination in Employment*. Toronto: Urban Alliance on Race Relations in Employment and Social Planning Council of Metropolitan Toronto.

———— and Carol Tator. 1994. 'Racism and the University', *Canadian Ethnic Studies* 26, 3: 74–90.

Hou, Feng, and T.R. Balakrisnan. 1996. 'The Integration of Visible Minorities in Contemporary Society', *Canadian Journal of Sociology* 21: 307–16.

Howard, Rhoda. 1998. 'Being Canadian: Citizenship in Canada', *Citizenship Studies* 2: 133–52.

Hu, Feng, and Garnett Picot. 2004. 'Visible Minority Neighbourhoods in Toronto, Montréal, and Vancouver', *Canadian Social Trends* (Spring): 8–13.

Hunt, Wayne A. 1996. 'The First Peoples and the Quebec Question', *Telos* 108: 139–48.

Ignatieff, Michael. 1994. *Blood and Belonging: Journeys into the New Nationalism*. New York: Farrar, Straus & Giroux.

Inuit Tapiriit Kanatami (ITK). 2002. *Suicide Prevention in Inuit Communities*. Ottawa: ITK.

Johnson, Genevieve Marie, and Reinhild Boehm. 1995. 'Aboriginal Canadian University Students: A Comparison of Students Who Withdraw and Students Who Continue', *Australian Journal of Adult and Community Education* 35, 2: 141–56.

Johnson, Melissa A., Alyse R. Gotthofer, and Kimberly A. Laufer. 1999. 'The Sexual and Reproductive Health Content of African American and Latino Magazines', *Howard Journal of Communications* 10, 3: 169–87.

Kalbach, W.E. 1970. *The Impact of Immigration on Canada's Population*. Ottawa: Dominion Bureau of Statistics.

Klos, Nancy. 1997. 'Aboriginal Peoples and Homelessness: Interviews with Service Providers', *Canadian Journal of Urban Research* 6: 40–52.

Krieger, Nancy, Diane Rowley, Allen A. Herman, Byllye Avery, and Monol T. Phillips. 1993. 'Racism, Sexism, and Social Class: Implications for Studies of Health, Disease, and Well-Being', *American Journal of Preventive Medicine* 9, 6 (suppl.): 82–122.

Kymlicka, Will. 1995. *Multicultural Citizenship: A Liberal Theory of Minority Rights*. Oxford: Clarendon Press.

Landrine, Hope, and Elizabeth A. Klonoff. 1996. 'The Schedule of Racist Events: A Measure of Racial Discrimination and a Study of Its Negative Physical and Mental Health Consequences', *Journal of Black Psychology* 22: 144–68.

Laroche, Mireille. 2000. 'Health Status and Health Services Utilization of Canada's Immigrant and Non-immigrant Populations', *Canadian Public Policy* 26: 51–73.

LaVeist, Thomas A., Chamberlain Diala, and Nicole C. Jarrett. 2000. 'Social Status and Perceived Discrimination: Who Experiences Discrimination in the Health Care System, How, and Why?', in Carol J. Hogue, Martha A. Hargraves, and Karen Scott Collins, eds, *Minority Health in America: Findings and Policy Implications from the Commonwealth Fund*

Minority Health Survey. Baltimore: Johns Hopkins University Press, 194–208.

Lee, David J., Kyriakos S. Markides, and Laura A. Ray. 1997. 'Epidemiology of Self-reported Past Heavy Drinking in Hispanic Adults', *Ethnicity and Health* 2, 1–2: 77–88.

Li, Peter S. 2003. *Destination Canada: Immigration Debates and Issues.* Toronto: Oxford University Press Canada.

Malin, Merridy. 2000. 'A "Whole of Life" View of Aboriginal Education for Health: Emerging Models', keynote address at the Australian Medical Association, Northern Territory, Conference 2000, 'Learning Lessons: Approaching Indigenous Health Through Education'. Available at: <http://192.94.208.240/Crc/General/CRCPubs/Malin_AMA_2000.PDF>; accessed 20 June 2001.

Massey, D.S., and N.A. Denton. 1993. *American Apartheid: Segregation and the Making of the Underclass.* Cambridge, Mass.: Harvard University Press.

Maxim, Paul S., Jerry P. White, Dan Beavon, and Paul C. Whitehead. 2001. 'Dispersion and Polarization of Income among Aboriginal and Non-Aboriginal Canadians', *Canadian Review of Sociology and Anthropology* 38: 465–76.

Maxwell, Bill. 2003. 'Rap's Excesses Come Home To Roost', *Tribune* (Welland, Ont.), 17 Oct., A6.

McConahay, J.B. 1981. 'Has Racism Declined in America? It Depends on Who Is Asking and What Is Asked', *Journal of Conflict Resolution* 25, 4: 563–79.

———. 1986. 'Modern Racism, Ambivalence, and the Modern Racism Scale', in J.F. Dovidio and S.L. Gaertner, eds., *Prejudice, Discrimination, and Racism.* New York: Academic Press, 91–125.

McNaughton, J. Craig. 1990. 'Are the Humanities in Canada Too Eurocentric?', *Society* 14, 2: 17–19.

Melancon, Hugues. 1997. 'A Pluralist Analysis of Indigenous Legal Conceptions before the Criminal Law Courts of Canada', *Canadian Journal of Law and Society* 12: 159–86.

Moreau, Sylvie, Cecile Rousseau, and Abdelwahed Mekki Berrada. 1999. 'Immigration Policies and the Mental Health of Refugees: The Profile and Impact of Family Separations', *Nouvelles Pratiques Sociales* 11, 1: 177–96.

Nakamura, Raymond M. 1999. *Health in America: A Multicultural Perspective.* Boston: Allyn & Bacon.

Office of the High Commissioner for Human Rights. 1969. *International Convention on the Elimination of All Forms of Racial Discrimination.* Available at: <www.unhchr.ch/html/menu3/b/d_icerd.htm>; accessed 18 Feb. 2006.

Oppenheimer, Valerie K., and Matthijs Kalmijn. 1995. 'Life-Cycle Jobs', *Research in Social Stratification and Mobility* 14: 1–38.

Ottaway, S.A., D.C. Hayden, and M.A. Oakes. 2001. 'Implicit Attitudes and Racism: Effects of Work Familiarity and Frequency on the Implicit Association Test', *Social Cognition* 19: 97–144.

Peikoff, Tannis Mara. 2001. 'Anglican Missionaries and Governing the Self: An Encounter with Aboriginal Peoples in Western Canada, 1820–1865', Ph.D. thesis, University of Manitoba.

Phipps, Etienne, Martin H. Cohen, Rorng Sorn, and Leonard E. Braitman. 1999. 'A Pilot Study of Cancer Knowledge and Screening Behaviors of Vietnamese and Cambodian Women', *Health Care for Women International* 20: 195–207.

Picot, Garnett, and Feng Hou. 2003. *The Rise in Low-income Rates among Immigrants in Canada* (Catalogue no. 11F0019–MIE). Ottawa: Statistics Canada.

Porter, John A. 1965. *The Vertical Mosaic: An Analysis of Social Class and Power in Canada.* Toronto: University of Toronto Press.

Quan, H., A. Fong, C. De Coster, J. Wang, R. Musto, T.W. Noseworthy, and W.A. Ghali. 2006. 'Variation in Health Services Utilization among Ethnic Populations', *Canadian Medical Association Journal* 174, 6: 787–91.

Rajaram, Shireen S., and Anahita Rashidi. 1999. 'Asian-Islamic Women and Breast Cancer Screening: A Socio-cultural Analysis', *Women and Health* 28, 3: 45–58.

Reed, Micheline, and Julian Roberts. 1999. 'Adult Correctional Services in Canada, 1997–98', in Canadian Centre for Justice Statistics, *The Juristat Reader: A Statistical Overview of the Canadian Justice System.* Toronto: Thompson Educational, 39–51.

Reitz, Jeffrey G. 1998. *Warmth of the Welcome: The Social Causes of Economic Success for Immigrants in Different Nations and Cities.* Boulder, Colo.: Westview Press.

——— and Raymond Breton. 1999. 'Prejudice and Discrimination toward Minorities in Canada and the United States', in Curtis et al. (1999: 357–70).

Roberts, Julian V., and Anthony N. Doob. 1997. 'Race, Ethnicity, and Criminal Justice in Canada', in Michael Tonry, ed., *Ethnicity, Crime and Immigration: Comparative and Cross-national Perspectives.* Chicago: University of Chicago Press, 469–522.

Rodlandt, Theo J.A. 1996. 'Ethnic Stratification: The Emergence of a New Social and Economic Issue?', *Netherlands Journal of Social Sciences* 32, 1: 39–50.

Rogers, Angie, Jane E. Adamson, and Mark McCarthy. 1997. 'Variations in Health Behaviours among Inner-City 12-Year-Olds from Four Ethnic Groups', *Ethnicity and Health* 2: 309–16.

Rollock, David, and Edmund W. Gordon. 2000. 'Racism and Mental Health into the 21st Century: Perspectives and Parameters', *American Journal of Orthopsychiatry* 70, 1: 5–13.

Rothermund, K., and D. Wentura. 2004. 'Underlying Processes in the Implicit Association Test (IAT): Dissociating Salience from Associations', *Journal of Experimental Psychology (General)* 133: 139–65.

Russell, Gerald L., Diane C. Fujino, Stanley Sue, Mang-King Cheung, and Lonnie R. Snowden. 1996. 'The Effects of

Therapist-Client Ethnic Match in the Assessment of Mental Health Functioning', *Journal of Cross-Cultural Psychology* 27: 599–615.

Russell, Peter. 1996. 'Aboriginal Nationalism: Prospects for Decolonization', *Pacifica Review* 8, 2: 57–67.

Ruttkay-Milkián, Eszter. 2001. 'Revival and Survival in Iugra', *Nationalities Papers* 29: 153–70.

Saldov, Morris. 1991. 'The Ethnic Elderly: Communication Barriers to Health Care', *Canadian Social Work Review* 8: 269–77.

Samson, Colin. 1999. 'The Dispossession of the Innu and the Colonial Magic of Canadian Liberalism', *Citizenship Studies* 3, 1: 5–25.

———. 2003. *A Way of Life That Does Not Exist: Canada and the Extinguishment of the Innu*. St John's and London: ISER Books and Verso.

Sears, Alan. 1990. 'Immigration Controls as Social Policy: The Case of Canadian Medical Inspection 1900–1920', *Studies in Political Economy* 33: 91–112.

Segura Escobar, Nora. 2000. 'Colombia: A New Century, an Old War, and More Internal Displacement', *International Journal of Politics, Culture, and Society* 14: 107–27.

Silove, Derrick, Ingrid Sinnerbrink, Annette Field, Vijaya Manicavasagar, and Zachary Steel. 1997. 'Anxiety, Depression and PTSD in Asylum-Seekers: Associations with Pre-migration and Post-migration Stressors', *British Journal of Psychiatry* 170: 351–7.

Simmel, Georg. 1964 [1905]. *The Sociology of Georg Simmel*, trans. and ed. Kurt Wolff. New York: Free Press.

Smith, Karen. 2003. 'New Racial Profiling Policy on Right Track', *Kingston This Week*, 21 May, 6.

Snowden, Lonnie R., Teh-wei Hu, and Jeannette M. Jerrell. 1995. 'Emergency Care Avoidance: Ethnic Matching and Participation in Minority-Serving Programs', *Community Mental Health Journal* 31: 463–73.

Spaulding, Richard. 1997. 'Peoples as National Minorities: A Review of Will Kymlicka's Arguments for Aboriginal Rights from a Self-determination Perspective', *University of Toronto Law Journal* 47: 35–113.

Spencer, N. 1996. 'Race and Ethnicity as Determinants of Child Health: A Personal View', *Child: Care, Health and Development* 22: 327–45.

Statistics Canada. 2001. *Census of Canada*. Ottawa: Statistics Canada.

———. 2003. *Longitudinal Survey of Immigrants to Canada: Process, Progress, and Prospects* (Catalogue no. 89–611–XIE). Ottawa: Statistics Canada.

———. 2004. *Juristat: Hate Crime in Canada* 24, 4. Ottawa: Statistics Canada.

———. 2005. *Population Projections of Visible Minority Groups, Canada, Provinces and Regions, 2001–2017* (Catalogue no. 91–541–XIE). Ottawa: Statistics Canada, Demography Division. Available at: <http://www.statcan.ca/english/freepub/91-541-XIE/91-541-XIE2005001.pdf>.

Stolcke, Verena. 1999. 'New Rhetorics of Exclusion in Europe', *International Social Science Journal* 51: 25–35.

Symons, Gladys L. 1999. 'Racialization of the Street Gang Issue in Montreal: A Police Perspective', *Canadian Ethnic Studies* 31: 124–38.

Tang, S.Y. 1999. 'Interpreter Services in Healthcare: Policy Recommendations for Healthcare Agencies', *Journal of Nursing Administration* 29, 6: 23–9.

Thomas, W.I., and Florien Znaniecki. 1971 [1919]. *The Polish Peasant in America*. New York: Octagon Books.

Trovato, Frank. 2001. 'Aboriginal Mortality in Canada, the United States and New Zealand', *Journal of Biosocial Science* 33: 67–86.

Waldram, James P., Ann D. Herring, and T. Kue Young. 1996. *Aboriginal Health in Canada: Historical, Cultural, and Epidemiological Perspectives*. Toronto: University of Toronto.

Warburton, Rennie. 1997. 'Status, Class and the Politics of Canadian Aboriginal Peoples', *Studies in Political Economy* 54: 119–41.

Wardman, D., K. Clement, and D. Quantz. 2005. 'Access and Utilization of Health Services by British Columbia's Rural Aboriginal Population', *International Journal of Health Care Quality Assurance* 18, 2 and 3: xxvi–xxxi.

Weinrath, Michael. 1999. 'Violent Victimization and Fear of Crime among Canadian Aboriginals', *Journal of Offender Rehabilitation* 30: 107–20.

Wen, S.W., V. Goel, and J.I. Williams. 1996. 'Utilization of Health Care Services by Immigrants and Other Ethnic/Cultural Groups in Ontario', *Ethnicity and Health* 1, 1: 99–109.

Whaley, Arthur L. 1998. 'Racism in the Provision of Mental Health Service: A Social-Cognitive Analysis', *American Journal of Orthopsychiatry* 68: 47–57.

Williams, David R. 1999. 'Race, Socioeconomic Status and Health: The Added Effects of Racism and Discrimination', in N.E. Adler, M. Marmot, B.S. McEwen, and J. Stewart, eds, *Socioeconomic Status and Health in Industrial Nations: Psychological and Biological Pathways*. New York: New York Academy of Sciences, 173–88.

———, Yan Yu, James S. Jackson, and Norman B. Anderson. 1997. 'Racial Differences in Physical and Mental Health: Socio-economic Status, Stress, and Discrimination', *Journal of Health Psychology* 2: 335–51.

Wortley, Scot, and Lysandra Marshall. 2005. *Bias Free Policing: The Kingston Data Collection Project—Final Results*. Available at: <www.police.kingston.on.ca>; accessed 1 Aug. 2006.

Wu, Z., M.J. Penning, and C.M. Schimmele. 2005. 'Immigrant Status and Unmet Health Care Needs', *Canadian Journal of Public Health*, 96(5): 369–373.

Yeo, Gwen. 1991. 'Ethnogeriatric Education: Need and Content', *Journal of Cross-Cultural Gerontology* 6: 229–41.

SEXISM AND GENDER INEQUALITY

Introduction

This chapter is about gender and sex, men and women, and gender inequality, stereotyping, discrimination, and socialization—all of which can be found in homes, schools, and work settings throughout this country.

Since this chapter is about issues associated with gender, we will also discuss some of the disadvantages associated with being a *man* in our society. Indeed, as we will see, norms of masculinity are as much of an impediment to men as norms of femininity are to women—especially if those men are elderly or disabled.

However, the principal focus here is on the disadvantages associated with being a *woman* in our society. Historically, women have suffered more disadvantages than men at school, in the workplace, and in the public realm. To a large degree, these disadvantages have been overcome in the past two decades. For example, formally, Canadians support rules that make it illegal for employers to limit or separate their employees by sex. Informally, however, many Canadians still discriminate against women or in favour of men. As we will see, gender stereotyping and discrimination, in various settings, hinder women far more than they do men.

The problem begins at birth. As parents, we tend to raise children who are genetically female as 'girls'. We raise children who are genetically male in a different way as 'boys'. Many aspects of our social institutions reinforce this differential socialization, ignoring the fact that tendencies towards masculinity and femininity are continuous, not discrete.

Yet, gender stereotyping and gendered socialization—based on a rigid two-gender model—occur at most levels of social life in Canada. Unfortunately, some of the outcomes of gender stereotyping go beyond job discrimination to include rape and other criminal and dehumanizing acts. Poverty is also a more common experience for women than for men. Canadian women experience sexism, prejudice, and harassment far more often than Canadian men. This chapter will explore these problems and others that affect, in varying degrees, over half the Canadian population.

Defining Sexism and Gender Inequality

Sexism includes discrimination and insulting attitudes and beliefs that stereotype people because of their gender. Sexism and gender stereotyping can be problems for both men and women. However, since males have traditionally dominated Canadian society, sexism has harmed women more than men. **Gender inequality** is any difference between men and women in gaining access to valued societal rewards. It can grow out of structural arrangements, interpersonal discrimination, or cultural beliefs.

Sex and Gender

Sex is a biological concept. From a purely biological standpoint, the Y chromosome must be present for the embryonic sex glands to develop in a male direction. Further, hormones must be present in both sexes for either males or females to reach sexual maturity. Most people are (mainly) male or female from the moment of conception, with biological differences between the sexes that are anatomic, genetic, and hormonal.

However, research has not revealed any simple split between the sexes or any direct link between genetics and the behaviour of each sex. Moreover, current thinking is that 'male' and 'female' are not entirely discrete biological categories. It would be more accurate to view them as opposite poles along a continuum of sexual variation. The value of such subtle thinking is obvious when we consider unusual cases. For example, consider the condition known as adrenogenital syndrome, in which an XX (46-chromosome) individual is exposed in the womb to abnormally high levels of androgens, a family of hormones that usually predominates in the development of masculine features (Crooks and Baur, 1999). The result is an intersexed appearance, with normal internal genitalia (ovaries, uterus, inner vagina) and an external phallus that is intermediate in size between a clitoris and a penis. Male or female? For practical purposes, the answer is socially determined, through socialization and social interaction.

Moreover, what biological differences that exist between men and women have few (if any) unavoidable effects on modern-day social life. Men and women have different reproductive functions, but there is no scientific proof there are biologically based psychological differences (such as a 'maternal instinct') between human males and females. And as women spend less and less of their lives bearing children, the reproductive difference becomes less socially relevant to a definition of people's roles.

Hormones and chromosomes are therefore only part of the story. In contrast to biological sex, **gender** refers to culturally learned notions of masculinity and femininity. From a social standpoint, gender is the social enactment of a biological difference. Males are treated as men because they play masculine roles, and females are treated as women because they play feminine roles. In socially neutral roles (such as friend, guest, traveller, or stranger), men and women still perform in gendered ways. However, since our sex organs and genes are not usually in view, biology per se is not directly relevant to any of these gendered social interactions.

All known societies have distinguished between male and female roles in some way. However, the precise distinctions made between men and women, and the resulting divisions of labour, have varied through time and across cultures. Gender distinctions are always socially constructed. They work within social institutions to decide the roles that men and women can enter and the kinds of experiences they will have within these roles. So what begins as a mere biological difference between sexes assumes a vast importance through the social construction of gender roles. Sociologists use the term 'gender' when referring to these sex-based social constructions, a practice that suggests that biology is largely irrelevant to understanding the social distinctions people make between males and females.

We have a hard time classifying the sex of people with mixed male and female features. Predicting their gender is even harder, since gender, unlike sex, is a purely social form, as we have said. It involves shared understandings of how women and men, girls and boys, should look and act. Gender is a label that includes a large variety of traits, beliefs, values, and mannerisms, and it defines how we should act in various social contexts. Like sex, gender is popularly (and wrongly) understood as comprising two mutually exclusive categories—'masculine' and 'feminine'—that neatly parallel the matching biological division between 'male' and 'female'.

Masculinity/Femininity

Views of the inherent difference between males and females are captured in a neat dichotomy found in our culture—and most others—that distinguishes masculinity and femininity. Not only is this dichotomy an oversimplification of the real differences between people, but it is also the source of many problems for both men and women.

Gender roles are learned patterns of behaviour that a society expects of men or women, and they are a widespread aspect of social life. By **masculinity**, then, we mean that package of qualities that people in our society expect to find in a typical man. By **femininity** we mean that package of qualities people expect to find in a typical woman.

So, for example, in our culture few men have been taught to become as nurturing as women have, so fathers typically behave differently from mothers with their children. Since gender is learned, gender roles vary from one culture to another. For example, housework is not everywhere, nor always, defined as a woman's activity, nor is housework always considered inherently degrading. In our own society, domestic service came to be seen as 'women's work' largely for historical and cultural reasons. In short, beliefs about masculinity and femininity are not linked to sex in the same way in all societies.

People learn their gender-based habits of behaviour through **gender socialization**. The socialization process links gender to personal identity—in the form of *gender identity*—and to distinctive activities—in the form of gender roles. The major agents of socialization—family, peer groups, schools, and the mass media—all serve to reinforce cultural definitions of masculinity and femininity. Consider the obvious difference between men's and women's interest in football. Men are more likely to play football and watch football games than women, but the difference doesn't end there. Men also use football playing and watching as occasions for male bonding or *homosociality*. Televised football games model a certain style of male talk and behaviour. Football is a good example of masculine behaviour in our society; other examples abound in business, warfare, sex, and various (other) recreations.

Risky Behaviour
Men are more likely than women to suffer accidents or death due to risky behaviours such as drinking, fighting, and dangerous driving.

In our own society, traditional notions of masculinity and femininity are breaking down. In addition, consciously designed social or state policies have altered gender roles in ours and many other societies. As a result, throughout the world women today are, in many respects, acting in ways people would have considered 'unfeminine' a mere generation or two ago. Fewer women continue to act in 'feminine' ways that have fallen into disrepute—for example, to serve as mistresses or paid companions who use their sexuality to attract and control men. Today, criticisms of such practices have less to do with their immorality or the dangers they pose to family life and more to do with the widespread sentiment that such practices are degrading to women, discriminatory, and associated with outmoded thinking about gender relations.

Interestingly, men suffer from gender stereotypes as much as women do. Just as the stereotype of women as dumb sex objects—personified by the lap dancer or topless waitress—undermines women's pursuit of respect and opportunity, so the stereotype of men as aggressive jocks and protectors of frail femininity—personified by football players and chivalrous knights—causes men to think twice about displaying their 'softer side'—their intellectual, emotional, or artistic dimensions. Besides reducing men's opportunities to live as they wish, this stereotyping can have serious effects for mental health and social relations.

Dramatizing male–female differences, with men being the wild and crazy members of humanity, encourages various risky, violent, and even criminal behaviours. Consider, for example, that men are more likely than women to drive recklessly. This, combined with the fact that men drive more often than women, means that men have more accidents, and more severe accidents, than women. Men also are more likely to drink too much and to drink and drive, with the expected outcomes of more drunk-driving accidents.

Men are also more likely to commit violent crimes and to be victimized in violent crimes. They are also are more likely to work in dangerous work settings and more likely to be victims of occupational accidents. In our society, as in many others, male anti-social behaviours are often associated with striving for a masculine self-image. Our culture expects masculine men to behave in dangerous and anti-social ways.

So, for example, young men who become unemployed often take to smoking and drinking heavily. Unemployment plays an important part in setting up lifelong patterns of dangerous behaviour in young men, but it is often because they are men that unemployment affects them so (Montgomery et al., 1998). Social practices that undermine men's health are often signifiers of masculinity, and instruments that men use to negotiate social power and status (Courtenay, 2000).

As a result, Canadian men suffer more severe chronic health conditions; have higher death rates for all leading causes of death; and die, on average, nearly five years younger than women (Keyfitz, 1988). Even the experience and expression of illness are gendered. Though men and women have similar overall rates of mental disorder, women more often develop symptoms of depression and anxiety, while men more often develop symptoms of alcoholism, drug abuse, and anti-social personality (Hankin, 1990).

Exceptions to Patterns of Male Dominance

There is much evidence, from across today's societies, of males having greater control, power, and status in many social situations. However, some anthropological studies emphasize that gender roles are not always arranged in this way. Some pre-industrial societies treated men and women equally. Many hunting-and-gathering societies were egalitarian. Some were cross-gendered, in the sense that women played 'male' roles.

Consider the examples of cross-gendered females in Native North American tribes and selected African cultures. According to Evelyn Blackwood and Saskia Wieringa (1999), a pattern of consistent gender socialization of males to superior roles was not present in some Native American tribes. Cross-gendered women were able to enter a 'male' role by various accepted cultural channels and took up adult male tasks when mature.

In these cultures, girls were encouraged to take on the different role if they expressed any interest in it as they grew up: 'Adults, acknowledging the interests of such girls, taught them the same skills the boys learned' (Blackwood and Wieringa, 1999: 143). This possibility arose from social organization based on egalitarian co-operation among autonomous individuals. Though gender roles entailed the performance of specific tasks, there was much overlap between the sexes. Kinship was based on mutually rewarding ties between men and women. Cross-gendered women could have sexual relations with other women and marry them. This cross-gendered role disappeared with Western cultural influence.

In short, the female cross-gendered role in certain North American tribes gave women an opportunity to assume the male role permanently and even marry women. Its existence challenges Western assumptions about gender roles. Further, in certain African cultures, women have had the highest status roles: 'In this part of the world more than any other in precolonial times, women were prominent in "high places". They were queen-mothers, queen sisters, princesses, chiefs and holders of other offices in towns and villages, occasionally warriors, and in one well-known case, that of the Lovedu, the supreme monarch' (Sudarkasa, 1986: 152).

As we think about the male-dominated gendered pattern in Canadian society and other modern societies like Canada, these studies should serve to remind us there is nothing unavoidable or certain about male dominance as defined through gender roles and gender socialization. Indeed, various other hunting-and-gathering societies, and even African societies that were horticultural or agricultural, show little of this. So why does the male dominance pattern occur so often in Canadian society and in other modern societies?

Factors That Reinforce Gender Inequality

Sociologically, the most important difference between the sexes is that most women can and do bear children, while men can't and don't. Gender researcher Nancy Chodorow, in the often-cited work, *Reproduction of Mothering* (1978), even explains women's subordination by the fact that women mother. If women and men shared equally in parenting, gender inequality would diminish, she argued. Today, gender inequality remains, as does motherhood.

To some degree, this basic difference between men and women gets played out differently in different societies. In most, however, mothers carry the main burden of child care and housekeeping; this, in turn, has enormous effects on other aspects of their lives. Until the recent past, this burden has limited women's education, work, income, political representation, and legal rights. So, we begin our discussion of gender inequality with an examination of women's family work. Following that, we will discuss women's education, work, income, political representation, and legal rights.

At Home

Reproduction and child-rearing continue to be mainly female activities in Canadian society, as they have been in most past cultures. Women's genes and hormones make child-bearing possible. However, child-bearing is no longer unavoidable. Effective birth control, by reducing the risk of unwanted pregnancy, has made the outcome of sexual intercourse more predictable and controllable than at any other time in history. As a result, men and women can lead more similar lives today than ever before. Today, women spend less time bearing and raising children than they did in the past. Other parts of their lives—especially education, work, career, and marital companionship—are more important today than they once were. Even sexual practices and sexual ideas, like the traditional double standard, have changed because of this contraceptive revolution.

However, the family household remains a workplace for women more than for men (see Table 5.1). Before industrial capitalism, it was men's workplace, too, but the separation of home and paid work largely brought this to an end (Tilly and Scott, 1987). Under this system, though each family has its own particular division of labour, what is remarkable is how similar this division is across families and even across nations. Domestic labour, in short, is gendered labour (for a good Canadian review, see Nakhaie, 1995). We still expect adult women to carry out more of the work than men, daughters to do more of the work than sons. This pattern also persists in caregiving. The primary caregiver is usually the wife, mother, or daughter. Women do more of the domestic work even if they engage in paid employment outside the home and are parenting infants, and even when they are taking care of sick or disabled family members.

A study comparing detailed data from Canada, the United States, Sweden, Norway, and Australia finds the factors shaping men's and women's participation in housework vary little across countries, despite variations in ideology and sex-role attitudes:

> Households that have the most egalitarian divisions of labour are those in which both husband and wife are employed outside the home, both hold liberal sex role attitudes, and . . . wives contribute a significant proportion of the household income relative to their husbands. The data also show support for a number of other individual-level factors. In particular, older women do a greater proportion of indoor tasks than younger women, and having children in the household increases women's share of housework. (Baxter, 1997: 239–40)

Table 5.1 Canadian Population 15 Years and Over, by Hours Spent on Unpaid Housework, 2001

	Males	Females
No hours	1,550,265	924,845
Less than 5 hours	3,486,140	2,139,030
5–14 hours	3,890,035	3,650,145
15–29 hours	1,786,960	2,929,165
30–59 hours	689,980	1,834,035
60 or more hours	223,405	797,360

Source: Statistics Canada (2002a).

Of course, families in each country do vary. In some studies, for example, remarried couples report a less complete or weaker version of gendered inequality than first-time married couples (Ishii-Kuntz and Coltrane, 1992). Couples who become parents in their twenties are more traditional in their gendering of domestic work than couples who make this transition in their thirties (Coltrane and Ishii-Kuntz, 1990). Women who cohabit do much less household work than women who are legally married (Shelton and John, 1993). And dual-career couples often renegotiate their domestic division of labour as outside work duties change (Gregson and Lowe, 1994).

Statistics Canada (1999: 5) estimates that women with partners do a daily average of 4.3 hours of 'household work and related activities', including cooking, housekeeping, maintenance and repair, shopping, and child-rearing, compared with 2.8 hours for men. Women usually do the chores that must be done daily, such as cooking and child care, while men are more likely to do the chores that need only occasional attention, such as mowing the lawn, automobile maintenance, and small household improvements (ibid.). Not by accident, women's tasks usually call for nurturing and sensitivity, while men's tasks often call for power tools. Women do more than their share of unpaid domestic duties. Women are equal with men only on measures of total workload and amount of employment training participation (Clark, 2001). Unpaid community work and family health care are still considered women's work, in our society as in others.

The Arrival of Children

With most women in the paid workforce, who looks after their children? Some families rely on daycare provided by professional caregivers. More, however, rely on babysitters who come to the parents' houses, on small-scale child-care operations, or on family members' voluntary care. Most babysitters are female, and few are male. Most non-household family members who 'help' with child care are female; only some are male. When researchers ask parents how they divide the responsibility of the household, they find women taking much more responsibility for the events or tasks of child care (Doucet, 2000; Tremblay, 2001). Thus, although men do take children to doctor's appointments, most often women will have made the appointments.

Women's lives become much more complicated with the arrival of children. Helena Willen and Henry Montgomery (1996) refer to this fact as the 'Catch-22' of marriage: wishing and planning for a child increases marital happiness, but achieving this wish reduces that happiness. The birth of a child and the resulting intense mother–child relationship strain marital relations (Erel and Burman, 1995). New parents are less happy with each other and experience more frequent, sometimes violent, conflicts with each other after the baby arrives (Crohan, 1996). For some, the conflict may begin even before the baby arrives.

With the arrival of children, wives have much less time for their husbands or for themselves, which may cause resentment. The birth of a child reduces by up to 80 per cent the activities wives do alone, or that parents do as a couple or with non-family members, until the child is school-aged (Monk et al., 1996; for Canadian evidence on this topic, see Cowan and Cowan, 1995).

This radical shift from spousal (adult-centred) activities to parenting (child-centred) activities creates an emotional distance the partners find hard to bridge. Romance and privacy decline. Sleepless nights increase. Mothers, the main providers of child care,

Dual-earner Families
According to the Vanier Institute of the Family, more than three out of four Canadian couples with children count on the earnings of both parents. A single wage is no longer enough to support a comfortable or even adequate lifestyle in urban Canada today.

change their time use much more than fathers. Especially after the birth of a first child, marital quality and quantity of time together decline immediately. Mothers report feeling angrier and more depressed than before (Monk et al., 1996; Cowan and Cowan, 1995).

The transition to parenthood increases gender inequality between partners (Fox, 2001). The social relationship between husband and wife changes. Wives, as mothers, devote more time to their infants and less time to their husbands. Husbands often resent this change, and wives may adopt a new, subservient way of dealing with husbands to reduce the resentment and conflict. This often produces resentment on the wife's side. As Bonnie Fox (2001: 11–12) summarizes the evidence:

> how a woman defines mothering is partly a product of negotiation with her partner. Because intensive mothering requires considerable support, it is contingent upon the consent and active cooperation of the partner, which makes for all sorts of subtle inequalities in the relationship. . . . [A] strong relationship between the father and his child . . . is partly contingent upon the woman's active creation of it. And in encouraging the relationship, women cater to their partners' needs more than they otherwise might.

Even the closest, happiest couples experience distress after having a baby, and few professional services are available to smooth this transition (Cowan and Cowan, 1995). After the early euphoria and depression of parenthood wears off, reality sets in. The spouses are often too busy to spend even limited 'quality time' with each other. For example, sexual activity falls off dramatically and never returns to its original level (see, e.g., Kermeen, 1995).

Typically, marital satisfaction, which decreases with the arrival of children, reaches an all-time low when the children are teenagers. The presence of children in the household, though pleasing in many respects, also increases the domestic workload for parents and increases conflict. Once the children leave home, creating what some sociologists have called an 'empty nest', many marriages improve to near-newlywed levels of satisfaction (Lupri and Frideres, 1981).

In part, this return to marital satisfaction is due to the decline in parental and other work responsibilities (Orbach et al., 1996). Many couples rediscover each other because they have more leisure time in which to become reacquainted. Thus, older couples show much less distress, less desire for change in their marriage, and a more accurate understanding of the needs of their partners than do younger married couples (Rabin and Rahav, 1995). They also have fonder memories of parenthood than people who have only recently gone through the process.

As Chodorow (1978) has written, for co-parenting to lead to gender equality, parenting must de-emphasize gender identity and concentrate instead on common human characteristics that transcend gender. This, in turn, requires a critical mass of men and women who define themselves in terms other than gender and value equality among people—a change that is yet to happen, as we can see from the literature on caregiving.

Caregiver Burden

Serious illnesses and disabilities also strain a family's capacity to function and the well-being of its members—especially the well-being of the main caregiver. Caregiving is an emotional, mental, and physical load. As more care is given, the caregiver's well-being decreases. This is a growing problem because of the aging of the Canadian population, which means that more adults—especially women—will be called on to provide care for their aging parents and spouses (Figure 5.1). As well, medicine and health technologies have become more successful in prolonging the lives of severely ill or disabled people. Family members today can expect to spend a larger fraction of their lives caring for other family members than was the case in the past.

Overall, unpaid caregivers to the sick and disabled—whatever the relationship or cause of disability—have a distinctive profile. Most are women, ages 30–59, and married. Most are the children, parent, or partner of the care recipient. The caregiver in an elderly couple is usually the wife. If a spouse is not available, an adult daughter usually takes over. Men typically offer occasional contributions, but are much less likely to help with such things as daily chores (Stoller, 1990). No wonder sons in our society tend to become caregivers to older parents only in the absence of an available female sibling (Horowitz, 1985). Most of the recipients they care for have multiple problems, often age-related. Except for caregivers whose relatives are in residential care, few receive any formal help, although many receive informal support from family and friends. Nearly half the caregivers report they have experienced major health problems of their own in the past year. Two-thirds say they feel exhausted at the end of each day. Half feel they have more to do than they can handle (Schofield and Herrman, 1993).

So women are far more likely than men to provide care. As a result, they suffer caregiving strain, work interference, income loss, and role strain (Fredriksen, 1996). When caregiving responsibilities are added to the regular demands of domestic work, parenting, and paid work, the dangers of caregiver burnout and family breakdown increase dramatically. Some women shift to part-time work, at least temporarily, when their caregiving loads become heavy (Walsh, 1999). Others make different short-term arrangements or take a leave of absence (Franklin et al., 1994). The result is a forced disruption in women's lives as paid workers, despite their skills, training, and goals (Pohl et al., 1998). This disruption can have serious long-term results for Canada/Quebec Pension

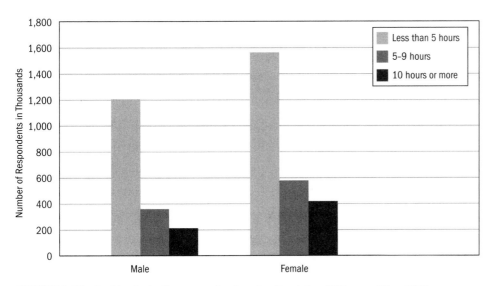

FIGURE 5.1 Who Provides Senior Care among the Canadian Population, 15 Years and Over, 2001
Source: Statistics Canada (2002b).

Plan benefits after retirement because these benefits are related to income earned in the workforce (Kingson and O'Grady-LeShane, 1993). Further, some women—especially single mothers—are forced to stay on welfare so they can meet their parental duties (Heymann and Earle, 1998).

Difficulties in balancing the demands of home and employment create great stress that, taken to extremes, contributes to life-threatening health conditions (see, e.g., Ginn and Sandell, 1997; Scharlach and Fredriksen, 1994). Working women experience large increases in stress when they are forced to alter their work schedules to meet the home care needs of an impaired, elderly family member (Orodenker, 1990).

The socialization of women to view themselves as especially responsible for caregiving makes guilt and shame potent added sources of stress if caregiving becomes difficult to do well. Even when faced with high care demands, women who are primary care providers use secondary providers merely to help in care tasks they are already carrying out (Stommel et al., 1995).

Individual psychosocial interventions, including respite programs, have been moderately effective in dealing with caregiver distress (Knight et al., 1993). Increasingly, the social, medical, and helping professions are learning how to intervene most effectively to support families that are dealing with chronic illness (Woods et al., 1989). Some families adapt to this stressor so well that functioning returns to normal. However, the stressor may still be present. Support from family, friends, and community agencies eases the impact of caregiving for some people. A sympathetic work environment also reduces physical and emotional strains (Lechner, 1993).

Support for the caregiver can come from two sources: other caregivers who provide help (that is, who take on some of the workload) and others who provide emotional support. Social networks often play a potent role in providing social support to families that are struggling to support severely ill or disabled family members. A family's ability to support its members is, in large part, influenced by its ability to get external support to moderate illness-related family stress. This is where networks of kin and friends can play an important part (Ell, 1996).

Caregiver stress, burnout, and psychosomatic symptoms may occur because of unresolved conflicts with or ambivalent feelings towards the ill or aged parent. As we have said, this duty tends to fall more often to daughters than sons. Subsequently, they experience more distress due to interference with work and strained relationships with the parents being cared for (Mui, 1995). So far, there is little information on the extent of this caregiving in the general population or on types of work interference (Carswick, 1997; Tennstedt and Gonyea, 1994). What is known is that spending large amounts of time providing attentive and personal care to an elderly parent with whom the child has a strained relationship is bound to take an extra toll on the caregiver's mental health. Family caregivers who put their relatives in nursing homes experience immediate relief from feelings of overload and tension. However, for many, a continuing concern and sense of guilt lead to long-term stress (Zarit and Whitlatch, 1993).

The problems that come with caring for a chronically ill parent, spouse, or other relative promise to become increasingly prevalent as lifespans lengthen (Blazer, 1982). These problems also come at a time when a decline in fertility rates has ensured that people have fewer siblings to share their duties with and fewer social supports to help them, despite cuts in the numbers of hospital beds and nurses.

Problems of Structural Sexism

Problems of *structural sexism*—that is, the ways social institutions outside the home treat men and women differently—and the problems that this different, unequal treatment poses for men and women reinforce one another. It would be hard to get rid of one without getting rid of them all.

Education

Education—especially university and college education—has opened many social and economic opportunities for girls and women. Before Confederation, young girls went to school along with the boys, but often family duties kept many of them from getting as much primary education as they wanted. Until 1862, young women had no chance to gain a higher education in Canada; then, Mount Allison University in New Brunswick enrolled its first female students. Shortly after, other Canadian universities and colleges opened their doors to female students.

In the early years of post-secondary education for women, many women—regardless of their interests and aptitudes—were urged to take general arts degrees or domestic science courses. Though women were allowed to become nurses, they were prevented from studying medicine. At the end of the nineteenth century, hospitals in Montreal refused to accept any female physicians. As a result, by 1893 all Canadian universities had closed their doors to women medical students. Most Canadian universities would not reopen their medical programs to women for another 50 years.

Though Elsie MacGill, the first Canadian woman to obtain a degree in electrical engineering, graduated from the University of Toronto in 1927, it wasn't until much later that women were entering male-dominated fields of study such as business, engineering, medicine, and law in noticeable numbers. By 1981, though women remained in the minority, census figures had recorded a dramatic increase in female enrolments in these fields (www.swc-cfc.gc.ca/dates/whm/2003/facts_e.pdf).

Increasingly, government and other bodies began to encourage young women to continue schooling and careers in non-traditional fields such as science and engineering. According to the most recent available data on the status of women in universities in Canada, in the academic year 1999–2000, women received 59 per cent of all post-secondary degrees, including 59.5 per cent of all bachelor and first professional degrees, 52.3 per cent of all master's degrees, and 40.7 per cent of all PhDs. Women were a clear majority of degree recipients in health professions (73.1 per cent), humanities (63.7 per cent), and social sciences (58.3 per cent), but continued to be a minority in engineering and the applied sciences, where they received only 24.1 per cent of all the degrees (www.fedcan.ca/english/pdf/issues/indicators2004eng.pdf).

In Canada, female enrolments in the university-level social sciences and humanities have been high for many years, and have reached or even exceeded parity with male enrolment in some traditionally male-dominated programs such as medicine and law. However, in recent years, women's numbers have made only slight progress in engineering, mathematics, and the physical sciences and women's enrolment in these fields remains relatively low (Statistics Canada, 2006; Normand, 1995). Table 5.2 and Figure 5.2 present an overview of male and female university enrolment.

Gender and Education
In the early years of the twentieth century, men were far more likely than women to get a higher education. Today the tables have turned. Is this good or bad?

Table 5.2 Full-time University Enrolment, by Level, 2000–1

	Women	Men	Total	Women as % of Total Enrolment
Bachelor's and first professional degree	280,821	208,638	489,459	57.4
Master's	24,702	23,031	47,733	51.8
Doctorate	11,114	13,301	24,415	45.5
Total enrolment	316,637	244,970	561,607	56.4

Source: <www.swc-cfc.gc.ca/pubs/women_men_2003/women_men_2003_6_e.html>.

A survey released by the Canadian Council of Professional Engineers (1999) found that although '24 per cent of all professional engineers born after 1970 are women' and 'women accounted for nearly 20 per cent of the students enrolled in Canadian undergraduate engineering programs during the 1998–99 academic year', low female entry rates into the engineering profession before the early 1980s mean that women account for fewer than 6 per cent of Canada's registered professional engineers. Among those enrolled in undergraduate mathematics and physical science programs in 1999, only 30 per cent were women. The gap between the sexes is even more dramatic in masters-level and doctoral-level programs, except in the social sciences.

The social benefits of education are dramatic for both men and women, but especially for women. Evidence collected in Canada and other industrial countries shows clearly that women who gain the highest levels of education come closest to job and income equality with men. As it is for racial minority groups and poor people, for

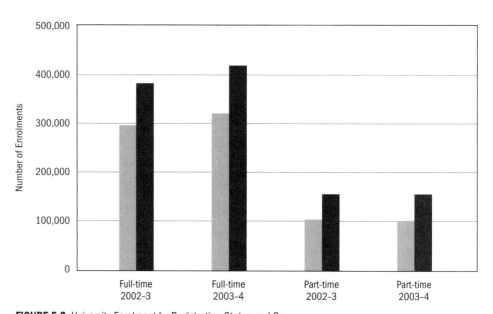

FIGURE 5.2 University Enrolment by Registration Status and Sex
Source: Data from Statistics Canada, 'University Enrolments by Registration Status and Sex, by Province', at: <www40.statcan.ca/l01/cst01/educ53b.htm> and <www40.statcan.ca/l01/cst01/educ53c.htm>; accessed 20 Nov. 2005.

Box 5.1   Social Policy: The Educational Gap

Today there is increased concern that, as girls and women move ahead educationally (and occupationally), increasingly boys and men are falling behind. Canadian boys, for example, are much more likely than girls to drop out of secondary school and less likely to pursue a university degree. This has led to increased research interest in whether boys and girls learn differently and, if so, how schooling can be changed to ensure that more boys and men get more education. An advocacy organization in Montreal, composed of educators, business leaders, city and provincial government officials, and community and parent representatives, reports the following:

Two out of three dropouts are male. There is already a considerable gap between boys and girls as early as elementary school.

■ This gap is most pronounced with regard to the language of instruction. For example, the results on the 1998 SAIP (School Achievement Indicators Program) reading test show that, among francophones in Quebec, 67 per cent of 13-year-old girls had demonstrated an acceptable level of reading skill (3 on a scale of 5), compared to 43 per cent of boys, a difference of 24 points. Among Quebec anglophones, the gap is somewhat less pronounced (18 points), but the results in English reading are weaker: 51 per cent of girls compared with 33 per cent of boys.

■ In 2000–1, 25 per cent of boys were academically delayed by the end of elementary school, compared with 17.8 per cent of girls, and this gap has persisted over the last 35 years.

■ In September 1997, among students aged 6 to 11, twice as many boys as girls exhibited learning or social maladjustments. As regards students with behavioural difficulties or disorders, the ratio was 5.5 boys for every girl.

At the secondary level, the difficulties observed are largely the same as in elementary school, the difference being that they follow a cumulative pattern that widens the gender gap year after year. For example, 31 per cent of all boys who left secondary school in 2000–1 had not earned their diploma, compared with 18.5 per cent of girls.

This gap between boys and girls is not a question of gender-based intellectual ability. Research tends to focus on the relationship, attitudes, and strategies that boys develop with respect to school and their role as students, socialization within the family and at school, learning rates, and social factors such as a child's or adolescent's circle of friends.

The difference between boys' and girls' academic success is apparent in all social classes, although it is more evident in disadvantaged areas. While girls from working-class backgrounds more readily perceive academic success as the key that will open doors for them, allow them to lead a satisfying professional life, and exert more control over their family life, boys from the same background tend to fall back on the prerogatives supposedly guaranteed by their masculinity. This is why girls are more likely to stake their future on education while boys do not always feel they have an interest in staying in school. Instead, they follow the traditional model, which emphasizes entering the job market as soon as possible, even if one's education remains limited.

Source: From 'The Gender Gap'. Montreal: Partnership Table for School Retention in Montreal, 2004, at: <www.perseverancescolairemontreal.qc.ca/english/gender.html>.

women higher education is an important way towards social equality in Canada today. Though it does not solve all the problems women face, education solves many.

A large part of the continuing problem of gender inequality in less developed parts of the world is educational. Families, governments, and economies simply do not give young women high priority in education and jobs in many parts of the world. As Figure 5.3 shows, women are particularly likely to be illiterate in sub-Saharan Africa, the Arab states, and South Asia (the Indian subcontinent).

Work

Throughout most of the twentieth century, women were still expected to be home-makers. Therefore, they were discouraged from taking on jobs that would prevent them from fulfilling their household duties. However, many women needed or wanted to work; and many companies wanted to hire women who wanted to work. One attractive feature, for employers, was that women could be paid less than men for the same work.

However, the range of available jobs in the paid workforce was narrow. During the first half of the twentieth century, women could find work as teachers, retail salespersons, or as domestic servants in higher-class homes. This was significantly interrupted by World War II, which allowed record numbers of women to enter factory jobs to replace men who were away at war. These jobs—hard, dirty, often unsafe and unhealthy—required women to work 60 or more hours per week, nearly double the working week today. Then, with war's end, the returning servicemen and their government expected their jobs to be waiting for them, and women, therefore, were expected to leave these jobs at which they had worked so hard and well. Many did just that, and were happy to return to the male breadwinner/female homemaker family model. But a precedent had been set, and many women sought to continue working as well.

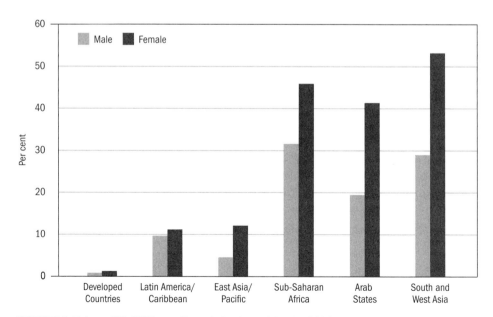

FIGURE 5.3 Estimated World Illiteracy Rates, by Region and Gender, 2004
Source: Adapted from UNESCO Institute for Statistics, www.unesco.org 'Adult (15+) Literacy Rates and Illiterate Population by Region and Gender' (Sept. 2006), using UN Population Division Population Estimates (2004 revision).

After a baby boom that saw record numbers of births between 1947 and 1962, which coincided with steady economic growth that made the male breadwinner model feasible and desirable for many families, women were once again looking for paid work. They faced many barriers in the labour market, including limited access to training and higher education, undiminished household responsibilities, and, often, simple discrimination. Even in the public service, women faced more hindrances than men, being obliged to quit their jobs when they married. Eventually, it became acceptable to hire married women, but women still faced elimination if they became pregnant.

There were many reasons people—especially men—thought it was right to limit women's labour force participation in these ways. Many felt that women should not compete for men's management positions, because—as women—they naturally lacked the skills and abilities needed for these jobs. Many men were ashamed to have others know their wives were working for pay; it implied that they were inadequate breadwinners and therefore lacking in ambition, ability, or manliness. Because men were expected to be 'the breadwinners', as recently as 20 years ago it was common for women to be paid less than men for doing the same work. And, because married women were expected to give their greatest attention to husbands and children, it was assumed that they could not possibly give enough concerted attention to difficult, time-consuming tasks at work.

Much has changed since then. First, the good news. We now understand that by excluding women from the most important jobs, we significantly limit the country's supply of human capital. Today, in many parts of the industrialized world, discrimination against women is illegal. Both women and men are encouraged to follow their educational and occupational talents to the maximum, in whatever field they have chosen. Statistics Canada shows that women accounted for 46 per cent of the total country's labour force participation for the year 2005 and 42 per cent of all full-time, full-year earners.

Today, women have access to a much wider variety of jobs and are not forced to leave if they get married or pregnant. Women are still dominant within the ranks of traditionally female occupations, such as secretary, sales clerk, bookkeeper and accounting clerk, cashier, nurse, elementary schoolteacher, general office clerk, and janitor and cleaning staff. Figure 5.4, for example, illustrates the female predominance in nursing. The difference is that many are now *choosing* to do these jobs. For various reasons, many women still enter jobs that are low-paid or that do not lead to promotions and career paths. Sometimes the content of the job attracts them. Sometimes they think the job will fit in with their family responsibilities. For any given woman, raising a family may take priority at one point in her life, and she may highlight her career later.

However, women continue to suffer disabilities in the workplace. If we look at the distribution of occupations, we still find fewer women than men in high-paying positions, and, on average, full-time working women still earn about 70 cents for every dollar earned by men in similar employment.

Besides, job prestige (and pay) may be tied to whether a job is considered men's or women's work. Office clerks in the early nineteenth century, for instance, were mainly male, and as a result, clerkships were valued jobs. When typewriters and other technological innovations made office work more routine, men abandoned the field and women moved in. The clerical job lost status and pay, and remains a low-status, low-paying position to this day. Perhaps other 'feminizing occupations' like pharmacy, law, and medicine will eventually suffer a similar decline in pay and prestige.

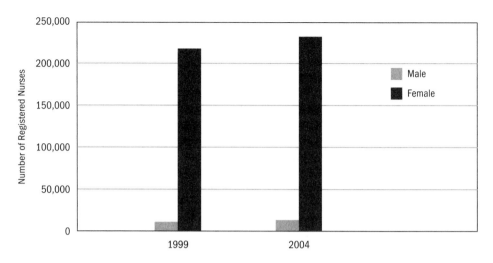

FIGURE 5.4 Nurses by Sex, 1999 and 2004
Source: Canadian Nursing Association, '2004 Workforce Profile of Registered Nurses in Canada', 2; at: <www.
cnanurses.ca/CNA/documents/pdf/publications/workforce_profile_2004_e.pdf>; accessed 16 Dec. 2005.
Reprinted with permission by Canadian Nurses Association/Association des infirmières et infirmiers du Canada.

In many workplaces, women do have an equal opportunity. However, in many others, they still hit a **glass ceiling** when they strive to advance. This term points to the fact that women face nearly hidden obstacles when it comes to advancing into the highest-status jobs. Women are less often hired into these jobs, in part because of an 'old boys' club' mentality and a belief (sometimes) that women are inferior.

To find out whether there is still a 'glass ceiling', we should look not at today's highest earners, but at people who are working their way up the corporate and professional ladders. The evidence suggests that women with higher education do as well as men with the same educational attainment and career goals—until they marry and have children (Jones et al., 1990).

At that point, their pay starts to dip in comparison with men's. At more senior levels, women may put off career plans to bear and raise children. If they do so, they will take longer to achieve more senior executive status. The existence of this 'Mommy track' shows that women themselves make choices about their lives, choices that obviously affect their career plans.

The large-scale entry of women into the paid workforce has had many benefits: for the Canadian economy, for Canadian women, and yes, for Canadian men. Over the years, women have been actively involved in labour organizations and groups that lobbied government for minimum wage legislation, shorter workweeks, and better, healthier work conditions. Today, both women and men have the choice to take time off, without penalty, to look after young children. Women, as paid workers, have done a lot to help humanize the Canadian work environment.

PAID WORK VERSUS HOUSEWORK
In the last few decades, throughout the industrial world, women's lives have changed dramatically. In particular, mothers of young children are now routinely working full-time and part-time in the paid workforce. For women, working outside the home has

many benefits. It contributes to their satisfaction, increases the likelihood of equal treatment within the home, and provides security in case of marital dissolution (Chafetz and Hagan, 1996). However, women continue to do most of the housework and child care.

This results in overload, culturally induced stress, and spillover. Let's look at each of these. (1) Overload means, simply and clearly, that women are saddled with too much work. Often they are physically and emotionally unable to keep up with the demands. (2) The workload and the failure to complete it carry guilt-inducing meanings in our culture. This 'guilt', however inappropriate, results in culturally induced stress. (3) The demands and stress from one domain—paid work, child care, housework—spill over into other domains of a woman's life, and this spillover affects the entire family.

The stress associated with the unequal division of domestic work is often intensified by the fact that women are as likely as or more likely than men to hold stressful jobs. Many of the jobs of women combine heavy continuing demands with a lack of decision-making authority (for example, sales, service, and clerical positions), and in some cases, as in nursing, this can lead to serious burnout. The combination of high demands and lack of workplace authority causes increased risk of stress and health problems, including cardiovascular disorders (Karasek and Theorell, 1990). Because women spend more combined time on paid work and domestic work than men, they experience overload attached to a greater variety of activities, especially during early parenthood (Michelson, 1985, 1988). Also, women often have to work more hours than men because of their lower overall earning power (that is, their hourly differences in earnings). Further, they are much more likely to face the demands of single parenthood.

What many women face today is a twenty-first-century work pattern with a twentieth-century division of labour at home. Arlie Hochschild (1998) has suggested that domestic labour is even less manageable and egalitarian than paid work. This may be why many women do not take advantage of corporate arrangements such as job sharing. If they spend less time at work, it simply means that they'll be doing more domestic labour.

INCOME

In 1945, Saskatchewan CCF MP Gladys Strum announced in Parliament that 'No one has ever objected to women working. The only thing they have ever objected to is paying women for working.' Unequal pay for men and women has been the norm in Canada for over a century and is only now starting to disappear.

Among young men and women with the same educational background in the same line of work, income differences are lessened significantly. For example, in 2000, Canadian university-educated women aged 25–9 who worked in the 10 most common occupations chosen by men of the same age group and qualifications earned about 89 cents for every dollar their male counterparts made. In four out of these 10 occupations, women made at least 90 per cent of what men earned (Statistics Canada, 2004).

Still, 90 per cent is not 100 per cent. As well, the most common occupations held by young women are lower paying than those men most commonly work in. The 10 most common occupations held by university-educated women aged 25–9 paid $37,185 on average. The 10 occupations most common to men of the same age group and education paid women an average of $41,509.

Thus, a large part of the gendered income difference today is because of the continued segregation of work. Gender segregation affects people's earnings even after controlling for human capital variables (such as education level), organizational features (such as industry or size of organization), and job characteristics (such as job level), suggesting the gender gap in pay is at least partly a result of the gendering of workplaces (Knudsen and Roman, 2000).

However, women also receive a lower return on their investment in a university education because of family responsibilities. In 1998, 62 per cent of men but only 49 per cent of women between the ages of 25 and 64 with a university degree were employed in professional or managerial positions (Clark, 2001: 8). This largely reflects women's loss of income and opportunities because of maternity leave, employment in part-time work, or move to another town or province to accompany a male partner. According to Statistics Canada, in 2005, 15 per cent of women employed part-time cited 'caring for children' as their reason for such working arrangements, versus 1 per cent of men in the same category.

In short, income equality flies out the window among men and women who parent children. Whatever their education, men and women have different experiences. The income-depressing effect of parenthood on women is great while the effect on men is zero. Family responsibilities continue to fall most heavily on wives and mothers, not husbands and fathers. For good reason, then, more and more women delay marriage, childbearing, or both in order to pursue higher education and high-paying careers.

FEMINIZATION OF POVERTY

Women are over-represented among the poor people of the world. Researchers have labelled this development the **feminization of poverty**. High rates of female poverty are usually the result of (1) women's occupational disadvantage in society, (2) women's overall subordinate position to men, and (3) women's economic difficulties following abandonment, divorce, or widowhood.

The National Anti-Poverty Organization (NAPO, 1999) calculates the figures for Canada to be as follows: 41 per cent of non-elderly unattached women live in poverty, while 35 per cent of non-elderly unattached men are poor. Not only are the women who head poor families affected by their impoverished state, but their children feel the results of poverty as well. Roughly one in six of Canada's children, or 1.2 million people under 18, live in poverty (Campaign 2000, 2005). The effects on children can be both direct—nutritional insufficiencies or a shortage of satisfactory clothing—or indirect, as when they are forced to assume tasks for which their parents have no time. Gender differences also increase with age. Older women are poorer and sicker, have less satisfactory housing and access to private transport, and are more likely to experience widowhood, disability, and institutionalization than are older men (Gibson, 1996).

Women overall, and single mothers in particular, are more likely to be impoverished than any other demographic group (Albelda and Tilly, 1997.) Various health consequences trouble women who are economically deprived, including increased vulnerability to infectious and other disease, arthritis, stomach ulcers, migraines, clinical depression, stress, vulnerability to mental illness, self-destructive coping behaviours, and increased risk of heart disease (Morris, 2002).

Politics and Gender

People have waged the 'battle of the sexes' for centuries (e.g., Wollstonecraft, 1992 [1792]), a struggle that has until recently been a lopsided victory for men. Only with the rise of the feminist movement and, thus, more progressive views have women made headway in achieving equal standing with men.

Much of this has been achieved through women's ability to vote and take part in various organizations that press for more rights. In earlier times, Canadian women lacked these opportunities. In 1849, all Canadian women were banned from voting in all elections. However, in the mid-1800s, women in Britain, the US, and Canada—among other nations—began to unite to gain political rights. This activism was the beginning of the women's suffrage movement.

In the 1800s, women began to receive more education and became more active in social movements, such as temperance, prison reform, and poor relief, which inevitably involved them in politics. This, combined with the idea of equality, an import from the American and French Revolutions, led to the birth of the women's **suffrage movement** in Canada. Suffrage, or the right to vote, quickly became the chief goal of the women's rights movement. Leaders of the movement believed that if women had the vote, they could use it to influence society in beneficial ways and to gain other rights. But the suffragists faced strong opposition. Most people who opposed women's suffrage believed that women were less intelligent and less able to make political decisions than men. Opponents argued that men could represent their wives better than the wives could represent themselves. Some people feared that women's participation in politics would lead to the end of family life.

Suffrage movements arose in several Western countries during the late 1800s and early 1900s, and ultimately these women accomplished what they sought. In 1893, New Zealand became the first nation to grant women full voting rights. In 1902, Australia gave women the right to vote in national elections. Other countries that agreed to women's suffrage during the early 1900s included Canada, Britain, Finland, Germany, and Sweden. In Britain, the suffrage movement began in the 1860s, but women did not win full voting rights there until 1928 (*World Book*, 2006).

Suffragist leaders brought new energy to electoral district activity and lobbying in the nation's capital. Other leaders appealed to young people, radicals, and working-class women and devoted their efforts to marches, picketing, and other forms of protest. The suffragists were often arrested and sent to jail, where many of them went on hunger strikes. They were persistent campaigners, lecturers, and demonstrators. By 1918, most Canadian women had gained the right to vote, but others were still barred for reasons of race, ethnicity, and religion, and women in Quebec did not gain the franchise in provincial elections until 1940. The job of ensuring universal suffrage wasn't completed for another two generations, with the introduction of the Universal Right to Vote in 1963 and the addition of the equality clause in the Canadian Charter of Rights and Freedoms in 1985 (www.swc-cfc.gc.ca/dates/whm/2003/facts_e.html).

By the middle of the twentieth century, China, France, India, Italy, Japan, and many other nations had given women the right to vote. To date, virtually every country in the world whose male citizens can vote has also extended the franchise to women. Only Saudi Arabia continues to deny women the right to vote (*World Book*, 2006).

Women's Rights and the Feminist Movement in Canada

Many of the changes in gender relations in Canada in the past century have stemmed from the extension to women of rights previously enjoyed only by men. As we can see from the chronology of important events in Box 5.2, the process of achieving equal rights for women was a long one, requiring much participation, activism, and risk-taking—especially by Canadian women.

Box 5.2   Historical Perspective: Some Facts and Dates in Twentieth-Century Canadian Women's History

1897   After a very long fight, Clara Brett Martin became Canada's first woman lawyer and the first woman to practise law in the entire British Empire. (1)

1909   The Criminal Code was amended to criminalize the abduction of women.

1916   Suffrage activist Emily Murphy became Canada's first woman judge (1)

1917   Over 35,000 Canadian women worked in munitions factories while Canadian men fought overseas in World War I. (1)

1918   After a long struggle, Canadian women (except First Nations women) obtained the right to vote in federal elections, after some limited women's suffrage was granted the year earlier. (3)

1921   Canada's first woman MP, Agnes Macphail, began several successful campaigns, including prison reform and the establishment of old age pensions.

1925   The federal divorce law was changed to allow a woman to divorce her husband on the same grounds that a man could divorce his wife—simple adultery. (2)

1929   The Judicial Committee of the Privy Council in the UK overturned a Canadian Supreme Court ruling that women are not 'persons' in law. The victory in the *Persons* case opened up federal court and Senate appointments to women.

1932   Dr Elizabeth Bagshaw started to direct Canada's first family planning clinic, which was illegal at the time.

1940   Quebec women obtained the provincial vote (3) and, in 1941, Quebec women were granted the right to practise law.

1943   There was a massive influx of women into the paid labour force, taking over many traditionally male jobs while men were away at war.

1951   Ontario enacted Canada's first equal pay legislation. Other provinces followed suit between 1952 and 1975. (2)

1952   Manitoba women were the first Canadian women permitted to serve on juries.

1954   A federal Women's Bureau was established (3)

1955   Restrictions on married women in the federal public service were removed. No longer would women public service employees be fired upon marriage. (3)

1960   Aboriginal women (and men) obtained the federal vote. (2)

1967   Women student protestors succeeded in integrating women into the University of Toronto's Hart House, for which women students paid fees but were restricted from entering. (2)

1968   The Presbyterian Church first ordained women.

1969   Women's liberation clubs were formed in some high schools, colleges, and universities, building on informal 'consciousness-raising groups' formed a few years earlier. (2)

1970   The groundbreaking *Report of the Royal Commission on the Status of Women* was published, calling attention to a wide variety of gender inequalities

1971   The federal government amended the Canada Labour Code to prohibit sex discrimination, reinforce equal pay for equal work, and establish a 17-week maternity leave. (2)

1973   The first rape crisis centres in Canada opened in Vancouver and Toronto, and Interval House, one of the first shelters for abused women, also opened in Toronto. (2)

1974   The RCMP hired its first woman member. (3)

1976   The remaining overt discrimination against female immigrants was removed from the Citizenship Act. (2)

1978 The law changed so that women could no longer be fired for pregnancy in federally regulated industries.

1981 1,300 women met to demand the inclusion of women's rights in the proposed new
Charter of Rights. By lobbying members of Parliament intensively, they brought about
the inclusion of women's rights in Canada's Constitution (sections 15 and 28 of the
Charter). (2)

1983 Rape laws were broadened to sexual assault laws, and for the first time it became a
criminal offence for a man to rape his wife.

1983 The Canadian Human Rights Act prohibited sexual harassment in workplaces under
federal jurisdiction. (3)

1985 The Indian Act was amended so that Aboriginal women who married non-status men
could retain their Indian status. (2)

1988 The first woman justice of the Supreme Court of Canada, Bertha Wilson, wrote one of
the majority judgements that struck down Canada's restrictive abortion law.

1993 Canada's refugee guidelines were changed to include women facing gender-related
persecution.

1999 The Supreme Court ruled that job standards and tests cannot be solely based on capabilities that would favour men.

Source: Morris (2000), based on materials in the following: (1) Prentice et al. (1988); (2) Armour and
Stanton (1990); and (3) Status of Women Canada (1992). Reprinted by permission of the publisher.

The suffrage movement, or the 'first wave' of feminism, made important gains for women's rights in Canada through the late nineteenth and early twentieth centuries. Early feminists, represented nationally by the Woman's Christian Temperance Union, the Young Women's Christian Association, the National Council of Women of Canada, and the Federated Women's Institutes, focused mainly on three sets of issues—political rights, legal rights, and social reform. These early feminists fought to place the 'woman's role on a more secure material footing' rather than attempt to shatter the traditional gender myths that considered the man to be the provider and the woman to be the nurturer (Brooks, 2007: 426).

True to these goals, the tactics Canadian feminists employed were cautious and moderate: 'Unlike their sisters in Great Britain and the United States, Canadian suffragists did not resort to such confrontational methods as chaining themselves to the fences surrounding Parliament, physically resisting the police, or hunger strikes' (ibid.). Their more moderate tactics were successful and brought women the vote. It was only in the last 35 years of the twentieth century that the 'second wave' of feminism began its attacks on the cultural and social bases of inequality. Without questioning gender roles, as the women's movement has done over several decades, it is unlikely that women would have made strides towards social and economic equality.

Granting women's demands in one area often led to granting demands in other areas. After the right to vote was granted in 1918, five determined suffragists—the so-called Famous Five—pushed for changes to the British North America Act that would deem women to be legal 'persons' who qualified for appointment to the Senate. In 1929, the declaration of personhood for women by the Judicial Committee of the Privy Council increased the likelihood that further rights would be forthcoming.

A turning point in gender equalization was the Royal Commission on the Status of Women, which began in 1967 and heard the concerns of individuals and organizations across the country. As well as considering the specifics of women's lives, the Commission also looked at some of the underlying causes of women's inequality. One outcome of the Royal Commission's work was the establishment of Status of Women Canada as a government agency. Since the Commission, women have continued to push for changes that would bring equality closer to reality.

The feminist ideology, or *feminism*, has been chief in stimulating and directing these political efforts. As with all political ideologies, feminism comes in various forms and comprises a variety of factions, each with a different and gradually more radical opinion on how the struggle for women's rights should continue.

The extreme position taken by some members of the feminist movement aside, women's political organizations have advanced our awareness and understanding of gender relations. Perhaps the greatest triumph of the women's movement has been to increase public acceptance of the fluidity of gender: the notion that men can be 'feminine' and women can be 'masculine'. Because of this ongoing shift in social attitudes, the ideas of biological sex and sociological gender are not as rigidly paired and opposed as they used to be. Also, gender studies have advanced awareness of existing levels of gender inequality. One hopes that the women's and men's movements will continue their instructional activities, with the result that this will bring society closer to flexible and tolerant understandings of gender roles and greater gender equality.

Feminism is a form of political activism that tries to change the conditions under which men and women lead their lives. Feminism, then, has an emancipatory goal—it aims to free people from oppression. If gender relations always reflect the larger pattern of social relations in a society, then changing gender relations requires changing those social relations as well. Feminism is one of the social movements that—alongside the anti-war, civil rights, anti-racism, and environmental movements—have in the last three decades reshaped modern politics. Like these other social movements in spirit and organization, feminism has looked for grassroots support, affirmed agency and spontaneity in politics, and dramatized its struggle outside the traditional party system using non-traditional electoral methods. Like these other movements, feminism has appealed to the social identity—the personal life experience—of its supporters. More than that, by arguing that 'the personal is political', feminism opened new domains of social life—sexuality, housework, child-rearing, and so on—to political debate and legislation. It also forced us all to examine the roots of our being as gendered subjects—that is, how we get to be, and think of ourselves as, men versus women or mothers versus fathers.

Men's Movements

Without the push from the women's movement, the men's movement would never have begun. It was only after female activism began to shatter traditional gender myths about women that men, in the later years of the last century, began to re-evaluate their own notions of masculinity. Only after women began to voice their dissatisfaction with the constraints that gender placed on them did men begin to examine their own gender and the costs of living a myth. Thus, some felt that gender oppresses all individuals; and that in the same way women needed to free themselves from the effects of patriarchy, men needed to free themselves from the damaging outcomes of masculinity. Many men came to feel frustration over the need to conform to masculine stereotypes.

Men are institutionally privileged, it is true; but they are privileged at a cost of shorter lives, emotionally shallow relations, and less time spent with loved ones. Moreover, not all men are similarly privileged, as categories of race, class, ethnicity, and sexual orientation cut across this gender status.

Mindful of this variety in men's lives, 30 years ago sociologist Arthur Shostak (1977) wrote that four questions had become central to the study of gender relations: (1) Do men know much about the issues being raised by the women's movement? (2) Are they ready to discuss these issues? (3) Are they ready to do anything in response? (4) Are they ready to try to know other males as brothers? Shostak concluded that while men were familiar with the complaints of the women's movement (due largely to TV), few were willing to make more than minor compromises. For example, they typically rejected reforms that threatened their job security as primary breadwinners.

Since then, there has been no decrease in what Collier (1996) has characterized as a complex crisis of masculinity. The masculine male role continues to be challenged by feminist, gay, lesbian, and queer critiques of heterosexuality. One result of this challenge has been the rise of men's organizations. During the 1980s and 1990s, at least two streams of male organization emerged: pro-feminist masculinity on the one hand, and a range of organizations that attempted to reawaken traditional masculinity on the other hand (Clatterbaugh, 2000). Competing discourses and social movements came to include (1) the mythopoetic men's movement; (2) the Christian Promise Keepers; (3) the men's liberation movement; (4) the men's rights movements; (5) the radical men's movement; (6) the social feminist men's movements; (7) a racialized masculine movement; and (8) a gay male liberation movement (Messner, 1997). Space allows only a brief discussion of these varieties.

On the political right, some men have been attracted to the 'mythopoetic men's movement', especially as represented by poet Robert Bly's *Iron John* (1990). In the late 1980s, this movement particularly appealed to a professional middle class arising since World War II by calling for a cultural revitalization of American masculinity. The narratives of the movement offered participants the power of stories, the power of status, and the power of essentialism (Mechling and Mechling, 1994). The goal of this mythopoetic movement is to produce 'fierce and tender men' (as noted in the title of a book on the topic by Jesser, 1996) by getting men to perform idealized male roles in the wild. The movement creatively reworks colonialist fantasies of non-Western societies and, in this way, forces participants to examine their own conflicting experiences of power (Bonnett, 1996).

Some analysts view this movement as progressive. Face-to-face, members of this movement are said to develop moral understandings of both a dominant (or hegemonic) masculinity and a counter-hegemonic masculinity. Members of the mythopoetic men's movement come to see themselves as opposing a form of gender identity that has limited and damaged both men and women. Their goal is to formulate a counter-hegemonic masculinity. They are also actively involved in critiquing a dominant culture that stresses the work ethic, professional success, and material achievement at all costs. As an alternative, they imagine lives that prioritize emotional growth, family life, love, creativity, and spiritual pursuits (Magnuson, 2001).

However, other analysts view this movement as regressive. Ferber (1997), for example, has noted a strong likeness between the mythopoetic men's movement and the white supremacist movement. For example, both movements reinforce broader backward-looking discourses about gender. They both frame gender in essentialist terms, view present-day American men as demasculinized, blame current social problems on this demasculinization, blame women and the women's movement for this demasculinization, and try to help men rediscover their lost masculinity and assert their rightful authority. Both movements encourage white men to see themselves as victims and argue that (white) men are the oppressed minority in today's world. In short, the mythopoetic movement contains contradictory and often regressive elements, despite its goal to change men's ways of thinking.

Similar tensions between progressive and regressive ideology are noted in the youth-oriented Straight Edge Movement—a male-dominated youth movement also struggling to create a more progressive masculinity. Despite its goal, this movement, too, reflects dominant constructions of masculinity (Haenfler, 2004). A strong collective identity provides members with 'structure', a basis for commitment, and guidelines for participation. Nonetheless, there is a continuing tension within the Straight Edge Movement between tolerance and militancy, inclusiveness and exclusivity. One aspect of Straight Edge proposes a progressive vision of manhood, another reflects dominant masculinity. These multiple expressions of masculinity that emerge within a single men's movement illustrate the problems of remaking manhood from a masculinist stance (Haenfler, 2003).

By far the most studied men's movement in this tradition is Promise Keepers, a men's evangelical movement. The goal of Promise Keepers is to rejuvenate 'godly manhood', which is marked by both expressive and instrumental characteristics (Bartowski, 2000). As Kelley-Moore (2001) notes, the Promise Keepers (PK) experienced growth and success in the 1990s. The PK ideological frame developed at the junction of two broader social trends: the men's movement and evangelical membership growth. PK has adopted evangelical issues to appeal to the growing evangelical audience, coupling traditionally conservative issues such as the abolition of pornography with emerging evangelical issues such as racial harmony. Simultaneously, PK has borrowed rhetoric from different factions of the men's movement, redefining issues of masculinity in a religious context and arguing for increased male–male interaction.

Although claiming to be apolitical, the Promise Keepers organization has mobilized hundreds of thousands of men into taking action that is political in its outcomes. Whether reclaiming the primacy of traditional family relationships, holding a 'Sacred Assembly' (its version of a Million Man March) of prayer in Washington, DC, in October 1997, or stressing the racial and ethnic equality of all men, this organization has had huge success in mobilizing men in the US. Despite financial troubles in the past few years, the organization carries on, now supported solely by donations. Promise Keepers remains a powerful influence on many men in the US. Also, it has expanded into other countries—including Canada—promoting an international agenda through Promise Keepers Global Ministries (Bernotsky and Bernotsky, 1999).

Why do men join the Promise Keepers? In a qualitative study of the conservative Promise Keepers movement, middle-class, mainly white, suburban fathers were interviewed in focus groups about their parenting experiences. Grounded theory analysis found the men were experiencing gender-role strain as they tried to conform to traditional masculine role norms. The Promise Keepers movement gave them an ideology and social support system that helped them become more involved fathers, while also reassuring them that they were the leaders of their families. With these supports, the men were able to build a more personally gratifying fatherhood identity (Silverstein et al., 1999).

Part of the success of Promise Keepers may be its organizational structure, which builds on two contradictory group structures—a large formal organization and multiple small informal groups—that work together smoothly. Lacking a centralized ministry, the Seven Promises of the Promise Keepers serve both to integrate members of the small groups and to preserve an ideal distance between the small groups and the formal organization (Schindler and Lena, 2000).

The somewhat contradictory PK gender discourses have resulted in four versions of godly manhood: the Rational Patriarch (traditional masculinity), the Expressive Egalitarian (men's liberationism), the Tender Warrior (poeticized manhood), and the Multicultural Man (interracial masculinity). PK leaders use rhetorical devices to manage the tensions and contradictions that surface within and among these discourses. However, fractures within the ideology remain. The multiple depictions of godly manhood, which contributed to a rapid rise of this evangelical men's movement during the 1990s, may also be one source of its recent decline (Bartkowski, 2001).

The pro-feminist approach is somewhat more consistent. It starts with the observation that—as members of particular classes, races, and other social groups—most men, like most women, are systematically mistreated and therefore oppressed in modern societies. While men are often the agents of the oppression of women, and in many senses benefit from it, their interests in the gender order are constructed by and within it and, hence, are open to change. Since in many ways men's human needs and capacities are not met within the gender orders of modern societies, they also have a latent 'emancipatory interest' in their transformation (New, 2001).

True, men and women may think differently about various topics. We can examine the male perspective on many issues, for example, dating, commitment, social interaction, sports, male friendships, and male–female relationships in the workplace, to clarify the way men think, as Wicks (1996) has done. But whatever the gendered differences, until men and women learn to communicate once again, and men learn to communicate their ideas, needs, and reactions to women's changing roles and their experiences of being men, the male–female divide will persist.

New critical approaches in masculinity studies are influenced by feminist, antiracist, and pro-gay politics, incorporating feminist and postmodernist notions of identity and stressing a variety of masculinities. By recognizing that men need women and vice versa, new writings on gender relations—though varied and often disagreeing—provide opportunities to transform masculinity and, therefore, men, and to create alliances that build community (Newton, 1998).

A prime example of the pro-feminist men's alliance with women has been around efforts to lessen violence against women (on this, see Milne, 2001). Flood (2001) argues, for example, that men's anti-violence activism is making an important contribution to ending violence against women. Men's groups focused on gender-based violence have emerged in over a dozen countries—for example, in Mexico (on this, see Garda, 2001). In such mobilizations, men's efforts to end men's violence embody partnerships across gender lines and increase gender justice.

In recent years, the close connection between male pro-feminism and feminism and the contradictions in pro-feminist theorizations of traditional masculinity have contributed to the decline of men's movements (Clatterbaugh, 2000). At the same time, there have been gains, however humble. For example, Singleton (2003), reporting on the findings from a qualitative study of two relationally centred men's groups, notes that the group involvement enabled participants to transcend traditional masculine modes of relating and form intimate and trusting relationships with other participants. The interviews show that this change is attributable to group processes, not merely the result of an ideological commitment to change.

In short, the so-called men's movement has been mainly reactive—not so much a force in promoting change as a response to change. In comparison with women, men—ideologically, socially, and electorally—have tended to resist liberal policies of almost every kind, while women have done the opposite. This is evident in issues as diverse as abortion, daycare, gay marriage, capital punishment, and sending troops overseas (though in fairness, this gender difference is more marked in the United States than it is in Canada, which is generally more liberal). So, in the end, it is the women's movement that has transformed Western societies in the late twentieth century. The men's movement, if it persists at all, will have to catch up.

Gender Stereotypes in the Media

Despite major advances in women's opportunities and rights during the twentieth century, portrayals of girls and women in the mass media, especially in television, keep harmful gender stereotypes alive. In this way, they continue to keep women from achieving full equality with men at home or at work (see, e.g., Merlo and Smith, 1994a, 1994b). In the mass media, we see gendered images all around us—gendered images of women and men, boys and girls. Even animals are presented as gendered (think about Disney cartoons, for example). These gendered images are paralleled in media advertisements for consumer items and in the items people end up buying—toys, clothes, cars, beer, and deodorant. The media often present items as proper for use by one or the other biological sex. Our culture assumes what male people and female people will typically want to do. Such assumptions produce a self-fulfilling prophecy: often our children turn out to be how we expect them to be.

Consider Saturday morning children's television: cartoon shows interspersed with commercials. Advertisers aim the commercials directly at girls or boys, typically matched to the show—Barbie dolls (or the equivalent) for girls, GI Joe figures (or the equivalent) for boys. These programs entertain children, but they also teach them which toys are for them, how we expect them as girls or boys to behave, and what we expect them, as gendered beings, to want in our society.

The messages from TV are clear. Ideal boys will fight physically and push aside others whom they do not respect, making decisions about themselves and for others weaker than them. Girls will fight verbally (if at all), play with dolls, and wait to be chosen or told what to do. Storybooks and movies carry similar messages. Years later, young women follow the men whom they feel have chosen them, trying to appear not too aggressive, not too successful, in case they are seen as a threat and rejected (Brinson, 1992; Furnham and Bitar, 1993; Salamon and Robinson, 1987).

Some have hailed the growing display of open sexuality in the mass media as liberating and empowering, for women as well as for men. Others, however, believe that some forms of sexually open display—for example, pornography—are not empowering. Pornography objectifies women by depicting women in dehumanizing ways. In doing so, it helps to uphold female submission and male domination. Like prostitution, pornography supports patriarchal culture and its gender hierarchy (Leuchtag, 1995).

Straight pornography and gay pornography can also objectify and dehumanize males. Degrading pornography denigrates all its subjects, whether female or male.

Others have celebrated the way current popular culture embraces the word 'girl' as a term of female empowerment, especially as it is applied to high-profile female athletes—hockey player Hayley Wickenheiser, for example, or speed skaters Cindy Klausen and Clara Hughes. Supposedly, the new 'girl culture' of these female athletes offers young women role models that are better than prior images of girls as vulnerable, doll-like, and helpless. The newer image promotes confidence, health, and authority, and that is all to the good (Geissler, 2001).

The popular media in general, though, are more likely to describe women by the number of children they have, men by their occupations or political affiliations. A woman who stresses politics in her life or a man whose priority is his children's care is more often pointed out as a curiosity rather than as a role model. These are only a few of the gender stereotypes that bombard us from the media (Livingstone, 1994; Media-Watch, 1991; Shaw and Martin, 1992).

Of course, members of some branches of the media see their role differently. They aspire to be forerunners and agents of change. Thus, they will purposely show the female engineer or the male nurse or elementary teacher not as curiosities but as experts in their fields, deliberately chosen as role models. Some programs and magazines also typically show an awareness of diversity in race and ethnicity. However, the rest of the media often stereotype these programs and magazines as 'educational' or 'feminist'. The public often receives them in the same terms; they are watched, read, or listened to by fewer people than other aspects of the media.

Some socially conscious agencies are also now trying to use commercial media (for example, television advertisements) to promote change. We will occasionally see, for example, male sports stars talking about problems of violence against women and trying to promote models of masculinity that are concerned, caring, and nurturing though strong. However, the idea of a rapid direct imitative influence of media images on viewers, and so on society, may be too simplistic. The media may reflect and reinforce culture more than they are able to easily change culture and society.

Research by Melissa Milkie (2002) shows that editors of girls' magazines share in the critique of the depiction of girls in the media, recognizing they should change images but cannot. In these accounts, the editors reveal struggles at the organizational and the institutional levels over altering narrow images of femininity. At the same time, these editors also undermine the critique by suggesting that the (good) reader is supposed to understand the images. Here, editors claim that they can change images but should not. Eventually, both sets of responses prevent the portrayal of women in the media from helping to redefine femininity in an empowering manner and undermine the power of girls' resistance to media images.

The mass media may not be the main cause of gender inequality in Canada, but they do play a major role in creating and upholding gender stereotypes. In this way, they help to perpetuate existing inequalities between men and women.

Theories of Gender Inequality

Like the other social issues discussed in this book, sexism and gender inequality have been viewed differently by proponents of different sociological approaches.

We will briefly review these views, starting with the structural-functionalist approach. Remember that structural functionalists ask of every social arrangement: *What function* does it perform for society as a whole? In this case, how does gender inequality contribute to the well-being of society as a whole? Functionalist theorists starting with Talcott Parsons (1951) would say that a gendered division of labour is the most effective and efficient way to carry out society's tasks. It may even have evolutionary survival value for the human race. Mothers, by their early attachment to the child (via pregnancy and breast-feeding, for example), are well-suited to raising the family's children. Since they are at home with the children anyway, mothers are also well-suited to caring for the household while the husband is at work outside the home.

Kingsley Davis and Wilbert Moore (1945) might also say that gender inequality arising from this arrangement is due to the higher social value most people place on expert paid work done outside the home. Given the need for skills and training, not everyone can be a doctor, lawyer, manager, plumber, and so on. By comparison, almost anyone can take care of children and keep the house clean.

Conflict theorists and feminist theorists, by contrast, always ask the question: *Who benefits* from a particular social arrangement? In this case, who is best served by gender inequality? Marxists would tend to answer this question by class relations: capitalism requires the low-cost social reproduction of a workforce from one generation to the next. Families are the best and cheapest way to raise new workers. Mothers have the job of keeping all the family earners and earners-to-be healthy—well-fed, housed, and cared for emotionally. They do this at no cost to capitalists who will benefit from the surplus value workers produce.

The Marxist approach assumes that working-class men and women are on the same side, both equally victims of the capitalist class. By contrast, the feminist approach assumes that women have a different experience from men and may be exploited by men of their own class, as well as by capitalists. Therefore, they see gender inequality as mainly serving the interests of men who, by lording it over their girlfriends, wives, and daughters, at least have someone subservient to them just as they are to their own bosses. The theory of patriarchy—that men are the main and universal cause of women's oppression—is compatible with Marxist analyses that view working-class women as being the victims of both class and gender oppression.

Symbolic interactionists, for their part, ask: *How* is an arrangement *symbolized*? For example, how is gender inequality negotiated, symbolized, and communicated in our society? The presumption is that inequalities arise where social differences have been symbolized, communicated, and negotiated—that is, made into something that is 'taken for granted' by the population at large. From this standpoint, people are always trying to understand and normalize social interaction through shared meanings. Thus, symbolic interactionists are concerned with the ways that gender differences become gender inequalities—for example, the ways that young women become 'objectified' and turned into sex *objects*. They would also want to understand how the double sexual standard, which has allowed men more sexual freedom than women, has been 'negotiated' so that many women go along with an agenda that, it would seem to many people, benefits males more than females.

Related to this approach, social constructionists always ask the question: *When and how* did the arrangement *emerge*? When, for example, did gender inequality emerge in a particular society, what events preceded this emergence, and what individuals or groups were especially instrumental in this process of 'moral entrepreneurship'? This approach is much more historically oriented than the symbolic interactionist approach to which it is related. So, for example, a social constructionist would note that gender inequality began to decline (a second time) in the 1960s and 1970s, largely because of the actions of the women's movement.

The women's movement was especially successful then because social protest (against the rich, against imperialists, and against racists, for example) was in the air throughout the Western world. Besides, the baby boom had already ended; there was now a need for two family incomes, and therefore a need for less child-bearing and more education for women. This new agenda—getting women out of the homes and into the marketplace—was aided significantly by the development of reliable birth control pills that made it possible for people to have sex without having babies. Cutting the links between gender, sexuality, and child-bearing was central to the emergence of women as full-fledged members of society. It also helped gay and lesbian people stake a claim to full social inclusion, for similar reasons.

Notably, all these explanations are compatible with one another. Each focuses on a different aspect of the rise, maintenance, and decline of gender inequality. Table 5.3 summarizes the main sociological perspectives.

Social Consequences of Gender Inequality

As one would expect, issues of gender are involved in most if not all aspects of Canadian social life. We have already discussed issues associated with education, work, and income

Table 5.3 Five Main Sociological Paradigms on Gender Inequality	
Structural Functionalism	■ Elements in society are all interrelated. ■ Inequality rewards effectiveness and efficiency. ■ Inequality is based on value consensus. ■ Gender inequality stems from what was at one time an effective household arrangement, which has failed to develop with the times.
Conflict Theory	■ Gender inequality results from struggle for economic and social power. ■ Capitalists benefit from gender inequality. ■ Gender inequality forces women to maintain the workforce without pay.
Symbolic Interactionism	■ Socialization and labelling shape gender identities. ■ Most variations between men and women are cultural and learned. ■ A gendered self develops out of a process of gradual socialization, which occurs at all levels of social life: women learn to do women's jobs and see themselves as suited for these tasks. ■ Values, media, religion, and language help maintain gender differences. ■ Double standards are considered normal.
Feminism	■ Gender inequality is almost universal. ■ This inequality is a result of patriarchal values and institutions. ■ Gender inequality favours men over women.
Social Constructionism	■ The creation of (in)equality is a social process. ■ It usually requires leadership and organization. ■ Some social periods are more conducive to this process than others.

that pose particular problems for women. In this section, we consider crime, violence, and self-esteem.

Crime and Violence

Using data from the General Social Survey, Statistics Canada reported in 2005 that 'While overall rates of violent victimization did not differ between men and women, men were at greater risk of physical assault. Women were at higher risk of sexual assault' (Statistics Canada, 2005c). Although men are sometimes the victims of rape and sexual assault, these vicious crimes are mainly directed towards women. Rape is devastating for the victim not only because of the physical and psychological violations, but also because the victim must come to terms with the fact that she was attacked solely because of her gender. Rape offenders, who are usually male, typically harbour misogynistic, sadistic attitudes towards their victims.

According to the Ontario Women's Directorate (2000), 83 per cent of all sexual assault victims in Canada during 1998 were women, while 98 per cent of the accused perpetrators were men. Young women are at particular risk: 24 per cent of single women aged 18 to 24 reported having been victims of date rape, while another 12 per cent of married women in that same age group reported at least one incident of violence by a marital partner in a one-year period, compared with an average of 3 per cent for all married or cohabiting women.

In 2005 Statistics Canada reported:

> Nearly one-third of all women who had sought temporary accommodation in a shelter for abused women on April 14, 2004 had stayed there at some time during the past . . . . On this date, there were 3,274 women and 2,835 children in such shelters, 82 per cent of them escaping abuse. The remaining women and children were there for other reasons such as housing, addictions, and mental health issues. Of all women who had stayed in shelters previously, 40 per cent had been there once in the previous year, 38 per cent had been there two to four times, and about 1 in 10 had been to the facility five times or more during the previous year. The largest proportion of women staying in shelters, just over one-third, were between 25 and 34 years old (Statistics Canada, 2005a).

Statistics Canada also reported in 2005 that, 'As in previous years, most homicides in 2004 were committed by someone known to the victim. Among solved homicides, half were committed by an acquaintance, one-third by a family member, and 15 per cent by a stranger' (Statistics Canada, 2005b). Though Canada's spousal homicide rate has generally been declining since the mid-1970s, women remain much more likely to be killed by their spouse than are men.

> In 2004, the spousal homicide rate against women was five times higher than the corresponding rate for men. . . . Those in common-law relationships were more at-risk than those living in legally married unions. In 2004, the homicide rate against persons living in common-law relationships was almost five times higher than the rate for those living in legal marriages. Among solved homicides involving victims aged 15 and older, one-half of all women were killed by someone with whom they

had had an intimate relationship at some point, either through marriage or dating. The comparative figure for men was 8 per cent. Men were far more likely to be killed by an acquaintance or a stranger. (Ibid.)

In our society, violence against women runs the gamut from verbal and psychological harassment to physical assault, sexual assault, and homicide. Research on criminal victimization in Canada (Sacco and Johnson, 1990: 21) shows that 'rates of personal victimization are highest among males, the young, urban dwellers, those who are single or unemployed . . . . Risk of personal victimization is also greater among Canadians who often engage in evening activities outside the home and among heavier consumers of alcohol.' Most recorded victimization is male victimization in public, but this is not the *female* experience of crime or victimization.

This issue of 'experience' is important. It puts into focus the concerns and fears with which women in our society must deal and men can ignore. Many women fear going out to a park at night, for example, or even to take a stroll in their own neighbourhood. Universities across Canada offer free, student-run 'walksafe' services where trained volunteer escorts accompany students, faculty, and community members across campus or to a nearby public transit stop after dark. Women are always aware of the potential danger of attack, which most men do not feel they need to consider.

Without ever taking a sociology course, young women soon learn the most dangerous, crime-prone (including violence-prone) people in Canadian society are young, single men. Less obvious is the fact that the danger to women is *least* likely to come from strangers outside the home. More often than not, it comes from intimates: from spouses, dates, male acquaintances, and workmates. In particular, family life has the potential for both physical and mental abuse since stronger family members have the power to take out their frustrations on weaker ones within the privacy of the home.

We have no reliable figures on *all* the violence that takes place, but domestic violence and rape are likely much more common than the official statistics reveal. For various reasons, the data on domestic violence are uncertain. For example, research done by York University's Institute for Social Research in 1992 has shown that women's reporting of sexual abuse on a survey is significantly affected by (1) whether another person is present at the interview, and (2) whether the respondent likes the interviewer. This evidence of an 'interviewer effect' on the reporting of abuse reminds us that *all* data are gathered in a social environment. All data are 'social facts' in more than one sense. Therefore, they are always open to debate and reanalysis.

Research on abuse also shows that violence often occurs after excessive drinking, as a spillover of work stress, or because of a loss of control over anger. But social structural effects are no less important than these psychological ones. For example, the state's attitude towards violence against women significantly affects domestic conditions women have to face everyday. Often, police are reluctant to intervene when neighbours call to complain of a noisy family dispute, or even if the wife or partner herself complains. Many people still think that family members should be allowed to work their problems out for themselves. Police and social workers, they believe, should stay out of the picture until there are overwhelming grounds for outside involvement.

The stigma of abuse also discourages many victims, particularly those with social reputations to protect, from leaving their tormenters. For example, the wealthy rarely use shelters and legal clinics, even though they may suffer from just as much domestic violence as other women. As a result, within wealthy neighbourhoods, the extent of domestic violence may be hidden.

Women as well as men commit violent acts. However, data indicate the chances of injury for male and female respondents differ significantly. Since men are usually stronger than women, wives are more often injured than are husbands, even when both partners are acting violently.

While women are slightly more likely to start a violent episode—usually by slapping, kicking, or throwing an object—men are more likely to respond with more devastating force—beating, choking, or threatening to use (or actually using) a knife or gun. As a result, nearly half of women (49 per cent) who report being abused by a previous spouse in the past five years in Canada suffered physical injury, compared with 21 per cent of men. Fully 19 per cent of these women and only 5 per cent of these men received injuries severe enough to need medical attention. In retrospect, 48 per cent of female victims and 13 per cent of male victims feared for their lives during the ordeal (Statistics Canada, 2001: 40).

One survey of self-reported domestic violence in Canada shows that (1) younger people are more violent to their spouses than older people; (2) unemployed people are more violent than employed people; but (3) people with less education and lower income are no more violent than those who are highly educated and who have higher incomes. There is also a relationship between a belief in patriarchy and wife battering. Husbands who believe men ought to rule women are more likely than other husbands to beat their wives. In turn, a belief in patriarchy depends on educational and occupational level (Lupri et al., 1994; Lupri, 1993).

Ethnicity is also a factor here. Some cultures in multicultural Canada and elsewhere are more patriarchal than others. Specifically, other things being equal, patriarchal beliefs appeal to lower-status, less-educated men, perhaps because they have so little control over other aspects of their lives.

The most revealing finding in this study is that high rates of domestic violence are associated with high levels of domestic stress. That is, the more stressful events a person reports experiencing in the previous year, the more violence will have taken place within the household. Still, even if stress and frustrations result in violence, they do not excuse it. The real problem underlying violence is not stress or frustration but the fact that some men find it acceptable to channel their frustrations into violence towards family members.

DATE RAPE AND SEXUAL INEQUALITY

Another important concern is 'date rape'. A survey conducted on 44 college and university campuses across Canada by sociologists Walter DeKeseredy and Katharine Kelly found that four women in five said they had been subjected to abuse by a dating partner. Overall, nearly as many men admitted having acted abusively towards their dates (DeKeseredy and Kelly, 1993).

The weight of the findings was attacked (Gartner and Fox, 1993) because the study listed a very wide range of behaviours under the heading of 'abuse'. These behaviours included insults, swearing, and accusations of flirting with others or acting spitefully, as well as violent and grotesque acts such as using or threatening to use a gun or knife, beating, kicking, or biting the dating partner. So it is best to separate the violent from the less violent abuses before we try to analyze the results.

When we do this, certain patterns fall into place. Women report violent abuse directed towards them more than twice as often as men admit to having been violently abusive, but with less violent or non-violent abuse, men and women admit them equally often. For example, 65 per cent of women reported being insulted or sworn at by a date, and 64 per cent of men reported having done that to a date. On the other hand, 11 per cent of women reported being slapped by a date, yet only 4 per cent of men reported slapping a date. Also, 8 per cent of women report being kicked, bitten, or hit with a fist, yet only 2 per cent of men reported having done any of those things. The data also showed that violent abuses on dates were not only physical, but sexual as well. As before, male respondents were only about one-third to one-half as likely to report having been sexually abusive as women were to report having been assaulted by a male date (DeKeseredy and Kelly, 1993).

Most instances of forced sex occur between people who know each other. The result is, too often, that women blame themselves for the experience. Because they know the assailant, they react passively to the sexual assault. Because they react passively, they blame themselves for not reacting more forcefully. A few even continue the dating relationship.

Historically, women who faced violence from intimates could not rely on police protection. Because the larger community saw domestic violence as a private matter, police were trained to respond accordingly. In doing so, they reflected the expectation of the community and the criminal justice system that officers should be involved in only the most extreme cases. Police were taught to either defuse the situation quickly and leave or try to mediate the 'dispute'. This reinforced a view of the victim and assailant as equal parties with equal power over each other's behaviour. Victims were left feeling confused and at fault. Having turned to the police for help, they were left blaming themselves for bothering to call.

Only recently have we come to understand that domestic violence is usually uneven. Even if men do not introduce the physical violence during an argument, once it is launched they tend to use more physical force than women do. Further, men and women often have different goals in using force. Women are more likely to leave an unsatisfactory relationship, while men are more likely to use force to prevent the partner from leaving. Women will use violence mainly to protect themselves. Men will also use violence to compel partners to give them sex. Only recently have law enforcement agencies and the public come to accept spousal rape as a criminal offence. In the past, many considered such behaviour, like spousal abuse, to be a private matter between husband and wife.

HARASSMENT

Another problem that women sometimes must deal with is **sexual harassment** in the workplace. In fact, according to Status of Women Canada, in 2000 women represented 78 per cent of all reported cases of criminal harassment (National Day of Remembrance, 2005). According to the Canadian Human Rights Commission (2004):

Harassment is any unwanted physical or verbal conduct that offends or humiliates you. Such conduct can interfere with your ability to do a job or obtain a service. Harassment—a type of discrimination—can take many forms, such as:
- threats, intimidation, or verbal abuse;
- unwelcome remarks or jokes about subjects like your race, religion, disability, or age;

■ displaying sexist, racist, or other offensive pictures or posters;
■ sexually suggestive remarks or gestures;
■ inappropriate physical contact, such as touching, patting, pinching, or punching;
■ physical assault, including sexual assault.

Harassment may involve a single incident or several incidents over the course of time. This creates a negative work environment that may interfere with job performance; it may also result in women being refused a desirable job, promotion, or training opportunity. The harasser may be a supervisor, a co-worker, or someone who provides service, such as a clerk in a government department.

It is impossible to know the full extent of gender-based harassment in Canada today, since much of it likely goes unreported. Harassment comes in at least two forms. First, sexual harassment may be the open demand by employers for sexual favours in exchange for promotion opportunities, salary increases, and preferential treatment, in other words, **quid pro quo sexual harassment**. The second type of harassment is subtler; it involves fostering a hostile and unpleasant work environment through sexist remarks, jokes, and insults. It is this second type of harassment that is least likely to be reported.

The Canadian Human Rights Commission (ibid.) reminds us that:

The employer is responsible for any harassment that occurs in the workplace. It is the employer's duty to:
■ make it clear that harassment will not be tolerated;
■ state a harassment policy;
■ make sure every employee understands the policy and procedures for dealing with harassment;
■ inform supervisors and managers of their responsibility to provide a harassment-free work environment;
■ examine and correct harassment problems as soon as they come to light, even if a formal complaint has not been received.

Enforcing these policies is an important first step. However, harassment occurs also in schools—sometimes in the form of 'bullying'—and in public spaces, where norms against harassment are harder to enforce.

STALKING

A rarer but more menacing form of harassment is stalking. Recently, stalking has emerged as a new form of criminal deviance in our society. This crime has gained much attention in recent years because it is common and is associated with gendered abuse and violence. Stalking is a form of relationship abuse that may evolve into violent physical, psychological, and sexual forms. In the year 2000, nine in 10 female victims of stalking in Canada were stalked by men (www.metrac.org/new/stat_sta.htm). In all US stalking cases for the year of 1997, stalkers made overt threats to about 45 per cent of victims; spied on or followed about 75 per cent of victims; vandalized the property of about 30 per cent of victims; and threatened to kill or killed the pets of about 10 per cent of victims (Tjaden, 1997).

Stalking often follows a relationship breakup or a rejection in a proposed relationship. Most stalkers are therefore former or imagined, rather than current, intimates.

Many stalking victims must resort to help from the authorities and seek restraining orders to protect themselves from the emotional abuse and prevent the stalking from intensifying into violence.

Self-Esteem Issues

Gender discrimination also carries social-psychological costs. For women, decreased self-esteem, increased depression, and other psychological problems often result from derogation by men, awareness of their subordinate status in society, or a failure to achieve the stereotypical ideal female body.

As we have already noted, one area in which this limitation occurs is in the choice of careers. Women are often reluctant to enter professions that involve dangerous, physically demanding work, such as firefighting or the military. By contrast, men are informally, and sometimes directly, cautioned against entering professions that undermine their masculinity, such as early childhood education or nursing.

To protect their self-esteem, women often seek to explain negative criticisms made to them about their work, their abilities, and so on to prejudice by male evaluators, whether the men actually believe in gender stereotypes or not (Crocker et al., 2000). This defensive strategy, although understandable, may lead some people to see prejudice where none exists. This becomes a problem when it leads a person to imagine that every member of the opposite sex (or of a different 'race', ethnic group, age cohort, etc.) is the 'enemy'.

Marriage counsellors and couples therapists have long noted that power differences can drive a wedge between partners. Trying to balance work, spousal/partner relations, and family life is difficult at the best of times. An unequal sharing of duties can create stress, frustration, and anger for the partner—usually a woman—who is doing more of the work. Consistently, research finds that men are more satisfied with current household task arrangements than women. This finding cannot possibly be surprising considering that men, on average, do much less work around the home.

In the past, this imbalance was believed to be solved if the couple agreed that the man contributed more than his share in another aspect of the relationship, such as the household finances, say, or parenting duties. Even today, some men feel it unnecessary to make an equal contribution to the domestic workload, reasoning that their earnings are contribution enough to the household. Increasingly, their partners are less willing to accept this premise. Modern views on love and intimate relationships are based on emotional, experiential, and intellectual compatibility. That, coupled with the increasing acceptance of divorce and ease of ending a marriage, means that partners who fail to nurture the relationship, or once too often take advantage of the significant other's willingness to compromise, may find themselves formerly married.

Body Image and Appearance Issues

Like it or not, people *do* judge books by their cover and strangers by their appearance. In judging appearance, people often look for points of likeness and familiarity that make them feel secure. Beyond that, they look for evidence of the cultural ideal. People admire others who look prosperous, healthy, and attractive, according to society's standards. Appearance features that approximate the ideal—not merely the familiar—are important because individuals want to fit in and be accepted. Such ideal features make up what we consider 'appearance norms'.

Society's dependence on and need for social norms—even appearance norms—teach us about deeper cultural ideals of beauty, propriety, and worth. Scarcity alone lends value to some physical qualities—for example, perfect facial features or flawless white teeth—but far from all. Our cultural ideals are manifested by the plentiful photos and media images that glorify so-called ideal men and women (see Box 5.3). To judge from these images of 'beautiful people', our culture idealizes youth, a slender toned body, and

Box 5.3 Social Construction: Body Image and the Media

Cultural ideals shape the way we think we should look. Throughout history, women's bodies have been 'moulded' to fit the ideal of the time.

Consider these media trends . . .

The Era	The Look of the Day for Women
1800s	A large body is a sign of health and fertility. Corsets narrow the waist and enhance the bust.
1890s	Actress Lillian Russell at 200 lbs or 91 kg is the most celebrated beauty of the time.
1910s	Paris designer creates slim sheath dresses, declares that breasts are "out".
1920s	Era of the flat-chested, slim-hipped flapper. First dieting craze of the 20th century begins.
1950s–1960s	Voluptuous full figured shapes of Marilyn Munroe and Jayne Mansfield are popular.
1967	British model Twiggy (5'6" or 168 cm and 91 lbs or 41 kg) arrives on the scene—and the diet industry explodes.
1970s–1980s	Models gradually become taller, thinner and begin to show toned muscle definition. Breasts make a fashion come-back.
Early 1990s	Waif-like figure of Kate Moss presents a wasted 'heroin chic' look and a pre-teen body.
Late 1990s	Tall, very thin models with no visible body fat and muscles highly toned by hours of working out. Large breasts remain in style—but are rare in this body type without the help of breast implants.

The average North American woman is 5'4" or 163 cm and 140 lbs or 64 kg	Models in the 1970s weighed 8 per cent less than the average woman. By the 1990s models weighed 23 per cent less.

2000 and beyond	Real bodies come in all shapes and sizes. . . . set your own trend!!!!

Today's advertisers go to huge lengths to sell products and to convince women that their bodies are never good enough. Female models are typically tall, thin, young, white, and they appear 'perfect'. More and more, male models are lean and muscular and equally 'perfect' in their appearance.

Reality Check
- Body features in the media are enhanced with props, lighting angles, and computer techniques.
- Shapes and sizes are altered.

- Blemishes, freckles, lines, wrinkles, skin folds, and any other unwanted features are edited out.
- Body features from photos of different people are combined to create the 'perfect' image.
- 'Body doubles' are common in films when body parts of lead actors don't measure up to the 'perfect' image.
- Photo images can be completely computer-generated to fit the look of the day.

The physical images presented in the media are flawless in every way. Nobody looks that 'perfect' naturally—not even the models themselves. The media message is that if you try hard enough, spend enough, suffer enough, you can have the look you want . . . that shaping your body will somehow bring you success and happiness.

Unhealthy Goals

The body does not follow fashion trends. If you have been persuaded to think that your body is not good enough, you may be trying to reach unrealistic and unhealthy goals.

- Too many young women aspiring to today's ultra-thin look literally starve themselves.
- Some are over-exercising or risking damage to their bodies with steroids.
- Plastic surgery and implants have their own health risks.
- The price of trying to achieve the 'perfect' look may include an eating disorder such as anorexia, bulimia, or compulsive overeating due to the extreme efforts required to maintain this over time.

Source: Region of Peel (Ont.), Peel Public Health, at: <www.region.peel.on.ca/health/commhlth/bodyimg/media.htm>. Adapted and reproduced with permission of Public Health, Region of Peel.

symmetrical, delicate facial features. Departures from these norms suggest poor genes, poor grooming, or a lack of self-discipline and self-worth.

To corroborate this fact, Spitzer and colleagues (1999) compared the body standards of North Americans aged 18 to 24. Data were collected from 11 national health surveys, from the 1950s to the 1990s, in Canada and the US. The researchers compared these data to *Playboy* centrefold models, Miss America Pageant winners, and *Playgirl* models, and found a growing difference between real bodies and ideal bodies in North America.

Since the 1950s, the body sizes of Miss America Pageant winners have *decreased* noticeably, and those of *Playboy* centrefold models have remained below normal body weight. Over the same period, the body sizes of average young adult North American women and men have *increased* dramatically, mainly because of an increase in body fat—the result of a spread of obesity in the general population.

Thus, since the 1950s, the body size and shape of average young adults became increasingly different from the ideal promoted by the media and in the popular culture. Further, male and female body images changed in opposite ways: ideal women became more petite, yet toned and physically fit, while ideal men bulked up (mainly through increased muscularity). The difference between real men and women in the general population remained small, since both men and women got bigger.

The media spotlight on body image is far more intense for women than for men. As a result, women tend to experience more insecurities about their bodies than men, and are much more likely to starve their bodies into submission through anorexia or bulimia. Though historically African-American women have not been as much afflicted by eating disorders because of a greater acceptance in their culture of fuller female figures, the tendency of mainstream culture to measure women's worth by their approximation to the slender, boyish supermodel figure has lately led even black women and girls to judge themselves physically inadequate (Williamson, 1998).

As with fashions in clothing and adornment, fashions in body size and shape change over time. For centuries, eating disorders among women have been the subject of discussion and debate. Anorexia has its roots as far back as the thirteenth century. People then canonized religious women as saints for their fasting practices. Scholars sometimes call these women 'holy anorexics'. Eating disorders have probably occurred in other societies, too. However, the reasons may have been different. In other cultures, young women who denied themselves food may have valued spiritual health, fasting, and self-denial much as our own society values thinness, self-control, and athleticism (Eating Disorder Recovery Centre, 2005).

Seventy years ago, Wallis Simpson—the woman for whom a king gave up his throne—declared that you can't be too rich or too thin. Today, people might disagree with the second part of that statement. Increasingly, people consider thinness to the degree that bones show through skin—whatever its merits for fashion, modelling, or ballet—unhealthy and unattractive. More than that, excessive thinness is often linked to eating disorders. For centuries, eating disorders resulting in too little weight among women have been the subject of casual discussion and debate, but little serious scrutiny or concern was paid these problems.

In the 1970s and 1980s, eating disorders finally received media attention with the death of singer Karen Carpenter from cardiac complications caused by anorexia nervosa. This was the first time the media focused attention on the life-threatening results of eating disorders and stopped viewing them as simply a group of 'benign' psychiatric illnesses. Anorexia and bulimia came to be seen as a result of women over-conforming to norms of slenderness and sacrificing their health for unattainable cultural goals of perfect thinness (see Box 5.4).

Fertility and Abortion Issues

Adolescent fertility is another big problem for women in North America. Factors predicting non-marital teenage pregnancy include two proximate determinants of pregnancy—contraceptive use and frequency of intercourse—as well as a history of school problems, drug use, fighting, living with parents, length of relationship with boyfriends, and best friends experiencing pregnancies (Gillmore et al., 1997). In short, young women without long-term goals and stable, cordial relationships are more likely to produce children in adolescence. The results are regrettable, for the children as well as for the mother: an end to the mother's education; a limit to the child's economic future; and, all too often, abortion, which effectively has become contraception of last resort. In 2002, for example, 35,077 pregnancies were recorded for young women ages 15–19, and of these 19,007, or 54 per cent, were terminated by abortion (see Figure 5.5).

Societies willing to address openly the sexual activity of teenagers and provide the information and contraceptive resources to prevent their child-bearing are less likely to experience serious problems with teenage pregnancy (Furstenberg, 1998). The blame does not all lie at the feet of the poor or minority communities that produce these teenage pregnancies in large numbers. For example, contrary to popular notions that the

---

Box 5.4 Personal Experience: 'My Child Is Starving Herself to Death'

These diary excerpts, written by Mara Kates, then 15 years old, are from a newspaper article by a mother and her daughter and describe something of the mindset of someone battling an eating disorder.

March, 2001

The doctor says that if I don't start eating, I will have to go into the hospital. I don't believe her. Hospitals are for sick people. I don't feel like I'm losing weight. In the mirror, I look the same. We don't even own a scale. I just get a rush from pushing my limits. The less I can eat in a day, the better I feel about myself. I love that I can survive on less than everyone else. I am special. Most people tell me how awful I look. My eating disorder is triumphant and keeps getting stronger. A few say I look good. That means I have to lose more weight. . . .

April, 2001

They put me in the hospital. I can't believe it. I'm not even sick. I feel like a fraud, taking a bed away from someone who really needs it. I hate my parents for making me stay here. I am jealous of the deathly ill patients. They must be more self-disciplined than me. It is like a competition of who's the best anorexic. . . .

Source: Kates and Kates (2003).

African-American community excuses teenage pregnancy, single parenting, and reliance on welfare, studies in the United States have shown that the girls' mothers and grandmothers express feelings of anger, frustration, and disappointment over the situation (Kaplan, 1997).

Patriarchy is, by its nature, pro-natal; it views women's primary responsibility as bearing and raising children. Many societies press women to bear as many children as they

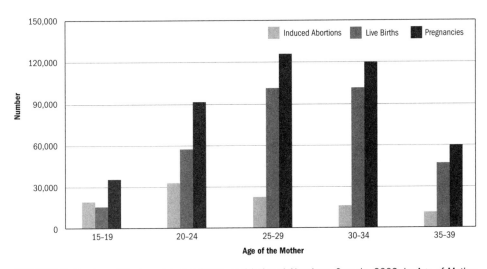

FIGURE 5.5 Number of Pregnancies, Live Births, and Induced Abortions, Canada, 2002, by Age of Mother
Note: Pregnancies include live births, induced abortions, and fetal loss.
Sources: Statistics Canada, (2003). Health—Pregnancy Outcomes by Age Group (catalogue no. 82-224): (total pregnancies), <www40.statcan.ca/l01/cst01/hlth65a.htm>; (live births), <www40.statcan.ca/l01/cst01/hlth65b.htm>; (induced abortions), <www40.statcan.ca/l01/cst01/health43.htm>.

can, stigmatizing them if they are childless (Inhorn, 1998). Yet, high rates of pregnancy often result in high rates of illness and mortality to a society. Each year around the world, half a million women die needlessly from pregnancy-related complications, worsened by poverty and remoteness (WHO, 2000). Many women, especially in developing countries, die during pregnancy and childbirth. The figure is highest in the least developed nations (1,000 deaths/100,000 live births, compared with 21/100,000 in developed countries). WHO reported that in 2000, 529,000 women died from pregnancy-related causes, and for each of these women, 20 more—a total of 10 million women—were left seriously injured or disabled (ibid.) These deaths, injuries, and disabilities are preventable, and they are symptomatic of women's vulnerability and the violation of their human rights. This fact turns women's health issues into a matter of social justice.

The same pro-natal patriarchal sentiments that support high rates of pregnancy also oppose abortion. The legalities of abortion affect women's lives in every society. For example, in Chile, where all abortion procedures are banned, illegal abortions are the leading cause of maternal death. However, poverty is an important factor in determining who is prosecuted for abortion in Chile. Poor, uneducated women have to rely on illegal abortionists who are illiterate, without medical training, and helped by friends or relatives. Wealthier women who can afford less risky procedures and private care can obtain the services of more expensive but better trained abortionists, while avoiding public hospitals that betray patient confidentiality (Casas-Becerra, 1997). Abortion providers in Latin America are subject to lack of medical support, the need for secrecy, and threats of violence, extortion, and prosecution (Rodriguez and Strickler, 1999). Policies that criminalize abortion promote fetal rights over maternal rights, are sexist, and serve to victimize poor pregnant women around the world (Gustavsson and MacEachron, 1997).

In South Asia, abortions are common among women of all socio-economic statuses. However, the quality of the procedure sought varies according to economic circumstances: most poor women use non-medical services or perform self-induced abortions, whereas non-poor women are more likely to seek trained medical personnel (Singh et al., 1997).

Research by demographers in Eastern Europe and elsewhere has shown high rates of abortion wherever good-quality birth control is unavailable to urban industrial people—that is, people who enjoy some sexual freedom and typically do not want large families. In Hungary, for example, many women were using abortion as their means of birth control and would have had 5, 10, or more abortions between ages 15 and 45. However, as sterilization, condoms, birth control pills, IUDs, and other reliable devices became easily available, the abortion rate dropped rapidly. This suggests that the need for abortion and its attendant risks decrease as people are helped and encouraged to use technologies for preventing pregnancy.

Sex Selection and Female Infanticide

In patriarchal societies such as India and China, females have long suffered grave risks of infanticide (the killing of infants), a practice that only recently has begun to decline. New technology that makes possible prenatal sex determination is likely to allow for—even encourage—the selective abortion of female fetuses. Legislation curbing prenatal sex determination and policy measures addressing societal female devaluation have had little effect, suggesting that female demographic disadvantage in India, for example, will continue (Sudha and Rajan, 1999).

Sex selection is an especially great danger in the People's Republic of China. The traditional preference for boy babies over girl babies, combined with the official 'one-child policy', encourages the disappointed parents of baby girls (or girls-to-be) to kill (or abort) their children to keep trying for a boy. Here is a case where a traditional cultural attitude (male preference) combines with modern statecraft (the one-child policy) and modern technology (ultrasound and other internal scanning equipment) to produce even worse harm—more savage sexism—than existed before.

Solutions: Policy and Institutional Changes

Many institutional policies are designed to protect women in their private lives and remove barriers that prevent women (and other marginal groups) from taking part to a full extent in public life. For example, discrimination in the workplace based on sex or gender is no longer tolerated in modern society, either by the judicial system or by most public opinion.

However, policies are not yet in place that would give women the same occupational freedom that men enjoy. For example, we know that the employment and child-bearing and child-rearing of many women have been affected by problems with child care. Analysis suggests that policies to increase the supply of child care or to lower its cost could increase female labour supply substantially, with an even greater rise among women most at risk of poverty and reliance on public assistance (Mason and Kuhlthau, 1989).

Finally, employment discrimination remains a problem. More effective workplace sexual harassment policies would likely improve women's work lives by preventing male chauvinism from impeding a woman's career ambitions. Canada's Employment Equity Act protects all workers in federal employment (and all people who work for an employer that employs 100 or more employees on or in connection with federal work) against discriminatory hiring procedures, whatever their gender, race, ethnicity, disability status, or sexual orientation, by ensuring that employee composition reflects the diversity of society. In specific relation to gender, this means the workforces of large companies and federal employees must have a roughly equal number of men and women in all levels of employment, at least in theory. In practice, the division is not nearly as exact, although the gap is closing.

Some critics argue that such 'quota systems' lead to decreased productivity, since the employer, constrained by employment equity laws, may occasionally be forced to pass over the most qualified candidate because his or her gender, ethnicity, etc. is already over-represented in the present workforce. Other opponents point out that, like anti-hate legislation, policies that force employers to act in a gender-neutral fashion will not end discrimination and, in fact, may serve to intensify it or drive it underground. These criticisms have some merit: since gender inequality remains a problem in society, the criticisms probably predict what will happen sometimes. Discrimination based on gender is unfair, it is socially harmful, and it has indirect and direct health results.

The process of finding and actualizing solutions will continue to be difficult and wrought with opposition, as society overcomes its inertia and undergoes the painful process of unlearning centuries' worth of outmoded gender socialization. The system has been skewed in favour of men for generations. In trying to correct this problem, having some policies that temporarily favour the marginalized group may be necessary until the playing field has been levelled. In especially patriarchal communities and societies, a resistance to changes such as reduced fertility, new family forms, more education for women, and gender equality at work and in politics may create a social crisis that could lead to political violence (Fargues, 1977).

Cross-national research makes clear that women's long-held concerns must be transformed into well-understood social problems before policy proposals are drafted and passed. Around the world, women have worked to place issues such as equal pay, affirmative action, educational equality, child care, abortion, domestic violence, and sexual harassment on the policy agenda. They have done so most directly and effectively in countries such as Norway, Sweden, and Finland, where women play a key role in politics and in the legislative process, largely through a history of effective mobilization in unions, social movements, and political parties (Bacchi, 1999; Tyyska, 1994). Canada has also made impressive progress, yet much more work remains to be done.

Concluding Remarks

Are gender inequality and sexism in Canadian society a 'real' problem or merely a socially constructed problem? On the one hand, there can be little doubt that 'moral entrepreneurship' by the leaders of the women's movement was critical in calling public attention to many of the issues associated with gender inequality—poverty, violence, discrimination, and so on. However, gender inequality was and is not merely a manufactured issue. It did exist prior to the first and second waves of the women's movement. And although there has been considerable improvement in Canada over the past two generations, gender inequality is still a fact of life for many women. We have seen that women suffer the material, psychological, and emotional outcomes of inequality and discrimination. They even suffer significant health problems—our touchstone for measuring the 'reality' of a social issue.

As we have seen, gender inequality is a social phenomenon. Gender discrimination and gender inequality are not due to the intrinsic or biological inferiority of one or the other sex. Instead, they are the result of political, economic, and ideological structures. Women have increasingly entered the workforce in both developed and less developed countries. Despite this, women are still subject to discrimination within the workforce. This discrimination often takes the form of sexual harassment and the 'glass ceiling'. Women who work for pay are also likely to face the double shift—heavy workloads both at the workplace and at home. Within the home, gender inequality extends across domestic work, child care, and caregiver duties with parents and spouses.

Socialization plays an important role in subordinating women. Socialization causes people to internalize values that, in turn, lead them to enforce and act out gender roles. This socialization occurs not only in the family, but also through the media, language, schools, and religion. Images of, views of, and beliefs about gender are learned both in childhood and through adult socialization.

In Canada, women still tend not to occupy positions of real power in political or legal spheres. Therefore, women's issues are often ignored or receive less political attention than they deserve. In other societies, where women are more powerful politically, gender issues are sometimes dealt with more firmly and thoroughly.

QUESTIONS FOR CRITICAL THOUGHT

1. Go to a toy store, or recall from memory the characteristics of the different aisles of toys. What do they look like? What toys are intended for girls and what toys are geared to boys? Do you think society has made any progress recently in moving towards more equal gender representation? Discuss in terms of gender socialization and identity formation.

2. There is a widely held belief that people creatively and actively shape their behaviour, making choices and acting by will. What role, if any, does agency play in socialization? Do people actively choose their paths, or are we just susceptible to the powerful macro forces of social norms?

3. Do you believe that a 'glass ceiling' still exists? Have any recent changes helped to alleviate this? Bring in insights about the 'Mommy track' from current events and look on the Statistics Canada Web site at <www.statcan.ca> for recent figures and statistics.

4. This text shows that social-psychological costs are another common outcome of gender discrimination and stereotyping. The media, and specifically advertising, are constantly under scrutiny for imposing their own set of ideals, which are often accused of being androcentric. Discuss the social-psychological costs of the media focus on a limited concept of ideal beauty, unattainable wardrobes, and airbrushed faces for woman's self-esteem.

5. Describe the impact the shift from agricultural to industrial societies had on the gendered division of labour.

RECOMMENDED READINGS

Lisa Adkins and Beverley Skeggs, eds, *Feminism after Bourdieu* (Oxford: Blackwell, 2004). This work explores the sociological thought of Pierre Bourdieu from a feminist lens to reanalyze gender and class, using concepts such as habitus, cultural capital, cultural field, symbolic violence, and reflexivity.

Donna Eder, with Catherine Colleen Evans and Stephen Parker, *School Talk: Gender and Adolescent Culture* (New Brunswick, NJ: Rutgers University Press, 1995). This fascinating study provides a comprehensive qualitative study of modern adolescents.

Cynthia Fuchs Epstein and Arne L. Kalleberg, eds, *Fighting for Time: Shifting Boundaries of Work and Social Life*. New York: Russell Sage Foundation, 2004. This collection explores the changes in time spent at work and the consequences of those changes for individuals and families. The authors examine how time interacts with factors such as professional and gender roles and the organization and control of work, as well as how individuals interpret the meaning of time and conform to or resist time norms.

Arlie Hochschild, with Anne Machung, *The Second Shift: Working Parents and the Revolution at Home* (New York: Viking, 1989). Using data from interviews, the authors explore the tensions in two-income families.

Michael Kimmel, *Manhood in America: A Cultural History* (New York: Free Press, 1996), and Kimmel, ed., *The Politics of Manhood* (Philadelphia: Temple University Press, 1995). The first work is pro-feminist, stressing men's and women's common interest in breaking out of the confines of traditional gender roles. Kimmel's edited collection concerns the debate between pro-feminist men—a left-liberal group—and the mythopoetic men's movement, which is socially and politically more traditional.

Chris Shilling, *The Body and Social Theory*, 2nd edn (Newbury Park, Calif.: Sage, 2003). This book, part of Sage's 'Theory, Culture and Society' series, offers a critical analysis of the sociological literature on the body, examining such issues as sexuality and bodily image, developments in genetic engineering, the role of the body in consumer culture, and social theories of the body.

Recommended Websites

The Men's Center.com

www.themenscenter.com/National/national11.htm#GEN-ERAL

This website provides a lengthy list of links to men's organizations with varied goals: political, spiritual, educational, and otherwise. Most of the organizations listed are centred in the United States.

Status of Women Canada

www.swc-cfc.gc.ca

Status of Women Canada is a federal government agency that promotes gender equality and the increased participation of women in political, social, cultural, and economic life in Canada. The website provides information on publications, programs, news, and related websites.

Canadian Research Institute for the Advancement of Women

www.criaw-icref.ca

The Canadian Research Institute for the Advancement of Women is a national not-for-profit organization committed to advancing women's equality through research. Founded in 1976, CRIAW is a bilingual, membership-based organization that seeks to bridge the gaps between the community and academe, and between research and action. CRIAW provides research grants, resource links, facts, and publications for researchers and interested individuals.

Ontario Women's Directorate

www.gov.on.ca/mczcr/owd/

The Ontario Women's Directorate is an agency committed to the full participation of all women in provincial affairs. Information on publications, resources, statistics, facts, and grants are provided.

The Canadian Women's Health Network

www.cwhn.ca

The Canadian Women's Health Network is a national organization that seeks to improve the lives of girls and young and older women in Canada and the world through the dissemination and collection of knowledge on areas that relate to women's physical and emotional health needs. Besides the information and reports the site provides, it also links women with existing programs across various communities.

Glossary

Feminization of poverty Women are clearly over-represented among the impoverished people of the world. In the West, economic liberalization and the dominance of the market have meant that those with the least earning power—single mothers with children—have suffered most.

Gender A social division referring to the social and psychosocial attributes by which humans are categorized as 'male' or 'female'. Biology is deemed somewhat irrelevant to understanding social distinctions between males and females. Gender encompasses the shared understandings of how women and men, girls and boys should look and act. It is a label that subsumes a large assortment of traits, beliefs, values, and mannerisms, and defines how we should practise social interactions.

Gender inequality The differential success of men and women in gaining access to valued rewards. This tends to stem from structural arrangements, interpersonal discrimination, and cultural beliefs.

Gender socialization The process by which people learn their gender-based behaviour. The socialization process links gender to personal identity in the form of gender identity and to distinctive activities in the form of gender roles. The major agents of socialization all serve to reinforce cultural definitions of masculinity and femininity.

Glass ceiling Women can have considerable success, but only up to the point of reaching top-level positions. For women at high levels of achievement, further advancement becomes especially difficult.

Quid pro quo sexual harassment The blatant demand by employers for sexual favours in exchange for promotion opportunities, salary increases, and preferential treatment.

Sexism Discrimination and derogatory attitudes and beliefs that promote stereotyping of people because of their gender. Sexism and gender stereotyping are two problems for both men and women that are most often experienced in institutions and social relationships.

Sexual harassment Any unwanted physical or verbal conduct directed towards a person that is offensive or humiliating.

Suffrage movement The central aim of many in the 'first wave' of the women's movement in the late nineteenth and early twentieth centuries was the right for women to vote in elections. With women's suffrage (i.e., voting rights), other goals—social reform, legal rights—would then be more readily attainable.

REFERENCES

Albelda, Randy, and Chris Tilly. 1997. *Glass Ceilings and Bottomless Pits: Women's Work, Women's Poverty*. Boston: South End Press.

Armour, Moira, and Pat Stanton. 1990. *Canadian Women in History: A Chronology*. Toronto: Green Dragon Press.

Bacchi, Carol Lee. 1999. *Women, Policy and Politics: The Construction of Policy Problems*. London: Sage.

Bartkowski, John P. 2000. 'Breaking Walls, Raising Fences: Masculinity, Intimacy, and Accountability among the Promise Keepers', *Sociology of Religion* 61, 1: 33–53.

———. 2001. 'Godly Masculinities: Gender Discourse among the Promise Keepers', *Social Thought and Research* 24, 1 and 2: 53–87.

Baxter, Janeen. 1997. 'Gender Equality and Participation in Housework: A Cross-National Perspective', *Journal of Comparative Family Studies* 28: 220–48.

Bernotsky, R. Lorraine, and Joan M. Bernotsky. 1999. 'Promise Keepers and the Politics of Gender and Religion: A Contemporary Men's Movement Prepares for the Next Century', American Sociological Association, conference paper.

Blackwood, Evelyn, and Saskia E. Wieringa, eds. 1999. *Female Desires: Same-Sex Relations and Transgender Practices across Cultures*. New York: Columbia University Press.

Blazer, Dan G. 1982. 'The Epidemiology of Late-Life Depression', *Journal of the American Geriatrics Society* 9: 587–92.

Bonnett, Alastair. 1996. 'The New Primitives: Identity, Landscape and Cultural Appropriation in the Mythopoetic Men's Movement', *Antipode* 28, 3: 273–91.

Brinson, Susan L. 1992. 'TV Fights: Women and Men in Interpersonal Arguments on Prime-Time Television Dramas', *Argumentation and Advocacy* 29, 2: 89–104.

Brooks, Stephen. 2007. *Canadian Democracy: An Introduction*, 5th edn. Toronto: Oxford University Press.

Campaign 2000, 2005. *Decision Time for Canada: Let's Make Poverty History, 2005 Report Card on Child Poverty in Canada*. Available at: <www.campaign2000.ca/rc/>.

Canadian Council of Professional Engineers. 1999. 'Women in Engineering'. Available at: <www.ccpe.ca/e/prog_women.cfm>; accessed 20 Feb. 2003.

Canadian Human Rights Commission. 2004. 'Harassment: What Is It and What To Do about It'. Available at: <www.chrc-ccdp.ca/publications/what_is_it-en.asp>.

Cranswick, Kelly. 1997. 'Canadian Caregivers', *Canadian Social Trends* (Winter): 2.

Casas-Becerra, Lidia. 1997. 'Women Prosecuted and Imprisoned for Abortion in Chile', *Reproductive Health Matters* 9: 29–36.

Chafetz, Janet Saltzman, and Jaqueline Hagan. 1996. 'The Gender Division of Labor and Family Change in Industrial Societies: A Theoretical Accounting', *Journal of Comparative Family Studies* 27: 187–219.

Chodorow, Nancy. 1978. *The Reproduction of Mothering: Psychoanalysis and the Sociology of Gender*. Berkeley: University of California Press

Clark, Warren. 2001. *Economic Gender Equality Indicators 2000*. Ottawa: Status of Women Canada. Available at: <www.swc-cfc.gc.ca/pubs/egei2000/egei2000_e.html>; accessed 15 Mar. 2003.

Clatterbaugh, Kenneth. 2000. 'Literature of the U.S. Men's Movements', *Signs* 25, 3: 883–94.

Collier, Richard. 1996. '"Coming Together"?: Post-Heterosexuality, Masculine Crisis and the New Men's Movement', *Feminist Legal Studies* 4, 1: 3–48.

Coltrane, Scott, and Masako Ishii-Kuntz. 1990. 'Men's Housework and Child Care: A Life Course Perspective', paper presented at the annual meeting of the American Sociological Association.

Courtenay, Will H. 2000. 'Constructions of Masculinity and Their Influence on Men's Well-being: A Theory of Gender and Health', *Social Science and Medicine* 50: 1385–1401.

Cowan, Carolyn Pape, and Philip A. Cowan. 1995. 'Interventions to Ease the Transition to Parenthood: Why They Are Needed and What They Can Do', *Family Relations* 44: 412–23.

Crocker, Jennifer, Kristin Voelkl, Maria Testa, and Brenda Major. 2000. 'Social Stigma: The Affective Consequences of Attributional Ambiguity', in Charles Stangor, ed., *Stereotypes and Prejudice: Essential Readings*. Philadelphia: Psychology Press, 353–68.

Crohan, Susan E. 1996. 'Marital Quality and Conflict across the Transition to Parenthood in African American and White Couples', *Journal of Marriage and the Family* 58: 922–44.

Crooks, Roberts, and Karla Baur. 1999. *Our Sexuality*, 7th edn. Toronto: Nelson Canada.

Davis, Kingsley, and Wilbert E. Moore. 1945. 'Some Principles of Stratification', *American Sociological Review* 10, 2: 242–9.

DeKeseredy, Walter S., and Katharine D. Kelly. 1993. 'The Incidence and Prevalence of Woman Abuse in Canadian University and College Dating Relationships', *Canadian Journal of Sociology* 18, 2: 137–59.

Doucet, Andrea. 2000. '"There's a Huge Gulf between Me as a Male Carer and Women": Gender, Domestic Responsibility, and the Community as an Institutional Arena', *Community, Work and Family* 3, 2: 163–84.

Eating Disorder Recovery Centre. 2005. 'Are Eating Disorders New?' Available at: <www.addictions.net/default.aspx ?id=15>.

Ell, Kathleen. 1996. 'Social Networks, Social Support and Coping with Serious Illness: The Family Connection', *Social Science Medicine* 42: 173–83.

Erel, Osnat, and Bonnie Burman. 1995. 'Interrelatedness of Marital Relations and Parent–Child Relations: A Meta-analytic Review', *Psychological Bulletin* 118: 108–32.

Fargues, Philippe. 1977. 'State Policies and the Birth Rate in Egypt: From Socialism to Liberalism', *Population and Development Review* 23, 1: 115–38.

Ferber, Abby L. 2000. 'Racial Warriors and Weekend Warriors: The Construction of Masculinity in Mythopoetic and White Supremacist Discourse', *Men and Masculinities* 3, 1: 30–56.

Flood, Michael. 2001. 'Men's Collective Anti-Violence Activism and the Struggle for Gender Justice', *Development* 44, 3: 42–7.

Fox, Bonnie. 2001. 'The Formative Years: How Parenthood Creates Gender', *Canadian Review of Sociology and Anthropology* 38: 373–90.

Franklin, Susan T., Barbara Ames, and Sharon King. 1994. 'Acquiring the Family Eldercare Role: Influence on Female Employment Adaptation', *Research on Aging* 16, 1: 27–42.

Fredriksen, Karen I. 1996. 'Gender Differences in Employment and the Informal Care of Adults', *Journal of Women and Aging* 8, 2: 35–53.

Furnham, Adrian, and Nadine Bitar. 1993. 'The Stereotyped Portrayal of Men and Women in British Television Advertisements', *Sex Roles* 29: 297–310.

Furstenberg, Frank F. 1998. 'When Will Teenage Childbearing Become a Problem? The Implications of Western Experience for Developing Countries', *Studies in Family Planning*, 29: 246–53.

Garda, Roberto. 2001. '"I Want to Recover Those Things I Damaged": The Experience of Men's Groups Working to Stop Violence in Mexico', *Development* 44, 3: 104–6.

Gartner, Rosemary, and Bonnie J. Fox. 1993. 'Commentary and Debate', *Canadian Journal of Sociology* 18, 3: 313–24.

Geissler, Dorie. 2001. 'Generation "G"', *Journal of Sport and Social Issues* 25: 324–31.

Gibson, Diane. 1996. 'Broken Down by Age and Gender: "The Problem of Old Women" Redefined', *Gender and Society* 10: 433–48.

Gillmore, Mary R., Steven M. Lewis, Mary J. Lohr, Michael S. Spencer, and Rachelle D. White. 1997. 'Repeat Pregnancies among Adolescent Mothers', *Journal of Marriage and the Family* 59: 536–50.

Ginn, Jay, and Jane Sandell. 1997. 'Balancing Home and Employment: Stress Reported by Social Services Staff', *Work, Employment and Society* 11: 413–34.

Gregson, Nicky, and Michelle Lowe. 1994. 'Waged Domestic Labor and the Renegotiation of the Domestic Division of Labor within Dual-Career Households', *Sociology* 28: 55–79.

Gustavsson, Nora S., and Ann E. MacEachron. 1997. 'Criminalizing Women's Behavior', *Journal of Drug Issues* 27: 673–87.

Haenfler, Ross Jay. 2003. 'Straight Edge: The Newest Face of Social Movements', *Dissertation Abstracts International, A: The Humanities and Social Sciences* 64, 4: 1430–A.

———. 2004. 'Manhood in Contradiction: The Two Faces of Straight Edge', *Men and Masculinities* 7, 1: 77–99.

Hankin, Janet R. 1990. 'Gender and Mental Illness', *Research in Community and Mental Health* 6: 183–201.

Heymann, Jody, and Alison Earle. 1998. 'The Work-Family Balance: What Hurdles Are Parents Leaving Welfare Likely to Confront?', *Journal of Policy Analysis and Management* 17: 313–21.

Hochschild, Arlie R. 1998. *The Time Bind: When Work Becomes Home and Home Becomes Work*. New York: Henry Holt.

Horowitz, Amy. 1985. 'Sons and Daughters as Caregivers to Older Parents: Differences in Role Performance and Consequences', *Gerontologist* 25: 612–17.

Inhorn, Marcia C. 1998. 'Infertility and the Quest for Conception in Egypt', in Robin Barlow and Joseph W. Brown, eds, *Reproductive Health and Infectious Disease in the Middle East*. Brookfield, Vt: Ashgate, 114–29.

Ishii-Kuntz, Masako, and Scott Coltrane. 1992. 'Remarriage, Stepparenting, and Household Labor', *Journal of Family Issues* 13: 215–33.

Jesser, Clinton. 1996. *Fierce and Tender Men: Sociological Aspects of the Men's Movement*. New York: Praeger.

Jones, Charles L., Lorna Marsden, and Lorne Tepperman. 1990. *Lives of Their Own*. Toronto: Oxford University Press.

Kaplan, Elaine Bell. 1997. *Not Our Kind of Girl: Unraveling the Myths of Black Teenage Motherhood*. Berkeley: University of California Press.

Karasek, Robert A., and Tores Theorell. 1990. *Healthy Work: Stress, Productivity, and the Reconstruction of Working Life*. New York: Basic Books.

Kates, Joanne, and Mara Kates. 2003. 'My Child Is Starving Herself to Death', *Globe and Mail*, 25 Jan., F8.

Kelley-Moore, Jessica A. 2001. 'Whose Promise Kept? Frame Construction within the Promise Keepers', *Sociological Focus* 34, 2: 199–211.

Kermeen, Patricia. 1995. 'Improving Postpartum Marital Relationships', *Psychological Reports* 76: 831–4.

Keyfitz, Nathan. 1988. 'On the Wholesomeness of Marriage',

in Lorne Tepperman and James Curtis, eds, *Readings in Sociology: An Introduction*. Toronto: McGraw-Hill Ryerson, 449–62.

Kingson, E.R., and R. O'Grady-LeShane. 1993. 'The Effects of Caregiving on Women's Social Security Benefits', *Gerontologist* 33: 230–9.

Knight, Bob G., Steven M. Lutzky, and Felice Macofsky-Urban. 1993. 'A Meta-analytic Review of Interventions for Caregiver Distress: Recommendations for Future Research', *Gerontologist* 33: 240–8.

Knudsen, Hannah K., and Paul M. Roman. 2000. 'Gender Segregation in Work Groups in the United States: An Analysis of Earnings', paper presented at the annual conference of the Southern Sociological Society.

Lechner, Viola M. 1993. 'Support Systems and Stress Reduction among Workers Caring for Dependent Parents', *Social Work* 38: 461–9.

Leuchtag, Alice. 1995. 'The Culture of Pornography', *Humanist* 55, 3: 4–6.

Livingstone, Sonia. 1994. 'Watching Talk: Gender and Engagement in the Viewing of Audience Discussion Programmes', *Media, Culture and Society* 16: 429–47.

Lupri, Eugen. 1993. 'Spousal Violence: Wife Abuse across the Life Course', *Zeitschrift fur Sozialisationforschung und Erziehungssoziologie* 13, 3: 232–57.

——— and James Frideres. 1981. 'The Quality of Marriage and the Passage of Time: Marital Satisfaction over the Family Life Cycle', *Canadian Journal of Sociology* 6, 3: 283–305.

———, Elaine Grandin, and Merlin B. Brinkerhoff. 1994. 'Socioeconomic Status and Male Violence in the Canadian Home: A Reexamination', *Canadian Journal of Sociology* 19, 1: 47–73.

Magnuson, Eric Paul. 2001. 'Reconstructing Masculinity and the American Dream: Cultural Transformation in the Mythopoetic Men's Movement', *Dissertation Abstracts International, A: The Humanities and Social Sciences* 61, 11: 4555–A.

Mason, Karen Oppenheim, and Karen Kuhlthau. 1989. 'Determinants of Child Care Ideals among Mothers of Preschool-Aged Children', *Journal of Marriage and the Family* 51: 593–603.

Mechling, Elizabeth Walker, and Jay Mechling. 1994. 'The Jung and the Restless: The Mythopoetic Men's Movement', *Southern Communication Journal* 59, 2: 97–111.

Media-Watch. 1991. 'Two Years of Sexism in Canadian Newspapers: A Study of 15 Newspapers', *Resources for Feminist Research* 20, 1 and 2: 21–2.

Merlo, Joan, M. Reidy, and Kathleen Maurer Smith. 1994a. 'The Feminine Voice of Authority in Television Commercials: A Ten-Year Comparison', paper presented

at the annual conference of the American Sociological Association.

——— and ———. 1994b. 'The Portrayal of Gender Role in Television Advertising: A Decade of Stereotyping', paper presented at the annual conference of the Society for the Study of Social Problems.

Messner, Michael A. 1997. *Politics of Masculinities: Men in Movements*. Thousand Oaks, Calif.: Sage.

Michelson, William. 1985. *From Sun to Sun: Daily Obligations and Community Structure in the Lives of Employed Women and Their Families*. Totowa, NJ: Rowman & Allanheld.

———. 1988. 'Divergent Convergence: The Daily Routines of Employed Spouses as a Public Affairs Agenda', in Caroline Andrew and Beth Moore Milroy, eds, *Life Spaces: Gender, Household, Employment*. Vancouver: University of British Columbia Press, 81–101.

Milkie, Melissa. 2002. 'Contested Images of Femininity: An Analysis of Cultural Gate Keeper Struggles with the Real Girl Critique', paper presented at a conference on Gender and Society.

Milne, Elisabeth-Jane. 2001. 'Key Websites and NGO Newsletters on VAW and Men's Groups', *Development* 44, 3: 133–6.

Monk, Timothy H., Marilyn J. Essex, Nancy A. Snider, Marjorie H. Klein, et al. 1996. 'The Impact of the Birth of a Baby on the Time Structure and Social Mixture of a Couple's Daily Life and Its Consequences for Well-Being', *Journal of Applied Social Psychology* 26: 1237–58.

Montgomery, Scott M., Derek G. Cook, Mel J. Bartley, and Michael E.J. Wadsworth. 1998. 'Unemployment, Cigarette Smoking, Alcohol Consumption and Body Weight in Young British Men', *European Journal of Public Health* 8, 1: 21–7.

Morris, Marika. 2000. 'Millennium of Achievements', *CRIAW Newsletter* 20, 1 (Winter).

———. 2002. *Women and Poverty*. Canadian Research Institute for the Advancement of Women (CRIAW). Available at: <www.criaw-icref.ca/Poverty_fact_sheet.htm#50>; accessed 23 Mar. 2003.

Mui, Ada C. 1995. 'Caring for Frail Elderly Parents: A Comparison of Adult Sons and Daughters', *Gerontologist* 35: 86–93.

Nakhaie, M.R. 1995. 'Housework in Canada: The National Picture', *Journal of Comparative Family Studies* 26: 409–26.

National Anti-Poverty Organization (NAPO). 1999. *Poverty in Canada: Some Facts and Figures*. Available at: <www.napo-onap.ca/nf-figur2.htm>; accessed 27 June 2001.

National Day of Remembrance and Action on Violence against Women. 2005. 'Fact Sheet: Statistics on Violence against Women in Canada', 6 Dec. Available at: <www.swc-cfc.gc.ca/dates/dec6/facts_e.html>.

New, Caroline. 2001. 'Oppressed and Oppressors? The Systematic Mistreatment of Men', *Sociology* 35, 3: 729–48.

Newton, Judith. 1998. 'White Guys', *Feminist Studies* 24, 3: 572–98.

Normand, Josée. 1995. 'Education of Women in Canada', *Canadian Social Trends* 39: 17–21.

Ontario Women's Directorate. 2000. 'Students and Teachers: Facts and Statistics for Students'. Available at: <www.gov.on.ca/mczcr/owd/english/students/facts.htm>; accessed 21 Jan. 2003.

Orbach, Terri L., James S. House, and Pamela S. Mero. 1996. 'Marital Quality over the Life Course', *Social Psychology Quarterly* 59: 162–71.

Orodenker, Sylvia. 1990. 'Family Caregiving in a Changing Society: The Effects of Employment on Caregiver Stress', *Family Community Health* 12, 4: 58–70.

Parsons, Talcott. 1951. *The Social System*. Glencoe, Ill.: Free Press.

Pohl, Joanne, Clare E. Collins, and Charles W. Given. 1998. 'Longitudinal Employment Decisions of Daughters and Daughters-in-Law after Assuming Parent Care', *Journal of Women and Aging* 10, 1: 59–74.

Prentice, Alison, Paula Bourne, Gail Cuthbert Brandt, Beth Light, Wendy Mitchinson, and Naomi Black. 1988. *Canadian Women: A History*. Toronto: Harcourt Brace Jovanovich.

Rabin, Claire, and Giora Rahav. 1995. 'Differences and Similarities between Younger and Older Marriages across Cultures: A Comparison of American and Israeli Retired Nondistressed Marriages', *American Journal of Family Therapy* 23: 237–49.

Rodriguez, Karen, and Jennifer Strickler. 1999. 'Clandestine Abortion in Latin America: Provider Perspectives', *Women and Health* 28, 3: 59–75.

Sacco, V., and H. Johnson. 1990. 'Violent Victimization', *Canadian Social Trends* 17 (Summer): 10–13.

Salamon, E.D., and B.W. Robinson, eds. 1987. *Gender Roles: Doing What Comes Naturally?* Toronto: Methuen.

Scharlach, Andrew E., and Karen I. Fredriksen. 1994. 'Elder Care versus Adult Care: Does Care Recipient Age Make a Difference?', *Research on Aging* 16: 43–68.

Schindler, Amy, and Jennifer Carroll Lena. 2000. 'Promise Keepers in Perspective: Organizational Characteristics of a Men's Movement', *Research in the Social Scientific Study of Religion* 11: 209–24.

Schofield, Hilary, and Helen Herrman. 1993. 'Characteristics of Carers in Victoria', *Family Matters* 34: 21–6.

Shaw, Donald L., and Shannon E. Martin. 1992. 'The Function of Mass Media Agenda Setting', *Journalism Quarterly* 69: 902–20.

Shelton, Beth Anne, and Daphne John. 1993. 'Does Marital Status Make a Difference? Housework among Married and Cohabiting Men and Women', *Journal of Family Issues* 14: 401–20.

Shostak, Arthur B. 1977. 'The Women's Liberation Movement and Its Various Impacts on American Men', *Journal of Sociology and Social Welfare* 4, 6: 897–907.

Silverstein, Louise B., Carl F. Auerbach, Loretta Grieco, and Faith Dunkel. 1999. 'Do Promise Keepers Dream of Feminist Sheep?', *Sex Roles* 40, 9 and 10: 665–88.

Singh, Susheela, Deirdre Wulf, and Heidi Jones. 1997. 'Health Professionals' Perceptions about Induced Abortion in South Central and Southeast Asia', *International Family Planning Perspectives* 23, 2: 59–67, 72.

Singleton, Andrew. 2003. 'Men Getting Real? A Study of Relationship Change in Two Men's Groups', *Journal of Sociology* 39, 2: 131–47.

Spitzer, Brenda L., Katherine A. Henderson, and Marilyn T. Zivian. 1999. 'Gender Differences in Population versus Media Body Sizes: A Comparison over Four Decades', *Sex Roles* 40, 7 and 8: 545–65.

Statistics Canada. 1998. *Canada Yearbook 2000*. Ottawa: Minister of Industry.

———. 1999. *Overview of the Time Use of Canadians in 1998*. Ottawa: Minister of Industry, Catalogue no. 12F0080XIE.

———. 2001. *Family Violence in Canada: A Statistical Profile 2001*. Ottawa: Minister of Industry, Catalogue no. 85–224–XIE.

———. 2002a. 'Population 15 Years and Over, by Hours Spent on Unpaid Housework, by Provinces and Territories' (2001 census), at: <www40.statcan.ca/l01/cst01/famil56a.htm>; accessed 16 Dec. 2005.

———. 2002b. 'Population 15 years and Over by Hours Spent Providing Unpaid Care or Assistance to Seniors, by Provinces and Territories' (2001 census), at: <www40.statcan.ca/l01/cst01/famil57b.htm>.

———. 2004. 'Overview: University Education, Experience Pay Off in Higher Earnings'. Available at: <www12.statcan.ca/english/census01/products/analytic/companion/earn/canada.cfm>.

———. 2005a. 'Shelter for Abused Women', *The Daily*, 15 June. Available at: <www.statcan.ca/Daily/English/050615/d050615a.htm>.

———. 2005b. 'Homicides', *The Daily*, 6 Oct. Available at: <www.statcan.ca/Daily/English/051006/d051006b.htm>.

———. 2005c. 'General Social Survey: Criminal Victimization', *The Daily*, 24 Nov. Available at: <www.statcan.ca/Daily/English/051124/d051124b.htm>.

———. 2006. 'University Enrolments, by Registration Status, Program Level and Classification of Instructional Programs (CIP), Annual (Number)' (E-Stat table no. 477–0011). Ottawa: Ministry of Industry.

Status of Women Canada, Canadian Committee on Women's History and Department of the Secretary of State of Canada. 1992. 'Towards Equality for Women: A Canadian Chronology', Women's History Month, Oct.

Stoller, Eleanor Palo. 1990. 'Males as Helpers: The Role of Sons, Relatives, and Friends', *Gerontologist* 30: 228–36.

Stommel, Manfred, Barbara A. Given, Charles W. Given, and Clare Collins. 1995. 'The Impact of the Frequency of Care Activities on the Division of Labor between Primary Caregivers and Other Care Providers', *Research on Aging* 17: 412–33.

Sudarkasa, Niara. 1986. '"The Status of Women" in Indigenous Africa Societies', *Feminist Studies* 12: 91–103.

Sudha, S., and S. Irudaya Rajan. 1999. 'Female Demographic Disadvantage in India, 1981–1991: Sex-Selective Abortions and Female Infanticide', *Development and Change* 30: 585–618.

Tennstedt, Sharon L., and Judith G. Gonyea. 1994. 'An Agenda for Work and Eldercare Research: Methodological Challenges and Future Directions', *Research on Aging* 16: 85–108.

Tilly, Louise A., and Joan W. Scott. 1987. *Women, Work, and Family*. New York: Routledge.

Tjaden, Patricia. 1997. *The Crime of Stalking: How Big Is the Problem?* Washington: US Department of Justice, Office of Justice Programs, National Institute of Justice, Nov.

Tremblay, Diane-Gabrielle. 2001. 'Polarization of Working Time and Gender Differences: Reconciling Family and Work by Reducing Working Time of Men and Women', in Victor W. Marshall, Walter R. Heinz, Helga Kruger, and Anil Verma, eds, *Restructuring Work and the Life Course*. Toronto: University of Toronto Press, 123–41.

Tyyska, Vappu Kaarina. 1994. 'The Women's Movement and the Welfare State: Child Care Policy in Canada and Finland, 1960–1990', Ph.D. dissertation, University of Toronto.

United Nations Development Program (UNDP). 1998. *Human Development Report 1998: Gender-Related Development Index*. Available at: <www.undp.org/hdr2000/english/presskit/gdi.pdf>; accessed 20 Feb. 2003.

Walsh, Janet. 1999. 'Myths and Counter-myths: An Analysis of Part-time Female Employees and Their Orientations to Work and Working Hours', *Work, Employment and Society* 13: 179–203.

Wicks, Stephen. 1996. *Warriors and Wildmen: Men, Masculinity, and Gender*. Westport, Conn.: Bergin and Garvey.

Willen, Helena, and Henry Montgomery. 1996. 'The Impact of Wishing for Children and Having Children on Attainment and Importance of Life Values', *Journal of Comparative Family Studies* 27: 499–518.

Williamson, Lisa. 1998. 'Eating Disorders and the Cultural Forces behind the Drive for Thinness: Are African American Women Really Protected?', *Social Work in Health Care* 28, 1: 61–73.

Wollstonecraft, Mary. 1992 [1792]. *A Vindication of the Rights of Woman*. London: Penguin.

Woods, Nancy Fugate, Bernice C. Yates, and Janet Primomo. 1989. 'Supporting Families during Chronic Stress', *Image: Journal of Nursing Scholarship* 2, 1: 46–50.

World Book. 2006. 'The History of Women's Suffrage', at: <www.worldbook.com/features/whm/html/whm010.html>.

World Health Organization (WHO). 2000. *Gender, Health and Poverty*. (Fact Sheet 251). Available at: <www.who.int/inf-fs/en/fact251.html>; accessed 22 Jan. 2003.

Zarit, Steven H., and Carol J. Whitlatch. 1993. 'The Effects of Placement in Nursing Homes on Family Caregivers: Short- and Long-Term Consequences', *Irish Journal of Psychology*, 14, 1: 25–37.

CHAPTER SIX

SEXUAL ORIENTATION AND HOMOPHOBIA

LEARNING OBJECTIVES

■ To understand the meaning of the terms 'homophobia', 'heterosexism', and 'transgendered'.

■ To know about the history and origins of homophobia.

■ To appreciate the significance of the gender binary to transgendered people.

■ To become familiar with the different theories of homophobia.

■ To be able to distinguish between innate homosexuality and homosexuality as a choice.

■ To discover the social and health consequences of homophobia.

■ To learn of possible solutions to the homophobia problem.

Introduction

This chapter is about sexual orientation and identity, discrimination and education, political rights and social protest. Views about sexual orientation vary around the world and across history. So do explanations of homosexuality and heterosexuality—with some people taking a biological or genetic ('nature') approach and other people taking a social or cultural ('nurture') approach to the topic.

It may help to start this story about sexual orientation in Canada by talking about another part of the world. Recently, the anthropologist Fernando Cardoso (2002) conducted ethnographic research in a small fishing village on the Atlantic coast of Brazil. Through fieldwork, participant observation, and long interviews, he found that men in the village range in sexual orientation from completely heterosexual to completely homosexual, with all points covered in between. In this community, every kind of sexual orientation is accepted. Even many 'straight' men regularly have sex with local 'gay' men.

This picture of sexuality is different from what we observe in Canada, for a variety of reasons. Generally, Canadians are not casual about the boundaries between homosexual and heterosexual relations. They expect people to be either homosexual or heterosexual and to act accordingly. In the past, many Canadians have also considered homosexual behaviour to be problematic. Over the last generation, Canadian public opinion about sexual topics has changed dramatically, however. Attitudes about same-sex intimacy and marriage have become more liberal. Today, few Canadians view homosexuality as immoral or worthy of criminalization, as many did in the past; this is particularly true of people with a first-hand familiarity with homosexuals. As sociologist John Alan Lee has written in *The Canadian Encyclopedia*:

> From Confederation to 1969, under Canada's criminal law, homosexuality was punishable by up to 14 years in prison. In 1969, the law was amended by exempting from prosecution 2 consenting adults of at least 21 years of age who engaged in these 'indecent acts' in private. Since then, the speed of social change in attitudes toward homosexuality has accelerated because of general tolerance (e.g., for common-law couples and single parents) and organized gay liberation campaigns.
>
> Many Canadians no longer consider homosexual acts 'indecent'. At the time of the 1985 edition of this encyclopedia, one province and several cities had enacted laws against discrimination on the basis of sexual orientation. By 1996 the majority of Canadian provinces had legislated against discrimination, as is also the case in the internal rules of numerous public and private institutions ranging from churches to universities to Canada Post to major banks. The Canadian military have gone much further than the American military's 'Don't ask, don't tell' policy by banning discrimination on the basis of sexual orientation. When the age of consent for vaginal and oral sex was lowered to 14 in the Criminal Code, consent for anal sex remained at 18, until a high court decided in 1995 that this distinction unlawfully discriminated against homosexuals.
>
> Source: <www.thecanadianencyclopedia.com/index.cfm?PgNm=TCEandParams= A1SEC822060>.

Canadian attitudes, laws, and practices relating to sexual orientation have changed rapidly and dramatically in the last few decades. In most of Canada today, most people consider outwardly *anti*-homosexual behaviour—not homosexuality—a social problem and a potential violation of hate laws or the Human Rights Code. To understand how and why Canadian attitudes to sexual orientation have changed, we need first to define our key terms: sexual orientation, gender binary, homosexuality, and homophobia, among others.

Sexual Orientation

Homosexuality is an attraction, physical and emotional, to people of the same sex. It is hard to say whether homosexuality is an act (or set of acts) or an identity—something occasional or regular or permanent. This very question has posed problems for the military, as we will see later. Families, too, have sometimes had to deal with the blurred distinction between behaviour and identity when, for example, a spouse of a heterosexual couple has cheated with a same-sex partner and questions have arisen about whether this signals the spouse's true identity or a passing sexual impulse.

Sexual orientation is defined here as sexual attraction to people of a particular sex (or sexes). The word **queer**, though once thought offensive by the gay community, has now been embraced by that community as an umbrella term to describe people who identify as anything other than heterosexual. However, the term is still not widely accepted in the heterosexual community. So, in this chapter, we will refer to the non-heterosexual community by the inclusive term 'lesbian, gay, bisexual, and transgendered', or LGBT. In much of the literature, however, the preferred acronym is **LGBTQ**.

The sexologist Dr Alfred Kinsey believed that the human sexual orientation lies on a continuum, with heterosexuality at one end and homosexuality at the other. Most people are neither entirely homosexual nor entirely heterosexual; in their sexual desires, they exist somewhere between the ends of the continuum. Kinsey also noted that not all people act on their sexual desires. Some people who think of themselves as heterosexual may feel some attraction to people of the same sex, yet for various reasons may not act on these desires. The same is true of people who identify themselves as homosexual yet may still feel an attraction to one or more people of the opposite sex. So, it is difficult to label people as being clearly and solely homosexual or heterosexual. This blurs the boundaries between homosexuals and heterosexuals and, for that reason, leads some people reactively to enforce the boundaries with special rigour.

The Gender Binary and Transgendered People

Most cultures of the world appear to code for only two sexes: male and female. Moreover, many societies consider gender a master status—one of the two most important bases of social differentiation (the other is age). Whether a person is male or female is central to their social identity. Since distinguishing between maleness and femaleness is so important in most societies the idea of changing or blurring genders, or crossing gender lines, troubles many people. When someone does not fit clearly into one of the two required categories, many members of society feel uncomfortable.

Within the rigid gender binary, identifiable women and men are expected to play particular roles. Usually, people expect women to act as caregivers; most cultures consider women more emotional and empathetic than men. People expect men, on the other hand, to be tougher and less in touch with their emotions. Some people also think men are better decision-makers and more rational thinkers than women (for more on this, see Chapter 5). In ideal dyadic relationships, we find two roles—a task leader and an emotional leader—usually defined by gender. Ideally, these gendered differences create a balanced reciprocal relationship between partners, with one assuming the role of the active giver and the other that of the passive taker. Ideally, in a heterosexual relationship, the man uses his unique strengths to support and protect the woman; in return, the woman uses her unique strengths to care for the male partner.

Of course, reality is more complex and interesting than that. First, heterosexual dyads vary in all sorts of ways. In some, both partners are protective and caring; in others, neither is. In some, the male provides protection and the female provides caring, while in others, the opposite occurs—particularly where significant differences in age or health are present. In short, we cannot predict couple behaviour or identities simply by looking at gender.

Second, many possible identities can exist between ideal-typical 'male' and 'female'. Some cultures—for example, in certain parts of the Dominican Republic and Papua New Guinea—include a third gender, which falls somewhere between male and female based on physical appearance (see Herdt, 1994). Ursula Le Guin (1969) hints at the difficulty we might have in understanding this subtlety in her classic science fiction novel, *The Left Hand of Darkness*. It deals with a race of people, the Gethenians, who are ambisexual and repeatedly pass through female and male phases. In that story, the earthling

Ai—accustomed to a gender binary—is never able fully to understand and appreciate their power and subtlety.

In our own society, even same-sex couples appear to follow the gender binary in many respects, working much the same way as opposite-sex couples. Sociological research finds many similarities between homosexual and heterosexual couples. For example, gays and lesbians select mates in the same ways as heterosexuals—for example, they tend to find partners who match them in age, race, education, and income (Jepsen and Jepsen, 2002). Likewise, the same factors contribute to partner satisfaction in the long-term relationships of both heterosexual and same-sex couples. Specifically, two factors predict satisfaction within these relationships: containment of relational conflict and psychologically intimate communication between partners (Gottman et al., 2003; Mackey et al., 2004).

Same-sex relationships and opposite-sex relationships also show role specialization and power inequalities. For example, the division of household labour is just as unequal when both members of the relationship belong to the same sex as when they are of opposite sexes. Gender inequality in domestic work is not merely a result of patriarchal culture, as shown by the similarity of arrangements in gay and lesbian couples. Unlike heterosexual couples, factors such as income, education, and time availability have little bearing on the distribution of tasks among homosexual couples (Illig, 1999). At the same time, these findings demonstrate just how powerful the patriarchal culture is. Even people in same-sex couples adopt the gender roles that are prevalent in their culture. Division of labour in gay and lesbian households is not based on gender; yet, typically, the division of household work is not egalitarian (Oerton, 1998). Often a pattern of primary breadwinner/primary caregiver emerges, and this is what defines the pattern of activities in the household.

These different roles are not static; they often change over time and some people may change their role from one relationship to another. Moreover, these complementary (dominant/submissive, active/passive, protecting/caring) roles repeatedly emerge in most dyadic relationships, whether opposite-sex or same-sex. However, some people fall outside the rigid gender binary: they do not fit easily into either of the socially or biologically defined roles of male and female. As a result, they also do not fit easily into the socially recognizable role dichotomies.

The prime examples are **transgendered** people, who feel that their social identity does not match their biological sex. They do not—cannot—identify with their birth gender. Besides genitalia, other features that are the opposite of one's biological gender can contribute to forming a transgendered identity. 'Transgender' is a broad term that denotes anyone whose gender identity falls outside the conventional gender boundaries. Because the term covers such a broad range of experience, many transsexual people—and many lesbian, gay, and **bisexual** people as well—have taken on the label of 'transgender'. As a result, the term can mean transsexual people who are pre-operative, post-operative, or non-operative (i.e., whether or not they have chosen surgical means to change their sex so that it conforms with their own sense of gender); cross-dressers (who are sometimes called transvestites); intersexed people; and people who, regardless of their gender or sexual orientation, are viewed by others as atypical of their gender.

Some people who identify as transgendered go through various medical procedures so they can *transition* into the sex they feel they ought to be. These treatments range from simple hormone therapy to complicated sexual reassignment surgery. For various

How Sexually Dimorphic Are We?

One researcher, whose conclusions are based on an extensive search of the medical literature from different countries for the years 1955-98, has found that 1 per cent of people have bodies that differ from 'standard' male or female, and that one or two of every 1,000 people receive surgery to 'normalize' genital appearance.

Source: <dspace.mah.se/bistream/2043/2952/1/Intersexuality,+and+its+medical+and+social+implications.pdf>.

reasons, not all transgendered people undergo surgery; some live, for example, as women with male genitalia. This may happen because they lack access to surgical procedures, or because they simply do not wish to change physically.

Like many minority groups, transgendered people gather in special places, including bars and community centres, to meet other transgendered people with whom they might share similar interests and experiences. Typically, transgendered people face much more discrimination than lesbians, gays, and bisexuals. As noted, society is uncomfortable with people who stand outside the rigid binary 'norm'. Since, for many, the thought of being attracted to someone of the same sex is hard to accept, transgendered people must deal with discrimination based on both attraction to someone of the same sex (should they identify as transgendered *and* homosexual) and their ambiguous gender status.

Many view transgendered people as part of the LGBT community; yet sometimes transgendered people feel that they are different from other segments of that community. Besides dealing with medical issues and discrimination issues that are different from those experienced by the rest of the gay community, transgendered people must also deal with different issues of identity and orientation. A transgendered person may identify as either gay or straight. For example, if a biological man undergoes surgery to become female, once the procedure is complete, she will want to live life as female. If she then chooses to identify as heterosexual, she may feel little attachment to the gay community, choosing instead to lead her life as any other heterosexual woman would.

Like other LGBT communities, the transgendered community is typically found in large urban centres. Many transgendered people move to big cities specifically to find their niche. As well, in big cities there is less discrimination than in smaller cities and towns, which are generally less familiar with people who are outside the mainstream.

Multiple Identities

By **sexual identity**, we mean the way a person thinks of himself or herself, in terms of whether that person is sexually and romantically attracted to members of the same gender. These identities refer to how people perceive themselves, rather than how someone else has labelled them. As we have seen, most societies assume or require us to be sexually and romantically attracted to members of the other gender. Failing to follow this rule may result in rejection, rude comments, verbal harassment, assault, rape, and even murder. As a result, it is a matter of great importance how one thinks of oneself sexually, especially when one's sex and one's gender identity are different.

Given the risks and costs associated with homosexuality, some people take a long time to figure out their own sexual identity. Others determine it more quickly but do not take the 'identity-appropriate' actions. Others still may have two sexual identities, one as a man and one as a woman. These issues are often confused and confusing. For instance, researchers may categorize bisexual-identified women and men as lesbians and gay men and transvestites as transsexuals. Not only does this confuse differences that exist within each of these categories, but it also blurs connections between the two categories. This confusion matters not only to the individuals who are misperceived in this way, but also to the communities to which they may (or may not) belong.

The postmodern study of power and sexuality has given strong support to the study of alternative sexualities, including homosexuality and homosexual practices. This approach has led to a growing recognition that multiple homosexual subcultures coexist. Rosenfeld (1999) identifies at least two distinct homosexual 'identity cohorts'. One cohort is composed of people who were 'born' as homosexuals before the gay liberation movement that began in the late 1960s, during a time when homosexuality was stigmatized and being openly gay posed much greater risks to personal safety and job security. The second cohort is composed of those who came to define themselves as homosexual through the gay liberationist discourse. Members of different identity cohorts have developed different understandings of the meaning of homosexuality, the threat posed by the heterosexual world, and the proper response to that threat. As a result, the actions that one cohort deems sensible may seem foolish to the other.

Coming Out

From a sociological perspective, the most important step in the sexual 'career' of an LGBT person is 'coming out'—disclosing his or her (until then secret) homosexual identity to family, friends, co-workers, etc. Usually, LGBT people delay coming out for some time after they have realized their sexual orientation is homosexual because they fear rejection, stigmatization, or worse.

This transition is sociologically important for a variety of reasons. First, until a person comes out, he or she has difficulty fully entering into the LGBT community—a major social transition from the heterosexual world to the homosexual world. Second, but equally important, sociologists understand that people's identities are linked to the social roles they play. They cannot fully enter into, or endorse, an identity for themselves until they fully embrace the role that it entails. So, coming out is as much a statement a person makes to oneself as it is a statement to one's partner, friends, family members, and the general community. Finally, the process of disclosure of minority sexual identity in organizations is important for the individual lesbian or gay man since it often concerns the discursive recognition and renegotiation of the individual's identity in a work environment, where the person earns his or her paycheque and has been—up to now—known as 'someone else' (Ward and Winstanley, 2005).

Sometimes, explicitly coming out is not necessary; disclosure can be more subtle. One study (Schmidt, 2003) examined the non-verbal strategies lesbians used to negotiate sexual identity disclosure in a corporate work environment. For example, many used 'coded speech', such as chatting casually but knowledgeably about gay issues, or silence—for instance, by refraining from office conversations about heterosexual romance—to subtly indicate the possibility of a lesbian orientation.

Other times, disclosure may not even be the best policy. How families handle secrecy and disclosure, for example, depends on the different social contexts in which lesbian women and gay men negotiate their sexual identities. In many situations, secrecy is not dysfunctional—it is preferable. Secrecy minimizes family disruption and stigma by association, and gives people control over the spread of information about their own gay or lesbian identity (Cameron and Hargreaves, 2005).

People who choose to hide their identities may take pains to avoid giving out any clues. They often practise strategies of impression management—an ongoing process by which LGBT youth make careful, planned decisions about whether they will disclose their sexual orientation, and, if they decide to disclose, to whom and how they disclose, and how they continue to monitor the presentation of their sexual orientation in different environments (Lasser and Tharinger, 2003).

Some LGBT people delay coming out for years. Others go so far as to marry and raise children with a person of the opposite sex, while recognizing their sexual preference is otherwise. They may not come out for decades, having led a life of secret wishes, desires, and (sometimes) activities all that time. Typically, this population faces serious dilemmas: coming out in mid-adulthood disrupts relationships and leads people to fear the loss of everything they have constructed. Many grieve the loss of a 'normal' adolescence. In short, coming out in mid-adulthood requires great courage and strength, but so does the lengthy delay of coming out (Johnston and Jenkins, 2004).

When people first come out, it is usually to their closest friends and/or closest family members—people whom the homosexual person feels will respect and accept their homosexual orientation, provide social and psychological support if needed, and keep the information secret until given permission to release it. Often the discloser feels liberated from secrecy upon coming out and may forge a stronger bond with the people to whom he/she has disclosed the information. At the same time, coming out can lead to stress and conflict with family members and friends who have trouble accepting the information. Sometimes it takes years to mend the relationships that are damaged at this time; some relationships are ruined forever. On the other hand, coming out strengthens some relationships or forges new ones to support the discloser's public entry into a new kind of life.

Just as the secretly homosexual person must struggle with 'coming out', in many cases, so too must their parents (Crooks, 2003). They must not only accept a reality that is new and perhaps morally unacceptable to them; they must also put a good face on it for their friends and relatives. Not all parents are able to do this—at least not very readily—and so are not immediately accepting and supportive of their children's sexual identities.

Not only do some families handle disclosure better than others do; some cultures handle it better than others. Disclosure also varies according to cultural group, with some groups being more inclined than others to disclose their secrets. One longitudinal study of multi-ethnic LGBT youth found that black and Latino youths were less likely than whites to feel comfortable with others knowing their sexual identity and, consequently, less likely to disclose that identity to other people (Rosario et al., 2004). This is connected to traditional notions about heterosexual masculinity and femininity in these groups—most particularly, to Latino or Hispanic notions of *machismo*.

Attitudes and Laws

As we have said, cultural definitions of what we mean by 'normal sexuality' and 'sexual deviance' change over time. Throughout history, sexuality has been one of the most debated and problematized of human activities. Most of the time, however, people ignore the sexual inclinations of others unless these are brought forcefully to their attention. For example, a great many people knew and accepted Oscar Wilde—the celebrated Irish playwright—as being gay long before anyone thought to charge and imprison him for this offence. It was the forceful efforts of John Sholto Douglas, the Ninth Marquess of Queensberry and disapproving father of Wilde's aristocratic lover, to discredit the playwright in court that made Wilde's homosexuality a public issue no one could ignore.

In ancient Greece, people considered sexual relations between two men a regular and 'normal' part of life. As a citizen, a Greek man who was old enough to vote was free to have sex with whomever he wished; this included having sex with young boys. The rule, however, was that a free man must adopt the position of the 'top' or insertive partner. To 'bottom', or receive, was socially acceptable only for a non-citizen, a woman, or a young boy. For a citizen to assume this bottom position would be considered dishonourable and improper. Besides, in ancient Greece, *behaviour* that we would consider homosexual today, such as anal sex between two males, was not assumed to reveal a person's sexual *identity* (see, e.g., Halperin, 1990). In the Greek mind, one could not readily infer sexual identity from sexual actions.

Many of the varied cultural attitudes about homosexuality changed—indeed, homogenized—with the spread of Christianity and the Catholic Church. In Christian Europe before the High Middle Ages, the Church largely ignored or tolerated homosexual behaviour. However, hostility and resentment towards homosexuals surfaced in the twelfth century. The writings of Thomas Aquinas spread the idea that homosexuality is unnatural and undesirable; it was then that those who considered themselves Christians came to condemn homosexual behaviour. In orthodox religious circles, this negative view has continued until the present day, influencing current attitudes on the subject.

Because of the stigma and shame that became attached to homosexuality in Christian countries, homosexual behaviour was forced underground, if not quite practised in secret. The behaviour was known to be common in many male-dominant milieus, for example, but authorities made little effort to uproot it. In England alone, homosexuality became associated with private boys' schools, prisons, the Queen's Navy, and the Boy Scouts, among other institutions. Cambridge University in the early twentieth century was known for its community of brilliant gay students, who included Lytton Strachey, E.M. Forster, and John Maynard Keynes among many others.

Ironically, this behaviour, though widespread, continued to elicit shame, so most people who engaged in homosexual activities hid them. For several reasons, the tendency to exclude, isolate, and vilify homosexuals in Britain, Canada, and other Christian countries began to change in the middle of the twentieth century. Beginning in the late 1950s and 1960s, newspapers and magazines began to focus more on homosexuality, and this focus unintentionally helped to attract isolated individuals to the growing homosexual communities.

In his book *Sexual Politics, Sexual Communities* (1998), John D'Emilio was among the first professional historians to detail the social experience of gay men and women in America. He dates the beginning of the homosexual subculture, as we know it today, to World War II. That war separated the sexes and, by bringing more people together in same-sex residential units, allowed homosexuals greater access to other homosexuals.

Of course, the formation of gay and lesbian communities had its roots much earlier in the growth of cities that were committed to human liberty. As the old German saying had it, *Stadtluft macht frei*—'City air makes one free'—because it relieved people from traditional medieval customs and obligations. This liberating role of cities was, in turn, a result of increased commercial and industrial activity. In a sense, then, LGBT communities were one of the many products of the rise of capitalism, industrialism, and secularism in the West.

In societies where these processes did not occur, homosexuality was slower to find acceptance. In the Islamic religion, which regulates all Islamic societies, homosexuality is considered a sin because it is sex outside marriage. In particular, Islam condemns anal intercourse—whether with males or females—as a major sin. (In the Judaic religion, which in important ways was a source of Islam as well as Christianity, Jewish homosexuals are just as much a part of the community as everyone else. However, the Torah objects to sexual acts between men, as follows: 'Thou shalt not lie with a man after the manner of a woman: it is an abomination.')

Of course, there is some division on the matter of homosexuality within the Jewish faith, just as there is within Christianity. Like fundamentalist Christians, Orthodox Jews tend to reject it because the Torah prohibits it. Reform Jews tend to accept it in the same way that, say, the United Church in Canada does.

Many countries have not been as progressive as Canada in their social attitudes and laws concerning homosexuals. In many countries, homosexual behaviour remains illegal or, at best, highly regulated. In several states of the United States, sodomy remains illegal. Countries with these restrictive 'morality laws' believe that homosexual behaviour is morally wrong and threatening to society. Other places where laws continue to restrict homosexual behaviour (to varying degrees) include the Dominican Republic, Brazil, Ghana, Sri Lanka, Kenya, India, and Sudan, to name a few. In these countries, punishments for homosexual relations include imprisonment, lashes, or death. In some countries, these laws only apply to homosexual relations between two men, however. Sri Lanka's law, for example, does not even mention lesbian relations.

In Confucian philosophy, which regulated China and societies affected by China, there was no explicit injunction against homosexuality unless the family forbade it. So long as it did not interfere with procreation—a familial duty—Confucianism did not forbid men from having erotic feelings for other men, nor did it forbid sexual relations between men. However, this did not prevent the development of restrictions on homosexual behaviour in Chinese communities like Singapore.

Anti-homosexual laws continue to prevail in many parts of the world. For example, in November 2005, a gay wedding took place in the traditionally homophobic United Arab Emirate of Dubai. Eleven pairs of men were due to be married before police interrupted the ceremony, arresting the 22 men who were involved. In the United Arab Emirates, homosexuality is banned and is punishable by imprisonment and lashings. The men who were arrested at this wedding were subjected to both punishments and psychological assessments. About this incident, the Minister of Justice and Islamic Affairs, Mohammed bin Nikhira Al-Dhahiri, commented that there was no room for homosexual acts in the UAE and that parents should be watchful of their children, to prevent them from involving themselves in 'deviant' sexual behaviour (Krane, 2005).

In Dubai, as in the rest of the Islamic world, homosexual behaviour is viewed as a risk to society and is in violation of Islamic *shariah* law, upon which Emirati law is based. After this wedding in Dubai, Al-Dhahiri was quoted as saying, 'It wasn't just a homosexual act. Now we're dealing with a kind of marriage. There was a ritual involved.' This statement implies a difference between homosexuality per se and a ritual. 'Ritual' suggests a new cultural norm that will challenge traditional norms in respect to homosexuality.

On the other hand, Western and Northern European countries such as Belgium, Sweden, and the Netherlands have been much more accepting in regard to the rights and freedoms of homosexuals. These countries have laws banning discrimination against homosexuals in areas such as housing, medical care, and the labour force. They also specify the same age of sexual consent for all people, gay or straight. In other countries that allow homosexual behaviour, often the age of sexual consent is older for homosexual relations than for heterosexual relations. As sociologists, we might ask why policy-makers believe that people should be older when engaging in homosexual sex, compared to heterosexual sex, and why (male) gay sex is thought to pose a problem while lesbian sex is not even addressed in many countries.

Homosexual Culture

Even before World War II, cities like San Francisco and New York began to attract homosexuals to 'the gay life'.

> The most enduring contribution of San Francisco to the social history of sexual minority subcultures has been its role in forging a political self-consciousness among gay, lesbian, bisexual and transgender peoples. . . . Among the factors most influential in forming a sense of collective identity and political purpose are: 1) the establishment of permissive social spaces (e.g., bars, bathhouses, nightclubs), 2) the founding of sexual identity-based political and social organizations, and 3) the consciousness-raising effect of demonstrations of social and political power, sometimes circulated through mass media. . . . Public visibility of gays and lesbians in bars and nightclubs facilitated the growth of social networks and planted the seeds for collective resistance against persecution meted out by the city's police force. (www.friendsof1800.org/context_statement.pdf)

After the repeal of prohibition in 1933, older vice districts in San Francisco changed into entertainment and tourism districts, providing a social environment where people could break sexual and gender rules with relative freedom. In North Beach—the city's main vice and tourist district—businesses emerged to satisfy a wide range of desires. There, homosexual and transgender populations were able to lead lives that blended in with the nighttime entertainments of tourists and heterosexual residents. This close association between tourism and sexual freedom gave the city a reputation as a 'wide open town' and encouraged San Francisco businessmen to support an urban arrangement that yielded financial profits.

Groups formed within the new homosexual urban communities to provide information and support for gays and lesbians. The Mattachine Society, for example, was a left-leaning group that called for the recognition of homosexuals as an oppressed minority. They promoted the idea of a homosexual culture in which members would be able to adopt positive values and take pride in their sexuality (D'Emilio, 1998). The Mattachines helped to bring together frightened men and women and provide them with an organizational network through which they could begin to form their own distinct culture.

The growth of gay communities coincided with reports that challenged the accepted definitions of sexuality. For example, the so-called Kinsey reports, published in the early 1950s and discussed near the beginning of the chapter, indirectly supported the emergence of an openly gay subculture.

The beginning of the modern gay rights movement can be traced to an 'enforcement' event in New York City's Greenwich Village in 1969. Throughout the 1950s and 1960s, underground gay bars and clubs had begun to shape the experience of community for gays and lesbians. In mainstream culture, however, homosexuality was still viewed as a deviant and dangerous lifestyle. Police would regularly raid known homosexual locales and arrest patrons merely for being at a homosexual establishment. In June 1969, New York City police raided the Stonewall Inn. However, unlike earlier incidents, this time the gay patrons fought back. For the first time, homosexuals showed resistance as a group, marking the start of what continues to be a long battle for the equal rights of LGBTs.

Like the gay and lesbian communities of New York City, the gay community in Toronto had been routinely victimized by police raids and discrimination. On 5 February 1981, during what became known as the Toronto bathhouse riots, the LGBT there fought back. Although the LGBT rights movement had been building for a decade, this event marked a turning point in the movement's history in Canada. A series of protests ensued, including one in which close to 2,000 people gathered at Queen's Park (the provincial legislative complex) in Toronto to express their outrage, forming what was then the largest gay demonstration in Canada. After that, many new gay organizations sprang up in Toronto and existing ones grew rapidly in size and power, with more access to resources. The City of Toronto commissioned a report to examine and improve the rocky relationship between the police and the LGBT community.

Since then, changes in the direction of tolerance have indeed taken place. Today, sizable gay and lesbian communities exist in various North American cities, including Toronto. Not only are these communities and their members increasingly visible, but they are increasingly outspoken as well. Pride celebrations and parades, occasions for the gay community to celebrate their sexuality and voice the demand for rights, take place in almost all the major cities of Canada.

These changes have brought new relations between the gay community and the larger society, and autonomous, non-repressive forms of social control have developed as well. For example, consider the governance of security in Toronto's gay village, a major global centre of lesbian/gay community life. Layers of private (both formal and informal) policing uneasily coexist alongside the actions of the public police and of regulatory officials such as municipal licensing officers. One can distinguish at least two kinds of spaces: the commercial spaces of bars and baths, which have their own unique ways of ensuring security, and the streets, particularly the legal spaces created through municipal and provincial permits during Pride Day celebrations. One notes a growing trend towards self-policing in both businesses and community events and a commercialization of security services that extends to the public police, since public police often work as 'paid duty officers' and act like security guards for the organization holding events (Valverde and Cirak, 2003).

The rise of homosexual communities in North America also coincided with the rapid growth of large cities after World War II. In Canada, urban growth was due both to the immigration of large numbers of European and then Asian immigrants and to the continuing population shift from rural to urban settings. Much of the urban growth in the US resulted from the northward migration of blacks from the 1920s through the 1940s. In the newly enlarged black communities, demands for civil rights exploded in the 1960s at the same time as protests against the war in Vietnam, the women's movement, and the gay liberation movement. Protest was in the air. The urban black communities in the US and the Canadian immigrant communities taught gays and lesbians something important about social mobilization: namely, the importance of *institutional completeness*—the creation of communities that are fully self-supporting and self-aware. They sensed that through institutional completeness ethnic *communities* survive, and through community survival ethnic *identities* survive. The same principle was applied in building large, diverse homosexual communities in Toronto, Vancouver, and elsewhere.

People who feel socially marginalized, excluded, or stigmatized by the main communities in society often form communities of their own. In response to problems of gaining acceptance from the wider community, everywhere LGBT groups are building their own communities. Consider a Canadian example. Supporting Our Youth is a grassroots program that builds community for lesbian, gay, bisexual, transsexual, and transgender youth in Toronto (Lepischak, 2004). Since 1997, Supporting Our Youth has followed principles of community development that stress broad participation, diverse skills, partnerships, coalition-building, and grassroots ownership. Accordingly, hundreds of adults and youth have worked together to develop arts, cultural, recreational, and employment training activities, as well as a mentoring and housing program.

Often, building an LGBT community is difficult and slow (Botnick, 2000). First, gay men may not always know what is truly in their best interest, since the dominant views about gay identity have been expressed by people outside of the gay movement. Second, gay men who are HIV (human immunodeficiency virus)-positive often engage in fewer social (and sexual) contacts than men who are HIV-negative, which makes them less likely to frequent gay venues. Third, service organizations generally dedicated to gay interests and service organizations specifically dedicated to HIV/AIDS issues—which should be able to co-operate in community-building—have ideological bases that are different enough to prevent such co-operation. Members of the gay community frequently internalize these ideological differences, which fall into two main categories: (1) whether and how to assimilate in the larger (heterosexual) population versus whether and how to assert a distinct identity; and (2) how to help the HIV/AIDS survivors in the community without making HIV/AIDS central to gay identity in the community and in the public mind. The divisiveness of many subgroups within the gay movement contributes to a further isolation of gays from each other, frustrating attempts at community-building.

Peacock and colleagues (2001) identified five subgroups within the supposedly homogeneous San Francisco gay scene. In each of these categories—which the researchers have labelled leather, men of colour, activists, men who go to clubs, and younger people—group members constructed a form of 'community' out of their own negotiated roles and criteria. This suggests that the 'gay lifestyle' may be no less varied and diverse than the 'heterosexual' lifestyle.

Another source of gay divisiveness results from social class differences. Murray (2001) notes that lesbian experiences in Jakarta, Indonesia, differ radically as a function of class position. Among the wealthy, lesbian status confers cultural and social capital. The poorer classes, however, view lesbianism simply as a form of deviance. Similarly, in North America, white middle-class people have increasingly populated the visible and political gay community. The middle-class lifestyle of community members requires economic and other resources that are often not available to the working class, limiting the membership of working-class gays in this community.

Data from the multi-city Urban Men's Health Study show that working-class men who are homosexually active are less likely than other active homosexuals to describe themselves as gay, are more likely to have heterosexual experience, and are less likely to be involved in the gay community (Barrett and Pollack, 2005). Other research has found that differences among gays and lesbians also revolve around ethnic identities (Ridge et al., 1999).

People in LGBT communities often experience and spend time in ways that are different from their heterosexual counterparts. Their uses of time and space develop in opposition to the institutions of family, heterosexuality, and reproduction, and LGBT subcultures develop as alternatives to kinship-based notions of community (Halberstam, 2003).

One example is the use of public sites for sex. Laud Humphreys's (1970) work found that public sex sites, such as bathhouses, are settings for quick, emotionally detached sex among men. According to his findings, most of the men do not identify as gay or bisexual. Recently, social historians have argued that these sites provided gay and bisexual men with settings that promoted the recognition of their communities prior to the Stonewall riots in New York, discussed earlier. Today, public sex sites continue to serve gay and bisexual men by allowing them a place to congregate with others like themselves (Brown, 2003).

Big-city communities are best at satisfying the needs for interaction and support among LGBT people. For example, in a classic study of New York male-to-female transsexuals on public welfare, Lloyd Siegel and Arthur Zitrin (1978) found that all the people they were studying lived with one or more transsexual friends. A transsexual community had come into existence, creating its own subculture. A city-wide informal network provided transsexuals with information about particular needs and reportedly worked to create a supportive environment for members. The community, made up of multiple cliques, was stable, cohesive, and sympathetic. Transsexual friends often accompanied transsexual clients to welfare centre interviews and provided other practical help. This subcultural community helped transsexual men to foster their identity as female, often without their having to undergo surgery.

Sociological Theories of Sexual Orientation

Structural Functionalist Theory

Structural functionalists focus on society's institutions and the functions they serve. From the functionalist standpoint, homosexuality threatens the survival of society because it does not typically result in reproduction or socialization of the next generation.

Functionalists might also note that homophobia has emerged as a form of scapegoating during periods of social upheaval. Through much of the twentieth century, homosexuals played a significant role as the incarnation of evil, decadence, or immorality. However, the symbolic universe started to change in the 1980s. With blurred gender performances and varied sexual customs, sexual preference has increasingly been viewed as a lifestyle choice. 'The homosexual' is vanishing as a popular incarnation of evil, and new symbolic incarnations of evil are taking their place—for example, terrorists and Muslim immigrants (Bech, 2002).

The changing of sex roles and the decline of traditional marriages in North America—characterized by a dominant male household head and a submissive wife—has made some people worry about the demise of 'the family'. Gender politics, sexual politics, and the multiplication of sexual identities have added to this confusion about the number of 'social types' and the proper relationships to be expected among them. From the functionalist perspective, anything that upsets clear role expectations and situation norms is socially disruptive.

Conflict Theory

Conflict theorists focus on the power struggles between people with less power in society and those with more. Conflict theorists believe the dominant group always imposes its own beliefs and values on the rest of society. So, for example, the dominant group presses everyone to accept heterosexuality—in the past this was done overtly, through restrictive laws and punishments against homosexuality and the teachings of social reformers; today, the mainstream media and advertising, as well as the public education system, implicitly and covertly hold up a heterosexual lifestyle as the norm. Society's institutions—its government, politics, education, even arts—display the power of the heterosexual majority. Indeed, it was not until 2005, arguably, that a major film, *Brokeback Mountain*, examined the subject of homosexuality as one possibility of 'normal' rather than as a subcultural phenomenon of aberration (*Cabaret*), anguish (*The Dresser*), or 'camp' fascination (*The Rocky Horror Picture Show*; *Priscilla, Queen of the Desert*).

Conflict theorists argue that homosexual people, as workers and family members, are no less subject to class-based social inequalities than heterosexuals. For example, homosexual families, as well as heterosexual ones, are affected by the wage gap between men and women and the struggle to provide adequate family care while holding a job. As we note in Chapters 8 and 9, on families and on work, a great many organizations are unresponsive to workers' caregiving responsibilities, and too many governments have privatized child-rearing responsibilities. To lessen the conflict between parenting and employment, society must support programs that ensure fairness for families in diverse circumstances, including homosexual families. To do this, it will be necessary to overcome the business community's resistance to any policy change that shifts the costs of reproduction from the private family household to the public economy (Glass, 2000).

In the late 1990s, a record number of Fortune 500 corporations began to extend equal benefits to all of their employees regardless of sexual orientation. Today, one-third of these huge organizations extend domestic partner benefits to their gay employees, despite a national refusal in the US to legalize same-sex unions. Moreover, their actions will likely influence the actions of smaller organizations. Because of their size and wealth, the largest and most powerful corporations act as leaders for the corporate community. A stated commitment to diversity issues influences these organizational changes. In many cases, the corporate climate proclaims domestic partner benefit policies as 'the right thing to do'—as good business sense in order to compete for the best employees. The domestic partner benefits movement reflects corporate America trying to upgrade its reputation by including gay issues as part of its diversity programs and policies (Davison and Rouse, 2004).

Changes in attitude like these are visible in all the major cities, where commerce and business have a foothold. Consider recent shifts in the treatment of gays and lesbians in Singapore. They reflect the island state's current effort to present itself as a centre for international business and a vacation place for the skilled, wealthy travellers who drive the global economy. For these reasons, the Singapore government—traditionally repressive about sexual matters—has taken steps towards greater official tolerance of gays and lesbians (Weiss, 2005).

Symbolic Interactionism

Symbolic interactionist theories pay attention to how sexual orientations are socially constructed. They look at the outcomes of labelling individuals as gay, straight, lesbian,

What Is Essentialism?
Essentialism is the belief that category members share important underlying properties that determine category identity and are responsible for other important characteristics of the category. Essentialist thinking affects how we view the natural world (e.g., how we categorize biological species). It also shapes the way we think about the social world (e.g., how we think about gender, race, mental illness, personality, and the self).

Source: <hebb.uoregon.edu/essential.html>.

bisexual, and so on, and at how these roles are internalized and then performed. Symbolic interactionists might argue that homophobia, and the rigid gender binary to which it is related, helps to organize social interaction in a society (like ours) in which so many tasks and roles are distinguished by gender. The main benefit of enforcing the rule that 'men are men' and 'women are women' is that everyone knows exactly how to behave. Identities are secure and unambiguous, as are social relationships based on gender.

The important point to understand here is that sexual identities, like gender identities and other social identities, are socially constructed. As we have seen, they vary from one society to another, and they vary over time. Societies differ in the degree to which sexual identities are conceived to be essential or fundamental and the degree to which they are viewed as immutable and uncontrollable (versus chosen). At the same time, rapid social change in people's attitudes and identities challenges our creativity as a society, as we scurry to invent, learn about, and enact new approaches to sexuality.

Table 6.1 outlines the views of the different theoretical perspectives on homosexuality.

Homophobia and Heterosexism

Homophobia is the fear or hatred of homosexuals. However, is 'homophobia' the right term for what we want to suggest? Usually, the word 'phobia' means an irrational, uncontrollable fear or hatred. Yet, the tendency we are considering under the label of 'homophobia' comes in various forms, ranging from social distance (for example, the unwillingness to form a close friendship), to stereotyping (for example, the view that all gays are the same), to religious injunctions, to bullying and harassment at school or work, to hate crimes including murder.

One basic feature of homophobia has been called 'essentialism'—the belief that all homosexuals have essentially or fundamentally the same 'basic' characteristics. Psychologist Gordon Allport (1954) proposed that any belief in group 'essences' constitutes part of a prejudiced personality, along with a rigid cognitive style that cannot accept ambiguity or changeability. Recent research confirms that essence-related beliefs about homosexuals are strongly associated with anti-gay attitudes (Haslam et al., 2002). People who tend towards essentialist thinking are usually hostile to homosexuals, even though they may not be hostile to other 'minorities'—women or Arab people, for example.

Recent research also suggests that essentialist beliefs about sexual orientation vary along two dimensions: the 'immutability' of sexual orientation and the 'fundamentality' of a classification of people as heterosexuals and homosexuals. *Immutability* refers to the belief that under no circumstances can one change a personal feature—in this case, homosexuality. In other words, homosexuality is like height. *Fundamentality* refers to the belief that a certain feature—in this case, homosexuality—is central to a person's entire character.

While related theoretically, these two dimensions are empirically distinct. Take, for example, a family physician in small-town Nova Scotia. Her identity as 'doctor' may be fundamental to her life—that is, it may be a master status—yet it is also entirely mutable—for example, she could retire and adopt a new master status such as 'philanthropist' or 'grandmother'.

Also, where homosexuality is concerned, 'fundamentality' and 'immutability' are negatively correlated with each other. Research finds that hostile attitudes towards lesbians and gay men are correlated positively with fundamentality but negatively with

Table 6.1 Five Main Sociological Paradigms	
Theory	**Main Ideas**
Structural Functionalism	■ Elements in society are all interrelated. ■ Homosexuality endangers the survival of society as it usually results in neither reproduction nor the socialization of children. ■ Homosexuality is now viewed as a lifestyle choice rather than, as in the recent past, an incarnation of evil to scapegoat. ■ Society is disrupted when clear role expectations are upset by changing sex roles and sexual identities.
Conflict Theory	■ Conflict and change are basic features of social life. ■ Homosexual people are just as subject to class-based social inequalities in the workplace as heterosexuals. ■ Many huge, influential corporations extend equal rights and privileges to attract good employees. ■ Changes in attitudes are visible in all the major cities where commerce and business make up a large part of the power structure.
Symbolic Interactionism	■ Socialization and labelling shape attitudes and the roles people adopt towards others. ■ Identities and gendered social relationships are secure and unambiguous when a rigid gender binary is enforced. ■ Rapid social change in attitudes and identities challenges society's creativity.
Feminism	■ Personal troubles and public issues are intertwined in social life. ■ Society's institutions, dominated by the heterosexual majority, display and impose a heterosexual lifestyle as the norm. ■ Homophobia is common among people who are sexist, chauvinistic, and homosocial. ■ Gay liberation has been linked to women's liberation.
Social Constructionism	■ Sexual and gender identities, and their social consequences, are socially constructed and variable. ■ Churches and political parties deflect criticism by focusing national attention on deviants. ■ People mobilize to form social movements and to influence public policy across societies and time—for example, in respect to gay marriage.

immutability (Hegarty and Pratto, 2001a, 2001b). Said another way, people are more likely to hold anti-gay attitudes if they think homosexuals have a choice in their sexual orientation. They are also likely to hold anti-gay attitudes if they think of homosexuality as an essential feature or 'master' status of a person.

Most gay rights activists agree with the idea that one is born gay, and therefore it is not a choice: homosexuality is immutable and uncontrollable. Other people continue to argue that homosexuality *is* a choice.

Some people also believe that homosexuality is largely a result of developmental factors—that a person's experiences while growing up can influence the way he or she identifies sexually as an adult. For example, they may believe that someone who has a negative heterosexual experience when young will become homosexual in later life. They may also believe that someone who has a positive homosexual experience when young will become homosexual in later life, or that someone with a dominant, domineering, or smothering mother who is dependent on the child, in combination with a weak or absent father, will likewise be more likely to develop a homosexual orientation. Finally, since our dominant culture promotes the idea that people can become who they want to be, some people even *believe* that they are heterosexual simply because they wish to be, whatever their original sexual tendencies.

As noted above, the idea that a person is born gay is widely accepted within the gay community, and it is an idea that is gaining acceptance and support from the heterosexual public. Comparing intrinsic homosexuality to the (assumed) intrinsic nature of heterosexuality has proved an effective way to 'explain' gay orientation to heterosexual people. That is, heterosexuals—at least in a secular society like ours—think of themselves as 'naturally' heterosexual, so by comparison they find it possible to think of homosexuals as 'naturally' homosexual.

An *attribution-value* theory of prejudice hypothesizes that people are prejudiced against groups that they feel have some negative attribute for which they are held responsible (Crandall et al, 2001). According to this theory, prejudice towards a group stems from two interrelated variables: attributions of controllability and cultural value. Thus, according to this theory, prejudice is more likely among people who hold gay men and lesbians responsible for their preferences and see a negative (cultural) value in homosexuality. Researchers tested this theory on a sample of Turkish undergraduates who completed a homophobia scale and answered questions about the supposed causes of homosexuality, attitudes towards homosexuality, and the respondents' own gender and sexual preferences. Most of the respondents in this sample expressed some prejudice against gay men and lesbians. As expected, both attributions of controllability and negative cultural values about homosexuality work together to explain the variation in homophobia. Moreover, respondents who think that homosexuality is controllable hold more negative attitudes towards gay men and lesbians than respondents who think that homosexuality is uncontrollable (Sakalli, 2002).

So, based on the research we have reviewed, popular prejudices could be undermined by showing that homosexuality is immutable—that is, unchangeable—and uncontrollable. Also, prejudices could be undermined by showing that homosexuality is not an essential feature or master status—only one of many human characteristics—and that it has value for the society and culture.

George Weinberg's introduction of the term 'homophobia' challenged traditional thinking about homosexuality and helped focus society's attention on the problem of anti-gay prejudice and stigma (Weinberg, 1972). The main limitation of the term 'homophobia' is its implication that anti-gay prejudice is a 'phobia'—that is, an irrational feeling based mainly on fear and, consequently, a defence mechanism. This approach is unable to account for historical changes in how society regards homosexuality and heterosexuality as the bases for social identities. If we are to gain a sociological (versus psychiatric) understanding of homophobia, we need a new vocabulary for discussing homophobic behaviour. To this end, Herek (2004) has defined three concepts that capture parts of the current notion of homophobia: (1) sexual stigma (the shared knowledge of society's negative regard for any non-heterosexual behaviour, identity, or community); (2) heterosexism (the cultural ideology that perpetuates sexual stigma); and (3) sexual prejudice (individuals' negative attitudes based on sexual orientation).

Several useful measurement efforts have grown out of this redefinition. For example, Morrison and Morrison (2002) have developed a modern homonegativity scale (MHS), which measures 'present-day' negative attitudes towards gay men and lesbians (that is, attitudes not based on traditional or purely moral objections to homosexuality). As hypothesized, scores on the MHS correlate positively with political conservatism, religious behaviour, religiosity, rural residence, and sexism. In short, while homosexuality was once considered a psychiatric disorder, today there is an increasing belief that homophobia (anti-homosexual behaviour) may be considered, if not a psychiatric disorder, at least a social problem (Jones and Sullivan, 2002).

Factors of Homophobia

There is no shortage of speculation about the causes of homophobia. True, it appears to be founded on faulty beliefs about homosexual people and about the essentiality and controllability of homosexuality. But where do these beliefs come from, how do they

---

Box 6.1   Historical Perspective: The Rise, Decline, and Comeback of Gay Films

In 1981, Vito Russo wrote a book called *The Celluloid Closet*, which became the Rob Epstein documentary of the same name in 1995. The film was a watershed moment in the popularization of 'gay studies'. Here on screen, and spliced together for the first time, were those top-hatted lesbians of the 1930s, the flouncing nellie boys making musicals in the 1940s, the 1950s closet cases saying lines so close to the bone that they seemed more like surgery than art. . . .

Perhaps Alla Nazimova's *Salome* from 1922 can be interpreted as the first film to be self-consciously homoerotic in intent, rather than an assortment of nancy-boy vaudeville cliches. Pretty soon, overtly gay films were coming thick and fast, and there was a bona fide 'pansy craze' in which camp actors like Franklin Pangbourne found many cheery roles.

It got to the point where a movie was even promoted as gay. In 1930, *The Dude Wrangler* was tagged as 'the story of a pansy cowboy—oh dear!' on its poster. That film has been lost and no print exists, and the lead actor was obliged to change his name.

The party soon ended. By 1934 the informal Hays code [a set of industry guidelines governing the production of American motion pictures between 1930 and 1967 that spelled out what was considered morally acceptable in the production of motion pictures for a public audience] became policed by the gimlet-eyed Production Code Administrator and vicious anti-Semite, Joseph Breen. Henceforth all references to 'perversion' were rigorously excluded. . . .

Then there were the Fifties: the Doris Day and Rock Hudson movies, the rush of Sapphic 'women in jail' exploitation flicks, and the arrival of teen culture pushing to the inevitable relaxation of anti-gay censorship as early as 1962. By January 1969, *Variety* was able to trumpet 'Homo 'n' lesbo films at Peak!'

Source: Clarke (2003). © *The Independent* (London).

arise, and why do some people hold them? In the social science literature, we find four main types of factors that appear to influence homophobia: openness to human diversity, openness to sexual diversity, familiarity with homosexuals, and membership in a homophobic culture.

Openness to human diversity. In looking for the social and sociological bases of authoritarian thinking, researchers (Adorno et al., 1969) unexpectedly found socio-psychological correlates of homophobia. They found that authoritarian people are more likely than other people to hate homosexuals, as well as blacks, Jews, and other ethnic, racial, and social minorities. This homophobic, racist orientation is rooted in a complex of superstitious beliefs and conservative political and economic views and conventional ideas. Other studies have confirmed the correlation between homophobia and political conservatism (Johnston, 1990).

Indeed, conservatism may possibly be the single best predictor of homophobia (Schatman, 1990). Among people who are religious, uneducated, and older, conservative political beliefs are the strongest predictor of homophobia (Seltzer, 1992). This relationship holds up among highly educated people as well. For example, politically conservative freshmen at an Ivy League university were found to hold more negative attitudes towards homosexuals—also, more traditional ideas about female sexuality and male dominance—than liberals (Lottes and Kuriloff, 1992; see also Larsen et al., 1980). Among heterosexual college students, homophobic attitudes are positively correlated with traditional social views and a reliance on conventional rules about human behaviour (Kurdek, 1988). Because of their conventionality, people with homophobic attitudes reject a wide variety of 'deviant groups' (King and Clayson, 1984).

Familiarity with sexual diversity. In a survey conducted by the Kinsey Institute (Klassen et al., 1989), Americans responded to statements designed to gauge their attitudes and beliefs about homosexuality, among many other sexual topics. Klassen and colleagues found *sexual experience* to be a determining factor. People who have had a wide variety of first- or second-hand experiences, that is, personal acquaintance with others who have had such experiences—whether with premarital sex, extramarital sex, or homosexuality—are less homophobic than people with a more limited 'lifetime sexual environment'.

Familiarity with homosexuals. Contact theory holds that interaction with members of minority groups makes members of the majority more accepting. As a result, people who live in communities where they are likely to meet many homosexuals are more accepting of homosexuality. The Kinsey study (ibid.) also found that people who are more familiar with homosexuality and homosexuals tend to score lower on the anti-homosexuality scale. This finding is supported by other research that shows the great importance of acquaintanceship or contact with known homosexuals in mitigating homophobia. Herek and Glunt (1993) report that personal contact with gay friends and relatives has more influence on attitudes towards gay people than any other social or demographic variable.

Using data from a 1996 national survey, researchers also found that community context has a strong effect on public attitudes towards homosexuals, rivalling the effects of education (i.e., more educated people are more accepting) and age (i.e., younger people are more accepting) (Overby and Barth, 2002). People in cities are less likely to be homophobic because in cities they are more likely to get to know homosexuals. The same has been found to be true in regard to racism.

Membership in a homophobic culture. Certain cultural characteristics contribute to the likelihood of homophobia. Hélie (2004) reports that in at least 83 countries homosexuality is a punishable crime; fundamentalist religion, an important cultural factor for homophobia, is often the source of such laws. Research shows that homophobia is related to **heterosexism**—a belief in the moral superiority of heterosexual institutions and practices. Morin and Garfinkle (1978) report that the best single predictor of antigay sentiment is sex-role rigidity: a belief in the essential difference between men and women and the need to keep women 'in their place'. As well, sex-role confusion and related anxiety may explain why men are more prejudiced against gays than are women, gay men elicit more negative reactions than do lesbians, and effeminate gay men are less threatening to most non-gays than are their 'macho' counterparts (Siegel, 1979; for a contrary view, see Millham and Weinberger, 1977).

The Role of the Media

People learn a great deal about their normative sexual roles and responsibilities through the mass media. In this sense, then, the media are responsible for teaching understandings of sexuality. Homosexuals, who were once left out of the media, are now being represented visibly. Currently, many popular television shows feature at least one gay character. Other television shows have dedicated episodes to gay issues. The daily news often includes one or more stories dealing with gay issues. As youth see these positive changes in the media, they have begun coming out at younger ages. LGBT youth can feel there is a place for them in society.·

Analysis of a random sample of *New York Times* advertising business news articles reveals the size of this change in the perception and pursuit of LGBTs as consumers of mainstream products between 1980 and 2000. Although all LGBTs experienced increased news coverage, gay men received twice the coverage of lesbians. Advertisers and the *Times* changed from stigmatizing and avoiding homosexuals to promoting stereotypes of gay affluence, commodifying social identity, and establishing a gay market niche. The increased visibility of gays and lesbians may not have granted them social legitimation but it does indicate social change in the status of homosexuality from deviant/stigmatized to selectively commodified (Ragusa, 2005).

Having said that, many people within the gay community feel they are still not being accurately represented in the media. They acknowledge that any representation at all is a step forward, but also note that television shows such as *Will and Grace* and *Queer Eye for the Straight Guy* promote a 'sanitized' image of gay men. The gay men portrayed on television are asexual, white, and well off; these qualities make them acceptable to the heterosexual public. This idea of the 'good gay' makes heterosexual viewers more comfortable with homosexuality, yet it may not be accurate in its representation of homosexual life. In addition, few lesbian women are represented in the mainstream media.

Another source of concern is continued interference with the development and mass distribution of gay and lesbian reading materials and pornography. In 2000, in the case of Little Sisters Book and Art Emporium, the Canadian Supreme Court was asked to decide whether gay male pornography violated the sex equality protections guaranteed by the Canadian Charter of Rights and Freedoms (see Box 6.2). Throughout this case, gay male activists and academics stressed the value of pornography for disseminating materials intended to promote safer sexual behaviour (for further information, see the documentary film *Little Sisters vs. Big Brother*). This case has just been resolved in favour of the appellants.

In short, there is an imperfect but improved public understanding of homosexuality, thanks to the media and other opportunities for increased familiarity. Traditional homophobia has declined significantly in the last two decades as a result. Yet, homophobia has

---

Box 6.2   Social Construction: Court Supports Bookstore's Fight against Censorship of Gay Books

A small Vancouver bookstore held a big celebration . . . after the country's highest court agreed the shop had been treated unfairly in a row over imported merchandise labelled obscene.

Little Sister's Book and Art Emporium has been battling with Canada Customs since it began seizing material in 1984.

The store, which specializes in gay and lesbian books, magazines and videos, argued that customs officers unfairly targeted its mail orders.

The owners said the authorities were making decisions about whether merchandise was obscene based on 'heterosexual values'.

. . . [T]he Supreme Court of Canada ruled that the obscenity laws can stand. But it struck down a provision of the Canada Customs Act.

In a 6-3 decision, the court said the onus belongs to the government to prove that material seized by Canada Customs is obscene, and that it should not be up to the importer to prove it is not obscene.

The judgement condemns the way gay erotica has been targeted at the border. But experts say its legal impact isn't as strong as its wording, because customs officers still have the power to detain material.

The three dissenting justices wanted to go further and strike down the entire customs legislation.

The Supreme Court found that Little Sister's suffered 'excessive and prejudicial treatment' at the hands of Canada Customs officers.

Canada Customs has confiscated 262 items destined for Little Sister's since 1984.

The court pointed out some of the books in question were imported by other mainstream bookstores without any problem.

Janine Fuller, manager of Little Sister's, called the ruling a victory for freedom of expression.

She said the case is an 'incredible indictment' against Canada Customs' 'unscrutinized tyranny at the border'.

Fuller added: 'Our community celebrates . . . yet again a victory that really announces that our community is moving way, way away from the marginalization that has so historically been part of who we are.'

The case first went before a judge in 1994. After several appeals, it finally landed before the Supreme Court.

The justices had to look at whether the seizures were subjective and arbitrary, and if they contravened the Charter of Rights and Freedoms.

They also had to decide if Canada Customs agents are properly equipped to be making those kinds of determinations in the first place.

Source: CBC News Online (2000).

far from disappeared; it continues to pose a problem for homosexuals as a form of prejudice that promotes discrimination and even violence.

Social Consequences of Homophobia

Despite an increased awareness and acceptance of homosexuality, many people still see heterosexuality as the ideal way of living. Because of this, many members of society continue to distinguish between people who do and do not satisfy this norm.

Consequences in the Family

Parents of homosexual or bisexual children may have a hard time accepting their children's sexual orientation. They may be disappointed because they have other expectations for their child or because their child's behaviour embarrasses them. Their reactions can lead to harsh words, broken relationships, and depression. Parents often believe that they want 'what is best' for their children and fear that, if gay, their child will miss valuable opportunities or suffer discrimination. Often, parents react with 'why did you do this to me?' when in fact a child's coming out has little to do with his or her parents (see Seidman, 2002).

In some cultures, homosexuality challenges traditional views of masculinity and the family may view it as dishonourable. Because of cultural ideas and traditions, children may feel great pressure to conform to heterosexist ideals. The negative ideas about homosexuality and the expectation that one must live up to the standards of one's family may cause children of these racial and cultural backgrounds to hide their sexual identity. Children fear their parents might disown them if they were to discover their true sexual orientation.

Canadian sociologist Michelle Owen has noted that, increasingly, same-sex families have disrupted or changed our dominant views of what 'normal' families are and what they do. Coming from a theoretical tradition known as queer theory, Owen argues that 'families headed by same-sex couples signal both a "normalization of the queer" and a "queering of the normal"' (Owen, 2001: 97). On one hand, many same-sex families want to be recognized as just like heterosexual families. On the other hand, the very situation of being a same-sex couple raising children resists the dominant model of family, because the dominant family model operates on the premise of gender difference. Since conventional family norms do not apply in the same way, gay and lesbian couples must renegotiate and recreate how family roles and responsibilities will be distributed.

Thus, same-sex couples 'normalize the queer' by forming families, raising children, and struggling to be recognized as being just like heterosexual families in their abilities to parent, to provide stability, and to be self-sufficient. At the same time, they 'queer the normal' because their very existence signals that families are defined as being heterosexual. Therefore, same-sex families force us to examine in new ways how we think of family, what we do as families, and what we want the family to be.

Generally, the involvement of policy or the state (with all of its agents and agencies) in marriage has been limited to laws about who cannot marry whom and what procedures must be followed to enter legal wedlock. There has been some resistance on the part of governments to become closely involved in the inner workings of marriage, which they see as largely a private family matter. From this standpoint, the ongoing political debate over whether gay and lesbian couples ought to be allowed to marry legally (despite the fact that same-sex marriage is legal in Canada as of 2005) and in religious ceremonies is revealing sociologically.

On the one hand, some (but not all) gay and lesbian couples want to have the responsibilities and entitlements, as well as the social recognition, that legal marriage provides. On the other hand, some worry that equating their unions with heterosexual marriages could rob gay and lesbian unions of their unique and valued aspects—among these, equality and sharing. Many gay and lesbian opponents of same-sex marriage see the institution as patriarchal and inequitable. They feel they have been lucky 'to escape the strictures of gender roles and religious dogma about marriage and prefer not to be subjected to [them]' (Schwartz and Rutter, 1998).

The argument to allow same-sex marriage is based on the idea that marriage is beneficial to society because it keeps people from depending on social assistance and keeps them healthier and happier. In short, it functions as a 'stabilizer' in society. This argument is the purely practical one of private support of people in families, no matter what kind of families they choose. It has the added advantage of taking the pressure off governments to help when spouses of whatever type are doing the caring.

As more countries accept or legalize gay and lesbian unions, the number of couples wishing to adopt a child or raise a child with two same-sex parents will naturally increase. Some individuals are concerned for the children of these unions, wondering if their development will be different from that of children of heterosexual parents. A common fear is that a child growing up in a homosexual household will also be homosexual. This fear is largely unfounded. Among lesbian couples, a mother's sexual orientation neither determines the child's gender development nor increases the likelihood of psychological problems (Mooney-Somers and Golombok, 2000). Rather, the quality of family relationships makes more impact on the child's well-being. The findings are similar for children raised by gay male-parent couples (Fitzgerald, 1999).

Until recently, most family studies ignored same-sex couple families and their parenting practices. This lack of research resulted in an incomplete picture of what families are and do. Though a larger fraction of the public is coming to accept homosexuals, attitudes towards gay parents still remain conservative, especially among older and rural people. Only around 20 per cent of Canadians surveyed in Miall and March's (2005) study, for example, were in favour of homosexuals adopting children, compared with the 92 per cent who supported adoption by traditional married couples. Research finds stereotypical views about homosexuality even among young, highly educated people. These views include the beliefs that homosexual parents create a dangerous environment for the child, provide a less secure home, and offer less emotional stability. As far as we know and contrary to popular belief, gay and lesbian parents raise fine, healthy children as often as heterosexual families do (Wainright et al., 2004).

Data are still rare on how many gay and lesbian couples are parenting children. Official definitions of family still often exclude gay and lesbian families. Moreover, some gay and lesbian couples are not 'out', preferring to keep their sexual preferences secret. During the 1980s, lesbian access to clinic-based donor insemination was limited because such access was thought to threaten both the traditional family and the medical definition of infertility. As a result, many people made insemination arrangements privately (Haimes and Weiner, 2000).

Lesbian couples would seem to be especially advantaged as parents. Apart from considerations of age, education, and health, lesbian couples have the luxury, for example, of deciding which partner will carry the child and how to create gender-unrelated parenting roles (Reimann, 1999). Also, as women, they would be more likely than men to have learned gender-related roles of nurturance. However, gay/lesbian families face great challenges in being accepted by law and society. One well-publicized case—Ms T in Alberta in 1997—brought out previously unspoken but strongly held attitudes towards raising children in same-sex families (Abu-Laban and McDaniel, 1998: 82). The province of Alberta judged Ms T, a woman who had successfully raised 17 foster children over many years, an unfit foster mother when authorities discovered that she had moved from a heterosexual to a lesbian relationship. They did not raise such questions about her capacity to parent when they saw her as heterosexual.

Harassment and Hate Crimes

Many studies have identified the classroom as a place where gender and sexuality are constructed. It is in the classroom that children first come to terms with the views of their peers about different sexual orientations.

Boys and young men at school often use homophobic terms with one another. But what do they mean by the use of these terms? Far from being indiscriminate terms of abuse, terms like 'faggot' tap a complex array of meanings that are precisely mapped in peer cultures, and boys quickly learn to use these homophobic terms against others. Significantly, this early, powerful use of homophobic terms occurs before puberty, before adult sexual identity, and before knowing much, if anything, about homosexuality. As a result, early homophobic experiences may well provide a key reference point for understanding imminent adult sexual identity formation—gay or not—because powerful homophobic codes are learned first (Plummer, 2001).

Bullying and harassment around the issue of sexuality are not trivial. Since 1982, there have been 28 cases of random school shootings in American high schools and middle schools. Researchers have found that most of the boys who opened fire were mercilessly and routinely teased and bullied. Their violence was in reprisal against the threats to their courage and self-confidence. Much of the specific content of the teasing and bullying was homophobic in nature. So, it would appear, there is a link between adolescent masculinity, homophobia, and violence (Kimmel and Mahler, 2003).

On 29 April 2004, Bill C-250 was passed, making it a crime in Canada to spread hate propaganda based on people's sexual orientation. Under this bill, sexual orientation is now included in the list of groups protected against hate crimes under the Criminal Code, a list that includes colour, race, religion, and ethnic origin.

Yet, hate crimes continue to be a problem for the homosexual community. Anti-homosexual harassment and violence are often described as 'hate' crimes perpetrated by homophobic people. However, there is little detailed international research evidence about the victims, perpetrators, and social contexts of such incidents. A study in Australia drew on evidence from 74 homicides with male victims that occurred in New South Wales between 1980 and 2000. Analysis of the fatal scenarios showed the significance of situational factors (such as alcohol, illegal drugs, and anonymous sexual cruising) as well as the 'hate' motive in this violence. Some perpetrators had serious drug use or psychological problems, and most killers were young men and boys from socially disadvantaged backgrounds. These crimes were usually linked to commonplace issues of male honour and masculine identity, sharpened by the perpetrators' low social status (Tomsen, 2002). Though not all hate crimes are fatal, this research shows the kind of background factors that can enter into their perpetration.

An interview study of the gay and lesbian victims of hate crimes found that most crimes are perpetrated in public settings by one or more strangers. However, victimization also occurs in other locales, and perpetrators can include neighbours, co-workers, and relatives. Victims' concerns about police bias and public disclosure of their sexual orientation are important factors in deciding whether to report anti-gay crimes, as are beliefs about the crime's severity and the likelihood that perpetrators would be punished (Herek et al., 2002). These concerns are typical among all victims of assault.

In another study of lesbian, gay, and bisexual people, nearly three in every four interviewed said they had been the victim of at least one homophobic incident. Speaking about the most serious incident they had experienced, victims of sexual assault reported significantly more post-traumatic stress symptoms than victims of any other acts or threatened acts. These assaults typically involved a known perpetrator—often, multiple perpetrators—and previous incidents of bias involving the same person or persons. Sexual and physical assault victims were more likely than other victims to report the incident to police and seek other types of help, owing largely to the psychological distress they had suffered (Rose and Mechanic, 2002). Thus, mental health organizations need to play a greater role in ameliorating prejudice against LGBT people and supporting social justice issues around the world (Dworkin and Yi, 2003).

Workplace Discrimination

Despite changing laws and changing attitudes, workplace discrimination against homosexuals continues. According to the Canadian Human Rights Code, it is against the law

Box 6.3   Social Policy: Force Tackles Transgender Issues

Rebecca Dittman has been pelted with bricks and attacked because she refuses to conform with 'normality'.

The 57-year-old was born a man but a decade ago she started to dress and live like a woman.

Since then she has become a target for thugs who have attacked her when she has been on a night out or walking home from work.

Rebecca, who lives in the city centre, said the transgender community needs to know that the police understand their problems. And she welcomed the special policy which will help protect them and make sure they are treated with dignity.

Rebecca, who works as an employment adviser, said: 'I have suffered abuse and been attacked but refuse to let people like that beat me.

'They are ignorant and I would never stoop to their level.

'The police are good and this is another positive step in the right direction. I would never expect them to just understand transgender issues immediately and I know they are complicated.

'But anything which can stop crime against people like me has to be looked at.'

Rebecca has helped devise the force's transgender policy and is also looking at setting up a Merseyside support group.

She said: 'We should never be afraid to report crime and should help the police all we can.'

Source: Dittman (2003).

to discriminate against a person based on his or her sexual orientation. Under this code, it is also illegal to discriminate against someone in a same-sex relationship. Many companies today claim to seek diversity in their employees. They stress that they are equal opportunity employers and that all minorities, including gays and lesbians, have an equal chance of being hired, promoted, and treated fairly once employed. These claims sound reasonable, yet many companies do not always follow through on their promises. As a result, many gays and lesbians feel a need to hide their identity while at work for fear of discrimination (Raeburn, 2004).

Many people in the business world receive training in how to deal with diversity in the workplace. Yet even with proper training, homophobic attitudes can persist, creating uncomfortable and sometimes dangerous work environments for gay employees. Homophobic attitudes may exist among employees, but they are not always overt. As a result, though the rules may ban discrimination against people who identify as gay or lesbian, many homosexual people still feel uncomfortable in the workplace. They fear an open admission of their sexual orientation might harm their workplace experience or hinder their career advancement.

The past decade has seen increased awareness about employment discrimination against gays and lesbians, but there has been limited research on the response of Canadian labour organizations to the workplace needs of gay and lesbian members. Data collected from more than 240 Canadian collective agreements suggest that larger, public-sector bargaining units with equality clauses in their collective agreements have most likely achieved an explicit ban against discrimination based on sexual orientation (Brown, 2003). Many other unions and workplaces provide no such protections.

Gay men and lesbians who experience discrimination in the workplace are sometimes unwilling to report it; such an action would often mean revealing their sexual identity to even more people. A desire for privacy is another reason for reluctance to report harassment. Most people want to keep their personal lives quiet, and reporting discrimination can mean publicizing one's private life to the entire office. Yet gay rights groups warn that if harassment goes unreported, nothing will ever change. Homosexuals who experience discrimination clearly have an important decision to make.

Police work offers an interesting example of the problem. Despite attempts to expand social diversity, a white, masculine, heterosexist ethos still dominates policing. As a result, the employment of lesbians and gay men as police officers may be especially threatening to members of this occupation. Within this context of potential hostility and homophobia, non-traditional officers must handle their presence on the police force with diplomacy. Researchers find that masculinity and femininity do not hold together in a cohesive, dichotomous manner for these officers. Instead, they highlight other characteristics to support their occupational competence. These officers see themselves as 'good cops'. Although gay and lesbian officers see their sexuality as an occupational asset, they also work harder to prove themselves as crime fighters (Myers et al., 2004).

As discussed at the outset, the debate about whether homosexual *behaviour* proves that a person *is* homosexual has become a political issue, for instance, in connection with the US military and its criteria for recruitment and dismissal. At present, someone who self-identifies as homosexual is denied entry into the US armed forces. Yet, a member of the army caught in the act of sodomy may be able to prove that he or she is not really homosexual, so exceptions are made. The 'don't ask, don't tell' policy was included in the 1994 Defense Authorization Act, part of President Bill Clinton's efforts to take a step

Don't Ask, Don't Tell

The Pentagon's principal justification for its 'don't ask, don't tell' policy continues to be that the presence of openly gay and lesbian personnel would interfere with the military's ability to accomplish its mission. In essence, the Pentagon's rationale is that heterosexual personnel have such antipathy for gay people that they would be unable and unwilling to serve with them. Moreover, the Department of Defense believes that it is powerless to prevent this hostility from interfering with the military mission.

Thus, the presumed focus of the problem is not really homosexual personnel. Rather, it is heterosexual service members and military leadership.

Source: <psychology.ucdavis.edu/rainbow/html/military.html>.

towards lifting the ban on gay people in the military. The law essentially allowed gay men and lesbians to serve in the military as long as they did not expose their sexual preference or exhibit homosexual behaviour. Those who do, however, are swiftly discharged.

Charles Moskos, a sociology professor at Northwestern University who helped to craft the US 'don't ask, don't tell' policy, believes that allowing *openly* gay people into the military—especially as front-line soldiers in combat—could cause the services to lose many more recruits who would be uncomfortable living in close quarters with them. He said the financial costs, mainly due to the loss of training 'investment'—an estimated $364 million in associated funds over the policy's first decade, according to a report released in February 2006—do not outweigh the costs of forcing people to live in intimate circumstances with openly gay people. He also said he believes many of the discharges are the result of people claiming to be gay to get an honourable discharge from service early (www.washingtonpost.com/wp-dyn/content/article/2006/02/13/AR2006021302373.html).

A study of the Canadian military addresses (and contradicts) some of the assumptions made by Moskos:

A new study of gays and lesbians in the Canadian military has found that after Canada's 1992 decision to allow homosexuals to serve openly in its armed forces, no negative consequences occurred. The study, titled 'Effects of the 1992 Lifting of Restrictions on Gay and Lesbian Service in the Canadian Forces; Appraising the Evidence', was sponsored by the Center for the Study of Sexual Minorities in the Military at the University of California, Santa Barbara.

Key findings are as follows:

- Lifting of restrictions on gay and lesbian service in the Canadian Forces has not led to any change in military performance.
- Self-identified gay, lesbian, and transsexual members of the Canadian Forces contacted for this report who have served since the ban was lifted describe good working relationships with peers in supportive institutional environments where morale and cohesion are maintained.
- The percentage of military women who experienced sexual harassment dropped 46 per cent after the ban was lifted. While there were several reasons why sexual harassment declined, one factor was that after the ban was lifted women were free to report assaults without fear that they would be accused of and subsequently discharged for being a lesbian.
- Before Canada lifted its gay ban, a 1985 survey of 6,500 male soldiers found that 62 per cent said that they would refuse to share showers, undress, or sleep in the same room as a gay soldier.
- After the ban was lifted, however, follow-up studies found no increase in disciplinary, performance, recruitment, sexual misconduct, or resignation problems.
- None of the 905 assault cases in the Canadian Forces from November 1992 (when the ban was lifted) until August 1995 involved gay bashing or could be attributed to the sexual orientation of one of the parties. (www.gaymilitary.ucsb.edu/Publications/CanadaPub1.htm) Used by permission of Aaron Belking and Jason McNichol.

In the civilian arena, it is clear what factors create a more comfortable environment for homosexual workers: support from top management, policies to prevent discrimination, the presence of LGBT employee networks, and a non-heterosexist organizational climate (Creed, 2004). Other marginalized groups—women, visible minorities, and people with disabilities—look for the same kinds of things in their workplaces. In addition, Ragins et al. (2003) state that gay and lesbian people are more likely to come out at work when the supervisor is of the same race as they are. Conversely, conditions that influence a person to stay 'in the closet' at work include a lack of racial balance and work teams that are composed mostly of men. Having to report to a male supervisor also increases the likelihood of staying in the closet, as people report experiencing more discrimination and homophobia under male supervisors.

Family Rights

Adoption and same-sex parenting are two related issues that same-sex couples must deal with. Currently, gay adoption is possible in every province but Alberta. Although much progress is still needed, Canadian law and attitudes are liberal about gay people compared with other places around the world.

So far, the research evidence argues neither for nor against lesbian parenting. Rosemary Barnes, former chief psychologist at the Women's College Hospital in Toronto, notes there are no visible differences between children raised by heterosexual mothers and those raised by lesbian mothers. Many gay and lesbian parents are rightly challenging the view that they are unfit parents. They do this by public acts of equal mothering, sharing parenting at home, and supporting each partner's sense of identity as a mother (Reimann, 1999). In time, both research and personal familiarity will convince Canadians that same-sex parents are no different from opposite-sex parents.

Many studies support the finding that gay and lesbian parents are just as capable in child-rearing as heterosexual parents. Children raised by homosexual parents do not have different behavioural and educational outcomes than children of heterosexual unions, nor do they feel any less loved or accepted by their parents (Mattingly and Bozick, 2001). Rather, the quality of family relationships affects the child's well-being. Further, there is no more chance of children growing up gay or lesbian in a same-sex family than in a heterosexual family (Mooney-Somers and Golombok, 2000; Fitzgerald, 1999).

Some critics of homosexual parenting argue that lesbian unions lack a proper father figure, which could affect the growth of the child. Besides fighting for their right to raise children, many gay and lesbian parents also wish to dispel gendered assumptions about mothering and fathering and the notion that mothers and fathers must necessarily share a household with their children (Donovan, 2000). Many children of same-sex unions feel they gained important insights into gender relations and broader, more inclusive definitions of family by growing up with same-sex parents (Saffron, 1998).

In Canada, for over a decade, most gay and lesbian couples have had the right to adopt children. Yet, as with many laws granting equal rights to homosexuals, there are complications with this law in practice. Gay couples who seek to become adoptive parents often meet discrimination, or at least discouragement. This is because many people still hold the view that a child should have both a mother and a father. Contrary to available evidence, they still assume that children who grow up with two parents of the same sex will not be socialized properly. There is also an unfounded concern that children of same-sex parents will turn out to be gay, too. Not only is there no basis for this concern, but we should be asking, if we view homosexuals as equal to heterosexuals, why should this matter?

Health Consequences

HIV/AIDS

When HIV/AIDS first became a major issue in the 1980s, the US government was reluctant to help communities in need. The virus seemed to affect only injecting drug users and 'men who have sex with men'—people who were popularly believed to have complete choice and control over their own risky behaviours. Given public levels of homophobia and the fact that HIV infection was seemingly not affecting heterosexuals, little was done to stem the growing epidemic. Doctors at the time were not only uninformed about how to deal with HIV infection, they were reluctant to learn about it, treat it, or help people who became HIV-positive.

In the early days, news reports called it a 'gay disease'. For a long time, people were unsure exactly how HIV was passed on and, therefore, how its transmission could be prevented. Large numbers of gay men in gay communities, in New York City, for example, were dying of the disease. AIDS activists such as Larry Kramer and Douglas Crimp tried to raise awareness about the sick and dying communities of gay men infected with the virus. Kramer's controversial articles, for example, called attention to the epidemic and pointed out that government inaction and silence were letting more and more people die.

Official indifference and lack of support and care outraged the gay communities. Many felt certain that if HIV were to affect heterosexual people in large numbers, the government would take action immediately. This state of outrage led to the formation of organizations for action and support, including the AIDS Coalition to Unleash Power (ACTUP), which is now one of the largest AIDS organizations fighting for awareness and research about HIV/AIDS. In New York City, posters with the slogan 'silence = death' appeared everywhere around the city.

Today, we know that HIV affects more than just the homosexual community (see Chapter 11). Television commercials, posters promoting the use of condoms, and news and other forms of media spread awareness of the problem. There is also greater awareness of the AIDS crisis in Africa and of rising HIV rates among young North American women. Members of the gay community were pioneers in promoting this awareness about HIV/AIDS through their activism, demanding more research, more access to drugs and treatment, and more protection of the rights of HIV-positive people. These actions have benefited all people infected with the virus, regardless of their sexual orientation. Regrettably, some groups of gay men have continued to practise unsafe sex. Studies have shown that gay men who reported more instances of social discrimination and financial hardship were more likely to take part in risky sex. It appears, then, that risky behaviours are an indirect result of homophobia, social oppression, and psychological distress (Diaz et al., 2004). Risk-taking or a lack of self-care is often characteristic of other oppressed peoples as well.

Use of Health Services

Health problems experienced by gay, lesbian, bisexual, and transgendered people may not be caused by homophobia in itself, but they may be worsened by the homophobia and heterosexism that exists among doctors and other medical professionals. Sometimes, ignorance of LGBT issues—not hostility—leads doctors and other health professionals to treat their LGBT patients insensitively and unprofessionally. Such institutionalized homophobia frightens many homosexual people. People who feel they will be judged or misunderstood are likely to visit the doctor less often, leading to poorer health.

Many LGBT people have reported experiencing homophobia or heterosexism from health-care professionals (see, e.g., www.mun.ca/the/research/bibliography.html; also, sogc.medical.org/guidelines/pdf/ps87.pdf). Consider also the results of a study of lesbian and gay parents seeking health care for their children within the Australian medical system. Though 89 per cent of respondents reported satisfaction with the health care received by their children, half of the parents feared disclosing their sexual orientation and more than one-quarter reported negative experiences with their children's health care because of their sexual orientation or family arrangement. This study shows that feared discrimination and homophobic attitudes remain a factor within the Australian health-care system (Mikhailovich et al., 2001).

Bergeron and Senn (2003) studied the use of health care among lesbians to find out how it was affected by comfort with health-care providers (HCPs) and disclosure of sexual identity. Surveys were completed by 254 Canadian lesbians recruited through snowball sampling and specialized media. Researchers found that higher education predicted higher levels of disclosure to HCPs and better use of health services. Feminism also predicted lower levels of internalized homophobia and higher levels of disclosure. Being more open about her sexual identity increased the likelihood a lesbian would disclose

---

Box 6.4 Personal Experience: Homosexual Seniors Facing Health-Care Problems

Gays and lesbians who grew up in the days when homosexuality was considered a mental illness are now seniors who face continued discrimination and self-imposed silence when it comes to accessing the health-care services they need, says a study released [in early 2006].

'People were once forced into psychiatric institutions', said Bill Ryan, one of the lead researchers in the study by the McGill University School of Social Work. 'Going to a doctor was a very fearful experience for many people.'

. . . Shari Brotman, co-author of the study, said many recalled medical treatment to 'cure' their homosexuality. 'Their relationship throughout their early lives with the health-care system was one of extreme discrimination and hostility', Brotman said. 'So they come to their older selves, requiring care, losing some autonomy . . . and they really are afraid to access the same system that treated them so badly when they were younger.'

Researchers spoke to seniors, their caregivers and health-care providers in Montreal, Vancouver, and Halifax. Their sample group was small—38 seniors, 31 health-care providers, and 21 caregivers—but the stories were similar, researchers said.

Lobotomies, shock therapy, and jail were once common reactions to same-sex attraction.

'You didn't want anybody to know', said Wilfrid Dube, a 71-year-old who spent much of his life in the closet. 'You were called sissy, teased. What I had to do was adapt myself, adopt the behaviours of people who were more masculine.'

And while much has changed, there are still a surprising number of stories of discrimination, Brotman said.

One woman told researchers that her home-care provider arrived with a Bible to 'save her'. Another was told she didn't need an annual pap smear because she was a lesbian.

Source: Moore (2006). Reprinted by permission of The Canadian Press.

her identity to HCPs, which in turn led to better health-care use. Finally, the more comfortable women were with their HCP, the more likely they were to seek preventive care.

Some transgendered people who feel that they should have been born the opposite sex, and consequently often feel neither wholly male nor wholly female, seek sexual reassignment surgery to remedy this condition. To receive it they must claim they feel they were born in the wrong body.

Sexual reassignment surgery is not the only medical issue facing transgendered people, however. Some children are born intersexed, with ambiguous genitalia. These could include, but are not limited to, Turner syndrome, 5-alpha reductase hermaphroditism, or androgen insensitivity syndrome. In cases like these, where the child may be born with both a vagina and a small penis but no testicles, for example, a difficult decision has to be made. Because our society works on a rigid gender binary, doctors and parents may feel that they must choose a single gender for the child and perform the surgery accordingly. Repeat genital surgeries are often needed as the child gets older, mainly for cosmetic purposes to make the genitals looks more 'normal'. The doctors who perform these surgeries believe that a child cannot develop properly with ambiguous sexuality, so the doctor and family must make a decision about whether the child is to 'become' male or female.

Solutions to the Homophobia Problem

As we have learned, a lot of political change has taken place in recent years. One of the greatest changes has been the establishment of sexual orientation as a personal realm protected from discrimination.

In *Vriend v. Alberta*, a 1997 Supreme Court of Canada case, Delwin Vriend, a lab instructor at King's University College in Edmonton, argued that he was unjustly fired from his job as a result of his sexual orientation. Sexual orientation is not included under the Canadian Charter of Rights and Freedoms, although gay and lesbian activists in the early 1980s sought specific inclusion in the Charter, or in the Alberta Individual Rights Protection Act as a basis for legal protection against discrimination. Vriend was successful in challenging this by proving that sexual orientation is similar to the other grounds stated in Section 15 of the Charter, such as race, religion, and sex, and should be protected as such. As a result, today no one can legally discriminate against homosexuals because of their sexual orientation, any more than they can discriminate against blacks because of their skin colour or against Jews because of their religion. Nonetheless, important legal precedent, such as was achieved in *Vriend*, is not quite the same as explicit constitutional protection, which women, ethnic groups, visible minorities, the disabled, and the elderly achieved in the 1982 Constitution Act.

Education and Policies

Norms and values change over time because of the constant interaction between individuals and major social institutions. This explains why some acts once considered sexually deviant—for example, homosexual acts—are increasingly accepted in the general population. In North America, gay men and lesbians are finally receiving legal rights and social acceptance. Yet the acceptance is slow in coming, as many people still fear and hate homosexuals. On occasion, homophobia can still lead to conflict and violence.

The activities of early leaders of the gay and lesbian community made room for new ways to think and talk about homosexuality at a time when very little was being said. Today, homosexuals are receiving new recognition and are being counted in Canadian society. The 2001 Canadian census included for the first time a question about same-sex relationships, a step forward in recognizing homosexuality as a part of Canada's diverse population. The census found 34,000 same-sex common-law couples that lived in every part of Canada, a statistic that has likely changed since Canada's subsequent legalization of same-sex marriages. The 2001 census also revealed that 15 per cent of lesbian couples and 3 per cent of gay couples are raising children. These data, although probably underestimating the extent of gay and lesbian couples, begin—finally—to number homosexual people among Canadian citizens.

Internationally, interest has revived in HIV/AIDS-related stigma and discrimination, triggered at least in part by a growing recognition that many people in seriously affected communities continue to respond harmfully to the epidemic. The stigmatization of HIV/AIDS-infected individuals feeds on, strengthens, and reproduces existing inequalities of class, race, gender, and sexuality. Individual efforts to alleviate stigma are, by their nature, of limited effectiveness. Programmatic approaches are needed to mobilize the resistance of stigmatized individuals and communities as a resource for social change (Parker and Aggleton, 2003).

The legislation and implementation of civil rights for sexual minorities are one step in this direction. When such rights are available, they are used. People who oppose anti-discrimination laws sometimes argue that gay rights claims are rarely filed and therefore legislation of this type is not needed. This has been shown to be untrue. An empirical analysis in the US looked at the number of filed sexual orientation complaints compared to the total number of gay people in the workforce to produce a measure of the prevalence of complaint-filing by gay workers. The same methodology was applied to race and sex discrimination cases in the same states for the same years. The study found that gays were just as likely to file sexual orientation complaints in states that had passed anti-discrimination laws as women or people of colour were to file sex- or race-discrimination complaints (Rubenstein, 2001). The message: if you build it, they will come.

Like many minority groups, homosexuals and lesbians have tried to educate the public, form organizations, change laws, and build their own communities with separate institutions to shed their caste-like status. Two kinds of organizations created by the gay community have been effective. The first are formed within the gay community for the gay community, such as formal and informal support groups. The second are organizations formed within the gay community to achieve political and social change by educating people outside the gay community. These organizations include Equality for Gays and Lesbians Everywhere (EGALE), Parents, Family, and Friends of Lesbians and Gays (PFLAG), and Gay and Lesbian Alliance Against Defamation (GLAAD), among many others. Their goals are to change policies and attitudes about people who identify as homosexual.

The finding that health care improves when women make the best use of available facilities led the Canadian Rainbow Health Coalition (CHRC) to create Rainbow Health: Improving Access to Care, a program designed to nurture partnerships between the health-care industry and health-care groups in the LGBT community. Organizations like this make fair and comfortable health care more accessible to LGBT people.

In the last few years, there has been an increased emphasis on education in the schools about homosexuality. Groups such as Teens Educating and Confronting Homophobia (TEACH) have attempted to teach their peers about being LGBT—a challenging task considering that the presentation may be many people's first meeting with an openly gay or lesbian person. Speakers present their 'coming out' stories to high school and university classes. Their goal is to get students to realize and understand that gay people deserve respect, as they are not very different from heterosexuals.

Some high schools have decided to include information on homosexuality in their sex education classes; many have urged their teachers to stop assuming that all their students are heterosexual. These changes in education are steps in the right direction, but discrimination and harassment of gay students is still an issue. Many high school or elementary students use the term 'that's so *gay*' when referring to something they dislike or they use the term 'faggot' to make fun of other students. Groups like TEACH work towards making young adults aware of the harmful, if unintended, effects of such casual use of homophobic language.

British Columbia has led the way in trying to solve the problem of homophobia in schools. Before 2005, the Ministry of Education had not taken any action to ensure the protection of LGBT students in schools. This meant, effectively, that there were no rules banning the harassment of LGBT students. To familiarize themselves with the problem, a Safe Schools Task Force travelled around the province, hearing about the school experiences of gay- and lesbian-identified youth. Their report noted that many LGBT students feel afraid going to school. With prodding by the homosexual community, in April 2005 the BC Ministry of Education established regulations to protect LGBT students in the public school system. It banned not only discrimination against LGBT-identified youth, but also discrimination against youth merely believed to be LGBT.

British Columbia is only one place where there are pressures for positive change. Similar problems are found in schools all across the country. One strategy being used in universities and other public spaces both in Canada and the US is the 'Safe Space' logo—a triangle filled in with the colours of the Gay Pride flag. Wherever it appears, this logo means this is a place where LGBT people can feel comfortable. The goal of the Safe Space campaign is to combat hatred and discrimination by symbolizing and advertising support. The Safe Space logo expresses acceptance by those who support the social equality of gay, lesbian, bisexual, and transgendered people.

Concluding Remarks

As we have seen, the LGBT community is comprised of people who differ in many ways. Yet, often they are viewed as just one deviant group.

Owing largely to the influence of religion, people have long stigmatized homosexuality as a sexual perversion, and some parts of Canadian society continue to do so; however, this is changing. It is hard to say whether changing attitudes have led to changing laws, or vice versa. Religion continues to play a huge role in popular views about homosexuality, especially outside Canada. Religious beliefs influence the political and social ideas people have about homosexuality and the laws that make homosexual behaviour easier or harder, safer or more dangerous. In religious societies, the dominant belief is that homosexuality is wrong or sinful. In these societies, people believe that a primary purpose of marriage is reproduction. Since gay couples cannot naturally bear children, they are abnormal and gay marriage should not be allowed.

Many more liberal Christian denominations and the liberal segments within other religious faiths, such as Judaism, openly accept LGBT communities into their fold. This has caused major rifts, however, in some churches and faith communities, perhaps most notably the Anglican Church: the African branch of the Church in particular called for the expulsion of the American Episcopalians over the issues of gay marriage, ordination of homosexual priests, and the appointment of a homosexual bishop. And, for many people who identify as homosexual, religion remains an important component of their lives. As such, gays and lesbians of faith still attend reform churches or synagogues where people of their sexual orientation are welcome.

In contrast to rural people, urban people are more accepting of homosexuals, and this acceptance includes a willingness to protect the civil liberties of homosexuals. Also, urban people are more willing to allow free expression to people with non-conformist political views and to support political activism. It is little wonder, then, that gay and lesbian people continue to congregate in cities, where they form their own communities. Other things being equal, people who know homosexuals personally are less homophobic than people who do not. In fact, personal contact with homosexual friends and relatives has more influence on attitudes towards gay men and lesbians than any other social or demographic variable.

Changes in how the media portray homosexuality have helped the gay community in becoming both less threatened and more open about who they are. As gays and lesbians mobilize, change is slowly taking place. With increased exposure in the media and more education, social attitudes, laws, and politics are changing to create an increasingly equal environment for LGBT people. Yet despite many encouraging changes in popular views on homosexuality, more research and education are needed. Political policies in Canada are shifting, but some social attitudes and practices remain homophobic.

QUESTIONS FOR CRITICAL THOUGHT

1. How does the LGBT community differ from other minority groups? How is it similar?

2. How does political change on issues concerning homosexuality (gay marriage, adoption rights, etc.) reflect social attitudes? Do you think opinions differ between age groups, sex, or race?

3. How are ideas of act and identity understood and negotiated both within the LGBT community and between the LGBT community and the heterosexual public?

4. In what ways has increased representation in the media helped the gay community? Can you think of any ways that it has hurt the community?

5. How have your own experiences with LGBT people (either yourself, or friends) shaped the way you feel about gay rights?

RECOMMENDED READINGS

John D'Emilio, 'Capitalism and Gay Identity', in D'Emilio, ed., *Making Trouble: Essays on Gay History, Politics, and the University* (New York: Routledge, 1992), 3–16. D'Emilio discusses how the elements of capitalism allowed for conditions where men and women could organize their personal lives around their attraction to their own sex. Capitalism, through the separation of work and home life as well as the separation of sex from procreation, permitted the formation of urban gay and lesbian communities, as well as the popularity of sexual identity politics.

Richard Goldstein, *Homocons: The Rise of Gay Right* (London: Verso, 2003). This is a quick and interesting read about the roots of radical gay activism and how activism has changed. It focuses on the debate between 'conservative' gays who claim that gay people are just like heterosexuals, and radical gays, who disagree. *Homocons* deals with the political dynamics between the heterosexual majority and LGBTs.

Janet E. Halley, *Don't: A Reader's Guide to the Military's Anti-Gay Policy* (Durham, NC: Duke University Press, 1999). This book offers a detailed and interesting analysis of the US military's anti-gay policy. Halley uses critical and cultural theory to examine the laws regulating homosexuality and homosexual conduct in the military, as well as what type of 'conduct', according to those who determine policy, reveals a *propensity* to be homosexual.

David M. Halperin, 'Is There a History of Sexuality?', in H. Abelove, M.A. Barale, and D.M. Halperin, eds, *The Lesbian and Gay Studies Reader* (London: Routledge, 1994), 416–31. This essay explores the idea of sexuality as a cultural creation. Halperin discusses the difference between modern-day Western understandings of sexuality and sexual orientation and compares them to those of the Athenians in ancient Greece.

JeeYeun Lee, 'Why Suzie Wong Is Not a Lesbian: Asian and Asian American Lesbian and Bisexual Women and Femme/Butch/Gender Identities', in Brett Beemyn and Mickey Eliason, eds, *LGBT Studies* (New York: New York University Press, 1996), 115–32. This essay explores the concepts of race and sexual orientation. Issues of self-representation, societal pressures, and allegiance to a certain identity are discussed.

Gayle Rubin, 'Thinking Sex: Notes for a Radical Theory of the Politics of Sexuality', in H. Abelove, M.A. Barale, and D.M. Halperin, eds, *The Lesbian and Gay Studies Reader* (London: Routledge, 1994), 3–44. This essay describes a 'value system' attributed to ideas concerning sexuality. Rubin explains how and why society views some behaviours as good or acceptable and other behaviours as wrong or immoral. While thinking has certainly changed since this paper was first published, Rubin's work is important for understanding how our society's notion of sexuality and sexual orientation came to be.

Steven Seidman, *Beyond the Closet: The Transformation of Gay and Lesbian Life* (New York: Routledge, 2004). This book is an account of gay people in North America. Through interviews with gays and lesbians of varying age groups Seidman depicts the different experiences of what it is like to be gay in a predominantly heterosexual world. His book acts as a 'story behind the numbers' for the situations of gay people and their encounters, and is essential for basic understandings of modern LGBT life.

Randy Shiltz, *And the Band Played On: Politics, People, and the AIDS Epidemic* (New York: St Martin's Press, 1987). This in-depth analysis of the AIDS epidemic discusses how it started and spread and the social, political, and institutional reactions to it, with special focus on how it affected gay communities, especially in the earlier 1980s when the virus was not yet fully understood.

Suzanna Danuta Walters, *All the Rage: The Story of Gay Visibility in America* (Chicago: University of Chicago Press, 2001). Walters evaluates representations of homosexuality in popular culture, focusing on film, television, and print advertisement, and argues that although gay people are welcomed in the popular media they are then denied full citizenship rights in real life.

RECOMMENDED WEBSITES

The Commercial Closet
www.commercialcloset.org

This website is an excellent source for tracking LGBT representation and visibility in popular culture. It has an extensive library of television commercials and advertisements where gay imagery (sometime overt, sometimes subtle) has been used by marketers, and thus is complementary to Walters's *All the Rage*.

Gay and Lesbian Alliance Against Defamation
www.glaad.org/

This organization's main focus is on media representations of gays and lesbians. It has encouraged local newspapers to include gay wedding announcements, and has organized other media campaigns to fight discrimination and promote equality. The website is aimed specifically at both straight and gay readers.

EGALE Canada
www.egale.ca/

EGALE is a national organization that advances equality and justice for lesbian, gay, bisexual, and trans-identified people and their families across Canada. The group's website offers up-to-date information about social and political policies affecting Canada's LGBT population. Articles concerning health care, education, politics, and employment can be found here.

Canadian Rainbow Health Coalition
www.rainbowhealth.ca/

This site is designed to provide health-care news and information for and about LGBT-identified people.

GLOSSARY

Bisexual Someone whose sexual orientation is towards people of both the same and opposite sexes. The attraction to both sexes does not need to be equal in strength.

Heterosexism Discrimination against homosexuals in favour of heterosexuals.

Homophobia Fear/hatred of homosexuals.

Homosexuality Sexual orientation towards people of the same sex.

LGBTQ Acronym for lesbian, gay, bisexual, transgendered, queer. One often speaks of the 'LGBTQ (or LGBT) community'.

Queer An umbrella term for gays, lesbians, bisexuals, transgendered people, or people who simply do not identify as 'straight'. This term was once deemed offensive but has more recently been 'taken back' by the community.

Sexual identity How a person self-identifies sexually, as gay, lesbian, straight, or transgendered.

Sexual orientation One's sexual attraction to a particular sex. Many feel that sexual orientation is fixed and is not a matter of choice.

Transgendered An umbrella term for any gender-variant people. This can include cross-dressers/transvestites and drag queens/kings.

REFERENCES

Abu-Laban, Sharon McIrvin, and Susan A. McDaniel. 1998. 'Beauty, Status and Aging', in Nancy Mandell, ed., *Feminist Issues: Race, Class and Sexuality*, 2nd edn. Scarborough, Ont.: Prentice-Hall Allyn and Bacon, 78–102.

Adorno, T.W., E. Frenkel-Brunswik, D.J. Levinson, and R.N. Sanford. 1954. *The Authoritarian Personality*. New York: Norton.

Allport, Gordon. 1979 [1954]. *The Nature of Prejudice*. Reading, Mass.: Addison-Wesley.

Almaguer, T. 1991. 'Chicano Men: A Cartography of Homosexual Identity and Behaviour', *Differences* 3, 2: 75–100.

Barrett, Donald C., and Lance M. Pollack. 2005. 'Whose Gay Community? Social Class, Sexual Self-Expression, and Gay Community Involvement', *Sociological Quarterly* 46, 3: 437–56.

Bech, Henning. 2002. 'Evil in Denmark', *Dansk Sociologi* 13, 3: 49–74.

Bergeron, Sherry, and Charlene Y. Senn. 2003. 'Health Care Utilization in a Sample of Canadian Lesbian Women: Predictors of Risk and Resilience', *Women and Health* 37, 3: 19–35.

Botnick, Michael R. 2000. 'Part 3: A Community Divided', *Journal of Homosexuality* 38, 4: 103–32.

Brown, Matthew Curtis. 2003. 'Thanks, Buddy: The Personal Aspects of Public Sex Sites', *Dissertation Abstracts International, A: The Humanities and Social Sciences* 64, 4: 1413–A.

Brown, Trevor. 2003. 'Sexual Orientation Provisions in Canadian Collective Agreements', *Relations industrielles/Industrial Relations* 58, 4: 644–66.

Cameron, Jan, and Katrina Hargreaves. 2005. 'Managing Family Secrets: Same-Sex Relationships', *New Zealand Sociology* 20, 1: 102–21.

Cardoso, Fernando Luiz. 2002. '"Fishermen": Masculinity and Sexuality in a Brazilian Fishing Community', *Sexuality and Culture* 6, 4: 45–72.

CBC News. 2000. 'Top Court Closes Chapter in Gay Bookstore Feud', 15 Dec. At: <www.cbc.ca/story/news/national/2000/12/15/little_sisters001215.html>; accessed 5 May 2006.

Clarke, Roger. 2003. 'The Thursday Book: The Pansy Cowboy in Hollywood's Closet', *The Independent* (London), 20 Mar.

Crandall, Christian S., Silvana D'Anello, Nuray Sakalli, Eleana Lazarus, Grazyna Wieczorkowska, and N.T. Feather. 2001. 'An Attribution-Value Model of Prejudice: Anti-Fat Attitudes in Six Nations', *Personality and Social Psychology Bulletin* 27, 1: 30–7.

Creed, W.E. Douglas. 2004. 'Ten Conversations about the Same Thing: Homophobia and Heterosexism in the Workplace', in P. Prasad, A. Konrad, and J. Pringle, eds, *Handbook of Workplace Diversity*. Thousand Oaks, Calif.: Sage, 1–41.

Crooks, Michelle M. 2003. 'Systemic Influences on Accepting and Supportive Parents of Gay Sons: Towards a Strengths Model', *Dissertation Abstracts International, A: The Humanities and Social Sciences* 64, 5: 1861–A.

Davison, Elizabeth L., and Joy Rouse. 2004. 'Exploring Domestic Partnership Benefits Policies in Corporate America', *Journal of Homosexuality* 48, 2: 21–44.

D'Emilio, John. 1998. *Sexual Politics, Sexual Communities: The Making of a Homosexual Minority in the United States, 1940–1970*, 2nd edn. Chicago: University of Chicago Press.

Diaz, Rafael M., George Ayala, and Edward Bein. 2004. 'Sexual Risk as an Outcome of Social Oppression: Data from a Probability Sample of Latino Gay Men in Three U.S. Cities', *Cultural Diversity and Ethnic Minority Psychology* 10, 3: 255–67.

Dittman, Rebecca J. 2003. 'Policing Hate Crime: From Victim to Challenger: A Transgendered Perspective', *Probation Journal* 50: 282–8.

Donovan, Catherine. 2000. 'Who Needs a Father? Negotiating Biological Fatherhood in British Lesbian Families Using Self-insemination', *Sexualities* 3, 2: 149–64.

Fitzgerald, B. 1999. 'Children of Lesbian and Gay Parents: A Review of the Literature', *Marriage and Family Review* 29, 1: 57–75.

Glass, Jennifer. 2000. 'Envisioning the Integration of Family and Work: Toward a Kinder, Gentler Workplace', *Contemporary Sociology* 29, 1: 129–43.

Haimes, Erica, and Kate Weiner. 2000. '"Everybody's Got a Dad": Issues for Lesbian Families in the Management of Donor Insemination', *Sociology of Health and Illness* 22, 4: 477–99.

Halberstam, Judith. 2003. 'What's That Smell? Queer Temporalities and Subcultural Lives', *International Journal of Cultural Studies* 6, 3: 313–33.

Halperin, David M. 1990. *One Hundred Years of Homosexuality and Other Essays on Greek Love*. London and New York: Routledge.

Haslam, Nick, Louis Rothschild, and Donald Ernst. 2002. 'Are Essentialist Beliefs Associated with Prejudice?', *British Journal of Social Psychology* 41, 1: 87–100.

Hegarty, Peter, and Felicia Pratto. 2001a. 'The Effects of Social Category Norms and Stereotypes on Explanations for Intergroup Differences', *Journal of Personality and Social Psychology* 80, 5: 723–35.

——— and ———. 2001b. 'Sexual Orientation Beliefs: Their Relationship to Anti-Gay Attitudes and Biological Determinist Arguments', *Journal of Homosexuality* 41, 1: 121–35.

Hélie, Anissa. 2004. 'Holy Hatred', *Reproductive Health Matters* 12, 23: 120–4.

Hennessey, Rosemary. 2000. *Profit and Pleasure: Sexual Identities in Late Capitalism*. New York: Routledge.

Herdt, Gilbert. 1994. *Guardians of the Flutes, Volume 1: Idioms of Masculinity*. Chicago: University of Chicago Press.

Herek, Gregory M. 2004. 'Beyond "Homophobia": Thinking about Sexual Prejudice and Stigma in the Twenty-First Century', *Sexuality Research and Social Policy* 1, 2: 6–24.

———, Jeanine C. Cogan, and J. Roy Gillis. 2002. 'Victim Experiences in Hate Crimes Based on Sexual Orientation', *Journal of Social Issues* 58, 2: 319–39.

——— and E.K. Glunt. 1993. 'Interpersonal Contact and Heterosexuals' Attitudes toward Gay Men: Results from a National Survey', *Journal of Sex Research* 30, 3: 239–44.

Humphreys, R.A.L. 1970, 1975. *Tearoom Trade: Impersonal Sex in Public Places*. New York: Aldine De Gruyter.

Illig, Diane S. 1999. 'Instrument Development for Assessing the Task Allocation by Lesbian and Gay Couples with Regard to Household and Familial Tasks', *Dissertation Abstracts International, A: The Humanities and Social Sciences* 60, 4: 1347–A.

Jepsen, Lisa K., and Christopher A. Jepsen. 2002. 'An Empirical Analysis of the Matching Patterns of Same-Sex and Opposite-Sex Couples', *Demography* 39, 3: 435–53.

Johnston, G.D. 1990. 'An Examination of the Psychological and Sociocultural Deterrents to Intimacy between Male Friends', Ph.D. thesis, California School of Professional Psychology.

Johnston, Lon B., and David Jenkins. 2004. 'Coming Out in Mid-Adulthood: Building a New Identity', *Journal of Gay & Lesbian Social Services* 16, 2: 19–42.

Jones, Mairwen K., and Gerard Sullivan. 2002. 'Psychiatric Disorder or Straight Prejudice? The Role of Education in Overcoming Homophobia', *Journal of Gay and Lesbian Social Services* 14, 2: 95–105.

Kimmel, Michael S., and Matthew Mahler. 2003. 'Adolescent Masculinity, Homophobia, and Violence: Random School Shootings, 1982–2001', *American Behavioral Scientist* 46, 10: 1439–58.

King, K.P., and D.E. Clayson. 1984. 'Perceptions of Jews, Jehovah's Witnesses, and Homosexuals', *California Sociologist* 7, 1: 49–67.

Klassen, A.D., C.J. Williams, and E.E. Levitt. 1989. *Sex and Morality in the U.S.: An Empirical Enquiry under the auspices of The Kinsey Institute.* Middletown, Conn.: Wesleyan University Press.

Krane, Jim. 2005. 'Dozens Arrested at Mass Emirates Gay Wedding', *Globe and Mail*, 26 Nov.

Kurdek, L.A. 1988. 'Correlates of Negative Attitudes toward Homosexuals in Heterosexual College Students', *Sex Roles* 18, 2: 727–38.

Larsen, K.S., M. Reed, and S. Hoffman. 1980. 'Attitudes of Heterosexuals toward Homosexuality: A Likert-type Scale and Construct Validity', *Journal of Sex Research* 16, 3: 245–57.

Lasser, Jon, and Deborah Tharinger. 2003. 'Visibility Management in School and Beyond: A Qualitative Study of Gay, Lesbian, Bisexual Youth', *Journal of Adolescence* 26, 2: 233–44.

Le Guin, Ursula K. 1969. *The Left Hand of Darkness.* New York: Ace Books.

Lepischak, Bev. 2004. 'Building Community for Toronto's Lesbian, Gay, Bisexual, Transsexual and Transgender Youth', *Journal of Gay and Lesbian Social Services* 16, 3 and 4: 81–98.

Lottes, I.L., and P.J. Kuriloff. 1992. 'The Effects of Gender, Race, Religion, and Political Orientation on the Sex Role Attitudes of College Freshmen', *Adolescence* 27, 3: 675–88.

Mackey, Richard A., Matthew A. Diemer, and Bernard A. O'Brien. 2004. 'Relational Factors in Understanding Satisfaction in the Lasting Relationships of Same-Sex and Heterosexual Couples', *Journal of Homosexuality* 47, 1: 111–36.

Mattingly, Marybeth J., and Robert N. Bozick. 2001. 'Children Raised by Same-Sex Couples: Much Ado about Nothing', Southern Sociological Society, conference paper.

Miall, C., and K. March. 2005. 'Open Adoption as a Family Form: Community Assessments and Social Support', *Journal of Family Issues* 26, 3: 380–410.

Mikhailovich, Katja, Sarah Martin, and Stephen Lawton. 2001. 'Lesbian and Gay Parents: Their Experiences of Children's Health Care in Australia', *International Journal of Sexuality and Gender Studies* 6, 3: 181–91.

Millham, J., and L.E. Weinberger. 1977. 'Sexual Preference, Sex Role Appropriateness, and Restriction of Social Access', *Journal of Homosexuality* 2, 4: 343–57.

Mooney-Somers, F., and S. Golombok. 2000. 'Children of Lesbian Mothers: From the 1970s to the New Millennium', *Sexual and Relationship Therapy* 15, 2: 121–6.

Moore, D. 2006. 'Homosexual Seniors Face Many Health Care Obstacles', *Expositor* (Brantford, Ont.), 20 Mar., A6.

Morin, S.F., and E.M. Garfinkle. 1978. 'Male Homophobia', *Journal of Social Issues* 34, 1: 29–47.

Morrison, Melanie A., and Todd G. Morrison. 2002. 'Development and Validation of a Scale Measuring Modern Prejudice toward Gay Men and Lesbian Women', *Journal of Homosexuality* 43, 2: 15–37.

Murray, Alison J. 2001. 'Let Them Take Ecstasy: Class and Jakarta Lesbians', *Journal of Homosexuality* 40, 3 and 4: 165–84.

Myers, Kristen A., Kay B. Forest, and Susan L. Miller. 2004. 'Officer Friendly and the Tough Cop: Gays and Lesbians Navigate Homophobia and Policing', *Journal of Homosexuality* 47, 1: 17–37.

Oerton, Sarah. 1998. 'Reclaiming the "Housewife"? Lesbians and Household Work', *Journal of Lesbian Studies* 2, 4: 69–83.

Overby, L. Marvin, and Jay Barth. 2002. 'Contact, Community Context, and Public Attitudes toward Gay Men and Lesbians', *Polity* 34, 4: 433–56.

Owen, Michelle K. 2001. '"Family" as a Site of Contestation: Queering the Normal or Normalizing the Queer?", in Terry Goldie, ed., *In a Queer Country: Gay and Lesbian Studies in the Canadian Context.* Vancouver: Arsenal Pulp Press, 86–98.

Parker, Richard, and Peter Aggleton. 2003. 'HIV and AIDS-related Stigma and Discrimination: A Conceptual Framework and Implications for Action', *Social Science and Medicine* 57, 1: 13–24.

Peacock, Ben, Stephen L. Eyre, Sandra Crouse Quinn, and Susan Kegeles. 2001. 'Delineating Differences: Sub-

Communities in the San Francisco Gay Community', *Culture, Health & Sexuality* 3, 2: 183–201.

Plummer, David C. 2001. 'The Quest for Modern Manhood: Masculine Stereotypes, Peer Culture, and the Social Significance of Homophobia', *Journal of Adolescence* 24, 1: 15.

Raeburn, Nicole C. 2004. *Changing Corporate America from Inside Out: Lesbian and Gay Workplace Rights*. Minneapolis: University of Minnesota Press.

Ragins, Belle Rose, John. M. Cornwell, and Janice S. Miller. 2003. 'Heterosexism in the Workplace: Do Race and Gender Matter?', *Group and Organization Management* 28, 1: 45–74.

Ragusa, Angela T. 2005. 'Social Change and the Corporate Construction of Gay Markets in the New York Times' Advertising Business News', *Media, Culture and Society* 27, 5: 653–76.

Reimann, Renate. 1999. 'Shared Parenting in a Changing World of Work: Lesbian Couples' Transition to Parenthood and Their Division of Labor', *Dissertation Abstracts International, A: The Humanities and Social Sciences* 59, 9: 3662–A

Ridge, Damien, Amos Hee, and Victor Minichiello. 1999. '"Asian" Men on the Scene: Challenges to "Gay Communities"', *Journal of Homosexuality* 36, 3 and 4: 43–68.

Rosario, Margaret, Eric W. Schrimshaw, and Joyce Hunter. 2004. 'Ethnic/Racial Differences in the Coming-Out Process of Lesbian, Gay, and Bisexual Youths: A Comparison of Sexual Identity Development over Time', *Cultural Diversity and Ethnic Minority Psychology* 10, 3: 215–28.

Rose, Suzanna M., and Mindy B. Mechanic. 2002. 'Psychological Distress, Crime Features, and Help-Seeking Behaviors Related to Homophobic Bias Incidents', *American Behavioral Scientist* 46, 1: 14–26.

Rosenfeld, Dana. 1999. 'Identity Work among the Homosexual Elderly', *Dissertation Abstracts International, A: The Humanities and Social Sciences* 60, 4: 1348–A.

Rubenstein, William B. 2001. 'Do Gay Rights Laws Matter? An Empirical Assessment', *Southern California Law Review* 75, 1: 65–119.

Saffron, Lisa. 1998. 'Raising Children in an Age of Diversity—Advantages of Having a Lesbian Mother', *Journal of Lesbian Studies* 2, 4: 35–47.

Sakalli, N. 2002. 'Application of the Attribution-Value Model of Prejudice to Homosexuality', *Journal of Social Psychology* 142, 2: 264–71.

Schatman, M.E. 1990. 'The Prediction of Homophobic Attitudes among College Students', Ph.D. thesis, University of North Texas.

Schmidt, Kathryn J. 2003. '"I Didn't Say Anything, but Everybody Knew": Sexual Orientation Disclosure through Tacit Understandings and Silence', Southern Sociological Society, conference paper.

Schwartz, Pepper, and Virginia Rutter. 1998. *The Gender of Sexuality*. Thousand Oaks, Calif.: Pine Forge Press.

Seidman, Steven. 2002. *Beyond the Closet: The Transformation of Gay and Lesbian Life*. New York: Routledge.

Seltzer, R. 1992. 'The Social Location of Those Holding Antihomosexual Attitudes', *Sex Roles* 26, 9 and 10: 391–8.

Siegel, Lloyd, and Arthur Zitrin. 1978. *Archives of Sexual Behavior* 7, 4: 285–90.

Siegel, P. 1979. 'Homophobia: Types, Origins, Remedies', *Christianity and Crisis* 39, 12: 280–4.

Supreme Court of Canada. 1997. *Vriend v. Alberta*.

Tomsen, Stephen. 2002. 'Victims, Perpetrators and Fatal Scenarios: A Research Note on Anti-Homosexual Male Homicides', *International Review of Victimology* 9, 3: 253–71.

Valverde, Mariana, and Miomir Cirak. 2003. 'Governing Bodies, Creating Gay Spaces: Policing and Security Issues in "Gay" Downtown Toronto', *British Journal of Criminology* 43, 1: 102–21.

Wainright, Jennifer L., Stephen T. Russell, and Charlotte J. Patterson. 2004. 'Psychosocial Adjustment, School Outcomes, and Romantic Relationships of Adolescents with Same-Sex Parents', *Child Development* 75, 6: 1886–98.

Ward, James, and Diana Winstanley. 2005. 'Coming Out at Work: Performativity and the Recognition and Renegotiation of Identity', *Sociological Review* 53, 3: 447–75.

Weinberg, George. 1983 [1972]. *Society and the Healthy Homosexual*. New York: St Martin's Press.

Weiss, Meredith. 2005. 'Who Sets Social Policy in Metropolis? Economic Positioning and Social Reform in Singapore', *New Political Science* 27, 3: 267–89.

AGING AND AGEISM

Introduction

This chapter is about younger people and seniors, youth, aging and ageism, retirement, and decline. The average age of Canadians is rising each decade, yet despite our growing awareness of older people and age variation, many Canadians openly practise **ageism**— direct or indirect discrimination against people based on their age. This includes refusing qualified and willing candidates for employment because of stereotypic attitudes towards older or younger people—indeed, towards any people who violate the age norms and expectations that are common in our society.

The topic of this chapter is unlike most of the other social problems or issues discussed in this book. After all, many people will never experience sexism or racism— because many people will never be women or members of racial minority groups. Many people will never be poor or unemployed or homosexual or caught in the middle of a war. But almost everyone will get to be elderly and almost everyone who gets to be elderly will experience ageism. So, this chapter is likely about you and what happens as you move from being young to being older, and then old.

We begin this chapter with a discussion of ideas about the progression through life that are associated with aging—in particular, ideas about 'the life course'. We introduce some ideas about age and aging, as both individual and societal processes, and further consider the notion of ageism. We see that age inequality exists in our society, in much the same sense that income inequality or racial inequality exists. Following a brief discussion of different theoretical approaches to the sociology of aging, we examine some of the main social and health effects of aging and ageism. We end with a consideration of possible solutions to the problems of aging and ageism.

Cross-Cultural Attitudes to Aging

In earlier times, advanced age brought respect, authority, and attention from others. It also brought jealousy and impatience. In Ireland, for example, sons waited for their fathers to die so they could inherit land, marry, and begin a family. Sometimes they had to wait until well into their thirties, forties, or older. As a result, marriages were late and birth rates were low. Because wives tended to be much younger than their husbands, they were more likely to become widows. Most importantly, the old enjoyed a high degree of control over their children and over young people overall (see Lasch, 1977).

As Western populations industrialized, children could more readily strike out on their own as earners. They no longer had to rely on their fathers. With increased mobility, young people married, set up their own households, and made themselves less available (or willing) to provide help. This transition, which unfolded throughout the West during the nineteenth and twentieth centuries, also began in the East in the second half of the twentieth century (see Gottlieb, 1993).

As people move from one stage in life to another, they switch roles. From student to employee or employer, single to married, without child(ren) to parent, married to divorced or widowed, worker to retiree. In every society, there are ages by which these changes are expected to occur. For example, in most parts of Canada, social norms are to marry by 30 and retire by 65. These changes are important to us. We carefully track and celebrate age in our society. We recognize birthdays, anniversaries, graduations, retirements, and other important age-based landmarks in our lives. We treat turning 18, 21, 30, 40, 50, and 65 as occasions worthy of gifts and cake (or alcohol).

Other cultures revere their elderly members as vessels of wisdom and authority. By contrast, Western culture reveres youth, and consequently the appearance of youth. In this context, members of our culture fear aging with its concomitant physical decline towards death. They view a receding hairline or crow's feet around the eyes as glaring reminders of aging and the imminent end. The culture tends to stereotype and exclude old people. In a culture that dreads aging and stereotypes elderly people, ageism affects many people who become old. Myths about the old abound, as do jokes about the elderly.

One common belief about aging is that most seniors are frail and ailing and that the majority need full-time care in nursing homes or other institutional settings. In truth, only 1.4 per cent of men and 1.7 per cent of women aged 65 to 74 live in a special-care institution, while the vast majority live alone or with family members (Novak, 1997; Statistics Canada, 1998). Another common but misguided belief is that most elderly people are senile or heading in that direction. In fact, most of them keep their cognitive and perceptual functions for many years. Alzheimer's disease, the most common form of neurological dementia, affects only 3 per cent of people aged 65 to 74. The prevalence rate rises to nearly 50 per cent only after people pass 80 years of age (Alzheimer's Disease Education and Referral Center, 1995).

Stereotypes of elderly people as isolated, depressed, weak and physically idle, mentally confused, and living in the past all perpetuate a negative image of aging and of being old. Because of our tendency to socialize with people whose age is similar to our own, most young people know few elderly people. As a result, they often believe that elderly people all have the same abilities, interests, needs, characteristics, or lifestyles. However, old people are no more homogeneous than young or middle-aged people.

In growing up, we learn negative attitudes towards aging and older people, gathered in part from the mass media and from jokes and cartoons. Many of these stereotypical images are myths. Nonetheless, if accepted as fact they can influence expectations about and reactions to aging and aged people, even among elderly people themselves. By shaping the popular views of older people, the media create a self-fulfilling prophecy in which elderly individuals begin to think and behave as people expect, thus reinforcing and lending

Box 7.1   Social Construction: Senior Sexuality and Media Myths

So where does the theory come [from] that sex rarely happens after age 50? Generally, it's driven by the stereotypes and attitudes of the Madison Avenue crowd that only mention sexual issues in the 50-plus generations in light of [erectile dysfunction]. They find it easier to assign the greatest 'sex appeal' to those with the firmest body parts and whitest teeth.

One can hardly blame them. First, most have no idea what older people find sexually appealing. They assume that ideas of sexual attraction remain the same throughout life and they find those qualities lacking in older adults. The assumption is, therefore, that if those qualities are lacking, there isn't any sexual attraction.

Second, older adults learn that there's more to being sexually attractive than simply a tightly compacted gluteus maximus. Older adults also find attraction at much deeper levels, and these are hard to portray in a 28-second commercial.

Older adults also see an attractiveness in character and loyalty, and we generally become more patient and tolerant of the foibles of others. Such attributes become an integral part of the basis for attraction, leaving other physical attributes far less important. We learn that while white teeth are nice, emotional maturity, intelligence, common sense, and the ability to carry on conversations are more important than perfect skin tone.

Older generations have also learned that no matter how cute someone is, there's always someone who's tired of taking his/her junk, there's always someone cuter, and going from relationship to relationship is just a lot of pointless and useless work. We've learned that there is no such thing as a perfect relationship and everyone has their issues.

These are the realizations and understandings that develop and become the stronger components of attraction; and it is attraction, not the volume or exact placement of collagen, that matters. It's why 'boomers' are finding that sex is more satisfying past age 50 because there is so much more to sex than they ever dreamed.

Source: Adapted from: <www.seniormag.com/caregiverresources/articles/caregiverarticles/relationships/senior-sex.htm>.

legitimacy to the stereotype. For example, they may come to believe that shows of sexual interest are inappropriate. Negative stereotypes can also devalue the status of elderly people. One result is a decrease in the frequency and quality of social interaction between young and old. Another is the granting of fewer social services to elderly people.

People in their sixties who would have been considered old a generation ago are considered middle-aged today; they are active, healthy, and socially involved. This demonstrates that aging is largely relative to other factors, including how the elderly are regarded. In a society obsessed with youthful appearance, people are given to obsessing about the march of time. No wonder many people (women in particular) worry that, after 25 (or 30, or 40) they are 'over the hill'.

The Idea of a 'Life Course'

Our ability to think usefully about aging is helped immeasurably by the sociological idea of the 'life course'. Sociologist Glen Elder (1999), currently considered the most eminent researcher studying this topic, states the life course approach rests on five main assumptions, and each is important to our understanding of age and aging.

First, directing us away from age-specific studies—studies only of elderly people, of infants, or of teenagers—is the observation that 'human development and aging are life-long processes' (Elder, 1999: 7). They start at birth and stop only with death. As people get older, their lives change. At each stage, certain concerns become supreme and others become trivial. Certain important life events are typically concentrated in certain periods of a person's life. Social institutions also play a part as gatekeepers. They divide and regulate life-course transitions, pushing people in and out of school, in and out of marriage, in and out of jobs, and so on (Heinz, 1996). They also set up, teach, and reward the social expectations connected with a life course. We cannot understand the ideas, actions, and beliefs of people at any given age without some understanding of how they got to that age—that is, their developmental pathway. This means that longitudinal studies are the best ways of understanding all people, and especially older people.

Second, Elder (1999: 9) notes that 'the developmental antecedents and consequences of life transitions, events, and behaviour patterns vary according to their timing in a person's life.' Simply, it makes a difference at what age you make a key life transition—whether you divorce at 25 or at 55, for example, or graduate from college at 20 or at 40. Earlier and later life transitions affect the ways people view themselves, not least because their self-image is often based on a comparison with others.

Third, 'lives are lived interdependently and socio-historical influences are expressed through this network of shared relationships' (ibid., 10). Since our lives are embedded in social relationships with others, we may find ourselves entering new statuses or speeding through the life course because of the actions of others. The teenage pregnancy of her daughter may make a woman a grandmother 'before her time', just as the early death of her spouse may make her a widow 'before her time'. Our degree of preparation for new roles and statuses is important for how we experience and perform those roles and statuses.

Fourth, 'the life course of individuals is embedded in and shaped by the historical times and places they experience over their lifetime' (ibid., 13). Coming of college age means something different in wartime (for example, in the 1940s) than it does in peacetime (as in the 1980s), in prosperity (the 1950s) than in financial depression (the 1930s), in a period of gender equality (the 1990s) than in one of male dominance (the 1890s). The historical period affects the opportunities available to us and the actions we are likely to take, and these in turn will affect other opportunities and actions throughout our lives.

Fifth, 'individuals construct their own life course through the choices and actions they take within the opportunities of history and social circumstances' (ibid., 15). In other words, though social forces influence our opportunities and actions, we continue to have a measure of choice in our own lives. This means that within any social category or historical period, we will find variations in the human life course, because people are free to choose different paths. At the same time, cultural values and social norms influence the range of people's choices. This produces predictable variations in the life course across regions and across ethnic, religious, and other subcultures, as well as between people with different personality types.

The life-course model is a useful way of viewing age and aging. It helps us to understand why all 20-year-olds are not the same, nor are all 50- or 80-year-olds. On the other hand, it also helps us understand why people have a fairly predictable sequence of life experiences as they move from 20 to 50 to 80, and why they feel uncomfortable when they deviate from that sequence.

However, age and aging are not merely about passage through social stages in the life course. John Mirowsky and Catherine Ross (1999) identify five aspects of age: maturity, decline, generation, survival, and life cycle. First, with age comes experience and maturity. This is expressed in greater law abidance, safer habits, a more orderly lifestyle, greater satisfaction, and a more positive self-image. Second, decline is also evident with age. Often with aging we see a build-up of failures, faults, injuries, and errors, which over time may gradually promote physical and mental decline.

Third, different age groups represent different generations, or cohorts, and in this way reflect historical events and trends. For example, twentieth-century trends included increased education, income, female employment, and life expectancy but decreased family size and rural residence (Bianchi and Spain, 1986). These trends are obvious in consecutive cohorts of people. Older people are, for example, on average less educated and more likely than younger people to have grown up in large families or rural areas.

Age groups within a society also represent survivorship. Aging means surviving from birth until today. However, the chances of survival vary over time. As historical cohorts, different age groups have to survive different dangers at different ages. For example, the polio epidemic of the 1950s posed different risks if you were an infant, a teenager, or a mature adult at the time. The older you were, the less risk you faced. Each period also brings new challenges to survival. In recent decades, HIV/AIDS has posed a new risk to young people. Increasingly, depression and depression-related risks (such as suicide and alcoholism) pose a growing risk. Severely depressed people die at two to four times the rate of others who are similar in age, sex, socio-financial status, pre-existing health problems, and apparent fitness (Bruce and Leaf, 1989).

Finally, life cycle refers to the age-related passage through a sequence of common roles. As people grow older, they typically advance from school to job to retirement, from single to married to widowed, and so on. Changes in marital, employment, and financial status go with aging. No wonder some have compared life to a journey, others to a river. Still others think of it as a life 'cycle', as though life repeats itself or returns to its origins, like a wheel. And others speak of a life 'course', meaning a route, path, or track, as though a predictable but not exactly repeated sequence of events awaits us between birth and death.

Fit Facts for Older Adults

- Physical activity decreases with age.
- The most popular physical activities among Canadian adults aged 20 years and older are walking, gardening and yard work, home exercise, swimming, and bicycling.
- Thirty-nine per cent of adults in Canada aged 65 years and older are overweight; an additional 13 per cent are considered obese.
- In Canada, approximately one in four women and one in eight men over 50 years of age have osteoporosis.
- By age 75, approximately one in three men and one in two women engage in no physical activity.
- In 1999, approximately $2.1 billion of the total direct costs to Canada's health-care system were attributable to physical inactivity.
- A 10 per cent reduction in the prevalence of physical inactivity among the Canadian population might reduce direct health-care expenditures by $150 million per year.

Source: *in motion.* Saskatoon Regional Health Authority. <www.in-motion.ca/older/facts.php>.

The way sociologists think about it, the life course is a patterned sequence of individual experiences over time, subject to varied social, historical, and cultural influences (Gubrium and Holstein, 1995). There is, in each society—indeed, in each social group—an expected life course, which fits (more or less) with the generally experienced life course (Handel, 1997). True, these life courses, ideal and actual, are not identical. The gap between the life courses we expect and those we experience may cause much distress. Living may sometimes mean 'breaking the rules' or failing to live up to age-related expectations.

Still, in spite of this gap, we all expect life to follow known patterns, and these patterns are age-related. Changing ages often means changing roles, locations, skills, and identities. With each new age of life, people are led to congregate with others of the same age, to carry out age-related activities and share age-related lifestyles. As a result, people change their friends and associates as they age and pass through life.

Early in life, we are most concerned about relations with our parents. Our childhood home is the culture and society we know best, and we measure everything else—our wishes, our hopes, our self-esteem—against what we have learned there. As we age, this changes radically. We become acquainted with a much larger world at school; the peers we meet there are much more varied than are our parents and siblings. For the first time, we feel moral confusion. The question we face is not 'Should I obey the rules?' but 'What are the rules?' In adolescence, our needs for peer acceptance are increasing when we are searching for an identity and purpose of our own. We often feel torn between the conflicting goals of finding our own true selves and gaining social acceptance as one of the crowd.

Much of growing up is learning age-related rules of behaviour. Drawing on their own experiences, elders often give young people advice about how to travel the life course. Often, parents tell their children not to marry before they can support themselves, which means finishing their education and getting started in a career. Speaking of the United States, Dennis Hogan (1981) calls this the 'normative pattern'. In large part, it has also applied in Canada and other Western societies.

Many factors conspire against this normative pattern. Economic recessions, for example, disrupt traditional patterns; they make it harder for young people to find work and achieve financial security. Under these conditions, getting married seems no more foolish than does not getting married. This aside, Hogan senses a continuing movement away from the normative pattern: a trend towards marriage before completing education and career-building, for example. Reasons for this change include the gradual lengthening of formal education, the growing availability of student loans and married-student housing, the increase in full-time and part-time work for students and their spouses, the rise of part-time education, and, of course, the increased protection from unwanted pregnancy that modern birth control provides.

Age Differentiation

Everyone reading this book has experienced the ages 0–16, yet sociologically speaking, childhood is a fairly recent social invention (Ariès, 1958). The spread of this idea of childhood coincided with the development of schooling, city life, and industrialization. When most people still lived on farms or in small villages, children helped out with the family work from an early age onward. Differentiation of roles and statuses by age was slight. People learned to do adult tasks and took on adult responsibilities as soon as they were able. It was with the spread and elongation of schooling that childhood came into being as a recognized separate stage of life.

A further differentiation of people by age resulted, in the nineteenth century, in the invention of adolescence, once more reflecting the lengthening of education and the movement of people into cities. Possibly, we will see even more age differentiation of young people in the twenty-first century, as people continue to extend their education and delay their entry into full adult earning status.

This creation of age groups, through age differentiation, meant an increased distinction, separation, isolation, and segregation of different aged people from one another. As well, with the invention of childhood came a mythologizing of children's innocence, ignorance, and purity. Adults liked to believe that children could be moulded like clay. People who were 'bad' adults had been born 'good' but must have been abused, neglected, or poorly socialized in childhood. Thus, a strong responsibility came to rest on the shoulders of adults to raise their children in a loving, protective way.

Basic Aspects of the Sociology of Age

From birth onward, an individual's physical and mental abilities gradually improve, then decline in a biological process known as **senescence**. However, exactly at what age and in what form the decline takes place varies widely from one person to another. Today, older people can look forward to a longer and healthier old age than in the past. Yet our culture has not fully kept up with these changes in the social definition of who is elderly and what elderly people are like, largely because with an increased interest in childhood, there had been a decreased interest in later adulthood.

Age Socialization

Because so many factors are involved, aging is hard to understand and hard for people to enact. Both through its programming and through advertisements, the mass media in Canada contribute to age socialization, which teaches us about age roles. However, the mass media oversimplify the process, with regrettable results. Typically, young people are presented as attractive, spirited, hip, humorous, sexy, and rash; middle-aged and elderly people are presented as the opposite, often for comic relief. Many prime-time television shows now have one token older person (over 45), just as they used to have one token black person. Elderly roles in commercials remain rare, with old people appearing almost only in advertisements for life insurance, age-related health-care items (such as adult diapers), and other products targeted specifically at the elderly market.

Because the popular media mislead us about aging, as they do about everything else—marriage, crime, politics, finances, and so on—most of us enter old age saddled with ignorance and wrong ideas. We have to figure out how to live as elderly people in a world made more complicated and cruel by media images. In large part, our age socialization is a matter of teaching ourselves and learning from our peers. However, this is no less true among adolescents in school and adults in the workplace. All of us learn our social roles through 'on-the-job' training.

Age Stratification

Every known society distinguishes people according to their age. Probably because chronological age is associated with physical and mental ability and with social experience, most social roles carry assumptions about age, however hidden these may be. In high-fertility societies, where young people are in abundance, old people are fairly rare, highly valued, and socially dominant. As fertility falls, the population grows older and old people become more numerous. Then a conflict often develops with traditional expectations about age and aging. Older people become more numerous but less powerful and less respected—sometimes even resented. As we have said, younger people come to dominate the social and cultural agenda.

In 1901, only 5 per cent of the population was aged 65 or older. Over the past century, this fraction has more than doubled to 12 per cent. Canada is expected to have about 14 per cent of the population aged 65 and older by 2011 and 22 per cent in 2031 (Statistics Canada, 1994). Though the Canadian population is aging rapidly, it is far from the oldest population. Many Northern and Central European populations have been aging for generations, with much higher proportions of elderly people than one finds in North America.

We might best describe Canada's **age pyramid** today as a diamond shape, with a small base among the youngest groups, spreading out gradually as age groups increase in size until ages 45–55, before tapering off into a high, thin peak around ages 80–90 (Statistics Canada, 2000b). A diamond shape reflects a population undergoing change—a triangle that is gradually becoming a rectangle as the birth rate slows. The wide middle of the diamond represents the large number of births during the baby-boom period. The pointed ends represent the small number of surviving older people (at the one end) and the small number of births in recent decades.

Regionally, Saskatchewan has the highest proportion of seniors aged 65 and over (15 per cent) of any other Canadian province or territory. Yukon, the Northwest Territories, and Nunavut have the lowest proportions, at 5, 4, and 3 per cent, respectively (Statistics Canada, 2001). Several factors contribute to the greying of a region. One is that young people migrate out of the area for financial, social, or other reasons. Another

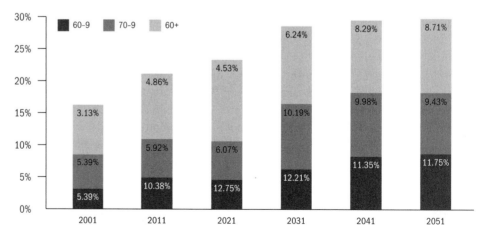

FIGURE 7.1 Population Projections for Canada, Percentage of the Population Aged 60 and Over, 2001-51 Source: Adapted from Statistics Canada, 'Population Projections for Canada, Provinces and Territories', 2000 to 2026, Catalogue no. 91-520, available at: <http://www.statcan.ca/english/freepub/91-520-XIB/0010191-520-XIB.pdf>.

factor is an influx of seniors into an area because of more favourable climate, suitable housing, and presence of resources, as is the case in Victoria, Vancouver, and the Okanagan Valley in British Columbia. However, the most important factor is the birth rate. Under good health conditions, a low birth rate means an old population, depicted by a rectangular age distribution. Some Canadian regions, in particular the northern territories, have higher birth rates (and lower life expectancies) than the national average, resulting in younger populations.

Age stratification theory focuses on the way social structures affect individual aging and the stratification, or vertical segregation, of people by age. It also analyzes the movement of age cohorts over the life cycle. Thus, people born in the same period usually experience the same role transitions around the same time, since they are subject to the same age-related rules and institutional arrangements.

Aging and ageism pose various problems for society. First, ageism, like discrimination based on race or gender, is repellent to a society like ours that is pledged, in principle, to judging people by what they do rather than who they are. We say we believe in rewards based on achievement, not ascription. Thus, ageism is a sign that we do not, as a society, live up to our own proclaimed values of justice and equality. Second, ageism poses practical problems for the victims of this discrimination. Like all discrimination, ageism has both material and psychological effects. Materially, it limits people's opportunities to get the jobs and incomes they may need to survive. Psychologically, ageism makes people feel rejected, excluded, and degraded. They feel they are less than they want and need to be as human beings.

Stereotyping aside, aging poses problems for a society. Generally, populations with a high proportion of very old or very young people—that is, low-fertility populations like our own, or high-fertility populations like, say, Iraq's—consume a high proportion of their national economy in the form of supports for dependent populations: health, education, welfare, housing, and so on. Populations with a high proportion in the workforce, aged 25–65, are able to invest more of their economy in development, savings, or war, without significantly reducing their spending on human capital.

Aboriginal Seniors

- Elderly Native people make up a relatively small proportion of Canada's Aboriginal population.
- The number of Aboriginal seniors is expected to triple between 1996 and 2016.
- The average life expectancy of Aboriginal people remains significantly lower than the Canadian average.
- The reported rate of heart problems, hypertension, diabetes, and arthritis is often double or triple the rate reported by Canadian seniors overall.

Source: <www.phac-aspc.gc.ca/seniors-aines/pubs/fed_paper/pdfs/fedpager_e.pdf>.

Sociological Theories of Aging

Structural Functionalism

As we have seen throughout this book, structural functionalists think that society is like a well-oiled machine, made up of supporting parts that together work as an efficient, productive whole. This perspective also views society as being only as strong as its weakest members.

One structural-functionalist theory of aging, first promoted by Elaine Cummings and William Henry (1961), is **disengagement theory**. This theory holds that elderly people are among the weakest members of the population and that society has, therefore, devised a means of displacing them from its central positions of power and influence. As people age, their bodies undergo physical and mental decline, Cummings and Henry note. Muscles weaken, bones become fragile, most perceptual abilities decline, and cognitive faculties become slower and diminish. Elderly people are also more prone to illness and disability. At work, elderly individuals are often less efficient than their younger, stronger, and more energetic counterparts. For the good of society and for themselves, disengagement theory argues, elderly people must finally give up their positions and withdraw to the edges of society, where they can prepare for their certain death.

Retirement from work serves several functions for society as a whole: (1) it empties a position, allowing someone from the next generation to move up the social hierarchy; (2) it allows the retiring member a moment of recognition—for example, a retirement party—for his or her contribution; and (3) it ensures that society replaces outdated skills and ideas with more useful ones. Though it may sound cold and cynical, structural functionalists stress that this change is both natural and crucial to society's effectiveness. Without such turnover, the economy would be less efficient and less equipped to compete globally.

Conflict Theory

However, many disagree with the assumptions of functionalism, especially with the assumption that the exclusion of older people from financially rewarding and socially important roles is good for society. Nor is age-related discrimination against the young necessarily useful to society, either. Conflict theorists believe that ageism does not serve society as a whole but is merely a form of inequality exercised by the younger majority to further its own interests.

Many scholars have criticized disengagement theory as too simplistic. It depicts humans as robots who contribute to the financial institution for many years before voluntarily delivering themselves to the dustbin of later life, waiting listlessly for death to overtake them in retirement communities. This view is wrong. Contrary to what disengagement theory predicts, many elderly individuals remain active, do not retire, and fight obsolescence. Elderly people rarely withdraw from society of their own will. Instead, employers and retirement rules push them out of the workforce. Without these pushes, many elderly people would remain active for as long as possible; active people are healthier, therefore people value being active. Even after retirement, many stay active as long as opportunities in the family and the wider community will allow. When elderly people disengage, it is often because of other people's wishes, not their own. This is the perspective taken by most conflict theorists.

Age groups hold different interests, and each group competes against the others to enlarge its yield of society's resources. A problem with this arrangement is the young and the old are less able to prevail since they lack the organization and the power that the middle-aged have to influence public policy. As a result, the interests and needs of elderly people and children are often ignored or set aside by middle-aged decision-makers.

Also, many assumptions about aging lead directly to the dependence of elderly people on the rest of society. These are false views that isolate age as the cause of dependence. In fact, financial help is needed for only a portion, not all, of the elderly population with physical and mental problems.

Symbolic Interactionism

Symbolic interactionists focus their attention on how we symbolize elderly people and enact aging in our society. They study how socially constructed definitions of age and aging affect a person's experience of growing old. The symbolic interactionists stress that age is a state of mind shaped by the labels society applies. For example, they might note that remaining happy and satisfied in the later stages of life depends largely on the perspective on aging accepted by the individual. Interactionists stress that satisfaction with aging means rejecting the definition of old age as disabling.

Activity theory (Havighurst and Albrecht, 1953) argues that, contrary to disengagement theory (which holds that people give up roles as they age), people in fact take on new roles as they age. Such continued activity preserves a sense of continuity, helps people preserve their self-concept, and contributes to greater life satisfaction. People who keep up a high level of activity age more 'successfully' than people who do not. This can be considered a symbolic interactionist theory because it relates role play to self-identity and psychological well-being.

Other symbolic interactionists have examined how society, and its media in particular, portrays elderly people. These portrayals both reflect society's stereotypes about older people and help reinforce those images. Women are chiefly targeted for elimination from the media because of age. As male lead actors continue to make Hollywood movies, same-aged women actors lose their marketability. They are no longer allowed to serve as compelling love interests since the largest group of ticket-buying moviegoers is young people in their teens and twenties, and in our society, while younger women might be paired with older men, it is rare for a younger man to be romantically involved with a significantly older woman.

Feminist Theories

The experience of aging is different for men and women, largely because, for women, aging is associated with a culturally defined loss of youth and glamour—a less critical concern for men. Women and men age differently owing to different biological constitutions. Research on medical interventions that affect the aging process, such as vitamin supplements and estrogen replacement therapy, is in its early stages. Women and men also bring different resources to old age. And they are subject to different expectations as young, middle-aged, and elderly humans (Ginn and Arber, 1995). Women in our culture dread getting older in a way that most men do not.

Today, women and men lead more similar lives, in the sense that both may aim for careers. However, their careers are likely to be in different sectors of the workforce. While in the workforce, most women earn less pay than men and are less likely to qualify for a private pension during the years in which they are working. Because of this, and because their spouses or partners usually die before them, women are at particular risk of finding themselves living alone on a meagre income in their senior years. As well, a reduced income and exhausted savings may mean that elderly women are forced to sell their family homes and move to rental or institutional homes. Besides their heavier weight of disadvantage in aging, older women have more domestic duties and social responsibilities than older men. They have a different role in the family division of labour. For example, unlike men, they play a vital role in kin-keeping through social networks and caregiving.

These social responsibilities over the entire life course carry important results in old age. The family caregiving roles women take on at younger ages often remove women from the labour force, again limiting their pension benefits (Moody, 2000). This limits their lifetime earnings and may result in poverty after retirement. At the societal level, this contributes to a 'feminization of poverty'. We will have more to say about poverty below.

Table 7.1 Five Main Sociological Paradigms on Aging	
Theory	**Main Ideas**
Structural Functionalism	■ All elements in society are interrelated. ■ Society is only as strong as its weakest members. ■ Disengagement theory accounts for the relegation of older people to the sidelines of society. ■ Retirement serves several functions.
Conflict Theory	■ Conflict and change are basic features of social life. ■ Age-related discrimination does not benefit society. ■ Elderly people do not disengage, they are pushed out of the workforce. ■ The most powerful groups in society command resources and are the 'decision-makers'. ■ False perceptions isolate age as the cause of independence.
Symbolic Interactionism	■ Social life involves continued interaction. ■ Socially constructed definitions of age and aging affect one's experience of growing old. ■ People take on new roles as they age (they do not disengage). ■ Media portrayals reflect and reinforce society's stereotypes about older people.
Feminism	■ Gender inequality is almost universal. ■ Aging affects men and women differently.
Social Constructionism	■ Views of aging are shaped by moral entrepreneurship. ■ Popular beliefs about aging are media myths.

Social Consequences of Aging

Retirement Income

After retiring from paid work, Canada's elderly support themselves in various ways: through government and private pensions, savings, and contributions by other family members. Canada's retirement income system currently consists of three tiers:

■ government benefit programs, such as Old Age Security (OAS), which in January 2006 was set at a maximum of $487.54 per month, and the Guaranteed Income Supplement (GIS).

■ the government-sponsored Canadian Pension Plan (CPP) and Quebec Pension Plan (QPP), which are based on a worker's income between the ages of 18 and 65 (the maximum CPP and QPP amounts in 2005 were $828.75 if taken at age 65).

■ personal savings, investment portfolios, and registered retirement savings plans (RRSPs).

Our current retirement income system is the result of efforts made over much of the twentieth century. In 1927, an Old Age Pension was introduced. After the Great Depression and World War II Canadians received a universal pension—the Canada Pension Plan and, in the 1960s, the Quebec Pension Plan. Finally, the government introduced the GIS in 1966 to supplement the incomes of seniors whose main source of income was the OAS. The monthly benefit varies according to marital status, pensioner's income, and spouse's income.

With the expansion and reform of retirement income programs in the 1970s and 1980s, Canada set up a public pension system that significantly improved the quality of life for seniors. This system remains intact today, despite pressures from an increase in the number of eligible elders and a larger public debt (from other sources). Increasingly, planners have had to think about ways to ensure the continued affordability of a universal pension plan.

Keeping up growth in Canada's standard of living will become more difficult as the population continues to age. This is because the share of the population that is working is projected to start to decline after 2010 as the baby-boom generation enters retirement age. Population aging will produce especially large increases in age-related government spending on universal public pensions and health care. More people of working age will be needed to help pay, through their taxes, for the pensions and benefits received by a growing number of elders—more generally, to preserve the Canadian standard of living.

Steps will be needed to increase Canadian productivity by fully integrating new immigrants and Aboriginal people into the labour market. Older Canadians who want to continue to take part in the labour market should not be prevented from doing so. Also, Canada will need to invest more heavily in those factors that contribute most to productivity: research, education and training, and financial infrastructure (roads, railways, airports, power systems, and so on).

Recognizing the need for readiness, more and more Canadians have been saving for old age. The financial reserves in Canada's main retirement programs—public government pensions, registered pension plans, and RRSPs—increased substantially during the 1990s. In total, by the end of 2001, Canadians had built up an estimated $1.15 trillion in the three main retirement programs, almost double the level of $593.6 billion in 1990, when measured in constant (inflation adjusted) dollars. Canadians had nearly $292.5 billion invested in RRSPs at the end of 2001, and about $64.7 billion in the C/QPP (Statistics Canada, 2003).

With these changes, the 'feminization of poverty' may have shown signs of slowing. Between 1991 and 2001, the gap in the number of men and women joining in registered pension plans narrowed significantly, from almost 1 million to less than half a million members. The increase in female membership is due to the growth in their labour force participation; the drop in membership among male workers is largely because of the recession of the early 1990s that led to many job losses among men especially (ibid.)

Careers and Mandatory Retirement

Until recently, in all industrial and post-industrial societies, most people's incomes have been gained from paid work, and most paid work has been organized into careers in large organizations: in government, large businesses, law firms, universities, and so on. The possibility of 'career mobility'—that is, financial and occupational promotion over the life cycle—has been age-related. It has also relied on one of two reliable sources of opportunity: continued financial growth or continued elimination of old people through death or retirement. In effect, elderly people through most of history have conveniently gotten out of the way of younger people, so younger people could also have careers.

This has all changed in recent years for three main reasons: lengthening of the average lifespan; a decline in financial growth; and the recent elimination of compulsory retirement. These problems have been intensified by the existence of tightly organized labour markets that strictly control access from the outside: in effect, promotion in a good career is only possible from the inside, and it is harder and harder to get inside a desirable labour market. These important points need some unpacking and elaboration.

The word 'career' originates in words that mean 'racecourse' and 'road for cars'. To say that a person has a 'career' implies he or she is rapidly moving towards a goal alongside, or in competition with, others. Ideally, no one starts ahead of anyone else, and no one fails to pass a marker. Some competitors progress faster than others; one competitor 'wins' the race and others 'place' or 'show'. A 'career' is like a life course in many respects (for example, there is predictable change over time) but unlike a life course in others (for example, people may be downwardly mobile in a career, but they cannot get younger; and people may move ahead at different rates in a career, but everyone ages at roughly the same speed).

That said, careers and aging are correlated, because most career mobility is based on seniority, or the length of tenure. Thus, other things being equal, the longer one works at an organization, the higher the salary and degree of authority, autonomy, and prestige. However, as the workplace becomes more specialized, seniority alone no longer guarantees advancement. The occupational structure is now finely stratified, so people can enter an organization or industry at different levels. Some positions require candidates to have an undergraduate education, while others within the same company or occupational field may require a graduate degree. Careers are patterned largely because of the workings of these 'internal labour markets'. These markets impose a high degree of control over who enters, at what level, through what stages people will move, and at what rate. The result is that, even today, society sorts people into different types of careers. Within each of these 'internal labour markets', career progress is still largely predictable and based on seniority. However, achievement becomes far more important than in the past. Moreover, seniority alone will not help one to jump from a lower internal market into a higher one. Thus, career mobility has been altered through industrial growth and differentiation, and through the rise of achievement as a basis for ranking. Modern professions (such as medicine and law) are especially notable for these features, including their ability to control career entries, reward systems, and conditions of work.

As we have suggested, careers are job-related pathways over the life course. Individually, careers reflect differences (and similarities) in opportunities and human capital. On the corporate level, they reflect linkages within firms, across firms, and across institutions. Just as careers tie together life events, so they also tie together institutional activities.

Just as we expect people to enter careers in particular ways, so we expect them to leave in particular ways. For example, we often expect them to leave paid work around the age of 65. However, high-level, high-seniority people are less likely than others to leave their job/career voluntarily—they are simply doing too well. For similar reasons, people in organizations or sectors of the economy that have high promotion rates are less likely to leave voluntarily than people in organizations or sectors of the economy with low promotion rates.

Thus, decisions to leave a job or career are dependent on career opportunities. People stay where the opportunities are best. Seniority in the firm is much more important than age for departure decisions. Thus, a 45-year-old, low-seniority worker is more likely to leave than a 45-year-old, high-seniority worker, or than a 60-year-old, high-seniority worker. This suggests that turnover is related more to the build-up of firm-specific skills than to life-cycle considerations. In these respects, women are different from men: women leave the organization for personal reasons more often than men, and less often for career reasons.

Compulsory retirement—the legal right of an employer to retire an employee, or the eligibility of an employee to receive various private and public pensions—has been a staple arrangement of industrial societies for well over a century. In Canada, where compulsory retirement was in place until 2005, employees of most public and private organizations routinely retired at age 65, if not earlier. (The age of voluntary retirement has been falling over the past century.) Since, for most workers, salaries had peaked a decade or more earlier, there was little financial incentive to stay on if they were offered a satisfactory retirement package.

Self-employed professionals (for example, doctors or lawyers) or business-owners (for example, shopkeepers) had much more choice about when they would retire. And since they received no benefits from a registered pension plan when they retired, their incentive to retire at age 65 or earlier was low: likely, their standard of living would be higher if they continued to work. Also, they tended to be more engaged in their work than wage-earning employees. For many, work was a vocation as well as a source of income and sociability.

Professionals who worked in large organizations—for example, university professors—found themselves in the undesirable position of being forced to quit a job they liked and accept a much reduced income, simply because they had reached the age of 65. So, it is not surprising that academics and librarians were first in challenging the compulsory retirement laws that applied to universities and other public organizations. In 2005, the Supreme Court ruled that compulsory retirement is a form of age discrimination and that it could no longer be practised. Immediately, universities and other large organizations recognized the need to adjust their operations because of this change.

Removing compulsory retirement will likely have major unintended consequences for everyone. For example, employers may be reluctant to hire older employees, since there will no longer be certainty about when those employees will leave. Older employees may no longer be kept on once their productivity starts to decline, since there is no longer any assurance that they will retire by age 65. However, attempts to fire unproductive employees would result in large numbers of human rights claims based on age.

Equally important, organizations that have previously organized jobs and careers around the seniority principle may start to rigorously monitor performance. If so, job security will likely decline (for example, the provision of tenure to faculty members may be replaced by five-year contracts). In that event, job uncertainty will reduce the attachment of workers to their organization and to one another. Job uncertainty may also lead workers to increase the behaviours that will earn them a renewed contract and lessen those that will not. So, for example, in the academic community, it may lead to (even) more emphasis on publishing and (even) less emphasis on undergraduate teaching.

However, the most immediate effect of ending compulsory retirement is likely to be a slowdown in hiring new younger workers—for example, new faculty members into universities. Remember that, unless there is expansion in an organization, there is only 'exchange mobility'. Then, there can be no promotion of people already inside the organization, and no entry of newcomers into the organization, unless there are departures. So, for example, a five-year or roughly 15 per cent (average) increase in the time senior faculty workers remain in their jobs will amount to a roughly 15 per cent drop in the number of new faculty members hired. This, in turn, will result in a delayed entry of new PhDs into teaching; more unemployment or underemployment for young PhDs; a pressure to reduce graduate training and advanced research in universities; and a drop in the entry of new ideas into university life (by means of new faculty members).

The compulsory retirement issue offers a clear example of how the interests of different age groups may be opposed. Younger workers benefit from continuing compulsory retirement, since (in a stagnant economy) it opens opportunities for employment and promotion. Older workers benefit from ending compulsory retirement, since this allows people to choose whether to continue doing work they like for a high salary. However, compulsory retirement is not the only issue that pits age groups against each other. The practice of inheritance has a similar effect.

Issues Associated with Inheritance

Wealth, property, power, and prestige all flow downward from older to younger generations. As older members of society retire from positions of power or die, they give up what they have amassed to their successors. Inheritance is the flow of property after death along kinship lines, usually from the older to the younger generation. In nearly all societies, unless other instructions are provided, it is assumed that close kin (spouses, parents, and children) will have first call on the property of the deceased person.

Cultures vary in whether the dominant inheritance pattern is one of **primogeniture**, that is, the eldest son gets everything, or whether the property is split among the surviving children. Historically, primogeniture has been a conservative strategy for ensuring the survival of the family by keeping the family's property intact. However, inheritance practices also influence marriage patterns, the quality of relationships between parents and children, and the quality of relationships between siblings. For

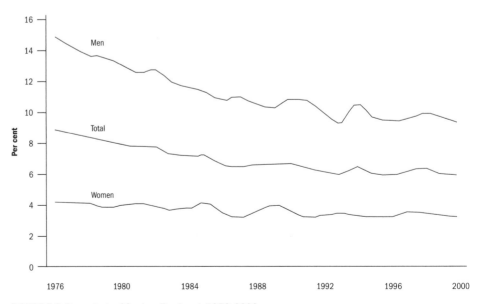

FIGURE 7.2 Percentage of Seniors Employed, 1976-2000
Source: Adapted from Statistics Canada data, at: <www.hc-sc.gc.ca/seniors-aines/pubs/factoids/2001/no08_e.htm>.

example, by giving all the family property to only one child, one almost ensures the inheritor will exercise power over the other children. Equally, the other children may have trouble getting set up financially, which in turn may limit their capacity to marry and raise children. It is especially under this winner-takes-all system of inheritance that one is likely to find bitter rivalries between the children of a family, and often a strong, though usually unconscious, wish by the inheritor to see his parent's death.

In societies where men and women are treated unequally, women may be barred from inheriting family property, yet they are expected to provide continuous care for their aging parents or in-laws. Even today in Canada, social expectations pressure daughters more so than sons to provide care to aging parents.

Filial responsibility is the moral responsibility of a grown child to look after his or her aging parent. Notions of filial responsibility, or filial piety, are especially marked in societies influenced by the teachings of Confucius (for example, China, Korea, and Japan). Recent social changes, associated with urbanization and industrialization, have weakened these traditional norms. With the nuclearization of the family, newlyweds in Asia have been setting up their own households, so daughters-in-law and mothers-in-law no longer share the same home. This has deprived mothers-in-law of a traditional source of caregiving (Kim, 1996).

POVERTY, WEALTH, AND SOCIAL CLASS

While many of Canada's elderly are poor, the problem is not as great in this country as in others. The low-income rate among the Canadian elderly population is 4.8 per cent, compared with 6.0 per cent in Sweden and 22.4 per cent in the United States (Ross et al., 2001). Still, financial strain remains a problem for many of Canada's elderly, in part because people are living longer and they are staying healthy, energetic, and active for longer periods of life.

Vital to the well-being of old people is their robustness. People's experience of old age reflects a variety of collected experiences up to that point. A history of employment instability, for example—that is, frequent unemployment and re-employment—leads to the build-up of large work experience shortfalls among inner-city minority people (Tienda and Stier, 1996). This has outcomes for later well-being: pensions will be smaller, health and well-being may be worse.

Most important of all to older people is their social connectedness. As Durkheim showed clearly in his book *Suicide* (1951), social integration is a matter of life and death. Not only does social integration reduce the wish of people to kill themselves, it also increases their likelihood to survive through the receipt of many social supports—material, physical, emotional, and spiritual. Children play a large part in helping their aging parents, just as aging parents play a large part in helping their children—when they live near each other.

However, social integration is not merely a matter of having children around. It also includes contact with and help from unrelated others—for example, neighbours, acquaintances, and friends. A good example of the dangers of social isolation is documented by the sociological study *Heat Wave* (Klinenberg, 2002), which documents the effects of a heat wave on two Chicago neighbourhoods in the summer of 2000. The mortality rate was higher in the less cohesive neighbourhood, and those most likely to die were elderly people living on their own. A similar situation arose during the flooding of New Orleans in 2005: those most likely to die were the poor, the sick, and the old.

Filial Piety in China
According to Chinese tradition, filial piety (hsiao) was the primary duty of all Chinese. Being a filial son meant complete obedience to one's parents during their lifetime and—as they grew older—taking the best possible care of them. After their death the eldest son was required to perform ritual sacrifices at their grave site or in the ancestral temple. A son could also express his devotion to his parents by passing the Civil Service examinations, winning prestige for the whole family. Most important of all, a son had to make sure that the family line would be continued.

Source: <www.wsu.edu:8080/~wldciv/world_civ_reader/world_civ_reader_1/filial.html>.

Health Consequences of Aging

Health outcomes of aging and ageism fall into several categories: physical outcomes of aging, psychological outcomes of aging and ageism, and elder abuse.

Physical Illness

Quality of life often declines in old age. One reason for this is senescence, the fact that physical and mental abilities naturally decline after a certain point in the aging process. Exactly at what age and in what form this decline takes place, however, varies from one individual to the next. Scientists are continuing to study the genetic and physiological processes involved in aging-related ailments.

Health problems often arise alongside and because of changes in the life course. Widowhood and divorce are associated with health problems, especially in men. Some research says that poorer health status is related both to retirement plans and to actual retirement for women, but not for men (Midanik et al., 1990). The loss of independence as one ages can also cause emotional and physical distress (Lazzarini, 1990).

People who are in good health in old age were often in good health during their youth. In other words, good health tends to continue, after we consider factors such as socio-economic status (SES) and health behaviours (Swallen, 1997) (see also Table 7.2). This being so, it is important for people, and for society as a whole, to develop strategies for 'aging well'. These include strategies for preserving health and independence, for improving quality of life, for developing coping strategies when needed, and for preventing or postponing disabilities during the later years (Perry, 1995).

Factors that increase the likelihood of a healthy old age include a strong constitution, an ability to cope with stressful events, and the availability of various social supports. Successful aging means more than avoiding disease and disability. It means preserving high physical and cognitive functioning, and continued engagement in social activities (Rowe and Kahn, 1997). Successful aging also means prolonging security, involvement, satisfaction, autonomy, integration, and creativity over the life course (Earle, 1999). Healthy older people remain active and engaged with others. Societies differ in the help they give old people to lead such lives.

Perceived health, in turn, is a good indicator of actual current health, but it is influenced by past health, current health, functional limitations, depression, and attitudes

Table 7.2 Average Annual Per Capita Expenditure on Health Care, by Age and Sector, 2000–1		
	Public	**Private**	**Total**
All age groups	$2,243.56	$930.69	$3,174.24
65+	$8,524.72	$2,309.30	$10,834.02
65–74	$4,975.16	$1,648.37	$6,623.53
75–84	$10,083.36	$2,451.91	$12,535.27
85+	$21,878.36	$5,256.59	$27,134.95

Source: Health Canada (2001: 22, Table 1.1). Adapted and reproduced with the permission of the Minister of Public Works and Government Services Canada, 2006.

towards aging (Erickson, 1997). Age, race, educational attainment, and financial status all affect the ways that people rate their own health (Peek, 2000; Peters and Rogers, 1997). People with poor psychosocial adjustment and poor perceived health pose particular problems to the health-care system. They cost more than people who are moderately or well adjusted. On the other hand, older poorly adjusted people are no more costly than younger poorly adjusted people (Watt et al., 1997).

Social and cultural factors mediate these relationships. A study by Becca Levy and Ellen Langer (1994) comparing mainland Chinese and American elderly people, for example, found the Asian group held more positive attitudes towards aging than their American counterparts. They also scored much higher on memory tasks, so much so that there was almost no difference in performance between young and old Chinese participants. Chinese elderly people also display a culture-specific strategy of not complaining about their health, even if miserable, thus perpetuating the stereotype of the Chinese elderly as having few life or health problems (Lam, 1994). Finally, though Chinese seniors prefer Western health care and Western-trained doctors, about half also use traditional Chinese care, owing to their religious beliefs and a preference for Chinese medicine (Chappell and Lai, 1998).

Home Care Issues

An aging, longer-living adult population leads to an increasing demand on the informal sector for care. Indeed, the national report, *Eldercare in Canada* (Keating et al., 1999), suggests the demographic imperative is upon us already. More than 20 per cent of Canadian seniors receive aid because of long-term health problems. Compared with 30 years ago, the elderly today are more likely to live independently. At the same time, more adult children in their fifties, besides being more likely to be divorced (and therefore not having a spouse present to assist with elder care), are more likely to have a surviving parent.

One result is the so-called 'sandwich generation', middle-aged adults caring for both elderly parents and for their own young children. Forty-two per cent of Canadian women ages 40–4 currently balance parental care, child care, and work outside the home.

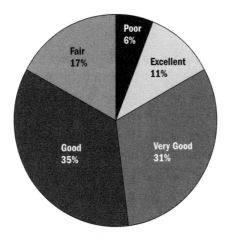

FIGURE 7.3 Self-Evaluation of Seniors' Health, 1999
Source: Adapted from Statistics Canada data, at: <www.hc-sc.gc.ca/seniors-aines/pubs/factoids/2001/no31_e.htm>.

Box 7.2   Social Policy: Aging and Health

Will the aging population burden the Canadian health-care system?

Actually, only a small proportion of seniors—about 20 per cent—are heavy users of formal health services. Most do not use the health-care system more than younger adults; some use it less. Although a large number of older Canadians suffer from one or more chronic conditions, ranging from arthritis to eye trouble, for the most part these do not prevent seniors from leading normal lives. According to surveys, less than half of seniors suffer from disabilities that limit daily activities; less than a third have severe problems that require formalized care. Despite people's fear of long-term institutional care in an old-age or nursing home, less than 10 per cent of seniors are in such institutions; more than 90 per cent of those 65 years and over live in the community. This helps relieve the load on the existing health-care system.

Seniors' health-care needs often require long-term help rather than expensive, short-term medical intervention. But Canada's health-care system is mainly designed to provide medical treatment for acute short-term illness or emergencies. Physicians look after patient visits, prescribe medication, order medial tests, and control admission to hospitals. Hospitals provide short-stay medical care. This system is not geared towards support services for those who need help to live on their own. Therefore, a substantial effort was made in the 1970s to develop home health care and community support programs. Services were gradually expanded for those who fell into the category between very sick and very healthy. Today many provinces offer a variety of services for seniors. Homemakers, meals-on-wheels, and home visits by nurses, therapists, social workers, and volunteers are vital not only for the seniors, but also for their family and friends. Less costly than the traditional medical system, community support services are a means of helping family and friends to provide care and to allow them to continue this assistance for a much longer period of time.

Source: <www.mta.ca/faculty/arts/canadian_studies/english/about/aging/>. Reprinted by permission of the publisher.

Broader changes include a shift from institutional to community-based care, a growing ideological commitment to elderly care by the state, and funding cuts by the federal government for such services (Rosenthal, 1997a). This Canadian trend to view elder care as a private matter rather than a public responsibility may have significantly negative outcomes in the future (Rosenthal, 1997b). Because of cuts to the health-care system, Canada, as well as other industrial nations with universal medical care, risks sliding back to the 'non-system' that exists in the US (Chappell, 1997). Yet public surveys repeatedly show that Canadians value public health care, desire good health and longevity, and view health as a public good, even while electing governments that impose cost reductions and ill-considered health-care reforms (Chappell and McDaniel, 1999).

SOCIAL SUPPORT FOR CHRONIC CAREGIVING

Social support makes an important contribution to the health of elderly people and others (for example, the housebound disabled) who often suffer from social isolation. The helpers in a social support network may include family members, friends, and informal community caregivers. As a result, network development and the establishment of support groups can be important to people's health (Gottlieb, 1985a, 1985b).

Political recognition of the role of informal caregivers emerged only in the 1990s. Evidence suggests that 75–85 per cent of seniors' total care comes from informal care arrangements (Chappell, 1996) and an equal proportion of Canadians report some self-care (Penning and Chappell, 1990). A study conducted in London, Ontario, found that just over 9 per cent of community-dwelling older persons are using or are in need of community services. Most older people manage without the aid of formal support services (Connidis, 1985). Need—specifically, functional inability—is the most significant correlate of health service use (Chappell and Blandford, 1987), though health, health beliefs, and marital status are also important predictors (Penning and Chappell, 1990).

Use of both the formal system and informal care occurs when seniors are in need and critical elements of their care network are lacking, or when they have an intact informal network but their health needs are high. The data point to the complementary nature of the two care systems, in a sharing of overall task load (Chappell and Blandford, 1991). Among care recipients with more severe health needs, those who do not use services and those using only in-home services have inadequate informal supports, more emotionally strained caregivers, and more functionally damaged care recipients, compared with users of out-of-home or both in- and out-of-home services (Biegel et al., 1993). The characteristics of caregiver need account for much of the variation in whether services are used, while family enabling factors are the most important predictors of the services used (Bass and Noelker, 1987).

Family composition (that is, number of children, number who are sons or daughters, and gender of the parent) affects whether a child will be the sole or primary helper for an older parent (Connidis et al., 1996). Geographic closeness is a major influence on contact frequency and form. Greater distance, as expected, decreases frequency of contact and the importance of matters discussed. Sisters have more face-to-face and telephone contact, and discuss important matters more frequently, than do brothers and brother–sister siblings, for example (Connidis, 1989). Marital status is more influential than parent status in affecting social support. Thus, divorced and single people are more likely than married people, and the childless are more likely than parents, to rely on formal support and paid help and less likely to rely on family (Connidis and McMullin, 1994).

CAREGIVER BURDEN

Long-term care for the elderly, disabled, or chronically ill can put great strains on a family's ability to function. Often, the main caregiver has to add caring to other heavy responsibilities (Keating et al., 1999). As a result, caregivers often have to make changes in social activities, change sleep patterns, or give up holiday plans (ibid., 69). Caregiving can also affect job performance (ibid., 86). Typically, caregiving creates a bigger burden for women than for men (ibid., 81). At some time in their lives, a large fraction of women in their forties and fifties can expect to be sandwiched between responsibilities to old parents and their other commitments (Rosenthal et al., 1989).

The 'caregiving family' in our North American culture contains both people who provide help and people who are *seen* as having some duty to provide help but do not. An idealized view of family caregiving is used to put pressure on families to provide more care, but this is not justifiable in reality (Keating et al., 1994). In fact, caregiving occurs in diverse household arrangements involving a multitude of caregivers, most of whom express a permanent commitment to the role. Although they often provide elderly—and especially disabled elderly—parents with many hours of care each day, wide variation is found in the incidence and severity of stress effects.

Informal and formal supports, though present, supply fairly little hands-on care, however (Noelker and Wallace, 1985). Often, most or all the care responsibilities, and attendant strains, fall on a single family member. Men and women are differentially involved in, and affected by, providing care to elderly family members. As noted above as well as in other chapters, women are almost twice as likely to provide elder care, and this difference increases when care involves five or more hours of help per week. Marital status, nature of sibling network, class, and ethnicity also influence the type and amount of care provided.

Women's disproportionate responsibility for elderly and other care has employment outcomes, such as forced or premature exit from the workforce and postponement of career re-entry or promotion (Martin-Matthews and Campbell, 1995). Elder care involvement is significantly associated with interference for paid work for women but not for men. Among women, family interference with work is related to job satisfaction and absenteeism. Among men, it is related to job costs and absenteeism. The difficulty in balancing the demands of home and employment produces great stress that, taken to extremes, contributes to life-threatening health conditions (see, e.g., Ginn and Sandell, 1997; Scharlach and Fredriksen, 1994). Working women experience significant increases in stress when they are forced to alter their work schedule to meet home care needs of an impaired, elderly family member (Orodenker, 1990). Women continue to be far more likely than men to provide care, and to suffer consequent caregiving strain, work interference, income loss, and role strain (Fredricksen, 1996).

Adult children with live-in parents have much more limited activity than those in separate living arrangements (Deimling et al., 1989). For example, men sharing households with their mothers-in-law are more likely to report interference in social lives, family vacation plans, time with wives and children, and relationships with other relatives (Kleban et al., 1989).

The extent, duration, and outcomes of family strains vary with the nature, severity, and duration of the illness. For example, informal caregivers for non-institutionalized parents with dementia report distress and heightened feelings of burden and depression because of the care recipient's aimlessness, aggressive behaviours, forgetfulness, and restlessness (Chappell and Penning, 1996). Strains also vary with the coping abilities and resources of the family; and the disease sufferer, whether a parent or child, old or young, male or female. Different coping techniques work best within different domains of caregiving (Gottlieb et al., 1996). So, different types of interventions may be needed to deal with these chronic stressors (Gottlieb, 1991).

Even after institutionalization, informal caregiving continues. This creates the need for collaboration between adult children and staff to improve the quality of care (Ross et al., 1997). Although much of the actual care burden is relieved, seeking out institutional care for an aging parent or partner is still a stressful experience for those who opt for it. Dawson and Rosenthal (1991) found that female seniors experienced mixed emotions when deciding to have their husbands placed in an institutional care facility. On the one hand, many initially experienced negative feelings—guilt, anger, sadness, resentment, loneliness, etc.—about having to do so. In the early weeks following the husband's admission, wives displayed poor physical health, low morale, and high levels of depression. At the same time, these emotions are tempered by feelings of relief over the end of exhausting home-based care and the knowledge that their loved ones were receiving excellent care. In addition, institutional care creates significant financial burdens on those who must pay for it. As well, some complain that staff at these facilities are unresponsive to their needs or requests.

Longer stays often have a negative impact on patient self-care and increase depression among caregivers (Sulman et al., 1996). In general, wives with better social support and better psychosocial health tend to be more satisfied with the care their spouse is receiving (Dawson and Rosenthal, 1991). However, wives of husbands who are only physically impaired continue to be heavily involved in care. They are more likely to be moderately to severely depressed, and express dissatisfaction with aspects of institutional care (Ross et al., 1997).

SOCIAL SUPPORT FOR CAREGIVERS

Social support is important not only for the well-being and morale of the elderly, disabled, and chronically ill. It is also important for the well-being and morale of their caregivers. Hardship is the dominant theme in this literature.

Caregiver burden and formal home health service use are only weakly related, in large part because of the mediating role of social support networks (Penning, 1995). Married women consider support from husbands and children a great benefit for caregiving, but the price of such support is competition between the demands of care and duties to family. For the unmarried women, not having such competing demands may be considered an advantage, but the cost is having less social support (Litvin et al., 1995). Equally, unmarried women caring for aged parents report significantly less socio-emotional support in caregiving and receive less satisfaction from their family and friendship networks than married women. This is especially marked if they do not have an intimate partner to serve as a supporter and confidant (Brody et al., 1995).

Individual psychosocial interventions—including respite programs—have been moderately effective in dealing with caregiver distress (Knight et al., 1993). Increasingly, the social, medical, and helping professions are learning how to intervene most effectively to support families that are dealing with chronic illness (Woods et al., 1989). But few family interventions have been rigorously evaluated. The results of a nationally funded research program entitled *Chronic Conditions and Caregiving in Canada: Social Support Strategies* have shown the effectiveness of interventions to provide social support for people with a wide variety of chronic conditions, and sometimes for their caregivers as well (Stewart, 2000). The authors of these studies found that support makes possible improvements in quantitative and qualitative outcomes, such as decreased loneliness, increased support seeking, reduced health service use, an expanded coping repertoire, and improved interaction with natural networks (ibid.). This supports the contention that effective and sustainable caregiving is an important social service that depends on social organization, community involvement, and social participation.

ISOLATED INDIVIDUALS

Informal care is more likely to occur when there are more sources for it. For example, having no adult children as a part of one's social network limits potential informal care (Havens and Chipperfield, 1990). However, little is known about the care experiences of socially isolated people. Some research has found that the childless elderly are more active seekers of a friend or other relative's companionship (Connidis, 1989a). They are less likely to have at least one close family member and have fewer close relatives than the elderly with children, but are no less likely to have a close friend or number of close friends. As such, they experience similar levels of well-being (McMullin and Marshall, 1996). However, it is also likely, but not certain, that elderly men receive less informal care than elderly women because they generally have less access to informal support

(Chipperfield, 1994). This may be because of the death of a spouse or the effects of divorce on men's relations with their grown children.

ETHNICITY AND SOCIAL SUPPORT

Isolation, caregiving, social support, and values related to care and illness vary from one ethnic culture to another. For example, in Winnipeg, Native Canadian elderly live with three times as many people in their households as non-Native elderly. They have more relatives and friends, and experience more interaction with them. Non-Natives have more interactions with their neighbours, however (Chappell, 1989).

Still, despite higher levels of social support, elderly Natives in Winnipeg experience lower levels of subjective well-being than non-Natives due to their relatively disadvantaged health and social circumstances (that is, lower socio-financial status) (Chipperfield and Havens, 1992).

Happiness and Mental Well-Being

Health status is correlated with happiness, life satisfaction, and general well-being. In turn, health status and well-being are both correlated with social integration and financial security. The same factors that contribute to life satisfaction contribute to good health and longevity (Lowry, 1984; Palmore, 1985). These include:

- nutritious diet;
- avoidance of obesity;
- exercise and recreation (see also Russell, 1990);
- avoidance of tobacco;
- moderate use of alcohol;
- work satisfaction;
- high SES or good income (see also D'Amato, 1987; Doyle and Forehand, 1984);
- marriage (see also D'Amato, 1987; Yahya, 1988);
- satisfying sexual activity.

Many people in their sixties and seventies are faced with retirement, the change to a work-free lifestyle, financial uncertainty, the loss of their spouse or partner, increased frequency of health concerns, a possible move to institutional or private care, and a growing awareness of the closeness of death. The quick succession of these events within a short period often makes the transition to elderly status a difficult one.

Social and family support continue to contribute to the life satisfaction of the elderly population (D'Amato, 1987; Levitt et al., 1985). Indeed, social integration is critical, whether in work or in leisure. What is important is not so much active involvement as affiliation (Duff and Hong, 1982; Lowry, 1984; Salamon, 1985) and the sense of being integrated into a community (Steinkamp and Kelly, 1985; see also Steinkamp, 1987). Among the elderly population, loneliness and boredom are especially likely to be associated with low satisfaction with life (Brown and Orlando, 1988; Doyle and Forehand, 1984). With fewer family and job concerns for them to think about, social and health concerns take on much greater importance.

The happiness of elderly people is determined in part by living arrangements. Living with a spouse is most preferred, followed by living alone and living with one's children. Marital status is enormously important to mental and physical health. Divorce later in life is harmful since it worsens the financial situation and raises the risk of mortality. Divorced elderly people are more likely to suffer from poor health than married, widowed, or single elderly people (Dooghe, 1996). Longitudinal research on widowhood shows that mental health, morale, and social functioning all decline with the death of a spouse. Even physical health declines for a period. Men are especially affected by the loss of a partner (Bennett, 1998).

People who engage in higher levels of religious activity tend to have better health outcomes, including better mental health (Levin and Chatters, 1998). The effects of religion on subjective health seem to be greatest for people who suffer from physical health problems. This suggests that religion comforts people (Musick, 1996). Religious involvement even reduces disability, depression, and the risk of dying in the month before an important religious holiday (Idler and Kasl, 1992). Religious involvement gives elderly people a sense of meaning and social integration, and it helps adjustment to the later stages of life (Broyles and Drenovsky, 1992). It may encourage people to help others, which also contributes independently to a higher subjective health rating (Krause et al., 1990). Perhaps for these reasons, church attendance has a statistically significant positive effect on subjective health, even when other possible explanatory variables are controlled for (Morris, 1997).

Elder Abuse

Living longer brings unprecedented opportunities but also presents serious social challenges (Daichman et al., 1998). One of these is elder abuse.

Elder abuse occurs in various settings. Typically, the older person is mistreated in the victim's own home by someone with whom he or she is intimately connected, such as a spouse, sibling, child, friend, or trusted caregiver. As well, elder abuse occurs at the hands of staff and professional caregivers in facilities for elderly people.

As the National Centre on Elder Abuse (2001) has shown, several categories of abuse occur across each of these settings, including physical abuse, sexual abuse, emotional or psychological abuse, neglect, abandonment, and financial or material exploitation. This last category includes improper use of an elderly person's savings, property, or assets without authorization or beyond the terms set out in a caregiver–patient contract; such offences may include stealing money or material possessions, forging signatures, and improper use of guardianship or power of attorney rights. The National Centre on Elder Abuse also stresses that self-neglect can be a problem among the elderly population. Self-neglect shows itself in an older person's refusal or failure to give himself or herself enough food, water, clothing, shelter, hygiene, medication (when responsibly prescribed), and safety precautions.

One study estimates that five times as many elder abuse incidents go unreported as are reported, with self-neglect the most frequent form of abuse and women the most frequent victims. Relatives report abuse most often, but also perpetrate abuse and neglect most often as well (Cyphers, 1999). Data on elder abuse have shown the typical (known) perpetrator of domestic elder abuse is the adult child or spouse of the victim, although older family members and non-relatives may also be perpetrators. Often, the abuser depends on the victim for shelter, financial aid, or emotional support. Also commonly associated with abuse of elders are histories of alcohol addiction by the abuser or of prior abuse by the victim.

Box 7.3 Personal Experience: Elder Abuse in Canada

Norma Stenson had been living in a retirement home in Brantford, Ontario, for just a month when her supplemental caregivers—who provide extra nursing care that is not provided by the home—first began to notice the signs.

'There were just little complaints', says Jean Bowen. Norma, a frail 87-year-old who has suffered several strokes, doesn't have an easy time communicating, but Bowen could tell she wasn't happy at Charlotte Villa Retirement Residence. Still, the home was considered to be one of the best in the city and she urged her client to give the facility the benefit of the doubt.

When the bruises kept appearing, Bowen and Norma's other caregiver, Lesley Anthony, approached the director of care at Charlotte Villa. They were given excuses: Norma had fallen out of her wheelchair; she had hit herself on the bed rail; she was lying. 'The director of care . . . hollered at me how I was too good to this woman, how I spoiled this woman, and it was about time that this lady gets treated the way the rest of them thought she should be treated', says Bowen.

Then employees at Charlotte Villa countered with complaints of their own, saying Norma had attacked a pregnant worker named Amanda LaPierre. She was accused of saying, 'I want to kill your unborn baby child', and of kicking LaPierre in the stomach.

'She hasn't put a sentence together in over seven years, so that was impossible', says Bowen. 'It was impossible for her to kick that high, it was impossible for her to even speak a whole sentence and threaten Amanda to begin with. It was just impossible—I mean, if she could talk, she would talk to me every day.'

With management at Charlotte Villa unwilling to acknowledge the abuse, Bowen and Anthony decided to take photos of Norma's bruises to the police. But they were told the photos proved nothing, and with Norma unable to speak on her own behalf, there was nothing they could do.

So Norma's two caregivers decided to take matters into their own hands, planting a hidden camera in her room.

Caught on camera was tape after tape of footage of Norma being thrown into bed, screamed at, threatened with fists and with a slipper. The video also revealed workers helping themselves to Norma's food and to money from her wallet.

Charges were laid against two Charlotte Villa employees: LaPierre, who was charged with four counts of assault and two counts of theft; and Shelley Grisdale, who was charged with one count of assault and two counts of theft.

LaPierre pleaded guilty but claimed self-defence, and was sentenced to two years of probation and 240 hours of community service. Grisdale's verdict has yet to be decided.

But abuse is happening to others too. Statistics Canada reports as many as 7 per cent of all seniors are abused. And seniors' advocates say our laws still need to catch up to the seriousness of the problem.

In Canada, not one province has regulations covering abuse in retirement homes. In Ontario, there is a group that tries to set standards for these communities, but membership and compliance aren't mandatory.

While Ontario's minister responsible for seniors has promised ORCA [Ontario Residential Care Association] that he will legislate changes in the system, for now, Ontario—like the rest of Canada—remains unregulated.

In the meantime, it remains difficult to tell what goes on behind the closed doors of retirement and nursing homes and many seniors—especially those who don't have family who can provide home care—are at the mercy of the system.

Source: <www.ctv.ca/servlet/ArticleNews/story/CTVNews/1076082613040_71491813/?hub=WFive>. From 'Help Me: Elder abuse in Canada': CTV Television Inc.

Box 7.4   Historical Perspective: Elder Abuse

The abuse of older people by family members dates back to ancient times. Until the advent of initiatives to address child abuse and domestic violence in the last quarter of the twentieth century, it remained a private matter, hidden from public view. Initially seen as a social welfare issue and subsequently a problem of aging, abuse of the elderly, like other forms of family violence, has developed into a public health and criminal justice concern . . . .

Mistreatment of older people—referred to as 'elder abuse'—was first described in British scientific journals in 1975 under the term 'granny battering'. As a social and political issue, though, it was the United States Congress that first seized on the problem, followed later by researchers and practitioners. During the 1980s scientific research and government actions were reported from Australia, Canada, China (Hong Kong SAR), Norway, Sweden, and the United States, and in the following decade from Argentina, Brazil, Chile, India, Israel, Japan, South Africa, the United Kingdom, and other European countries. Although elder abuse was first identified in developed countries, where most of the existing research has been conducted, anecdotal evidence and other reports from some developing countries have shown that it is a universal phenomenon. That elder abuse is being taken far more seriously now reflects the growing worldwide concern about human rights and gender equality, as well as about domestic violence and population aging.

Source: <www.who.int/violence_injury_prevention/violence/global_campaign/en/chap5.pdf>.

Safety

Many elderly people so fear being victimized that often they become voluntary prisoners in their own homes. However, except for purse snatching, pickpocketing, and home burglary, fewer crimes are committed against elderly persons than against any other age group. Strangers do not victimize elderly people as often as is commonly believed or as media reports tend to suggest. One reason for this lower rate of victimization is that elderly people go out less often at night, in part, perhaps, because they are more fearful of doing so (see Figure 7.4). And, as the preceding discussion on elder abuse indicates, many incidents of violence against the elderly occur at home and involve family members who have their own problems or who can no longer cope with the stress of providing care to an older relative.

Solutions for Problems of Aging

As we have mentioned throughout this chapter, many conditions contribute to well-being in old age, including financial prosperity (or at least security), marriage and parenthood, good health and physical functioning, a sense of autonomy and personal control, a sense of connectedness to a support network and to the community, and a more general sense of purpose or meaning. In this last respect, one finds repeatedly that people who are older, more religious, married, and healthy are the people most satisfied with their lives. In surveys, older people typically report being happier than younger people (although the differences are not great) (Wood, 1990).

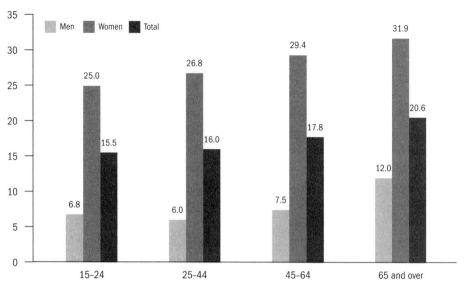

FIGURE 7.4 Percentage Feeling Very or Somewhat Unsafe When Walking Alone in Their Neighbourhood after Dark, 1999

Source: Adapted from Statistics Canada data, at: <www.hc-sc.gc.ca/seniors-aines/pubs/factoids/2001/no11_e.htm>.

Informal and Formal Social Supports

Solving the problems of aging will involve strengthening the individuals and institutions that provide social integration: caregivers, families, support networks, and community organizations.

As children enter middle life and their parents enter their later years, intergenerational interactions may increase, especially if an elderly parent becomes dependent on a child for support. This shift from independent parent to dependent parent represents a shift in power and responsibility from parent to offspring. Depending on the quality of the relationship between parent and child throughout life, this onset of dependence may provide an occasion to repay the parent for past debts or to seek revenge for real or imagined injustices.

At the same time, the need for aging parents to support middle-aged children who have become unemployed or divorced is also on the rise. Several factors influence the frequency and quality of these relationships, including the older generation's own need for independence or support, the intergenerational interaction patterns set up early in the life of the family, the social class and cultural background of the family, the gender of the offspring, and the location and type of living arrangements (Connidis, 1989a). Said another way, unfolding relations between children and their aging parents will reflect various factors that include the larger culture (for example, notions of filial responsibility), the ethnic culture, family traditions, long-standing relations between parents and particular children, the availability of children (especially daughters), and the financial ability of children to care for their dependent parents.

All four types of social support—informational, tangible, emotional, and integrating—mitigate the impact of stress on elderly individuals (Krause and Markides, 1990). There is by now a huge literature on social support networks as they affect elderly, chronically ill, and other dependent people. Men rely emotionally on spouses, while women diversify their emotional supports when possible (McDaniel and McKinnon, 1993). Social contacts with friends are related to well-being; thus, fewer contacts lead to lower well-being (Lennartsson, 1999).

Some of the support provided is instrumental, some of it emotional. Instrumental support and subjective social support protect elderly people against decline. Subjective social support buffers the harmful effect of depression on risk of physical decline (Hays et al., 1997). Both types of support are needed; neither can compensate for the lack of the other (Ikkink and van Tilburg, 1998). More resourceful and diversified networks, including friends and neighbours, are consistently associated with better scores on measures of basic and instrumental activities of daily living and self-rated health than are narrow family-focused networks (Litwin, 1998).

Increasingly, researchers have become aware that we need supports both to preserve the health of elderly people and to support the health of caregivers. Patients have to play their part, doctors theirs. The supporting cast of friends and relatives also has an important role to play in this culturally scripted drama. Chronic illness can often be stigmatizing and cause social isolation for the sufferer (Warner et al., 1998). The elderly sick person's attitudes towards illness and medical care are important. Cancer patients, for example, have much regard for their doctors and expect a lot from them. They want doctors to provide professional support, information, help in learning coping strategies, regular updates from other professionals, and education about the nature of the disease they are trying to defeat.

Trust depends on the degree to which patients see their doctors as competent, responsible, and caring. Trust can be established through a continuous, consistent, and open doctor-patient relationship that allows opportunities for response, patient instruction, and patient participation in decision-making. The importance of trust also extends beyond the patient's relationship with his or her doctor. For example, a larger social network is more important for sick people who are less trusting than average. Because they are distrustful, they use the resources available in their networks less efficiently. For people who are more trustful, and therefore better able to mobilize support from their networks, network size is less important.

Social supports help caregivers and patients, whether it is a doctor, a group, a network, or a technology that delivers the support. Social support pushes sick people away from harmful behaviours towards healthy ones. Thus, social support is a form of social control and a means of influencing behaviour and delivering benefits. One way it does this is by influencing sick people to comply with the treatment advice they receive from their doctors.

Technology and Support Groups

Since elderly people and their caregivers cannot get all the support they need from doctors, support groups, or social networks, technology may have to play a greater role.

In recent years, researchers have studied the possible uses of communication technologies, such as the telephone and the Internet, as means of delivering social support. In one study of caregivers to patients with Alzheimer's disease, researchers tried two types of intervention. One intervention used the telephone to create discussion groups. Four or five caregivers held regularly scheduled, sympathetic conversations with one another over the telephone. The other intervention delivered taped informational lectures over the telephone. After three months, caregivers in both programs showed less psychological distress, more satisfaction with the support they were receiving, and more sense that they were receiving social support. After six months, however, these gains had leveled off or declined. Caregiver burden and social conflict increased again. Of the two programs, participants learned more by listening to the informational lectures. However, they contacted family and friends more while waiting to enter a peer conversational network (Goodman, 1990).

Health professionals have also set up telephone support groups for AIDS caregivers. Use of the telephone offers people a sense of privacy not available with face-to-face group meetings. It also offers support to people who are isolated because of the stigma associated with HIV/AIDS and the lack of support networks in their communities. In one telephone-based program, semi-structured groups of caregivers used conference calls to share information about resources and coping strategies. After eight such calls, participants reported having valued the group experience (Meier et al., 1995). However, the other results were mixed. Measures of social isolation and self-efficacy improved, but measures of social support and coping did not. Said another way, the caregivers felt more effective than before, but they still did not know what to do or who would help them do it (Rounds et al., 1995).

Like telephone-mediated groups, computer-mediated groups have the potential to help people who are unable or unwilling to take part in traditional face-to-face support groups. They do away with the barriers of time and distance, can be of any size, and provide for an increased variety and diversity of supports. Membership is anonymous, participants can express themselves in writing, and the arrangement offers potential training experiences for group leaders. As a result, health professionals have adapted computer technology to a variety of self-help and mutual-aid groups. These have included computer-based 12-step groups for problems with alcohol, narcotics, eating, gambling, compulsive sexuality, relationships, smoking, and more.

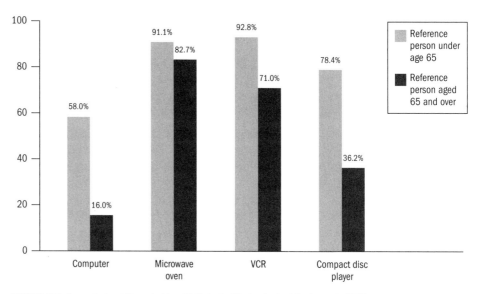

FIGURE 7.5 Percentage of Households with Selected Technological Equipment, 1998
Source: Adapted from Statistics Canada data, at: <www.hc-sc.gc.ca/seniors-aines/pubs/factoids/2001/no29_e.htm>.

Where addiction is the problem, on-line communication provides more access to support, a growth in or spreading around of dependency, and more attention to the needs of people with unusual concerns. Social status becomes irrelevant, since participation in on-line chat rooms and message boards can be anonymous. Reluctant group members are more likely to join in, relational communications improve, and people with interpersonal difficulties find themselves opening up more readily.

Possible disadvantages of going on-line include destructive interactions and lack of clear and accountable leadership. The same elements that promote ease of on-line communication, especially anonymity and invisibility, can also promote recklessness and cruelty. This may lead to even more social isolation, ostracism, or stigmatization for some. Beyond that, populations without computer access will not benefit from this form of available support. Lastly, the existing research has yet to make conclusive evaluations of its benefits and about user satisfaction.

Personal Efforts to Adapt

Some elderly people have a harder time than others making use of services and supports. Because of low levels of education, language problems, and lack of job skills, many elderly members of ethnic groups, especially those who came to Canada during the 1940s, are now retired without a pension. They may also underuse social and health-care services due to a lack of knowledge about such programs or because they cannot be served in their own language. Further, they may be unwilling to enter long-term care institutions because of differences in language, customs, beliefs about medical practices and death, food preferences, or the need for privacy.

Elderly people need to learn how to age effectively. Some role changes, such as marriage and retirement, are common and predictable, and individuals can begin planning to help themselves adjust to these major life events. Other changes, however, such as widowhood or becoming a father at the age of 55, may occur unexpectedly. Still others, though expected, can be stressful and can lead to an identity crisis or loneliness and to a decreased quality of life. One example is the empty nest syndrome, which occurs when children leave home for university or marriage.

Thus, aging always involves change—in friendships, health, financial status, role relationships, and more. Changes in daily routines can create stress because of the constant need for coping with a new life situation. Anticipatory socialization can ease later-life role changes. Important aids in making these age-related changes include the social support of friends and family, the development of personal coping skills, and the presence of older peers who serve as role models (George, 1980).

Widowhood is one of the most problematic of all changes because it can occur suddenly and endure for many years; and widowhood is mainly a women's issue. In 2001, 45 per cent of all Canadian women over 65 years old were widowed, compared to only about 13–14 per cent of men. What's more, at all ages widows—numbering 1.25 million in total—are four times more numerous than widowers—numbering only 300,000 (Statistics Canada, 2004).

The reasons for the large difference include the greater life expectancy of women, the fact that husbands are typically two to three years older than their wives, and men's greater inclination to remarry after the death of their spouse. Thus, not only do more women experience this tragic life event, they also live longer in the role of widow. Even a woman

10 Tips for Aging Successfully
1. Don't retire. Get a part-time job or volunteer.
2. Have a social support network before emergencies strike.
3. Relationships are essential. Keep close ties to family and friends.
4. Reliance and adaptability: maintain a flexible attitude.
5. Keep playing for a healthy, happy outlook towards life.
6. Eat healthy and exercise. Quit bad habits.
7. Keep learning.
8. Positive attitudes are essential for successful aging.
9. Maintain independence.
10. Storytelling: Successful agers are able to tell stories about themselves and share them with their families. Reliving these stories helps them find purpose in their life.

Source: Adapted from <www.aging.missouri.edu/seniors/tips.php>.

who becomes a widow at the age of 80 can expect an average of 9.7 more years of life as a single person (www.statcan.ca/english/freepub/84-537-XIE/tables/pdftables/caf.pdf).

A large body of research literature has shown that the death of a spouse is one of the most stressful role changes in the life cycle and the most stressful in the later years (Martin-Matthews, 1991). Most of the literature has focused on the experience of widows. However, the few studies of widowers suggest that while they are not often faced with financial burdens, widowers have more difficulty in adapting to their new role, as shown by higher suicide rates, higher rates of remarriage, and higher rates of mortality following bereavement.

People have little opportunity to prepare for the change from married person to widow or widower unless their spouse has been ill for a long time. Adjustment to widowhood normally begins with a stage of mourning, which may last up to two years. Unlike in earlier times, there is no formal mourning period, and mourning clothes to represent the new status are seldom worn in this society.

Research has highlighted the importance of developing a social support network around the widowed person. The bereavement process is easier if the survivor has a friendship group containing age peers who have already been widowed. They have in effect created community-based 'widow-to-widow' programs to provide emotional and social support. After the immediate and acute period of grief and mourning, the widowed person must begin to rebuild a new identity and lifestyle—being alone, having no spouse to share thoughts and feelings with, cooking for one person, losing friends who were more closely tied to the deceased spouse, managing financial affairs alone, and, for a widow who loses the pension rights of the deceased spouse, living on a reduced income.

While adjustment is initially difficult, most eventually make a successful changeover. However, though they may adjust to the loss of their spouse as a person, they may not cope as well with the results of being widowed—the loss of income, of companionship, of friends, and, for men especially, of a homemaker. Many widows become closer to their children or move into a social circle comprising other widows.

One of the most difficult adaptations for older widows is the beginning of new intimate or sexual relationships, especially if female friends, children, or siblings disapprove. Still, social values and norms have changed in recent years, and cohabitation or remarriage has become a more socially acceptable alternative for the elderly widowed person. At the same time, with the onset of the women's movement, fewer older women are likely to remarry merely to play nurse, cook, and homemaker. Future generations of older widows will probably also have more personal financial and social resources, so they will not have to remarry for sheer financial survival.

Government Legislation

There is much disagreement about the extent of the state's duty to support retired individuals. This issue is especially significant because of the impoverished status of many older adults, especially elderly widows, and because of fears that public old age security funds and private pension plans may become bankrupt in the future (Brown, 1991).

Income after retirement depends on the individual's pattern of lifetime employment (regular or sporadic), place of employment (whether it offers a private pension), income while in the labour force, and pattern of savings, investments, and expenses over the life course (see Figure 7.6).

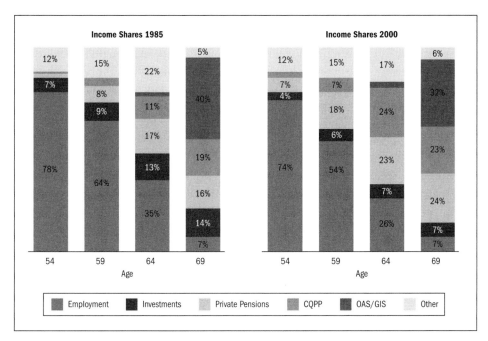

FIGURE 7.6 Income of Seniors, by Source, 1985 and 2000
Source: Statistics Canada, 2001 Census, at: <www.labour-info-travail.org/docs/A-POP%20AGING%20LIFE-HUNSLEY.ppt>.

From a demographic perspective, there is no evidence to suggest that fertility rates will increase or that life expectancy will decrease significantly any time soon. The median age of the population will therefore continue to rise, to as high as 41 years in 2006 and 48 years in 2031. This means that 20 to 25 per cent of the population will be over 65 years old when you reach 50 years old (if you are now in your early twenties). Statistics Canada notes that 'Canada's population is aging fast and senior citizens would outnumber children in about a decade, according to new population projections. In all growth scenarios . . . seniors aged 65 and over would become more numerous than children aged less than 15 around the year 2015. This would be an unprecedented situation in Canada. By 2031, the number of people aged 65 and over would range between 8.9 million and 9.4 million, depending on the scenario selected, while the number of children would range between 4.8 million and 6.6 million' (Statistics Canada, 2005).

Future generations of seniors can be healthier, more physically and mentally active, more independent, and more satisfied with their life than the current elderly population. This optimistic scenario is based on the belief that personal, private, and government interventions will create a more viable system in which to age. This elderly-friendly environment would include creative social policies and programs; improved private-sector products and services; changing attitudes towards health, nutrition, physical activity, and stress; political involvement and empowerment; new attitudes towards retirement and leisure; and innovative long-range financial planning during the early and middle years of adulthood. It remains for us to bring about these changes.

Canadians will also have to focus on creative fiscal management of private and public pension funds. This will mean dealing with the issue of compulsory retirement, examining choices for both early and late retirement as labour surpluses and shortages occur overall or in specific regions or occupational groups. Finally, they will have to address such ethical issues as the right to die, the creation of living wills, guardianship for the dependent elderly, empowerment of the elderly population, and equity across genders, races, ethnic groups, and religions in developing policies and the delivery of services.

The role of elderly people may change drastically if they are once again needed by the economy. With an increasingly aged population, a relative lack of suitable workers creates a vicious cycle of smaller revenues to support larger pension expenses. One possible solution is to promote a privately funded and managed pension system to reinforce the possible shortfall of the public system, as Mexico began to do in 1997. Replacing the Mexican public pension system with a system of compulsory private pension plans for all working Mexicans has eased the problem of preserving a government-sponsored benefit plan. Such procedures can boost the country's insurance sector while providing more secure pensions for employees (Souter, 1997).

Lobbying Efforts by Elderly People

As a varied group, elderly people have experienced widely different lives and have not voted with a common voice. However, through such voluntary organizations as the United Senior Citizens of Ontario, One Voice, CARP, the National Academy of Older Canadians, and the Fédération de l'Âge d'Or du Québec, Canada's older adults have been making their concerns known to politicians, business, and younger voters. Such lobby groups play an invaluable role in promoting the interests of elderly people.

Currently, the largest lobby group for the elderly population in Canada is CARP. This set of initials once stood for the Canadian Association of Retired Persons, but because of the changing characteristics of its membership, the group's name was changed to Canada's Association for the Fifty-Plus (CARP, however, remains the preferred acronym). Formed in 1984 by the husband-and-wife team of Murray and Lillian Morgenthau, CARP was initially comprised of 10 friends who met around kitchen tables to share their experiences of being elderly. Currently, CARP is a non-profit organization and refuses funding from government bodies. It has a membership of more than 400,000 and a mandate dedicated to promoting the rights and quality of life of mature Canadians. In addition, the organization publishes an award-winning magazine and gives its members discounts for homes, cars, medical expenses, retirement planning, and health insurance.

CARP fights for an improved quality of life for seniors and helps make policy-makers and the public aware of elderly people's unique perspective on social, financial, and political issues. Among its many actions, CARP has organized several national forums on scams and frauds against seniors, on home care, and on the environment, and addressed health-care issues such as long-term care, hospital closures and mergers, the national health strategies, and the funding, availability, cost, and taxation of drugs. CARP has also persuaded the federal government to change the legislation on registered retirement income funds (RRIFs) to remove the 90-year age limit and allow increased withdrawals, and has identified and combatted incidences of ageism and elder abuse. Finally, CARP has helped to design strategies to provide safe, affordable living accommodations and transport for seniors, and has held seminars and released many reports, publications, and videos on various topics of interest to the elderly population (CARP, 2001).

Like racism and sexism, ageism is now considered an inappropriate form of discrimination. Government policies have, therefore, been enacted in an effort to ensure that age does not act as a barrier to equal opportunity. Regulators have applied these to the work environment, where older people have traditionally been overlooked in hiring and promotions. However, the burden of proving age discrimination is difficult. It is well documented that age is associated with increased risk of serious health complications. Therefore, the line between failing to meet valid qualifications for the position and being dismissed or overlooked because of discriminatory attitudes is often difficult to detect.

Protecting Rights and Limiting Risks

Vulnerable seniors may have difficulty making their wishes heard and respected by family or caregivers. The right of seniors to make choices that involve risk is limited by the effects of their decisions on others. In short, at some point individual freedom must give way to collective rights.

Respecting a senior's right to choose is not limited to a rule of non-interference; when caregivers defer to the senior's choice they are, in fact, protecting those values and beliefs that give meaning and purpose to the senior's life. Seniors, especially older or disabled seniors, may be more exposed to risk of harm than other adults. The risk of harm may be compounded by the presence of chronic diseases or by varying mental incapacities. So, caregivers may be tempted to overrule the wishes of vulnerable seniors to protect them from possible harm. The problem of respecting individual freedom versus protecting a senior from harm arises in many situations. For example:

- Should seniors who express a desire to continue living in their own homes be allowed to do so even if their health or their behaviour exposes them to serious harm?
- Do seniors have the right to refuse treatments that could restore or preserve their health?
- Should seniors with sensory, perceptual, or intellectual disabilities be prevented from driving a car? (Newsletter of the National Advisory Council on Aging, 2006)

In these and other domains, the rights of seniors must be balanced with the needs and rights of other people. Respecting seniors' right to make choices that involve risks does not mean withdrawing care and support. At the heart of the problem is a difference in wishes between the senior and the caregivers. Assessing true risk is often influenced by personal fears or desires. Caregivers, who often fear the worst, can increase the risk.

Making a valid assessment sometimes calls for expert testing. Competency assessments, for example, consist of a series of mental tests managed by health professionals to find out if an individual can understand and reason well enough to care for himself or herself. People found to be unfit may lose the right to decide for themselves (ibid.).

However, there are several problems in using competency assessments to decide if seniors can exercise the right to live at risk. The professional conducting the competency test can choose how strict a test to use, depending on the professional's view of the likelihood the senior's decisions and actions could harm the senior or others. Furthermore, a person's competency may rise and fall over time. A senior who is not mentally competent today may be competent next week and vice versa. Should this person's freedom to make decisions be forever revoked by a single assessment?

Competent seniors are legally entitled to refuse treatments or other health-care interventions. In cases where the senior is terminally ill, it may be easier for health-care professionals and family members to accept his or her decision not to begin a course of treatment that would serve only to prolong suffering. However, when the treatment or intervention could almost certainly restore the senior's health and functional capacities, it may be tempting to try to ignore the senior's wishes (ibid.).

When patients refuse potentially lifesaving treatments, caregivers may question their mental capacity to consent to treatment. In Ontario, seniors who have refused treatment and who have subsequently been found to be mentally incapable of consenting to treatment are entitled, through the Consent to Treatment Act, to have an advocate inform them of their right to have the incapacity finding reviewed by a tribunal. Responsible caregivers would not simply abandon the incompetent senior who refused a helpful treatment.

The abuse or mistreatment of seniors has been recognized as yet another symptom of family violence. A major obstacle to intervention against elder abuse is the reluctance of these seniors to report the abuse. Adult protection legislation is challenged by many seniors and professional groups. Measures are needed to safeguard individual liberties; these include the right to legal representation, the right of competent people to refuse help, and the requirement that any intervention be minimally intrusive and restrictive.

In hospitals and long-term care institutions, physical restraints are commonly used to prevent falls, stop wandering or aggressive behaviour, and protect medical devices, such as feeding tubes. Restraints may include bedrails and cloth or leather straps. Some contest their use on clinical grounds, because they do not decrease injuries from falls or wandering and because restraint may lead to other physical problems, such as muscle weakening. If restraints are proposed and the patient is mentally competent, informed consent must be gained before they are applied; if the person refuses, restraints are not applied and the person must sign a disclaimer absolving the institution of liability for any resulting injury. Refusing restraint in this case would be the same as refusing treatment.

The ability to drive a car safely may decrease following age-related physical or mental decline. Safe driving programs for seniors, such as the Canada Safety Council's 'Fifty-five Alive' program, teach older drivers strategies to compensate for decreased abilities and discuss when seniors should voluntarily quit driving. Because of the danger to others posed by unsafe driving, there are legal qualifications to the right to drive in every province based on age or on health status. For example, in Ontario, drivers aged 80+ must take a written and practical driving test as well as a vision test each year to have their licences renewed. If family and friends notice that driving is hindered, they may have the moral responsibility to persuade the senior to stop driving, to prevent him or her from using a car, or, depending on the province, they may be required by law to report the senior's impediments to licensing authorities.

The freedom to make choices in life is a primary source of personal dignity and a cornerstone of a democratic society. To uphold the right of competent people to live at risk is to reaffirm this value. Yet the principle of dignity of the person also applies to those who can no longer make personal choices. An ethical course is to restrict individual freedom only if necessary and only as much as necessary (ibid.).

The Right To Die

Today, Belgium, the Netherlands, and Switzerland are the only nations with assisted-suicide laws. As well, the state of Oregon allows assisted suicide. Oregon's Death with Dignity Act, like the European statutes, lays out an elaborate set of procedures for assisted suicide. A patient must be over 17 and must have a life expectancy of fewer than six months. The patient must communicate a request to die to a doctor orally and in writing. Two doctors must confirm the diagnosis and state that the patient is not clinically depressed. These kinds of stipulations, or variations on them, are necessary reassurances that an assisted-suicide law would never be used impulsively, against best medical opinion or the wishes of the patient. The Oregon law has been used sparingly. Between 1998 and 2004, 208 people died using the terms of the Death with Dignity Act, fewer than 1 per cent of all terminally ill patients (*New England Journal of Medicine*, 2005).

Most Oregonians approve of the assisted-suicide statute. However, this support is not shared by the rest of the country, nor by the federal Bush administration, which has attempted in recent years to overturn the law. In January 2006, however, the US Supreme Court upheld Oregon's Death with Dignity Act by a 6–3 decision. Supporting justices stated that an effort by former US Attorney General John Ashcroft to threaten Oregon's doctors with loss of federal prescription-writing privileges exceeded his authority. By ruling as it did, the Court affirmed that it would not intrude on a state-sanctioned law. On the other hand, 38 states have laws forbidding assisted suicide, and several others treat assisted suicide as a crime under common law.

Assisted suicide remains illegal in Canada. The Criminal Code statute prohibiting the strategy was narrowly reaffirmed by the Supreme Court of Canada in the 1993 Sue Rodriguez case. A subsequent Senate committee also narrowly recommended against any change in the law. In practice, however, decisions about assisting death—that is, ending life ahead of the natural process taking place—are made all the time in hospitals, hospices, and private homes. When these decisions become publicly known, the practitioners suffer the penalties, which may include being charged with murder. In a society eager to protect the rights associated with life, many consider it appropriate to offer individuals 'the right to death', or death with dignity—meaning a swifter, less painful death.

However, this is a thorny issue and dignity may lie in the eyes of the beholder. Sue Rodriguez said in an interview shortly before her death that if she had not been divorced and still had a significant partner that she likely would be making a different decision about assisted death. The lack of a loving, or at least willing, caregiver has a great impact on people's desire to live and die; and ill or injured women are more likely than ill or injured men to suffer desertion or rejection by their spouse. So, offering people assisted death as a socio-legal option may tend to justify existing gender (and perhaps other social) inequalities. Nonetheless, as the Canadian population continues to age, and ever more Canadians may be kept alive through drugs and mechanical means, the debate over assisted suicide in this country continues to re-emerge. It is helpful to caregivers and medical personnel when people make known their wishes and arrange appropriate powers of attorney before they are faced with serious and terminal illnesses.

There is a great deal more that could be said on this topic. What constitutes 'dignity', for example? That is a concept that varies from religion to religion and from individual to individual; how can it become part of legislation? What position is a caregiver put in when a person with dementia is an enthusiastic supporter of the 'right to death', has the means of suicide close at hand, and the caregiver is in a position to inherit or to earn significant wealth through caregiving and/or when the person dies? The situation is not simplified by a tremendous joie de vivre still obvious in the demented person. If the demented person succeeds in killing her/himself, may not the caregiver be mistaken for the murderer? What are the rights and protection available to the caregiver? Consider, too, that making it easy for the unimaginative and uncaring to hasten death removes the opportunity for others more caring and creative to continue to offer and learn of supportive ways to minister to the dying.

Perhaps a later edition of this book will be able to report that medicine and social services can offer people more alternatives than they do today, and that individuals themselves see more alternatives as being socially, culturally, and philosophically viable. For example, perhaps people can imagine living under circumstances that are currently unthinkable. And perhaps, families will be better integrated, more supportive, and less preoccupied with competing concerns than they are today. Certainly, as we said in the Introduction, sociologists tend to favour life over death. Humans continue to struggle, often alone, with the difficult ethical and practical issues of aging and infirmity.

Concluding Remarks

Medicine, disease control, and biotechnology have led to large increases in life expectancy in the past century or so. As scientists improve their knowledge of how the human body ages and deteriorates, they will likely be able to design treatments and drugs that can compensate for or delay these processes. Not only will people live longer, they will also experience a better quality of life in the later stages of life. Though we are unlikely to discover a magical fountain of youth any time soon, medical technology may at least be able to reduce the significant difference in physical and mental functioning between young adults, middle-aged people, and the elderly population.

The mass media, in both programming and advertisements, are the main vehicle of socialization about the meaning of age in Canada. In part, the media are giving viewers what they want. What appears on television, in movies, and in print is a reflection of what society values and derides. However, the media are also an active force shaping how we view the world. Largely, the media promote images of elderly people that are outdated, disrespectful, and ridiculous.

These images support ageism, which in turn often leads to discrimination in the workplace and subsequent financial disadvantage of elderly people. This discrimination includes compulsory retirement and the placement of elderly individuals in low-paying positions. Elderly people may not receive the financial support they need because ageism in the political realm discourages those with political power from spending resources on programs designed to help the elderly population. Ageism may also lead to emotional and physical abuse. Stereotypes associated with ageism may be the reason that we sometimes institutionalize elderly individuals unnecessarily. It also may be why institutions set up to support elderly people can be underfunded. Once institutionalized, elderly individuals are often neglected socially since institutions tend to place them in more isolating situations. Elderly people may also experience physical malnutrition and be prescribed unnecessary drugs.

From the functionalist perspective, aging is a social problem because the institutions of modern society are failing to meet the needs of the dependent aged. Conflict theorists view the problems of the elderly population as stemming from older people's lack of power to shape social institutions to meet their needs. Symbolic interactionists believe elderly people are stigmatized because they do not conform to the images, ideals, and norms of a youth-oriented culture. Feminist theorists note that among the elderly population, the most financially disadvantaged are women, minorities, and those who live alone.

The jobs of successful aging and age reform cannot be left to governments and voluntary associations alone, but these agencies, along with informal and formal social networks, are important for successful aging. Also, elderly people need to learn to play a role in their own well-being. Various studies have confirmed that social contact with friends and relatives improves physical and mental well-being among elderly people. Social relationships can markedly improve quality of life by reducing stress and increasing positive health practices. For example, they can foster awareness of health-care alternatives and of the importance of compliance with treatment. People who lack social and community ties are likely to die earlier than those with more extensive social activities. More media attention to health promotion among elderly people will go a long way to solving age-related problems.

We have seen that aging is unavoidable and that every society takes note of this in its own culturally meaningful way. Increasingly, however, every society has to deal with the public responsibility for increased longevity and reduced family care.

QUESTIONS FOR CRITICAL THOUGHT

1. There is a widespread discomfort and fear associated with growing old. As mentioned in the text, while some cultures revere their elderly members Western culture seems to worship the appearance of youth. Discuss the role of the media and mention specific products that appeal to this fear of aging. For instance, even in *Seventeen* magazine, targeted at pre-teen adolescents, there are advertisements for firming creams. Why, in your opinion, does Western culture so prioritize looking young and feeling fit? Is this obsession dangerous? Or is it just a reflection of insecurities of the influential baby-boom cohort as they are aging?

2. Often, elderly individuals feel that they are absent from and misrepresented in popular media and feel that their selective presence in commercials for such products as denture cleaners unfairly represents who they are. Further, Grandpa Simpson in the popular television series *The Simpsons* is depicted as senile, belligerent, and often terrified. What do you feel is the impact of this portrayal on people's opinions of elderly people, and how do you feel this affects elderly people themselves as they watch these commercials and shows? Discuss this using examples and references.

3. The text outlines physical, sexual, and emotional or psychological abuse, neglect, abandonment, and financial exploitation as forms of abuse particular to the elderly. Using the Internet as a tool, find examples, whether in news stories or on websites that deal specifically with elder abuse. Is there one type of abuse that seems most prevalent? Are there patterns that occur (for example, who is being abused and who is abusing)? What do you feel are possible solutions or remedies to the examples you found? In other words, could the abuse have been avoided?

4. The text suggests that elderly people and their caregivers cannot get all the support they need from doctors, support groups, or social networks. It is at this point that technology begins to play a greater role. In recent years, the Internet has had an increasing role as a means for delivering social support. Go on the Internet and find support websites for elderly people seeking companionship, answers, and help. What are the main features of these sites, and what services do they provide? Also, outline in your discussion possible drawbacks to Internet support groups.

5. There is constant controversy over the government's role in providing for the aging cohort of the population. What, in your opinion, is the purpose of government interventions such as social policies, financial planning programs, and improving products and services? What do you feel the government's role is, if any, in changing popular opinion and attitudes surrounding elderly issues?

6. Do you agree with a compulsory retirement program? Why or why not?

RECOMMENDED READINGS

Vern L. Bengtson and Ariela Lowenstein, eds, *Global Aging and Challenges to Families* (Hawthorne, NY: Aldine de Gruyter, 2003). This volume in the 'Life Course and Aging' series focuses on the emerging consequences of global aging for families and for the well-being of elders in those families. Examined is the change over recent decades in the expected, traditional life course of individuals, especially in industrialized societies. Contributors also examine worldwide changes in families and family structures over the past 50 years.

David Cheal, ed., *Aging and Demographic Change in Canadian Context* (Toronto: University of Toronto Press, 2002). The contributors to this collection carefully examine the economic and demographic challenges likely to emerge as Canada's population ages.

Christopher Faircloth, ed., *Aging Bodies: Images and Everyday Experience* (Walnut Creek, Calif.: AltaMira, 2003). This book attempts to bridge the gap between geriatrics and gerontology by reinserting the physical aging body and its lived experiences back into gerontology's study of aging. Focus is on everyday experience and the social and personal impact of its imagery, highlighting medicalization, gender/sexuality, and the body as consumer.

Walter R. Heinz and Victor W. Marshall, eds, *Social Dynamics of the Life Course: Transitions, Institutions, and Interrelations* (Hawthorne, NY: Aldine de Gruyter, 2003). This volume from the 'Life Course and Aging' series takes an international comparative approach in applying the life course theoretical framework to issues of work and career.

Stephen Katz, *Cultural Aging: Life Course, Lifestyle, and Senior Worlds* (Peterborough, Ont.: Broadview Press, 2005). Katz looks at how modern life course regimes have been defined historically by the professional sciences and the way that aging identities have been affected by Western consumer lifestyle markets.

Barry D. McPherson, *Aging as a Social Process: An Introduction to Individual and Population Aging*, 4th edn (Toronto: Oxford University Press, 2004). A comprehensive discussion of theories of aging and trends for individual and population aging in Canada. This volume also features material consequences of individual and population aging, including health consequences.

RECOMMENDED WEBSITES

National Center on Elder Abuse

www.elderabusecenter.org

The NCEA website offers publications, assistance, and information. It provides a number of links to subject areas relating to publications, elder-abuse laws, statistics, conferences, research, and a number of other topics related to the issue of elder abuse.

The Care Guide

www.thecareguide.com

The Care Guide is a resource centre providing information and knowledge to empower both consumers and providers of seniors' housing and health care. It offers considerable information to seniors who are looking into housing, as well as medical information relevant to seniors.

Canadian Association on Gerontology

www.cagacg.ca

The Canadian Association on Gerontology (CAG) is a national multidisciplinary scientific and educational association established to provide leadership in matters related to the aging population. CAG seeks to improve the lives of older Canadians through the creation and dissemination of knowledge of gerontological policy, practice, research, and education.

GLOSSARY

Age pyramid Graph used to illustrate the composition by age and sex of a given population.

Ageism Direct or indirect forms of discrimination against the young, the elderly, or other groups on the basis of their age.

Disengagement theory Holds that the elderly are among the weakest members of the population and that society has therefore devised a means of steadily displacing them from its core to its periphery.

Filial responsibility The moral responsibility of a grown child to look after his or her aging parent.

Primogeniture A system of inheritance in which the eldest son gets everything.

Senescence The process in which physical and mental abilities gradually decline with aging.

REFERENCES

Alzheimer's Disease Education and Referral Center. 1995. Alzheimer's Disease Fact Sheet. Available at <www.alzheimers.org/pubs/adfact.html>; accessed 27 Jan. 2003.

Ariès, Philippe. 1958. *Centuries of Childhood: A Social History of Family Life*, trans. Robert Baldick. New York: Vintage Books.

Bass, David M., and Linda S. Noelker. 1987. 'The Influence of Family Caregivers on Elders' Use of In-Home Services: An Expanded Conceptual Framework', *Journal of Health and Social Behavior* 28, 2: 184–96.

Bennett, Kate Mary. 1998. 'Longitudinal Changes in Mental and Physical Health among Elderly, Recently Widowed Men', *Mortality* 3: 265–73.

Bianchi, Suzanne M., and Daphne Spain. 1986. *American Women in Transition*. New York: Russell Sage Foundation.

Biegel, David E., David M. Bass, Richard Schulz, and Richard Morycz. 1993. 'Predictors of In-Home and Out-of-Home Service Use by Family Caregivers of Alzheimer's Disease Patients', *Journal of Aging and Health* 5, 4: 419–38.

Brody, Elaine, Sandra J. Litvin, Christine Hoffman, and Morton H. Kleban. 1995. 'On Having a "Significant Other" during the Parent Care Years', *Journal of Applied Gerontology* 14, 2: 131–49.

Brown, Robert. 1991. *Economic Security in an Aging Population*. Toronto: Butterworths.

Brown, W., and D. Orlando. 1988. 'Enhancing Life Satisfaction for Older Adults', *Journal of Applied Sociology* 5: 73–87.

Broyles, Philip A., and Cynthia K. Drenovsky. 1992. 'Religious Attendance and the Subjective Health of the Elderly', *Review of Religious Research* 34: 152–60.

Bruce, M.L., and P.K. Leaf. 1989. 'Psychiatric Disorders and 15-Month Mortality in a Community Sample of Older Adults', *American Journal of Public Health* 79: 727–30.

CARP. 2001. What Is CARP? Available at: <www.fiftyplus.net/CARP/about/main.cfm>; accessed 8 July 2001.

Chappell, Neena L. 1996. 'Editorial', *Canadian Journal on Aging* 15, 3: 341–45.

———. 1997. 'Health Care Reform: Implications for Seniors. Introduction', *Journal of Aging Studies* 11, 3: 171–5.

——— and Audrey A. Blandford. 1987. 'Health Service Utilization by Elderly Persons', *Canadian Journal of Sociology* 12, 3: 195–215.

——— and ———. 1991. 'Informal and Formal Care: Exploring the Complementarity', *Ageing and Society* 11, 3: 299–317.

——— and David Lai. 1998. 'Health Care Service Use by Chinese Seniors in British Columbia, Canada', *Journal of Cross-Cultural Gerontology* 13, 1: 21–37.

——— and Susan A. McDaniel. 1999. 'Health Care in Regression: Contradictions, Tensions and Implications for Canadian Seniors', *Canadian Public Policy* 25, 1: 123–32.

——— and Margaret Penning. 1996. 'Behavioural Problems and Distress among Caregivers of People with Dementia', *Ageing and Society* 16, 1: 57–73.

Chipperfield, Judith G. 1994. 'The Support Source Mix: A Comparison of Elderly Men and Women from Two Decades', *Canadian Journal on Aging* 13, 4: 434–53.

——— and Betty Havens. 1992. 'A Longitudinal Analysis of Perceived Respect among Elders: Changing Perceptions for Some Ethnic Groups', *Canadian Journal on Aging* 11, 1: 15–30.

Connidis, Ingrid. 1985. 'The Service Needs of Older People: Implications for Public Policy', *Canadian Journal on Aging* 4, 1: 3–10.

———. 1989a. *Family Ties and Aging*. Toronto: Butterworths.

———. 1989b. 'Contact between Siblings in Later Life', *Canadian Journal of Sociology* 14, 4: 429–42.

——— and Julie A. McMullin. 1994. 'Social Support in Older Age: Assessing the Impact of Marital and Parent Status', *Canadian Journal on Aging* 13, 4: 510–27.

———, Carolyn J. Rosenthal, and Julie Ann McMullin. 1996. 'The Impact of Family Composition on Providing Help to Older Parents: A Study of Employed Adults', *Research on Aging* 18, 4: 402–29.

Cummings, Elaine, and William Henry. 1961. *Growing Old: The Process of Disengagement*. New York: Basic Books.

Cyphers, Gary C. 1999. 'Elder Abuse and Neglect', *Policy and Practice* 57, 3: 25–30.

Daichman, Lia Susana, Rosalie A. Wolf, Gerald Bennet, Bridget Penhale, and Elizabeth Podnieks. 1998. 'Action on Elder Abuse: An Overview', *Australasian Journal on Ageing* 17, 1 (suppl.): 17–18.

D'Amato, T.J. 1987. 'Factors Causing Variation in the Life Satisfaction of the Elderly', *National Journal of Sociology* 1, 1: 54–72.

Dawson, Pam, and Carolyn J. Rosenthal. 1991. 'Wives of Institutionalized Elderly Men: The First Stage of the Transition to Quasi-widowhood', *Journal of Aging and Health* 3, 3: 315–34.

Deimling, Gary T., David M. Bass, Allen L. Townsend, and Linda S. Noelker. 1989. 'Care-related Stress: A Comparison of Spouse and Adult-Child Caregivers in Shared and Separate Households', *Journal of Aging and Health* 1, 1: 67–82.

Dooghe, Gilbert. 1996. 'Effects of Divorce at an Advanced Age', *Tijdschrift Voor Sociale Wetenschappen* 41: 406–28.

Doyle, D., and M.J. Forehand. 1984. 'Life Satisfaction and Old Age: A Reexamination', *Research on Aging* 6: 432–48.

Duff, R.W., and L.K. Hong. 1982. 'Quality and Quantity of Social Interactions in the Life Satisfaction of Older Americans', *Sociology and Social Research* 66: 418–34.

Earle, Leon D. 1999. 'Celebrating the International Year of Older Persons: Younging Longer or Ageing Younger?', *Journal of Family Studies* 5: 258–65.

Elder, Glen H., Jr. 1999. 'The Life Course and Aging: Some Reflections', Distinguished Scholar lecture given at the annual meeting of the American Sociological Association. Available at: <www.unc.edu/~elder/asa/asacharts.pdf>; accessed 25 Mar. 2003.

Erickson, Mary Ann. 1997. 'The Life Course and Physical Health: Perceived Health, Health Events and Health Trajectories', American Sociological Association, conference paper.

Fredricksen, Karen I. 1996. 'Gender Differences in Employment and the Informal Care of Adults', *Journal of Women and Aging* 8, 2: 35–53.

George, Linda. 1980. *Role Transitions in Later Life*. Monterey, Calif.: Brooks/Cole.

Ginn, Jay, and Sara Arber. 1995. '"Only Connect": Gender Relations and Ageing', in Arber and Ginn, eds, *Connecting Gender and Ageing: A Sociological Approach*. Buckingham, UK: Open University Press, 1–14.

———— and Jane Sandell. 1997. 'Balancing Home and Employment: Stress Reported by Social Services Staff', *Work, Employment and Society* 11, 3: 413–34.

Goodman, Catherine. 1990. 'Evaluation of a Model Self-Help Telephone Program: Impact on Natural Networks', *Social Work* 35: 556–62.

Gottlieb, Beatrice. 1993. *The Family in the Western World: From the Black Death to the Industrial Age*. New York: Oxford University Press.

Gottlieb, Benjamin H. 1985a. 'Assessing and Strengthening the Impact of Social Support on Mental Health', *Social Work* 30, 4: 293–300.

————. 1985b. 'Social Networks and Social Support: An Overview of Research, Practice, and Policy Implications', *Health Education Quarterly* 12, 1: 5–22.

————. 1991. 'Social Support and Family Care of the Elderly', *Canadian Journal on Aging* 10, 4: 359–75.

————, E. Kevin Kelloway, and Anne Martin-Matthews. 1996. 'Predictors of Work Family Conflict, Stress, and Job Satisfaction among Nurses', *Canadian Journal of Nursing Research* 28, 2: 99–117.

Gubrium, Jaber F., and James A. Holstein. 1995. 'Life Course Malleability: Biographical Work and Deprivation', *Sociological Inquiry* 65: 207–23.

Handel, Gerald. 1997. 'Life History and Life Course: Resuming a Neglected Symbolic Interactionist Mandate', American Sociological Association, conference paper.

Havens, Betty, and Judith Chipperfield. 1990. 'Does Informal Care Relate to Ethnic Diversity or Social Isolation?', International Sociological Association, conference paper.

Havighurst, Robert, and Ruth Albrecht. 1953. *Older People*. New York: Longman, Green.

Hays, Judith C., W.B. Saunders, E.P. Flint, B.H. Kaplan, and D.G. Blazer. 1997. 'Social Support and Depression as Risk Factors for Loss of Physical Function in Late Life', *Aging and Mental Health* 1: 209–20.

Health Canada. 2001. *Building on Values: The Future of Health Care in Canada*, Final Report of the Commission on the Future of Health Care in Canada (Romanow Report), Nov. Available at: <www.cbc.ca/healthcare/final_report.pdf>.

Heinz, Walter. 1996. 'Life Course and Social Change in Germany: The Interchange between Institutions and Biographies', American Sociological Association, conference paper.

Hogan, Dennis P. 1981. *Transitions and Social Change: The Early Lives of American Men*. New York: Academic Press.

Idler, Ellen L., and Stanislav V. Kasl. 1992. 'Religion, Disability, Depression, and Timing of Death', *American Journal of Sociology* 97: 1052–79.

Ikkink, Karn Klein, and Theo van Tilburg. 1998. 'Do Older Adults' Network Members Continue to Provide Instrumental Support in Unbalanced Relationships?', *Journal of Social and Personal Relationships* 15, 1: 59–75.

Keating, Norah, J. Fast, J. Frederick, K. Cranswick, and C. Perrier. 1999. *Eldercare in Canada: Context, Content and Consequences*. Ottawa: Statistics Canada, Catalogue no. 89–570–XPE.

————, Karen Kerr, Sharon Warren, Michael Grace, et al. 1994. 'Who's the Family in Family Caregiving?', *Canadian Journal on Aging* 13, 2: 268–87.

Kim, Myung-Hye. 1996. 'Changing Relationships between Daughters-in-Law and Mothers-in-Law in Urban South Korea', *Anthropological Quarterly* 69, 4: 179–92.

Kleban, Morton H., Elaine Brody, and Claire B. Schoonover. 1989. 'Family Help to the Elderly: Perceptions of Sons-in-law Regarding Parent Care', *Journal of Marriage and the Family* 51, 2: 303–12.

Klinenburg, Eric. 2002. *Heat Wave: A Social Autopsy of Disaster in Chicago*. Chicago: University of Chicago Press.

Knight, B.G., S.M. Lutzky, and F. Macofsky-Urban. 1993. 'A Meta-analytic Review of Interventions for Caregiver Distress: Recommendations for Future Research', *The Gerontologist* 33, 2: 240–8.

Krause, Neal, Berit Ingersoll-Dayton, Jersey Liang, and Hideihiro Sugisawa. 1990. 'Religion, Social Support, and Health among the Japanese Elderly', *Journal of Health and Social Behavior* 40: 405–21.

———— and Kyriakos Markides. 1990. 'Measuring Social Support among Older Adults', *International Journal of Aging and Human Development* 30: 37–53.

Lam, Lawrence. 1994. 'Self-Assessment of Health Status of Aged Chinese-Canadians', *Journal of Asian and African Studies* 29, 1 and 2: 77–90.

Lasch, Christopher. 1977. *Haven in a Heartless World: The Family Besieged*. New York: Basic Books.

Lazzarini, Guido. 1990. 'Paths of the Elderly', *Studi di Sociologia* 28: 371–85.

Lennartsson, Carin. 1999. 'Social Ties and Health among the Very Old in Sweden', *Research on Aging* 21: 657–81.

Levin, Jeffrey S., and Linda M. Chatters. 1998. 'Religion, Health, and Psychological Well-Being in Older Adults', *Journal of Aging and Health* 10: 504–31.

Levitt, M.J., T.C. Antonucci, M.C. Clark, J. Rotton, and G.E. Finley. 1985. 'Social Support and Well-Being: Preliminary Indicators Based on Two Samples of the Elderly', *International Journal of Aging and Human Development* 21:61–77.

Levy, Becca, and Ellen Langer. 1994. 'Aging Free from Negative Stereotypes', *Journal of Personality and Social Psychology* 66: 989–97.

Litvin, Sandra J., Steven M. Albert, Elaine Brody, and Christine Hoffman. 1995. 'Marital Status, Competing Demands, and Role Priorities of Parent-caring Daughters', *Journal of Applied Gerontology* 14, 4: 372–90.

Litwin, Howard. 1998. 'Social Network Type and Health Status in a National Sample of Elderly Israelis', *Social Science and Medicine* 46: 599–609.

Lowry, J.H. 1984. 'Life Satisfaction Time Components among the Elderly: Toward Understanding the Contribution of Predictor Variables', *Research on Aging* 6: 417–31.

McDaniel, Susan A., and Allison L. McKinnon. 1993. 'Gender Differences in Informal Support and Coping among Elders: Findings from Canada's 1985 and 1990 General Social Surveys', *Journal of Women and Aging* 5, 2: 79–98.

McMullin, Julie Ann, and Victor W. Marshall. 1996. 'Family, Friends, Stress, and Well-being: Does Childlessness Make a Difference?', *Canadian Journal on Aging* 15, 3: 355–73.

Martin-Matthews, Anne. 1991. *Widowhood*. Toronto: Butterworths.

———— and Lori D. Campbell. 1995. 'Gender Roles, Employment and Informal Care', in Sara Arber and Jan Ginn, eds, *Connecting Gender and Ageing: A Sociological Approach*. Buckingham, UK: Open University Press, 129–43.

Matcha, Duane A. 1997. *The Sociology of Aging: A Social Problems Perspective*. Needham Heights, Mass.: Allyn & Bacon.

Meier, Andrea, Maeda J. Galinsky, and Kathleen A. Rounds. 1995. 'Telephone Support Groups for Caregivers of Persons with AIDS', *Social Work with Groups* 18, 1: 99–108.

Midanik, Lorraine T., Krikor Soghikian, Laura J. Ransom, and Michael R. Polen. 1990. 'Health Status, Retirement Plans, and Retirement: The Kaiser Permanente Study', *Journal of Aging and Health* 2: 462–74.

Mirowsky, John, and Catherine E. Ross. 1999. 'Economic Hardship across the Life Course', *American Sociological Review* 64: 548–69.

Moody, Harry R. 2000. *Aging: Concepts and Controversies*, 3rd edn. Boston: Pine Forge Press.

Morris, David C. 1997. 'Health, Finances, Religious Involvement, and Life Satisfaction of Older Adults', *Journal of Religious Gerontology* 10, 2: 3–17.

Musick, Marc A. 1996. 'Religion and Subjective Health among Black and White Elders', *Journal of Health and Social Behavior* 37: 221–37.

National Centre on Elder Abuse. 2001. 'The Basics: What Is Elder Abuse?' Available at: <www.elderabusecenter.org/basic/index.html>; accessed 27 Jan. 2003.

New England Journal of Medicine. 2005. Available at: <www.compassionandchoices.org/documents/20050422_PASuicide_15.pdf>.

Newsletter of the National Advisory Council on Aging. 2006. 9, 2 (June). Available at: <www.naca.ca/expression/9-2/exp_9-2_e.html>.

Noelker, Linda S., and Robert W. Wallace. 1985. 'The Organization of Family Care for Impaired Elderly', *Journal of Family Issues* 6, 1: 23–44.

Novak, Mark. 1997. *Aging and Society: A Canadian Perspective*, 3rd edn. Scarborough, Ont.: Nelson Thompson.

Orodenker, Sylvia. 1990. 'Family Caregiving in a Changing Society: The Effects of Employment on Caregiver Stress', *Family Community Health* 12, 4: 58–70.

Palmore, E.B. 1985. 'How to Live Longer and Like It', *Journal of Applied Gerontology* 4, 2: 1–8.

Peek, Chuck W. 2000. 'Correlates of Dynamic Profiles of Self-Rated Health', Southern Sociological Society, conference paper.

Penning, Margaret. 1995. 'Cognitive Impairment, Caregiver Burden, and the Utilization of Home Health Services', *Journal of Aging and Health* 7, 2: 233–53.

———— and Neena L. Chappell. 1990. 'Self-care in Relation to Informal and Formal Care', *Ageing and Society* 10, 1: 41–59.

Perry, Daniel. 1995. 'Researching the Aging Well Process', *American Behavioral Scientist* 39: 152–71.

Peters, Kimberley, and Richard G. Rogers. 1997. 'The Effects of Perceived Health Status and Age on Elders' Longevity', *International Journal of Sociology and Social Policy* 17, 9 and 10: 117–42.

Rosenthal, Carolyn J. 1997a. 'The Changing Contexts of Family Care in Canada', *Ageing International* 24, 1: 13–31.

———. 1997b. 'The Care of Canadian Families for Their Aging Members', *Lien social et politiques* 38, 78: 123–31.

———, Sarah H. Matthews, and Victor W. Marshall. 1989. 'Is Parent Care Normative? The Experiences of a Sample of Middle-aged Women', *Research on Aging* 11, 2: 244–60.

Ross, David P., Katherine J. Scott, and Peter J. Smith. 2001. *Canadian Fact Book on Poverty—2000*. Ottawa: Canadian Council on Social Development.

Ross, Margaret M., Carolyn J. Rosenthal, and Pamela G. Dawson. 1997. 'Spousal Caregiving in the Institutional Setting: Task Performance', *Canadian Journal on Aging* 16, 1: 51–69.

Rounds, Kathleen A., Maeda J. Galinsky, and Mathieu R. Despard. 1995. 'Evaluation of Telephone Support Groups for Persons with HIV Disease', *Research on Social Work Practice* 5: 442–59.

Rowe, John W., and Robert L. Kahn. 1997. 'Successful Aging', *Gerontologist* 37: 433–40.

Russell, R.V. 1990. 'Recreation and Quality of Life in Old Age: A Causal Analysis', *Journal of Applied Gerontology* 9, 1: 77–90.

Salamon, M.J. 1985. 'Sociocultural Role Theories in the Elderly: A Replication and Extension', *Activities, Adaptation and Aging* 7, 2: 111–22.

Satariano, William A. 1997. 'Editorial: The Disabilities of Aging—Looking to the Physical Environment', *American Journal of Public Health* 87: 331–2.

Scharlach, Andrew E., and Karen I. Fredriksen. 1994. 'Elder Care versus Adult Care: Does Care Recipient Age Make a Difference?', *Research on Aging* 16, 1: 43–68.

Souter, Gavin. 1997. 'Costs, Restrictions Criticized in Mexico's Pension Reform', *Business Insurance* 31, 33 (18 Aug.): 33.

Statistics Canada. 1994. *Population Projections for Canada, Provinces and Territories, 1993–2016* (Catalogue no. 91–520). Ottawa: Statistics Canada.

———. 1998. *Canada Yearbook* (Catalogue no. 11–402–XPE). Ottawa: Statistics Canada.

———. 2000a. *Commission on the Future of Health Care in Canada*. Available at: <www.theglobeandmail.com/special/romanow/stories/numbers.html>.

———. 2000b. 'Age Pyramid of the Population of Canada, July 1, 1974 to 2004'. Available at: <www.statcan.ca/english/kits/animat/pyca.htm>; accessed 3 July 2001.

———. 2001. 'Population by Age Group'. Available at: <www.statcan.ca/english/Pgdb/People/Population/demo31a.htm>; accessed 3 July 2001.

———. 2003. *The Daily*, 17 Nov. Available at: <www.statcan.ca/Daily/English/031117/d031117a.htm>.

———. 2004. *The Daily*, 22 July. Available at: <www.statcan.ca/Daily/English/040722/d040722b.htm>.

———. 2005. *The Daily*, 15 Dec. Available at: <www.statcan.ca/Daily/English/051215/d051215b.htm>.

Steinkamp, M.W. 1987. 'Social Integration, Leisure Activity, and Life Satisfaction in Older Adults: Activity Theory Revisited', *International Journal of Aging and Human Development* 25: 293–307.

——— and J.R. Kelly. 1985. 'Relationships among Motivational Orientation, Level of Leisure Activity and Life Satisfaction in Older Men and Women', *Journal of Psychology* 119: 509–20.

Stewart, Miriam J., ed. 2000. *Chronic Conditions and Caregiving in Canada: Social Support Strategies*. Toronto: University of Toronto Press.

Sulman, Joanne, Carolyn J. Rosenthal, Victor W. Marshall, and Joanne Daciuk. 1996. 'Elderly Patients in the Acute Care Hospital: Factors Associated with Long Stay and Its Impact on Patients and Families', *Journal of Gerontological Social Work* 25, 3 and 4: 33–52.

Swallen, Karen C. 1997. 'Do Health Selection Effects Last? A Comparison of Morbidity Rates for Elderly Adult Immigrants and US-Born Elderly Persons', *Journal of Cross-cultural Gerontology* 12: 317–39.

Tienda, Marta, and Haya Stier. 1996. 'Generating Labor Market Inequality: Employment Opportunities and the Accumulation of Disadvantage', *Social Problems* 43: 147–65.

Warner, Camille D., Marie R. Haug, Carol M. Musil, and Diana L. Morris. 1998. 'Illness Narratives and Health Diaries of Older Adults', American Sociological Association, conference paper.

Watt, Susan, Jacqueline Roberts, and Gina Browne. 1997. 'Age, Adjustment, and Costs: A Study of Chronic Illnesses', *Social Science and Medicine* 44: 1483–90.

Wood, F.W., ed. 1990. *An American Profile: Opinions and Behavior, 1972–1989*. Detroit: Gale Research.

Woods, Nancy Fugate, Bernice C. Yates, and Janet Primomo. 1989. 'Supporting Families during Chronic Stress', *Image: Journal of Nursing Scholarship* 2, 1: 46–50.

Yahya, H.A.Q. 1988. 'Factors Influencing the Satisfaction of Muslim Organization Members in a University Town in the United States (Lansing, Michigan)', *Journal Institute of Muslim Minority Affairs* 9: 280–95.

FAMILY

Introduction

This chapter is about husbands and wives, parents and children, marriage and separation, family life and work life, divorce and violence. Essentially, family life is about three main social relationships: between spouses or partners, between parents and children, and between siblings. In this chapter, we will discuss the concerns that many people have about modern family life. As we will see, an important feature of family life is that family members interact with each other on a micro level. At the same time, the macro level of society plays a large part in framing the circumstances—economic, political, legal, religious, and otherwise—that shape these interactions.

Many people with family problems face a double difficulty: the problems themselves, and the shame and guilt that arise from believing that no one else has similar problems. We begin this chapter by examining some of the disabling myths people hold about family life. We then set these myths against the backdrop of real Canadian families, noting the difference. We briefly discuss the role of sex and sexuality in family life, recognizing that families have always regulated sexuality. We then review competing sociological theories about families. After considering the social problems that families face, we judge the health problems associated with family life. We finish with some thoughts about the ways that family problems might be corrected.

Family life is central to our society. It is the family that produces and socializes the next generation of citizens. Families provide the emotional support and economic security that people, and societies, need. People have always relied on families, especially in hard economic times. Because families are so important, problems in family living become important social problems for society as a whole.

Today, more than ever, we lack clear strategies about the best ways to fulfill our family duties or deal with the failings of other family members. There is no sure guide to good spousal, parental, or sibling behaviour. We are in a time of change, and sorting out modern family life is made more difficult by the survival of myths about an imaginary golden age of family life.

Different Kinds of Families

Families vary from one society to another, just as they vary within our own society. In most societies families exist within larger social networks—within kinship groups and clans. The members of a household—the husband and wife, parent and child, brother and sister—are thoroughly integrated into a larger web of kin, including uncles, aunts, cousins, grandparents, grandchildren, and their lives cannot be understood without reference to this larger web and the community at large.

A *kinship group* is a group of people who share a relationship through blood or marriage and have positions in a hierarchy of rights over the property. Kin relationships may also control where the members must live, whom they can marry, and even their life opportunities. The definition of a kin relationship varies between societies, but kin relationships are important everywhere.

Some societies trace kin relationships through the male line, so any individual's relationships are determined by his or her father's relationships; we call such kinship systems *patrilineal*. Others count relationships through the female line; these are *matrilineal* systems. Still others count relationships through both lines; they are *bilateral* kinship systems.

If the kinship system is patrilineal, a person gains a position in the community just by being the child of his or her father. In a matrilineal kinship system, on the other hand, a person has certain property rights as the child of his or her mother. However, that kinship system is independent of which sex holds more authority in society; men can be the dominant sex even in a matrilineal society. In this case, the person whose kinship link is most important to a child is not the biological father but the mother's brother, as among the Ashanti in West Africa or several North American Aboriginal societies.

Our family system follows the Western pattern, in which property is also typically inherited along the male line. Where families settle down is traditionally determined by the husband's job, not the wife's, although this too is changing. However, our society also has certain *matrifocal* characteristics. Because women have been defined as the primary kin-keepers—the people who preserve family contacts—children usually have stronger ties with their mother's kin than with those of their father (Rosenthal, 1985; Thomson and Li, 1992: 15). Children also keep closer contacts with their mothers when their parents grow old (Connidis, 2001). When parents of grown children live separately, fathers are less often visited, called, and relied on than are mothers.

Our society is neither matrilineal nor patrilineal—it is bilateral. This means that relatives of both of our parents are thought of as kin. We have maternal and paternal aunts, uncles, grandparents, cousins, and so on. Bilateral descent fits well with an equalitarian authority structure where father and mother have a roughly equal say in family matters.

In many societies, including our own, a household usually consists of parents and their unmarried children. In others, what we consider the **family** is embedded in a much broader web of kinship relations, and a household will include many kin. These two main forms of family household are referred to respectively as the nuclear family and the extended family. The **nuclear family** is the most common family household in our society. It consists of one or two generations living together—typically, one or two parents and their children. The nuclear family is a *conjugal* family, in which priority is given to marital ties over blood ties. The basic relationship is between spouses, not between one or more spouses and their parents, siblings, or more distant kin. Western families are *neolocal*, i.e., marriage brings with it the expectation that each of the partners will leave the parental home and establish a new residence, forming another independent nuclear family.

An **extended family** is one in which two or more generations of relatives live together. It may include grandparents or grandchildren, and uncles, aunts, and cousins. The extended family is a *consanguine* family, since preference is given to blood ties over marital ties. Consanguine families stress relationships between parents and their children, among siblings, and with other 'blood-related' members of the kin group.

Each of these family forms has its pros and cons. The extended family usually serves as one big productive unit, with all able-bodied members contributing to the family's common good. The members of this unit co-operate in such productive activities as agriculture, craft work, hunting and gathering, building shelters, and other activities related to subsistence.

However, the nuclear family has some advantages over the extended family. For example, such a family is not forced to remain in any particular location. Because it is small it can move easily to take advantage of job opportunities in another part of the country or in another country. It follows, then, that the rise of a middle class and industrial society helped shape the nuclear family as a private institution. Britain and the North American colonies were among the first areas to display this form of organization.

Yet, the nuclear family also has its drawbacks. It offers its members too few people to rely on in times of financial trouble or emotional stress. Family members are liable to expect too much from each other if they have no one else to turn to. This reliance puts strain on relationships between spouses and between parents and children.

This change in family composition has important outcomes for the many immigrants to North America who have often left members of their extended family behind. For example, Korean families in North America are moving towards nuclear family; as a result, many family traditions, such as filial duty, may soon disappear. This change to a nuclear family structure also weakens people's connections with their extended kin in Korea and with Korean culture as well (Kauh, 1999; Schwarz et al., 2006).

Recent decades have seen a growing variation in family and household types in Canadian society, due largely to the large number of immigrants and varied ethnic traditions. Though neolocal, heterosexual, nuclear-family households are the most common form, other forms of family life are also common. Increasingly, we are becoming familiar with single-parent families, empty-nest families, families that bring together two sets of children from earlier marriages, and family households based on a cohabiting relationship or on same-sex relationships.

Sociologists have adopted some new approaches to studying family life in a diverse and fluid society. One method, the life course approach, follows the variety of social and interpersonal dynamics of close relations and examines how they change throughout our lifetimes (Elder, 1992; Klein and White, 1996; Kohli, 1986). It notes how, over time, families change to meet new needs, such as those created by the arrival, care, or departure of children.

Another new approach is to look at family relations from the perspectives of different family members. This recognizes that different family members have different interests and experiences as members of any given family. Because different family members often have different interests, it is often inappropriate to speak of 'the family' as though it has a single interest and acts in a unified way.

Up until the 1970s (and beyond), much family research was done from an adult male perspective (Eichler, 2001; Giddens, 1992; Luxton, 1997). For example, a popular phrase of the time that has stuck is 'bedroom communities', which describes suburban communities in which families lived and women often worked at home. These were living communities and could be seen as 'bedrooms' only from the vantage point of men who worked elsewhere. What do family life and changes in close relations among adults look like from the viewpoint of children? They look markedly different, as we are now discovering (Marcil-Gratton, 1993; Mason et al., 2003). Children live in many and varied kinds of families while still dependent; changes in family are happening earlier in their lives than those of children in times past. Looking at the shifting of close relations among adults from the viewpoint of children's lives gives us a new and important perspective on families.

Yet another new approach is to collect data in new ways so that family diversity can be studied over time. One example is Statistics Canada's Longitudinal Survey of Children and Youth (Willms, 2002: 71–102, 359–77). This survey follows individual children as they grow up, interviewing them and their families every two years. Data are collected on family changes, schooling, health, and a whole range of variables that affect children's lives. Findings from this survey have taught us much about family life in Canada. For example, we now know that the negative effects on a child's mental or physical health, or school readiness and achievement, of living with a single parent are due to more than simply the effect of the low incomes such families often face. The good news from this longitudinal research is that good parenting can largely overcome these harmful effects.

Studying families in a context of change reminds us to stay away from any simple definitions of family, or theories about family life that assume that all families are the same, and stay the same, regardless of their historical context. Consider, for example, how family members may be differently affected by changes in the economy. Young adult children may stay in school longer because they cannot find jobs, or cannot find jobs that pay enough for them to have their own apartments or homes. Similarly, children in families may be differently parented because of changing policies on parental leave, enabling younger ones to have full-time parents for a period in their early lives, compared to older siblings where the parents returned to work soon after birth.

Myths of the Family

Throughout the period that makes up the supposed golden age of the family, television and Hollywood—ever the sentimentalists—promoted the image of an ideal family. In shows such as *Leave It to Beaver* (1957–63), *Ozzie and Harriet* (1952–66), *I Love Lucy* (1951–7), *Father Knows Best* (1954–62), and *The Donna Reed Show* (1958–66), television actors played out peaceful family scenes to the delight and disbelief of audiences. Father was the breadwinner, Mother the bread-maker. The phrase 'till death do you part' was

Table 8.1 Proportion of Common-Law Couples, Selected Countries, Canada and Regions

Country	Reference Year	As a Percentage of all Couples
Sweden	2000	30.0
Norway	2000	24.5
Iceland	2000	19.5
Finland	2000	18.7
Mexico	2000	18.7
New Zealand	2001	18.3
France	1999	17.5
United States	2000	8.2
Canada	2001	16.0
Quebec	2001	29.8
Other provinces/territories	2001	11.7

Source: Adapted from Statistics Canada (2004).

taken literally then, as it is today by somewhat smaller numbers of people of several faiths. Storylines made no mention of prior marriages, divorces, and separations, let alone children born to unmarried women. The children were clean-cut, respectful, and eager in school. They may have broken some rules, but when they did, parental discipline was fair and loving and the children learned their lessons.

This ideal remained prominent and desirable to many North Americans at the time. The ideal was old and well-established, deriving from long, even ancient, traditions buttressed by religion, founded on particular notions of personal, economic, social, and national strength. The traditions, furthermore, became strongly reinforced and enforced through laws that persisted for thousands of years.

That said, we understand now that these traditions were patriarchal—that is, significantly skewed in favour of men over women. They were pronatalist, heterosexist, and resistant to ideas of people leading alternative lifestyles. They systematically denied the existence of domestic violence—chiefly, violence against women—covert contraception practised by women in their own interest, and psychological and physical mistreatment of children. Many marriages survived solely because divorce was virtually impossible. In reality—not ideology—some brides were pregnant and some marriages ended in separation or divorce. Some parents abused alcohol or drugs, some spouses beat their partners, and some teenagers ran away from home. Actual domestic life was frequently loving and peaceful, to be sure, but it was also often conflictual, stressful, messy, and occasionally prone to violence—even in the idealized 1950s.

In North American culture today, the 'ideal' family is still based on a formal marriage between two people of different sexes who have come together freely to build a monogamous and enduring relationship that includes reproduction and the rearing of children. Many members of the public still view alternatives to this as 'departures' from the ideal, if not even as statistically deviant. Single-parenting, stepfamilies, common-law relationships, and same-sex couples may be growing in familiarity (and therefore acceptance), but they remain departures from the cultural ideal.

Box 8.1   Historical Perspective: American Women, Marriage, and the Pill

American society in the 1950s was geared towards the family. Marriage and children were part of the national agenda. And the Cold War was in part a culture war, with the American family at the centre of the struggle. . . .

Embedded in the propaganda of the time was the idea that the nuclear family was what made Americans superior to the Communists. American propaganda showed the horrors of Communism in the lives of Russian women. They were shown dressed in gunnysacks, as they toiled in drab factories while their children were placed in cold, anonymous daycare centres. In contrast to the 'evils' of Communism, an image was promoted of American women, with their feminine hairdos and delicate dresses, tending to the hearth and home as they enjoyed the fruits of capitalism, democracy, and freedom. . . .

In the 1950s, women felt tremendous societal pressure to focus their aspirations on a wedding ring. The US marriage rate was at an all-time high and couples were tying the knot, on average, younger than ever before. Getting married right out of high school or while in college was considered the norm. A common stereotype was that women went to college to get a 'Mrs' (pronounced MRS) degree, meaning a husband. Although women had other aspirations in life, the dominant theme promoted in the culture and media at the time was that a husband was far more important for a young woman than a college degree. Despite the fact that employment rates also rose for women during this period, the media tended to focus on a woman's role in the home. If a woman wasn't engaged or married by her early twenties, she was in danger of becoming an 'old maid'. . . .

If remaining single in American society was considered undesirable, being single and pregnant was totally unacceptable, especially for white women. Girls who 'got in trouble' were forced to drop out of school, and often sent away to distant relatives or homes for wayward girls. Shunned by society for the duration of their pregnancy, unwed mothers paid a huge price for premarital sex. In reality young women were engaging in premarital sex in spite of the societal pressure to remain virgins. There was a growing need for easy, safe, effective, reliable and female-controlled contraceptives. . . .

Not only did most married women walk down the aisle by age 19; they also tended to start families right away. A majority of brides were pregnant within seven months of their wedding, and they didn't just stop at one child. Large families were typical. From 1940 to 1960, the number of families with three children doubled and the number of families having a fourth child quadrupled. . . .

This was also the era of the 'happy homemaker'. For young mothers in the 1950s, domesticity was idealized in the media, and women were encouraged to stay at home if the family could afford it. Women who chose to work when they didn't need the paycheque were often considered selfish, putting themselves before the needs of their family. . . .

But even for happy homemakers, pressures were mounting. In a departure from previous generations, it was no longer acceptable for a wife to shut her husband out of the bedroom. Starting in the 1950s sex was viewed as a key component of a healthy and loving marriage. Without an effective female-controlled contraceptive, young wives faced three decades of child-bearing before they reached menopause. . . .

By the late 1950s, both single and married American women were ready and waiting for a new and improved form of birth control. When the Pill was introduced, the social factors affecting women's reproductive lives contributed significantly to the warm reception women across the country gave the Pill.

Source: PBS (2001).

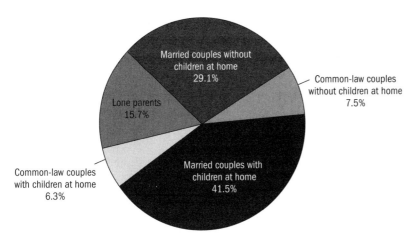

FIGURE 8.1 Structure of Canadian Families, 2001
Source: Adapted from Statistics Canada (2002).

Patriarchy and Family Values

By **patriarchy**, we mean male dominance that is justified in a society's values and therefore tied to the ideology of gender. Most known societies are patriarchal to some extent, a fact that has never been satisfactorily explained. Perhaps the universality of patriarchy is due to the universality of social differentiation by sex, which is due to the fact that men are typically larger and stronger than women—this gives them an advantage and a greater social value vis-à-vis the imperatives of wresting from the earth shelter and a living, in a sometimes unco-operative geography. Perhaps it is due to the physical vulnerability and dependence of women under conditions of frequent pregnancy and childbirth. If the latter, it follows that with the worldwide decline in childbearing, we can expect to see a worldwide decline in patriarchy. In fact, this change has been observed. An increase in women's educational and job opportunities makes it possible for lower fertility to translate into less male domination.

Like class inequality, the degree and form of inequality between the sexes varies a great deal from one society to another. So, too, does the cultural justification for gender inequality. In many societies, the excuse is sacred (based on religious texts and teachings). Some of the major religions of the world—Catholicism, branches of Judaism, and Islam among them—give different and less powerful roles to women than to men. However, other major religions, including denominations of Christianity, other branches of Judaism, Buddhism, Hinduism, and Taoism, preach and attempt to practise gender equality.

Many of the dominant beliefs of Canadian society today include women's right to choose contraception, divorce, and have a legal abortion; the increasing need for women of all cultures to work outside the home; and an increasing acceptance of gay relationships and marriage. However, the patriarchal nuclear family remains a powerful ideological image in our society and serves to control and socialize race, class, gender, and sexual orientation (Chambers, 2000). In North America, an influential source of mythology about family life in recent decades has come from fundamentalist Christians and social conservatives. The term *family values* was first used in the United States in the mid-1960s to describe a set of moral guidelines for defining the structure and role of a family and its members, supported by appeals to tradition.

Most often, 'family values' simply means a conservative ideology that supports traditional patriarchal morality or values—a social ideology that supports traditional gender roles and opposes feminism, birth control, and divorce. This world view sometimes also opposes the rights of families comprised of gay, lesbian, bisexual, and transgender persons and, by extension, opposes same-sex marriage. Other concerns of those who are socially conservative or seek to live a faith-based life include abortion, pornography, extramarital sex, and the effects on children of high levels of profanity, violence, and sexuality in the media. These values are evident at the many evangelical websites on the Internet and celebrated—in sermon and song—by the many evangelical programs broadcast on television every week. A thorough demonstration of these concerns can be found at the Focus on the Family website (www.family.org).

A growing number of Canadians—especially educated urban Canadians—take an opposite position on these issues, supporting the normalization of single-parent families, same-sex monogamous marriage, and unmarried monogamous couples (i.e., cohabitation), for example. However, even Canadian society has been influenced by the family values of the American conservative right, through the influence of the Bush presidency, television evangelism, and the efforts of lobbying and agencies such as Focus on the Family.

Contemporary sociologists have tried to disabuse people of beliefs that support unfair or abusive relationships between men and women, parents and children, and heterosexuals and homosexuals. We do so through research that tries to discover the truth about modern family forms and processes.

Basic Aspects of Canadian Families

In reality, families are more different and more varied than the traditional 'family values'-influenced media suggest. In place of an idealized nuclear family, we find a wide variety of families and more tolerant attitudes towards different family types. Increasingly, these varied, atypical, and even deviant families are finding their way into the mass media. Gradually, we are all coming to know and accept the fact that family life comes in a great many forms. And this increased public diversity of family lives is evident throughout the industrial world. In many respects, Canadian families today are similar to families in other Western societies, such as the United Kingdom, France, and the United States.

Like most urban industrial societies, Canadian society is organized around married couples. Society provides less protection for the property rights of partners in common-law relationships than for those of legally married partners, for example. Yet, Canadian family policies differ from those of other countries, and they often vary from one province to another.

Sociologists use different definitions of 'family' for particular purposes. For purposes of the census, the Canadian government defines the economic family as 'a now-married couple (with or without never-married sons or daughters of either or both spouses), a couple living common-law (again with or without never-married sons and/or daughters of either or both partners), or a lone parent of any marital status, with at least one never-married son or daughter living in the same dwelling' (Statistics Canada, 2001a). A broader sociological definition of the family, one that sociologists generally support, is 'a group of individuals, related by blood, marriage, or adoption, who support one another financially, materially, and emotionally' (see, for example, Murdock, 1949). This definition does not take into consideration same-sex partnerships between people who are not related by blood, legal marriage, or legal adoption. To include these relationships, sociologists recast the term 'family' to focus on social processes that typify marriage, such as financial, material, and emotional support.

As we mentioned, the most common forms of family structure in Canada today are nuclear families and extended families. The nuclear family arrangement is the norm for families in industrialized countries like Canada. Until recently, adult children in industrial societies have tended to be economically independent—they form their own households after starting a family, separate from their own parents, siblings, and extended kin. The most recent data, from the 2001 census, reveal a boomerang phenomenon, however, with 58 per cent of Canadian young people ages 20–4 and almost a quarter of those aged 25–9 living in the parental home. Reduced job opportunities have reduced the chance of neolocality for many young people, however strong the motivation may be to establish their own homes.

By contrast, the extended family is a nuclear family that lives with other kinfolk under one roof. The kinfolk are most commonly drawn from grandparents, aunts, uncles, and dependent nephews and nieces. Extended-family households are often found in pre-industrial societies. There, the agricultural basis of survival often means that a larger household, with more workers to help grow and harvest the crops, is better able to support the entire family. In Canada, extended families are common among newly arrived ethnic groups. Often, they place a strong value on upholding intergenerational ties with elders. However, overall, the occurrence of extended families in North America declined rapidly in the twentieth century.

Variety occurs even within the nuclear family structure. For example, in Canada and elsewhere, the percentage of families with a traditional two-parent structure is declining. Today, nuclear families include married couples without children, cohabiting couples (living in a common-law relationship), single parents (never-married persons or divorced), same-sex families, and blended families (remarriages in which one or both partners have one or more child from a previous relationship).

Most Canadian families, 70 per cent in 2001, are classifiable as a 'married-couple union.' However, this group has declined in size since 1981, when 83 per cent of all families were based in legal marriage (Statistics Canada, 2002). Alongside the decreased rate of marriage, we see a matching increase in common-law unions. Statistics Canada defines a common-law couple as 'two persons of opposite sex who are not legally married to each other, but live together as husband and wife in the same dwelling' (ibid.). The common-law union is the fastest-growing family category today: the proportion of common-law families increased from 5.6 per cent to 14 per cent between 1981 and 2001. Although historically Canadians frowned on couples who lived together without marrying, today the stigma against non-marital cohabitation has lessened if not disappeared (Vanier Institute, 2000). On this matter, Statistics Canada (2002) reports:

> The trend toward common-law was again strongest in Quebec, where 508,520 common-law families represented 30 per cent of all couple families in that province. A recent study based on Statistics Canada's General Social Survey showed that common-law unions have become more and more popular in Quebec, and that trend has started to take hold among younger people in other provinces. Still, while younger Canadian men and women are more likely to start their conjugal life through a common-law relationship (about 40 per cent of men and women aged 30 to 39), most will eventually marry (roughly 75 per cent) if trends observed in 2001 were to continue.

The Decline of Multigenerational Families

Taken as a whole, the evidence suggests that the shift towards independent residence of the aged is a worldwide phenomenon. According to the consensus of scholarly opinion, the simplification of the living arrangements of the aged during the twentieth century has resulted primarily from an increase in the resources of the aged, which has enabled increasing numbers of elderly to afford independent living. [However, one researcher, Steven Ruggles,] suggests the opposite: he argues that the decline of the multigenerational family occurred mainly because of increasing opportunities for the young and declining parental control over their children.

Source: <www.un.org/esa/population/publications/bulletin42_43/ruggles.pdf>.

Sex and Sexuality

Families typically begin through bonds formed between partners. In the beginning, this process is driven as much by sexuality as by the wish to satisfy social goals, such as to have companionship and achieve economic security. In a society like ours, in which most mating is based on romance, sexuality is central to the norms for mating and family formation.

The *Oxford English Dictionary* offers multiple definitions of 'romance', which is so central to our comprehension of modern mating and marriage. These definitions include: '1 a pleasurable feeling of excitement and wonder associated with love. 2 a love affair. 3 a book or film dealing with love in a sentimental or idealized way. 4 a quality or feeling of mystery, excitement, and remoteness from everyday life. 5 a medieval tale dealing with a hero of chivalry, of the kind common in the Romance languages.' Definitions 1, 2, and 4 come closest to what we are trying to say here. In Canadian society, people are expected to experience these kinds of romance before marrying. Sexual intercourse is also expected to flow from, and stimulate, these feelings of premarital and early marital romance.

Sexuality continues, over the course of family life, both to enhance a partner relationship and to create conflict; sexuality both enlivens and endangers family life. On the one hand, many couples come together to form a family because of sexual attractions between them. However, the intensity of the initial passion normally subsides after the first few years and stable feelings of love and involvement of a more durable kind help the couple ride out the many storms that come up as they learn to live and work together. Their relationship may have been based on a 'romantic' notion of love, a concept that is found mainly in societies that allow females as well as males to give and withhold love freely.

As a result, the power of romantic love and sexual passion to bring couples together and keep them together is at odds with a belief in sexual equality. In reality, people have to consider a variety of factors—some of them very practical—before committing to marriage, however dreamy the relationship may be. And, in reality, romantic love and sexual passion are often not strong and persistent enough to keep former lovers from breaking up. When people are truly and equally free to form and dissolve unions based wholly on their romantic feelings, more unions are bound to break up.

Marriages are less secure in 'romantic', i.e., modern as opposed to traditional, societies. Marriages based on choice and passion are always at risk of ending through the discovery of new choices and new passions. In this dichotomy of different types of love resides the challenge of modern marriage. The 'puzzle' resides in the difficulty of clearly defining 'choice', 'romantic', 'love', 'passion', and the loci of 'control' in the society and in the individual. One thing is certain, however: gender equality means more freedom for women, more sexual expression, and more romantic—rather than (male-dominated) coercive or chivalric—relationships.

Cross-national research has found that societies that allow premarital sex for both men and women rate romantic love higher than societies that have a double standard or that disapprove of female sexuality outside marriage (de Munck and Korotayev, 1999). Said another way, societies that treat female sexuality the same as male sexuality tend to view romantic love and passionate sex as being central to marriage.

Same-Sex Couples

Same-sex relationships are discussed in Chapter 6, and there is no need to repeat the same material here. Suffice to say that many gay and lesbian people are deeply embedded in family structures as parents, children, siblings, aunts, uncles, grandchildren, and so on (O'Brien and Goldberg, 2000). Yet in most industrialized countries, gays and lesbians are unable to marry legally since marriage continues to be defined as a union between a man and a woman. There are signs that this is changing. Indeed, the legal treatment of lesbian and gay families in the United States and Canada has been changing since the late 1970s, as is obvious in child custody, access, and adoption cases in which sexual orientation was a factor (Arnup, 1999). By challenging the definition of 'spouse' and applying to the courts to formalize their relationships with their children by adoption, lesbian parents have challenged the normative content of spousal relations and the law itself as a gendering strategy (Gavigan, 1999). Such challenge, of course, was instrumental in the former federal Liberal government passing Bill C-38, the Civil Marriages Act, on 20 July 2005. This Act validates the legality of marriage between same-sex couples, though it remains to be seen if it can stand the test of a recently elected Conservative government intent on holding a free vote in the House of Commons on same-sex marriage. For other significant changes that have impacted on the legal status of same-sex relationships in Canada and elsewhere, see Box 8.2.

Fertility and Child-bearing

Child-bearing for a woman today is much less frequent than it was in the past, the result of a slow and (almost) consistent decline occurring over more than a century. Data from the Population Division of the United Nations Department of Economic and Social Affairs (Associated Press, 2005) show that fertility rates have declined significantly even in developing countries. Following a long-term trend among rich nations, the fertility rate in developing countries has dropped below three children per woman for the first time. This decline came about as people across developing nations are waiting longer to marry and have children, and are using family planning, including contraception, more regularly. With the fertility rate in 20 developed countries now below the replacement rate, the world is seeing a major and unprecedented decline in fertility levels. In the world's 192 countries, the number of women between the ages of 25 and 29 who are single rose from 15 per cent in the 1970s to 24 per cent in the 1990s. For men, the increase was from 32 per cent to 44 per cent.

Government policies have played a central role in changing reproductive behaviour. The UN report cites support by 92 per cent of all governments for family planning and widespread backing for the distribution of contraceptives. According to the report, the use of contraceptives worldwide rose from 38 per cent to 52 per cent of women in their child-bearing years. In the developing world, the numbers also rose, from 27 per cent to 40 per cent (ibid.).

THE CHINESE ONE-CHILD POLICY

The strictest policies on fertility control are exercised in the People's Republic of China, where a one-child policy is in effect. China represents what we might call a 'coercive (or involuntary) model' of fertility decline. Sixty years ago, before the People's Revolution,

Box 8.2   Social Policy: Same-Sex Rights and Laws—Canada and the World

Canada Timeline

1969   Amendments put forward by Justice Minister Pierre Trudeau pass into the Criminal Code, decriminalizing homosexuality in Canada.

1999 (May)   The Supreme Court of Canada rules same-sex couples should have the same benefits and obligations as opposite-sex common-law couples and equal access to benefits from social programs to which they contribute.

1999 (25 Oct.) Ontario is the first province to legally recognize same-sex unions. Instead of changing Ontario's definition of spouse, the government creates a new same-sex category, changing the province's Family Law Act to read 'spouse or same-sex partner' wherever it had read only 'spouse' before. Bill 5 also amends more than 60 other provincial laws, making the rights and responsibilities of same-sex couples mirror those of common-law couples.

2000 (11 Apr.) Parliament passes Bill C-23, the Modernization of Benefits and Obligations Act, which gives same-sex couples the same social and tax benefits as heterosexuals in common-law relationships. The definition of 'common-law relationship' is expanded to include same-sex couples.

2003 (17 July) Ottawa introduces historic legislation that would allow gay couples to marry, called The Act Respecting Certain Aspects of Legal Capacity for Marriage. According to the draft bill, 'marriage for civil purposes is the lawful union of two persons to the exclusion of all others.'

2005 (28 June) The Liberals' controversial Bill C-38, the Civil Marriages Act, passes a final reading in the House of Commons. It gives same-sex partners the same legal recognition as other married couples, but protects religious freedoms. The bill became law when it received royal assent on 20 July 2005.

World Timeline

1885 (6 Aug.)   The British Parliament votes to make homosexual acts a criminal offence.

1930s   Adolf Hitler takes power in Germany and launches a campaign against Jews and other groups. Thousands of homosexuals are sent to concentration camps. Gay men are identified with pink triangles and lesbians are identified with black triangles.

1961   Illinois repeals its sodomy laws, making it the first state in the US to decriminalize homosexuality between consenting adults in private. The law takes effect in 1962. Connecticut follows in 1969 with the law taking effect in 1971. In the 1970s other states decriminalize homosexuality.

1967 (27 July) England and Wales decriminalize private homosexual acts between consenting adult men over the age of 21, except for those in the military and police. Scotland and Northern Ireland would follow in 1980 and 1982, respectively.

1989 (1 Oct.)   Denmark becomes the first country to legally recognize same-sex partnerships, essentially sanctioning gay marriages via the Danish Registered Partnership Act.

2001 (1 Apr.)	The Netherlands jumps to the forefront when its lower house of parliament enacts the world's most comprehensive legal recognition of gay rights. The Dutch law allows same-sex couples to marry and gives them the same rights as heterosexuals when it comes to adopting. The only restrictions to the new law are that same-sex couples can only adopt Dutch children, and foreign same-sex couples can't come to the Netherlands to marry unless one of them lives there.
2004 (24 May)	Australian Prime Minister John Howard asks Parliament to define marriage as a union between a man and a woman. The government also takes steps to block gays from adopting children from overseas. However, homosexuals would be allowed to name their partners as beneficiaries for pension and death benefits.
2004 (2 Nov.)	In the US national election, voters in 11 states pass amendments to state constitutions banning same-sex marriage.
2004 (9 Dec.)	New Zealand passes the Civil Union Bill to recognize unions between homosexual couples and unmarried heterosexuals, giving them the same rights as married couples in child custody, taxes, and welfare.
2005 (30 June)	The Spanish parliament makes gay marriage and adoption legal. The law also allows people to inherit the property of their same-sex partner.

Sources: CBC News Online (2005a, 2005b); BBC News Online (2005).

China had a huge population with a high fertility rate. The government saw a need to modernize and industrialize China as quickly as possible. This included laws fixing the equal rights of women and changing women's conditions of work and marriage.

As part of this, the Chinese government addressed child-bearing directly by means of compulsory permits for marriage and pregnancy. In 1971, it began its 'wan, xi, shao' (or 'later, longer, fewer') campaign, which asked people to marry later, leave a longer space between births, and bear fewer children in total. Then, in 1980, it legislated the one-child-per-couple policy. To clarify, there is no explicit law in China preventing couples from having more than one child. However, coercive and occasionally repressive strategies are used by the government to increase compliance. For example, couples who have pregnancies 'authorized' by local and regional authorities may be eligible for rewards, including financial support, extended maternity leave, and housing, education, and employment supplements. Conversely, those who defy the unofficial policy risk economic penalties, the loss of government benefits, and public censure. As well, the regulations allow some families, including rural couples whose first offspring is a girl, or urban couples who are both products of the one-child policy, to apply to the state for permission to have a second child.

A survey carried out in 1983 showed that these policies had achieved rapid and dramatic success. In 1965, the average Chinese woman had been bearing an estimated 6.1 children in her lifetime—the same rate we see in Central Africa today. By 2005, 40 years later, total fertility was down to 1.7 children—less than the population replacement (or zero growth) level (CIA, 2005)

So, within two generations, Chinese marriage and fertility patterns had changed rapidly from those of a developing country to those of a Western industrial country. Combined with other policies, this coercive fertility policy changed Chinese women's lives. Those born in the 1920s (for example) had received little or no education, married young, produced many children, and worked in the fields when not bearing children. Today, many Chinese women are afforded many more options, in terms of family structure, careers, and life in general.

Coercive family planning can be viewed as one of many preventive health programs. Fertility decline reduced the health risks and costs associated with pregnancy and childbirth. And by reducing the number of children, it also reduced the number of parenthood experiences (or years spent in parenthood) and the attendant joys and stresses.

At the same time, China's coercive one-child policy carries obvious costs. First, the Chinese traditionally shun daughters because China has historically been a patrilocal society. Many Chinese women who become pregnant suffer pressure to abort their child: first, if they are not married or not allowed to be married; second, if they are married but not permitted to have a child; and third, if they are allowed to have a child but don't want to have a daughter. (In China, as elsewhere, ultrasound technology makes it possible for women to know the sex of their unborn child.)

A high rate of abortions, under still primitive health-care conditions, increases women's health risks and health costs for the society. This adds to an already high estimated rate of abortion, infanticide, and child murder in China. Estimates of murdered children, especially daughters, run into the hundreds of thousands (Gendercide Watch, at: www.gendercide.org/case_infanticide.html).

By contrast, a voluntary program of family limitation, such as those of Brazil or India (for example, the sterilization program started by Indira Gandhi), works more slowly but is more humane. The key to this strategy is to lower the infant mortality rate, reduce the economic value of children, and make available an improved lifestyle to people who consume less of their income raising children. Successful experiences in Kerala (India) and elsewhere show that improving the social and economic status of women also reduces fertility.

THE CANADIAN PATTERN

Historical records show a strong decline in the Canadian birth rate from the mid-nineteenth to the mid-twentieth centuries in average numbers of children born (Gee, 1986). Women born between 1817 and 1831 had about 6.6 children, compared with 1.7 children for women born between 1947 and 1961. Our grandmothers and great-grandmothers had more children, on average, than we do today, and they spent a much larger portion of their lifetime bearing and raising children. Today we spend less of our lives occupied with parenting, both because we live longer and because our patterns of entering parenthood have changed. For instance, Gee (ibid.) found that Canadian women born between 1831 and 1840 spaced their first and last births an average of 14 years apart (often, with many births between). This compares with an average of only 1.8 years between first and last births for women born between 1951 and 1960.

The decline in numbers of children born into families was largely because of the changing social and economic circumstances in which families lived. As Canadian society industrialized, people needed fewer children to work on the farms. Children cost more to raise in towns and cities than they do on farms. Children in cities changed from an economic resource to an economic liability.

This century-long downward trend in child-bearing continued with only a brief interruption—the baby boom between 1947 and 1967. Today, the average number of births per woman is roughly 1.5, an all-time low. Most Canadians continue to enter parenthood in their mid- to late twenties, though increasingly, more couples are choosing to delay this life stage. On this, Statistics Canada (2005a) reports, 'Nearly one half of the women who gave birth in Canada were age 30 and older . . . . In fact, in Ontario and British Columbia, mothers age 30 and older were already in the majority. This reinforces the long-term trend among Canadian women: they have been waiting longer and longer to start families.'

More people today are parents than in the past, but they have fewer children overall, start later, and compress parenting into less of their lifetimes. This, and other social and economic changes, opens the door for women to combine paid work with families.

Entering Parenthood Today

Widespread use of contraception has been a key factor in the decline of both the Canadian birth rate and average family size—but it is not the cause of this decline, only the means. People have to want to limit their fertility if they are to have smaller families. Then, the widespread use of effective contraception allows a separation of sexual intercourse from risks of pregnancy, which changes both the practices surrounding sex and the view of entering parenthood.

As a result, many people now see the entry into parenthood as a distinct choice—neither inevitable or inescapable nor necessarily ideal. This view has serious social implications, especially for single women who become mothers. The view that child-bearing can be considered a choice tends to lead some people to presume that single women are solely responsible if they become pregnant and have children, with all its outcomes and risks.

Typically, contraception rates are higher where literacy is higher and women receive more education, social and economic opportunity, and general empowerment. As a result, contraceptive use varies throughout the world, as it does in Canada. Europe, especially Czechoslovakia and Western/Northern Europe, has the highest use of contraception in the world. By contrast, low contraceptive rates occur in Pakistan (8 per cent), Haiti (7 per cent), Senegal (11 per cent), and Kenya (17 per cent) (*Statistical Record of Women*, 1991).

CONTRACEPTIVE USE ACROSS THE WORLD

Worldwide, 61 per cent of all women of reproductive age who are married or in a consensual union are using contraception (UN, 2003). The level of contraceptive use is higher in the more developed regions, where 69 per cent of the 170 million women aged 15–49 who are married or in a consensual union are using contraception. In the less developed regions the equivalent figure is 59 per cent of the 873 million women of reproductive age who are married or in union. The level of contraceptive use is lowest in Africa. Only 27 per cent of the 117 million women of reproductive age who are married or in union in Africa are using contraception. By contrast, the percentage using contraception is fairly high in Asia (64 per cent of 689 million women who are married or in union) and in Latin America and the Caribbean (71 per cent of 82 million women who are married or in union) (ibid.).

Nine out of every 10 women using contraception rely on modern methods. The most commonly used modern methods are female sterilization (21 per cent of women

Contraception
Worldwide, 61 per cent of all women of reproductive age who are married or in a consensual union are using contraception. This percentage amounts to 635 million of the more than 1 billion women aged 15–49 who are married or in union. In the more developed regions, 69 per cent of those women use a method of contraception, while in the less developed regions 59 per cent do.
Source: United Nations, Department of Public Information, News and Media Services Division, press release POP/902, 21 Apr. 2004. At: <www.un.org/esa/ population/publications/ contraceptive2003/WallChart _CP2003_pressrelease.htm>.

who are married or in union), IUDs (14 per cent), and oral pills (7 per cent). Modern methods are more effective at preventing pregnancy and must generally be obtained from family planning services or suppliers, or, in the case of sterilization, by surgery. Short-acting and reversible contraceptive methods are more popular in developed countries, whereas longer-acting and highly effective clinical contraceptive methods are more commonly used in developing countries. In developed countries, contraceptive users rely mostly on oral pills (used by 16 per cent of women who are married or in union) and condoms (used by 13 per cent). In contrast, female sterilization and IUDs, used by 23 per cent and 15 per cent of women who are married or in union, respectively, are the mostly commonly used methods in developing countries (ibid.).

Traditional methods—most commonly, rhythm (abstinence during the fertile phase of the woman's periodic cycle) and withdrawal before ejaculation—are more popular in developed countries than in developing countries; they are used by 13 per cent of couples who are married or in union in developed countries compared with just 6 per cent in developing countries. The higher prevalence of use of traditional methods in developed countries accounts for much of the difference in contraceptive use between developed and developing countries (ibid.).

Contraceptive use has increased substantially over the past decade. The percentage using contraception increased by at least 1 percentage point per year in 56 per cent of all developing countries, and by at least 2 percentage points per year in 16 per cent of all developing countries. In Africa, the percentage of contraceptive users increased from 17 per cent in 1990 to 28 per cent in 2000; in Asia, from 57 per cent to 65 per cent; and in Latin America and the Caribbean, from 62 per cent to 74 per cent. The percentage of contraceptive users remained fairly stable in developed countries, where contraceptive prevalence is already high (ibid.).

Unmet need for family planning remains high in developing countries, despite the recent accelerated growth in the use of contraception. In sub-Saharan Africa in particular, an average of 23 per cent of women of reproductive age who are married or in union are believed to need family planning because they report that they want no more children or want to delay the next pregnancy by two years or more, but are not using contraception. In North Africa, Asia, and Latin America and the Caribbean, the unmet need for family planning is lower, at around 16 per cent. In Europe, that percentage is 6 per cent on average.

The spread among women of literacy, education, and empowerment leads to a rapid change in contraceptive practices. Contraception is even taking hold in traditionally religious high-fertility areas of the world. In southern Italy, for example, widespread access to contraceptive measures and a rapid rise in the median age of marriage has caused a decrease in expected births (Dalla Zuanna et al., 1998). Often, the decline in expected pregnancies makes unexpected pregnancies seem more problematic and, ironically, societies come to view both unplanned pregnancy and falling fertility as problems.

ENTERING PARENTHOOD YOUNG

Increasingly, public concern is focused on 'children having children'. Statistics Canada reports that 'During the last quarter century, there has been an overall decline in the teenage pregnancy rate in Canada, perhaps reflecting the availability of contraceptives, and the increased awareness of unprotected sex' (Dryburgh, 2001). In the late 1990s, the rate increased a little, but it remains much lower in Canada than in the United States (Baker, 1996).

Teen pregnancy rates vary enormously across the industrialized West. Teen pregnancy, for example, is rare in Sweden, where child-bearing among women below age 18 has almost disappeared. By contrast, the United States has the highest rate of unmarried teen pregnancy in the world—one-third of live births in 1990 were to teenaged mothers, for example (Baker, 1996).

Given their easy access to reproductive control, why would young men and women in North America 'choose' to reproduce? One unsubstantiated theory is that teens are confused by the messages of some religious groups, which may discourage contraceptive devices or measures. Another unproven possibility is that deeply ingrained cultural taboos against premarital sex lead most young people to not 'come prepared'. Meanwhile, the popular media show teens an exciting sexualized world where sexual activity is associated with adult freedom that appears to include neither self-control nor contraceptive measures.

A social stigma remains associated with single-motherhood. Some believe that teen pregnancy is a social problem that starts with not enough parental support. Young people with less support from their families are more likely to involve themselves in risky behaviours, including unprotected sex (Hanna and Jones, 2001).

A study in which pregnant or parenting adolescents were interviewed found four other factors that predict sexual behaviour that could lead to teenage pregnancy: pres-

---

Box 8.3   Social Construction: Why Do Teens Have Sex?

LINDSEY TANNER
Associated Press

CHICAGO—Teenagers whose iPods are full of music with raunchy, sexual lyrics start having sex sooner than those who prefer other songs, a study suggests. Whether it's hip-hop, rap, pop or rock, much of popular music aimed at teens contains sexual overtones, and its influence on their behaviour appears to depend on how the sex is portrayed, researchers found.

Songs depicting men as 'sex-driven studs', women as sex objects, and with explicit references to sexual acts are more likely to trigger early sexual behaviour than those where sexual references are more veiled and relationships appear more committed, the study found.

The study found that teens who said they listened to lots of music with degrading sexual messages were almost twice as likely to start having intercourse or other sexual activities within the following two years as were teens who listened to little or no sexually degrading music. Among heavy listeners, 51 per cent started having sex within two years, versus 29 per cent of those who said they listened to little or no such music.

Exposure to lots of sexually degrading music 'gives them a specific message about sex', said lead author Steven Martino, a researcher for Rand Corp. in Pittsburgh. Boys learn they should be relentless in pursuit of women and girls learn to view themselves as sex objects, he said. 'We think that really lowers kids' inhibitions and makes them less thoughtful' about sexual decisions and may influence them to make decisions they regret, he said.

The study, based on telephone interviews with 1,461 participants aged 12 to 17, appears in the August [2006] issue of *Pediatrics* . . . .

Source: *Globe and Mail*, at: <www.theglobeandmail.com/servlet/story/RTGAM.20060807.wsexy0807/BNStory/specialScienceandHealth/>. Copyright © 2006 The Associated Press. All rights reserved. The information contained in the AP News report may not be published, broadcast, rewritten or redistributed without the prior written authority of The Associated Press.

ence of a family member with a drinking problem, physical assault by a family member, (early) age of first drunkenness, and (early) age at first consented sexual experience (Kellogg et al., 1999). Cross-national research suggests that another source of the problem may be cultural. In large part, the problem is caused by extensive sexualization of the mass media combined with insufficient sexual education in the schools and poor access to contraception in the community.

In recent years, concern about adolescent single-parenting remains, despite a 50 per cent decline in the number of teen births. Part of the reason for concern is that adolescent motherhood is associated with socio-economic disadvantages for the mother and poor outcomes for the child. As well, '[l]ow birth weight has long been a public health concern because of its relationship to poor infant health and mortality, [and] it is mothers at the lower and upper ends of the age spectrum who have the highest rates of low birth weight babies' (Statistics Canada, 2005a).

Canadian research (Dahinten and Shapka, 2004) using data from the National Longitudinal Survey of Children and Youth finds a clear pattern of improvement in children's outcomes as mother's age at child-bearing increases. Also, teen mothers typically suffer disadvantages. For example, the average family income of mothers who had a first child as a teen was $25,000—half the national average. Their education was lower than that of older mothers. Teen mothers are much more likely to be single parents and not work outside the home.

For these and other reasons, teen mothers report lower levels of family functioning than older mothers. One in four teen mothers reports being depressed—twice the prevalence of mothers who had their first child in their late twenties (ibid.). Child-bearing during older adolescence strongly influences the likelihood that the resulting child will display a behavioural disorder, especially during preschool years, and have poor receptive vocabulary on entry to school (however, these effects are only partially attributable to the age of the mother).

People who enter parenthood unexpectedly are likely to find the parenting role stressful and their children difficult. Beyond this, adolescent women often have little understanding of the developmental milestones in their infants' behaviour. These mothers are themselves still forming their own identities, which can further aggravate the stress of parenting. Outside support often helps an adolescent mother to handle the demands her child poses. Researchers report that adolescent mothers receiving an intensive family support program provide higher-quality care for their infants than mothers who receive less intensive support (Luster et al., 1996). As well, societal support is also increasing. The Vancouver School Board, among others, currently offers the Teen Mothers Program, allowing adolescent mothers to complete their secondary school education while their children receive daycare arranged by the school board (see the Vancouver School Board website: www.vsb.bc.ca).

We know far less about the fathers of babies born to teen mothers. Using birth records, Millar and Wadhera (1997) found that more than 75 per cent of births to teen mothers involved men who are older, by an average of 4.1 years. A quarter of fathers are six or more years older than the teenage women they impregnated. These findings raise many questions about responsibility for pregnancy and contraception.

Likely, employment opportunities influence the father to stay with or leave the pregnant woman: he is more likely to stay if he can find a job to support the mother and child. Some contend that at the macro or societal level, teen pregnancy results from not enough educational opportunity, job opportunity, or career ambition, and perhaps a limited access to birth control and abortion services; and, at the micro level, that the problem of teen pregnancy results from poor parenting, including poor parental communication, the setting of a poor example, and poor guidance and backing. However, economic and other social factors beyond the control of the parent(s) are significant factors in teen pregnancy. Sexual coming of age among the poor is as fraught with difficulty as every other aspect of impoverished life.

Theories of the Family

As in other areas of sociology, the analysis of family life varies according to the perspective of the analyst. Different approaches to the study of families provide different explanations of why families evolve as they do and why problems arise in families.

The Structural-Functionalist Perspective

Functionalists view the family as a central institution in society. They see the family as a microcosm of society, with individual family members coming together in a unified and productive whole (Lehmann, 1994). In Talcott Parsons and Robert Bales's functionalist analysis (1955), the family's division of labour is the key to its success. In a traditional family, the husband of the household performs an instrumental role as the breadwinner, decision-maker, and source of authority and leadership, while the wife fulfills an expressive role as homemaker, nurturer, and emotional centre of the family. Though these roles of the husband and wife have changed since the 1950s, functionalists still view the family institution as accomplishing several important functions, including the regulation of sexual behaviour and reproduction, the provision of physical (food, shelter) and psychological (nurturance, learning) needs of its members, and the socialization of children.

Functionalism today surfaces in arguments about the naturalness or inevitability of certain family forms. For example, psychiatrists Ronald Immerman and Wade Mackey (1999) argue that almost all marriage systems across the world support monogamous pair bonding. In communities where people have multiple partners, sexually transmitted diseases increase. So do a variety of societal dysfunctions, such as out-of-wedlock births, infant morbidity, violent crime, and lower educational attainment. These outcomes reduce the ability of the community to compete with other societies that have maintained pair bonding. This, in turn, reduces the survival capacity of the community.

Others make structural arguments to show that cohabitation is inferior to traditional (legal) marriage. Linda Waite (2000) argues that cohabiting relationships are often less permanent, fail to provide the many benefits that marriage offers to both participants, are less likely to involve extended families, and provide less support for the cohabiting partners during a crisis.

Conflict and Feminist Theories

Unlike functionalists, conflict theorists do not assume that families operate as units, perform functions, or accomplish tasks for the good of society. Conflict theorists take a historical approach and focus on political and economic changes.

They note that with industrialization, families moved from being self-sustaining economic units (e.g., a farming household) to consumption units (e.g., a dual-income household that purchases shelter, food, clothing, services, and luxuries). In doing so, they

Child Care in Canada

- Statistics Canada found that, in 2002–3, 54 per cent of Canadian children received some care from someone other than their parents. That's up from 42 per cent in 1994–5.
- About 30 per cent of those children were enrolled in a daycare centre as their main care arrangement, but a growing number are now being cared for by relatives.
- Over the same eight-year period, the proportion of children cared for by a relative grew from 8 per cent to 30 per cent.
- The proportion of children who were looked after in someone else's home by a non-relative fell from 44 per cent to 30 per cent.
- The growth in the use of daycare is even more pronounced in rural areas. In 1994, 36.5 per cent of rural children were placed in some form of daycare. By 2001, that rate had grown to 50.5 per cent.

Source: CBC News Online (2005c).

became dependent on outside sources of income to meet their survival needs. This meant that working-class men had to sell their labour power to the bourgeoisie in exchange for an income. In this process, women gained exclusive control over (or, more accurately, were relegated to) the home, becoming responsible for child-rearing, food preparation, and the provision of emotional support. However, as both conflict and feminist theorists emphasize, women did this work without financial remuneration, despite the importance of the tasks. This amounted to exploitation of women that benefited their husbands' employers. Thus, sexual inequality increased under industrial capitalism. In short, gender inequality arises out of economic exploitation, not the need of 'society' or even of a given family for task differentiation based on gender.

There are historical reasons for this development, and for the association of this development with the rise of industrial capitalism. Feminist theorists argue that, just as factory workers depend on capitalists for a living wage, wives depend on their husbands. This dependence easily turned into subordination. Women have historically endured not only economic reliance on men in the household, but also political and social inferiority. For example, women did not receive the right to vote in Canada until 1918. The ideology of gender perpetuates the notion that men and women are fundamentally different, thereby justifying an unfair social order that benefits males over females. Though these patriarchal tendencies are very old, the capitalist economy affirmed them by providing men with preferential access to the labour market.

Symbolic Interactionism

As we have seen, interactionists focus on the micro level of sociological phenomena. With respect to families, symbolic interactionists study the ways members of a family interact with one another and how they resolve conflicts within the boundaries of their roles in the family. An important part of this process is the creation and revision of myths about family.

Like people in any social relationship, couples enter a marriage as separate individuals with distinct identities. However, as time passes, a married couple builds a shared definition of their family—its goals, identity, and values. They may even change their views about themselves as individuals to make them more consistent with the family subculture (Berger and Kellner, 1964). For example, a couple may develop stories about how they met and fell in love that are congruent with their current beliefs about their relationship. As children are born and the family grows larger, they may again revise their stories and identities to incorporate new roles and goals.

Symbolic interactionists also study how people view the institution of marriage overall and how they come to imbue it with values and meaning. Although modern Western culture stresses that love is the basis of a solid marriage, this has not always been the case. For much of the history of marriage, love—although undeniably experienced both within and without the bounds of wedlock—was not a necessary factor in deciding who wedded whom. Instead, people often based marriage on economic interests, complementarity of goals (including reproduction, inheritance, and so on), and companionship. They intended marriage to weld two people into a single economic unit of production, consumption, and reproduction. Only in the modern era have personal attraction and romantic love (as opposed to money or convenience) become the assumed basis for choosing a mate.

Table 8.2 Five Main Sociological Paradigms of the Family

Theory	Main Ideas
Structural Functionalism	■ Elements in society are all interrelated. ■ Families provide nurture and socialization. ■ A gendered division of domestic labour is functional. ■ The family is a central institution in society. ■ The family is a microcosm of society—individual family members come together in a unified and productive whole (Lehmann, 1994). ■ The familial division of labour is the key to a family's success (Parsons and Bales, 1955). ■ The regulation of sexual behaviour and reproduction, the provision of physical and psychological needs of members, and the socialization of children are important family functions. ■ Modern functionalism argues that certain family forms are natural or inevitable.
Conflict Theory	■ Social reproduction in families supports capitalism. ■ Families maintain the workforce without pay. ■ It should not be assumed that families operate as units, perform functions, or accomplish tasks for the good of society. ■ Families must be understood historically and placed in the context of political and economic changes. ■ Families are no longer self-sustaining economic units, but are consumption units dependent on outside sources of income for survival. ■ Working-class men had to sell their labour power to the bourgeoisie in exchange for an income, while women gained exclusive control over the home with responsibility for child-rearing, food preparation, and emotional support. All this work by women was without financial remuneration, despite the importance of the tasks, which amounted to exploitation of women that benefited their husbands' employers. Thus, sexual inequality increased under industrial capitalism. ■ Gender inequality arises out of economic exploitation, not the need of 'society' or even of a given family for task differentiation based on gender.
Feminism	■ The domestic division of labour is arbitrary. ■ Just as factory workers depend on capitalists for a living wage, wives depend on their husbands; the dependence is easily turned into subordination. ■ Women have historically endured not only economic reliance on men in the household, but also political and social inferiority. ■ The capitalist economy affirmed old patriarchal tendencies by providing men differential access to the labour market.
Symbolic Interactionism	■ Families involve continued interaction. ■ They are maintained by shared myths and beliefs. ■ Their main role is to socialize the next generation. ■ A married couple builds a shared definition of their family—its goals, identity, and values.
Social Constructionism	■ Family life is shaped by moral entrepreneurship. ■ Popular beliefs about families are media myths. ■ The development and use of family ideologies need to be studied and understood. ■ Moral entrepreneurs appeal to people's interest in and concern about their family lives, and so channel popular anxieties into hostility against minority groups—single mothers, gays and lesbians, and divorced people, to name a few.

Social constructionists focus on the development and use of family ideologies such as the 'family values' promoted by right-wing religious leaders and conservative politicians in the United States. By appealing to people's interest in and concern about their family lives, these moral and political entrepreneurs channel popular anxieties into hostility against such groups as single mothers, gays and lesbians, and divorced people. These antipathies produce support for political initiatives that reduce social welfare spending and coerce the behaviour of other minorities—for example, urban blacks in the United States or Aboriginals in Canada. By implication these groups become a focus for part of the outcry against those who are accused of failing to lead moral family lives or instill family values in their children.

Social Consequences of Family Life

Stressful elements in family life such as abuse, employment and unemployment, and divorce all have serious social and health outcomes that can affect the individual, his or her family, and society as a whole. Every family has problems to deal with. In this section, we will discuss some of the more common issues faced by families and their social outcomes.

A higher cost of living than one or two generations ago prevents most families from surviving comfortably on a single income. The desire of families after World War II for more and more of the products of industrialization and technology, coupled with the wartime acceptance of women working outside of the home, established a cycle of demand and affluence that encouraged suppliers to keep raising prices higher and higher. Eventually, the second income no longer provided luxuries but became vital to providing the revised norm of 'minimal' comfort. As a result, today usually both parents have to work to make enough money to cover the necessities, pay for the occasional luxury, and perhaps save enough for their children's post-secondary education and their own retirement. The demands of employers for workers' time are often in direct conflict with the needs of the family.

Findings from a major study of time stress among working parents suggest the size of the problem. When asked, 'Do you ever consider yourself a workaholic?', one-third of surveyed fathers and one-fifth of mothers answered yes. One out of three said his or her partner was a workaholic. Many admitted they experienced a problem of 'time famine' (Hochschild, 1997: 199–200).

A study of female hospital workers and their families finds spillovers from both paid work to the home and, to a lesser extent, from the home to work (Wharton and Erickson, 1995). Simple exhaustion is one of the most important impacts of work on family life. Work-induced emotional exhaustion—along with work overload and mood shifts—profoundly affects a person's state of mind. Along with family conflict, emotional exhaustion increases the likelihood that work will interfere with family life by disrupting spousal and parenting relationships (Leiter and Durup, 1996).

Since spillover produces a tendency for parental withdrawal from family activities after difficult workdays, parents reporting high work-to-family spillover are less knowledgeable about their children's daily lives. This applies only to fathers, however. Bumpus (2001) finds that fathers' (but not mothers') work-to-family spillover is associated with decreased knowledge about children's experiences. This relationship is mediated by marital love and father–child acceptance: when fathers report a high spillover, their marriages are on average less happy, which in turn is predictive of a less accepting father–child relationship and less knowledge about children's experiences. Said another way, parents are less knowledgeable when fathers' jobs are highly demanding and when they have younger boys or are less happily married. The negative effects of fathers' work stress are made worse by poor marital quality and having a younger son (Bumpus et al., 1999)

Data from the US Child Outcomes Study (Zaslow et al., 1999) point to more positive child outcomes across various measures of development for children of employed mothers in families with some history of welfare receipt. Employment yields an income that reduces family poverty, thus improving child health and educational outcomes. It also increases the mother's independence and equality, which improves her mental well-being. Employment, as well as income and control, benefits the mother's mental health (Davies and McAlpine, 1998).

Managing a career is difficult for women, especially if they are mothers of young children. As a result, many educated women today delay marriage, preferring to go to school, work, and achieve financial independence before bearing children. Others avoid marriage altogether, opting instead to have a career and aim for only those personal relationships that do not hinder their professional lives. The higher we look in the occupational hierarchy, in professional or managerial jobs, the more likely we are to find women who never married, who married and divorced, who married early but did not have children, or who married late and had few if any children (Houseknecht et al., 1987; Heathcote et al., 1997).

Whatever their education and career goals, women who marry and bear children usually face a **double shift**: modern women's dual roles as both breadwinners and homemakers. Several factors put particular pressure on the boundary between work and home life: (1) a spouse who often works overtime, (2) a bad work schedule, (3) a heavy workload, and (4) a troubled relationship with the boss. These work–home conflicts produce emotional exhaustion, psychosomatic health complaints, and sleep deprivation (Geurts et al., 1999). Parenthood and employment are not separate categories, but are woven together throughout life. More research needs to be done on the social and policy implications of making work and parenthood compatible.

Divorce

At the beginning of the twentieth century, divorce was rare in Canada. In 1900, a mere 11 divorces were registered (Snell, 1983, cited in Eichler, 1997: 10). People widely disapproved of divorce, as expressed both in religion and popular opinion and in the law that restricted it. Until 1968, adultery was the only ground for divorce. The Divorce Act in 1968 brought about a massive change in family behaviours. This law allowed judges to grant divorces on the grounds of 'marriage breakdown' after a couple had been separated for at least three years. Between 1968 and 1970, the number of divorces nearly doubled (Oderkirk, 1994). An amendment to the Divorce Act in 1985 reduced the minimum period of separation to one year.

In 1968, before the reforms, a marriage that finally ended in divorce lasted an average of 15 years. The liberalization of divorce laws shortened the process. At the beginning of the twenty-first century, the average was 12.7 years. Based on 1996 divorce rates, we expect 37 per cent of current Canadian marriages to end in divorce. In 2003, 70,828 Canadian couples divorced, up 1 per cent from 2002 and in step with the growth of population (Statistics Canada, 2005b). Canadian divorce rates are higher than

The Double Shift

People simply cannot afford to live without a full wage and often the only thing stopping women with children working more is lack of affordable childcare. . . . [W]orking women carry a double burden of being seen as the primary child carers and as a consequence suffer low pay and [fewer] opportunities in the workplace. But what is crucial is that most women see the benefits from waged work as being more than solely financial. Work increases social contact with other adults and a sense of collective experience . . . . Source: Judith Orr, 'Working Mothers: The Double Shift', Socialist Review no. 206 (Mar. 1997). At: <pubs. socialistreviewindex.org.uk/ sr206/orr.htm>.

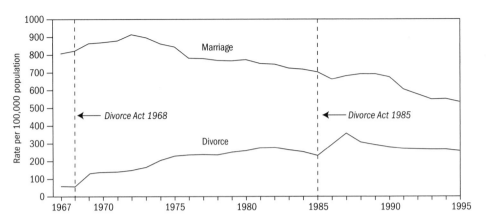

FIGURE 8.2 Canadian Marriage and Divorce Rates, 1967–95
Note: By 1995 cohabitation was becoming common enough that divorce was no longer a completely useful measure of union dissolution.
Source: <www.divorcerate.org/divorce-rates-in-canada.html>. Adapted from Statistics Canada, 'Marriage and Conjugal Life in Canada', 1991, Catalogue no. 91-534.

one finds in other Western nations: 2.6 divorces per 1,000 people, compared, for example, with 2.2 in Sweden and 2.0 in Germany, based on 1996 data (Ambert, 2002). However, the American divorce rate is nearly twice that of Canada. In 1996, there were 4.3 divorces per 1,000 people in the United States.

CONSEQUENCES OF DIVORCE

Divorce affects men and women differently because of gender inequalities in the wider society. Economically, divorce affects women much more negatively than men. A formal separation lowers women's standards of living by 73 per cent on average, but raises men's by 42 per cent (Mahoney, 1995: 18). Forty per cent of ex-wives lose half their family income following the separation compared to less than 17 per cent of ex-husbands (Arendell, 1995: 38). Custody of children is usually granted to mothers, compounding the economic burden on women. So, for women, not only is income reduced after the divorce, but that smaller income often must go towards caring for one or more dependants as well.

Taking on the role of primary caregiver also consumes a lot of time. Lone working mothers often report severe time stress and a feeling of being overwhelmed by responsibilities. Combining work, child-rearing, and household maintenance leaves little time to develop a social life. The alternative, giving up custody to the father, is usually unacceptable to the mother because she loves and wishes to be close to her children. As a lesser consideration, she would face the disapproving eye of a patriarchal society if she gave up custody.

Following a separation or divorce, men are usually better off financially than are women because they were the dominant income earners during the marriage and they continue to have larger salaries or wages after the divorce. Although their ex-wives' incomes are no longer available to them, the decrease in expenses partially offsets this loss. As well, men experience more freedom following a divorce, since children of a marriage usually live with the mother. Thus, men have more opportunities to work, travel, return to school, and explore other relationships.

The negative impact of divorce on children has also been well-documented. Much of the effect of divorce on children can be predicted by conditions that existed before the separation occurred, and 'at least as much attention needs to be paid to the processes that occur in troubled, intact families as to the trauma that children suffer after their parents separate' (Cherlin et al., 1991: 1388). Family and personal distress caused by conflict, poverty, or unemployment leads to less effective parenting—a complex notion that involves inadequate surveillance, lack of control over the child's behaviour, lack of warmth and support, inconsistency, and displays of aggression or hostility by parents or older siblings.

Depression is common among children of divorce, as are declines in academic performance, higher rates of emotional problems, and increased chance of anxious or anti-social behaviour (Roizblatt et al., 1997). These problems can continue into adulthood. Amato and Keith (1991), for instance, report that adult children of divorced parents register poorer psychological well-being (in the form of depression and low self-reported life satisfaction); lower educational attainment, income, and occupational prestige; an increased risk of undergoing a divorce themselves; and poorer physical health.

The debate over divorce and children's well-being has been especially fierce. Extreme positions on whether it causes harm have not given a clear picture of the results of growing up in a single-parent family or stepfamily (Cherlin, 1999).

Lone Parenthood

Single-parent families and young (teen) parents are at the highest risks of poverty and other disadvantage. Having said that, many women—and possibly men—are consciously deciding to parent alone and may be doing an excellent job.

Of the 1.1 million single parents enumerated in 1996, 58 per cent were separated or divorced, 22 per cent were single or never married, and 20 per cent were widowed. The vast majority, 83 per cent, were women (Vanier Institute, 2000: 70). Of Canadian marriages that dissolved in 1995, child custody was a concern in roughly 70 per cent of cases. In more than two out of three of these cases, judges granted mothers sole custody of their children (ibid.).

As we saw in Chapter 1, poverty is a continuing social problem, and the gender difference regarding custody is significant because female-headed lone-parent families are more likely to suffer from lower incomes—indeed, poverty—than are male-headed lone-parent families or two-parent families. In 1998, lone-parent families headed by women made up the largest fraction of all low-income families. Female-headed families were more than twice as likely as male-headed families to be living in poverty (42.0 per cent versus 17.5 per cent) (Glossop and Mirabelli, 2002).

The number of Canadian lone-parent families has increased dramatically since the 1970s—almost 250 per cent between 1971 and 1996, compared with an overall increase of only 55 per cent in the total number of Canadian families (Vanier Institute, 2000). These rates mark a return to percentages seen in the early decades of the twentieth century. In 1931, for example, 14 per cent of Canadian families were headed by one parent, compared with a similar 15 per cent in 1996 (ibid.). However, the reasons for lone parenthood have changed. In the first half of the twentieth century most single-parent households were a result of the death of a spouse. In the second half of the century, they were mainly the result of separation, divorce, or non-marriage (Oderkirk and Lochhead, 1992).

Caring for the Elderly

Canada's population is aging as the result of lowered fertility and general increases in life expectancy for both men and women. In 2000, 12.5 per cent of the Canadian population was 65 years old or older (Bélanger et al., 2001: 9). With continued declines in fertility, this percentage will continue to rise. The same trend can be seen in all Western societies, especially in Europe.

With the greying of the population, concerns have increased about the costs of caring for an aging population (McDaniel, 1994). In the last few decades, governments have made an effort to move elder care outside institutional settings, making it increasingly the responsibility of informal caregivers, most often female family members (McDaniel, 1996). Health-care services previously offered in institutional settings are now being performed in community health centres, day clinics, and people's own homes. This has created a difficulty for elderly people, especially in rural Canada. Alongside limited formal health-care supports in these areas, depopulation, aging communities, smaller family sizes, limited community resources, and volunteer burnout have resulted in fewer informal community supports (Blakley, 1999).

This development, in turn, has led to widespread concerns that the middle-aged children of elderly parents will be 'squeezed' or 'sandwiched' by the multiple roles and duties associated with dependent children, elderly parents, and work (Martin-Matthews, 2000). Women show greater engagement with caregiving and more willingness to travel to provide help, even to the point of moving residentially (Hallman and Joseph, 1999). Living nearby and being without siblings may force men into being more involved in the care of aged parents (Campbell and Martin-Matthews, 2000a, 2000b).

Elder care can drastically affect personal time for other family relationships, as well as for work and leisure. As we saw in Chapter 7, 42 per cent of Canadian women aged 40–4 care for elderly parents while raising their own children and working outside the home. In fact, however, until parents reach the age of 75, the flow of support favours the children: they receive more help from parents than they give to them (Spitze and Logan, 1992). Using data from Canada, the United States, the United Kingdom, West Germany, and Japan, Harald Kunemund and Martin Rein (1999) found that the giving of services by older people to their adult children increases the chance they will receive help from them. In this way, generous welfare systems that give resources to elderly people help to increase rather than to undermine family solidarity.

Most Canadian seniors continue to live on their own well into advanced age, and most of the care they receive comes not from their children, but from other members of the same generation, usually a spouse (Martin-Matthews, 2000). Friends and neighbours may also provide essential help when seniors live alone (Martel and Legare, 2000).

The Boomerang Effect

In her recent book *The Boomerang Age* (2005), Canadian sociologist Barbara Mitchell notes that important domestic changes are taking place in the lives of young adults in Western industrialized societies. Today's young people often move through a larger variety of family-related roles, statuses, and living arrangements.

Among the most prominent changes is the rise of 'boomerang kids'—young adults returning to the parental home after their first entrance into the adult world. According to the General Social Survey in 2001, 33 per cent of men and 28 per cent of women between the ages of 20 and 29 have returned home at least once after previously moving away. The number of young adults returning home has been increasing year by year, reaching 41 per cent in 2001. As the *Globe and Mail* reported, there is increasing evidence of a 'crowded nest' syndrome. About 41 per cent of young Canadians aged 20–9 were living with their parents in 2001. Twenty years ago, the proportion was only 27 per cent. Statistics Canada analysts offer several explanations: adult children returning home after failed marriages, delayed marriage, more people in their twenties still in school, and the difficulty of those young adults in finding jobs (*Globe and Mail*, 2002).

Boyd and Pryor (1989) report that couples who thought that their children had grown up and 'flown away' are now discovering the family home (nest) being refilled with adult children who are returning to school (or have never left school), having trouble finding or keeping jobs, getting separated or divorced, or even having children of their own.

The return of grown children to their parental home, usually for financial reasons, is an especially vivid example of the generational transfer of wealth from older to younger adults. Children move back home with their parents after an often lengthy period on their own as students, workers, and, often, married people. A significant shift in occupational opportunities or marital status may be enough of a jolt to the young person's finances to send him/her back into the family nest (Mitchell et al., 2000). Parental satisfaction with the arrangement is greater when children provide support in return, are more autonomous, and are closer to completing adult roles (Mitchell, 1998). Normatively, adulthood involves completing one's education, finding a job that pays an income, mating with a partner, setting up a separate household, and (often) producing children.

The future may become like the past: some families live in refilled nests only out of need and do not see themselves as creating anything new, merely pooling housing and resources to survive. Others, however, may see huge creative possibilities in refilled nests, such as for child care by grandparents while parents work; for sharing housework among more family members; for reducing environmental problems by having fewer accommodations; for developing new ways of intergenerational caring for elders.

Domestic Violence

Family or domestic violence includes domestic and intimate-partner abuse, child and adolescent physical and sexual abuse, and elder abuse (discussed in Chapter 7). Such violence is responsible for a significant portion of intentional injury recorded in Canada. As such, it is a major social and health problem (Kaplan, 2000).

Child abuse can take the form of physical or mental harm, sexual abuse, neglect, or maltreatment. Of these, neglect is the most common form of reported child abuse. Children also run the risk of sexual abuse, more commonly by a stepfather or a boyfriend of the mother than by their biological father. Stepfathers are seemingly less controlled by the same culturally imposed incest taboos than are biological fathers (Blankenhorn, 1995).

Abused children often display anti-social behaviour, aggression, low self-esteem, depression, and poor school performance. In adulthood, self-destructive behaviours often continue, including depression, low self-esteem, anxiety, and an increased risk of alcohol or drug abuse and suicide. Children who witnessed or were victims of physical abuse have an increased risk of becoming abusers themselves when they enter adulthood (Gelles and Conte, 1991).

Cross-National Data on Intimate-Partner Violence during Pregnancy

- The proportion of women ever pregnant and physically abused during at least one pregnancy exceeded 5 per cent in 11 of 15 international sites surveyed.
- The lowest figure was 1 per cent in Japan and the highest was 28 per cent in provincial Peru.
- Between a quarter and half of the women who were physically abused during pregnancy were kicked or punched in the abdomen.
- Between 11 and 44 per cent of ever-abused ever-pregnant women reported being assaulted during pregnancy except in Japan, where the figure was 8 per cent.
- In all countries surveyed, over 90 per cent were abused by the biological father of the child the woman was carrying, most of whom were living with the woman at the time.
- While the majority of those beaten during pregnancy had experienced physical violence before, between 13 per cent (Ethiopia) and approximately 50 per cent (urban Brazil and Serbia and Montenegro) said they were beaten for the first time during pregnancy.
- The majority of women who experienced violence both before and during a pregnancy in all countries reported that, during the last pregnancy in which they were abused, the violence was the same or somewhat less severe or frequent than before the pregnancy.
- The results support findings from both developing and industrialized countries that pregnancy can be a time of increased protection from violence, but this is not consistent across all cultures.

Source: WHO (2005).

Even after controlling for other socio-demographic variables, poverty, substance abuse, and (young) maternal age are strong predictors of confirmed reports of all types of child maltreatment. Young mothers and impoverished mothers are at particular risk of abusing their children. This suggests that we need a comprehensive approach to the problem of child abuse, one that lessens the economic stress on young mothers while improving their parenting skills (Lee and George, 1999).

In regard to partner abuse, also discussed in Chapter 5, both married and unmarried couples inflict violence on each other. One study found severe violence to be five times more likely among cohabiting couples than among married couples (Yllo and Straus, 1981). Further, Douglas Brownridge and Shiva Halli (2001) have found that Canadian women who cohabit, those who cohabited with someone other than their husband before getting married, and those who did not cohabit before marriage differ in the prevalence of their victimization by violent partners. Research confirms that cohabitors are still more likely than spouses to engage in violent relationships (Jackson, 1996).

Other variables likely to distinguish men who batter their wives are the presence of alcohol abuse, low education, frequent arguments with the spouse, and frequent drug use. Abusing husbands typically also have a (childhood) background of family violence and marital arguments (Coleman et al., 1980).

Many women have trouble leaving an abusive relationship or even seeking help when they are in the abusive relationship. As women, they typically earn less than their husbands, so, in the absence of alternative support networks, leaving is often not a financially viable option. Should they divorce, they are often left with the care of the children and a lack of financial child support from the children's father. Thus, the co-dependency of abused people is as often a financial problem as it is a psychological or emotional one.

Often, psychologically and physically abusive men fear the loss of their partner, whom they consider their sexual and emotional property. Men are more likely to batter—or kill—to protect what they think of as their sexual property, whereas women are likely to batter or kill only to protect themselves. Men are also prone to kill themselves after killing their 'property'. Women kill their partners because the partner has battered them systematically and they fear being battered even more. Compared with non-battered women, battered women use more violence, receive lower levels of social support, and experience higher levels of self-blame. Battered women, therefore, are more likely to use violence against their spouse when they feel they are receiving little social support, and even if they feel they are to blame for the conflict (Barnett et al., 1996).

Same-sex relationships are also subject to partner abuse. Lesbians and transsexual people are not always comfortable in women's shelters, as they may experience homophobic violence from heterosexual women. Shelter clients, for their part, having escaped from abusive relationships with a man, may not feel safe being with a transsexual person.

Box 8.4   Personal Experience: Women and HIV

Women are not 'victims, vessels and vectors' of HIV but leaders helping to turn the tide of the epidemic, the 16th International AIDS Conference heard on Monday in Toronto. Louise Binder, who founded and co-chairs the Canadian Treatment Action Council, shared the success stories of women and girls from around the world at the Aug. 13–18 event, which has lured more than 30,000 participants from around the world.

Binder, a lawyer who was diagnosed with HIV, pointed out that a major part of the HIV pandemic stems from power imbalances between men and women, such as in marriages where the women may not be willing or able to insist their husbands use condoms. She pointed to the courage of a woman who asked an HIV prevention conference in 1991 why, if people can be put on the moon, no one has found a way for women to protect themselves. Binder said the question led two other women to put the wheels in motion to develop a microbicide, a virus-killing gel that can be put into the vagina before sex. There are now 92 potential microbicides in development, including five in clinical trials in 19 countries. 'Staring in the face of massive injustice, women are at the forefront of success', Binder said.

Binder shared a number of success stories involving women, including:

- In Rwanda, where 4,500 HIV-positive women were each given a chicken and two roosters. The women—nearly half of whom were raped during the genocide of the early 1990s—used it to gain a source of protein and products to sell as they received treatment with antiretrovirals, peer education, counselling, and testing services. The combined approach had a 90 per cent adherence rate.
- In South Africa, a program to reduce violence against women by their intimate partners reduced the risk of violence by 55 per cent, helping cut HIV infections. It combined training on gender roles, domestic violence, and HIV by engaging men and youth. It also showed how combining HIV with other health issues and using education, training, employment, and economic security for women is urgently needed 'to save this generation of girls and women and the next ones', Binder said.

Binder said that applying the 'lived experience' of women and girls shows HIV is the result and not the cause of inequity, and challenges the myth that cultural and religious practices pose insurmountable barriers.

Source: CBC News Online (2006).

As well, lesbians have little safety from their violent partners in a women's shelter that is open to women. Gay men have no shelters they can use other than homeless shelters, which offer little security from abusive partners and no long-term housing.

Health Consequences of Family Life

Research shows that marriage usually adds to people's health and happiness, especially for men, and especially when contrasted with divorce and separation. However, what matters is the stability and quality of the relationship, not its legal status. Some common aspects of family life are not healthy at all.

So, for example, a recent study (Choi, 2006) found that being married compared to being single was associated with lower odds of mortality. However, this effect was mainly indirect, in the sense that marriage buffers the harmful effects of poverty and other disadvantage. When the moderating effect of marriage on the SES-health association was tested, being married compared to being single was found to protect against the negative effects of lower income on survival and worsened functioning, particularly for men. Even being in a high-disagreement marriage (compared to being single) was found to buffer the income-mortality gradient for men. However, among the married, both men and women who experienced an increase in marital disagreement were more vulnerable to the negative effects of education and income stratification on their health.

A Canadian study (Strohschein et al., 2005) likewise confirmed the mental health advantage of marriage and revealed that the short-term effects of moving into and out of marriage on psychological distress are similar for men and women. However, again, the quality of the marriage matters a great deal. There is also some evidence that staying unhappily married is more detrimental than divorcing, as people in low-quality marriages are less happy than individuals who divorce and remarry. They also have lower levels of life satisfaction, self-esteem, and overall health than individuals who divorce and remain unmarried (Hawkins and Booth, 2005).

Divorce and Remarriage

Some health problems, especially those that are psychological in nature, commonly affect divorced adults and children of divorce. As we have said, divorce increases the risk of poverty for many women, resulting in health risks linked to poor nutrition, unsanitary living conditions, and lack of access to health-care services. Far more common are emotional problems resulting from divorce. Usually these are short-term difficulties arising from the stressful change in adapting to a new living arrangement. Rates of psychiatric care, suicide rates, accident rates, and post-marital stress are all higher among divorced men than women, although women are more likely than men to report emotional problems such as depression (Ambert, 1982; Gove, 1970).

Some observers have added that research on emotional problems among divorcees should be treated with some caution because divorced individuals who experience emotional problems after the divorce may already have had emotional problems before the divorce. These problems may have led to marriage dissolution rather than the other way around (Rushing, 1979).

Divorce is an emotionally draining and stressful experience. This is not surprising because divorce results in the loss of a sexual partner and companion, possible decrease in contact with children, lower financial standing, single parenthood, and so on. Children of divorced parents have more substance-using friends and fewer coping and social skills than children whose parents are married (Neher and Short, 1998). Some research suggests that parental divorce increases the risk of poor mental health in adulthood (Cherlin et al., 1998).

One contentious issue concerns the circumstances under which it is in the child's best interest for parents to separate rather than stay together. An investigation by Jaap Dronkers (1996) examined whether serious conflicts between non-divorced parents have a stronger negative effect on the well-being of their children (in terms of use of drugs, illness, violence and crime, mental health, etc.) than living in a single-mother family caused by divorce.

Three of Dronkers's findings are relevant to the current discussion. First, the well-being of children living in single-mother families was higher than that of children living in two-parent homes marked by a great deal of parental conflict. Second, the well-being of children living in single-mother families with a low level of parental conflict and with a high degree of contact with the non-residential father was still lower than that of children living in two-parent families with an equally low level of parent conflict. Finally, the degree of parental conflict after divorce was more important for the well-being of the children than was contact with the departed father. These results suggest that, as measured by well-being outcomes, divorce may the best alternative for children, depending on the parental conflict in the marriage. Conflict is bad for children—worse than divorce, it seems.

Researchers have also linked health outcomes to single parenthood for both mothers and their children. Teenage women and unmarried women are less likely to seek prenatal care and more likely than older women and married women to smoke, drink alcohol, and take drugs. Often, negative health effects are caused by the poverty that many teenage mothers find themselves living in. As well, the need for two incomes among married households has created a shortage of time, which may lead indirectly to further health problems for families. Sylvia Hewlett links the time crunch experienced by today's working parents with a lack of child supervision and, as a result, higher rates of developmental impairment; young people today are more likely to 'underperform at school, commit suicide, need psychiatric help, suffer a severe eating disorder, bear a child out of wedlock, take drugs, be a victim of a violent crime' (Hewlett, 1991: 81).

Work as a Family Health Problem

As we have noted, paid work is a key source of stress. Questionnaire data from nearly 80,000 employees from 250 work sites in the United States reveal the greatest sources of stress in people's lives are job, finances, and family (Jacobson et al., 1996). Once they become parents, men and women approach the workplace in different ways. Fathers are more likely to work extended hours when possible. Mothers work shorter hours and need more flexibility in their working arrangements. Mothers working full-time are more likely to ask for and receive parental leave from their employers than are either mothers working part-time or fathers.

When work increases the stress on a husband, it increases the likelihood of hostile marital interactions. In that way, stress reduces the quality of both marital and family functioning (Larson et al., 1994). As work increasingly interferes with family life, both emotional and practical supports within the family weaken.

Solutions to Family Problems

Work–Family Solutions

Many families suffer from the conflict between work life and family life. Currently, efforts are being made to solve this problem, with variable success. Arlie Hochschild finds, however, that even within family-friendly companies that offer their workers various programs designed to increase the time available to spend with family, few employees took advantage of the programs.

Even though many workers state a wish to cut back on their 'workaholism' and spend more time with spouses and children, 'programs that allowed parents to work undistracted by family concerns were endlessly in demand, while policies offering shorter hours that allowed workers more free or family time languished. . . . Only flex-time, which rearranged but did not cut back on hours of work, had any significant impact on the workplace' (Hochschild, 1997: 25–6).

Three explanations have been offered to account for these worker preferences. One is that workers cannot afford to cut back on work hours, despite their wishes to the contrary. This is most obviously true among lower-tier workers whose combined household incomes bar either partner from scaling back to meet family needs. However, this theory does not explain why top-level executives, whose salaries are large enough to allow the adoption of a shorter workweek, also choose against such policies as job-sharing and part-time work.

A second explanation is that workers choose not to use family-friendly programs because they are afraid of being laid off. Although company policies often encourage employees to spend more time with their families, workers doubt the sincerity of such offers, especially since the policies are devised by top-level executives concerned with public relations and company image and are carried out by practical-minded middle managers and supervisors concerned with meeting quotas, budgets, and deadlines. This argument implies that family-friendly programs are often mere ornaments designed to soothe external critics but not to solve workers' problems.

A third explanation is that despite what workers say about wanting to spend more time with their families, they find the time spent at work is often more pleasant and rewarding than time spent at home. In her three-year study of a top US company, Hochschild (1997) found that the duties of home life—caring for the children, sharing household duties, trying to preserve intimacy and love with one's spouse, and so on—were often very stressful. As a result, one's family becomes in many ways like work—in fact, a 'second shift'.

For these reasons, work-based solutions to the family–work issue are helpful, but they must be fine-tuned, made more widely available, and accepted more widely by workers and management. At the same time, families need to seek new answers through reorganizing domestic work.

Caregiving Solutions

Caregiving is a fundamentally social activity, and increasingly, it is a family activity. Social support networks are important for caregivers and care recipients alike. Clear and continuing communication between informal and formal caregivers, on the one hand, and health-care and social service providers, on the other, is a necessity. Family and community organization is central to good caregiving.

Rosalie Kane and colleagues (1999) followed the experiences of family caregivers of older people hospitalized for stroke or hip fracture in three US cities. The researchers studied the families for one year after the hospitalization, tracking the demands that providing care placed on the families and how families responded to those demands. They found the primary caregiver—often aged 65 or older—regularly spent 20 hours or more every week caring for the relative. What surprised the researchers was the variety of ways that families reorganized to meet these new demands.

Perhaps the most striking information to come from this study was that the difficulties that caregivers reported facing were related less to specific task performances than they were to dealing with feelings, managing time, and adjusting to changing relationships and life plans. This tells us that understanding how caregiving affects a family and its organization might significantly contribute to efforts to help families deal with the many problems associated with long-term care. Once we understand how some families effectively reorganize to provide care, it will become possible to help other families trying to do the same.

Researchers must seek information that may lead to solutions to problems of family organization and restructuring around home-care duties. As well, researchers must determine how much and what kinds of public support—services and funding—families need in order to provide their members with desirable levels of health care, and they must communicate this information to relevant policy-makers.

Solutions to Family Violence

We can learn a great deal from research about the best ways to intervene to solve problems of family stress and violence. First, violence is a major factor causing women to leave their marriages and children to leave their parents' home. Second, programs that attempt to address abuse directly—such as civil restraining orders, treatment programs for batterers, and policies requiring mandatory arrest and no dropped charges—are usually not effective in solving the problem of domestic violence (Davis and Smith, 1995), but they are a necessary first step in protecting the woman and any children in the family. By contrast, treatments aimed at reducing alcohol and drug abuse may make a long-term difference to the likelihood of future violence (O'Farrell and Murphy, 1995; Brannen and Rubin, 1996).

Third, problems like stress and violence require active solution-making. If we want to reduce family stresses, we must create a society that is family-friendly, with increased social support and practical assistance to working parents with small children. Fourth, research shows us that the health and social service provisions are inadequate. Fifth, research shows us that personal lives, and families, are increasingly diverse. Recently arrived immigrant and refugee women, for example, have needs that differ markedly from battered women in the general population by involving language, cultural, and immigration issues (Huisman, 1996). Gay men and lesbians are less likely than heterosexual women to use battered-women services that were designed for male–female relationships.

In the end, however, we must recognize there will be no major decline in the violence against family members until societies reduce the stresses on family members, place greater personal value on all people, and treat all people with respect and dignity—especially children, women, elderly people, and sexual and visible minorities. Societies must also reject the cultural justifications for domestic violence and deprive violent people of opportunities to hide or repeat their behaviour. Ending domestic violence is a societal project no less complex than dealing with unemployment, illiteracy, AIDS, or any other recognized social problem.

Individual Solutions

Families can be helpful in overcoming life's troubles. To make the home more sympathetic and less stressful, husbands and male common-law partners can increase their presence in the domestic area. They can accept that just earning an income is not a sufficient contribution to their family's well-being. A complete and equal contribution will also have to include providing help in raising the children, performing household chores, and supporting their partners' ambitions.

The stresses of divorce include economic hardship, periods where parents are undergoing adjustment, interpersonal conflict, and parental loss. Developing resources and protections can reduce the negative effect of these stresses. Higher levels of coping support a greater optimism about the future, fewer financial problems, greater confidence in parenting ability, and a more satisfactory relationship with the former spouse (O'Leary et al., 1996).

Factors that reduce the adverse effect of divorce on children include a strong and clear sense that both parents still love them, an understanding that they are not to blame for the divorce, and regular visits with the non-custodial parent. Children of divorce may need some help with irrational beliefs about divorce and with feelings of sadness, guilt, and anxiety (Skitka and Frazier, 1995). Involved and caring parents can help a child adjust to divorce. Parental distance, on the other hand, is likely to produce maladjustment. Parental conflict has a bad effect in both intact and divorced families.

At the same time, we must not exaggerate the extent or permanence of harm done. In some instances, divorce may be in the best interest both of the spouses and of their children. Though divorce may sometimes cause problems, it also often solves problems. It may even bring benefits. People whose parents divorced during their adolescent years display a much higher moral development than those whose unhappy parents did not divorce (Kogos and Snarey, 1995). Underlying the development of moral judgement is an increased perspective-taking, developed in children of divorce who witness differences in opinions between their parents.

Violence is a major factor causing women to leave marriages. Often, violence continues throughout the separation and divorce process, affecting negotiations for assets and custody (Kurz, 1995). At the societal level, legal protective measures need to be put in place to ensure that this isn't the case. Where these support mechanisms are insufficient, victims of violence need to come forward and seek help. They may have to leave the home and relationship to do so.

Concluding Remarks

There can be little doubt that many people have turned their backs on the traditional, idealized family of 50 years ago. Today, people are getting married later in life and having fewer children. The fraction of childless couples has also increased. Closely related to this trend has been an increase in the number of couples who cohabit. The divorce rate has increased dramatically in the last few decades. Yet most young people continue to come together in long-term relationships and work to make them survive.

Although more women have been entering the workforce, women still do more housework than men in dual-income households. This so-called double shift has harmful health outcomes, and places stress on the relationships between spouses and between parents and children.

As we have seen, families often have to deal with serious problems. The negative consequences of divorce, both emotional and financial, tend to be greatest for women and children. One-seventh of all Canadian families are single-parent households. Women head about 90 per cent of these single-parent families, which are more prone to financial and emotional strain. However, most families, single-parent or not, are experiencing financial and emotional strain these days. Family violence is more common than many people recognize. Although women and men are just as likely to take part in violence, women are the ones hurt most often.

QUESTIONS FOR CRITICAL THOUGHT

1. It is an unfortunate fact that teenage mothers constitute a significant portion of single parents. They are young and alone in struggling to support their child, and also lack the earning power of men and are at much greater risk of impoverishment than single fathers. The Internet provides a wealth of information on teenage pregnancy, offering social support, resources, and statistics, as well as personal testimonies. Isolate one such case and record what it must be like for that specific teenager to be a single mother. What issues does she deal with every day? Who is there for support? What is the role of the father in raising the child? Imagine a day in the life of a teenage parent.

2. A myth of suburbia has permeated society's collective consciousness since the 1950s. A nostalgic wish for block parties, green grass, a new car, and nourishing dinners brought steaming from the kitchen by a smiling mother shaped the ideology of the perfect nuclear family for decades. However, a lot has changed with the portrayal of the family since then. Examine a TV show like *The Simpsons* and ask yourself if this is an accurate portrayal of the family in the twenty-first century. If it is, how so? And if not, where is it wrong? Be detailed in your analysis by considering the roles of specific characters within the family. How are family relationships portrayed?

3. Families around the world were not created equal. The families in many cultures do not fit Westernized notions of who is considered 'family'. Look in anthropological studies and research family structure in different cultures. Who lives in the household? Are the structures matrilineal or patrilineal? Contrast with our own dominant notion of family.

4. Undoubtedly women today are pursuing post-secondary education and seeking occupational careers and financial independence. However, most women still want to raise families and play a major role in child-rearing. For some, the daycare that would be necessary for both parents to be at work all day is not an option. Thus, there is a conflict for women between wanting to raise a family and aiming for a full-time career where starting a family may be seen as a disadvantage to the company. How might this conflict be resolved? Should the government further develop maternity-leave programs? Or is this just an unavoidable conflict for females? How has the role of 'supermom' changed with more women in the labour force?

5. Most often, abusive situations are not reported by the victims. Why do women choose not to report such events? Discuss how statistics might not be as representative as they claim to be. Research a trauma hotline; contact the hotline and ask what kind of calls they get and how they help victims of domestic, sexual, drug, or alcohol abuse.

RECOMMENDED READINGS

Lourdes Benería and Shelley Feldman, eds, *Unequal Burden: Economic Crisis, Persistent Poverty, and Women's Work* (Boulder, Colo.: Westview Press, 1992). The contributors draw connections between some of the social problems we have addressed within the family as they relate to the international economy. Most interesting among the articles is one regarding the Mexican debt crisis, in which Benería relates the debt crisis to familial adaptations through increased women's work and a change in the actual social problems that develop within families.

Cynthia Fuchs Epstein and Arne Kalleberg, eds, *Fighting for Time: Shifting Boundaries of Work and Social Life* (New York: Russell Sage Foundation, 2004). This work explores the changes in time spent at work and the consequences of those changes for individuals and families.

William N. Eskridge Jr, *Equality Practice: Civil Unions and the Future of Gay Rights* (New York: Routledge, 2002). Eskridge describes the evolution of gay rights movements and the development of statutes legalizing civil unions for same-sex couples. State recognition of same-sex unions in Denmark, the Netherlands, Canada, Germany, and France are described, with interview data from legislators and state officials.

Marion Lynn, ed., *Voices: Essays on Canadian Families* (Toronto: Nelson Canada, 1996). This volume offers contemporary Canadian families an analytical mirror in which to view themselves. The articles emphasize the meaning of trends in the Canadian family and the attitudes that accompany these changes.

Meg Luxton, *More Than a Labour of Love: Three Generations of Women's Work in the Home* (Toronto: Women's Press, 1980). Luxton's work shows some of the changes in Canadian rural society in the last 100 years, using interviews from Flin Flon, Manitoba. She includes insightful chapters regarding women's feelings towards the sexual exchange in their marriage as well as a chapter on housework. The technological changes associated with these two areas of women's family life cause fewer attitudinal changes than one might expect.

Richard A. Settersten, Frank F. Furstenberg, and Ruben G. Rumbaut, eds, *On the Frontier of Adulthood: Theory, Research, and Public Policy* (Chicago: University of Chicago Press, 2005). This work shows that traditional transitions into adulthood in post-industrial societies—leaving home, finishing school, starting work, and having a family—are becoming more prolonged, ambiguous, and disordered. Historical and contemporary data are drawn from longitudinal studies in the US, Canada, and Western Europe.

Kath Weston, *Families We Choose: Lesbians, Gays, Kinship* (New York: Columbia University Press, 1991). Looking at the contemporary experiences of gays and lesbians in the United States, Weston develops a new and looser concept of the family, which she sees exemplified in the gays and lesbians she interviews.

Chester A. Winton, *Children as Caregivers: Parental and Parentified Children* (Boston: Allyn & Bacon, 2003). Children can develop into caregivers in their family in two ways: (1) as parents to their siblings (parental children) or (2) as parents to their impaired parents (parentified children). This can happen in families with substance abuse problems, large size, single parents, military members, immigrants, incarcerated members, and physical or mentally ill members. Some caregiving by children is normative, especially in non-European cultures, but excessive parentification is destructive.

Recommended Websites

National Clearinghouse on Family Violence

www.hc-sc.gc.ca/hppb/familyviolence

The National Clearinghouse on Family Violence (NCFV) is a resource centre for those seeking information about violence within the family. It provides a number of publications that deal with violence against children, women, and older adults. The NCFV website also allows visitors to search its online library for books and video aids on family violence.

Family Service Canada

www.familyservicecanada.org

Founded in 1982, Family Service Canada is a not-for-profit national voluntary organization representing the concerns of families and family service agencies across Canada. It provides a wide range of services and programs to individuals and families, designed to assist and strengthen people in their relationships, both in times of crisis and in day-to-day living.

Childcare Resource and Research Unit

www.childcarecanada.org

The Childcare Resource and Research Unit seeks to further the idea of publicly funded, not-for-profit early childhood daycare. It provides information on past, current, and future research projects on child care, and also provides links to governmental policies in other countries regarding child care. The CRRU website also provides a resource section containing past CRRU publications, print and web resources, and links relating to the topic of child care.

Glossary

Double shift Modern women's dual roles as breadwinner and homemaker.

Extended family More than two generations of relatives living together in a household. The arrangement often includes grandparents, aunts, uncles, and dependent nephews and nieces.

Family A group of people related by kinship or similar close ties in which the adults assume responsibility for the care and upbringing of their natural or adopted children.

Members of a family support one another financially, materially, and emotionally.

Nuclear family A family unit comprising one or two parents and any dependent children who live together in one household separate from relatives.

Patriarchy Male dominance that is justified in a society's system of values. This dominance is tied to the ideology of gender and can be found in practically every society.

References

Amato, Paul R., and Bruce Keith. 1991. 'Parental Divorce and Adult Well-Being: A Meta-analysis', *Journal of Marriage and the Family* 53: 43–58.

Ambert, Anne-Marie. 1982. 'Differences in Children's Behavior towards Custodial Mothers and Custodial Fathers', *Journal of Marriage and the Family* 44: 73–86.

———. 2002. *Divorce: Facts, Causes, and Consequences*, rev. edn. Ottawa: Vanier Institute of the Family. Available at: <www.vifamily.ca/cft/divorce/divorcer.htm>; accessed 24 Mar. 2003.

Arendell, Terry. 1995. *Fathers and Divorce*. Thousand Oaks, Calif.: Sage.

Arnup, Katherine. 1999. 'Out in This World: The Social and Legal Context of Gay and Lesbian Families', *Journal of Gay and Lesbian Social Services* 10, 1: 1–25.

Associated Press. 2005. 27 Jan. At: <www.religiousconsultation .org/News_Tracker/UN_says_fertility_rate_declining. htm>.

Baker, Maureen. 1996. 'Introduction to Family Studies: Cultural Variations and Family Trends', in Baker, ed., *Families: Changing Trends in Canada*, 3rd edn. Toronto: McGraw-Hill Ryerson, 3–34.

Barnett, Ola W., Tomas E. Martinez, and Mae Keyson. 1996. 'The Relationship between Violence, Social Support, and Self-Blame in Battered Women', *Journal of Interpersonal Violence* 11: 221–33.

BBC News Online. 2005. 'Canada Senate Backs Gay Marriage', 20 July. <http://news.bbc.co.uk/1/hi/world/americas/ 4699411.stm>; accessed 9 Jan. 2006.

Bélanger, Alain, Yves Carrière, and Stéphane Gilbert. 2001. *Report on the Demographic Situation in Canada 2000* (Catalogue no. 91–209–XPE). Ottawa: Statistics Canada.

Berger, Peter, and Hansfried Kellner. 1964. 'Marriage and the Construction of Reality', *Diogenes* 46: 1–32.

Blakley, Bonnie M. 1999. 'The Impact of Health Care Reforms on Elderly Caregivers in Rural Canada', Society for the Study of Social Problems, conference paper.

Blankenhorn, David. 1995. *Fatherless America: Confronting Our Most Urgent Social Problem*. New York: Basic Books.

Boyd, Monica, and Edward T. Pryor. 1989. 'The Cluttered Nest: The Living Arrangements of Young Canadian Adults', *Canadian Journal of Sociology* 14, 4: 461–77.

Brannen, Stephen J., and Allen Rubin. 1996. 'Comparing the Effectiveness of Gender-Specific and Couples Groups in a Court-Mandated Spouse Abuse Treatment Program', *Research on Social Work Practice* 6: 405–24.

Brownridge, Douglas A., and Shiva S. Halli. 2001. 'Marital Status as Differentiating Factor in Canadian Women's Coping with Partner Violence', *Journal of Comparative Family Studies* 32: 117–25.

Bumpus, Matthew F. 2001. 'Mechanisms Linking Work-to-Family Spillover and Parents' Knowledge of Their Children's Daily Lives', *Dissertation Abstracts International, A: The Humanities and Social Sciences* 61, 8: 3368–A.

———, Ann C. Crouter, and Susan M. McHale. 1999. 'Work Demands of Dual-earner Couples: Implications for Parents' Knowledge about Children's Daily Lives in Middle Childhood', *Marriage and the Family* 61, 2: 465–75.

Campbell, Lori D., and Anne Martin-Matthews. 2000a. 'Caring Sons: Exploring Men's Involvement in Filial Care', *Canadian Journal on Aging* 19: 57–79.

———. 2000b. 'Primary and Proximate: The Importance of Co-residence and Being Primary Provider of Care for Men's Filial Care Involvement', *Journal of Family Issues* 21: 1006–30.

CBC News Online. 2005a. Indepth: 'Same Sex Rights—Canada Timeline', 29 June. At: <www.cbc.ca/news/background/samesexrights/timeline_canada.html>; accessed 9 Jan. 2006.

———. 2005b. Indepth: 'Same Sex Rights—World Timeline', 21 July. At: <www.cbc.ca/news/background/same-sexrights/timeline_world.html>; accessed 9 Jan. 2006.

———. 2005c. Indepth: 'Childcare in Canada', 6 May. At: <www.cbc.ca/news/background/daycare/>; accessed 9 Jan. 2006.

———. 2006. At: <www.cbc.ca/story/canada/national/2006/08/14/aids-women-binder.html>.

Central Intelligence Agency (CIA). 2005. *The World Fact Book 2005*. Washington: CIA. Available at: <www.cia.gov/cia/publications/factbook/geos/ch.html>.

Chambers, Deborah. 2000. 'Representations of Familism in the British Popular Media', *European Journal of Cultural Studies* 3: 195–214.

Cherlin, Andrew J. 1999. 'Going to Extremes: Children's Well-Being and Social Science', *Demography* 36: 421–8.

———, P. Lindsay Chase-Lansdale, and Christine McRae. 1998. 'Effects of Parental Divorce on Mental Health throughout the Life Course', *American Sociological Review* 63: 239–49.

———, Frank F. Furstenberg Jr, P. Lindsay Chase-Lansdale, Kathleen E. Kiernan, Philip K. Robins, Donna Ruane Morrison, and Julien O. Teitler. 1991. 'Longitudinal Studies of Effects of Divorce on Children in Great Britain and the United States', *Science* 252 (7 June): 1386–9.

Choi, Heejeong. 2006. 'Socioeconomic Status, Marriage, and Physical Health: The Moderating Effects of Marriage on Socioeconomic Status-Health Associations', *Dissertation Abstracts International, A: The Humanities and Social Sciences* 66, 8: 3107–A.

Coleman, H.H., M.L. Weinman, and P.H. Bartholomew. 1980. 'Factors Affecting Conjugal Violence', *Journal of Psychology* 105: 197–202.

Connidis, Ingrid. 2001. *Family Ties and Aging*. Thousand Oaks, Calif.: Sage.

Dahinten, V.S., and J.D. Shapka. 2004. 'The Adolescent Children of Adolescent Mothers: Behavioural and Academic Trajectories', Society for Research on Adolescents, Baltimore, conference presentation.

Dalla Zuanna, Gianpiero, Stefano Gavini, and Angela Spinelli. 1998. 'The Effect of Changing Sexual, Marital and Contraceptive Behaviour on Conceptions, Abortions, and Births', *European Journal of Population* 14, 1: 61–88.

Davies, Lorraine, and Donna D. McAlpine. 1998. 'The Significance of Family, Work, and Power Relations for Mothers' Mental Health', *Canadian Journal of Sociology* 23: 369–87.

Davis, Robert C., and Barbara Smith. 1995. 'Domestic Violence Reforms: Empty Promises or Fulfilled Expectations?', *Crime and Delinquency* 41: 541–52.

de Munck, Victor C., and Andrey Korotayev. 1999. 'Sexual Equality and Romantic Love: A Reanalysis of Rosenblatt's Study on the Function of Romantic Love', *Cross-Cultural Research* 33: 265–77.

Dronkers, Jaap. 1996. 'The Effects of Parental Conflicts and Divorce on the Average Well-Being of Pupils in Secondary Education', American Sociological Association, conference paper.

Dryburgh, Heather. 2001. 'Teenage Pregnancy', *Health Reports* 12, 1: 1–9.

Eichler, Margrit. 1997. *Family Shifts: Families, Policies, and Gender Equality*. Toronto: Oxford University Press.

———. 2001. 'Biases in Family Literature', in Maureen Baker, ed., *Families: Changing Trends in Canada*, 4th edn. Toronto: McGraw-Hill Ryerson, 51–66.

Elder, Glen H., Jr. 1992. 'Models of the Life Course', *Contemporary Sociology* 21: 632–5.

Gavigan, Shelley A.M. 1999. 'Legal Forms, Family Forms, Gendered Norms: What Is a Spouse?', *Canadian Journal of Law and Society* 14: 127–57.

Gee, Ellen M. 1986. 'The Life Course of Canadian Women: An Historical and Demographic Analysis', *Social Indicators Research* 18: 263–83.

Gelles, Richard, and Jon R. Conte. 1991. 'Domestic Violence and Sexual Abuse of Children: A Review of Research in the Eighties', in Alan Booth, ed., *Contemporary Families: Looking Forward, Looking Back*. Minneapolis: National Council on Family Relations, 327–40.

Geurts, Sabine, Christel Rutte, and Maria Peeters. 1999. 'Antecedents and Consequences of Work–Home Interference among Medical Residents', *Social Science and Medicine* 48: 1135–48.

Giddens, Anthony. 1992. *The Transformation of Intimacy: Sexuality, Love, and Eroticism in Modern Societies*. Cambridge: Polity Press.

Globe and Mail. 2002. Available at: <www.theglobeandmail.com/special/census/2001/stories/families/20021022main.html>.

Glossop, Robert, and Alan Mirabelli. 2002. *The Current State of Canadian Family Finances, 2002 Report*. Ottawa: Vanier Institute of the Family. Available at: <www.vifamily.ca/PR/releases/state02pr.htm>; accessed 15 Mar. 2003.

Gove, W.R. 1970. 'Sex, Marital Status, and Psychiatric Treatment: A Research Note', *Social Forces* 58: 89–93.

Hallman, Bonnie C., and Alun E. Joseph. 1999. 'Getting There: Mapping the Gendered Geography of Caregiving to Elderly Relatives', *Canadian Journal on Aging* 18, 4: 397–414.

Hanna, Deborah H., and Kirsten G. Jones. 2001. 'The Impact of Social Support on Youth Risk-Taking Behaviors', Southern Sociological Society, conference paper.

Hawkins, Daniel, and Alan Booth. 2005. 'Unhappily Ever After: Effects of Long-Term, Low-Quality Marriages on Well-Being', *Social Forces* 84, 1: 451–71.

Heathcote, J., K. Cauch-Dudek, and D. Rhyne. 1997. 'The Professional Lives of Women in Gastroenterology: A Canadian Comparison Study with Men', *Gastroenterology* 113, 2: 669–74.

Hewlett, Sylvia. 1991. *When the Bough Breaks: The Cost of Neglecting Our Children*. New York: Basic Books.

Hochschild, Arlie Russell. 1997. *The Time Bind: When Work Becomes Home and Home Becomes Work*. New York: Henry Holt.

Houseknecht, Sharon K., Suzanne Vaughan, and Anne Statham. 1987. 'The Impact of Singlehood on the Career Patterns of Professional Women', *Journal of Marriage and the Family* 49, 2: 353–66.

Howard-Hassmann, Rhoda E. 2001. 'Gay Rights and the Right to a Family: Conflicts between Liberal and Illiberal Belief Systems', *Human Rights Quarterly* 23: 73–95.

Huisman, Kimberly A. 1996. 'Wife Battering in Asian American Communities: Identifying the Service Needs of an Overlooked Segment of the U.S. Population', *Violence Against Women* 2, 3: 260–83.

Immerman, Ronald S., and Wade C. Mackey. 1999. 'The Societal Dilemma of Multiple Sexual Partners: The Costs of the Loss of Pair-Bonding', *Marriage and Family Review* 29, 1: 3–19.

Jackson, Nicky Ali. 1996. 'Observational Experiences of Intrapersonal Conflict and Teenage Victimization: A Comparative Study among Spouses and Cohabitors', *Journal of Family Violence* 11: 191–203.

Jacobson, Neil S., John M. Guttman, Eric Gortner, Sara Berns, and JoAnn Wu Shortt. 1996. 'Psychological Factors in the Longitudinal Course of Battering: When Do the Couples Split Up? When Does the Abuse Decrease?', *Violence and Victims* 11: 371–92.

Kane, Rosalie A., James Reinardy, Joan D. Penrod, and Shirley Huck. 1999. 'After the Hospitalizatioin Is Over: A Different Perspective on Family Care of Older People', *Journal of Gerontological Social Work* 31: 119–41.

Kaplan, S.J. 2000. 'Family Violence', *New Directions for Mental Health Services* 86: 49–62.

Kauh, Tae-Ock. 1999. 'Changing Status and Roles of Older Korean Immigrants in the United States', *International Journal of Aging and Human Development* 49, 3: 213–29.

Kellogg, Nancy D., Thomas J. Hoffman, and Elizabeth R. Taylor. 1999. 'Early Sexual Experiences among Pregnant and Parenting Adolescents', *Adolescence* 34, 134: 293–303.

Klein, David M., and James M. White. 1996. *Family Theories: An Introduction*. Thousand Oaks, Calif.: Sage.

Kogos, Jennifer L., and John Snarey. 1995. 'Parental Divorce and the Moral Development of Adolescents', *Journal of Divorce and Remarriage* 23: 177–86.

Kohli, Martin. 1986. 'Social Organization and Subjective Construction of Life Course', in A.B. Sorenson, F.E. Weinhert, and L.R. Sharrod, eds, *Human Development and the Life Course*. Hillsdale, NJ: Erlbaum, 271–92.

Kunemund, Harald, and Martin Rein. 1999. 'There Is More to Receiving Than Needing: Theoretical Arguments and Empirical Explorations of Crowding In and Crowding Out', *Ageing and Society* 19, 1: 93–121.

Kurz, Demie. 1995. *For Richer or for Poorer: Mothers Confront Divorce*. New York: Routledge.

Larson, Jeffrey H., Stephan M. Wilson, and Rochelle Beley. 1994. 'The Impact of Job Insecurity on Marital and Family Relations', *Family Relations* 43: 138–43.

Lee, Bong Joo, and Robert M. George. 1999. 'Poverty, Early

Childbearing, and Child Maltreatment: A Multinomial Analysis', *Children and Youth Services Review* 21: 755–80.

Leger Marketing. 2001. 'Canadian Perceptions of Homosexuality'. Available at <www.legermarketing.com/english/set.html>; accessed 20 Mar. 2003.

Lehmann, Jennifer M. 1994. *Durkheim and Women*. Lincoln: University of Nebraska Press.

Leiter, Michael P., and Marie-Josette Durup. 1996. 'Work, Home, and In-between: A Longitudinal Study of Spillover', *Journal of Applied and Behavioural Science* 32, 1: 29–47.

Lindell, Marianne, and Ingegerd Bergbom Engberg. 1999. 'Swedish Women's Partner Relationship and Contraceptive Methods', *European Journal of Women's Studies*, 6, 1: 97–106.

Luster, Tom, Harry Perlstadt, Marvin McKinney, Kathryn Sims, and Linda Juang. 1996. 'The Effects of a Family Support Program and Other Factors on the Home Environments Provided by Adolescent Mothers', *Family Relations* 45, 3: 255–64.

Luxton, Meg, ed. 1997. *Feminism and Families: Critical Policies and Changing Practices*. Halifax: Fernwood.

McDaniel, Susan A. 1994. 'Health Care Policy in an Aging Canada: Forward to the Past?', International Sociological Association, conference paper.

———. 1996. 'The Family Lives of the Middle-Aged and Elderly in Canada', in Maureen Baker, ed., *Families: Changing Trends in Canada*, 3rd edn. Toronto: McGraw-Hill, 195–211.

Mahoney, Rhona. 1995. *Kidding Ourselves: Breadwinning, Babies, and Bargaining Power*. New York: Basic Books.

Males, Mike. 1994. 'Bashing Youth: Media Myths about Teenagers', *Fairness and Accuracy in Reporting (FAIR)* (Mar.–Apr.). Available at: <www.fair.org/index.php?page=1224>.

Marcil-Gratton, Nicole. 1993. 'Growing Up with a Single Parent: A Transitional Experience? Some Demographic Measurements', in Joe Hudson and Burt Galaway, eds, *Single Parent Families: Perspectives on Research and Policy*. Toronto: Thompson Educational Publishing, 73–90.

Martel, Lauren, and Jacques Legare. 2000. 'L'orientation et le contenu des relations réciproques des personnes âgées', *Canadian Journal on Aging* 19: 80–105.

Martin-Matthews, Anne. 2000. 'Gerontology in Canada: A Decade of Change', *Contemporary Gerontology* 7, 2: 53–6.

Mason, Mary Ann, Arlene Skolnick, and Stephen D. Sugarman, eds. 2003. *All Our Families: New Policies for a New Century*, 2nd edn. New York: Oxford University Press.

Millar, W.J., and S. Wadhera. 1997. 'A Perspective on Canadian Teenage Births, 1992–94: Older Men and Younger Women?', *Canadian Journal of Public Health* 88, 5: 333–6.

Mitchell, Barbara A. 1998. 'Too Close for Comfort? Parental Assessments of "Boomerang Kid" Living Arrangements', *Canadian Journal of Sociology* 23: 21–46.

Mitchell, Barbara A., Andrew V. Wister, and Ellen M. Gee. 2000. 'Culture and Co-residence: An Exploration of Variation in Home-Returning among Canadian Young Adults', *Canadian Review of Sociology and Anthropology* 37: 197–222.

Murdock, George P. 1949. *Social Structure*. New York: Macmillan.

Neher, Linda S., and Jerome L. Short. 1998. 'Risk and Protective Factors for Children's Substance Use and Antisocial Behavior Following Parental Divorce', *American Journal of Orthopsychiatry* 68: 154–61.

O'Brien, Carol-Anne, and Aviva Goldberg. 2000. 'Lesbians and Gay Men Inside and Outside Families', in Nancy Mandell and Ann Duffy, eds, *Canadian Families: Diversity, Conflict, and Change*, 2nd edn. Toronto: Harcourt Canada, 115–45.

Oderkirk, Jillian. 1994. 'Marriage in Canada: Changing Beliefs and Behaviours, 1600–1990', *Canadian Social Trends* 33: 3–7.

——— and Clarence Lochhead. 1992. 'Lone Parenthood: Gender Differences', *Canadian Social Trends* 27: 16–19.

O'Farrell, Timothy J., and Christopher M. Murphy. 1995. 'Marital Violence before and after Alcoholism Treatment', *Journal of Consulting and Clinical Psychology* 63: 256–62.

O'Leary, Micky, Janet Franzoni, and Gregory Brack. 1996. 'Divorcing Parents: Factors Related to Coping and Adjustment', *Journal of Divorce and Remarriage* 25, 3 and 4: 85–103.

Parsons, Talcott, and Robert F. Bales. 1955. *Family Socialization and Interaction Process*. New York: Free Press.

Public Broadcasting System (PBS). 2001. 'The Pill. People & Events: Mrs. America: Women's Roles in the 1950s'. At: <www.pbs.org/wgbh/amex/pill/peopleevents/p_mrs.html>.

Roizblatt, Arturo, Sheril Rivera, Tzandra Fuchs, Paulina Toso, Enrique Ossandon, and Miguel Guelfand. 1997. 'Children of Divorce: Academic Outcome', *Journal of Divorce and Remarriage* 26, 3 and 4: 51–6.

Rosenthal, Carolyn J. 1985. 'Kinkeeping in the Familial Division of Labor', *Journal of Marriage and the Family* 47, 4: 965–74.

Rushing, W.A. 1979. 'Marital Status and Mental Disorder: Evidence in Favor of a Behavioral Model', *Social Forces* 58: 540–56.

Schellenberg, E. Glenn, Jessie Hirt, and Alan Sears. 1999. 'Attitudes toward Homosexuals among Students at a Canadian University', *Sex Roles* 40: 139–52.

Schwarz, Beate, Gisela Trommsdorff, Uichol Kim, and Young-shin Park. 2006. 'Intergenerational Support: Psychological and Cultural Analyses of Korean and German Women', *Current Sociology* 54, 2: 315–40.

Skitka, Linda, and Michele Frazier. 1995. 'Ameliorating the Effects of Parental Divorce: Do Small Group Interventions Work?', *Journal of Divorce and Remarriage* 24: 159–79.

Snell, James G. 1983. '"The White Life for Two": The Defence of Marriage and Sexual Morality in Canada, 1890–1914', *Histoire Sociale/Social History* 16, 31: 111–28.

Spitze, Glenna, and John R. Logan. 1992. 'Helping as a Component of Parent–Adult Child Relations', *Research on Aging* 14: 291–312.

Statistical Record of Women Worldwide. 1991. Detroit: Gale Research.

Statistics Canada. 1997. 'Formation of First Common-Law Unions', *The Daily*, 9 Dec.

———. 2000. *Family Violence in Canada: A Statistical Profile 2000* (Catalogue no. 85–224–XIE). Ottawa: Statistics Canada.

———. 2001a. 'Changes to Family Concepts for the 2001 Census'. Available at: <www12.statcan.ca/english/census01/Meta/fmlycncpts.cfm>; accessed 24 Mar. 2003.

———. 2001b. 'Divorces'. Available at: <www.statcan.ca/english/Pgdb/People/Families/famil02.htm>; accessed 12 July 2001.

———. 2002. *2001 Census Families Time Series*, 6 Nov. At: <www12.statcan.ca/english/census01/Products/Analytic/companion/fam/canada.cfm>; accessed 13 May 2005.

———. 2004. 'Analysis Series, 2001 Census', *Profile of Canadian Families and Households: Diversification Continues, 2001 Census,* Catalogue no. 96F0030XIE2001003, pp. 3–5. At: <www12.statcan.ca/english/census01/Products/Analytic/companion/fam/contents.cfm>; accessed 9 Jan 2006.

———. 2005a. 'Births', *The Daily*, 12 July. Available at: <www.statcan.ca/Daily/English/050712/d050712a.htm>.

———. 2005b. 'Divorces', *The Daily*, 9 Mar. At: <www.statcan.ca/Daily/English/050309/d050309b>.; accessed 23 June 2006.

Strohschein, Lisa, Peggy McDonough, Georges Monette, and Qing Shao. 2005. 'Marital Transitions and Mental Health: Are There Gender Differences in the Short-Term Effects of Marital Status Change?', *Social Science and Medicine* 61, 11: 2293–303.

Tepperman, Lorne, and James Curtis. 2003. 'Orientations toward Outgroups', unpublished paper.

Thomson, Elizabeth, and Min Li. 1992. *Family Structure and Children's Kin*. NSFH Working Papers No. 47. Madison: Center for Demography and Ecology, University of Wisconsin.

United Nations. *World Contraceptive Use 2003*. New York: UN Department of Economic and Social Affairs Population Division. Apr. Available at: <www.un.org/esa/population/publications/contraceptive2003/wcu2003.htm>.

Vanier Institute of the Family. 2000. *Profiling Canada's Families II*. Ottawa: Vanier Institute of the Family.

Waite, Linda J. 2000. 'The Negative Effects of Cohabitation', *The Responsive Community* 10, 1: 31–8.

Wharton, Amy S., and Rebecca J. Erickson. 1995. 'The Consequences of Caring: Exploring the Links between Women's Job and Family Emotion Work', *Sociological Quarterly* 36, 2: 273–96.

Willms, J. Douglas, ed. 2002. *Vulnerable Children: Findings from Canada's Longitudinal Survey of Children and Youth*. Edmonton: University of Alberta Press.

Wilson, James Q., and Richard J. Herrnstein. 1987. *Crime and Human Nature*. New York: Simon & Schuster.

World Health Organization (WHO). 2005. *WHO Multi-Country Study on Women's Health and Domestic Violence against Women: Summary Report of Initial Results on Prevalence, Health Outcomes and Women's Responses*. Geneva: WHO. At: <www.who.int/gender/violence/who_multicountry_study/summary_report/en/index.html>; accessed 9 Jan. 2006.

Yllo, K., and M.A. Straus. 1981. 'Interpersonal Violence among Married and Cohabiting Couples', *Family Relations* 30: 339–47.

Zaslow, Martha, Sharon McGroder, George Cave, and Carrie Mariner. 1999. 'Maternal Employment and Measures of Children's Health and Development among Families with Some History of Welfare Receipt', *Research in the Sociology of Work* 7: 233–59.

CHAPTER NINE

WORK AND UNEMPLOYMENT

LEARNING OBJECTIVES
- To know some basic facts about work and unemployment.
- To appreciate aspects of work and employment that may be considered as social problems.
- To understand the role of multinationals in the global economy.
- To make the connection between bureaucratization and unemployment.
- To know the major sociological theories about work and unemployment.
- To be able to explain the role technology plays in unemployment and work.
- To be aware of health outcomes of work and unemployment, and possible solutions.

Introduction

This chapter is about employment and unemployment, workers and workplaces, productivity, labour, industry, profits, manufacturing, and health. In particular, it is about work in Canada under capitalism.

Modern technology is an important part of the modern Canadian workplace. Increasingly, Canadian companies need fewer, better-educated, and more highly skilled workers to run the machinery of production. One result is less job security. Yet, in important ways, work under capitalism has not changed in a century. Despite automation, modern workplaces still have human relations problems. We have already discussed the problem of gender inequality in the workplace. In this chapter, we will discuss class exploitation and class conflict in the workplace.

Modern society has not removed the class structure, though it has blurred class distinctions. The division between social classes, first highlighted by Karl Marx, who distinguished between the owners of the means of production and the working class, or the bourgeoisie and the proletariat, continues in our post-industrial, service- and information-based society. And, perhaps for the reason Marx suggested—the need for a reserve army of labour to keep wages down—modern work has not erased unemployment. People who are forced out of work by mass layoffs are usually workers on the lowest rungs of the occupational ladder. Ironically, these workers who are the most in need of a stable income are the first to lose their jobs whenever a recession occurs.

However, in a few important ways, work *has* changed in the past half-century. For example, work has become more flexible, family-friendly, and woman-friendly. It is now easier for people to work at home. Flextime, another new arrangement, allows employees to decide when they begin and end the workday. Researchers are still debating whether these are genuine improvements in working life or mere window dressing.

Comparative Economic Systems

Work becomes a social problem when it makes workers unhappy, harms their health, or supports other social problems, such as racism, sexism, and material inequality. This section will focus on different types of economic organization and how they affect the workplace. We will expand on unemployment as a social problem in later sections.

Capitalism and Socialism

Throughout the last century, two economic approaches controlled the world's economy: capitalism and socialism. **Capitalism** refers to the economic system in which private individuals or corporate groups own the means of production and distribution and invest private capital to produce goods and services to be sold for profit in a competitive market. **Socialism** is an alternative economic and political ideology that flourished in the nineteenth and twentieth centuries. It favours public ownership of the means of production and distribution and investing public capital in producing goods and services.

For those who defend socialism—generally Marxists—the capitalist system is just one step in humanity's historic development. They argue that from the early days of human civilization social inequalities were established based on an individual's relationship to material wealth. As societies became more industrialized and capitalistic, imbalances in the relations of production between social classes—that is, between those who had the wealth to purchase and control the engines of production, and those who did not—became entrenched in social structures, institutions, and economic organizations. As well, according to this viewpoint, capitalism itself contains certain internal contradictions based on the market structure and the way in which the bourgeoisie exploits the labour of the working class while keeping economic surpluses for itself. Marxists state that these contradictions will only be resolved when the members of the proletariat rise up and seize the means of production. By doing so, the working class can redistribute wealth according to a more equitable scheme for the well-being of the society as a whole. This economic system—without individual property rights over the means of production, and organized for the benefit of society as a whole—is called socialism. Marxists consider this to be the last stage in the development of economic structures.

Those who oppose socialism, on the other hand, consider capitalism to be 'the end of history' (Fukuyama, 1992). They argue that socialist societies are inefficient because the common will never drives people to work as hard as their own individual interests and benefits. In the view of capitalists, the market system ensures maximum efficiency because it maximizes the competition between firms, corporations, and individuals. This competition also guarantees that resources are assigned in the best way, because production for profit always follows the consumers' demand. Most importantly, supporters of capitalism state that the contradictions pointed out by Marxists will be solved as the system develops.

The Great Population Shift

Until the Industrial Revolution, most of the world's population was rural. However, by mid-nineteenth century, half of the English people lived in cities, and by the end of the century, the same was true of other European countries. Between 1800 and 1950 most large European cities exhibited spectacular growth. At the beginning of the nineteenth century there were scarcely two dozen cities in Europe with a population of 100,000, but by 1900 there were more than 150 cities of this size.
Source: <www.ecology.com/archived-links/industrial-revolution/index.html>.

Currently, most modern economies remain capitalist in the sense that the means of production are owned by individuals, but they are influenced by socialist ideas in the matters of distribution of wealth and public investment. This influence is stronger in some countries (for example, Sweden and Canada) and weaker in others (for example, Japan and the United States).

Under capitalism, private individuals own and run the means of production for profit. As we have noted, socialism emphasizes public ownership, stresses the needs of the whole society over the wishes of individuals, and, most importantly, proposes sharing the economic surplus among the workers. In theory, it proposes that goods and services be spread equally among members of society as dictated by their needs. Socialists argue that since many human needs can be satisfied only through co-operation with others, it is in everyone's interest to work together to serve the collective interest, thus bringing about prosperity.

Arguments have been made for both sides. Capitalist societies have tended, on average, to achieve a higher average standard of living than socialist nations. However, the variation between rich and poor is also far wider under the capitalist system than under the socialist system. In the twentieth century, countries such as Canada, Germany, France, and Sweden have adopted strategies that include elements of both capitalism and socialism. Of all developed countries, the United States continues to resist socialism most vigorously. As a result, the standard of living is slightly lower in Canada than in the United States, as shown by (among other things) the value of the Canadian dollar compared with the American dollar. On the other hand, material inequality in Canada is not as severe as the extremes of poverty and degradation found in the United States (for example, in urban ghettos).

Industrialism and the Industrial Revolution

Since the late eighteenth century, industrialism has transformed the way we work. In pre-industrial societies, people worked collectively in mainly agricultural settings. Because of the small, localized scale of rural communities and the interconnectedness of people's experiences, work was largely inseparable from family and personal life. People led similar lives and held similar moral, religious, and political beliefs.

Two major economic developments changed this, the agricultural and the industrial revolutions. Early in the eighteenth century the agricultural revolution allowed farmers to produce a surplus large enough to sustain a large number of manufacturing workers, or proletarians. In other words, the agricultural revolution allowed enough food to be produced that many people could work outside food production.

This great number of non-farmer workers and the technological developments, such as the steam engine, that occurred, especially in the United Kingdom, made possible the Industrial Revolution. This new system of production introduced innovations in agricultural practices, further increasing efficiency. The new factory system allowed a large surplus also in the manufacturing areas, beginning especially with the textile and steel industries. These surpluses in most economic activities, along with the presence of large number of workers paid with wages, increased dramatically the complexity of the market and laid the foundations for the emerging capitalist system.

During the Industrial Revolution, machines began to replace human hands and tools, while steam (and later, electrical) power began to replace human exertion as the source of energy. As the manufacturing process became more complex, jobs became more specialized. Early in the twentieth century, Henry Ford invented the assembly line. Cities began to grow rapidly as people came together in factory towns to seek work in return for wages. Prior to industrialization, family life and work life had been carried out in the same place—often on a farm. Now, the two realms of activity became distinct and exclusive, the one still located at home, the other in a factory or office. This began a new marked separation of men and women, men's work and women's work, adult work and children's formal education.

The Global Economy and Post-Industrialism

In the late twentieth century, industrialism evolved into post-industrialism. Post-industrialism is characterized by the shift from a manufacturing-intensive economy to an economy based on services and information. With the development of computer-based and telecommunications technology, production has become a mainly automated process, with information as both the main input and output.

With post-industrialism, geography, distance, and national borders have lost much of their meaning as barriers in communication. Technology has allowed information to flow across these distances quickly, cheaply, safely, and easily. Other factors have increased the flow of information, products, and people. They include multinational trade agreements, such as the North American Free Trade Agreement (NAFTA), the European Union, MERCOSUR, which includes several countries in South America, and the more recently proposed Free Trade Area of the Americas (FTAA), and international economic organizations, such as the World Trade Organization (WTO), the World Bank, and the International Monetary Fund (IMF). These agreements, while benefiting relations between countries, have been laced with political agendas.

Trade agreements are aimed at removing tariffs for import and export. International organizations pressure less developed countries to open their borders to global trade, dangling the promise of foreign investments and economic prosperity. When this happens, corporate multinationals find it easier to gain access to raw materials in foreign countries, to employ cheap labour overseas, and to steer clear of government controls over workers' rights and environmental pollution. Many believe this process benefits rich nations at the expense of poor ones, and large multinational organizations at the expense of smaller organizations and nation-states. As a result, free trade and other features of globalization have been the focus of massive organized protests at such international forums as WTO meetings (e.g., Seattle, 1999), G-8 summits (e.g., Genoa, Italy, 2001), the Organization of American States (Quebec City, 2001), the World Economic Forum (Davos, Switzerland, 2001), and the International Monetary Fund and World Bank (Washington and Prague, 2000). Notably, large civil protests against the forces of globalization have been reined in to a considerable extent since the terrorist attacks on the US in September 2001.

In the end, global capitalism has supported the growth of huge multinational corporations with revenues larger than the GDPs of most nation-states. They are the dominant political and economic force in the post-industrial world. Sometimes, they produce jobs and new wealth. In other instances, they destroy jobs—leading to unemployment—and put more wealth in the pockets of the already wealthy.

Technological Dualism

The explosion of telecommunications and computer technology in the last quarter of the twentieth century resulted in the growth of jobs needing skilled workers with advanced educations and professional training.

The pace of development has been unrivalled in any other period in history. For workers, this means that skills are becoming outdated faster than ever, and constant upgrading is needed to remain competitive in a continuously changing job market. However, not everyone can achieve this. This spirited self-improvement is largely limited to those with the financial and educational means to do so and those who work in a sector of the economy that wants and promotes such changes. For workers mired in low-wage, dead-end positions—in the retail industry, for example—the market may not force them to rapidly adapt to technical change, but neither does it offer many opportunities for greater self-improvement and wealth.

Workers in the manufacturing industry are increasingly being threatened with job cuts made possible by the automation of production. Computer-controlled machinery benefits corporate managers for several reasons. First, it removes human error in jobs that are boring and repetitive. Second, high-tech machines can manufacture products with greater uniformity and precision than can human workers. Third, computerization replaces humans with machines that can run continuously, resulting in significant cost-effectiveness.

Fourth, computerization and mechanization reduces human conflict between workers and bosses by reducing the number of humans involved. It makes the control of productive workers far easier, too. Computing devices do not demand an income, never go on strike (although they do break down), never tire of or get bored by their work, and can work around the clock. Rather than employing dozens of workers to run a production floor, managers and owners can now hire only a few well-trained employees to program, supervise, and maintain the otherwise robotic manufacturing process.

As technology continues to transform the workplace, more efficient and less costly machines take over tasks once done by human labour. A common assumption is that automation and mass production create unemployment for some individuals and leave others—almost always those of the working and middle classes—to work in monotonous and deskilled jobs that lack autonomy and challenge. Critics of capitalism argue that the owners of the means of production are the only ones who benefit from technological change in the workplace. Their view is that much technological innovation has been bad for workers because machines take their jobs. There is, however, some belief and evidence to the contrary.

Research in the United Kingdom, for example, studied the spread of microelectronics throughout the manufacturing industry and surveyed workers about the impact of the new technology on their jobs. Fewer than half reported a significant change in their work. Overall, the average net decrease was only about two jobs per factory per year, mainly unskilled positions. Among new-technology adopters, the losses were larger in factories that enthusiastically embraced the most advanced applications. Over the same period, however, technology non-adopters lost about three times as many jobs as technology adopters. The number of jobs increased, not decreased, in the plants that were open to mechanization and technology (see Daniel, 1987; Newton and Lockie, 1987; Northcott et al., 1985; Northcott and Walling, 1988).

Technology has also affected social interaction and social bonds. The benefit of telephones, fax machines, e-mail, and Internet chat rooms is the convenience of allowing people separated by great physical distances to remain in real-time contact with one another, either over a wire or in cyberspace. On the downside, however, these and other technological inventions have reduced the need for face-to-face contact. Often, we have replaced activities that once involved human interaction with a machine. Because of the expectations that technology has created, everything must now be accessible and instant. This has changed, among many other things, the way in which we work.

For example, in terms of their impact on jobs, the answering machine largely replaced the secretaries and office switchboard operators, automatic teller machines (ATMs) largely replaced bank tellers, and on-line shopping websites largely replaced salespeople. Technology has also allowed for different ways of working, including telework, job sharing, work from remote locations, and teleconferencing, just to name a few. This has in turn affected the way we interact with one another and with the work experience itself.

Developing the Different Sectors of the Modern Economy

For analytical purposes, different types of work, characterized by different types of technology and different relations of production, can be separated into five main 'sectors' of the economy. Every modern economy, Canada's included, has these five major sectors (or more). The *primary sector* contains those jobs that are connected with the capture or extraction of primary resources from the environment. Examples include farming, logging, trapping, mining, and fishing. Primary production of this kind was the most common work activity of Canadians until the twentieth century. Canadian economic historian Harold Innis stressed that Canadian geography and its rich resource base ensured the country developed around its primary sector (e.g., Innis, 1930). Political, social, and cultural history largely followed developments in the primary economic sector.

Historically, this sector of the economy has used the simplest technology and been characterized by the simplest relations of production. In the last half of the last century, however, many family farms went out of business. The rise of huge, corporate, often multinational 'agribusinesses' meant the adoption of more complex, costly technology and more sophisticated labour-management relations. Other primary production sites—mines, logging sites, and fisheries—also became larger and more technologically complex. For industries throughout the primary sector, global markets determined job security more than ever.

After 1850, with the rise of industrial technology, the *secondary (manufacturing) sector* became the driving force in Canada's economy. Work in this sector involved processing raw materials to produce usable goods. Much of this was done in large factories, using technology and materials provided by the factory owner(s). As sellers of their labour-power, a large number of workers in this sector formed and joined labour or trade unions.

After 1945 and even more dramatically after 1970, Canadian manufacturing changed fundamentally, because of powerful new technologies—especially those that could be computerized—and the transfer of production to low-wage nations, a process also known as globalization. Traditionally strong Canadian industries have been those that grew out of Canadian primary production—pulp and paper (from forestry) and metal-smelting (from mining), for example. With the automation and globalization of this sector, job security has decreased through layoffs and the transfer of jobs to other countries. Another result of this growing turbulence has been a drop in union membership and bargaining strength.

Around 1900, a *tertiary (service) sector* started to grow dramatically. Work in this sector is involved with the recording, storage, and communication of information in offices; with professional and personal services, such as law, medicine, chiropractic, hairdressing, and computer repair; and sales, service, and other clerking in shops. This sector has expanded explosively since the mid-twentieth century, with growth in the information-based economy and a strong consumer culture. Computerization has been especially significant in developing this work.

However, as might be obvious from the list of jobs in the service sector, there is a great variation and even polarization of tertiary workers. This is caused by the presence of a few highly skilled, well-paid jobs (such as doctor and lawyer) and many low-skilled, poorly paid jobs (sometimes referred to as 'McJobs'). Although high-end service work often requires long hours, the advantages of high pay, high prestige, and relative job security often outweigh the negatives. In contrast, the experience of low-end service work is full of negative features, with sometimes too-long or too-short hours, low pay, little prestige, no job security, and few positive features.

Often, low-end service jobs, like high-end ones, also demand emotional labour, the regulation of one's emotional state through the suppression or invention of feelings. At low-end work sites, the general lack of trust between workers and bosses, displayed by close direction and surveillance, adds to the high stress levels and emotional drain among workers.

The fourth (*social reproduction*) sector contains the socially necessary labour that is not performed in exchange for money. Usually, this work—cooking, cleaning, child care, and so on—is done in family households, most often by women. The labour force in this sector is not officially recorded as a part of the economy and receives little recognition and no pay. In effect, the work done here is free work contributed directly to the family but indirectly to the capitalist system, which benefits from this unpaid labour. This free labour is worth billions of dollars to the economy, as will be obvious if you consider what would happen if women and other family members decided to no longer perform this labour for free and it had to be bought at market prices.

Though technological innovations have also changed work in this sector over time—for example, through the development of cheap electrical home appliances—from a technological perspective, this work is to a large degree pre-industrial. Social reproduction continues to rely on individualized personal relationships and emotion-work, just as it did two centuries ago. What is problematic today is the competition many people—especially, women—experience between their paid jobs in the third sector and their unpaid jobs in the fourth sector.

A fifth sector is the so-called *informal economy*. This sector includes work that may not be legal and whose earnings are not reported to the government. It may include a barter system, where goods and services are exchanged informally without the use of cash, and it usually includes the 'black market' where anything—rare foods, drugs, weapons, animal body parts—can be bought and sold for the right price. An informal economy exists in every society. Currently, it is particularly prevalent in Africa, in response to contracting opportunities in the formal economy, and in Russia, where the formal economy has been in turmoil since the collapse of communism in 1991.

Less is known about technology and labour relations in the informal or underground sector. Often, it is low-tech work organized through personalistic relations between the bosses, workers, and customers. In this respect, the informal economy is pre-industrial, like the organization of work in feudal times.

The Bureaucratization of Work

Besides factories and cities, bureaucracies are a defining feature of modern work life. Bureaucracies are large, complex organizations employing specialized workers who work within the context of what Max Weber (1947) called *a legal-rational authority* structure. This form of authority is distinguished by thorough written rules governing how people are to perform their jobs. Bureaucratic work is usually performed in offices.

Bureaucratic organization is well suited to the pursuit of profits: it is usually prudent, cautious, and shrewd. Bureaucracies as a whole are rarely impulsive or petty, as despots and dictators might be. Furthermore, a bureaucratic organization can grow large yet remain controlled from the top. Growth is much more limited in organizations that rely on personal attachment and duty, such as family businesses (or workplaces in the fifth sector, discussed earlier).

Another facet of modern bureaucracy is the legal idea of 'limited liability', which allows a corporation to manage investment and profits impersonally, in a way that protects both the owners and the workers. Under this legal principle, organizational officers are protected (usually) from lawsuits arising out of the legal operation of their company. In principle, bureaucracies distinguish between the rights and duties attaching to a position and the characteristics of the person who (temporarily) holds a position of authority. The impersonal connection between officeholders and the organization also makes bureaucracy different from patronage and other personalized systems, such as organized crime.

Industrialization and capitalism favoured the rise of bureaucracies. Bureaucracies are good at controlling large workforces—even highly educated and differentiated workforces. As organizations grow, their differentiation usually increases. Problems of co-ordination and control—formalization, decentralization, and supervision—are bound to arise. Often, reorganization is needed, especially if the number of personnel is large and growing rapidly. As industrial enterprises grow with the mechanization of work, control structures (that is, for management and administration) usually grow as well.

Structurally, every member of a bureaucratic organization is enmeshed in a network of **reporting relationships**. The ideal **bureaucracy** is a Christmas-tree-shaped structure that repeatedly branches out as you go down the hierarchy. At the bottom of the hierarchy many people have to (1) carry out orders from above, (2) report work-related information up the tree to their superiors, and (3) uphold linkages between the organization and its client or customer base. At the top of the hierarchy, only a few people get to (1) issue orders to their subordinates, (2) process information received from below, and (3) preserve linkages between the organization and other organizations—political, economic, and social. Also, those at the top of this organization are to share information between the heads of planning, manufacturing, shipping, public relations, and other sectors of the organization.

In theory, all information in a bureaucratic organization is stored and communicated in writing. All written information is reported up the ladder and workers never leak work-related information outside the organization or to superiors other than their own. For example, a shop supervisor is expected to hear about a problem related to shipping, sales, or customer satisfaction only after this information has made its way up the structure from the bottom to the top. In an ideal world, most employees of a large bureaucracy would be encouraged to be strangers to one another.

Reality offers a different picture of bureaucratic organization. Below the surface, those near the bottom of the organization can carry out actions that defy, oppose, or sidestep the rules and roles of the organization. More generally, below the surface of the ideal or formal structure—which prescribes how a bureaucracy ought to work—there inevitably exists an informal structure. This informal organization is developed through communication based on trust. Trust is formed through friendship, acquaintance, and gossip about third parties that strengthen existing ties. People have stronger attachments to other workers than they do to 'the organization', an abstract entity.

Good decision-making depends on the flow of reliable information to the right people. To ensure this, a good organization has a structured chain of command, where it is clear who is to get information from whom and who is to give orders to whom. In these respects, bureaucratic organizations achieve great clarity. And whatever its size, any organization can be tall and narrow, or flat and broad. These variations are achieved by shifting the number of levels and the span of control at each level. Clear patterns of information flow may seem trivial until you consider the possibilities for error.

The 'tall' (many-level) bureaucracy—with a clear chain of command and information flow—effectively controls vast numbers of workers and transfers vast amounts of information up and down the chain. Could a flat organizational structure do better? Other things being equal, the better organization should produce better outcomes: higher profitability, more satisfied customers, and more satisfied employees, for example. Given two companies of (roughly) the same size, which organizational structure works better?

By definition, organizations with a flat and broad structure have few 'middle managers', which means that a higher percentage of employees meet the public. In turn, this should result in better service to retailers and more feedback from customers about what is liked and disliked. And finally, this should facilitate a faster response to criticisms and faster introduction of new products. In short, the flat-and-broad organization *should* be more responsive and adaptable. A short communication distance means less chance that incoming information will get distorted or lost as it travels from the bottom level up to the boss. So, the boss should get more accurate and faster information from her/his front-line workers in such an organization.

Finally and conversely, the maximum distance downward is also just a few steps. This means less distortion of commands coming from the top. Because of familiarity and nearly direct contact, employees should develop a stronger loyalty to the company. Morale is high; so is productivity.

Since the advantages of flat organization are obvious, you might wonder why all businesses (also, governments, armies, and so on) do not follow this pattern. The reason is because flat/broad structures are less able to supervise and control their workers than tall/narrow structures. A flat structure—with little supervision of the workers—is fine under some conditions, such as when subordinates are competent and motivated to please their boss, and when they identify with the goals of the organization. Then, workers can be trusted to work hard and well, without much supervision.

The conditions that make this possible include: clear rules and expectations; enough money to select and train good workers; job security; a career ladder to reward good service; and corporate stability that justifies workers' investment of loyalty in the company. All these are features of what economist Richard Edwards (1979), in his book *Contested Terrain*, has called the 'bureaucratic control' of workers. Under this 'bureaucratic' system, control is internalized. Workers obey the rules without much supervision because they believe in the rules and expect obedience to pay off in future rewards. Since control is internalized, it doesn't have to be externalized (in the form of close supervision). This allows for a flat structure and all the benefits of a flat structure.

However, bosses who favour 'lean and mean' management have largely destroyed the possibility of flat structuring. In recent decades, more and more organizations have 'downsized'—that is, fired and laid off workers, or cut their pay and benefits. Many organizations have also erased job security. These acts have reduced workers' willingness to invest their loyalty in the company in return for future rewards. Workers have a hard time imagining a career there, or even—given the rise in mergers and bankruptcies—imagining the company will survive. So, with the weakening of internalized organizational loyalty, more externalized control is needed, and that means more middle managers and taller organizational structures.

Theories of Work and Unemployment

As in other areas of sociological research, sociologists employ different theoretical approaches when studying work and unemployment. The four broad theoretical perspectives of structural functionalism, conflict theory, feminism, and symbolic interaction all provide interpretations for work and unemployment.

The Structural-Functionalist Perspective

The structural-functionalist perspective asks, as always, *What function* does work perform? This perspective stresses that, along with the family, work is the most basic of social institutions. Functionalists believe that everyone needs love, work, and hope. Work is especially important because it lets people acquire the material necessities of life—food, water, shelter, and clothing—for themselves and their families.

Not only does paid work give workers an opportunity to satisfy their physical needs, it also allows them to satisfy their emotional needs. These include the wishes to be a productive and valued member of society, to gain recognition and praise, and to interact and co-operate with others. Thus, work has social purposes. It provides a basis for social interaction, social solidarity and cohesion, and the sharing of lifestyles and meanings. The workplace, ideally, lets people exercise all of their social and creative impulses while earning a living.

Conflict and Feminist Theory

Conflict theorists, by contrast, ask, *Who gains the advantage* from the current system of work? The competing interests of different classes lead inevitably to conflict. Karl Marx (e.g., 1936 [1887]) claimed that class relations under capitalism cause all the conflict within and between societies. To his mind, the members of a capitalist society can be divided into two factions. The ruling class, or bourgeoisie, comprises the wealthy owners of the means of production, and the working class, or proletariat, comprises the labourers who work for the bourgeoisie. One group wants to hire labour for the lowest possible price; the other wants to sell its labour for the highest possible price.

Given their opposed interests, the two classes are locked in a conflict that plays itself out largely in the workplace. In this 'contested terrain' (to use economist Richard Edwards's term), there can never be peace and co-operation, or a universally accepted definition of efficiency, because the interests of workers and capitalists are opposed. From this point of view, the workplace is not a place for sociability and creativity; it is a place for repression and mistreatment, in which some groups of workers are even more vulnerable than others. In this system, low-end workers—the most vulnerable workers, those most in need of a stable income—are often the first to lose their jobs when the economy goes into a slump.

According to conflict theory, the power elite also uses the situation of unemployment to boost profits. In *Capital*, Karl Marx stated that capitalism inevitably creates unemployment. As economic growth creates new jobs, wages go up and the profits for the capitalists go down. As a result, capitalists stop investing, creating the conditions for a recession. This leads to periodic cycles in the economic system that leave workers unemployed as capitalists try to control the rate of profits. Indeed, unemployed workers are thought to be necessary for those periods of prosperity because they serve as a supply of labour—what Marx called the 'reserve army of labour'—for the increasing demand of industries.

Unemployment also allows industrialists to threaten workers if their demands are considered to be too high. Workers who protest too hard in times of high unemployment will find themselves replaced by people from the great pool of the unemployed. In this way, the bourgeoisie uses the unemployed as a way of quashing employee unrest. Workers are less likely to demand higher wages if they fear they will be replaced by cheaper labour.

Feminist theorists also ask, *Why don't women benefit* from the capitalist organization of work? They note that Canadian women are still disproportionately engaged in work that has little or no pay—that is, in social reproduction. As a result, capitalists profit from the hard work of women even more than they profit from the hard work of working men; and men, who usually occupy higher-paid jobs than women, often profit at the expense of women. The result is job dissatisfaction, a lack of job control, and a rising prevalence of depression and other psychosomatic illnesses among women.

Symbolic Interactionism

Symbolic interactionists, as always, ask the question, *How* are jobs and job differences *symbolized*, negotiated, and communicated? They focus on the meanings of work and unemployment for the individual. Work, especially in a modern, individualistic culture, provides a major part of our identity. Because a person's line of work is so central to his or her identity, others often use it as a source of information. 'So what do you do for a living?' is the second most popular question asked whenever two strangers strike up a conversation (behind only 'Hi, what's your name?').

Whether true or not, it is commonly believed that knowing one's occupation (for example, nun or rock musician) can provide clues to that person's character, personality, and interests. Many people also treat occupational titles as status symbols, basing their assessments of an individual largely on the prestige and income associated with the work that he or she does.

Social Constructionism

Finally, related to this approach, social constructionists always ask: *How* did the arrangement *emerge*? An example of this would be the work by Richard Edwards on the historical evolution of management practices, from simple (or direct) control to technological control to what he calls bureaucratic control. This evolution of management strategies and ideologies reflected changes in the work done and technology used in the workplace. Even more, it reflected changing worker strategies to thwart managerial practices of control. As one means of control no longer worked, another would be invented and taught to new generations of managers.

Also, social constructionists would be interested in the evolution of popular thinking about work. In the 1950s and 1960s, the dominant concern was with alienating work—how work in large organizations turns people into robots. In the 1970s and 1980s, the dominant concern was the exploitation of workers here and abroad, the possibility of computers replacing humans in the workplace, and with securing more leisure. Since then, alongside the rise of globalism, the principal concern has been job insecurity, job loss (that is, the export of jobs to low-wage countries), and the spillover effects of bad work lives into people's health and family lives.

Note that all of these explanations are compatible with one another. Each focuses on a different feature of work and unemployment. A summary of this information is contained in Table 9.1.

Social Consequences of Work

As we have already seen in earlier chapters, work and unemployment are connected to a great many other social problems. We will touch on a few of these in this section.

Gender Discrimination

Despite a steady advance in gender equality over the past several decades, discrimination against women remains an important problem. Gender stereotyping and inequality continue in the workplace. Because the issue of sexism was discussed in detail in Chapter 5, this section will only briefly remind us of some facets of this problem.

The 'glass ceiling' that results in earning differences between women and men, and other gender-related workplace concerns, such as harassment, are discussed at length in Chapter 5. The problem of gender inequality in the workplace is important because the income earned at work affects a person's access to the necessities of life, education of children, and leisure. Women are over-represented in the lower end of the occupational marketplace, where dead-end and/or part-time work dominates. Low wages and job instability often mean that even full-time workers must live in poverty.

Stereotypes persist of women as nurturing and emotional and of men as more dominant and rational. As a result, female workers are expected to be the primary caregivers. This expectation has carried over into the world of work, often resulting in women being excluded from occupations that require higher education and skill development. For these and other reasons, women are still under-represented in leadership positions.

For women, employment does not always mean an escape from poverty. The types of available jobs are part of the problem. 'Women's work'—clerical jobs, sales, light manufacturing, and the catch-all category 'service work'—tends to pay poorly. In general,

Table 9.1 Five Main Sociological Paradigms on Work

Structural Functionalism	▪ Work is a basic human need. ▪ Everyone profits when everyone works. ▪ Work is the most basic of social institutions. ▪ Everyone needs love, work, and hope. ▪ Work provides a basis for social interaction, social solidarity, and cohesion.
Conflict Theory	▪ Capitalists benefit from the current organization of work. ▪ Globalization produces job insecurity in Canada. ▪ Work promotes social inequality. ▪ Work is a place of repression and mistreatment. ▪ Unemployment is used by power elite to boost profits. ▪ Unemployed people depress wages, provide a reserve army of labour.
Symbolic Interactionism	▪ Work can be organized in a variety of ways. ▪ Socialization and labelling shape the content and perception of different jobs. ▪ Meanings are found in work and unemployment. ▪ Work provides a major part of our identity. ▪ People treat work as a status symbol, and jobs are used as a method of making judgements. ▪ Chronic unemployment is a learned trait—a culture of poverty that perpetuates a sense of learned helplessness.
Feminism	▪ Women continue to be disadvantaged at work. ▪ Patriarchy operates in the workforce. ▪ Women are paid less than men for the same jobs and work in lower-paying sectors. ▪ Capitalists benefit from the hard unpaid work of women.
Social Constructionism	▪ The organization of work is an evolving social process. ▪ It reflects changes in technology and worker-management conflict. ▪ The structure of work evolves based on relations between workers and employers. ▪ Technology is a new force in the evolution of work organization.

women's work not only pays less than men's, but is also less inflation-proof. The occupational segregation of women in our society makes for a vital difference between women's poverty and men's. For men, poverty is often a result of unemployment and is curable by getting a job. But for the large number of female 'working poor', concentrated in the low-wage stratum of the workforce, a job may not expel poverty, only reduce it.

Another important issue women face at work is that, especially on a global scale, women's household labour is unrecognized as work that deserves compensation. Even when cash changes hands, the involvement of women is usually discounted or not included at all in national statistics. Yet, in rural areas, women not only prepare but also grow most of the family food, and it is mainly girls and women who collect water, fuel for cooking, and fodder for domestic animals. Women's unpaid household labour may account for as much as one-third of the world's economic production. When unpaid

Box 9.1   Historical Perspective: Counting Women's Work in the 1911 Census of Canada

[In collecting information for the 1911 Census of Canada,] every person ten years of age and over was to have an entry in column 17—Chief Occupation or Trade.

Women who performed housework in their own homes, without earning a salary or wages, and who were not employed outside the home, were to have 'none' entered under 'Chief Occupation or Trade'. However, those working at housework for wages were to have the appropriate employment title entered (such as 'servant', 'cook', 'chambermaid', etc.) as appropriate, with a description after of the place where they worked, such as 'private family', 'hotel', or 'boarding house'. A woman who, in addition to housework in her own home, regularly earned an income from another occupation, either in her own home or outside, was to have that other occupation stated in column 17, with the place of employment entered in column 22. For example, a woman who regularly brought in laundry was to be entered as 'laundress' or 'washerwoman', in column 17, with the location of her work described in column 22.

Members of the Census and Statistics Office did not necessarily agree with the exclusion of those performing housework in their own home: 'It may here be noted that in every census, women performing household duties in their own homes, have not been regarded as being "gainfully employed" and are therefore not included in the statistics of occupations. This restriction is more or less arbitrary as in the agricultural class, particularly, the female portion of the family often performs as large a proportion of the work about the farm as does the male portion and is therefore entitled to be classed as "gainfully employed".'

For individuals who performed piecework at home, the type of work performed was entered, whether the individual was employed under contract with a manufacturer or under any other such agreement. These individuals were to be classed as 'employees'. The term 'clerk' was to be avoided whenever a definite occupation could be specified. Thus, someone that sold goods in a store was to be recorded as a 'salesman' or 'saleswoman'. A worker in an office was similarly to be distinguished as a 'stenographer', 'typewriter', 'accountant', 'bookkeeper', 'cashier', etc., rather than simply 'clerk'.

Despite these instructions, the Census and Statistics Office found that the use of 'indefinite terms' by enumerators made it impossible to develop detailed employment statistics. For example, with workers in a carriage factory, some enumerators would specify the various trades employed in the factory, while others would simply designate all the employees as 'carriage builders'.

Source: Library and Archives Canada, at: <www.collectionscanada.ca/archivianet/1911/006003-100.04-e.html>. Reproduced with the permission of the Minister of Public Works and Government Services Canada (2006).

agricultural work and housework are considered with wage labour in developing countries, women's work hours are estimated to exceed men's by 30 per cent (UN Population Fund, 2000: 38).

Racial and Ethnic Discrimination

Another widespread and institutionalized form of discrimination in the workplace is ethnic and racial prejudice, as we saw in Chapter 4. Workers who belong to ethnic and racial minorities are especially disadvantaged in their search for jobs, in the incomes they receive once hired, and in opportunities to advance based on merit. In part, these problems are because of stereotypes—employers are unwilling or unable to imagine that certain types of people can do good work. Equally important, these problems are due to weak social networks, as we will see later in this chapter. People with more **social capital** are in a better position to hear about good jobs, and employers are more likely to hear about them.

Poverty and Wealth Inequalities

Work also influences the widening income gap between the haves and the have-nots. Even as corporations post record profits to the benefit of their well-paid executives and shareholders, 'downsizing' continues to leave many lower- and middle-class labourers underemployed or unemployed. The clear division between haves and have-nots, first noted by Marx when he distinguished between the bourgeoisie and the proletariat, continues in our post-industrial, service- and information-based society. The capitalist drive to take full advantage of profits and reduce production costs creates an outlook in which company executives are eager to ignore or override the needs and rights of workers if doing so promises greater corporate wealth.

Work–Family Concerns

As gender roles, demographics, and families have changed, the dual-income household has emerged as the norm in Canada and elsewhere. These changes have had effects on both the workplace and the family. A once-patriarchal and male-dominated workforce has come under pressure to provide for women's career goals and needs for financial independence. These changes progressed steadily throughout the twentieth century, but as we saw in Chapter 5, women still have much ground to make up if real equality is to be achieved.

Parents must now learn the difficult daily task of balancing work, family, and personal needs, often with neither the financial means to pay for child care nor the traditional help of extended-family support networks. One major problem of the new century is in figuring out how families can organize themselves most effectively to deal with the multiple problems of work, companionship, child-rearing, and, increasingly, elder care, as we have seen in Chapters 7 and 8.

Worker Dissatisfaction and Alienation

In an ideal world, work is invigorating, satisfying, and socially useful. It fulfills the individual's need for meaningful labour and society's need to get work done. In reality, however, many jobs are not stimulating and challenging. They are repetitive, boring, and often not even socially useful.

At least as far back as Marx, thinkers have noted that industrialization and the resulting division of labour have separated the worker from the work process, from the object he or she produces, and from his or her co-workers. This experience of **alienation** involves feelings of powerlessness, meaninglessness, normlessness (anomie), estrangement, and social isolation in the workplace. Specialized work roles mean that each individual worker is given few responsibilities, performing narrowly defined tasks

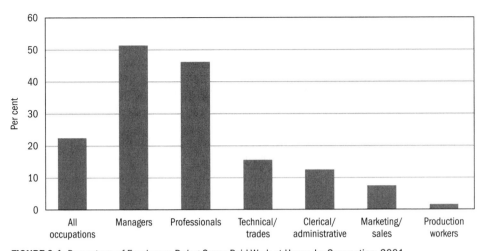

FIGURE 9.1 Percentage of Employees Doing Some Paid Work at Home, by Occupation, 2001

Note: Some employment areas, such as public administration, are excluded.

Source: Adapted from Statistics Canada, 'The Canadian Labour Market at a Glance', 2005, Catalogue no. 71-585, available at: <http://www.statcan.ca/english/studies/maxine/71-222-XIE/2006001/chart-l68-big.htm>.

lacking in variety and challenge, often below his or her full intellectual, physical, and emotional potential, as demanded by the employer. Sociologists have disagreed about the origins of these problems: Marx attributed them to capitalism, Durkheim (1964 [1893]) to specialization, and Weber to rationalization.

Whatever the source, these problems are made worse in tall, hierarchical bureaucracies in which workers at the bottom have no control of, or say in, the work process. Often, employees become just another cog in the wheel, mindlessly churning out the products wanted by their employers as part of a factory line, clerical office, filing department, or retail shop. In extreme cases, this narrow range of tasks is repeated daily for years, even decades. The result is a decline in worker loyalty and production, since employees are no longer dedicated to doing an especially good job. Many studies have shown that low levels of work satisfaction result from these work circumstances (Langfred and Moye, 2004; Stanton et al., 2002; Sikora, 2002).

To be sure, not everyone needs complete control and stability in a job for the work to be enjoyable and fulfilling. Still, surveys show that several factors consistently are related to job satisfaction. The list includes safe working conditions, job security, challenging and stimulating work content, pleasant and like-minded colleagues, respect and consideration from superiors, and opportunities for creativity, initiative, and advancement. Also, it is important that the worker's expectations of the job match the work experience. When the two diverge, resentment, job dissatisfaction, and alienation arise. Perhaps most importantly, people crave some measure of autonomy and control over their work.

Vulnerable Populations

Sex Workers

Whatever the power of personal experiences that incline a person towards sex work, it can still only be possible under specific cultural conditions. Sex work is built on a sexual double standard, widespread poverty, and a gendered labour market. Consequently, as we saw in Chapter 1, poor women and children, especially in societies without a social welfare net, are most likely to be engaged in sex work.

In India, for example, women suffer from the double standard of morality that governs a profitable sex trade. Despite the financial vulnerability that leads them to enter sex work and the health hazards they suffer, Indian sex workers endure stigmatization because they must sell their bodies to live. In particular, 'floating' sex workers who return to their families after work suffer from the sense of leading a discreditable double life.

Throughout history, sex workers have fallen into three categories. In the lowest category are those of the streets. In the middle category are those who work in brothels or bordellos. At the top are the courtesans. Present-day escort services fall somewhere between the top and bottom categories of traditional sex worker: they are mobile (like streetwalkers) but work by appointment and are often well-paid (like geishas).

In Canada, sex work itself is not illegal. However, one can be arrested for related offences such as communicating (solicitation) offences, bawdy house offences, or procuring (pimping) offences. Even in jurisdictions where sex work is illegal, places to find sex are well known. There, sex workers gather in so-called 'red-light districts'. These districts may come and go: the unstable location of sex work in a city results from the interplay between the ordering strategies of the police and community protestors and the resistive tactics adopted by sex workers. These strategies depend on whether the society believes in the legalization or criminalization of sex work. With decriminalized sex work, distinctive red-light or brothel districts are created to isolate sex work from more socially approved activities and people and to keep women from walking the streets, propositioning potential clients (Hubbard and Sanders, 2003).

Sex work entails relations between a sex worker, her client, and her pimp. Street-level sex work includes both pimp-controlled and independent entrepreneurial sex work. Pimp-related violence is common towards women involved in pimp-controlled sex work (Williamson and Cluse-Tolar, 2002). Even so, the social bonds between pimps and sex workers follow certain rules. As with other forms of vice and crime, public violence is bad for business, so efforts are made to control sex work activities without much violence, or at least to reserve violent methods of control for when it can be delivered in private.

Even protected sex workers are at risk, however. Guidroz (2001) examined two types of sex industry work—escorts and telephone sex work—to explore sex workers' gendered work experiences in the sex industry. The escorts' and telephone sex operators' lives are affected by their work and many report feeling isolated. The work also involves emotional labour—a characteristically female activity. The power imbalance in the relationship between sex worker and client is obvious everywhere. Lastly, poorer women are more vulnerable and less able to negotiate safe sex (Gysels et al., 2002).

In many countries, female sex workers must switch daily between the roles of mother and sex worker. As a result, they are constantly subjected to society's double standard for women (Castaneda et al., 1996). Sex workers divide their lives between the mother/saint and traitor/sex-worker roles. Rationalizations of those who wish to legalize sex work include justifying it as a better-paying employment opportunity for women and as a type of social service. These practical considerations, however, are frequently drowned out by moral outcries. Because of these difficulties, sex workers have had difficulty mobilizing for their own protection and advancement. Some sex workers have tried to improve their health and social standing by forming social movements. For the first time, sex workers are politically organizing and expressing their claims and grievances in the public debate about sex work—a debate from which they are usually excluded (Mathieu, 2003).

Usually, people enter the sex trade because they can see no other choice. To confirm this, Nixon and colleagues (2002) studied data from three western Canadian provinces and found that young women tend to enter sex work out of financial necessity. Once there, many experienced violence with such consistency that it almost seemed 'normal'. Many sex workers, here and elsewhere, grew up in harsh and even abusive families. Often, they have limited educational backgrounds or have not completed high school, thus making their exit from sex work into other types of work even more difficult.

Survey results (Kramer and Berg, 2003) show that both white and minority women engaging in sex work experienced high rates of physical and sexual abuse in childhood, as well as parental substance abuse. The result is a spread of sex work among adolescents with its attendant problems (Bamgbose, 2002). Gaudette et al. (1996) state that the average age in which a sex worker enters the sex trade is 14. As is the case throughout the industry, adolescent sex workers vary: some are in brothels while others are streetwalkers, call girls, and casual, part-time, or floating sex workers. Among sex workers in many countries, parental substance abuse, neglect, and emotional, physical, and sexual abuse are common in the girls' lives. They run away from turbulent home lives and are trapped by the illegal world of underground sex work.

Some people just drift into selling sex, which can be casual or professional, implicit or explicit. Wojcicki (2002) describes the practice of *ukuphanda*, a Zulu verb that describes the sex-for-money exchanges that take place outside commercial sex work in some parts of South Africa. Women who exchange sex for money in taverns do not self-identify as commercial sex workers and are less stigmatized. Unlike commercial sex work, which is associated with short skirts and other revealing clothes, sex-for-money exchange in the taverns is viewed as more private, ambiguous, and informal. Women who work as informal sex workers, or *phandela imali* ('try to get money'), are understood to use the sex-for-money exchange to survive financially.

Thus, it may be easy in some places and circumstances to drift into sex work; often, it is far more difficult to leave. Manopaiboon et al. (2003) studied Thai women's ability to leave sex work and the factors influencing their lives after leaving. All but one of the 42 current and former female sex workers surveyed had quit sex work at least once before. Women's ability and decisions to leave sex work are determined mainly by four factors: financial situation, link with a steady partner, attitudes towards sex work, and HIV/AIDS experience. Most women assume their risk for HIV infection to be lower after leaving sex work, yet three of the 17 HIV-infected women were infected after having left, presumably from their steady partners.

Everywhere in the prosperous West, sex workers are being sourced from Eastern European, Asian, and Latin American countries. The rapid expansion and diversification of the international sex trade can be credited to several factors. Among them are the simultaneous rise in service occupations, temporary work, and corporate-fuelled consumption; an increase in labour migrations, tourism, and business travel; the connection between the information economy and the privatization of commercial consumption; and new forms of gender, sexuality, and kinship (Bernstein, 2002).

Young women suffer the assaults of war, and in addition face the intensifying levels of sexual and domestic violence, poverty, and social dislocation that war brings. As well,

Trafficking for the Sex Trade

Human Rights Watch has identified consistent patterns—fraud, deception, isolation, debt bondage, and threat and use of physical force—used in the trafficking of women. Often, corrupt officials facilitate this trafficking. The Future Group, an NGO founded to combat human trafficking, warned a House of Commons committee in November 2006 that the 2010 Vancouver Winter Olympics could create an explosion in human trafficking for the sex trade, and today Eastern European women, after having been promised good jobs in Canada, are forced to pay off their travel debt by working in the sex trade.

they may be preyed on by international criminal rackets exploiting the invisibility of poor young women in war zones for illegal sexual, domestic, and industrial labour—part of the tragic underbelly of development that yields billions of dollars annually.

Child Labour

Child labourers are a second vulnerable workforce. The International Labour Organization (ILO) has estimated that 250 million children between the ages of 5 and 14 worked in developing countries in 1996—at least 120 million working full-time. Africa and Asia together account for over 90 per cent of total child employment. In sub-Saharan Africa, almost one child in three children below the age of 15—or a total of 48 million children—is engaged in work. Latin America and the Caribbean have roughly 17.4 million child workers. Fifteen per cent of children work in the Middle East and North Africa. By contrast, roughly 2.5 million children are working in industrialized and transition economies (Human Rights Watch, at hrw.org/children/labor.htm).

Child labour is especially common in rural areas where the capacity to enforce minimum age rules for schooling and work is lacking. Most children in rural areas work in agriculture or as domestics, while urban children tend to work in trade and services, with fewer in manufacturing and construction. Though children are poorly paid in these jobs, they still serve as major contributors to family income in developing countries. The lack of good schools also encourages parents to send their children to work rather than school. Rigid cultural and social views about children and childhood may also limit educational goals and increase child labour (ibid.).

Working children are the objects of extreme exploitation, toiling for long hours at low pay. Furthermore, three-quarters (171 million) work under risky conditions in mines, with chemicals, or with dangerous machinery. Not surprisingly, this exposure leads to lasting physical and psychological harm. Working at rug looms, for example, may leave children disabled with eye damage, lung disease, stunted growth, and a vulnerability to arthritis as they grow older.

Many children work in order to attend school, so abolishing all child labour may only hinder their education. However, in general, improving the financial condition of struggling families would free children from full-time labour. Sometimes, a child's work can be helpful to him or her and to the family. Working and earning can be a positive experience in a child's growing up, not least by teaching important lessons in responsibility, independence, and the value of a dollar. This depends largely on the child's age, the conditions in which the child works, and whether work prevents the child from going to school. Invariably, exploitative child labour hampers the child's development and preparation for adult life in a post-industrial world.

Without an education and a normal childhood, some children are reduced almost to slavery. Some are kidnapped and forced to work. Many are beaten or subjected to other severe physical abuse. An extreme form of child labour, bonded labour, takes place when a family receives a small advance payment (sometimes as little as $20) to give a boy or girl over to an employer. Usually the child cannot work off the debt, nor can the family raise enough money to buy the child back. Bonded child labour is widespread in countries around the world; millions of such children work in India alone.

Currently, there is no international agreement defining child labour, making it hard to isolate cases of abuse, let alone abolish them. However, eliminating child labour is one of the four fundamental principles of the ILO's Declaration on Fundamental Principles and Rights at Work. ILO Convention 182 calls for the prohibition and immediate action to expel the worst forms of child labour. It defines a child as a person under 18 years old, and 'worst forms of child labour' as: all forms of slavery or practices similar to slavery such as the sale and trafficking of children, debt bondage and serfdom, forced or compulsory labour, including forced or compulsory recruitment of children for use in armed conflict; the use, procuring, or sale of a child for prostitution, pornographic performances, or illicit activities—especially, for the production and trafficking of drugs. In short, it calls for an end to all work that is likely to harm the health, safety, or morals of children (ibid.; also International Labour Organization, at www.ilo.org/public/english/standards/ipec/about/factsheet/faq.htm).

By contrast, work by children in Canada is regulated and the worst forms of child labour are banned. Free primary and secondary schooling are universally available, and school attendance is compulsory until at least age 16. In addition, the federal, provincial, and territorial governments have adopted many laws banning or restricting the employment of children to ensure that their participation in work does not affect their health and development or interfere with their schooling. At the national level, the Federal Committee Against the Commercial Sexual Exploitation of Children was created specifically to examine programs underway across Canada to fight the exploitation of children and youth in the sex trade (for more on this, see Canadian Strategy Against Commercial Sexual Exploitation of Children & Youth, at sen.parl.gc.ca/lpearson/htmfiles/hill/17_htm_files/Committee-e/Exploit_EN.htm).

Unemployment and Its Effects

Types of Unemployment and Their Measurement

Researchers distinguish between discriminatory and structural unemployment. **Discriminatory unemployment** is unemployment resulting from discrimination against particular groups, such as ethnic minorities and women. **Structural unemployment** results from social and economic factors that affect workers equally across all groups. These factors include corporate layoffs, capital flight (caused by corporate mergers and the move of operations to another geographic region—so-called 'runaway plants'), and automation (replacing human labour with machinery).

Researchers base their measures of unemployment on the percentage of the workforce currently without jobs, actively seeking employment, and available to work. This definition excludes women who work as homemakers without pay and **discouraged workers**, i.e., those who have turned their backs on the traditional work system and abandoned efforts to work for pay. These discouraged workers consist disproportionately of women and racial minorities. Other people do not take part in the labour force because they are in school, retired, injured, sick, or otherwise unable to work.

Because of these exclusions, most official unemployment rates understate the true percentage of the unemployed. This in turn underestimates the size of the unemployment problem. Official employment rates also do not distinguish between full-time and part-time work, nor do they recognize odd jobs, temporary work, and other forms of underemployment as different from full-time work. A person who reports working as little as one hour per week is formally considered 'gainfully employed'. This, too, lessens the visible problem of unemployment. So, in the end, our estimates of unemployment provide too rosy a picture of the world.

Predictors of Unemployment

Some explanations of unemployment focus on the social and financial environment in which jobs are lost; others focus on the individuals who lose their jobs. In the former category, research has been done on the causes and effects of downsizing. For example, researchers found that downsizing cut out about 60 per cent of the workforce and one-quarter of the job titles in the British Columbia sawmill industry, largely in response to an economic recession in the early 1980s. Job loss tended to affect the youngest workers most severely (Ostry et al., 2000).

Other researchers focus on the characteristics of people who lose their job or are at particular risk of losing their job in a recession. Often they focus on human capital characteristics, such as educational attainment or particular job-related skills. Age itself predicts unemployment. Older workers (over age 40) who have been laid off find it harder than younger workers to get a job, especially in work, like construction, that demands physical strength. Family characteristics play a part, too. For example, single marital status predicts unemployment after a layoff among construction and forest workers (Liira and Leino, 1999). Parental divorce, low parental emotional involvement, and parental unemployment (for males only) predict the unemployment of youth (de Goede et al., 2000).

Box 9.2   Social Policy: Mandatory Retirement

One year from today [12 December 2005], mandatory retirement will be illegal in Ontario, Labour Minister Steve Peters announced.

'This is another step to modernize working conditions for the people of Ontario', said Peters. 'Mandatory retirement is a discriminatory practice that makes no sense in a time when we're all living longer, healthier, more active lives. Ending it is the right thing to do.'

The Ending Mandatory Retirement Statute Law Amendment Act was approved by the legislative assembly in an overwhelming 60–5 vote on December 8 and was given royal assent by Lieutenant-Governor James Bartleman . . . . It takes effect [on 12 December 2006], to allow employers time to adjust their workplace policies and practices.

'We want to give Ontarians time to get ready for the change. Some employers, for instance, may need to adapt their human resources policies and practices to comply with the law', said Peters. 'We would urge employers to consider the legislation when dealing with employees coming up on age 65 in the next year.' People are healthier and living longer, so it is unfair to insist that they stop working simply because they turn 65, he said. Ending mandatory retirement allows workers to decide when to retire based on lifestyle, circumstance, and priorities. [Figure 9.2 shows retirement trends in the Canadian workforce over the period 1976–2003.]

The Ontario Human Rights Code will protect people aged 65 and over from age discrimination for most employment purposes. The legislation also amends a variety of other statutes that have provisions connected to mandatory retirement.

Source: Government of Ontario, at: ogov.newswire.ca/ontario/GPOE/2005/12/12/c6207.html?lmatch =?=_e.html>. © Queen's Printer for Ontario, 2005. Reproduced with permission.

Some have argued that health problems often predate and cause unemployment. Unhealthy lifestyle behaviours, such as smoking and heavy use of alcohol, are correlated with unemployment, for example (Liira and Leino, 1999). Poor physical health may result in unemployment, even among youth (Hammarstrom and Janlert, 1997). A study of job mobility over a five-year period in the Netherlands found that health problems were significantly associated with a higher risk of mobility out of employment in 1991 and a lower likelihood of mobility into employment in 1995. The least healthy people remained economically inactive over the period studied (Van de Mheen et al., 1999).

To some degree, the effects of illness on working life depend on the duration of a disability. In one study, over half of the workers who became limited in activities of daily living as adults had unemployment spells lasting less than two years. Few disabled people who remained outside the workforce for four years re-entered it (Burchardt, 2000). More than half of the non-working disabled reported that economic, social, and job-based barriers contributed to their inability to work, and one-fourth of working disabled people reported having been discriminated against in the last five years (Druss et al., 2000). Mental as well as physical health is linked to transitions to early retirement or other unemployment (Wray, 2000). Above-average mental health plays a protective role in keeping workers in the workforce rather than laid off, on sick leave, or unemployed.

However, health problems do not always lead to long-term unemployment. Specific health conditions, such as asthma or visual impairment, may be associated with work limitation, yet they are not among the main determinants of continuous unemployment (McCarty et al., 1999; Yelin et al., 1999). The risk of unemployment for chronically ill people largely depends on active labour market policies—specific efforts made by government to stimulate employment, job training, and worker mobility. Employment protections also play a role, as shown by lower rates of unemployment and inactivity in Sweden than in Britain (Burstrom et al., 2000).

Social Consequences of Unemployment

As unpleasant as work can be, the alternative is often even worse. Since everyone needs money to buy what they need and most people can get money only by working, unemployment deprives most people of the basis for material survival. Unemployment also

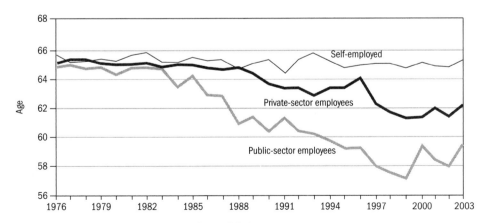

FIGURE 9.2 Median Age at Retirement, by Class of Worker
Source: Adapted from Statistics Canada, Labour Force Survey, CANSIM database, http://cansim2.statcan.ca, table 282-0051.

takes a toll on society at large. With people out of the workforce, the economy cannot reach its utmost potential for production. Another reason unemployment affects the overall economy is the cost of preserving a social support network to help those who are between jobs.

From a social-psychological perspective, unemployed people are often marked with the stigma of being lazy and unwilling to work. Some think that unemployment insurance and welfare undermine the work ethic that has motivated so many others to succeed in life. People who see themselves as masters of their own fate hold those who are unemployed responsible for their own condition and do not think that they deserve public aid. On the other hand, people who see themselves (and others) as victims of forces beyond their control are able to believe that those who are unemployed due to ill health, discrimination, recession, or corporate downsizing deserve help.

The aid made available to unemployed people varies with the duration and causes of unemployment. Those who are physically disabled receive the most help, since people consider them the blameless 'deserving poor'. Chronically unemployed people are sometimes considered the 'undeserving poor'. This thinking runs on the assumption that, after a while, unemployed people should have taken retraining or moved to another city and found a new job. People who have failed to do this have failed to act in their own interests. As a result, they receive less generous and secure help. Social assistance payments to continuously unemployed people fail to meet living expenses, especially for people who live in large cities like Toronto and Vancouver where the cost of living is high.

Many believe that if social relief payments were to exceed the minimum-wage level, unemployed people would be reluctant to get off welfare and take a job, even though hundreds of thousands cannot find a job despite actively searching. Some abide by the notion that only motivation is at issue: anyone who tries to can find a job. This supposition ignores the evidence of discrimination against racial minorities and disappearing work for the less educated. Certain groups, such as female single parents of small children, cannot afford to pay the daycare costs that would allow them to take a job. Others, such as the physically disabled, cannot find a job that fits their abilities.

Health Consequences of Work

Workplace Safety Issues

Health and safety hazards in the workplace are an obvious social problem. For example, in 1998, 798 Canadian workers died because of an occupational injury and another 793,666 were injured on the job. In 2004, the number of workplace deaths in Canada had risen to 928: 'the Canadian Centre for the Study of Living Standards investigated safety at workplaces in rich nations around the world. Canada's rate of workplace fatalities—7 deaths per 100,000 workers—tied for top spot as the worst. Canada's record for reducing workplace fatalities over the previous 20 years stood alone as the worst' (CBC News, 2006). This dismal record is explainable, in part at least, by the extent to which Canada, relative to other wealthy countries, is still reliant on the dangerous work of resource extraction—logging, fishing, oil drilling, mining—and on heavy manufacturing.

A report on industries under federal jurisdiction showed that, in 2002, 1,020,699 employees suffered occupational injuries in Canada. Though many of these injuries were minor, roughly one-third were classed as disabling, resulting in significant losses in hours worked (www.sdc.gc.ca/en/lp/lo/ohs/statistics/images19982002/oicc9802.pdf).

Some industries are more dangerous than others. The manufacturing sector, in particular, is a dangerous place to work, accounting for nearly 30 per cent of the total occupational injuries reported in Canada in 1998. Incidence rates were highest among the logging and forestry, construction, and manufacturing industries, and lowest within the finance and insurance sector. In general, the occupations with the highest risk of occupational injury or death are those that involve semi-skilled manual labour, such as equipment operator and installer, manufacturer, and machine assembler. The occupations with the lowest risk of work-related injury or death are senior management executive and business and finance professions (HRDC, 2000).

These official statistics often underrate the severity of the health risks in dangerous workplaces since they measure only directly observable medical conditions. Many other job-related injuries and deaths can result from years of exposure to poor air quality and toxic or carcinogenic (cancer-causing) substances. Biological hazards in the workplace include viruses, bacteria, fungi, and parasitic organisms. Dangerous chemicals include liquids such as gasoline and mercury, paint and pesticide vapours, and toxic gases such as ammonia. Environmental hazards include radiation, ultraviolet and microwaves, extreme temperatures and humidity, and not enough interior lighting. These hazards may be known and accepted parts of the job. Firefighters, for example, are at a higher risk of developing cancer than the average person, a direct result of their constant exposure to toxic smoke and burning materials. However, most of the people who enter this profession have been made aware of the dangers in advance.

Sometimes, however, the hazards are a result of company negligence. Many workers do not enjoy the luxury of preventive technologies, or even an awareness of the harm that can be caused by hazards in their workplaces. For example, James Coleman (1994) points out that although people had been aware of the dangers of asbestos exposure since 1918, the industry did not try to protect workers until as late as the 1960s. As a

Top Workplace Hazards

- Falls
- Machinery (e.g., hoists and cranes)
- Moving vehicles
- Overexertion
- Collapsing platforms or equipment
- Explosions and fires
- Electrical hazards
- Confined space
- Hazardous chemicals
- Falling objects
- Workplace violence
- Burns

Source: The Ontario Workplace Safety and Insurance Board, at: <www.wsib.on.ca/wsib/wsibsite.nsf/publicprint/TopWorkplaceHazards>.

Box 9.3 Personal Experience: How Work Can Affect Health

Reorganization at work can make a manageable illness unmanageable as new time structures become untenable. Productivity speedups due to reorganization, promotion, or layoffs of co-workers wreck time structures. Several individuals had found it hard to handle their workload before a change increased it. Afterwards, they could not handle it. A corporate takeover had left a middle-aged salesman responsible for covering a larger area and for making higher profits in a tighter market. He felt that these changes contributed to his heart disease:

> I worked for Healthtech Pharmaceuticals and we sold blood therapeutic products. And I felt like I was a used car salesman at times, because everything was based on price and I would be running all around the countryside delivering vials of blood here and there and the other place, getting prices from the company, kind of fibbing to the company, telling them that my competition was lower so they would give me a lower price, you know. And, I was working out all kinds of deals. It was really traumatic.

Source: Charmaz (1997: 174). Copyright © 1991 by Kathleen C. Charmaz.

result, of the half-million labourers exposed, at least 100,000 will die of lung cancer, 35,000 from mesothelioma, and 35,000 from asbestosis. Even today, workers continue to be exposed to dangerous levels of asbestos, sometimes with the full knowledge of corporate management.

Work Stress

Another health-related feature of employment that is increasingly being studied is work-related stress. This can lead to the neurological condition called 'burnout' as well as other significant physical and mental health outcomes. When the demands of the job exceed the abilities, resources, or needs of the worker, job stress occurs.

Workplaces can be stressful at times, the result of work overload, conflicts with the boss or workmates, a lack of control over the work process, or sheer boredom from the repetition of work (see Box 9.4). Some of the signs of stress employees may experience as a result will include sleep disorders, high blood pressure, headaches, ulcers, and an an inability to concentrate or relax. According to the Canadian Mental Health Institute (cited at epilepsyontario.org/client/EO/EOWeb.nsf/web/Stress+in+the+Workplace):

1. Workplace stress is the most common form of stress experienced by Canadians.
2. Of Canadian adults 30 years of age and older, 43 per cent feel overwhelmed by their jobs, according to the Heart and Stroke Foundation's Annual Report Card on Canadians' Health.
3. Canadian workers view job stress as more prevalent than work-related injury or illness.
4. Canadians are not alone: job-related stress has been identified by the World Health Organization as a 'worldwide epidemic'.
5. Not all stress is bad: without some degree of stress, people become bored and depressed. However, ill health can occur when our response to stress is not channelled properly.
6. It is estimated that 40 per cent of employee turnover is due to job stress.
7. Job stress is a major factor in employee absenteeism. Statistics Canada calculates the annual cost of work time lost to stress at $12 billion.
8. Workplace stress has been shown to cause backaches, migraines, and substance abuse, all of which contribute to poor job performance.
9. Chronic stress can lead to hypertension, depression, and susceptibility to other common physical illnesses.
10. Less obvious results of workplace stress are the feelings of frustration, anger, and hopelessness that affect stressed employees.

Statistics on hours spent at work cannot capture either the full amount of time spent working or the stress associated with work. It is possible to be 'at work' without working. One could be at home, yet preoccupied with job issues. It is possible to work 10 hours a day in a leisurely fashion yet do less work and feel less stressed than someone who works seven intense hours a day. Increasingly, for example, professional and managerial workers are expected to take their work home with them and to be on call as needed. The continuous availability of these workers to one another—through telephone, voice mail, fax, and e-mail—means that we need subtle and comparable measures of work, and of stress, if we are to make international comparisons.

Box 9.4   Social Construction: Bosses Define the Work Experience

A bad boss can do more than just pass you over for a promotion or give you a minuscule pay raise. He or she can also raise your risk of depression, heart disease, and stroke, some experts say. . . .

A bad boss who causes stronger anger, anxiety, headaches, and backaches is most likely to be doing so by giving unclear directions and orders, said Scott Schieman, a sociology professor at the University of Toronto.

Schieman surveyed 1,800 employees across the United States from February to August to determine correlations between workplace conditions and mental, emotional, and physical health. The professor is still compiling data, but preliminary findings show a distinct trend: a boss who nags an employee and/or casts blame for something that is not an employee's fault erodes emotional well-being and causes more stress and depression.

A separate study, 'The Contribution of Supervisor Behaviour to Employee Psychological Well-Being', provides further support for the idea that a bad boss leads to poor emotional health. When an employee rated a supervisor's behaviour above average, there was a 63 per cent probability the employee's score of psychological well-being would also be above average, according to this study by Brad Gilbreath and Philip Benson of the Indiana University–Purdue University Fort Wayne.

But a bad relationship with the boss can lead to more than psychological ailments. Nadia Wager, a psychologist at Buckinghamshire Chilterns University in the United Kingdom, found in a 2003 study of health-care workers that a bad boss is associated with high blood pressure and higher risk of stroke. Nurses working for managers who showed little respect, fairness, or sensitivity had higher blood pressure than those who worked for managers assessed as considerate and empathetic. Wager found the risk of heart disease increased 16 per cent; and stroke 38 per cent. Now she's studying the link between bad bosses and depressed workers . . . .

Schieman suggested three strategies for creating a positive workplace:

Provide an environment where employees can contribute and create a better environment.

Treat employees like people.

Be aware of what's happening around you.

Source: Prashad (2005). Reprinted with permission—Toronto Syndication Services.

The health effects of prolonged workplace strain are obvious and serious. After reviewing 14 studies, Paul Landsbergis and colleagues (1993) reported that a clear connection exists between job stress and heart disease. The pressures of high demand—that is, the need for someone to be 'on call' and responsive all the time—can be offset by high control over the work environment. However, when the tasks are demanding but the employee lacks control over the situation, stress may encroach on both productivity and health. Prime examples of people in these types of occupations are waitresses, nurses, schoolteachers, and social workers—note that they are overwhelmingly 'women's occupations'. Most of the people in these occupations who report stress and burnout reveal that their wish to help others and solve problems is 'frequently thwarted by the need to deal with an excessive number of clients, limited resources, and administrative policies that make it difficult to be effective' (Krahn and Lowe, 1993: 362).

Job Insecurity

Chronic job insecurity can also produce adverse physiological changes in people's bodies because of increased stress and worry (Ferrie, Shipley, et al., 2001). Insecure jobs can be as damaging to health as unemployment. This fact leads us to infer that employment and unemployment are points on a continuum (Hallsten et al., 1999).

Job insecurity can have enormous physical, mental, and financial effects on people's lives (Ferrie, 1997; Ferrie, Martikainen, et al., 2001). A study of Swedish police inspectors threatened with unemployment, for example, traced chemical changes in their bodies over a three-year period, reflecting worry about employment and symptoms of burnout during the reorganization of a police district. Reports of lowered work satisfaction, a perceived decline in the ethical and moral standards of the organization, and favourable changes in the employment status and work environment all registered noticeably in blood samples taken before and after the reorganization (Grossi et al., 1999).

Because of this negative effect of uncertainty, people can suffer from recessions even if they are not immediately affected. The trade cycle affects the health mainly of people with jobs to lose. Distress and dissatisfaction increase during economic recessions because of increased job demands and ever less adequate pay (Tausig and Fenwick, 1999). Young job-holders report more physical and psychological symptoms during a recession than they do during a boom. The effects of a recession on young people's—especially young women's—health are mediated by pessimism about the future, high work demands, and financial problems (Novo et al., 2001). Among men, recessions increase the prevalence of binge drinking, even among those who remain employed (Dee, 2001). Similarly, people who live in communities where the unemployment rate is high are at a greater risk of ill health even if they are employed full-time (Bellaby and Bellaby, 1999).

Job insecurity reduces people's sense of control over their environment and their opportunities for positive self-evaluation. These experiences have harmful health outcomes that cut across genders, educational levels, income levels, marital status, and other social categories (McDonough, 2000). However, one study found that job insecurity has a more unfavourable effect on the health of educated employees than on the health of the less-educated (Domenighetti et al., 2000).

Along similar lines, people in organizations where layoffs have occurred because of downsizing and who have maintained personal contact with laid-off workers are more likely to experience job insecurity, and more symptoms of poor health, depression, and eating changes than are people who have no such contact. People who have been laid off and rehired suffer more work-related injuries and illnesses and miss more work days than people who were employed throughout the same period (Grunberg et al., 2001).

Exploitation of Workers

What happens in the workplace has even more impact on a person's health than success or failure in finding a job and keeping it. The health outcomes of employment are directly contingent on the quality of work. The highest levels of health risk are found among dissatisfied workers, the lowest levels among satisfied workers (Graetz, 1993). Two conditions influence a person's experience of stress and depression on the job. One is job strain: a combination of high demand and low control at work. The other is job injustice: high effort with low reward (Tsutsumi et al., 2001). Both relate to the problem that Marx called alienation.

An example of job injustice would be workers in some (typically, non-unionized) occupations that pay below minimum wage, offer no overtime or benefits, and entail 50 to 60 hours of work per week in unsafe and crowded factories.

Conditions are even worse in developing countries, where unemployment rates are higher and unions are weak or non-existent. Some workers, including many children, are paid only a fraction of the country's official minimum wage. Often governments are unwilling to legislate better working conditions because they do not want to scare off foreign capitalists who are willing to move their factories to these low-wage countries.

In recent years, protestors in Canada and other developed countries have called on consumers to recognize the extent of worker exploitation abroad and to understand that this exploitation—though outside their immediate view—has consequences for their own lives. As long as workers are exploited in developing countries, Canadian consumers will be able to buy logo-branded clothing, smart household furnishings, and up-to-date electronic items for low prices. As workers, however, we should know the result is continued exploitation abroad and the movement of high-paying jobs from Canada to low-wage countries. In addition, inequitable and oppressive conditions have arguably contributed to global unrest, which inevitably has impacts on all countries. It remains to be seen whether Canadians, as consumers and as voters, will take suitable action.

Indicators of Health

Aspects of work and unemployment have serious effects on health. Statistics Canada uses the following as determinants of health:

1. Unemployment rate
2. Long-term unemployment
3. Youth unemployment
4. Low-income rate
5. Children in low-income families
6. Average personal income

Source: Statistics Canada, at: <dissemination.statcan.ca/english/freepub/82-221-XIE/defin.htm#top>.

Health Consequences of Unemployment

Unemployment, also, can have significant health outcomes. Research shows that unemployment causes a wide range of social and personal pathologies. Although inadequate employment can be depressing, unemployment also—and even more so—deprives people of money, meaning, and sociability (Dooley et al., 2000).

Mortality

Unemployed people are at a higher risk of death from causes associated with unhealthy lifestyles. Specifically, unemployment produces anxiety and depression, which can lead to increased smoking, alcohol consumption, and drug use. Over the long term, these habits increase the risk of cirrhosis, bronchitis, emphysema, and various forms of cancer (Pasarin et al., 1999). A review of the literature on mortality and morbidity rates shows a causal link between unemployment and mortality from cardiovascular disease and suicide (Jin et al., 1997).

Unemployment does not usually cause death in the short term, except by linkages to suicide, homicide, and driving accidents (Martikainen and Valkonen, 1998). The longer the period of unemployment, the more physical and psychological health problems emerge. For example, unemployment in 1973 among women and men in Sweden showed an association with higher than expected mortality by 1996 among people under age 70 (Nylen et al., 2001), even after controlling for social, behavioural, work-related, and health-related factors (for example, smoking, alcohol, and lifestyle behaviours). Unemployment also raised the risks of death among young people studied over a shorter period. For example, among young Australian men studied over a five-year period, being out of school but unemployed was associated with a higher risk of death (Morrell et al., 1999).

Unemployment is not the only disturbing life event that interacts with existing psychological problems (for example, hopelessness, psychological distress, or drug abuse) to raise the risk of suicide, but it is an important one (Foster et al., 1999). Most research finds that unemployment increases the risk of suicide (Brown et al., 2000; but also see Goldney et al., 1995; Hagquist et al., 2000). Unemployment increases the risk of a wide variety of suicide attempts, including deliberate self-poisoning (Carter et al., 1999), often carried out on repeated occasions. Suicide rates for unemployed people are clearly and consistently higher than those for employed people (Preti and Miotto, 1999). The connection between unemployment and suicide can be noted on both the individual level and through ecological (community) analysis. The latter shows that areas experiencing the lowest increase in unemployment rates experience the lowest increase in rates of suicide (Crawford and Prince, 1999).

Suicide rates have always been higher for men than for women, though women make more suicide attempts. Men are more likely to succeed because of the more lethal means they use, because of their higher levels of alcohol and drug use, and because they are less likely to seek medical or psychiatric help when they are feeling suicidal (Russell and Judd, 1999). The associations between unemployment and suicide, in both men and women, are stronger for young people. The factors influencing suicide influence men and women to the same degree (Gunnell et al., 1999).

Substance Abuse

Unemployment increases the risk of consumption of alcohol, tobacco, and other drugs, especially in young men (Fillmore et al., 1998; MacDonald and Pudney, 2000; Montgomery et al., 1998). Alcohol abuse, associated with unemployment, is correlated with a heightened risk of death by suicide, violence, and driving accidents (see, e.g., Stefansson, 1991).

Increased alcohol consumption is one of the mechanisms connecting unemployment and suicide (Hintikka et al., 1999). Unemployment increases the risk of alcohol abuse, and re-employment reduces the prevalence of alcohol abuse (Claussen, 1999a, 1999b). In turn, alcohol abuse increases the risk of violence, especially family violence (Rodriguez et al., 1997). If we control for alcohol use, unemployment has no effect on family violence. Alcohol abuse also increases the likelihood of fatal car crashes at night; insofar as unemployment reduces the frequency of car accidents, it is because those without jobs no longer spend time on the road commuting to and from work (Gonzalez and Rodriguez, 2000).

Drug and alcohol dependence is associated with both lower employment rates and fewer hours of work. In particular, co-morbidities—multiple drug dependencies—play a critical role in the link between substance use and employment (Bray et al., 2000).

Psychological Consequences: Depression and Anxiety

More than anything else, unemployment affects health by increasing anxiety and depression (Comino et al., 2000; Montgomery et al., 1999; Viinamaki et al., 1993, 1996; Ytterdahl, 1999). Job loss typically arouses defensive feelings, lowers self-esteem, and creates doubt about the future. It often causes people to become passive and to withdraw from social life, further harming their mental health (Underlid, 1996). Unemployed people report more stress, boredom, doubt, and dissatisfaction with themselves and their lives than do the gainfully employed (Gien, 2000). Typically, unemployment causes people's resources to dwindle, having a negative impact on their views of themselves, their aging, and the possibility of leading a productive life (Schmitt, 2001).

It is easy to understand why unemployed people become depressed. Work is not only instrumental for fulfilling material needs—for most adults it is a human need in itself. Most people have a psychosocial need for work (Nordenmark and Strandh, 1999).

However, some people feel unemployment more keenly than others. People who are committed to work for non-financial reasons have the highest risks of poor mental health after losing their job (Nordenmark, 1999a). People with strong feelings of commitment to being employed feel especially distressed if they are unemployed for extended periods (Hannan et al., 1997). Also, people who lose a stimulating job and have only a weak attachment to other activities, such as housework and leisure, are especially likely to miss their job.

Unemployed people in low-unemployment areas are also more likely to be depressed, especially if they have a college-level education (Turner, 1995). Further, people who believe the world is 'just' experience job loss more negatively, with more depressive symptoms, than people who do not expect justice in events that impact their lives (Benson and Ritter, 1990).

Researchers disagree about whether unemployment has the same effects on women and men. Some researchers find that men feel job loss as more existentially threatening than do women, explaining a higher frequency of depression among unemployed men (Lahelma, 1992; Ytterdahl and Fugelli, 2000). Women, it is argued, have less of their self-identity defined by paid work and can usually invest themselves in housework, if necessary, though unemployment for women also involves a loss of personal identity (Desmarais, 1991). Others note that women can suffer great distress from unemployment, even after giving birth when they are much involved in their maternal role (Saurel Cubizolles et al., 2000). Thus, some have concluded that, in responding to unemployment, women and men are more similar than they are different (Nordenmark, 1999b), though they may show their distress in slightly different ways. Job loss results in anxiety disorders in women, while unemployed men often fall victim to substance abuse and depression and anxiety. When a spouse loses a job, women more often than men suffer both from the financial outcomes and from increased marital conflict (Avison, 1996).

Unemployment produces distress, fatalistic attitudes, feelings of a lack of control over one's life, and feelings of personal inefficacy. Poor mental health, in turn, reduces the likelihood of finding a job. Depression caused by unemployment may lead to continued unemployment. Conversely, success in finding a job is predicted by a positive attitude and an active way of dealing with unemployment (Schaufeli, 1997).

Other Health Problems

Unemployment and its social and health outcomes carry secondary effects one might not imagine:

■ Unemployment predicts higher smoking rates. Higher smoking rates increase the risk of sudden infant death syndrome (SIDS)—an otherwise unexplained death of an infant during sleep (Mehanni et al., 2000).
■ Unemployment increases the risk of domestic violence; factors involved include alcohol abuse, drug use, intermittent employment, and recent unemployment (Kyriacou et al., 1999).

- Unemployment among husbands increases stress and illness in wives and the incidence of low birth weights in babies born to pregnant wives (Catalano, Hansen, and Hartig, 1999).
- Unemployment, by increasing anti-social behaviour, increases the incidence of foster-home placements for children in families that lose jobs or income (Catalano, Lind, and Rosenblatt, 1999).
- Unemployment of all household members is associated with the risk of a pre-term birth within the first 22 to 32 weeks of pregnancy (Ancel et al., 1999).
- Unemployment reduces the likelihood that a woman will have a periodic cervical (pap) smear, increasing the likelihood that doctors will fail to detect cervical cancer early (Rohlfs et al., 1999).
- Unemployment increases the risk of obesity because of increased fat consumption, reduced exercise, and increased alcohol consumption (Karvonen and Rimpela, 1997; Sarlio-Lähteenkorva and Lahelma, 1999).

Thus, unemployment sets in motion a long line of mental and physical health problems, which in turn make it harder for a person to find and keep a job.

Entering unemployment is a drastic form of downward social mobility, which substantially impacts a person's future mobility chances. Unemployment often results in ill health. The longer the unemployment period, the more physical and psychological health problems are likely to arise (Buffat, 2000). The more health problems a person has, the harder it is to find a good job. In short, ill health increases the risks both of becoming and of remaining unemployed (Korpi, 2001).

Solutions

Unemployment leads to poverty and ill health. This tells us that a society that does not invest money in jobs for the poor will have to invest money in more health-care and social welfare programs, and possibly more law enforcement and jails as well. Losing a job decreases a person's well-being—his or her confidence, self-esteem, and health. In the end, we all pay for this social problem. The chronically unemployed often put a heavy burden on health, social support, and welfare assistance programs.

There are no quick and easy solutions to the various problems associated with unemployment and work, but there are some practical choices.

Unemployment Interventions

Interventions for the problem of unemployment might take the form of reducing the number of people who experience unemployment, reducing the stresses of unemployment, strengthening individuals' life skills and psychosocial resources, and providing counselling and clinical interventions (Avison, 2001). Job-creation programs can reduce some unemployment. Here, it is important that job creation occurs mainly in full-time, stable, and skill-intensive fields. Such 'good' positions are less likely to result in a return to unemployment further down the road. Jobs that are temporary and fail to build new skills and contacts are a waste of effort.

As well, since education is the best weapon against unemployment, governments should ensure that schooling is made available to as many people as possible. Schooling opportunities are especially needed by those whose financial condition might otherwise prevent them from getting higher education, including poor people, rural people, disabled people, and Aboriginal people. This initiative should include adult education programs, which can be another effective tool for increasing the chance of re-employment and career advancement.

Labour unions, which historically have been effective tools in pressuring employers to provide better wages and working conditions for employees, have experienced a decline in recent years. Initiatives that support unions and political parties that promote working-class interests, such as the New Democratic Party in Canada and equivalent parties abroad (for example, the traditional Labour Party in Britain), are key to ensuring that wages and working conditions remain on the legislative agenda.

No one has taken responsibility for the health problems of unemployed people. Existing and newly created institutions will need to take responsibility for delivering treatment to people who suffer from unemployment-related health problems (Schiffer, 1999). Doctors need to know how to identify and track the factors that simplify or impede return to work; this implies a change in the way doctors are trained (Guirguis, 1999). People need to be taught job-search skills, helped to prevent declines in mental health, and helped to cope with involuntary unemployment (Turner et al., 1991).

While they are without a job, people need money to live on. However, the support they receive also makes a difference. Unemployed people who receive means-tested benefits (such as welfare) are more likely to be depressed than people who receive unemployment benefits (Rodriguez, 2001; Rodriguez et al., 1997; Rodriguez et al., 2001).

Unemployment hurts people's health, especially when it humiliates them and makes them insecure. Welfare benefits are best when they provide income security without making demands of the recipient. Means testing humiliates benefit recipients and therefore does nothing to reduce the harm of unemployment. By contrast, benefits that replace lost income, as is the practice in Sweden, provide income security without humiliating the recipient (Strandh, 2001). Such a policy is both fair and economically efficient, since it keeps the working-age population healthy even when they are unemployed. As a result, organizations committed to redistributive policies, such as social democratic parties, are more successful in improving the health of populations (Navarro and Shi, 2001).

Workplace Health and Safety

To reduce the number of annual occupational injuries and deaths, governments will have to obligate employers to respond to the health and safety concerns of their workers more effectively. It will likely cost more to do business this way, which is why the government will have to take the initiative and impose penalties for non-compliance. Already, there is strong evidence of support for such changes. In recent years, closer public and media scrutiny, combined with constant pestering by anti-corporate and human rights groups, has forced some companies to improve their workplace conditions, especially in the overseas factories of transnational organizations. More of the same pressure, with resulting changes to the workplace, is needed at home as well as abroad.

Increasingly, workers and lobby groups want more than a minimally hazard-free work space. They want a higher standard of quality of life at work. In response, many of today's more progressive employers, aware of the link between employee well-being and corporate profitability, are offering workers on-site health education and medical care. Some have begun to outfit their workplaces with gyms, swimming pools, and other recreational facilities, as well as provide their workers with lunchtime yoga classes and healthy food options in the cafeteria. These attempts to improve employee health and fitness, whether sincere or self-serving, can help ensure that work itself does not become a health risk.

Job Satisfaction

If we accept the view that a happy worker is a productive worker, then it is in the employer's best interest to ensure that job satisfaction levels remain high. This means designing jobs, careers, and workplaces that provide meaning and stimulation, and opportunities that allow workers to apply the full scope of their abilities. The most satisfying work allows workers to take part in consequential decision-making. It also allows room for workers' needs and commitments outside the workplace. Communication among workers should also be encouraged, as should harmonious employee–employer relations. Regardless of the particular strategy or incentive chosen by the employer, any attempt to improve job satisfaction will necessarily involve an awareness of what people wish to gain from working.

Extrinsic concerns are important, so income, recognition, promotions, and benefit packages all need to be shared in a way that mirrors both personal performance and company prosperity. Equally or more important, however, are the intrinsic benefits of work, which vary from job to job and from worker to worker. Indeed, job satisfaction is an intricate, subjective, and possibly inseparable mix of **intrinsic and extrinsic rewards**. Some people, for instance, crave a high degree of independence and lack of structure (for example, freelance writers or entrepreneurs), while others find themselves most comfortable and happiest in a job that is rule-bound and rigidly defined (for example, chartered accountants).

To maximize job satisfaction, executives, administrators, and workers must recognize that a paycheque is important but not enough. To keep workers happy, employers must be able to match employee interests with job characteristics while providing benefits and perks that make work intrinsically satisfying.

Individual Solutions

We have seen that an unemployed person may be in danger of becoming fatalistic, passive, and depressed. This must be avoided at all costs. Jobs must be sought, and for this to happen the unemployed person must fight the negative psychological effects of unemployment. Some training programs based on cognitive behavioural therapy have been effective in preparing people for this (Proudfoot et al., 1999). Problem-focused coping and cognitive restructuring programs lessen emotional distress (Grossi, 1999). Interrupted career group therapy encourages people to discuss their feelings of jealousy, shame, inferiority, rage, and humiliation associated with their unemployment. Some participants in this type of therapy benefit from the technique and are able to resume their career-building efforts; the rest cannot (Ronningstam and Anick, 2001).

Though networking is important in finding a job, networking intensity—increasing personal actions such as contacting friends, acquaintances, and referrals to get information, leads, or advice on getting a job—does not increase a person's chance of achieving re-employment rapidly, compared with other methods (Wanberg et al., 2000). Job-search intensity—engaging a high degree of commitment, persistence, and focus—predicts re-employment status, though not necessarily re-employment quality (Wanberg et al., 1999).

Most of the readers of this textbook are already doing the single most important thing to obtain a good job and income, and to minimize the risks of unemployment, at least for a very long period: that is, getting a college or university degree. People with higher education are the least likely to be unemployed at any particular time, or, if unemployed, to stay unemployed for long.

One might take note of the current trends of job growth, and shortages of trained people, in the areas of teaching, nursing, and other applied health services. If some of these areas of work are of interest, one can prepare for the work through courses, with the knowledge there will likely be jobs out there to be had over the near future. Sources of information on labour market expansion and contraction include newspapers and magazines, Internet sources, government resources, and college and university courses on work in sociology and economics.

Social supports are important in buffering the effect of unemployment and financial strain on health and emotional well-being. In particular, partner and family support are important immediately after the loss of a job (Shams, 1993). Social support and contact with close friends can have a moderating effect on nervous symptoms in women but less so in men (Hammer, 1993). The presence of a confidant significantly reduces the odds that unemployment will result in depression, anxiety, and other illnesses (Harrison et al., 1999).

Concluding Remarks

A small elite mostly controls the level of employment and unemployment in any society, ours included. For example, this elite controls private bureaucracies that employ large numbers of people. Employment and workplace problems can arise when these elites act exclusively in their own interest and not also in the interest of their employees.

Workplace problems include racial and gender discrimination, difficulties juggling work and family, technological advances, and worker exploitation. Some lines of work, such as sex work, can be extremely taxing and dangerous, and attach stigma to the workers. Workplaces can also be hazardous and extremely stressful. Such problems can lead to worker dissatisfaction, stress, and health problems. Even so, the alternatives associated with unemployment can be worse.

Unemployment can cause health problems, depressive disorders, and consequently a higher mortality rate. Solutions to unemployment can come either from the community or the individual. Accessible education, financial support for the unemployed, and a positive attitude towards re-employment possibilities are paramount. Companies also need to be more sensitive to workers' needs to ensure their health and job satisfaction.

QUESTIONS FOR CRITICAL THOUGHT

1. Take a quick survey to discover which kind of jobs give people the most stress. Which jobs have the highest wages and highest prestige? Using the data you collect, consider how peoples' perceptions of jobs support a neo-conservative approach to economics and public policy. For example, if financial managers are thought to have high stress, high wages, and high prestige, should they be let off easy for white-collar crime?

2. Evaluate the conflict perspective view on unemployment. Does the interpretation ring true? How would you criticize or elaborate on it?

3. This chapter argues in part that work means something quite different for men than it does for women. For example 'pink-collar' workplaces such as the service industry are not as often unionized as 'blue-collar' workplaces are. Review the occupations of 10 or 20 people you know well. Is it fair to say that the work of the women has different meaning than that of the men?

4. In your view, should prostitution be viewed as a form of work (i.e., sex work), a type of social deviance, or a sign of personal or social pathology? Give arguments for each of these views, and suggest whether they are compatible with one another.

5. How are family life and gender inequality in the workplace connected? Discuss.

RECOMMENDED READINGS

Morton Beiser and Feng Hou, 'Language Acquisition, Unemployment and Depressive Disorder among Southeast Asian Refugees: A 10-Year Study', *Social Science and Medicine* 53 (2001): 1321–34. Although unemployment increases the risk of mental health difficulties, this study looks at the mediating effects of language facility among Southeast Asian refugees resettling in Canada. English-language proficiency did not mediate depression or employment rates, but after 10 years in Canada, English-language proficiency had become a factor, especially among refugee women.

Barry Glassner, *Career Crash: America's New Crisis—And Who Survives* (New York: Simon & Schuster, 1994). This text uses ethnographic methods and interviews to examine how men and women have reinvented their relationship to work. Glassner shows how work is a major component of the structure of self-identity. He notes that career crashes among baby boomers are common, and so baby boomers are forced to re-evaluate their relationships to work and to other members of the community.

Selahadin A. Ibrahim, Fran E. Scott, Donald C. Cole, Harry S. Shannon, and John Eyles, 'Job Strain and Self-Reported Health among Working Women and Men: An Analysis of the 1994/5 Canadian National Population Health Survey', *Women and Health* 33, 1 and 2 (2001): 105–24. Using the Canadian national population health survey of 1994–5, this article examines the association between high-strain jobs and self-rated health. High-strain jobs were classed in terms of decision latitude and psychological demands. Among both men and women, high-strain jobs predicted worse self-rated health.

J. Lait and J.E. Wallace, 'Stress at Work: A Study of Organizational-Professional Conflict and Unmet Expectations', *Industrial Relations* 57 (2002): 463–90. Anyone who has worked in service and anyone who plans to do so should know that the pleasure of interpersonal contact can also be a stressful way to make money. Using data from a survey of service providers in Alberta, this study tests a management-stress model; the model posits that organizational conflict and bureaucratic conditions result in service providers' stress. Interestingly, decreasing service providers' control over their work does not increase their job stress.

Victor W. Marshall, Philippa J. Clarke, and Peri J. Ballantyne, 'Instability in the Retirement Transition: Effects on Health and Well-Being in a Canadian Study', *Research on Aging* 23 (2001): 379–409. This study looks at the little-researched, yet increasingly common, transition between post-retirement work and full retirement. The subjects are a group of early retirees from a Canadian telecommunications corporation, and ill health is found to be associated with instability.

Peggy McDonough, Vivienne Walters, and Lisa Strohschein, 'Chronic Stress and the Social Patterning of Women's Health in Canada', *Social Science and Medicine* 54 (2002): 767–82. Social roles and socio-economic position do affect women's health, but why? This research uses data from a 1994 Canadian national probability sample of women between the ages of 24 and 64. Employment, marriage, and living with children enhanced women's lives, as did income and education. This article is one of many in this volume of *Social Science and Medicine* on women's health, socio-economic status, and work.

Richard Ogmundson and Michael Doyle, 'The Rise and Decline of Canadian Labour / 1960 to 2000: Elites, Power, Ethnicity and Gender', *Canadian Journal of Sociology* 27 (2002): 413–54. Unions are thought to have declined in importance of late, although labour leaders are still powerful. Among the changes in labour have been an influx of women and a decrease of people of British origin. Interestingly, however, there has not been an increase in visible minority groups within labour.

Paul Ryan, 'The School-to-Work Transition: A Cross-national Perspective', *Journal of Economic Literature* 39, 1 (2001): 34–92. Looking at results alone in seven advanced economies and focusing on young people without post-secondary education, Ryan examines the flows of unemployment and their duration, and the effects of social disadvantage on unemployment.

Michel Tremblay and Denis Chênevert, 'Managerial Career Success in Canadian Organizations: Is Gender a Determinant?', *International Journal of Human Resource Management* 13 (2002): 920–41. The future of Canadian women at work is of critical importance. Using research on 3,060 Canadian managers, the importance of human capital, family context, socio-economic origin, work investment and reward expectations, and structural factors were analyzed. Successful female managers are found to be successful for different reasons than are successful male managers.

RECOMMENDED WEBSITES

Human Resources Development Canada
www.hrdc-drhc.gc.ca

Human Resources Development Canada (HRDC) provides information for employers and employees and for the unemployed. Labour publications and information pertaining to children, youth, and senior citizens are also available, as are reports about employment trends in Canada.

International Labour Organization
www.ilo.org

As the website of the US branch of this international organization indicates, the ILO is 'a specialized agency of the United Nations', it 'brings governments, workers and employers together to promote decent work', and it 'transfers knowhow to 138 countries through technical co-operation'. In recent years, it has focused its attention particularly on the effects of globalization.

Canadian Labour Congress
www.clc-ctc.ca

The Canadian Labour Congress (CLC), the umbrella organization of organized labour in Canada, promotes decent wages and working conditions and improved health and safety laws. It also lobbies for fair taxes, strong social programs, job training, and job-creation programs. Considerable information is provided on topics ranging from social and economic labour policies to anti-racism and human rights links.

Canadian Centre for Occupational Health and Safety
www.ccohs.ca

The Canadian Centre for Occupational Health and Safety promotes safe and healthy working environments by providing information and advice. This website covers products and services provided by the CCOHS, education and training programs, resource links, and general information about workplace safety.

GLOSSARY

Alienation Marx noted that industrialization and the division of labour have separated the worker from the work process, from the object he or she produces, and from his or her fellow workers. This experience involves feelings of powerlessness, meaninglessness, normlessness, estrangement, and social isolation in the workplace.

Bureaucracy A large, complex organization employing highly specialized workers who work within the context of what Max Weber called a legal-rational authority structure.

Capitalism The economic system in which private individuals or corporate groups own the means of production and distribution. Capitalists invest capital to produce goods and services, which they sell for profit in a competitive free market.

Discouraged workers Those people who are not actively seeking employment. Specifically, they are thought to have turned their backs on the traditional work system and to have abandoned any desire to be gainfully employed. Most discouraged workers are qualified to work only within the secondary job market. They consist disproportionately of women and racial minorities.

Discriminatory unemployment Unemployment resulting from discrimination against particular groups, such as ethnic minorities and women.

Extrinsic rewards When work rewards the worker with money, prestige, respect, and social recognition.

Intrinsic rewards When work rewards the worker with the feeling of a 'job well done'.

Reporting relationships   A network in a bureaucratic organization that enmeshes each individual worker into a Christmas-tree-shaped structure that repeatedly branches out as you go down the hierarchy. Thus, at the bottom of the hierarchy many people have to (1) carry out orders from above, (2) report work-related information up the tree to their superiors, and (3) uphold linkages between the organization and its client or customer base. At the top of the hierarchy, a few people (1) issue orders to their subordinates, (2) process information received from below, and (3) uphold linkages between the organization and other organizations—political, economic, and social.

Social capital   Some people have more education, income, and social status; often these people have larger networks of acquaintances with more varied people among them. Sociologists call having larger, more varied, and more powerful networks 'having greater social capital'.

Socialism   An alternative economic and political ideology that flourished in the nineteenth and twentieth centuries. It favours the public ownership of the means of production and distribution, and the investment of public capital in producing goods and services.

Structural unemployment   Results from social and economic factors that affect workers equally across all groups, such as corporate downsizing, capital flight (caused by corporate mergers and the move of operations to another geographic region—'runaway plants'), and the automation of work processes (that is, the replacement of human labour with mechanical equipment).

REFERENCES

Ancel, P.Y., M.J. Saurel Cubizolles, G.C. Di Renzo, E. Papiernik, and G. Breart. 1999. 'Social Differences of Very Preterm Birth in Europe: Interaction with Obstetric History', *American Journal of Epidemiology* 149: 908–15.

Avison, William R. 1996. 'What Determines Health? Summary of the Health Consequences of Unemployment', National Forum on Health. Available at: <www.nfh.hc-sc.gc.ca/publicat/execsumm/avison.htm>; accessed 23 Jan. 2003.

Avison, William R. 2001. 'Unemployment and Its Consequences for Mental Health', in Victor Marshal, Walter R. Heinz, Helga Kruger, and Anil Verma, eds, *Restructuring Work and the Life Course*. Toronto: University of Toronto Press, 177–200.

Bamgbose, Oluyemisi. 2002. 'Teenage Prostitution and the Future of the Female Adolescent in Nigeria', *International Journal of Offender Therapy and Comparative Criminology* 46, 5: 569–85.

Bellaby, Paul, and Felix Bellaby. 1999. 'Unemployment and Ill Health: Local Labour Markets and Ill Health in Britain, 1984–1991', *Work, Employment and Society* 13: 461–82.

Benson, D.E., and Christian Ritter. 1990. 'Belief in a Just World, Job Loss, and Depression', *Sociological Focus* 23: 49–63.

Bernstein, Elizabeth. 2002. 'Economies of Desire: Sexual Commerce and Post-Industrial Culture', *Dissertation Abstracts International, A: The Humanities and Social Sciences* 63, 2: 778–A.

Bray, J.W., G.A. Zarkin, M.L. Dennis, and M.T. French. 2000. 'Symptoms of Dependence, Multiple Substance Use, and Labor Market Outcomes', *American Journal of Drug and Alcohol Abuse* 26: 77–95.

Brown, G.K., A.T. Beck, R.A. Steer, and J.R. Grisham. 2000. 'Risk Factors for Suicide in Psychiatric Outpatients: A 20-Year Prospective Study', *Journal of Consulting and Clinical Psychology* 68: 371–7.

Buffat, J. 2000. 'Unemployment and Health', *Revue médicale de la Suisse romande* 120: 379–83.

Burchardt, Tania. 2000. 'The Dynamics of Being Disabled', *Journal of Social Policy* 29: 645–68.

Burstrom, B., M. Whitehead, C. Lindholm, and F. Diderichsen. 2000. 'Inequality in the Social Consequences of Illness: How Well Do People with Long-term Illness Fare in the British and Swedish Labor Markets?', *International Journal of Health Services* 30: 435–51.

Carter, G.L., I.M. Whyte, K. Ball, N.T. Carter, A.H. Dawson, V.J. Carr, and J. Fryer. 1999. 'Repetition of Deliberate Self-poisoning in an Australian Hospital-Treated Population', *Medical Journal of Australia* 170: 307–11.

Castaneda, Xochitl, Victor Ortiz, Betania Allen, Cecilia Garcia, and Mauricio Hernandez-Avila. 1996. 'Sex Masks: The Double Life of Female Commercial Sex Workers in Mexico City', *Culture, Medicine and Psychiatry* 20, 2: 229–47.

Catalano, Ralph, Hans Tore Hansen, and Terry Hartig. 1999. 'The Ecological Effect of Unemployment on the Incidence of Very Low Birthweight in Norway and Sweden', *Journal of Health and Social Behavior* 40: 422–8.

———, Samuel L. Lind, and Abram B. Rosenblatt. 1999. 'Unemployment and Foster Home Placements: Estimating the Net Effect of Provocation and Inhibition', *American Journal of Public Health* 89: 851–5.

CBC News. 2006. 22. Apr. Available at: <www.cbc.ca/news/background/workplace-safety/>.

Charmaz, Kathy. 1997. *Good Days, Bad Days—the Self in Chronic Illness and Time*. New Brunswick, NJ: Rutgers University Press.

Claussen, Bjørgulf. 1999a. 'Alcohol Disorders and Re-employment in a 5-Year Follow-up of Long-term Unemployed', *Addiction* 94: 133–8.

———. 1999b. 'Health and Re-employment in a Five-Year Follow-up of Long-term Unemployed', *Scandinavian Journal of Public Health* 27, 2: 94–100.

Coleman, James. 1994. *The Criminal Elite: The Sociology of White-Collar Crime*, 3rd edn. New York: St Martins Press.

Comino, E.J., E. Harris, D. Silove, V. Manicavasagar, and M.F. Harris. 2000. 'Prevalence, Detection and Management of Anxiety and Depressive Symptoms in Unemployed Patients Attending General Practitioners', *Australian and New Zealand Journal of Psychiatry* 34: 107–13.

Crawford, M.J., and M. Prince. 1999. 'Increasing Rates of Suicide in Young Men in England during the 1980s: The Importance of Social Context', *Social Science and Medicine* 49: 1419–23.

Daniel, W. 1987. *Workplace Industrial Relations and Technical Change*. London: Frances Pinter and Policy Studies Institute.

Dee, Thomas S. 2001. 'Alcohol Abuse and Economic Conditions: Evidence from Repeated Cross-sections of Individual-Level Data', *Health Economics* 10: 257–70.

de Goede, M., E. Spruijt, C. Maas, and V. Duindam. 2000. 'Family Problems and Youth Unemployment', *Adolescence* 35: 587–601.

Desmarais, Danielle. 1991. 'Linking Unemployment, Health and Employment in Women's Accounts of Unemployment: Understanding as a Prerequisite to Social Intervention', paper presented at the annual meeting of the Sociological Practice Association/ISA Working Group in Clinical Sociology.

Domenighetti, Gianfranco, Barbara D'Avanzo, and Brigitte Bisig. 2000. 'Health Effects of Job Insecurity among Employees in the Swiss General Population', *International Journal of Health Services* 30: 477–90.

Dooley, David, Joann Prouse, and Kathleen A. Rowbottom-Ham. 2000. 'Underemployment and Depression: Longitudinal Relationships', *Journal of Health and Social Behavior* 41: 421–36.

Druss, B.G., S.C. Marcus, R.A. Rosenheck, M. Olfson, T. Talielian, and H.A. Pincus. 2000. 'Understanding Disability in Mental and General Medical Conditions', *American Journal of Psychiatry* 157: 1485–91.

Durkheim, Émile. 1964 [1893]. *The Division of Labor in Society*, trans. George Simpson. New York: Free Press.

Edwards, Richard. 1979. *Contested Terrain: The Transformation of the Workplace in the Twentieth Century*. New York: Basic Books.

Ferrie, Jane E. 1997. 'Labour Market Status, Insecurity and Health', *Journal of Health Psychology* 2: 373–97.

———, P. Martikainen, M.J. Shipley, M.G. Marmot, S.A. Stansfeld, and G.D. Smith. 2001. 'Employment Status and Health after Privatization in White Collar Civil Servants: Prospective Cohort Study', *British Medical Journal* 322: 647–51.

———, M.J. Shipley, M.G. Marmot, P. Martikainen, S.A. Stansfeld, and G.D. Smith. 2001. 'Job Insecurity in White-Collar Workers: Toward an Explanation of Associations with Health', *Journal of Occupational Health Psychology* 6: 26–42.

Fillmore, Kaye Middleton, Jacqueline M. Golding, Karen L. Graves, Steven Kniep, E. Victor Leino, Anders Romelsjo, Carlisle Shoemaker, Catherine R. Ager, Peter Allebeck, and Heidi P. Ferrer. 1998. 'Alcohol Consumption and Mortality, I. Characteristics of Drinking Groups', *Addiction* 93: 183–203.

Foster, T., K. Gillespie, R. McClelland, and C. Patterson. 1999. 'Risk Factors for Suicide Independent of DSM-III-R Axis I Disorder: Case-Control for Psychological Autopsy Study in Northern Ireland', *British Journal of Psychiatry* 175: 175–9.

Fukuyama, Francis. 1992. *The End of History and the Last Man*. New York: Free Press.

Gaudette, Pamela, Bob Alexander, and Chris Branch. 1996. 'Children, Sex and Violence: Calgary's Response to Child Prostitution', *Child & Family Canada*. Available at: <www.cfc-efc.ca/docs/cwlc/00000826.htm>; accessed 29 Oct. 2004.

Gien, L.T. 2000. 'Land and Sea Connection: The East Coast Fishery Closure, Unemployment, and Health', *Canadian Journal of Public Health* 91, 2: 121–4.

Goldney, Robert D., Anthony H. Winefield, Marika Tiggerman, and Helen R. Winefield. 1995. 'Suicidal Ideation and Unemployment: A Prospective Longitudinal Study', *Archives of Suicide Research* 1: 175–84.

Gonzalez, Luque J.C., and Artalejo F. Rodriguez. 2000. 'The Relationship of Different Socioeconomic Variables and Alcohol Consumption with Nighttime Fatal Traffic Crashes in Spain: 1978–1993', *European Journal of Epidemiology* 16: 955–61.

Graetz, Brian. 1993. 'Health Consequences of Employment and Unemployment: Longitudinal Evidence for Young Men and Women', *Social Science and Medicine* 36: 715–24.

Grossi, G. 1999. 'Coping and Emotional Distress in a Sample of Swedish Unemployed', *Scandinavian Journal of Psychology* 40: 157–65.

———, T. Theorell, M. Jurisoo, and S. Setterlind. 1999. 'Psychophysiological Correlates of Organizational Change and Threat of Unemployment among Police Inspectors', *Integrative Physiological and Behavioral Science* 34, 1: 30–42.

Grunberg, L., S.Y. Moore, and E. Greenberg. 2001. 'Differences in Physiological and Physical Health among Layoff Survivors: The Effect of Layoff Contact', *Journal of Occupational Health Psychology* 6: 15–25.

Guidroz, Kathleen. 2001. 'Gender, Labor, and Sexuality in Escort and Telephone Sex Work', *Dissertation Abstracts*

International, A: The Humanities and Social Sciences 62, 6: 2252–A.

Guirguis, S.S. 1999. 'Unemployment and Health: Physician's Role', *International Archives of Occupational and Environmental Health* 72, suppl.: S10–13.

Gunnell, D., A. Lopatazidis, D. Dorling, H. Wehner, H. Southall, and S. Frankel. 1999. 'Suicide and Unemployment in Young People. Analysis of Trends in England and Wales, 1921–1995', *British Journal of Psychiatry* 175: 263–70.

Gysels, Marjolein, Robert Pool, and Betty Nnalusiba. 2002. 'Women Who Sell Sex in a Ugandan Trading Town: Life Histories, Survival Strategies and Risk', *Social Science and Medicine* 54, 2: 179–92.

Hagquist, C., S.R. Silburn, S.R. Zubrick, G. Lindberg, and G. Ringback Weitoft. 2000. 'Suicide and Mental Health Problems among Swedish Youth in the Wake of the 1990s Recession', *International Journal of Social Welfare* 9: 211–19.

Hallsten, L., G. Grossi, and H. Westerlund. 1999. 'Unemployment, Labour Market Policy and Health in Sweden during Years of Crisis in the 1990s', *International Archives of Occupational and Environmental Health* 72, suppl.: S28–30.

Hammarstrom, Anne, and Urban Janlert. 1997. 'Nervous and Depressive Symptoms in a Longitudinal Study of Youth Unemployment: Selection or Exposure?', *Journal of Adolescence* 20: 293–305.

Hammer, Torild. 1993. 'Unemployment and Mental Health among Young People: A Longitudinal Study', *Journal of Adolescence* 16: 407–20.

Hannan, Damian F., Sean O'Riain, and Christopher T. Whelan. 1997. 'Youth Unemployment and Psychological Distress in the Republic of Ireland', *Journal of Adolescence* 20: 307–20.

Harrison, J., S. Barrow, L. Gask, and F. Creed. 1999. 'Social Determinants of GHQ Score by Postal Survey', *Journal of Public Health Medicine* 21: 283–8.

Hintikka, J., P.I. Saarinen, and H. Viinamaki. 1999. 'Suicide Mortality in Finland during an Economic Cycle, 1985–1995', *Scandinavian Journal of Public Health* 27, 2: 85–8.

Hubbard, Phil, and Teela Sanders. 2003. 'Making Space for Sex Work: Female Street Prostitution and the Production of Urban Space', *International Journal of Urban and Regional Research* 27, 1: 75–89.

Human Resources Development Canada (HRDC). 2000. *Work Safely for a Healthy Future: Statistical Analysis: Occupational Injuries and Fatalities Canada*. Available at: <info.load-otea.hrdc-drhc.gc.ca/~oshweb/naoshstats/naoshw2000.pdf>; accessed 23 Jan. 2003.

Innis, Harold A. 1930. *The Fur Trade in Canada: An Introduction to Canadian Economic History*. New Haven: Yale University Press.

Jin, Robert L., Chandrakant Shah, and Tomislav J. Svoboda. 1997. 'The Impact of Unemployment on Health: A Review of the Evidence', *Journal of Public Health Policy* 18: 275–301.

Karvonen, Sakari, and Arja H. Rimpela. 1997. 'Urban Small Area Variation in Adolescents' Health Behaviour', *Social Science and Medicine* 45: 1089–98.

Korpi, Thomas. 2001. 'Accumulating Disadvantage: Longitudinal Analyses of Unemployment and Physical Health in Representative Samples of the Swedish Population', *European Sociological Review* 17: 255–73.

Krahn, Harvey J., and Graham S. Lowe. 1993. *Work, Industry, and Canadian Society*, 2nd edn. Scarborough, Ont.: Nelson Thompson Canada.

Kramer, Lisa A., and Ellen C. Berg. 2003. 'A Survival Analysis of Timing of Entry into Prostitution: The Differential Impact of Race, Educational Level, and Childhood/Adolescent Risk Factors', *Sociological Inquiry* 73, 4: 511–28.

Kyriacou, D.N., D. Anglin, E. Taliaferro, S. Stone, T. Tubb, J.A. Linden, R. Muelleman, E. Barton, and J.F. Kraus. 1999. 'Risk Factors for Injury to Women from Domestic Violence against Women', *New England Journal of Medicine* 341: 1892–8.

Lahelma, Eero. 1992. 'Unemployment and Mental Well-Being: Elaboration of the Relationship', *International Journal of Health Services* 22: 261–74.

Landsbergis, Paul A., Susan J. Schurman, Barbara A. Israel, Peter L. Schnall, Margrit K. Hugentobler, Janet Cahill, and Dean Baker. 1993. 'Job Stress and Heart Disease: Evidence and Strategies for Prevention', *New Solutions* 3, 3: 42–58.

Langfred, C.W., and N.A. Moye. 2004. 'Effects of Task Autonomy on Performance: An Extended Model Considering Motivational, Informational, and Structural Mechanisms', *Journal of Applied Psychology* 89, 6: 934–45.

Liira, J., and Arjas P. Leino. 1999. 'Predictors and Consequences of Unemployment in Construction and Forest Work During a 5-Year Follow-up', *Scandinavian Journal of Work, Environment and Health* 25, 1: 42–9.

McCarty, C.A., M. Burgess, and J.E. Keeffe. 1999. 'Unemployment and Underemployment in Adults with Vision Impairment: The RVIB Employment Survey', *Australian and New Zealand Journal of Ophthalmology* 27, 3 and 4: 190–3.

MacDonald, Z., and S. Pudney. 2000. 'Illicit Drug Use, Unemployment, and Occupational Attainment', *Journal of Health Economics* 19: 1089–15.

McDonough, Peggy. 2000. 'Job Insecurity and Health', *International Journal of Health Services* 30: 453–76.

Manopaiboon, C., R.E. Bunnell, P.H. Kilmarx, S. Chaikummao, K. Limpakarnjanarat, S. Supawitkul, M.E. St Louis, and T.D. Mastro. 2003. 'Leaving Sex Work: Barriers, Facilitating Factors and Consequences for Female Sex Workers in Northern Thailand', *AIDS Care* 15, 1: 39–52.

Martikainen, Pekka, and Tapani Valkonen. 1998. 'The Effects of Differential Unemployment Rate Increases of Occupation Groups on Changes in Mortality', *American Journal of Public Health* 88: 1859–61.

Marx, Karl. 1936 [1887]. *Capital: A Critique of Political Economy*, trans. Samuel Moore and Edward Aveling. New York: Modern Library.

Mathieu, Lilian. 2003. 'The Emergence and Uncertain Outcomes of Prostitutes' Social Movements', *European Journal of Women's Studies* 10, 1: 29–50.

Mehanni, M., A. Cullen, B. Kiberd, M. McDonnell, M. O'Regan, and T. Matthews. 2000. 'The Current Epidemiology of SIDS in Ireland', *Irish Medical Journal* 93, 9: 264–8.

Montgomery, Scott M., Derek G. Cook, Mel J. Bartley, and Michael E.J. Wadsworth. 1998. 'Unemployment, Cigarette Smoking, Alcohol Consumption, and Body Weight in Young British Men', *European Journal of Public Health* 8, 1: 21–7.

———, ———, ———, and ———. 1999. 'Unemployment Pre-dates Symptoms of Depression and Anxiety Resulting in Medical Consultation in Young Men', *International Journal of Epidemiology* 28: 95–100.

Morrell, Stephen, Richard Taylor, Susan Quine, and Charles Kerr. 1999. 'A Case-Control Study of Employment Status and Mortality in a Cohort of Australian Youth', *Social Science and Medicine* 49: 383–92.

National Institute for Occupational Safety and Health. 1999. *Stress . . . at Work* (Catalogue no. 99–101). US Department of Health and Human Services, Centers for Disease Control and Prevention. Available at: <www.cdc.gov/niosh/pdfs/stress.pdf>; accessed 23 Jan. 2003.

Navarro, Vicente, and Leiyu Shi. 2001. 'The Political Context of Social Inequalities and Health', *Social Science and Medicine* 52: 481–91.

Newton, Keith, and Norm Lockie. 1987. 'Employment Effects of Technological Change', *New Technology, Work and Employment* 2, 2.

Nixon, Kendra, Leslie Tutty, Pamela Downe, Kelly Gorkoff, and Jane Ursel. 2002. 'The Everyday Occurrence: Violence in the Lives of Girls Exploited through Prostitution', *Violence Against Women* 8, 9: 1016–43.

Nordenmark, Mikael. 1999a. 'Employment Commitment and Psychological Well-Being among Unemployed Men and Women', *Acta Sociologica* 42: 135–46.

———. 1999b. 'Unemployment, Employment Commitment, and Well-Being: The Psychological Meaning of (Un)employment among Women and Men', Ph.D. thesis, Umeå University (Sweden).

——— and Mattias Strandh. 1999. 'Towards a Sociological Understanding of Mental Well-Being among the Unemployed: The Role of Economic and Psychological Factors', *Sociology* 33: 577–97.

Northcott, Jim, Michael Fogarty, and Malcolm Trevor. 1985. *Chips and Jobs: Acceptance of New Technology at Work*. London: Policy Studies Institute.

——— and A. Walling. 1988. *The Impact of Microelectronics; Diffusion Benefits and Problems in British Industry*. London: Policy Studies Institute.

Novo, Mehmed, Anne Hammarstrom, and Urban Janlert. 2001. 'Do High Levels of Unemployment Influence the Health of Those Who Are Not Employed? A Gendered Comparison of Young Men and Women during Boom and Recession', *Social Science and Medicine* 53: 293–303.

Nylen, L., M. Voss, and B. Floderus. 2001. 'Mortality among Women and Men Relative to Unemployment, Part-time Work, Overtime Work, and Extra Work: A Study Based on Data from the Swedish Twin Registry', *Occupational and Environmental Medicine* 58: 52–7.

Ostry, Aleck, Steve A. Marion, L. Green, Paul A. Demers, Kay Teshke, Ruth Hershler, Shona Kelly, and Clyde Hertzman. 2000. 'The Relationship between Unemployment, Technological Change and Psychosocial Work Conditions in British Columbia Sawmills', *Critical Public Health* 10: 179–91.

Pasarin, M., C. Borrell, and A. Plasencia. 1999. 'Two Patterns of Social Inequalities in Mortality in Barcelona, Spain?', *Gaceta Sanitaria* 13: 431–40.

Prashad, Sharda. 2005. 'Bosses Define the Work Experience', *Toronto Star* (Ont. edn), 5 Nov., D1.

Preti, A., and P. Miotto. 1999. 'Suicide and Unemployment in Italy, 1982–1994', *Journal of Epidemiology and Community Health* 53: 694–701.

Proudfoot, J., J. Gray, J. Carson, D. Guest, and G. Dunn. 1999. 'Psychological Training Improves Mental Health and Job-Finding among Unemployed People', *International Archives of Occupational and Environmental Health* 72, suppl.: S40–4.

Rodriguez, Eunice. 2001. 'Keeping the Unemployed Healthy: The Effect of Means-Tested and Entitlement Benefits in Britain, Germany, and the United States', *American Journal of Public Health* 91: 1403–11.

———, K.E. Lasch, P. Chandra, and J. Lee. 2001. 'Family Violence, Employment Status, Welfare Benefits, and Alcohol Drinking in the United States: What Is the Relation?', *Journal of Epidemiology and Community Health* 55: 172–8.

———, ———, and June P. Mead. 1997. 'The Potential Role of Unemployment Benefits in Shaping the Mental Health Impact of Unemployment', *International Journal of Health Services* 27: 601–23.

Rohlfs, Izabella, Carme Borrell, M. Isabel Pasarin, and Antoni Plasencia. 1999. 'The Role of Sociodemographic Factors in Preventive Practices: The Case of Cervical and Breast Cancer', *European Journal of Public Health* 9: 278–84.

Ronningstam, E., and D. Anick. 2001. 'The Interrupted Career Group: A Preliminary Report', *Harvard Review of Psychiatry* 9: 234–43.

Russell, D., and F. Judd. 1999. 'Why Are Men Killing

Themselves? A Look at the Evidence', *Australian Family Physician* 28: 791–5.

Sarlio-Lähteenkorva, S., and E. Lahelma. 1999. 'The Association of Body Mass Index with Social and Economic Disadvantage in Women and Men', *International Journal of Epidemiology* 28: 445–9.

Saurel Cubizolles, M.J., P. Romito, P.Y. Ancel, and N. Lelong. 2000. 'Unemployment and Psychological Distress One Year after Childbirth in France', *Journal of Epidemiology and Community Health* 54: 185–91.

Schaufeli, Wilmar B. 1997. 'Youth Unemployment and Mental Health: Some Dutch Findings', *Journal of Adolescence* 20: 281–92.

Schiffer, J. 1999. 'Concept on Health Promotion about the Unemployed in Switzerland', *International Archives of Occupational and Environmental Health* 72, suppl.: S23–5.

Schmitt, E. 2001. 'Significance of Employment and Unemployment in Middle and Advanced Adult Age for Subjective Perception of Aging and Realization of Potentials and Barriers of a Responsible Life', *Zeitschrift fur Gerontologie und Geriatrie* 34: 218–31.

Shams, Manfusa. 1993. 'Social Support and Psychological Well-Being among Unemployed British Asian Men', *Social Behavior and Personality* 21, 3: 175–86.

Sikora, Patricia B. 2002. 'Enlarging the View of Participation in Organizations: A Proposed Framework and Analysis via Structural Equation Modeling', *Dissertation Abstracts International* 63–02B: 1091.

Stanton, Jeffrey M., Peter D. Bachiochi, Chet Robie, Lisa M. Perez, and Patricia C. Smith. 2002. 'Revising the JDI Work Satisfaction Subscale: Insights into Stress and Control', *Educational and Psychological Measurement* 62, 5: 877-895

Stefansson, Claes Goran. 1991. 'Long-Term Unemployment and Mortality in Sweden, 1980–1986', *Social Science and Medicine* 32: 419–23.

Strandh, Mattias. 2001. 'State Intervention and Mental Well-Being among the Unemployed', *Journal of Social Policy* 30: 57–80.

Tausig, M., and R. Fenwick. 1999. 'Recession and Well-Being', *Journal of Health and Social Behavior* 40, 1: 1–16.

Tsutsumi, A., K. Kayaba, T. Theorell, and J. Siegrist. 2001. 'Association between Job Stress and Depression among Japanese Employees Threatened by Job Loss in a Comparison between Two Complementary Job-Stress Models', *Scandinavian Journal of Work, Environment, and Health* 27, 2: 146–53.

Turner, J. Blake. 1995. 'Economic Context and the Health Effects of Unemployment', *Journal of Health and Social Behaviour* 36: 213–29.

Turner, J. Blake, Ronald C. Kessler, and James S. House. 1991. 'Factors Facilitating Adjustment to Unemployment:

Implications for Intervention', *American Journal of Community Psychology* 19: 521–42.

Underlid, Kjell. 1996. 'Activity during Unemployment and Mental Health', *Scandinavian Journal of Psychology* 37: 269–81.

United Nations Population Fund. 2000. *State of World Population 2000: Lives Together, Worlds Apart: Men and Women in a Time of Change*. Available at: <www.unfpa.org/swp/2000/english/index.html>; accessed 23 Jan. 2003.

Van de Mheen, H., K. Stronks, C.T.M. Schrijvers, and J.P. Mackenbach. 1999. 'The Influence of Adult Ill Health on Occupational Class Mobility and Mobility out of and into Employment in the Netherlands', *Social Science and Medicine* 49: 509–18.

Viinamaki, Heimo, Kaj Koskela, and Leo Niskanen. 1993. 'The Impact of Unemployment on Psychosomatic Symptoms and Mental Well-Being', *International Journal of Social Psychiatry* 39: 266–73.

———, ———, and ———. 1996. 'Rapidly Declining Mental Well-Being during Unemployment', *European Journal of Psychiatry* 10: 215–21.

Wanberg, Connie R., R. Kanfer, and J.T. Banas. 2000. 'Predictors and Outcomes of Networking Intensity among Unemployed Job Seekers', *Journal of Applied Psychology* 85: 491–503.

———, ———, and M. Rotundo. 1999. 'Unemployed Individuals: Motives, Job-Search Competencies, and Job-Search Constraints as Predictors of Job Seeking and Reemployment', *Journal of Applied Psychology* 84: 897–910.

Weber, Max. 1947. *The Theory of Social and Economic Organization*, trans. A.M. Henderson and Talcott Parsons. New York: Free Press.

Williamson, Celia, and Terry Cluse-Tolar. 2002. 'Pimp-Controlled Prostitution: Still an Integral Part of Street Life', *Violence Against Women* 8, 9: 1074–92.

Wojcicki, Janet Maia. 2002. 'Commercial Sex Work or Ukuphanda? Sex-for-Money Exchange in Soweto and Hammanskraal Area, South Africa', *Culture, Medicine and Psychiatry* 26, 3: 339–70.

Wray, Linda A. 2000. 'Does Mental Health Affect Transitions out of the Labour Force in Older Workers?', paper presented at the annual meeting of the American Sociological Association.

Yelin, E., J. Henke, P.P. Katz, M.D. Eisner, and P.D. Blanc. 1999. 'Work Dynamics of Adults with Asthma', *American Journal of Industrial Medicine* 35: 472–80.

Ytterdahl, T. 1999. 'Routine Health Check-ups of Unemployed in Norway', *International Archives of Occupational and Environmental Health* 72, suppl.: S38–9.

——— and P. Fugelli. 2000. 'Health and Quality of Life among Long-term Unemployed', *Tidsskrift for Den Norske Laegeforening* 120: 1308–11.

CHAPTER TEN

Health, Illness, and Health Care

LEARNING OBJECTIVES

- To know the biomedical and biopsychosocial definitions of health.
- To understand different ways to measure population health.
- To appreciate the basic facts of Canadian and global health threats.
- To know how globalization and air travel affect the nature of disease.
- To learn about the major areas of concern regarding Canada's health-care system.
- To appreciate what is meant by deinstitutionalization, medicalization, and depersonalization.
- To know the social determinants of health and illness.
- To understand how public health interventions improve population health.
- To discover different ways to address the problems in Canada's health-care system.

Introduction

This chapter is about the health of Canadians and of the global community, the diseases and illnesses that threaten health, and the health-care system that is designed to treat these conditions.

In one sense, illness is the most immediate form of *personal problem* that we face. The throbbing ache of arthritis, the fever and chills of a malarial infection, the torment of schizophrenia—these physical and neurological pains of an illness are felt by the sufferer alone. Family and friends may sympathize, but in the end the experience of sickness and internalizing the identity of being 'sick' are borne by the individual (see Box 10.1).

At the same time, health and illness are *social problems* for several reasons. First, many diseases and illnesses are common, affecting millions of people. Second, as we will see, health and health-care resources are unequally distributed throughout society. Some groups are more likely than others to become ill, struggle to meet their health-care needs, and die too soon. One of the main areas of research in the field of **medical sociology** is studying the social factors that promote illness and contribute to health inequalities. Other areas focus on the institution of medicine and explore the social construction of 'illness' and 'health', the economics and politics of health-care delivery, and the features of physician–patient interaction. Finally, inequalities in health and health care are social

Box 10.1 Personal Experience: 'It felt like my identity was being stripped away'

It was a routine mammogram, but when the X-ray was done, the radiologist asked for a magnified view of my right breast. She needed to get a better look at something. . . . She tried to be reassuring, but her eyes were fixed on the floor as she suggested that I undergo a biopsy. I could feel the fear rising. I knew I was in trouble. After all, I was a doctor too.

But on that day, without warning, I switched roles and became a patient. . . . The biopsy led to surgery that ultimately confirmed I was suffering from invasive breast cancer.

In many ways, where Dr Marla ended and just Marla began was poorly defined. My profession was inextricably woven into the very fabric of who I was—someone taught to be a clear thinker and problem solver whose decisions are based on evidence, even if it's just the best that science can offer at the moment.

. . . I did not want the disease to define me, but clearly it has in many ways, some perceptible and some not. I am not the same woman who walked through the doors of mammography that fateful day. For one thing, the treatment meant that I couldn't practise medicine. I did not want to abandon this role I felt so comfortable with—I felt like my identity was being stripped away.

People ask if this fight has gone better for me because I'm an informed patient. I really don't know. . . . There are so many decisions that have to be made—and made quickly. The various treatment options were outlined, along with the potential benefits and side effects, but ultimately I had to make the choices that I hoped were right for me. . . . It's something you have to figure out yourself: what treatments are right for you, what your comfort level is, what risks you're willing to take.

. . . Today, my chemotherapy is behind me. The surgeries I elected to have rather than radiation are over, and I have gone back to my office and a career I love. So how have I changed? In many ways, I am the same—juggling a zillion work balls and loving the return. But in so many other ways, I am different. The only word I can think of to describe it is mindful. I am so much more mindful of the decisions I make, my family, my children and how I choose to live my life.

Source: Adapted from Shapiro (2005).

problems because, as we see at the end of this chapter, improving the health of whole populations will require the efforts of governments and other large institutions.

Defining and Measuring Health

Definitions of Health and Illness

According to the **biomedical view of medicine**, which has been dominant in industrial societies since early in the twentieth century, health is the absence of illness. By this standard, health is a 'passive', default state of normalcy; illness, an 'active' problem in need of treatment. This emphasis on illness is partly due to the Western medical profession's focus on curing the sick rather than preventing sickness from occurring in the first place. In the biomedical model, the doctor is like a mechanic and the human body is like a machine to be fixed. Most of the time, the machine runs smoothly. Only when something goes wrong—a broken spark plug, a failing kidney—are the professionals called in to mend or replace the faulty part and get 'the machine' working again.

The biomedical approach has been dominant largely because its focus on reducing diseases to their basic biological processes has yielded major medical advances for the past century. Our current ability to treat a wide range of physical and psychological problems owes much to the rigorous approach to medical problems that the biomedical model inspired.

However, defining health in strictly somatic terms is inadequate in several ways. For instance, people can be less than perfectly healthy without showing outward symptoms of discomfort—for example, a seemingly fit individual can have a dangerously high cholesterol level. Also, there is a growing recognition that the symptoms of biologically identical illnesses vary with differences in personal history, socio-economic condition, and cultural background, requiring physicians to 'treat the patient rather than simply the disease'.

More recent ideas about health have therefore moved away from a solely physiological model towards a more holistic understanding. Here, health is viewed almost synonymously with **well-being**—that is, as a state of existence characterized by happiness, prosperity, and the satisfaction of basic human needs. By this reasoning, health is not simply the absence of illness or injury. The World Health Organization (WHO), for example, defines **health** as 'a state of complete physical, mental, and social well-being', a definition that has gone unchanged since the organization's formation after World War II (WHO, 1946). Health Canada takes an equally broad stand on the meaning of health, viewing it as a state of social, mental, emotional, and physical well-being that is influenced by a broad range of factors, including biology and genetics, personal health practices and coping skills, the social and physical environments, gender, socio-economic factors such as income and education, and cultural practices and norms (Joint Working Group on the Voluntary Sector, 1999).

These various definitions represent the **biopsychosocial view of health and illness** (Engel, 1977; also see White, 2005). As the name implies, this perspective recognizes that health and disease are products of the interaction of body, mind, and environment, and not just of biology alone. As well, it reminds us that health is not an all-or-nothing condition. A person may be healthy in some respects (e.g., passing an annual physical checkup) while being unhealthy in others (e.g., suffering at the same time from anxiety disorder). The relative contributions of each factor—mind, body, and social environment—vary from condition to condition and from case to case. The challenge is to determine the role of each factor and tailor interventions—medical as well social—accordingly.

Cultural and Ethnic Variations in the Perception of Health and Health Care

In defining and measuring health, we must also recognize that views about health, well-being, illness, and suffering vary by culture and ethnicity. These views in turn can affect how symptoms are recognized and interpreted (i.e., whether or not they are seen as indicative of a medical problem) and whether health-care services are sought (Anderson et al., 2003). For example, attitudes to body weight vary among ethnic groups. In Canada, we often hear about the desirability of thinness, of watching the intake of fat, starches, and junk food, and minimizing disease risk. However, Filipino immigrants tend to value weight gain, eating lots of fat and rice, and in this way hope to increase disease resistance (Farrales and Chapman, 1999).

Another example is pain, the body's way of indicating that something is wrong. At the biological level, pain is a natural physiological response of the nervous system. Overlying this is the subjective socio-cultural interpretation of pain, which varies from individual to individual and culture to culture. For example, in North America and elsewhere, stereotypes of acceptable masculine behaviour influence how men respond to painful stimuli (for example, the stoic 'take it like a man' approach).

Many studies have examined ethnic differences in pain tolerance, focusing especially on variations between African Americans and those of European ancestry. This body of research, which includes laboratory pain studies and clinical observation studies, concludes that blacks tend to be more sensitive to pain than whites (see Edwards et al., 2001). However, these results should be interpreted cautiously, since it is difficult to determine whether they reflect physiological differences, cultural norms, or researcher bias. Differences in pain reported in clinical settings may be due to a tendency of physicians to underestimate the severity of pain felt by ethnic minorities following trauma, when compared to white patients. For this reason, doctors are also more likely to underprescribe pain management medication to these groups (e.g., Todd et al., 1994).

Cultural variations also influence attitudes towards medical care. Some Eastern philosophies take a holistic approach to health, viewing sickness as a sign of a fundamental imbalance of one's body, mind, spirit, and environment. Similarly, various Aboriginal traditions in North America, Australia, and elsewhere consider the connection with the land as a sacred and inseparable component of well-being. Canadians with these cultural backgrounds, especially recent immigrants who are less acculturated than others, may view mainstream medical practices with doubt and thus be less willing to seek care in institutional settings such as hospitals. Instead, they may choose to practise home remedies or consult with holistic medical practitioners who share their beliefs about the causes and cures of sickness. This preference may be reinforced where past discrimination—inside and out of the health-care setting—has resulted in a general distrust of Western institutions, language barriers hinder access to mainstream health care, and a large ethnic or cultural community supports alternatives to Western medicine (Ngo-Metzger et al., 2003; Ma, 1999; Suchman, 1965).

Measuring Health and Illness

Epidemiology is an applied science that examines the causes, distribution, and control of disease in a population. Epidemiologists use various techniques to study the patterns of health and illness in society, drawing on the knowledge of many disciplines, including medicine, public health, sociology, psychology, and economics, among others.

Rather than trying to directly assess vague concepts such as 'well-being', most epidemiologists measure health with standard quantitative indicators. One of the most common is **life expectancy**, the average number of years remaining to a person at a particular age, given current age-specific mortality rates.

Global life expectancy has increased dramatically as a result of advances in medicine, public health, and technology. Fifty years ago, worldwide life expectancy was 47 years; by 2005, it had increased to 65 years (UN, Population Division, 2005). However, important disparities in life expectancy still exist between rich and poor nations. Japan, for instance, continues to lead the world, with an average life expectancy in 2005 of 82 years, while Botswana has the lowest, at barely 37 years (ibid.).

Today, Canadians enjoy one of the highest life expectancies in the world—82 years for women and 77 years for men (Statistics Canada, 2004). Again, however, life expectancies vary geographically and demographically. For example, the Richmond Health Service Delivery Area in British Columbia has the highest life expectancy in the country at 83.4 years, higher even than in Japan. At the other end is the Région de Nunavik in Quebec, where life expectancy of 66.7 years, the lowest in Canada, is similar to the average lifespan measured in Egypt and the Dominican Republic (Statistics Canada, 2005b). Life expectancies, generally, are lowest in Canada's northern and rural communities, where rates of poverty, alcohol abuse, smoking, and suicide are all above national means.

In addition to life expectancy, epidemiologists examine **mortality rates** (typically measured as deaths per year per thousand people). The **maternal mortality rate** refers to the number of deaths of women due to complications during pregnancy, childbirth, or abortion. It is a problem clearly linked to global poverty, with 99 per cent of all pregnancy-related deaths worldwide occurring in developing countries (see Figure 10.1). There, maternal mortality is the leading cause of death and disability among women of reproductive age (15–49 years), with an estimated 515,000 women dying annually. At least 15 million more suffer injury, infection, and disability due to unsafe obstetric practices, unhygienic environments, inadequate maternal nutrition, and other threats to healthy child-bearing. In total, roughly one in four adult women living in developing nations—over 300 million people—are thought to have suffered some form of adverse health condition rising from complications during pregnancy and childbirth (UNICEF, 2001).

The **infant mortality rate** (number of deaths of children under one year of age per 1,000 live births) and the **under-five mortality rate (U5MR)** are two other statis-

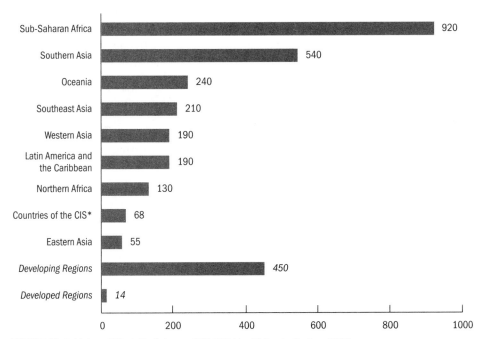

FIGURE 10.1 Maternal Mortality Rate per 100,000 Live Births, by Region, 2000

*Commonwealth of Independent States, which consists of 'transitional economy' nations in Asia and Europe, including Russia, China, and others.

Source: UN (2005). The United Nations is the author of te original material.

Maternal Mortality Begets Infant Mortality
Among children under five years of age, the risk of death is doubled for those whose mothers died during childbirth (WHO, 2003c).

tical indicators of population health, focusing on society's youngest and most vulnerable members. Globally, the infant mortality rate was estimated at 54 deaths per 1,000 live births in 2004, while the U5MR was roughly 79 deaths per 1,000 live births; again, both indicators are highest in the developing world. At the national level, war-ravaged Sierra Leone had the world's highest U5MR in 2004, at 283 deaths per 1,000 live births. By contrast, Canada's U5MR rate during the same year was six deaths per 1,000 live births (UNICEF, 2005).

The **morbidity rate** indicates the extent of disease in a population. Morbidity can be reported according to its *incidence*, the number of new cases in a given population during a given period of time, or its *prevalence*, the total number of cases of a disease in the population at a particular point in time. Diseases can also be categorized as *endemic*, or constantly present within a population; *epidemic*, being a local or national outbreak; or *pandemic*, an epidemic of international or global proportions. Like mortality rates, morbidity rates vary according to social variables such as sex/gender, racial grouping, and social class. The interactions between health status and these social factors are discussed later in this chapter.

The Epidemiological Transition

Examining long-term national trends in mortality and morbidity during socio-economic development reveals a general pattern referred to as the **epidemiological transition** (Omran, 1971). During this transition, the nature of illness shifts from diseases of acute infection and nutritional deficiency characteristic of developing societies to chronic non-communicable illnesses characteristic of developed societies. The epidemiological transition is caused by socio-economic growth and advances in public health, especially improved water sanitation, waste disposal, and housing. This in turn causes a decline in mortality among infants, who are most vulnerable to communicable illnesses such as malaria and tuberculosis (WHO, 1996). With fewer deaths among children, more people survive to adulthood and suffer the types of chronic health problems—'lifestyle' conditions such as diabetes or smoking-induced lung cancer, or degenerative conditions such as Alzheimer's disease—common among adults and the elderly.

Research indicates the epidemiological transition is neither uniform nor unidirectional. Within a country, several stages of transition may be occurring at the same time in different geographical regions or demographic subgroups, with wealthier segments experiencing increases in non-communicable diseases while poorer segments continue to battle poor nutrition and communicable diseases. As well, many developing nations experience a 'double burden' during the transition, wherein citizens suffer from both new non-communicable diseases and lingering communicable diseases at the same time. So, the transition process is complex and shaped by continually shifting demographic, social, economic, environmental, and biological conditions. Even in developed societies like Canada, new waves of infectious disease are continually emerging, as is evident from the continued threat of AIDS, SARS, and influenza in the twenty-first century (WHO, 1996).

Threats to Canadian and Global Health

Global health has improved dramatically in recent decades, yet major threats to health and well-being remain. Some conditions, such as infectious pandemics, move with great speed and visibility and result in catastrophic levels of death, disability, and suffering.

Others, such as mental illness, exist as hidden epidemics that nevertheless exact huge social, economic, and human costs. In most cases, the socially and economically vulnerable are the groups most at risk of health problems.

The AIDS Pandemic

'Rare cancer seen in 41 homosexuals'—so read the headline from the 3 July 1981 edition of the *New York Times*, among the first mainstream media reports about what would become known as acquired immune deficiency syndrome (AIDS). Yet despite exponentially rising infection rates throughout the 1980s, AIDS was too often labelled—and thereby dismissed—in those early days as a disease for 'them' rather than 'us', an affliction limited to three socially marginalized populations: homosexuals, injection drug users, and Haitians. According to a US Centers for Disease Control (CDC) spokesperson interviewed in the *New York Times* article, 'the best evidence against contagion is that no cases have been reported to date outside the homosexual community or in women' (Altman, 1981).

Today, we know better. By the end of 2005, an estimated 40.3 million people worldwide, including 17.5 million women and 2.3 million children under 15 years of age, were living with the human immunodeficiency virus (HIV), the pathogen commonly viewed as the cause of AIDS. Nearly five million people were infected in 2005 alone. The number of global AIDS-related deaths is equally staggering—25 million since 1981, with 3.1 million in 2005 alone (UNAIDS, 2005). Globally, AIDS is the leading cause of death among adults ages 15–59, and the fourth leading cause of death overall (WHO, 2005a).

HIV is transmitted via the exchange of bodily fluids. Infection occurs mainly through unprotected sexual intercourse, sharing of intravenous needles, perinatal transmission (from an infected mother to a fetus or newborn), infusion of tainted blood products, and, in rare cases, through the breast milk of an infected mother. Worldwide,

Box 10.2   Social Construction: AIDS and Its Metaphors

In her classic essay *AIDS and Its Metaphors*, Susan Sontag describes how the social meaning of disease is constructed out of society's insecurities, and how the metaphors of military invasion and plague-as-punishment are used to situate the medical condition in the public consciousness.

Sontag notes with some distress, for instance, how the language of war is used to describe the threat of AIDS: 'Military metaphors have more and more come to infuse all aspects of the description of the medical situation. Disease is seen as an invasion of alien organisms, to which the body responds by its own military operations, such as the mobilizing of immunological "defenses," and medicine is "aggressive," as in the language of most chemotherapies' (Sontag, 1989: 9). So, when we speak of AIDS, we often use terms like the body under 'siege', the immune system 'fighting back', and most openly, 'the war against AIDS'.

Sontag also argues that the metaphors used for AIDS have two sources: 'As a microprocess, it is described as cancer is: an invasion. When the focus is transmission of the disease, an older metaphor, reminiscent of syphilis, is invoked: pollution' (ibid., 17). Often, the language of infectious disease takes on moralizing overtones: 'AIDS is understood in a premodern way, as a disease incurred by people both as individuals and as members of a "risk group"–that neutral-sounding, bureaucratic category which also revives the archaic idea of a tainted community that illness has judged' (ibid., 46).

heterosexual intercourse is the primary mode of HIV transmission (Gayle, 2000), while in Canada, homosexual intercourse between two men carries the highest risk (Public Health Agency of Canada, 2005).

AFRICA

Sub-Saharan Africa remains the region hardest hit by AIDS, with an estimated 25.8 million currently infected. The area is home to about 10 per cent of the world's population but nearly two-thirds of all those living with HIV. Women account for 57 per cent of all sub-Saharan African adults currently living with the disease. In 2005, 2.4 million people in this region died as a result of AIDS, while another 3.2 million were newly infected (UNAIDS, 2005). Infection rates exceeding one-fifth and in some cases one-third of the national population have been recorded in Swaziland, Botswana, Lesotho, South Africa, and Namibia (Ministry of Health and Social Welfare Swaziland, 2005; UNAIDS, 2005).

Amid the tragedy, however, are small but promising signs of hope. Intense public health and medical interventions have recently begun to show results in some African nations. In Zimbabwe, for example, HIV prevalence among pregnant women fell from 26 per cent in 2002 to 21 per cent in 2004, a trend that has been credited at least in part to changes in sexual behaviour, such as higher rates of condom use and a decrease in the number of casual sexual partners (UNAIDS, 2005; Mahomva, 2004). The delivery of anti-retroviral medications to the developing world, while still failing to meet the need, has also improved largely due to efforts by governments and pharmaceutical corporations in the developed world to provide these drugs for free or at a fraction of their cost (see Table 10.1).

EMERGING CRISES IN ASIA AND EASTERN EUROPE

In the developing countries of Asia, Eastern Europe, and Latin America, injection drug use is emerging as the primary cause of HIV infection. Poverty, low education, unemployment, and poor access to health care worsen the problem and frustrate attempts at delivering public health interventions. Although prevalence rates in these regions are still low, their large population sizes mean that even small percentage increases in prevalence translate into huge numbers of new infections.

Data from India, Russia, Ukraine, and elsewhere confirm high rates of infection among injection drug users and other high-risk groups (EuroHIV, 2005; MAP, 2005b; Ukrainian AIDS Centre, 2005). In Jakarta, for example, the estimated effect of injection

Table 10.1 Coverage of Adults in Low- and Middle-Income Countries on Anti-Retroviral (ARV) Treatment for HIV/AIDS, by WHO Region, June 2005

Region	Estimated Number of People Receiving Treatment	Estimated Need (ages 0–49)	Coverage
Sub-Saharan Africa	500,000	4,700,000	11%
Latin America and the Caribbean	290,000	465,000	62%
East, South, and Southeast Asia	155,000	1,100,000	14%
Europe and Central Asia	20,000	160,000	13%
North Africa and the Middle East	4,000	160,000	2.5%

Source: WHO (2005b).

drug use is such that the city can expect a total of 110,000 HIV infections by 2010 given current incidence rates, compared to only 2,000 if the current injection drug problem did not exist (cited in MAP, 2005a). Of particular concern is the intersection of injection drug users with the commercial sex trade, which serves as a channel for the spread of AIDS from marginalized high-risk groups into the general population (State Council AIDS Working Committee and UN Theme Group, 2004). For instance, a survey conducted among sex workers in Ho Chi Minh City, Vietnam, found that more than half of the sex workers who also injected drugs were HIV-positive, compared to only 8 per cent of those who were drug-free (UNAIDS, 2005). In China, Yang and colleagues (2005) found that more than half of all female drug users surveyed had also at some point traded sex for money and that female injection drug users were the least likely to use condoms.

CANADA

The scale of the AIDS problem in Canada is small in comparison to the prevalence rates experienced by countries in the developing world, but it is not trivial. According to the Public Health Agency of Canada's Centre for Infectious Disease Prevention and Control (CIDPC), roughly 60,000 Canadians have tested positive for HIV since reporting began in 1985. More than 13,000 have died from AIDS since 1980 (see Figure 10.2) (Public Health Agency of Canada, 2005). Due to under-reporting by the public and other limitations on data collection, however, these figures likely underestimate the true extent of AIDS in Canada.

The AIDS epidemic in Canada has occurred in several waves, each concentrated in specific populations. The first epidemic chiefly affected what the official literature calls 'men who had sex with men' and those who received tainted blood products. The current phase of the epidemic, which began around 1997, chiefly affects injection drug users, men who have sex with men, women, and Aboriginal populations (Health Canada, 2005). In recent years, the proportion of new infections due to injection drug use has declined, while the proportion due to sexual intercourse has increased. Some experts worry that 'AIDS fatigue' and 'condom fatigue' are setting in among younger

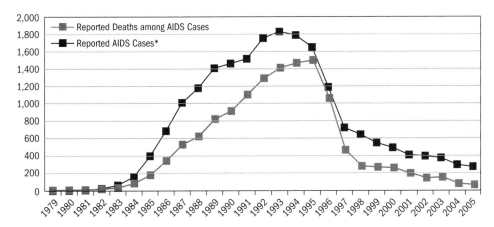

FIGURE 10.2 Number of Reported AIDS Cases and AIDS-Related Deaths in Canada, 1979–2005
*As reported to the Centre for Infectious Disease Prevention and Control (CIDPC), Public Health Agency of Canada.
Source: Public Health Agency of Canada (2006). Adapted and reproduced with permission of the Minister of Public Works and Government Services Canada, 2006.

Canadians who have no memory of the AIDS panic in the 1980s and early 1990s and who have grown tired of constant urging to practise safer sex.

SARS, Pandemic Influenza, and the 'Globalization' of Infectious Disease

The AIDS pandemic is a stark reminder that infectious disease remains a major health problem throughout the world. Malaria, a disease almost exclusive to the world's poorest nations, claims over one million lives each year and is estimated to have slowed annual economic growth in Africa by 1.3 per cent. Tuberculosis, once believed to be eradicated, has made a comeback in recent years (UN, 2005).

The World Health Organization also estimates that, every year, somewhere in the world a new infectious disease emerges that is previously unknown in humans and for which we have no natural immunity (WHO, 2003c). AIDS is unique among recent global epidemics in that its primary modes of transmission—unprotected sexual intercourse, needle-sharing, and perinatal transmission—do not support rapid mass infection. Infectious illnesses with more opportunistic transmission and incubation profiles, however, create extra risks in our increasingly interconnected world.

A striking example of how contemporary globalization has increased the risks posed by emergent communicable viruses is the 2003 outbreak of severe acute respiratory syndrome (SARS). The epidemic has been called 'a product of globalization' in view of the fact that its rapid spread from Guangzhou, China, to Singapore, Hanoi, Toronto, and elsewhere was facilitated by the movement of people along international air travel and trade routes (So and Pun, 2004: 5).

By the end of the outbreak in July 2003, 8,422 cases of SARS and 916 SARS-related deaths had been officially reported in 30 countries, including places as far from southern China as Kuwait, South Africa, Canada, and Brazil (WHO, 2003b). Global economic costs due to lost trade and declining tourism were estimated in the tens of billions of dollars, including a $1.5 billion loss for Canadian businesses (Conference Board of Canada, 2003). The SARS outbreak led to a renewed awareness of the connection between global health risks and the interdependent nature of the modern world. The volume and speed of global commerce and international air travel—as many as 700 million tourist arrivals per year, according to one estimate (Gössling, 2002)—have increased the risk of major infectious pandemics.

Scientists have since expressed concerns that SARS was merely the forerunner to an even larger global pandemic, one that is likely to involve a new strain of highly virulent influenza. Major influenza outbreaks occur in human populations about three or four times per century, the most recent being the 1918 Spanish flu, the 1957 Asian flu, and the 1968 Hong Kong flu. The deadliest of these, the 1918 outbreak, killed an estimated 30,000 to 50,000 people in Canada and 20–50 million people worldwide, more than the number of combined military and civilian deaths during World War I. Like SARS, influenza was also spread along travel routes, carried by infected soldiers aboard naval personnel ships criss-crossing the Atlantic Ocean (Canadian Pandemic Influenza Plan, 2004).

Mental Health and Mental Illness

Mental health refers to the ability of individuals to feel, think, and act in ways that improve the quality of daily functioning, the range and depth of social relationships, and the ability to adapt to life changes. Conversely, a **mental disorder**, according to one definition by Health Canada, is a condition 'characterized by alterations in thinking, mood, or behaviour (or some combination thereof) associated with significant distress and impaired functioning over an extended period of time' (Health Canada, 2002b:16). Although *mental disorder* and *mental illness* are often used interchangeably, some reserve the term **mental illness** for clinical diagnoses requiring medical and psychotherapeutic treatment. Mental illnesses and disorders should not be confused with the momentary feelings of loneliness, sadness, or emotional agitation that we all experience. What chiefly distinguishes mental illnesses from more ordinary feelings of psychological malaise are their duration and intensity, both of which are at levels sufficient to interfere with daily functioning.

Mental disorders and illnesses are social problems because they often interrupt the normal functioning of families, groups, and other social institutions. At the same time, their causes are still poorly understood, which contributes to a general sense of unease and stigmatization by the public (Phelan et al., 2000).

The most widely accepted categorization system for mental illness is the American Psychiatric Association's (APA) *Diagnostic and Statistical Manual of Mental Disorders* (*DSM-IV*) (American Psychiatric Association, 1994). The most common categories of mental illnesses are anxiety disorders; mood disorders, including depression and bipolar disorder; schizophrenia and other forms of psychosis; dementias, including Alzheimer's disease; eating disorders, including anorexia nervosa and bulimia; and personality disorders, such as obsessive compulsive disorder (OCD).

Although the causes are not yet fully understood, most experts now agree that most mental illnesses arise from a complex interaction of genetic/biological, psychological, and social/environmental factors. Major social disruptions, such as wars or natural disasters, can promote the development of mental illness through traumatic stress and the breakdown of social order. Other experts contend that the individualistic nature and accelerated pace of life in modern industrialized societies promote mental health problems by eroding traditional sources of social stability like family and religion.

OCCURRENCE AND IMPACT OF MENTAL ILLNESSES IN CANADA AND WORLDWIDE

In industrialized nations, major depression, bipolar disorder, schizophrenia, and OCD account for four of the 10 leading causes of mental illness (Murray and Lopez, 1996). Globally, mental illness, together with alcohol and drug addiction, comprises the leading cause of disability, accounting for one-third of total years lived with a disability among adults 15 years and older. Unipolar depressive disorders make up the single largest category of non-fatal disabling conditions and are the third leading cause of lost years of productivity (WHO, 2004). Depression alone is expected to become the world's second leading cause of disability by 2020 (Statistics Canada, 2003).

In Canada, mental disorders have a combined lifetime prevalence rate of approximately 20 per cent, meaning one person in five—or roughly 6 million Canadians—will experience a mental illness at some time in their lives. Among young adults aged 15–24, the age group at which most mental illnesses first appear, the risk is about one in four (Offord et al., 1996). The most common diagnoses are anxiety disorders, followed by depression and other mood disorders.

Often, the presence of one mental illness predisposes an individual to other mental health problems, for example, depression and anxiety. This condition is known as **co-**

morbidity. According to a major US study of mental illness involving nearly 10,000 adults, 45 per cent of those who experienced mental illness within the past 12 months had suffered from more than one disorder during that time (Kessler et al., 2005). Stephens and Joubert (2001) estimate the economic costs of mental health problems in Canada—the direct costs of treatment (including psychological and social work services not covered by public health care) and the indirect costs due to lost productivity—at $14.4 billion. This analysis does not include the tremendous psychic and social costs to family members who care for sick relatives.

Mental illness cuts across all social groups and classes. However, not everyone is equally at risk. Overall rates of most mental illness are higher among women than among men, while substance dependence is higher among men (see Statistics Canada, 2003; Mathers et al., 2003; Health Canada, 2002b). When one-year prevalence rates for both mental health disorder and alcohol and drug addiction are pooled, a roughly equal number of men and women are affected—1.2 million or 10 per cent of the male population versus 1.4 million or 11 per cent of the female population (Statistics Canada, 2003).

Mental health is also poorer among marginalized ethnic and cultural groups, especially Aboriginal populations. Shah (2004) reports that Aboriginal communities have suicide rates that are much higher than those for the general population. Suicide in turn is highly correlated with depressive and mood disorders. One study of suicide in the Northwest Territories and Nunavut found that 50 per cent of suicide victims between 1981 and 1996 had a history of depression or emotional distress, 46 per cent had a history of alcohol abuse, and 28 per cent had sought help for social or mental health problems (Isaacs et al., 1998).

Some think that the relationship between mental disorders and social class can be explained by **social selection** and various 'downward drift' hypotheses. These propose that mental illnesses prevent some people from functioning effectively, resulting in poorer educational outcomes, higher rates of unemployment, increased downward social mobility, and consequent over-representation among the lower classes (e.g., Goldberg and Morrison, 1963). Others have proposed **social causation** theories, which argue that stresses associated with life in the lower social classes—featuring poverty, unemployment, discrimination, family fragmentation, the absence of social supports, etc.—promote frustration and despair while they erode coping abilities, and contribute to the onset of mental health problems among vulnerable individuals and groups (Hudson, 2005; Clarke, 2001).

Issues in the Treatment of Mental Illnesses

The diagnosis and treatment of mental illness are hindered by the stigma still attached to mental health problems. Stigma arises from incomplete knowledge and a common tendency to exclude and isolate people who are different (and therefore potentially threatening). Thus, many people do not even realize they are experiencing a mental disorder, or if they do, they may keep it a secret, fearing that disclosure to family, employers, and doctors will result in embarrassment and rejection. Currently, many Canadians who suffer from mental illness or substance dependency do not seek treatment from a health professional (Statistics Canada, 2003). The higher rate of substance abuse among men is thought to reflect a tendency to 'self-medicate' rather than seek help when emotional problems arise, due to the common view that men should be psychologically strong and that mental illness is a sign of weakness. Overcoming discrimination against the mentally ill remains one of the most important goals of mental health advocacy.

Another problem hindering the successful treatment of the mentally ill is **deinstitutionalization**, the movement of treatment away from large mental institutions into smaller community-based settings. Deinstitutionalization became popular in North America during the 1960s and 1970s due to shifting public attitudes regarding involuntary commitment, a policy that allowed the state to confine patients to mental residences without their consent. In 1961, sociologist Erving Goffman published a classic critique of US psychiatric care, in which he characterized mental hospitals as being examples of **total institutions**, which control and regulate all aspects of life for those confined within their walls or their organizational structure. Goffman argued that much of the abnormal behaviour observed among mental patients was a result of institutionalization rather than of the 'illness' itself (Goffman, 1961). He and others condemned mental institutions as practising inhumane forms of social control to keep an unpleasant social reality out of sight. These criticisms resonated particularly with the broader cultural movement of the 1960s towards greater individual and social freedoms. Policy-makers began to argue for the delivery of care at the community level, where (they thought) everyday contact with other members of society would encourage higher levels of integration and stability for the mentally ill. New anti-psychotic drugs that controlled symptoms and allowed patients to lead more independent lives outside the mental institution furthered the argument that community-based mental health care could succeed.

However, deinstitutionalization has since been denounced as a well-meaning but flawed strategy that has failed to improve the lives of the mentally ill. Community mental health services never received as much funding as was promised, with the result that patients were released from mental hospitals—which, for all their flaws, were at least structured environments—into an indifferent and sometimes hostile society (Sigurdson, 2000). Too often, the effect of deinstitutionalization was simply to increase levels of homelessness and even imprisonment—another type of total institution. In the US, more mentally ill people are currently housed in prisons than in all the state hospitals combined (Jones and Connelly, 2002). In addition, the public is more likely today than 50 years ago to view the mentally ill as violent and unpredictable, in spite of the promise of deinstitutionalization to 'normalize' the sick (Phelan et al., 2000). In the end, this policy appears to have been mainly a government cost-reduction measure, one that in effect marginalized the poor and vulnerable and downloaded the cost of care to the local level.

Obesity

Throughout the world, obesity and excess weight are increasing at an alarming rate (WHO, 1998). The primary causes are energy-dense, nutrient-poor diets high in saturated fats and sugars, and sedentary lifestyles with little physical activity or exercise. Also to blame are larger portion sizes, increased television viewing, and an urban environment that encourages driving over walking (Frank et al., 2004; Cameron et al., 2003; Caballero, 2001). As Figure 10.3 illustrates, however, weight-related problems are the result of a complex network of factors.

Is obesity a social problem? Historically, a round figure signified success and social standing for both men and women. It indicated that a person ate well and had little need to experience hard manual labour; as examples, think of Winston Churchill, King Henry VIII, or the plump and curvaceous nudes that Rubens painted. What we see in the Western media—lean and well-toned body types—is a social construction of nor-

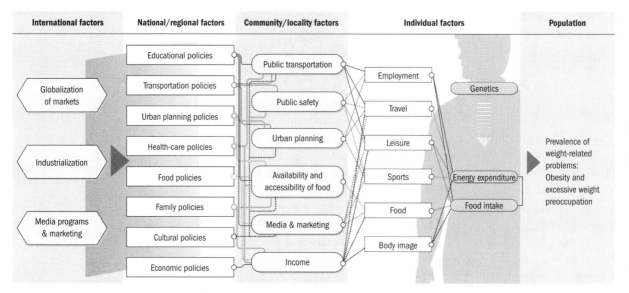

FIGURE 10.3 The Causal Network of Weight-Related Issues

Source: ASPQ (2003). Weight problems in Québec: Getting mobilized, Groupe de travail provincial sur la problématique du poids (GTPPP) [Online] http//www.aspq.org/view_publications.php?=17 accessed 5 mar 2006

mative beauty, an illusion rather than a real depiction of modern North Americans. And, in many cultures today, especially in the developing world, plumpness is still considered a sign of wealth and power.

However, obesity has also been linked to a long list of chronic physical health outcomes that became apparent only as the threat of infectious illnesses waned and life expectancies increased. These conditions include type 2 diabetes mellitus, arteriosclerosis, coronary artery disease, hypercholesterolemia, hypertension and stroke, gallbladder disease, kidney failure, osteoarthritis, and some forms of cancer (Hsu, 2006; WHO, 2005d; CIHI, 2004a; Flegal et al., 2002). For this health reason alone, we can view obesity and overweight as genuine social problems threatening to reach epidemic levels among adults and children worldwide.

Moreover, obesity can also exact lifelong psychosocial costs. Obese children are often the targets of discrimination and ridicule by school-age peers, which can lead to emotional harm. As obese children enter adolescence and adulthood, self-esteem and body image may also suffer (Must and Strauss, 1999). In addition, social bias continues to be a common problem, particularly in the media-saturated developed world, where fashion advertisements and television characters spread unrealistic views of 'normal' body images. Discrimination based on weight has been documented in school settings, workplaces, and even in health professional offices (see Stunkard and Sobel, 1995).

The most common measure of 'obesity' is the **body mass index (BMI)**, defined as weight in kilograms divided by the square of height in metres (kg/m²). 'Overweight' is defined as a BMI measurement over 25 kg/m², while 'obesity' is defined as a BMI measurement over 30 kg/m². Using these definitions, researchers estimate that, globally, at least 700 million people are at present overweight, including 17.6 million children under the age of five; and at least 300 million more are clinically obese (WHO, 2005d). Surveys have found rising rates of obesity in almost all developed regions, including Canada (see Rennie and Jebb, 2005; CIHI, 2004b; Matsushita et al., 2004; Cameron et al., 2003; Flegal, 1999).

Obesity is a Canada-wide problem, with rates increasing particularly in Atlantic Canada and the Prairie provinces (CIHI, 2004a). However, provincial region per se has not been identified as a separate risk factor for obesity, once we control for factors like education and socio-economic status (Le Petit and Berthelot, 2005). The direct costs (related to health-care expenditures) and indirect costs (associated with economic output lost due to illness, injury-related work disability, and premature death) of obesity to the Canadian economy are estimated to total $4.3 billion per year (Katzmarzyk and Janssen, 2004).

WHO estimates that at least 115 million people in the developing world—particularly those living in urban centres—suffer from obesity-related problems (Mendez et al., 2005; WHO, 2003a). Ironically, both under-nutrition and overweight are dietary problems for the poor. Some of the factors associated with the rise of obesity in the developing world, including urbanization, lower infant mortality and increased life expectancy, mechanization and lower energy-expending labour, the growing popularity of television viewing and other sedentary activities, and the growth of Western-style 'fast-food culture', are particularly common among poor people (Block et al., 2004; Caballero, 2001; Townsend et al., 2001).

Obesity rates in Canada

1979: 14 per cent of Canadian adults and 3 per cent of children ages 2–17 were considered obese.

2004: 23 per cent of Canadian adults and 8 per cent of children ages 2–17 were considered obese

(Statistics Canada, 2005a).

Health Care in Canada

Many view Canada's public health-care system, commonly referred to as medicare, as emblematic of our national identity and values. In fact, medicare is an umbrella term for 13 separate but linked health insurance plans, which are administered separately in each of the provinces and territories. The federal government establishes national standards for health-care delivery through the Canada Health Act, provides a share of funding to the provinces, and delivers health-care services directly to on-reserve Native populations, federal penitentiary inmates, war veterans, and members of the RCMP. Otherwise, health care is under the control of the provinces. For more information on the development of medicare in Canada, see Box 10.3.

While medicare remains a cornerstone of Canada's social welfare system, our publicly funded health care is showing signs of strain. Some of the major areas of concern about health care in Canada include cost, access, coverage, quality of care, and alternative treatments and health systems.

Cost

Canada (and Canadians) spent an estimated $142 billion on health care in 2005, a more than tenfold increase from 30 years ago (CIHI, 2005b). This amount is equal to roughly 10 per cent of our national GDP, comparable to spending levels in other Organization for Economic Co-operation and Development (OECD) countries. Among OECD members, the US operates by far the most costly health-care system, whether measured as a percentage of its GDP (13 per cent) or in terms of health expenditure per capita (US$5,635 versus US$3,003 in Canada) (OECD, 2005). In Canada, about 70 per cent was paid by various levels of government; private-sector contributions, including private health insurance and out-of-pocket expenses, made up the remaining 30 per cent (CIHI, 2005b).

Public health-care funding is always controversial, since there is never enough money to go around. As a government-delivered service, medicare is primarily funded

Box 10.3   Historical Perspective: The Evolution of Medicare

1919   Prime Minister William Lyon Mackenzie King proposes the idea of publicly funded health-care insurance and a universal health-care system in Canada.

1947   Saskatchewan's CCF government, led by Premier Tommy Douglas, implements the Saskatchewan Hospitalization Act, which guarantees free hospital services for all provincial residents.

1957   Ottawa passes the Hospital Insurance and Diagnostics Services Act, which commits the federal government to pay 50 per cent of the costs of any provincial program that delivers publicly funded hospital care.

1962   The Saskatchewan government passes the Medical Care Insurance Act to extending health coverage to include physician services, sparking a three-week strike by 90 per cent of the province's doctors to protest against 'creeping socialism'. Two years later, the Hall Royal Commission on Services recommends establishing a national medical insurance program based on the Saskatchewan model.

1966   Lester B. Pearson's federal Liberal government passes the National Medical Care Insurance Act, which articulates four principles of public health care—universality, comprehensiveness, portability, and public administration—that provincial plans must meet to qualify for federal funding.

1971   All provinces have established health-care systems based on the four principles, giving rise to a national health insurance plan known.

1977   Ottawa and the provinces negotiate the Established Programs Financing Act (EPF), which replaces the 50:50 cost-sharing formula with block funding for health insurance and post-secondary education based on a per capita funding model. Health-care transfer amounts are pegged to gross national product (GNP) growth rates.

1984   Federal commitment to medicare is renewed by the passing of the Canada Health Act, which adds a fifth principle of health-care delivery—accessibility to medically necessary services regardless of financial circumstances. Provincial governments can be penalized for allowing hospital user fees and extra-billing practices by physicians.

1986   The Mulroney government amends EPF funding levels; increases in transfer amounts are now calculated based on a formula of GNP minus 2 per cent.

1990   Bill C-69 freezes EPF levels for three years, after which future EPF growth will be based on a new formula of GNP minus 3 per cent.

1991   Bill C-20 freezes EPF levels until 1994. Federal transfers can now be withheld from any provincial or territorial government that contravenes the Canada Health Act.

1995   Federal health-care funds are subsumed under the new Canadian Health and Social Transfer (CHST). Ottawa's priorities shift towards debt reduction, resulting in significant cuts to its share of health-care funding (to as low as 16 per cent of the total) over the remainder of the decade.

2000   The Alberta legislature passes Bill 11, allowing the contracting out of in-patient medical and surgical services requiring overnight stays to private, for-profit hospitals. Premier Ralph Klein asserts that the plan will reduce wait times and improve health-care delivery throughout the province.

2002   The Commission on the Future of Health Care in Canada, headed by former Saskatchewan Premier Roy Romanow, calls for renewed federal funding, a limited pharmacare program, expanded coverage of home care, and other reforms.

2005   The Supreme Court of Canada strikes down a Quebec law prohibiting people from buy-
       ing private health insurance to cover procedures already offered by the public system.

2006   In response to the Supreme Court ruling, the Quebec government announces in Febru-
       ary 2006 a new public-private health-care initiative allowing hospitals to subcontract
       with private clinics to deliver some non-essential services—paid for by the province—if
       patients face a wait time of longer than six months in the public system.

Sources: Heeney (1995); Rachlis and Kushner (1994).

by compulsory taxation. The Alberta, British Columbia, and Ontario governments also charge their residents a health premium, revenue from which is invested in health-care delivery. The provincial and federal governments often battle about how much funding the latter should contribute, with agreements seldom satisfying everyone. Debates aside, everyone agrees about two things: the portion of provincial budgets spent on health care is rising, so less money is available for education and social programs; and, therefore, the status quo is unsustainable. Yet proposed solutions, including privatization, which is discussed at the end of this chapter, remain highly controversial.

Access

For many Canadians, access to health care is hindered mainly by long wait times for diagnostic tests and surgical procedures. In one survey of health-care users who had difficulties seeing specialists or getting non-emergency surgery, more than three in five cited long wait times as an important issue. Wait times vary by province. In Newfoundland, for example, more than 20 per cent of those who sought to visit a medical specialist waited more than three months, while only 8 per cent waited this long in Prince Edward Island (Sanmartin et al., 2004). In his 2002 report entitled *Building on Values: The Future of Health Care in Canada*, former Saskatchewan Premier Roy Romanow concluded that 'long wait times are the main, and in many cases, the only reason some Canadians say they would be willing to pay for treatments outside of the public health care system' (Commission on the Future of Health Care in Canada, 2002: 173).

Another way to measure access to health care is to look at unmet needs. Between 1994–5 and 2000–1, the percentage of Canadians aged 12 and older who reported having unmet health-care needs increased from 4.5 per cent to 12 per cent (Sanmartin et al., 2002). Chen and Hou (2002), examining National Population Health Survey (NPHS) data from 1998–9, report that about 1.5 million Canadian adults had experienced unmet health-care needs in the previous 12 months. Not surprisingly, people with unmet needs were more likely to have low household incomes.

A third problem related to health-care access is the shortage of health-care professionals. Canada currently ranks twenty-sixth out of 30 OECD countries in the number of practising physicians (2.1) per 1,000 people (OECD, 2005). According to a 2004 Decima poll, five million adults were unable to find a general practitioner or family physician for themselves or their families during the past 18 months. Shortages are particularly acute in rural communities, where one-fifth of the Canadian population reside but only 16 per cent of all family practitioners and less than 3 per cent of all specialists practise.

The Five Principles of Medicare

- *Universality*, by which all Canadians are entitled to insured services on uniform terms and conditions;
- *Comprehensiveness*, by which all medically necessary health-care services provided by physicians or in hospitals are insured;
- *Portability*, by which insured benefits are transferable across all provincial and territorial boundaries;
- *Public administration*, by which all provincial and territorial health insurance plans operate on a public, not-for-profit basis; and
- *Accessibility*, by which all Canadians should have reasonable access to insured services without direct charge.

The average travelling distance to see a family practitioner is only 0.7 km in big cities, but 34 km in the smallest rural towns and 202 km in the territories; and the average distances to a psychiatrist are 2 km, 144 km, and 957 km, respectively (CIHI, 2006).

The main causes of doctor shortages are cutbacks to medical school enrolments in the mid-1990s; a failure to accept the credentials of foreign-trained physicians; and a steady loss of Canadian-trained doctors to other countries—the so-called 'brain drain' (CMA, 2006). Many of the doctors available in Canada are working at capacity. About 40 per cent of Canadian doctors currently accept new patients only under specific circumstances (e.g., referrals from other physicians), while another 20 per cent are not accepting any new patients at all (National Physician Survey, 2005). A nationwide shortage of nurses further adds to Canada's health-care staffing problems.

Coverage

Canada's medicare program guarantees universal coverage for medically necessary procedures by paying almost all the costs related to hospital and physician services. However, it does not cover the costs of prescription medicines, most dental care and vision care, non-physician health services, and long-term home care.

The cost of medicines is a growing concern for both the public and policy-makers. Drugs have become the fastest-growing category of health-care spending in Canada, at $25 billion in 2005 (CIHI, 2005b). Several factors—an aging population, longer life expectancy, rising rates of chronic illnesses, and reductions in the number and length of hospital stays owing to medical advances—have contributed to the growing demand for medications. Currently, medicare only covers drugs taken during in-hospital treatment. Provincial drug insurance plans subsidize some costs, but the level of coverage varies widely from province to province. For example, pharmaceuticals are free in Yukon only for seniors over 65 or for those at least 60 and married to someone 65 or older. In British Columbia, the Fair PharmaCare Program is available to all BC residents, with costs varying by net family income, and a complicated formula determines the payment of drug costs. For those not covered by their provincial plans, prescription and over-the-counter medications obtained outside hospitals are paid for largely through employer health insurance plans and out-of-pocket expenditures.

In an attempt to free up money for vital care areas such as cancer and cardiac treatments, some provinces have also removed some 'non-essential' services, such as chiropractic care, adult eye exams, and some physiotherapy services, from medicare coverage. Critics assert that the savings achieved by delisting services now will be cancelled out later by increased pressure on the public system. People with minor health issues will delay seeking treatment no longer covered by medicare until they develop into major problems requiring long and costly services.

Quality of Care

Modern medicine is a delicate blend of science and art in which some error is to be expected. At the same time, patient safety is of growing concern in Canada and abroad. **Medical (clinical) iatrogenesis** refers to any state of diminished physical or mental health caused by medical intervention by a physician, therapist, or pharmacist. Many iatrogenic conditions are the result of human error, though they can also result from the accidental side effects of treatment.

The prevalence of medical iatrogenesis in Canadian hospitals was estimated in 2000 by the Canadian Adverse Events Study, which involved randomly selected patients from 20 hospitals across the country. An **adverse event** was defined as 'an unintended injury or complication that results in disability at the time of discharge, death or prolonged hospital stay and is caused by health care management rather than by the patient's underlying disease process.' The adverse event rate was found to be 7.5 per 100 hospital admissions. Thirty-seven per cent of the adverse events were judged by the researchers to have been preventable, including 9 per cent of cases in which the patient died as a result of adverse event complications. As a result of adverse events, 255 patients in the study required an additional 1,521 days in hospital (Baker et al., 2004). By comparison, a US study of 30,000 medical records in New York state found that adverse events occur in 3.7 per cent of hospitalizations, while an Australian review of over 14,000 hospital admissions found an adverse event incidence rate of 16.6 per cent (Wilson et al., 1995; Brennan et al., 1991).

There is general agreement that better safeguards and accountability measures are needed to help health-care systems to perform at better levels. Some provincial physician and surgeon accreditation organizations oblige their members to reveal harm to patients as part of their ethics code or standards of practice. However, no national laws or uniform guidelines currently require that physician errors and adverse events be reported to patients. Kalra et al. (2005) note several persuasive reasons for timely disclosure, including the need to safeguard public trust in the medical profession, respect patients' rights to information about treatment outcomes, and reduce the risk of malpractice liability arising from violations of informed consent.

> **Adverse Events in Canada**
> According to the *Health Care in Canada 2004* report, nearly one in four Canadians (5.2 million people) reported that they or a family member experienced a preventable adverse event in 2003 (Gagnon, 2004).

Complementary and Alternative Health Care in Canada

Unlike much of mainstream Western medicine, which aggressively focuses on treating or curing the somatic aspects of disease, complementary and alternative medicines take a different approach. Though varied, all forms of complementary and alternative health care share the belief that the body is capable of healing itself and that the role of therapy is to facilitate this healing through holistic and patient-centred treatment. Common healing practices include chiropractic, acupuncture, massage therapy, herbal remedies, traditional Chinese medicine, homeopathy, and naturopathy. Some people also consider prayer and vitamin consumption as forms of alternative care. As with all biopsychosocial approaches to health and illness, alternative health care focuses on achieving overall well-being rather than simply curing a disease.

Sociologist Terri Winnick (2005) argues that the Western medical profession has responded to the growth of complementary and alternative health care in three distinct phases. In the 'condemnation phase' of the 1960s and 1970s, medical journal authors exaggerated the risks of alternative medicines and lobbied for government suppression of non-Western healing practices. During the 1980s, in response to growing consumer use of alternative health care, the medical establishment entered a 'reassessment phase' and began to consider both the merits of alternative health care and the shortcomings of conventional care. With the 'integration phase' of the 1990s, the medical establishment shifted away from blunt efforts to ban alternative health care to more subtle strategies. One such approach has been to insist that the efficacy and safety claims of alternative health practices be subjected to scientific scrutiny, which despite an appearance of seeming 'neutrality' is based on Western medical principles (Kelner et al., 2004).

In 2003, 20 per cent of Canadians 12 years and older used some alternative health care, up from 15 per cent in 1995. Chiropractic was the most commonly used service, followed by massage, acupuncture, and homeopathy/naturopathy. Women tend to consult alternative health-care providers more often than men. The use of alternative care is also higher in the western provinces and lower in Atlantic Canada, due partly to broader health-care coverage for these services in BC and the Prairie provinces. However, even the most generous provincial health insurance plans cover only some of the costs of alternative services, resulting in high out-of-pocket expenses. As a result, use of alternative health care is positively correlated with household income and education levels (Park, 2005).

Surveys reveal that people use alternative health care for a number of reasons. Many health-conscious individuals do so as a preventive measure, to maintain their good health rather than cure an illness. Users also seek alternative care to supplement conventional medical treatment for chronic conditions such as back problems, migraines, and arthritis. Some people first try these alternative approaches after having been disappointed by conventional Western medicine—whether because of long wait times, adverse side effects to prescription drugs, or an unsympathetic patient–physician relationship.

In most cases, however, people use alternative health care in conjunction with classic Western medicine and other health-enhancing options (York University Centre for Health Studies, 1999). The increasing popularity of alternative health care may also be attributable to North America's growing immigrant populations, who bring with them the knowledge, beliefs, and skills of traditional medical and healing practices from their respective cultures and blend these with the biomedical approach common in the Western world (Zhang and Verhoef, 2005; Ma, 1999).

Sociological Theories of Health, Illness, and Health Care

Medical sociology is among the more interdisciplinary and applied of sociology's subfields. Often, research in this area aims directly at finding answers to program or policy questions; in doing so, it relies on the sharing of knowledge and methods with medicine, psychiatry, biological science, economics, and political science. At the same time, roots in sociology and social theory ensure that its primary focus remains the social aspects of health and illness.

Structural Functionalism

For structural functionalists, good health is considered the normal, desirable state of an individual; good health allows a person to be functional and productive, which benefits society. Sickness, on the other hand, is considered a deviant state of being that threatens the ability of society to function effectively. Widespread illness—during an epidemic, for instance—can undermine a society and wreaks havoc on its social, economic, and political infrastructure. Structural functionalists therefore stress the role of social institutions and relationships in maintaining the health of society's members.

The social institution primarily responsible for a population's health is the health-care industry, which includes physicians, nurses, pharmacists, allied health professionals, and health administrators, and material structures such as hospitals, clinics, laboratories, and dispensaries. As well, societies devise procedures for isolating the ill and reintegrating them back into society when they are 'well'. Talcott Parsons's concept of the 'sick role', discussed below, is the classic statement of this perspective.

Conflict Theory

Conflict theorists see health and medical services as 'goods' that are unequally distributed among different social groups. According to this view, health inequalities are largely the result of income, economic, and social inequalities that expose vulnerable populations to harm and hinder access to medical services and health-affirming lifestyles.

The connection between social conditions and health is well established. In *The Conditions of the Working Class in England*, political philosopher Friedrich Engels (1845) showed how the deplorable conditions of disadvantage in Manchester—substandard housing, lack of sanitation, inadequate diet and clothing, oppressive work environments, etc.—affected the city's death rate. Three years later, the German physician Rudolf Virchow, often credited as the 'father of modern pathology', concluded in a state-commissioned investigation of a typhus epidemic in the Prussian province of Upper Silesia that the root causes of the outbreak were regional poverty, poor education, and inept government policy-making. He famously remarked that 'medicine is a social science and politics is nothing else but medicine on a large scale' and asked, 'Do we not always find the diseases of the populace traceable to defects in society?' (Rather, 1985).

More recent work confirms Virchow's statements. There is now ample evidence that people who are socially, economically, and politically disadvantaged—including women, the elderly, visible and ethnic minorities, the homeless, and others—suffer worse health than their more well-off counterparts (e.g., Marmot, 2005; Mackenbach and Bakker, 2003).

Symbolic Interactionism

Symbolic interactionists ask questions like: What does it mean to be diagnosed (i.e., labelled) as 'sick'? What is the 'meaning' of a given medical condition? Can this given condition even be legitimately considered a 'medical problem'? Researchers who adopt this theoretical perspective remind us that the concepts of 'health' and 'illness' vary from one society to another and are constructed by groups in keeping with their needs, values, and beliefs.

Mainly, symbolic interactionists examine micro-sociological issues connected with health. For example, they might look at the ways medical and nursing schools teach students their new 'professional' identities, or the ways doctors and patients talk during medical visits, following a predictable script that reflects the power difference within these relationships.

Table 10.2 summarizes the outlooks of the three sociological approaches on health, illness, and medicine.

Social Aspects of Medicine and Health

The Doctor–Patient Relationship

Sociologists have studied the relationship between doctors and patients through a variety of theoretical lenses. Functional theorist Talcott Parsons (1951) formulated the concept of the **sick role** to explain how societies deal with their ill members. The sick role is a socially constructed temporary identity that individuals may adopt during times of illness in order to withdraw from 'normal' society and recover without being subject to

Table 10.2 Summary of Theoretical Perspectives on Health and Illness

Structural Functionalism	■ Health is normative, and is maintained by social institutions and structural relationships. ■ Health care is a social institution responsible for maintaining the well-being of all members in society. ■ Illness is a form of deviance that threatens the ability of society to function. ■ The ill adopt a 'sick role', allowing them to temporarily withdraw from society while they recuperate.
Conflict Theory	■ Problems in the delivery of health care result from the capitalist economy, which sees medicine as a commodity that can be produced and sold. ■ People struggle over scare resources (medical treatments). ■ Health, health care, and research are affected by wealth, status, and power or the lack thereof.
Symbolic Interactionism	■ Unique meanings and experiences are associated with specific diseases and with being labelled as 'sick'. ■ What constitutes 'health' or 'sickness' varies from culture to culture. ■ Crises in health care are socially constructed notions and can be used to promote certain political objectives.

blame. To receive the benefits of this socially negotiated role (e.g., going on sick leave), the patient must be willing to accept several 'conditions': he or she must want to get better, voluntarily seek medical assistance, and comply with the physician's orders. In turn, the doctor must adopt the matching role of an objective and emotionally detached professional who will use her or his skills and expert knowledge to return the patient to full health, so that the patient can shed the sick role and rejoin society. Although the patient is a subordinate actor in this performance, the nature of the doctor is complementary rather than domineering. Both the patient and the doctor are needed to assign social meaning to the other (Clarke, 2001).

Functionalist theories assume that the doctor–patient relationship is based on consensus and a shared understanding. For conflict theorists, differences in the social statuses of doctors and patients result inevitably in contradictory needs and wishes (e.g., Friedson, 1970). To maintain their elite status, physicians use hard-to-understand technical language (i.e., 'medical-speak'), a terse and domineering interview process during medical visits, and other measures that keep up a 'competence gap' (Turner, 1987).

Another characteristic of the doctor–patient relationship is the process of **depersonalization**, whereby physicians learn to view their patients narrowly, in terms of their clinical symptoms. From the patient's perspective, this experience may be cold and unpleasant. However, there are good reasons for doctors to avoid emotional attachment, including the need for professional objectivity, clinical efficiency, and protection of their own mental well-being. Many doctors face daily exposure to human suffering and death, particularly in high-stress specialties like emergency medicine, oncology, and neonatology. Uncontrolled emotionalism would complicate rather than assist life-and-death decision-making. Doctors' frequent use of humorous—and often crude—medical slang (e.g., using 'vegetable garden' to mean a hospital's coma ward, or CTD, 'circling the drain', to refer to a patient who is close to death) to describe their patients also helps doctors to cope with otherwise heartbreaking and emotionally exhausting medical cases (Fox et al., 2003).

Medicalization and Professionalization

The term **medicalization** is used to describe the process whereby the medical profession extends its domain of expertise by applying medical thinking to traditionally non-medical aspects of life. For example, medicalization has been documented in areas as diverse as childhood (e.g., attention deficit hyperactive disorder), aging (e.g., menopause, baldness), sexual performance (e.g., erectile dysfunction), sleep (e.g., insomnia and sleep medications), and consumerism (e.g., compulsive shopping disorder). Most recently, road rage fell under the protective wing of the medical profession when researchers argued in the June 2006 issue of the *Archives of General Psychiatry* that aggressive, abusive driving behaviour is best understood—and treated—as intermittent explosive disorder.

According to medical sociologist Irving Zola (1972), medicalization encompasses four components:

1. an expansion of what in life and in a person is relevant to medicine;
2. the maintenance of absolute control over certain technical procedures by the mainstream medical profession;
3. the maintenance of almost absolute access to certain areas by the medical profession;
4. the spread of medicine's relevance to an increasingly large portion of living.

Closely related to medicalization is the **professionalization** of the medical industry, whereby physicians established autonomous control over the institution of health care and elevated their collective status to become authoritative judges of disease and gatekeepers of medical service (Starr, 1982). Important developments in this process include the standardization of medical school curricula, the creation of professional bodies such as the Canadian Medical Association (CMA), and the spread of biomedical visions of health and illness into mainstream culture.

Social constructionists view these twin processes—medicalization and professionalization—as instruments of social control exercised by the medical establishment (Turner, 1987). According to this perspective, doctors, by virtue of their elite professional social status, have established a monopoly over the body as a site for the projection of illness and disease. For example, Ann Oakley (1979, 1980) and others have written critically of the Western medical establishment's medicalization of childbirth. Arguing from a feminist perspective, they claim that the process of childbirth, once considered a natural biological act, has been redefined as medically hazardous and therefore in need of clinical intervention. This redefinition 'decreases the control of the birthing woman, fails to improve the physical and emotional outcome of the birth, and even alienates the woman from a potentially powerful experience' (Fox and Worts, 1999: 327–8).

Conrad (2005) and others have noted that medicalization and professionalization have evolved as a result of the growing dominance of market forces in recent years.

Increasingly, the process is being driven by political and corporate interests rather than mere professional elitism. Feminist scholars have argued, for instance, that the legitimization of 'female sexual disorder' as a mental problem is the result not of new scientific discoveries but of economic self-interest by the medical and pharmaceutical industries. Certainly, many sexual problems are legitimate and have real health consequences. However, Hartley and Tiefer (2003), among others, have argued for a rejection of biological approaches in favour of explanations that highlight the social, political, and economic causes of sexual ill health among women and focus on prevention rather than cure.

The Social Determinants of Health

What determines the health of populations? Of course, lifestyle behaviours (smoking, diet, exercise, etc.) play a role in personal well-being. Health-conscious decisions such as quitting smoking and joining a gym can yield noticeable gains. But research confirms that major improvements in population health over the past century have mainly been the result of improved socio-economic conditions rather than improved individual behaviours (Raphael, 2002). Others, pointing to flaws in the health-care system, argue that poor health is the result of not enough access or funding. But health inequalities still exist where universal, publicly funded health care is provided, so access alone is not the problem. Likewise, though the United States spends more on health care per citizen than any other country, it still lags significantly behind other developed nations in most health indicators.

In recent years, social scientists have turned towards examining the effects of various social, economic, and political factors—together commonly referred to as the **social determinants of health**—on population health outcomes. Some researchers have adopted a *materialist* approach, arguing that disadvantaged populations suffer from higher levels of total exposure to negative conditions over their lifetimes, resulting in poorer health outcomes than more advantaged groups. This exposure can directly hinder physical and social development. Indirectly, it can create extra stress and encourage unhealthy behaviours like alcohol abuse and smoking. *Neo-materialists* agree that material conditions are important, but also point to important social structural contributors (including income inequalities, systemic racial and gender discrimination, and cuts to government social spending) as playing a key role in health disparities.

Finally, *social comparison* theories have been developed to explain the observed health inequalities that exist even among relatively well-off people. The best example of this phenomenon is found in the Whitehall studies of British civil servants (described in detail in Chapter 1). Since the groups in question were all white-collar and at least middle-class, differences in health status cannot be attributed to material deprivation. These workers experienced subtly different opportunities and varying degrees of control over their life decisions; both affected health through accumulated psychological stress.

A mountain of research has followed the Whitehall studies (e.g., Marmot, 2005; Wilkinson and Marmot, 2003). Europe in general and the United Kingdom in particular have been particularly open to the notion that health status is closely and subtly related to the social environment and that health policies must harmonize with social policies. Canada, too, has been active in theorizing about the social determinants of health but has been less successful in translating academic research into government policies.

In 2002, York University in Toronto hosted a conference entitled 'The Social Determinants of Health across the Lifespan'. One outcome of this event was the identification of 11 key social determinants of health in Canadian society. Many of these factors, and their links to health problems, are discussed in more detail in other chapters; here, we only review briefly what the literature has to say about each topic.

1. *Early life.* The benefits of healthy development begin at the earliest stages of life. For example, exposure to cigarette smoke, alcohol, and environmental pollutants can impair fetal development, setting the stage for poor health throughout the lifespan. In contrast, programs that provide parenting education and adequate nutrition for young mothers and their infants help to ensure the best start to life (Wilkinson and Marmot, 2003). Governments are also beginning to realize that healthy child development is a national interest; for this reason, more countries are funding early childhood education and care.

2. *Education.* Educational attainment in adolescence and early adulthood is also linked to health outcomes later in life. A solid education helps build the skills, resourcefulness, and sense of mastery that prove useful when dealing with problems later in life. Even a basic education can mean better access to steady jobs, a home in a safer neighbourhood, and the ability to understand health information. In fact, worldwide, literacy is a more sensitive predictor of health status than is education level, income, ethnic background, or any other single socio-demographic variable (Ronson and Rootman, 2004).

3. *Food security.* It is often assumed that malnutrition and starvation are problems of the developing world only. In fact, many Westerners go hungry every day. In 2005, more than 820,000 Canadians used a food bank in a typical month. Welfare recipients and the working poor, many of whom are single parents, are the most frequent users. Nationwide, food bank use has increased 118 per cent since 1989 (Canadian Association of Food Banks, 2005). However, food insecurity is more than simply lacking enough food to eat; it is also 'the inability to acquire or consume an adequate diet quality . . . or the uncertainty that one will be able to do so' (MacIntyre, 2004: 174). Thus, as we saw earlier, obesity is another major problem for the poor, in both the developed and developing worlds.

4. *Housing.* Renters have lower average incomes than homeowners, yet face a national shortage of affordable rental housing. This shortage means a difficult choice for the poor: either live in substandard housing conditions—for example, in illegally converted basement apartments or deteriorating apartment complexes—or rent costly apartments that leave little after-rent income for food, clothing, and other necessities. In addition to obvious health and social implications, the shortage of affordable housing can also be 'a major impediment to business investment and growth' (TD Economics, 2003).

5. *Employment security and work conditions.* As we saw in an earlier chapter, work and unemployment can have serious health consequences. Many factors besides pay level distinguish good jobs from bad ones. They include job security; high control and low demand in work responsibilities; opportunities for growth and personal challenge; work–life balance; environmentally and physically safe conditions; and appropriate managerial acknowledgement of workers' efforts. Note that these positive factors are all more abundant in higher-prestige occupations, which are usually dominated by white, middle-class males. Conversely, at the bottom of the job hierarchy, unskilled manual labour and service industry positions are disproportionately filled by women and ethnic minorities.

6. *Income inequality.* Income and economic inequality, discussed in Chapter 2, are key determinants of health disparity. Research has consistently shown that as one moves up the income hierarchy, health status improves. If this trend were restricted to the poor, one might imagine that the conditions of poverty—poor housing, inability to buy healthy food, and so on—are the cause of the problem. However, researchers have

shown that health inequalities exist along the entire income spectrum, even among the richest members of society (e.g., Marmot, 2004). The fact that even CEOs can have better health than the vice-presidents just below them on the corporate hierarchy indicates that inequality itself is as much a problem as material deprivation.

7. *Social exclusion.* Social exclusion refers to the marginalization of some groups in society from the economic, social, cultural, and political resources that affect quality of life. Social exclusion is created and maintained by unequal social structures, processes, and relationships, such as unemployment, high crime rates, and poor housing. As Galabuzi (2004) points out, social exclusion is both a process and an outcome.

Research finds a clear link between exclusion and health. Women, the poor, ethnic minorities, and people with mental and physical disabilities tend to experience poorer socio-economic and health outcomes because of their marginalized statuses. Exclusion reduces access to education and work opportunities, health-care services, and technological and social innovations. Exclusion can also lead to racially segregated neighbourhoods and occupational categories.

8. *Aboriginal status.* Compared to the general Canadian population, Aboriginal communities have higher rates of mortality, infant mortality, suicide, potential years of life lost, infectious disease, and many chronic illnesses. Aboriginal people are also more likely to smoke, abuse alcohol and drugs, gamble to excess, suffer from food insecurity, be overweight, and have unprotected sex; and they are less likely to be immunized or get physical exercise (Shah, 2004).

9. *Social safety net.* The social safety net includes unemployment insurance benefits, welfare payments, publicly administered pension plans, universal health-care access, job training, and other community programs and services provided by the state as a system of supports for those who for a variety of reasons are unable to cope on their own. The existence of this net reduces the negative health effects of unemployment, poverty, racial and social exclusion, and other social problems.

10. *Health-care services.* Health-care services are obviously related to health outcomes. Unequal access to health care, which research has shown to be particularly prevalent among poor and marginalized people, contributes to society's health disparities. Unless the problems currently affecting Canada's medicare program are solved, differential health outcomes will become more pronounced over time.

11. *Gender.* The participants of the York University conference determined that gender and its social construction are important social determinants of health. However, because gender interacts with each of the other determinants in complex ways, its connections to health are often addressed within these other discussions.

Historically, men have controlled women's bodies—as fathers, husbands, and, more recently, employers. As the earlier discussion of the medicalization of childbirth showed, they have also controlled women's bodies as physicians, by defining how women's symptoms and experiences might be interpreted medically. It is easy to find, in such assumptions, 'scientific' legitimacy for the sexual objectification of women, for women's secondary social status and low self-esteem, and for the tendency to dismiss women's health complaints as unfounded. Throughout the mid- to late twentieth century, articles in women's magazines often trivialized potentially important and serious mental symptoms and subordinated women's health problems to those of others around them, especially their male partners. Depression, for instance, was viewed as a women's mental health disability and a form of 'gendered incompetence' (Beal and Gardner, 2000).

Even today, 'women's' illnesses and health conditions are often considered more trivial or shameful than men's. Consider menopause. Women going through menopause often view their physical symptoms as embarrassing or disruptive. They struggle to conceal and control the changes, to keep up appearances (Kittell et al., 1998). In Japan, a menopausal woman is sometimes blamed for her condition and condemned as selfish or lacking in willpower. Canadian research has shown that some doctors view the conditions associated with menopause as psychiatric problems, owing to a multiplicity of losses and the lack of a meaningful occupation (Kaufert and Lock, 1998).

12. *Social environment.* A final health determinant, not specifically noted by the scholars at the York University conference, is the social environment. Our environment is complex and includes harmful natural elements, such as pollutants and contaminants in the air, water, soil, and food that can increase the risk of cancer, asthma, and other serious health problems. The social environment also refers to neighbourhood quality, which is influenced by rates of crime and deviance, level of community cohesion, and shared sense of civic responsibility. Finally, the social environment includes elements of the built infrastructure, such as the quality of housing and public spaces and the availability of public transportation and bicycle lanes (Wilkinson and Marmot, 2003).

Solutions to Problems in Health Outcomes and Health-Care Delivery

Public Health Promotion

Most of the improvements in global population health and well-being over the past century and a half are due not to advances in medicine, pharmaceutical agents, or lifestyle changes, but to socio-economic development and public health programs that focused on preventive medicine rather than treatment or cure (e.g., Marmot, 2004). The **population health perspective**, a framework for understanding health and illness in society, emphasizes the importance and benefits of preventive health care. It acknowledges that preventive actions are not only the most effective way to improve health indicators at the societal level, but they are also the most economically cost-effective. As the twenty-first century unfolds, health-care delivery in Canada and internationally will likely continue the trend of prevention over treatment.

Primary prevention refers to steps people take to prevent a disease from occurring. Louria (2000) identifies four aspects to the primary prevention of infectious diseases: (1) immunization; (2) a well-functioning public health infrastructure; (3) prudent use of antimicrobial medicines; and (4) 'the amelioration of the societal variables that provide the milieu in which emerging and re-emerging infections arise and flourish'—that is, improving the social determinants of health.

The need for better health promotion is particularly urgent in the developing world. Disseminating information about causes, consequences, and prevention is vital to controlling outbreaks of communicable diseases. For example, AIDS education among Indian commercial sex workers in recent years has resulted in promising declines in HIV infection rates in some areas. A concentrated effort to educate prostitutes in Kolkata's Sonagachi red-light district about ways to prevent STD transmission has resulted in condom use rates as high as 85 per cent and a subsequent decline in HIV prevalence among sex workers from 11 per cent in 2001 to 4 per cent in 2004 (NACO, 2004). Similar grassroots efforts in the Indian state of Tamil Nadu have reduced the frequency of unprotected sex between truck drivers and prostitutes from 14 per cent in 1996 to 2 per cent in 2003, with fewer men paying for sex and more condom use by those who did (MAP, 2005b).

Effective public health delivery requires adaptation to local circumstances and acknowledging that the target individuals are whole human beings. Consider the vastly differing approaches taken by two Southeast Asian countries in dealing with the HIV/AIDS epidemic. In Myanmar, women found possessing a condom face imprisonment, as the contraceptive is considered evidence of prostitution. Not only does this severe policy fail to stem the transmission of HIV between sex workers and clients, it further intensifies the problem by discouraging non-prostitutes from practising safe sex. By contrast, in Laos, efforts to contain the spread of HIV/AIDS among sex trade workers are pragmatic and creative. Careful attention to the social hierarchy led researchers to recognize the influential, almost maternal role that *mamasans* (female brothel-owners) played within the industry. By giving *mamasans* incentives to provide condoms and sex education to their 'staff', higher rates of condom use soon resulted.

Finally, research points to the importance of information-sharing between governments and international bodies. For example, China has been criticized for trying to cover up the extent of the SARS epidemic in its southernmost regions during the early stages of the 2002–3 outbreak. This delayed a response by the World Health Organization and other health agencies with the resources and expertise to contain infectious diseases. Epidemiologists generally agree that early detection and response are crucial to the effective control of communicable diseases, so it is likely that this delay cost lives. How many lives were lost this way cannot be estimated.

Improving Health in the Developing World: Honouring Global Commitments

Improving global health will require co-ordinated reforms that address underlying social inequalities that complicate efforts to deliver health prevention, screening, and treatment programs. As UNAIDS recently stated with respect to the current AIDS epidemic:

> Bringing AIDS under control will require tackling with greater resolve the underlying factors that fuel these epidemics—including societal inequalities and injustices . . . stigma, discrimination, gender inequality and other human rights violations. It will also require overcoming the new injustices of AIDS, such as the orphaning of generations of children and the stripping of human and institutional capacities. These are extraordinary challenges that demand extraordinary responses. (UNAIDS, 2005: 5)

In 2000, the United Nations adopted the Millennium Development Goals, an unprecedented agreement between all 191 member nations and participating international agencies to co-ordinate efforts to wipe out poverty and improve global health by 2015 (see Table 10.3). Three of the eight goals explicitly address population health needs; the others address issues like poverty, development, and vulnerability to disease that affect population health. Together, they form the central objectives of the UN development agenda, for the first time addressing jointly the related issues of peace, security, fundamental freedoms, and human rights.

Table 10.3 The United Nations Millennium Development Goals	
Goal 1:	Eradicate extreme poverty and hunger.
Goal 2:	Achieve universal primary education.
Goal 3:	Promote gender equality and empower women.
Goal 4:	Reduce child mortality.
Goal 5:	Improve maternal health.
Goal 6:	Combat HIV/AIDS, malaria, and other diseases.
Goal 7:	Ensure environmental sustainability.
Goal 8:	Develop a global partnership for development.

Source: UN (2005). The United Nations is the author of the original material.

In the five years since the Millennium Development Goals were stated, some targets have been met while others have fallen behind schedule. Achievements in some areas—better access to safe drinking water, lower child mortality rates, and global increases in girls' primary school enrolment—have been tempered by such setbacks as the continuing HIV/AIDS pandemic and higher rates of hunger in Southeast Asia and sub-Saharan Africa. More must be done to meet these goals. For example, five diseases—pneumonia, diarrhea, malaria, measles, and AIDS—account for over half of all deaths globally among children under five years old (see Figure 10.4).

Many of these deaths can be prevented through inexpensive interventions, such as encouraging the breast-feeding of infants and increasing the availability of antibiotics, vaccines, and oral rehydration salts (UN, 2005). According to UNICEF's *State of the World's Children 2006* report, at the current rate of progress, meeting the target of reducing child mortality by two-thirds will not happen until 2045, 30 years beyond the established date for this goal to be achieved. As a result of the delay, 50 million children will

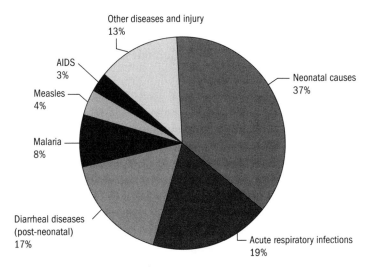

FIGURE 10.4 Causes of Death among Children under Five, Worldwide, 2000–3
Source: UN (2005). The United Nations is the author of the original material.

not receive access to adequate nutrition; 70 million, to cleaner water; and 170 million, to improved sanitation (UNICEF, 2005).

Meeting the Millennium Development Goals is slowed by a lack of funds. In 1970, the developed nations of the UN agreed to give 0.7 per cent of their respective gross domestic products (GDP) to development aid, a target established by an international commission led by former Canadian Prime Minister Lester B. Pearson. Commitment to achieving this target was reaffirmed at UN summits in 1992 and 2002. By 2005, total development aid in dollars had reached an all-time high, but remained at a historic low as a percentage of the donor countries' combined GDP. That is, giving to poor nations had not kept up with increases in the wealth of the wealthy nations (OECD, 2005). Only five nations—Denmark, Luxembourg, the Netherlands, Norway, and Sweden—have met or exceeded the 0.7 per cent mark; however, at least eight others have committed to doing so by 2015 (UN, 2005). The Canadian government currently gives about 0.26 per cent of its GDP to foreign aid, and has pledged to increase this amount in the future in order to bring Canada up to the OECD average. To date, however, it has yet to commit to the goal of 0.7 per cent by 2015, arguing that doing so would be fiscally irresponsible.

Health research funding must also overcome biases. This is especially true of the so-called '90/10' research gap, which refers to the estimate that 90 per cent of global spending on medical and pharmaceutical research is aimed at finding treatments for diseases that affect only 10 per cent of the world's (wealthiest) population. As a result, much of the research on diseases in developing nations—malaria, tuberculosis, typhoid fever, etc.—is severely underfunded. Various humanitarian aid programs, many supported by private donors and corporations, have tried to correct this imbalance. For example, the Global Fund to Fight AIDS, Tuberculosis, and Malaria, a unique funding agency comprised of governments, international aid agencies, private foundations, and corporate donors, has pledged over US$6.1 billion to finance health initiatives through 2008 (Global Fund to Fight AIDS, Tuberculosis, and Malaria, 2005). Similarly, the Bill and Melinda Gates Foundation had committed nearly US$9.3 billion as of December 2005 to numerous global health and education initiatives, particularly in the developing world (Bill and Melinda Gates Foundation, 2006).

Box 10.4 Social Policy: A Canadian Commitment to Fighting AIDS in Africa

Beginning in August 2003, the World Trade Organization allowed developed countries to approve the production of lower-cost generic versions of patented medicines by a firm other than the patent holder for the express purpose of export to developing countries. Canada was the first country to execute the WTO's decision through Bill C-9, also known as the 'Jean Chrétien Pledge to Africa' in recognition of the former Prime Minister's commitment to this issue.

This pledge is part of Canadian efforts to fight epidemic diseases in developing countries. Legislative changes, which permit Canada to respond to the need for safe and effective medicines in developing countries, were the result of consultation with multiple stakeholders, including representatives of the pharmaceutical industry and non-governmental organizations such as Médecins Sans Frontières and Oxfam.

Source: Adapted from Industry Canada (2005).

Health-Care Reform in Canada

The debate over health-care reform in Canada is complex and often divisive. Its focus primarily is on access and the role for-profit health services can or should play in Canada's putatively universal system.

Health-care access in underserviced areas, particularly in northern Canada, is one critical area in need of improvement. Among the Romanow Report's 47 recommendations was a call for targeted funding to improve care for Canadians living in smaller communities in rural and remote areas.

International medical graduates, who traditionally have provided health-care services in areas that have had trouble recruiting domestically trained medical school graduates, are one potential source of well-trained physicians. For instance, they make up over half of all physicians in Saskatchewan and Newfoundland and Labrador (Audas et al., 2005). Efforts are underway to reduce the bureaucratic hurdles that immigrants face in obtaining a licence to practise medicine in Canada. Medical school initiatives, such as BC's Northern Medical Program (a partnership between the University of British Columbia and the University of Northern British Columbia) and the Northern Ontario School of Medicine, are another possible source. Programs such as these are designed specifically to produce young doctors who are trained to deliver health-care services in northern, remote, and Aboriginal communities and in francophone communities in English-speaking Canada.

Telehealth—the use of computer and communication technologies to aid health-care delivery—is a growing industry that may revolutionize the medical profession's ability to service its patients. Diagnostic images, such as X-rays and MRI scans, and pathology images, such as diseased tissue and blood samples, are now routinely sent electronically from rural or remote locations for review by specialists hundreds of kilometres away. Similarly, video-conferencing technology now allows medical consultations, mental health assessments, and observation of surgical procedures for educational purposes to take place over vast geographic distances.

Managing Costs: Is For-Profit Health Care the Answer?

Cutting across the various challenges facing Canada's medicare system—including cost, access, and quality of care—is the debate over privatization. The typically heated and divisive nature of the debate is not surprising, since in survey after survey most Canadians cite the universal health-care system as our most cherished social program and a source of national pride.

It should be noted that much of Canada's health-care system is already 'privatized'. The for-profit/not-for-profit debate is not about whether (or how much) private money should be spent on health-care services. As noted earlier, 30 per cent of health-care spending in Canada already comes from private sources, either through out-of-pocket expenses or health insurance. Nor is the dispute over whether services should be privately delivered. Already, most physicians practising in Canada operate as private entrepreneurs, billing their provincial governments for services provided to the public. Also, most hospitals in Canada are administered as not-for-profit private institutions. In essence, medicare is a health insurance program that uses public money to pay for privately delivered care.

Tommy Douglas

'Courage, my friends; 'tis not too late to build a better world.'

Tommy Douglas (1904–86), widely regarded as the 'father of medicare', was Premier of Saskatchewan (1944–61) and leader of the federal New Democratic Party (1961–71). In 2004 he was selected 'greatest Canadian' in a widely publicized CBC poll.

The Canada Health Act does not explicitly ban private health insurance; it limits private health-care insurance to services not covered by the public insurance plan. By stating that all 'medically necessary' treatments by physicians and in hospitals must be delivered through the public system, medicare exercises a monopoly over health care in the country. Canada is currently the only OECD country that so staunchly divides health-care services into public and private spheres.

The debate over 'privatization' is therefore a debate over whether health care is a private commodity or a public good. The champions of privatization argue that the various 'crises' of cost and access plaguing medicare can be eased by ending the state monopoly on health care in Canada. A for-profit health-care system governed by free-market principles, it is claimed, will inspire more efficient delivery models, provide more access and options for treatment, and produce economic benefits through job creation. Supporters also argue that as a matter of individual rights, people who can afford more choices in care should be permitted to exercise them. Finally, proponents note that many industrialized countries, including Australia, France, and the Netherlands, operate publicly funded health-care systems while allowing their citizens to upgrade their services through a privatized health insurance scheme.

On the other side, opponents of privatization argue that allowing for-profit medicine into the health-care regime would result in a two-tier system. The for-profit tier would provide better-quality services to the rich and the not-for-profit tier would suffer from decreased funding, burned out health-care professionals, and poorer service overall. The quality of public health care in Canada would suffer from the gradual loss of health professionals and funding dollars to the private for-profit tier. The need to turn a profit would lead some private health administrators to cut corners and limit services to lucrative procedures.

The international body of literature on for-profit versus not-for-profit medicine is abundant, with each side of the debate able to cite empirical evidence to support its own arguments. Also, as Chodos and MacLeod (2004:11) have noted, 'there is such commitment to entrenched positions that there seems to be little room for compromise, or even a shared understanding of what the terms of the debate are.' The arguments for and against health-care privatization are too complex to be addressed in detail here. Interested students are encouraged to consult the vast literature (as a starting point, see the recommended readings at the end of this chapter).

In recent years, British Columbia, Alberta, Quebec, New Brunswick, and Nova Scotia have authorized health-care initiatives that may violate the Canada Health Act. The *Chaoulli* ruling by the Supreme Court of Canada in June 2005, which held that Quebec's ban on private health and hospital insurance was inconsistent with the province's Charter of Human Rights and Freedoms, marks the latest—and perhaps most legally serious—challenge to the survival of medicare. The case was brought up through the courts by Dr Jacques Chaoulli, a Quebec doctor, and George Zeliotis, a patient who waited a year before receiving hip replacement surgery. At the heart of the matter is the issue of whether forcing a person to endure long wait times for a medically necessary procedure—by banning alternative delivery of service outside the public system—violates the right to security of the individual. While agreeing that unreasonable delay indeed violated the Quebec human rights charter, the Quebec courts argued that this violation was justified by an overriding public interest—namely, ensuring that the health-care system remains universally available to all. On appeal, however, the Supreme

Court disagreed, ruling 4–3 that the ban on private health insurance to cover medically necessary treatment is unconstitutional. As Chief Justice Beverley McLachlin and Justice John C. Major wrote in their majority opinion, 'access to a waiting list is not access to health care.' How profoundly this ruling from Canada's highest court will alter medicare remains an open question.

Concluding Remarks

Throughout this text, we have stressed a population health approach to the study of social problems. One recurring theme has been: 'Does a given social condition negatively affect population health, and if so, does that make the social condition a *social problem*?'

The current chapter turns this theme on its head by asking a different question: 'What are the social causes and consequences of health problems?' It directly adopts a population health perspective that focuses on how social structural variables influence the physical, psychological, and social well-being of large groups of people.

We learned first that the concepts of health and illness are viewed differently by different groups, and that we must begin any evaluation of population health issues with a consideration of cultural values and beliefs. We also learned that some groups are more vulnerable to health threats—infectious diseases, obesity, injuries—than other groups, and these different levels of risk are usually stratified by economic and social inequalities.

At the same time, the health-care system, the purpose of which is to improve societal well-being, is troubled by serious shortcomings that further threaten population health. Again, not all social groups feel the effects of these health-care inadequacies, if they even recognize that such inadequacies exist. Some problems—for example, the nationwide shortage of specialist physicians and nurses—will likely have consequences for everyone; other structural inequalities—such as increasing opportunities to bypass hospital waiting lists or the ability to travel to the US or elsewhere for immediate treatment—ensure that the impact will be least disturbing for the social elite. The health-care system is also a social institution, and so it contains socializing elements and processes, such as medicalization and professionalization. Finally, we explored some possible solutions to current health problems, both globally and locally.

QUESTIONS FOR CRITICAL THOUGHT

1. Is there an ethical obligation to provide potentially life-saving medicines for free or at cost to those in the developing world who would otherwise be unable to afford them? If so, where does that obligation lie—with the pharmaceutical companies, the affluent Western world, the global community, or all of the above?

2. How is mental illness treated in the media, including fictionalized portrayals on television and in film, as well as journalistic accounts in the news? Are conditions stigmatized and stereotyped or treated as realistic and potentially treatable health problems?

3. On average, those who engage in health-adverse behaviours such as smoking or consuming a fat-laden diet are at a higher risk of developing chronic illnesses and therefore impose a greater burden on the public health-care system compared to those who take preventive steps to protect their health. Should these and other health-adverse behaviours be more heavily taxed as a way to raise the additional funds needed to pay for the eventual treatment of the illnesses they cause?

4. Where does Canada's medicare system stand in comparison with those of other developed nations? Is our approach to publicly funded health care sustainable, or should we look to others for a better model? In answering these questions, compare Canadian health policies, funding structure, and outcomes with those of other countries.

5. Once dismissed as 'pseudo-science' by the Western medical establishment, complementary and alternative medicines have gained much ground with the public and have attracted renewed interest from mainstream medicine as well. As Canada becomes ever more ethnically diverse and different ideas about the roots of health and illness grow in popular consciousness, how might this increased acceptance of alternative therapies change the way public medicine is delivered and funded in Canada in the future?

RECOMMENDED READINGS

Canada Health Act, R.S. 1985, c. C-6. Available at <lois.justice.gc.ca/en/C-6>. The Canada Health Act provides the statutory framework for Canada's publicly funded health-care system.

Dennis Raphael, ed., *The Social Determinants of Health: A Canadian Perspective* (Toronto: Canadian Scholars' Press, 2004). This book summarizes the reports presented at the 2002 'Social Determinants of Health across the Lifespan' conference held at York University, and provides a good overview of Canadian research to date on the social determinants of health.

Erving Goffman, *Asylums: Essays on the Social Situation of Mental Patients and Other Inmates* (New York: Doubleday, 1961). In this classic sociological text, the author discusses the concept of total institutions, outlines the 'moral career' of the mentally ill patient, and critiques institutionalized mental health care.

David A. Karp, *Speaking of Sadness* (New York: Oxford University Press, 1996). This book, written by a sociologist who himself had battled with depression, uses in-depth interviews with other depression sufferers to gain insights into the meanings of mental illness, issues of treatment and coping, and the role of society in shaping the experience and understanding of depression.

World Health Organization (WHO), *The World Health Report* (Geneva: World Health Organization). Available at <www.who.int/whr/en>. This annual report of the WHO offers a comprehensive, quantitative assessment of global health, focusing on a different theme each year. Past themes have included mothers and children, AIDS, and mental health.

RECOMMENDED WEBSITES

Canadian Institute for Health Information
www.cihi.ca

This independent, non-partisan, not-for-profit organization publishes essential statistics, analyses, and reports on Canadian health and health-care issues.

Public Health Agency of Canada
www.phac-aspc.gc.ca/ph-sp/phdd/index.html

This website provides an excellent overview of the federal Public Health Agency's approach to population health. It includes information on the social determinants of health, program and service initiatives, project funding, and international collaborations and partnerships.

World Health Organization
www.who.int

The website of the United Nations' public health arm and the international community's leading intergovernmental agency for global health provides epidemiological status updates by country and health topic, as well as a huge collection of data sheets, reports, and other publications.

GLOSSARY

Adverse event An unintended injury or complication directly related to medical intervention that results in death, disability at the time of discharge from hospital, or prolonged hospital stay.

Biomedical view of medicine A medical perspective that emphasizes Western scientific principles, defines health as the absence of illness, views the human body as a machine that sometimes requires repair, and promotes the use of therapeutic intervention (e.g., drugs, surgery) to 'cure' disease and injury.

Biopsychosocial view of health and illness A medical perspective that considers health and disease as products of the interaction between body, mind, and environment.

Body mass index (BMI) Weight in kilograms divided by the square of height in metres (kg/m^2); 'overweight' is defined as 25 kg/m^2 and 'obesity' as 30 kg/m^2.

Co-morbidity The predisposition of an individual with an illness to additional health conditions.

Deinstitutionalization The trend towards moving the locus of treatment for mental patients away from large institutions into smaller community-based settings.

Epidemiological transition An observable epidemiological pattern whereby the nature of population illnesses shift from diseases of acute infection and nutritional deficiency characteristic of developing societies to chronic non-communicable illnesses characteristic of developed societies.

Epidemiology An applied science that examines the causes, distribution, and control of disease in a population.

Health 'A state of complete physical, mental, and social well-being' (WHO).

Infant mortality rate Number of deaths of children under one year of age per 1,000 live births.

Life expectancy The average number of years remaining to a person at a particular age, given current age-specific mortality rates.

Maternal mortality rate The number of deaths of women due to complications during pregnancy, childbirth, or abortion, typically measured as deaths per year per 1,000 live births.

Medical (clinical) iatrogenesis Any state of adverse physical or mental health caused by the effects of medical intervention by a physician, therapist, or pharmacist.

Medicalization The process whereby the medical profession comes to be viewed as being relevant to an ever-widening range of traditionally non-medical aspects of life.

Medical sociology The field of sociology that examines the social context of health, illness, and health care.

Mental disorder A condition 'characterized by alterations in thinking, mood, or behaviour (or some combination thereof) associated with significant distress and impaired functioning over an extended period of time' (Health Canada).

Mental health The capacity for individuals to feel, think, and act in ways that enhance the quality of daily functioning, the range and depth of social relationships, and the ability to adapt to both positive and negative life changes.

Mental illness Clinical diagnosis of mental disorder requiring medical and/or psychotherapeutic treatment.

Morbidity rate The extent of disease in a population, reported by incidence (the number of new cases in a given population during a given period of time) and/or its prevalence (the total number of cases of a disease in the population at a particular point in time).

Mortality rate The death rate of a given disease or population, typically measured as deaths per year per 1,000 people.

Primary prevention Proactive steps taken to prevent a disease from occurring.

Professionalization When used to refer to the medical industry, the gradual process whereby physicians established autonomous control over the institution of health care and elevated their collective status in society to become authoritative judges of disease definitions and gatekeepers of medical services

Social determinants of health The complex causal relationships between various social, economic, and political factors and population health outcomes.

Telehealth The use of computer and communication technologies to facilitate health-care delivery across geographic space.

Total institutions Organizations, such as a mental institution or prison, that isolate, control, and regulate all aspects of life for those individuals confined within their walls or organizational structure.

Under-five mortality rate (U5MR) Number of deaths of children under 5 years of age per 1,000 live births.

Well-being A positive state of existence characterized by happiness, prosperity, and the satisfaction of basic human needs, and not simply the absence of negative conditions, such as illness or injury.

References

Altman, Lawrence. 1981. 'Rare Cancer Seen in 41 Homosexuals', *New York Times*, 3 July.

American Psychiatric Association. 1994. *Diagnostic and Statistical Manual of Mental Disorders*, 4th edn. Washington: American Psychiatric Association.

Anderson, Laurie M., Susan C. Scrimshaw, Mindy T. Fullilove, Jonathan E. Fielding, Jacques Normand, and the Task Force on Community Preventative Services. 2003. 'Culturally Competent Healthcare Systems: A Systematic Review', *American Journal of Preventative Medicine* 24, 3S: 68–79.

Audas, Rick, Amanda Ross, and David Vardy. 2005. 'The Use of Provisionally Licensed International Medical Graduates in Canada', *Canadian Medical Association Journal* 173, 11: 1315–16.

Baker, G.R., P.G. Norton, V. Flintoft, R. Blais, A. Brown, et al. 2004. 'The Canadian Adverse Events Study: The Incidence of Adverse Events among Hospital Patients in Canada', *Canadian Medical Association Journal* 170, 11: 1678–86.

Bill and Melinda Gates Foundation. 2006. Available at: <www.gatesfoundation.org/default.htm>; accessed 29 Jan. 2006.

Block, Jason P., Richard A. Scribner, and Karen B. DeSalvo. 2004. 'Fast Food, Race/Ethnicity, and Income: A Geographic Analysis', *American Journal of Preventative Medicine* 27, 3: 211–17.

Brennan, T.A., L.L. Leape, N.M. Laird, L. Hebert, A.R. Localio, A.G. Lawthers, J.P. Newhouse, P. C. Weiler, and H.H. Hiatt. 1991. 'Incidence of Adverse Events and Negligence in Hospitalized Patients. Results of the Harvard Medical Practice Study I', *New England Journal of Medicine* 324, 6: 370–6.

Bull, Chris, ed. 2003. *While the World Sleeps: Writing from the First Twenty Years of the Global AIDS Plague*. New York: Thunder's Mouth Press.

Caballero, Benjamin. 2001. 'Symposium: Obesity in Developing Countries: Biological and Ecological Factors (Introduction)', *Journal of Nutrition* 131 (Suppl.): 866S–70S.

Cameron, Adrian J., Timothy A. Welborn, Paul Z. Zimmet, David W. Dunstan, Neville Owen, et al. 2003. 'Overweight and Obesity in Australia: The 1999–2000 Australian Diabetes, Obesity and Lifestyle Study (AusDiab)', *Medical Journal of Australia* 187, 9: 427–32.

Canadian Association of Food Banks (CAFB). 2005. *HungerCount 2005*. Toronto: Canadian Association of Food Banks.

CBC. 2005. 'Banning the Butt: Global Anti-smoking Efforts'. Available at: <www.cbc.ca/news/background/smoking/smokingbans.html>; accessed 29 Jan. 2006.

Canadian Institute for Health Information (CIHI). 2002. 'Health Conditions—Injuries'. Available at: <secure.cihi.ca/cihiweb/dispPage.jsp?cw_page=statistics_topic_e>; accessed 5 Jan. 2006.

———. 2004a. *Improving the Health of Canadians*. Ottawa: CIHI.

———. 2004b. *Overweight and Obesity in Canada*. Ottawa: CIHI.

———. 2005a. *Major Injury in Canada*. Ottawa: CIHI.

———. 2005b. *National Health Expenditure Trends 1975–2005*. Ottawa: CIHI.

———. 2006. *Geographic Distribution of Physicians in Canada: Beyond How Many and Where*. Ottawa: CIHI.

Canadian Medical Association (CMA). 2006. 'Statistical Information on Canadian Physicians'. Available at: <www.cma.ca>; accessed 15 Jan. 2006.

Canadian Pandemic Influenza Plan. 2004. Ottawa: Her Majesty the Queen in Right of Canada.

Chen, Jiajian, and Feng Hou. 2002. 'Unmet Needs for Health Care', *Health Reports* 13, 2: 23–34.

Chodos, H., and J.J. MacLeod. 2004. 'Romanow and Kirby on the Public/Private Divide in Healthcare: Demystifying the Debate', *HealthcarePapers* 4, 4: 10–25.

Clarke, Alan. 2001. *The Sociology of Healthcare*. Essex, UK: Prentice-Hall.

Commission on the Future of Health Care in Canada. 2002. *Building on Values: The Future of Health Care in Canada—Final Report*. Ottawa.

Conference Board of Canada. 2003. *The Economic Impact of SARS*. Ottawa: Canadian Tourism Research Institute, Conference Board of Canada.

Conrad, P. 2005. 'The Shifting Engines of Medicalization', *Journal of Health and Social Behaviour* 46, 1: 3–14.

——— and A. Angell. 2004. 'Homosexuality and Remedicalization', *Society* 41, 5: 32–9.

Devereaux, P.J., Peter T.L. Choi, Christina Lacchetti, Bruce Weaver, Holger J. Schünemann, et al. 2002. 'A Systematic Review and Meta-analysis of Studies Comparing Mortality Rates of Private For-Profit and Private Not-For-Profit Hospitals', *Canadian Medical Association Journal* 166, 11: 1399–1406.

Edwards, Christopher L., Roger B. Filligim, and Francis Keefe. 2001. 'Race, Ethnicity, and Pain', *Pain* 94: 133–7.

Engel, George L. 1977. 'The Need for a New Medical Model: A Challenge for Biomedicine', *Science* 196: 129–36.

Engels, Friedrich. 1987 [1845]. *The Conditions of the Working Class in England*. New York: Penguin.

EuroHIV. 2005. *HIV/AIDS Surveillance in Europe: End-Year Report 2004* (No. 71). Saint-Maurice, France: Institut de Veille Sanitaire.

Farrales, Lynn L., and Gwen E. Chapman. 1999. 'Filipino Women Living in Canada: Constructing Meanings of Body, Food, and Health', *Health Care for Women International* 20: 179–94.

Flegel, K.M. 1999. 'The Obesity Epidemic in Children and Adults: Current Evidence and Research Issues', *Medicine and Science in Sports and Exercise* 31 (suppl. 11): s509–14.

———, M.D. Carroll, C.L. Ogden, and C.L. Johnson. 2002. 'Prevalence and Trends in Obesity among US Adults, 1999–2000', *Journal of the American Medical Association* 288: 1723–7.

Fox, Adam T., Michael Fertleman, Pauline Cahill, and Roger D. Palmer. 2003. 'Medical Slang in British Hospitals', *Ethics and Behavior* 13, 2: 173–89.

Fox, Bonnie, and Diana Worts. 1999. 'Revisiting the Critique of Medicalized Childbirth: A Contribution to the Sociology of Birth', *Gender and Society* 13, 3: 326–46.

Frank, Lawrence D., Martin A. Andresen, and Thomas L. Schmid. 2004. 'Obesity Relationships with Community Design, Physical Activity, and Time Spent in Cars', *American Journal of Preventative Medicine* 27, 2: 87–96.

Friedson, Eliot. 1970. *The Profession of Medicine: A Study of the Sociology of Applied Knowledge*. New York: Dodd, Mead, and Company.

Gagnon, L. 2004. 'Medical Error Affects Nearly 25% of Canadians', *Canadian Medical Association Journal* 171, 2: 123.

Galabuzi, Grace-Edward. 2004. 'Social Exclusion', in Raphael (2004: 235–51).

Gayle, Helene. 2000. 'An Overview of the Global HIV/AIDS Epidemic, with a Focus on the United States', *AIDS* 2 (suppl. 2): S8–17.

Global Fund to Fight AIDS, Tuberculosis, and Malaria. 2005. Available at: <www.theglobalfund.org>; accessed 11 Dec. 2005.

Goffman, Erving. 1961. *Asylums: Essays on the Social Situation of Mental Patients and Other Inmates*. New York: Doubleday.

Goldberg, E.M., and S.L. Morrison. 1963. 'Schizophrenia and Social Class', *British Journal of Psychiatry* 109: 785–802.

Gössling, Stephan. 2002. 'Global Environmental Consequences of Tourism', *Global Environmental Change* 12, 4: 283–302.

Groupe de travail provincial sur la problématique du poids (GTPPP). 2004. *Weight Problems in Quebec: Getting Mobilized*. Montreal: ASPQ. Available at: <www.aspq.org/view_publications.php?id=17>; accessed 5 Mar. 2006.

Hartley, Heather, and Leonore Tiefer. 2003. 'Taking a Biological Turn: The Push for a 'Female Viagra' and the Medicalization of Women's Sexual Problems', *Women's Studies Quarterly* 31, 1–2: 42–54.

Health Canada. 2002a. *Economic Burden of Illness in Canada, 1998*. Ottawa: Health Canada.

———. 2002b. *A Report on Mental Illnesses in Canada*. Ottawa: Health Canada.

———. 2005. 'HIV and AIDS'. Available at: <www.hc-sc.gc.ca/dc-ma/aids-sida/index_e.html>; accessed 11 Dec. 2005.

Heeney, H., ed. 1995. *Life before Medicare: Canadian Experiences*. Toronto: The Stories Project.

Homedes, Nuria. 1995. 'The Disability-Adjusted Life Year (DALY): Definition, Measurement and Potential Use', Human Capital Development and Operations Policy Work Paper, World Bank.

Hsu, Chi-Yuan, Charles E. McCulloch, Carlos Iribarren, Jeanne Darbinian, and Alan S. Go. 2006. 'Body Mass Index and Risk for End-stage Renal Disease', *Annals of Internal Medicine* 144, 1: 21–8.

Hudson, Christopher G. 2005. 'Socioeconomic Status and Mental Illness: Tests of the Social Causation and Selection Hypotheses', *American Journal of Orthopsychiatry* 75, 1: 3–18.

Industry Canada. 2005. 'Coming Into Force of the Jean Chrétien Pledge to Africa', media release, 13 May. Available at: <www.ic.gc.ca>; accessed 5 Mar. 2006.

Isaacs, Sandy, Susan Keogh, Cathy Menard, and Jamie Hockin. 1998. 'Suicide in the Northwest Territories: A Descriptive Review', *Chronic Diseases in Canada* 19, 4: 152–6.

Joint Working Group on the Voluntary Sector. 1999. *Building the Relationship between National Voluntary Organizations Working in Health and Health Canada: A Framework for Action*. Ottawa: Health Canada.

Jones, Greg, and Michael Connelly. 2002. *Mentally Ill Offenders and Mental Health Care Issues: An Overview of the Research* (topical briefing). Annapolis, Md: State Commission on Criminal Sentencing Policy.

Kalra, Jawahar, K. Lorne Massey, and Amith Mulla. 2005. 'Disclosure of Medical Error: Policies and Practice', *Journal of the Royal Society of Medicine* 98, 7: 307–9.

Katzmarzyk, Peter T., and Ian Janssen. 2004. 'The Economic Costs Associated with Physical Inactivity and Obesity in Canada: An Update', *Canadian Journal of Applied Physiology* 29, 2: 90–115.

Kelner, M., B. Wellman, H. Boon, and S. Welsh. 2004. 'Responses to Established Healthcare to the Professionalization of Complementary and Alternative Medicine in Ontario', *Social Science and Medicine* 59, 5: 915–30.

Kessler, Ronald C., Wai Tat Chiu, Olga Demler, and Ellen E. Walters. 2005. 'Prevalence, Severity, and Comorbidity of 12-month *DSM-IV* Disorders in the National Comorbidity Survey Replication', *Archives of General Psychiatry* 62, 6: 617–27.

Le Petit, Christel, and Jean-Marie Berthelot. 2005. *Obesity: A Growing Issue*. Ottawa: Statistics Canada Catalogue no. 82–618–MWE2005003. Available at: <www.statcan.ca/bsolc/english/bsolc?catno=82-618-M2005003>; accessed 4 Jan. 2006.

Ma, Grace X. 1999. 'Between Two Worlds: The Use of Traditional and Western Health Services by Chinese Immigrants', *Journal of Community Health* 24, 6: 421–37.

MacIntyre, Lynn. 2004. 'Food Insecurity', in Raphael (2004: 173–86).

Mackenbach, Johan P., and Martijntje J. Bakker. 2003. 'Tackling Socioeconomic Inequalities in Health: Analysis of European Experiences', *Lancet* 362: 1409–14.

Mahomva, Agnes. 2004. 'Trends in HIV prevalence and Incidence and Sexual Behaviour', presentation to the UNAIDS Reference Group on Estimates, Modeling and Projections, Harare, 15–17 Nov.

MAP (Monitoring the AIDS Pandemic Network). 2005a. *MAP Report 2005: Drug Injection and HIV/AIDS in Asia*. Washington: MAP Secretariat.

———. 2005b. *MAP Report 2005: Sex Work and HIV/AIDS in Asia*. Washington: MAP Secretariat.

Marmot, Michael. 2004. *The Status Syndrome: How Social Standing Affects Our Health and Longevity*. New York: Henry Holt and Company.

———. 2005. 'Social Determinants of Health Inequalities', *Lancet* 365: 1099–1104.

Mathers, Colin D., Christina Bernard, Kim M. Iburg, Mie Inoue, Doris Ma Fat, et al. 2003. *Global Burden of Disease in 2002: Data Sources, Methods and Results*. Geneva: WHO.

Matsushita, Y., N. Yoshiike, F. Kaneda, K. Yoshita, and H.

Takimoto. 2004. 'Trends in Childhood Obesity in Japan over the Last 25 Years from the National Nutrition Survey', *Obesity Research* 12, 2: 205–14.

Meehan, Amy, A. Chindanyaki, S. Naidoo, L. Didier, G. Ramjee, et al. 2004. 'Prevalence and Risk Factors for HIV in Zimbabwean and South African Women', Fifteenth International AIDS Conference, Bangkok, 11–16 July, Abstract MoPeC3468.

Mendez, M.A., C.A. Monteiro, and B.M. Popkin. 2005. 'Overweight Exceeds Underweight among Women in Most Developing Countries', *American Journal of Clinical Nutrition* 81, 3: 714–21.

Ministry of Health and Social Welfare Swaziland. 2005. *9th Round of National HIV Serosurveillance in Women Attending Antenatal Care Services at Health Facilities in Swaziland: Survey Report*. Mbabane: Ministry of Health and Social Welfare Swaziland.

Murray, Christopher J.L., and Alex D. Lopez, eds. 1996. *The Global Burden of Disease: A Comprehensive Assessment of Mortality and Disability from Diseases, Injuries, and Risk Factors in 1990 and Projected to 2020*. Cambridge, Mass.: Harvard University Press on behalf of the World Health Organization and the World Bank.

Murray, Christopher J.L., Alex Lopez, and Dean T. Jamison. 1994. 'The Global Burden of Disease in 1990: Summary Results, Sensitivity Analysis and Future Directions', *Bulletin of the World Health Organization* 72, 3: 495–509.

———, Joshua A. Salomon, Colin D. Mathers, and Alan D. Lopez, eds. 2002. *Summary Measures of Population Health: Concepts, Ethics, Measurement and Applications*. Geneva: WHO.

Must, Aviva, and Richard S. Strauss. 1999. 'Risks and Consequences of Childhood and Adolescent Obesity', *International Journal of Obesity* 23 (suppl. 2): s2–11.

NACO (National AIDS Control Organization). 2004. *State-Wise HIV Prevalence (1998–2003)*. New Delhi: Ministry of Health and Family Welfare.

———. 2005. 'HIV Estimates—2004'. New Delhi: Ministry of Health and Family Welfare. Available at: <www.nacoonline.org/facts.htm>; accessed 11 Dec. 2005.

Nantulya, Vinand M., and Michael R. Reich. 2002. 'The Neglected Epidemic: Road Traffic Injuries in Developing Countries', *British Medical Journal* 324: 1139–41.

National Physician Survey (Joint collaboration of the College of Family Physicians, the Canadian Medical Association, and the Royal College of Physicians and Surgeons). 2005. Available at: <www.cfpc.ca/nps>; accessed 14 Jan. 2006.

Ngo-Metzger, Quyen, Michael P. Massagli, Brian R. Clarridge, Michael Manocchia, Roger B. Davis, et al. 2003. 'Linguistic and Cultural Barriers to Care', *Journal of General Internal Medicine* 18, 1: 44–52.

Oakley, Ann. 1979. 'A Case of Maternity: Paradigms of Women as Maternity cases', *Signs: Journal of Women in Culture and Society* 4, 4: 607–31.

———. 1980. *Women Confined: Towards a Sociology of Childbirth*. Oxford: Martin Robertson.

Offord, David R., Michael H. Boyle, Dugal Campbell, Paula Goering, Elizabeth Lin, et al. 1996. 'One-Year Prevalence of Psychiatric Disorder in Ontarians 15 to 64 Years of Age', *Canadian Journal of Psychiatry* 41, 9: 559–63.

Omran, Abdel R. 1971. 'The Epidemiological Transition: A Theory of the Epidemiology of Population Change', *Milbank Quarterly* 29: 509–38.

Organization for Economic Co-operation and Development (OECD). 2005. *OECD in Figures*. Paris: OECD.

Park, Jungwee. 2005. 'Use of Alternative Health Care', *Health Reports* 16, 2: 39–42.

Parsons, T. 1951. *The Social System*. Glencoe, Ill.: Free Press.

Phelan, Jo C., Bruce G. Link, Ann Stueve, and Bernice Pescosolido. 2000. 'A Public Conception of Mental Illness in 1950 and 1996: What Is Mental Illness and Is It To Be Feared?', *Journal of Health and Social Behavior* 41, 2: 188–207.

Public Health Agency of Canada. 2006. *HIV and AIDS in Canada: Surveillance Report to June 30, 2005*. Ottawa: Surveillance and Risk Assessment Division, Centre for Infectious Disease Prevention and Control, Public Health Agency of Canada.

Rachlis, M., and C. Kushner. 1994. *Strong Medicine: How to Save Canada's Health Care System*. Toronto: HarperCollins.

Raphael, Dennis. 2002. *Social Justice Is Good for Our Hearts: Why Societal Factors—Not Lifestyles—Are Major Causes of Heart Disease in Canada and Elsewhere*. Toronto: Centre for Social Justice Foundation for Research and Education.

———, ed. 2004. *The Social Determinants of Health: A Canadian Perspective*. Toronto: Canadian Scholars' Press.

Rather, L.J., ed. 1985. *Rudolf Virchow: Collected Essays on Public Health and Epidemiology*. Canton, Mass.: Science History Publications.

Rennie, K.L., and S.A. Jebb. 2005. 'Prevalence of Obesity in Great Britain', *Obesity Reviews* 6, 1: 11–12.

Ronson, Barbara, and Irving Rootman. 2004. 'Literacy: One of the Most Important Determinants of Health Today', in Raphael (2004: 155–70).

Salomon, Joshua A., Daniel R. Hogan, John Stover, Karen A. Stanecki, Neff Walker, et al. 2005. 'Integrating HIV Prevention and Treatment: From Slogans to Impact', *Public Library of Science (PLoS) Medicine* 2, 1: e16.

Sanmartin, Claudia, François Gendron, Jean-Marie Berthelot, and Kellie Murphy. 2004. *Access to Health Care Services in Canada 2003*. Ottawa: Statistics Canada.

———, Christian Houle, Stéphane Tremblay, and Jean-Marie

Berthelot. 2002. 'Changes in Unmet Health Care Needs', *Health Reports* 13, 3: 15–21.

Sanvictores, Kyle M., A. Banasa Williams, Jason A. Chen, and Paul N. Sy. 2002. *Fred and Claire*. Toronto: Chang, Cornejo, and Co.

Shah, Chandrakant P. 2004. 'The Health of Aboriginal Peoples', in Raphael (2004: 267–80).

Shapiro, Marla. 2005. 'It Felt Like My Identity Was Being Stripped Away', *Globe and Mail*, 15 Oct., F6.

Sigurdson, Chris. 2000. 'The Mad, the Bad and the Abandoned: The Mentally Ill in Prisons and Jails', *Corrections Today* 62: 70–8.

So, Alvin Y., and Ngai Pun. 2004. 'Introduction: Globalization and Anti-globalization of SARS in Chinese Societies', *Asian Perspective* 28, 1: 5–17.

Starr, Paul. 1982. *The Social Transformation of American Medicine: The Rise of a Sovereign Profession and the Making of a Vast Industry*. New York: Basic Books.

State Council AIDS Working Committee Office and UN Theme Group on HIV/AIDS in China. 2004. *A Joint Assessment of HIV/AIDS Prevention, Treatment and Care in China*. Beijing: State Council AIDS Working Committee Office and the UN Theme Group on HIV/AIDS in China.

Statistics Canada. 2003. *Canadian Community Health Survey: Mental Health and Well-being*. Ottawa: Statistics Canada Catalogue no. 82–617–XIE. Available at: <www.statcan.ca:80/english/freepub/82-617-XIE/index.htm>; accessed 2 Jan. 2006.

———. 2004. *Deaths, 2002*. Ottawa: Statistics Canada Catalogue no. 84–F0211–XIE. Available at: <www.statcan.ca/english/freepub/84F0211XIE/2002/index.htm>; accessed 10 Dec. 2005.

———. 2005a. 'Canadian Community Health Survey: Obesity among Children and Adults', *The Daily*, 6 July. Available at: <www.statcan.ca/Daily/English/050706/d050706a.htm>; accessed 28 Nov. 2005.

———. 2005b. 'Health Indicators', *The Daily*, 1 Feb. Available at: <www.statcan.ca/Daily/English/050201/d050201a.htm>; accessed 26 Dec. 2005.

Stephens, Thomas, and Natacha Joubert. 2001. 'The Economic Burden of Mental Health Problems in Canada', *Chronic Diseases in Canada* 22, 1: 18–23.

Stunkard, Albert J., and Jeffrey Sobal. 1995. 'Psychosocial Consequences of Obesity', in Kelly D. Brownwell and Christopher G. Fairburn, eds, *Eating Disorders and Obesity: A Comprehensive Handbook*. New York: Guilford Press.

Subramanian, S.V., and I. Kawachi. 2004. 'Income Inequality and Health: What Have We Learned So Far?', *Epidemiological Reviews* 26: 78–91.

Suchman, E.A. 1965. 'Social Patterns of Illness and Medical Care', *Journal of Health and Human Behaviour* 6: 2–16.

Szasz, T.S. 1961. *The Myth of Mental Illness: Foundations of a Theory of Personal Conduct*. New York: Hoeber-Harper.

TD Economics. 2003. *Affordable Housing in Canada: In Search of a New Paradigm*.

Todd, K.H., T. Lee, and J. R. Hoffman. 1994. 'The Effect of Ethnicity on Physician Estimates of Pain Severity in Patients with Isolated Extremity Trauma', *Journal of the American Medical Association* 271: 925–8.

Toews, L.K. 2006. *Laurel and Jazz*. Toronto: Sunnyside.

Townsend, M.S., J. Peerson, B. Love, C. Achterberg, and S. P. Murphy. 2001. 'Food Insecurity Is Positively Related to Overweight in Women', *Journal of Nutrition* 131, 6: 1738–45.

Turner, B. 1997. *Medical Power and Social Knowledge*, 2nd edn. London: Sage.

Ukrainian AIDS Centre. 2005. 'HIV Infection in Ukraine', *Information Bulletin* 24. Kiev: Ukrainian AIDS Centre.

UNAIDS. 2004. *Report on the Global AIDS Epidemic*. Geneva: Joint United Nations Program on HIV/AIDS (UNAIDS).

———. 2005. *AIDS Epidemic Update: December 2005*. Geneva: Joint United Nations Programme on HIV/AIDS (UNAIDS) and World Health Organization.

UNICEF. 2001. *Progress Since the World Summit on Children: A Statistical Review*. New York: UNICEF.

———. 2005. *The State of the World's Children 2006: Excluded and Invisible*. New York: UNICEF.

United Nations (UN). 2005. *The Millennium Development Goals Report 2005*. New York: UN.

———, Population Division. 2005. *World Population Prospects: The 2004 Revision Population Database*. Available at: <www.esa.un.org/unpp>; accessed 10 Dec. 2005.

White, Peter, ed. 2005. *Biopsychosocial Medicine: An Integrated Approach to Understanding Illness*. Oxford: Oxford University Press.

Wilkinson, R., and M. Marmot. 2003. *Social Determinants of Health: The Solid Facts*, 2nd edn. Geneva: WHO.

Wilson, R.M., W.B. Runciman, R.W. Gibberd, B.T. Harrison, L. Newby, and J.D. Hamilton. 1995. 'The Quality of Australian Health Care Study', *Medical Journal of Australia* 163, 9: 458–71.

Winnick, Terri. 2005. 'From Quackery to 'Complementary' Medicine: The American Medical Profession Confronts Alternative Therapies', *Social Problems* 52, 1: 38–61.

Woodhandler, Steffie, Terry Campbell, and David U. Himmelstein. 2003. 'Costs of Health Care Administration in the United States and Canada', *New England Journal of Medicine* 349, 8: 768–75.

World Health Organization (WHO). 1946. Preamble to the *Constitution of the World Health Organization* as adopted by the International Health Conference, New York, 19–22 June; signed 22 July 1946 by the representatives of 61 states (Official Records of the WHO, no. 2, p. 100) and entered into force 7 Apr. 1948.

——. 1996. 'The Epidemiological Transition', *Eastern Mediterranean Health Journal* 2, 1: 8–20.

——. 1998. *Obesity: Preventing and Managing the Global Epidemic*. Geneva: WHO.

——. 2002. *The Injury Chart Book: A Graphical Overview of the Global Burden of Injuries*. Geneva: WHO.

——. 2003a. 'Controlling the Global Obesity Epidemic'. Available at <www.who.int/nut/obs.htm>; accessed 4 Jan. 2006.

——. 2003b. 'Severe Acute Respiratory Syndrome (SARS): Status of the Outbreak and Lessons for the Immediate Future'. Geneva: WHO, 20 May.

——. 2003c. *The World Health Report 2003: Shaping the Future*. Geneva: WHO.

——. 2004. 'Global Burden of Disease Estimates'. Available at: <www.who.int/healthinfo/bodestimates/en/index.html>; accessed 5 Jan. 2006.

——. 2005a. *Health and the Millennium Development Goals*. Geneva: WHO.

——. 2005b. *Progress on Global Access to HIV Antiretroviral Therapy: An Update on '3 by 5'—June 2005*. Available at: <www.who.int/3by5/en/index.html>; accessed 9 Mar. 2006.

——. 2005c. 'Disability Adjusted Life Years (DALY)'. Available at: <www.who.int/healthinfo/boddaly/en>; accessed 27 Dec. 2005.

——. 2005d. 'Obesity and Overweight'. Available at: <www.who.int/dietphysicalactivity/publications/facts/obesity/en>; accessed 2 Jan. 2006.

——. 2005e. 'Ten things You Need To Know about Pandemic Influenza'. Available at: <www.who.int/csr/disease/influenza/pandemic10things/en/index.html>; accessed 31 Dec. 2005.

Yang, Hongmei, Xiaoming Li, Bonita Stanton, Hongjie Liu, Hui Liu, et al. 2005. 'Heterosexual Transmission of HIV in China: A Systematic Review of Behavioural Studies in the Past Two Decades', *Sexually Transmitted Diseases* 32, 5: 270–80.

York University Centre for Health Studies. 1999. *Complementary and Alternative Health Practices and Therapies: A Canadian Overview*. Toronto: York University Centre for Health Studies.

Zhang, Jinjin, and Marja J. Verhoef. 2005. 'Illness Management Strategies among Chinese Immigrants Living with Arthritis', *Social Science and Medicine* 55, 10: 1795–1802.

Zola, Irving K. 1972. 'Medicine as an Institute of Social Control', *Sociological Review* 20: 487–504.

CHAPTER ELEVEN

POPULATION, URBANIZATION, AND ENVIRONMENT

LEARNING OBJECTIVES

- To find out about the history of the world's population.
- To learn what is meant by the demographic transition.
- To understand competing perspectives of population growth.
- To appreciate the historical impact of technology on human populations.
- To know the historical founding theories of urban sociology.
- To discover the social significance of neighbours and neighbourhoods.
- To know about the historical and social significance of suburbanization.
- To gain an understanding of urban issues such as heavy traffic, sprawl, and gentrification.
- To find out about the environmental issues of metropolitan areas.
- To understand issues such as climate change, desertification, and ozone depletion.
- To differentiate sociological perspectives on urban life and environmental issues.
- To appreciate the social and health consequences of continued unsustainable consumption.
- To learn of possible solutions to urban and environmental problems.

Introduction

This chapter is about population, urbanization, and the environment. It examines the interactions between human society, the built environment, and the natural world and the problems that emerge from these interactions. It brings together three central topics of modern sociology—population studies, urban sociology, and environmental sociology. Two common threads run through these fields of study—the first is that each topic directly addresses the physical and material backdrops of social life; the second is that human ingenuity (or more concretely, technology) is both at the root of a variety of social problems and the source of potential solutions to these problems.

Let us begin by acknowledging that the problems discussed so briefly in this chapter are highly complex, and we cannot hope to do justice to them in so short a space. Instead, we aspire only to introduce some of the more pressing issues as starting points for further exploration, and encourage readers interested in learning more about these problems to pursue them in the appropriate sources.

Further, let us note that population growth, long thought of as a demographic problem, can also be a benefit. For instance, without population growth in human history, there would not have been agricultural growth. The denser a population is, the more intensive cultivation becomes (Boserup, 1965). In turn, agricultural surplus and population density make possible social differentiation, institutional growth, and, eventually, industrialization.

Finally, let us consider the view, put forth by economic theorist Julian Simon (1996) and others, that human beings are 'the ultimate resource'. Simon's body of work—a direct rebuff of the Malthusian perspective, described below—remains controversial, and some of his own theories about the infinite fecundity of the planet have since been disproved as overly simplistic. Still, one element of his central thesis is difficult to refute: that the human species has, throughout its short history, proven immensely creative in the face of adversity.

Therefore, to solve the problems associated with population, we may not need *fewer* people but, instead, better-equipped and better-educated people; not necessarily *less* use of non-renewable resources, but more effort and creativity in using them and finding substitutes (as humanity has done throughout its history); and not a *suspicion* of technology, but rather a commitment to using technology for the good of humanity. The problems we discuss in this chapter are not population, urbanity, and environment per se—they are the human failure to manage these raw materials more creatively and effectively. Humanity, then, is the problem we are discussing, and a better organized humanity is the solution.

Still, we must recognize that humankind faces important population-related problems. One set of problems relates to imperfections in how societies are organized, which in the twenty-first century primarily means how urban cities are organized. A second set of problems relates to humanity's inefficient relationship with the natural world, resulting in a growing list of environmental concerns, such as global warming, air and water pollution, the depletion of certain key resources, and the gradual extinction of living species. The continued growth of the world's population only exacerbates these problems, by adding to their magnitude and intensity even as initial solutions are proposed.

To clarify connections among the central topics in this chapter—population, the built environment, the natural environment, and technology—it is useful to imagine life 100,000 years ago. At that time, everyone lived in small bands. The human population of the world existed solely as nomadic hunters and gatherers, living off whatever the surroundings offered and moving to more fertile regions when food became scarce. As far as we can tell, people led lives that were short but healthy. These nomads probably had enough to eat. To judge from hunter-gatherer peoples living today, they were also sociable, co-operative, and contented. At some point, however, humans developed tools and skills that enabled them to farm the land, and all this began to change (see, e.g., Lee, 1979).

Humans first began to artificially transform the natural environment into a built environment with the invention of agricultural tools and practices. Farming, by providing a steady supply of food, allowed people to settle down. With settlement came a rapid rise in child-bearing, longevity, and population size. These changes, in turn, led to increases in social differentiation, inequality, and conflict. People began to separate themselves from the natural world and to make efforts to dominate it. Technology, which helped them do that, also brought new social and health problems. A growing population, which succeeded for a while in conquering the environment, also carried unforeseen side effects. It increased human reliance on technology and began to transform the natural environment (see, e.g., Farb, 1978).

Severe damage to the environment, through technology and urban growth, began about two centuries ago, with industrialization in the West. Since then, governments have often ignored environmentally harmful practices, perhaps because the industries responsible for much of the pollution in our skies, land, and water also power the economy. In less developed countries, environmental damage has occurred mainly because governments are trying to attain the wealth that older industrial countries enjoy.

To understand society's impact on the planet, we must first consider the driving force behind this impact: humanity itself. We begin, then, with a brief discussion of some of the issues addressed by demography and population studies.

World Population in Context

The history of the world's population unfolded in two general stages: an extended period of slow population growth from the time when the first primitive humans appeared to approximately the mid-eighteenth century; and a relatively brief period of explosive growth from about 1750 until the present day. According to one estimate, human population growth prior to the modern era was barely a hundredth of a per cent per year (Coale, 1974). Since then, the world's population has increased exponentially, with particularly rapid growth in the period since the beginning of the Industrial Revolution in the late 1700s. Between the year 1 AD and 1750, it is estimated that population size doubled only once, from 300 million to 750 million. In the last 250 years, the world's human population has doubled three times, surpassing 6 billion prior to 2000. As estimated by the United Nations, the world population reached 6.5 billion in 2005 (Population Reference Bureau, 2006).

Even though the global population continues to increase, worldwide growth rates peaked in the 1970s and have been in decline for several years now. Currently, the growth is around 1.3 per cent per year and is expected to decline to 0.5 per cent by 2050. Population growth will occur unevenly around the world, with most developed nations, including Canada, experiencing zero or even negative growth. Italian demographer Massimo Livi-Bacci (1992: 202) predicts that 'developing countries will account for approximately 95 per cent of world population increase in the period 1990–2025. . . . [As a result] between 1950 and 2025 the developed country share of world population will decline from 33.1 per cent to 15.9; Europe's share will decline still faster, from 15.6 per cent to 6.1.' European countries whose populations were among the world's largest in 1950—Germany, the United Kingdom, Italy, France, Spain, and Poland—will be off the list of largest countries in 2025. Newcomers to the list will include Ethiopia, Zaire, and Tanzania. As Livi-Bacci points out, 'though relations between countries are conditioned primarily by political, cultural, and economic factors, large changes in their relative population sizes are bound to have an effect' (ibid.).

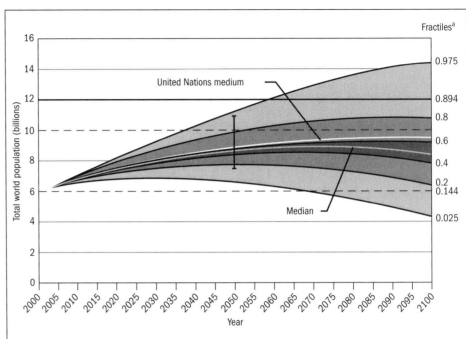

There has been enormous concern about the consequences of human population growth for the environment and for social and economic development. But this growth is likely to come to an end in the foreseeable future. Improving on earlier methods of probabilistic forecasting, here we show that there is around an 85 per cent chance that the world's population will stop growing before the end of the century. There is a 60 per cent probability that the world's population will not exceed 10 billion people before 2100, and around a 15 per cent probability that the world's population at the end of the century will be lower than it is today. For different regions, the date and size of the peak population will vary considerably.

ᵃ Forecasted distributions of world population sizes (fractiles). For comparison, the United Nations medium scenario (white line), and 95 per cent interval as given by the NRC on the basis of an ex post error analysis (vertical line in 2050) are also given.

FIGURE 11.1 Population Projections into the Twenty-Second Century
Source: Lutz et al. (2001). Copyright 2001. Reprinted by permission from Macmillan Publishers Ltd.

The Demographic Transition

The **demographic transition** refers to a shift in demographic patterns from high birth and death rates to low birth and death rates. The demographic transition occurs in parallel with a society's socio-economic development. During the first stage of the demographic transition, when the society is still in its pre-modern phase, the number of births and deaths are both high but equal, resulting in a steady population size with only minimal growth. Stage two usually arrives as the population enters the early stages of urbanization and industrialization, when socio-economic advances result in declining death rates. During this period, birth rates remain high, resulting in explosive population growth and a young population profile. In stage three, birth rates begin to fall as well, slowly reaching levels comparable to the death rate. As a result, the population continues to grow but the rate of increase slows down. By stage four, when a society has reached a post-industrial phase of development, population is once again stable, with rates of births and deaths equal again and at historic lows. At this point, with low birth rates, the overall population begins to age.

Table 11.1 Canadian Demographics: Population and Growth Components, 1851–2001 (thousands)[a]

Period	Census population at the end of period	Total population growth[b]	Births	Deaths	Immigration	Emigration
1851–61	3,230	793	1,281	670	352	170
1861–71	3,689	459	1,370	760	260	410
1871–81	4,325	636	1,480	790	350	404
1881–91	4,833	508	1,524	870	680	826
1891–1901	5,371	538	1,548	880	250	380
1901–11	7,207	1,836	1,925	900	1,550	740
1911–21	8,788	1,581	2,340	1,070	1,400	1,089
1921–31	10,377	1,589	2,415	1,055	1,200	970
1931–41	11,507	1,130	2,294	1,072	149	241
1941–51[c]	13,648	2,141	3,186	1,214	548	379
1951–6	16,081	2,433	2,106	633	783	185
1956–61	18,238	2,157	2,362	687	760	278
1961–6	20,015	1,777	2,249	731	539	280
1966–71[d]	21,568	1,553	1,856	766	890	427
1971–6	23,450	1,488	1,760	824	1,053	358
1976–81	24,820	1,371	1,820	843	771	278
1981–6	26,101	1,281	1,872	885	678	278
1986–91	28,031	1,930	1,933	946	1,164	213
1991–6	29,611	1,580	1,936	1,024	1,118	338
1996–2001	31,021	1,410	1,705	1,089	1,217	376

[a]Numbers may not add up evenly because of rounding.

[b]Total population growth is the difference in census population counts at the end and beginning of each period.

[c]Beginning in 1951, Newfoundland is included.

[d]Beginning in 1971:

- The population estimates are based on census counts adjusted for net undercount, and the reference date is July 1 instead of census day (the 1 July 1971 population adjusted for net census undercount is 21,962,100).
- Immigration figures include landed immigrants, returning Canadians, and the net change in the number of non-permanent residents.
- Population growth calculated using the components will produce a different figure than is reported in table. Beginning in 1971, an independent estimate of emigration is produced. Prior to 1971, the emigration figures are 'residual' estimates and include the errors in the other three growth components—births, deaths, and immigration—as well as errors in the census counts.

Source: Adapted from Statistics Canada at: <www40.statcan.ca/l01/cst01/demo03.htm>; accessed 26 July 2006.

Historical evidence shows that the 1870s were a watershed in world history. In that decade rates of child-bearing in Western European, Northern European, and North American countries began their steep, never-to-be-reversed downward trend. This change marked the beginning of the end of high fertility for the human race, a pattern that has since spread to Southern and Eastern Europe, Latin America, Asia, and Africa, and continues today. In 2001, the continent of Africa still had a total fertility rate of 5.2 childbirths per woman, much higher than the world's average rate of 2.8. However, there is every sign in Africa of a continuing decline in child-bearing through increased use of birth control.

Contrasting Perspectives on Population Change

THE MALTHUSIAN POSITION

Modern scientific theories about population growth and its effect on societies begin with the ideas of Thomas Malthus (1959 [1798]). Malthus reasoned as follows: a population growing exponentially (that is, through a series such as 1, 2, 4, 8, 16, etc.) at a constant rate adds more people every year than the year before. Consider a population of 1,000 women and 1,000 men. Each woman marries and has four children. If all survive, in the next generation there are roughly 2,000 women and 2,000 men. If all of those women have four children each, then in the next generation there are roughly 4,000 women and 4,000 men. With a constant pattern of four births per woman, the population doubles every generation (roughly 30 years). In only 300 years, the original population of 2,000 has grown to a million people! (As you can verify, this is due to 10 doublings.)

On the other hand, Malthus said that increases in the food supply are only additive, or arithmetic (that is, in a series such as 1, 2, 3, 4, 5, etc.). Limits on available land, soil quality, and technology all constrain the growth in food supplies. Malthus believed that there is a real risk of populations outgrowing the food supply. So the chance of running out of food poses a real threat to humanity. For that reason, checks (or limits) are needed to keep population growth in line with growth in the food supply. Welfare schemes to help the poor by redistributing wealth are futile, said Malthus. If we feed the hungry, they will procreate until they run out of food and are hungry again.

The only sure solutions are positive checks and preventive checks. **Positive checks** prevent overpopulation by increasing the death rate. They include war, famine, pestilence, and disease. **Preventive checks** prevent overpopulation by limiting the number or survival of live births. They include abortion, infanticide, sexual abstinence, delayed marriage, and contraceptive use. Among these preventive options, the pious Reverend Malthus approved of only delayed marriage and sexual abstinence.

Today, people who believe that there is still a 'population problem' make some of the same arguments Malthus did two centuries ago. Neo-Malthusians believe the world is becoming overpopulated, that population growth will outstrip agricultural growth, and that this population burden will permanently harm the environment. World population is still growing. Even allowing for slower growth, experts predict that in 30 years the current population of 6.5 billion people will be nearly three billion larger. With population growth come new challenges, including increased competition for non-renewable resources, the need to feed, nurture, and educate a larger proportion of young people, increased pressures on the health and welfare systems, and the need for governments to prevent and deal with economic and natural disasters.

Neo-Malthusians argue that humanity cannot rely on social or scientific innovations—for example, more equality, better government, or new technology—to increase the planet's ability to sustain the growing population. Therefore, humanity must take measures now, for environmental and social reasons, to lower world fertility rates and reduce the pressures a surging human population puts on the planet's ability to sustain its inhabitants.

Demographic transition theorists predict that worldwide modernization and the spread of cheap, safe contraception will cause fertility to continue dropping, as it has done for the last century or so. Some societies might follow China's example and promote below-replacement fertility through a one-child policy.

CRITICISMS OF THE MALTHUSIAN PERSPECTIVE

It is not clear, however, that the planet's carrying capacity will unavoidably be strained by population increases. Some note that Malthus was incorrect in supposing that food supplies can increase only arithmetically. Long-term food production trends reveal that in technologically advanced societies, food production has increased at a faster rate than the human population owing to better seeds, fertilizers, and growth techniques. Past warnings of an impending global food shortage by the end of the twentieth century have been proven unwarranted. Writing in 1949, the eminent demographer Alfred Sauvy described potential overpopulation as a 'false problem' and argued against attempts at global population control (Sauvy and Demeny, 1990). He suggested examining countries on a case-by-case basis to see whether they lack the raw materials and natural resources that can support a larger population. Otherwise, we run the risk of underpopulating a country (such as Canada) that could support a much larger population.

Demographer Joel Cohen (1995) notes that a fundamental problem may lie in the notion of a single 'carrying capacity' for the planet. This concept, he argues, does not translate well from the plant or animal models on which it was based to human societies, since humanity—because of its ingenuity, resourcefulness, technological inventiveness, ability to adapt, awareness of the future, and stubborn free will—is constantly defying standard ecological models of population behaviour. Population sustainability is tied not only to reproductive trends, but also to countless economic, political, and social processes. Thus, the question of 'How many people can the planet support?' must be prefaced by the question of 'How do we want to live?'—that is, at what level and distribution of material and environmental well-being; using what form of political, economic, and demographic arrangements; and by whose standards of acceptable stability, risk, and value system? Depending on the conditions that we choose for humanity, the Earth either may sustain far more than the present population or has already surpassed its maximum capacity threshold.

Some even argue in favour of a more extreme and controversial position—that Earth is almost infinitely resourceful, and that only limits on human creativity prevent our species from tapping into this unending wellspring of raw materials (see, e.g., Simon, 1996). Proponents of this **cornucopian view of nature** argue that the solution is to increase, rather than decrease, global population size. Since human ingenuity is the 'ultimate resource', what the world needs most is more people to think up new and better ways to grow food, build shelters, and generally advance human civilization.

The Future of World Population

Demographers continue to debate the merits of different theories of population growth. For this reason, it is difficult to foresee the future of the world's population and predict whether it will thrive or worsen through strife and competition. All that can be said with certainty is that population processes should not be left unchecked. Regional, national, and global population sizes should be monitored closely, and as much as possible subjected to human control, for the greatest long-term benefit of humanity and the planet's biodiversity.

In the end, 'population problems' such as high fertility and high rates of immigration are social problems in societies that have not worked out ways of putting their populations to good use. Population problems are urban problems in societies that are struggling to organize their members in ways that balance efficiency with quality of life. And population problems are environmental problems in societies that do not know how to protect their natural environments in the face of increased population pressure. In this sense, urban and environmental problems—which the remainder of this chapter will examine—arise not because of too many people or technological menace, but because of poor social organization.

Urban Sociology: A Primer

Cities, as Max Weber (1958 [1921], 1981 [1924]) pointed out, are among humanity's great social inventions. Most important, cities make possible a range of experiences that are unavailable in smaller rural areas or small towns. The sheer size and heterogeneity of city populations allow for specialization and diversity in the goods and services on offer.

Yet, for all that, city life has been surrounded by controversy since the beginning. Some have hailed cities as affording liberty, especially the freedom to think and act as one wishes. Others have viewed cities as lacking in neighbourliness and community spirit. They have depicted city-dwellers as lonely atoms, deprived of purpose and control.

Much of twentieth-century American sociology examined these competing views of cities. At first, research on cities was skewed by the dominance of research on the city of Chicago, owing to the overwhelming presence of the Department of Sociology at the University of Chicago. During the heyday of this department, roughly 1900–40, Chicago was a living laboratory for the study of city populations, especially the poor, the marginal, and the stigmatized. In the last half of the twentieth century, the main goals of urban sociologists broadened to understand a wider variety of cities, and especially the topics of suburbanization, urban renewal, and the development of enormous cities in the Third World.

According to a United Nations Development Program international survey of mayors, the number-one urban problem in the world today is unemployment. The second most serious problem is insufficient solid waste disposal; the third—which may be related to unemployment—is poverty (International Survey of Mayors, 2002). Many of the high-profile social problems people associate with urban centres—crime, poverty, and racial segregation, for instance—are found in rural areas as well, though these problems are particularly pronounced in cities (see, e.g., Higley, 1995). Such urban problems are discussed in detail in other sections of the book (for instance, see Chapter 1 on poverty and homelessness). In this chapter, we will focus on urban problems related to social organization, particularly on the intersection of urban growth, the built environment (e.g., neighbourhoods, streets, buildings, etc.), and social well-being.

Contrasting Images of Urban Life

City life is appealing to many people. Perhaps the attraction is urban architecture, the constant kinetic energy, the allure of cosmopolitan sophistication. Even the sheer congregation of lives is exciting, with its dense mass of strangers who live side by side, each expecting civility but not necessarily friendship from their neighbours. Cities are hectic, yes, but many people believe the freedom afforded by city life is worth the psychic costs. Cities are great accumulations of people, capital, knowledge, and institutions. Just about every activity is possible in a city, and perhaps this sense of possibility makes urban life so alluring.

For theorist Henri Lefebvre, the urban lifestyle is a way of being-in-the-world. The urban is an *oeuvre* (i.e., creation) produced anew everyday by its inhabitants. The 'everyday' is both the residual of organized and planned life and the product of the social whole (Boudreau, 1998). High rates of population growth show that urban areas are interesting, desirable places to live.

Yet for all the glamour and excitement that major cities offer, urban life has its problems. Some people manage to avoid these problems. Experiences of city life vary widely from one person to the next depending on each person's position in the social structure: racial, class, gender, and age characteristics, for example. A social problem affecting some people in the city may have no serious consequence for many others. This said, most city-dwellers are at least aware of some common city problems—crime, poverty, pollution, and traffic congestion, for example.

The earliest sociological theories about cities and city life—by Ferdinand Tönnies, Louis Wirth, and Georg Simmel, and others—were first developed more than a century ago. For example, Tönnies (1957 [1887]) asked, what social bonds tie together people in small, stable communities, compared with large, fluid communities? For Tönnies, the movement from rural to city life meant a loss of **Gemeinschaft**—the typical characteristics of rural and small-town life, including a stable, homogeneous group of residents with a strong attachment to one particular place. Socially, the Gemeinschaft is marked by dense networks, centralized and controlling elites, multiple social ties, intimacy, and emotional meaning. With everyone constantly observing each others' behaviour, someone deviating from the prevailing social norms would feel social pressures to conform.

In contrast, Tönnies notes, the ties among people in a city take the form of a **Gesellschaft**. In urban settings, residents have different personal histories and impersonal brief relationships. They interact around similar interests, not similar characteristics, moralities, or histories. Social networks in cities are less connected, less centralized, less cliquish, and less redundant.

Following Tönnies's lead, early American sociology considered cities anonymous and stressful. In his article 'Urbanism as a Way of Life' (1938), Louis Wirth explained that cities unavoidably foster less social integration or cohesion than smaller communities due to their immense population size, variety, and fluidity. A large population ensures that most people will not know one another, nor feel tied to one another in ways that control deviance and support co-operation. A high degree of variety—in values, norms, and interests—can generate confusion if not outright conflict, when irresolvable differ-

Jane Jacobs on Cities
Great cities are not like towns, only larger. They are not like suburbs, only denser. They differ from towns and suburbs in basic ways, and one of them is that cities are full of strangers.
Source: Jacobs (1993 [1961]:30).

ences collide. Fluidity means people are forced into many interactions with strangers. To partially counteract the uncertainty of these interactions, they develop means of control—informally, social norms of behaviour such as distancing and civil inattention, and formally, such as the police—to deal with socially unacceptable behaviour or to pacify strangers in public places.

The German sociologist Georg Simmel (1950) was among the first to sense how life in a large city affects people psychologically and emotionally. City life is too stimulating, Simmel wrote. Strangers surround us on all sides. We experience countless strange noises, smells, sights, dangers, and opportunities. Walking a city street, we must pay constant attention to our environment. In the end, sensation overload takes its toll on our nervous systems.

Research supports at least some of these suppositions. The tempo of life *is* faster in a large city—more costly, arousing, and engaging than in a small town. People walk faster, talk faster, and even eat faster, mostly because more people must crowd into the same spaces every hour. City people also make more noise: the larger the city, the more car horns there are for irritated people to honk. In these various ways—through isolation and stresses on mental health—the city enslaves people who may have expected to gain freedom through city life.

The Importance of Neighbours and Neighbourhoods

Tönnies was wrong to suppose that cities lack communities or community sentiments, or that city-dwellers would not care about such sentiments. As sociologist Claude Fischer showed, cities are collections of communities each with its own subculture. People want to live alongside other people they consider like themselves in important ways. Largely as a result, residential segregation by race, ethnicity, and social class is a common feature of life in North American cities (Emerson et al., 2001) and has an enormous impact on people's social relations and social identities. This voluntary assortment of people into urban communities based on culture, language, and ethnicity, and on resulting distinct identities, is a major source of Canada's continuing multiculturalism. It is also an antidote to the randomizing and anonymizing of large cities.

Despite the tendencies of mass education and the mass media to make everyone similar, neighbours and neighbourhoods are still important today as sources of personal identity and difference. The importance that people attach to their neighbourhoods can be seen in reactions of NIMBYism ('not in my backyard') under certain circumstances— for example, to the placement in their neighbourhood of public housing, halfway houses, or treatment facilities for recovering drug addicts (Oakley, 1999). To a large degree, it is precisely because cities are *not* agglomerations of undifferentiated strangers, and because people feel so strongly about keeping strangers and people unlike themselves at a distance, that cities have trouble solving typical problems such as homelessness and fear of victimization.

Sociological Theories of Urban Life

STRUCTURAL FUNCTIONALISM

Some structural functionalists would view social problems in the city as resulting naturally from growth and specialization. For example, more wealth in cities means more theft and robbery; higher density equals more intense competition for resources; and more privacy translates into more private vice, such as drug use.

Other structural functionalists focus on those tendencies of the city—its size, variety, and fluidity in particular—that promote social disorganization, weak social controls, and consequent deviance and distress. From this perspective, social problems such as crime, addiction, and mental illness are foreseeable consequences of urbanization. They are functional in the sense that they are the normal price to be paid for the positive aspects of city life; they contribute to the survival of the city by promoting integrative reactions.

Pre-industrial societies were mainly small, rural settlements in which members shared the same experiences and developed similar values, norms, and identity. Émile Durkheim (1964 [1893]) called this *common conscience*. Moreover, the lives of these people were often interconnected in a tight, homogeneous social order, which Durkheim called **mechanical solidarity**. The new social order was based on interdependent, though not necessarily intimate, relationships. Under this **organic solidarity**, no member of society was entirely self-sufficient; all people were dependent on others for survival and prosperity.

CONFLICT THEORY

Unlike functionalists, conflict theorists always ask whose interests are served by the actions of the dominant groups in society and by their ideology. These theorists attribute urban problems such as homelessness and poverty not to the effects of size, variety, and fluidity, but to the workings of capitalism. By their reckoning, cities suffer problems because it is in no powerful group's interest to prevent this from happening.

Unlike functionalists, conflict theorists believe that solving urban problems will require more than simply addressing economic stagnation. Unequal power, competing class interests, capital investment decisions, and government subsidy programs mediate the growth of cities. The distribution of urban wealth, not merely its creation, determines whether the majority of city-dwellers will live or die, stay or leave. The flight of well-off residents from the inner city to distant suburbs suggests a lack of interest in solving these problems among those who have the power to do so.

SYMBOLIC INTERACTIONISM

Symbolic interactionists study the ways people experience city life on an everyday basis. One of the earliest writers to take this approach was Simmel (1950). As noted earlier, he argued that cities were so inherently stimulating and quick-paced that to prevent sensory overloading, inhabitants needed to reduce their sensitivity to events and people around them.

However, symbolic interactionists tend to doubt that everyone in the same structural setting has the same experience. Herbert Gans (1982), among others, has focused on how the meaning of city life varies among groups and subcultures. A subculture is a group of people who share some cultural traits of the larger society but who, as a group, also have their own distinctive values, beliefs, norms, style of dress, and behaviour. Subculture membership allows individuals who are otherwise isolated within an impersonal city to form connections with their neighbours. An ethnic community is an example of a subculture, as are skinheads and youth gangs. The corporate elites, who have determined the future of urban areas, are also by this view a subculture.

Social and Health Problems Related to Urbanization

Contrary to what some people might first imagine, cities existed thousands of years ago. Babylon, Jerusalem, Byzantium, Alexandria, Athens, and Rome were all large and important cities in the pre-modern era. The Maya and Inca, in Central and South America, developed large city-states, and nearly a thousand years ago, Cahokia, in present-day Illinois, 'was bigger than contemporaneous London, England' (Dickason, 2002: 29). Paris, London, Venice, and Florence were established as world cities long before massive economic developments in the late eighteenth century kick-started rapid **urbanization**, the process by which a large portion of the human population came to shift from rural to urban homes (see Sjoberg, 1965; Weber, 1958 [1921]).

However, modern cities are new in human history, only a few centuries old. With the rise of the urban mode of life came a focus on efficiency, a high standard of living, liberty, diversity, and innovative ideas and lifestyles. Modern cities are a prime example of a social organizational strategy, an organic solution to the problem of how to co-ordinate a growing human population. Said more simply, modern cities are creative efforts by humanity to deal with large numbers of varied, mobile people concentrated in a small space. Thus far, however, a great many of the organizational strategies devised by city governments have been flawed, resulting in problems such as overcrowding, epidemics and sanitation issues, inner-city poverty, housing shortages and homelessness, traffic and noise problems, and a tension-filled pace of life.

Let's define our terms. Statistics Canada defines an 'urban area' as one with a population of at least 5,000 and no fewer than 400 persons per square kilometre. All territory outside an urban area is considered rural. The term used for cities is 'census metropolitan area (CMA)', defined as a region with an urban core comprising at least 100,000 population. But while these definitions suffice for Canada, they do not apply as well to other nations. For example, in highly populated countries such as India, virtually all areas have a density of more than 400 persons per square kilometre, yet many do not display any other characteristics associated with 'urban' life. For these countries, the criteria for 'urban' versus 'rural' may require a higher density, or may include other factors such as economic output (i.e., agricultural or non-agricultural). When comparing across countries or reporting on regional or global trends, the United Nations simply allows that 'urban' is whatever each nation defines it as. We shall defer to this practice in the discussions that follow.

Size, then, is a defining feature of cities. However, the problems of urban life we will discuss are problems not of population size per se, but of the way that population is organized. To illustrate this point, consider that the Vancouver region is home to slightly more than 2 million residents, a population roughly the size of the Asian country of Bhutan. Clearly, however, the pressures facing these two regions are vastly different and, to a significant degree, the result of their divergent modes of social organization. As an urban centre, the typical problems Vancouver grapples with include petty crime, inner-city prostitution and drug abuse, skyrocketing rent prices, and public transit funding—issues that are likely low on the priority list of the average mountain-dwelling Bhutanese, but very likely familiar to other urban inhabitants around the world.

Urbanization in the Developing World

Some time within this decade, for the first time in human history, a majority of the world's population will be residents of cities. Thus, the twenty-first century will become humanity's first 'urban century', a consequence mainly of the pace of urbanization in the developing world (United Nations Population Division, 2006). Historically, the emergence of cities has reflected an increasing complexity in regional development. Cities, as we have learned, are economic engines. They foster new businesses and attract foreign investments and tourists. The development of cities in the world's poorer regions, then, is a promising sign of economic growth.

Unfortunately, the pace of urban growth in the developing world is outstripping the ability of many local and state governments to provide the infrastructure (for example, the roads and communication networks) needed to house, employ, and support the influx of people into their cities. Many cities are experiencing the serious social and health hazards often associated with overcrowding, poor sanitation, slum developments, and a lack of clean water—the same urban problems that plagued Western industrial nations in the eighteenth and nineteenth centuries. Also, many mega-cities are expanding chaotically, without any co-ordinated urban planning or management. This lack of overall vision will likely increase urban problems in the future. Already, seven of the 10 largest cities in the world are located in developing countries. By 2050, it is estimated that Tokyo will be the only urban centre on that list from the developed world; India alone will have three cities in the top 10 (also see Figure 11.2).

Suburbanization

In North America, the period of prosperity following World War II changed the urban landscape dramatically. During the post-war economic boom, spending and birth rates

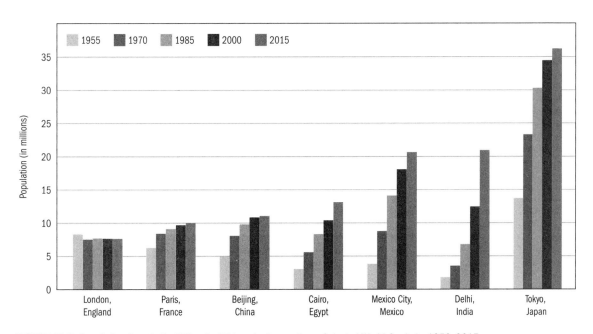

FIGURE 11.2 Population Growth (in Millions) of Urban Agglomerations, Selected World Capitals, 1950–2015
Note: 'Urban agglomeration', as defined by the UNPD, refers to the 'de facto population contained within the contours of a contiguous territory inhabited at urban density levels without regard to administrative boundaries. It usually incorporates the population in a city or town plus that in the suburban areas lying outside of but being adjacent to the city boundaries.'
Source: United Nations Population Division, *World Urbanization Prospects, 2003 Revision Population Database.* Available at <esa.un.org/unup>; accessed 4 March 2006. The United Nations is the author of the original material.

were high, unemployment was low, and families prospered. The purchase of homes outside the urban core exploded in the 1940s and 1950s, causing land developers to extend residential housing into outlying regions. In this way, the modern suburb was born.

Suburbanization is the process by which lower-density housing spreads into once-rural regions surrounding the city core. This process greatly expanded the geographic size of cities. For instance, Chicago's population has increased only 4 per cent in the past 20 years, yet its spatial geography has increased by 46 per cent between 1980 and 2000.

The first people to move to the suburbs were mainly wealthy middle- to upper-class whites. This movement increased the racial and ethnic segregation of minorities in urban centres. Further, as wealthier residents migrated to the outskirts of the city, their property taxes went with them, leaving the city's centre with less revenue for schools, roads, and other services. Then as now, suburbanites who work in the city use the city's services, such as road, water, and sewer systems, but do not pay for them. As a result, while the suburbs flourished amid a surplus of property tax income, downtown areas stagnated and dried up. With the huge expansion of road and highway infrastructure in the post-war years, truck transport of goods and of the inputs and outputs of manufacturing made the need for business to locate close to fixed railway lines of little importance relative to earlier years. This factor, combined with the cheaper land values and lower property tax rates in the suburbs, led business and industry to move from the downtowns and inner cities, taking much-needed jobs away from urban cores. In many places today, the traditional functions of cities—as employment, recreational, and cultural centres—have been relocated to individual urban villages, pods that are ever farther away from the central cities (Garreau, 1991). The best-paying new jobs in Canada are often located in suburban cities: Mississauga (outside Toronto), Kanata (outside Ottawa), and Richmond (outside Vancouver).

Yet, while economic activity blossoms in formerly remote fringe towns, the people most in need of a stable income and a decent place to live—the urban poor—continue to suffer, unaided and unable to take advantage of these opportunities. Financial institutions have also abandoned troubled urban areas. Some banks and insurance companies, for example, have redlined certain 'undesirable' metropolitan areas, literally drawing red lines on a map and making loans and providing insurance on one side of the line and not on the other.

In a cruel twist of irony, the latest threat to impoverished neighbourhoods in the downtown core is the return of affluent residents into the area. As noted above, the upper- and middle-class flight to the suburbs emptied out many North American downtown centres, leaving working-class families and individuals to struggle in economically and culturally withered neighbourhoods. However, in recent years, the once-forgotten inner city has experienced rejuvenation and has once again become a desirable place to live. Downtown housing markets have become flooded with demand, due largely to an influx of upwardly mobile young adults seeking a cosmopolitan alternative to the staid suburban lifestyle of their childhood. One of the results of this urban renaissance has been the *gentrification* of impoverished inner-city neighbourhoods (Box 11.1).

Sprawl

Some social scientists have attacked urban sprawl as an inefficient and ineffective urban form that contributes to a variety of social and environmental ills. At the same time, oth-

Box 11.1 Historical Perspective:
The Trajectory of Neighbourhood Gentrification

Gentrification is the process whereby established working-class neighbourhoods, usually in the inner city, are converted into middle- and upper-class neighbourhoods. This is typically accomplished through the renovation of existing buildings and landscapes into middle-class homes and the introduction of businesses and services catering to higher-income residents. The process results in higher property values and taxes and the gradual displacement of the poor.

Researchers have noted that the process of gentrification frequently follows a common trajectory, beginning when artists and other cultural producers, seeking work spaces and cheap rents, move into traditionally working-class inner-city neighbourhoods. Over time, their work—rich in cultural capital and Bohemian cachet—attracts the attention of middle-class consumers of art (Bourdieu, 1984). As this population, comprised of professionals and capitalists, moves into the area, they bring with them upscale interests and investment dollars, which drive up the cost of living. The cultural producers, no longer able to afford the neighbourhood and anyway repelled by the influx of middle-class influences, move on to other areas within the city, beginning the cycle once more (Ley, 1996, 2003; Florida, 2002).

For some, gentrification is an essentially positive force, an economic, social, and aesthetic 'rehabilitation' of a once run-down, stagnant neighbourhood. Although the dislocation of the relatively poor is usually acknowledged by the defenders of gentrification, this social cost is justified by the salvation of valuable real estate, the injection of private investments, and resuscitation of the local tax base. For others, the process is tinged with class discrimination, a type of economic genocide in which the vibrant and diverse working-class collective of artists, labourers, and other interesting characters are pushed out of their communities, replaced by banal middle-class interests (Atkinson, 2003). Often, the poor are forced to relocate in less desirable neighbourhoods, resulting in the further segregation and concentration of poverty (Fong and Shibuya, 2000). Ironically, as the urban boom continues to reverse the residential trends of the past half-century, the suburban pockets surrounding the revitalized central core are becoming the new 'undesirable' neighbourhoods. A recent United Way study of poverty in the Greater Toronto Area (GTA) reported that in 1981, the former City of Toronto—which comprises the high-density central urban core—was home to approximately half of all high poverty neighbourhoods. By 2001, its share had declined to 23 per cent, while the surrounding suburban municipalities in the GTA accounted for 77 per cent. Increasingly, these impoverished suburban 'outer cities' are populated by single parents, new immigrants, and members of visible minority groups (United Way of Greater Toronto/Canadian Council on Social Development, 2004).

ers have accepted it as a new paradigm in today's urban life (Dear, 2001; Schmidt, 1999; Dear et al., 1996). Urban sprawl is most often characterized as haphazard or unplanned growth, resulting in undesirable land-use patterns. It includes such patterns as scattered development, 'leapfrog' development, strip or ribbon development, and continuous low-density development (Redburn, 2002). In Canadian cities, large low-density, low-rise bedroom suburbs dotted by strip malls, shopping centres, and industrial parks epitomize suburban sprawl, and much of the nation's best agricultural land has been and continues to be lost to urban sprawl.

More than any other single factor, the spread of the personal automobile allowed suburbanization to take place by allowing residents to commute long distances every day between where they lived and where they worked. The vast highway programs of the 1950s and 1960s fostered massive migration to the suburbs and a corresponding deterioration of urban centres, though more so in the United States than in Canada.

The prevalence of auto-centred transport systems largely determines a nation's pattern of transportation and urban sprawl (Freund and Martin, 2000). Today, many developing nations are adopting Western standards of 'automobility' but face unique problems such as unequal access, inadequate roads, and the cost of importing oil. These nations represent a major new market for automobiles as well as an environmental threat. China, for example, faces a shortage of arable land that will be further compromised by auto-centred transport systems. Similar problems beset South Africa, Mexico, India, and other countries (ibid.).

Los Angeles is a particularly vivid and well-known example of the sprawl problem. Until recently, the history of California has been characterized by spectacular growth in all aspects: population, economic output, housing construction, and the global impact of its cultural values. Yet this growth has come at the price of sprawl and traffic congestion, distressed older neighbourhoods, air pollution, inadequate urban services, and a decline in quality of life.

However, not everyone criticizes this outcome or sees it as a failure to achieve another kind of order. Some view the evolution of economics, politics, and culture in Los Angeles—historically depicted as outside the mainstream of US urban culture—as having successfully established a new style of urban life. In contrast to the Chicago School, this emerging Los Angeles School of urban sociology regards LA as a model for many of the emerging urban centres in North America and around the world, all of them characterized by dispersed patterns of low-density growth, multicultural and ethnic enclaves, and an array of urban centres in a single region (Dear, 2001; Hise et al., 1996).

Traffic

Another major problem mainly affecting urban centres in both the developed and developing world is vehicular traffic. At present, many car users choose the car over alternative modes of transport because it is more convenient, it saves time, and public transport, even when it is a feasible alternative, is deemed to be bothersome. In most North American cities, cars are given more priority than pedestrians or bicycles, as reflected, for instance, in the amount of parking space devoted to cars. In Paris and Amsterdam, two cities famous for their metropolitan charm and pedestrian-friendly streetscapes, there is only one parking space for every three people living in the central area. By contrast Houston, with its sprawling web of highways slicing through the urban core, allots 30 spaces per resident (Lowe, 1995: 131). Similarly, the parking lots of major suburban shopping centres are usually larger than the malls themselves (Duany et al., 2000: 13).

The problems related to traffic are many. As we learned in the previous chapter on health, hundreds of thousands of people worldwide suffer death or injury in traffic-related accidents each year. Generally, traffic accidents are caused by our increased dependence on autos and the supremacy of the automobile over social space. When auto traffic is dense, as in cities, accidents are bound to occur. However, human behaviour is also to blame. For instance, the use of cellphones by drivers unnecessarily increases the risk of a collision 4–16 times. Analysis of 699 drivers who were involved in motor vehicle collisions that caused substantial property damage but no personal injury found that 24 per cent had used a cellular telephone during the 10-minute period before the collision

(Redelmeier and Tibshirani, 1997: 455). The continued popularity of larger, heavier SUVs also increases the risk of injury and death for people who are struck by vehicles.

Congestion is another problem caused by traffic. Canadians are travelling farther and farther to get to their workplaces—for example, a median distance of 9.6 kilometres in 2001 for workers in census metropolitan areas. Not surprisingly, as commuting distances increase, more workers choose to drive rather than take public transit or other modes of transportation (e.g., bicycles, walking). However, even when the distance to work is less than five kilometres, the car remains favoured over any other single mode of transportation (see Figure 11.3). Moreover, as the rate of growth of new work opportunities in suburban areas outpaces the growth in downtown business districts, more and more workers are travelling across town to get to work, a journey they usually make by car. In most large metropolitan areas, as many as 90 per cent of workers commute by car,

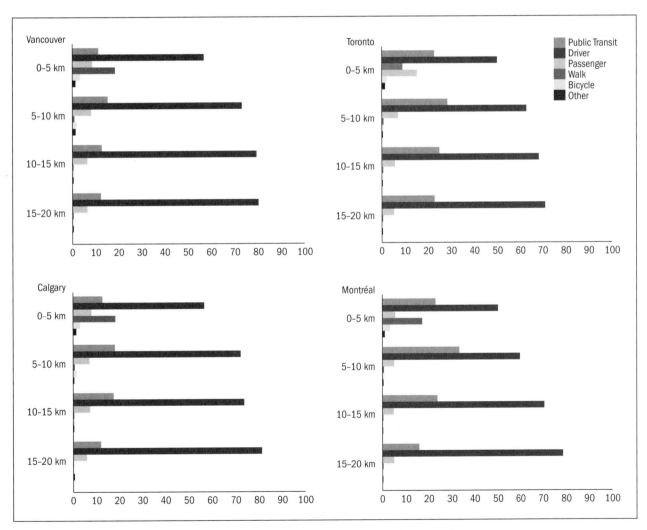

FIGURE 11.3 Percentage Distribution of Workers by Commuting Mode and Distance in 2001, Selected CMAs
Note: Some individuals reside in a different CMA from that in which they work.
Source: Heisz and LaRochelle-Côté (2005). Adapted from Statistics Canada, 'Trends and Conditions in Census Metropolitan Areas', Catalogue no. 89-613, no. 007, available at: <http://www.statcan.ca/english/research/89-613-MIE/89-613-MIE2005007.pdf>.

either as a driver or passenger, when their job is located 20 or more kilometres outside of the city centre (Heisz and LaRochelle-Côté, 2005).

The cost of traffic congestion—in lost time, wasted fuel, and higher insurance rates—is considerable and mounting fast. Related to the growth of congestion is the increase in air pollution, noise, and lack of green space in and around cities. Automobile and truck exhaust releases a huge amount of carbon monoxide into the air, contributing to the global warming problem; the other greenhouse gases produced by cars (and other machines) all help to create the thick, dirty cloud of smog that can be seen hanging over many car-heavy cities.

Traffic also interferes with people's enjoyment of their neighbourhoods. The high-speed, multi-lane roads that cut through residential areas are often too dangerous for children to cross alone, resulting in their dependence on parents to drive them everywhere: to and from school, sporting and recreational events, visits to friends' homes, and more. In a study comparing 10-year-olds in a traditional, light-traffic, small Vermont neighbourhood with their counterparts in a new Orange County, California, suburban development, those in Vermont enjoyed three times more mobility than their Californian peers (cited in Calthorpe, 1993: 9). In short, traffic has a negative effect on neighbourhood cohesion and community integration.

Human and Environmental Health

Health problems, to be found in all populations, are most concentrated in urban areas. This is in part the result of a large number of people gathering in a small area. Rates of illness and disease are bound to go up merely due to population size. At the same time, city life is particularly stressful, and this, too, poses health problems. The rush of traffic, the pace of change, the cost of living, jostling with strangers, the fear of victimization, economic competition, the noise—all of these characteristics are common in the city, and all are stress-inducing. Though people can manage the occasional experience of acute stress, chronic exposure to high stress levels can lead to serious health problems, including heart disease and a weakened immune system. The homeless and the mentally ill, two populations who suffer particularly high levels of poor health, are also concentrated in urban inner cities. For instance, in a 2002 Toronto Daily Bread Food Bank survey of their clients' self-reported health, over 40 per cent rated their health as fair or poor relative to others of their age. By comparison, when middle-income earners were

Table 11.2 Food Bank Clients' Self-Evaluations of Health

	1993 (%)	2002 (%)	2006 (%)
Rated health excellent	17.2	11.8	12.3
Rated health very good	16.2	17.2	18.9
Rated health good	30.2	28.6	30.1
Rated health fair	19.0	24.4	22.8
Rated health poor	12.5	16.4	15.9

Source: Daily Bread Food Bank (2002, 2006).

asked the same question, only 12 per cent rated their health as fair or poor (Daily Bread Food Bank, 2002; see Table 11.2).

Another urban health concern is the massive amount of sewage, litter, and solid waste produced by the millions of people crowded into a small area. For example, of the 162 sites in Chicago that are considered highly polluted, 98 (60 per cent) are in the predominantly African-American South Side neighbourhood. As well, all 10 of the city's communities with the highest levels of lead poisoning (caused by toxic levels of lead in the paint used in residential buildings) are made up of at least 70 per cent minorities (Cohen, 1992). This correlation between social class, neighbourhood racial composition, and pollution level, replicated in surveys of cities around the world, has been labelled by some researchers as a form of **environmental racism**. It is the result of several factors: fewer public services—sanitation workers, garbage disposal units, road maintenance crews, and so on—being devoted by local governments to the undesirable areas; a perception among corporate polluters that the local residents lack the political clout to prevent the dumping of industrial trash in their communities; and a shared sense of general demoralization by the economically deprived residents that reduces the likelihood of any concerted effort to preserve and improve the neighbourhood.

Environmental problems often result from human inefficiency and waste. For example, industrial pollution reflects inefficiencies in the manufacturing process, the result of by-products created when the raw materials used in production are not fully converted into usable end products. The causes and consequences of these problems involve entire populations, not only those organized into cities. Therefore, we turn now to problems arising from humanity's impact on the natural world.

Canadian and Global Environmental Problems

Unlike most other social problems, environmental issues are global in their consequences. They affect us all in a way that many social problems, such as alcohol and drug abuse or race and ethnic relations, may not.

Still, as with other social problems, there are important connections between social problems of the natural environment and the economic organization of society. Often, those in power generate the most environmental damage, through harmful industrial practices and wasteful individual lifestyles, while those lacking an economic or political voice pay an unequal toll in their personal health and social well-being. Again, the problem here is not simply humankind's consumption of natural resources, but rather the heartless and indefensible exploitation of these resources for short-term and self-interested gains.

Air Pollution

In large cities around the world—whether Los Angeles, Paris, Budapest, or Beijing—smog has become a major problem. There and elsewhere, the air is thick and the sky yellowish-grey near major thoroughfares. Emissions from cars and trucks, mixed with other chemicals released by industrial processes and other forms of fuel combustion, create high levels of pollution by releasing carbon monoxide, sulphur dioxide, and lead into the atmosphere. In Taipei, Tokyo, and other large Asian cities, one often sees people walking on the street—or, ironically, driving motor scooters—with their faces covered by masks to strain out the air pollutants. This daily exposure to air pollution has become a universal urban sensation, part of humanity's sensory experience of the world.

The Health Impact of Air Pollution
In 2004, air pollution was linked to approximately 1,700 premature deaths and 3,000–6,000 hospital admissions in the City of Toronto (Bray et al., 2005).

In principle, nature can repair itself. Through the process of photosynthesis, trees and other vegetation cleanse the air of the carbon dioxide that humans and other organisms produce, replacing it with breathable oxygen. However, the available amount of greenery—trees and other vegetation—limits these natural processes and their ability to process air. Trees and bushes can remove only so much pollution per day, and when the level of pollutants exceeds what they can remove, pollutants build up in the atmosphere, making the air potentially dangerous to breathe.

Ozone Depletion

The ozone layer is a thin veil in the stratosphere that shields Earth against the sun's harmful ultraviolet (UV) radiation. Without this protective layer, UV rays would seriously damage most of the life on the Earth's surface. Unfortunately, certain industrial chemicals—including chlorine chemicals, halons, and the chlorofluorocarbons (CFCs) used in most refrigerators, aerosol cans, and solvents—have weakened the ozone layer, allowing UV rays to go through it. This is the ozone depletion problem. Ozone declines of varying severity have been detected at several middle latitude locations and over the Arctic Circle. The damage has been most severe, however, in the Antarctic region where, by 2003, an area of extreme thinning within the ozone layer (the ozone 'hole') had grown to a record size of 29 million square kilometres (larger than the landmass of Canada, the United States, and Mexico combined) and had begun to stretch into more densely populated areas of South America. However, a combined global effort to reduce industrial chemical pollutants over the past decade appears to be having an effect. The National Institute of Water and Atmospheric Research in New Zealand reported in late 2004 that the Antarctic ozone hole had shrunk 20 per cent from the previous year, prompting some experts to predict guardedly that the ozone layer, at least in that region of the world, is beginning to recover.

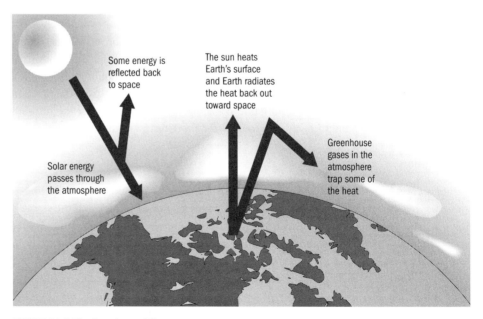

FIGURE 11.4 The Greenhouse Effect

Global Warming

Climate change, as caused by global warming, is possibly the single biggest environmental threat that humanity faces today because people can do little to reverse the process. All we can do is slow down the change. Certain greenhouse gases, such as CFCs, carbon dioxide, and methane, tend to accumulate in the atmosphere, trapping the heat reflected off the Earth's surface. This causes global temperatures to rise. The process is known as the greenhouse effect (see Figure 11.4).

As students of global warming might have predicted, 2005 was the world's warmest year on record, surpassing the previous mark set in 1998. The five warmest years in human history have all occurred in past eight years (NASA, 2006). The 1990s were estimated to be the warmest decade in the past millennium. As well, experts have noted that the high temperatures in 1998 were driven by an unusually strong El Niño effect, making its record at the time a meteorological abnormality. However, the 2005 El Niño episode was relatively weak and had little effect on overall global temperatures. Therefore, the record temperatures of 2005 cannot be blamed on the El Niño weather phenomenon.

These patterns of climate change have been attributed to the greenhouse effect (WMO, 2000). Even a small increase in global temperatures can lead to elevated sea levels and devastating changes in precipitation rates. Such climate changes, in turn, harm the natural vegetation and wildlife of local ecosystems, alter the crop yields of agricultural regions, and allow deserts to take over fertile regions. As a striking example of the effects of global warming, Greenpeace recently reported that small islands in Kiribati in the Pacific Ocean have entirely disappeared as a result of rising sea levels (Greenpeace, 2001).

As of July 2006, 164 of 168 participant countries have both signed and ratified the Kyoto Protocol (the four holdouts are Australia, Croatia, Kazakhstan, and the United States). Canada did not ratify until December 2002, and even then it did so in the face of a vocal opposition. The United States, for its part, has called the Kyoto Protocol irresponsible because a reduced use of fossil fuels (which lead to greenhouse gas emissions) required by the accord would hinder the American oil industry and economic growth more generally. Moreover, few signatory countries are currently on track to meet the emissions reduction targets set out within the accord. In late 2005, the US, Australia, China, India, Japan, and South Korea—which together account for approximately half of the world's greenhouse gas emissions—agreed to sign an alternative international agreement known as the Asia-Pacific Partnership on Clean Development and Climate (AP6), which allows member nations to set targets for reducing emissions individually, without a mandatory enforcement scheme. In 2006, Canada's federal Conservative government announced cuts to environmental funding meant to move Canada towards the Kyoto Protocol goals and indicated a desire to adopt the AP6 agreement instead. At present, the Kyoto Protocol appears to be dying by a thousand small cuts.

Water Pollution and Scarcity

Water pollution is another environmental problem, and it is largely caused by technological and industrial practices. Fertilizers, waste from industrial plants, oil spills, and acid rain have all polluted much of the world's drinking water. For example, the Great Lakes, a major source of fresh water in North America, have experienced much pollution. Pollutants from the surrounding regions—heavily farmed rural areas and densely populated

Species Extinction

- Of the Earth's estimated 10 million species, 300,000 have become extinct in the past 50 years.
- 3,000 to 30,000 species disappear each year (between 8 to 82 per day), which is 1,000 and 100,000 times the natural rate (www.healthyworld.org/species.html; accessed 5 Jan. 2006).

urban areas—have found their way into the lakes, poisoning the water, promoting the extreme growth of algae, and killing the aquatic life. Today, most of the beaches along the shores of the Great Lakes are too polluted for authorities to allow swimming. Similar conditions have been reported at points all along the North American seacoasts.

Global water use—especially for agricultural purposes, as well as for explosive population growth in arid regions such as the US Southwest that cannot naturally support high population densities—has increased greatly in the past 50 years. Such use further strains the supply of clean, drinkable water, and Canada has been among the worst water abusers. Among the 29 members of the Organization for Economic Co-operation and Development (OECD), the most developed industrial nations, 'only Americans use more water than Canadians.' As Boyd (2001) notes, 'Canada uses 1,600 cubic metres of water per person per year. This is more than twice as much water as the average person from France [uses], three times as much as the average German, almost four times as much as the average Swede, and more than eight times as much as the average Dane. Canada's per capita water consumption is 65 per cent above the OECD average.'

More and more countries are experiencing 'water stress', a level of supply that is so low that each person has available an average of only 1,000 to 2,000 cubic metres of water per year. Other countries are at the level of 'water scarcity', defined as a level of supply that is less than 1,000 cubic metres of water per person per year. By contrast, Canada's per capita per year water availability is 120,000 cubic metres (IFPRI, 1997).

Deforestation

As noted above, trees remove carbon dioxide from the air and convert it to oxygen. However, as forests have been continuously harvested, mainly by commercial logging operations, the rate of carbon dioxide removal from the atmosphere has markedly decreased. Up to 30 per cent of the atmospheric accumulation of carbon dioxide, which is directly responsible for global warming, is due to deforestation, according to an estimate by the World Resources Institute (1998: 1).

Forests are also vital to the health of a region because they help to protect the thin layer of fertile topsoil from wind erosion. Widespread clear-cutting of wooded areas for harvesting or to make room for expanding farmland and ranching often results instead in the expansion of deserts. When this happens, the rich topsoil may be worn out too quickly or carried away by wind. Deforestation of the world's rain forests also results in the dislocation of indigenous peoples and the loss of many animal and plant species. In extreme cases, peoples themselves risk extinction because of deforestation.

Sometimes it helps us to think about the future by running history backwards. Once upon a time, the barren Sahara Desert in Africa was woodland, and all of the parched and sandy beach land around the Mediterranean Sea was covered with trees. Today, there are few trees there and the land cannot be farmed; it can only be used for grazing, fishing, or tourism. Perhaps the same will happen, in time, to BC's Vancouver Island or the vast wooded interior of New Brunswick and northern Ontario. At the same time, damage done to the environment is not necessarily irreparable and permanent. The land along Canada's vast coastlines need not become like the Mediterranean, nor its interior woodlands like the Sahara Desert. The future health of Canada's vast forests can still be retained, but to do so requires a program of sustainability and rejuvenation that must be started today.

Waste Disposal and Pollution

The mass production process also creates useless by-products that need disposal. People produce a great deal of leftover paper, clothing, food, metals, plastics, and other synthetics. These materials are used and then thrown away. Canadian governments and businesses alone generate millions of tonnes of garbage each year.

There are two main methods of waste disposal: landfills and incinerators. As well, many products produced by today's industries that end up in these sites consist of plastics and other synthetic materials. Unlike organic materials, which decompose naturally in a short period if suitably disposed of, plastics can survive in one piece indefinitely when left in a landfill site. Another option is to burn the plastics, along with other forms of waste, using incinerators. However, this process converts many synthetics into hazardous chemicals, which are then released into the air as pollutants.

Compared to citizens of the developed world, citizens of developing countries use relatively few resources and recycle the resources they do use. This is usually more out of necessity than out of environmental consciousness. City authorities in the developing world, however, appear set on duplicating the solid waste management systems of developed countries while giving little consideration to those people who make their living from picking waste (Paccione, 2001). It is possible that when these cities begin to develop economically, they will be less environmentally friendly than the average North American city is today.

Non-renewable Resources

All industrial societies use massive amounts of energy because energy—petroleum, coal, natural gas, nuclear, hydroelectricity—powers technology. The first three of these cannot be renewed once we have exhausted the planet's supplies; nuclear energy produces radioactive waste as a primary by-product, which poses serious disposal problems, security concerns, and long-term health uncertainties; and hydroelectric power, in the form of massive dams and flooding, alters ecosystems, destroys species, and displaces humans who happen to be in the way. The US Energy Information Administration (2001) estimates that the world's energy consumption will increase from 382 quadrillion British thermal units (382×10^{15} BTUs) in 1999 to 607 quintillion (607×10^{18}) BTUs in 2020. As US President George W. Bush stated during his State of the Union address in early 2006, 'America is addicted to oil.' The same could be said of most Western industrial nations, including Canada.

Already we are beginning to suffer the economic consequences of the world's declining fossil fuel reserves, with gas prices in Canada and elsewhere increasing significantly since the early 1980s. The exchange of Western money for Middle Eastern oil results in a huge transfer of funds from the West to Arab and other developing countries. Recently, the issue of 'peak oil' has emerged as a major topic of concern within the global geopolitical debate. Crude oil reserves are limited—once oil is taken from the ground, it cannot be replenished. Also, what remains in the ground is deeper down and more difficult and expensive to remove. As well, as supplies slowly dwindle, control over the remaining petroleum reserves—most of which are located in the Middle East, with the Alberta oil sands accounting for a significant secondary source—will become increasingly entangled with political, military, and economic interests. The term 'peak

Box 11.2 Social Construction: Is the World Running Out of Oil?

Crude oil is a finite resource, and like most finite resources, the production of oil follows a bell curve. Once the peak of the production curve is reached, the rate of production will plateau and begin to decline. This phenomenon, termed 'peak oil', was first explicated in 1956 by an American geophysist, M. King Hubbert. Hubbert predicted at the time, to the amused skepticism of his colleagues, that oil production in the United States would peak sometime between 1965 and 1970, and global production sometime around 2000. As it turned out, US oil production peaked in 1971, so the first part of Hubbert's prediction was close to the mark.

However, not everyone agrees with the Hubbert peak theory. Though few would disagree that oil is a finite resource, critics contend that the methodology used to predict US production trends does not apply on a global scale. As a result, the growing public panic over potential $5/litre gas prices and the 'end of civilization' may be unwarranted.

In fact, the worldwide peak did not occur in 2000, perhaps because Hubbert's model could not have taken into account the 1973 and 1979 energy crises. But since nobody knows how much oil is left in the ground, nobody can say with certainty when the actual peak will occur. Some experts contend that the point was reached sometime within the past few years, while others say it will happen in a year or two. Another estimate, by the Association for the Study of Peak Oil and Gas, puts the global peak at around 2010. Yet other industry insiders, including the US Energy Information Agency, insist that the theoretical peak will not happen for decades.

What everyone agrees is that oil production will some day peak, if it has not peaked already, and from that point on, each barrel of oil taken from the ground will be increasingly difficult—and expensive—to extract. Given the dependency of the advanced industrial world's economies on cheap energy and the growing energy demands of developing nations such as China and India, this means that in the foreseeable future everything will cost more—from the fruit and vegetables that travel halfway across the continent to reach our dinner tables to all the services we rely on, including our water supplies and medical care. Alternative energy production—wind farms, solar panelling—will become vital in the future, but unless growth in these industries is bolstered by a commitment from ordinary citizens to cut back on personal energy consumption, the looming energy crisis—if and when it occurs—could be devastating.

oil' refers to the theoretical point at which world oil production reaches its maximum level and then begins to decline. From that time on, oil will become an ever-scarcer resource. According to most expert projections, the global peak period has either already occurred or will occur within the next decade (for more on the peak oil controversy, see Box 11.2).

Current reliance on non-renewable energy sources is also devastating the environment. Used as a substitute, coal (when burned) contributes substantially to the carbon dioxide and sulphur dioxide production that increases global warming and acid rain. But since first becoming aware of the potential energy crisis, some people have given thought to renewable energy sources, such as hydroelectric, solar, wind, and geothermal energy. Of these alternative options, the least expensive and therefore most widely used is hydroelectric power. Even so, hydroelectricity is not without its drawbacks, mainly in the form of environmental damage caused to the local wildlife, waterways, and ecosystems by the massive dams that we must construct to harness the water's energy.

Sociological Theories of Environmental Problems

The Structural-Functionalist Perspective

Functionalists are not surprised that modern people's values and activities have contributed to the pollution of our natural surroundings and the overharvesting of resources. Several types of cultural ideologies help support these ecologically harmful practices. One example, mentioned earlier, is the *cornucopia view of nature*, by which people view nature as a storehouse of resources that exists only for the use of humans—especially, currently living humans. Another environmentally unfriendly belief is the *growth ethic*, which is especially popular in North America. This view, linked closely with *materialism*, celebrates the (imagined) ability of technology to easily solve all the problems in the world, including those that technology itself has caused. This promotes the belief that things will always get better and therefore encourages us to discard just about everything in favour of the production and consumption of new items. Finally, the Western notion of *individualism*, which recommends personal goals and desires over collective interests, is the driving force behind the tragedy of the commons, to be discussed later.

Conflict Theory

A conflict theorist will emphasize that when environmental problems arise, they tend to hurt the poor more often and more severely than the rich. Over 90 per cent of disaster-related deaths, for instance, occur among the poor populations of developing countries, while developed nations experience 75 per cent of disaster-related economic damage since there is more of value to lose in materialist, developed societies. This will mean that an agricultural drought in Canada's prairie region, for example, may result in reduced crops but almost no deaths. In Pakistan or Indonesia or Ethiopia, by contrast, a drought can lead to catastrophic famine and many deaths. Of the 25 per cent of the world's population currently living in regions prone to natural disaster, most live in less developed countries (Smith, 2001: 26–7).

Sociological research shows that disasters result more often from 'the spread of capitalism and the marginalization of the poor than from the effects of geophysical events' and offers possible solutions that involve 'the redistribution of wealth and power in society to provide access to resources rather than . . . the application of science and technology to control nature' (Smith, 2001: 50–1). The scale of destruction caused by the South Asian tsunami of December 2004, for example, would have been lessened had the region's protective coastal mangrove forests not been significantly destroyed earlier to make room for aquaculture farms and upscale tourist resorts, and had the coral reefs not been slowly decimated by years of unsustainable fishing methods. The rich alone possess the economic means to protect themselves from the health consequences of locally occurring disasters, such as floods and hurricanes. The wealthy are also more often able to physically remove themselves from an area once disaster occurs, permanently or temporarily moving to where they can weather the storm. For instance, the loss of life and structural damage caused by the flooding of New Orleans by Hurricane Katrina in 2005 was concentrated mostly in poor, mainly black neighbourhoods whose residents were unable to leave before the storm landed. Moreover, much of the destruction would have been ameliorated if coastal swamplands, which act as a sponge, had not been destroyed for real estate development.

Symbolic Interactionism

The symbolic interactionist perspective studies how the meanings and labels learned through social interaction affect environmental problems, with a particular focus on how they alter people's perception of these problems.

Here, the social constructionist framework is particularly relevant. Sociologists who approach environmental problems from this perspective ask why and how certain environmental problems enter the public consciousness: what kinds of 'claims' make the great-

Table 11.3 Summary of Sociological Perspectives on Urban and Environmental Problems

Theoretical Perspective	Main Points
Structural Functionalism	■ Urban and environmental problems result naturally from population growth, density, and specialization.
	■ City life is anonymous and atomizing, and tends to promote social disorganization and weak social controls.
	■ Cultural ideologies support ecologically harmful practices (e.g., materialism and the growth ethic emphasize the triumph of progress and ingenuity, and encourage the discarding of the old in favour of consuming new innovations.
Conflict Theory	■ Social structure benefits some individuals at expense of others.
	■ Urban deprivation, including poverty, homelessness, and unemployment, are the by-products of capitalism.
	■ Unequal power, competing class interests, capital investment decisions, and government subsidy programs mediate the growth of cities.
	■ Environmental problems negatively affect the poor more often and more severely than the rich.
	■ The solution to urban and environmental problems is through redistribution of wealth.
	■ Collective action by underclass is needed to gain political attention to their needs.
Symbolic Interactionism	■ How are urban life and environmental issues imbued with meaning?
	■ The focus is on the lived experience of urbanites.
	■ To prevent sensory overload, inhabitants must reduce sensitivity to events and people around them.
	■ Subculture membership moderates how urban life is experienced.
	■ How are environmental issues constructed as 'problems'?
	■ Environmental polluters manipulate symbols to protect themselves from criticism.
	■ Marketing products with labels such as 'environmentally friendly' or 'green' soothe consumers' concerns about potential ecological harm from consumption of products.

est impact, and under what circumstances. For instance, sociologists Clay Schoenfeld, Robert Meier, and Robert Griffin (1979) have looked at how environmental issues have become a 'problem' in the public's eye. How and why, for example, does the greenhouse effect become a widespread public concern one year, and AIDS or women's rights or child labour in India become a concern another year?

The symbolic interactionist perspective also offers insights into how environmental polluters manipulate symbols to protect themselves from criticism. Many companies and businesses, increasingly sensitive to greater public awareness over their impact on the environment, have attempted to boost their image and profits by using a public relations strategy known as 'greenwashing'. This technique involves redesigning and repackaging their products as 'environmentally friendly' or 'green', playing to (some) consumers' wish to help solve the environmental problem by purchasing ecologically friendly items.

Social Aspects of Environmental Problems

The Tragedy of the Commons

The tragedy of the commons is sometimes used to explain why people knowingly pollute and damage the environment with seemingly no regard for their actions. The **tragedy of the commons** refers to what happened when medieval English lords opened their uncultivated pastures to allow commoners to freely graze their herds. These open fields became known as the commons. Soon the cattle in these areas were so numerous that the pastures could no longer sustain them. As competition for pasturage increased, each commoner was faced with a difficult choice. On the one hand, he could add more cows to his own herd, which would lead to greater personal yields but would also create an additional burden on the pasture and all those who used it. On the other hand, he could limit his personal gains and let others share the benefits. This conflict between the interests of the individual and the interests of the group occurs regularly, creating problems of depletion of non-renewable resources and accumulating levels of pollution.

Technological Dualism

Usually, we think of technology in terms of machinery and gadgets. However, **technology** can be viewed more broadly as the expression of human knowledge and ingenuity as applied to the solution of a problem. This definition covers the vast array of humanity's past and present interventions, from the development of primitive stone tools to the construction of a deepwater oil platform, from early farming techniques to genetically enhanced drought-resistant crops, from the Gutenberg printing press to wireless broadband Internet, and from the first settled villages constructed out of mud and straw to the glass-and-steel skyscrapers of today's mega-cities. If environmental problems reflect the consequences of humanity's flawed attempts to manipulate the natural world around them, then technology represents both the means by which those interactions took place and a potential source of correctives to the resulting problems.

Technology is inherently neither good nor bad. Technological innovations have both positive and negative effects. Like all other human achievements, how we apply these innovations determines whether they will have positive or negative effects on

Box 11.3 Personal Experience:
World's First Biogas Train Fuelled by Cows

In Sweden, if you are travelling between the cities of Linköping and Västervik, you have the option to make the journey via a passenger train fuelled by cows.

Actually, the train is fuelled by biogas, i.e., methane produced by the bacteria-induced fermentation of organic matter. The source of the organic matter is cows that are already destined for slaughter. Once butchered, the organs, fat, and entrails are collected and allowed to stew for a month, at which point the methane produced is drawn off and stored, ready for use.

Nor is it just trains that have been converted in this way. The 65-bus fleet in Linköping is also powered by biogas, as are the city's taxis, garbage trucks, and a number of private cars. Experts regard bioethanol and biodiesel as 'carbon-neutral', because they generate fewer carbon emissions and the crops that provide the source material for these fuels also absorb greenhouse gas-causing carbon dioxide as they grow. This biogas, when properly processed and purified, burns cleaner than coal and is similar to natural gas in its chemical properties.

Currently, the train between Linköping and Västervik costs 20 per cent more to run on methane than on the usual diesel. But with both fuel prices and air pollution on the rise, biogas presents both an economically and environmentally sustainable long-term alternative. As for fuel economy, the energy conversion is not too shabby—one cow can produce enough biogas to power the train 4 km.

Source: Franks (2005).

society. Box 11.3 provides an example of how technological innovation can be used to benefit humanity, in this case through the development of alternative, cleaner-burning sources of fuel.

The automobile exemplifies both the good and the bad of technology. This invention has simplified travel across vast distances, offering the freedom to determine one's own pace and destination and providing the convenience of a speedy mobile private space. Today, the automobile allows you to travel in one hour a distance that would previously have taken more than a day to complete on foot, or half a day on horseback. On the other hand, cars and trucks have contributed dangerous levels of carbon monoxide and smog in the atmosphere, promoted global warming, and encouraged suburban sprawl. Today, thanks to traffic congestion, it is sometimes faster to travel through urban centres by foot than by car.

Health Consequences of Environmental Problems

Environmental problems have harmful health consequences. This is particularly striking in the poorer regions of the developing world. The World Health Organization (1999) estimates, for instance, that 'poor environmental quality is directly responsible for 25 per cent of all preventable ill-health in the world today, with diarrheal diseases and respiratory infections heading the list.'

These health consequences are socially structured, too: a majority of all the preventable ill health that results from environmental conditions affects children; further, children and adults living in rural and semi-urban areas are more affected than people in urban areas (WHO, 1997; see also Aronwitz and Cutler, 1998; Helfgott, 1988). Even in developed nations, pollutants, chemicals, and other environmental hazards constantly bombard people. A major Canadian example occurred during the summer of 2000, when an outbreak of E. coli bacteria in the water supply of Walkerton, Ontario, killed seven people and infected thousands more. Although a board of inquiry looking into the deaths eventually blamed insufficient government regulation and human error, this event proved that water supplies in even the most technologically advanced regions are not safe from environmental contamination.

The list of health consequences is too long to present here, but consider just a few examples. The number of asthma cases treated in hospital emergency departments increases after a period of severe air pollution. Noise pollution, most apparent in dense urban environments and a result of our industrialized lifestyle, has been shown to contribute to hearing loss. The thinning of the ozone layer has meant an increase in the amount of harmful UV rays that penetrate the atmosphere. This has resulted in a parallel increase in the number of skin cancer cases, particularly melanomas, which have increased 15 times in prevalence in the past 60 years. This upsurge in UV-caused cancer accounts for eight out of every 10 skin cancer deaths.

The use and haphazard dumping of ecologically harmful chemicals into the local environment have allowed persistent organic pollutants (POPs), such as pesticides, to accumulate in the food chain and, eventually, in human food supplies. Chronic exposure to POPs in our food and air has resulted in an alarming buildup of harmful synthetic chemicals and heavy metals in our bodies, a phenomenon that has been termed **body burden** (Coming Clean, 2006). On a global scale, climate change resulting from global warming has led to a rise in the occurrence of droughts and famines, particularly in Africa and in regions along the equator, and to increases in the number of floods.

Not everyone is affected to the same degree. For example, age makes a difference. Children in both developed and developing nations are especially vulnerable to chemical, physical, and biological pollutants in the environment since their immune systems are only partly developed. Indoor air pollution caused by fossil-fuel combustion (for cooking and heating) is responsible for respiratory infections that cause 20 per cent of the deaths among children under five years of age. Diarrheal diseases claim another 2 million children a year, mainly because of unclean drinking water and lack of hygiene. Ailing and elderly members of society are also at a higher than average risk because of their declining health status.

The technologies people have devised to improve our material conditions and advance our collective quality of life can also have adverse health implications. These technologies include nuclear power plants, automobiles, x-rays, food preservatives, breast implants, and pesticides. As we suggested above, industrialized societies are also experiencing more and more technological emergencies, including accidents involving hazardous materials or nuclear power and mass transportation (for example, airplanes, buses, and trains).

Another, more controversial, example of technology having potential adverse health consequences is agricultural biotechnology, the union of molecular biology research, applied engineering, and farming. Although farmers have for generations experimented with natural cross-pollination and selective breeding techniques to improve the genetic stock of their crops, agricultural biotechnology in recent years has developed into both a field of genetic science and a multi-billion dollar global industry. Biotechnology firms have harnessed genetic engineering and genetic modification (GM) techniques to produce, for instance, slower-ripening tomatoes and pest-resistant

Skin Cancer in Australia
Australia has the highest rate of skin cancer in the world. With only 0.3 per cent of the world population, it accounts for 6 per cent of all lethal forms of skin cancer diagnosed globally.
Source: Australian Academy of Science (1997).

corn and potato crops. However, many critics are concerned that a failure to consider the long-term health effects of this new technology may lead to the creation of new allergies and other, more serious forms of technology-induced disease. Others have raised environmental concerns, noting that the agribusiness industry's practice of monoculture—where entire fields are planted over multiple growth cycles with a single GM crop—destroys diversity and soil health, contaminates the genetic pool of non-GM crops, and may create harmful complications in the developmental cycle of other species. Already, for example, studies have shown that populations of monarch butterfly larvae have been harmed by eating genetically modified corn (WHO, 1999). Concerns over the unknown medium- and long-term consequences of GM foods on human and environmental health led the European Union to impose in 1998 a six-year moratorium on new GM crops. When the ban was lifted, the EU implemented a series of strict regulations requiring food packaging labels to clearly identify the presence of GM ingredients and for these GM ingredients to be carefully traced through the production process. These regulations are opposed, however, by powerful agriculture lobbyists in the US, who claim that EU labelling regulations violate international free trade agreements. Whether or not the artificial manipulation of other species will, in the future, introduce novel human health problems remains to be seen.

Most important of all, in a highly technological society like ours, technological problems—even disasters—are predictable and almost inevitable. In that sense, we are sure to experience what sociologist Charles Perrow (1999) has called 'normal accidents'. To prove this point, Perrow examined a variety of technological disasters, including the nuclear accidents at Three Mile Island in Pennsylvania and Chernobyl in Ukraine, and, more generally, nuclear power as a high-risk system for producing energy. He also examined detailed records on aircraft accidents, marine accidents, and accidents at dams, mines, petrochemical plants, and elsewhere.

For Perrow, the 'villains' in all these cases of catastrophe are system complexity, on the one hand, and subsystem coupling, on the other. Conventional engineering tries to ensure safety by building in extra warnings and safeguards. However, this approach fails because it increases system complexity. Adding to complexity not only makes system failure more likely, it creates unexpected new kinds of accidents. Said simply, more complex systems have more chances of failing and more ways to fail. In addition, the more tightly connected (or coupled) a system's parts, the more inevitable that one part's failure will trigger another failure. Thus, simplicity and loose coupling are preferable from a safety standpoint, but complexity and tight coupling are increasingly the norm. Technological catastrophes are often blamed on human error, but invariably such error is only the social side of a built-in technological risk.

Solutions to Population, Urban, and Environmental Problems

Population Control

We have emphasized thorough this chapter that a growing global population size is not in itself a social problem. However, overpopulation in the developing world and underpopulation in the developed world are problems because they reveal flaws in the organization and migration of human populations.

Industrialization, urbanization, education, mass literacy, and the emancipation of women were all key parts of the voluntary reduction in child-bearing in recent history. Invariably, birth rates have fallen wherever women have received more education, delayed marriage, and generally enjoyed more social, economic, and political equality with men. Several developing societies—among them Costa Rica, Sri Lanka, and Kerala State in India—have enjoyed notable success in lowering the birth rate. In these places, low mortality and fertility rates are the result of a long process that began with fairer income distribution, better nutrition, more education and autonomy (especially for women), higher rates of political awareness and participation for all, and universal access to health services. Also, income and land redistribution gave people more sense of involvement in their own lives—hence, more to gain from changing their fertility decisions. This is particularly true of women, who with more education and autonomy are no longer as reliant on children for social status and income security.

In Canada today, by any standard, there are not too many people for the land to support. Nor is the population growing too quickly through high rates of fertility. Yet some people view high rates of immigration as a population problem and a social problem. Immigration has recently become an explosive political issue. Many people inside the country want the chance to bring their relatives over to Canada. Many outside the country want a chance to get in. However, whenever the economy weakens, many native-born Canadians resist the push for more immigrants. Some even want the immigration rate cut back.

Should immigration be more limited? As usual, there are conflicting views on this question. People who argue that immigration should be more limited make three main points that focus on economic, cultural, and social issues respectively. (In Australia, many now also make the case against immigration on a fourth, ecological ground, arguing that immigration speeds population growth, which in turn speeds environmental degradation.) First, they claim that immigration poses an economic problem in a slow-growing economy. Second, they say that immigrants pose a problem of assimilation and cultural unity, an issue we discussed in Chapter 4. Third, they raise the concern that high rates of immigration produce problems of social cohesion and conflict. (For general discussion of these issues, see Banton, 1992; Dei, 1996; Reitz, 1994, 1998.)

People who want to limit or reduce immigration on economic grounds argue that immigrants use too many public services. Health care is particularly important for older immigrants, educational services for younger immigrants, and welfare for unemployed immigrants. On the one hand, critics complain that too many immigrants fail to get (or keep) jobs, so they increase the unemployment rate. On the other hand, they complain that too many immigrants take jobs away from native-born Canadians in a tight job market. Increasingly, immigrants come from countries and cultures that are different from the dominant white North American culture. As with rapid population change because of high rates of fertility, rapid change stemming from high rates of immigration strains a society's capacity to adapt.

High rates of immigration press a society to rapidly acculturate the new immigrants or, alternately, to adopt multiculturalism policies that some reject. Often, immigrants develop a self-protective strategy that the sociologist Raymond Breton has called institutional completeness (Breton, 1964). This tactic gives the impression of clannishness, but that is not the goal. Institutional completeness is a measure of the degree to which an immigrant ethnic group gives its own members the services they need through its own institutions. The success of these services may evoke the envy of poor native-born people.

Because population per se is not the cause of urban problems or environmental damage, population control alone cannot solve these problems. However, social organization is harder to improve and social problems are harder to solve when a population is large and growing rapidly. This is because so much effort and money are diverted to dealing with population issues—for example, the care and education of the young, and the creation and maintenance of housing, roads, and other infrastructure—that money is not available for new initiatives (for example, job creation, or research and development).

Economic and Political Solutions to Urban Stagnation

High unemployment, crumbling infrastructure, little access to business capital, and loss of hope all pose major challenges to inner cities. These problems have often arisen because of the political, economic, and social abandonment of troubled and stigmatized city centres, so the solutions may have to include reversing these trends. For an example of the type of policy commitments needed, see Box 11.4.

Box 11.4   Social Policy: A New Deal for Canadian Cities

As the world continues to urbanize, cities will become even more important as a nation's economic and cultural engines. Keeping Canada's metropolitan centres competitive on the world stage will require major policy commitments, both fiscal and political. The following information is taken from the Department of Finance Canada's so-called New Deal for Cities and Communities, *devised in 2005 under the Martin government.*

Under the New Deal, federal, provincial, territorial and municipal governments will work together with other stakeholders to develop long-term strategies for improving our communities. In combination with full rebate of the goods and services tax introduced last year, the measures announced in Budget 2005 will provide Canadian communities with more than $9 billion in funding over the next five years.

Budget 2005 delivers on the Government of Canada's New Deal for Cities and Communities commitment through:

1. Gas tax revenue sharing: Over the next five years, the Government of Canada will provide $5 billion to municipalities to support environmentally sustainable infrastructure projects such as public transit, water and wastewater treatment, community energy systems and the handling of solid waste. This funding will come from the sharing of federal gas tax revenues, and will be distributed to provinces, territories and First Nations on a per capita basis.
2. Renewing existing infrastructure programs: Budget 2005 commits to renewing the Canada Strategic Infrastructure Fund, the Municipal Rural Infrastructure Fund, and the Border Infrastructure Fund.
3. Green municipal funds: Budget 2005 more than doubles funding for the Green Municipal Funds, with new funding totaling $300 million. These funds, which are administered by the Federation of Canadian Municipalities, provide grants, low-interest loans, and innovative financing to increase investment in infrastructure projects that deliver cleaner air, water and soil, and climate protection.

Source: Reproduced with the permission of the Minister of Public Works and Government Services Canada, 2007.

Empowerment zones, enterprise communities, and other economic incentives may help to attract private corporate industries back to the central cities. A program initiated in the United States—the formation of urban empowerment zones—targets tax breaks, development grants for housing projects, and job-creation programs at economically stagnated urban cores. Four key principles guide these initiatives: (1) a strategic vision for change, (2) community-based partnerships, (3) economic opportunity, and (4) sustainable community development. In Detroit, for instance, the automotive industry, with big players like General Motors and DaimlerChrysler, has pledged billions of dollars towards the city's empowerment zone. Such programs would likely meet with success in Canada as well.

Increasingly, large cities are trying to make a global impact and participate fully in the global economy. Success will require establishing new governmental institutions to manage public resources, reduce social and racial inequalities, and constrain urban sprawl; create an environment that accelerates and nurtures economic activity; and build mechanisms of social responsibility for industry and finance (Moberg, 1997). Geographer Richard Florida (2002) has also emphasized the need for a city to attract creative professions, including architects, scientists, writers, information technology specialists, and designers of various types, if it is to thrive in the new idea-driven global information economy.

Urban Planning

The decentralization of cities and the uncontrolled rate of suburban sprawl have contributed significantly to the urban and environmental problems described in this chapter. The spread of characterless bedroom communities in the suburbs and of segregated poverty in the downtown core can be halted if land developers are forced to build mixed-use neighbourhoods, however. The principle of mixed-use construction is that communities should be built so that all necessities—occupational, commercial, and recreational—are within easy reach of one's home, either on foot or by public transit (Rybczynski, 1995). In certain respects, this is like the 'institutional completeness' we described above, but it is based on neighbourhood, not ethnicity. Urban theorist Jane Jacobs (1993 [1961]) described this blending of 'primary uses' as one of the four conditions needed to generate diversity in a city's streets; the other conditions are short city blocks, a mingling of buildings that vary in age and condition, and a sufficient density of people in the area to sustain the neighbourhood's businesses and institutions.

However, mixed-use developments are often prohibited by strict building regulations that separate the various aspects of daily life. Until the middle of the twentieth century, this segregation applied only to incompatible land uses (for example, residential and industrial), in order to promote health, safety, and general public welfare (Rybczynski 1995). Today, it applies to every use and there are signs that it has become oppressive. For instance, a Los Angeles study found that residents in both middle- to upper-income and low-income communities desired more diversity and services, such as markets, drugstores, and libraries, than present zoning codes allowed. These same respondents ranked sociability and friendliness as their first and second most desirable characteristics of an ideal community (Lowe, 1995).

Mixed-use communities also promote less reliance on cars for transport, which has environmental benefits. For instance, the city council of Vancouver was advised by its own 1990 *Clouds of Change* report to improve air quality by curtailing the use of motor vehicles and encouraging more density through multi-unit residential developments. Among the specific recommendations were proposals to 'decentralize commercial and community services to reduce travel distance, creating self-contained communities with a better balance between employment and population' and to 'encourage the development of high-quality walking and bicycling facilities, including alternatives to private automobile use' (Vancouver Task Force on Atmospheric Change, 1990: 11–12).

Urban developers and government officials need to pay closer attention to these types of report. In a study examining why some of New York City's parks and plazas consistently attract larger crowds than others, sociologist William Whyte (1996) found that people simply congregate wherever there are places to sit down. For Whyte, the only thing more surprising than the obviousness of his own conclusion was the fact that the provision of seating was in fact often overlooked by designers of public space.

Improving the urban quality of life also requires a commitment from all levels of government to recycling and composting programs, the design of energy-efficient homes, and new policies that reduce the number of garbage bags disposed of per home. Regulatory monitoring accompanied by higher levels of water treatment to raise quality would deal with inadequate water sanitation. Full public transportation should also be subsidized provincially and federally, and municipalities should explore alternative urban transportation models. For example, the popularity of bicycling is growing as a viable form of transportation in many cities, particularly in Europe, where bicycles account for up to 30 per cent of all trips made within city boundaries (Gardner, 1998). Bikes have the benefit of being easy to use, cheap to fix, and health-inducing. In addition, bicycle riding reduces the number of casualties caused by traffic every year.

Urban Health Promotion

The 'Healthy City', a common concept in developed societies, has only recently been adopted in developing countries. From 1995 to 1999, the World Health Organization supported healthy city projects (HCPs) in Cox's Bazaar, Bangladesh; Dar es Salaam, Tanzania; Fayoum, Egypt; Managua, Nicaragua; and Quetta, Pakistan.

Throughout the developing world, urbanization has brought significant health problems. Infectious diseases common in rural areas combine with urban problems such as pollution and stress. The urban poor are particularly victimized and health services simply cannot cope. An HCP attempts to integrate preventive health care into all the other planning and development decisions. It attacks the causes of ill health, most of which are beyond the reach of curative medicine.

Trudy Harpham, Salma Burton, and Ilona Blue (2001) evaluated four of these projects, the first major evaluation of HCPs in developing countries. Using various methods, the researchers found that in these cities, municipal health plan development—one of the main components of the healthy city strategy—was limited. Evaluations of HCPs in Europe arrived at similar conclusions. Despite an increased understanding of the links between environment and health, the political commitment to the HCPs was limited, perhaps because most of the municipalities had not requested the projects. Consequently, the projects had little influence on written or expressed municipal policies. These findings highlight the importance of motivating senior policy-makers to address urban and environmental problems.

Environmental Policies

Environmental problems, because of their broad, snowballing nature, are difficult and expensive to solve. Still, all levels of society must plan remedies because of the seriousness of the problems and their costs for humanity and the planet. At the highest levels, national and international policies need to be formulated to ensure that we follow a common, co-operative path. Under this approach, governments should try to establish policies that will make it profitable for industries to clean up the environment and exercise ecologically friendly practices. We must also demand greater preparedness of emergency response organizations, including local government, fire, and police departments and special response teams.

Post-materialist Values

A theory proposed by Ronald Inglehart, a political scientist at the University of Michigan, argues that there is wide public support for solving the problems of technology and environment we have discussed here. He puts this new environmental activism down to a culture shift that originates in a generation accustomed to prosperity. Inglehart (1990; see also Tepperman, 2001) argues that people who grow up in prosperous and secure conditions develop high personal and social goals. These include the goals of belonging, self-esteem, and self-actualization. Throughout the Western world, the post-war generation grew up with these goals.

Over time this generation replaced earlier generations as voters and in elite positions of influence. In the West, according to Inglehart, the result is a new political culture. The new generation's goals have increasingly come to define the political agenda of Western democracies. The new political culture links a variety of political, social, and economic views. As a result, it represents a new outlook on life. It is post-materialist in the sense that it places less importance on personal wealth, economic development, and economic determinants of social life. In this respect the new outlook is also post-Marxist. The new post-materialist culture contains political attitudes and potentials for action. It encourages more political involvement, and more protest, than the materialist culture did. However, much of this activity occurs outside the framework of elections and traditional political parties.

Inglehart's research examines anti-establishment, grassroots politics and skepticism about material progress. One major part of this post-materialist shift is the growing support for environmentalism and for movements that seek solutions to these problems. Linked as they are to preferences for specific political issues and parties, these 'new' needs produce 'new' political behaviours, including shifts in goals and partisanship. Post-materialists, who also report higher levels of material satisfaction, are said to be more politically active than materialists (Inglehart, 1977).

If Inglehart's theory is valid, the problems we have discussed in this chapter are already on the way to being solved. New environmentalist movements and political parties will gain ever more support, form governments, and ban environmentally unsound practices. Human life will become healthier and happier. However, evidence does not entirely support the theory's predictions (on this, see Tepperman, 2001). Some say that Inglehart's approach is surprisingly simple or naive—a one-dimensional view of political culture that pits materialism against post-materialism. Some say that we cannot assume that a shift in cultural values towards environmentalism will translate into political action. We need only to look at the negative North American political response to the Kyoto agreement to know that warm fuzzy feelings about the environment do not necessarily equal committed political action when elected officials must also contend with competing economic and political interests in a highly complex world.

We may not be able to rely on a new political culture of post-materialism to bring about environmental or technological change, to improve our health and well-being. People will have to mobilize to consider, discuss, protest, and enact new policies. And a number of factors, including global capitalism, stand in the way. So long as 'the commons' is not understood to include the entire planet, 'the tragedy' will continue to play itself out as those with power and influence seek personal short-term gain over longer-term equity.

Individual Strategies

Actions by average citizens, in groups, are clearly called for, of course, because of the dire consequences for future generations of the problems of technology and the environment. As with several other social problems discussed in this book, individuals can have significant consequences for these problems only through sustained organized activity by many people leading to changes in social policies and collective values. There are actions that each individual can take with respect, for example, to personal fertility planning, environmental practices, and restrained and enlightened use of technology. But given the magnitude of the problems, only widespread adoption of these practices in the general population will have significant impact.

To live an environmentally friendly, technologically uncluttered life means to make major sacrifices in convenience and cost. The simplest 'green' activities include recycling household items such as newspapers and aluminum cans instead of throwing them in the trash, and turning off lights and water taps when they are not being used. Other options, more inconvenient and costly but also more eco-friendly, include choosing to bicycle, carpool, or use public transit instead of driving from one place to another, and purchasing organic foods (which are not treated with pesticides) and energy-efficient fluorescent light bulbs, the use of which has to date saved the equivalent of about 100 coal-burning power plants.

Concluding Remarks

As mentioned at the beginning of this chapter, the topics discussed here—population growth, urban problems, and the degradation of the environment—are all complex, and each could justify its own textbook, let alone chapters within a book. However, these topics are related in several important ways. First, issues of population size feed naturally into discussions of urban and environmental problems, since the latter are fuelled in part by the former. Second, traversing all three subjects is the notion of human ingenuity (and its manifestation, technology), which has been both the cause and frequently the solution to the urban and environmental troubles facing the world today. Third, each represents a separate component of the material backdrop of social life. To borrow Shakespeare's metaphor of human life as a play, the human population represents the world's actors; our cities, the set; and the natural environment, the stage upon which everything plays out.

Finally, the topics discussed in this chapter are unique in that they will outlive any one individual and, therefore, serve as legacies to later generations in a way that other social problems (e.g., drugs or crime) do not. Ultimately, our collective choices will determine the outcome of these population-related problems—that is, whether the urban centres of the future are energizing and beautiful or stagnant and bland, and whether global environmental problems are worsened by human intrusion or improved by human ingenuity and by human choices that take into account the well-being of others. Just as we must take collective responsibility for these present problems, so, too, must we draw upon collective efforts to find their solutions.

QUESTIONS FOR CRITICAL THOUGHT

1. China is famous for its so-called 'one-child policy', with governmental policy formally reducing the birth rate of one of the most populous countries in the world. Generally, this is seen as very successful. However, some believe it may produce more problems than it solves (for example, a proliferation of rules, the creation of an all-powerful state, infanticide). What are some other drawbacks to such a policy, or do you believe the advantages outweigh the possible disadvantages? Do you feel other countries should adopt such a law?

2. It seems as though in a big city there is something for everyone. Pick a certain subculture, such as the gay and lesbian community or ethnic enclaves, and explore its presence in your city. Are certain services, facilities, restaurants, bars, and shops concentrated in a certain area? Do they share similar characteristics? Where are they found? Discuss how living in a big city makes for greater opportunity for subcultures to emerge and flourish.

3. Everything around us, from banking to movie-ticket sales, is becoming automated. People's jobs are being replaced by machines, and human interaction seems to be a nostalgic idea of the past. Read sociologist Georg Simmel's essay 'Metropolis and Mental Life' (1950 [1917]), paying special regard to his ideas about people's becoming calculating and rational actors. Link his theory to the time-saving technologies automation provides. What would Simmel say about this apparent shift away from personalized and intimate relationships?

4. There is no doubt that suburbanization is a major force permeating the modern urban landscape. What effect has this had on your own life? Do you live in a suburb? If so, how often do you go into the city centre, and for what reasons? What do you think about the myth of suburbia? Does living near the city centre offer a different lifestyle than suburban living? Discuss using specific examples and figures.

5. Along with deforestation comes the displacement of indigenous peoples and many animal species from these natural habitats. Also, peoples and species may be at risk of extinction because of such activities. Chart out the advantages and disadvantages of deforestation. Do you feel it is an ethical practice? Should the government set limits? Research specific examples to back up your claims.

RECOMMENDED READINGS

John W. Bennett, *Human Ecology as Human Behavior: Essays in Environmental and Development Anthropology* (New Brunswick, NJ: Transaction, 1993). Bennett proposes solutions to the problem of relations between humans and our environment. Taking a macro perspective, he claims that the most useful analysis is not to look at human actions individually as the source of environmental degradation; instead, he advocates an analysis of the historical, cultural, and economic contexts in which humans create these problems.

Stephen Dale, *McLuhan's Children: The Greenpeace Message and the Media* (Toronto: Between the Lines, 1996). This book is a good and entertaining resource for those interested in the symbolic interactionist perspective, which is concerned with the construction of an environmental problem. Dale also addresses the political implications of constructing a claim of environmental damage.

Mary Douglas and Aaron Wildavsky, *Risk and Culture: An Essay on the Selection of Technological and Environmental Dangers* (Berkeley: University of California Press, 1982). The authors examine the connections between the structure of human societies and the environment in which we live.

Tim Flannery, *The Weather Makers: How Man Is Changing the Climate and What It Means for Life on Earth* (New York: Atlantic Monthly Press, 2006). This popular work offers a layman's guide to the current status of global climate change, energy consumption, and the geopolitical implications of our looming environmental problems.

Mario Polèse and Richard Stren, eds, *The Social Sustainability of Cities: Diversity and the Management of Change* (Toronto: University of Toronto Press, 2000). This book uses 10 case studies of cities across Canada, the US, Europe, South America, and Africa to explore how urban centres can use policy reforms to promote levels of cohesion, inclusiveness, and social sustainability among their inhabitants.

RECOMMENDED WEBSITES

World Wildlife Fund

www.worldwildlife.org

The World Wildlife Fund (WWF) is dedicated to protecting the world's wildlife and wildlands. Its conservation efforts are directed towards three global goals: protecting endangered spaces, saving endangered species, and addressing global threats.

Environment Canada

www.ec.gc.ca/envhome.html

Environment Canada's mandate is to preserve and enhance the quality of the natural environment, including water, air, and soil quality; to conserve Canada's renewable resources; to conserve and protect Canada's water resources; to

monitor weather systems (meteorology); to enforce the rules made by the Canada–US International Joint Commission relating to boundary waters; and to co-ordinate environmental policies and programs for the federal government.

Canadian Technology Network

ctn.nrc.ca

The Canadian Technology Network links federal and provincial government labs and agencies, universities, community colleges, industry associations, technology centres, and economic development agencies. Together, these organizations provide innovative Canadian companies with quick and personal access to expertise, advice, and information about how to meet technology and related business challenges.

GLOSSARY

Body burden The buildup of synthetic chemicals and heavy metals in our bodies as a consequence of POPs (persistent organic pollutants) in the food chain and thus in human food supplies.

Cornucopian view of nature Nature is seen as an almost endless storehouse of resources that exist only for use by humans, especially by those currently living.

Demographic transition Shift in a population or society from high birth and death rates to low birth and death rates.

Environmental racism Certain social groups and areas within a city, most often minority groups, the marginalized, and the poor, are discriminated against as a result of several factors, including fewer public services being devoted by local governments to undesirable areas and a perception on the part of polluters that local residents are so politically weak that they are unable to mount successful NIMBY campaigns against polluting industries or government.

Gemeinschaft Social situations in which those involved treat one another as ends rather than as means; primary relationships based on sentiment, found most often in rural life.

Gentrification The restoration and upgrading of deteriorated urban property by middle-class or affluent people, often resulting in displacement of lower-income people.

Gesellschaft Social situations in which those involved treat one another as means rather than as ends; secondary relations based primarily on calculation and individual interest, found most often in city life.

Mechanical solidarity Durkheim's term for the kind of tight, homogeneous social order typical of a pre-industrial, primarily rural society.

Organic solidarity Durkheim's term for the new social order of industrial society, which was based on interdependent, though not necessarily intimate, relationships.

Positive checks Part of Malthusian theory, these prevent overpopulation by increasing the death rate. They include war, famine, pestilence, and disease.

Preventive checks In Malthusian theory, these prevent overpopulation by limiting the number or survivals of live births. They include abortion, infanticide, sexual abstinence, delayed marriage, and contraceptive technologies.

Suburbanization The process by which housing spreads almost unhindered into once rural regions surrounding the city core. This greatly expands the geographic size of cities, and there is a noticed shift of the affluent out of the urban centre to these surrounding areas.

Technology The manifestation of human knowledge and ingenuity applied to the solution of a problem or need.

Tragedy of the commons A market system based on the capitalistic belief that economies work best when left alone, with each self-interested actor seeking what is personally best, leads to the situation where this agglomer-ated self-interest works against the common good by polluting, destroying, and exhausting bodies of water, the air, the land, ecosystems, and, especially, renewable resources such as fish and forests.

Urbanization The growth in the proportion of the population living in urbanized areas. There is also an increasing appearance in rural and small-town areas of behaviour patterns and cultural values associated with big-city life.

REFERENCES

Aronowitz, Stanley, and Jonathan Cutler, eds. 1998. *Post-Work: The Wages of Cybernation*. New York: Routledge.

Atkinson, Rowland. 2003. 'Introduction: Misunderstanding Saviour or Vengeful Wrecker? The Many Meanings and Problems of Gentrification', *Urban Studies* 40, 12: 2343–50.

Australian Academy of Science. 1997. Nova: Science in the News. Available at: <www.science.org.au/nova/008/008key.htm>; accessed 12 Nov. 2006.

Baer, Douglas, James Curtis, and Edward Grabb. 2001. 'Has Voluntary Association Activity Declined? Cross-national Analyses for Fifteen Countries', *Canadian Review of Sociology and Anthropology* 38: 249–74.

Banton, Michael. 1992. 'The Nature and Causes of Racism and Racial Discrimination', *International Sociology* 7: 69–84.

Beaujot, Roderic. 1991. *Population Change in Canada: The Challenges of Policy Adaptation*. Toronto: McClelland & Stewart.

Bell, David, and Lorne Tepperman. 1979. *The Roots of Disunity: A Look at Canadian Political Culture*. Toronto: McClelland & Stewart.

Boserup, Ester. 1965. *The Conditions of Agricultural Growth: The Economics of Agrarian Change under Population Pressure*. Chicago: Aldine.

Boudreau, Julie-Anne. 1998. 'Inhabitants of a Megacity: The Urbanity of Citizens for Local Democracy', paper presented at the annual meeting of the International Sociological Association.

Bourdieu, Pierre. 1984. *Distinction*. Cambridge, Mass.: Harvard University Press.

Boyd, David. 2001. *Canada vs. the OECD: An Environment Comparison*. Victoria, BC: Eco-Research Chair, University of Victoria. Available at: <www.environmentalindicators.com/htdocs/PDF/CanadavsOECD.pdf>; accessed 25 Mar. 2003.

Bray, R., et al. 2005. *Report on Public Health and Urban Sprawl in Ontario: A Review of the Pertinent Literature*. Toronto: Environmental Health Committee, Ontario College of Family Physicians. Available at: <www.ocfp.on.ca/local/files/Communications/Current%20Issues/Urban%20Sprawl-Jan-05.pdf>; accessed 29 Oct. 2005.

Breton, R. 1964. 'Institutional Completeness of Ethnic Communities and the Personal Relations of Immigrants', *American Journal of Sociology* 70, 2: 193–205.

Burman, Sandra, and Margaret Naude. 1991. 'Bearing a Bastard: The Social Consequences of Illegitimacy in Cape Town, 1896–1939', *Journal of Southern African Studies* 17: 373–413.

Caldwell, Gary, and Daniel Fournier. 1987. 'The Quebec Question: A Matter of Population', *Canadian Journal of Sociology* 12: 16–41.

Calthorpe, Peter. 1993. *The Next American Metropolis: Ecology, Community, and the American Dream*. New York: Princeton Architectural Press.

Coale, Ansley J. 1974. 'The History of the Human Population', in *The Human Population*. New York: Scientific American, 15–25.

Cohen, Joel. 1995. *How Many People Can the Earth Support?* New York: Norton.

Cohen, Linc. 1992. 'Waste Dumps Toxic Traps for Minorities', *Chicago Reporter* 21, 4: 6–9, 11. Available at: <www.chicagoreporter.com/1992/04-92/0492WasteDumpsToxicTrapsforMinorities.htm>; accessed 27 Feb. 2003.

Coming Clean. 2006. 'Body Burden'. Available at: <www.chemicalbodyburden.org>; accessed 8 Feb. 2006.

Curtis, James E., Douglas E. Baer, and Edward G. Grabb. 2001. 'Nations of Joiners: Explaining Voluntary Association Membership in Democratic Societies', *American Sociological Review* 66: 783–805.

Daily Bread Food Bank. 2002, 2006. *Poorer People, Poorer Health: The Health of Food Bank Recipients, Spring Food Drive*. Toronto: Daily Bread Food Bank.

Daniel, W.W. 1987. *Workplace Industrial Relations and Technical Change*. London: PSI/Frances Pinter.

Davis, Kingsley. 1988. 'Social Science Approaches to International Migration', *Population and Development Review* 14 (suppl.): 245–61.

Dear, M.J. 2001. *From Chicago to L.A.: Making Sense of Urban Theory*. Thousand Oaks, Calif.: Sage.

————, H.E. Schockman, and G. Hise, eds. 1996. *Rethinking Los Angeles*. Thousand Oaks, Calif.: Sage.

———— and S.M. Taylor. 1982. *Not on Our Street: Community Attitudes to Mental Health Care*. London: Pion.

Dei, George J. Sefa. 1996. *Anti-Racism Education: Theory and Practice*. Halifax: Fernwood.

Dickason, Olive Patricia. 2002. *Canada's First Nations: A History of Founding Peoples from Earliest Times*, 3rd edn. Toronto: Oxford University Press.

Duany, Andres, Elizabeth Plater-Zyberk, and Jeff Speck. 2000. *Suburban Nation: The Rise of Sprawl and the Decline of the American Dream*. New York: North Point Press.

Emerson, Michael O., George Yancey, and Karen J. Chai. 2001. 'Does Race Matter in Residential Segregation? Exploring the Preferences of White Americans', *American Sociological Review* 66: 922–35.

Farb, Peter. 1978. *Man's Rise to Civilization: The Cultural Ascent of the Indians of North America*, 2nd edn. New York: Bantam.

Florida, Richard L. 2002. *The Rise of the Creative Class: And How It's Transforming Work, Leisure, Community and Everyday Life*. New York: Basic Books.

Foot, David K. 1982. *Canada's Population Outlook: Demographic Futures and Economic Challenges*. Toronto: Lorimer.

Franks, Tim. 2005. 'Cows Make Fuel for Biogas Train', BBC News on-line, 24 Oct. Available at: <news.bbc.co.uk/2/hi/science/nature/4373440.stm>; accessed 4 Mar. 2006.

Freund, Peter, and George Martin. 2000. 'Driving South: The Globalization of Auto Consumption and Its Social Organization of Space', *Capitalism, Nature, Socialism* 11, 4: 51–71.

Gans, Herbert. 1982. *The Urban Villagers: Group and Class in the Life of Italian-Americans*, 2nd edn. New York: Free Press.

Gardner, Gary. 1998. 'When Cities Take Bicycles Seriously', *World Watch* 11, 5: 16–22.

Garreau, Joel. 1991. *Edge City: Life on the New Frontier*. New York: Doubleday.

Greenpeace. 2001. 'Pacific in Peril'. Available at: <www.greenpeace.org>; accessed 14 May 2001.

Harpham, Trudy, Salma Burton, and Ilona Blue. 2001. 'Healthy City Projects in Developing Countries: The First Evaluation', *Health Promotion International* 16, 2: 111–25.

Hawkins, Freda. 1972. *Canada and Immigration: Public Policy and Public Concern*. Montreal and Kingston: McGill-Queen's University Press.

Heisz, Andrew, and Sébastien LaRochelle-Côté. 2005. *Work and Community in Census Metropolitan Areas, 1996–2001*. Ottawa: Statistics Canada.

Helfgott, Roy B. 1988. *Computerized Manufacturing and Human Resources: Innovation through Employee Involvement*. Lexington, Mass.: Lexington Books.

Henripin, Jacques. 1974. *Immigration and Language Imbalance: Green Paper on Immigration*. Ottawa: Manpower and Immigration.

Higley, Stephen Richard. 1995. *Privilege, Power and Place: The Geography of the American Upper Class*. Lanham, Md: Rowman & Littlefield.

Hise, Greg, Michael J. Dear, and H. Eric Schockman. 1996. 'Rethinking Los Angeles', in Dear, Schockman, and Hise, eds, *Rethinking Los Angeles*. Thousand Oaks, Calif.: Sage, 1–14.

Inglehart, Ronald. 1977. *The Silent Revolution: Changing Values and Political Styles among Western Publics*. Princeton, NJ: Princeton University Press.

————. 1990. *Culture Shift in Advanced Industrial Society*. Princeton, NJ: Princeton University Press.

International Food Policy Research Institute (IFPRI). 1997. 'Report Finds World Water Supplies Dwindling While Demand Rises; World Food Production, Health, and Environment at Risk', press release. Available at: <www.ifpri.org/pressrel/030997.htm>; accessed 25 Mar. 2003.

International Survey of Mayors. 2002. Available at: <magnet.undp.org/docs/urban/maysur.htm>; accessed 28 Feb. 2003.

Jacobs, Jane. 1993 [1961]. *The Death and Life of Great American Cities*. New York: Random House.

Kalbach, W.E. 1970. *The Impact of Immigration on Canada's Population*. Ottawa: Dominion Bureau of Statistics.

Kay, Jane H. 1997. *Asphalt Nation: How the Automobile Took Over America and How We Can Take It Back*. New York: Random House.

Klonglan, Gerald E., George M. Beal, Joe M. Bohlen, and E. Walter Coward Jr. 1971. 'Conceptualizing and Measuring the Diffusion of Innovations', *Sociologia Ruralis* 11, 1: 36–48.

Lachapelle, Réjean. 1980. 'Evolution of Ethnic and Linguistic Composition', in Raymond Breton, Jeffrey Reitz, and Victor Valentine, eds, *Cultural Boundaries and the Cohesion of Canada*. Montreal: Institute for Research on Public Policy, 15–43.

Lavoie, Yolande. 1972. *L'émigration des Canadiens aux États-Unis avant 1930*. Collection Demographie canadienne 1. Montreal: Presses de l'Université de Montréal.

Lee, Richard B. 1979. *The !Kung San: Men, Women and Work in a Foraging Society*. Cambridge: Cambridge University Press.

Ley, David. 1996. *The New Middle Class and the Remaking of the Central City*. Oxford: Oxford University Press.

————. 2003. 'Artists, Aethesticisation and the Field of Gentrification', *Urban Studies* 40, 12: 2527–44.

Li, Peter S. 2003. *Destination Canada: Immigration Debates and Issues*. Toronto: Oxford University Press.

Livi-Bacci, Massimo. 1992. *A Concise History of World Population: An Introduction to Population Processes*, trans. Carl Ipsen. Cambridge, Mass.: Blackwell.

Lowe, Marcia. 1995. 'Reclaiming Cities for People', in Sue Zielinski and Gordon Laird, eds, *Beyond the Car: Essays on the Auto Culture*. Toronto: Steel Rail Publishing, 129–36.

Lucas, Rex. 1972. *Minetown, Milltown, Railtown: Life in Canadian Communities of Single Industry*. Toronto: University of Toronto Press.

Lutz, Wolfgang, Warren Sanderson, and Sergei Scherbov. 2001. 'The End of the World Population Growth', *Nature* 412: 543–5.

Malthus, Thomas R. 1959 [1798]. *Population: The First Essay*. Ann Arbor: University of Michigan Press.

Ministry of Finance Canada. 2005. *Budget 2005: A New Deal for Canada's Communities* (informational pamphlet). Available at: <www.fin.gc.ca/budget05/pamph/pacome.htm>; accessed 4 Mar. 2006.

Moberg, David. 1997. 'Chicago: To Be or Not to Be a Global City', *World Policy Journal* 14: 71–86.

NASA. 2006. '2005 Warmest Year in Over a Century'. Available at: <www.nasa.gov/vision/earth/environment/2005_warmest.html>; accessed 5 Feb. 2006.

Neptis Foundation. 2002. *Toronto-Related Region Futures Study: Interim Report—Implications of Business-As-Usual Development*. Toronto: Neptis Foundation.

Newton, Keith, and Norm Lockie. 1987. 'Employment Effects of Technological Change', *New Technology, Work and Employment* 2, 2.

Northcott, Jim, Michael Fogarty, and Malcolm Trevor. 1985. *Chips and Jobs: Acceptance of New Technology at Work*. London: PSI.

——— and Annette Walling. 1988. *The Impact of Microelectronics*. London: PSI.

Oakley, Deirdre A. 1999. 'Keeping Homeless Individuals Homeless: City Politics and the Zoning of Permanent Housing for Street Alcoholics', paper presented at the annual meeting of the American Sociological Association.

Paccione, Michael. 2001. *Urban Geography: A Global Perspective*. New York: Routledge.

Perrow, Charles. 1999. *Normal Accidents: Living with High Risk Technologies*, 2nd edn. Princeton, NJ: Princeton University Press.

Population Reference Bureau. 2001. *World Population Data Sheet, 2001*. Washington: Population Reference Bureau.

———. 2006. Available at: <www.prb.org>; accessed 5 Feb. 2006.

Porter, John. 1965. *The Vertical Mosaic: An Analysis of Social Class and Power in Canada*. Toronto: University of Toronto Press.

Putnam, Robert D. 2000. *Bowling Alone: The Collapse and Revival of American Community*. New York: Simon & Schuster.

Redburn, David E. 2002. 'Urban Sprawl in the Upstate of South Carolina: Do City and County Residents' Attitudes Diverge?', paper presented at the annual meeting of the Southern Sociological Society.

Redelmeier, Donald A., and Robert J. Tibshirani. 1997. 'Association between Cellular-Telephone Calls and Motor Vehicle Collisions', *New England Journal of Medicine* 336: 453–8.

Reitz, Jeffrey G. 1994. *The Illusion of Difference: Realities of Ethnicity in Canada and the United States*. Toronto: C.D. Howe Institute.

———. 1998. *Warmth of the Welcome: The Social Causes of Economic Success in Different Nations and Cities*. Boulder, Colo.: Westview Press.

Rogers, Andrei, John F. Watkins, and Jennifer A. Woodward. 1990. 'Interregional Elderly Migration and Population Redistribution in Four Industrialized Countries: A Comparative Analysis', *Research on Aging* 12: 251–93.

Rybczynski, Witold. 1995. *City Life: Urban Expectations in a New World*. Toronto: HarperCollins.

Sauvy, Alfred, and Paul Demeny. 1990. 'Alfred Sauvy on the World Population Problem: A View in 1949', *Population and Development Review* 16: 759–74.

Schmidt, Robert R. 1999. 'An Analysis of the Causes and Consequences of Urban Sprawl on the Las Vegas Valley', Ph.D. thesis, University of Nevada at Las Vegas.

Schoenfeld, A. Clay, Robert F. Meier, and Robert J. Griffin. 1979. 'Constructing a Social Problem: The Press and the Environment', *Social Problems* 27: 38–61.

Sears, Alan. 1990. 'Immigration Controls as Social Policy: The Case of Canadian Medical Inspection 1900–1920', *Studies in Political Economy* 33: 91–112.

Simmel, Georg. 1950 [1917]. *The Sociology of Georg Simmel*, trans. Kurt Wolff. New York: Free Press.

Simon, Julian L. 1996. *The Ultimate Resource 2*. Princeton, NJ: Princeton University Press.

Sjoberg, Gideon. 1965. *The Preindustrial City, Past and Present*. New York: Free Press.

Smith, Keith. 2001. *Environmental Hazards: Assessing Risk and Reducing Disaster*, 3rd edn. New York: Routledge.

Statistics Canada. 2002. 'English-French Bilingualism'. Available at: <www12.statcan.ca/english/census01/products/analytic/companion/lang/bilingual.cfm>; accessed 24 Mar. 2003.

Tepperman, Lorne. 2001. 'The Postmaterialist Thesis: Has There Been a Shift in Political Cultures?', in Douglas Baer, ed., *Political Sociology: Canadian Perspectives*. Toronto: Oxford University Press, 15–36.

Tönnies, Ferdinand. 1957 [1887]. *Community and Society (Gemeinschaft und Gesellschaft)*. New York: Harper and Row.

United Nations Population Division (UNPD). 2006. *World Urbanization Prospects: The 2003 Revision Population Database*. Available at: <esa.un.org/unup>; accessed 6 Feb. 2006.

United States Energy Information Administration. 2001. 'World Primary Energy Consumption (Btu) 1990–1999, Table E1'. Available at: <www.eia.doe.gov/emeu/iea/tablee1.html>; accessed 30 Jan. 2003.

United Way of Greater Toronto/Canadian Council on Social Development. 2004. *Poverty by Postal Code: The Geography of Neighbourhood Poverty, City of Toronto, 1981–2001*. Toronto: United Way of Greater Toronto.

van de Walle, Etienne, and John Knodel. 1980. 'Europe's Fertility Transition: New Evidence and Lessons for Today's Developing World', *Population Bulletin* 34: 6.

Vancouver Task Force on Atmospheric Change. 1990. *Clouds of Change: Final Report of the City of Vancouver Task Force on Atmospheric Change*, vol. 1. Vancouver: City of Vancouver.

Vining, Daniel L. 1989. 'The "Demographic Problem" in Israel', *Mankind Quarterly* 30, 1 and 2: 65–9.

Weber, Max. 1958 [1921]. *The City*, trans. Don Martindale and Gertrud Neuwirth. New York: Free Press.

————. 1981 [1924]. *General Economic History*. New Brunswick, NJ: Transaction Books.

Wellman, Barry, and Keith Hampton. 1999. 'Netville On-line and Off-line: Observing and Surveying a Wired Suburb', *American Behavioral Scientist* 43: 475–92.

Whyte, William H. 1996. 'The Design of Spaces from City: Rediscovering the Center', in *The City Reader*, edited by 483–90. New York: Routledge.

Wirth, Louis. 1938. 'Urbanism as a Way of Life.' in Richard T. Legates and Frederic Stout, eds, *On Cities and Social Life*. Chicago: University of Chicago Press, 60–83.

World Health Organization (WHO). 1997. *Health and Environment in Sustainable Development: Five Years after the Earth Summit*. Geneva: WHO.

————. 1999. *Report on Infectious Diseases*. Geneva: WHO. Available at: <www.who.int/infectious-disease-report/index-rpt99.html>; accessed 23 Feb. 2003.

World Meteorological Organization (WMO). 2000. 'WMO Statement on the Status of the Global Climate in 1999' (WMO No. 913). Available at: <www.wmo.ch/web/wcp/wcdmp/statement/html/913-1999.html>; accessed 14 May 2001.

World Resources Institute. 1998. *Climate, Biodiversity, and Forests: Issues and Opportunities Emerging from the Kyoto Protocol*. Baltimore: World Resources Institute.

CHAPTER TWELVE

WAR AND TERRORISM

LEARNING OBJECTIVES

- To learn basic facts about war.
- To know definitions of war.
- To understand the role religion may play in war and terrorism.
- To see how gender socialization affects attitudes towards violence.
- To appreciate the contribution of world systems theory to understanding war and terrorism.
- To be able to identify what each of the different theoretical perspectives adds to the academic study of the violence of war.
- To understand the social and health outcomes of war.
- To discover possible solutions to global war and terrorism.

Introduction

This chapter is about war and terrorism, conflict and combat, soldiers and civilians. At no point in recorded history has there been a complete absence of conflict between groups of humans. It seems that when people are around, wars occur. There are no societies that are known to have avoided war. Thus, warfare appears to be a human universal.

Yet, Canada is an especially un-warlike nation. Compared with the US military, the Canadian Forces are few, underfunded, and stuck with old equipment. It would be unreasonable to assume the wish to wage war is a human universal; most Canadians lack such a desire. Canadians go to war only when they are pushed into it, usually by loyalty to a close ally like Britain, as occurred during both world wars. Despite loyalty to our ally the United States, few Canadians served in Korea in the early 1950s, and no Canadian troops were sent to Vietnam or (more recently) Iraq. Their presence in Afghanistan, on the other hand, has begun to cause political doubt in some quarters as Canadian soldiers are wounded and killed in action. Elsewhere, in Rwanda, Canadian forces sought to serve a peacekeeping role, and for many years they have filled this role with success in such places as Egypt, the former Yugoslavia, and Cyprus.

We cannot understand warfare without understanding politics and statecraft since, as the early nineteenth-century Prussian military thinker Karl von Clausewitz (1993 [1833]) wrote, 'war is not merely a political act, but also a real political instrument, a continuation of political commerce, a carrying out the same by other means.'

A Snapshot of the Canadian Forces and National Defence

■ The budget for national defence is approximately $14 billion (in 2005-6).

■ The Department of National Defence is the third largest employer in Canada and the largest single public-sector employer.

■ There are more than 110,000 Canadian military personnel in Canada and around the world, including approximately 61,500 Regular Force and 24,500 Primary Reserve, 4,000 Canadian Rangers, and 21,000 civilian personnel.

■ More than 1,300 Canadian Forces personnel are deployed on 17 international operations in 16 countries.

Source: From the Canadian International Policy Statement 2005. Available at: <www.dfait-maeci.gc.ca/cip-pic/ips/infokitdnd-en.asp>; accessed 2 Jan. 2006.

Some political conditions make war more likely to break out. For example, a ruling party's need to deflect domestic criticism by focusing national attention on external enemies, real or imagined, increases the likelihood of war. In other words, one role of conflict with an outside group—as in a war—is to increase social cohesion and conformity within the nation. Warfare clarifies the social boundaries between insiders and outsiders, loyal citizens and traitors.

Just as some groups are more warlike than others, some periods of history have also been more warlike than others. This suggests that sociological variables likely explain this variation. So even if we can never find ways to erase war, we can hope to find ways to reduce war's frequency.

As we shall see, the scale and nature of war has changed with the rapid pace of technological innovation. In the last century, it has become possible to kill thousands with the push of a button, at long distances without seeing the faces of victims. War has psychological and cultural as well as political and financial aspects. In times of war, politicians use a special language to legitimize combat and reduce the emotional impact of the massive numbers of deaths that will follow. Propaganda plays a large part in storytelling about wars and helps to increase public engagement. In their recruitment materials, the military always stresses honour, courage, and sacrifice for the greater good as defining characteristics of the 'ideal soldier'.

As we shall also see, globalization has affected warfare as it has affected everything else. With around-the-clock news coverage, e-mail, and telecommunications networks, we are made endlessly and instantaneously aware of events in other parts of the world. In addition, causes affecting the outbreak of wars, such as ethnic conflicts, resound throughout the world, through the diasporic networks of immigrants that we discussed in Chapter 4.

These and other changes in warfare have been examined by various sociological approaches, and different conclusions have been reached. War continues to have important social and health outcomes. Though often good for the economy, war is bad for living things; with the pursuit of nuclear, chemical, and bacterial weapons, it is likely to get worse. Though social problems related to poverty and conflict may often be improved by warfare in the short run, in the long run everyone suffers.

We shall also see that the health outcomes of war are varied and vast. Moreover, though researchers have studied the effects of war on soldiers in the medical literature since the US Civil War, only within the past few decades have they studied civilian suffering from military conflicts. Research on civilians caught in a war finds that exposure to terrorism leads to psychiatric difficulties in later life. Added to the visible losses of lives and limbs, spouses and parents, are the less visible injuries: the losses of opportunities and futures. To begin then, we note that wars—and their associated glories and horrors—are both widespread and recurrent over time.

War as Recurrent and Widespread

War—the pattern of large groups of people systematically trying to kill one another—is a common and persistent fact of human life. One has to wonder why people have repeatedly undertaken war in the face of massive human casualties, property damage, and public expense. Because of war's persistence, peace scarcely has a real meaning except in short outbursts.

Consider the last century. In *The Age of Extremes* (1994), historian Eric Hobsbawm divided the twentieth century into three periods based on their levels of warfare and violence: the first period had two large-scale global conflicts; the second had relative peace (or at least the relative absence of warfare) for about two decades; and the last period saw the revival of international and intranational hostilities. In Hobsbawm's words, people of the twentieth century:

> lived and thought in terms of world war, even when the guns were silent and the bombs were not exploding.... For those who had grown up before 1914 the contrast was so dramatic that many of them refused to see any continuity with the past. 'Peace' meant 'before 1914': after that came something that no longer deserved the name. (Hobsbawm, 1994: 6)

For innocent civilians caught in the middle, the effects of war can be devastating. Unlike soldiers, who can at least justify their participation as military personnel, civilians are not prepared or trained to fight. Nonetheless, they are often forced participants in the horrors of war.

For both people in uniforms and for civilians, war is a repeated nightmare. To understand its repetition, we need to understand war's roots in politics, ideology, and religion. Only then will we start to understand why people let their children go off by the hundreds of thousands to be killed in battle.

Politics, the State, and Warfare

The Role of the State

Within any social unit—family, school, community, state, or otherwise—any conflict over resources is a political conflict. In conflicts of every type, the state has a special part to play: it always watches and seeks to control the ways that other groups compete.

The state is a set of public organizations that makes and enforces decisions binding every member of a society (Weber, 1946). It includes an elected government, civil service, courts, police, and military. At one extreme of political life, we find the authoritarian state, which tries to fully dominate civil society and penetrate everyday life. Compared with our Canadian government, the authoritarian state is extremely repressive.

Fascist authoritarian states typically appear when a landed aristocracy remains in power during industrialization, keeping the middle class small, weak, and disorganized (Moore, 1967). With the aid of the military, the Church, and the bankers, the landed aristocrats control the state in their own interest. Military support for the ruling party or dictator is central to most if not all authoritarian political states. Typically, military officers and institutions are culturally sympathetic to the goals of authoritarian regimes such as order over liberty and tradition over modernity. They also see opportunities for enrichment and career advancement by supporting war and by supporting authoritarianism. Thus, warfare is a secondary effect of the connection between the military and the state in authoritarian regimes.

In their need to stifle rebellious elements like the peasantry and workers, authoritarian regimes often use warfare to promote patriotic cohesion and justify cracking down on political dissidents as 'traitors'. The dominant cultural imagery of authoritarian regimes—including various representations of past glory, racial purity, defence of the fatherland (as by the Nazis) or motherland (as by the Soviets), mythical figures, and national heroes—brings war to the forefront as a measure of the nation's courage, pride, and strength. Thus, war is viewed as an activity that carries a glorious past onto new glories. By contrast, non-authoritarian regimes normally use economic or sporting competition to pump up a national sense of achievement.

In Canada, the military has never played an important role in maintaining the status of the ruling elite, compared with many African and South American countries (for example, Nigeria, Brazil, and Paraguay). There and in other countries with less stable economic and bureaucratic elites, the military dictator or junta (that is, ruling group) is a fixture of political life. More often than not, military dictators and juntas draw their strength from the help, co-operation, or tacit approval of bureaucratic and economic elites in other, more developed societies.

A society like Canada's, in which power is shared among competing political, bureaucratic, and economic elites, is likely to have difficulty mobilizing the will and the assets to make war. For this reason, decentralized leadership is likely to be less warlike than centralized or, especially, dictatorial leadership.

Another factor influencing politics and war is ideology. An **ideology** is a system of beliefs that 'explain' how society is or should be organized. Ideologies are important for social change because they motivate and control people. Before people can change their political order, they must imagine a new order worth working towards. People must have faith in that vision of the future and in the political leaders whom they expect would carry out that vision.

Box 12.1 Social Policy: The Canadian Forces and International Operations

The Canadian Forces must remain capable of participating in a wide range of operations overseas, particularly when dealing with the complex, fluid and dangerous environment of failed and failing states. These will include:

- *combat operations*, such as those conducted during the Kosovo air campaign and with the United States in Afghanistan;
- *complex peace support and stabilization missions*, such as those carried out with NATO in Bosnia and with the International Security Assistance Force in Afghanistan;
- *maritime interdiction operations*, such as those conducted in the Persian Gulf after the first Gulf War, and as part of the campaign against terrorism;
- *traditional peacekeeping and observer operations*, such as those carried out by the UN in the Middle East for many years, and, more recently in Ethiopia/Eritrea;
- *humanitarian assistance missions*, such as those conducted by the Disaster Assistance Response Team in Honduras, Turkey and, more recently, Sri Lanka; and
- *evacuation operations* to assist Canadians in countries threatened by imminent conflict and turmoil, as we have done in Haiti.

In the new security environment, the Canadian Forces could find themselves in situations where they are conducting several of these operations simultaneously in one theatre.

Source: Defence Policy Statement: Contributing to a Safer and More Secure World, 2005. Reproduced courtesy of the Department of National Defence, with the permission of the Minister of Public Works and Government Services, 2007.

In recent years, organized religions and religious leaders have gained more power than they had in much of the twentieth century. This rebirth of religion testifies largely to the downfall of communism, an ideology and political system that had tried to destroy organized religion, which Karl Marx had viewed as 'the opiate of the masses' (see Tucker, 1978). In many parts of the world today, fundamentalist religions are gaining power—Christian fundamentalism is politically important in the United States, Jewish fundamentalism in Israel, and Islamic fundamentalism in Pakistan and other Islamic states in Africa and Asia.

Fundamentalist religions seek to control the minds, hearts, and loyalties of their members, and fundamentalist religious leaders can have significant political influence. This was true of Billy Graham in the United States through seven presidencies in the last half of the twentieth century, as it was in somewhat different fashion with Ayatollah Ruhollah Khomeini in Iran during the late 1970s and early 1980s, and, more recently, with the Taliban government and rebel terrorist Osama bin Laden in Afghanistan. In some cases fundamentalist movements and their leaders are created or propped up by capitalists outside the country to prevent the election to power of liberal, socialist, or Marxist critics of capitalism.

To be sure, fundamentalism is an extremist religious position that diverges significantly from the more moderate belief systems of many of the world's faithful. Indeed, many religious activists work in less violent ways to change the political order. Catholic nuns, for example, have campaigned for increased status for women and an end to spousal abuse; many leading religious figures have campaigned for peace; and in a few outstanding cases, a single individual, as spokesperson for a religious movement, has become associated with a civil cause. Looking to the recent past, anyone who has heard of South Africa's successful move to racial equality knows the name of Archbishop Desmond Tutu, and anyone who has heard of the US civil rights movement knows about the achievements of Dr Martin Luther King.

In many societies, the Church—like the military—was until recently a major social institution that not only controlled large amounts of land and wealth, but also controlled ideology and popular thinking. In these societies, the Church was a major means of upward social mobility, and for those who reached the top, a means of political influence. In countries like Canada, where religion and politics are constitutionally separate, there is no church that enjoys this degree of political or ideological power.

Though there is no state church in the United States, in recent years fundamentalist Protestantism has exercised a disproportionate political influence at the highest political levels. This fact points both to the more important role of religion in American culture and to the superior organization of American religion through the formation of cults, sects, and churches—all of which are protected in the US Constitution far more than they are in Canada.

The Role of Social Movements

In every society, people mobilize to influence public policy, forming social movements when membership reaches a critical mass. From a social constructionist viewpoint, they are practising moral entrepreneurship and mobilizing assets to get their messages across.

Social movements are more numerous and more successful at some times than at others, though there are contending theories about how and when this works. One theory—**relative deprivation theory**—argues that movements arise when many people

al-Qa'ida (also spelled al-Qaida and al-Qaeda):
- means 'the base' in Arabic;
- founded in 1988 by Osama bin Laden, a Saudi-born millionaire;
- a terrorist organization that supports the activities of Muslim extremists around the world.

Source: Jacobs et al. (2003).

feel deprived in comparison with other people. They perceive a gap between the social rewards they are getting and those they are entitled to get, and feel cheated when they compare their own lives with those of others. These people want to join a **social movement** whose goal is to change the distribution of social rewards. Compared with absolute deprivation—a serious, visible, and lengthy lack of social rewards—relative deprivation is largely subjective and even temporary. Yet relative deprivation is more likely than absolute deprivation to produce social movements.

By this standard, social movements gain the strongest support when there is a 'revolution of rising expectations' (Runciman, 1967). That is, people typically protest under improving conditions, not grinding, desperate poverty. Improving conditions make it easier for people to protest because they are not so fully preoccupied with the struggle to survive. Also, when people's lives improve, their expectations for change often grow faster than the rate at which change is taking place. A sense of deprivation causes feelings of frustration and discontent. Such feelings are necessary for social movements to emerge. Still, they are not enough by themselves to start a movement. Many discontented people never join, let alone form, social movements. Before a movement forms, leaders must satisfy another condition, resource mobilization.

Resource mobilization theory addresses the methods leaders use to put forward their views. This theory looks not at why people want to promote or resist social change, but at how they launch social movements. It acknowledges that discontent is necessary to spark a social movement. Yet discontent is a constant of human life, always lurking in the background, waiting to express itself. Without assets, discontent can never express itself as a social force. It remains hidden or comes out in non-political, personal pathologies—as random violence, mental illness, heavy drinking, domestic violence, and so on.

Important elements in political organization include assets such as effective leadership, public support, money, legal aid, ties with influential officials and public personalities, and access to the mass media. Occasionally, political organizing also means acquiring and learning to use weapons. Without access to such key assets, discontented people cannot change society or resist the powerful, so they rarely attempt it. Thus, the success or failure of a social movement hinges on access to key assets, and not necessarily a change in levels of contentment.

World System Theory

Politics occurs between states as well as within them. One theory that examines the relations between states in a global system is **world system theory** (see Wallerstein, 1976, 2004). This theory explains the uneven pace of development in the world by looking at the unequal relations between different countries. Industrial core states take much of the raw materials and cheap labour they need from less developed peripheral states. Because they are financially and politically dominant, core states have the power to extract an economic surplus from the periphery. Investors from the core states effectively control the economies of peripheral states. As a result, profits made in the periphery drain out of the local economy and flow back to the core.

Core states are frequently accused of engaging in **imperialism**, the exercise of political and economic control by one state over the territory of another. Throughout history, this has often been accomplished through military means. However, domination does not always require military conquest and colonization. In fact, under the right conditions, economic imperialism is far safer, less costly, and usually more stable than military or political imperialism. This is precisely how first Britain and then the United States have controlled Canada. And, between 1945 and the fall of the Soviet Union, the battle for hegemony between capitalism and communism was more often economic, political, and cultural than it was military. In this respect, MTV, Coca-Cola, and McDonald's were important means of infiltrating and co-opting foreign populations.

With the increased imbalance in political affairs since 1989, military imperialism has once again resurfaced in Iraq and elsewhere. David Harvey (2005), in his book *The New Imperialism*, notes the diversity of different forms of imperialism and argues that the recent move towards a militarized neo-conservative imperialism in the United States, as shown in the unilateral determination to invade Iraq, suggests weakness rather than strength in the US's quest to maintain its dominant position in the world.

Globalization Processes

Globalization is the end point of world system-building—the construction of a single world market. Globalization is also the trend of increasing interdependence between the economies and societies of the world. Some view it as just another name for US imperialism; others view it as the highest stage of what Émile Durkheim (1960 [1893]) called organic solidarity, or interdependence based on difference. The global economy as it exists today is a form of world social organization with six defining features. To understand the current state of global politics and war, we must recognize these characteristics:

1. There is *global economic interdependence*. This means that most societies trade goods and services with one another. People are all buyers and sellers in a single world market.
2. A driving force for change is *scientific and technological innovation*. New methods for producing goods and services are continuously developed.
3. The key actors in a global economy are *'built' or corporate entities*, especially multinational corporations (like General Motors, IBM, Toyota, and Exxon). Individuals, small local firms, and even nationwide businesses lose in the competition for international markets.
4. *Cultures and polities are polycentric*—that is, they are found in and influenced by activities in many nations. More cultures today are dispersed, with centres of activity throughout the world.
5. A changing 'world culture' *homogenizes human ambitions*, narrowing the variety of wishes and lifestyles. More people everywhere act like Americans. Likewise, Europeans think and act like the French, English, and Germans—the dominant actors in the European Union.
6. Most relevant to this discussion, *economic globalization forces nation-states to change*. With less influence over the culture and economy, governments have less influence over the people they rule. With these changes come political stresses and upheavals and the formation of new social movements and ideologies.

Hybridization

As mentioned above, the key actors in a global economy are multinational corporations. Currently, multinational corporations control half the world's total economic production. Multinationals, consequently, have huge political importance. Some have budgets larger than most countries. They gather and spend huge amounts of money, create and cancel many jobs. As a result, multinationals are important members of every financial community, yet they are loyal to none. They move their operations wherever they can to increase their profits, regardless of the results left behind for the countries in which they did business.

Globalization does not, however, erase the role of traditional cultures, nor does it reduce the number of world cultures:

> As the changing pattern of world trade intensely shapes our national living standards and the vitality of our local communities, it is also dramatically transforming the social and cultural foundations of many so-called 'developing' nations. The rapidity of these changes, with heightened fears over preserving their national sovereignty, environmental standards, and traditional cultural values, is contributing to growing social and political movements in developing countries to resist the growing political and culture influence of multinational corporations. (Harper and Leicht, 2002)

As states and local cultures influence the uses made of foreign cultural products, the result is a new 'hybrid', or crossbreed, of the two cultures. This hybridization is dialectical, a result of opposing currents. According to political scientist Benjamin Barber (1996), there is on the one hand a 'McWorld' influence—Western cultural homogenization and the dominance of consumerist capitalism. This brings uniformity and secular cultural detachment from a nation's own history and identity. On the other hand, there is a 'Jihad' influence—a reaction against Euro-Americanism. Named after the Islamic word for a holy war against infidels, the Jihad influence (the phrase is used in this context to refer to any form of religious or tribal fundamentalism, and does not necessarily imply Muslim involvement) brings conflict, even war. Neither influence—McWorld or Jihad—can prevail because each represents hundreds of millions of people and each reflects a genuine cultural commitment. The two impulses are locked in conflict in many less developed societies.

The Nature of War and Terrorism

Having set the political and economic context, we can now discuss the character of warfare and terrorism in the twenty-first century.

Definitions

Most people consider **war** to be an armed conflict between two countries or between groups within a country. However, many would also expand the definition of war to include undeclared battles, guerrilla wars, covert operations, and even terrorism (Wright, 1964). Many countries—among them the United States, whose 'military-industrial complex' was first brought to public attention by President Dwight Eisenhower—even have a war system, in which units of their social institutions, such as economies and governments, and their cultural practices promote warfare as a normal aspect of life—even if no war is being waged at that particular moment (Cancian and Gibson, 1990).

War, at the least, is an institution of **collective violence**. Collective violence is organized group violence used to promote an agenda or resist an unjust other. Unlike **interpersonal violence**, which is more episodic, unorganized, and impulsive, modern warfare relies on unemotional killing and advanced technology. Because of advances in military technology over the past century, people can now wage wars against enemies thousands of kilometres away, so the killers and the killed may never even see one another face to face. As well, the weaponry used in modern combat is exponentially more deadly than even a century ago. Arrows, rifles, and swords require proximity to the target and usually claim only one life per shot or swing. In contrast, a single precision-guided missile released by a B-52 bomber many thousands of feet above the war zone can kill hundreds of enemy soldiers. The nuclear bomb dropped on Hiroshima in the last days of World War II is estimated to have killed 80,000 people instantly. No wonder, then, the twentieth century was the bloodiest hundred years in the history of human warfare.

Though people may be able to agree on an expanded definition of war, they may still disagree about the causes of wars and about the ways we might prevent them. For example, people still argue about the causes and effects of the two world wars of the twentieth century. They argue even more about the nature, causes, and effects of terrorism.

Terrorism: The Poor Man's War

Terrorism may be best viewed as a 'poor man's war', a war that is fought by new rules. Terrorism can be defined as:

> the calculated use of unexpected, shocking, and unlawful violence against non-combatants (including, in addition to civilians, off-duty military and security personnel in peaceful situations) and other symbolic targets perpetrated by a clandestine member(s) of a subnational group or a clandestine agent(s) for the psychological purpose of publicizing a political or religious cause and/or intimidating or coercing a government(s) or civilian population into accepting demands on behalf of the cause. (Hudson and Den Boer, 2002: 1)

A dispassionate formal definition of the term is difficult because terrorism is an ideological and value-laden term, as well as a description of events. An even broader, simpler definition characterizes terrorism as any act by an individual or by a group that is intended to undermine the lawful authority of a government or state.

There have been many global terrorism acts during the past hundred years. It was through terrorism that the Irish were able to force British troops out of what is today the Republic of Ireland. By means of terrorism, the Mau Mau tribe forced the British out of Kenya, and Jewish settlers forced the British to give up Palestine (now Israel) to United Nations supervision. Continued terrorism in Chechnya has cost the Russian Federation many lives and many millions of rubles. Continued acts of terrorism in Sri Lanka and the Democratic Republic of Congo have pitted tribal or ethnic groups against another, with many subsequent deaths but as yet no resolutions. We learn from these many examples that terrorism is, by now, a well-established means by which weak or under-resourced groups achieve their nationalistic goals against far stronger opponents. In sum, terrorism is a no-holds-barred war between David and Goliath.

War Casualties and Conflicts

One in four children worldwide lives in [an area of conflict]. Some 17 million children have been displaced by war, and more than 2 million children have been killed due to armed conflict since 1990. More than 1 million children have been separated from their parents or orphaned. More than 50,000 children have lost both of their parents due to conflict in Sudan alone.

In Sudan, women and girls are raped when they leave camps to fetch water and firewood. Liberian refugee children who were forced to become soldiers still face the risk of re-recruitment every day. In Iraq, an increasing number of children have been left to fend for themselves on the streets, making them targets for trafficking and sexual abuse.

Source: Save the Children, at: <www.savethechildren.org/one_world/index.asp>.

Types of Terrorist Activities

- *Bombings:* account for half of all terrorist activities, via automobiles, trucks, or individuals who are suicide bombers.
- *Hijackings:* the seizing of planes, buses, or other vehicles to threaten to kill hostages if demands are not met or simply to kill non-combatants.
- *Chemical attacks:* intentional public release of toxic chemicals that affect the central nervous system or other forms of bodily harm.
- *Biological attacks:* the release of harmful bacteria, viruses, toxins into an enemy or civilian environment; also known as 'germ warfare'.
- *Nuclear attacks:* potential (no nuclear terrorism has occurred to date) use of bombs to release harmful radioactive substances.
- *Cyberterrorism:* use of computer technology to sabotage information systems, such as the extraction or alteration of sensitive information or the spreading of computer viruses through networks.

Source: Adapted from Jacobs et al. (2003).

The roots of terrorism can be found in the religious, ethnic nationalist, political, economic, and social differences that prevent people from living together in peace. There is no evidence to suggest a single motive behind the use of terrorism, but the most accepted theory is that participants feel that violence is the best course of action, after all things are considered. A rational cost-benefit analysis—not reckless impulse—leads them to this conclusion, often because of various frustrating or limiting social, political, and economic conditions. Many of the suicide bombers in the Middle East have come from both oppressed and relatively impoverished circumstances, and one factor in accepting suicide is the promise of large cash payments to their families by states, wealthy sympathizers, and a variety of organizations. Valerie Hudson and Andrea Den Boer (2002) report that terrorists, and especially their leaders, are mainly men from middle- to upper-class backgrounds, typically with a higher than average education. They have specific skills and strong political motivation. Increasingly, terrorist organizations in the developing world recruit younger members. Often the only role models these young people have to identify with are terrorists and guerrillas.

Experts view terrorism as only a different form of soldiering, with the usual motives: to protect home and country. As Jeffrey Simon (2001: 338) writes, 'what limited data we have on individual terrorists suggests the outstanding common characteristic is normality.' As in the formation of social movements, the formation of terrorist groups relies on social networks to recruit members. Because terrorist activities are necessarily organized and carried out in secret, social networks are important as a source of social control over the recruits, to ensure their reliability (see, e.g., Erickson, 1981, on secret organizations).

State-sponsored terrorism is the state-sanctioned use of terrorist groups to achieve foreign-policy objectives. In the eyes of the current US government, there are seven countries on the 'terrorism list': Cuba, Iran, Iraq, Libya, North Korea, Sudan, and Syria (US Department of State, 2003). Of the seven countries, five are Middle Eastern or other Islamic nations with mainly Muslim populations. Other governments and groups might compile different lists. In the eyes of some, the United States itself might be viewed as a state that sponsors terrorism, with the aim of destabilizing foreign governments and undermining progressive political movements.

In certain areas, state sponsorship remains an important driving force behind terrorism. This is likely true in Israel, the West Bank, and the Gaza Strip today, where 'state-sponsored groups gain instant access to money, sophisticated weapons, training, false passports, safe passage, and protection both before and after their attacks' (Simon, 2001: 328). The American Central Intelligence Agency (CIA) has often been involved as a go-between, providing these kinds of assets to the citizens of various Central and South American countries.

The irony of state-sponsored terrorism is that while it can be a powerful form of clandestine warfare, it can also be vulnerable to shifts in the international political arena. On various occasions, developing world rebel groups, like various governments, have found themselves suddenly deprived of support from the foreign sponsors that they had relied on. For example, Iraq's Saddam Hussein was enlisted by the United States as an ally against Iran, only to be villainized later. Various religious fundamentalists, including the Taliban and even Osama bin Laden, also received support from the United States and its allies to undermine the Russians, only to be dropped and defamed later.

Many efforts have been taken by governments to safeguard their citizens against terrorist attacks. Often, these measures involve tightening domestic security, sometimes at the expense of civil liberties. Because terrorism frequently involves the use of technology, even advanced weaponry, there is some reason to believe that preventing future attacks will involve improving the technology used to detect terrorist plots. Radiation detectors at seaports, chemical scanners in airports, and software to intercept and monitor Internet 'chatter' are only a few examples of advanced technologies being used in the current 'war on terror'. One recurring theme that we will revisit throughout this chapter is the role of technology in modern warfare, in all its forms.

However, science and technology cannot solve what is finally a social and political problem. Improved technologies are not guarantees against future terrorist strikes or criminal sabotage. No amount of enhancements to detection and counterterrorism techniques will fully secure a country against attack. Terrorists will continue to adapt their tactics to exploit weaknesses in homeland security measures. Finally, note that on 11 September 2001 the terrorists used low-tech weapons to take over the planes, which they then used as high-tech weapons. It takes little imagination to see how dedicated terrorists might easily and calamitously bring about mass death by infiltrating a city's water or subway system, the ventilation in a skyscraper, or a country's food distribution network.

What this means is that we must concentrate on changing the motives of terrorists, because we cannot control their opportunities. Without understanding terrorist motives, no war against terrorism can succeed. Preventing future attacks will mean considering the historical, political, economic, and other factors that lead normal humans to see mass terror as proper and death by martyrdom as appealing.

To fully understand the complexity of this topic—how hard terrorism is to define, to explain, and to prevent—consider the disagreement about what was for Americans a cataclysmic warlike event: the terrorist attacks on the World Trade Center and the Pentagon on 11 September 2001.

Civilian Casualties

Ninety per cent of modern war casualties are civilians—primarily women and children.

Source: Save the Children, at: <www.savethechildren.org/news/releases/legislation_oct31.asp>.

The Case of 9/11

Intellectual opinion is strongly divided on the causes of and cures for terrorism. This comes out clearly in sociological analyses of the attacks on the World Trade Center and Pentagon.

According to Seyla Benhabib (2002), the 11 September 2001 terrorist attacks defied conventional categories of war, international law, and nation-statism. Non-state actors, such as al-Qaeda, carry out Islamic jihadist terrorism with no clear political goals other than destruction. These elements challenge the United States, its allies, and international bodies such as the United Nations to come up with new responses in the areas of international law, multilateralism, and foreign policy that do not shore up repressive regimes simply for the sake of oil.

Various factors support terrorism, in Benhabib's view. The failures of modernity and modernization, and the worldwide discrediting of communism, have created an ideological vacuum in the Middle East that radical Islam has rushed to fill. Meanwhile, globalization has helped erode the distinction between sacred and secular spheres in the Islamic world while spreading the 'decadent' values of the West by media images, travel, and migration.

Robin Blackburn (2002) is most concerned about US politics and its pretense. He notes that Congress granted President George W. Bush almost unlimited power to carry out the vaguely defined 'war on terror'. This has strengthened the administration's already obvious leaning towards unilateralism and given the presidency imperial powers, despite the potential for multilateralism to quash al-Qaeda and its affiliated terrorist groups. Past US policy decisions to strengthen Saudi Arabia, Pakistan, and anti-communist Afghani 'freedom fighters' all backfired. All three have supported al-Qaeda and other Islamic jihadists.

Blackburn urges Washington to engage diplomatically with Iran. Other potential allies are Pakistan and Uzbekistan. Most important, a multilateral approach through the United Nations must displace US crusading, not only to eradicate terrorism, but also to foster economic and democratic reform in the Middle East and promote global disarmament.

Echoing these sentiments, Carl Boggs (2002) notes that US history is full of military conquest, territorial enlargement, and forceful power-seeking. Today, he writes, the United States preaches international order, democracy, and human rights. Yet in recent memory and currently it has conducted precision-strike military campaigns in Grenada, Nicaragua, Haiti, Serbia, Sudan, Somalia, Afghanistan, Panama, and Iraq; exported weapons to 'unfriendly' nations; stockpiled and used weapons of mass destruction; and tested more nuclear weapons than any other country. The United States, animated by a neo-liberal ideology, also exercises control over international funding bodies and militarized drug wars. In Boggs's view, terrorism and increased authoritarianism in other countries are merely unexpected results of such US militarism.

David Held (2002) notes the 9/11 terrorist attacks violated not only Western values, but also cosmopolitan (that is, basic and universal) human rights principles that transcend borders and ethnic differences. However, responding to these attacks militarily is impractical against an enemy that does not act in the name of a state. The United States needs to work with the UN and other alliances to shore up the role of international law in fighting terrorism, regardless of its source. It should also help to create tribunals to prosecute terrorist acts as war crimes. At the same time, Islamic countries need to recognize their duty to curb rather than promote anti-democratic, anti-modern ideologies. The entire international community must recommit to world order.

Patricia Ticineto Clough (2002), for her part, is troubled by the popular position that the United States should strike back against those connected to the planning and execution of the terrorist attacks. She suggests that American citizens should have expected these attacks because of the extent of economic injustice throughout the present-day world. Strategies aimed at intensifying national security are problematic and potentially dangerous. For Clough, a more fruitful approach may be to question current global practices, especially American ones.

John Michael (2002) also examines the misleading metaphor of 'the West and the rest (Islam)' that structures official statements about the 9/11 attacks and the responses to them. Such language allows Americans to view opposition to the United States as the product of the Islamic world's misinterpretation of Western values and opposition to modernity rather than a rational response to US policies of imperialist domination and military aggression. This formula keeps American citizens from critically examining grievances against destructive political and military actions carried out by the United States. Not surprisingly, the identification of the 'enemy' as Islamic civilization has also produced a backlash against Muslims in the United States, as well as in Canada and Western Europe. It seems ironic and hypocritical to speak out against this backlash, as some American politicians have done, while continuing to condemn the supposedly wrong values of Islamic culture.

Victor Wallis (2002) argues that the US government is using the 11 September terrorist attacks to support an agenda of global domination and that it is linking the destruction of the World Trade Center to opposition to the World Trade Organization. Paradoxically, the terrorist network al-Qaeda—the perpetrator of a devastating attack against the imperialist centre—is also a product of imperialism.

S. Ravi Rajan (2002) also sees fault on both sides. Characterizing the perpetrators and planners of the terrorist atrocities as genocidal criminals, Rajan feels it is an insult to compare them to revolutionary anti-colonial freedom fighters. However, Rajan also fears the principles of democracy and freedom have been undermined in the name of increased security. Other trends in world history related to this terrorist incident are just as frightening as the attack itself, he writes, including the persistence of imperialism, the backing of evil leaders by Western governments, and the gradual dilution of democracy.

America since 9/11

Whatever the causes, the effects of the terrorist attacks of 9/11 for Americans in particular have been many and severe. First, civil rights have been cut short: the American government—never shy about spying on its own citizens—has undertaken to wiretap phone calls and monitor e-mails to find signs of terrorist planning. Security has been increased at every airport and border checkpoint into the country, and citizens who wish to leave and re-enter the United States will be obligated to carry new biometric identity cards. Since so many Canadians cross into and out of the United States every week, the Canadian government is considering the issuance of similar identity cards that are compatible with American scanners. Each new discovery of a terrorist plot to detonate airplanes—most recently (at time of writing) in August 2006 in and around London, England—leads to intensified security measures on planes flying into the United States. Where this tightening of security measures will end is impossible to guess.

When people are frightened, they take shortcuts—often, by acting first and thinking afterwards. So, racial profiling has also increased in the United States, with the aim of identifying and detaining people—especially young men—who look like they might be Arab terrorists. For most people, this activity has had no serious effect. However, for some suspected terrorists it has resulted in detention for extended periods without charge and without trial. President Bush has used his emergency powers to override constitutionally protected civil liberties. Some of these liberties, such as habeas corpus—the right of an accused to hear the charge against him—date back to the Middle Ages, so the freedom clock is being turned back over 500 years in response to fears about another terrorist attack.

Similarly, torture is being routinely practised in American detention centres where the suspected terrorists are being held without charge, without trial, and without conviction. Torture, it appears from manuals provided to American soldiers, is to be considered a standard method of interrogation where terrorist plans are suspected. In this respect, too, the United States has turned back the clock; torture has not been systematically practised—or at least officially condoned—in 'developed' societies (such as the US, Britain, and Canada) for at least three centuries.

An investigation by the United States Army begun in January 2004 revealed acts of torture in Abu Ghraib Prison in Iraq (formerly, the Baghdad Correctional Facility), including photographs that confirmed that American military police, CIA officers, and military contractors had abused prisoners during 2003. In April of 2004, a televised news report and a magazine article reported the story. The resulting political scandal seriously damaged the public image of the United States and its allies.

Defenders of the US government claimed the abuses were a result of independent actions by low-ranking personnel. Critics of US foreign policy argued the actions showed a general American disrespect towards Arabs. They also claimed that authorities had either ordered or tacitly excused the abuses. The Department of Defense responded by removing 17 soldiers and officers from duty, charging seven of them with dereliction of duty, maltreatment, aggravated assault, and battery.

It is doubtful that these actions repaired the damage the Abu Ghraib photographs had done to America's standing, especially in the minds of millions of Iraqis and Arabs, among others. Until recently, human rights organizations, such as Amnesty International and the International Red Cross, have continued to demand information about the treatment of prisoners detained in other military prisons, such as at the Guantanamo Air Base in Cuba, and the use of prisons on foreign soil—in Syria and elsewhere—to carry out acts of torture that are banned in the US (an unofficial policy referred to as 'extraordinary rendition').

However, the legal situation of detainees changed suddenly and dramatically when, on 29 June 2006, the United States Supreme Court ruled that military trials arranged by the Bush administration for detainees at Guantanamo Bay are illegal. The Bush administration had argued that neither military courts martial nor American civilian courts were appropriate for trying the Guantanamo detainees because much of the evidence would involve sensitive issues of national security.

The Court found that these trials—known as military commissions—for people detained on suspicion of terrorist activity do not conform to any act of Congress. The justices also rejected the government's argument that the Geneva Conventions regarding prisoners of war do not apply to those held at Guantanamo Bay. The commissions, which comprised five senior military officers, were generally held in private, and little media coverage was allowed. Though defendants were represented by both military and civilian lawyers, human rights groups have said the military commissions were overly secretive and little better than kangaroo courts. The ruling reversed a decision by a lower court that said the trials could go ahead.

A prime example of this practice, and one that involves Canada, was the detention and secret deportation of Syrian-born Canadian Maher Arar, who was held captive without trial and allegedly tortured in a Syrian prison for over a year before being returned to Canada. This kidnapping and unlawful imprisonment, engineered by the US government with co-operation from Canadian authorities (especially the Canadian Security Intelligence Service, or CSIS), was deemed justifiable because Arar was suspected of having links to al-Qaeda (accusations that were never substantiated). There are many who believe that this erosion of civil liberties in the United States, as well as in Britain and Canada, has been a more odious outcome of the terrorist acts of 9/11 than the destruction of the Twin Towers.

Much more can be said about this sensitive issue, and the situation is unfolding too rapidly for timely textbook coverage. For example, on 2–3 June 2006, raids by police and security agencies in Ontario in the greater Toronto area resulted in the arrest of 17 alleged members of an Islamic terrorist cell. Canadian authorities allege the men arrested had been planning a series of major terrorist assaults on targets in southern Ontario. The suspects were charged under the anti-terrorism legislation passed by Parliament in December 2001 in response to the 9/11 attacks in the US. The arrests marked one of the largest anti-terrorism sweeps in North America. It remains to be seen whether the interests of national security will be invoked to justify the suppression of evidence or sources of evidence, or the use of non-conventional legal tactics.

Other events around the world in the last two years—such as the London bombings by homegrown terrorists, the Madrid bombings, and the Mumbai train bombings—illustrate the geographic spread of these problems. Everywhere, issues of security, protection, and detection are bumping up against concerns about free speech, civil liberties, and the needs for normal social and economic interaction. The fact that much of this global terrorism is orchestrated from outside the country using local people as the active agents further complicates problems of policing and prosecution.

The Nature of Warfare

As we can see from this brief discussion of terrorism, the nature of warfare has changed dramatically. No longer do contending armies square up against each other on a battlefield and let the strongest, largest, bravest army prevail while civilian curiosity-seekers and picnickers look on, as was the case at the Battle of Waterloo and in some instances during the American Civil War. No longer do we rely much on hand-to-hand fighting with simple weapons of death: knives, spears, and maces. No longer do warriors hide behind fortress walls while besieged by airborne rocks and fire-tipped arrows. No longer do most warriors see whom they are killing, and many of those they kill are not opposing forces but civilians. Warfare has become more impersonal and, in this sense, sanitized—cleansed of human emotion on the part of the aggressors. More and more, wars are battles between technologies in which ordinary people are often innocent victims. Wedding parties in Iraq have been annihilated by American weaponry; picnickers in Gaza have been killed by Israeli missiles. Secrecy, deception, and torture are the order of the day.

Not only has the nature of warfare changed over time, but so have the settings in which conflicts take place. At the beginning of the twenty-first century, there were an estimated 40 active military conflicts in the world, many of them intranational. Many wars are being 'played out on the terrain of subsistence economies; most conflict involves regimes at war with sectors of their own society—generally the poor and particular ethnic groups' (Summerfield, 2000: 232). As well, with the growing popularity of terrorist tactics that target civilian populations rather than military personnel, warfare has shifted from secluded outposts and isolated bases to crowded urban centres.

As a result, the numbers of civilian casualties have risen steadily since the middle of the twentieth century (Renner, 1993a). Researchers estimate that civilian deaths accounted for 75 per cent of all war-related deaths in the 1980s and almost 90 per cent in the 1990s. War has also become increasingly urban, as the daily civilian deaths in Baghdad, the July 2006 train bombings in Mumbai, and the Israeli–Hezbollah conflict in the summer of 2006 illustrate dramatically. Direct atrocities against civilians, including execution, torture, disappearances, and sexual violation, have also increased.

One of the most common causes of war is dispute over natural resources, such as land, oil, and water. In some circles, the two Gulf wars were waged primarily over control of Middle East oil reserves. Joyce Starr and Daniel Stoll (1989: 1) argue that soon 'water, not oil will be the dominant resource issue of the Middle East.'

Another common cause of war is defence against possible hostile attacks from others—in other words, pre-emptive war. When Germany invaded Poland at the onset of World War II, Britain and France declared war on Germany out of fear that their geo-

Box 12.2 Social Construction: Counting Terrorist Attacks

There were nearly 3,200 terrorist attacks worldwide [in 2004] the Bush Administration said yesterday [6 July 2005], using a broader definition that increased fivefold the number of incidents that Washington had previously tallied for 2004. In figures published in April, the US State Department said that there were 651 significant international terror incidents, with more than 9,000 victims.

But under the newer, less-stringent definition of terrorism, which counts domestic attacks without an international element, the National Counterterrorism Center (NCTC) reported 3,192 attacks worldwide, with 28,433 people killed, wounded, or kidnapped.

Iraq, with 866, had the most attacks against civilians and other non-combatants, according to the report. Under the April figures, Iraq was considered to have suffered 201 attacks in 2004. The new tally included attacks on Iraqis by Iraqis, a category previously excluded because it was not considered international terrorism. But attacks against coalition forces were omitted, because soldiers are considered combatants. Insurgent attacks on Iraqi police, deemed non-combatants, were included.

The Bush Administration's terrorism figures have been the subject of repeated controversies. Last year the State Department withdrew its annual report on global terrorism after claiming that terrorism incidents had been declining for three years and that 190 cases reported in 2003 represented the lowest total since 1969. American officials trumpeted the report as evidence that the US was winning the War on Terror. But the document was found to be full of errors, and officials acknowledged that it had vastly understated the number of attacks.

This year the State Department decided not to publish the terrorism figures in its annual report. It handed the responsibility to the new NCTC. John Brennan, its interim director, said that the methodology that produced the April statistics was so flawed that the numbers were unreliable.

Source: *The Times* (London), 7 July 2005, at: <www.timesonline.co.uk/article/0,,3-1684077,00.html>. © Tim Reid NI Syndication Limited (July 7, 2005).

graphic nearness and opposing ideological stances would make them the next logical targets of attack. Japan bombed Pearl Harbor because it wished to avoid a later confrontation with the US naval fleet in the Pacific.

War Crimes

Despite the saying that 'all's fair in love and war', signatory nations of the Geneva Conventions have formally declared that at least some actions are unacceptable even in the madness of war. Having atrocities committed during war defined as war crimes may seem strange, given the fundamental ambition of combat—to kill your enemies—and the barbarous way warriors typically carry out much of the killing. However, many nations hold the view that slaughtering soldiers is an acceptable cost of war but the intentional slaughter of civilians is an indefensible horror. These distinctions are socially and politically, if not morally, meaningful.

Acts of political violence—including war crimes—differ from other kinds of violence in that representatives of one political or national group inflict such violence to perpetuate or change the relative political status of another political or national group or to prevent that group from achieving the changes its members want (Kanaaneh and

Netland, 1992). Rationalizations are commonly devised to explain away the extent of violence, its effects, or its lack of fairness.

These rationalizations begin by distinguishing between 'us' and 'them'. A group defined as outsiders or strangers is easily defamed and attacked—easily viewed as a means to an end, or fully expendable. The most horrific manifestation of this is **genocide**, the systematic and planned execution of an entire national, ethnic, racial, or political group. The most notorious case of genocide was the attempted extermination of Jews and gypsies by Nazi Germany during World War II. Many others—including Slavs, homosexuals, and mentally retarded people—were also murdered. In all, six million Jews were killed, many in concentration camps like Auschwitz, where an estimated one million died.

Though many vowed after 1945 that such an atrocity should never be allowed to happen again, genocides continue to occur, in the former Yugoslavia and in Rwanda, to name the most notorious cases. However, the world now has procedures for dealing with genocidal war criminals.

In 2001, Slobodan Milosevic, the president of Yugoslavia during the 1998–9 conflicts in Kosovo in Yugoslavia's republic of Serbia, was extradited to the International Criminal Tribunal for the former Yugoslavia (ICTY) in The Hague, Netherlands, and indicted for committing war crimes against ethnic Albanians. Among other things, the prosecutor accused him of ordering soldiers to dump at least 50 Kosovo Albanians into the Danube River in 1999, approving the deaths of hundreds of others, displacing up to 700,000 more, and carrying out other 'ethnic cleansing' policies while in power. Milosevic was the first sitting head of state to ever face international war crimes charges. However, he died in prison before his trial was concluded, and thus before a verdict was rendered.

Issues involving the prosecution of war crimes fall into at least four categories: assigning responsibility for criminal acts; trying and punishing the criminals; bringing about national reconciliation; and ensuring that a nation remembers its criminal past and learns from it. The International Criminal Court (ICC), which Canada was instrumental in establishing and which opened on 1 July 2002, sets up a permanent, international court to prosecute war crimes and crimes against humanity. Some countries, however, most notably the United States, have refused to be participants in this international forum for justice because they do not want to cede any of their own jurisdictional control and because they claim their own soldiers (or leaders) might be apprehended and tried unfairly.

On the whole, the calls for international war crime tribunals, which are established on an ad hoc basis in contrast to the permanency of the ICC, are sporadic because of tensions between selfishness and idealism within liberal states. Also, the war crimes tribunals are physically unable to process hundreds of thousands of trials. Nevertheless, these tribunals are superior to acts of vengeance by the aggrieved parties. Right actions following wrongdoing, such as changing institutions, reparations, or giving apologies, may help to bring about healing and peace (Bass, 2002).

This is fine as a grand principle. On the ground, it may be more difficult to reorganize people's lives after a genocidal episode. Babic (2002) studied 180 war migrants, including returnee Croats, returnee Serbs, and refugees-immigrants in one county in Croatia. He found the coexistence of the hostile Croats and Serbs remains a problem, both for groups of war migrants in local communities and for the state of Croatia. The returnees are burdened with memories of the recent conflict, human and material losses, and issues of forgiveness and compromise. Ironically, all three groups confirm that, *before* the war, they each valued peaceful coexistence. The groups today differ in who they think is responsible for the war.

At a recent Toronto conference on war, Aersi Aafi from Somalia and Pradeepa Kandasamy from Sri Lanka spoke about the way war affects children and their later adjustment to life in Canada. Children who experience war close up continue to suffer psychological trauma even when the war is faraway in time and space. For instance, Aafi is often afraid of authority figures—including his Canadian teachers—because of his experiences with authority figures in Somalia. Because of post-traumatic stress disorder (PTSD) symptoms like these, victims of war further isolate themselves from normal Canadian life (Keung, 2005).

National self-examination has been a continuing problem after wars and war crimes, but nations approach their history in different ways. The Federal Republic of Germany (West Germany), for example, was slow to admit its role in the Holocaust. While the interpretation remained mainly the same throughout the existence of the German Democratic Republic (East Germany, 1949–90), the main focus in the Federal Republic of Germany changed several times. At first, textbooks to a certain extent argued Nazi positions (under conservative nationalist policy) on many questions of national interest, engagement, and expansion. Gradually, authors changed their underlying theories about National Socialism. The theory of 'totalitarianism', that is, of Communism and National Socialism as hostile twin brothers, was officially promoted in West Germany. There, placing the Nazi period (and crimes) in the context of German history and society was not seriously discussed before the 1980s.

For all victims and analysts of political violence, the Nazi Holocaust remains the benchmark against which all other crimes against humanity are judged and led to the Nuremberg war trials of 1945–6, when a number of German military and political officials were tried and convicted of war crimes by an international military tribunal. The Holocaust example doubtless was instrumental in the development of the concept of 'war crimes'.

Rape as a Weapon of War

Despite prohibitions outlined in the Geneva Conventions, rape, assault, and enforced prostitution of women have all continued during armed conflicts. For example, in the years of World War II, the Japanese military forced up to 200,000 young women into prostitution as 'comfort women' for military personnel, with many eventually dying of sexually transmitted diseases and torture. During the recent conflicts in Bosnia-Herzegovina and Rwanda, and in most other hostile actions as well, roving bands of soldiers raped, beat, and even killed women (Amnesty International, 1995).

Buchanan (2002) notes especially the problem of 'gendercide'—genocidal acts committed against women as women and men as men—as human rights violations. Gendercide against women typically involves rape, which has come to be recognized as a war crime. Against men, such crimes involve the selective separation of young civilian men 'of military age' (that is, 18–45 years) from old men, children, and women of all ages for punishment, torture, and execution.

Formerly, many believed that rape was an unintended consequence of invasion by foreign soldiers—as occurred in Berlin in 1945, when Soviet soldiers overran the defeated city. For centuries, warriors have considered captive women to be part of the booty of warfare. However, today many believe that a systematic campaign of rape against civilian women is designed to humiliate and break the resolve of an enemy nation, and in some African conflicts it has been used intentionally to spread HIV. It also destroys families by turning husbands, fathers, and brothers against the young women—wives and daughters—who have been raped. Finally, when rape results in pregnancy, it changes the ethnic composition of a conquered society—a further source of humiliation and conflict that will continue for at least a generation. In some countries, such as Korea, which over the years has been occupied by Mongolian, Chinese, Japanese, and American troops, this has resulted in the subsequent shunning and social isolation of people of mixed race (see Greenfeld, 2006).

International feminist activists and women's organizations have played an important role in recent prosecutions of war crimes committed against women, especially rapes and sexual enslavement (Cooper, 2002). Feminists successfully pressured the UN to label crimes against women as prosecutable human rights abuses and to include female prosecutors and judges in tribunals. Indeed, Louise Arbour, who became a Supreme Court of Canada justice and currently is the UN High Commissioner for Human Rights, was Chief Prosecutor of War Crimes at the International Criminal Tribunal for Rwanda and the former Yugoslavia in The Hague from 1996 to 1999 and indicted Slobodan Milosevic, among others, for war crimes. In 2001, the ICTY convicted three Bosnian Serb men for their role in the mass rape of Muslim women in the city of Foca during the conflict in Bosnia-Herzegovina.

Environmental Destruction

The wilful destruction of the environment as a strategy of war, as practice for war, or as punishment for the defeated occurred at least as early as Roman times, and it has persisted to the present. Roman armies routinely destroyed crops and salted the earth to ruin the land's fertility. A millennium later, the Russians burned their own crops and homes not once but twice, to prevent the invading armies of Napoleon and, later, Hitler from making use of them. In a different but no less destructive manner, Allied navies during World War II routinely used the whales of the North Atlantic for target practice (Mowat, 1984).

When the Allied forces pushed the Iraqi forces out of Kuwait in 1991, the Iraqis set fire to 732 of the country's roughly 900 oil wells, producing one of the worst environmental disasters in history. Black smoke from the fires blocked out the sun and produced record low temperatures along a 950-kilometre tract of land. Rescue operations recovered over 22 million barrels of oil, but more is thought to have leaked from the destroyed oil fields into the local environment, contaminating soil and water supplies. Saddam Hussein also ordered the release of an estimated 11 million barrels of oil into the Arabian Gulf, damaging the local marine life.

Military operations also harm the environment during peacetime. According to Martin Calhoun, the US military is the largest producer of dangerous materials in that country, and 'decades of improper and unsafe handling, storage and disposal of hazardous materials while building and maintaining the world's most powerful fighting force have severely polluted America's air, water and soil' (Calhoun, 1996: 60). Disposal is a major problem, and the drafters of disarmament treaties often have trouble suggesting a safe place for disposal of missiles, mines, bombs, and nuclear warheads.

> ### Box 12.3 Historical Perspective:
> ### Old Chemical Weapons Lie on Ocean Floor
>
> Inspectors from the Department of National Defence (DND) have discovered that Canada is guilty of dumping chemical weapons off the coast of British Columbia just after World War II. Research revealed that the canisters and munitions full of deadly mustard and phosgene gas were tossed into the Pacific Ocean just 160 km from Vancouver Island, about 2.5 km below the water. Two other ocean dumps have also been found off the east coast. The DND states that ocean dumping was a common practice after the wars, and that it is no longer legal after the London Protocol banned it in 1972. Canada participated in testing mustard gas, a deadly blistering agent that causes choking, on humans and used it for training in World War II. Internationally, most countries leave dumping sites undisturbed. The DND is attempting to discover the damages this dump will or has caused; however, the whole project, which may not even be possible, will cost millions.
>
> Source: Baron (2005).

Population Control

As Thomas Malthus (1959 [1798]) pointed out over two centuries ago, war—along with disease and starvation—is a 'positive check' on population (for more on Malthus's theory of global populations, see Chapter 11). Whether or not we choose to view war in this benignly clinical way, there can be no doubt that, to a dramatic degree, wars have reduced the population of humanity. In the thousand years between AD 1000 and 2000, wars killed about 175 million people. Of these, 111 million were killed in the twentieth century alone, owing to the increased scope and efficiency—the industrialization—of warfare in that century. An estimated 9 million were killed in World War I and another 61 million—over half of them civilians—were killed in World War II. The Soviet Union alone lost over 25 million people in World War II (on this, see Coupland and Meddings, 1999; Rummel, 1992, 1994, 1998).

UN and other projections estimate that had these 70 million people not been killed in World Wars I and II, the world's population today would have been 6.95 billion instead of 6.24 billion. Thus, the deaths of 70 million people in two world wars prevented the births of 710 million people who, but for these wars, would have been alive today. Among the 710 million people who were never born, there might have been another Einstein, Mozart, Shakespeare, or Picasso; another Mother Teresa; or even your own uncle or cousin. Under some circumstances, you yourself might not have been born.

Theories of War and Terrorism

Given warfare's universal quality, it is no surprise that something so complex and consequential would have theoretical explanations at different levels of analysis—psychological as well as sociological.

Psychological Perspectives

Competition between groups is a natural phenomenon that can develop over time into hostile forms if the assets fought over are rare or if superiority and victory are central to the groups' identities. Jordan Peterson (1998) argues, for example, that the horrible acts committed during World War II can be understood in terms of adherence to group ideology (then, Nazi ideology and a belief in the 'Final Solution'). Such behaviour is helped by a denial of contradictory information and of moral reservations and by an inability to think independently outside prescribed boundaries (Peterson, 1998).

Other social psychologists examine how otherwise 'normal' and mild-mannered citizens can change during wartime into soldiers able to kill and injure others seemingly without hesitation or remorse. Philip Zimbardo (1971) states that taking on a role, such as 'soldier', causes a person to internalize that role's identity. Similarly, ordinary citizens called on to defend their country can readily identify themselves as 'soldiers' temporarily. They take on a role that justifies the brutal slaughter of their enemies. The degree of role socialization to violence is, of course, even greater among career soldiers whose entire adult lives have been spent in the military.

In his classic study, Zimbardo simulated a prison in the Stanford University psychology department, assigning student volunteers at random to play the role of guards and prisoners. To the guards, he gave uniforms, billy clubs, and whistles; to the prisoners, prison outfits and jail cells. After only one day, all participants had become engrossed in their roles. 'Guards' cruelly ridiculed and degraded their 'prisoners'; prisoners suffered anguish and rebelled against their captors. Intense social conflict emerged, forcing Zimbardo to end the experiment after only six days, a week earlier than planned.

In another classic experiment, Stanley Milgram (1974) enlisted Yale University students ostensibly to take part in a study on learning and memory, but he was really studying the role of authority in preserving obedience among subordinates. The research reflected Milgram's wish to learn how the atrocities of World War II, especially the Holocaust, could have been committed by German soldiers who claimed they were only 'following orders'.

Subjects were recruited for Milgram's study through newspaper ads and direct mail; participants included men from all educational backgrounds between the ages of 20 and 50. In each instance, the participant and a confederate of the experimenter, who was an actor pretending to be another participant, were told by the experimenter that they would be participating in an experiment to test the effects of punishment on learning. In each instance, the participant was led to believe that he had randomly drawn the task of teaching the other participant a series of word pairs, aided by electric shocks to stimulate learning.

The 'teacher' was given a 45-volt electric shock from the electro-shock generator as a sample of the shock that the 'learner' would supposedly receive during the experiment. The teacher was then given a list of word pairs he was to teach the learner. The teacher began by reading the list of word pairs to the learner and the learner would press a button to indicate his response. If the answer was incorrect, the learner would receive a shock, with the voltage increasing with each wrong answer. If correct, the teacher would read the next word pair.

The experimenter led subjects to believe that for each wrong answer, the learner would receive actual shocks. After the confederate was separated from the subject, the confederate set up a tape recorder integrated with the electro-shock generator, which played pre-recorded sounds for each shock level. With each test, the shock level was increased. At 135 volts, some test subjects paused and began to question the purpose of the experiment. If the subject still wished to stop after all four successive verbal prods, the experiment was halted. Otherwise, it was halted after the subject believed he had given the maximum 450-volt shock three times in succession—a shock level that participants understood could be fatal.

In Milgram's first set of experiments, 27 out of 40 experimental participants administered the experiment's final 450-volt shock, though many were quite uncomfortable in doing so. No participant absolutely refused to give further shocks before the 300-volt level. In subsequent experiments using a similar methodology, the percentage of participants who were prepared to inflict fatal voltages remained remarkably constant, between 61 and 66 per cent, regardless of time or location.

While many celebrated this experiment's ingenuity for showing the willingness of ordinary people to mindlessly inflict pain—even to the point of murder—others were critical. Among many researchers, the experiment provoked a hostile response. Most modern scientists would consider the experiment unethical today, though it resulted in valuable insights into human psychology. What's more, the participants learned a lot about themselves from this study: 84 per cent of former participants surveyed later said they were 'glad' or 'very glad' to have participated and 15 per cent chose neutral.

Sociological Perspectives

THE STRUCTURAL-FUNCTIONALIST PERSPECTIVE

As we have said repeatedly, structural functionalists believe that most elements in society exist to serve some purpose. Conflict and violence are the results of a system malfunctioning—for example, some system needs for integration and consensus not being met. From this standpoint, wars may occur because groups or societies do not know how to resolve their conflicts peacefully. They lack shared values or institutions for lawfully resolving disagreement. They lack the leadership and assets to bring peace. By this reckoning, war results from the breakdown of peace. Wars may even arise because military institutions and activities hold great importance within the society and culture.

Ralf Dahrendorf, in his classic work *Class and Class Conflict in Industrial Society* (1959), notes that violence, as a means of conducting conflict, diminishes through the regulation of conflict. There is less violence when conflict is more regulated, even if the causes of conflict—for example, oppositions between authority holders and those subject to authority—continue to exist.

For conflict to be regulated, according to Dahrendorf, parties must recognize the conflict as an inevitable outgrowth of conflicting interests, must be organized into groups, and must agree to rules under which the conflict will take place. Such rules protect the survival of both parties, reduce potential injury to each party, introduce some predictability into the actions of each party, and protect third parties from undue harm.

This suggests a framework for analyzing violent crimes and violent acts more generally. It assumes that violence is a means of conducting conflict in the absence of ground rules and shared assumptions. Conditions of trust and mutual understanding are needed for people to conduct social life—even competitive or conflictual social life. Note that this theory contains elements of the conflict approach: most particularly, a recognition of the normality of conflict based on competing interests. However, in addition, the theory includes aspects of the functionalist approach, with its emphasis on the way that agreed-on procedures can channel competition into peaceful, non-conflictual forms.

Once in motion, a large-scale conflict increases social cohesion and group identity. Internal squabbles between political parties, ethnic communities, special interest groups, and so on are put aside, at least temporarily, as the entire nation bands together in a show of patriotism to defeat a common enemy. Only when this common enemy is no longer a threat to national well-being do the internal conflicts resume. Sometimes the solidarity between allies created through the defence of shared interests lasts for a while even after the war is over.

CONFLICT THEORY

Conflict theorists state that wars are struggles between opposing groups over power, limited assets, or ideological domination taken to their logical, violent conclusions. Just as social classes may battle one another for economic position within a society, so nation-states and interest groups within the society may go to war with one another. The difference is that they routinely use weapons and kill one another.

Conflict theory stresses the ways in which war benefits some groups—most notably, corporations, politicians, and the military—but not others. The 'military-industrial complex', a term first introduced in warning by US President Dwight D. Eisenhower in 1961 as he left office, refers to the close relationship between the military and the private defence industry and their combined control of the political agenda. The sociological and structural underpinnings of this combination of power were earlier analyzed by C. Wright Mills in his classic work, *The Power Elite* (1956). In Canada, for example, the current Conservative Minister of National Defence, Gordon O'Connor, was a career officer in the Canadian military, retiring as brigadier general, and then worked as a defence industry lobbyist for several major military suppliers until he entered politics in 2004. In the US, several leading figures in the Bush administration, notably Vice-President Dick Cheney and Defense Secretary Donald Rumsfeld, had previously been involved with companies that profit from war. Corporations contracted by the Pentagon to design, develop, and make weapons are guaranteed profits even if they overrun their budgets. It is sensible, therefore, for these companies to ensure that global conflicts and threats to national security continue so they can run the highly profitable war machine. Also, as Cynthia Enloe (1987: 527) notes, 'government officials enhance the status, assets, and authority of the military to protect the interests of private enterprises at home and overseas.'

Industrialists, politicians, brokers, and black marketeers, among others, make enormous fortunes from war and weapons of war. This has an important effect on the class structure of society. According to one estimate, governments throughout the world were collectively spending $1 trillion per year, or roughly $2 million (US) per minute, to finance various military efforts by the end of the 1980s (Brown et al., 1992). These costs included the salaries of military personnel, research into and development of weapons and combat technology, the purchase and manufacture of artillery and wartime machinery, and veterans' benefits. Of course, this also means that $1 trillion was *not* being spent globally on health care, education, infrastructure, or social services.

SYMBOLIC INTERACTIONISM

Symbolic interactionists examine the ways in which cultures socialize people to adopt certain attitudes towards war and conflict. Adult members of society encourage aggression and the resolution of conflicts through physical force as early as childhood, mostly in boys.

Symbolic interactionists also study the language and labels of war. Thus, propaganda techniques are employed by the government, businesses (for example, munitions manufacturers), the military, and 'patriotic organizations' (such as veterans' groups) to describe the current global 'war on terror' as a 'justified war' against 'evil' terrorism. In particular, the media play an important role in the spin-doctoring of this message. In times of war, leaders use a special language to legitimize combat and reduce the emotional impact of the deaths that will follow. Soldiers on both sides are not 'murder victims', they are 'casualties'. A missile does not blow up an enemy barracks; it 'services the target'. The unplanned but 'unavoidable' killing of innocent civilians is reported in official documents as 'collateral damage'. Nuclear missiles are not weapons of mass destruction, they are 'peacekeepers'.

THE FEMINIST PERSPECTIVE

Masculinity and militarism have had a close relationship over time and across cultures, and the 'meanings attached to masculinity appear to be so firmly linked to compliance with military roles that it is often impossible to disentangle the two' (Enloe, 1987: 531). The association between masculinity and militarism begins in childhood socialization. For instance, in Western culture, boys wage make-believe wars with GI Joe figurines, while girls are much more likely to play with dolls and act out domestic routines such as baking and child-rearing.

With only a few exceptions through the history of Western culture, it has been mainly men who have fought wars. This is due in part to women's smaller physical stature, to the nature of warfare (which has traditionally involved much face-to-face, close range, physical combat), and to men's greater tendency towards aggression and violence. Some say that a protective chivalry or paternalistic sexism towards the 'lesser sex' is also involved in men's largely exclusive role in warfare; men try to protect women, they argue.

As already noted, rape is one major result of war for women. On a more positive note, major wars have also allowed women greater entry into the workforce, both as soldiers and as civilians, to replace the men recruited for war. During World War II, this meant opening new job opportunities for women, who up to then had been limited to a narrow range of traditionally female jobs. Now they found themselves working in 'essential' industries such as engineering, metals, chemicals, vehicles, transport, energy, and shipbuilding (Summerfield, 2000).

SOCIAL CONSTRUCTIONISM

This approach stresses the role of moral entrepreneurs in mobilizing support for social causes—for waging wars, for instance. As has recently come to light, false propaganda and misinformation produced by the US administration were used to gain support from American citizens for the 2003 invasion of Iraq. The so-called facts used to justify this unilateral pre-emptive war—such as the presence of weapons of mass destruction, and the claimed co-operation between Osama bin Laden and Saddam Hussein—have since been exposed as deceptions and red herrings. Remarkably, however, once such a war has begun, public awareness of politically motivated lies—to the extent the public is even aware of the deception or believes it to be true—changes nothing when the propaganda machine continues to proclaim the necessity of war to secure the 'homeland' against 'evildoers'.

Such propaganda also supports the vilification of certain groups during wartime. As an example, consider the effects of Canada's War Measures Act on Canadian race relations (and vice versa). The War Measures Act was originally legislated in 1914 as a response to anxieties connected with World War I. This legislation was used during two world wars and, in particular, was used to justify the unjust treatment of Japanese Canadians during and after World War II. Using this Act, the Canadian government uprooted Japanese Canadians from their homes, placed them in internment camps, and had their properties confiscated; some were even deported (Kage, 2002).

The War Measures Act was imposed after the bombing of Pearl Harbor on 7 December 1941 helped to rally (non-Japanese) Canadians around patriotic slogans and shared views of internal and external danger. Fearing for their safety and well-being, Canadians united against the Japanese and against Japanese Canadians. At the same time, singling out Japanese Canadians and confiscating their property suited some Canadians even more than others. Non-Japanese Canadians on the west coast had felt threatened by the presence of the Japanese community for decades owing to a scarcity of jobs.

Enacting the War Measures Act gave these non-Japanese Canadians more access to limited assets—for example, land, jobs, and businesses. The war and the War Measures Act helped to justify derogatory and racially hostile views that already existed. In short, it made racism acceptable in Canada. Also, it blamed the Japanese Canadians for racially hostile sentiments that they had played no part in creating.

Social Consequences of War

The two most socially consequential facts about warfare are: first, it kills many people; second, it costs much money. The rise in both casualty rates and military expenditures in

Table 12.1 Five Main Sociological Paradigms	
Structural Functionalism	■ Elements in society are all interrelated.
	■ War and terrorism reinforce group identity and increase social cohesion as well as conformity.
	■ Increased employment and production of weapons lead to economic benefit.
Conflict Theory	■ Conflict and change are basic features of social life.
	■ War and terrorism reflect struggles between opposite groups over power, limited resources, or ideological domination.
	■ Only some groups benefit, namely corporations, politicians, middlemen, and black marketeers.
Symbolic Interactionism	■ Socialization and labelling shape attitudes and the roles people adopt towards war efforts and conflicts.
	■ In times of war, leaders use propaganda and euphemistic language to legitimize combat and to reduce the emotional impact of death.
Feminism	■ In Western culture, men have fought in wars primarily.
	■ War is seen as misguided protective chivalry or paternalistic sexism toward the 'lesser' sex.
	■ Consequences of war: women are raped, forced into prostitution.
Social Constructionism	■ Propaganda legitimizes war and reduces the emotional impact of death.
	■ Political parties deflect criticism by focusing national attention on real or imagined enemies.
	■ People mobilize to form social movements and to influence public policy.

modern warfare is partly due to the larger scale of conflict and partly due to the advanced technology used in waging war. In addition, for many people, warfare shatters morale and the fabric of civic society.

Although it is true that countries or groups internal to them who emerge as the victors undergo a general improvement in spirits, for many people war will always be a gruelling and haunting experience. For instance, many Vietnam veterans returned to the United States disillusioned, unable to find purpose in the conflict and to understand the lack of sympathy from fellow Americans on their return.

Effects on the Economy

Wars sometimes bring economic benefits. For example, Canadian participation in World War II led to increased employment and production, helping to end the financial downturn of the Great Depression. After the war, North America, which did not experience the devastation visited upon many European and some Asian countries, rode the financial momentum through the next several decades, experiencing prosperity and growth in all parts of society. Canadians, the strongest trading partner of the United States, also enjoyed a financial boom during and after the war: the gross national product (GNP) doubled, industry developed exponentially, and consumer spending rose with the baby boom generation (Girvan, 2000). Losers of the war, especially Germany and Japan, suffered significant setbacks to their economies for many years after the conflict ended.

Wars also lead to scientific and technological innovations that benefit society in peacetime. Military research on laser-based defence made it easier to develop laser surgery; experimentation with nuclear weaponry allowed for the widespread development of nuclear power stations; the airline industry's technological innovations were made possible largely through the work of military defence departments; and the Internet grew out of research sponsored by the US military as a possible emergency communications network in case of nuclear war. In this sense, innovations in weaponry are social innovations as well as engineering feats.

This raises the question of whether the bloodiness of warfare in recent decades—indeed, in the twentieth century more generally—is ascribable to an increased bloodthirstiness—a motivation to inflict maximum harm—or merely to an increased ease of inflicting maximum harm through lethal technology. On the one hand, one does not require cutting-edge weaponry to effect massive casualties. The Nazi Holocaust, for example, needed few technological innovations. Mainly, it was a feat of social engineering: to kill so many civilians in so few years needed organization and dedication. Similarly, during 9/11, the al-Qaeda hijackers used simple box-cutters to commandeer the aircrafts used to topple the World Trade Center and damage the Pentagon. On the other hand, the enormous harm perpetrated by Americans in Vietnam and elsewhere since—through aerial 'carpet bombing' and other forms of long-distance attack—demonstrates modern technology's ability to inflict maximum harm without much risk. Indeed, some US pilots during the 'shock and awe' thrust upon Iraq in 2003 were based in the American Midwest—they flew to Iraq to drop their tons of bombs and were back home in time for the Little League game or the family barbecue the next day. In general, the twentieth century has taught that people will use the most extreme weapons they can devise to win a war.

Effects on Children

Increasingly, wars are being waged with the help of child soldiers. Though the United Nations Convention on the Rights of the Child states that children under the age of 15 are not to be used as soldiers, children were used as soldiers as recently as the Rwandan

Table 12.2 The 15 Top Military Spenders, 2005

Military expenditure in MER dollar terms						Military expenditure in PPP dollar terms[a]		
Rank	Country	Spending ($ b.)	Spending per capita ($)	World share (%) Spending	World share (%) Popul.	Rank	Country	Spending ($ b.)
1	USA	478.2	1,604	48	5	1	USA	478.2
2	UK	48.3	809	5	1	2	China	[188.4]
3	France	46.2	763	5	1	3	India	105.8
4	Japan	42.1	329	4	2	4	Russia	[64.4]
5	China	[41.0]	[31.2]	[4]	20	5	France	45.4
Sub-total top 5		**655.7**		**65**	**29**	**Sub-total top 5**		**882.3**
6	Germany	33.2	401	3	1	6	UK	42.3
7	Italy	27.2	468	3	1	7	Saudi Arabia[bc]	35.0
8	Saudi Arabia[bc]	25.2	1,025	3	0	8	Japan	34.9
9	Russia	[21.0]	[147]	[2]	2	9	Germany	32.7
10	India	20.4	18.5	2	17	10	Italy	30.1
Sub-total top 10		**782.7**		**78**	**51**	**Sub-total top 10**		**1,057.2**
11	Korea, South	16.4	344	2	1	11	Brazil	24.3
12	Canada[c]	10.6	327	1	0	12	Iran[b]	23.8
13	Australia[c]	10.5	522	1	0	13	South Korea	23.4
14	Spain	9.9	230	1	1	14	Turkey	17.8
15	Israel[c]	9.6	1,430	1	0	15	Taiwan	13.4
Sub-total top 15		**839.8**		**84**	**53**	**Sub-total top 15**		**1,159.8**
World		**1,001**	**155**	**100**	**100**	**World**		..

MER = market exchange rate; PPP = purchasing power parity; [ ] = estimated figure. [a] The figures in PPP dollar terms are converted at PPP rates (for 2003), calculated by the World Bank, based on comparisons of gross national product. [b] Data for Iran and Saudi Arabia include expenditure for public order and safety and might be a slight overestimate. [c] The populations of Australia, Canada, Israel, and Saudi Arabia each constitute less than 0.5% of the total world population.

Source: From: <www.ipb.org/pdf/15Major%20MSpenders04.pdf>, using the following: *SIPRI Yearbook 2005,* Appendix 8A; PPP rates: World Bank, *World Development Report 2005: A Better Investment Climate for Everyone* (Washington, 2004), table 1, 'Key indicators of development', 256–7, and table 5, 'Key indicators for other economies', 264; 2005 Population: United Nations Population Fund (UNFPA), *State of the World Population 2005* (New York, 2005), at: <unfpa.org/swp/>. Petter Stålenheim, Damien Fruchart, Wuyi Omitoogun, and Catalina Perdomo, 'Military Expenditure' *SIPRI Yearbook 2006.* Oxford University Press.

Child Victims of War

Recent developments in warfare have significantly heightened the dangers for children. During the last decade, it is estimated that child victims have included:

- 2 million killed
- 4–5 million disabled
- 12 million left homeless
- more than 1 million orphaned or separated from their parents
- some 10 million psychologically traumatized.

Source: United Nations Children's Fund, The State of the World's Children 1996 (New York: Oxford University Press, 1995).

war (*c.* 1994–6). Human Rights Watch (n.d.: 88) estimates that roughly 250,000 child soldiers are currently fighting in more than 30 wars around the world. This is not counting the large numbers of children who have enlisted themselves in civil wars, as part of liberation armies in Ireland, Palestine, and elsewhere.

This use of children in warfare has been promoted, unwittingly, by technological innovation—specifically, by the development and manufacture of lightweight automatic weapons. These weapons are light enough for a young child to carry and are easy to use (Human Rights Watch, n.d.: 91). Since more people are able to handle these weapons properly, armies are able to grow faster.

Effects on Later Generations

War affects not only those who fight in them, but also civilians even those who are sheltered from the physical horrors of combat. The Lost Generation and the Beat Generation provide good illustrations of the effects of global warfare on social cohesion. The term Lost Generation was coined by Gertrude Stein, a member of the expatriate American circle in 1920s Paris, to refer to the group of American and British citizens (Ernest Hemingway and Ezra Pound among them) who had rejected the traditional conventions of their homelands during and after World War I for the more appealing lifestyle of the Left Bank. Hemingway's *The Sun Also Rises* (1926) depicts the lassitude of this generation.

Just as World War I shattered the world view of the Lost Generation, so, too, did World War II for those who came of age in the late 1930s and early 1940s. The Beat Generation, as they came to be called, were just as out of love with the post-World War II lifestyle as the Lost Generation was with that of the post-World War I era. However, unlike their predecessors, the Beats were not raised in an optimistic, flourishing environment like that of the pre- and post-World War I years, but in the crushing gloom of the Great Depression. Beat writers and poets captured the disillusionment and cynicism of their compatriots in such literary works as Jack Kerouac's *On the Road* and Allen Ginsberg's *Howl*.

Health Consequences of War

One estimate is that military conflicts in the twentieth century have led to the deaths of over 100 million soldiers and civilians—more than the total number of casualties in all previous wars in human history combined (Porter, 1994). Other estimates vary according to whether we include the deaths stemming from war-related famine and disease. Michael Renner (1993b) calculated that 75 per cent of all military deaths since the reign of Julius Caesar had taken place in the twentieth century. Thus, Hobsbawm's characterization of the twentieth century as the 'age of total war' is not far from the truth.

If these numbers seem appalling, they pale in comparison to the possible death tolls humanity would achieve were a full-scale nuclear war to break out. Currently, the nuclear weapons in major military arsenals are more than 4,000 times as powerful as the atomic bombs dropped on Japan. George Friedman and Meredith Friedman (1996) estimate that a nuclear war today would kill 160 million people instantly. Another billion would perish in the first few hours because of radiation poisoning, environmental devastation, and massive social chaos, while hundreds of millions more would die slowly over the ensuing years.

Exposure to war also increases the risk of health problems and lowers life expectancy. One archival study of World War II veterans who either remained in the United States or served overseas found that combat experience increased the risk of physical decline or death in the 15 years after the war. Military rank and theatre of engagement with the enemy did not affect the trend (Elder et al., 1997).

Just as death is an unavoidable outcome of war, so, too, are physical and psychological injuries. The number of military personnel and civilians who are injured or maimed during a war usually exceeds the number of deaths. Indeed, one common military strategy is to maim rather than kill the enemy since it takes more assets to care for the wounded than to discard their bodies. Anti-personnel land mines are especially suited to this vicious task, since they are largely undetectable by civilians or enemy troops without proper equipment and do not need a soldier present to 'pull the trigger'. Cambodia has been called the 'land of the one-legged men', referring to the more than 30,000 individuals—mostly rural farmers—whose limbs have been severed when they accidentally detonated a hidden mine (Stover and McGrath, 1992). Three decades of continuous war in that country have resulted in an estimated 4 to 6 million anti-personnel mines and unexploded ordinances littering the countryside (Cambodia Mine Action Centre, 2006).

Many troops from the Gulf War of 1991 reportedly contracted a disease that has become known as 'Gulf War syndrome'. As many as 100,000 US soldiers and at least 150 Canadian soldiers have been affected by this mysterious illness, the symptoms of which include fatigue, headaches, immune system depression, reproductive problems, and aching joints and muscles (National Gulf War Resource Center, 2001). It is still unclear what the causes of this illness are, how it may be prevented, and what the cure is.

Box 12.4   Personal Experience:
Daily Living Conditions in Iraq Dismal, UN Survey Finds

12 May 2005—Daily living conditions in Iraq are dismal, with families suffering from short water and electricity supply, chronic malnutrition among children and more illiterate young than ever before, a new report by the United Nations Development Program (UNDP) and the Iraqi government shows.

'While many aspects of living conditions in Iraq are dismal, most reflect the courage, endurance and determination of the Iraqi people to overcome the hurdles they are facing', [the] UN Deputy Special Representative stated. Iraqi questioners, trained by a Norwegian research NGO, asked 22,000 households in 18 governorates about their housing, infrastructure, population, health, education, work, income and the status of women . . . . Although a large percentage of the population in Iraq is connected to water, electricity and sewage networks, the supply has been too unstable to make a difference to people's lives. Almost a quarter of the children between 6 months and 5 years suffer from chronic malnutrition. In a country where 39 per cent of the people are younger than 15, the young today are more illiterate than preceding generations. Young men with a high school education or better are suffering from 37 per cent unemployment. The survey not only allows for a good understanding of socio-economic conditions in Iraq, but will also be a building block for further analysis that will certainly benefit the development and reconstruction processes in Iraq.

Source: <www.un.org/apps/news/story.asp?NewsID=14255&Cr=Iraq>. The United Nations is the author of the original material.

Surviving a war physically unscathed does not guarantee complete well-being. Many veterans of war suffer the slow torture of psychological disorders. Much of the mental health literature on the effects of war focuses on **post-traumatic stress disorder (PTSD)**, which researchers had previously studied under labels such as 'shell shock', 'con-centration-camp syndrome', 'survivor syndrome', and 'war neurosis' (Summerfield, 2000).

Although negative psychological reactions to the rigour and insanity of war were initially considered an expression of cowardice, we now recognize PTSD as a common form of distress produced by a traumatic experience, especially by crime victimization, sexual assault, or military combat. Symptoms include nervousness, sleep disturbances, disruption of concentration, anxiety, depression, irrational fear, and flashbacks triggered by loud noises like thunder. Paul Witteman (1991) estimates that 479,000 of the 3.5 million veterans of the Vietnam War suffer from severe PTSD, while another 350,000 have moderate symptoms. Researchers have also linked PTSD to higher rates of drug use and suicide among veterans.

Another study, of the Lebanese civil war (1975–90), revealed that malingering and general anxiety disorder (GAD) decreased in the general population during the years of combat, but drug abuse, neuroses, and psychotic reactions such as anti-social personality disorders increased overall (Baddoura, 1990). J.R. Walton, R.L. Nuttall, and E.V. Nuttall (1997) found that children born into the Salvadoran civil war suffered psychological effects, with those who experienced the highest personal-social impact of the conflict having the poorest mental health.

Victims of terrorism are especially at risk of psychological trauma because of the unexpected and severe nature of the event, and because civilians are usually sheltered from such levels of violence and death. Henk Van der Ploeg and Wim Kleijn (1989) studied the long-term effects of being taken hostage by terrorists in the Netherlands. They found that one-third suffered from PTSD and GAD, and that 12 per cent of the hostages and 11 per cent of their family members still needed professional therapy even nine years after the incident.

Solutions: Seeking Peace in a World of Conflict

Military conflict has occurred so consistently throughout human history that it is unlikely we can propose any practical solution to overturn centuries of human practice. Of the social problems discussed in this book, war is among the oldest. It is a 'final, supreme problem'—a result of greedy ambition and desperation bred by an inability to solve other social problems. Still, if we cannot end all warfare, at least we can develop policies to help reduce conflict and preserve peace. As with other social problems that are unlikely to go away—alcohol and drug abuse, for example, or trafficking in sex—the best we can hope to do is carry out a strategy of harm reduction so that the problem has as few negative social and health outcomes as possible.

The Scale of War

The scale, or magnitude, or warfare expanded drastically in the twentieth century com-pared to earlier centuries. In World War I (1914–18), an estimated 65 million people served in the armed forces of all the combatant countries and roughly 8.5 million of these were killed, along with 6.6 million civilians (www.spartacus.schoolnet.co.uk/FWWdeaths.htm). In World War II (1939–45), another estimated 62 million people served in the armed forces of all the combatant countries and this time roughly 24.5 million of these were killed, along with 37 million civilians (en.wikipedia.org/wiki/World_War_II_casualties). These huge numbers do not even include deaths due to the Nazi Holocaust; victims of Japanese war crimes; deaths related to the Soviet annexations in 1939–40; and civilian losses in the immediate post-war era (1946–7) due to famine and disease.

What is evident from these figures is that, in World War II, both more soldiers and more civilians were killed than in World War I. This change was largely due to an increase in killing power of military technology—an increase that reached its zenith with the development of the atomic and hydrogen bombs. Since the end of World War II, two trends have been observed. First, a vastly larger proportion of war casualties have been civilians, not soldiers—continuing the earlier trend. Second, fewer countries and fewer uniformed service people have been fighting the world's wars. Increasingly, wars since 1945 have involved troops from relatively few countries, have been border wars or civil (i.e., internal) wars, and/or have drawn upon non-professional, civilian fighters (e.g., relatively untrained terrorists).

This latter phenomenon can be characterized as the shrinking scale of warfare. In the past, wars were often formal and co-ordinated campaigns waged by well-organized military units involving thousands of soldiers and war machinery. By contrast, wars today increasingly take the form of **low-intensity conflicts (LICs)**, which involve a smaller army of guerrillas, terrorists, or civilians. LICs are less-organized campaigns characterized by small-arms combat, bombings, ambushes, murders, and massacres. Martin van Creveld (1991) estimates that around 120 LICs have been waged since World War II, with the frequency expected only to rise in the future. In this context, the large current war in Iraq, like earlier wars in Vietnam and in Afghanistan, are exceptions, though they are nowhere near as large as World War II in scope and fatalities.

Like warfare, terrorism is often motivated by causes such as promoting an ideology, is blind to borders, and can, therefore, be directed at both domestic and transnational targets. As we have seen, improvements in social and economic conditions are likely to incite more social movements. The activities of these movements will be largely determined by assets at their disposal. Thus, one means of harm reduction is to limit the global production and sale of arms.

Arms Reduction

In most societies in human history, warfare consisted of only a few thousand or even just a few hundred armed people squaring off against each other. The combatants went at each other with knives, sticks, arrows, spears, clubs, swords, and eventually guns. Early European warfare, for example, was highly stylized: like Roman warfare a millennium earlier, it followed certain set rules of combat. Often people stood, crouched, or proceeded slowly and collectively against an opposing force. Under these circumstances, few civilians were killed. It's true that some warring societies—the fabled Goths, Huns, Vikings, and Vandals among them—were notorious for killing, raping, pillaging, and enslaving the people they conquered, but this was not the norm in warfare. For the most part, killing was confined to small numbers of combatants in highly scripted circumstances of battle.

As we have already noted, with the coming of the twentieth century the scope of battle increased; both more combatants and more civilians were killed by ever more potent weapons. Thus, a chief concern in recent decades has been to find ways to reduce the number and types of weapons in people's hands, and especially to find ways of protecting civilians against weapons and their misuse.

A prime example of this effort has been the Landmines Convention that Canada and Lloyd Axworthy were instrumental in achieving. Landmines have been widely and indiscriminately used around the world as a means of killing foot soldiers and spreading fear among enemy combatants and civilian populations. Often, they have remained in place after wars have ended and have killed many unsuspecting civilians. The Convention on the Prohibition of the Use, Stockpiling, Production and Transfer of Anti-Personnel Mines and on their Destruction, known as the Ottawa Convention, opened for signature on 3 December 1997. By the end of 1998, fully 133 countries had signed the Convention, and 55 of those had ratified it a year later. The Convention came into legal force in March 1999. Many countries contributed funds to making this Convention work: Canada alone contributed $2.8 million for mine-action projects in seven countries in Central Europe, Africa, and the Middle East. An example of the work done with this money includes demining activities in Cambodia, where over 32,000 mines were removed and 10,000 people, as a result, were able to return to fields where they could now safely grow rice. (For more on this topic, see Cameron et al., 1998; and w01.international.gc.ca/MinPub/Publication.asp?publication_id=375588&Language=E).

Other efforts have been made to limit the production and sale of small arms. As the United Nations has noted, 'small arms and light weapons destabilize regions; spark, fuel and prolong conflicts; obstruct relief programs; undermine peace initiatives; exacerbate human rights abuses; hamper development; and foster a "culture of violence"' (disarmament.un.org/cab/salw.html).

International co-operation on this matter took a giant step forward when the United Nations held a Conference on the Illicit Traffic in Small Arms and Light Weapons in All Its Aspects in July 2001. On that occasion, the participating states agreed to adopt a Program of Action to Prevent, Combat, and Eradicate the Illicit Trade in Small Arms and Light Weapons, in All Its Aspects. This agreed-on program includes a number of measures to legislate, destroy weapons, and co-operate in tracing illicit arms. Most recently, in the 2005 World Summit Outcome Document (A/60/L.1) the General Assembly reiterated its support for the implementation of this Program.

From 26 June to 7 July 2006, member states met at a United Nations conference to review progress made in carrying out the Program. To this end, the UN has been consulting broadly on procedures to collect and circulate information received from member states—including national reports and national legislation on small arms and light weapons—and to support practical disarmament measures.

Arms are big business. In 2004, the eight top arms exporters in the world were—in descending order—the United States, Russia, France, the United Kingdom, Germany, Canada, China, and Israel. The United States that year exported $18.5 billion worth of weapons—four times as much as its nearest competitors, Russia and France (at roughly $4.5 billion each) and 20 times as much as sixth-place Canada (which shipped a 'mere' $900 million worth). Military sales accounted for fully 18 per cent of the US national budget—by far the highest proportion of any nation in the world—which helps to explain the claim that, in the US, there is a military-industrial complex with huge political as well as economic power.

Every year, according to current estimates, over $900 billion are spent on arms. In 2002, 2003, and 2004, India and China were the biggest arms buyers. Almost every industrialized country in the world has a domestic arms industry to supply its own military forces. In addition, some countries have a sizable domestic trade in weapons. An illegal trade in small arms is common in many countries and regions of the world—particularly those affected by political instability. Often, the legal arms trade feeds an illegal arms trade, with legally purchased weaponry being resold for illegal purposes. In this way, the arms industry poses global problems due to its (often secret) business practices (en.wikipedia.org/wiki/Arms_trade).

The Control Arms Campaign, founded by Amnesty International, Oxfam, and the International Network on Small Arms, estimates that there are over 600 million small arms in circulation in the world, with over 1,135 companies based in more than 98 different countries occupied manufacturing them. The result is an average of over 500,000 deaths every year, roughly one death per minute. Many people see the supplying of weapons for conflict as immoral and dangerous behaviour that carries little personal, national, or corporate risk. In this way, the global arms industry enables a few to profit from war and death by prolonging wars that might otherwise dwindle to an end if the arms supply dried up (ibid.).

During the 1960s, the United States and Russia were engaged in an international arms race to amass a dominant military arsenal. However, with the development of nuclear weaponry, any war between countries that both possessed nuclear warheads would result in both sides—as well as many others on the periphery—being devastated beyond recognition. This principle of **mutually assured destruction (MAD)** was what held nations back from all-out war. If starting a war meant losing it, then, theoretically, it would be in nobody's interest to start one.

Citing the presence of new threats to national security that have emerged since the end of the Cold War, mainly from 'rogue nations' undeterred by the threat of MAD, the United States has argued for the need for a new arms treaty that reflects the current state of global hostilities. President George W. Bush has proposed to rehatch the Strategic Defense Initiative (SDI), better known as 'Star Wars', first presented by President Ronald Reagan in the 1980s. Some fear that embarking on this strategy will have the effect of reversing decades of progress on reducing the world's stockpile of weapons and possibly even spark a new global arms race, including the weaponization of space. As the US's neighbour to the north and one of its closest military and economic allies, Canada would be directly involved in any push by the US to increase North America's defence capabilities, including the establishment of the controversial continental missile defence shield.

In March 2003, the United States embarked on war against Iraq, aided only by the United Kingdom, Australia, and several dozen small countries (Albania, Ethiopia, and others), against the wishes of the United Nations. (The American government called its allies in war 'the willing states', while an unnamed comic has renamed them 'the billing states'.) This act has led some to wonder which are the rogue nations in the world—the so-called 'axis of evil' (Iraq, Iran, and North Korea, as the American government has said) or the United States and its partners in warfare.

Redistributing Economic Assets

Some believe that terrorism and warfare will be reduced, and peace ensured, only by redistributing economic assets more equally among nations and among people within nations. We know that disparities in wealth and assets have been and are causes of many wars, past and present. Thus, we can probably reduce conflict through a more equal distribution of assets. However, it is unlikely that prosperous nations will readily agree to lower their standards of living at home to benefit less wealthy societies.

Redistributing economic wealth from core nations to peripheral nations does not guarantee that poorer nations will have a better standard of living. There must be proper rules to ensure that citizens will benefit from aid funds. Otherwise, politicians and state elites may appropriate the funds to further their own interests at the expense of their citizens. In addition, aid funds must be targeted for social development, not for military spending—much of US foreign aid, for example, has been targeted for arms to client states such as Saudi Arabia and Israel, just as it was in the past to Saddam Hussein in Iraq, to Osama bin Laden and freedom fighters against the Soviet invasion of Afghanistan, to the Shah of Iran, and to numerous dictatorial regimes in Latin America.

At the same time, sometimes the money for foreign aid, in the form of loans, is never moved into the peripheral countries because of strings attached to the loans. Often, through such agencies as the World Bank and the International Monetary Fund, core countries tell peripheral countries how to spend the loan money. For example, a Canadian loan with strings attached might tell farmers in a peripheral country to spend some portion of the loan money buying farm equipment from Canadian companies. This stimulates the Canadian economy, but may or may not help the peripheral country the loan was supposed to help. In effect, the aid money never leaves the core country. If farmers were allowed to spend the aid money on local businesses, it would help the peripheral country, since their local economy would be stimulated.

The Role of International Peacekeeping Bodies

Another harm-reduction and risk-reduction strategy has been to form an international body dedicated to peacekeeping and preventing global conflict. The most prominent organization attempting to carry out this task has been the United Nations. UN peacekeepers have been patrolling war-torn regions since 1948, when the UN Truce Supervision Organization was created to monitor the ceasefire agreed to by Israel and its Middle East neighbours.

Canadians have been active peacekeepers in the world since 1956, when then Secretary of State for External Affairs (and eventual Prime Minister) Lester B. Pearson sent Canadian forces to Egypt. Seeing a chance to ease tensions around the Suez Canal conflict, Pearson suggested creating a worldwide peacekeeping force to oversee the withdrawal of armed forces from the area and serve as a long-term barrier between Egypt and Israel. The United Nations mission, led by Canadians, was a success, and resulted in Pearson winning the Nobel Peace Prize in 1957.

Since the use of peacekeeping troops in Suez, there have been 60 UN peace operations involving more than 750,000 military, police, and civilian personnel. Missions have served all over the world, creating buffer zones in Cyprus and the former Yugoslavia, bringing aid to Haiti and Rwanda, and providing observers to conflicts in Angola and El Salvador.

Peacekeepers assume that their neutrality will allow them to insert themselves between combatants, to act as a safeguard. In theory, their presence provides a physical and psychological barrier against shots being fired. In practice—for example, in Rwanda during the mid-1990s—the peacekeeping force had no such effect and could not prevent bloodshed. Peacekeeping also assumes that fighters on all sides are sincere in their wish for peace. When this is not the case, violence can break out, as occurred in the former Yugoslavia, where broken ceasefires led to general fighting in 1995 and the first withdrawal of UN troops.

Yet, the need for UN peacekeeping has risen dramatically since the end of the Cold War. In the first 40 years of operation, UN peacekeepers carried out only 18 campaigns. Since 1990, however, 42 operations have been undertaken. As of March 2006, there were 15 active UN peacekeeping operations in the world, involving nearly 90,000 military, police, and civilian personnel from at least 107 countries and annual costs of approximately $5 billion (US). There have been human costs as well: since 1948, 2,242 UN peacekeepers have been killed while on duty (UN, 2006).

Interventions by UN peacekeeping forces have undoubtedly prevented wars and saved lives. However, UN actions have not been enough to eliminate wars, many of which were conducted under 'the watch' of the United Nations. To this list, we can add the 2003 invasion of Iraq by the United States, Britain, and others, which was launched in spite of extensive efforts by the UN to preserve diplomacy and peace. Most recently, as we write in August 2006, the United Nations has agreed to play a role in enforcing a ceasefire between Israel and the Hezbollah forces located in Lebanon, in hopes of bringing about a resolution to the bloodshed that reigned on the border of Israel and Lebanon through the months of July and August.

Concluding Remarks

Some have thought of war as the natural sign of innate aggression. The opposing view is that people are not born to be violent or aggressive, but that we learn to act so. According to this latter explanation, war is a result of social organization and cultural tradition and a response to cultural symbols.

We could think of the arms race as a symbolic show of power and as a means of securing peace through mutual deterrence. However, the negative outcomes include the obvious potential for mass destruction and the enormous monetary cost. The assets spent to produce and preserve armaments could instead be assigned to relieving other social problems. This is especially true in countries of the developing and less developed world, where the need for these assets is more prominent.

Terrorism can exist for different reasons. Common forms are revolutionary terrorism, in which rebels wage war on the state, and repressive terrorism, in which the state wages war in an attempt to repress its citizens. Other forms include transnational terrorism or terrorism by autonomous agents.

Massive economic inequalities exist between nations. Relative deprivation breeds resentment, and resentment can foment aggression. War will pose a problem for humanity so long as there are wide inequalities in wealth and power between nations, wide differences in beliefs and interests, and weaknesses in bodies—such as the United Nations—that are charged with keeping the world's peace.

QUESTIONS FOR CRITICAL THOUGHT

1. Think of the some of the war movies you have seen recently (for example, *Saving Private Ryan*, *The Thin Red Line*, or *Black Hawk Down*). How do those movies portray war? Did you leave the theatre with feelings of patriotism or with a sense that war is awful and should be avoided at all costs, or was it a combination of both? Do you feel Hollywood can be realistic in its depictions of war, or will war films always be susceptible to dramatization for the sake of story rather than truth? What responsibility, if any, does the filmmaker have in making a war movie, both to war veterans and to the general public?

2. With the proliferation of Internet technology spanning the globe, more of the world's peoples are gaining access to information they never had before. The people of less developed countries are seeing the standard of living of others and often wondering why they have been left out. In the 1980 movie *The Gods Must Be Crazy*, an African tribe discovers a Coke bottle, symbolic of Western culture and all the amenities they lack, and the people begin to quarrel among themselves over possession of the bottle. What are the implications of this? How will countries that may not be able to afford the Western culture cope with their inability to achieve this goal?

3. It is a known fact that girls are usually given Barbies and other dolls as small children and that boys are given GI Joe figures and other war toys. In your opinion, how much do you think toy socialization affects violent and aggressive tendencies in adulthood? Do you prefer a biological approach, with testosterone as the explanatory variable, or is the root cause of aggressiveness to be found in socialization? If toys and gender differentials in socialization might be to blame, what should we do about it? Is banning action figures and war toys an option?

4. Research the Nuremberg trials, which occurred after the Holocaust, in which Nazi officials were tried for their genocidal behaviours during World War II. How do these trials illustrate that war crimes are not to be tolerated? What can we learn from this in order to prevent catastrophic events such as the Holocaust from ever occurring again?

5. The remaining time for survivors of some of the major world wars and conflicts is limited. Do you have friends or close relatives who were in a war? Next time you see them, ask them about their experiences of warfare, such as where they were, how they felt, and who they lost, and try to see the world through their eyes. Research post-traumatic stress disorder (PTSD) further and try to imagine how traumatizing these events were to the individual and how scary PTSD symptoms must be. Keep a journal of your experiences.

RECOMMENDED READINGS

Rabab Abdulhadi, 'The Palestinian Women's Autonomous Movement: Emergence, Dynamics and Challenges', *Gender and Society* 12 (1998): 649–73. This article details the women's movement in Palestine and describes the interactions of femininity, religion, and military uprising.

Cynthia Enloe, *The Morning After: Sexual Politics at the End of the Cold War* (Berkeley: University of California Press, 1993). Enloe examines international relations and gender issues by looking at the connections between militarism and masculinity. She grounds her ideas in the everyday experiences of women worldwide.

Arturo Escobar, *Encountering Development: The Making and Unmaking of the Third World* (Princeton, NJ: Princeton University Press, 1995). In his examination of global inequality, Escobar focuses on the many perspectives of Third World development. He argues primarily that powerful nations wish to maintain their dominance over the developing world, not aid it.

Franklin L. Ford, *Political Murder: From Tyrannicide to Terrorism* (Cambridge, Mass.: Harvard University Press, 1985). This is a thorough historical analysis of the use of political murder. Ford focuses on 155 specific murders to discern the larger pattern.

Edward S. Herman and Noam Chomsky, *Manufacturing Consent: The Political Economy of the Mass Media*, new edn (New York: Pantheon Books, 2002). This now-classic text describes government's use of the media in constructing the apparent consent of the population. Using examples of wars in the Americas, the authors question journalistic integrity as well.

RECOMMENDED WEBSITES

United Nations

www.un.org

The purposes of the United Nations are to maintain international peace and security; to develop friendly relations among nations; to co-operate in solving international economic, social, cultural, and humanitarian problems and in promoting respect for human rights and fundamental freedoms; and to be a centre for harmonizing the actions of nations in attaining these ends.

Canadian War Museum

www.warmuseum.ca

The Canadian War Museum represents a living memorial to those men and women who served in Canada's armed forces. Its website is also a resource base for research and the dissemination of information and expertise on all aspects of the country's military past, from the pre-Contact era to the present. It preserves artifacts of the Canadian military experience and advances Canadian military history.

International Policy Institute for Counter-Terrorism (ICT)

www.ict.org.il

The ICT is a research institute and think-tank dedicated to developing innovative public policy solutions to international terrorism. The ICT applies an integrated, solutions-oriented approach built on a foundation of real-world experience. It provides information, seeks to raise awareness, advises decision-makers, and continues to develop research on the issue of counter-terrorism.

GLOSSARY

Collective violence Often organized by a group of individuals or a social movement, this type of violence is used to promote an agenda or resist an oppressive other.

Globalization The integration on a world scale of economic activities and peoples by units of private capital and improved communications technology and transportation. In other words, globalization is the trend of increasing interdependence between the economies and societies of the world.

Ideology A system of beliefs that explain how society is, or should be; any system of ideas underlying and informing political action. In a Marxist sense, ideological ideas justify and legitimate subordination of one group to another.

Imperialism The exercise of political and economic control by one state over the territory of another, often by military means. Developing countries are often the focus of imperialistic and exploitive activities that stifle their own development and concentrate their resources and labour for the profits of advanced capitalist countries.

Interpersonal violence Violent interactions occurring between individuals, such as murders, rapes, and domestic and child abuse.

Low-intensity conflicts (LICs) Conflicts involving smaller armies of guerrillas, terrorists, or civilians. LICs are less-organized campaigns characterized by small-arms combat, bombings, ambushes, assassinations, and massacres.

Mutually assured destruction (MAD) The fear of destroying one's own people acts as a deterrent to acts of aggression. For example, the detonation of a nuclear warhead could clearly result in all sides being decimated and is often used as a threat rather than as a real option.

Post-traumatic stress disorder (PTSD) A form of psychological distress produced by a traumatic experience such as crime victimization, sexual assault, or military combat. Symptoms include nervousness, sleep disturbances, disruption of concentration, anxiety, depression, irrational fear, and flashbacks triggered by loud noises like thunder or even a car's backfiring.

Relative deprivation theory The feelings felt and the judgements reached when an individual or members of a group compare themselves to others who are better off materially. It is not absolute standards that are important in making such judgements, but the relative standards or frame of reference in terms of which people make judgements. These sentiments can be argued as brewing social movements.

Resource mobilization theory Emphasizes the critical role that material resources play in forming social movements. In this perspective, social movements are not founded on hysteria and frustration, but are based on rationality, leadership, and organization.

Social movement Any broad social alliance of people who seek to effect or block an aspect of social change within a society. While they may be informally organized, they may in time lead to the formation of formal organizations such as political parties and labour unions. Examples of social movements include political movements, labour movements, the women's movement, ecological movements, and peace movements.

War Violent, usually armed conflict between states or people. This includes armed conflict, undeclared battles, civil conflicts, guerrilla wars, covert operations, and even terrorism. It is often argued that warfare is a culturally influenced phenomenon rather than simply biologically determined (instinctual aggressiveness). This would explain why some countries and cultures are more prone to warfare.

World system theory A conception of the modern social world that views it as comprising one interlinked entity with an international division of labour unregulated by any one political structure. Developed by Immanuel Wallerstein (e.g., 1976), this theory seeks to explain the uneven pace of development in the world by looking at the unequal relations between different countries.

REFERENCES

Amnesty International. 1995. *Human Rights Are Women's Right.* New York: Amnesty International USA.

Babic, Dragutin. 2002. 'The Croatian Government and Programs Regarding the Return of War Migrants: Between Plans and Realizations—The Experience of the Brod-Posavina County', *Migracijske i etnicke teme* 18, 1: 63–83.

Baddoura, C. 1990. 'Mental Health and War in Lebanon', *Bulletin de l'Académie nationale de médecine* 174: 583–90.

Barber, Benjamin. 1996. *Jihad vs. McWorld.* New York: Times Books.

Baron, Ethan. 2005. 'Old Chemical Weapons Lie on Ocean Floor', *Montreal Gazette*, 15 Nov., A15

Bass, Gary Jonathan. 2002. 'Stay the Hand of Vengeance: The Politics of War Crimes Tribunals', *International Studies Review* 4, 1: 129–39.

Benhabib, Seyla. 2002. 'Unholy Wars', *Constellations* 9, 1: 34–45.

Blackburn, Robin. 2002. 'The Imperial Presidency, the War on Terrorism, and the Revolutions of Modernity', *Constellations* 9, 1: 3–33.

Boggs, Carl. 2002. 'Overview: Globalization and the New Militarism', *New Political Science* 24, 1: 9–20.

Brown, Lester R., Christopher Flavin, and Hal Kane. 1992. *Vital Signs 1992: The Trends That Are Shaping Our Future.* Washington: Worldwatch Institute.

Buchanan, David. 2002. 'Gendercide and Human Rights', *Journal of Genocide Research* 4, 1: 95–108.

Calhoun, Martin L. 1996. 'Cleaning Up the Military's Toxic Legacy', *USA Today Magazine* 124: 60–4.

Cambodia Mine Action Centre. 2006. Available at: <www.cmac.org.kh>.

Cameron, Maxwell A., Robert J. Lawson, and Brian W. Tomlin, eds. 1998. *To Walk Without Fear: The Global Movement to Ban Landmines.* Toronto: Oxford University Press.

Cancian, Francesca M., and James William Gibson. 1990. *Making War, Making Peace: The Social Foundations of Violent Conflict.* Belmont, Calif.: Wadsworth.

Clough, Patricia Ticineto. 2002. 'Posts Post September 11', *Cultural Studies—Critical Methodologies* 2, 1: 15–17.

Cooper, Sandi E. 2002. 'Peace as a Human Right: The Invasion of Women into the World of High International Politics', *Journal of Women's History* 14, 2: 9–25.

Coupland, Robin M., and David R. Meddings. 1999. 'Mortality Associated with Use of Weapons in Armed Conflicts, Wartime Atrocities, and Civilian Mass Shootings: Literature Review', *British Medical Journal* 319: 407–10.

Dahrendorf, Ralf. 1959. *Class and Class Conflict in Industrial Society.* Stanford, Calif.: Stanford University Press.

Department of National Defence. 2005. 'Defence Policy Statement: Contributing to a Safer and More Secure World', May. Available at: <www.forces.gc.ca/site/reports/dps/main/05_e.asp#2_1>; accessed 14 Aug. 2006.

Durkheim, Émile. 1960 [1893]. *The Division of Labor in Society.* Glencoe, Ill.: Free Press.

Elbaum, Max, and Bob Wing. 2002. 'Some Strategic Implications of September 11', *Socialism and Democracy* 16, 1: 161–4.

Elder, G.H., Jr, M.J. Shanahan, and E.C. Clipp. 1997. 'Linking Combat and Physical Health: The Legacy of World War II in Men's Lives', *American Journal of Psychiatry* 154: 330–6.

Enloe, Cynthia H. 1987. 'Feminists Thinking about War, Militarism, and Peace', in Beth Hess and Myra Marx Ferree, eds, *Analyzing Gender: A Handbook of Social Science Research.* Newbury Park, Calif.: Sage, 526–47.

Erickson, Bonnie H. 1981. 'Secret Societies and Social Structure', *Social Forces* 60, 1: 188–210.

Friedman, George, and Meredith Friedman. 1996. *The Future of War: Power, Technology, and American World Dominance in the 21st Century.* New York: Crown.

Girvan, Susan, ed. 2000. *Canadian Global Almanac 2000.* Toronto: Macmillan Canada.

Greenfeld, Karl Taro. 2006. 'The Long Way Home', *Sports Illustrated*, 15 May.

Harper, Charles L., and Kevin T. Leicht. 2002. *Exploring Social Change: America and the World*, 4th edn. Upper Saddle River, NJ: Prentice-Hall.

Harvey, David, 2005. *The New Imperialism.* Oxford: Oxford University Press.

Held, David. 2002. 'Violence, Law, and Justice in a Global Age', *Constellations* 9, 1: 74–88.

Hemingway, Ernest. 1926. *The Sun Also Rises.* New York: Simon & Schuster.

Hobsbawm, Eric. 1994. *The Age of Extremes: The Short Twentieth Century 1914–1991.* London: Abacus.

Hudson, Valerie M., and Andrea Den Boer. 2002. 'A Surplus of Men, a Deficit of Peace: Security and Sex Ratios in Asia's Largest States', *International Security* 26, 4: 5–38.

Human Rights Watch. n.d. 'Stop the Use of Child Soldiers!' Available at: <www.hrw.org/campaigns/crp/index.htm>; accessed 17 Feb. 2003.

Jacobs, Dale W., et al. 2003. *World Book: Focus on Terrorism.* Chicago: World Book.

Kage, Tatsuo. 2002. 'War Measures Act: Japanese Canadian Experience', workshop held at a meeting on Immigration and Security, Our Voices, Our Strategies: Asian Canadians against Racism, 7–9 June, University of British Columbia, Vancouver.

Kanaaneh, Moslih, and Marit Netland. 1992. *Children and Political Violence: Psychological Reactions and National Identity Formation among the Children of the Intifada.* East Jerusalem: Early Childhood Resource Center.

Keung, Nicholas. 2005. 'Images of War Linger with Students', *Toronto Star*, 31 Mar.

Malthus, Thomas R. 1959 [1798]. *Population: The First Essay.* Ann Arbor: University of Michigan Press.

Michael, John. 2002. 'Intellectuals and the Clash of Cultures', *Socialism and Democracy*, 16, 1: 137–43.

Milgram, Stanley. 1974. *Obedience to Authority.* New York: Harper and Row.

Mills, C. Wright. 1956. *The Power Elite.* New York: Oxford University Press.

Moore, Barrington. 1967. *Social Origins of Dictatorship and Democracy: Lord and Peasant in the Making of the Modern World.* Boston: Beacon Press.

Mowat, Farley. 1984. *Sea of Slaughter.* Toronto: McClelland & Stewart.

National Gulf War Resource Center. 2001. '1999 Gulf War Statistics', available at: <www.ngwrc.org/Facts/index.htm>; accessed 31 July 2001.

Peterson, Jordan B. 1998. 'Individual Motivation for Group Aggression: Psychological, Mythological, and Neuropsychological Perspectives', in Peterson, ed., *Personality and Its Transformations: Selected Readings.* Montreal: P.S. Presse, 1–32.

Porter, Bruce D. 1994. *War and the Rise of the State: The Military Foundations of Modern Politics.* New York: Free Press.

Rajan, S. Ravi. 2002. 'Democracy, Security, Citizenship', *Capitalism, Nature, Socialism* 12, 4: 1–2, 170–2.

Renner, Michael. 1993a. *Critical Juncture: The Future of Peacekeeping.* Washington: Worldwatch Institute.

———. 1993b. 'Environmental Dimensions of Disarmament and Conversion', in Kevin J. Cassidy and Gregory A. Bischak, eds, *Real Security: Converting the Defense Economy and Building Peace.* Albany: State University of New York Press, 88–132.

Rummel, R.J. 1992. 'Megamurders', *Society* 29, 6: 47–52.

———. 1994. 'Power, Genocide and Mass Murder', *Journal of Peace Research* 31: 1–10.

———. 1998. *Statistics of Democide: Genocide and Mass Murder Since 1900.* Piscataway, NJ: Transaction.

Runciman, W.G. 1967. *Relative Deprivation and Social Justice: A Study of Attitudes to Social Inequality in Twentieth-Century England.* London: Routledge & Kegan Paul.

Simon, Jeffrey D. 2001. *Terrorist Trap: America's Experience with Terrorism*, 2nd edn. Bloomington: Indiana University Press.

Snyder, Charles McCool. 1962. *Dr. Mary Walker: The Little Lady in Pants.* New York: Vantage Press.

Starr, Joyce R., and Daniel C. Stoll. 1989. *U.S. Foreign Policy on Water Resources in the Middle East.* Washington: Center for Strategic and International Studies.

Stover, Eric, and Rae McGrath. 1992. 'Calling for an International Ban on a Crippling Scourge—Land Mines', *Human Rights Watch* 10, 2: 6–7.

Summerfield, Derek. 2000. 'War and Mental Health: A Brief Overview', *British Medical Journal* 321: 232–5.

Tucker, Robert C. 1978. 'Introduction', in Karl Marx and Friedrich Engels, *The Marx-Engels Reader.* New York: Norton.

United Nations. 1998. *50 Years of United Nations Peacekeeping Operations.* Available at: <www.un.org/depts/dpko/dpko/50web/2.htm>; accessed 31 Jan. 2003.

———. 2001. 'United Nations Peacekeeping Operations: Background Note', July. Available at: <www.un.org/peace/bnote010101.pdf>; accessed 31 July 2001.

———. 2006. 'United Nations Peacekeeping Operations: Background Note', 28 Feb. Available at: <www.un.org/depts/dpko/dpko/bnote_htm>; accessed 28 Mar. 2006.

United States, Department of State. 2003. 'Patterns of Global Terrorism 2002'. Available at: <www.state.gov/s/ct/rls/pgtrpt/2002/>; accessed 15 May 2003.

van Creveld, Martin. 1991. *The Transformation of War.* New York: Free Press.

Van der Ploeg, Henk M., and Wim C. Kleijn. 1989. 'Being Held Hostage in the Netherlands: A Study of Long-term Aftereffects', *Journal of Traumatic Stress* 2, 2: 153–69.

von Clausewitz, Carl. 1993 [1833]. *On War*, trans. Michael Howard and Peter Paret. New York: Knopf.

Wallerstein, Immanuel. 1976. *The Modern World-System: Capitalist Agriculture and the Origins of the European World-Economy in the Sixteenth Century.* New York: Academic Press.

————. 2004. *World-Systems Analysis: An Introduction*. Durham, NC: Duke University Press.

Wallis, Victor. 2002. 'A Radical Approach to Justice for 9/11', *Socialism and Democracy* 16, 1: 156–61.

Walton, J.R., R.L. Nuttall, and E.V. Nuttall. 1997. 'The Impact of War on the Mental Health of Children: A Salvadoran Study', *Child Abuse and Neglect* 21: 737–49.

Weber, Max. 1946. *Max Weber: Essays in Sociology*, trans. and ed. H.H. Gerth and C.W. Mills. New York: Oxford University Press.

Witteman, Paul A. 1991. 'Lost in America', *Time*, 11 Feb., 76–7.

Wright, Quincy. 1964. *A Study of War*. Chicago: University of Chicago Press.

Zimbardo, Philip. 1971. 'The Psychological Power and Pathology of Imprisonment', statement prepared for the US House of Representatives Committee on the Judiciary, Subcommittee No. 3: Hearings on Prison Reform, San Francisco, 25 Oct.

CHAPTER 13

SOCIAL PROBLEMS IN THE FUTURE

LEARNING OBJECTIVES

- To learn what 'futures studies' are.
- To understand the contributions of the first futurist, Thomas Malthus.
- To discover what past theorists have predicted for our future.
- To appreciate the changing definition of social problems.
- To know about the trends in social problems that may continue into the future.
- To understand the controversy surrounding genetic manipulation.
- To appreciate the problem posed by gambling.
- To learn about the implications for the future of cyberspace.
- To see both the positive and negative effects of globalization.
- To understand the sociology surrounding rumour.
- To learn how contagion leads to the marginalization of some groups.

Introduction

This chapter is about predictions and trends, sociology and futures studies, the links between past and future, and how people viewed the future in the past. In this chapter, we wonder what the future will bring. Methodically studying and predicting the future has important practical value. As we shall see, **futures studies** help us think about the future more clearly. Futures researchers track technical innovations, value shifts, geopolitical trends, economic developments, demographic patterns, and other changes. Using these data, they consider possible alternative futures, then use them as part of strategic planning initiatives.

In this chapter, we will examine the ways in which people today think about the future and how people thought about the future in the past. If we are going to think about the future in useful ways, we need to avoid the mistakes people made in the past. If we can do so, we can make better predictions. By making better predictions, we can prepare better for the future.

This is not to say that we can hope to predict the future perfectly. The bad predictions of the past suggest that we cannot. Besides, we cannot even hope to prepare perfectly, no matter how good our predictions may be. However, where social organization is concerned, preparing is always better than being taken by surprise. Today, in working to build a better society, we can take advantage of the methods devised by the field of futures studies, which urges us to imagine desired futures and then work towards them.

As we shall see, some social problems of the past will likely persist and new problems will emerge in the future. A future without problems is unthinkable, if only because we humans continue to create new problems as we go along. A few likely types of problems come easily to mind. Like much else in the past 100 years, the problems of the future will probably involve science and technology, travel and communication, war and inter-group conflict. Since we will likely continue to live in a global society, humanity's problems will be (increasingly) global in scope. Though worldwide health is continually improving, concerns about health will continue to grow. Medical technology will continue to improve, but new illnesses will continue to develop.

Most important, since we are increasingly reliant on information and technology, our problems will be concerned ever more with information flow, the abuse of technology, and the failing of technology. **Cyberspace**—the notional location of most of our information in the future—will be the source of new social problems, especially problems of social control and misinformation. Rumours and contagion, especially where they spread troublesome misinformation, will pose critical problems—even (possibly) creating problems of war and panic.

We end this chapter with a call for modest optimism about the future of humanity and the future of social problems. Like hamsters on treadmills, we might continue to move ahead in absolute terms. However, we will stay more or less where we are in relative terms, since our expectations will rise with our abilities to meet them. Our capacity to solve social problems—to improve society in absolute terms—will need better social science. This, in turn, will need a reassessment of what we think sociology can do and of how it should be done. The chapter ends with a call for better measurements of basic social processes.

Thinking about the Future

The future is always before us yet always a day away from being the past. Think how much the world has changed in the last half-century. As we moved out of the shadow of possible all-out nuclear war with the Soviet enemy in the 1950s and 1960s, national concern over military conflict declined. Then people worried increasingly about domestic concerns such as the economy and unemployment, health and aging, and the environment. There has been no 'peace dividend' as far as worrying is concerned. We continue to imagine, find, and create new social problems.

A recurring theme in this book has been the interconnectedness of social problems. None of the social problems we have discussed stands alone; each is related to other problems. And as we have shown, all have health effects. What this complexity suggests, in part, is that a change in one area of social life will affect other areas. Another important aspect of the social problems we have discussed is their historical basis. Most problems today are the result of long-standing neglect and simmering conflict.

Consider as an example the current problem of conflictual relations between Quebec and the other provinces in Canada, which we can trace back to the early history of relations between the French and English in Canada three centuries ago. Or consider the problem of race relations between blacks and whites in the United States, which dates back nearly 400 years to that country's practice of slavery. Even today, echoes of these earlier periods in Canadian and US history are heard in the relationships between ethnic and racial groups in the two countries. These examples clearly suggest, as do many other social problems, that effective solutions to social problems will often be slow in coming.

At the same time, social problems change. For example, as we saw in Chapter 3 on alcohol and drug abuse, what people consider an unlawful substance, the use of which is therefore a social problem, can shift markedly over time. Cocaine and opium were once considered proper medicinal and recreational drugs but now are strictly banned by the criminal justice system. Public officials considered marijuana use legal, then illegal; today we have tight limits on legal access to marijuana for strictly therapeutic purposes and the prospect of the effective decriminalization of marijuana use. Not all social problems have a long history, however. On the contrary, people are, for various reasons, always creating new problems.

The dynamic nature of social problems—a result of their relationship with one another and with the past—poses difficulties not only for people actively working to improve social conditions, but also for researchers trying to foresee the social problems of the future. And, as we shall see, the organization of sociological research also makes precise forecasting difficult, though there are ways we can improve that. Our goal in thinking about the future is not, strictly speaking, to foresee the future (this is impossible) but to map out alternative futures. This, finally, is what futures studies are about.

What Is Futures Studies?

'Human futures are unpredictable and it is futile to think that past trends will forecast coming patterns' (Gould, 1999: 145). The only exception to this general rule may be that 'technology might offer some opportunity for predicting the future—as science moves through networks of implication, and each discovery suggests a set of subsequent steps. From these data they create scenarios of possible alternative futures, which are then used as choices within strategic planning initiatives' (University of Houston–Clear Lake, 2001).

To claim an ability to predict accurately the details of the future would be rash. Nevertheless, it is both practical and possible to make reasonable guesses about the world of tomorrow, for two reasons. The first is that anticipating future events allows people today to prepare better for events in the future. As the global panic (which, fortunately, proved unwarranted) induced by the threat of the Y2K computer failure has shown, a lack of preparation can have strong economic and social effects. (Computer systems, because of human short-sightedness, had not been designed to account for dates past the year 1999, which, it was anticipated, would necessitate practically insurmountable reprogramming.) Second, the decisions we make today can shape and alter the future. Defining the world we want can help us to work actively towards it. Occasionally we are successful in that effort.

Wendell Bell, one of the leaders of this field in social research, notes four key assumptions made in futures studies: (1) 'time is continuous, linear, unidirectional and irreversible. Events occur in time before or after other events and the continuum of time defines the past, present and future' (1997: 140); (2) 'not everything that will exist has existed or does exist' (141), meaning that the future will bring novel events, processes, and structures that have no precedent in history; (3) 'futures thinking is essential for human action' (142), referring to the fact that all significant human actions need anticipation and an awareness of a future goal; and (4) 'in making our way in the world, both individually and collectively, the most useful knowledge is 'knowledge of the future'' (143–4).

Alternative Forecasting Methods

The future is filled with doubt. Since we can have no hard facts about the future, we have only estimates and opinions. In this sense, all forecasts are opinions about the future. Yet, we need to know as much as possible about the future if we are to prepare for it adequately. Forecasting, whether in regard to climate change or next week's weather, aims to help today's decision-making and planning by encouraging people to think about the ways they can adjust the present to prepare for the future. Every prediction, as part of a forecast, is an invitation to introduce change. However, whatever methods we

Table 13.1 Five Main Sociological Paradigms Related to Futures Studies	
Structural Functionalism	■ Futures studies look into alternative futures and identify the most probable social trends. ■ Forecasting contributes to today's decision-making and planning by helping politicians to devise social policies. ■ Looking to the future encourages people to reflect on current patterns of events and make adjustments in preparation for the future.
Conflict Theory	■ Different forecasting and simulation methods produce different insights into the nature and probability of occurrence of certain events that may favour one population subgroup over another. ■ Various interest groups compete for government support by raising and perhaps exaggerating the acuity of particular concerns.
Symbolic Interactionism	■ Gossip and rumour may spread misinformation and create moral panic or fear. ■ The rise of cyberspace and virtual communities hides many social factors (e.g., gender, race, and class) that often prevent similar people from interacting with one another.
Feminism	■ Despite ongoing efforts made by women to overcome gender discrimination, inequalities in wage and job opportunities will continue to persist. ■ Modern mothers must learn to negotiate a fine balance between work and family responsibilities as their participation in the labour force increases.
Social Constructionism	■ The future is a social construct, a form of propaganda designed to evoke a particular set of behaviours. ■ Media portrayals of social problems and trends exert a large influence on people's perspectives of society, may spark social movements, and contribute to policy-making.

use, there will always be uncertainty until the period of the forecast has passed; so forecasting demands patience. Second, we can never forecast every element of every scenario, since some elements are less understood than others; so forecasting demands humility. Third, giving policy-makers forecasts will help them devise new social policies. These new social policies, in turn, will change the future, thus changing the accuracy of the prediction. Consequently, forecasting often may change the future and prove the forecast wrong, making it hard for us to evaluate the forecasting method.

Forecasting methods fall into several main categories. David Walonick has identified a number of these methods, including the genius method, trend extrapolation, consensus methods, simulation methods, cross-impact matrix method, scenario-building, decision trees, and combining forecasts (Walonick, n.d.). We will discuss several of these briefly.

So-called *genius forecasting* is a method that relies mainly on intuition and insight; a prime example would be the forecasts provided by H.G. Wells, some of which are discussed below. Many genius forecasts turn out wrong, but others turn out right. As Malcolm Gladwell (2005) has recently argued, we all make very rapid intuitive judgements, decisions, and predictions all the time, and many of them turn out to be correct. Some individuals produce consistently accurate forecasts by this method, and their forecasts are useful because they are reliably accurate, even if we don't understand how they achieve their accuracy.

Likely, the reason genius forecasting works as well as it does is because it builds on our own experiences. In this respect, it is a personal form of 'trend extrapolation'. *Trend extrapolation* examines trends and cycles in historical data; it uses mathematical techniques to predict the future from the past—for example, to predict the birth rate in Canada in 2050 from the birth rates between 1950 and 2006. The strength of this method is that it roots the future firmly in historical experience. The weakness is that, with this method, the further out we try to forecast, the less certain the forecast becomes. That is because conditions change, and some processes change quickly and repeatedly. The stability of the environment is a key factor in controlling whether trend extrapolation will be a suitable forecasting model.

So-called 'data-smoothing' methods separate the historical data into trends: seasonal and random parts. Mathematical models based on the observed trends use smoothing constants, coefficients, and other features that must be chosen by the forecaster, making this method something of an art. Largely, the choice of these features determines the outcome of the forecast. So, once again, the quality of the forecast depends largely on the expertise, experience, and intuition of the forecaster.

Forecasting complex systems often involves seeking expert opinions from more than one person. These are so-called *consensus methods* of forecasting. 'Judgemental forecasting' usually involves combining forecasts from more than one source. 'Informed forecasting' begins with a set of key assumptions and then uses a combination of historical data and expert opinions. 'Involved forecasting' seeks the opinions of all those directly affected by the forecast. These techniques produce better forecasts than can be arrived at from a single source by compensating for defects in a given forecasting technique.

The best-known 'consensus method' is the Delphi method. In a series of iterations, experts offer judgements on the likelihood of certain outcomes, then evaluate the answers given by their peers. This approach is intended to produce a rapid narrowing of opinions among experts. It provides more accurate forecasting than group discussions, is more reliable than judgements by individual geniuses, and makes better use of expert knowledge than mathematical trend extrapolation. However, this method needs the co-operation of many experts over an extended period; often, therefore, it is impractical.

Simulation methods use analogs to model complex systems. For example, game analogs may be used to model the interactions of players in imagined social interac-tions—for example, in the studying of negotiation and bargaining. Mathematical analogs have been successful in forecasting outcomes, especially in the physical sciences. Many of these models use advanced statistical techniques (known as multivariate analy-ses) to model complex systems involving relationships between two or more variables. Multiple regression is the mathematical analog of a systems approach, and it has become the primary forecasting tool of economists and social scientists.

Ironically, strong correlations between predictor variables create unstable forecasts, where a slight change in one variable can have a large effect on another variable. In a multiple regression (and systems) approach, as the relationships between the compo-nents of the system become stronger and more numerous, our ability to predict any given component decreases. This was one of the criticisms levelled at what was perhaps the most famous future simulation in social science history: the 'limits to growth exer-cise' developed under the auspices of the Club of Rome (Meadows and Meadows, 1972). We will discuss this study shortly.

The *scenario method* is a narrative forecast that describes a potential course of events. Recognizing the interrelationships of system components, it considers events such as new technology, population shifts, and changing consumer preferences. Scenarios, writ-ten as long-term predictions of the future, force decision-makers to ask: (1) Can we sur-vive the worst possible scenario? (2) Will we be happy with the most likely scenario? (3) Are we able to take advantage of the best possible scenario?

Scenario modelling leads directly to a need to make choices and decisions, and this in turn leads to models of decision-making. *Decision trees* are graphical devices to help illustrate the relationships between choices. Computer technology has made it possible to create very complex decision trees, with many subsystems and feedback loops.

Every decision can be expected to produce a variety of outcomes, some desired and some undesired; and each of these outcomes will have an assignable value to us. Deci-sion theory, using decision trees, is based on the idea that the expected value of an out-come variable can be calculated as the average value for that variable. In other words, the value of a decision is the 'value' of the outcome it produces, calculated as the total of all estimated positive and negative outcomes in the decision tree.

It should be clear by now that no single forecasting technique suits all situations. As a result, as Walonick (n.d.) points out, *combining* various individual forecasts yields the most accurate forecasting. However, combining quantitative and qualitative forecasts reduces accuracy. Researchers have not yet discovered which combinations of methods yield the best forecasts.

The goal of forecasting is obviously to be as accurate as possible. An accurate fore-cast enables us to plan the use of our resources efficiently and effectively. However, the usefulness of a forecast is not always related to its accuracy. The value of a forecast depends on various things, including the type of information being forecast, our confi-dence in the accuracy of the forecast, the magnitude of our dissatisfaction with the fore-cast, and the variety of ways we can adapt to or modify the forecast. Each forecasting situation must be evaluated individually regarding its usefulness.

As we noted earlier, if a forecast results in an adaptive change, then the accuracy of the forecast might be modified by that change. Suppose the forecast is that our business will experience a 10 per cent drop in sales next month. The way we contemplate the future is an expression of our desire to create that future—an expression of our present thoughts. In this sense, then, the future is invented, not predicted. And if reality is an illusion, then the future is also an illusion.

We predict the future based on knowledge, intuition, and logic. Sometimes forecasts become part of a creative process, and sometimes they don't. When two people make

---

Box 13.1 Social Construction: Future Business Trends

The following piece shows that forecasters who see capitalism as the status quo project the foreseeable future in terms of business as usual, aided by technology that makes global business easier and faster, all of this resting on a value consensus that supports global capitalism.

Complex and real-time changes will become the norm for business in the twenty-first century. Business leaders need to develop a capacity to envision future opportunities as well as challenges.

Technology will be the major enabling force for business in the future, transforming supply chains, value nets, business models, work styles and opening up new global markets for expansion.

THE GLOBAL INTELLIGENT MARKETPLACE
Future supply chains will possess the super efficiencies of knowledge management, customer data mining, and be linked to Marketplace to Marketplace, M2M commerce. Deeply personalized artificial intelligence (AI) enabled decision support systems that connect vendors, suppliers and producers will produce an elegant network of commercial efficiency for customers.

PRICE ELASTICITY AND FLUID MARKETS
Real-time anywhere wireless communications will explode competition and open markets worldwide. New marketplaces will revolve around one-minute product offers, predicative demographics, Internet product development polls and other Net-economy innovations.

E-CASH—THE NEW CURRENCY OF THE GLOBAL ELECTRONIC ECONOMY
The 'wallet' of the future is a smart wireless media appliance, transaction portal, personal computer, and communication device. Markets will be fluid, very flexible and personalized based on loyalty commitments, dynamic and digitally cash-ready.

THE DIGITAL LIFESTYLE
The wireless revolution is just beginning. The next generation of consumers, the kids of today, will have less barriers to frustrate their adoption of technology. As communications and commerce merge, as technology becomes pervasive and invisible, tomorrow's consumers will forge new lifestyles.

SMART PORTALS, ENGINES OF THE B2B UNIVERSE
The integration of knowledge management, ERP, collaborative workspace, intelligent media, and the Internet.

GLOBAL DIVERSITY
We will all have to learn to deal with a multicultural world of different values and lifestyles. China will become the largest market in the world.

Source: From 'Business Futures' by Dr. James Canton, Institute for Global Futures, at: <www.globalfuturist.com>. Copyright © 2006 Dr. James Canton.

mutually exclusive forecasts, both of them cannot be true. At least one forecast is wrong. Does one person's forecast create the future while the other does not? The mechanisms involved in the construction of the future are not well understood on an individual or social level. Because of the power of a prediction to affect the future, prophecy itself may be part of a self-interested quest for power.

If the future is a social construct, are predictions of the future a form of propaganda, designed to evoke a particular set of behaviours? Some believe that the desire for control is hidden in all forecasts. Since decisions made today are based on forecasts, forecasts may be ways to control today's decisions. In this respect, forecasting is a type of agenda-setting, a way of forcing everyone to think about the future, and make decisions, in particular ways. Since forecasts can and often do take on a creative role, is it necessary to discuss the ethics of making forecasts that involve other people's futures?

Each person has the right to create his or her own future. On the other hand, a social forecast might alter the course of an entire society. There are no clear rules involving the ethics of forecasting. For this reason, social forecasting must specifically address relevant physical, cultural, and societal values. Also, forecasters must examine their own personal biases, which are likely to influence the forecasting process. As we have said, even the most rigorous forecasting techniques build on judgements that can dramatically alter the forecast.

Ideally, we will find ways to use forecasting to create socially desirable futures: for example, sociologists might favour peaceful coexistence, ecological sustainability, and a fairer distribution of the world's assets. However, not everyone views desirable futures in the same way; the idea of a *desirable future* is a subjective concept. If a goal of forecasting is to create desirable futures, then the forecaster must ask the ethical question of 'desirable for whom?' At least, forecasters should try to engage as many people as possible in the forecasting process to increase their understanding and accuracy. This would have the effect of empowering people who might be affected by the forecast. By involving these people, they could become co-creators of their own futures.

What Past Experts Predicted about the Future

History has recorded many instances in which highly regarded thinkers made wildly inaccurate guesses about the progress of human society. The Roman engineer Sextus Julius Frontinus, for example, confidently declared in the late first century that 'inventions have long since reached their limit, and I see no hope for further development.' Nor is this form of thinking limited to the pre-modern era. In 1899, Charles Duell, the commissioner of the US Patent Office, seriously considered closing down the Office to save the government money, reasoning, 'everything that can be invented has been invented' (Wilson, 2000: 21).

Any discussion of futures research in the modern sense must start with the work of Thomas Malthus (1959 [1798]). Malthus foresaw population problems in the future based on the premise that populations grow exponentially while food supplies grow additively (see the discussion in Chapter 10). He pointed out that any exponential series, however slowly it grows, eventually overtakes any arithmetic series, however quickly it grows. Many of Malthus's predictions about the impending overpopulation of the planet were off target, since he failed to foresee the degree to which humans have since been able to improve food production and limit birth rates. However, though our current circumstances have turned out to be less dire than expected, Malthus was on the right track in forecasting that world population, starvation in the developing world, and the depletion of natural resources will become serious problems in our time.

Malthus was not the only thinker to make accurate guesses about the future. In 1888, newspaper columnist David Goodman Croly predicted with remarkable insight that by 2000 'women throughout the world will enjoy increased opportunities and privileges. With this new freedom will come social tolerance of sexual conduct formerly excused only in men. In addition, because of the availability of jobs, more women will choose not to have children' (cited in Margolis, 2000: 35).

Similarly, a British *Daily Mail* writer accurately prophesied in 1928 that by century's end, the Prime Minister would be female, women would wear trousers and act as power brokers, the average life expectancy would be 75, and home cooking would be carried out by a machine that, as described in the late 1920s, sounded much like the modern microwave oven (ibid.).

One of the best, and least known, sets of predictions was made by H.G. Wells shortly after the beginning of the twentieth century. In his book of 'anticipations' about the new century, Wells (1902) correctly predicted that much that would occur in the century would be connected with new marvels of transport (trains, cars, and airplanes) and communication (the radio and telephone). With speedier transport and communication, he foresaw, would come decentralization—for example, the growth of suburbs, long-distance shopping, and more contact over distances for business and pleasure.

Other early writers predicted that by the twenty-first century, 'the US population will have risen to about 330 million [the figure today is around 295 million], and nine out of ten Americans will be living in supercities or their suburbs.' About communications technology, they wrote, 'cities, like industry, will tend to decentralize; with instant communications, it will no longer be necessary for business enterprises to cluster together' (*Time*, 1966: 42). A half-century ago, futurists also speculated on what sounds uncannily like our modern-day Internet: 'One thing that they almost all will want is electronic information retrieval: the contents of libraries and other forms of information or education will be stored in a computer and will be instantly obtainable at home by dialing a code' (ibid., 33).

Still, even as late as the mid-twentieth century, many futures researchers made predictions that were wildly off target. In the 1960s, futures researchers imagined that work would be almost non-existent by the year 2000. They even believed that people at the turn of the millennium would have so much leisure time at their disposal and the need for workers would be so small that people would have to be paid not to work. The logic was simple and, at the time, compelling. Only 40 per cent of the US population worked outside the home in the 1960s. Expecting that figure to decline further as automation increased and production became more efficient seemed logical.

Researchers then expected that Americans would nearly end poverty and class inequality by the twenty-first century, and that everyone would live in modest financial comfort. In large part, they relied on technological innovations to bring about such radical social change: with machines fully developed, there would not be enough work to go around for humans. 'Moonlighting will become as socially unacceptable as bigamy', they wrote (ibid.). The magic of technology would also solve the problems of a growing world population.

Faith in technology has been a staple of the modern world for at least two centuries. Indeed, much of the science fiction genre is premised on the great hope of science to create human utopias, and conversely, the potential malevolence of technology to thwart

---

Not Novel

Most predictions tell us less about the future than about the time at which the prediction was made. *Nineteen Eighty-four* is a surer guide to 1948, when Orwell was writing his novel, than to his dated hell. Naturally, someone at Random House believes that Jules Verne's [recently discovered] *Paris in the Twentieth Century* ... is 'an astonishingly prescient view into the future'. We could hardly expect them to bill it as 'a fairly interesting view into the past'.

... Verne foresaw [for 1960 Paris] a bureaucratized, inert, technologically efficient and passively oppressive state in which only three professions remained: those of financier, businessman, and industrialist. Science and moneymaking rule, the arts are despised and Victor Hugo is forgotten. ...

Source: Julian Barnes, 'Back to the Future', New York Times, 26 Jan. 1997. At: <www.nytimes.com/books/97/01/26/reviews/970126.26barnest.html>.

our arrogant ambitions. To end Third World famines, some futurists imagined the following solution: 'Huge fields of kelp and other kinds of seaweed will be tended by undersea "farmers". Frogmen will live for months at a time in underwater bunkhouses. The protein-rich undersea crop will probably be ground up to produce a dull-tasting cereal that eventually, however, could be regenerated chemically to taste like anything from steak to bourbon' (ibid., 32). A 1950 illustration in *Popular Mechanics* predicted the 'housewife of 2000' would 'happily be doing her daily housecleaning with a garden hose, since everything would now be made of plastic' (Wilson, 2000: 236). Not only did this picture overestimate a love of polymer furniture at the turn of a new century, it also importantly failed to foresee the vast changes in views about 'women's work'.

One researcher in the past even predicted that a giant nuclear power station built on Mount Wilson, overlooking Los Angeles, could probably heat the surrounding air and raise it, with the infamous LA smog layer, safely into the upper stratosphere, while drawing sea winds and rainfall onto the mainland to irrigate the desert and transform it into arable greenspace (*Time*, 1966).

Trends in beliefs—in religion or politics, for example—are also difficult, if not impossible, to predict. H.G. Wells, for example, who foresaw suburbs and air travel, could not foresee the Nazi Holocaust or the emancipation of women. Without the Holocaust, there would have been no state of Israel. Without the emancipation of women, there would have been no work–family conflict. Likewise, people could not imagine the fall of Communism until the dismantling of the Berlin Wall or the disintegration of the Soviet Union actually occurred.

Our failures to make accurate predictions teach us an important lesson about futures studies—radical, unpredictable changes in human life can occur. When they do, entire generations of future forecasting suddenly look absurd for their lack of insight. While futures researchers often err on the side of wild abandon in their predictions, just as often they err on the side of timidity and lack of imagination. Thus, we are not good at predicting our future. That said, we continue to try.

A Key Study: The Limits to Growth

The most elaborate, rigorous, and imaginative study in forecasting problems of the future was the 'limits to growth study' carried out at MIT in the 1970s. This study illustrates some of the techniques, and methodological problems, associated with forecasting the future. It also suggests the power and accuracy of expert system modelling. As to the long-term accuracy of the results, this remains uncertain 30 years later, but there are reasons for thinking this study was going in the right direction.

The limits to growth 'world model', devised by researchers at MIT in the early 1970s, was designed to examine five major trends of global concern—quickening industrialization, rapid population growth, widespread undernourishment, depletion of non-renewable resources, and a worsening environment (Meadows et al., 1972). Like every model, this one is imperfect and oversimplified. However, the researchers felt it was developed enough to be useful to decision-makers. Besides, the elements portrayed in this model are so basic and general that the researchers did not expect their broad conclusions to change much with further revisions (see Figure 13.1).

Computer simulations led the researchers to judge that if the present growth trends in world population, industrialization, pollution, food production, and resource depletion continue unchanged, humanity would reach the limits to growth on this planet within

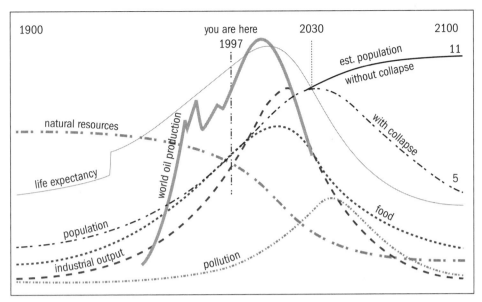

FIGURE 13.1 A Graphic Depiction for the Alternative Doomsday Scenarios Presented in *Limits to Growth*
Source: From *Beyond the Limits* by Donella H. Meadows, Dennis L. Meadows, Jorgen Randers, and Jan Tinbergen (London: Earthscan, 1992), p. 133. Reprinted by permission of Earthscan and SLL/Sterling Lord Literistic, Inc. Copyright by Earthscan, 1992.

the next 100 years. Most likely, the result would be disastrous: a sudden and uncontrollable decline in both population and industrial capacity. Having accidentally overshot the capacity for human life on earth, humanity would die of starvation or pollution.

To 'overshoot' means accidentally to go beyond allowable limits. People overshoot limits every day: for example, they eat too much at a meal and get an upset stomach. Or, they get too aggressive during an argument and risk a friendship. Most instances of overshooting cause little harm or occur often enough that people learn to avoid them or to lessen their effects. Sometimes, however, the potential for disastrous overshoot arises. We are facing one such possibility today, in the unprecedented growth in the planet's population and material economy (Meadows et al., 2004). The situation confronts us with various issues never before experienced on a global scale. So, we lack the strategies, the institutions, the cultural norms, and the habits needed to cope. If a deep correction is not made soon, however, a crash is certain and it may occur while many of us are alive to see it. No matter how fine its technology, its economy, or its leadership, a system of accelerating growth will inevitably overshoot the limits. A capitalist-industrial system devoted to ever-increasing production and profit-making is bound to do so.

In every version of the model, growth ends well before the year 2100. Depending on certain assumptions, the end could come slightly sooner or later, and would be accompanied by one or more of a lack of food, a lack of raw materials, and an excess of pollution. Assuming no major change in the present system—that is, inaction—population and industrial growth will crash into a wall sometime within the next century.

But the outcome need not be disastrous. We have the chance of a purposeful correction that could lead to a sustainable, plentiful future for all the world's peoples. It is possible to alter these growth trends and set up ecological and economic stability that is sustainable far into the future. In this imagined state, the basic material needs of each

Forecast of the World Population by 2300

1. If the world fertility for every country averages around two children per woman (the medium scenario), then world population would rise from today's 6.3 billion persons to around 9 billion persons in 2300.
2. Low 1.85 children/women and high 2.35 children/woman scenarios of world population in 2300 range between 2.3 billion persons and 36.4 billion persons.
3. According to the medium scenario, Africa's share of the world population would double, from 13 per cent of the world population in 2003 to 24 per cent in 2300. Europe's share would be halved, from 12 per cent today to 7 per cent in 2300. India, China, and the US would continue to be the most populous.
4. The world population will continue to age rapidly; the median age in the world will rise from 26 years in 2003 to nearly 50 years in 2300.

Source: United Nations, at: <www.un.org/News/Press/docs/2003/pop881.DOC.htm>; accessed 7 Apr. 2006.

person on earth would be satisfied and each person would have an equal opportunity to realize his individual human potential.

If we blindly put our faith in technology to solve the problem, however, we risk failing to take effective action to solve it. No doubt technology can help solve the problem. Many technological developments—recycling, pollution control devices, and contraceptives, to name a few—will help to prolong the future of humanity if they are combined with deliberate checks on growth. At the same time, the blind adoption of new technology is no solution. Responsible adoption means first asking: What will be the side effects, both physical and social, if this technology is introduced on a large scale? What social changes will be necessary before this technology can be used properly? How long will it take to develop the needed technologies?

The 'limits to growth' simulation, known as 'World3', was part of a search for a model of a sustainable world system. This imagined world would continue indefinitely without a sudden and uncontrollable collapse and would satisfy the basic material needs of all its people. In doing so, it would help solve the global population problem. The rapid growth in world population is a recent event, a result of humanity's successful decrease of worldwide mortality. To restore a global population/environment balance, either the birth rate must be brought down to equal the new, lower death rate or the death rate must rise again. All the 'natural' constraints to population growth work in the second way, by raising the death rate.

But stabilizing population growth alone is not enough to prevent overshoot and collapse. If population and industrial development slowed to zero growth almost immediately, with no other changes, the first result would be high levels of food, industrial output, and services per person. Eventually, however, the global system would deteriorate because of resource shortages, which would lessen industrial output. With improved technologies but the same production goals, resources would still be gradually exhausted. However, the rate of depletion would slow enough to allow time for humanity to adjust to changes in resource availability, through industrial change and technological innovation.

All the evidence available to us suggests that of the three alternatives—unrestricted growth, a self-imposed limit to growth, or a nature-imposed limit to growth—only the last two are possible. Relying on a nature-imposed limit to growth, however, means accepting a higher death rate. The emergence of new infectious pandemics, say, or a series of apocalyptic natural disasters would keep the population down to a manageable size; however, a nature-imposed limit to growth, though possible, is intolerable.

Thus, humanity is left with only one real choice. Achieving a self-imposed limit to growth would need much effort and we would have to learn to do many things in new ways. A self-imposed limit would tax the inventiveness, flexibility, and willpower of the human race. No one can predict what institutions humanity might develop under these new conditions. It seems possible, however, that a society released from struggling with the many problems caused by growth may have more energy and inventiveness available for solving other problems.

Only population and capital need to be constant in this imagined equilibrium (zero-growth) state. Any human activity that does not need a large flow of non-renewable resources or degrade the environment might continue to grow forever. In particular, those activities that many people find satisfying—education, art, music, religion, athletics, and social interaction, for example—could thrive. And, since the quantity of industrial output would never change, every improvement in production methods could result in more leisure for the population. As a result, technological advance would be both necessary and welcome in the equilibrium state.

In the more than 30 years since this study was published, humanity has not begun to approach this utopian equilibrium condition. The world's use of materials and energy has continued to grow. Rising oil prices, climate change, declining forests and fisheries, and the depletion of fresh water—all of these are simply symptoms of the overshoot. Though we are still some distance from collapse, there are signs that we have already overshot our environmental limits. Falling resource stocks and rising pollution levels are the first clues. Here are some other symptoms:

- Capital, resources, and labour are sidetracked to activities that were formerly provided without cost by nature (e.g., air purification, water purification, flood control, pest control).

- Capital, resources, and labour are diverted from goods production to exploit scarcer, more distant, deeper, or more dilute resources (e.g., Alberta oil sands, offshore drilling for oil and natural gas).

- Technologies are invented to make use of lower-quality, smaller, more scattered, less valuable resources, because the higher-value ones are gone (e.g., fishing down the food web, as in Newfoundland and Labrador).

- Natural pollution cleanup agents fail and result in rising levels of pollution.

- Capital depreciation exceeds investment and maintenance is postponed, so there is a decay in capital stocks, especially long-lived infrastructure (e.g., roads, schools, hydro lines).

- Demands grow for the military or industry to secure and defend resources that are increasingly concentrated in fewer, more remote, or increasingly hostile regions (e.g., Iraq).

- Investment in human resources (e.g., education, health care, shelter) is postponed to meet immediate consumption, investment, or security needs, or to pay debts (e.g., the erosion of the welfare state).

- Debts become a rising percentage of annual real output.

- Goals and acceptable levels of wellness for health and environment are eroded.

- Conflicts increase, especially conflicts over sources or sinks.

- Consumption patterns shift as the population can no longer pay the price of what it really wants and, instead, buys what it can afford.

- Respect for the instruments of collective government decline because they are used increasingly by the elites to preserve or increase their share of a declining resource base.

- Chaos grows in natural systems, with 'natural' disasters more frequent and more severe because of less resilience in the environmental system (Meadows et al., 2004).

Efforts to prevent further movement towards disaster will need pertinent, timely, and accurate information suggesting new rules and goals. However, systems strongly resist changes. Entrenched political, economic, and religious cliques will try to prevent rule changes; innovators will be ignored, ridiculed, or silenced. Only innovators, however—by seeing the need for new information, rules, and goals, communicating about them, and trying them out—can make the changes that transform systems (ibid.).

This, at any rate, was the message of the MIT group, whose model called forcefully for 'limits to growth'. One answer was *Models of Doom*, a book by an interdisciplinary team at Sussex University's Science Policy Research Unit (Jahoda et al., 1975). This book examined the assumptions of the MIT world models and a preliminary draft of the

Cornucopian Wagers Catastrophist

In 1980, Julian Simon, an economist and cornucopian, and Paul Ehrlich, a biologist and catastrophist, decided to put their money where their predictions were. Ehrlich had been predicting massive shortages in various natural resources for decades, while Simon claimed natural resources were infinite.

Simon offered Ehrlich a bet on the market price of metals. Ehrlich would pick a quantity of any five metals he liked worth $1,000 in 1980. If the 1990 price of the metals, after adjusting for inflation, was more than $1,000 (i.e., the metals became scarcer), Ehrlich would win.

Simon won the bet, and Ehrlich sent him a cheque for $576.07. Though they tried, they could never agree on any other bets on the future—their terms of reference were too different.

Source: Adapted from <www.overpopulation.com/faq/People/julian_simon.html>.

technical reports of Meadows et al. Based on computer simulations, it showed that forecasts of the world's future are sensitive to a few key assumptions and suggested the MIT assumptions were unduly pessimistic. Further, the Sussex scientists claimed that the MIT methods, data, and predictions were biased and faulty, and did not accurately reflect reality. The Sussex scientists criticized the MIT approach for its lack of concern with politics, social structure, and human needs and ambitions. They assert that changing social values, not a part of the MIT computer input, can significantly affect the growth of the world's population and resources. Nevertheless, these critics agreed with Meadows et al. (1972) about the urgency of the challenge. They agreed that dealing with foreseeable physical limits and sharing the fruits of growth equitably will require radical political and social, as well as technological, changes.

Critics such as Julian Simon (1996) and Bjørn Lomborg (2001) have questioned the assumptions of the 'limits to growth' model. First, they criticize the assumption of finite natural resources. They also state the limits on agriculture are invalid since they are based on the limit of the amount of land. However, this is wrong, since the model does allow more food to be grown with the same amount of land but with increases of other agricultural inputs (such as fertilizer). Moreover, even if the finite natural resource assumption is removed, the model still shows a collapse because of pollution. Also, critics of the critics have argued that Julian Simon, an economist, and Bjørn Lomborg, a political scientist, lack the needed scientific credentials. Their books have been heavily criticized by environmental scientists.

The main problem with the MIT study is its claim to precision and accuracy. Complex non-linear feedback systems are inherently unpredictable, and they are not controllable. We can only hope to understand them in the most general way. The goal of foreseeing the future exactly and preparing for it completely is unrealizable. The idea of making a complex system do just what you want it to do can be achieved only temporarily, at best. Also, small errors in measurement, or small changes in the estimated parameters, can produce huge changes in the system outcomes—making the simulation model as volatile as the world itself.

This suggests that the proper goal of futures research is not prediction and control: it is scenario-building. The future cannot be predicted, but it can be imagined and brought into being. Systems cannot be controlled, but they can be designed and changed. Living successfully in a world of systems demands a subtle ability to sort out truth from error, use our reason, and consult our morality. Visions of the future are short-lived snapshots viewed through a glass darkly: poorly understood near-future states with some unknown chance of happening, seen in the roughest outline. We will never be able to forecast the future and its social problems accurately; but we may be able to shape it if we use our ingenuity.

Changes in What the Public Sees as Social Problems

What people consider a serious social problem can also change, often in response to changes in social, political, and economic conditions. A social problems textbook from 1898, for instance, listed 'Dumping Garbage', 'Over-Production', 'Public Debts and Indirect Taxation', and 'Slavery' among its chapter headings (George, 1898). Another text, published only 18 years later, already showed concern over some of the harmful social conditions that continue to affect the world today, including 'Unemployment', 'Crime and Punishment', 'The Liquor Problem', 'Poverty', and 'The Conservation of Natural Resources' (Towne, 1916). Obviously, many of these problems are still with us today.

Box 13.2 Personal Experience: Immigrants Experience Work Inequality

Zainab Taiyeb, recently from Pakistan, didn't get paid an hourly wage for her door-to-door sales work: like others doing this kind of work, she was only paid a commission on what she sold. At Rogers, she wasn't given a contract; she was told she was 'self-employed' and that she would have to wait three weeks for her first paycheque. At the end of the first month, Taiyeb was owed $1,500.

When she didn't get her cheque, she and 14 other workers who hadn't received their pay confronted their employer. He said he was a subcontractor and that he couldn't pay them, because Rogers still hadn't paid him. 'When I demanded to be paid, along with the other workers, I was given $20', says Taiyeb. 'Can you imagine? I had worked for one month and was given $20. It was so insulting. I cried that day.'

Increasingly, workers like Taiyeb are hired through temporary help agencies or subcontractors to sell products and services, sew clothes, or make parts for companies that, on paper, they don't work for. Indeed, gone are the days when a worker can assume [she or he] will be hired directly by a company. And, for an increasing number, gone are the days of job security, decent wages and benefits. In Ontario, one in three jobs [is] part-time, contract or temporary. Workers like Taiyeb are facing a new world of work that is rampant with on-the-job injuries and violations of basic workers' rights. It is also a new world of work where old forms of organizing for justice just don't work.

Fly-by-night operations shut down when workers try to organize. Subcontractors claim bankruptcy and open the next day in the same place, with the same machinery, but under a different name. Workers are moved from one workplace to another without notice, or just not called back for more work. Meanwhile, deadbeat bosses knowingly and repeatedly hire workers, especially immigrant workers (who are told they need to put up with precarious work in order to get 'Canadian experience'), with no intention of paying them their wages. According to the Ministry of Labour's own statistics, $505 million of unpaid wages were owed to over 110,000 workers in Ontario from 1990 to the present day. This is just the tip of the iceberg. The majority of employment standard violations never make it to the ministry.

Source: Adapted from Berinstein (2004).

From the time of the Russian Revolution in 1917 onward, Western capitalist societies worried about Soviet Communism and the dangers of subversion and war. Soviet Communists worried about Western capitalism and the dangers of subversion and war. Between 1917 and 1967, through two world wars and two minor wars (Korea and Vietnam), a global depression, and hunts for traitors in the Soviet Union (in the 1930s) and the United States (in the 1950s), people on both sides waited for the worst—all-out war—to happen. It did not, and as the risk of all-out nuclear war with the Russians receded, national concerns over military conflict declined. Growing domestic considerations like the economy and unemployment replaced them. North America rode a technology-driven, record-breaking boom in the marketplace through the 1990s, and then crime and other social issues became the main social problems in the eyes of the public.

Since the widely publicized major terrorist events of September 2001, concerns about war and subversion have surfaced again, especially in the United States. In the foreseeable future, we can expect to see high prominence given to terrorism, treason, and national security in the public mind.

Trends in Social Problems Projected to the Near Future

Many predictions by today's leading futures researchers will be proven, a century down the road, to have been wrong. Others will have come close to the reality of 2100, and a few may even have hit the bull's eye.

Noted thinker Noam Chomsky is pessimistic about the prospects of futures research: 'The record of prediction in human affairs has not been inspiring, even short-range. The most plausible prediction is that any prediction about serious matters is likely to be off the mark, except by accident' (Chomsky, 1999: 30). However, the goal of futures studies is only partly to paint a picture of what life may be like for later generations. Its more important task is to imagine a desirable alternative future for people to work towards, a future that is actively shaped by the decisions of people living today. With this goal in mind, let us consider the likely future of several different categories of social problems.

The Future of Family Life

As we saw in an earlier chapter, families can be defined in various ways: narrowly, as in the nuclear family (husband, wife, and young children), or broadly, as in the extended family, which includes everyone related by blood, marriage, or adoption. By family, we can mean people of common ancestry, those living under one roof, or those having common characteristics or properties.

As sociologist Neena Chappell (2002) points out, the essential features of families—their nurturing and encouraging roles as well as their socialization roles for the next generation—have remained intact into the twenty-first century and are likely to do so in the foreseeable future. Families remain a basic social institution of society, providing emotional support, identity confirmation, and socialization. In fact, the core family roles have become even more important given recent changes that have reduced the role of government in the economy. New family forms are changing to allow the continuation of these essential roles under new circumstances.

Even in our individualistic and materialistic Western society, family members care for one another. To do this, family caregivers give up their own leisure time and sometimes sacrifice jobs and careers. No evidence indicates that families are moving away from providing this care. Indeed, societal changes such as globalization and the political-economic dominance of neo-liberalism have strengthened the traditional role of the family. Families continue to offer a refuge from the demands of work life, especially families facing various difficult economic and political circumstances. Advanced technology extends the choices individuals and families have for becoming involved with one another despite great geographic distances. We can expect this trend to continue into the future.

Problems of Family and Work

As society adjusts to the increased participation of women in the workforce and to changes in family life (such as fewer children and higher rates of divorce), some specific social problems we have discussed—for example, balancing family responsibilities with career ambitions and the time constraints of mothers—may be better worked out. For other work–family conflicts, we will need to develop more creative solutions that are flexible and constantly changing.

Box 13.3 Societal Progress

We believe that the question of whether progress objectively exists can be approached scientifically. An analysis of progress should be based on a well-founded theoretical framework, such as the theory of evolution, which at least in our interpretation seems to imply a preferred direction of advance towards increasing complexity and intelligence. Moreover, the theory should be based on empirical measures, comparing the overall 'well-being', 'happiness', or 'quality of life' of past and present generations. The problem is how to quantify an abstract and subjective concept such as 'quality of life' (QOL). We believe that such quantification is possible, by looking at more concrete and objective factors, which can be shown to contribute to QOL.

The sociologist Ruut Veenhoven and his coworkers have developed an extensive 'World Database of Happiness', which collects the data from hundreds of polls and questionnaires in which people were asked how satisfied they are with their life. These data for different countries were correlated with a number of other variables, such as GNP per head of the population, education level, freedom of expression, etc. Not surprisingly, life satisfaction turns out to have clear positive correlation with most of the factors, which we would intuitively consider as 'good':

- health, life expectancy
- level of education, literacy
- access to information
- average wealth
- democracy, political and individual freedom
- safety
- equality between classes and between the sexes

Note that these basic values or determinants of happiness, which come out of an empirical analysis, are remarkably similar to the values formulated in the Universal Declaration of Human Rights.

When on the other hand we look at statistics, which trace the development of these factors over time, we find that on average they all have undergone spectacular increases during the past century, and continue to increase. For example, life expectancy is still going up with some 3 years for every 10 years that passes, depending on the country in which you live. Even less tangible factors, such as general intelligence as measured through IQ tests seems to go up with some 3 points per decade, for the 20 or so countries for which data are available (the Flynn effect). We can only conclude that empirically all major indicators of progress (sometimes grouped together in combined indicators, such as the Human Development Index, the International Index of Social Progress or the Physical Quality of Life Index) seem to be increasing unabatedly for the world as a whole. Together with a theory explaining the mechanism of this on-going improvement this should prove that progress is an objective reality.

Source: Reprinted with permission from Principia Cybernetica Web <http://pespmc1.vub.ac.be/PROGRESS.html>

To reduce family conflict, the socialization of men and women will need to continue to change, as will the organization of workplaces. Change in the latter, in particular, may need strong political will by lawmakers to extend pay- and employment-equity legislation to cover more types of workplaces and to develop stronger sanctions against employers who treat their workers unfairly. Change of this kind, however, is complicated by an increasingly tough global market that has the tendency to drive pay and working conditions downward, leaving little room for creative workplace solutions to home problems.

Said another way, capitalists have little motivation to improve working conditions in Canada when they can move the workplace to South America or Asia and pay less for the same work. They do not do so as a whole because they need consumers at home who can afford to buy their products.

Problems of Class Inequality

For various reasons, it seems unlikely that social equality will be reached in the foreseeable future. Inequality is firmly entrenched in our society. As well, many of our political and ideological beliefs encourage unequal economic statuses, and economic inequality (like religion, ethnicity, and regionalism) has a long history in our culture. Given its ubiquity, it is unlikely that inequality will be eliminated in the near, or even distant, future. Still, as a human rights principle, it is worth striving towards, and though it may not be eradicated entirely it can at least be reduced.

As to how much inequality can be changed, the political will of governments or lawmakers to legislate change is central. Legislating greater equality will meet strong objections from the wealthy, who benefit from maintaining the status quo. However, taking our lead from futures research, work in the present can influence the future, and people who value equality must continue to work hard on such problems.

Problems that remain on the horizon as contributing to class inequality include the rise to power of multinational corporations and the effects of these corporations on labourers in less developed countries. The migration of jobs from North America and Europe to nations in Latin America, Africa, and Asia represents an improvement in the incomes of people in these countries. However, it also spreads sweatshop conditions around the world, creates global dependency on industrial capitalism, and pits labourers in developing countries against those in the industrialized world.

Environmental Damage

The degradation of the environment is a growing social problem. Many scientists and theorists believe that unless changes are made today, environmental problems will become more severe and their effects more intense in the future. Already, the world's temperature has increased, especially in the 1990s and since. This has led to more frequent droughts and famines, higher rates of skin cancer, and more extreme weather conditions throughout the year.

F. Sherwood Rowland, whose early warnings of the effects of chlorofluorocarbons (CFCs) on ozone depletion in 1974 earned him a Nobel Prize in chemistry, hypothesizes that:

> the global prevalence of smog will rise in the next century because more and more people will use cars. The twenty-first century will therefore begin with three major atmospheric problems firmly entrenched globally: stratospheric ozone depletion, the greenhouse effect from increasing carbon dioxide and other trace gases with accompanying global warming and urban and regional smog. My expectation in the coming decades is that the climatic consequences from continued greenhouse gas emissions will be more and more noticeable, and much more ominous. (Rowland, 1999: 209–10)

Box 13.4 Canada and Sustainable Development

The following represents a selection of commitments that Environment Canada chose for inclusion in its *Sustainable Development Strategy 2004–2006*. They are from the broader *Johannesburg Plan of Implementation*, which outlines 602 commitment paragraphs resulting from international negotiations at the 2002 World Summit on Sustainable Development.

Changing Unsustainable Patterns of Consumption and Production

■ Encourage and promote the development of a 10-year framework of programs in support of regional and national initiatives to accelerate the shift towards sustainable consumption and production.

■ Enhance corporate environmental and social responsibility and accountability.

■ Encourage relevant authorities at all levels to take sustainable development considerations into account in decision-making, including on national and local development planning, investment in infrastructure, business development, and public procurement.

■ Prevent and minimize waste and maximize reuse, recycling, and use of environmentally friendly alternative materials, with the participation of government authorities and all stakeholders.

■ Renew the commitment, as advanced in Agenda 21, to sound management of chemicals throughout their life cycle and of hazardous wastes for sustainable development as well as for the protection of human health and the environment, using transparent science-based risk assessment procedures and science-based risk management procedures, taking into account the precautionary approach, as set out in principle 15 of the Rio Declaration on Environment and Development.

Protecting and Managing the Natural Resource Base of Economic and Social Development

■ Halve, by the year 2015, the proportion of people who are unable to reach or to afford safe drinking water, as outlined in the Millennium Declaration, and the proportion of people without access to basic sanitation.

■ Develop integrated water resources management and water efficiency plans by 2005.

■ Improve water resource management and scientific understanding of the water cycle through co-operation in joint observation and research, and for this purpose encourage and promote knowledge-sharing and provide capacity-building and the transfer of technology.

■ Encourage the application by 2010 of the ecosystem approach, noting the Reykjavik Declaration on Responsible Fisheries in the Marine Ecosystem and decision V/6 of the Conference of Parties to the Convention on Biological Diversity.

■ Advance implementation of the Global Program of Action for the Protection of the Marine Environment from Land-based Activities and the Montreal Declaration on the Protection of the Marine Environment from Land-based Activities.

■ Enhance co-operation at the international, regional, and national levels to reduce air pollution, including transboundary air pollution, acid deposition and ozone depletion.

■ Negotiate within the framework of the Convention on Biological Diversity, bearing in mind the Bonn Guidelines, an international regime to promote and safeguard the fair and equitable sharing of benefits arising out of the utilization of genetic resources.

Health and Sustainable Development

■ Launch international capacity-building initiatives, as appropriate, that assess health and environment linkages and use the knowledge gained to create more effective national and regional policy responses to environmental threats to human health.

■ Reduce respiratory diseases and other health impacts resulting from air pollution, with particular attention to women and children by strengthening and supporting efforts for the reduction of emissions through the use of cleaner fuels and modern pollution control techniques.

Means of Implementation
■ Support the use of education to promote sustainable development.

Institutional Framework for Sustainable Development
■ Implement the outcomes of the decision on international environmental governance adopted by the Governing Council of the United Nations Environment Program at its seventh special session and invite the General Assembly at its fifty-seventh session to consider the important but complex issue of establishing universal membership for the Governing Council/Global Ministerial Environment Forum.
■ Continue to promote coherent and co-ordinated approaches to institutional frameworks for sustainable development at all national levels, including through, as appropriate, the establishment or strengthening of existing authorities and mechanisms necessary for policy-making, co-ordination, and implementation and enforcement of laws.
■ Make progress in the formulation and elaboration of a national strategy for sustainable development.

Source: Environment Canada's Sustainable Development Strategy 2004–2006. Available at: <http://www.ec.gc.ca/sd-dd_consult/SDS2004/sdspart5_e.htm>.

Technological Haves and Have-Nots

Thomas J. Watson, then chairman of IBM, is widely quoted as having said in 1943: 'I think there is a world market for maybe five computers.' Though there is no evidence he ever actually said this, the statement is widely repeated to underline the explosive spread of computers in the last 65 years (www.answers.com/topic/thomas-j-watson). His alleged statement remains believable because, in 1943, one of the world's first computers, the US military-built ENIAC (Electronic Numerical Integrator and Computer), cost nearly $500,000 (US) and weighed 30 tonnes. No one foresaw the use of semiconductors for miniaturization. Today, people carry enormously powerful computers in the palms of their hands.

This change is just one dramatic demonstration that technological inventions are almost always initially inaccessible to the average person. Gradually, as demand for the new product becomes obvious and production methods become cheaper and more efficient, costs decline to the point where the invention becomes widely available to most, if not all, people. Often supply comes to drive demand for the new technology. (No one 20 years ago would have imagined how much our lives would be controlled by e-mail and voice mail, for example. Yet here we are, working faster and living faster because of these new technologies and the expectation that we will use them.)

Around the world, the benefits of technological innovation are enjoyed first by the wealthiest people in the wealthiest nations. Then, slowly, the new technology spreads to the lower social classes and the rest of the world's population. Thus, hundreds of millions of computers are being used in the world today, yet people in poorer societies have few computers per capita. The most advanced machines continue to be available to only a small percentage of privileged buyers.

With computers, as with other technologies in the past, those in power steer the spread of technologies in ways that will further improve the quality of their own lives and the lives of others in the privileged social classes. Significant funding is directed at research and development for the latest in technical gadgetry, while technological solutions for poverty and homelessness (for example, affordable housing) remain largely unexplored. As technological development continues, the **digital divide** between the technological haves and have-nots continues to widen.

One application of technology that will likely gain popularity in the future is the use of **cyberterrorism** and cyberwarfare, especially by rogue nations and militant groups lacking the military firepower to threaten their enemies on a traditional battlefield. Specific tactics may include hacking or electronically jamming the enemy's computer and communications systems; using electromagnetic-pulse weaponry to destroy electronic devices; and infecting computer equipment with viruses (World Future Society, 2001).

Genetic Manipulation

Some predictions about the future of humanity hinge on the use of **genetic manipulation** to improve the quality of human life. Already, scientists have mapped out the human genome, the DNA material that contains the genetic instructions that fix hair, eye, and skin colour, height, physical build, tendency to various diseases, and, perhaps, personality or temperament.

Many ethicists and researchers are worried about human cloning and the use of embryos made expressly for research purposes. The dominant concern is that without enough government and institutional guidelines for ethical behaviour in genetic research, humanity risks abusing the new technology in as-yet-uncontrollable ways. This concern is justified: over the past century, every powerful technology has been used at one time or another to dominate, terrorize, or destroy political enemies.

Never before have humans been able to control the future of their species to such a degree. This is a social problem because manipulating a person's genetic code not only changes how that individual develops, but can also potentially alter the human gene pool permanently for future generations. So decisions that people make today about the application of genetic research to the general population can have unforeseen effects on future members of the human population. The results could extend to the ways in which parents control the sex and racial characteristics of their unborn children, or how genetically altered individuals interact with non-genetically altered people. Health issues may include redefinitions of illness and disability to consider such characteristics as height, body type, skin colour, and clarity of vision.

Statehood and Globalization

Globalization makes it possible to help more people, but it also increases the danger that inequality among citizens will grow. We saw this problem in the digital divide: where computers are concerned, the haves and the have-nots are gaining social and economic benefits at increasingly different rates. More government involvement is needed to ensure strong human and social capital for all Canadians. One critical issue facing governments is how to fight vested interests and create policies that are for all citizens. However, money alone will not be enough; governments need to provide imagination and organization as well. For example, the Commission on the Future of Health Care in

What Is Cyberterrorism?

To the best of my knowledge, no attack so far has led to violence or injury to persons, although some may have intimidated their victims . . . as acts of civil disobedience, analogous to street protests and physical sit-ins, not as acts of violence or terrorism. This is an important distinction. Most activists, whether participating in the Million Mom's March or a Web sit-in, are not terrorists. My personal view is that the threat of cyberterrorism has been mainly theoretical, but it is something to watch and take reasonable precautions against.

Source: Dorothy E. Denning, testimony before the Special Oversight Panel on Terrorism, Committee on Armed Services, US House of Representatives, 23 May 2000. At: <www.cs.georgetown.edu/~denning/infosec/cyberterror.html>.

Canada (2002)—the Romanow Commission—showed that the health-care system needs reorganization, co-ordination, and a redistribution of funds, not more dollars.

Governments also have a role in both national and individual identities, especially during globalization when there is concern that nations' identities become diluted and individual lives become determined by global forces outside their own and their country's control. The extent to which Canada is a nation of many ethnicities (Table 13.2) emphasizes this fact, as well as the extent to which we are connected to the wider world.

With globalization and the spread of American media, Canadian cultural values and attitudes may be less different from American values and attitudes than they used to be. This need not be interpreted as an Americanization of Canadians. Nonetheless, Canadian culture has always been at risk because of the nearness and the relative size, wealth, and power of our neighbour to the south. A major challenge for Canadian governments is ensuring genuine public participation to increase the likelihood that Canadian values will be heard and represented. Ways must be found to increase and capitalize on citizens' political skills.

The Problem of Aging

One thing that can be predicted with reasonable certainty is the continued aging of human populations. Even today there is concern about how a shrinking base of workers will be able to support the growing elderly population in Canada. With aging, the population distribution takes on the shape of an inverted pyramid and the ratio of dependent elderly people to working-age people increases. As we discussed in Chapter 11, this aging is the result of continued drops in fertility and, secondarily, of increased longevity. Whether the younger generations can continue to support an aging population and whether the health-care system can cope with demands for better care for everyone remain to be seen. Table 13.3 suggests how Canada's population balance will change over the next half-century according to a medium-growth scenario.

How society deals with the aging population will decide the future social problems that will be associated with it. Several possibilities present themselves. First, the child-bearing population could be encouraged to increase the number of children they produce. This policy would be unlikely to have much effect given continuing declines over the past century, as well as socio-economic values (such as individualism, family economics) and opportunities (such as urban careers) that work against large family sizes. Second, Canada's immigration laws could be loosened to allow more young immigrants from countries with high fertility. Such a policy, however, would not be likely to win support from Canadians currently in the workforce, who would see it as increasing competition for jobs. Third, a larger fraction of the national budget could be invested in health care. This policy would call for either higher taxes (which are unpopular) or reduced spending in other areas, such as education (also unpopular and, in the long run, harmful to the nation's productivity). Fourth, new ways to raise money might be found—for example, by selling land or water to the United States. However, this policy only works for a short time, as you can sell your heritage only once. Fifth, through ingenuity or sheer good luck, wonderful new drugs or technologies might be invented; patents for their use and taxes on their sale would provide funds to support health care. However, this is not as much a policy as it is a wish. We cannot rely on good fortune. So in the end, it may be necessary for people to lower their health-care expectations or pay more of the cost of their own care. This may require the elimination of compulsory retirement so elderly people can earn enough for their own health

Table 13.2 Canadian Population by Selected Ethnic Origins (2001 Census)			
	Total Responses	Single Responses	Multiple Responses
Total population	29,639,035	18,307,545	11,331,490
Ethnic origin			
Canadian	11,682,680	6,748,135	4,934,545
English	5,978,875	1,479,525	4,499,355
French	4,668,410	1,060,760	3,607,655
Scottish	4,157,210	607,235	3,549,975
Irish	3,822,660	496,865	3,325,795
German	2,742,765	705,600	2,037,170
Italian	1,270,370	726,275	544,090
Chinese	1,094,700	936,210	158,490
Ukrainian	1,071,060	326,195	744,860
North American Indian	1,000,890	455,805	545,085
Dutch (Netherlands)	923,310	316,220	607,090
Polish	817,085	260,415	556,665
East Indian	713,330	581,665	131,665
Norwegian	363,760	47,230	316,530
Portuguese	357,690	252,835	104,855
Welsh	350,365	28,445	321,920
Jewish	348,605	186,475	162,130
Russian	337,960	70,895	267,070
Filipino	327,550	266,140	61,405
Métis	307,845	72,210	235,635
Swedish	282,760	30,440	252,325
Hungarian (Magyar)	267,255	91,800	175,455
American (US)	250,005	25,205	224,805
Greek	215,105	143,785	71,325
Spanish	213,105	66,545	146,555
Jamaican	211,720	138,180	73,545
Danish	170,780	33,795	136,985
Vietnamese	151,410	119,120	32,290

Source: Adapted from Statistics Canada, Census of Population (last modified 25 Jan. 2005). At: <www40.statcan.ca/l01/cst01/demo26a.htm>; accessed 8 Apr. 2006.

care. Governments, for their part, may have to reject demands for further health-care improvement out of public funds.

The Uses and Misuses of Information

Of all the changes that will bear on the future of societies, and on the future of social problems, none is likely to have more impact than cyberspace and the information that resides there. In that sense, in shaping social problems of the twenty-first century, nothing will be more real in its effect than virtual reality. This is because in an **information economy** such as ours, information is a major source of wealth and power, and more and more information is coming to reside in cyberspace.

Table 13.3 The Age Structure of the Canadian Population, 1996–2051, Medium-Growth Scenario				
Year	0 to 14	15 to 64	65 and over	Total
		Thousands		
1996	5,992	20,098	3,582	29,672
2000	5,869	21,018	3,863	30,750
2006	5,527	22,400	4,302	32,229
2016	5,241	23,477	5,702	34,420
2026	5,382	23,056	7,753	36,191
2036	5,203	22,765	9,067	37,035
2051	5,053	22,440	9,366	36,860
		Percentage		
1996	20.2	67.7	12.1	100.0
2000	19.1	68.3	12.6	100.0
2006	17.1	69.5	13.3	100.0
2016	15.2	68.2	16.6	100.0
2026	14.9	63.7	21.4	100.0
2036	14.0	61.5	24.5	100.0
2051	13.7	60.9	25.4	100.0

Source: Adapted from Statistics Canada, *The Daily*, 13 Mar. 2001, at: <www.statcan.ca/Daily/English/010313/d010313a.htm>.

THE RISE OF CYBERSPACE

We are now living in what some have called the **Information Age**. We have more information about more ideas than at any other time in history. We use this information and exchange it. Information is a commodity, to be bought and sold. Five centuries ago, scholars could determine the proper body of knowledge within any literate society. It was still possible for someone to imagine becoming an expert—a knowledgeable person—in everything. (People have thought of the Renaissance scholar Erasmus in these terms, and some would speak of Leonardo da Vinci the same way.) Even 50 years ago, scholars could still distinguish the boundaries of knowledge—what was known and knowable from what was not.

However, today the demarcated body of knowledge is far beyond the reach of a single person, so we need detailed specialization even within fields (for example, within chemistry, anthropology, or literature). This idea of the demarcated body of knowledge—of what educated people should know—has also been produced by technology of the day, as has the question of 'knowledge ownership'.

Until the invention of the printing press, people did not have an idea of authorship in the modern sense. In Europe, monks spent lifetimes copying old manuscripts, which many believed to be the word of God. However, most knowledge or information—about growing crops, blacksmithing, weaving, or any of the other activities that were part of everyday life—was passed on orally and/or by observation from person to person. The printing press changed this by making possible the rapid copying of what had previously taken months or years. Knowledge was now a thing that people could share among strangers, and printers sought material to print. Still, the idea of authorship took several centuries before it gained its modern form (Eisenstein, 1979; Rose, 1993). With the notion of authorship, or of the ownership of knowledge, came ideas about standards for knowledge. Eventually the standard, in the popular mind, became what was printed.

The ownership of knowledge is important, both for its own sake and for its market value. Increasingly, technology has made the borrowing, stealing, sampling, and reproduction of knowledge possible for everyone, through computers, scanners, photocopiers, fax machines, and, of course, printing presses. The Internet further affects this relationship between consumers, producers, and knowledge, changing the whole way we view information and changing the relations of its production.

Business use of the new technology allows a shift in the location of 'work' to 'home' and allows companies to further spread their roles among many locations, whether these are towns, regions, or countries. The new electronic marketplace is made up of people who have probably never physically met each other but who share beliefs and ideologies, give support, and exchange ideas regularly. The result is a creation of worldwide virtual communities—communities of interest and shared viewpoints that are unhampered by distance or by many social factors (age, race, gender, class) that often keep otherwise similar people from meeting or interacting with one another.

The Internet, unlike other information media, is not centralized and not restricted: anyone who can gain access to a computer and modem can take part. Community nets (or 'freenets') are developing in many towns and cities, often with terminals installed in public libraries, to give access to those who do not have computers at home or work. Pages for specialized groupings—women, African Canadians, bikers, and so on—are rapidly increasing in number. However, centralization, censorship, and monitoring of the Internet—always possibilities on the horizon—may hinder both access and the spread of ideas among 'alternative' groups and communities. Without vigilance by users, the Internet could go from being an anarchic network of information providers and communicators to a means of surveillance.

THE SOCIAL ORGANIZATION OF CYBERSPACE

Not only does the Internet ease information-sharing, commerce, and social support, it also allows people to create and try out new identities. The virtual community, mediated by computers and populated by real and invented identities, provides cybersurfers with a new sense of community. In virtual associations, people may have multiple selves but they share a common goal and common identity. Cyberspace offers people unparalleled opportunities to meet and grow emotionally close to total strangers who may be at a considerable distance (Merkle and Richardson, 2000).

New technologies enable more fluid changes in language use that are largely free of indicators (for example, age, sex, or physical appearance), which limit self-expression. The 'self-disclosure' may be candid, masked, or downright devious. Many report adopting bogus names and identities for their interactions. Deception is part of the fun of cyberspace, a type of social gaming. Thus, some males take on the identities of females, and vice versa. The possibilities for play and deception are almost infinite. For example, women can experience ungendered interaction for the first time. Bodily features, such as sex or physical attractiveness, are simply irrelevant in cyberspace—at least in principle. In turn, this means people in cyberspace can create new social and sexual relationships. One result is what some have called 'emotional adultery' (Collins, 1999).

Cyberspace has the potential to blur the distinction between reality and fantasy. However, strange to say, people in cyberspace often behave just the same as ever. For example, many Internet communicators still behave in traditionally gendered and even sexist manners when they have information about the gender of the people with whom they are interacting. Interestingly, research (Kendall, 1998) on people's self-presentation in MUDDS (chat rooms organized for game playing) finds that gender continues to structure social interactions in remarkably conventional ways. At least in the early stages of contact, men in cyberspace tend to act in traditionally male ways, emphasizing the sexual aspects of their relations with women.

The ability to depict oneself in various identities creates a 'zone of confusion' between reality and common-sense notions of the imaginary. There is a danger that the Internet promotes emotionally disconnected or superficially erotic contacts. Participants on-line may experience ambivalent feelings about self-presentation. On the one hand, they may wish for involvement and for a presentation of real, not merely realistic, selves. On the other hand, they may fear self-revelation and lack an ability to trust those they contact. The exercise of social control is almost impossible in cyberspace. As a result, on-line communities develop with more free riders, and problems arise in setting up boundaries and defining membership. Conflicts develop between competing communities, and even among members of the same community. Internet technology, some believe, is resulting in decreased human interaction and community cohesion.

At the same time, the growing influence of cyberspace has resulted in increased power for large corporations and larger power disparities between races, classes, and gender. Commercial, military, and professional contexts are driving virtual technology towards better uses in entertainment and military training. However, few benefits are being seen for most ordinary people. Concentration and commercialization undermine the democratic potential of new communications systems. And outside the Internet, life goes on as it did before. A politics of digital inequality is now surfacing, and questions are arising about the basic conditions of access, capability, and distribution in cyberspace.

At first, the creation of the Internet led to utopian fantasies of citizen empowerment and the revitalization of democracy. Some observers call it the 'Californian ideology'—the belief that the use of new information technologies will create a new democracy that allows everyone free expression in cyberspace. However, dominant economic, social, and political forces in society are struggling, with some success, to capture and regulate the Net (Barbrook and Cameron, 1996). Virtual reality has come to resemble the real world; ordinary, everyday politics have captured cyberspace. Websites, blogs, and mass mailings are easily established to publicize partisan views and simulate popular support. Today, every variety of human is found in cyberspace, flogging every idea and product. Humanity is no better than before, just more virtual.

Based on ethnographic and survey evidence from four election seasons between 1996 and 2002 of the role of digital technologies in the production of contemporary political culture, Howard (2005) reports that democracy is 'deeper' in terms of the diffusion of rich data about political actors, policy options, and the diversity of actors and opinion in the public sphere. However, he also reports that citizenship is 'thinner' in terms of the ease with which people can become politically expressive without being substantively engaged.

However, the new forms of virtual community, and the technological and cultural resources needed for participation in them, are likely to create new forms of division and, therefore, barriers to universal access. Given society's social and racial polarization, only some people have access to the new technologies. A reliance on unregulated market forces will create social distance between the 'information rich' and the 'information poor'. Global inequalities of access to information technology mean an increase of disadvantage for many people and countries, reinforcing existing power structures.

What interaction occurs now and will occur in cyberspace in the future? What kinds of social classes exist in cyberspace? What sociological ideas should be used to explain this? We can probably apply existing knowledge to understand what is going on. Imagine cyberspace as a new frontier in which strangers exchange information and practice impression management on one another in a context rooted in three ways. First, these participants are themselves the members and products of certain genders, classes, races, and childhood experiences. Second, their interactions are all rooted in a particular historical moment. Whatever they may fantasize, the participants live at a particular time and place that offers particular opportunities and constraints.

Third, and specifically, the interests, goals, and technologies of large organizations—chiefly, states and private enterprises—establish boundaries to their interactions. In cyberspace, General Motors and the Pentagon, for example, will continue to protect their own turf and promote their own interests. They will not be transformed politically by the new technology—to think otherwise is to be a 'technological determinist'; rather, they can be expected to use the new technology to their own existing purposes. In future, as at the present, everything will depend on what information people are able to get. And, as we have said, the powerful and wealthy will try to control what people know. This issue leads to a discussion of information diffusion and two particular forms of diffusion: rumours and contagion.

Rumour, Contagion, and Moral Panics

In an information society, all social, economic, and political life depends on the quality of the information available. This makes the withholding, piracy, and distortion of information more problematic than ever. One foreseeable social problem of the future concerns rumours and contagion, two deviant forms of information flow that can have powerful outcomes for societies of the future.

Rumour

In the summer of 1986, during an intense drought, rumours spread through the Dordogne region of France. Allegedly, cloud seeding that was intended to prevent hail and was sponsored by large agricultural enterprises—by Spanish 'tomato barons'—had miscarried, and this had caused the drought. Similar rumours about the Spanish 'tomato barons' had surfaced in 1985 and earlier, during equally severe droughts (Brodu, 1990).

The rumours all contained inaccurate information. While cloud seeding is infamously ineffective at producing rain, there is no evidence that it can prevent rain. Such rumours appeal to people in a time of drought because of popular superstition and the general unreliability of techniques for controlling the weather. Nevertheless, other factors enter as well. These rumours have a political content that is just barely hidden below the surface. There is a reason the French rumour mongers blamed Spanish

---

The Digital Divide

Yet, however important income is . . . [u]nderstanding barriers to access and use of new technologies remains important. While there is ample evidence that affordability is critical, it certainly does not explain the still-sizable proportion of non-users at the highest income levels. . . .In the end, the issue of the digital divide, like all others, will come down to outcomes and impacts. As Castells put it: 'The fundamental digital divide is not measured by the number of connections to the Internet, but by the consequences of both connection and lack of connection' (*The Internet Galaxy*, 2001: 269). Source: George Sciadas, *The Digital Divide in Canada* (Statistics Canada Catalogue no. 56F0009XIE), at: <www.statcan.ca/english/research/56F0009XIE/56F0009XIE.pdf>.

'tomato barons'. After all, the French and Spanish people have been military and economic rivals for over 500 years. Besides, the alleged wrongdoers were barons—people of wealth and standing. Rumours often contain allegations of wrongdoing by the powerful against the powerless. By studying rumours, we learn something valuable about society, and about people's fantasy lives.

Sociologists view rumours as 'improvised news' (Shibutani, 1966). From this standpoint, rumours are closer to other forms of individual and collective information-seeking than they are to dreaming and escapism: a **rumour** is information provided to solve an ill-defined problem. In creating a rumour, members of society draw on their limited stock of cognitive resources, but in a purposeful manner. Rumours that build on stereotypes or ideal images are more likely than other rumours to gain currency in the media and in public debate and are more resistant to denial. The most 'successful' rumours match what people hope or fear will come true rather than what has really happened. The power of the rumour is not in its outburst, but in its making visible otherwise invisible relations.

Contagion

Like rumours, popular anxieties can spread rapidly. Often they reflect anxieties about immoral behaviour. For example, during World War I, across Great Britain, young women were seemingly so attracted to men in military uniform that they behaved in what people considered indecent and sexually dangerous ways. People called the outbreak of wickedness 'khaki fever'.

This wartime loss of social control caused public anxiety over young women's social and sexual behaviour. 'Khaki fever' appeared to infect not only the morally lax poor, but even young women from the normally upstanding middle class. Today, we understand that this fear of 'khaki fever' was symptomatic of a change from the secretiveness of the nineteenth century to a more open public display of feminine sexuality in the twentieth century. In turn, the growing openness of sexual display went with a growing social and sexual independence for women (Woollacott, 1994).

This supposed 'outbreak' of female sexuality illustrates many elements of **contagion**. Most importantly, with contagion a new behaviour spreads rapidly. People fear that immorality is 'catching', or infecting everyone. The fear is itself contagious, producing what sociologists now call a moral panic.

Contagion, like contact, comes from the Latin word for 'touching'. It refers to the passing on of something—whether information, behaviour, or disease—by direct contact or touch. Contagion is merely one form of diffusion. It is also a form of diffusion about which people have old and deep beliefs. The magical law of contagion, a traditional belief, holds that properties, both physical and moral, can be transferred through contact, so some essence passes from source to recipient. Even today, some people act as though they fear that poverty or mental or physical deformity may be catching. This helps to explain the stigmatization of some groups.

All forms of diffusion, contagion included, have certain common features. Compared with information that is broadcast, information that is diffused relies on connection. For diffusion to occur, a relevant exposure link must connect the people involved. The person receiving it must accept the object of diffusion—for example, a rumour. Having once received the rumour, the recipient continues to have it indefinitely. The same rumour (or other object of diffusion) cannot diffuse twice to same person. These basic features of diffusion are also basic features of contagion, and, like diffusion, contagion is strongly locational. It spreads information spatially, from near the source to farther away. Therefore, the object of contagion shows concentration in space. Over time, the concentrations gradually grow, spread out, and move.

Many view contagion as the unreflective, irrational adoption of a trivial or worthless new behaviour. Thus, contagion is a disparaging view of diffusion and innovation, associated with mass or popular rather than elite behaviour. Unlike much other innovative behaviour, contagious behaviours are supposedly impulsive (not rational), possibly destructive (not adaptive), ambiguous (not predictable), and group-driven (not fitted to individual needs). In this view, contagion relies on what we might call a snowball effect. A mass or crowd of undifferentiated, irrational actors collects through contagion and then behaves in mindless ways.

Thus, contagion is a form of diffusion that produces group activity that is disapproved by others. This is largely how people viewed 'khaki fever' at the time. Like a contagious disease—measles or the common cold—a contagious behaviour follows special rules. First, it requires the simultaneous actions of multiple senders to build up a critical mass of influence on the receiver. Second, receivers vary in their openness to the message; some are not merely indifferent, they actively resist it. This not only prevents their adoption of the information, but may even discourage the information sender from making further attempts. Senders are likely to stop their efforts after a certain time. The message 'dies out'—that is, loses its currency—or the sender becomes discouraged and does not attempt to send the message. People stop trying to change other people's behaviour when they feel they have made themselves look like idiots.

Some social flow processes—epidemics, protest movements, and popular fads, for example—only happen if a few people become involved and remain involved. If the new information or behaviour does not catch on, the spread will decline and die out. Epidemics are most common in populations in which uninfected people have a high average vulnerability and a frequent rate of contact with infected (or information-bearing) individuals.

What is remarkable about collective behaviour is that different people with different motives may produce the same behaviour. Moral panics arise when people come to believe in the existence of a threat from new forms of deviance. However, irrationality is not essential or primary to collective behaviour; outsiders often wrongly assume it. For example, ordinary people respond effectively when people in authority fail to do so. Formal organizations and government often fail to mobilize as quickly as expected because of flaws in emergency response planning. Typically, communication defects, not motivational defects, undermine response efficiency and lead to co-ordination problems.

There are good sociological (that is, organizational) reasons for seemingly irrational behaviour. Take the crowd crush at Hillsborough Stadium in Sheffield, England, in 1989. Ninety-six people were crushed to death at an English FA Cup semifinal game between Liverpool and Nottingham Forest, when police opened gates to alleviate crowding outside Hillsborough Stadium. The resulting rush of people onto the already filled terrace sections trapped fans against riot control fences ringing the field. A belief that gaining access to the soccer game being played there was both possible and desirable motivated this crush, despite a shortage of space and tickets. Conduciveness was created through media hype, poor distribution of tickets, and a market distinguished between ticket holders and non-ticket holders. Confusion about the possibility of gaining access to the match contributed to the general belief that access could be gained by force. Media hype, poor organization, and peers all pushed towards action. Poor police and stadium security weakened the social control (Lewis and Kelsey, 1994).

Another explanation of the coincidence of irrationality and catastrophe is not that normal people become beastly, but that beastly people come to appear normal. At the outbreak of wars, for example, psychopaths and other social outcasts are able to shift attention away from their problems and express politically violent emotions against internal and external enemies. Also, disasters and emergencies of other kinds are likely to bring the beasts out of the woodwork without turning normal people into beasts.

Contagion, then, is diffusion that is especially important to sociologists, especially in an information society, because it addresses the question of how individuals link and eventually form large groups capable of collective action. Out of pairs—through aggregation—come networks, movements, parties, and other large organizations. Central to this transformation is the flow of information, which we have been calling diffusion, and the aggregative that is contagion. Like other forms of diffusion, contagion passes information through networks of contact, although important information may also pass by broadcast.

This change, like others we have discussed, often passes through stable networks of relations. As we have seen, wrong information, in the form of stereotypes and rumours, can produce much social harm. It is our job as educated people to learn the difference between facts and fantasies. It is our job as sociologists to learn how to understand and, if possible, control the creation of fantasy. If we fail to do so, the information society will become a misinformation society, and moral panics will be more common than not. Eventually, most 'information' will lose credibility.

The Need for Modest Optimism

It would be fitting to end this book on a note of optimism that we will eventually be able to foresee and solve our social problems better than we can today. What are the chances that we will be able to do this in future, and what do we need to do as sociologists to make this possible?

The answer to this question becomes clearer when we consider our knowledge, or lack of it, about the basic social processes that underlie social problems. Consider, for example, our understanding of the flows—diffusion, migration, mobility, renewal (or turnover), for example—that are the basis of all social organization. We know that these flows have certain common elements: source, length, volume, rate. They move through channels and are subject to flooding and damming.

We know that flows are locational changes over time. Sometimes they are changes in the social system, and sometimes they are so great that they bring about changes of the social system. We know that flows are both markers and makers of social structure. In effect, what we call social structure is merely frozen change—flows caught in a moment of time.

Time is the backdrop for studying both change and structure. This means that as sociologists, we need to have a clear understanding of what we mean by correlation, causation, and theory. Time is of the essence in any social theory. To study flows in time is to study all of the central issues in social science. But what do we actually know about the timetable of everyday flows? We must end this book by confessing that we know very little about the everyday processes that make up the larger processes and structures that we call social problems.

Here are some things sociologists will, eventually, have to find out.
How long it takes for:

- a rumour to pass through a town
- a fad or fashion to die out
- migrant families to assimilate
- a person to find a mate
- a chat room to form in cyberspace
- a jury to decide a murder case
- what the half-life is of a job search; a spy network; a household
- what the age structure (or life expectancy, or average age) is of 100 websites in cyber-space; 100 social support networks in Quebec; 100 best-selling books in English.

Here are some other difficult, but somewhat easier, problems to which we need to find the answers. Under what conditions it will take half as much time as usual for:

- a rumour to pass through a town
- a fad or fashion to die out
- a secret to be exposed.

What the best length of time is for:

- a person to find a mate
- a chat room to form in cyberspace
- a jury to decide a murder case.

How we might speed up:

- the completion of a job search
- the discovery of a spy network
- the building of a social support network.

How we can double the rate of renewal of:

- the Canadian system of beliefs
- the 100 best-selling books in English
- information technology used in British Columbia.

To answer these questions, sociologists will need to go about 'normal' science in a different way. Some essential features of normal science include the adoption and clear definition of key concepts; the development and sharing of reliable measurement tools (e.g., scales); and the collective debate of findings—especially disconfirmatory findings.

We have to start doing this and sociology will come around to this view in due course. In these respects, sociology's professional associations, top journals, leading grad-uate schools, and chief funding agencies will play a central role. Finding the answers to these hard and easier questions will take general agreement on research strategies and research priorities. In a mature science, researchers do not continuously reopen old questions—e.g., Is the world flat after all? Is it possible to specify the temperature at which water boils?—to indulge new political and cultural inclinations. There is an assumption that empirical reality operates according to laws that can be discovered (only) through concerted systematic observation. As to whether we will eventually be able to foresee and solve our social problems better than we can today, the chances are good in the foreseeable future. We know what we need to do as sociologists to make this possible, and all that remains is the doing of it.

In the first chapter of this book we noted that sociology has historically been a moral discipline. Sociologists who study social problems often think of themselves as engaged in a moral enterprise whose goal is to improve human societies through social change. Seven value preferences guide their inquiries: life over death, health over sickness, knowing over not knowing, co-operation over conflict, freedom of movement over physical restraint, self-determination over direction by others, and freedom of expression over censorship (Alvarez, 2001).

We have demonstrated in this book that sociology—social science more generally, and systematic research most generally of all—has made progress in each of these areas. We know more than we did a decade or a century ago. Our progress is slow and we forget some of what we knew as we move forward, so our progress is lurching, unsteady, and uncertain. Modern societies, it turns out, are not as liberating as people living 200 or 500 years ago expected they would be. Leonardo da Vinci, Erasmus, John Stuart Mill, and Voltaire would be surprised and not necessarily pleased with many of the things to see in an average Canadian city today. Some changes would seem like a parody of their hopes and aspirations.

Yet the dream of human betterment through science and knowledge remains. A majority of people still look to science and technology for entertainment, comfort, safety, and reduced drudgery at work and home. Though religious fundamentalism prevails in some parts of the world and among some people in many societies, giving people a needed sense of identity and hope for their own future, we do not believe that disaster—a fall from grace and banishment from Eden—is an inevitable result of knowledge. We believe that knowledge is generally better than ignorance and that more people knowing the truth is better than fewer—only priests and gods—knowing the truth.

Fear and ignorance, as we have seen in our discussion of diffusion, are the context within which lies and errors spread. They support stigma, stereotyping, discrimination, vilification, and warfare. There are many sources of fear, not least the deprivation and violence that flow from vast social inequality. It is difficult, therefore, to do much about fear by writing or reading a book. Ignorance, however, is something we can address, and begin to remedy, by spreading information. Freedom of expression is not only a good in itself, one of our seven guiding values; it is also a means to achieving the other six.

This book has not presented the answers or solutions to our most pressing social problems, but it has asked many of the most pertinent questions and has suggested where the relevant research is headed. Much more needs to be done, as we have seen. The readers of this book are prime candidates for doing this needed work. We hope that you are inspired, not turned off, by the importance of the work before us. Given the hopes of humanity, we have no choice but to make the effort.

Concluding Remarks

Knowledge is, to some extent, empowering. As we have seen, wrong information, in the form of stereotypes and rumours, can produce a great deal of social harm. It is our job as educated people to learn the difference between facts and fantasies. It is our job as sociologists to learn how to understand and, if possible, control the creation of fantasy, in the belief that understanding public issues is better than not understanding them. Armed with a greater understanding of the social problems we face, we can pursue solutions through both individual and collective actions. Individual solutions are often easier to achieve, but in the end collective solutions are the only road to long-lasting changes.

As this book has shown, there are a few master problems—in particular, inequality and exclusion, ignorance and misinformation—and they play out in many combinations and historical variations. Our future as a species will depend on our ability to understand and moderate the more harmful versions of these problems. Cyberspace in particular offers us various exciting, challenging, and dangerous opportunities: to create virtual communities that have no visible location, to participate in world events almost instantaneously, and to observe human life in every part of the world. Cyberspace reduces the constraints of space and time to nearly zero. In doing so, it plunges us into a larger, more crowded frog pond than any we have ever known before. Can we handle the challenge?

As with all technological advancement in the last two centuries, the development of cyberspace makes it more likely that we can build a better mousetrap and a better gas chamber; we can cure our deadly diseases and create new ones; we can tell each other more truths and more lies—more quickly (and persuasively) than ever before. How we will survive this ordeal by information remains to be seen.

Nothing shows more clearly than cyberspace the opportunities and dangers that face humanity when new information technology produces 'new societies' without tradition or regulation. Nothing shows more clearly than futures studies the desire of humanity to imagine and, through imagination, to control the future.

QUESTIONS FOR CRITICAL THOUGHT

1. Can you think of a social problem (one not in the text) that will not likely be solved in the near future? Why will this be so? Can you think of one that will not be an issue in the near future? Why will it not be?

2. Future predictions are often used to determine several possible alternative futures. What are some alternative futures regarding the social issues surrounding environmental damage?

3. How has the advent of the Internet affected your life? Do you find that you have more or less information available? Is this information easier or harder to locate? Has its quality gone up or down?

4. The rate at which information spreads is related to its content. Consider the daily newspaper versus tabloids. How many people, for example, know the reasons for the conflict in the Middle East compared with those who are up to date on who's dating whom in Hollywood? Can you think of any other current examples?

5. Knowing how rumours and contagions spread, what are some ideas on ways we can counteract or slow down this flow?

RECOMMENDED READINGS

Daphna Birenbaum-Carmeli, Yoram S. Carmeli, and Rina Cohen, 'Our First "IVF Baby": Israel and Canada's Press Coverage of Procreative Technology', *International Journal of Sociology and Social Policy* 20, 7 (2000): 1–38. This article compares the Israeli and Canadian responses to IVF technologies. Using the news coverage in each country, the authors cite the difference in the two nations' cultures as an explanation of their differing levels of enthusiasm regarding IVF technology—Israeli enthusiasm is much greater, given that country's more strongly pro-natalist culture.

Neena L. Chappell and Margaret J. Penning, 'Sociology of Aging in Canada: Issues for the Millennium', *Canadian Journal on Aging* 20, suppl. (2001): 82–110. As Canada's population ages, one critical question is how Canadian society can cope with the new strains on our health-care system and family relations.

Crystale Purvis Cooper and Darcie Yukimua, 'Science Writers' Reactions to a Medical "Breakthrough" Story', *Social Science and Medicine* 54 (2002): 1887–96. After a *New York Times* story boosted the hopes of cancer patients, 60 science writers from the United States, Canada, and Great Britain posted e-mail messages to the discussion list of the National Association of Science Writers over a period of 12 days in a discussion on the issue of news coverage of medical 'breakthroughs'. The article analyzes these messages and finds suggestions for the future news coverage.

Jim Dator, 'Futures Studies and Sustainable Community Development', paper presented at the First World Futures-Creating Seminar, Renewing Community as Sustainable Global Village, Aug. 1993, Goshiki-cho, Japan; available at <www.soc.hawaii.edu/future/dator.html>. One of the creators of educational television in Ontario (TVOntario), Jim Dator went on to found the Hawaii Research Center for Futures Studies at the University of Hawaii and served as president of the World Futures Studies Federation. His long list of books and papers includes recent works on environmental and sustainability issues.

Johan Galtung and Sohail Inayatullah, *Macrohistory and Macrohistorians: Perspectives on Individual, Social, and Civilizational Change* (Westport, Conn.: Praeger, 1997). The essays in this volume focus on historians—from Ibn Khaldhun to Oswald Spengler and from Piritim Sorokin to Arnold Toynbee—who have helped shape our way of conceiving of ourselves.

Sohail Inayatullah and Susan Leggett, eds, *Transforming Communication: Technology, Sustainability and Future Generation* (Westport, Conn.: Praeger, 2002). The contributors argue that to create sustainable futures, new ways must be found to make communication inclusive, participatory, and mindful of future generations.

Richard Slaughter, 'A New Framework for Environmental Scanning', *Foresight: The Journal of Futures Studies, Strategic Thinking and Policy* 1, 5 (1999); available at <members.ams.chello.nl/f.visser3/wilber/slaughter2.html>. Current president of the World Futures Studies Federation, director and foundation professor of foresight at the Australian Foresight Institute at Swinburne University, Slaughter has been primarily interested in questions of methodology, that is, how we can know the future and how we can shape it.

RECOMMENDED WEBSITES

Environment Canada
www.ec.gc.ca

This government website offers information on current environmental issues in Canada and abroad. There are links to various programs for Canadians that can help with the environment.

Greenpeace
www.greenpeace.ca

Greenpeace is an activist organization that operates to preserve the earth's natural environment. Along with causes Greenpeace works on, this website has information about current environmental issues and discussion of their effects in the future.

NASA
www.nasa.gov

The National Aeronautics and Space Administration in the US, in addition to space exploration, also researches a wide variety of up-and-coming technologies.

World Health Organization
www.who.int

The World Health Organization is the health agency of the United Nations. It sets out to achieve the highest level of health for people around the world. The site contains information about current and future health issues around the world.

World Bank

www.worldbank.org

A supporter of globalization, the World Bank helps poor and developing countries fight poverty and establish economic stability and growth based on the neo-liberal belief in free markets and private enterprise. The World Bank website has readings, statistics, and general information about globalization.

GLOSSARY

Contagion A passing on of something, whether information, behaviour, or disease, by direct contact or touch.

Cyberspace The abstract location where information is said to be exchanged in the Information Age.

Cyberterrorism A means of attack that relies not on physical damage, but on crippling the enemy's technology and communications infrastructure.

Digital divide The separation between those who have access to technology ('haves') and those who do not ('have-nots').

Futures studies The area of research concerned with the forecasting of possible future scenarios in order to prepare for and shape what may come.

Genetic manipulation The altering of genes to produce a more desirable physical makeup.

Globalization The denationalization of politics, markets, and legal systems leading to the formation of a global economy, as well as the homogenizing and/or dispersal of cultures and peoples through communications and improved transportation.

Information Age A historical time—the present—in which information of all forms is quickly and easily accessible via the Internet and computers.

Information economy An economy in which information is treated like any other commodity and can be bought, sold, traded, and so on.

Rumour A type of information diffusion in which the content is not pure misinformation but is conceived for a purpose with limited reliability.

REFERENCES

Alvarez, Rodolfo. 2001. 'The Social Problem as an Enterprise: Values as a Defining Factor', *Social Problems* 48: 3–10.

Barbrook, Richard, and Andy Cameron. 1996. 'The Californian Ideology', *Science as Culture* 6, 1: 44–72.

Bell, Wendell. 1997. *Foundations of Futures Studies: Human Science for a New Era*, vol. 1. New Brunswick, NJ: Transaction.

Berinstein, Juana. 2004. 'The Fight for Jobs with Justice', *Our Times: Canada's Independent Labour Magazine* (Oct.–Nov.).

Brodu, Jean-Louis. 1990. 'A Rumor of Drought', *Communications* 52: 85–97.

Chappell, Neena. 2002. 'Home and Families in the Future', paper presented at the World Congress of the International Sociological Association, Brisbane, Australia.

Chomsky, Noam. 1999. 'Language Design', in Griffiths (1999: 30–2).

Collins, Louise. 1999. 'Emotional Adultery: Cybersex and Commitment', *Social Theory and Practice* 25, 2: 243–70.

Commission on the Future of Health Care in Canada (Romanow Commission). 2002. *Building on Values: The Future of Health Care in Canada: Final Report*. Ottawa: Health Canada.

CTV. 2004. 'Family Trends Include Fewer Marriages', 29 Nov. Available at: <www.ctv.ca/servlet/ArticleNews/story/CTVNews/1101752621646_9716182>; accessed 6 Apr. 2006.

Eisenstein, Elizabeth L. 1979. *The Printing Press as an Agent of Change: Communications and Cultural Transformations in Early Modern Europe*, 2 vols. Cambridge: Cambridge University Press.

George, Henry. 1898. *Social Problems*. New York: Doubleday and McClure.

Gladwell, Malcolm. 2005. *Blink: The Power of Thinking without Thinking*. New York: Little, Brown.

Gould, Stephen Jay. 1999. 'Unpredictable Patterns', in Griffiths (1999: 145–6).

Griffiths, Sian, ed. 1999. *Predictions*. New York: Oxford University Press.

Howard, Philip N. 2005. 'Deep Democracy, Thin Citizenship: The Impact of Digital Media in Political Campaign Strategy', *Annals of the American Academy of Political and Social Science* 597: 153–70.

Jahoda, Marie, K.L.R. Pavitt, H.S.D. Cole, and Christopher Freeman. 1975. *Models of Doom: A Critique of the Limits to Growth*. London: Chatto and Windus.

Kendall, Lori. 1998. 'Meaning and Identity in Cyberspace: The Performance of Gender, Class, and Race Online', *Symbolic Interaction* 21, 2: 129–53.

Lewis, Jerry M., and Michael L. Kelsey. 1994. 'The Crowd Crush at Hillsborough: The Collective Behavior of an Entertainment Crush', in Russell R. Dynes and Kathleen J. Tierney, eds, *Disasters, Collective Behavior, and Social Organization*. Newark: University of Delaware Press, 190–206.

Lomborg, Bjørn. 2001. *The Skeptical Environmentalist: Measuring the Real State of the World*. Cambridge: Cambridge University Press.

Malthus, Thomas R. 1959 [1798]. *Population: The First Essay*. Ann Arbor: University of Michigan Press.

Margolis, Jonathan. 2000. *A Brief History of Tomorrow: The Future, Past and Present*. London: Bloomsbury.

Meadows, Donella H., Dennis L. Meadows, Jorgen Randers, and William W. Behrens III. 1972. *Limits to Growth*. New York: Universe Books.

———, Jorgen Randers, and Dennis Meadows. 2004. 'Facing the Limits to Growth', *AlterNet*, 18 June. Available at: <www.alternet.org/story/18978>; accessed 31 Mar. 2006.

Merkle, Erich R., and Rhonda A. Richardson. 2000. 'Digital Dating and Virtual Relating: Conceptualizing Computer Mediated Romantic Relationships', *Family Relations: Interdisciplinary Journal of Applied Family Studies* 49, 2: 187–92.

Rose, Mark. 1993. *Authors and Owners: The Invention of Copyright*. Cambridge, Mass.: Harvard University Press.

Rowland, F. Sherwood. 1999. 'Sequestration', in Griffiths (1999: 208–11).

Shibutani, Tamotsu. 1966. *Improvised News: A Sociological Study of Rumor*. Indianapolis: Bobbs-Merrill, 1966.

Simon, Julian. 1996. *The Ultimate Resource*, 2nd edn. Princeton, NJ: Princeton University Press.

Time. 1966. 'The Futurists: Looking Toward A.D. 2000', 25 Feb., 32–3.

Towne, Ezra Thayer. 1916. *Social Problems: A Study of Present Day Social Conditions*. New York: Macmillan.

University of Houston–Clear Lake. 2001. 'What Is Futures Studies?' Available at: <www.cl.uh.edu/futureweb/futdef.html>; accessed 2 Feb. 2003.

Walonick, David S. n.d. 'An Overview of Forecasting Methodology'. Available at: <www.statpac.com/research-papers/forecasting.htm>.

Wells, H.G. 1902. *Anticipations of the Reaction of Mechanical and Scientific Progress upon Human Life and Thought*. New York: Harper.

Wilson, David A. 2000. *The History of the Future*. Toronto: McArthur and Company.

Woollacott, Angela. 1994. '"Khaki Fever" and Its Control: Gender, Class, Age and Sexual Morality on the British Homefront in the First World War', *Journal of Contemporary History* 29: 325–47.

World Future Society. 2001. 'Forecasts'. Available at: <www.wfs.org/forecasts.htm>; accessed 22 Aug. 2001.

Appendix

The Sociological Study of Social Problems

Although few students reading this book will pursue a career in social science research, all readers will benefit from understanding the processes by which such research is conducted. Without such an understanding, they cannot hope to decode the information provided in newspapers, magazines, and television. Often social science findings are reported in the media in such a way as to produce the most attention-grabbing headlines. To remain well informed, then, it is necessary to look beyond the results as filtered and presented by the media and interest groups and to understand the research as it was originally conducted by the investigators. The following, then, is a brief overview of the ways in which sociological research on social problems is performed.

Stages of a Research Study

The first step in conducting a research study of any kind, sociological or otherwise, is to come up with a research question: 'What do I want to investigate?'

Sometimes the topic of study is derived from the researcher's personal interests or life experience. For instance, a sociologist whose parents divorced when he or she was still a child may want to explore the factors that contribute to an increased risk of marital separation, or the effects of divorce and custodial battles on the mental health of young people. Other researchers are motivated by a desire to enhance the collective understanding of human nature or to improve the social environment around them. They may seek the answers to questions such as 'What is the most effective way to dispense emergency treatment and resources to victims of a natural disaster?' or 'How do a patient's race and ethnicity affect the quality and quantity of treatment in an inner-city medical clinic?' Still others are contracted by government ministries or private companies to answer a specific question, the answer to which has important consequences for policy making.

Regardless of their content, the best research questions are specific enough that they can be answered by a well-designed study generating a manageable amount of data over a reasonable period of time, but also broad enough that the results have some significance and applicability to the real world.

Having formulated a research question, the investigator's next step is to review the literature, that is, the published material that documents what is already known about the topic. A review of past research not only helps narrow a researcher's own research project, but also provides ideas about how to conduct the study.

Once the researcher has a good understanding of the current state of research in the topic of interest, she or he may formulate a hypothesis, an educated guess about how one or more variables affect others. Variables are any measurable events, characteristics, or properties that have the capacity to change in value or quality.

In any scientific study, variables must be operationally defined; that is, it must be made clear how variables will be described and measured by the investigator. For instance, the term family may refer to immediate family members (that is, father, mother, and their biological and adoptive children) or it may also include extended relatives (aunts, uncles, grandparents, nephews, nieces, and so on) depending on the researcher's topic or research problem. Similarly, some characteristics may be subjectively defined by different research subjects. Thus, it is necessary to formulate a standard definition of what is meant by a term before a study is conducted. 'Patriotism', for example, might be measured by subjects' responses to the question 'How important is your nationality to your overall sense of self-identity?' or by the amount of knowledge that they possess about their country of residence.

Hypotheses are statements about how a dependent variable (DV)—the variable of interest that the researcher is attempting to explain—is affected by an independent variable (IV)—the variable that the researcher believes will explain the changes to the dependent variable. In a study of the effects of marital separation on the mental well-being of children, the IV might be types of family background; the DV is the children's mental health. In many sociological studies, several IVs are measured and assessed against one or more DVs, an indication of both the complexity of the subject material and the research task that the sociologists face.

Types of Research Methods

Once the researcher has formulated a research question and derived a hypothesis, the next step is to actually perform the study and collect data to analyze. The majority of sociological research is conducted using one of four research methods or some combination of them.

EXPERIMENTS

When most people think of scientific experiments, they envision a researcher in a white lab coat, surrounded by test tubes and Bunsen burners in a laboratory. In truth, experiments are much more varied than what the stereotype might suggest; they include any procedure that involves the manipulation of the IVs and the observation of the effects on the DVs.

To ensure that the experimental manipulation was indeed the cause of the changes observed in the DV, such studies are often carried out using several groups of subjects, some of which receive the experimental treatment(s)—that is, the IVs—and a control group comprising similar individuals who do not receive the treatment. The latter may receive a placebo, an inert substance or procedure that mimics the effects of receiving a treatment but none of the effects of the treatment itself. Thus, any variance between the DVs measured among the experimental and control groups can be attributed to the only factor that differed between them—the type of IV treatment(s) they received.

The primary strength of the experimental method is that it provides good evidence for a causal relationship between IVs and DVs. Unfortunately, experiments can only be performed with small groups in artificial laboratory settings, and only where other factors can be held constant while the IV is being manipulated. Thus, this research approach has two weaknesses: first, it is difficult to generalize experimental findings beyond the lab to the larger population in natural settings, and, second, the experimental method can only be applied to a small percentage of research studies that lend themselves to highly controlled study conditions.

SURVEYS, INTERVIEWS, AND QUESTIONNAIRES

Surveys, which elicit information from subjects through a series of questions, are probably the most popular method of data collection among social scientists. However, because it would be impossible and tedious to administer a survey to every single member of the population of interest (for example, children of divorce, single mothers, Canadians), most survey research is performed using a sample of those being studied. In order for the results to be generalizable beyond the small group who actually complete the study, great efforts must be made to ensure that the sample is representative of the entire population—that is, that it is a representative sample. Thus, to arrive at a representative sample of, say, Canadians, a researcher would have to ensure that the proportions of men, women, age groups, racial and ethnic groups, religious groups, socio-economic classes, and regions in the survey accurately reflect their proportions in the real world.

After a representative sample is selected, the researcher can choose to either interview each subject or provide the subjects with pre-constructed questionnaires. Interviews are advantageous for several reasons. One is that interviewers can clarify questions for subjects and pose follow-up questions to elicit further information. As a result, interviews are particularly suited to studies in which a significant amount of detailed knowledge is required. Another benefit of the interview method is that the researcher can study groups that are typically inaccessible using other forms of data collection. For example, Thomas Plate's study of the advantages and disadvantages of a career in the criminal underworld (1975) was performed almost exclusively through informal interviews; it would have been more difficult to elicit the same data had he been restricted to administering pencil-and-paper questionnaires to the burglars and hit men who comprised his subjects.

However, because interviews are based on face-to-face interaction between the interviewer and the interviewee, some drawbacks are also present. The most significant is the lack of anonymity afforded to the subject, a concern that becomes especially important when the topic is of a sensitive, threatening, or embarrassing nature, as in studies of drug use, economic resources, sexual abuse, or sexual orientation and sexual behaviour. Many subjects may therefore choose not to participate, while others may censor or alter their responses or even lie to reflect socially desirable habits. A second disadvantage of interviews is the cost that comes with paying trained interviewers to perform the time-consuming work. The time constraint also means that only a small sample of subjects can be interviewed; the results may therefore not be generalizable to the larger population.

Precisely for these reasons, many social scientists opt instead to gather information about their study populations by means of formalized questionnaires. The main advantages of questionnaires correspond to the weaknesses of interviews. Questionnaires are cheaply, easily, and quickly administered to a large number of people. Also, questionnaires can be completed anonymously and in privacy, increasing the likelihood of receiving a frank and honest set of data.

FIELD RESEARCH

A third method of data collection, field research, involves observing and studying a target population in its natural setting. Rather than having the subjects come to them, researchers who use this approach go to their subjects. Field research is performed in many settings, including schools, prisons, large corporations, small neighbourhoods, tribal communities, and among the homeless. The obvious benefit of this research method is that the behaviours, values, rituals, customs, beliefs, symbols, and emotions observed are more genuine, in that they are the result neither of manipulation of other variables (as is often the case with experiments) nor of artificial and blunt probing (as is often the case with surveys).

The two general types of field research, participant and non-participant observation, each have their own particular advantages and disadvantages. Participant observation, as its name suggests, has the researcher collecting information about the group he or she is studying while participating in their social activities. The main benefit of this approach is the wealth of insight that can be harnessed from an 'inside' look at the population of interest. Since the researcher is actively participating in the local customs, habits, rituals, and norms, she or he can often pick up on the nuances of the culture that might otherwise go unnoticed.

As well, researchers conducting field research must be wary of inadvertently altering their subjects' behaviour merely because of their own presence and status as strangers. By integrating themselves into the group and gaining the trust of their subjects, participant observers minimize the effects of their intrusion into a foreign culture. However, because they become so fully immersed in the practices and beliefs of the host population, these researchers run the risk of losing objectivity and constructing a biased interpretation of observed events. As well, as with in-depth interviews, the small sample size of participant observation may preclude any generalization of findings.

Participant observation offers an insider's perspective. Non-participant observation, in contrast, is the practice of viewing and studying a group from an outsider's perspective, without any significant direct interaction between researcher and subject. This method is desirable if information about a specific group is required but any direct contact would likely disrupt the natural flow of activity and prejudice any resulting observations. In additional to the drawbacks that non-participant research shares with participant observation—potential for researcher bias, small sample size—a further disadvantage is the loss of insight that comes from direct interaction with subjects.

SECONDARY DATA RESEARCH AND ANALYSIS

In addition to the methods described above, which result in primary data—information accumulated at first hand and specifically for a given study by probing a representative sample of subjects—social scientists occasionally analyze secondary data—information that has already been gathered by another researcher or organization, or that exists in historical documents and official records.

The main benefit of secondary data analysis is that it can be performed without disturbing the subjects who originally provided the source material. As well, it can be used in cases in which the subjects refuse to participate or are unavailable for interview (for example, subjects in a historical sociological study who are now deceased). For these reasons, another name for this method is unobtrusive research. The primary drawback is that because the data was collected by a separate agency or researcher, often for an unrelated purpose, the information may not be entirely complete, accurate, or in accordance with the present researcher's specific needs.

Concluding Remarks

Today, there is no single model of analysis in social science, but rather a set of more or less closely related approaches for exploring data and the links between macro and micro levels of reality.

In his fascinating book *Once Upon a Number* (1998), the great popularizer of mathematics John Allen Paulos points out some differences and similarities between stories and statistics. Statistics, typically, address generalities: the characteristics of large populations and large trends, for example. These generalities are so large that we can scarcely hope to picture individuals who personify them. Largely for this reason, statistics often leave people cold; nonetheless, they capture the 'truth' about a population because they are usually based on an unbiased sampling of that population. They are about people just like us, yet they fail to move us. Maybe this is part of the reason people are so willing to believe that statistics are easily manipulated into telling us great lies.

By contrast, the best stories are particular, not general; they sketch particular people caught in particular dramas at a particular time and place. Despite their particularity, stories often capture our interest in a way that statistics do not. Stories also tell 'truths' about the human condition. In the end, every population is just the sum and the product of the unique stories that make it up. Clearly, statistics and stories are just two sides of the same coin, the forest and the trees respectively. Both are true, and both speak to different parts of our need to know the truth.

And just as statistics have a mathematical logic, so too do stories. They have logical structures in the same sense that pieces of music (for example, sonatas and symphonies) do. Good authors (and good composers) know these standard forms and genres of exposition. Their skilful manipulation is largely the reason why people respond to them emotionally, as they often do. It is unclear whether these forms are, in some sense, essential and universal—whether, for example, every successful love story (or sonata) will necessarily have the same structure, wherever and whenever it is written—or whether they all merely reflect particular features of a time, culture, or civilization. In either event, successful stories are no more random than the social statistics describing a crime rate or a population of families. There is order in good writing just as there is in society itself.

These points are important for two reasons. First, they affirm the essential compatibility of statistical analysis and storytelling, quantitative and qualitative analysis, 'scientific' and 'interpretive' approaches to reality. More than ever, social scientists in every discipline recognize the need to bring these approaches together in their respective research enterprises. We rely on all of these skills and insights in discussing social problems in this book. Second, like statistics and stories, people's lives reflect both public issues and personal troubles—the duality that C. Wright Mills (1959) stressed in defining 'the sociological imagination'. There is no good sociological analysis of social problems without recognizing this duality.

References

Mills, C. Wright. 1959. *The Sociological Imagination.* London: Oxford University Press.

Paulos, John Allen. 1998. *Once Upon a Number: The Hidden Mathematical Logic of Stories.* New York: Basic Books.

Plate, Thomas Gordon. 1975. *Crime Pays! An Inside Look at Burglars, Car Thieves, Loan Sharks, Hit Men, Fences, and Other Professionals in Crime.* New York: Simon & Schuster.

Index